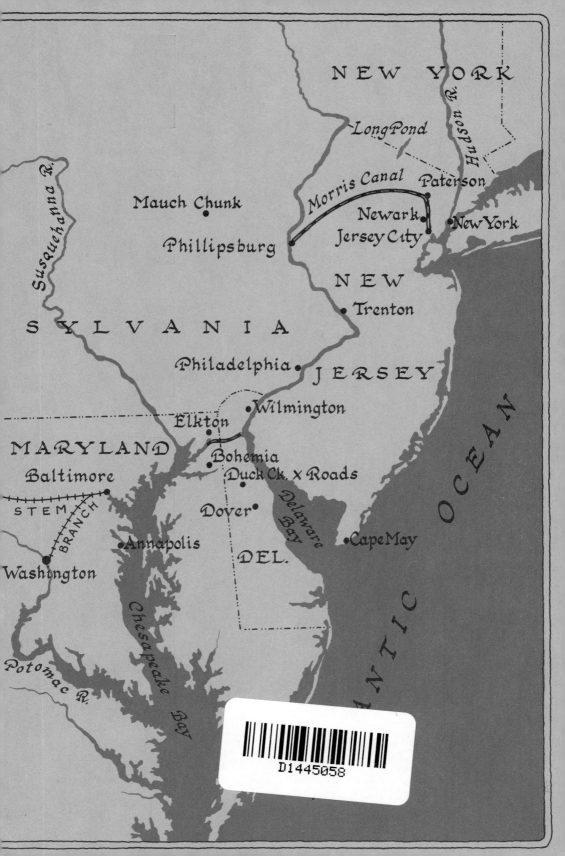

Louis McLane:

Federalist and Jacksonian

Louis McLane, 1784–1857. Oil, circa 1829, variously attributed to John F. Francis and to William E. West. The University of Delaware, gift of Mrs. George L. Batchelder, Jr.

Louis McLane:
Federalist and Jacksonian

JOHN A. MUNROE

RUTGERS UNIVERSITY PRESS
NEW BRUNSWICK, NEW JERSEY

Library of Congress Cataloging in Publication Data

Munroe, John A   1914–
    Louis McLane: Federalist and Jacksonian.

    Bibliography: p.
    1. McLane, Louis, 1786–1857. 2. United States—
Politics and government—1783–1865. I. Title.
E302.6.M137M86   973.5′092′4 [B]   73–17240
ISBN 0–8135–0757–X

To Dorothy

Contents

Illustrations

Foreword

Much about Louis McLane, including the date of his birth and the nature of his politics, has been unknown or incorrectly surmised by historians. About twenty years ago, in preparing an essay that I read to the Pacific Coast branch of the American Historical Association, I set about looking for his papers. I had then little more than a score of interesting letters to his colleague at the Delaware bar, James A. Bayard, the younger, lent me by the kindness of Bayard's granddaughter, Mrs. Florence Bayard Hilles. Although I soon heard that the McLane papers had been destroyed in the Baltimore fire of 1904, I was encouraged by finding a small set of them in the possession of a McLane descendant, Mrs. George Batchelder, Jr., of Beverly, Massachusetts, and by her I was led to McLane's granddaughter, Mrs. D. K. Este Fisher, then an octogenarian. Mrs. Fisher promptly answered that she was too old to begin an interest in genealogy but received my protestations on behalf of history and turned them over to her son, who kindly guided me to what proved a rich lode of McLane ore. This was the collection of family papers stored in a Bekins warehouse in Denver by the Reverend James Latimer McLane, since deceased but then rector of an Episcopal church in Los Angeles. While I was busy assimilating these papers, which were, like the others, previously unknown to historians, one more sizable McLane collection came to light. This was another set of McLane letters found in a Baltimore closet after the death of a sister of Mrs. Fisher. These discoveries caused me to cast aside my earlier essay and undertake a full-scale biography.

It would be easy to picture Louis McLane as a Federalist driven by the collapse of his party to abandon politics for business. Although there may be a snippet of truth in this picture, McLane was in a peculiar situation, for he was a party leader in a state the Federalists never lost. They did, however, change their labels as they sought to fit into the second American party system, and McLane, seeking to direct the change, failed to carry his party with him. Old political enmities made the local scene uncomfortable for him at the same time that his choler, his ambition, and his intelligence brought him into new conflicts in Washington at exalted heights where only the dominant or the patient can long sustain themselves. McLane's attempt to dominate failed; he had little patience, and so he retreated to private life, awaiting a call that never came. One new opportunity was only barely missed when Buchanan's change of mind in 1846 cost McLane appointment to the first place in Polk's cabinet. Yet it is difficult to believe that the cry of "McLane and Oregon" could have carried this bold man up the final step to the pinnacle he sought.

The career of Louis McLane was multifaceted, involving many aspects of politics, diplomacy, finance, and business. Appearing first on the national scene as a Congressman representing a small state and a weak minority party, McLane rose by his talents and industry to the chairmanship of the most important committee in the House of Representatives, despite the steadfast Federalism that won him six consecutive elections from 1816 through 1826. After brief service in the Senate he was sent to the United States' most important diplomatic post abroad, as minister to London. Returning triumphant, he served brief but important terms in Jackson's cabinet as Secretary of the Treasury and Secretary of State, and for a very short period he was the dominant figure in that cabinet. After retreating to private life, he moved to New York on accepting the presidency of the Morris Canal and Banking Company, which was then more interested in its Jersey City bank, with a Wall Street branch, than in its canal. From New York McLane moved to Maryland as president of the Baltimore & Ohio Railroad Company. And there in Maryland McLane remained until his death twenty years later, except for a brief return to diplomacy when he undertook a critical second mission to England in 1845.

It is hoped that this exposition of Louis McLane's career casts new and fresh light on many of the important developments in our country in that silver age when McLane flourished. To the author it has been a challenge not only to utilize unused and even unknown materials but also to attempt to understand and lay bare the struggles of a man with the forces of his environment. McLane's activities were never scandalous and only rarely sensational, but they were often exciting and their elucidation may prove of permanent value.

My chief indebtedness is to the assistance given me in one form or another by four McLane descendants, Mrs. George L. Batchelder, Jr.,

Mr. D. K. Este Fisher, Jr., the late Reverend James Latimer McLane, and his son Louis McLane. Other McLane relatives who have assisted me include the late Louis McLane Hobbins and Mrs. Hobbins, Mrs. Thomas Hurst and her grandson Allan McLane Hurst, Mr. L. McLane Fisher, and Mrs. Sophie-L. Brocklebank. The late Jess D. Otley and Mrs. Otley, who restored Bohemia, and their successors on that estate, Mr. and Mrs. W. Harrison Mechling, have shown me many courtesies.

Over almost two decades I was assisted by so many people in various libraries and archives that I despair of naming them all. It is safe to say that almost every member of the reference staffs of the University of Delaware Library, the Delaware State Archives, the Historical Society of Delaware, and the Eleutherian Mills-Hagley Foundation has helped me at one time or another. I particularly wish to thank Ruth Alford, John M. Dawson, Leon de Valinger, Jr., Dale Fields, Walter J. Heacock, John B. Riggs, E. Berkeley Tompkins, and Marie Windell, as well as John A. H. Sweeney (of the Winterthur Museum) and Charles Coleman Sellers.

I owe the Fund for the Advancement of Education and the Ford Foundation gratitude for a year of freedom from teaching in which, while roaming the country, I came upon many of the papers which formed the basis of this study. The University of Delaware furnished research funds on various occasions, especially for typing, and granted occasional leaves to further my work. I am grateful to four student assistants for their help in taking notes: Marie Donaghy, Jane N. Garrett, Joseph McNeal, and Harry Rinker.

My colleague Stephen Salsbury has put me greatly in his debt by his kindness in reading and criticizing my entire manuscript, and in a form even longer than it has now. Richard P. McCormick, Norman B. Wilkinson, and the late Marshall Knappen read small sections of my work, and Ralph D. Gray and Ralph Ketcham were helpful in calling my attention to manuscripts I might otherwise have missed.

John A. Munroe

University of Delaware
August, 1973

Louis McLane:

Federalist and Jacksonian

1

The Old Collector
and His Son

The Borough of Wilmington in the State of Delaware owed its life to its harbor. Down every street a gentle grade led to a river, the Christina (then called Christiana), a tributary of the Delaware. The Christina River and the harbor it formed were for a third of a century the domain of a cranky, courageous, spirited old man named Allen McLane.

The borough that was the seat of his power from 1797 to 1829 was a cluster of buildings inside one of the arms of a V that was formed by the conjunction of two water courses. The stream forming the nearer arm, the Christina, to the right of the borough as one looked down from the hills behind, was slow, circuitous, and navigable. The left arm of the V was the Brandywine, shallow, rocky, and precipitous.

The Christina wound its course through the farms and marshes of New Castle County past Wilmington to join the Delaware River; it was essentially a highway by which country produce left the farm and necessities and luxuries were imported, often via the great port of Philadelphia on the Delaware. The Brandywine was navigable only near its mouth, where it joined the Christina, just east of Wilmington and just west of the Delaware. Its falls were its fortune—no one great, spectacular fall, but dozens of small useful falls, one succeeding the other as the creek carried a dependable current southeastward from the hills of Pennsylvania. Fertile land, navigable water giving access to a major port, Philadelphia, and, via the Delaware, directly to the world, and water power to turn mills and manufacture natural products—wheat or wood or wool —these were the bases of Wilmington's modest prosperity.

Behind Wilmington, to the west at the open end of the V, were the

3

low hills of the Piedmont's edge. Before it, to the east, lay the Delaware, and, by the Delaware, the world. The streets coaxed boys to the sea to make their fortunes; the river brought the world's goods to local merchants.

II   THE COLLECTOR OF THE CUSTOMS

Like Philadelphia, Wilmington is built in rectangular blocks back from a river. On the river front were the wharves and near them the shops of chandlers and other merchants dependent on the river traffic. Among the shops, near the wharves, at 16 East Water Street, was the seat of the major dignitary of the harbor, the Collector of the Customs for the District of Delaware.[1]

The office made any collector a person of consequence in his community. Collectors in great ports were, in effect, heads of large business houses who employed dozens or even hundreds of clerks and received a larger compensation than cabinet members. Wilmington was not a great port, but the compensation received by its collector was quite respectable. In 1801 the figure was $3,262.96, the adequacy of which may be gauged by comparison with the salary of the Vice-President ($5,000), the Chief Justice ($4,000), the Attorney General ($3,000), and the District Judge ($1,200).[2]

To be sure the collector's income was less dependable than that of these salaried officers. Whereas Chief Justice Marshall was reasonably sure of his $4,000 a year and District Judge Gunning Bedford, Jr., of his $1,200, the collector had no such assurance. Only $250 of his 1801 compensation was in salary;[3] all the remainder represented fees and commissions. He received a fee at every entrance and clearance of a vessel from his port: two dollars and a half, for instance, if the vessel was of one hundred tons or more burthen. He received twenty cents for every permit to land cargo, forty cents for every bond taken, twenty cents for every bill of health. Besides such fees, the collector of Delaware enjoyed a commission of 3 percent of all the money he collected as tariff duties or tonnage dues.[4]

The money that flowed through the port collectors provided the federal government's chief source of funds in all but a few years prior to the twentieth century. And because the collectors were responsible officials with staffs adequate for their essential tasks, they were called upon by the federal government for many other local services.

The main task of the port collectors was to police the entry and departure of all ships and their cargoes and to estimate and receive payment of tariff duties, or store the goods while taking bond for payment.

They granted permits for the unloading and delivery of goods, employed weighers, gaugers, measurers, and inspectors, as well as the sailors needed to man any boats required for the collection of duties. They also provided scales and other equipment for evaluating imports, and secured the use of warehouses for goods that were to be stored and bonded for the delayed payment of duties.[5]

Whenever the country became involved in an international controversy, the responsibilities of the customs collectors were greatly increased. The enforcement of the Embargo Act of 1794, the suspension of trade with France in 1798, the Embargo of 1807, the Non-Intercourse Act of 1809, and the Embargo of 1812 depended largely upon the collectors. And by the Alien Act of 1798 the collectors became the official registrars of all incoming aliens, sharing with the district court clerks the responsibility for registering all resident aliens.[6]

In times of calm as well as of crisis, the collectors were assigned additional new duties. Frequently they were employed to collect information for the Secretary of the Treasury. Alexander Hamilton, in 1791, had asked collectors to send him such documents as they could gather concerning commerce, fisheries, navigation, and manufactures. Albert Gallatin, in 1809, requested information about American manufactures and the methods to foster and protect them. In 1829 the collectors were called on to gather statistics concerning the manufacture of salt.[7]

A miscellany of other duties came to the collectors. In 1790 they were declared pension agents and directed to pay the military pensions then being assumed by the federal government. In 1798 they were ordered to collect from every ship arriving from a foreign port twenty cents a month for every seaman employed, and to use these funds for the care of sick and disabled seamen. Under this law the collectors became the virtual directors of marine hospitals, and so they remained for almost a century. They were also ordered to observe all restraints, including quarantines, imposed by health laws of the states; and when in 1819 the first federal law regulating immigration required minimum supplies of water and provisions to be carried on immigrant ships, enforcement was quite naturally left to the collectors.[8]

If the collectors had many duties, they also had a great deal of influence. They were a focal point of federal patronage in every port. In 1801, for example, the collector at Wilmington employed an unnamed number of clerks and ten inspectors, some of whom functioned also as weighers, gaugers, and measurers.[9] Not in that year, probably, but in later years he had the use of a boat, and therefore a few seamen enjoyed jobs through him. He placed advertising in some local paper of his choice; he rented warehouses for the storage of goods seized or goods bonded for the later payment of taxes; he hired counsel to press cases in court.

The collector of Wilmington, declared Hezekiah Niles in 1804, had more "power & influence, as an officer than even our governor." From the collector's own wealth and from "the Number of men he now imployes in his Off[i]c[i]al cappacity," declared Peter Jaquett in the same year, "he is inabled to take to the Election 50 Votes." According to another contemporary, the collectorship in 1829 was the most reputable federal post in Delaware.[10]

Numerous claimants sought the post whenever there seemed the chance of a vacancy, even under a Federalist administration.[11] Yet the very numbers of claimants helped defeat their object. "Why," wrote Senator Thomas Clayton in 1825, "cannot the people of Wilmington unite on some one man?"[12] The result was that though many people sought the post one man retained it for thirty-two years.

III   AN OLD CONTINENTAL SOLDIER

The collector of Wilmington was an important figure in the community not only because of the office he held but because of his own character and history. "In the name of God Amen!" he began his will: "I Allen McLane of the Borough of Wilmington in the State of Delaware, Collector of the Customs of the United States for the Delaware District and friend and soldier of the American Revolution."[13]

In a letter ten years before he died, the collector described himself as "an Old Continental Soldier" and told how he and his military comrades "waided through a Seven Years War, waisted our Patrimony and fortunes, and was Disbanded with Broken Constitutions and broken hearts, returned to our famillies to waid through the vile mire of Dependence, [the] Scoff of some and ridicule of Others."[14] Only in its implication of a broken constitution does Allen McLane's statement seem to be untrue. Or, if his constitution was broken, it remained formidable, for he lived to be eighty-two and at that age visited Washington to see the inauguration of his last military idol, Andrew Jackson.

He was certainly an old Continental soldier, the veteran of a hundred skirmishes on land and sea. In a war of seven years he had been in every major engagement and dozens of minor ones from Long Island to Virginia. By his own testimony the war had wasted his patrimony, and after disbandment he had known the pains of dependence as he struggled for a living. Scoff and ridicule had been and were his. When he was in his eighty-second year, a partisan Wilmington newspaper attacked him unmercifully: "What can be more disgusting," asked the editor of this anti-Jackson sheet, "than to see this old dotard [Allen McLane], with one foot in the grave, boring steam-boat passengers with importunities to hear extracts from Wilkinson's [General James Wilkinson's] Memoirs, into which the name of the imbecile old man has by some accident crept." [15]

But scoff and ridicule were not the whole of his reward. "I have," he declared in 1815, "by Industry acquired Houses and lots" worth ten thousand dollars. Though he lived long and made a number of gifts to children and grandchildren, his estate after his death was valued at $5,365.[16]

Nor was his only reward financial. His long life brought him many honors as one of the last surviving officers of the Revolution. He attended fêtes at Yorktown and Richmond in 1824.[17] He dined in Baltimore with other Revolutionary veterans in 1826.[18] When Lafayette revisited America in 1824 and came on his triumphal progress to the boundaries of Delaware, there, at the head of the welcoming committee, according to Lafayette's secretary, "General Lafayette recognized with pleasure Captain McLane, who commanded with great intrepidity under his orders, a company of partizans during the campaign of Virginia, and who at this time in spite of his 80 years of age, came to receive him on horseback, wearing the revolutionary hat and feather." When, in the next year, Lafayette toured the battlefield of Brandywine, where he had been wounded, his escort was led by the oldest Revolutionary veterans of the area, of whom one was "Colonel McLean." [19]

Of all the joys of pride that Allen McLane experienced toward the close of his life, the greatest, unquestionably, arose from the repute of one of his sons, "the never-enough-to-be-admired" Louis, whom he had named for the King of France out of a soldier's gratitude to an ally.[20] For Louis, by the time of his father's death, had been a Representative, was a Senator, and perhaps the highest post of all was not beyond him.

John Quincy Adams heard the story of Louis's naming but thought it was for the King of France's son, not the King himself, that Louis McLane was named. So "Louis the Dauphin" Adams called him, and he intensely hated the rising young man.[21] However his name originated, "the Dauphin" was a good title. Louis McLane was, his father hoped, to succeed him in the reputation and eminence the old man had gained through a hundred battles in nearly a hundred years.

IV   ANCESTORS

The best prospect in Scotland, said Dr. Samuel Johnson, in crushing retort to Boswell, is the road to London. Had Dr. Johnson been less unfriendly to America, he might have admitted that the road to the New World also offered the eighteenth-century Scot a bright prospect. It was this prospect, undoubtedly, that drew the McLanes to America from the bleak soil of the Inner Hebrides.

For the McLanes were Highlanders, members of the Clan Maclean that based its strength on the islands of Mull and Coll. The collector's father is said to have been born Allan Maclean on Coll or Mull in about 1719,[22] but whatever the ancestral spelling of his name, he signed it Allen McLeane when he made out his will in 1775, a year before he died.[23] By family legend he migrated first to the Isle of Man, then to Ireland, and then to America in 1740 or a few years earlier.[24] With him came an older brother Neil—Neil was the third son and Allen the fourth, apparently— but Neil returned to Scotland.

Whether he came from Ireland or directly from Scotland, it was not strange that Allen McLeane settled in Philadelphia, for Philadelphia was a major entry port for Scottish immigrants in the eighteenth century. Great numbers of them went westward, to take up land in the valleys at the foot of the Appalachians, but Allen McLeane married a girl from the Falls of the Schuylkill, Jane Erwin, daughter of Samuel Erwin, a Scotch-Irish immigrant farmer, and stayed to practice his trade of skinner and leather-breeches maker near the colonial metropolis. Allen and Jane had at least three children. The youngest, a daughter, Anne, born in 1754, married Isaac Lewis, a lawyer of Philadelphia. The other two children were boys, Allen and Samuel.[25]

Both boys learned the trade of their father, but Samuel the middle child, born in 1750, seems to have followed it consistently. He lived in Philadelphia, where he was an officer in the militia, but like his brother he married a Kent County girl. Elizabeth Miller McLane was the daughter of a Presbyterian minister and sister of a distinguished physician (Dr. Edward Miller) and a distinguished scholar (the Reverend Samuel Miller). It was generally thought that Samuel McLane had married above his station.[26]

A family legend declares that the elder brother changed the spelling of his name to Allen McLane during the Revolution, in order to avoid any chance of confusion with the British Colonel Sir Allan Maclean.[27] This distinguished officer played a major role in saving Canada from the American invasion of 1775; to the collector he was a renegade Scot serving a Hanoverian usurper.[28] Although this story fits Allen McLane's character (and from this point the spelling of his name that he adopted and consistently used will be employed), some change in the spelling had probably occurred already. Samuel, in 1768, signed his name McClane, but eventually accepted McLane as the spelling. Many other variants of the Scottish name—McClean, McClain, and McLain, for example—were used in America, but Allen McLane clung to this spelling of his name, though otherwise his spelling was, if still original, quite inconsistent. His descendants retained the last name as he passed it on, but they changed the spelling of the first name to Allan, and thus the name appears on this McLane's gravestone in Asbury churchyard, Wilmington.

V PHILADELPHIA TO DUCK CREEK

Allen McLane was born in or near Philadelphia on August 8, 1746.[29] By his own testimony he visited Europe when he was twenty-one and returned to settle in the Lower Counties [30]—that is, the three counties lying below Pennsylvania on the Delaware River, counties that were added to William Penn's American property in 1682 by the Duke of York. Though Penn desired to merge them with his province in one government, they strongly protested against a merger with rapidly growing Quaker Pennsylvania because it would leave them in a minority position; and Penn reluctantly granted them their separate assembly in 1704. Still, one governor served both colonies, and their political connection supplemented by their geographical and economic propinquity on the Delaware encouraged a population flow back and forth between them.

It was not unusual for a young Philadelphia artisan to move to the rich and neighboring rural county of Kent, where fertile wheat fields were augmenting the wealth of Dickinsons and Rodneys and Chews. Nor, since Allen McLane was a demonstrably bold fellow in other sorts of business, was it odd that this newcomer should court and marry Rebecca, the young second daughter of the sheriff of Kent, James Wells.[31]

Though in terms of money and education, Allen was probably as well off as his bride's family, Scots and Scotch-Irish were looked down upon in the Lower Counties as pushing newcomers, and perhaps there were those who thought Rebecca Wells demeaned herself by her marriage. The Wells family had long been settled in Kent County, where it was, however, not much different from Allen McLane and his parents in its economic status. Before 1767, when James Wells was elected sheriff, he is mentioned in Kent County records as an innkeeper at Dover.[32]

At about the time of his wedding, which was January 1, 1770, Allen settled at Duck Creek Cross Roads, now Smyrna, a small market town at the northern edge of Kent County in a rich agricultural region. Annually Duck Creek shipped forty thousand bushels of corn and wheat, plus barley and lumber, to Philadelphia, New York, Boston, and the Wilmington area in the years Allen McLane settled there. Residents called the little stream a "bold and . . . valuable water," but bars of sand and silt that greatly hindered navigation were constantly forming near its junction with the Delaware.[33]

Duck Creek was not only a center of trade in the late eighteenth century but also a center of religious ferment. Most of the people of the area were Anglicans, but a shortage of clergy left them unchurched until Methodist preachers arrived in the 1770's to take up the slack. The greatest of the Methodist missionaries, Francis Asbury, spent more time in Kent County than anywhere else, finding the people "attentive and affected, so that, although they are rude and unpolished, yet God is able, even of these unseemly stones, to raise up children unto Abraham." [34] Duck Creek became an early Methodist stronghold, the site of many of the annual meetings of the Philadelphia Methodist Conference.[35] Here, in 1773, Rebecca Wells McLane, in Allen's words, "Joined the Religious Sect Denominated Methodist Episcopal Christian Church." [36]

Through her Methodism we have one of our rare pictures of the historically elusive Rebecca and her family. Mrs. Freeborn Garrettson, sister of Robert and Edward Livingston and wife of a famous American Methodist itinerant, tells of coming to a quarterly meeting at the "little village" of Duck Creek and of lodging there with the McLanes. "A long table," she wrote, "was set and elegantly spread with every thing you could wish. The lady received and welcomed us with the affection and tenderness of a sister. She appeared to be around six or seven and thirty, and very interesting. I found in her one of those persons to whom my spirit became united at first sight." [37]

If Mrs. Garrettson gauges the age of Rebecca McLane correctly, she cannot have been more than fifteen when Allen married her, for this visit took place some time between 1793 and 1797. And it would be astonishing to find that Rebecca looked much less than her real age, for her life had been filled with tragedy. "She told me," Mrs. Garrettson's account continues, "she had been the Mother of 14 children, three of whom only survived. But oh she said, I had a dear and only Brother, and if ever I prayed for myself, I prayed for him, but alas he is gone—he took away his own life," and while Mrs. McLane was telling the story, both ladies dissolved into tears.

When Rebecca McLane recovered, she continued, "Oh, said she, my dear Mrs. Garrettson, my affliction was so great that I had almost lost my confidence, I was almost overwhelmed. And my poor afflicted Mother —he was her darling, a more dutiful child never lived."

Mrs. Garrettson visited Rebecca's mother, who apparently lived not with her daughter but nearby. She "found her dressed, sitting in a chair with a fan in her poor withered hand of the use of which she was entirely deprived as well as of her feet, by the injudicious treatment of an ignorant physician." While Mrs. Garrettson sat by her, Mrs. Wells told "a tale of sorrow and her fan was frequently raised to her face to hide her tears. Mr. Asbery, said she, was with me this morning—his prayer and his advice I hope never to forget."

The next day Mrs. Garrettson called on both Rebecca McLane and her mother to say farewell. The "afflicted old lady . . . wept on my bosom, . . . thanking me a thousand times," the caller wrote. "I almost tore myself from her. With my heart greatly softened I returned to dear Mrs. McLane—she threw her arms about my neck and in a flood of tears cried out, I do love you most affectionately."

Mrs. Garrettson and her husband were both deeply moved as they left Smyrna and drove off to Dover. "It was almost too much," she wrote in closing her account, the most intimate view we have of the family into which Allen McLane married.[38]

VI   THE SUFFERING LIFE

It seems likely that his wife's piety led Allen McLane to join the Methodists, though his adherence was not constant. In 1786 he gave the Methodists a lot in Smyrna for the construction of Asbury Church,[39] and at about this same time he was an active sponsor of the construction of a Methodist college, called Cokesbury—for Thomas Coke and Francis Asbury—at Abingdon, in Harford County, Maryland. When John Dickinson made a gift to this college, McLane was one of the trustees to administer it.[40]

In moving from Smyrna to Wilmington in 1797, Allen left a Methodist stronghold for a city in which the Methodists were a small and contemptuously treated minority. The forty-nine white and thirty-two black Methodists were tormented by "sons of Belial" who surrounded the church during evening meetings and raised such commotion that women feared to attend.[41] A committee of three members, including Allen McLane and his son-in-law, Edward Worrell, inserted a note in the Wilmington paper on September 24, 1800, to the effect that legal measures would be taken against offenders if "the infidel rabble" continued to disturb Methodist worship by such antics as "breaking the windows, stoning the preachers, [and] casting nauseous reptiles, insects, and other filth in at the windows among the female part of the congregation."[42]

As his position on this committee might indicate, Allen McLane was the leading member of the Wilmington Methodist society. Francis Asbury, for whom the church was named, stayed with him when he came to Wilmington, at least as long as the collector's wife lived.[43] He baptized the collector's sons, and then in time he baptized their firstborn, old Allen's grandsons. "These people," Asbury wrote in his journal, "have not forgotten the holy living and dying of their mother, nor her early and constant friend, the writer of this journal." [44]

It was Rebecca Wells surely who was the strong support of religion in the McLane home. After her death on May 11, 1807, the religious ties of the McLanes seem clearly weakened. "She lived the Suffering life of a . . . Christian," the collector noted in his Bible; "[and] died in the faith, praising God." But he could not refrain from adding another note: "[She] was interd in the Methodist Church Graound, [where] he Erected a tom[b] stone of Marble that cost 350 dollars—to her memory."

Before Rebecca died, Allen must have broken with the Methodists for a time. One of their sons told of the family's attending "a celebrated Camp Meeting" near Dover in July, 1806. Over three hundred tents were erected to house about seven thousand people, and half as many more rode in from the neighborhood each evening. The emotional atmosphere must have deeply affected the ardent old collector, but his son gave no indication of being moved by the scene. "Doctor Chandler," he wrote, "presided, and when I left them on Sunday night at 12 o Clock, he had recruited (as he termed it) 843 new soldiers and promoted 325 old ones: e.i. there had been 843 persons *converted* and 325 sanctifyed!!! Father and Mother were both there, and from Fathers conduct there, I believe he will once more become a member of the methodist connection!" [45] Fortunately, we know more precisely what the collector's conduct was like from the reminiscences of one of the ministers: Allen McLane "was there on his knees wrestling with the Angel of the Covenant, with tears rolling down his cheeks for a clean heart, and he was made pure in heart and enabled to see God." [46]

VII   THE PARTISAN LEADER

"Friend and soldier of the American Revolution," is the way Allen McLane described himself in his will, written thirty-eight years after the Revolution was over. He could not, of course, forget this great event of his life. Otherwise, his was essentially a modest career, though punctuated, because of his impetuosity, with some stormy scenes.

When the Revolutionary War began, Allen McLane and his young wife were living at Duck Creek Cross Roads, where he had bought five acres of land in 1772 and was plying his trade as a leather-breeches maker.[47] At the call of Congress, seventy-one out of eighty male residents formed a military association, among them McLane, who armed himself at his own expense.[48] In September, 1775, he was appointed lieutenant and adjutant of a "Battalion of Foot Militia" raised in northern Kent County, but in October he set out for Virginia with a note from his commanding officer, Caesar Rodney, identifying him as "a warm friend to American Liberty." [49]

His first battle was at Great Bridge, outside Norfolk, on January 1, 1776. For the next several years there were few major actions he missed. He was in the Battle of Long Island as a volunteer with the Pennsylvania infantry.[50] In the following campaign he fought in the engagements at White Plains, Trenton, and Princeton. His greatest fame, the foundation of his legendary reputation, was won as a commander of partisan troops, foot and horse, some of them Indians, operating around Philadelphia just outside the British lines in 1777 and 1778. So closely did he scout the enemy that in June, 1778, when at last they left Philadelphia, he was in the city before they cleared it and captured a laggard captain and forty men at Dock Street bridge. Since his mother's family came from the Falls of Schuylkill, Allen McLane was well acquainted with the terrain where tales of his derring-do in fifty-some engagements are almost endless.[51] A remarkable escape from British dragoons was memorialized on canvas by James Peale.[52] At least two historical novelists have used Allen McLane as a swashbuckling character in their fiction.[53] Anecdotes about his adventures that circulated widely may have been elaborated in an old veteran's memory, but the basic character of the rough, tough captain seems true.

A characteristic story has McLane addressing his men during the hardships of the Valley Forge winter: "Fellow soldiers!" he is said to have harangued them, "you have served your country faithfully and truly. We have fought hard fights together against a hard enemy. You are in a bad way for comfortable clothes, and it almost makes me cry to see you tracking your half-frozen, bloody feet on the cold, icy ground. But Congress can't help it, nor can I. Now if any of you want to return home, to leave the army at such a time as this, you can go. Let those who would like to go step out four paces in front—but the first man that steps out, if I don't *shoot him* my name is not McLane!" [54]

From 1778 to 1781, McLane served, intermittently, on the siege lines outside New York, much as he had earlier near Philadelphia. His most famous adventures while on this duty were at Stony Point and Paulus Hook (Jersey City), British strongholds on the west shore of the Hudson, where McLane's skillful reconnaissances led to the success of bold assaults.[55]

For a time he was attached to Morgan's riflemen; in 1778 he accompanied John Sullivan's expedition against the Iroquois as far as Sunbury; in the fall of 1780 he was with Baron von Steuben and the Marquis de Lafayette in Virginia; in 1781 he was at Yorktown. In his record there was even a naval interlude, for in 1781 he sailed to Haiti as commander

Allen McLane's escape from British dragoons. Oil, by James Peale. *Photograph courtesy of Frick Art Reference Library.*

Allen McLane, 1746–1829. Oil, attributed to Charles Willson Peale. Maryland Historical Society. *Photograph courtesy of Frick Art Reference Library.*

of marines on the privateer *Congress*. At Cap François he informed Admiral de Grasse of Washington's situation, and on the way home participated in a four-hour engagement as the *Congress* captured a British sloop.[56]

Even when McLane left the battlefields for rest or recruiting, he was likely to get into a fight. For instance, he aided in the defense of four British barges that John Barry had captured and run ashore at Port Penn, Delaware, in the winter of 1777–78.[57] In October, 1779, he was in the center of the so-called battle of Fort Wilson, caught in James Wilson's house in Philadelphia when it was attacked by a mob blaming merchants and lawyers for skyrocketing prices.[58] And even when he retired to Duck Creek, at the war's end, McLane took up his musket and joined some neighbors in repelling a Tory captain who had sailed up the creek and seized two shallops loaded with wheat. He ended the war as he began it, a volunteer militiaman.[59]

Nor had he advanced far in rank, considering the length, the quality, and the reputation of his service. He was commissioned a captain in January, 1777, and so he remained till his retirement, when he was made brevet major, an honorific title. Though most writers refer to him as "colonel," this rank was not truly his until 1794, when he was appointed lieutenant colonel in the Delaware militia.[60]

His slow advance in rank was a sore point with McLane. The circumstances that allowed him opportunity for daring adventures and independent action also worked against his promotion. He commanded small partisan companies, unattached or but informally attached to larger units, and Washington opposed any enlargement of such independent forces as would have opened the way to advancement. At one time McLane's company was attached to the Delaware regiment, but the regimental officers objected to the introduction of a veteran captain into their organization because his claims to promotion would interfere with the ambitions of their deserving juniors, who had already been denied promotion because the regiment was small. He was then transferred to Light-Horse Harry Lee's legion, a very unhappy assignment for McLane.[61]

McLane and Lee had quarreled over Lee's gambling when they were collecting provisions on the Delmarva Peninsula, and though Lee may have forgotten the incident, McLane had not.[62] It probably rankled McLane that Lee, ten years his junior, outranked him and was wealthier, better educated, and of a higher social standing than he. The greatest immediate difficulty was the loss of freedom of action. With Lee there would be a sufficiency of action, but McLane would be fighting Lee's battles, taking Lee's orders, enhancing Lee's fame. The situation was not made easier by the character of Lee, who was brave, daring, and intelligent, but unstable, a gambler and dreamer whose life became a bitter tragedy that led to self-imposed exile.

In 1780 McLane appealed to Pennsylvania to "comprehend" him in its establishment, explaining that though he had entered the army when living in Delaware he was now a Pennsylvanian again, having sold his property in Delaware and moved to Philadelphia after that city was evacuated by the British. And though attached to Lee's legion, he was the only officer in it not provided for by some state.[63]

Pennsylvania was no more eager than Delaware to make room for McLane in its table of organization. He was a veteran officer with a good record, he was eager for a promotion that he deserved, but these states were unable to gratify the wishes of all the good officers to whom they were already committed.

A direct appeal to General Washington for promotion, addressed through Lee, had already failed.[64] Hope bloomed briefly when Congress and the Board of War authorized enlargement of Lee's infantry. However, Washington, angered at this enlargement of an independent legion without his approval, again turned down the promotions Lee proposed, including McLane's.

When a New York Congressman wrote on McLane's behalf, Washington made it clear that he had a high opinion of McLane and that his opposition was chiefly to the promotion of a young legionary, whose advancement Lee could be counted on to press if McLane were promoted. And though McLane was deserving, there were hundreds of captains who were senior to him.[65]

After Yorktown, McLane turned to the Virginia government for some compensation as a retired officer of Lee's legion, but he found that Henry Lee had settled the legion's accounts with Virginia without making any claim for him. The half pay received from Congress was of so little value that he agreed in 1783 to give it up in return for five years' pay in full, trusting that this arrangement would serve to set him up securely in the commission business. He bartered his commutation certificates (which represented the five years' pay due to him) for merchandise to stock a store in Duck Creek, and more money soon went after the first. In 1784 he received a final repayment for money advanced in recruiting troops and an allowance for pay depreciation—a total sum of $2,945, which was not, he declared, worth more than $300 in specie, less than his expenses in getting the settlement. In 1785 he received a warrant for "300 Acres of Land on the moon which he sold to two Specks . . . for 90 dollars." [66]

At Duck Creek, in Kent County, Allen McLane found that no automatic preference was accorded him because of his Revolutionary activity. In a private letter of 1785 a native of Kent County spoke of "the hard struggles the revolutionists have had to support their measures in this country" (meaning Delaware) and insisted that "they must have even yielded to superior numbers, had not the tide of the continent swept them along." [67] No wonder that McLane found the people not disposed to trade with "an old Revolutionary Charactor." He was even sued for seizure of horses and provisions while patrolling the enemy lines at Philadelphia but appealed to Washington and received a letter explaining that he had been ordered "to stop all improper intercourse between the City and Country and to seize supplies of every kind." "To the best of my knowledge," Washington wrote, "Capt. McLane made no improper use of the power with which he was vested." [68]

VIII   IN POLITICS

Despite such troubles, McLane persisted with his business. He imported rum and sheeting and sugar. He exported corn and wheat and other country produce. And he met various vexations: his vessels—shallow-draft sloops, shallops, that brought his goods from Philadelphia—were caught in the ice; his debtors were slow to pay; proper storage space was wanting or expensive; crops failed and ruined his market.[69]

Yet, or perhaps because of such troubles, he found time for politics. Men of Scottish stock in Delaware generally did. The Scots (most frequently they were Scotch-Irish) were such active politicians that Delaware politics often seemed to be a battle between them and the English. Since most of the former were Presbyterians and the latter, before the Revolution, Anglicans, the contest could also be described as one between the Presbyterian party and the Church party. Neither term was quite correct. Some Presbyterians and some Anglicans would be found in each of the opposing political factions at every election—but the bulk of the Presbyterians were on the opposite side from the bulk of the Anglicans. Partly this was so because the Anglicans represented an older group of settlers, those who had been in this colony through several generations. The Scotch-Irish, on the other hand, were the main immigrant group of the mid-eighteenth century. Because they understood the language when they arrived and because they often, indeed usually, were better educated than natives of America, they were able to profit from their interest in public affairs and push forward into prominent positions.

Since many of these exiles from Ireland bore with them to America deep grievances against the English government, they were particularly inclined to support revolution against the status quo. Native Delaware Anglicans, on the other hand, little disturbed by English rule, almost unfettered by English control, enjoying self-government without even a resident English governor, were not so quick to see the virtues of revolution, not so sudden to take a rebel side in any crisis.

These were the tendencies to be observed in political alignments, not the rules. And the alignments could switch any day or month or year, for there were no organized parties. Factions there were, cliques that fought each other for offices and power. Before the Revolution the Court party was the faction in office, and the Country party sought to take its place. Since the Anglicans had been dominant, the Court party was also the Church party. Since the immigrants were seeking power, the Country party was also the Irish party. And in their attitude to revolutionary effort to secure independence, the Anglicans of Delaware were apt to pause, to hesitate, to favor conciliation, to play a conservative role; whereas the Irish Presbyterians breathed blood and thunder, sought a hasty severance of connections, and seemed quite radical in their zeal.[70]

It was natural that Allen McLane, a newcomer to Delaware of Scottish descent and Revolutionary ardor, should enter politics with the Country faction, the Presbyterians, the radicals. A legislature controlled by this faction made him a justice of the peace in June, 1785, and in the fall of that year he won election to the house of assembly, the lower chamber of the legislature. For a newcomer to Delaware he won election astonishingly easily, polling 688 out of a total of approximately 1,100 votes and standing third among the list of seven assemblymen chosen by the county-wide balloting.[71] If Tories were as numerous in Delaware as was claimed and if "an old Revolutionary Charactor" was boycotted by them to the extent that he believed, McLane could hardly have done so well at the election. He outpolled John Patten, another Revolutionary figure, a former lieutenant colonel of the Delaware regiment. Patten, who stood sixth among the victorious candidates for the house of assembly, was later to become the first Republican Congressman from Delaware. And McLane outpolled Dr. James Tilton, an outspoken Dover physician who was already a member of the Continental Congress.

One political post led to another. McLane was not reelected to the legislature in 1786; records do not show whether he was a candidate, but it was a year of conservative victory. In November, 1787, however, he was chosen by his county as delegate to the state convention that was to consider adoption of the federal Constitution. The convention met in Dover, Monday, December 3, and unanimously ratified the federal Constitution at the end of the week. This action made Delaware the first state to ratify the Constitution.[72]

In the next year, 1788, the legislature elected Allen McLane to the privy council, an elected body of four men with terms of three years who served as a collective constitutional guardian upon the actions of the chief executive, called the president. Early in 1789, in the election of Representatives to the first Congress of the United States under the new Constitution, Allen McLane received a sizable number of votes, 90, in New Castle County. The number of votes he got was remarkable because it placed him second in the poll, the top man in New Castle having only 162 votes, and also because McLane did not reside in New Castle.[73] In 1791, McLane was back in the legislature, again a representative from Kent, and when the new legislature met, he was elected speaker of the lower house.

His election to preside over the house of assembly signaled McLane's change of alignment in Delaware politics. In 1785 McLane had been elected to the assembly by the votes of the Country party; now in 1791 he was returned by the Court party, which had dominated Kent County for the last few years. None of the Kent County delegates elected with him to the assembly in 1785 were his colleagues in the convention of 1787 or the assembly of 1791. The anti-Presbyterian Court party's sway in Kent was so complete that in 1794 a Republican complained that no Presbyterian had been chosen to the legislature from Kent for nine years —or since 1785.[74]

In 1804, a Revolutionary veteran jealous of Allen McLane's political standing attempted to explain it. After the Revolution, he said, George Read, a New Castle lawyer who was the dominant figure in Delaware politics, decided he would have to get all the Tory votes to maintain control of the state. The Tories, said the writer, would naturally be on Read's side politically, but they were disfranchised by a Revolutionary law called the Test Act, which demanded from each voter an oath that he would support the Revolution. All those who refused to take it— Loyalists and neutrals—were disfranchised.

Knowing that these disfranchised voters were in a 3-to-1 majority in Kent and Sussex counties, and nearly equal to the rebels in the third Delaware county, Read got the Test Act repealed, and then, to put the best face on affairs, appointed three Revolutionary veterans to head the Tories of each county at the next election: his brother-in-law, Lieutenant Colonel Gunning Bedford, in New Castle; Captain McLane in Kent; and a Captain Nathaniel Mitchell in Sussex. The Tories rallied so well to Read's party, this calumniator goes on, that at the next election they produced more votes than there were eligible voters in Kent and Sussex. Of course, they won the legislature, and "by this Great Majority of Torys on the Legislator they Where enabled to do What they Pleased, and thier first Act was to Appoint McLain Thier Spaker and Counsler to the Govener. . . ." In these offices McLane "rigidly obayed" the orders of

Read "and would not suffer a Singel Officer of the late Regement or a Wig to fill any office in this State, but assisted his Master to persicute them. . . ." Perhaps the worst charge this enemy leveled at McLane was not intended to be so critical: McLane cannot write well, he complained, "and altho Some of Us are not Good Clerks, yet any of Us are eaquel to Mr. McLain." [75]

The story that George Read picked him as a Kent County leader is, at its best, too simple to explain McLane's politics. Read was an intelligent and able politician who would see the obvious advantages of having a man of Scottish name and Revolutionary record to bolster a party that generally lost the votes of the Scots and the veterans. But other factors existed to throw McLane into Read's arms. Probably McLane's marriage was a factor. McLane's father-in-law was a sheriff, which suggests that he was a member of the Court party. Delawareans inherited their politics as they did their religion, and the Wells family, though only in-laws, were the closest Delaware relations that Allen had.

We can speak more definitely of the influence of religion than that of family on Allen McLane's politics. He was a Methodist, and all of the leading Methodists in Delaware became Federalists. The Federalists in Delaware were the English party, the Church party, as opposed to the Scotch-Irish or Presbyterian party. Delaware Methodists were largely of English stock and former Anglicans. In Delaware early Methodism, though an offshoot of Anglicanism, had arisen in harmony with the old church. Anglicans and Methodists, remaining friendly, both looked with some disfavor on the immigrant Presbyterians.

Furthermore, Delaware Federalists developed from the moderate or conservative party, the party that was the less vigorous in support of measures for independence or measures tending to upset the status quo ante bellum. Their opponents were the more ardently Revolutionary party, the more radical in respect to the issues of independence. The early Methodist preachers were Englishmen who remained loyal to their King, to whose constitutional system John Wesley himself had counseled obedience. Delaware Methodists tended to be neutral or lukewarm in their attitude toward the Revolution, and they found the Court party, the Federalists that were to be, the more sympathetic to their position. Allen McLane was lukewarm in neither politics nor religion, but when the Revolution was over, his religion helped draw him into a political alignment that his Revolutionary record made unexpected.

Most of the veteran officers of Delaware, and particularly the veteran officers of the famous Delaware regiment, became active in the party opposing the Federalists, the Republican party. John Patten, a Revolutionary major and once McLane's commanding officer, was the first Republican Congressman from Delaware; Colonel David Hall was the first Republican governor; Caesar Augustus Rodney, son of Captain Thomas Rodney, was the first Republican Senator. The first president of the Delaware Cincinnati, the society composed of officers of the Revolutionary army, was Dr. James Tilton, the violent Republican who wrote a scurrilous biography of the Federalist leader George Read. When Tilton resigned the office, he was succeeded by John Patten, who retained it till the Delaware society became defunct in approximately 1800.

The Republican sympathies of the Delaware officers, many of them Presbyterians, are obvious: at a July 4 banquet in 1796, the Cincinnati toasted the French Republic, the Dutch Republic, "the patriots of Ireland," equality, and "the extinction of Monarchy in essence as well as in name." [76] Federalist celebrants would not have been likely to offer any of these toasts. How McLane behaved at these meetings, if he attended them, we may wonder. He was a member of the Cincinnati, and, after the Delaware society's collapse, he transferred his membership to Pennsylvania, where he probably found the order more Federalist in tone.

McLane had little reason to feel any close kinship to the officers of the Delaware regiment. They had never been very friendly to him. His company had been allied to the Delaware regiment for a very brief period only, and even that brief association seems to have been against the wishes of the Delaware officers. When Allen McLane called upon old comrades to certify to his Revolutionary exploits, it was usually men from other states upon whom he called.

If various factors led Allen McLane to the Federalist party, it is clear that he clung to the party and offered it his service and that of his son because it served him well. In 1789, at the organization of the new government, he received an appointment from President Washington as marshal of the District of Delaware, district being the name given to the area of jurisdiction of a federal judge, which in most cases in 1789 was a whole state—and so it was in Delaware.[77] This office brought McLane only a small revenue—$86.34 in the year ending October 1, 1792—but it did not demand his full time; he did not need to abandon either his business in Smyrna or his home.[78]

Besides his commission business and his federal appointment, Allen McLane found time for other activities. He continued to serve as a justice of the peace, and earned some money through the fees falling to that office.[79] He served as a militia officer in Kent County, commanding the fourth militia regiment till he moved to Wilmington to assume the collectorship. He was an early member and in 1803 became president of the leading Delaware abolition society.[80]

IX   THE MC LANE HERITAGE

Most of their fourteen children were born while the McLanes lived in Smyrna. The firstborn was James Allen McLane, who died in April, 1773, and was buried in the old Presbyterian graveyard at Duck Creek.[81] Then there followed in fairly rapid succession Anne, Jane, Elizabeth, Rebecca, Louis, Samuel, a second Louis (the first having died), Mary, John, a second Anne, Allen, a second Mary, and "Betsy," who was probably a second Elizabeth.[82]

There were many heartaches in the McLane household as eleven of these children died in infancy. The only children to survive were Rebecca, the second Louis, and Allen. Rebecca was the oldest of the three, born in February, 1779, in Dover, which had been Mrs. McLane's home. She remains a rather faint figure in the background of the McLane story, rarely mentioned, never described. She was married before she was seventeen, in January, 1796, to Edward Worrell, and by him she had at least five children: George Washington (a proper name for the first grandchild of a Revolutionary veteran), Edward, Rebecca, Elizabeth, and Priscilla.

Edward Worrell, Rebecca's husband, became a man of some prominence in Wilmington, Delaware. Perhaps he moved there with his father-in-law. At any rate, we know he was employed by Allen McLane in the customs house and that he was also an active member of the Methodist church. In 1810 he became cashier of the Bank of Delaware, the oldest bank in Wilmington and in the state, and he held this position till he died in 1830.[83]

Poor Rebecca McLane Worrell became an invalid, and her trouble was such that the McLanes preferred never to mention it. Letters of her brother Louis note an early illness and indicate she made a complete recovery by December, 1805.[84] In April, 1815, however, she was admitted as a paying patient to the Pennsylvania Hospital in Philadelphia, and her trouble was diagnosed in the hospital records as "insanity." Her father conveyed property to his oldest grandson in trust for Rebecca, and when her husband made his will in 1829, he provided a trust for her under the care of the managers of the Pennsylvania Hospital.[85] Rebecca did not die until 1851, but there is scarcely a reference to her in the surviving correspondence of her brothers, nephews, and nieces.

The youngest of Captain McLane's children, another Allen, also suffered from invalidism of a sort. Though he received a good education, married well—in the usual meaning of the term—and was admitted to a respectable profession, the practice of medicine, at which he seems to have had real ability, and though he showed considerable vigor both in politics and business, he was, in worldly terms, a failure. Again and again he lost his practice, in politics he never rose far, his finances were frequently in a precarious state, and his boys, once they attained maturity, sought new homes in the West. Drink was Dr. Allen's curse, surviving records indicate, the crippling influence that kept his various endeavors from being successful.

The older of Captain McLane's sons, the middle of the three surviving children, was Louis, who was born in Smyrna on May 28, 1784, a date often given incorrectly in reference books as 1786.[86] Neither his brother's curse nor his sister's seems to have affected him. Various complaints beset him all his days, and although he felt he was doomed to an early death, he lived an active, responsible life, and died at the age of seventy-three. His life was a responsible one not only because of the weighty positions he filled—Representative, Senator, minister to England, bank president, railroad president, Secretary of the Treasury, Secretary of State—but because of the family he reared—thirteen children, of whom twelve lived to adulthood, with a number proving to be of remarkable vigor and acuteness of body and of mind. One of his sons became a Congressman, a governor, and a diplomat—minister to China, Mexico, and France. A second became president of the greatest express company and one of the greatest banks in the West—Wells, Fargo and Company and the Bank of Nevada. A third son became the president of the premier American steamboat company in the Pacific—the Pacific Mail Steamship Company. Two other sons won a measure of distinction, and several of the daughters married or begot distinguished men—one son-in-law was General Joseph E. Johnston, and a grandson was Dr. Allan McLane Hamilton, called "the alienist," a precursor of the psychiatrist.

From his father and perhaps also remoter ancestors among the Hebridean McLanes or the more obscure Erwins or Wellses, Louis did inherit a choleric temper, a vigorous spirit, and an ardent ambition. Probably it was less a matter of biological inheritance than of environmental influence, for Captain Allen would have provided lessons in pugnacious quarrelsomeness enough for several sons. Louis was not born at the time of his father's daring and often obstreperous feats in the Revolution, but tales of them were familiar to Louis from his boyhood. He was reared amid business and political quarrels, and in his teens his father was embroiled in patronage struggles and tax suits growing out of his official position.

To stories of Allen's Revolutionary ardor were added accounts of recent exploits. There was the tale James Bayard told Richard Bassett, of how Allen McLane was visiting in the House of Representatives in the winter of 1798, when Representative Roger Griswold, a Federalist, caned Representative Matthew Lyon, a stormy Vermonter, while General Daniel Morgan, another Federalist, prevented interference. A man standing beside McLane wanted to go to Lyon's aid, but McLane stopped him. "Some words ensued, and the fellow told Allen, he would spit in his face. Allen demanded his name and place of abode. The man gave his name and said he lived over the mountains. Well Sir, said Allen, I tell you if you spit in my face you will never go over the mountains again. Allen was highly enraged and he told me since that if the fellow had spit on him, he would have killed him on the spot." [87]

With such a father, it is not surprising that little of his mother's meek Methodist resignation rubbed off on Louis McLane. But if his father's pugnacity and quick-triggered pride were unhappy inheritances, the fighting spirit, the grit and determination that came with them, served Louis well. So did the physical resilience that carried him through wearing positions and trying situations, not without illnesses, for he had many, but with the strength to survive illness, travel, worry, and responsibility and live to seventy-three.

And there were many more elements of value in the heritage of Louis McLane from his father. There was, for one, the Federalist party. Allen was an ardent, a vigorous, even a furious Federalist, and his services to the party gave his son a claim upon it. In any other state it would have been of doubtful value for a young man reaching the age of maturity as late as 1805 to have a claim for the support of the Federalist party. Not so in Delaware. This was the Federalist state paramount, and for decades to come the Federalists, under their own or other names, would control its politics and its offices. As a Federalist, Louis McLane won six successive state-wide congressional elections in Delaware between 1816 and 1826. Federalism opened to him the path to Washington and to a national reputation. Had he been reared a Republican in Delaware, his chance of advancement would have been much slighter.

Another element in McLane's heritage, difficult to measure in its political effect, was the Methodist religion of his parents. To be sure, he seems to have felt little of their enthusiasm or their faith; his correspondence gives little hint of his personal views. Louis could be profuse in pious references to the Almighty, but he did not remain religious in any denominational sense. His protestant spirit came to be deeply disturbed when Catholicism entered his family, years later, but one wonders whether he did not find Methodism too crude, whether he did not set it aside with the unexpressed scorn that made him so very careful of the orthography of which his father knew nothing.

If the religious message of Methodism was wasted on Louis, his father's Methodism furthered Louis's career in a practical, worldly way, for as he established himself as a Wilmington lawyer it gave him a corps of rural sympathizers and potential supporters at the polls. It is impossible to say to what extent the Methodists did support Louis. In his campaigns the bulk of his support came not from Wilmington, where he lived, but from Kent and Sussex counties, rural, downstate Delaware. These counties were the home of Methodism, but they were the bulwark of Federalism too. At the least, his father's well-known connection with Asbury and other eminent Methodist preachers, his status as one of the leading Methodist laymen, must have helped Louis get started up the political ladder.

Similarly, Louis's Kent County birth and his maternal relations must have helped his political career, but such help cannot be measured. The fame of his father's Revolutionary military career was a heritage of perceptible value to Louis. In spite of the fact that many Delawareans were Loyalists or neutrals in the war, politicians considered it of great value to have a name on their ticket that brought recollections of heroism in the time of crisis. Four times the Republicans ran Joseph Haslet for governor, apparently not so much for any virtues of his own as because he was his father's son, the son of Delaware's most notable martyr of the Revolution, the colonel who stayed with Washington to fight and meet death at Princeton, although the other members of his regiment, their time expired, had gone home. Caesar Augustus Rodney, another prominent Delaware Republican, was the nephew and namesake of the Revolutionary governor, Caesar Rodney. With John Patten, David Hall, and Caleb Bennett, all veterans, available to the Republicans, the Federalists were particularly glad to have on their ticket a name associated with patriotic military exploits.

Nor did McLane's Scottish name harm his career. On the contrary, it helped him. Even though there was a considerable anti-Scottish and anti-Irish feeling in Delaware, it was prevalent mainly among Federalists, men who would set aside minor prejudices to support their party. In nominating McLane, Federalists were following a maxim of Delaware politics, choosing a candidate who would pull some votes from the opposition. And while the name McLane would draw some Presbyterian votes, its association with Methodism helped hold the votes of the rural English stock.

Another heritage of value rested in old Allen's friends. Three Senators, Richard Bassett, James Bayard, and William Hill Wells, were closely associated with Allen McLane and inclined to oblige his son. Wells may have been distantly related to Louis through his mother. Bassett and the McLanes had Methodist connections, and Bayard, no Methodist, was Bassett's son-in-law and Allen's principal political patron. Through such friends Allen undoubtedly got his son Louis a commission as a midshipman, and then, when the sea turned out not to be the life for Louis, it was in James Bayard's law office that Louis learned his profession.

Not the least advantage Allen was able to bestow on his sons was the substantial property he amassed as collector, particularly in the years after 1797. It enabled him to send the boys to school at the Newark Academy, and the younger one to Princeton College, and to support them in the study of law and medicine. Through his life Allen was able to make a number of substantial gifts to his children and grandchildren, and at his death he left Louis five properties in Wilmington and all his personal estate. With this bequest to Louis came one rather rare and unusual item that was potentially the greatest prize—all his rights and interest in the ships *Good Friends, Amazon,* and *United States,* and their cargoes—these ships being those involved in the litigation called the Amelia Island cases (of which more later). In view of the size of Louis McLane's family and of the small income, in relation to necessary expenditures, allowed by the government to Congressmen, diplomats, and cabinet members, his father's help and promises of future help were of great importance.

Louis McLane may also have derived from his father an acute sense of the closeness of the family circle. Although Allen marched off to war and left his wife to rather slim resources for many years, this action derived from his ardent patriotism, rather than from any want of family responsibility. He seems to have been an affectionate, responsible husband and father, albeit often rough in his ways. And his son Louis was so much his boast that his paternal adulation became a subject for raillery in the community and abroad.[88]

Louis too showed affection and regard for the members of his immediate family circle. He gave his wife the sincere flattery of making her his political confidante. He watched with pride and love the development of his children, and rejoiced in their material successes, though his bad temper cost him some loss of their love. Unlike his father, he possessed both manners and features that were regular and even distinguished, but his interior spirit was rough and fiery and violent, and his anger could not always be repressed even within his family, though here surely his love was centered.

Even the place of his birth was of advantage to Louis McLane. To be of Scottish and English descent, Methodist in religion, Federalist in politics, son of a military hero, and a Wilmington lawyer of downstate birth —this was a formula for success in the politics of the Delaware of McLane's day. Though Louis McLane might move with merchants and manufacturers, such as the millers of the Brandywine, he still had a claim to a rural heritage, to an understanding and fellowship with the rural gentry and yeomanry who were the major and dominant class in Delaware.

His birthplace, though a town, was very modest indeed. The name Duck Creek Cross Roads betrays its rural nature; Smyrna, which it became in 1806, is the mark of its pretensions. The town grew on a tract called "Gravesend," where James Green began selling lots in 1768 because two roads met here. One from a landing on Duck Creek proceeded across the Delmarva Peninsula to the Eastern Shore of Maryland; the other ran from Dover, the county seat, north toward New Castle and Wilmington. Here on four and a half acres of land that Allen McLane, "leather-breeches maker," bought of James Green on January 4, 1772,[89] it is likely that Louis McLane was born twelve years later, and here he lived till his parents moved to Wilmington in 1797.

How the McLane children were educated while the family lived at Smyrna is not known. The village had not more than one hundred houses, and in spite of what the gazetteers call its "brisk trade" with Philadelphia,[90] it had no established school. Perhaps a clergyman supplemented his salary by schoolkeeping; perhaps the McLanes and other families combined to "board around" a hired teacher; perhaps some of the townsmen had "bought" a teacher, for it is said that Kent farmers used to watch for immigrant ships coming up the Delaware, and then ride up to New Castle and buy the indenture of some lettered Scotch-Irishman whom they could put to teaching their children.

X   DUCK CREEK TO WILMINGTON

More problems than his children's education bothered Allen McLane during his residence in Smyrna. His commission business did not prosper as he hoped; his post as marshal brought him many responsibilities "but no profit." Indeed, he complained to Washington, "the office . . . taking all things in to Consideration brings me in Debt. I cannot Get men of integrety to assist me as Deputy marshall if I wont Give them all the fees. . . . I have to neglect all other Concerns to attend to the duties of the office which laies at Extream parts of the State." [91] The "extream parts" of Delaware were, of course, not very far apart, but roads were bad, travel in wet weather could be unpleasant, and the necessity of serving a writ in the southern part of Sussex County or northwestern New Castle could be a most annoying interference with his other business at Smyrna. The compensation for serving any writ, warrant, or attachment was only two dollars, plus five cents a mile for travel.[92] Consequently Allen besought the President to "add some appointment of profit," for which he would be quite willing to move, if necessary even out of Delaware to his native Pennsylvania.[93]

In 1797 the collectorship of customs at Wilmington fell vacant upon the death of George Bush, a Revolutionary veteran. Former Senator Bassett hastily recommended his fellow Methodist, Allen McLane, for the place, and on February 27 President Washington announced the appointment. It was the last service the old general could perform for his partisan captain, for in five days Washington was to retire from the Presidency. And, strangely, it almost amounted to giving McLane a partisan command over again, for it placed him on the front lines of the commercial wars that were to rage through the next fifteen years.

It also forced him to abandon his home and his business in Smyrna. "Wilmington," Washington told McLane, "will be your place of Residence Settled by Law, which I apprehend you will find a more healthy situation than [where] you have resided Since the peace." [94]

The point was well taken. Kent County, where Smyrna was located, was notoriously sickly. In the "inland part," a physician explained, "heat and stagnation occur to exalt the noxious exhalations of our low grounds." So this physician, Dr. James Tilton, like Allen McLane, moved from Kent to Wilmington, which lay, thanks to its hilly surroundings, in "as healthful a district of country as any in America." [95] Allen McLane, with thought of his eleven lost infants, could sigh amen.

And so, as he declared in his memoirs, he sold his livestock at a disadvantage and moved from a sickly climate to a healthy one. His new position took his full time, and he could no longer serve as magistrate and merchant on the side. Indeed, Washington, in his letter announcing the appointment, expressed a kindly personal wish that Allen might find it to his advantage to abandon his other pursuits for the support of his family.[96]

But he could remain active in politics. He had, of course, new powers of patronage. And he also had new obligations to the party and the persons who had provided for his promotion. Allen was vigorous and he was loyal, and his vigor and loyalty were placed at the service of his party at the very time when party strife was becoming more severe than it had ever been before.

If as marshal, McLane had been useful as a despatch carrier through Delaware for the Federalists,[97] repeating in party strife one of his duties in revolutionary war, as customs collector, he was even more useful, for his position by the water made him a natural medium between the Federalist administration upstream in Philadelphia and the party downstream in Delaware. For example, he reported at length to Secretary of State Timothy Pickering on a visit Senator George Logan made to John Dickinson at Wilmington in the fall of 1798. McLane described those who attended a "Jacobin" conference with Logan at Dr. Tilton's house and reported on Logan's statements there. He even noted what Logan had declared in a barbershop. Wilmington was a "hopeless sink of Jacobinism," in McLane's words, but he would at least keep watch on it.[98]

In the 1800 campaign the Federalists were reported to have sent Allen McLane back into Kent County to rouse the people against Jefferson by spreading a report that the Democratic Republicans would, if they won, "drown all the men, women, and children in Kent and Sussex." [99] Like a proper Federalist, Allen McLane subscribed to a set of William Cobbett's heartily pro-English American essays, published in London in 1801 as *Porcupine's Works.*[100] At home, he gave his support to W. C. Smyth, an experienced Wilmington newspaperman, who began a new Federalist paper called the *Monitor* in 1800.[101]

Republicans, of course, reviled both McLane and the *Monitor.* The *Monitor's* editor, Smyth, was called McLane's

> . . . black-letter'd dog,
> Whom he retains, as Codrus does his hog,
> To chew his husks and take his filth away,
> And belch it out again for weekly pay.[102]

Hezekiah Niles, a Delaware Republican who later gained fame for the weekly journal of public affairs he published in Baltimore, declared that McLane was cunning and crafty, "of immense injury to us," with influence, by reason of his office, greater than that of the governor.[103] Another Republican declared that McLane was "the most active and bitter Enemy" to the Jeffersonian party in Delaware; "from the Wealth he had Acquiered by his Numerous offices and the Number of Men he now imploves in his official cappacity, he is enabled to take to the Election 50 Votes Which being always imployed against Us makes a difference of 100 Votes. . . ." [104]

Other enemies sought to belittle his Revolutionary record. The author of a satirical poem, *The Wilmingtoniad,* called McLane "wriggling Hispo" and offered to

> . . . tell the world with what consummate skill,
> He pilfer'd fowls and geese, from Dick and Will,
> With what amazing courage, sword in hand,
> He drove the unarm'd baker from his stand,
> His *oven* storm'd, seiz'd all his pyes and bread,
> And left the scent of brandy in their stead.[105]

Such was their enmity for Allen McLane that it is no wonder the Delaware Republicans expected, and sought, his replacement after Jefferson became President and the national government ceased to be Federalist. The collector held office without term, entirely at the favor of the President, and for that reason Jefferson's approval was soon besought.

Indeed, Jefferson's favor was courted even before he became President. In view of the ardent part McLane had played in the Federalist struggle against Jefferson and the Republicans in 1800 and before, the outcome of the presidential election of that year was sad news for him. Still, the identity of the new President was not certain when the election was over. Jefferson and his running mate, Aaron Burr, were tied, and the choice between them had to be made by the House of Representatives—there being, in these pre-Twelfth Amendment days, no separate ballot for President and Vice-President. Selection between Jefferson and Burr would have been a simple matter had Republicans controlled the House, but they did not. In the election they had won the new House of Representatives, but a President would be chosen by the old lame-duck House that had been elected in 1798 to serve from March 4, 1799, to March of 1801. To complicate matters, the Representatives did not vote as individuals, but as state delegations, each state being allowed one vote.

For a time the Federalists sought to throw the election to Burr, but their best—or worst—efforts succeeded only in preventing Jefferson from getting the necessary majority, and thus prevented any choice. Some Federalist Representatives were satisfied with this or any result that would keep Jefferson from election; others, affected either by Hamilton's advice to prefer Jefferson to Burr or by unwillingness to negate the new Constitution, determined to withdraw their opposition and permit Jefferson's election. Among the latter was James Bayard, whose influence was important because as Delaware's sole Representative, he cast the whole state vote.

But before Bayard acted, he wanted some terms from Jefferson, some assurance that the public credit and the Navy would be maintained, and that subordinate public officers, not involved in policy making, should not be replaced on the ground of their politics. When he approached Samuel Smith of Baltimore, a leading Republican, Bayard specified George Latimer and Allen McLane, customs collectors at Philadelphia and Wilmington respectively, as the officials he wished to protect.[106] Smith, by his own testimony, took the query to Jefferson, and reported back to Bayard that Jefferson thought such officials should not be removed from office for their politics unless they had improperly forced their subordinate officers to vote contrary to their judgment. Furthermore, Major Joseph Eggleston, a Virginian who had served in Lee's legion, had already spoken to Jefferson on McLane's behalf and given him such high character that he would not be displaced.[107]

Jefferson later denied that he ever made any bargain with Bayard during the election, and there is no need to doubt his word. Smith confessed he put Bayard's queries to Jefferson without the latter's being aware of his object. Then he told Bayard what Jefferson had indicated concerning his future conduct, without hinting that he was not an authorized spokesman.[108] For Allen McLane, the result was all the same. Bayard and others had sought to protect him in his post, and Jefferson had decided he was a meritorious officer and should not be removed. "I have direct evidence that Mr. Jefferson will not [remove every official]," Bayard wrote the collector; "I have taken good care of you, and think if prudent, you are safe." [109]

In fact, McLane had already taken care of himself, for it was he who had appealed to Major Eggleston, who in turn had spoken to Jefferson.[110] Once Jefferson was in office the attack on McLane was resumed, but the collector again brought influential men to his defense. He secured a recommendation from the Reverend Samuel Miller, now of New York, but son of a Presbyterian minister in Dover and member of one of the leading Republican families. Miller, who became famous for his voluminous published works, particularly a remarkable *Brief Retrospect of the Eighteenth Century*, was possibly encouraged to support Allen by being a brother-in-law of Allen's brother Samuel. This must not have struck him as of much importance, for he said "I am under no personal obligation to Captn. McLane, nor do I sustain any connection with him." He quickly confessed that Allen had "been a very decided and indeed warm *federalist*." (The emphasis is Miller's.) But yet, "in his present office, he has been, as is acknowledged on all hands, remarkably faithful, active, vigilant, and unwearied; —insomuch that the whole business of the customs, in the port over which he presides, has been on a footing, since he came into office, far more advantageous, than ever before." Therefore Miller supposed it "would subserve the interests of republicanism in Delaware" more to keep him in office than to remove him.[111]

Apparently Jefferson decided to get at the truth of the charges against McLane, and so appointed persons in Delaware to inquire carefully into them. McLane made a very shrewd choice in seeking a lawyer to plead his case; he engaged Caesar Augustus Rodney, the leading spirit in the Delaware Republican party, an able young attorney whose career would be capped by his appointment as Jefferson's Attorney General in 1807.[112]

With help from Eggleston, Bayard, Miller, and Rodney, McLane's collectorship weathered the political gale of 1801. "I was his counsel," Rodney boasted; "the charges were not supported; and so he retained his office." [113]

But the Republican furies turned upon McLane again in 1802. Then the first Republican governor of Delaware, David Hall, a veteran officer of the Delaware regiment that had not accepted McLane, forwarded to Jefferson a petition from Kent County for McLane's removal. "I know of no Character more obnoxious to the republicans of this State than Mr. McLane," declared Governor Hall, "no one who has taken more undue means to crush the republican Interest. . . . A removal of this man from office . . . would . . . be very gratifying to every Republican in the State of Delaware." [114] A Republican nominating convention and the Kent County grand jury supported Hall.[115]

"Oh, that monster envy!" exclaimed McLane, and to demonstrate his integrity he sent another long defense to Gallatin, enclosing endorsements of his military career from some of what he called "the first Military Characters." [116] Jefferson was impressed and declared that since McLane had been acquitted of various charges in 1801, his status would not be questioned officially unless some "new act" were charged against him "inconsistent with his duties as an officer," such as electioneering against the administration.[117]

In 1803 and in 1804 contention over McLane's post broke forth again. Jobs were at the root of the controversy, McLane explained: "Here lays the whole matter. The Collector of the Revenue in this District provides for a Deputy, a temporary Surveyor at New Castle, a temporary Surveyor at Lewis Town, an Inspector at Wilmington, a weigh master, Guager, measurer, etc." McLane's enemies, on the other hand, screamed that Jefferson must be clearly told that the administration was losing elections in Delaware because all the offices, federal and state, were filled by its enemies. But the many administration supporters who hungered for McLane's job only canceled each other out. None of them got it. McLane remained collector for another quarter of a century.[118]

XI   THE EDUCATION OF A MC LANE

The continual efforts of Delaware Republicans to seize Allen McLane's position must have had their effect on Allen's sons. They were reared in an atmosphere of deadly hatred between their father and the Delaware Republicans; they could hardly be aught but Federalists in state politics. On the other hand, the national Republican administration supported Allen; Jefferson and his successors kept the collector in office despite his enemies. So it is not strange that Louis McLane was able to become an ambivalent politician, a Federalist at home—that is, in Delaware—but a friend of the Republican administrations abroad.

These years, the first decade after Allen became collector, were years of apprenticeship for Louis. For a time, possibly even before his family moved to Wilmington in 1797, Louis studied at the Friends School there, the oldest school still existing in Delaware. The facilities for educating his children were a factor in inducing Allen McLane to move to Wilmington, he said, and it is likely that in John Webster, the teacher at Friends School, Louis was fortunate.[119] Very little is known of Webster, but he did teach a number of young men who rose in the world, including at least three Senators; and when he turned bookseller for a time he had the originality to place rhymed advertisements in the local papers, advertising works for adults—as in the following:

> Among the Books you'll find there are,
> Choice Sermons wrote by Doctor Blair,
>   With Bates on Man's Redemption;
> The Voyage of Cook—when sails unfurl'd
> Had wafted him around the world—
>   Well worthy your attention.

And works for children—as in the following:

> The History of Giles Gingerbread,
> With pictures and a cover red,
>   Tom Jones without a mother,
> Likewise Tom Thumb's folio,
> Who mounted on his bird could go
>   From one place to another.[120]

Was it ignorance, sophistication, or the demands of rhyme that placed Tom Jones between Giles Gingerbread and Tom Thumb?

What conditions were like in Webster's school we do not know, but we have some evidence that physical strength was prized both in teacher and pupils, for we know that a decade earlier, one John Filson, returning from the Army to schoolteaching in Wilmington found himself unable to continue in his profession because a wound in the right arm made it impossible for him to enforce discipline. Thereupon he gave up his school and went to the Kentucky frontier, where he became a companion of Daniel Boone. Indians, apparently, were less savage than the boys of Wilmington.

One account survives of rough practices in Webster's school—a tale of his being "barred out" by the boys. This folk practice, most memorably described by Augustus Longstreet in his *Georgia Scenes* and therefore not peculiar to Wilmington, was a means of getting a holiday—if it worked. The boys, arriving at the school before the teacher, would take possession of it as a fort, closing and fastening doors and windows however they could and forbidding him entrance. If the teacher could not force his way in, he was compelled by custom to grant a holiday. But if he could break in, every boy got a thrashing.[121]

From one rough school, Louis McLane went to another. On May 3, 1799, he was appointed a midshipman on the frigate *Philadelphia,* and he entered the service the day after Christmas that year, when he was fifteen and a half years old.[122] Appointment as midshipman was then the road to a naval career; there was no naval academy until the 1840's. And such appointments—and such careers—were more available than heretofore because the Federalist administration of John Adams was building a navy for the quasi-war with France, a commercial conflict that raged as an outgrowth of the wars following the French Revolution.

The *Philadelphia* was a new frigate of thirty-six guns, built from funds contributed by Philadelphia merchants for the new Navy. Its commander, like the ship, came from the Quaker City. He was Stephen Decatur, son of a French immigrant and his Rhode Island wife, and father of another Stephen Decatur whose heroism made the name famous—and, oddly, it was the destruction of this same frigate *Philadelphia,* after it had fallen to the Tripolitanians, that was the son's most famous exploit. But now the *Philadelphia,* under Decatur, and with young McLane aboard, set sail on her first voyage for the Guadeloupe station in the Lesser Antilles. This position had been decided upon early in the war with France for several reasons—for the protection of American shipping, for attacks on French shipping, and to keep French maritime forces busy here with less opportunity to raid shipping on the American coast.

Decatur reached his station in May, 1800, but for more than a half year he had no important engagements. Finally, at the beginning of December, a French privateer was seized, and in the few months following and previous to the *Philadelphia*'s departure for her home port, several more prizes were taken, for a total of five.[123]

In spite of the successes of his initial voyage, Louis McLane was not destined for a naval career. When he returned to Philadelphia, he was furloughed from April, 1801, to the end of the year, and was granted another furlough on January 16, 1802, that was ended by his resignation, in February of the same year.[124] All ships had been recalled from West Indies stations in the spring of 1801, for the war with France was over, settled by a new treaty. Furloughs, consequently, were easily secured, but at least the second furlough was granted on the basis of ill health. A family memoir declares he left the Navy in deference to his mother's wishes,[125] and this may well be, but it is likely that his health was a factor in his resignation. Although he was to live long, he suffered from numerous minor maladies, not the least painful of which was seasickness. Whenever in later life duty sent him to Europe, as it did on three occasions, he became violently seasick when his ship crossed the bar in leaving the harbor of New York, and he continued miserably sick until he got ashore in England. If the same weakness afflicted him at fifteen as at forty-five, it is no wonder he sought first a long furlough and then release—particularly after a voyage that lasted eleven months and continued right through the hurricane season.

When he left the Navy, Louis enrolled at the Newark Academy, a chartered school of colonial and Presbyterian origin that was, in due course, to become the University of Delaware. In 1802 the Reverend John Waugh was the principal. He had found the academy closed and the building padlocked when he came to Newark, in 1799, and by his own responsibility broke the lock and entered and reopened the school. The trustees, at their next meeting, examined Waugh's students, found his work good, and gave him their blessing, and a small stipend besides.[126] Soon it was again, as it had been before the Revolution, the leading classical school in Delaware.

Just what McLane studied at the Newark Academy is a mystery, as is the precise time of his stay there. The town of Newark was a small crossroads community thirteen miles southwest of Wilmington, near the right angle made by the Mason-Dixon Line at the tristate corner of Maryland, Pennsylvania, and Delaware. Here McLane must have boarded in a private home, since the academy had no dormitory. His tuition cost his father twenty dollars a year, and he stayed perhaps for as long as two years, from 1802 to 1804; his stay can hardly have been longer, and it may have been shorter. Since this was the only formal schooling Louis McLane received after he first left home to enter the Navy at fifteen, the evidence of his later letters and speeches suggests that Waugh was an excellent teacher and Louis a good student.

XII   THE YOUNG LAWYER

In 1803 or 1804 Louis left the academy and returned to Wilmington to read law in the office of James A. Bayard. This was then the customary way of preparing to practice law. There were no law schools in the vicinity; so a would-be lawyer arranged—usually his parents paid a fee for this privilege—to read with an accomplished practicing lawyer. Perhaps Bayard waived the requirement of a fee in McLane's case; he had many ties with Louis's father—of politics, for both were Federalists; of business, for Bayard was employed by McLane in some of his legal problems as collector; of more personal relations, for Bayard had sought to protect McLane against Jefferson and had even fought a duel that grew out of his defense of the collector's salary against the efforts of a Rhode Island Representative to reduce it; and even of religion, though not Bayard's but that of his father-in-law, Richard Bassett, who was an even more ardent Methodist than McLane.

Surely Bayard's office was a proper place for the collector's law-inclined son to be in the early years of the nineteenth century. James Bayard was an ornament of the Delaware bar and of Delaware politics. Florid, clever, and spirited, he was at once gay and cynical, an admirer of numerous luxuries of life—food, cards, wine, sports. He made friends and aroused admiration wherever he went, at his practice in Delaware, or at his post in Congress. In 1803 he had just relinquished a position in the House of Representatives that he had held for six years, longer than any Delawarean after him, until his new law clerk in time should assume this position. Bayard had not resigned his seat; he had been defeated in a campaign for reelection by his good friend and stout Republican rival, Caesar A. Rodney. But the defeat was not altogether a disappointment to Bayard. Failure or success in the campaign, he told Rodney, was a choice between "the homely drudgery of making money and . . . the refined and elegant pursuit of attaining honor and reputation." The successful man in the election was in another sense the loser.[127]

There was but one other young man studying law with James Bayard when Louis McLane entered the office. This was George Strawbridge, already a Princeton graduate but still just under nineteen years old, a few months younger than Louis. Strawbridge had already studied with Bayard for a year. Soon the number of students was doubled, for Louis McLane and George Strawbridge were joined by John Barratt and William H. Ward.[128] Barratt came from a family connected with the McLanes —and the Bayard-Bassetts—through Methodism, for the Barratts were among the leading followers of Francis Asbury in Kent County. Ward came from Cecil County, Maryland, where his relatives were among the principal landholders in Sassafras Neck, across the Bohemia River from the estate of Bayard and his father-in-law.

The following year, as George Strawbridge remembered it, "passed in much harmony with us." Strawbridge left the office twelve months later and went to lower Delaware to begin an independent practice.[129] Louis McLane remained in Bayard's office until 1807, when he was admitted to the bar.

We have but a few mementos of these years in his life. One is from July, 1805. A young lawyer named John Fisher—Judge Fisher he was to be—gave the July 4 oration at a Democratic-Republican celebration in Wilmington, and he wrote his brother-in-law, Caesar A. Rodney, of his success. The Federalists, he wrote, had had to call off their July 4 celebration because of a death in the family of their intended speaker. Yet only two Federalists had come to hear the Republican oration. These two were the young law clerks, Louis McLane and John Barratt, who probably were lured across Market Street from Bayard's office to the town hall. They left as soon as Fisher stopped speaking.[130]

Between 1805 and 1807 Louis's brother Allen was at Princeton College, and we get our clearest picture of Louis from the letters of advice he was sending Allen. The letters make Louis sound quite stuffy, but they cannot be taken at face value; it is difficult for an older brother to counsel a younger one. And Louis was certainly full of advice. "In future be more carefull," he told Allen, who did not seem to know the difference between "ultimo" and "instant" in dates; "you who have learned the lattin language should be ashamed." Do not be "too precipitant" in determining your vocation. "Be ambitious, be resolute and determined, and dont suffer yourself to be ranked in the line of mediocrity in your class without a single effort to get higher." [131]

When Allen's *style* and diction" do not please Louis, he advises, "Get some desertation on letter writing, or get some letter writer, and attend to his diction." A year later Louis repeats the same theme: we should neglect no chance to correct our errors and improve our style; "I will not acknowledge any vanity when I say, that you have greater cause for amendment than myself." In my letter are "few, if any orthographycal errours: and if I could say as much for yours I would still be silent. Is it possible that there is no dictionaries in Nassau Hall? . . . Let me assure you Allen that you greatly need their assistance. . . ." Yet omitting to write was not one of Allen's faults; Allen may be the only college boy in history asked to write home less often. Because of "the expense of postage" from Princeton to Wilmington and since illness in the family compels us "to write to you by almost every mail," Louis advised him, "you had better not write so often as you have done, but reduce the number of your epistolary days to one in the week at any rate, if not to less. . . ." Allen took Louis's advice so seriously that six weeks later Louis scolded him for not writing.[132]

The letters furnish other clues to Louis's character and tastes. "Reed Birds and Rail," he told Allen, will be "in their Zenith" at the time of your fall vacation; "a dish of reed birds, is always to me a very agreeable repast." His taste for hunting Louis shared with his father, but his recreational reading was a different matter.[133]

It is not likely that the collector shared Louis's taste for Laurence Sterne or Horace. "You have the 2 vol. of my Horace at College," Louis reminded Allen, "and as my regard for that book is great, and my demand at present greater . . . dont forget to bring it with you. . . ." And when in 1807, Louis was bothered by tumors near his eyes, he found a literary metaphor from *Tristram Shandy*, which was ever a favorite with him: "the severity of one of them," meaning the tumors, "must cut my letter as short as my Uncle Toby's pipe." [134] With his taste for *Tristram Shandy*, maybe young Louis was not very stuffy.

More serious illnesses disturbed the peace of the McLane family than the tumors near Louis's eyes. His mother suffered in the winter of 1806–07 an illness that grew gradually worse. In December, 1806, Louis referred to "the natural delicacy of our beloved Mother's constitution" which could not long resist disease; unless she is soon relieved, he wrote Allen, we will "sustain the most serious loss which God has designed for us." Gloomily, he looked ahead to the death of both their parents: "if the deprivation of *one* of those only sincere friends, guides, and protectors . . . is felt so sensibly, how much more so will be the effect of a total loss of both." The moral: get to work, Allen; remember how you have broken past resolutions and neglected your studies.[135]

When his mother seemed somewhat improved in health, Louis felt "a relish for society" and decided to visit Philadelphia for a week. From there he forwarded to Allen a five-dollar bill from their mother as "a Christmas gift," reminding Allen that this might be the last such gift from "the best of mothers." [136] It was the last such gift. On May 11, Rebecca Wells McLane died.

Obscure though she is in history, she had, it would seem, some influence, a softening, kindly influence, upon her son. His memories of her were warm, fond memories, and his picture of the loving unity of a family was drawn from his recollections of his mother and of the warmth and unity she gave to the stormy collector's family. Louis came to be a man of close attachments to his children and particularly to his wife, and by her side, as perhaps he had remembered the situation in his mother's home, he built the hearth that was the center of his personal, intimate, domestic life.

But except for his domesticity, the ways of Louis McLane in his political, religious, and social life might have shocked his mother. He wandered far from the simplicity of her Methodism. Only a few years earlier, a Methodist governor, Richard Bassett, had attacked the practice of dueling as a devilish snare that severe laws should drive from the state.[137] Yet in August of 1807, three months after his mother's death, Louis McLane fought a duel with John Barratt, his fellow student in the law office of James Bayard.

John Barratt, grandson of the donor of Barratt's Chapel near Frederica, Delaware, was apparently a belligerent young man, for he is reported to have fought many duels. What caused the quarrel between him and Louis McLane, the two young Federalists who have been previously seen together attending John Fisher's July 4 oration in 1805, is not precisely known; the dispute arose out of a former duel in which Barratt had been a second. Louis was his father's son and not a man to allow a slighting remark or action to go unnoticed. "Be resolute and determined" was his counsel.

Pistols were the weapons employed. Louis's first shot grazed Barratt near the waist; Barratt's shot went astray. A second exchange of shots followed. This time Louis came closer to his target. His fire nicked Barratt's left hand as it was placed on his right breast. And Barratt's second shot wounded Louis near the groin.[138]

Apparently the wounds were speedily healed, and probably the dispute was too. A few months later in December, 1807, Louis McLane and John Barratt were both admitted to practice at the New Castle bar. And for the decade that followed, from 1807 to 1817, Louis lived the life of a young lawyer—practicing in the courts, making some investments in real estate and some tentative ventures in business, beginning to participate in party politics, marrying and starting a family. To these engagements war threatened a serious interruption in 1812, but the war passed without removing Louis far from his home or his family.

2

A Rising Young Federalist

On the Eastern Shore of Maryland, Bohemia was a river and a hundred, a house and a history. The history told of a man legendary by Louis McLane's time, Augustine Herrman, of Prague. Awarded a large tract of land by Lord Baltimore in repayment for drawing a map of the colony, Herrman named his new estate Bohemia Manor, for his native province; and the river that flowed by the southern part of his estate likewise came to be known as the Bohemia.

Use of the name spread. When Cecil County, in which Herrman's manor lay, came to be divided into areas called hundreds, the land just north of the Bohemia River became Bohemia Manor Hundred, and the land south of the river, plain Bohemia Hundred.[1] Augustine Herrman's grandson, Richard Bassett, the Delaware politician who had recommended Allen McLane for appointment as collector, had his country home on Bohemia Manor, and so did Bassett's son-in-law, James A. Bayard, Louis McLane's legal preceptor. Across the Bohemia River, in a house that was itself called Bohemia, dwelt a family named Milligan.

The house was built between 1743 and 1745 for John Baldwin, Gentleman, high sheriff and magistrate of Cecil County. In 1751 he deeded the property (one thousand acres, of which eight hundred and fifty were cultivated) to his son-in-law George Milligan, who extensively remodeled it.[2] For a time the house was known as Milligan Hall, but by 1772 it was called Bohemia, the name it still bears. A brick house, built on a rectangular, nearly a square plan, it has matching façades front and rear, one façade facing the water, which all old Eastern Shore mansions saluted, and one facing the lane up which rode neighbors on Sassafras

Neck (between the Bohemia and the next stream southward, the Sassa-fras), Wards, Veazeys, and Formans, for instance.

On the river side were falling gardens and Dolls Spring, a trysting place for the young in heart. On the lane side the old kitchens swept forward to the right like a large forearm, joined to the house by a brick arcade. From the garret a bull's-eye window looked out through the triangular eave pediment front and rear. Below it, in the center of each façade, three windows were grouped in a Palladian effect. A central hall behind the door on the lane side boasted a beautiful squared staircase with an unusual banister of varied lattice designs. High overhead a plaster eagle held the chain for a lantern suspended from the second-floor ceiling. Other decorative plaster figures abounded through the house.[3]

II   "A JUDGE OF FEMALE MERIT"

The part of Maryland where Milligans and Bayards and Bassetts lived was tied not only to Chesapeake Bay society but also to the Philadelphia-dominated Delaware valley to the northeast. For this northern Eastern Shore, planted in wheat and corn, in some ways had less in common with the tobacco country around Williamsburg and Annapolis than with the wheat country of neighboring Chester and New Castle counties of Pennsylvania and Delaware. Then too it was on the main road leading north toward Philadelphia. Baltimore was growing rapidly at the begin-ning of the nineteenth century, and as it grew it exerted its own attrac-tion upon the northern Eastern Shore. But in the eighteenth century when Annapolis was Maryland's metropolis, Philadelphia had hardly a rival in this region.[4] And thus it was that Cecil County planters and merchants often played major roles in the society of Philadelphia and satellite communities such as Wilmington.

George Milligan, a lowland Scot from Ayrshire, was a merchant at Chestertown, a small port on the Eastern Shore. His son Robert, after studying abroad at St. Andrew's and the Middle Temple, established himself at Philadelphia, either as a merchant or as a lawyer. Here he en-tertained George Washington at dinner in 1787, and here in 1789 Mathew Carey published an announcement of Milligan's marriage to Sally Jones in his magazine *The American Museum*.[5]

"I quite long to see Bob's choice," one Eastern Shore belle wrote an-other: "he is so good a judge of female merit that I think she must be clever." [6] Sally Jones came from Delaware, where her father had an estate on Drawyers Creek, St. Georges Hundred, that was called Mount

Jones. Sally's mother, born Lydia Cantwell, represented one of the most distinguished of Delaware colonial families.[7]

Through the next few years, Robert and Sally Milligan divided their time between Bohemia and Philadelphia. They were people of substance; Robert's thirty-four slaves made him one of the major slaveholders in Cecil County, where the largest holding was only sixty-seven slaves.[8] After Sally died in 1796, Robert bought a house in Wilmington, a halfway point between his Philadelphia business and his plantations, Bohemia and Mount Jones, the latter of which he bought from Sally's brother in 1797. Robert Milligan's sister Catherine, a maiden lady, came to live with Robert's motherless family and take charge of the children.[9]

After Robert Milligan died in 1806, Catherine bore complete responsibility for her four nieces and nephews. Parentless they were, but not penniless, for there was an ample inheritance for each child. The older son, George Baldwin Milligan, received the Maryland lands and $3,000 to boot. The younger son, John Jones Milligan, and the two daughters, Catherine and Lydia, were bequeathed their father's Delaware plantations, including Mount Jones.

There were other legacies. "I give to my dear daughter Kitty," wrote Robert Milligan, "the gold watch of her blessed mother," and "to my dear Lid one hundred and twenty dollars to buy herself such a Watch as pleases her." A codicil to the will made one final legacy to Robert Milligan's friend James Bayard: "a handsome double barreled fowling piece . . . as a small testimony of . . . friendship." The will, dated 1806, the year of Milligan's death, was signed by James Bayard, who drafted it, and two other witnesses. One of them was Bayard's young clerk, Louis McLane.[10]

III THE MILLIGAN SISTERS AND THEIR MARRIAGES

The Milligan sisters, Catherine and Lydia, were not only wealthy; they were pretty, too. When their brother George visited Washington City in February, 1812, James Bayard reported to George's aunt and guardian: "George has been here some time and had his full share of the gaiety and dissipation of the place. He has dined with the two Ministers, and the President and seen all the best company of the city. He will probably take to himself the whole credit of being very well received in all societies into which he has gone, but I can tell him he owes a good part of it to the fame of the pretty Sisters he is known to have in Wilmington." [11]

The pretty sisters whose fame had spread to Washington did not long remain unattached. Lydia (Lid, as her father called her) was married to Joseph Sims, Jr., of Philadelphia, on June 28, 1812. The elder Joseph

Sims was one of the great merchant princes of Philadelphia with a splendid town house at Ninth and Chestnut Streets in the city and a country home, Laurel Hill, on a bluff overlooking the Schuylkill.[12]

Somehow Lydia Milligan's marriage to Joseph Sims, Jr., was unfortunate. "The beautiful Mrs. Joseph Sims—most unhappily married," as Lydia, who had no children, was described by a later Milligan, is the tone of a number of references to her.[13] Lydia kept the affection of her family, though they did not hold Joseph in high regard. After accompanying Joseph, his wife, and his parents on a trip to New York and the Falls of the Passaic, Lydia's sister wrote: "I believe his Father and Mother will be happy to get rid of him, for he really behaves most scandalously to both." [14]

Lydia's elder sister, the "dear daughter Kitty" of Robert Milligan's will, probably had a much happier and certainly a much busier life. Her fame too had spread abroad. If she was the slightest bit less remarkable than Lydia for her beauty, she was yet "the most agreeable of women." [15] And she was intelligent; her letters are proof of this, and if more proof were needed, it would be found in her husband's willingness to inform her of all affairs of the day, of his secret hopes and opinions. And this from a man who normally kept his own counsel.

Kitty's husband, of course, was Louis McLane. Very likely their meeting came about through James Bayard, who was legal counselor to both the McLanes and the Milligans, and more than that, for he was Louis McLane's preceptor at the law, while to Kitty and her brothers and sister he was almost a guardian. A friend and neighbor of the Milligans whether at Bohemia or in the city, Bayard took young George Milligan with him as a secretary when he went to St. Petersburg and Ghent in the years 1813 to 1815 to negotiate a peace with Britain. But since the Milligans lived chiefly in Wilmington after Robert's death, a meeting between Kitty and Louis McLane could not have been difficult.

Yet Louis was almost pledged elsewhere before he became engaged to Kitty Milligan. Ann Van Dyke, a daughter of the Nicholas Van Dyke who had been a Representative and would be a Senator, had been the object of Louis's attention. She would have made a very appropriate match for Louis, too.

In a June wedding in 1812 his brother Allen, now out of Princeton and a young physician, was married to Catherine Read, daughter of George Read, of New Castle, the district attorney. This was quite a good marriage for the collector's son. Catherine's father was a son of another George Read, famous as a signer of both the Declaration of Independence and the Constitution, as a chief justice of Delaware, and long the most influential politician of the state. To be sure her father was hardly

Bohemia. Entry hall. Photograph circa 1960. *Courtesy of Mrs. J. D. Otley.*

Bohemia. South Façade. Photograph circa 1960.

her grandfather's equal—except in one respect, for he made himself memorable in the annals of New Castle by building what was—and is— the old river town's grandest house.

If any New Castle family could be put forward as a rival to the Reads, it very likely was the Van Dykes. One Nicholas Van Dyke of New Castle had been a governor and a Congressman in the Revolutionary genera- tion. His son Nicholas not only followed the father's path to Congress, but like his father—and like George Read—built a notable New Castle house.[16] If a second McLane had married a Van Dyke after his brother had married a Read, wags might have talked of the McLane taste for New Castle domestic architecture.

On June 30, 1812, Louis McLane formally solicited Van Dyke's per- mission to court Ann, who was then seventeen. Their association at the wedding of his brother and Catherine Read, Louis explained, had caused his feelings to ripen "into a sentiment of affection" which he had neither "the inclination or power to resist." He suspected that Ann knew how he felt.[17]

Without knowing how Nicholas Van Dyke responded to McLane's letter, we suspect that the courtship went forward for a time. And then, suddenly, there came a change. Late in the night of September 11, 1812, Van Dyke made a copy of the letter just referred to, as is indicated by a notation on the copy. Something agitated the cultured Van Dyke so that he misspelled "night" in the endorsement; is it not likely that Van Dyke was moved to copy McLane's letter with its protestation of affection by news that McLane had changed his mind and was jilting Ann for an- other girl?

Some New Castle gossip has survived from the fall of 1812 that seems to confirm this hypothesis. "Matters are in forwarding for the Union of Mr. Lewis [McLane] and Miss M[illigan]," Mrs. George Read reported to an absent son. "Miss V. D____ Does not appear to feel her Disapoint- ment. She is More Dressy and gay than Ever. . . . Mr. V____ and Mr. McL. seem as good *friends* as *Ever*. What do you think [of] this for- bearance[?] he must truly be a Christian in forgiving his Enemies." [18] The implication is clear that Ann Van Dyke is the injured person, and that Louis McLane has jilted her.

Ann was not handsome, her closest friend admitted, but of a lively, pleasant disposition and a cultivated mind. The term "cultivated mind" does not usually mean much in nineteenth-century eulogies, but Ann's case is different, for there are several indications that Nicholas Van Dyke's home was a center of intellectual interests transcending what was ordinary in the homes of successful lawyers in his day. The Van Dyke home, for instance, may have had an influence on the shaping of the novelist and playwright Robert Montgomery Bird, who was Van Dyke's ward. The social position of the Van Dykes is clearly indicated by the fact that Washington was in attendance at a Van Dyke wedding in 1784 and Lafayette at another in 1824.[19]

Poor Ann was not long for this world. "In her affluent home," her friend wrote, "was everything to make life desirable, but all could not save her from sorrow and disappointment." Can this be a reference to the disruption of her romance with Louis McLane? All we know is that her health slowly declined and that her father, fearing her end was near, had her sit for a portrait by Gilbert Stuart. Ann died in 1814.[20]

Whether or not Louis McLane was guilty of jilting Ann Van Dyke (and the fact that he and her father were not very friendly in the years to come may be evidence on this point), he showed good choice in the marriage he did make. Catherine Mary Milligan was a prize: wealthy and well connected (and it is not likely that Louis overlooked these details), but also attractive, agreeable, kindly, and intelligent. With Senator Bayard present, they were married in Wilmington on December 29, 1812, by Bishop William White, of the Episcopal Church, of which she was a member.[21]

IV   LEGAL BUSINESS: THE SUSQUEHANNA CASE

"Be ambitious, be resolute and determined," young Louis McLane had advised his brother; "dont suffer yourself to be ranked in the line of mediocrity in your class without a single effort to get higher." [22] An elder brother's advice is often better than his action, but Louis McLane was ambitious, resolute, and determined, unwilling "to be ranked in the line of mediocrity." And a decade after he had given this advice he had more reason than ever before to abide by it. For now he was not only the heir of a Revolutionary hero, the son of the collector of Wilmington; he was also the protégé of the great James A. Bayard, the husband of Catherine Milligan, and the father of a growing family. His first child, a daughter, named Rebecca Wells McLane for Louis's mother, was born October 2, 1813, and his second child, named Robert Milligan McLane for Catherine's father, was born on June 23, 1815. And in rapid succession came other children: Catherine, named for his wife; Louis, named for himself; Sally Jones, named for his mother-in-law; Lydia Sims Milligan, for his wife's sister; Allan, for his father; and so on to a total of thirteen. Moreover, of the thirteen only one died in infancy—a vastly different record from that of Louis McLane's parents, who had fourteen children but lost eleven.

The pressure of his responsibility to this growing family was upon

Louis McLane ever after through all the active years of his life. For he had been twenty-eight when he was married, twenty-nine when his first child was born, and when he retired, he still had young children at home, the youngest a boy of fourteen, born when Louis was fifty.

Because of his father's position, Louis McLane had a decided advantage over other beginning young lawyers. The Embargo and Non-Intercourse Acts gave the collector of Wilmington opportunity to seize ships coming up the Delaware before they reached the jurisdiction of the collector of Philadelphia. Shrewd importers could see an advantage in retaining the collector's son as their attorney when threatened with confiscation of their vessels or their goods.

For instance, when Thomas Cope, an important Philadelphia merchant, was forced to come to New Castle in June of 1812, because his ship the *Susquehanna* had been seized by Allen McLane for violation of the embargo, he engaged as his attorney "young Read, son of the dist. Atty." From New Castle Cope went to Wilmington to see the collector. "He rece[ive]d us rather cooly at first," Cope wrote, "but a little pleasant conversation induced a favourable change."

"It seems," Cope's journal continues, "he has also a son an Atty—now absent—expected home in a day or two. Engaged him in our service by leaving the father a fee for him. Parted in much mutual good humor." [23]

Four days later, Cope returned to Wilmington and had an interview with Louis. "His appearance and deportment," Cope noted, "please me." On the other hand, "the more we see of G. Read, district atty, the more we are persuaded of his want of principle. It is understood to be his practise to extort money by filing or threatening to file capriciously a great many libels against a Cargo, each of which if prosecuted to judgement will cost ab[ou]t $200."

After assessors had reported the cargo, which cost £3,300 sterling, to be worth $39,000, "Read proposed thro McLane . . . that if we," Cope and his partner, "would give him one thousand dollars, he would consent to the appointment of another set of values and file but two libels." Cope "indignantly rejected" the proposition, and another was made; Read would consent to file but two libels and permit another valuation if Cope would pay him the legal fees on ten libels, or $170. "Otherwise he will oppose us all in his power."

"Having no alternative," Cope consented to these terms. A new assessment valued the cargo at $20,000 less than before—at $19,000, instead of $39,000. "Both the Collector and his son," wrote Cope, "speak in high terms of reproach of the base conduct of the district Atty. This is the more remarkable as another of the Collectors sons was a few days since, married to Reads daughter." [24]

Happily, Louis McLane came through this incident retaining the respect of his client. Incidentally, the cargo of the *Susquehanna* was probably worth as much as the first assessors thought. "We sold the Cargo this day," Cope exulted on July 16, 1812, "at public auction at a very large profit. Salt $1.59 a bushel. The queensware generally from 6 to 9 hundred advance on the Sterling. Callicoes that cost from 5 to 7½ from 45 to 56 cts. per yard." [25]

V   LEGAL BUSINESS: THE AMELIA ISLAND CASES

Another law case of 1812 turned out to be the most important one in Louis McLane's life. On this occasion too the fact that he was the collector's son influenced his entrance into the case. But this case, and other litigation that it led to, dragged on through the courts for almost thirty years before a final settlement. And in the end Louis McLane, as the defendant, was a main party to the litigation as well as the single individual best rewarded by it.

The initial stages of this long dispute are known as the Amelia Island cases. They had their inception in an action of Collector Allen McLane in April, 1812. In that month the ship *Good Friends*, belonging to the wealthy merchant Stephen Girard, of Philadelphia, was seized by one of Allen McLane's men as she came up the Delaware and taken to New Castle while libels were filed for forfeiture of ship and cargo under the Non-Intercourse Law.

The *Good Friends* had left England in 1811, loaded with dry goods at the orders of Girard, who was attempting thereby to withdraw some of the large sums he had deposited with the Baring Brothers, chief English bankers for American business, on account of sales he had made in northern Europe. By the Non-Intercourse Act, Girard could not import from England, and therefore he had ordered the *Good Friends* to proceed to the old smugglers' haven, Amelia Island, a portion of what was then Spanish East Florida that lies in the river separating Florida from Georgia. Girard intended to keep his ship and cargo in safety in this port just outside the United States until developments in the Napoleonic Wars, then at their height on the Continent, or a change in American laws made it possible for him to dispose of the goods at a profit.

But suddenly turbulence broke out on this frontier. An abortive attempt was made to annex East Florida to the United States, much in the way slices were being cut off Spanish West Florida. George Matthews, commander of the American troops that seized Amelia Island, ordered the *Good Friends* and two other American ships, the *Amazon* and the *United States*, that had similarly sought refuge in these waters, to leave port lest their presence invite attack from pirates or Spaniards. And Matthews wrote to the collector at Philadelphia explaining the circumstances.[26]

But Allen McLane seized the *Good Friends* coming up the Delaware in April, 1812, and after her the *Amazon* and the *United States*, before they could reach the jurisdiction of the Philadelphia collector. The owners of the ships were very much disturbed because they stood to lose everything by forfeiture if they could be convicted of violating the Non-Intercourse Law; and this was quite likely, since the East Florida annexation movement ended in a fiasco and the United States government disavowed any responsibility for General Matthews's acts.[27] They were naturally quite angry with McLane and willing to listen to unfriendly gossip to the effect that, though a vigilant officer, he was selfish and enjoyed doing injury.[28]

Everyone agreed that Allen McLane was vigilant. And no one could deny that his own interests as well as those of the government might profit—and in a very large way, monetarily—from his vigilance. For in the case of a forfeiture, the collector received one half the value of the ship and cargo forfeited. In the case of the three ships from Amelia Island, this could amount to a princely sum. The *United States*, valued at $9,000, was the most valuable ship, but had the least valuable cargo, $12,617.60. On the other hand the value of Girard's *Good Friends* and her cargo was estimated at $303,458.85. And the *Amazon* and her cargo were valued even higher, at $320,624.73. In other words, the total value involved in the Amelia Island cases was $645,701.18. Of this Allen McLane's share, if forfeiture was approved by the courts, was $332,850.59.[29]

Such sums were worth the best legal talent that could be secured. Girard at once retained Caesar A. Rodney as his Delaware attorney, and later added Nicholas Van Dyke and one of the Reads to his counsel.[30] It was up to the collector to look to the prosecution, and to that end he made a contract with James Bayard on April 21, two days after the seizure of the *Good Friends*. Bayard was to seek to secure condemnation of the *Good Friends* in federal court. If the effort was successful, Bayard was to be recompensed by one half of whatever the collector should recover. A day later, April 22, the agreement was amended to admit Louis McLane to it, Bayard, the collector, and the collector's son each now being promised one third of the proceeds.[31]

Although the federal district judge was Rodney's brother-in-law, his decision was against Rodney's client, Girard, who immediately appealed the case. At the same time he petitioned Congress for relief, and Congress, feeling the laws were unfair to these victims of George Matthews's assumption of authority at Amelia Island, remitted the forfeiture on condition that the shipowners pay double the normal duties on the goods imported, as was required by a law of July, 1812—for whether or not the owners were innocent, the goods had been brought into the country and sold here.[32]

Not until 1819 did Girard finally give in and pay the double duties on the *Good Friends,* which amounted to $87,724.25, plus many thousands of dollars interest. Allen McLane claimed half of this money, but had not been able to justify his claim before the courts when he made out his will in 1821. In it he declared he had assigned to Louis all his right, title, and interest in the fines incurred by the owners of the *Good Friends, Amazon,* and *United States* and their cargoes. But the litigation resulting from the seizures lasted twenty more years, a total of almost three decades from the time the controversy began.[33]

VI   ROKEBY

In the Amelia Island cases, Louis McLane's chief interest was as successor to his father's claim. He did little work himself on the cases beyond preparing for the original trial in the district court in the fall of 1812 under Bayard's direction.[34] But generally he enlarged his own practice with cases large and small, including, among the more famous of them, Peter Bauduy's suit against the du Ponts which began in 1816 and continued, in one form or another, for more than a decade. By 1822 he was fourth in seniority of the fourteen attorneys practicing in New Castle County. By 1827 he was one of the attorneys employed by such an important enterprise as the Chesapeake and Delaware Canal Company.[35] Yet almost from the beginning Louis McLane's legal career was interrupted by his business and political interests, till finally his appointments to England and then to Jackson's cabinet caused him to give up the law altogether.

Real estate speculations also engaged some of Louis McLane's attention. His first purchase of real estate was made in November, 1812, a month before his marriage. In partnership with Outerbridge Horsey, a Federalist attorney who was then Bayard's Delaware colleague in the Senate, McLane purchased, for $10,000, an acre of land on West Street, Wilmington, that had previously belonged to a tanner and may have been his tanyard.[36] It seems likely that Louis's father backed him in this venture, and if the purchased property was a tanyard, there is a pattern of interest to be found in that purchase and in his next real estate investment.

His next purchase was a millsite called Rokeby, on the Brandywine and just below the Hagley Yards of E. I. du Pont. Again he had a partner associated with him; this time it was his new brother-in-law—Louis had been married only three months—George B. Milligan. It was a tract of land of over one hundred and fifteen acres that the two young men bought in March, 1813, for $13,250, largely on the west bank of the Brandywine and extending from Squirrel Run (the stream the visitor crosses now in going to the Hagley Museum) to Pancake Run to the southeast. A small strip of land across the Brandywine on the east bank (down the slope from the present Du Pont Experimental Station) was also in the tract.[37]

On the west bank, in the main Rokeby property, Vincent Gilpin had operated a gristmill; and Louis McLane and George Milligan, after purchasing it from his widow and children, rented part of the property as a cotton factory. But first they erected a new stone mill near Gilpin's old gristmill, aided in this enterprise by the $2,596.59 they received for selling nineteen acres—the land on the east side of the Brandywine and a strip south of Squirrel Run—to E. I. du Pont.[38] Rokeby Mill was probably just below the present Breck's Mill on the Brandywine. Eleven or twelve dwellings near it constituted a little village, probably the one that is now called Henry Clay, in tribute to the champion of protective tariffs.[39]

No complete list exists of the tenants who rented from McLane and Milligan. Originally a man named Massey was to run the business. In 1815, Isaac Briggs listed "Rokeby Cotton Works" as his address, when McLane, E. I. du Pont, and other local mill owners, sent him to Washington to lobby for higher tariffs on textiles.[40] A year later Delaware papers announced the dissolution of Thomas Little and Company, cotton manufacturers at Rokeby. In 1818, *Niles' Register,* describing a great explosion at the Du Pont powder works, declared "McLane's mill" was safe, except for broken glass.[41]

In 1820 "A Farmer" protested in a Dover newspaper that Louis McLane was a factory owner and as such naturally supported all measures in Congress that favored the few over the many, a contention McLane's friends were quick to refute. Louis McLane, they said, had given up his interest in the factory before he voted on the 1820 tariff.[42] However, they were wrong. McLane still had his interest in the factory, now rented to John D. Carter, who employed twenty-three men, twenty-two women, and thirty-four children, according to the 1820 census.

Carter complained that the demand for cotton goods was "trifling" and all sales "forced," but he was optimistic and, despite a flood in 1822, stuck to his work until his lease expired in 1823.[43] McLane tried to sell the mill and then again rented it.[44] Eventually he found a more permanent tenant in William Breck, who married a granddaughter of Victor du Pont.[45] Breck employed sixty hands in the mill in 1832.[46] In that same year McLane advertised Rokeby for sale for $25,000, almost double what he had paid.[47] No one would buy at this price, so in 1835, when he was moving from Delaware, he sold Rokeby to Breck and a partner, for $16,500.[48] In the sale, Louis also acted for George Milligan, then living in Louisiana, whose power of attorney he held.[49]

VII   THE FARMERS BANK

Louis McLane's connection with manufacturing was never very direct. He bought Rokeby and he built a cotton mill, but he rented the mills to other people and was never active in the management of any mill himself. His ventures in banking engaged him more directly.

In the beginning he was merely an investor, in banking as in milling. In 1811 he was a stockholder in the Bank of Delaware, of which his brother-in-law, Edward Worrell, was cashier.[50] In 1813 he became a member of the first board of directors of the Wilmington branch of the Farmers Bank of Delaware.[51]

The Farmers Bank itself was an interesting institution. Unlike its rivals in Wilmington, the Bank of Delaware and the Bank of Wilmington and Brandywine, it bore an official state connection beyond mere incorporation. The Farmers Bank of the State of Delaware, to use the full title, was the official state bank. The state had invested in it by purchasing one fifth of its capital stock of $500,000 when it was chartered in 1807. Its main office was in Dover, with branches in the other county seats, Georgetown and New Castle. As a demand grew in Wilmington for more banking facilities, the Farmers Bank's charter was amended, in 1813, to allow it to open another branch in Wilmington, and it was of this branch that Louis McLane became a director.

Each branch had its own president. The first president of the Wilmington branch was John Rumsey. In 1815, after two years as president, Rumsey shifted offices to become cashier, and Louis McLane assumed the presidency. The cashier probably had a fulltime job; certainly the president did not. He presided over a board of directors which met, however, not only to determine major policies but also to decide many specific questions of daily or weekly procedure—what loans to make, for instance.

With the state holding one fifth of the stock, it is not surprising that men of political prominence often occupied the presidencies. Henry Moore Ridgely, a Kent County Federalist and president of the central office of the Farmers Bank for its first forty years, was also a delegate to the federal House of Representatives in 1815 when Louis McLane was elected president of the Wilmington branch. McLane himself was chosen to his first political office while he held this post, and his successors in it included such prominent local politicians as his brother, Dr. Allen McLane, and his legal protégé, James A. Bayard, son of the famous Federalist Senator of the same name, who died in the summer of 1815.[52]

But this is not to say that presidencies in the Farmers Bank were held as political spoils, or that prominent politicians were made presidents as a matter of course. Four fifths of the stock was held and four fifths of the directors were chosen by individual investors. And they sought for the presidency young men of professional or business interests—lawyers, physicians, merchants, manufacturers—men who could be counted on to make wise decisions and ensure good dividends. Such men, of course, and particularly if they were lawyers, were apt also to win political preferment, but political office followed rather than preceded banking posts. So it was that Henry Ridgely was chosen Representative and later Senator after he had become president of the Farmers Bank. James A. Bayard was president of the Wilmington branch bank years before he occupied any prominent political post. And Louis McLane's election to the branch presidency preceded his political preference by a year. He became president in 1815, and though he was elected to Congress in 1816, he retained his bank post until 1818.[53]

It may well be that Louis's influence, which is to say the patronage of Louis's father, the collector, saved his bank. In 1816 notes from the Wilmington branch were refused in the markets and publicly cried down by the town crier. But the collector came to the rescue, announcing that the customs house would receive these notes.[54] Thus once again old Allen's federal office was employed to assist his friends, including his fellow Federalists—Henry Ridgely and Louis.

In Wilmington the Farmers Bank office was located on the west side of Market Street, just above Third. Farther up Market Street and on the other side Louis in 1815 bought the former residence of Jonathan and Rumford Dawes, merchants, and of Judge Gunning Bedford, Jr.[55] The Dawes house (606 Market), a three-story brick, was said to have been the headquarters for officers of French troops quartered in Wilmington during the Revolution and was then considered by some to be the stateliest house in the borough.[56] Lawyer, millowner, and banker, Louis was now an established person of some local importance, the son of a recognized hero, the husband of a remarkable woman, the father of two children by the time the year 1815 and the second war with Britain were at an end. He was ready now for a political career; in years to come this career was frequently bolstered by reference to his wartime activities.

VIII   THE COLLECTOR AND THE WAR OF 1812

The war with Britain that began in 1812 is popularly believed to have been responsible for the death of the Federalist party. Leading members of the party, this thesis suggests, opposed the war, sympathized with Britain, and finally entertained ideas of secession from the Union rather than persevere in the war. To whatever extent some Federalists were correctly categorized by this thesis, it did not pertain to the Federalists of Delaware in general, nor to the McLanes in particular.

The author of a campaign biography of Louis took up this point a quarter of a century later. Federalists, he explained, were divided into prowar and antiwar elements, and generally the prowar element was the smaller. "Such a division existed in Delaware," he continued, "though it must be remembered to the credit of this federal little state that an overwhelming majority of the people of both parties warmly espoused the side of the Country, and yielded a patriotic support to the Gov[ern-ment]." [57]

This eulogist goes on to say that in 1812 Democrats opposed to Madison's reelection planned an alliance with antiwar Federalists behind DeWitt Clinton, and that "in connection with this scheme a convention of certain prominent statesmen of the Federal party from various parts of the Union informally assembled at *New York.*" Louis McLane was invited there to represent Delaware, but "he declined uniting in an opposition to Mr. Madison's reelection," refusing even to attend the meeting, and determining rather "to yield a cordial and active support to the gov. in the prosecution of the war."

This was the general attitude of the Delaware Federalists, to whom James Bayard had given the cue. In the Senate he had opposed most of the measures that led to war and had opposed the war itself, but once the war was begun Bayard voted for all measures—taxes, men, ships—that would aid its successful prosecution. Bayard and other Delaware Federalists wasted little time on recriminations against the government for involving the country in war; they leveled their attacks on the government for not more effectively prosecuting the war. Since all Delaware was coastline, it was easy to see and popular to observe that the federal government could not adequately defend the coast either with men or with ships. Therefore Delaware Federalists found themselves in the popular position of being able to insist that Republican administrations should take much more vigorous action against the British than they seemed either willing or capable of undertaking.

As early as 1807, at the time of the *Chesapeake-Leopard* affair—an unprovoked and unresisted attack by a British upon an American ship off Cape Henry—Bayard, Federalist and consequently reputedly pro-British though he was, declared that it was impossible to be an American and not feel enraged upon this occasion. And old Collector McLane wished that he (instead of nonresisting Commodore Barron) had been captain of the *Chesapeake:* "Methinks had I have been a long side of the Leopard, with the Chesapeake's crew, we should not have been Barren or unfruitful." Indeed he had immediately sprung to the colors. He and other "old fellows of 45 and upwards" formed a volunteer company; "revenge is our pass word," he explained.[58]

As the years passed, old Allen's anger grew. "Is it possible," he expostulated in February, 1812, "that the people of America will bear any more with impunity from those oppressors on the land, and tyrants on the seas." When the war broke out, he was placed in charge of the defenses of Wilmington. An old political enemy, Hezekiah Niles, was moved to praise Allen McLane as "a seventy-sixer and as true as steel," leading "a veteran band of gallant hearts." [59]

Soon old Allen was offering gratuitous advice to all who would listen, including the President and members of his cabinet.[60] "Trust not in the professions or promises of Britain," he advised Secretary of State Monroe.[61] With his unerring instinct for landing on the scene of fighting, he was in Washington in August, 1814, when the British army suddenly struck at the capital. He submitted a plan of battle to President Madison, his Secretary of War, and his commanding general, but the British swept the American militia from their path and entered Washington despite the collector.[62]

IX   LOUIS AND THE WAR

A son of the fire-eating collector could hardly remain neutral in the war. Yet Louis did not do very much. He was, of course, courting when the war began, married before a year of war had passed, the father of one child and anticipating the arrival of another when peace was restored. But the collector had been older when he marched off to fight the English in 1775, and had been married for several years to boot.

The two wars, of course, were not alike. Americans, at least nationalistic Americans, seemed less called upon for personal participation in 1812 than in 1775. The British were not present tyrants to be ousted, but foreign enemies off somewhere in the distance, in ships at sea, on the far Canadian frontier. A young lawyer (especially one prone to seasickness) would hardly be expected to rejoin the Navy, or even to march off to Canada. If the British should carry the war to American hearths, then things would be different—and then things were different for Louis McLane.

And yet, it is obvious that the two McLanes were not alike either. For the father had never waited for the British to come to his hearth; he had marched off to Virginia. Neither wife nor child was permitted to keep him at home.

The son was more sophisticated, less crude, less wild, less ardent—less erratic. Instead of marching away to the war, this young bachelor joined a volunteer artillery company commanded by Caesar A. Rodney. Bayard had pushed Rodney into organizing the company: "as we are now at war," the Federalist Senator had written his political rival but personal friend, "we must defend ourselves; & I think you ought to bestir yourself in organizing a military force." [63]

The Wilmington Artillery Company was the force organized by Rodney. Its intent was defensive, but when Baltimore was threatened in 1814, its services were offered to the defenders of the Maryland metropolis. Off they started on foot, and Louis McLane had his first real taste of campaigning since the cruise of the *Philadelphia,* over a decade earlier.

The first night's camp was at Newport, up the Christina, and from there Louis addressed his bride of a year and a half: "The habilaments of a soldier set quite easily on me, and tho the roads were heavy, and our march rapid I feel as if I could set out again in the morning with more spirits than I left the spot where all my best affections are."

Being in a mess with his fellow attorney, Senator Outerbridge Horsey, and with his brother, Dr. Allen McLane, he should, as he expressed the expectation, "do Well," but he wanted Kitty to send his old hat after him. "The moment I feel fatigue," he assured her, "I shall take my seat in the stage and precede my company for Baltimore." [64] Why walk to Baltimore if the stage was running?

But Louis did not have much need for his old hat or the stage, for when the company reached Elkton, at the head of the Chesapeake navigation and about one fourth of the way to Baltimore, they were met by letters from General Sam Smith, commanding the Baltimore defenses, who countermanded their march on the ground that the forces already gathered were more than could be adequately cared for. [65]

With this taste of campaigning behind him, Louis joined some fifty men of Wilmington and New Castle who met at the Green Tree Tavern, formed themselves into a corps of flying (light) artillery, and elected officers. At the first ballot, George Read was unanimously elected captain, Louis McLane, first lieutenant, and James McCullough, Jr., second lieutenant. Brigadier General John Stockton of the Delaware militia recommended these elected officers to the governor as men who would "do credit to any appointment the Gov. will give," [66] and the officers were officially commissioned by the governor on September 15.[67]

Through the fall of 1814, Louis busied himself with a number of military functions. He interviewed General Joseph Bloomfield and Governor Simon Snyder of Pennsylvania when the latter came to Delaware to look after some Pennsylvania troops that were camped near the Brandywine. He ordered caps; [68] he traveled to Philadelphia to report on his light artillery corps to General Edmund P. Gaines.[69] For his service from November 28, 1814, to February 11, 1815—two months and fifteen days— he received $170.95, and of this sum part was an allowance for a servant (not a soldier) named John Louis that he shared with the second lieutenant, and part was an allowance for the use of two horses. His second sergeant, it may be worth noting, was his brother-in-law, John J. Milligan.[70]

But Louis's outstanding national service was not to be as a partisan fighter like his father but as a diplomatist and politician. It is symptomatic of this difference between the father and the son that whereas the old collector planned campaigns on the Delaware and, at sixty-six, managed to be near the battlefield at Bladensburg, the young attorney distinguished himself primarily by a speech he made to the Wilmington Artillery Company on July 5, 1813.

In the Episcopal Church, Holy Trinity, called Old Swedes because it had been built by the Swedish Lutherans who founded Wilmington, the volunteer militiamen assembled to hear this speech. Nearby on the Christina was Fort Union, their particular charge, and a flag for this fort had just been presented to them by the ladies of Wilmington. The speech that McLane made was highly patriotic, grandiloquent, effusive, from its beginning salutation, "Fellow-Soldiers and Fellow-Citizens!" to its oratorical conclusion, a tribute to the martyred Captain Lawrence and an injunction to take him as a model, and "if we fall, to fall like him— TO BE IMMORTAL!" [71]

But amidst all the homage that he paid to great men and great deeds, McLane introduced some Federalist notes. The Republican administration, he charged, in giving up neutrality had broken with the policies of Washington. "It is not for *Us*, as *Soldiers*," he added, on the same theme, "to make our conduct dependent upon our investigation into the policy of this war, or the causes which the government had to embark in it. We will refer that to the mild moments of peace, and to our men in council. . . . *We* are *soldiers* and not *politicians*. . . . As *such* we contend, not for the administration, but for the nation." [72]

He had no sympathy at all for talk of secession. "The true patriot should look to the dissolution of the Union as contemporaneous only with that of the world. . . . He should cling to it as the plank in the storm. . . . It would be next to treachery to link its fate with party schemes. . . ." But it seemed quite fair to Louis to get in a partisan word for the Navy, the pet of the Federalists: "This nation is formed for a naval Power, because the bold enterprise of her sons, makes them nautical from their birth. . . . The true policy [obviously not the Jefferson-Madison policy] of the government would direct the resources of the nation to the advancement of her naval power." [73]

Such Federalist sentiments were either ignored or discounted by the Republicans of Wilmington, which means a majority of the voters of Wilmington and quite probably a majority of the artillery company. The address was ordered to be published by the company "for the benefit of ourselves and our fellow citizens." [74] Louis McLane was glad to oblige them with a written copy. Publicity for himself and for his sentiments, patriotic and Federalist, was appreciated. It would be helpful in a political career in Delaware, where, almost alone in the Union, patriotism and Federalism were still not only popular but frequently conjoined in the minds of voters.

X DELAWARE FEDERALISM

From the time he returned to Wilmington to study law, Louis McLane must have known he was going into politics. His father had been active in politics and, as collector, held an office of great practical political importance. His legal preceptor, James Bayard, was the most prominent Federalist politician in Delaware and even in the Senate of the United States.

Louis could be reasonably sure not only of a political career but of going to Congress. At one time or another most Delaware lawyers went to Congress. For example, the first Wilmington directory, in 1814, lists nine lawyers with offices in Wilmington.[75] Of these, five went to the House of Representatives, four to the Senate. And downstate, in Kent and Sussex counties, a lawyer's chances were even better, for there were fewer lawyers to share the spoils, and yet there was insistence that no one area should monopolize the choice positions.

No matter where a man lived in Delaware, his political opportunities were greatest if he was a Federalist. Of the eight men elected governor of Delaware from the adoption of a new constitution in 1792 to the end of the War of 1812, all but two were Federalists. Of the ten men elected to the United States House of Representatives from its establishment in 1789 to the end of the War of 1812, all but two were Federalists. Of the nine men elected to the United States Senate in the same period, every one was a Federalist.[76] This senatorial choice, of course, indicates the prevailing sympathy of the Delaware legislature, officially entitled the General Assembly, which chose the Senators.

The odd thing about the position of the Federalist party in Delaware was not its strength prior to the War of 1812; there were other states in which it showed great strength in that period. It was the source of Federalist strength in Delaware that was odd, particularly in view of the general impression regarding the relative appeal of the Federalist and the Republican parties. For in Delaware, the Federalist party was the agrarian party, the rural party, the backwoods party. The Republicans could usually carry one Delaware county, New Castle, while the Federalists carried the other two.

New Castle County was the most urbanized, most actively commercial, most industrial part of Delaware. And its largest community, its chief port and manufacturing center, was Wilmington, which was also the stronghold of Jeffersonian Republicanism in Delaware. Justice Samuel Chase, of the United States Supreme Court, was unduly worried about the rise of Republicanism in Delaware in 1800, but though wrong in his general appraisal of the popularity of the somewhat pro-French and therefore to him seditious party, was right in detail as to the center of its strength. At a circuit court he told Gunning Bedford, Jr., the district judge, "that a highly seditious temper had manifested itself in the state of Delaware among a certain class of people, particularly in New Castle County, and more especially in the town of Wilmington." [77]

Delaware Federalism was peculiar not only in the geographical distribution of its constituency but in the degree of its organization and in the longevity of its political control, even of its life as an organized statewide party. The first of these factors undoubtedly contributed to the latter, which can be demonstrated by the political life of Louis McLane. Here, let us note that although the Federalist party lost its dominant position, if indeed it was dominant, in every other state within two or three years after the War of 1812, it continued to thrive in Delaware and to win elections for more than a decade after that war until finally it lost its identity in the rise of new parties that accompanied the political rivalry between John Quincy Adams and Andrew Jackson in 1828.

It is easier to describe than to explain the extraordinary popularity and persistence of Federalism in Delaware. To some extent this popularity and persistence developed by accident. The leaders of Delaware politics in the early 1790's were admirers of Washington and of his policies, and the state was conservative, inclined to hew to its leaders and adhere to established patterns of loyalty, not at all likely to rebel against the existing order. Perhaps this was because the state lacked both a newly settled western frontier and a large metropolis; the growth of either might have encouraged a rebellion to set aside the status quo and give the new and rising frontier or city a greater measure of influence in state affairs. Though woodlands back from the rivers remained to be cleared, the best land throughout the state was occupied for generations before 1789. Delaware was settled, demographically and emotionally, and was willing to stand pat. The one large new immigrant group in the eighteenth century were the Scotch-Irish, and they did become Republicans and challenge the existing order; the largest and most rapidly growing city was Wilmington and it became the Republican stronghold. But the Scotch-Irish and Wilmington could not carry the state, could not upset the equilibrium that was the strength of the Federalist party in Delaware.

And then, besides, the Federalist party in Delaware proved highly adaptable. Although in general it was the party of stand pat, the conservative party, the party that maintained old ways, old notions, old prejudices, old patterns, its leaders were willing to learn and to adapt themselves, where they must, to new conditions and new necessities of life. They were adaptable in terms of legislation—though their strength rested in rural Delaware, they would eventually give Wilmington and its manufacturers most of the laws they wanted. They were adaptable in organization—though the Republicans were the first to adopt such devices as county mass meetings, hundred and county committees, state conventions, the Federalists were not far behind. Even their name they could change when necessary; so when Federalists became unpopular they became Federal Republicans.

And they were the popular party. Their strength rested in the yeomanry of Delaware, the common man. Solidly rooted in two of the three counties at a time when the three were approximately equal in population, the Federalists had only to get out the vote in their own enclaves to win. And they did do so, often to a very surprising degree. Hezekiah Niles estimated that Sussex County had sometimes turned out as much as 90 percent of its eligible voters.[78]

The fact that the Federalist party's origins were rooted in nationalism must account for some of its appeal to Delawareans. Delaware was so small that it could harbor no ideas of independence, of pursuing a course separate from its neighbors. Once Delawareans were assured by the federal structure of the government and by equality in the Senate of continued control of their own local affairs, they rallied enthusiastically to the Constitution. The first state to ratify the Constitution, Delaware acted by unanimous vote of its convention and without any organized opposition. Delaware's size and geographical location, sharing a river and a peninsula with her neighbors, made her citizens quite conscious that their future opportunities would be best served by a high degree of interstate relationship. A Delaware merchant or miller, even a Delaware farmer, had little chance of advancing far if his products and his markets, his business, were restricted to the bounds of Delaware.

The original Delaware Congressmen saw this and rallied to the support of Washington's government and Hamilton's plans for a progressive and vigorous national policy. And even though the popular support of Delaware Federalism was rooted in the yeomanry, men who might not themselves recognize the sociopolitical motivations that directed Delaware's course, the leaders in Delaware politics were closely tied to the mercantile aristocracy of Philadelphia, where the name of Thomas Jefferson is still not overwhelmingly popular.[79] Delaware Federalists such as George Read, Richard Bassett, James Bayard, Henry Latimer, William Hill Wells, Henry Moore Ridgely, and Allen McLane had close relatives and friends in Philadelphia and tended to ally themselves politically to the leaders of that city's mercantile community. The yeomanry of Delaware were too close to the city to be stirred into political rebellion easily by tall tales of the monstrous crimes of the bankers of Chestnut Street.

And, finally, the strength and longevity of Federalism in Delaware can be partly explained by the fact that it was never seriously weakened by schemes for treason or disunion during the War of 1812. However much the Delaware Federalists might feel the war was unnecessary and a result of the mistaken policies of a bumbling administration, Delaware was too nationalist to consider treason, too central to think of secession. All the errors and failures, everything discreditable about the war, Delawareans blamed upon the Republican administration; all successes, everything that was creditable, could be scored, they felt, to the Federalists. The Navy was particularly the child of Federalist policy, and the successes of native sons such as Thomas Macdonough and Jacob Jones sounded particularly sweet to Delawareans. The peace brought an end to the rigors and dangers of British invasion—Lewes had been bombarded and the British raids along the Chesapeake had been too close for comfort— and a share of the credit for it could be given Delaware's Bayard.

If anything, in its purely local effects the war strengthened Delaware Federalism. But developments elsewhere were such that Delaware Federalism would soon become a unique relic of a past time, subject to attrition from national politics.

XI   THE ELECTION OF 1816

Such was the party, such was the political system, that nourished young Louis McLane. As the collector's son, as James Bayard's law clerk, he was stamped a Federalist from his youth, fed on the Federalist sentiments we have seen even in his ultrapatriotic July 5 speech in 1813.

He had to begin his political life, of course, in a humble role—as an electioneer, a speaker at the hustings, a committeeman. And so the first view of Louis McLane in politics comes in a meeting at Brandywine Village, the mill town where the road to Philadelphia crossed the Brandy-wine, now long absorbed into Wilmington. It was 1810 and Louis was twenty-six years old, short, dark-visaged, already with three years of experience at the bar. The Federalists were being pressed hard; accused of too great a friendship for England, they were victims of the war-mongering spirit that was abroad.

To try to turn the fury of this jingoism upon their opponents, they concentrated their attack upon the Emperor Napoleon, as was made apparent in a rhymed announcement of free transportation to the polls:

> We've chartered a federal republican boat
> For our friends and the friends of old England at heart.
> Who detest from their souls that arch fiend Bonaparte.

And so at the Brandywine Village meeting where there was much drink-ing—drinking was, indeed, a characteristic of Delaware political rallies—the two speakers, Senator Outerbridge Horsey and "Little Louis Mac-spang," leveled so much of the invective at the French bogeyman that an opposition paper said Bonaparte seemed to be running for governor of Delaware. The fact that McLane followed Senator Horsey as one of two main speakers indicates that he was already being given assignments of importance in his party, even if the opposition press called him by a demeaning name.[80]

His next political appearance may seem more routine, but it gave him an equally important role; his first appearance was as a public speaker at a festive rally, his second was as a writer, perhaps even a shaper of party policy, at an organizational meeting. On August 29, 1812, the Fed-eralists of New Castle County held their annual pre-campaign meeting at Christiana Bridge and there determined to hold hundred elections for the choice of delegates who would meet in September to form a county ticket. The meeting also chose a committee of five leading Fed-eralist lawyers—James M. Broom, James Booth, Kensey Johns, Nicholas Van Dyke, and Louis McLane—to prepare resolutions critical of recent measures of the Madison administration. At the same time, Louis's younger brother Allen was appointed to the party "committee of vigi-lance" for New Castle Hundred.[81]

It is of no particular significance that in the election that fall Louis received one vote for Representative.[82] Not until 1815, after the war was over, was Louis a candidate for political office. In that year he was on the Federalist ticket for assemblyman from New Castle County. Each county had seven members of the state house of representatives, the lower house of the General Assembly. These members were chosen annually on a countywide ticket, each elector voting for seven candidates, without any requirement as to residence more specific than in the county itself. Since 1811 there had been a polling place in each hundred; previously all voters had gone to the county seat. Normally, the entire legislative ticket of one party—the Republican party in New Castle, the Federalist in Kent and Sussex—would be elected, though occasionally, particularly when there was a schism within the dominant party, a mixed delegation would be chosen.

In this year, 1815, the normal course was taken: the Republican ticket swept New Castle County. Its lowest candidate, Victor du Pont, ran ahead of the leading Federalist.[83] The Federalists did elect a state senator from New Castle County, but here they were aided by a division among the Republicans.[84] Defeat in the election was no blow to Louis McLane's standing in his party, because Federalists were expected to lose in New Castle County. In the next year, 1816, his party ran him for a more important post, for United States Representative, and in doing so it was doubtless moved by the hope that McLane could reduce the normal Republican plurality in the county where he made his home. Whatever the reason he was run, it took a bit of luck to get him on the ticket.

The previous Delaware congressional election, in 1814, had been swept by the Federalists, who had sent Thomas Clayton, son of a former Senator, and Thomas Cooper, of Sussex County, to the House of Representatives. In the new Congress these Representatives voted for a law that became very unpopular, the Compensation Law, which raised the salaries of Congressmen from six dollars a day while Congress met to a fixed sum of $1,500 a year.

On August 6, 1816, the Federalist nominating committee met in Dover to choose a state ticket—a candidate for governor and two candidates for United States Representatives. The committee, or conference, consisted of only nine men, three "conferees" selected in each county by a county conference. When these conferees met, some of them were strongly of the opinion that Clayton and Cooper should not be renominated because their votes on the Compensation Law would make them a drag on party success. Jacob Stout, of Kent County, who was presiding, declared he was for Clayton's renomination regardless and that Clayton would not allow himself to be put aside; "if not taken up, he would run on his own bottom." Thomas Cooper, on the other hand, is reported to have said he could not get 50 votes in all Kent County because he had supported the Compensation Bill.[85]

In spite of Jacob Stout's opposition, the conferees decided not to consider Clayton and Cooper for the new ticket. Then they unanimously
selected Caleb Rodney, a Lewes merchant and brother of the governor,
Daniel Rodney. The second choice was not so easily made. Since Rodney
came from Sussex, it was obviously desirable to have the other man
come from upstate, but in this case that could mean Kent or New Castle.
Louis McLane was suggested, perhaps because he was born in Kent
(Smyrna) but lived in New Castle County (Wilmington). There were
other names suggested, including that of Thomas Clayton, who was proposed by Stout. But Clayton was not considered since Cooper had already
been dropped, and the conferees selected McLane over another Kent
County man. It was later declared that in the final selection McLane
had a majority of the votes of the Kent conferees, including Jacob
Stout's.[86]

Thomas Clayton, however, was not the man to be passed over lightly.
In a public letter he explained that two years earlier he had been persuaded to abandon a lucrative law practice to serve his state in Congress.
Having a family of young children, he did this reluctantly. He was elected
with "a larger majority than any other man ever received in this State,"
yet now he had experienced a "public degradation," being rejected by
his party because he voted to pay Representatives enough to live on in
an expensive city. If the compensation is not raised, he argued, "no one
who is not rich can serve you." His county, too, was unfairly passed over,
with most of the major offices going to Sussex and New Castle. Consequently, he solicited votes as an independent candidate for Congress.[87]

A few days after the appearance of this announcement of candidacy,
Clayton's supporters convened at Camden, Kent County. If Republicans
did not, as Clayton's opponents claimed, make up over half the crowd,
they must at least have rejoiced at the Federalist quarrel.[88] A few weeks
later Clayton appeared at a meeting of Sussex Federalists in Georgetown,
but after hearing him, the meeting resolved to support the whole Federalist ticket and to reject any suggestion that a second state nominating conference be held.[89]

Clayton's independent fight was hampered by Cooper's unwillingness
to take any active part. Federalist politicians throughout the state drew
together to combat this threat to their dominance. Kent County was
counseled to put aside its grievances and support the party, not individuals, if the party was to survive.[90] This county had had its share of offices
and had been offered the opportunity of naming the gubernatorial nominee but had refused. The party nominees were good men: Caleb Rodney,
a merchant of sound sense, and McLane, a respectable attorney and pupil
"of our departed friend Bayard." Many schismatic efforts had been begun

in the past, including one aimed to defeat Clayton's father, but the party had survived by holding together firmly, for all such independent candidacies as Clayton's were "vanity, ambition and vexation only." [91]

Upstate, in New Castle County, the manufacturer E. I. du Pont worried about the election. He cared nothing for Thomas Clayton and his claims, but he was intimately concerned in the success of the Republican ticket and particularly of the candidacy for Congress of his friend and attorney, Caesar A. Rodney. Rodney and a young Dover lawyer of New England rearing, Willard Hall, were the Republican candidates for the House, but du Pont seems not to have known that two men could be elected. He saw the election solely as a struggle between Louis McLane and Rodney, and he was very partial to the latter. Finding himself in Washington on business a few days before the election, he besought his wife by mail to get his workmen to the polls—to vote for Rodney, of course— and even to give them election day off, with pay. "Ask Dautremont and Dalmas to use all their influence with all the workmen to get those who can vote to vote for Rodney. . . . If any of them are ill or lame, . . . get them horses." Rodney's election over McLane is important to us and to all manufacturers, du Pont wrote, in some anxiety that he could not himself get home to vote; "if Rodney loses his election by one vote I will never forgive myself and he will never forgive me." [92]

Rodney was beaten. With two men to be chosen he ran third—by 48 votes, as it turned out, but the early returns must have particularly chagrined du Pont, for they indicated he had lost by only 3 votes, or even less. [93]

Why du Pont feared McLane's election so much is hard to fathom on any grounds other than historical ones. Louis McLane was du Pont's neighbor on the Brandywine at Rokeby, and with his interest in milling and his Federalist philosophy was likely to be as friendly to manufacturing as anyone could wish. But when du Pont came to Delaware in 1802, he had found the Federalists in general very friendly to England and unfriendly to such liberal French immigrants as his father and himself. It was the Federalist administration of John Adams, toward which Louis McLane's father and his legal preceptor, Bayard, were friendly, that had sought by statute to discourage du Pont's father from migrating to America. [94] As recently as the 1813 election, Federalist handbills and papers had stigmatized the du Ponts and their workers as "Alien ennemies —Friends to Bonaparte Marat & Robespierre—Imported manufacturers— Scouring of the earth—Scrappings of Gutters." [95] Moreover in this very year, 1816, Louis McLane had served as attorney for Peter Bauduy, du Pont's erstwhile partner, and as such had brought suit against du Pont in chancery court. [96]

Reason enough, then, for du Pont's preference for Rodney, an old Republican friend of France, Attorney General for Jefferson. It was sad that the absence of du Pont's vote helped defeat Caesar A. Rodney, but it did not mean victory for McLane. After all, two men were being chosen, and Louis came in first with 3,580 votes, outdistancing his running mate, Caleb Rodney, who collected but 3,410. Both Rodneys—they were cousins—were defeated, for Caesar A. Rodney's 3,476 votes were bettered by the 3,524 received by his running mate Willard Hall. And so it would be McLane and Hall, both young and new to Congress, who would now represent Delaware in the popular chamber at Washington.

An analysis of the voting shows that McLane's victory did not arise, as might have been expected, from his ability to attract what otherwise might have been Republican votes in his home county of New Castle. In fact he came in last of the six major candidates (including the two candidates for governor) in New Castle. John Clarke, the successful Federalist candidate for governor, who lived in Appoquinimink Hundred in the southern part of this county, received 1,090 votes in New Castle to McLane's 1,026. On the other hand, Louis McLane ran ahead of his running mate, Caleb Rodney, in both Kent and Sussex. Since McLane was born in Kent, he might be expected to pick up some votes there, but Sussex was Caleb Rodney's home county. Perhaps this odd result in which each of these two candidates fell behind in his own county can be explained by some very local jealousies; such would be easy to imagine in the case of McLane, the belligerence of whose collector father was notorious. But McLane's downstate popularity may also be owing to some positive reasons for support—for instance, to the Revolutionary fame of his father, or, more likely, to his family's Methodism, for Kent and Sussex were Methodist strongholds. In Sussex McLane received only 52 votes less than John Clarke, who was the only Federalist candidate for governor, whereas Thomas Clayton received 140 votes as an independent Federalist candidate for Representative and Thomas Cooper received 103 votes for the same office.

It was the independent candidacy of Clayton and Cooper that weakened the Federalists sufficiently to permit a Republican, Willard Hall, to be chosen to Congress with McLane. Clayton's 486 votes and Cooper's 390, while an unimpressive total, weakened the Federalist congressional ticket sufficiently to admit a Republican to Congress. On the other hand, a Federalist, without factional intraparty opposition, was elected governor with a plurality of 551 votes.[97] McLane, very likely because of his father's Methodist connections, was able to sustain the independent candidacy of Clayton and Cooper (Cooper apparently did no campaigning himself, but got votes as a result of Clayton's activity) and Caleb Rodney was not.

In winning his first election to office, Louis McLane had shown he possessed the first essential of a successful politician, the ability to get votes. In winning his first election, Louis McLane had also acquired a formidable enemy in state politics in Thomas Clayton, the man whose rejection—"public degradation," Clayton felt it to be—had given McLane a place on the ticket.

It was all the worse that this had happened to a Clayton and in Kent County, where, according to a commentator in 1809, "offices run in the blood of families and descend from father to son." "Were not," he asked, "the fathers, brothers, uncles, etc. of the most of the present office holders, office holders also?" [98] Though defeated now, the Clayton clan would be heard from again.

3

A Villager in Washington

I DOWN THE CHESAPEAKE

At Frenchtown, no town at all but a mere landing on Elk River, travelers from the North and East completed a short land journey across the neck of the Delmarva Peninsula and boarded a steamboat for Baltimore. There was an old post road to Baltimore through Elkton, a little to the north, but wide estuaries that were the northern fingers of the Chesapeake —the Bush, the Gunpowder, and the North East rivers—as well as the broad Susquehanna, interposed difficulties, and the bay journey was usually preferred.

At the end of November, 1817, Louis McLane sailed down the Elk River and into national life. A romantic melancholy seized him, overcoming for the moment his dreams of congressional distinction. Looking about from the deck of his ship he saw to the west the peninsula called Elk Neck, rugged and wooded. But to the east, on the side toward home, his ship slowly slipped past inviting coves and creeks, past fine houses and fertile fields beside Back Creek, and the Bohemia, and the Sassafras. Here was Bohemia Manor, home of his friends, the Bayards, and of his enemy, Thomas Clayton. Here were the comfortable retreats of Senator Outerbridge Horsey and General Thomas Marsh Forman, of Georges and Veazeys and Wards. Up the road from Ford's landing stood Kitty's old home, Bohemia, and it and all this land struck Louis McLane as a symbol of a sylvan peace and prosperity, a way of life that he was foolishly passing by.

He chose to see all his prospects bleak, his "fond anticipations blighted." His investments had failed. Wed in a war that had proved a boon to the manufacturers of his Wilmington and its vicinity, he had plunged into real estate speculations that had seemed destined to make any imaginative man rich in a short time. Probably with Kitty's inheritance as well as his own earnings, and in partnership with Kitty's brother, he had bought Rokeby. But the mill was hardly in his hands when British importations deflated textile prices and ruined American millers.[1]

And as his prospects of fortune died, his responsibilities grew. Three children, Bec and Bob and Kit, were home with their mother because their father must go off to Washington and could not afford to take his family along. And with what prospects did he go? As a Federalist to a Republican Congress. As a Representative from a tiny state unable to exert much influence on the giant Union. As a young man of thirty-five who had failed in finance and now seemed to be pinning his political future to a declining cause. In the last House there had been sixty-seven Federalists; in the assembling House there would be but forty. In Massachusetts, New York, Maryland, Virginia, and North Carolina their number was shrinking. In the delegations of Vermont, New Hampshire, New Jersey, Georgia, South Carolina, and most of the new western states there were no Federalists at all.[2]

How happy he might have been had he invested in some handsome spot upon this bold water! "The thought ever rushed upon me," he wrote Kitty, "that a great portion of my days might yet be destined to be passed on this stream." If he could do it, he would rush home from Congress, gather up the fragments of his shattered fortune, and compose his mind in the bosom of his family. How could he, in such a temper, seek society or friends in Washington? "Friendships are hollow," he concluded, and fashionable society "poisonous." [3]

II   THE ANTI-YANKEE FED

Nothing "can lighten the gloom of my heart," wrote Louis from Miss Heyer's boardinghouse in Washington. Here, probably by prearrangement, he had joined a dining group, or mess, of four Pennsylvanians, the four last relics of Federalism in their state. Joseph Hopkinson and young John Sergeant, both of Philadelphia, were the prominent men of the group and those who most appealed to Louis. For the village Federalists, Isaac Darlington, of West Chester, and Levi Pawling, of Norristown, he cared little.[4] And if Isaac and Levi were of little moment to Louis, he positively scorned their New England Federalist brethren—Elijah, Jeremiah, and Ebenezer; Zabdiel, Ezekiel, and Uriel. "Pedlars," sons of the "universal Yankee nation," from whom deliver me!

"Recollect the girl herself is a Yankee," he told Kitty as they gossiped by mail about a Boston belle and her wealthy but awkward suitors; "until

I have demonstrative proof, I will not believe that either pure love or honourable disinterestedness can mingle in the veins of either sex." [5]

Whatever had so predisposed Louis against his Yankee colleagues? Perhaps it was a heritage from the law office of James Bayard, brilliant, skeptical, wine-bibbing Bayard, who could find few personal cronies among his severe Calvinistic colleagues. Perhaps it was a prejudice of a more personal origin, deriving from his jealousy of transplanted New Englanders, the Wilmington attorney, John Wales, the editor of the opposition paper, Moses Bradford, and his Democratic colleague, Willard Hall. "I mean to recommend him," he wrote of Hall, "to purchase with the surplus of his pay, a tin cart, and trade his way back to Delaware, in the only capacity in which he should either go to or from that state." [6]

Or perhaps his anti-Yankee spirit was more subtly born, out of his Celtic ambition and its object, from his longing to be a landed gentleman of the Chesapeake, like James Bayard and like Kitty's father, Bayard's friend, Robert Milligan. It was Bohemia that Louis McLane sought, a rural retreat and the money to maintain it and the prestige and public position that should belong to its proprietor. But he could not altogether peacefully pursue his ends; as the collector's son, the son of an old guerrilla fighter, he saw enemy campfires in the distance, he suspected ambuscades nearer at hand, treacherous Tories, pernicious rivals, unreliable friends. His father had fought against hussars on land and smugglers on the river; Louis could not advance without a constant mental battle, at the least, against all possible menaces to his security, which meant particularly his home and family, his reputation and his prospects. Bohemia was his object: to be Bayard-like, gentlemanly, spirited, high-toned. Yankees were not. And besides, Bradford and Hall, two Yankees in Delaware, opposed him.

III   VILLAGER IN WASHINGTON

However high-toned he aspired to be, however melancholy his misfortunes made him, Louis McLane was a villager, son of a civil servant, a young Celt plunged now in high society. He affected disdain for it, his penury embarrassed him, he missed Kitty and her gay assurance, but he was entranced by what he saw.

Entranced, but disturbed by some things and shocked by others. He departed early from his first big Washington party, at the French minister's, and from his lonely bedchamber poured out to Kitty a tale of the "dancing, singing, carousing, eating, drinking, and wild wonder" he had seen. The "mode of dressing . . . was both shocking and infamous. I could not describe to you certain parts of their dress, or rather the want of dress, without offending your delicacy. Two of these shameless fair ones had *oustripped* all the rest, and whilst most of the others put on some apology for a covering to the bosom, these defied all such useless drapery, and actually came without any." [7]

Even the kindly Bayard connection, Mrs. Samuel H. Smith, shocked Louis by her "freedom of manners and conversation unbecoming her sex." "For instance," he wrote Kitty, "she had heard when out, of the melon-cholly fate of the Princess Charlotte, and gave us the News—in plain words she said she had died in child bed, and lost the child. . . ." [8] In his amazement at such forthright speech, Louis forgot how to spell melancholy—a remarkable error for him.

In a month Mrs. Smith had retailed to an eager, shocked Louis the Washington gossip of the past decade. "I have seen enough of Washington myself," he told Kitty, "to believe . . . that tho' a lady may retain her absolute virtue, without a very large share of ugliness, awkwardness, or discretion, she cannot long preserve the reputation of it." [9]

But at the "palace," as he called the President's home, all Louis's wide-eyed wonderment was in approbation of the presidential reception on New Year's Day. The large rooms were filled by a crowd of as many as five hundred at one time, including the most distinguished men in the country. A band of "musick" played in the large entrance hall. In four magnificently furnished rooms behind it the guests were received and given refreshment. The mirrors and chairs were most striking, but the whole scene was of astounding splendor.

The two chief actors in the scene won his complete respect. "The President was the same plain honest gentlemanly looking personage which he at all times appears to be." Mrs. Monroe was in a light satin dress with matching hat ornamented by a feather and artificial flowers, and had a "small bunch of artificial flowers set on her left side just below the bosom—the whole giving her an air of youth and beauty. . . ." "Graceful and dignified, tho' easy and very lady like," she "preserved most admirably the character of her station" and yet looked very little older than her daughter who stood beside her.[10]

IV EMINENT MEN

Not all of the great and prominent figures in Washington won Louis McLane's admiration. For one of the most powerful of men, the great Speaker of the House, Henry Clay, he conceived an intense and passionate dislike. So intense was it that it gives evidence of Louis's sensitivity and easy resentment, the irritability he may have acquired from his father; for his dislike of Clay grew out of a small matter.

In gloomy mood when he reached Washington, McLane was slow to call upon the Speaker, though in his first letter to Kitty he told her of his intention of doing so as soon as his despondency was relieved. Clay was offended, McLane heard, "and therefore played shy—and I followed suit." When Clay called on McLane's mess, Louis did not return the call for several weeks—"leaving him to see his attentions were just as indifferent to me, as he might please to make them." This was being "high-toned," in Louis's mind. "The truth is, my dear Kit, that C. himself is very much of a drum on the floor, and his wife as much of a squash at a tea party, . . . and ugly as the Devil." [11]

The result was that Clay only barely spoke when they met and Louis felt snubbed. In burning rage he wrote Kitty that he had only "hearty curses" and "sovereign hate" to offer the Speaker, "a Mad Politician," who played as fast and loose with the fortunes of his country as with his own fortune at cards.[12] But on the floor of the House Clay won McLane's praise in spite of himself, and in his second session he admitted to Kitty that Clay was the best speaker he had ever heard: "I confess I never knew Clay's power before." [13]

Few of his fellow Congressmen won McLane's respect. In fact, he was "strikingly disappointed" in the personal appearance of the Congressmen generally, but there was little chance to judge of their intellectual powers in the dull opening weeks.[14] John Forsyth, of Georgia, who was one day to succeed Louis at the head of Jackson's cabinet, seemed now to have no "capacity beyond an inordinate desire to hear his own voice." [15]

Visiting in the Senate, Louis was little more impressed. Vice-President Tompkins was awkward in the chair—Louis never said this of Clay—and although Rufus King's oratory came up to expectations, it was not to be compared to James Bayard's. As to Bayard, indeed, he was a nonpareil; "I meet with none who will bear a comparison." [16]

Yet the man was present in Washington who was to replace Bayard as Louis's idol. This was William H. Crawford, the giant Georgian who had been runner-up to Monroe in the Republican nominating caucus of 1816 and who now bided his time at the head of the Treasury Department until Monroe's terms were ended. McLane probably saw Crawford first at the same party where the décolleté had shocked him. In writing Kitty, he lavished praise on the Secretary: "For dignity and grandeur of appearance Crawford surpassed every man I saw. His is indeed a front upon which it would seem every God had set his seal."

By contrast John Quincy Adams was "an interesting man, but cold and reserved to an excess." [17] McLane had made his choice years before he was called upon to cast a ballot for one of these two or General Jackson. Jackson he did not meet this winter, not till 1819, and then he was disappointed in the general's appearance, disappointed that he showed nothing of the "ferocious, cruel temper" he was charged with, but instead such a "modest, amiable face" as was seldom seen—a tall man (tall to Louis, that is) and slender, "considerably gray, with a face strongly marked with the lines of care and hard service." [18] An honorable man, a great patriot, a distinguished soldier, Louis thought, but not a Crawford!

The Supreme Court and its great attorneys also elicited Louis's admiration. In February he stopped at the court to hear William Wirt, the Attorney General, and was so spellbound that he forgot he was on his way to the House and missed the day's events there. Wirt "made out of a dry legal subject one of the ablest arguments I ever heard," Louis wrote his young brother-in-law, describing the Attorney General as a "large clumsy looking man, of a cadaverous hue, prodigiously large head, ill looking nose, high wrinkled forehead, and small blue eyes, with rather a melancholy expression. His voice is enchanting, naturally soft and easy, but he swells it to the highest pitch without any great effort, and it is never harsh." [19]

It was a great disappointment to Louis that illness prevented him from hearing more of the arguments before the Supreme Court, arguments in which Webster and Hopkinson as well as Wirt set the whole town to talking of their brilliance. Robert Goodloe Harper, a famous Baltimore lawyer, shed tears as he repeated to Louis a part of Webster's conclusion, and Louis almost sobbed too at his disappointment in missing the forensic duel.[20]

Yet not the least of Louis's admiration was reserved for the famous old Virginian, reared, it was said, on Federalism and madeira and faithful to both, who presided over the Court. John Marshall seemed no longer in the body than the five-foot, five-inch McLane, but Marshall's small body was set on legs that were "two poles of almost immeasurable length." On them he walked unlike anyone else, striding along "like a wild man who never saw the light of civilization." "Slovenly to a fault," he seemed to wear the same shirt for a month. His voice was "infamous, drolling, fine and finicking, and yet with all these imperfections," declared Louis, "he holds your mind completely enchained whenever he attempts to investigate his subject. He is really a most wonderful man." [21]

V   THE ONE-PARTY HOUSE

If the House of Representatives did not awe Louis McLane, it was because he did not immediately understand the significance it had assumed in the government. Under the leadership of Clay, Speaker since his arrival and now presiding for his fourth biennium, the House, and the

Senate too, had come to rival the Executive in the initiation of policy. Indeed the President himself owed his nomination to a caucus of Republican Congressmen, in which House members, being more numerous, carried more weight than the Senators. Standing committees, appointed by the Speaker, with fairly continuous membership, had become important agencies of government, not only initiating most legislation, but often supervising the operation of executive departments.[22] During this very session a member of the Supreme Court observed that the Executive had no longer a commanding influence; "the House of Representatives has absorbed all the popular feeling and all the effective talent of the country." [23]

The intentionally gentle leadership of the past President, James Madison, and of the new President, James Monroe, allowed the House to gain and to consolidate such authority. And at the same time the collapse of the Federal party allowed the House a unity that it had not known since its earliest years. The forty Federalists remaining in the House no longer were considered a unit in anything more than name. Occasionally it suited their individual wishes to vote together, but more often they followed their sectional interests. No formal organization at all existed among them, and because they were so few that they were no longer feared, committee assignments were given them with no special regard to their party.

"Nothing like the present state of things has been experienced since the adoption of the Constitution," declared the noted Portsmouth lawyer Jeremiah Mason. "For the last sixteen years (I think I may say twenty) the government has been carried on by party spirit. What is now to be substituted?" [24] Opposition to the President did arise, particularly over the South American policy of the administration, but at the end of the session the Secretary of State could write of it: "the divisions heretofore so keen and bitter, between federalists and republicans, were scarce perceptible." [25]

VI   A MAIDEN SPEECH (THE ANDERSON CASE)

The House that Louis McLane entered in December, 1817, contained two future Presidents, William Henry Harrison and John Tyler, Jr., as well as Richard M. Johnson, a future Vice-President. More distinguished in its early deliberations, however, were William Lowndes, a tall South Carolinian who was chairman of the Ways and Means Committee; John W. Taylor, of upstate New York, chairman of the Committee on Elections; and Thomas Newton, of Norfolk, longtime chairman of the Committee on Commerce and Manufactures. Two eminent statisticians were in the House, Adam Seybert, of Pennsylvania, and Timothy Pitkin, of Connecticut. General Joseph Bloomfield was in the New Jersey delegation, and in the Maryland, General Samuel Smith, a Baltimore merchant-politician. Samuel Ingham and Henry Baldwin, of Pennsylvania, and Philip P. Barbour, of Virginia, as well as John Forsyth, of Georgia, were members destined to be better known.

Carefully Louis surveyed the personnel and the customs of the House, while he nervously awaited a proper occasion for his debut. In his first recorded vote he joined a decisive majority of 161 to 5 in favor of repealing the excise taxes enacted during the war.[26] The next day he commanded the attention of the House for a moment by moving that a committee look into the expediency of authorizing the Secretary of the Treasury to subscribe for stock in the Chesapeake and Delaware Canal Company.[27] He had been appointed fifth on the Committee on Commerce and Manufactures—a proper assignment for the proprietor of a mill on the Brandywine and the son of a customs collector.[28] But the mill just now was one reason for his despondency, and when he rushed home for a Christmas visit, he had not only cases in common pleas court to tend to but the more worrisome matter of raising money to meet the interest due on the Rokeby mortgage.[29]

The visit home relieved his mind and allowed him to concentrate his attention on affairs in the House. His first speech gave him particular concern, because he was painfully eager to make a mark by it. "If a new member falls off, or fails to arrest attention," he wrote Kitty, "he is not listened to again." That being so, a man of pride—this was Louis—cannot decide "to risk the chances of debate . . . in a day or a month."

Many of the old members, he noticed, jumped up at once, contesting to deliver quarter-hour speeches in which they all said the same thing; then they busily prepared for the press speeches quite different from those just delivered. So "in a day or two, you will have before you all the speeches that were, *not delivered.*" [30]

But Louis was convinced that this was not the way to distinction. Not the number of speeches but the force of what was said gave a man "weight and respectability" in Congress.[31] Parties being nearly extinct, declamation was out of season; "when a man speaks, it is expected that he will speak for effect and not for parade, and there is no feeling to uphold him, but what he creates for himself." [32]

Louis probably did not perceive how fortunate it was for him, inasmuch as he represented a party in a woeful minority, that he appeared in Congress at this time when "effect" and not "parade" or party feeling made a speaker's reputation. Federalist as he was, the very insignificance of his party assured him a hearing on his merit alone, with little partisan prejudice. Party prejudice, in fact, never did hinder his rise till he aimed for the very highest position in the House.

The Anderson case finally brought him forth. John Anderson, a Revolutionary veteran from Kentucky, visiting Congress to plead a private claim of his own and also as agent for several claimants for losses in the Michigan Territory in the War of 1812, offered a bribe to the chairman of the Committee on Claims, hoping a common membership in the Masonic fraternity would permit him this intimacy. The chairman—Lewis Williams, of North Carolina, then in the early years of a long service which in time made him the senior member of the House—was indignant, and reported the offer. Clay ordered the sergeant at arms to seize Anderson, and the House debated not only what punishment he deserved but a more significant point, what powers the House had to seize and punish.

The hesitance in Congress to act, the feeling that constitutional power was lacking, roused the Federalist in McLane. He went to Congress on Saturday, January 10, his courage screwed to the speaking point, but his debut was necessarily postponed because he could not get the floor.[33] On Monday, however, his turn came, and when it did, he chose to open his congressional speaking career with an exposition of Federalist dogma, the faith that he had learned at the knees of his father and at the office of Bayard. The House did have power to seize and punish without doubt, he argued: "We live in an age when Constitutional scruples and doubts of the powers of Congress have become fashionable, and it is not unworthy of remark that these doubts multiply as we recede from the times in which the instrument was formed, and lose sight of those men who assisted in its formation, when, and by whom, it is fair to infer its spirit and meaning were at least as well understood as they can be at the present day." By the disposition to lop off the branches of authority one by one, Congress might soon be left "a naked trunk," without a limb for the exercise of its functions.[34]

Whether or not the Republican Congress was disturbed by McLane's outspoken plea for "a liberal and reasonable construction of the Constitution," it voted to hold Anderson and bring him to the bar for a reprimand by the Speaker.[35] To Louis this was a triumph, for, as he told Kitty, three fourths of the members, before the debate was begun, would have voted to free Anderson. It added to his pique against Clay that the Speaker let Anderson go after a reprimand instead of returning him to the custody of the sergeant at arms.[36] But Clay's action saved the House any further problems of jail-keeping.

VII   AGAINST CLAY: SPEECH ON EXPATRIATION

The reception of his speech gave Louis self-confidence. He had been quite nervous beforehand. "The task of speaking for the first time on the floor of this House," he explained to his brother-in-law, after it was all over, "is one of the most painful I ever undertook." Though "afraid to play about" his subject very much, he had "endeavoured to inforce it like a lawyer, with the best powers of reasoning" he could command.[37] But now he felt triumphant. He had gained standing, had been "rescued . . . from the indiscriminate herd of new members." [38]

Further consolation would come as his and Kitty's friends at home read his speech in the Federalist paper of Wilmington, the *Delaware Gazette.*[39] While others, including Hopkinson and Sergeant, wrote out new speeches for the papers, he abhorred the labor of writing (perhaps there was an affectation of dilettantism in this letter to Kitty) and was satisfied to correct the notes that Joseph Gales, publisher of the *National Intelligencer,* had taken. But he craved a compliment, and asked Kitty to let him know what her aunt and sister thought of it.[40]

What Kitty's aunt and sister thought of the speech we do not know, but some compliments did come; a correspondent of the New York *Commercial Advertiser* reported that McLane had distinguished himself by his elegant language, his graceful manner, and his lucid and convincing arguments.[41] Friend John Bellach and Chancellor Nicholas Ridgely wrote their congratulations from Delaware—though Bellach, with a Quaker frankness that McLane did not admire, said he thought Louis was on the wrong side.[42] The episode furnishes evidence of Louis's driving ambition, and in his own words he testifies to other characteristics—to a "quick pride" which prevented him from making impudent remarks in debate, remarks that Kitty warned against for fear they might lead to a challenge and a duel; [43] and to a kind of fastidiousness or bad temper, which he confessed in admitting his inability to put up with the conceits of an unnamed Congressman's wife.[44]

Not from Federalism, but from his more instinctive feelings, his pride, and his temper, arose the stimulus for his next major speech in Congress. It was against a project of Henry Clay, an expatriation bill allowing Americans to shed their nationality easily and go off to serve the Spanish-American rebels against Spain. It was against Clay that he spoke, and, oddly, for a narrow interpretation of the Constitution.

It was, of course, not the first demonstration that attitudes toward the Constitution were apt to be affected by other feelings. Many Federalists, in opposition now for more than two decades, had come to be chronic protestants against strong executive action of the sort their party had defended in the 1790's. So now McLane declared that only the individual states could permit men to give up citizenship. But he did not confine himself to the constitutional issue; the bill, he thought, was unwise as well as unconstitutional.

Its purpose, he declared, was to get around a provision in our Spanish treaty allowing Spain to treat as a pirate any American assisting the rebels.

By allowing Americans to cast off their citizenship easily, the bill encouraged them to fight against Spain and was covertly anti-Spanish and an abrogation of neutral status. And suppose a crisis arose for our own country and military conscription was needed; would not such a bill as this encourage draft-dodging?

A Virginian rose to point out that no son of the Old Dominion would ever seek to avoid serving his country in time of war; maybe Delawareans would. And this, of course, brought Louis back to his feet to defend the conduct of the people of Delaware in the last war and to disclaim any desire to revive "party heat." He had, he realized too late, given any Republican who wished it a fine chance to taunt the Federalists for New England secessionism and the Hartford Convention.[45]

The bill was defeated and Louis reveled at this victory over the hated Clay. Besides, it brought him still more recognition, and from people whose good opinion he was gratified, almost exalted, to hear. "Hopkinson and *Webster* have told me I came off with their entire approbation," he wrote Kitty, underlining Webster's name, for whereas Hopkinson and he slept in adjoining rooms, Webster's was a new name in his correspondence. Louis's venom against Yankees could be cast aside on occasion, as it was for this famous advocate who had come to Washington to attend not Congress but the Court. For Kitty's own eye—"I have a delicacy upon this subject, which I could not overcome to any other than yourself, who I am always happy in considering the best part of myself"—and therefore not to be read or repeated to anyone: he was proud to say Webster had asserted that he, Louis McLane, was the only speaker in the long debate "who asserted the true principles upon the subject." [46]

A week later he asked Kitty again to pardon his vanity; in writing her he assumed he was addressing his own heart and communicating with himself. And always when he entered "the painful ordeal of publick debate" or any "struggle for some publick consideration," he thought how keenly she would feel his disappointment, and therefore she was entitled to share his success. The occasion: the Secretary of State, John Quincy Adams, sent Louis a request to prepare his expatriation speech for printing in the administration paper, the *Intelligencer,* "as truely illustrative of this great subject." [47]

VIII   THE LABORS OF CONGRESS:
COMMITTEES, VOTES, ILLNESS

His speeches might bring him quick returns in prestige, but in the long run Louis McLane's standing depended upon less sensational facets of his work in Congress—the votes that he cast on important measures, the skill with which he pushed the immediate needs of his constituents, the diligence and ability he displayed in committee work. As a speaker, McLane was what he sought to be, effective rather than brilliant. As a Congressman, he won distinction not only for his effectiveness on the floor but for the understanding he exhibited of whatever particular business became his responsibility and the efficiency with which he could steer matters entrusted to him through Congress.

This was the sort of ability, however, that it took time to develop. He had no resounding successes with the business, largely local, that he undertook in his first session of Congress. As a Federalist, he had no hesitancy in presenting a petition for tariff protection from the Delaware Society for the Promotion of American Manufactures or petitions calling for federal aid, in the form of stock subscriptions, to the Newark and Stanton Turnpike Company and the Chesapeake and Delaware Canal Company.[48] He took the floor twice to explain "at some length" the national utility of the canal, but the success of this struggle was still several years in the future.[49]

Years later he could boast he had supported every internal revenue bill that had come before Congress in his time, and his Federalist bias in favor of federal aid to internal improvements was displayed not only in bills that gratified his own constituents but in his support of a specific program of road repairs in Alabama and Tennessee and in a general statement of the authority of Congress to build roads and canals for the postal service, interstate commerce, and national defense.[50] He was confident of his judgment on the important question of internal improvements and probably equally decided but more concerned about his vote on a less significant matter, the compensation of Congressmen.

This matter was of major importance to McLane, for it was the issue that had brought him to Congress. The Federalist state convention had dropped his predecessors and chosen him because their support of increased compensation had endangered their chance of reelection by an unsophisticated electorate that would but slowly learn to appreciate the cost of public service. So there was no question but that McLane must vote for reduced compensation if the subject came up, as it did. Still it must have been ironic that this issue was raised in the days before Christmas when Louis's own financial problems were most on his mind. "I have made up my mind—and cannot I think be diverted. . . ."[51] The words "I think" indicate some weakness in his resolution. But he had no choice. Down the line he went on the recorded vote, supporting every proposition for reduction, both of per diem allotment and of mileage, but he must have been greatly relieved when a compromise figure was arrived at—eight dollars a day and eight dollars for every twenty miles traveled.[52]

A large majority supported the bill finally, though he did not, but he was glad to tell Kitty that there was little discussion of this troublesome issue on either side except for one or two "fools." [53]

Aside from some "select committees," committees chosen for some special and limited purpose, the Committee on Commerce and Manufactures was McLane's only assignment. Early in the session there is no indication what effort this required of him, but by March he appears quite active. The illness of Newton, the chairman, threw the work on other members, and McLane seems to have borne a large share—most of it, he claimed, and from the reputation he was to gain later for committee work this is not unlikely, though it is not clear why the chairman's labors should have devolved on a freshman Congressman who was but fifth on the committee.[54] Yet in March he reported several times to the House from the committee, a chore commonly, but not always, performed by the chairman.[55] The first of these reports was most important, for it was a bill regulating passenger ships, and McLane's interest in it may have been aroused by the story of the *Aprill* from Rotterdam, which lay off New Castle in January disposing of a cargo of three hundred Dutch or German redemptioners. These were the sole survivors of an emigrant band of over one thousand, the rest having perished either in the port of embarkation or on the high seas.[56]

Unfortunately, McLane's health broke down as the session continued. It was the first of a series of afflictions that upset him during every congressional session. Of course there was no diagnosis in dependable terms. This year it was "rheumatick pains" of which Louis complained; at other times he was afflicted by colds, "dyspepsy," and fevers. After a few years of such ailments he became convinced that his was to be a short life and suggested that the great mortality in Washington required that physicians be provided for Congress as they were for the Army and the Navy.

Even when his rheumatic pains subsided in March, 1818, he was left too enfeebled for the labors of a Congress which was meeting every day from eleven till five or six without refreshment—"unless," he explained to Kitty, "I follow the example of many others and lounge about either in or out of the house, without regard to the business." [57] His illness, his labors, and his loneliness countered whatever reluctance he felt at leaving Congress before the session was over, as he had to do to tend to his legal business in the courts of Delaware. "I shall rouse you from your morning pillow on All fools day," Kitty was promised, "and for once, act the part of a wise man on that anniversary, by seeking the comforts bestowed by wife and children, and attending to the call of business, instead of the windy empty frothy oratory for which Congress Hall is so famous." [58]

IX   REELECTION, 1818

Congress Hall had exerted its fascination on McLane and drew him back despite the "windy empty frothy oratory" he despised, or affected to despise. After a season devoted to domestic comforts and "the call of business," Louis made no known protest when, early in August, the Federalist state convention nominated him for reelection. For the second congressional seat, occupied by the Republican Willard Hall, the Federalists nominated Thomas Clayton, the man they had ditched in 1816.[59] Obviously the party was willing to forgive Clayton for his independent campaign in 1816, even though it had cost them the loss of one seat. Or, if not quite forgiving Clayton, they would take him back on the ticket to unite all Federalist strength possible in these days when the old party of Hamilton and Adams was collapsing in other states.

A few days later the Democratic-Republicans (the terms used were "Democratic Republican conferees" and "Federal conferees") nominated their candidates: Willard Hall and George Read, the district attorney who was the father-in-law of Dr. Allen McLane.[60] "The congressional candidates on both sides," the Republican paper said, "are gentlemen of talents and character." Yet the election did not stir the people of Delaware into turning out in great numbers at the polls.[61]

New Castle County was an exception. The Republicans made efforts to add to their normal majority here, especially appealing to "Sons of Erin" to vote for all Republicans and against the party of the Alien, Sedition, and Naturalization Acts, the pro-English Federalists.[62] The Irish voters probably did respond; in this county the Republican majority increased, and so did the total vote.

Downstate, however, the number of votes declined drastically—by about one third. Such a result in the Federalist stronghold would have spelled catastrophe for McLane's party had not the Republican vote decreased even more than the Federalist vote. The cause may have been that a gubernatorial contest was not on the ballot; in 1819, when there was a gubernatorial election, the number of voters rose to its previous high level.[63]

When the official returns were complete, it was clear that Louis McLane had been elected to Congress again, by a bigger majority, if by a smaller total vote, than in 1816. Again, as in 1816, he had led all the candidates in Kent and Sussex. He and his party were, of course, aided by the fact that this time Clayton was with them instead of being the leader of an independent ticket of party dissidents.

In view of this, it was remarkable that Thomas Clayton was not elected. But Willard Hall, the Dover Yankee, was again returned to Congress as a Republican colleague of McLane. The suspicion naturally arises now—as it arose in 1818—that some Federalists cut Clayton to punish him for running independently in 1816. The Republican press accused McLane's friends of such action, and Louis not only had the Federalist paper deny this but rushed off a personal denial to a friend in Kent, Clayton's county. "I have myself on all occasions advocated Mr. C's nomination, and I know that my father is even unusually zealous in support of the ticket." (The old collector was apparently still an effective Federalist politician.) Louis suspected that the Read faction spread these rumors in an attempt to elect George Read by driving a wedge between McLane and Clayton.[64] If so, they were unsuccessful. In the long run, the Reads were friendlier to McLane than the Claytons were.

X   DOMESTIC ARRANGEMENTS: THE OLD GENT

Dr. Allen McLane never enjoyed high respect from his older brother. When Kitty was pregnant again in the fall of 1818, Louis advised her to consult a Dr. Gibbons, proposing "that both he and Allen may be in the house, the latter to save his feelings, the former to officiate in case of need." [65]

Apparently Kitty's third child, named Catherine for her, had died in the spring or early summer of this year, leaving but two children, Rebecca, who was now five, and Bob, who was three. In the winter Louis had "thanked . . . God that I have yet been saved the agony of loss of children"; [66] now his attachment to the remaining children and their mother became even greater than it had been. When he left home without kissing Bob good-bye, the thought of his neglect haunted him all the way to Baltimore, two days distant on this trip.[67]

Such attachment to his family made it all the harder for Louis to forego taking them, or at least Kitty, with him when he left for the new session of Congress in November, 1818. Never had he calculated on such a separation; repeatedly, during the previous winter, he had declared he would not tolerate such a separation again. And if Louis found the situation difficult to bear, it must have been far worse for Kitty. In the many winters she was doomed to remain at home bearing and nursing and caring for children while her husband was away at Congress—seven of the twelve winters from December, 1817, to the spring of 1829—Kitty complained very little, but occasionally her longing for company, and to be away from the noise of children, found its way into her letters.

The first winter had been hard on her not only because of the financial reverses that had kept Louis from taking her to Washington but also because of the fact that her father-in-law was staying with her. The old collector in many ways was a lovable man: he would make great pets of children, he would delight in superintending the laying in of a supply of ice, he would load the house with turkeys if the mood seized him. But Kitty found him hard to live with, a strange and erratic creature moved suddenly by the oddest quirks and fancies.

Louis knew that his father was not a restful man to have in the house.[68] "I assure you my Dear Kitty," he wrote, "I will devote my life to make you amends for the situation in which I have placed you this winter." "As the spring approaches the old Gent. will be thinking of his garden; if so encourage him for heavens sake to go to it, for . . . we must keep separate establishments." Indeed Louis came to fear, from the odd tone of the collector's letters, that his mind might be deranged. In his letters to Louis, the collector enclosed letters from time to time to people of importance in Washington, but Louis, concerned as he was, never delivered them.[69]

"The old Gent." could write so much, unhandy penman though he was, because he had clerks, or at least one clerk, at his disposal in the customs house. He had an income too, and property—he owned three of the four corners at Second and French Streets, Wilmington, and seven or eight houses in the area—acquired by his remarkable diligence in enforcement of the commercial laws and restrictions, particularly in the times of the Embargo and Non-Intercourse Acts. He also had some remarkable claims against the government and wealthy merchants for ships and cargoes that he seized in those times for law violations. Cope's *Susquehanna* and the ships from Amelia Island have already been referred to. In 1815, before his first election to Congress, Louis had defended his father in a suit resulting from another seizure in 1812, that of the *Superior*.[70] Another prize of value, the schooner *Mary*, was of such worth that the collector's claims to it were specifically devised to Dr. Allen in a will made in 1821.[71]

"The old Gent." was odd and impulsive, a creature of humors who might at times seem deranged, but in the long run it was "the old Gent." who paid the bills. He was the financial resource on which the McLane edifice was built, but he was headstrong, too independent to be counted on at any one moment, a man to be coaxed and cajoled but not to be led. In the end, though, he came through.

At some time in these years, he made over to Louis all his enormous claims in the Amelia Island cases, claims for double duties on the rich cargoes of the *Amazon*, the *United States,* and the *Good Friends.* When making out his will in 1821, the collector testified that he had already made gifts "to a large amount" to his daughter Rebecca Worrell, her husband, and son, and "to a considerable amount" to Louis and Dr. Allen and their children. And in that will, after specific gifts of property to his two sons, the collector made Louis his residuary legatee.[72]

Considering his pride in Louis, his interest in public affairs, and his demonstrated generosity, it is not surprising that the collector had come to the assistance of Louis and Kitty in the winter of 1817–18 when they wished to be in Washington together. But he did such things only in his own time, and he did not come forward until they had given up hope of such help and Louis was trying to sell a slave named Jim—probably a slave of Kitty's—to raise the needed money.[73] "I have no other means," he wrote Kitty. "Break the subject to the old man delicately, as if to sound him, and see what he says. It would be cruel to keep us separated till May." [74]

When Kitty turned to the collector, she found him in a kindly mood, and he advanced $300 at once, enough to equip her and all three children,[75] but it was now February and too late. Louis had enlisted Mrs. Smith to help him search for rooms, but he could find only one suitable place, a boardinghouse called Queen's where some rooms were being vacated in the middle of the month. When Caroline Bayard, the Senator's daughter, decided not to accompany Kitty, Louis decided she must not come. He explained he could not consent to make her the only lady in a "Mess of gentlemen, not remarkable for their polish or intelligence." She would not get to Washington, anyway, till March 1, and he had to be home by April 10 to attend court. "It would hardly be worth while to incur the additional expense of 5, or 600$ which your dress, board and travelling expenses would amount to for four or five weeks. . . . Better give up the idea of coming on, this winter." [76]

This must have been dreadfully disappointing news for her. Just three weeks earlier, a Quaker friend had written Louis: "The prospect of visiting thee at Washington . . . delights Kitty exceedingly." [77] So now Louis had to assure Kitty: "I will sooner surrender my seat in Congress, than spend another winter in Washington, absent from you and the children." [78]

But by the time the next winter arrived, Kitty, expecting a child, was doomed again to stay at home.

XI   RETURN TO CONGRESS—FALL, 1818

It was again the mess at Miss Heyer's on Capitol Hill that Louis Mc-Lane joined when he arrived in Washington in November, 1818. He found Capitol Hill almost deserted, most of the members having "fled to a more central part of the city" and some to Georgetown. He longed to follow them, for although he enjoyed the company of Joseph Hopkinson and John Sergeant at Miss Heyer's, he preferred not to be with others of her guests—namely Nicholas Van Dyke (with whom McLane's relations had been strained ever since the abrupt termination of his suit for Ann Van Dyke's hand) and Levi Pawling—and he disliked his room, which was "cold, open, small and uncomfortable."

The mess that he felt tempted to join was one organized by Senator Harrison Gray Otis and including David A. Ogden, Federalist lawyer from New York, "a gentleman," Louis explained to Kitty, "whose private establishment is perhaps the first in our Country." He would also have enjoyed the company of two other New York Congressmen, Rensselaer Westerlo and Philip J. Schuyler, both wealthy Hudson valley squires, but they had brought their wives and were residing in Georgetown.[79]

Since early in the previous session McLane had felt attracted to Otis and to Rufus King, of New York, who were the high priests of Federalism in the Senate in these, its declining years.[80] But his attitude toward Otis was not one of undiluted admiration. When he first saw Otis at a party, Louis described him as playing "the part of a pert little fop, chuckling with the girls, saying smart things, and looking round for the gaze of admiration, with which he was seldom gratified." [81] Otis would have been gratified, however, by the impression he made on Louis when the latter dropped into the Senate to hear him speak: "A neater and for its length a more beautiful address I never listened to. His enunciation is excellent, his manner extremely graceful, his language pure and impressive, brilliant without being tawdry, and splendid without bombast." [82]

At the end of November, a congressional investigation took McLane from Washington, and when he returned on New Year's Day, it was not to Miss Heyer's but to a new mess, where he shared the company of Otis and Ogden. Kitty too had moved, temporarily. She was still in Wilmington, but she had gone to the home of her aunt to await the coming of her next child.

XII THE SECOND BANK

The congressional business that took Louis from Washington through December, 1818, was of great significance to his career. Yet this business that was now to spur his rise and some day to precipitate his fall had hardly occurred to him when Congress opened.

All that mattered to him then, he wrote Kitty, was "the Del. & Ches. Canal." Otherwise the session did not promise to be either very busy or very interesting. "I mean," he wrote, "to be at home much more during this than the last winter, and so make all the amends in my power for the separation." [83]

The beginning of the session was smooth enough. Louis was reappointed by Clay to the Committee on Commerce and Manufactures, and moved up from fifth to third on this committee, after Chairman Newton and scholarly Dr. Adam Seybert, of Pennsylvania.[84] His first recorded vote was for a bill granting Illinois statehood.[85] His first remarks on the floor were made two days later on November 25, when he moved the tabling of a resolution to investigate the Bank of the United States.[86]

The matter did not seem sufficiently important to be given space in the letter he wrote Kitty that day. From it he would seem obsessed by thoughts of Kitty's welfare—he pines over their separation and counsels her to take exercise, such as walks to Eden Park and along the Brandy-wine—and of his personal business interests with her brother George, probably the Rokeby investment.[87] The motion in Congress, however, was prompted by the situation that was threatening the success of the McLane-Milligan venture at Rokeby.

Through the country in the fall of 1818 financial difficulties grew, prompted by a tight money market, and inability to raise capital to begin new endeavors or sustain old ones. A manufacturing mania had been encouraged by the Napoleonic Wars, which distracted European competitors of the United States, and by an American commercial policy and an American war of 1812–1815, which decreased importations, hampered trade, and thereby made Americans economically more self-reliant than they were accustomed to being. Like George Milligan and Louis McLane, other men had hoped to get rick quick; like Louis McLane, other men had been "wrung . . . by the effects of ill fated speculations"[88]— and some of them had no fathers or friends to fall back upon. When new money could not be borrowed to meet old notes, some men blamed themselves for contracting debts, some blamed the times that made it hard to pay them, and some blamed the lenders who would not increase the debts or postpone the payment.

Banks were lenders, and so men blamed banks and most particularly they blamed the largest bank in the country—potentially, by its charter, the largest bank in the world—the Bank of the United States. This, the second institution to bear the name, had been chartered in 1816 on a motion by John C. Calhoun and had opened for business in Philadelphia in January, 1817. Like its predecessor, it was a commercial bank, permitted to establish branches where it chose, and also a central bank, agent for the United States government, which owned one fifth of its stock and appointed one fifth of its directors.

Poorly managed under the presidency of William Jones, a Republican politician and bankrupt merchant of Philadelphia, it had sought, in the late summer of 1818, by contracting its loans to retrieve its early errors in making credit too easy. The contraction of its loans was at the least inconvenient and at the worst disastrous to its borrowers, and thus the Bank raised a third class of enemies to the two it already had: (1) those, like John Taylor of Caroline or Thomas Jefferson, who were unfriendly to banks in general, and particularly unfriendly to a national bank, and (2) those who opposed this bank because it competed with or constricted the operation of other banks—an example of this latter group being the numerous New Yorkers who resented the power of the Second Bank, a Philadelphia institution. With so many enemies, the progress of the Bank was bound to be challenged soon.

When the challenge came on November 25 in the form of a motion to investigate the Bank, it was moved by a New Yorker, John C. Spencer, an upstate lawyer who was the son of Chief Justice Ambrose Spencer, then the autocrat of New York politics. McLane was the only person to rise and speak to Spencer's motion, and he did so to warn against hasty action. He knew, he said, that there were rumors concerning certain transactions of the Bank, but the Secretary of the Treasury had previously been asked—by the Senate, at the last session—to report on its activities. That report would soon arrive and might furnish all the desired information. At any rate, an investigation should not be undertaken hastily when founded only on rumor. His motion that Spencer's resolution be tabled and printed was accepted without objection, even from Spencer, who observed only that he wished the inquiry he had suggested to be considered again very soon.[89]

Acceptance of McLane's motion was a measure of the respect the House paid him after only one session, as well as of McLane's ability to express effectively the opinions and doubts of his colleagues. When Spencer's motion was taken up again on November 30, McLane moved it be amended by striking out all reference to specific details to be investigated and making the inquiry broad and comprehensive. He thought that some of the information Spencer wanted related to activities over which Congress had no power, and that an inquiry into some details, such as the names of borrowers from the Bank, was objectionable in itself, and meaningless, too, unless the inquiry also looked into the names of all who had applied for loans and been refused, and, further still, into their character and solvency in order to judge whether the Bank based its loans on any unfair prejudices.

Though Spencer opposed McLane, Louis was undoubtedly happy that one of the acknowledged leaders of the House, William Lowndes, came to his aid. Lowndes argued that the broad and comprehensive statement of the inquiry that McLane desired was preferable to Spencer's specified details in order that the statement of the inquiry might not seem to be loaded with allegations. The House agreed, accepting McLane's amendment 85 to 64.[90]

When Clay came to appoint the committee of investigation, it was as natural for him to include McLane as it was to make John Spencer, the originator of the inquiry, chairman. It was a further indication of McLane's standing that he was not named second on the committee but third, after Spencer, of course, and also after William Lowndes. Joseph Bryan, of North Carolina, and John Tyler, of Virginia, were named to fill out the committee, but Bryan asked to be excused from serving because he was a stockholder in the Bank, and William Burwell, of Virginia, was appointed to his place.[91]

XIII   THE BANK INVESTIGATION COMMITTEE

Louis McLane had been a stockholder in the Bank of the United States, but for some reason, very likely because of other necessities, he had disposed of his holdings early in 1817.[92] In Delaware the largest stockholders in the Bank were Republicans, not Federalists. McLane's late Republican rival for Congress, George Read, was the largest private shareholder in Delaware, having 147 shares in July, 1818. Victor du Pont, a leading Republican legislator, had 130 shares, and McLane's Republican colleague in Congress, Willard Hall, was one of five Delawareans owning 100 shares each—among them being Federalist Senator Van Dyke. No McLanes are listed as shareholders in July, 1818 (when a list is available because a dividend was paid), but Read, of course, was father-in-law to Louis's brother, and Kitty's Aunt Milligan, with whom Kitty was staying, was the holder of 29 shares. The largest stockholder in Delaware was the bank with which Louis had been affiliated, the state-owned Farmers Bank, holder of 250 shares in the Bank of the United States.[93]

Besides his onetime interest as a stockholder, Louis had had other reasons to be concerned with the Bank of the United States at the time of its establishment. When it was chartered by Congress in 1816, he was president of the Wilmington branch of the Farmers Bank, and he thought it of first importance to his bank to prevent the establishment of a branch of the national Bank in Wilmington: "There is not business for it, unless by the prostration of some other Institution, and here will be our chief danger." [94] It would be highly desirable to have his bank employed as the agent, or branch in Delaware, of the United States Bank—and political influence might help, plus the fact that the collector already employed the Farmers Bank—but better far to have no agency at all for the United States Bank in Delaware or even that one of the Farmers Bank's rivals be employed as that agent, rather than have a branch of the national Bank established here.[95] In view of these observations, it is odd that in January, 1817, Louis became one of a committee appointed to petition for an office of the Bank of the United States in Delaware, but perhaps his intention was to see that his bank became that office.[96]

By the fall of 1818 when the Spencer committee was appointed to investigate the Bank of the United States, Louis no longer was an officer of the Farmers Bank, having been replaced as branch president the previous January. But his banking experience qualified him to give competent service on the Spencer committee.

If McLane was especially fit to understand the problems of the everyday operations of a bank—for in this day bank presidents and directors met very frequently and passed upon many details, including all loans—another member of the Spencer committee, William Lowndes, was peculiarly well qualified to observe the Bank's activities as a fiscal agency for the United States Treasury. Not only was he chairman of the Ways and Means Committee but he was author of the Sinking Fund Act, which provided for the retirement of the national debt. Though he was a Republican who had gained national attention as a War Hawk in 1811 and 1812, he had married into a Federalist house—his wife was the daughter of Thomas Pinckney, Federalist candidate for Vice-President in 1796—and in his independent course he had espoused many policies dear to Federalists: a tariff, a national bank, and a large navy. His ability, his recognized position (he had refused several foreign missions and, before Calhoun's appointment, had turned down the War Department in 1817), and his opinions made it easy for McLane to look up to him—so did his physical stature, for being six and a half feet tall, he towered more than a foot over Louis.

The committeemen were all young; not one was forty. Lowndes, serving in his fourth Congress, was only thirty-seven. William Burwell, the veteran of the committee, was serving in his seventh Congress but was only thirty-eight. The other three members were in their first Congress.

Young as they were, the committeemen all brought some prestige to their work. Spencer, the chairman, had come to Congress with some élan through being his father's son; he had, moreover, once been secretary to Daniel Tompkins, now the Vice-President. William Burwell boasted a more distinguished clerkship; he had been secretary to President Jefferson. The youngest member of the committee was destined to rise highest in politics. John Tyler had made a good impression on McLane as a debater in the previous winter: "Tyler . . . bears off the palm of oratory from his state . . . —quite a youth [six years younger than patronizing Louis], but manly and at the same time easy, and unaffected." [97]

XIV   THE BANK REPORT

Despite their chairman's reputation for a short temper, members of the Spencer committee apparently worked together fairly harmoniously—and worked hard, too. Soon after appointment they set off for Philadelphia to examine the records and the officers of the Bank. Working daily from ten in the morning till four or five in the afternoon, they waded through innumerable folios, perplexed themselves with banking terms and calculations, and interviewed all the available directors and other personnel of the Bank. Avoiding the social life of Philadelphia, they refused all invitations to dinner except on Sundays. Their one known outing was a dinner on December 15 with one of the government-appointed directors, a young Republican man of letters named Nicholas Biddle, who also had at his table Joseph Bonaparte, the exiled King of Spain, and J. D. Le Ray de Chaumont, another French exile, now president of the Agricultural Society of New York.[98]

Louis McLane, of course, may have seen more of Philadelphia and Philadelphians than the other members of the committee, for this city was the home of many of his relatives and friends—of his father's connections, the McLanes and the Erwins; of Kitty's in-laws, the Simses and Levys—indeed his village of Wilmington and his life to this time were on the Philadelphia periphery. But no notes of his survive from this visit, no comments on what may have been his first encounter with Nicholas Biddle.

After two weeks the committee left Philadelphia, and Louis was able to spend Christmas with his family, comforting Kitty in her season of waiting. The day after Christmas he left for Baltimore—spending a night en route at Elkton and walking across the frozen Susquehanna on foot, the Frenchtown-Baltimore water route being out of the question at this season—and with Burwell and Spencer he spent four days investigating the Baltimore branch of the national Bank, interrogating its president, one James A. Buchanan, and its cashier, made famous by a lawsuit, James W. McCulloch. While McLane and his colleagues were in Baltimore, rather comfortably fixed at Gadsby's Hotel, Lowndes and Tyler singly investigated the Washington and Richmond branches.[99]

As he returned to Washington on New Year's Day, 1819, McLane rejoiced that "the mechanical part" of the investigation was over; the "tug of War" was yet to come.[100] By January 16 the Spencer committee report was completed and presented to the House. "The effect," Louis wrote home, "was great and unexpected. Its tenor was unlooked for, and its development of transactions wholly unanticipated."[101] Supported by a mass of documents and other data, the report disclosed abundant cases of mismanagement and fraud, or as Rufus King, a friend of the Bank, put it, "the dishonorable and injurious proceedings of the Confederacy of Speculators in Balto. and Philadelphia." [102] The committee felt that the charter had been violated in four instances but did not recommend any congressional action, either because they could not agree on a proper course or because a majority felt it was enough that the Secretary of the Treasury already possessed the power to remove government deposits from the Bank.[103]

The worst faults of the Bank were not direct violations of its charter, but a failure to live up to its responsibilities. Controlled by adventurers like William Jones, rather than by men of the standing of its largest stockholder, Stephen Girard, it had joined in the prevailing speculative mania, lent wildly and unwisely, and done nothing to limit the loans of its eighteen branches. When finally its offices recognized that they had overextended themselves, the Bank was forced to curtail its activities very severely, and the effect of its operations was entirely opposite that of a properly functioning central bank, which should check expansion and ease contraction. The worst frauds occurred at the Baltimore branch and were not thoroughly exposed till several months after the committee had reported. It was known that one of the Baltimore investors in the Bank had taken 1,712 shares in 1,712 different names to assure himself many times the maximum of 30 votes permitted to any one stockholder. Only later was there a full revelation of the extent of the chicanery practiced by this stockholder, George Williams, and the two Baltimore officers, Buchanan and McCulloch, who had embezzled much more than a million dollars.[104]

If the congressional committee did not expose all the fraud, it at least began the exposure. On the day the report was made, Rufus King, who had not yet heard it, declared he understood that it deeply affected "the reputation of the Pres. & Cashiers of the Bk. U.S., of Buchanan, McCulloch, & George Williams, and without hearing particulars, the general impression is most disadvantageous to the character of a majority of the Directors." [105]

Already some changes had occurred: the Bank stock had fallen below par and Jones had resigned the presidency. In the House, three alternate courses of action were proposed: (1) that the charter be repealed; (2) that issuance of a writ of *scire facias* be ordered, looking toward a forfeiture of the charter; (3) that the charter be amended to prevent fraud. The committee itself was divided on the extent of the charter violation. "On this point," Louis explained to Kitty, "I am in the minority with Mr. Lowndes": that is, Lowndes and McLane both felt the violations were not so serious as to warrant destruction of the Bank.[106] A majority of the committee did agree to censure Bank officials for mismanagement and speculation, but the only recommendation made was to forbid anyone from voting more than 30 shares, whether they were in the names of other people or in his own name. What further action should be taken, if any, was left to Congress.[107]

McLane confessed privately that he had great uncertainty in deciding for himself the course that Congress should take.[108] But on February 22 when he followed Tyler and Lowndes in the debate, he gave no hint of any indecision. He confessed—he even emphasized—that the existence of abuses in the Bank's management was undeniable. But was "total extinction" the only remedy? Did not the reasons that had led to the chartering of the Bank in the first place remain valid? The most important, in his view, were the need for a national currency and the inexpediency of relying on state banks.[109]

Probably it was fortunate for the Bank that this session of Congress closed on March 3, before the Baltimore frauds were fully known. As it was, all proposals to destroy the Bank were rejected by the House, and only remedial legislation was passed.[110] McLane had the satisfaction of seeing that the course for which he, Lowndes, and John Sergeant, the Bank's attorney, had been the principal spokesmen, was the one followed.

XV   JACKSON'S FLORIDA CAMPAIGN CONSIDERED

Another congressional controversy of the winter of 1819 that did not involve McLane so directly as the Bank question but was also of special interest to his career was the controversy over General Andrew Jackson's invasion of Florida. Florida was then a weakly held Spanish possession from which Indians and brigands of all sorts raided nearby settlers and passing seamen. In pursuing bands of Seminole Indians, Jackson had crossed the Florida border and captured the Spanish forts at St. Marks and Pensacola. Since Pensacola was the capital of Spanish West Florida and since Jackson had captured the governor with the city, the Spanish government protested vigorously. And so did the British, not to the invasion, but to the court-martialing and execution of two captured royal subjects, Ambrister and Arbuthnot, whom Jackson felt to be instigators of Indian attacks.

All the cabinet except Adams had been united in deprecating Jackson's actions, and the House Military Affairs Committee reported to the floor a resolution of censure. When the debate began, Louis's feelings were mixed: "Jackson's conduct cannot, I think, in the whole be approved," he wrote Kitty; "tho', in as much, as in the result it has been beneficial to the Country, I am inclined to ascribe all the hostility toward Jackson, to private resentment, and other feelings than those founded on the public good. But the contest is among those in whose squabbles I feel no interest." [111]

According to John Quincy Adams, the chief defendant of Jackson in the administration, it was William Crawford who led the movement for censure.[112] If this was so, McLane had not yet been enlisted in the band of Crawford's followers. "Mr. Monroe," McLane wrote, "appears to be so destitute of active supporters that he has great need to fear the result of the next caucus. But it is not a matter of much importance to me." [113]

Henry Clay also joined in the attack on Jackson in a speech so forceful that McLane forgot his hatred of the Speaker in his admiration of his oratorical skill. Yet Louis was not himself persuaded: "I feel interested enough to appreciate the argument on both sides, and to endeavour to form at least a sound judgment upon a subject of momentous concern to Genl. Jackson at any rate." [114] In fact, he was leaning toward Old Hickory's side; after all, no harm had been done to this country—how could the general's former services be forgotten and his feelings sacrificed "in his old age." This sentiment would have delighted Collector McLane.

And so too must the collector have been delighted by the stories Louis heard about the general—of his fire and intrepidity in battle, of his kindness and affection in camp, of the devotion his soldiers felt for him. If Louis was, as he says, "perpetually from a sense of duty, and regard for my friends, resisting an inclination to participate" in the debate, it must have been to Jackson's side that his inclination led him.[115] The regard for his friends which kept him out of debate does not necessarily mean he would have been opposed to them; he may merely mean he was sparing them from any obligation of friendship to hear another speech in what was already an overlong discussion.

"Our ears," he complained, "have unintermittingly dinned with the noise of ranting speakers and pygmy statesmen." As he was writing, Charles Fenton Mercer, of Virginia, spoke to an empty house. Only fifteen members were in their seats, and of them only five or six, members of Mercer's mess who were being polite, were listening to him.[116] When the vote was taken on February 8, McLane and a large majority rejected the resolutions censuring Jackson.[117] "The result once more crowned the hero of New Orleans with the laurels of victory." [118]

XVI   THE AMELIA ISLAND CASES

Louis McLane's dissatisfaction with the long-winded debates on the invasion of Florida was augmented by the anxiety with which he awaited news of Kitty's accouchement in Wilmington. He not only worried about whether she would have Dr. Gibbons in addition to his brother, he also fretted as to whether Lydia Sims, Kitty's sister, would get to Wilmington, as she was supposed to do, in time to be with Kitty at their aunt's house.[119] Lydia and her husband were living at this time on a farm called Oaklands, probably part of Lydia's Milligan inheritance, in the southern part of New Castle County. But Lydia, with Rebecca, who had been visiting her, got to Wilmington in time to write Louis on January 20, 1819, that his second son had been born.

Rejoicing to hear "we are blessed with a new pledge of our lives & hopes," [120] Louis fretted that business detained him several days before he could run home to see the new baby.[121] After a week with Kitty he returned to Washington on February 5 for the last month of the session. If he could succeed in carrying his bill for aid to the Chesapeake and Delaware Canal, he promised, his greatest inducement to come to Congress would be removed and he could not be forced to separate himself from Kitty again.[122] In this mood, he was disturbed when Kitty neglected to write for a few days. "Louis the second," he scolded her, "engrosses so much of your time that Louis *le grand* comes off poorly." [123]

Besides the Bank controversy, which lasted through February, "Louis *le grand*" had his time engrossed by private business, the nature of which is not entirely known. As always, he had a number of private memorials to present and private bills to urge upon Congress.[124] There were "several pieces of business in the offices" which, as he wrote on January 24, he was bound to complete before he went home to see the baby.[125] Quite likely these were pension claims, similar to the one that had caused him to remark, a little earlier this month, "There are already more applications than there were soldiers at any time during the War of the Revolution." [126]

The most important piece of private business for Louis McLane arose suddenly in February, when he learned that Stephen Girard had at last determined to pay double duties on his Amelia Island ship, the *Good Friends,* which Collector McLane had seized in the spring of 1812. He had to give up a dinner party at the British minister's, he explained to Kitty on February 11, in consequence of the sudden arrival of Charles J. Ingersoll, United States attorney at Philadelphia, "whose business was too urgent to admit of delay, and with whom I was compelled to spend the evening preparing the business for the Treasury. If this should result well, it will be of infinite greater importance to us, than all the gaieties of Washington for a century." [127]

This matter that kept Louis occupied at least a week was worth between $50,000 and $100,000 to his father and himself. The Amelia Island cases would have been worth much more to the collector—half the total value of the three confiscated ships and their cargoes—if Congress had not remitted this drastic penalty in return for payment of court costs and double the normal duties on imports. Girard, Edward Thompson, and the other owners had recovered their ships years ago, but the original forfeitures still were hanging over them because they never had paid the double duties.

Extended less help by District Attorney Read than he needed and further hampered by the death in 1815 of his chief legal reliance, James Bayard, Collector McLane, upon whose initiative the whole prosecution depended, was slow in pressing the suits. In November, 1817, the federal district court supported McLane's claims, and in September, 1818, the circuit court affirmed the district court's decrees.[128] Girard at last resigned himself to paying the duties, which he thought were quite unjust, but Ingersoll claimed that interest must also be paid on them, which caused further delay.

The sum was so large that personal appeals were contemplated, if not actually made, to the highest officials. Edward Thompson, co-owner of the *Amazon,* wrote Girard in December, 1818, of his desire to negotiate the claim in Washington before an appeal could be heard by the Supreme Court: "As Mr. Crawford is determined on running for the President he will of course be visiting his old neighbors &c. &c., and when he is absent I am of opinion with Mr. Rodney, will be the best time."[129] Why Thompson and Caesar A. Rodney thought Crawford's absence gave them an advantage in negotiating is not clear, but either the negotiation failed or Girard decided not to depend on it. President Monroe himself was informed of Girard's decision by his friendly Delaware correspondent, Caesar A. Rodney, Girard's attorney: "Mr. Girard concluded to pay the additional duties on the cargo of his ship Good Friends. . . . Tho' I retain my opinions on the subject of his case, I would not discourage his terminating the unpleasant dispute with the government. . . . He is an important man in Pennsylvania, & has done much to support the credit of the country, at a critical moment; and should the times require it, would step forward again."[130]

Girard's payment of $53,245.20, added to the $47,810.87 he had paid in March, 1813, at last settled the case of the *Good Friends* as far as he was concerned. In August of this same year, 1819, Edward Thompson paid $16,558.57, as his share of the additional duties on the *Amazon.*[131] He too was now removed from the case, but it remained for Collector McLane to secure his personal share of the double duties, which amounted to approximately the whole of the two 1819 payments. Why Louis and his father were so long delayed in securing their share is not entirely clear. Perhaps they doubted their chance of succeeding in a claim to share the double duties. Probably they first relied upon negotiation. At any rate they do not seem to have begun suit for this sum until 1822, which is a year after the collector made the entire case over to Louis in his will. But the circuit court decreed against the collector, and another decade elapsed before the Supreme Court in January, 1832, reversed the circuit court decision and awarded one half of the double duties to Louis, as the collector's representative.[132]

And though that is ahead of our story, it is not the end of this litigation, which still had years before it.

XVII THE GAIETIES OF WASHINGTON, 1819

Despite the fact that there seemed to be "more gaiety & entertainment perpetually in operation" than he had previously observed in Washington,[133] McLane's business, particularly respecting the Bank and the Amelia Island ships, kept him from attending many social affairs. In the third week of February, 1819, he was invited to a party every night. There were so many parties, he wrote Kitty, that a man who "dipped as deeply into them as he is requested to do, would have no time to attend to anything else."[134]

On Monday evening he had Archibald Hamilton, a fellow attorney from Wilmington, as a dinner guest at his mess, and from there ("to save my credit & character") went to a party given by Mrs. Bagot, wife of the British minister, made his "bow," and left in half an hour.[135] He passed up parties on Tuesday and Wednesday evenings, the latter given by the Monroes at "the Palace," but apparently dined with Crawford and then attended Mrs. Crawford's party on Thursday evening. Mrs. Adams's invitation for Friday he declined, but of course he had to attend the dinner on Saturday given by his mess for the members of the cabinet and the resident foreign diplomats. This affair was in repayment of debts of hospitality and went off "most pleasantly," Louis thought. "After our dinner, and when the champaign had enlivened us most delightfully," he reported to Kitty, "we went forth . . . to Madame de Neuvilles, where an immense crowd had assembled——. In the midst of such a crowd I deemed it most prudent to take my champaign home, rather than allow it to evaporate amid the gaiety of the levee, and accordingly did not remain more than half an hour."[136] He intended to pass up the Washington "Birth Night Ball" but to go the next night to see the "splendour of the ancient aristocracy," as exhibited by Mrs. Thomas Peter, a granddaughter of Mrs. Washington and a staunchly Federalist patriot who, with her severely corseted daughters, America and Columbia, sneeringly referred to the Republicans as "our present rulers," as though a restoration of a Federalist line was imminent. "As this is likely to be something out of the ordinary," Kitty was promised, "I shall not fail to be a spectator of the scene." [137]

When Louis got home in March, there was much to be told to his lonely but lively helpmeet—tales of the oratorical skill of William Pinkney in the Supreme Court, of the failures of James Tallmadge and John Holmes in the House, of the gambling of Henry Clay, of the bloody Mason-McCarty duel, of the domestic manners of the Senator Outerbridge Horseys and the Harrison Gray Otises, of the political intrigues, the amorous scandals, and the fashionable apparel of Washington.[138] While Louis played with the baby and gave Bec and Bob the kisses he had promised them, Kitty determined she must, if conditions were favorable, her condition particularly, come along to Washington in the fall and see all the wonderful goings-on for herself.

4

Missouri—and
Making One's Way

I KITTY GOES TO WASHINGTON

Kitty did get to Washington at last. In the fall of 1819, she and her entourage—the children, some servants, and her friend Caroline Bayard, the Senator's daughter—joined Louis in the capital. It was a gay winter in Washington, and sociable, chatty Kitty must have enjoyed the change from the last two lonely winters in her own village.

"Take care that so fascinating a dame be not kidnapped from thee," a friend had joshed Louis in a previous winter when there was a prospect Kitty would come.[1] Kitty was far too attached to Louis to be stolen away, but she could be entranced by the excitement of the city. And Louis could share her excitement. At last what he had longed to do through the past two winters was possible. He could take his wife on his arm through the grand saloon at the great parties; he could present her to the distinguished society of Washington; after a party or visit or debate, he could chat with her to whom alone he was able to pour forth his convictions and his fears.

"I have been so much occupied since my arrival here, in the ceremony of visits, parties, and some little publick business," he explained to Caroline Bayard's brother, "that I have been obliged to deny myself the pleasure of writing."[2] It was squiring Kitty and Caroline about the city, of course, that left time for only a "little publick business." But the time could be afforded at the beginning of Congress, when committees and business generally were less demanding than after the session was well under way.

Congress kept Louis engaged daily from eleven to three or four in the afternoon, and if he had to attend a committee meeting, he would be off

96

to the Capitol earlier. If Kitty followed the fashion, she stayed in their rooms with the children till noon, when she could sally forth in a carriage with Caroline Bayard and make morning calls any time up to three, sometimes merely leaving cards by a footman. Or they might proceed to the newly reopened House chamber, where they would be welcomed as spectators, but hardly as auditors, for the otherwise splendid room was so constructed that only with the utmost difficulty could even a loud orator be heard by all.[3]

If neither calling on friends nor visiting the House attracted them, Kitty and Caroline might go to the Senate, where they were sure to find friends among the members to welcome them to the sofas outside the bar of the chamber. On days when the number of guests exceeded the number of seats available for them, gallant Vice-President Tompkins even allowed some of the ladies onto the floor, despite the displeasure of many of the Senators.[4] Another fashionable resort was the Supreme Court once its session had begun, for there the ladies would come on the arms of gentlemen to hear performances by Wirt, Pinkney, Webster, and others of the nation's most distinguished advocates.[5]

If these amusements palled, Kitty and Caroline might visit some of the one hundred and twenty-nine shops in Washington. J. Stettinius, for example, offered many kinds of cloth, handkerchiefs, hosiery, and rugs. Ann Sawyer advertised new winter fashions in millinery from New York and also a mantua maker just come from England and acquainted with the latest London fashions.[6] Bookshops offered a variety that may have appealed to Kitty and Caroline, and Louis too, for they were readers, their favorite writer being the author of *Waverley*. Many a quiet hour in Washington may have been devoted to Walter Scott's long romantic novels, for his early thralldom over the McLanes and Milligans, transplanted Scots, is attested by the name they gave their mill on the Brandywine, Rokeby being the title of one of Scott's narrative poems. *Ivanhoe*, *The Heart of Midlothian*, and *The Pirate*—these three novels, at least, were eagerly read in the McLane circle upon their appearance.[7]

Shakespeare was also known well to the McLanes, and Laurence Sterne's *Tristram Shandy* lent metaphors to Louis's correspondence— "chapter on accidents" and "Uncle Toby's Pipe," for instance.[8] Louis, if not Kitty, had a taste for history, and was reading—or at least borrowing—Robert Watson's *Philip II* in 1821;[9] years later he waited for each of Macaulay's volumes.[10] When he was obliged to fill a page in Kitty's memory book, he chose a passage from the prose of Lord Bolingbroke's *Reflections upon Exile* rather than the customary poetry, noting that prose was more fitting for him. Perhaps his youthful enthusiasm had been ephemeral; or maybe he had never cared for Rokeby anyway, and had merely acquiesced in the name to please George Milligan, or Kitty.[11]

Squiring the ladies gave Louis little time for reading in the winter of 1819–20. Evening parties were given almost every night, and as the season wore on they became more rather than less frequent. "This city and the publick business will wear its best garb in February when the Supreme Court will be in session," Louis explained, for then was the height of the fashionable season, with both Congress and Court operating to attract the fair and the important of all America.[12]

All winter the President's home was open every other Wednesday evening to anyone who chose to attend. On the intervening Wednesdays Secretary Adams and his wife entertained, by invitation only, but it seems certain that Kitty and Louis were invited, since Louis had always been invited in the past when he was alone. The other cabinet ministers also entertained, as did some of the wealthy private citizens, such as the anachronistic Mrs. Peter; but the monarchical elegance of the parties of the foreign ministers offered Kitty a special thrill.[13]

When Kitty was with him, Louis's familiar correspondence was so much reduced that many details of his personal life, which were in other years set forth in detail, did not now come to be recorded. So it is that Louis does not mention where he and Kitty stayed in Washington this winter, but it seems likely that it was at Crawford's boardinghouse in the mess he had shared the previous season with the Otises and Rufus King, as well as with Thomas Van Swearingen, of Virginia, Thomas Baily, of Maryland, and others. Their close associates included the John Elliotts, Elliott being a Senator from Georgia, the family of Senator James Brown, of Louisiana, and the John D. Dickinsons, of New York—not to be confused with the family of the famous John Dickinson of Delaware. Two Virginia bachelors, Charles Fenton Mercer and John Randolph of Roanoke, were also among the intimates of the McLanes.

Louis was irritated by Caroline Bayard's "fullsome affection" for Mercer and her inability to conceal it, particularly as he saw Mercer as a "conceited little bladder" and a confirmed jilt, unworthy of and indifferent to Caroline. Mercer called on them nightly (it seems likely he was a fellow boarder), but twice when he called he was "much more than *tight.*" Caroline also admired Randolph, whose company they all enjoyed. His departure from their mess, soon after they had arrived in Washington, would have left them inconsolable, Louis declared, only half in jest, had not this "wonder of wonders" occasionally given them his company still "in some of his happiest moments." [14]

However odd may seem this association between a Delaware Federalist and an undiluted Virginia Republican, it was based on a reciprocal enjoyment of each other's society. Randolph declared on first meeting McLane that this was the finest young newcomer he had seen in Washington by a long sight.[15] When returning home in April, 1820, he sent for Louis, "made many professions of regard, and was rather flattering," not least by his presentation of "a very neat little picture of Genl. Washington, set in a frame," as a gift to the McLane baby, Louis, Jr., who was to be told, "as soon as he becomes old enough to understand it, . . . that it is an Easter present from John Randolph of Roanoke." He also tried to be helpful in a project McLane was considering, that of moving to Baltimore to enlarge his practice.[16]

The erratic Virginian was not altogether happy. "His mortification at what he considers his failure on the Missouri Question," Louis wrote in February, "has thrown him into a fever of body and mind, and until he recovers from this, he is bad society for anybody." [17] Randolph himself testified to the oppression this subject cast on his spirits, when he wrote Louis, in May, as he was about to go abroad: "I long to talk to Miss Caroline about Ivanhoe. Do you know that Garth and Womba with their Dog-Collars around their necks brought up Missouri Question to my mind. I am persuaded they were happier in those days of slavery than in these of Pauperism and Gin and Radical reform. No slavery so intense, so scorching, so heart breaking as that of the manufacturing and paper systems."

And this strange, lean boy-man concluded his note with a couplet,

> Fare thee well, & if forever,
> Still forever, Fare thee well.[18]

II   THE FIRST MISSOURI DEBATE, 1819

The Missouri Question oppressed more men and less sensitive men than John Randolph. Yet in its initial stages it was singularly unexciting to the country at large. Only months after the session of Congress in which it was raised did it become a popular issue of controversy, but then it became a dress rehearsal of the greater sectional conflict that was to come and as such it appalled thoughtful men.[19]

In this controversy, as in other public issues, Louis McLane took a moderate position not unsuitable for a representative from a border state who was at once the son of an abolitionist and the son-in-law of the second largest slaveholder in Cecil County. When he adopted a position, however, he expressed himself with such conviction, and fought for his views with such vigor, as had his father, that opponents became to him villains and blackguards, foul-hearted enemies to all wisdom and good. If he was a persuasive statesman, and his career in Congress, in the cabinet, and in a foreign mission seems to indicate that he was, his success rested as much on the fact that he became himself persuaded of the justice and righteousness of his views as it did upon the moderation and intelligence on which his views were based. Yet this ardor with which he embraced a position was, if useful, also self-destructive. It filled him with baleful thoughts of all who opposed him; it destroyed his ease, his happiness, and, far too often, his friendships.

The Missouri controversy began quietly. In November, 1818, a year before Kitty came to Washington, the House was considering a resolution for the admission of Illinois to statehood, when James Tallmadge, Jr., of New York, a veteran of only one congressional session, rose to oppose the resolution on the grounds that the Illinois constitution provided insufficient safeguards against slavery. His opposition was brushed aside, as a majority, including McLane, voted for the admission of Illinois.[20]

Tallmadge's opposition to the expansion of slavery was not to be dismissed so easily. When statehood for Missouri was considered in February, 1819, Tallmadge again moved an amendment, one that consisted of two parts, the first prohibiting the further introduction of slaves and the second setting free at the age of twenty-five all slaves born in Missouri after its admission to statehood. McLane voted against the first part of the amendment and refrained from voting on the second part—whether purposely or accidentally, as by absence from the floor, the sources do not say. Both passed, narrowly, and when the House was called to vote on engrossing the newly amended Missouri resolution, McLane was in the majority.[21] Apparently at the moment the admission of Missouri was more important to Louis than any question about the expansion of slavery.

His feelings may well have been mixed. In Wilmington, his home, and in Smyrna, his birthplace, abolitionism had long been popular. In the local abolition movement, Methodists in general had been active, and among the Methodist abolitionists his father particularly and his father's friend Richard Bassett had been leaders. Louis himself was at one time counsel for an abolition society.[22] On the other hand, McLane's admiration of the Eastern Shore planting and slaveholding gentry, typified by the Bayards and the Milligans, helped moderate whatever abolition sentiments he absorbed from his lower middle class Methodist father.

In January, 1819, when Congress discussed Jackson's invasion of Florida, McLane grew disgusted at a series of ranting speeches on "scalps, broken heads, and butchered women and children." The worst of all was a long "empty harangue" on this subject by James Tallmadge, who by it "lost the standing" he had previously acquired and plunged to the level of those "to whom no one listens who can get out of the noise." [23] Perhaps the scorn he felt for Tallmadge helped turn Louis against Tallmadge's proposal of an amendment to the Missouri statehood bill. When another New Yorker, John W. Taylor, proposed to ban slavery in the Arkansas Territory, Louis entered the debate by proclaiming his abhorrence of slavery, even "in its mildest form." He cited "his earliest education and the habits of his life," as alike opposed to slaveholding; indeed "he would unite with gentlemen in any course within the pale of the Constitution for the gradual abolition of slavery within the United States."

The importance of McLane's speech, however, rested neither in these pious declarations of his personal dislike of slavery nor in his main argument that Congress had no constitutional right to impose such a restriction as Taylor proposed—for slavery existed in Arkansas and was protected by the clause of the Louisiana Purchase Treaty guaranteeing the property of the inhabitants. The importance of, or at least the interest in his speech, rests in his suggestion of a compromise. Though he was speaking on an amendment to the bill organizing Arkansas Territory, the problem of restricting the expansion of slavery had just been raised in the case of Missouri, and whether in Missouri or in Arkansas the problem was the same, except that in one case a state government was concerned, and in the other a territorial government.

McLane did not go so far as to propose a specific line dividing slave and free territory, but he did propose some line. It had always been "a favorite policy with him," he explained, to fix a line west of the Mississippi, north of which slavery could not be tolerated, and he hoped this might soon be done on principles of fair compromise, particularly since he had heard some gentlemen from the South and West say such a line would be satisfactory to them. [24]

The compromise was not yet forthcoming, and in the next few days he cast a series of votes against all proposals to restrict slavery in Arkansas or Missouri. [25] Yet the issue did not appear of great significance to him. In the extant letters to Kitty written after Tallmadge first proposed his restrictive amendment on February 13, Louis makes not one reference to it or to this controversy. Some letters are lost, of course—only three survive for the last two or three weeks of this session—but other issues such as the Bank investigation and the censure of Jackson were mentioned through letter after letter. The Senate turned down the Tallmadge amendment, and the Missouri bill was lost when the Fifteenth Congress adjourned for good in March, 1819.

III   THE SECOND MISSOURI DEBATE:
INSTRUCTIONS FROM HOME, 1820

By fall when the new Congress convened and Kitty came to Washington, the public was excited about Missouri. Beginning with a meeting in Burlington, New Jersey, on August 30, an anti-Missouri crusade was under way with numerous town meetings—particularly in the Middle States, at Trenton, New York, Philadelphia, Lancaster, West Chester, Mount Holly—addresses, committees of correspondence, petitions, circulars, and other publications. Quakers and Federalists were active in the movement from the beginning—Joseph Hopkinson, McLane's old Federalist messmate was at the original Burlington meeting—and in a state with as many Federalists and Quakers as Delaware something was bound to be heard of the excitement stirred up over slavery expansion.[26]

As the opponents of slavery expansion gathered support, Louis McLane became more vehement in his opposition to any restriction on slavery in Missouri. The result was to open a gap between McLane and the greater part of the northern Federalists—men such as Hopkinson, Boudinot, King, and Otis—to intensify rivalries already existing among the Federalists in Delaware, and to throw McLane into closer accord with southern Congressmen and with Northerners who sought to work with the South in favor of compromise and for the diminution of sectional antagonisms. In a sense, it was the Missouri controversy that set McLane on the road that took him first to Crawford and then to Jackson, just as the Bank controversy, also in the winter of 1819, demonstrated the Federalist Achilles heel that ultimately hampered his success with his new friends.

At the opening of 1820, McLane's letters betray his new concern over "the famous Missouri question," as he described it to James Bayard.[27] "I have reinvestigated the subject since my arrival here," he wrote Caesar A. Rodney from Washington, "and am perfectly confirmed in my first impression; It is in no degree a question of Slavery. It is simply whether Congress can take from the people of any one State the right of self-government, or the enjoyment of any political right secured by the Constitution . . . and possessed by the other States." A territory was something else again, he continued: "I have no hesitation to restricting the extension of Slavery into it, but, being bound by Treaty to incorporate it into the Union when it has the requisite population, it would appear strange if we could impose or even require terms which suppose a discretion in Congress to admit or reject. . . . I cannot surrender my conscience to any man or any number of men." [28]

Talk of surrendering his conscience must have been prompted by knowledge of the deliberations of the General Assembly of Delaware. In that body a representative named Joshua Gordon Brincklé, a friend of young John M. Clayton's, presented on January 5, 1820, the second day of its session, a petition from seventy-four citizens of his county, Kent, "praying the legislature to instruct our Senators and request our representatives in Congress to use their voice and influence in favour of the restriction of slavery in the proposed State of Missouri and the Territory of Arkansas." [29]

Brincklé's action may have been prompted by sources outside Kent. Rufus King is known to have advised Massachusetts to instruct its Senators to vote against slave expansion, and Brincklé may have been influenced by King or others he met in Washington in the course of his services as commissioner for the settlement of Delaware claims against the United States for expenditures in the War of 1812.[30] Possibly Thomas Clayton was stirring up sentiment in Kent to make trouble for McLane and others of his rivals in the party—seeking an issue on which they could be dropped from office as the salary bill had caused him to be dropped from the ticket in 1816. This is pure supposition, but Kent had been a stronghold of abolitionism since the days of Warner Mifflin and John Dickinson, so the collection of signatures to the petition should not have been difficult.

The action that the legislature took was a matter of such interest to Louis McLane that thirty-four years later, long after he had retired, he inquired about the composition of the 1820 General Assembly. Specifically, he asked who voted for and who against the resolution prepared as a result of the Kent petition, his question being motivated by a speech on Nebraska by Brincklé's friend, John M. Clayton, who told the Senate that any restriction on slavery in the territories was unconstitutional.[31]

The petition Brincklé presented to the 1820 legislature was not neglected. A committee under his chairmanship reported two resolutions which, after changes made on the floor, principally suggested by the rich Federalist landholder and former United States Senator William Hill Wells, were sent to McLane and his three Delaware colleagues in Congress. "Resolved," the General Assembly agreed, "that it is . . . the constitutional right of the United States in Congress assembled, to enact and establish as one of the conditions for the admission of a new State into the Union, a provision which shall effectively prevent the further introduction of slavery into such State; and that a due regard to the true interests of such State, as well as of the other States requires that the same should be done." [32]

"I cannot surrender my conscience," McLane had said, and his Federalist colleagues, Senators Horsey and Van Dyke, felt as he did. Van Dyke laid the resolution on the table of the Senate and proceeded, according to McLane, who was not usually very friendly to Van Dyke, to make "a very able argument . . . on the constitutional question and in opposition to the restriction." [33] The three men joined in a reply to Speaker Caleb Rodney of the Delaware senate, who had forwarded the resolutions to them; they acknowledged receipt of the instructions but avowed their inability to comply because their oath to observe the Constitution precluded their participating in action they thought unconstitutional.[34] And this was precisely what they thought of any attempt to restrict Missouri's freedom to decide for itself on slavery.

Willard Hall, the one Republican in the Delaware delegation, refused to join with his colleagues in their letter to the legislature. He thought— or so it seems from his voting record, for he never spoke in Congress— that the restriction was entirely constitutional, and he voted for it and for every bill to restrict slavery. His political persuasion does not explain his vote, but his New England origin may. He was a reformer, an active promoter of public education, thrift, sabbatarianism, and most of the causes of his day.[35]

Louis McLane was no reformer, but he was sensitive to "the peculiar situation" in which the legislature's instructions placed him. To explain his position he rose in the House on February 7, conceding no right of Delaware's legislators to instruct him, but admitting that their opinions must be given serious attention. He regretted that he would not vote as they wished, but he had reviewed his opinion and he still thought Congress lacked the power to restrict slavery in Missouri—and he explained at length why he thought so. He urged the advocates of restriction to compromise, to "yield something to a spirit of harmony" and "put this unpleasant subject to sleep forever," to accept a slave Missouri to get territories "unpolluted with slavery" which would in due time become, of their own desire, nonslaveholding states. The compromise, he insisted, could not bind future states, but if these areas did not have slaves when they were territories they would be very unlikely to allow slavery to be introduced when they became states.[36]

On February 19 McLane again was on his feet advocating compromise. The Maine statehood bill, already passed by the House, had been returned from the Senate with amendments providing for the admission of Missouri and for the exclusion of slavery from the territory north and west of Missouri. McLane liked every one of these proposals, but he would not accept them in one bill, because he did not want to make the admission of Missouri conditional upon the admission of Maine. This may seem a small point, but it was basic to his position, which was the unconstitutionality—by reason of the Louisiana Purchase Treaty—of denying statehood to Missouri.[37]

The House acted just as McLane desired. It rejected the compromise measure from the Senate which connected Missouri to Maine, and then passed the two admission bills separately. In passing the Missouri bill, the House first, by a very narrow margin, defeated the restriction on slavery in Missouri which the Delaware legislature had recommended, but replaced it by the compromise proposal from the Senate forbidding slavery in the territory north and west of Missouri. For every one of these actions McLane voted, and when the famous Missouri Compromise was a reality in March, 1820, he had a right to feel triumphant.[38]

It added to his joy, of course, that Kitty was with him to see his triumph. After she left Washington in late March to visit her sister Lydia at Oaklands and then return to Wilmington to wait for the next baby, Louis had to reduce his exultation to writing to share it with her. For instance, he sent her a St. Louis newspaper with an account of his part in the debate, and with it a revealing comment: "We from the North who opposed the restriction may be denounced" by "Fanaticks, Demagougs, ignorant old women, and finikin, young ones of a fastidious sensibility," but "the most valuable of both sexes will not fail to see the best interests of society" were served by our action.[39] Probably he was responding to some report Kitty gave him of the unfriendly reaction of her friends and relatives, such as Aunt Milligan and Lydia ("ignorant old women" would take care of Aunt Milligan, though "finikin young ones" is less likely to be meant for Lydia), but the significant phrase is the use of the term "we from the North."

Most scholars working on the Missouri Compromise are apt to consider Delawareans Southerners, because Delaware was a slave state. But most Delawareans, in McLane's time and today, think of themselves as Northerners—not Yankees, of course—but Middle States Northerners. And so thought the people of Cecil County, Maryland, including the Milligans of Bohemia. McLane might prefer the Southerners, he might even ape their ways, but he did not think he was one of them.

IV   ENEMIES AT HOME

Nevertheless, the attitude of some Delawareans to his part in the Missouri controversy angered Louis McLane. His home in Wilmington was in the midst of his enemies, for Wilmington was a city dominated in politics by Republicans and in business by Quakers. The Wilmington Republicans were likely to be opponents, at least, of the expansion of slavery, and, at most, abolitionists; the Wilmington Quakers were certain to be both.

On January 15, 1820, a town meeting in Wilmington, addressed by Caesar A. Rodney, passed resolutions in favor of the legality and the wisdom of banning slavery in Missouri.[40] McLane wrote Rodney that the meeting caused him mortification—probably referring to the difficult position in which he was placed by instructions to seek a restriction on Missouri that he thought unconstitutional. "The restriction upon Missouri," he tried to persuade Rodney, "cannot promote the cause of emancipation, but will encourage a political cabal at the expense of the Constitution." This last idea, which he later suggested on the floor of the House, he bulwarked by quoting John Holmes that the restriction "is a hobby got up by some skilful rider, and the head of the pony was turned to the Presidential chair." [41] Possibly he had DeWitt Clinton in mind, since Tallmadge was a Clintonian, but it is difficult to say. Rodney answered that in view of his convictions, he could not have played truant from the Wilmington meeting nor have said less than he did—he might have said more.[42]

The response from Rodney and from others in Wilmington was not gratifying. Louis wrote John Milligan that he did not speak on the Missouri question "without the fullest preparation and a due sense of the responsibility I was encountering in a debate which I am sure has never been exceeded in ability by any that has ever taken place under the Government." To try to draw his young brother-in-law into the right path, he warned him that the speech of Rufus King (the Federalist leader and his own messmate!) was unmanly and seditious. As to his own speech: "I succeeded to my best expectations; and I now put all the efforts of the growling faction in Del. at defiance." [43]

Probably Louis hoped less to win John to this point of view than to unsettle John's determination, and to bid defiance, through John, to some of his Wilmington enemies. A year earlier Louis complained to Kitty that John Wales, a "Yankee Pettifogger," was telling, with exaggerations, a story of Henry Clay's gambling that he could only have heard from John Milligan, who got it from Louis. "Suppose Clay were to hear it." Certainly he would blame Louis McLane for its circulation. "He wd. no doubt think, if not say—it is true, but this Gent. need not have been so busy spreading it over the country." [44]

The Yankee, John Wales, was one of the chief of the "growling faction" McLane complained about, and he did not hesitate to name him along with Joseph Bringhurst and another Quaker in a letter to John Milligan in March. Again he bid them defiance, and used John as his medium. Except for Wilmington, where this little group would exert its "pigmy malignity," he did not think his stand on the Missouri question would hurt him with the voters. "I have great confidence in the mass of the people, and I believe, tho' they may differ with me, that they will not consent to sacrifice me." He had determined to retire from public life, he said, but not now: "I do not like to go out with a rope about my neck, or to sneak from a contest got up by such enemies." So much for this "contemptible little cabal in Wilmington!" [45]

It was a brave front that Louis presented to his brother-in-law, but to Kitty he confessed he was out of sorts. Why should he work hard to secure legislation for men—the Quaker millers of the Brandywine were probably the ones he had principally in mind—who used every means in their power in injure him? "They would take my services and return hostility." [46]

The abuse of Wilmingtonians led him to give serious consideration to moving to Baltimore. [47] Both Sam Smith and John Randolph were encouraging, and Randolph tried to secure for McLane the aid of William Pinkney, the most foppish but most eloquent member of the Baltimore bar. Louis was interested, though he knew that if he moved he would have to start all over and build a practice on his own exertions. "I am fully sensible of the trial that would await my removal to Bal. but does not our situation in Del. justify the risk?" [48]

So he felt in April. But by summer he was fighting for reelection. One enemy was punished when Joseph Bringhurst, through Louis's efforts, lost his position as Wilmington postmaster and was replaced by a more friendly Republican, Nicholas G. Williamson. "By all means take care to keep the old man within bounds," Louis warned Kitty as he told her the news. [49] It was the old collector he meant, and he must have feared that the pugnacious and indiscreet veteran would revel in Bringhurst's fall so loudly that all would know Louis's agency therein. The collector was bound to rejoice. This Bringhurst had satirized the collector as "wriggling Hispo," who had sought to

> . . . tell the world with what consummate skill,
> He pilfer'd fowls and geese, from Dick and Will. [50]

And so on. Of course, the collector would exult. Could Kitty keep him in bounds?

V REELECTION, 1820

Although Louis contemplated removal to Baltimore, where he might gain a larger practice and by it be better able to meet the financial needs of his growing family (including four children after the birth of Sally

Jones McLane, named for Kitty's mother, in September), he could not make his mind up to it as long as his political prospects were fair in Delaware. Maryland was a larger state and therefore offered a politician more substantial backing, promised him more attention, than tiny Delaware. But Delaware had elected McLane to office, and returned him to that office as long as he sought it. Would Maryland do as much? So it was that his political success in Delaware and the political ambition that made him value that success caused him to postpone for a decade a chance at professional advancement that was always tempting. When finally he did succumb to the temptations of Baltimore wealth, it was not as a lawyer, for his legal ambitions had by then been sacrificed to politics.

For a while in 1820, his chance of winning reelection seemed doubtful. His party was nationally almost extinguished; only seven Federalists remained in the Senate, and but twenty-seven in the House.[51] Massachusetts was the only other state in which his party was still dominant, and it was so much on the decline even there that politicians consented to the separation of Maine, which had become a Republican area, in order to preserve "a snug little Federal State," as they said, "for the rest of our lives." [52]

Nowhere did a Federalist candidate contest Monroe's bid for reelection to the Presidency. There was opposition to him within the Republican party, but no one wished openly to oppose Monroe because one reelection had become a matter of course, and no one wished to hazard his chance for the 1824 nomination by a premature start. A nominating caucus of Republican Congressmen had been convened in April at the call of Sam Smith, possibly with some intent of dropping Vice-President Tompkins from the ticket, but only forty-six of over two hundred delegates attended and it was thought best to make no nomination at all.[53]

In Delaware, as in the nation, the Federalist party seemed to be in serious danger of losing its identity. Young John M. Clayton, not long out of Yale and Judge Reeve's law classes at Litchfield, Connecticut, but already setting forth in politics as clerk of the state senate, found, as he looked about him, that "the old party distinctions seem to be in great measure laid out of sight." In Sussex, he reported, a "union ticket"— that is, a ticket combining Federalists and Republicans—was being recommended.[54]

Friends of a union ticket had, in fact, spoken for it at the Republican state convention. Sussex appointed a delegation to this convention which was half composed of dissident Federalists, but when they sensed that only Republicans would be considered for the ticket, "the federal union conferees"—that is the Sussex delegation—withdrew from a turbulent meeting, and a completely Republican ticket was chosen: John Collins, of Kent, for governor, and Willard Hall and Caesar A. Rodney, for Representatives. The ticket was not adopted without objection, however. Two votes, supposed to be Victor du Pont's and George Read, Jr.'s, prevented Hall's renomination from being made unanimous, even among the delegates remaining after the Sussex secession. And Read, secretary of the convention, refused to countersign the proceedings in anger at the failure of his efforts to get a union ticket.

The union ticket that Read wanted was simply the ticket as adopted, except for McLane instead of Hall. Read was Louis's brother's brother-in-law, but probably his reasons were firmer than the ties of such a distant in-law relationship. Victor du Pont had no such connection with McLane; his support of Louis and opposition to Hall arose primarily from McLane's support of tariff protection and Hall's unfriendliness to that hope of the manufacturer in a time of depression. Obviously there was a schism among the New Castle County Republicans, and by helping in the replacement of Bringhurst by Williamson as postmaster Louis McLane had thrust himself into the intraparty quarrel. In doing so he had little to lose; he won some friends and only confirmed the hatred of old enemies. The new postmaster, Nicholas Williamson, had helped precipitate the union party movement among the Republicans of Sussex, his native county, by going to Georgetown, the county seat, as "an embassador from N. Castle county of his own accord" and persuading the Republicans that their New Castle brethren wanted McLane on the ticket.

After the failure of the McLane movement at the Republican convention—by this time the term Democrat was more commonly used—and the secession of the Sussex delegation, the seceders met in Georgetown and adopted their own ticket, substituting McLane's name for Caesar A. Rodney's, but accepting Collins and Hall.[55] This union ticket in Sussex was an odd one, for it contained no Sussex County men; in fact, in accepting McLane it rejected the two Federalist candidates who were from Sussex—Jesse Green, the candidate for governor, and John Mitchell, the second Federalist nominee for Representative.

If the movements for a union ticket worried some Democrats, they were symptoms of a strengthening of the Democratic party by an infusion —some Democrats would have preferred to say an invasion—of Federalists. Probably Louis McLane himself, embittered by the attitudes on Missouri of Federalists like Otis and King, would have been glad to swing over to the Democratic ranks if he could have done so while retaining his high position in politics and a consonant influence in party affairs. Certainly he did not have the influence he desired in Federalist affairs, and he lamented this state of things as he looked over his party. But by the

action of the 1820 state Democratic convention, his overtures to the
Delaware Democrats were rejected. Party distinctions were declining,
as John M. Clayton saw, but the parties were too nearly even in Delaware
to allow the old tags and prejudices to be forgotten, even if impersonal
issues had almost ceased to exist.

The Federalist party in Delaware, said a friendly critic, "now exhibits
the melancholy prospect of a venerable oak shattered and bending before
the tempest." [56] Officially the name Federalist had long been modified.
Though everyone refered to it as the Federalist (or, more often, Federal)
party, it had formally become the Federal Republican party. Even within
the party there was criticism of its candidates. John Mitchell, who had
been sheriff of Caroline County, Maryland, was objected to as a newcomer.[57] Opposition to Mitchell and Green in their own county, Sussex,
had led to their being dropped from the union ticket just discussed.[58]
McLane's friends had to defend his votes on Missouri and the tariff. Hall,
they said, privately favored the tariff, as did McLane, but sidestepped the
issue by not voting and now was vote-mongering by claiming that the
tariff taxed everyone to aid "a few speculators on the Brandywine." "A
Farmer" who charged that McLane was a factory owner was answered
that Louis had given up his interest in a factory before he voted on the
tariff. His defender was the *Delaware Gazette,* the Federalist paper of
Wilmington and McLane's public voice, which should have known
whereof it spoke. But it was stretching the truth: McLane and George
Milligan still owned Rokeby but did not themselves operate the mills.[59]
The tariff, which was unpopular downstate, was very popular on the
Brandywine; so for local consumption the *Gazette* issued handbills bearing a command: "Don't give up the Federal Ship Industry."

At the same time the *Gazette* defended McLane's vote on the Missouri
question. "Frown indignantly upon the first dawning of an attempt to
alienate one portion of the Union from another," its readers were
counseled. Louis McLane, it declared, disliked slavery. He owned no
slaves himself, the *Gazette* went on to say, and he had freed slaves that
his wife had inherited, worth $3,000—perhaps so, but Louis had tried to
sell Jim to bring Kitty to Washington in his first winter there.[60]

This was a last-minute plea, reaching the voters as they went to ballot,
but the McLanes had sought to bolster Louis's position on Missouri
weeks earlier by a letter to the Reverend Ezekiel Cooper, once his own
minister at Asbury Methodist Church, Wilmington, now the well-known
superintendent of the Methodist Book Concern. It was Louis's brother,
Dr. Allen McLane, who wrote to Cooper. Is it true, he asked, that the
Missouri question was raised at a recent session of one of the Methodist
conferences but since it "did not appear to them to involve the abstract

question of *Slavery* but depended upon a Constitutional Question, they declined making any Publick expression of thier [*sic*] feelings in relation to it?" [61] Probably Cooper never answered; at least no statement by him was openly used in the campaign.

The McLanes, however, need not have worried about the election. Louis had been right when he told John Milligan his Missouri vote would not hurt him in Delaware. Probably it was no help to him either, though the national prominence his speeches in Congress were winning must have made Delawareans proud of him. Louis was reelected; his colleague Willard Hall, who had followed the legislature's instructions on Missouri, was defeated. Yet, fending off any premature conclusion that they were rebuking their legislators on the Missouri question, the Delaware voters replaced Hall with Caesar A. Rodney, who agreed with Hall on Missouri and had taken a prominent part in the Wilmington rally for restrictions on slavery expansion. Rodney not only replaced Hall; he came in first in a four-man race for two seats. In this, his third campaign for Congress, Louis for the first time did not lead the poll, but he salvaged a measure of triumph in that besides being reelected, he received the highest number of votes he had ever had.

As usual the Democrats carried New Castle and the Federalists carried Sussex, but, what was not usual, the Democrats also carried Kent. This meant a signal Democratic victory in Federalist Delaware. Democrat John Collins was elected governor by a majority of 445, whereas a year before, Federalist Henry Molleston, who had since died, had won election by a majority of 638, a good margin in a total vote of only 7,014.[62] Rodney led the congressional race in New Castle, Hall in Kent, and McLane in Sussex. It it interesting to note that while Rodney and Hall carried their home counties, McLane carried the one farthest from his home. But he did outrun his ticket in his home county, standing third there, while he lagged behind in Kent, where he was last. There were his enemies, dating back to his supplanting of Clayton in 1816, and he complained to a Sussex friend: "I have been very badly treated in Kent. The persecution against me there is wholly undeserved." [63]

Louis was being overcritical. He trailed his Federalist running mate in Kent by only 34 votes, and the spread from first to fourth man there was only 93. In New Castle, on the other hand, there was a spread of over 600 votes, and in Sussex McLane, the top man, led Hall, the fourth, by 941. Sussex was responsible for McLane's election and Rodney's too, giving the latter a 300-vote margin over Hall, and in doing so Sussex turned out a whopping big vote.[64]

Rodney's victory margin undoubtedly was enhanced by his standing in the party. He had been chosen as a special commissioner to Buenos

Aires in 1817, and since returning from that expedition he had made a
pilgrimage to Monticello, which reawakened memories of his old Republican eminence as Attorney General to Jefferson and Madison.[65] His
victory now must have been sweet recompense for his loss to Hall by one
vote in 1816.

Louis respected Rodney's stature—and his service as attorney (and
political protector) for the collector—by carefully disclaiming attacks on
him that had appeared in the *Gazette*.[66] But a Washington acquaintance
of them both warned Rodney to be wary of the McLanes. If they do not
play fair with you, he wrote, "your patronage of them should forever
cease"—referring, probably, to the fact that it was Rodney, as chief dispenser of Democratic patronage in Delaware, who might have the collector dismissed. "I am sure, if they could elevate Louis, they would immediately abandon you; so little principle do I believe any of them
possess. Louis is the most honorable man among them in my opinion, and
on him even, it will be necessary to keep an eye." [67]

VI   THE THIRD MISSOURI DEBATE, 1821

November of 1820 saw McLane back in the District and again at
Crawford's boardinghouse in Georgetown. He was unhappy at Crawford's, for both the table and house had "fallen off": "every thing looks
dirty and gloomy, and I am cooped up in the third story, in a room to
which the access is exceedingly difficult, if not dangerous." The only
"genteel" men staying there were Rufus King and Otis, thought McLane,
and a remarkably good servant, James Green, was "the only redeeming
quality" about the place. He would not hesitate to move, however, for
"a little money" would purchase good service anywhere and he was going to be obligated to bring another colored boy, Frank, to Washington,
in order to please the boy's mother. It would also be more to his taste to
be with Southerners—with John Randolph, for example, and General Sam
Smith, or with Thomas Newton, Governor Barbour, Robert S. Garnett,
and Hugh Nelson; he liked their "proud chivalrous spirit," their freedom
from "grovelling meanness" and "creaking envy." [68]

And, besides, a new assignment made it inconvenient for him to reside
in Georgetown. A new Speaker, John W. Taylor, of New York, chosen
after twenty-two ballots to fill the place Clay resigned, had named Louis
McLane to an important committee assignment, to second place—after
Sam Smith—on the Committee of Ways and Means.[69] This was a distinct
promotion from the Committee on Commerce, and if it was but a second
place to which Louis was appointed, still it was higher than the position
of his friend William Burwell, of Virginia, who had been in third place

on this committee when McLane first appeared in Congress, and now, three years later, was in third place still.

The labors of the Ways and Means Committee were greater than he expected, for the committee normally met three mornings a week.[70] This was cause enough to move closer to the Capitol, as he did some time around the 1st of January, 1821, to a mess that included the most staunch southern Old Republicans—Randolph, now deplorably subject to nervous hypochondria, taking to his bed for forty-eight hours at a time and finding pleasure only in drink; and Nathaniel Macon, Randolph's plain North Carolina friend and, like Randolph, a leader of the House in early Jeffersonian days. McLane described Macon as a "fine-hearted, honest old gentleman," and declared he took more pleasure in his company than in that of any of the mess except John Elliott, a Senator from Georgia, kind and "well-bred, tho' weak as water." [71]

This winter when he shared a mess with Randolph and Macon was the season when McLane first met a new member from Missouri who was to become the grand figure of the Senate and its senior—Thomas Hart Benton. Already he was "renowned," or so Louis described him to Kitty—"a man on no ordinary scale. Intelligent and improved in a very great degree he most certainly is, and I think combines with all, a strong, manly genius of no common cast. His person and appearance is even better than his mind, and will or I am mistaken make a figure in Washington." [72] Yet his warmest sympathy was won by men of less fame; by the dying William Burwell, for whom he asserted "a very warm friendship"; and by Hutchins Gordon Burton, Virginia-born Representative from North Carolina, on whom McLane bestowed, lightly perhaps, the accolade, "the best man in the Nation." [73]

To Missourians, North Carolinians, and Virginians, McLane was drawn closer by the role he chose in the renewed debate over Missouri. In the summer of 1820 Missouri had written a constitution which it now presented to Congress as a preliminary to the recognition of its new state government. Northern Congressmen, led by John Sergeant, objected to this constitution because of a provision in it instructing the legislature to prohibit the entry of free Negroes and Mulattoes. Since they were citizens in some states and since the federal Constitution guaranteed to citizens of each state the privileges of citizens of every other state, Sergeant and most northern Representatives demanded the repeal of a clause they thought unconstitutional.[74]

To McLane, the outlook was bleak. He was sure that the old anti-Missouri troops would rally to the old banners, and prevent Missouri's admission.[75] There was a dreadful note of preparation about this odious subject: "God only knows to what consequences it is to lead." [76]

On December 12 he entered the debate with a two-hour speech in defense of the Missouri constitution, a speech made from notes prepared the night before.[77] He never found time to write his speech out—not even, as so many Congressmen did, to write what he wished he had said—so we are dependent on the notes made by Gales, the reporter; though corrected by McLane and "pretty full" in his opinion, they were still, to the friendly eyes of John Randolph, only a skeleton of his speech, stripped of the meat.[78]

McLane felt, of course, that the Missouri question should never have been revived. The new Missouri constitution did not forbid the entry of free Negroes, but merely instructed the legislature to do so. If to forbid such entry was unconstitutional, the legislature ought not to act; if it acted anyway, its action, being unconstitutional, would be void. Then why all this excitement? He doubted that free Negroes had the legal status of citizens in any state; even the right to vote was no proof of citizenship. "I am an enemy to slavery," he declared, but, he added, "I am an advocate for some discrimination." [79]

Two Yankees soon rose to assure him that Negroes were citizens in some states, in Vermont and Massachusetts certainly,[80] but this correction did nothing to dampen his spirits. Thank Heaven, he told Kitty, he had had more than usual success in his speech, both in his own opinion and in the opinion of others. But he was tired and feeling unwell.[81]

Perhaps he made a quick trip home at Christmas time. If so, he was back in Washington by December 30, when a violent cold confined him to the boardinghouse, where he remained for at least ten days.[82] By January 12 he was back in the debate, insisting that Missouri should be referred to as a state in the journal of the House, which would then serve as an acknowledgment that the debate over the Missouri constitution was only a technical dispute and not in any way a denial of Missouri's claim to statehood.[83] His motion was lost by the casting vote of Speaker Taylor.

On February 1 McLane offered to amend the resolution admitting Missouri by two provisions intended to satisfy Representatives who were disturbed by the possibility that a Missouri ban upon the entrance of free Negroes would abridge the rights of citizens of other states. Proviso one declared that nothing in the Missouri constitution should oblige the state legislature to pass any law depriving citizens of other states of their rights; proviso two declared that no Missouri law should be construed to deny to citizens of any one state rights extended to citizens of other states.[84] Congressmen congratulated McLane on his "candor" and on his "spirit of amity," but did not support him; his amendment was defeated, 88 to 77.[85]

McLane's proposals were among many that were offered,[86] but such recalcitrance was shown on both sides that no proposal succeeded till the matter was taken in hand by Henry Clay. The diplomatic Kentuckian, who had recently resumed his seat, now as a private member and not as Speaker, persuaded his colleagues to accept a compromise formula that was not vastly different from McLane's proposal, except that Missouri was required formally to agree not to deny to the citizens of any state the privileges guaranteed them by the federal Constitution.[87]

No Delawareans were present in the House to help or hinder the passage of this final compromise of the Missouri controversy on February 26. Willard Hall, who earlier in the session had been opposed to the admission of Missouri unless its constitution was changed, resigned from the House and returned to Delaware in January. Having been defeated for reelection, he chose to accept the position of secretary of state under John Collins, Delaware's new Democratic governor, rather than serve out his term.[88]

Louis McLane had also left Washington before the vote on Clay's compromise. He had been sick and confined to his room, he explained to Victor du Pont on February 20: "so incapable am I of attending properly to my public duties that I shall set out tomorrow for home." [89]

VII   THE COLLECTOR VISITS

The winter of 1820–21 was, to hear him tell of it, a bleak time for Louis McLane. For one thing, he missed Kitty, at home nursing the new baby. Her thousand good qualities, he assured her, made him "the happiest of men," [90] but it was all the worse for so fortunate a man to be separated from such a jewel. He could, for a time, assuage his remorse at Kitty's absence, his longing for "dear little Bob," "sweet little Lou," and "Miss Bec," in the "loathsom" duties of his office. "If I indulged the chief pleasure I have here," he explained to Kitty, "I should be perpetually thinking of and writing to you. . . . I partake scarcely at all of the pleasures and gaieties as they are miscalled, of this empty pageant." [91]

His unhappiness was compounded by long spells of illness. He had complained of ill health in Washington before, but in previous years he mixed dire tales of being a melancholy invalid with accounts of "rambles" on horseback or afoot.[92] "As I found no calculations for this world upon sanctimonious demeanor, or religious devotion," he had once explained to Kitty, "I am not much in the habit of shutting myself up in a church at Washington. I passed the last Sunday in writing to you, and making a long walk over the hills." [93]

This winter his duties and his health combined to keep him indoors. He was not altogether alone, however; his father had come to Washington and, Louis said, "renewed his youth." The old collector was so active, indeed, that he put his son to shame; "I bear the reproach," Louis wrote, "which is often made to me that my father is a younger man than I." [94]

The collector's appearance in Washington was probably not the result of any sudden whim to join Louis and with him see the great men of the nation. Instead, though nothing in the correspondence fortifies this opinion, the trip was probably motivated by a law passed in the previous spring. This was the Tenure of Office Act of 1820, which established a four-year term for customs collectors. Previously old Allen McLane and his fellow collectors had enjoyed indeterminate terms, and if they lived under the hazard of sudden dismissal, custom gave them the comfort that they would be left undisturbed in their offices for life.

Now this was changed. Every four years the collectors (as well as district attorneys and many other government officials) would need a new appointment, and pity the collector who had no friend at court.

All depended, of course, on how the new power would be used by the Secretary of the Treasury, in whose jurisdiction the collectors fell. If the Secretary automatically recommended the reappointment of all collectors in good standing, tenures might be as long and as certain as ever. Yet the law, which had been quietly adopted, aroused much uncertainty. With whom, for instance, need a collector be in good standing? With the President? Or with the Secretary of the Treasury?

John Quincy Adams, the Secretary of State, suspected it was the latter. Indeed he saw the law as a measure that would enable Secretary of the Treasury William H. Crawford to build a machine of officeholders that he could ride to the Presidency in 1824. There was, Adams noted, a second law passed on May 15, 1820, that also concerned the civil service—a law permitting the Secretary of the Treasury to use summary process at his discretion against delinquent collectors. This meant two weapons for Crawford, reappointment for those who had his favor, and prosecution for the unfriendly and unwary. [95]

The jealous Adams could hardly be expected to admit that these laws might also encourage a more responsible and more efficient customs service than the country had known. How would they be used? To establish efficiency or to strengthen a Crawford faction?

Adams's concern was shared by the collector of Wilmington, as his presence in Washington evidenced. "He plays his cards very well here," observed Louis, who aided his father's cause by taking Sunday dinner *en famille* with the Crawfords. The company was good—Nathaniel Macon, Governor Barbour, of Virginia, and Representative Burton, of North Carolina—and the family very agreeable. The children, one of them named for Macon, were delightful and played around the company all day "in the old style," and Mrs. Crawford was unpretentious and kind with none of the airs of Mrs. Adams. Louis, who had been accepting few invitations out, stayed till late at night, even though he was to return on Saturday to a more formal party.[96]

By this time all was well with the collectorship. Louis reported that "the old gentleman," his father, had stayed so long only because of the cold weather, and that he would be leaving as soon as the steamboats would run.[97] But imprudent exposures, as Louis viewed them, soon brought his father low. "The poor old Gentleman [he was seventy-four] has been at last overtaken, and has been handled pretty severely"; yet it "will now require more pains to keep him here till he is strong enough to travel, than it took before he was sick, to get him off." [98] He was a contrary old man.

Still, Louis was not inclined to be critical, for the session was ending very well. The collectorship was secure, his Missouri speech had been a success, his new position on the Ways and Means Committee gave him added prestige, and he had gained two influential friends in the cabinet, Secretaries Crawford and Thompson.

Smith Thompson, the Secretary of the Navy, and his wife, who had been born into the wealthy and influential Livingston family of New York, were, along with the English and French ministers, the social leaders of Washington this winter. They had taken "a separate and private establishment" near the late Commodore Decatur's.[99] There early in the session Louis McLane paid "a morning call" on them, and afterwards he reported to Kitty that they were handsomely fixed with a "dashing" interior.[100] It was not till January that Louis accepted any invitations, and when he did, it was those of Thompson and the British minister that he favored: "the former I like very much and the latter they say surpasses in style and entertainment everything yet seen here." [101]

Thompson, like Crawford and Adams, was an eager aspirant to the Presidency, and McLane was a rising young Congressman whose support any candidate would be glad to attract. The interest of Thompson and Crawford gave McLane great expectations. "I could whisper in your ear some very pleasant things—which are not among the greatest improbabilities," Louis told Kitty, as he chatted, in his correspondence, of the lack of leadership in Congress.[102]

VIII   FAMILY PROBLEMS AND LEGAL PRACTICE

Some disappointments had to be faced before McLane's expectations could be realized. Having now been elected to the House of Representatives three times, he might have hoped to be sent to the Senate to replace

Outerbridge Horsey, whose term was expiring. But the Delaware General Assembly, though both houses were Federalist, had made no choice at all.

In this decision it is likely that once again Thomas Clayton's enmity was employed against McLane. For when the lower house of the Assembly appealed to the upper for a joint meeting to choose a Senator, it was Clayton and his Kent colleague, Jacob Stout, who voted with the Democrats to prevent such a meeting and therefore prevent any election.[103]

There were also family problems to be discussed with Kitty. There was the intemperance of his brother, the doctor, to be regretted. To Louis intemperance seemed "the worst evil which besets our path," and Allen's succumbing to it, even relapsing after reflection and mortification, was all the more to be regretted in that his "sainted Mother" had "in this as in *all* other respects" performed her parental duty of warning her children against the dangers of drink.[104]

Kitty's family also displeased Louis. He thought her brother-in-law, Joseph Sims, was "over rated—both as to his head and heart." [105] Her aunt and guardian in Louis's opinion was a sycophant, worshiping wealth and power.[106] John Milligan's engagement to Martha Levy, daughter of a Philadelphia lawyer, won Louis's approval because he wanted to see John settled and because somehow the marriage was expected to relieve George Milligan of part of his load of debt.

Whatever George Milligan's debts were, they had so disturbed him that the death of a Miss Pearce, a neighbor and possibly a sweetheart, was looked upon as only another shocking blow to his nervous system.[107] His troubles were multiplied in February, 1821, when a flood on the Brandywine destroyed the dam and some of the works at Rokeby.[108] Before another year had passed, George Milligan had fled his native heath and sought relief from his debts and his disease in a long voyage and in new opportunities in Louisiana.

Disasters at Rokeby were hard on Louis McLane as well as on George Milligan, but the former had two other sources of financial strength to fall back upon, his father, reappointed collector in the spring of 1821, and his law practice, which began to flourish whenever he could afford time to it. By 1821 he was one of the more senior members of the bar, according to service, and the published reports indicate that he was being called into a fair share of the important cases at the New Castle courts.[109]

One case that took Louis to chancery court in August, 1821, was part of a long litigation, begun in 1816 and extending for more than a decade. It was the suit of Pierre, or Peter, Bauduy against E. I. du Pont for payment of a commission on all sales of gunpowder to 1815.[110] Bauduy, a Haitian Frenchman, had been a partner of du Pont, but they fell out after the marriage of Bauduy's son and du Pont's daughter was terminated by the death of the former.

The suit against du Pont that Bauduy and McLane initiated was the first in a series of legal actions that were before the courts for at least fourteen years. Eventually they were settled largely to the satisfaction of du Pont, who had ploughed most of his profits back into the firm instead of distributing them to stockholders.[111] For a time McLane also represented another complainant, the widow of one of du Pont's French connections.[112]

By 1821 the Bauduy-du Pont litigation had reached a mature stage, with few new developments to come. Bauduy had returned to the West Indies, leaving his interests in the gunpowder business to his two sons-in-law, brothers named Garesché.[113] Probably Bauduy's departure soothed ruffled feelings, for despite McLane's advocacy of their enemy's cause, the du Ponts, or Victor, at least, had sought to aid him politically in the 1820 contest and they were for the moment on excellent terms with him. Almost his last action before he left Washington had been to recommend Victor du Pont's young son Samuel for appointment as a midshipman in the Navy.[114]

As he practiced law in Delaware in the spring and summer of 1821 it was difficult for Louis McLane not to forget himself in political speculations. Opposed to him in the Bauduy case, for instance, were Delaware Attorney General James Rogers, United States Senator Nicholas Van Dyke, and his own new colleague in the House of Representatives, Caesar Augustus Rodney.[115] A high percentage, indeed, of the men McLane associated with at the Delaware bar were former members of Congress: Thomas Clayton, Henry M. Ridgely, Willard Hall, Thomas Cooper, and William Hill Wells, besides Van Dyke and Rodney. Still others were to be sent to Congress for the first time in the future—Kensey Johns, Jr., John Wales, and two young lawyers who were one day to become nationally famous, James A. Bayard, the younger, and John M. Clayton. Over half of the twenty-two lawyers practicing in the Delaware courts in the spring of 1822 had been or were to be members of the federal Congress, most of them Senators.[116] Politics, even national politics, must have been as common a subject of conversation for the assembled Delaware lawyers as coffee and madeira were staples in the diet of Louis McLane.

And on summer evenings, in the garden of his house at 606 Market Street, a few doors above the town hall that his client, Peter Bauduy, had designed, Louis must often have whispered to Kitty—in a low tone so the children would not hear—"some very pleasant things, . . . not among the greatest improbabilities."

5

A Man of Reputation

I POSSIBILITIES

McLane expected great things for himself in the new Congress. In four years he had come far. From a young and unknown delegate representing a tiny state and a moribund party he had risen by 1821 to a position of intimacy with important members, of influence in debate, and of consequence in committee.

In December, on his return to Congress, he might be chosen as a committee chairman, or to succeed John Taylor as Speaker. Could not such "pleasant things" have been whispered to him in the previous winter when he attended dinners and parties at Smith Thompson's and William Crawford's? And a senatorship from Delaware was vacant; Outerbridge Horsey's term had expired in March, 1821, and not yet been filled by the legislature. He could be Glamis, and Cawdor—and king thereafter.

II NOT GLAMIS

Glamis was first—the speakership of the House of Representatives. John W. Taylor, an upstate New Yorker, who was Speaker of the last Congress, succeeding Clay when he returned to Kentucky, was certain to face opposition. He had been an able Speaker, but never a popular one. For example, his conduct of his office had affronted Secretary of War Calhoun, who felt that Taylor had, by his appointments, strengthened House opposition to the War Department program.[1] Furthermore, a number of southern Representatives still held malice for Taylor because of his leadership in the attempt to restrict slavery in Missouri. And, to cap Taylor's troubles, many of his New York colleagues determined to cause his down-

120

fall on an issue of state politics—because he had supported DeWitt Clinton's legislative ticket in his home county after having given assurances a year earlier that he was no Clintonian.[2] Clinton was the stormy petrel of New York politics for a decade, and the forces that rallied against him in 1821 were disinclined to show any mercy to his friends.

But if not Taylor, who would be the new Speaker? Clay was out of consideration; having left Congress for his law practice at home to bolster his finances, he would not return till after the new Congress was organized. The other giant of the House, William Lowndes, of South Carolina, had been Taylor's chief opponent for the post in 1820, but was unwilling to be considered for it now and stayed away from Congress for a time.[3] Lowndes would have suited Calhoun very well, but if his fellow South Carolinian would not run, Calhoun, though leading a campaign against Taylor, had no candidate for his place.

In friendly loyalty some members turned to the veteran soldier and merchant from Baltimore, Sam Smith, chairman of the Ways and Means Committee. But though Smith had long been prominent, he was liked as a man more than he was esteemed as a statesman, and many Representatives glanced past him to the second man on his committee, the younger and more vigorous Louis McLane. To Southerners his votes and speeches on the Missouri question had endeared him. To Calhounites he was unobjectionable on any grounds related to the military establishment; as befit a Revolutionary partisan's son, he had consistently voted to support the armed forces.[4] To anyone willing to overlook his Federalist background and to choose a Speaker for his personal qualities, McLane was an attractive candidate, relatively young, vigorous, able, efficient, and unconnected with any one of the old cliques within Jefferson's party.

But, of course, he was not within the party. If a true Jeffersonian were sought, Congressmen might still find him in Delaware in the person of McLane's new colleague. Caesar Augustus Rodney was one of the founders of the Republican party. He had been a member of the Democratic Society in Philadelphia in the 1790's, a Republican Congressman from Delaware in the next decade, and Attorney General of the United States from 1807 to 1811, when he quit in a huff at Madison's failure to promote him to the Supreme Court. Yet he remained a faithful party member and returned to Congress in 1821 with a holy aura of party venerability surrounding him. "An able man," declared Hezekiah Niles, "an old friend, and, perhaps, deserving the character of a *statesman* as well as any member of the house."[5] Samuel Ingham, a Calhoun man, gave assurances that Rodney would get strong support in Pennsylvania as a candidate worthy of the support of the old Republican party.[6]

When the House convened on December 3, 1821, 81 votes were necessary for election as Speaker. On the first ballot John Taylor, who had made his peace with Secretary of State Adams and with Adams's help, had strong New England support, received 60 votes; his nearest rivals were Rodney with 45 votes, McLane with 29, and Smith with 20. A second ballot followed, without a choice, and a third and a fourth, and so on to a total of seven. Taylor picked up votes constantly till he was but four short on the last ballot of the day. But it was obvious that he could never have come so near election if his opposition had been united. The 94 votes polled by Rodney, McLane, and Smith on the first ballot were more than enough for the choice of any one of them.

Yet these votes could not be united on any one of the three. Rodney did pick up strength through the first five ballots, till he stood just nine votes shy of the needed 81. But McLane's support fell off after the second ballot and vanished on the seventh. Smith never showed much strength. His early support fell off at once, and though there was a movement back to him at the end of the day, his high total, on the seventh ballot, was but 26.

After a night's rest, the voting was resumed on December 4, with more members present and 87 votes necessary for a choice. Evidently the night had been spent in more than rest, for the opposition to Taylor now concentrated its strength on a new candidate with such success that after five more ballots he was elected. The new candidate, and new Speaker, was Philip P. Barbour, of Virginia.

Unlike the two original favorites, Taylor and Rodney, Barbour was a supporter of the presidential aspirations of William H. Crawford and took the southern position against a protective tariff and against restrictions on slavery in Missouri. To Hezekiah Niles it seemed that a minority, mainly composed of Southerners, had blocked the choice of Taylor or Rodney in order to have their way and secure a Speaker dear to their heart.[7]

Louis McLane viewed the election differently. He knew that two cabinet members, Calhoun and Smith Thompson, were leading the attack on Taylor, but he was dismayed that they, particularly Thompson, who had been so very friendly, would not take him up as Taylor's successor. Apparently he had counted on Thompson's support, but at a meeting between Thompson and the majority of the New York delegation, it had been decided to support Rodney first, and then McLane if Rodney could not win.[8] Very likely this agreement originated with the New York members, not Thompson, but Thompson agreed to it, and in Louis's mind he was not to be forgiven. "I promise Mr. Secy. Thompson . . . that he will gain no friends by the part he was pleased to act, and if he dreaded Taylor he shall have more to dread this winter." McLane was alluding to his new appointment as chairman of the Naval Affairs Committee; despite his threat he worked smoothly with the Navy Secretary in the ensuing winter.

Nor was McLane happy with Rodney. "The only effect of his being a candidate was to defeat my election and this it did effectually. He is now mortified in proportion to the hope he allowed himself to entertain of his success which was very great." [9] Less prejudiced observers saw that the competition between McLane and Rodney had produced their defeat.[10] "The Southern men," John D. Dickinson, of Troy, New York, explained to John Quincy Adams, "would not vote for Rodney, and others would not vote for McLane." [11]

Some Southerners opposed Rodney for one of the reasons they opposed Taylor; Rodney, like Taylor, was in favor of restricting slavery in Missouri. Furthermore, some who knew Rodney opposed him, with some reason, as "a man of no industry, or application to business." [12] So although Rodney came closer to election than McLane, McLane, who was a man of industry, method, and application, and who supported the South's position on Missouri, might have had the better chance to be chosen Speaker except for his own Achilles heel. Unlike Taylor, unlike Barbour, unlike Smith, unlike Rodney, unlike the overwhelming majority of Congressmen, McLane was no Republican, no Democrat. He belonged to the wrong party, and dead though it might be, it was not forgotten. "The truth is," Louis admitted, "that there was no resisting the spirit of Democracy which was got up, and which proscribed every thing like federalism." [13]

III   NOT CAWDOR

But in Delaware there was no prejudice against Federalism—at least no proscription of "every thing like federalism"—and therefore Louis McLane hopefully awaited his legislature's choice of a new United States Senator. "If our Legislature do me justice," he told Kitty, "I shall be brought . . . into a less active scene." This would not be altogether to his advantage; in leaving the House he would relinquish the influential position it had taken six years to gain. "But still," he explained, in contemplating the possibility of promotion, "it would relieve me from the envy of low intriguers at home, and leave me more at liberty to act a disinterested part in Publick life, should I conclude to remain there. On that account my election to the Senate would [be] a source of gratification to me." [14]

Unfortunately for Louis, there were other Delawareans who found similar gratification in the thought of election to the Senate. One such dreamer was his old Kent County antagonist Thomas Clayton, and if Louis's adherents are to be believed, Clayton's plans had been carefully laid for this event. Having prevented any senatorial election in the winter of 1821 when the choice would have fallen on some Federalist other than himself, he sought so to control the fall elections that he would hold the balance of power between the two parties—to his own advantage, of course. In October, 1821, the Federalists carried Sussex and the Democrats New Castle, as expected, but Kent chose a third ticket made up by Clayton of some Federalists, some Democrats, and some independents. In the state senate, where Clayton himself sat, and in the house, the Kent delegation held the balance between solidly Democratic and solidly Federalist delegations from New Castle and Sussex respectively.[15]

The success of Clayton's plans depended upon his getting some Democratic votes. The Kent Democrats, of course, owed him support for his help in their election, but he hoped for New Castle votes too. He might have had them, but for two developments—a Democratic schism in the New Castle elections and the appeal of a Democratic candidate for the United States Senate. In New Castle the regular Democratic legislative ticket was defeated by a slate of independent Democrats, who had Federalist support.[16] Since the New Castle County Federalists were opposed to Clayton, any influence they had with the new legislators would be used against him. The Democratic candidate for the United States Senate was Representative Caesar A. Rodney, whose popularity was attested by his success in the recent congressional election.[17]

"Rodney is certain of his election to the Senate," Louis McLane reported to Kitty, "and has the folly to tell everybody so who sees him." [18] In his jealousy McLane was titillated by rumors that the corpulent Rodney was bedfast for a week as a result of overindulging his fondness for oysters.[19]

As the legislators gathered in Dover in January, 1822, tempers became so strained that Rodney's brother-in-law and Thomas Clayton got into a fracas involving name-calling and at least one blow. One report said Clayton was drunk, and the affair may have hurt him.[20] At any rate, Clayton apparently decided to bide his time, and when he received only 7 votes on the first ballot in the General Assembly, he withdrew from the contest. Rodney had 10 votes on the first ballot, McLane had 2, and 10 votes went to Federalist Thomas Cooper, Clayton's former colleague in Congress. On the second ballot McLane gained 2 of the Clayton votes and Rodney 5, for a total of 15, a bare majority.[21] The result made Rodney "the first *democratic* Senator ever elected into the Senate of the U. States from Delaware." [22]

A few days later the Democrats rewarded the Clayton faction for their help, when Democratic Governor John Collins appointed Clayton's closest confederate a judge.[23]

IV DOMESTICITY AND LONELINESS

McLane had despaired of his chances before the election took place. "The old oysterman," meaning the overindulgent Rodney, "will win," Louis told Kitty.[24] And to his brother-in-law he later explained: "I was never so sanguine as you appear to have been of my election to the Senate." He did not blame Thomas Cooper for seeking the post with backing from the Sussex Federalists: "Cooper was impressed with the belief that Clayton was his friend and that all his disaffection was made to restore the old cast offs; . . . I doubt very much if the result would have been different had Cooper not have been nominated. . . . The folly consisted in going into the election in the absence of a *Sussex Member*, whose presence, if he had been there, would have rendered Rodney's election impossible by making *16* necessary to a choice; in that case my election would have been certain. . . . I do not *much* regret the result, except that it proves 'this world was made for Caesar.' "[25]

Despite the fact that he underlined "much," the disclaimer of regret sounds like sour grapes. So does his assurance to Kitty that his greatest disappointment in the election lay in his inability to rid himself of his responsibilities in the House in order to run home and be with her during her expected confinement.[26]

Providentially falling ill, Louis came home anyway. "Visited once more with my old disorder," he explained, "I stood it at Washington for ten days rather than encounter the cold ride home; but when they finally determined to assail me with the Lancet and blue pills I took a hack and resolved to undergo that regimen where I could have more comfort than at Washington." He arrived in Wilmington on January 18, resolved to stay till he recovered, and longer if Kitty was still confined.[27]

For another child was due. It was the imminence of the arrival of this new "recrute" that had kept Kitty from Washington this winter. "He is a steady fellow that will not be hurried," she had written Louis, "but will quietly wait his allotted time—for which *I* do not thank him."[28] The recruit arrived January 30 and was a girl, who was named Lydia for her Aunt Lee, who was Kitty's only attendant when the baby came. Three physicians, including Allen, hurried to the house at 606 Market in a few minutes, but the circumstances of the arrival gave the family "a serious fright."[29]

Though not altogether well, Louis soon had to hurry off, through a snow storm, to Washington, for he had responsibilities there which he could not altogether shirk. He was, for the first time, chairman of a stand-ing committee, the naval committee, an appropriate assignment for a former midshipman.[30] He had also been appointed to a committee to reapportion seats in the House in accordance with the 1820 census, and on this committee, to his chagrin, he was unable to prevent a reapportionment which cost Delaware one of its two seats.[31]

The reapportionment bill was passed in his absence, which was, however, particularly noted, two members, Rochester and Cambreleng, both of New York, taking the occasion to pay McLane a compliment.[32] Indeed, though defeated for the speakership, McLane was enlarging his already high reputation in Congress.

One of McLane's first appearances on the floor for this committee was to present the petition of John B. Timberlake, a purser, praying certain allowances in the settlement of his accounts.[33] The subject is of no significance, but the petitioner is, in an oblique way; he was the first husband of that Peggy O'Neale whose second marriage was to upset a cabinet and thus pave McLane's way to the highest positions he ever attained.

In a more significant appearance, McLane won the backing of the House in insisting that an attack on the naval establishment be transformed into a polite request that his committee inquire into the expediency of a reorganization. To be a defender of the Navy was, of course, a proper role for Federalist McLane, particularly when the antagonist was a western Democrat, John Cocke, of Tennessee, but besides this historical note there is a modern tone to McLane's speech. "There appeared to be," he said, "a rather unfair, if not an ungenerous proceeding creeping into the practice of this House; which is, that, when gentlemen want information from any Department . . . , they should preface it with an argument calculated to affect and even to criminate public officers, founded on an assumption of facts proposed to be inquired into, and followed by consequences almost as serious in the public mind as if the facts assumed were known to be true—when it very often happened that the facts, being obtained from the proper authority, were not as had been supposed." [34]

That the House backed McLane, the Federalist, rather than Cocke, the Democrat, was in part a tribute to McLane's personal standing among his colleagues. He continued to hold his old friends and to make new ones. When Victor du Pont, a Delaware state senator, visited Washington in December, 1821, McLane gave a dinner for him and invited John Randolph, Nathaniel Macon, Speaker Barbour, John Nelson of Maryland, and Hutchins Burton. "The day passed off most agreeably" for Louis, and he told Kitty, "I hope Dupont goes home with a pretty strong impression of my standing here." [35]

A stronger impression of the standing of McLane, or rather of McLane's mess at Strother's boardinghouse, was made on those like Kitty who knew that the Vice-President had applied to enter it and been refused. Kitty, of course, heard the tale from Louis, thus: "The Vice President arrived here the evening before last, and made application to be admitted into our mess. We have the subject under consideration, rather to find a pretence to exclude, than to deliberate to admit. He bears the most evident and conclusive marks of a sot, and the apprehension is that his habits may interfere with our pleasure, which is now as complete as it could well be." [36]

Vice-President Daniel Tompkins unfortunately had, as Louis reported, taken to drink in these years, moved to it, probably, by financial reverses. Still he was the Vice-President and he had been a general and governor of New York. Kitty, therefore, regretted that she had missed seeing him when he called on her in Wilmington on Christmas Eve. She had sent Bob to the door to say she was indisposed under the impression it was some tiresome Philadelphia folks who were visiting in Wilmington. [37]

But Louis reassured her: "You . . . lost nothing by not seeing him, for as he was tipsey when he arrived here, it is probable he was in the same condition when he called on you. . . . These unfortunate habits of his, have rather tended to encrease his freedoms and impudence with ladies than otherwise and on this account too, you have nothing to regret." [38]

The Vice-President was drawn to the mess at Strother's not by McLane's presence but because of the number of New Yorkers who were there. Presiding over it—in the sense that he had the largest family present and therefore took up the most room—was Representative John D. Dickinson, with his wife and pretty daughter Julia. [39] The Dickinsons gave McLane a taste of domestic warmth in his loneliness and made him more comfortable in Washington than he had ever been before without Kitty. [40] When Louis bought a grand piano as a Christmas present for Rebecca—he got it at an auction for $160 but knew it had once been Mrs. Decatur's and bought by her in England for $600—he had Julia Dickinson try it out. [41] Then, to await the spring thaw and the opening of water transportation, he had it moved into the Dickinsons' parlor, where one night the Dickinsons invited "Miss DeWolf and some other wild animals," along with the members of the mess, "and had quite a pleasant dance." Miss DeWolf, Louis reported to Kitty, thoughtful as he usually was of her lonely eagerness to hear tales of capital society, was pretty, genteel, innocently sweet, and very, very rich, but her wealth was tainted by the way it was made— her father was an African slave trader. Though this wealth was "clean cash, and the object of all lovers of pelf, . . . the crimes of Dives taint the ermine and gold." [42]

Churchill Cambreleng of New York, and the elegant, dashing Joel Poinsett of South Carolina, with whom Cambreleng, a North Carolinian

by birth, shared quarters, were among the new members who won
McLane's favor early in this session, while George McDuffie, also of
South Carolina, aroused his dislike.[43] And of the belles it was Miss Sophia
Otis, daughter of Harrison Gray Otis, who won Louis's heart—or would
have, as he said, had it not already been so firmly attached to Kitty.[44] The
Otises, of course, were not new friends. They had called on Kitty in
Wilmington on their way, to the delight of Kitty's brother George (about
to leave on another voyage to Louisiana), who had previously become
one of the pack of admirers of Sophia.[45]

The Otises helped persuade Louis to leave Strother's house for Crawford's, in Georgetown, where they were taking rooms. And though ultimately Louis became quite annoyed with Otis, for a short period he was
very close to this family, visiting frequently, and picking up from Miss
Sophia delectable bits of gossip for Kitty.[46]

V FRIENDS AND COLLEAGUES

The reigning belle in Washington this winter was not Julia Dickinson
or Sophia Otis but a granddaughter of Thomas Jefferson, and in connection with her McLane made his first reference to a man whose destiny
was for the next decade to be closely tied to his own. This young lady,
Louis explained to Kitty, was "the same probably who once was exhibited in Philadelphia," and then he added, "I should not be surprised
if Mr. Van Buren were to put in there; especially as he would be apt to
be dazzled with the connection." [47]

And so the gay, affable, clever, self-taught Dutch attorney and widower
from upstate New York came into McLane's friendship with an aura
about him of party orthodoxy and near-subserviency to a leader image
that aroused some jealousy in McLane from the beginning. Yet they
quickly became friends, for on the very day of this reference Van Buren
and McLane went together to Georgetown (this is before McLane moved
there) to spend Sunday evening with the Otises.[48]

Throughout the winter Louis McLane exhibited a continuing interest
in linking Van Buren's name romantically with various ladies of Washington society—for Kitty's benefit, of course. At one time or another Mc-
Lane connected the New York widower's name with a Miss Stewart (no
truth to this rumor, McLane added), Miss Sophia Otis, a Mrs. Pearson
("Miss Kitty Worthington that was"), and Miss Virginia Mason, daughter of General John Mason, who owned an island in the Potomac.[49] Mc-
Lane's interest was not merely to find news to send Kitty; it reflects the
intimacy that developed rapidly between him and Van Buren.

"I was almost immediately strongly attracted towards him," Van Buren wrote of McLane in his memoirs, "and our intimacy rapidly grew into a friendship that withstood exposure to many storms." [50] McLane testified to the same ripening friendship when he told Kitty that Harrison Gray Otis seemed out of humor because his place in carriage rides and walks with Rufus King had been taken by Van Buren, and that Otis might be further upset—"after all he is a confounded fool and trifler"—by observing "a little too much of that sort of intimacy he does not like between VB and me." [51]

A few days later McLane purposely tormented the wealthy Yankee: "I handed one of my business letters, rather amusing, to Van Bueren, and we exchanged observations in pencil on the paper. . . . Otis said at last after observing us very closely, 'is that a letter from Mrs. M L?' no said I, certainly not—I only read parts of Mrs. McLanes letters to Mr. VB— and this knocked him up." Of course, Louis told Kitty, I read no parts of your letters to anyone except a hundred times to myself.[52]

Besides Otis and Van Buren, Benjamin Gorham (a wealthy Massachusetts widower who was courting Sophia Otis), Senator Elijah Mills (also of Massachusetts), Charles Fenton Mercer, Jeremiah Cosden (of Cecil County, Maryland), an unidentified Schuyler, and Stephen Van Rensselaer composed the Georgetown mess that McLane had joined in January, 1822. "A sort of supernumerary" was the mammoth, almost grotesque, Dixon Lewis, of Alabama, the largest man in Congress.[53]

Van Rensselaer, among his messmates, won McLane's quick approval— "a most amiable man." When the Otises left the mess to move into Washington, two new members were accepted, Henry R. Warfield, of Maryland, and James Buchanan, "whom you have not seen," Louis explained to Kitty, "and suffer no great deal on this account." So much for another future rival! Yet if it were not for "contemptible little Mercer," McLane felt, the mess "would do very well." [54]

Perhaps it was his dyspepsia that made McLane so choleric—the illness that had given him excuse to fly home in January never fully left him, or if it did, it was only to be succeeded by new infirmities. "I have still great hopes," he wrote in the spring, "after I shall be released from this miserable hole, of being able soon to get into the mocha and madeira list, and when I do I shall take ample vengeance upon this temporary privation." [55] On another occasion he barely resisted: "I was strongly tempted, and even ventured to put a little old wine on my tongue but the horrors [of] dyspepsia in Washington stopt the current, and I easily summoned resolution enough to resist the dose." [56]

Louis missed his coffee and his wine, and even more he missed his beloved home—he gave careful directions about the garden (order some peach trees, a nectarine, two cherry, a May Duke and a large Montmorency, a pear, and some grape vines),[57] about papering the hall ("get the landscape paper for 75¢ per piece"), and about a new front door ("I should like the door and *fan* especially to be very *plain;* it will best suit the old House"). And in a fit of exasperation he exclaimed: "I would give the world if you would take some pride in your house, or reflect that I have a full portion of it." [58]

But most of all he missed Kitty. After Lydia's birth at the end of January, 1822, and his return to the capital, McLane was sustained for weeks by the expectation that his pretty wife would soon join him. Much of his free time was spent inquiring about rooms they might take and discovering the rent to be paid, the company to be enjoyed, the comforts to be had.[59]

Yet Kitty did not recover her strength very rapidly. A succession of maladies kept her from Washington all spring and even finally drove her to Philadelphia to seek rest with the Simses at Laurel Hill and a cure at the hands of that wonderfully well-named Philadelphia medical man, Dr. Physick, who was also consulted by Louis on his own behalf. Despairing and lonely, Louis considered retiring from politics. Your "vile *creeps,* or chills and fevers," he told Kitty, "harass me as much as they do you." [60]

"There is nothing in the honors of publick life," he decided, "that can compensate a man *really* happy as I am at home, for the loss of that home." Since his "cheif and almost only substantial enjoyment" was in his "domestick circle," why stay in Congress when a further reduction in congressional stipends threatened to make it impossible for him ever to support his family in Washington? [61] However, he was withholding an announcement of his withdrawal from public life till he could "come to an understanding" with Kitty on the subject. "I should like to have your deliberate and candid opinion." [62]

When in the spring fine weather came, Louis wished he could leave the "most abominable of all . . . abominable places" to saunter with Kitty on his arm "along the banks of the Brandywine," enjoying that stream's beauties while their "sweet chicks" ran "gamboling ahead." Though the session of Congress had begun with so much promise for Louis's ambition, it had been dull and disappointing to him. Except, that is, for the presidential contest. It was a whirlpool in which the candidates were perpetually tossed about; "sometimes one is uppermost, and sometimes another." He had made his choice, he had declared it, and happily his candidate seemed most buoyant in the whirlpool.[63]

VI   THE CRAWFORDITE

From his first month in Congress, Louis McLane had been very favorably impressed by the Secretary of the Treasury, William Harris

Crawford, but not for several years did he enter the Crawford camp. Indeed, in his first four years in Washington—that is, in the Fifteenth and Sixteenth Congresses—McLane was on two major issues distinctly opposed to Crawford's faction: first, in the winter of 1818–19, McLane was a supporter of Jackson against censure for his Florida campaign; and, second, McLane opposed various measures to reduce the size of the Army, measures that pitted the Treasury, and its desire for economy, against the defense plans of John C. Calhoun, the Secretary of War.

Not until the Seventh Congress had convened in the fall of 1821 did McLane commit himself to Crawford. The reasons for this commitment are not entirely clear. According to McLane, Crawford was the best man and the most likely candidate. There is no doubt that McLane admired Crawford as a stateman in a way that he never esteemed his next leader, Andrew Jackson. To McLane, Jackson was a great soldier, a hero, but seldom or never did he let enthusiasm carry him to such praise of Jackson's statesmanship.

"The course remaining for Federalists," Rufus King had counseled his party in 1816, "is to adhere to the integrity of their Principles; . . . and the Republicans . . . being sure to divide among themselves, the Federalists will be able to assist the true interests of Freedom and of Justice by giving their influence to the least wicked Section of the Republicans." [64] Support of Crawford represented just such a policy to McLane—identification with, to put the worst front on it, "the least wicked Section of the Republicans."

It seemed to McLane, also, that the Crawfordites were the faction most likely to triumph in the presidential contest. From one view Crawford was the heir apparent, for he had been runner-up to Monroe for the Republican nomination in 1816, just as Monroe had been runner-up to Madison in 1808; in fact, a change of six votes at the Republican caucus in 1816 would have nominated Crawford over Monroe. Despite the appearance of a number of rival candidates, Crawford still seemed to be the leading contender; his will be "the high road or I am much deceived," McLane wrote in February, 1822. [65]

High road or not, it was a road of gratitude. By the Tenure of Office Act of 1820, the collector's job had been made dependent upon the Secretary of the Treasury; Crawford had reappointed old Allen McLane as collector in 1821, and Louis was not likely to be altogether thoughtless of this kindness. Crawford's rivals and Crawford's friends were also such as to influence McLane's course.

It was odd, Federalist as he was, for McLane to have become associated with the old Republican or radical wing of the Democratic party, but so he had. Nathaniel Macon and John Randolph, central figures in this group, were men who had much appeal for McLane—perhaps because they, like the Federalists, objected to many administration policies and personalities, but also because of their character as men. Of his delight with the strange Virginian, for instance, McLane wrote as follows in the winter of his decision for Crawford: "Randolph came and breakfasted with our mess this morning, and is infinitely more gay, and entertaining than ever, and surpasses really almost any idea that we could form of him." [66]

Crawford's chief rivals in 1822 were men distasteful to McLane. Henry Clay, who seemed at the moment the chief antagonist, had borne Mc-Lane's dislike ever since McLane entered the House in December, 1817. John Quincy Adams and Calhoun were other objects of his enmity, particularly after the speakership contest in December, 1821, when Adams supported Taylor, and Calhoun, though opposing Taylor, refused to take up McLane.

The contest for Speaker seems to have been the turning point. Before December, 1821, there is no indication that McLane would support Crawford for President. After that date the evidence is plentiful. On January 4, 1822, McLane declared that Calhoun's "partizans fight shy of me, knowing as they do pretty well that I fight under different banners." [67] What those banners were is made clear by Kitty's letter of January 5, responding to earlier, doubtless lost letters of Louis—or perhaps to what she had learned from Louis in conversation when he had run home for a quick visit in mid-December. Adams's friends were multiplying in Philadelphia, Kitty reported she had learned from her brother John; there they did not properly esteem "the integrity of *that strong man* who presides over the Treasury department." [68] Since this idea of Crawford's great merit was not John Milligan's, Kitty must have taken it from Louis.

VII   THE COOK COMMITTEE

An opportunity to show his colors came to McLane in February, 1822, when he was appointed to a special committee of the House on the examination of the land offices.[69] The chairman of this committee was Daniel P. Cook, of Illinois, the solitary representative of his young state and a stubborn man. In Congress on January 3 Cook had asked that the Secretary of the Treasury be required to report how the land offices were examined prior to January 1, 1818, and how they had been examined since then.[70] Though his motives were rooted in the factional political quarrels of his own state, his action might have wide repercussions for it threatened the reputation and therefore the prospects of the Treasury Secretary.

Since the beginning of 1818, Secretary Crawford had been employing special agents instead of Treasury clerks, as heretofore, to investigate the account books and the cash balances of the land offices. The Treasury explained that the change was made because the business of the land offices had grown and clerks could no longer be spared for the work. However, as Cook knew, the use of special agents offered a fresh opportunity for patronage to an aspiring politician like Crawford. Cook also knew that one of these agents in 1821 was Senator Jesse B. Thomas, an Illinois rival of Cook's and of Cook's father-in-law, Senator Ninian Edwards.[71]

Adams and Calhoun were delighted at this attack on Crawford's patronage system, particularly because they felt that Thomas was "canvassing for Crawford" in his travels from land office to land office.[72] With the encouragement of Crawford's enemies, Cook, though a small, frail young man, kept pertinaciously pecking away at the Treasury Department until the Speaker appointed a committee to investigate his charges.[73]

But the Speaker, Philip Barbour, was a Crawford partisan and unlikely to appoint men who would give Crawford anything less than a fair deal. After Cook to the committee, Barbour named Jonathan Russell (of Massachusetts), a bitter enemy of Cook's friend Adams; Louis McLane and Andrew Stevenson (of Virginia), both emerging leaders of the Crawford faction; Cadwallader Colden, grandson and namesake of the learned colonial deputy governor of New York; David Trimble, a Kentucky Democrat; and, to round out the committee and give it prestige, the respected but ailing William Lowndes.[74]

The committee set to work gathering information from the Treasury and also from other executive departments. Cook grounded his criticism of the employment of Senator Thomas to inspect land offices on two bases: first, on the constitutional provision forbidding Congressmen from holding other office under the federal government, and, second, on an act of April 21, 1808, forbidding Congressmen from entering into contracts with the United States.

There was no gainsaying Thomas's employment. But after diligent search and careful inquiry of other departments of the government, the committee found several precedents and came to the conclusion that such partial and temporary employment as Crawford had extended to Thomas came under the prohibition neither of the constitutional nor of the statutory provision. Furthermore, the better to shield Crawford from partisan attack, the committee found that not only such Republican saints as Jefferson and Madison had employed members of Congress in similar fashion (to treat with Indian tribes), but also Crawford's rivals Adams and Calhoun had indulged in similar practices—Adams in contracting with a Congressman-publisher to print the laws and Calhoun in employing two Congressmen as War Department counsel and a third Congressman as superintendent of a fortification. (Calhoun promptly denied that the first two men—one was Caesar A. Rodney—were members of Congress when employed as counsel, and explained that the third man was hired by a local military commandant without any report of his identity reaching the Secretary.) [75]

When Daniel Cook presented his committee's report on March 29, 1822, he was visibly unhappy. "It completely *cooks* Mr. Cook," reported a North Carolina Crawfordite, Romulus Saunders; "the little serpent wreathed and twisted in its perusal—it is a statement of facts and reasoning highly satisfactory to the friends of Mr. Crawford." And, Saunders added, "it is from the pen of Mr. McLane of Delaware." [76]

McLane's words came sourly to Cook's tongue, when, for instance, the report declared that the committee, though recognizing the right of Congress to conduct this inquiry, could not "recognise either its justice or dignity in conducting *ex parte* investigations into breaches of highly penal statutes, and the commission of misdemeanors amenable by the laws to a different tribunal"—that is, a court of law. "Such precedents might lead, in worse times, to consequence of a ruinous and most troublesome character. . . . They would be very apt to be seized upon to produce public excitement, and be perverted to the purposes of ambitious men and individual resentments." [77]

The committee's conclusion refuted Cook's charges completely: "the employment of Mr. Thomas to examine the land offices originated in a desire honestly to discharge an important public duty" and "the peculiar importance of the trust at the time, and the character and elevation of the individual employed, were calculated rather to invite than forbid the selection." (According to Crawford the principal inducement for hiring Thomas was an expectation that he could secure to the United States a large amount of public money in the Bank of Vincennes when it stopped payment, which service he performed and without compensation.) [78] But Cook was too bold to be thus dismissed; he broke precedent by announcing that the committee was not unanimous.

This remark brought the true author of the report to his feet. Louis McLane was tired and ailing and eager to be home for the Delaware supreme court session on April 1. His committees had kept him particularly busy through this March. "I fear my engagements on the Crawford committee will render my return impossible," he had told Kitty,[79] but the Naval Affairs Committee also thrust a burden of work upon him. Indeed, before Cook reported, McLane had on the same day presented a plan for a permanent Navy peace establishment. True to his Federalist heritage, he defended a naval force of capital ships as "the best defence for this country and that on which it must ultimately rely, not only for the protection of our commerce but to prevent the actual invasion of the soil." [80] Such ardent advocacy of the Navy might be interpreted as a gage of battle thrown at Calhoun, sponsor of an expensive plan of military fortifications.

And now, after Cook's attempt to weaken the report by revealing committee disagreement, McLane quickly fired a salvo for Crawford. He was sorry that Cook felt it necessary to break with custom by revealing his vote in the committee, for every committee member might feel called on to do likewise. But since the precedent was broken, perhaps it could be revealed that Cook, the chairman, had been the only committee member not agreeing to the report.

It was embarrassing to Cook to have it known he had no support in his own committee, but Speaker Barbour completed the victory of the Crawfordites by refusing to consider accepting a minority report from Cook. Put in the position of one seeking to overturn sacred precedents, the young Illinoisan sputtered his defense: "he would rather abandon his seat—he would rather never have set foot in this House, than do a dishonorable act or even an act of unkindness to any of his fellow-members." McLane, having his victory, could now be soothing. He "disclaimed any intention . . . to alarm [Cook's] feelings . . . or impeach his motives. He considered it an act of justice to the committee to state the facts of the case, and he had done no more." [81]

Three weeks later Louis explained to Kitty that he had "neither the inclination or the power" to engage in the increasingly boisterous debates. "Of the former perhaps I feel a little now and then, but am so defective in the latter, that I am obliged to refrain. . . . The Crawford report . . . seems to have had a pretty conclusive effect here, among all parties. . . . The friends of Mr. Crawford rest satisfied that justice has been done to an honest man." [82]

Cook was impressed by McLane, if not by Crawford. In the next Congress he outlined to his father-in-law the policy he would take in debate: "There are none of the opposition but Forsyth, and McLane of Delaware, that I will meet, as deserving my special notice. This will be taking high ground, to be sure. . . ." [83]

VIII   CLOSE OF A SESSION

Committed to Crawford more decidedly than ever before by his report for the Cook committee, McLane became increasingly critical of the administration—as it was influenced by Crawford's rivals—during the final weeks of Congress in the spring of 1822. "The President is becoming unpopular," he opined on April 16, "and . . . Randolph's observation is likely to be verified, that he will go out of office, with as much unanimity and greater earnestness than that with which he came in." [84] And two days later: "The poor old President finds himself wofully beset; deserted by all his old friends, he is obliged to seek new ones." [85]

There were in these days some lyrical moments like those of a morning in April when Louis McLane on his White Fury (he was always fond of horses, but not always able to afford keeping a horse in Washington—he sold this "gallant grey" in April for a hundred dollars) [86] and Crawford on his horse rode "7 or 8 miles up the County." It was an interesting ride, Louis told Kitty. Politics must have made it so, for he had not a word to say of scenic beauties or of any other subject but the one: "He is now wofully beset [apparently McLane liked this phrase] by the Calhoun Party, and I fear is in some danger; tho' more from the indiscretion of his friends, than his enemies." The danger was, he explained, that the violent radicals who supported Crawford were so eager to reduce the expenses of government that they would hurt the popularity of their candidate in the process. (McLane was not only being a practical politician in realizing that spending can make popularity, and economy the opposite; he was also revealing his Federalist lack of sympathy for one of the main elements among Crawford's supporters, the old radical strict-construction, limited-government Republican faction, whom he admired as persons but condemned for their political philosophy.) "It is a great pity Mr. Crawford had not some prudent man of his own party, (for they will allow a man of no other to do it) to take the lead—if he had, his chance could not be defeated." [87]

Ah, if only Louis McLane were a Democrat.

Meanwhile other men and other parties were at work, winning the President to their side. "I suspect," Louis told Kitty on May 4, "Mr. Crawford has incurred the displeasure of Mr. Monroe, who has put his patronage in the hands of Calhoun. . . . But I trust the good ship, will yet reach the port in safety, and ride triumphant in a harbour for which she is so well qualified." [88]

That very evening, a Saturday, Congress stayed late in session, trying to hurry its business to a close. The hall looked beautiful, and "the galleries were grand with much of the fashion and the beauty of the city." But at the night session a villain appeared—or so McLane said: "Calhoun made his appearance for the first time this session and took advantage of the night to carry on his intrigue. The hour was well chosen for purposes so dark." McLane "gave out at a little after 9, and returned home," only to worry there about Calhoun. "He has little chance I think of success for himself, but will probably, or at least I begin to fear so, break down Mr. *Crawford* by forming a Coalition with *Clay,* whose prospects seem to me to begin to brighten." Then a note to his father which has omens of a future connection: "Tell him that his *honest, independent* friend [William] Duane," publisher of the influential *Aurora* in Philadelphia, and father of a future cabinet associate of Louis McLane, "has sold himself to the Secretary of War, who has the settlement of his accounts." [89]

IX   REELECTION, 1822

As a committed Crawfordite, McLane never forgot the importance of the role he might play in the presidential election—even if he did frequently threaten to abandon public life, particularly when he met political defeat or was disheartened by new physical maladies, whether his own or Kitty's. The Apportionment Act of 1822 in reducing Delaware's representation in the House to a single member had given that member a particular and a critical importance. The Federalist party had had no candidate for the Presidency since 1816. In 1820 the Democrats had been united by a unanimous if, in some quarters, grudging acceptance of Monroe's right to a second term. But in 1824 the party was likely to be split by a many-sided contest, with the probability that no one man would win a majority of the electoral votes. In that case, the Constitution ordained, the election should go to the House of Representatives, where the delegates, voting as state blocs, one vote per state, would choose among the three leading candidates by a majority vote. One Representative from Delaware, therefore, would be as important, as influential, as twenty from a more populous state. Not only McLane himself but his friends in the Crawford camp, too, would want him to stay in Congress.

The advantages of his position had occurred to McLane in January, 1822, just as he "despaired of all hope" of election to the Senate. "After all," he concluded, "at my age, and under the present circumstances of the country, the House of Representatives is the most eligible and if three years hence, the choice of presi't. should devolve on that body, as it probably will, the member from Delaware would have great advantages." [90]

And Kitty—good, faithful, and intelligent, if biased, wife—gave him the encouragement he wanted: You can keep your seat in the house "as *long* as *you* choose to occupy it; for there can be no doubt, that they have no man, who could make any stand against you." [91] One of the du Ponts "compared your friends wishing to put you in the Senate to Lownd's, Making him President —— that tho you had standing to justify any wish of theirs, yet they might overlook your real interest." [92]

Continued illness made Louis find fault with Congress and the capital: "This wretched place has been the grave of more talent and worth than it can ever atone for, and it would be well indeed if with surgeons for the Army, the Government would also supply Physicians for Congress." [93] But a few days of rest at home healed his spirit. "The noisy little brood . . . running about the house" at 606 Market Street, visits from his impatient, querulous, capricious, choleric father, talks on politics, law, and literature with young Jim Bayard (who thought Kitty resembled Brenda in Scott's *Pirate*),[94] and most especially the good company of Kitty, now well enough at least to go out daily for a ride—these domestic joys put Louis into the mood of a kind, joshing, loving parent (the inheritance from his tender mother dominating that from his crotchety father) who could call his firstborn child home from a Philadelphia visit in great good humor: "We are both sick enough, to require you to be very amiable, and interesting, to laugh and sing at command, and never to cry, or to pout, two of your old accomplishments, which I shall expect you to leave on the Banks of the Schuylkill, never to be practiced again. I hear a great deal of your good behavior and lady like airs in Philadelphia, and I shall expect to have proof of them all, when we have the happiness, to see you once more at home." [95]

Rested, healed in body and in spirit, the furious campaigner, the fiery old collector's son, rose again to do battle for fame and power when another election time arrived. Once again—as always in Delaware—he was a Federalist candidate ("they have no man who could make any stand against you," Kitty had said), coupled with Daniel Rodney, of Lewes, a Federalist Rodney running to fill the time remaining in his cousin Caesar's seat. The Democrats, of course, were not prepared to accept Kitty McLane's conviction; they nominated Dr. Arnold Naudain, a Kent County physician, to contest with Louis for the single House seat allotted to Delaware in the new Congress of 1823—hoping, very likely, that a Kent candidate would cut deeply into the usual Federalist majority downstate, as Willard Hall, a Kent resident, and Caesar A. Rodney, a Kent native, had done in previous elections.

McLane's partisans may have found it more necessary to defend him before the minority of Federalists in New Castle County than before the majority downstate in Sussex. At least a broadside that survives is obviously directed to the mercantile, urban north of Delaware, defending McLane's vote on the Missouri Compromise as an expression of his conscience and declaring that he pleased the people of Delaware in all his other votes—for the old soldier and the veteran (pension bills), for the manufacturing interests (tariffs), for internal improvements (particularly the Chesapeake and Delaware Canal). He had opposed the "Southern influence," the unknown author of the broadside declared, with reference apparently to economic measures. And though he obeyed his constitutional oath in opposing restrictions on slavery in Missouri, both his education and his family led him to oppose slavery.[96] Indeed, there were no slaves (though two free colored servants) in the McLane household in 1820.[97]

Another anonymous friend who claimed to be "A Naturalized Irishman" used rhyme to implore other Irish voters—and in Delaware parlance at the time "Irish" referred to anyone from the emerald isle, decidedly including the large number of Presbyterian Scotch-Irish, generally Democrats—to support only "those . . . fit to guide"—that is, the Federalists, presumably—and,

> While thus they act, give them your vote and voice
> And hail McLane—the people's friend and choice.[98]

The McLane propaganda apparently had its effect. Louis not only carried Sussex County by his usual large plurality—he held a 2-to-1 lead there with the voters turning out in their usual fantastic numbers—but he narrowed the Democratic plurality in New Castle to only 370 votes out of 2,400, decidedly the best showing he had ever made.[99] This gave him statewide a plurality of 650 votes, much the best he had done, and all the more remarkable in that it occurred in the face of an unprecedented Federalist defeat.

"Contrary to all expectation and almost without a precedent," as a Federalist paper put it, the Democrats captured Kent County as well as New Castle. Both houses in the new legislature would be controlled by Democrats, and Joseph Haslet, the Democratic candidate, had been elected governor. "In this instance the federalists of this state have met with a more serious loss than it has ever before been their lot to experience." Democratic governors had been elected before and once the Democrats had controlled the legislature, but never both at one time. The only important positions salvaged by the Federalists were the congressional seats, won by McLane and Daniel Rodney.[100] Since Rodney's plurality was less than half the size of McLane's, it looked as if Kitty was right when she assured Louis, "they have no man who could make any stand against you." No one, that is, since Caesar A. Rodney had been promoted to the Senate.

X   THE FRIENDSHIP OF VICTOR DU PONT

Caesar A. Rodney did not stay in the Senate long. Early in 1823 he resigned to sail to Buenos Aires as the first American minister to the young republic on the River Plate. The resignation gave the Democrats, who now controlled the legislature, an opportunity to choose two Senators, a replacement for Rodney and a successor to Federalist Nicholas Van Dyke, whose term expired in March. But the Democrats flubbed their opportunity. They could agree on Willard Hall to fill one of the posts, but they could not agree on a second choice.

A majority of Democrats wanted Dr. Samuel H. Black, a progressive farmer and physician of New Castle County, and a minority supported George Read, Jr. The Black-Read feud began before Rodney's resignation was received, and the followers of Black refused to allow Hall's election to one seat till their man had been elected to the other. He never was. Democrats for Black, Democrats for Read, and Federalists still true to Van Dyke made the race a three-sided one in the legislature, with Black a consistent leader but never gaining the majority needed for election.[101]

Whether policies or personalities were the original issue, both became involved, and Victor du Pont was the villain or hero of the affair, according to how it was viewed. Caesar A. Rodney explained to President Monroe that the failure to elect was due to "the intrigue of Victor du Pont, who succeeded in inducing" two other legislators—one the former acting governor, Charles Thomas—"from the Republican ranks," assisted by the Wilmington postmaster, Nicholas Williamson.[102] "Mr. Dupont openly boasts that he keeps *'the keys* of the State in his hands,' that he can permit the Election of a Senator when he pleases," Rodney had been told by a friend in Dover.[103] In retaliation the Black forces defeated a resolution du Pont sponsored—a resolution successfully passed the previous year—in favor of the protection of Delaware manufactures.[104]

Perhaps Victor du Pont was motivated by no personal antagonism to Dr. Black but by a quarrel on principles—as, for example, by a fear that Black would not stand staunchly for a protective tariff. Du Pont confessed that in 1820 he and "many others who stand high in the republican ranks" had voted for "what was then called the 'Manufacturers' Democratic ticket for Congress, Messrs. Rodney and McLane." "I am," Victor continued, "no fanatic in religion or politics; I . . . would without hesitation vote for a federalist of superior merits, particularly for a seat in Congress, where federalism and democracy have not been known or even talked of or dreamt of for a number of years." [105]

The du Pont-Read faction in the legislature in 1823 does look like a disguised group of Democrats for McLane. Du Pont was now on very friendly terms with Louis—they were both landlords on the Brandywine, and as befit proper Brandywiners, both were staunch protectionists; Louis had helped Victor's son Samuel, a future admiral, with appointments in the Navy; [106] and in Washington McLane occasionally helped direct gunpowder orders to Victor's brother Eleuthère Irénée.[107] Read was the father-in-law of Louis's brother, and Williamson, the Wilmington postmaster and reputed intriguer with du Pont, had received his post with McLane's help.

No wonder McLane chortled in glee at the outcome—the total failure of the Democratic legislature to elect any Senator: *"Dupont* and *Thomas* deserve immortal honor, for their conduct in the Legislature."[108]

XI CHAIRMAN OF WAYS AND MEANS

Daniel Rodney, a former governor of Delaware and a distant cousin of Caesar A. Rodney, was twenty years older than Louis McLane. When Daniel Rodney went to Congress, his son George Brydges Rodney, a young graduate of Princeton and a Congressman-to-be, visited Washington and was quite impressed with "the high standing" accorded Louis McLane in the House: "He appears to have very great weight with the members," George confided to his diary, "for when he begins to speak they collect about him and pay great attention to his words."[109]

Young George Rodney was not mistaken. On the heels of his election victory in 1822, Louis McLane had attained his highest standing in the House. For Speaker Barbour had moved Louis from the Naval Committee back to Ways and Means—from a chairmanship, true, to only a second position, but this was but a nominal demotion. Old General Smith, chairman of the Ways and Means Committee, was leaving the House to accept appointment to the Senate, and consequently before the month of December, 1822, was over, McLane's second place had become a first place: Louis McLane, Federalist from Delaware, had become chairman of the Ways and Means Committee. Was it not a favor from one Crawfordite (Barbour) to another, a consolation prize for the loss of the speakership? And yet, considering McLane's short service (five years), youth (thirty-eight), and Federalism, was this not also a tribute to the respect felt in the House for his ability, a reward due "a man of talents and a gentleman"?[110]

Kitty must have felt it was. Sending Rebecca off to school in Philadelphia, where her grandfather could look in on her occasionally in his infrequent peregrinations along the Delaware, Kitty took the rest of her brood, Robert, Louis, Sally, and Lydia—to Georgetown, where they took rooms. Soon she was enjoying the society of Washington—visiting ladies such as Mrs. Senator Brown, of Louisiana, whom she had met in previous Washington seasons; attending parties, such as one given by Mrs. Stephen

Pleasonton, wife of the fifth auditor; [111] sending her friends descriptions of the fashionable and elegant, such as Mrs. Decatur, widow of the naval hero.[112]

Before she was long in Washington, Kitty, to her exultation, found herself and Louis at a large and stylish dinner at the President's house (not yet called the White House)—"the first one this season." In the company were the highest officials of the government; Vice-President Tompkins, now accompanied by his wife, was there, and so were the Calhouns, who looked, Kitty thought, as if they hoped soon to be living in the presidential palace themselves. And, of course, there was Louis's hero—ergo Kitty's—William Crawford. To Kitty's delight he sat next to her and "had a great deal to say." He advised her to send Bob and Lou to a southern college and "said Delaware was far North enough." While he talked, Kitty, hopeful for his future, observed that he no longer wore a wig and that he was looking better than ever before [113]—and it is to be assumed that Kitty, like Louis and others, had always thought Crawford made a good appearance.

But it was Louis, not Kitty, who most often sat beside the great in this busy Washington winter of 1822–23. Even in the evening he was frequently out in all-male company, while Kitty had to stay at home. In daytime, of course, he was very busy. Besides the very great business of his committee—the appropriation bills—Louis was intensely interested in a proposal of the Committee on Manufactures to raise the tariff—so much so, he wrote a friend, that he subjected himself "to censure from all the departments, and with all the South, for postponing the Appropriation Bills . . . to give the Tariff a full chance." [114]

Even though he risked his popularity in the House for the sake of the tariff, he was criticized at home for his failure to do more for it. This criticism hurt McLane; it was "vile slander," he declared, to accuse him of "hostility to the manufacturing interest." He had objections to details in the new tariff bill, as he did in the case of the one Henry Baldwin, of Pittsburgh, had unsuccessfully sponsored in 1820, but he had supported Baldwin's bill "throughout" and would give the same support to this one. He would not make a major speech on it because its enemies wanted to protract debate, the better to defeat it in this short session, and its friends decided that those who had spoken for Baldwin's tariff would allow other advocates a turn now. "I was the more ready to yield to this course," McLane explained, "from the feeble state of my health, and the burthens of the Committee of Ways and Means, as much as it can bear."

Besides, there was little he could add to what he had already said to Congress on the tariff: "My speech three years ago . . . has made up all the speeches which have been delivered yet on that subject." [115] He was referring to a speech of April 28, 1820, in the debate on Baldwin's tariff, a speech that had brought him many compliments at the time, when even the respected Carolinian, William Lowndes, confessed he listened to McLane with "attention and pleasure," disagree though he did.[116] In this speech McLane had spoken decisively for protection, protection enough to "inspire the capitalists with confidence," so they would not withdraw money invested in manufactures—money of the kind he and George Milligan had invested in Rokeby. A tariff to him was a "purely national" policy, not sectional or class legislation but for "the best interests of all parts of the community." Nor did he advocate it for revenue; other sources of money must be found: "I value it only for the protection it would afford to the labor of the country."

He could pay tribute at once to "the enlightened independence" of Secretary Crawford, who "candidly exposed the extent of our wants," and to his own Federalist saint, Hamilton, who "portrayed with a prophetic hand the true course of national policy." "Desolating wars" in Europe have given us exclusive advantages and disguised our true situation. Now that "those wars have terminated" me must stimulate our industy as foreigners stimulate theirs. The need is great; he has seen the stimulus war gave to industry "upon the banks of the Brandywine," and now if he "did not feel too keenly," he "could delineate the melancholy reverse which . . . enfeebles the hand of labor and paralyzes every species of enterprise."

Did men say that manufacturing led to crime and vice, destroyed families? It was not so. It gave new opportunities for a better life. Nowhere was there less vice and criminality than in "the manufacturing establishments in the vicinity" of his residence, "and particularly those located upon the Brandywine. In those establishments there are hundreds of poor children employed, and I am sure that the utmost attention is paid to their moral habits, and a system of schools and education have been founded, through the liberality of their employers, which yield them a fund of instruction which they could never hope to acquire from the poverty of their parents." What if some hands were drawn from the farms: "We cultivate too much poor land" anyway.[117]

XII   A CLASH WITH RANDOLPH

Though in 1823 the efforts of McLane and other tariff men were in vain, 1824 was another story. In the latter year McLane's advocacy of a protective tariff involved him in a public controversy with his friend John Randolph.

The clash occurred on April 12, 1824. "A proposition was made to re-

duce the duty on sugar," Louis explained, and "seeing a strong probability of its succeeding," he jumped up to defend the tariff.[118] (Though
Delaware had no sugar crop, McLane, like other tariff advocates, was
sensitive to the concerns of his pro-tariff colleagues in Louisiana.) Mc-
Lane's speech "brought out" Randolph, who declared McLane's argument
was suicidal, destroying itself. In his turn, McLane, angered that his
argument was being ridiculed, stung more, however, by Randolph's
manner than by his words, began an irate reply. Randolph tried to interrupt; he regarded McLane as a friend and insisted "that he intended
not the least disrespect or offence." Although McLane may have re-
strained his reply somewhat, he did not stop it. He granted that Randolph meant no personal offense; remedy for that would lie outside
the House. But he objected to the manner of Randolph's speech; granting "the gentleman from Virginia had displayed a good head, . . . he
would not accept that gentleman's head, to be obliged to take his heart
with it." [119]

The remark stung Randolph and, in McLane's words, "affected the
House." [120] The slender Virginian's reply was faint and most respectful
as he apologized for the zeal that had made his remarks disagreeable
to McLane: "For that gentleman I have never expressed any other sentiment but respect—I have never uttered, or entertained, an unkind feeling towards that gentleman, either in this House or elsewhere, nor do
I now feel any such sentiment towards him. . . . He appears to have
considered my remarks as having a personal application to himself. . . .
He has been pleased, Sir, to say something, which, no doubt, he thinks
very severe, about my head and my heart."

And then John Randolph displayed the wit that, with his erratic wildness and his odd learning, made him a notable figure in Congress for
three decades: "How easy, Sir, would it be for me to reverse the gentleman's proposition, and to retort upon him that I would not, in return,
take that gentleman's heart, however good it may be, if obliged to take
such a head into the bargain.

"But, Sir, I do not do this. I never thought it; and, therefore, I cannot
be so ungenerous as to say it; for Mr. Speaker, who made me a searcher
of hearts? of the heart of a fellow-man, a fellow-sinner? . . . Sir, I dismiss the gentleman to his self-complacency; let him go; yes, Sir, let him
go, and thank his God that he is not as *this* publican." [121]

XIII　THE 1824 TARIFF

Humility was not one of McLane's virtues. Esteem McLane though
he did, his colleagues hugely enjoyed Randolph's retort, which they re-

peated amid chuckles in all the congressional boardinghouses. Senator Rufus King, the venerable Federalist from New York, came to Randolph and told him, so Randolph reported, "all the Georgetown mess were loud in their praise of my reception of McLane of Delaware's attack upon me . . . ; that the Patroon [Van Rensselaer] was delighted. . . . Tattnall of Georgia . . . told Mr. Macon that nothing could be more dignified or gentlemanly than my reply, and that it was just what it ought to have been." [122]

McLane's self-complacency did not altogether blind him to this reaction. "It is but right," he explained, with an uncharacteristic openness, to his brother-in-law, "I should state that opinions are somewhat divided on one part of the business—some thinking I went too far, others that my observations were merited." But Randolph must be clearly shown that a man will not quail before his attacks and that a challenge will come in a moment if he departs from respectful manners. Otherwise he is capable of the wildest charges. "*I* know Mr. R. well eno' to know that there is but one course of management, and that I shall always pursue upon like provocation." [123]

Yet if Randolph won the repartee, McLane won the vote. The sugar duty he defended was accepted by the House on April 12, despite any faults that might have resided in McLane's logic, and on April 16 the new tariff passed the House and moved on to the Senate.[124] Before the end of May it was through the Senate, signed by President Monroe, and become the law of the land.

Even before the tariff had passed Congress Randolph tried to calm McLane's irritation, but he was not immediately successful. Seeing off a friend on the steamboat on May 5, McLane caught sight of Randolph but kept away from him, "tho' he evidently desired a salutation." [125] Two days later Randolph opposed McLane in a House debate. "He assailed my Bill," Louis reported home, "in the wildest strain" but "he treated *me* most respectfully." When Louis defended the bill—it was for an appropriation to provide awards under the Florida Cession Treaty— he replied specifically to other opponents, but "pointedly avoided" Randolph, who later went to the Senate chamber and complained to Van Buren of McLane's treatment of him. With his usual suavity, Van Buren persuaded McLane to restore good fellowship as long as there was no danger of "future attack from the Crazy Knight." McLane denied harboring any ill feeling toward Randolph—"if I did, his present state would extinguish it," for "Randolph is deplorably crazy." [126]

Apparently McLane, despite his promise, found no opportunity in the next few days to exhibit his forgiveness of Randolph. On his arrival at the House on the morning of May 13 he found a letter from the eccentric

Virginian and he heard at the same time that Randolph had set off for Europe, "wild as a maniac." The letter enclosed some papers of the collector's and furnished the occasion for the letter from Randolph, who spoke affectionately of the old man, desired his best wishes given to Kitty, and subscribed himself McLane's obedient servant. "I sincerely regret now," Louis confessed, "that he will leave the country without my seeing him. If I can do so safely, I will address him an answer, and say all I can, without a sacrifice of my own pride."

The quarrel was apparently on McLane's conscience. He admired Randolph's wild talent for debate: "His last blow was at the Beaumarchais claim against which and Beaumarchais himself he delivered the most bitter and masterly phillipic I ever heard. The claim was rejected by an overwhelming vote, and he retired from the House in full triumph." And admiring Randolph as he did, McLane was bound to be flattered by the man's friendliness and somewhat concerned at his own conduct: "He is a strange man, but his senses are evidently deranged, and I fear his present condition is attributable to his rencontre with me. Would to Heaven it had never occurred!" [127]

Yet after he thought it over, McLane decided not to answer Randolph's letter.[128] The quarrel was not made up until the fall, at the opening of a new session of Congress, when McLane found Randolph "so attentive . . . as to be troublesome." [129]

XIV   INTERNAL IMPROVEMENTS

McLane's advocacy of a protective tariff was coupled, as for a good Federalist it should have been, with an equal interest in government aid for internal improvements. "It is for us," he had argued in his tariff speech of April 28, 1820, "to adopt a system of policy which shall draw [our resources] forth, and make them active, and which shall protect the home labor against foreign competition, and which shall provide the home market accessible by roads and canals." [130]

Roads and canals always won his support. Many times he gave his vote and occasionally his voice to appropriations for the great national road being constructed from Cumberland, Maryland, through Wheeling, in the Virginia panhandle, and on westward into the old Northwest. He not only supported construction of the road but opposed all bills to divest the federal government of responsibility for it by turning it over to the states through which it ran.[131]

In his first eight years in Congress, Louis McLane supported every internal improvement bill that came before Congress, or at least every one on which a recorded vote was taken. In January, 1824, when speaking on a bill providing for government support to surveys for roads and canals, he made his position clear, declaring himself in favor of "a liberal interpretation" of the Constitution. "Ours," he said, "is a limited government; limited as to objects confided to its administration." But for such objects "its authority is supreme, and unlimited as to means necessary for their accomplishment." The power not just to survey but to construct roads and canals he found "incident to . . . the commercial power of the government," and he thought it "too late in the day to contend" that the government did not possess this power. The power to regulate commerce between the states implied for him "a vigilant and active power."

To regulate, he argued, meant to "afford reasonable facilities." For foreign commerce we provide lighthouses, buoys, quarantine laws, embargoes, and so forth; for land-borne commerce rights of way are needed. "Has this great nation," he continued, "been organized with the dimensions of a giant to handle the instruments of a pigmy?" [132]

When he had finished, John Randolph and George Tucker voiced Virginia's objections. Let us pay off our debts if we have so much money, said Randolph, while Tucker disagreed on constitutional grounds with McLane, charging him with confusion in "political abstractions and technical distinctions" despite "the good sense for which he is so distinguished." [133] It was for his good sense, of course, that Virginia Republicans esteemed McLane; his "political abstractions" could seldom please them.

But the survey bill passed. When it had, and when John Todd, of Pennsylvania, moved that the House take up the discussion of his proposal for a protective tariff, John Randolph demurred, saying, "Sufficient for the day is the evil thereof." [134]

XV   THE CANAL

Through his twelve years in Congress Louis McLane's pet project, among the various internal improvements that he sponsored, was the Chesapeake and Delaware Canal. Sponsoring government aid to this canal was, of course, a service to his constituents, but it fitted into his "political abstractions" or "system of policy," and perhaps it helped to shape his policy on internal improvements. In his speech of January 28, 1824, on surveys for roads and canals, for instance, he had concluded by proposing that the federal government need not use its full power to construct roads and canals. Its objects, he said, "will be better accomplished by allowing individual enterprise, under the auspices of the State governments, to take the lead."

By "individual enterprise, under the auspices of the State governments," he meant chartered companies and particularly the Chesapeake and Delaware Canal Company, which was chartered by Delaware, Pennsylvania, and Maryland. If the federal government can buy bank stock (the Bank of the United States), he argued, why not canal or turnpike stock? And if canal or turnpike stock, why not stock in the Chesapeake and Delaware Canal? [135]

This, indeed, was what he had been urging for six years. The first motion he is recorded as making in Congress (on December 12, 1817) was to encourage a government subscription to stock in the Chesapeake and Delaware Canal.[136] One of his first speeches, made March 16, 1818, was to the same end.[137] And before he left Congress, in March of 1829, his last congressional victory was won when President Adams signed a bill appropriating $150,000 to the purchase of stock in the Chesapeake and Delaware Canal.[138]

But this was not his only success in his long battle for the canal, which itself had a long history. Begun in 1804 under the direction of Benjamin Latrobe, construction of the canal was soon discontinued for lack of funds. The chief interest in the canal came from Pennsylvania, not Delaware, and specifically from Philadelphia, because Philadelphians thought that by means of such a canal rafts or barges that floated goods down the Susquehanna River to the Chesapeake Bay might be lured away from the Baltimore market to the Delaware River and Philadelphia. Delawareans, particularly those from downstate, saw little advantage to themselves from the canal. What selfish interest Delawareans did have in it, declined after the revived company decided to adopt a lower route cutting directly to the Delaware River, near Pea Patch Island, rather than a northern route terminating near Wilmington or at New Castle.

In acting as spokesman for the canal company, Louis McLane was serving the mercantile community of the Delaware valley, of which he was a part as a Wilmington lawyer and as a customs collector's son, rather than the bulk of his Federalist constituents, the farmers of Kent and Sussex. He was, moreover, carrying on an interest of his legal preceptor, James Bayard, who had been a director of the canal company and doubly interested in its welfare as a Delaware attorney and as a Maryland planter whose lands were near the Chesapeake terminus of the canal. Though the canal was intended to take some of the Susquehanna trade from Baltimore and Baltimoreans consequently viewed it with alarm, it would profit the upper Eastern Shore of Maryland—and especially the region of Cecil County where the Bayards and Milligans owned land—by opening an easier and cheaper route to Philadelphia for their crops.[139]

For a time all hope of assistance from Congress was abandoned, because differences of opinion about the proper route for the canal became known in 1821 and destroyed confidence in the company.[140] But the company secured new private subscriptions and promises of assistance from the states concerned—of $100,000 from Pennsylvania, $50,000 from Delaware, and $25,000 from Maryland—and came back to Congress with petitions and memorials requesting help. As Joseph Hemphill, a Representative from Philadelphia, explained in urging the House to authorize a $300,000 federal stock subscription, Delaware and Maryland could hardly be expected to do any more for the canal. Even were internal improvement funds divided among the states, these two would not wish to spend their share on the canal, for its value was national; "many of the states," said Hemphill, "would be more benefitted by the canal than Delaware, through which it principally passes." [141]

This time the bill made progress. As the climax of its legislative life approached, McLane came to Hemphill's aid. This was "not an experiment hastily adopted," he pointed out; "it is the project of half a century, . . . grown up under the auspices of the most enlightened, scientific, and practical men for that period of time." He urged again "that the best mode of applying the resources of the government to great national works" was "to come in aid of individual skill and enterprise, where practicable, rather than to execute the work by the government." He explained how little interest some parts of Delaware and Maryland had in this work—and James Buchanan supported him—and he argued again that this was a truly national work, even as "important in a military point of view" as some fortifications.

To those who urged delaying appropriations for this canal till a whole system of internal improvements was adopted, he protested that this project was under way and could not be arrested to wait for the development of any scheme. To those who objected to undertaking expensive projects before the war debt was liquidated, he answered, "no man . . . seriously believes that our present debt is in the least degree alarming, or even to be regretted." And finally he appealed for help on his record: "He had been the uniform advocate, ever since he had the honor of a seat on this floor, of internal improvements. He had always given his humble aid in behalf of every national object, whether in the East or the West. He hoped he would, on this occasion, meet with similar liberality from others, . . . for no one state, but for the nation at large." [142]

The House could honestly doubt only one part of this statement— that the aid he gave was always "humble." The debate went on for another day, with some acknowledgment of McLane's "clearness and ability" and his "very able argument," before the House finally passed the subscription bill on January 21, 1825.[143] The Senate passed the bill too, after a debate in which Nathaniel Macon, old Republican Speaker of the House in Jefferson's day, rose "to take his last farewell of an old friend that he had always admired and loved— . . . the constitution of the United States." [144]

When news of the bill's success reached Philadelphia, Henry D. Gilpin, son of one of the first sponsors of the canal, hurried to Washington to receive the federal subscription on behalf of the canal company as well as to "see the *coronation*" of a new president.[145] He arrived in one day by traveling fast, hiring a hackney coach from Baltimore to Washington. In the capital he strolled up Pennsylvania Avenue, where he ran into McLane, "who was extremely kind and polite." By arrangement, they met again in the evening in the House of Representatives. McLane introduced Gilpin to various distinguished members and onlookers, the latter including President-elect Adams. Then McLane took Gilpin to the Senate and introduced him to the prominent men there, till finally Gilpin became sleepy and made his way back to Williamson's Hotel.[146]

For the kindness shown him, Gilpin felt very grateful to McLane, "whose reputation," he reported, "is I think quite equal if not superior to any member here." Yet it would hardly have pleased Louis to learn that Gilpin admired the new Vice-President more than anyone he had seen in Washington.[147]

Or perhaps Louis did not much care about John C. Calhoun by Inauguration Day, 1825. His venom by this time was transferred to another set of men, to the combination that had defeated his candidate for the Presidency. Calhoun had stood aside from the contest. Adams and Clay were the villains whose alliance had won the prize McLane's favorite had sought for eight years.

6

The Crawford Campaign

I . "AM I A FEDERALIST?"

Am I a Federalist? Louis McLane asked himself in the spring of 1823. "To be frank," he wrote to Martin Van Buren, "when I look round and see those men of the party which was, but is no more, yet panting in the walks of ultraism, or something worse, and by the aid of silly disaffection, and idle distinctions grasping, with vain efforts, at the shadow of power, whose substance is irretrievably beyond their reach, I doubt exceedingly, whether I have any other claim to federalism, than that, which the honor of being claimed and cherished as such by the best, and opposed by the worst citizens of my own little native state affords me. . . . If the lapse of a few months finds us both espousing the same principles, advocating the same cause, and advancing the same leader, you must give me at least as much credit for orthodoxy, as will be allowed to 'young Mr. Calhoun' and those worthy coadjutors, who . . . mean to take the palace by a *coup de main*. . . ." [1]

"The same principles, . . . the same cause, and . . . the same leader" —it was easy for McLane to equate himself and Van Buren on all three points. They did have the same leader—Crawford—but were their principles and was their cause the same? McLane, however he branded himself, was a Federalist of the old school, fast bound to the principles he had learned in James Bayard's office. He was for a high tariff, a national bank, internal improvements, a national debt, a strong army and navy, an adequately paid civil service, a strong central government, liberal construction of the Constitution; he was even for Alexander Hamilton. But in Congress the pitiful remnant of Federalists no longer were the staunch defenders of these policies. "Panting in the walks of ultraism

151

. . . and by the aid of silly disaffection," they, or many of them, had be-
come known as opponents of whatever measures the Republicans pursued.
Since through the years many Federalist policies had gained favor with
Republicans, and all Republicans—excepting John Randolph, Nathaniel
Macon, John Taylor of Caroline, and very few besides—had adopted some
Federalist policies, the Federalist opposition, so far as it clung to opposition, came to oppose many of its old principles. McLane's principles were
too strongly embedded in his Gaelic nature to allow him so to twist himself; what is more, his ambition was so great and his sense so practical
that he could not tolerate a foolish and idle "grasping . . . at the shadow
of power," when by another course its substance was within his reach.

Finding that his principles did not keep him from rising in a Congress
where the Republican party was shredded into many factions, grouped
around men rather than principles, Louis McLane came consciously to
feel that his principles were no bar to any political goal he set for himself (though his party might be) and even unconsciously to suspect that
principles did not matter in politics, that character and esteem were all
in all.

In this frame of mind he could hoodwink himself—or let Van Buren's
suavity persuade him—into believing that he and Van Buren could be
united in "espousing the same principles" as easily as in "advancing the
same leader." It was not so. By believing it was so, McLane cost himself
much heartache and many bitter regrets a decade later. McLane was
ambitious; he admired men of character, breeding, and manners, men
of the sort that the Chesapeake Bay society of James Bayard and Bohemia admired; in his ambition and his admiration he could lose sight
of the political principles of his associates. He thought of himself as a
moderate, reasonable man, and his self-complacency was so great that
he had little doubt of his ability to bring the men he admired to his
point of view in at least a good share of the questions between them.
His years of success in House debates (the members crowding round to
hear him, as George Brydges Rodney saw; the respect without superior
and almost without equal, that Henry Dilworth Gilpin noticed) had intensified his confidence and led him falsely to believe that he could go
almost where he chose, whatever the banners he bore, and be a leader.
But lurking beneath his calm reason, his moderate good sense, were the
principles imbibed in his youth and so much a part of him that they
would not down but would appear at a critical moment, a Federal
burden to retard his rise.

II   THE FEDERALISTS AND WILLIAM CRAWFORD

In the spring of 1823 other Federalists than McLane were doubtful of the value of retaining their party's identity. Jeremiah Mason, one of the most distinguished lawyers in New England, saw no point in maintaining the party even in the localities where it still had strength: "Since the dissolution of the Federal party [nationally]," he wrote to a friend, "I have not been able to see any general benefit from retaining its name and nominally supporting its principles in a single State. It may have been convenient to individuals, and possibly beneficial to that State at large. However that may be, it has certainly been injurious to neighboring States, by impeding by its example the amalgamation of parties." [2]

McLane became more doubtful than ever of the value of his Federalist connections in the following winter, when the Delaware Federalists chose a new senatorial slate that he did not approve. That the Federalists were in control of the Delaware legislature in January, 1824, and in a position to elect Senators was due to their political success in the fall of 1823. They had made a remarkable comeback. At the very time when Otis was losing a contest for the governorship of Massachusetts—a loss that marked the collapse of the Federalist party in its last New England stronghold [3]—Samuel Paynter, the Federalist candidate, defeated David Hazzard, a Democrat, for the Delaware governorship made vacant by the death of Democrat Joseph Haslet, who had been elected in the Democratic triumph of 1822. And whereas Haslet had won the office by a majority of only 20 votes, Paynter's Federalist majority was of 300 votes, featured, as usual, by a terrific outpouring of Federalist votes in Sussex County. For that matter, the election was marked by great interest—or at least by a large number of votes—throughout the state, for the number of voters was more than 10 percent higher than in 1822 in every county. [4]

In other words, the old Federalist party was reviving in Delaware at the very time its corpse was being interred in its other strongholds. "We are perfectly aware," a Delaware Democrat testified in September, 1823, "that we have a strong and crafty party to contend with, . . . for believe me . . . , I have never known so much activity and exertion used by the Federalists at any former period." [5]

For a time Louis McLane thought the Federalist revival might lead to his promotion. "On the subject of the Senator's appointment," he wrote young James Bayard, "I have concluded to accept it if it be offered me. In my state of health the labors in the H. of R. are exceedingly severe, and call for professional sacrifices which are too serious while I remain at the bar." [6] But in a few days he changed his mind because of the importance of his House seat to the Crawford party in the coming presidential election. "If the election go to the House," he explained, "Del. will probably hold the balance, and this consideration, if the vote be in my hands, may prevent such a resort. If I go to the Senate, the Ways and Means go into the hands of Ingham and McDuffie, Cr-----d's deadly enemies, and my services lost in the House."

If he could not go to the Senate, however, he was still very much interested in the choice that Delaware would make for the two Senate seats that had been left vacant in 1823. Louis hoped that Van Dyke, his fellow Federalist, would not be reelected—"his devotion to Adams ought to be sufficient" grounds—and suggested Thomas Cooper and Henry Ridgely, both former Congressmen, for the vacancies.[7]

Greatly to his dismay the Federalist Delaware General Assembly not only reelected Van Dyke but also chose McLane's chief enemy, Thomas Clayton. McLane's wrath boiled over. "How," he asked James Bayard, "can you reconcile the late proceedings at Dover with your sense of propriety? Is it worth while for men of real worth to use their characters to sustain the power of a party whose leaders employ it to their injury?" Why should he remain a Federalist? "In these times when party distinctions are everywhere going out, . . . I feel very little inclination to sacrifice myself, to preserve these distinctions at home, merely to prop the artificial importance of a few men, who wield them for my destruction."

Thomas Clayton, of all men! This was the choice of his enemies, surely. "I am prepared . . . to rebel. . . . I will not serve a party who cherishes these leaders. . . . I am satisfied the party is not worth preserving." [8] But, he added, "I will not act rashly." Nor did he.

The great, overriding issue to Louis McLane in the winter of 1823–24 was the election of William Crawford to the Presidency. For seven years a Crawford machine, in which McLane had lately become an important cog, had been preparing to take its leader to the post of chief executive in 1824. But in the fall of 1823, a fright was thrown into Crawford's followers when he suddenly became seriously ill and partially paralyzed. By the time Congress convened in December, 1823, he was reported to be convalescing, but the convalescence was very slow and apparently never complete.

The Crawford machine, geared for its major effort in 1824, could not easily be thrown off its track. Crawford's illness led some of his followers to desert him for another candidate; it is surprising, not that he was deserted, but that he was loyally supported by so many. However, Crawford's attack came so long—more than a year—before the election that his followers had every reason to hope that if it did not terminate fatally he would have completely recovered long before the election took place. (In these times, of course, the presidential candidates did not mount campaigns in the sense of traveling about the country making speeches and seeing large crowds of people; therefore Crawford did not need to be fully recovered weeks before the election.)

Besides, some of his adherents felt they had no other place to go. Old Republicans who supported Crawford as most nearly representing the simple agrarian republican virtues they associated with Thomas Jefferson could not turn from Crawford to Adams, Clay, or Calhoun—all supporters of the Bank of the United States or worse. Nor could they turn to Jackson, half damned to them as a military man, and not endeared to those who studied his voting record as a Senator in the 1823–24 session.

Other men, Louis McLane among them, had turned to Crawford partly out of dislike of his chief rivals. McLane thought Adams, Clay, and Calhoun almost equally distasteful; somehow he was slow to admit Jackson to the ranks of prime contenders. In December, for instance, McLane was sure that only "a union of the friends of Adams and Calhoun with Clay" could defeat Crawford.[9] Such a union he did not expect. "Crawford will be the President if he lives," McLane argued, but he was not sure Crawford would live: "his Physicians . . . pronounce him out of danger, but his situation is extremely distressing." [10]

The hopes of other candidates were brightened by Crawford's illness. Clay, reappearing in the House, was restored by an overwhelming vote to the Speaker's chair. According to a North Carolina Congressman, efforts were made to induce Clay to drop McLane from the chairmanship of the Ways and Means Committee, "but it would not do." [11] Clay's independence and good, fair judgment in committee assignments accounted in part for his popularity in the House.

It was important, of course, to the Secretary of the Treasury that the Ways and Means Committee be led by a man well disposed to him. McLane's loyalty to Crawford caused him to neglect his own law practice through the early months of 1824. "I sicken at the sacrifices my publick station requires of my private concerns," McLane asserted, and he was not being merely dramatic; the Treasury Report had just come to his committee and its "many important financial suggestions" would "occupy every moment" of his time, making it impossible for him to represent his clients in court.[12]

The next month, February, 1824, saw two important developments in the presidential contest. One was a nominating caucus, the traditional device of the Republicans for choosing a candidate for President. By the caucus of 1808, the Republicans had picked Madison—rather than Monroe or Clinton—as the successor to Jefferson. By the caucus of 1816 they had made Monroe—rather than Crawford—their candidate to succeed Madison. The 1824 caucus had been awaited by Crawford for eight years; here he should vanquish his rivals and stand forth as the Republican candidate and therefore the certain victor, for what party was there to challenge the Republicans?

But Crawford's opponents spurned a caucus and made a virtue of necessity by declaring the caucus to be obnoxious, an undemocratic device by which a small group of men, the members of Congress, could dictate to the American people their choice as President.

When Senator Jesse Thomas suggested that John Quincy Adams become the vice-presidential candidate on the Crawford ticket, the Secretary of State replied that he could not accept a caucus nomination, not even for the Presidency.[13] A similar appeal by Crawford's friends to Clay was also repulsed; [14] Clay "will hold on so long as to be able to do us no good," one Crawfordite reported.[15]

Louis McLane could not attend the caucus on February 14; he was not a Republican. But he was disappointed that few even of the Republican Congressmen showed up—only sixty-six out of two hundred and sixteen. And, therefore, though Crawford was easily nominated for President—and the veteran Republican Albert Gallatin for Vice-President— it was a doubtful nomination, by only a minority of the party.[16] When would "the friends of Crawford find out," a Kentuckian asked, "what everybody else seems to have found out (that *he* cannot be elected either by the people or the House of Representatives)"? This Kentuckian, George M. Bibb, saw things more clearly than McLane: "the most knowing," Bibb reported, "say that the substantial controversy is now between Adams and Jackson, and by a union of the slaveholding states with Pennsylvania Jackson may be elected." [17]

Bibb knew that Pennsylvania was committed to Jackson and that thereby Calhoun's hope of election had been destroyed. Calhoun's supporters in Pennsylvania, including George Dallas, a future Vice-President, and Samuel Ingham, a future Secretary of the Treasury, had arranged for a state nominating convention, which was expected to give momentum to the Calhoun campaign. But Jackson's popularity grew so rapidly in the Keystone State that the Calhoun leaders adopted a policy of expediency. At a Philadelphia town meeting on February 18, Dallas called for support of Jackson. When the state convention met at Harrisburg on March 4, Jackson received 124 out of 125 votes, and Calhoun received only 87 votes for Vice-President.[18] It was against Calhoun's will, according to Gallatin, that "Ingham, the most adroit political jockey of the day, has succeeded in making [Jackson] the horse on whom Calhoun is to ride and to reach the Presidential chair, after the next term." [19]

Louis McLane was one of the first men to note Calhoun's defeat: "Calhoun is off," he wrote James Bayard, "and is now endeavoring to carry his forces to Jackson." But McLane still felt—or said he felt—that Crawford would win.[20]

"The moon," wrote Daniel Webster, "does not change so often as the prospects of these candidates." And where Republicans competed so fiercely and evenly with each other, Federalists, and Federalist votes, were bound to be esteemed. "One thing is observable," declared Webster, "they are all, just now, very civil toward Federalists. We see and hear no abuse of us except in some places in New England."[21]

III   THE EDWARDS INVESTIGATION

One Federalist who ran into abuse from a transplanted part of New England was Louis McLane. The transplant was John Quincy Adams, who was irritated when McLane wrote directly to President Monroe to ask his opinion whether the office of Fourth Auditor could be abolished, the latest incumbent having died. The cabinet decided a direct application to the President from a committee chairman would set a dangerous precedent, even if the Treasury Secretary's illness rendered him unable to reply. "Discussion between the President and committees of either House of Congress can never be proper," wrote Adams in his diary, "and are never sought but by Chairmen of committees disaffected to the Executive."[22]

So many members of the administration sought the Presidency that everyone seemed disaffected to someone else. The Crawford party felt its nominee as choice of the caucus was the official, ordained, rightful heir to the throne; since Monroe withheld his blessing they deemed him an enemy and most of his cabinet with him. Adams was quite right about McLane's disaffection, at least as far as John Quincy Adams was concerned. "Tell your neighbor," McLane wrote to John Milligan, "that his friend J.Q. will not be President, and that he will be at liberty to stone me for a false prophet if mine be not."[23]

McLane's candidate was still in poor physical condition in April, 1824, when McLane was thus defending him. He had recovered sufficiently to make a visit to the House, presumably to encourage his supporters, but his apearance was not altogether reassuring. One observer—not a friend of Crawford—thought his appearance proved he was not physically fit to be President: "He has lost entirely the use of one eye—and sees so imperfectly with the other, as not to know any person whose name is not announced to him. . . . He walks slowly and like a blind man."[24]

Perhaps it was Crawford's condition that gave Daniel Cook the idea that McLane was wavering. Cook's father-in-law Ninian Edwards had attacked Crawford—first anonymously under the signature "A.B." in a Washington paper, and then openly in a memorial addressed to the Speaker—and Cook expected "vindictive assaults" upon himself from Crawford's "bullies." But, promised Cook, as the chief representative of Edwards, he would use "discretion and calmness"; he would himself debate only with the two leading Crawfordites in the House, McLane and John Forsyth, of Georgia. "This will be high ground to be sure," declared the Illinoisan, but he thought "McLane . . . not disposed . . . to *go very far* in his defence of Mr. Crawford." "This," he added, "I infer from some circumstances that I deem conclusive." [25]

Was McLane's support for Crawford wavering? In view of the candidate's health, such would not have been surprising. Perhaps McLane might entertain private doubts, but, except for Cook's view there is no evidence, public or private, that McLane's pro-Crawford sentiments were waning.

On April 12, 1824, just five days before Cook expressed his doubts, McLane wrote to James Bayard, his chief political and legal protégé in Delaware not only to cheer him regarding the campaign—"Mr. Crawford's prospects are brightening everywhere"—but to declare that the needs of the Crawford campaign would govern his own decision as to reelection— he would decline running only if he could depend on Delaware to replace him with another Crawford man in case the election went to the House. [26]

One may doubt McLane's sincerity in the latter remark, or even suspect him of self-deception, but he seems a consistent supporter of Crawford. On April 22, he protested that a committee appointed by Clay to investigate Ninian Edwards's charges against Crawford was reporting too often; he was, he said, wholly in favor of investigation of these charges, but daily or weekly reports of the committee's proceedings were unnecessary. [27] Nor did he object to going on record in Crawford's defense at this critical period in the campaign; after he spoke, in fact, he sent a sketch of his remarks to the editor of the *National Intelligencer* so that the "views of Crawford's friends" could be printed in a report of the debate. [28]

If he feared the committee was unfriendly to Crawford, he would blame the Speaker who appointed it. Since McLane had long borne a grudge against Clay, he reveled at a victory over him in May, 1828, when the Speaker entered the debate to oppose, "with all his influence and eloquence," a bill McLane reported for funding the debt assumed with the acquisition of Florida: "I have great reason to thank him for his course, as it only afforded me an opportunity of meeting him in argumentative debate, and the result added a new triumph to my measures—My bill was ordered to a third reading by a vote of 105 to 53. He was excessively mortified at his minority." [29] McLane might have mentioned that he had some distinguished support in the debate, since Churchill Cambreleng, Edward Livingston (newly returned to Congress this session), James Buchanan, John Forsyth, and Daniel Webster also spoke for the bill.[30] But as Randolph (who opposed it) had said, humility was not one of Louis McLane's virtues.

However confident of Crawford's success McLane may have been, he did not ignore the danger to Crawford's reputation from Edwards's charges. He was sure Crawford was "pure and innocent," but on top of the illness, these charges, pressed to the hilt by Crawford's enemies, would certainly be injurious "unless his innocence not only exist, but be clear as noon day." [31]

When Crawford submitted an answer to Edwards's charges—which were, essentially, that Crawford had mismanaged public funds—McLane hailed it as a "triumphant refutation"—he liked the phrase so much he used it in at least two letters. He admitted the answer had deficiencies in its presentation—after all, it was written by a clerk and Crawford's illness prevented his giving much help. But it clearly proved—to McLane—that his hero was "a great, a good and a wise man, honestly engaged in promoting the true interests of his country." [32] In the long run, he hoped, this "abortive, but wicked persecution" might help Crawford; he felt sure the committee would recognize Crawford's innocence and make a favorable report.[33]

His assurance was justified. The committee was composed not, indeed, of Crawfordites, but still of able, intelligent men, including Livingston, Randolph, John Floyd, John W. Taylor, and Daniel Webster, chairman, and its report—not submitted till June—finally exonerated Crawford. He might have been guilty of some loose practices; on the other hand Edwards was discredited for his deceit. He had denied his identity with "A.B." until confirmed by the Senate in a diplomatic appointment as minister to Mexico; then he had restated and acknowledged all of A.B.'s charges. They boomeranged in the end, for Edwards resigned his post and retired from politics, while Crawford escaped with no serious loss of standing.[34]

In the midst of victory, however, McLane showed a trace of despair. "Crawford's friends are. . . . as confident as ever," Daniel Webster noted, early in May.[35] But the Georgian's health did not continue to improve; instead he suffered a relapse and was bedridden again. McLane, moreover, heard pessimistic reports from home, from Kitty, who wrote: "They all seem to dispare of Crawford here, at least those I see—James Bayard most especially . . . says he sees no possibility of his success— John [Milligan] too seems to have taken up this idea strongly—I find

Saunders the carpenter, a most violent Jackson man & was just beside himself." [36]

Confidentially, Louis answered, his worries for Crawford had increased. Jackson could not win; of that he was certain. But Adams might. For Crawford might die. If only he could get to Dr. Physick in Philadelphia or Dr. Pattison in Baltimore.[37]

IV   FRIENDS IN WASHINGTON, 1824

While he worried about Crawford's health, McLane also found time for concern about his own. His chief problem was dyspepsia, rendered all the worse by, on the one hand, his love of good food and good wine and, on the other hand, the boardinghouse regimen to which he was condemned in Washington for part of every year. Tell McLane, his sister-in-law wrote in January, 1824, "that while he labours to kill himself . . . I pray for his digestion." [38]

The latest McLane child, Allan, had been born in June, 1823, and therefore Kitty was able to spend the succeeding winter in Washington with Louis. Rebecca, the oldest, was sent off to Mme Sigoigne's school in Philadelphia, where her grandfather, the collector, who visited the city often, could look after her. Bob, the oldest boy, was sent as a boarding student to Bullock's school in Wilmington.

The other children went to Washington with Kitty, as they had the previous year, but the season was a little disappointing in its lack of gaiety.[39] Another congressional lady, Mrs. Edward Livingston, found Washington duller than Kitty did: "Washington is certainly the dullest-looking town I have ever seen. It is neither a village nor a city, but unites the inconveniences of both without the advantages of either. . . . People are seldom brought together except in immensely crowded assemblies, where it matters little whether a man is a fool or not, provided he can fight his way through."

But Mrs. Livingston found one exception to her condemnation, and it was a house and a circle in which the McLanes were frequently entertained, the gay, widowed Mrs. Decatur's: "she has small evening parties, where you meet by turn every person of distinction in Washington— foreign ministers, chargés d'affaires, etc, etc. To be admitted into her set is a favor granted to comparatively few, and of course desired by all."

But Kitty from the "humble village" of Wilmington would find Washington more enchanting than the lady from New Orleans. And Mrs. Livingston admitted, "This is the best time for the wife of a member of Congress to visit the seat of government—she is sure of the most flattering reception." [40] Both of these ladies saw Washington differently from Rachel

Jackson, who, just a year later, referred to it as a "great city," where "the extravagance is in dressing and running to parties." [41]

Louis McLane was too busy to go to many parties. One evening, weary of his work, he went to an oratorio, but he regretted it. It was, he said, "a style of music rather above my untutored taste. . . . Mrs. Gales, Miss Lee, and that Kentucky fright who lives with them, appeared to be the chief female singers, of whom Miss Lee excelled the others, and really sang very well." [42]

As soon as Kitty and the small children left him to return to Wilmington, Louis longed to reunite his family, to take "fine walks over the hills" with Bob, to kiss "that fat faced Allen" every morning, to hear what Lou thought of school and what Sally learned, to be once again with one he recognized to be "a wife much beyond my merits." [43] He had tea every day with the Cuthberts but took his breakfast—his beloved Mocha —in his room. [44] Coffee was such a delight to Louis that Kitty, in trying to entice him home for his health's sake, promised him not only "a clean and quiet house . . . to rest in," but also "a better cup of coffee than anyone else can give." [45] His dyspepsia made Louis practice moderation; it was news when he could tell Kitty, "I am getting along pretty well with Dyspepsy, and ventured yesterday upon three glasses of Poinsetts twenty years old wine, with, at least, no disadvantage." [46]

Alfred Cuthbert, William Archer, and Martin Van Buren were three of McLane's closest congressional friends in these years. Cuthbert came to Wilmington with Louis after Congress adjourned—apparently to join his wife, who had been visiting in Philadelphia. [47] Archer and the Patroon, Stephen Van Rensselaer, were with Louis in May, 1823, in Philadelphia, where Louis tried vainly to get Van Buren to join them. [48] In the spring of 1824 most of the references to Van Buren in letters that passed between Louis and Kitty are hints half in jest about this merry widower's attentions to (and intentions toward) the ladies. [49] "V.B. is quite the Ladies man," reported Louis, "and makes many sly visits to Kalarama [Kalorama, where Mrs. Stephen Decatur was living], and other widowed houses in and about Georgetown." [50] "I hope," Kitty responded, "V.B. will not tarry too long at Kalarama; let him remember how Ulises resisted, and yet, how he was seduced by sweet music." [51]

The "sweet music" that threatened to seduce Louis McLane was neither the siren's song nor any widow's wiles—he assured Kitty that any service he rendered Mrs. Decatur in Congress was from a sense of duty to his old commander, not from gallantry: "there is no love intrigue in the way." [52] But, oh, to be a great figure in the land, esteemed abroad, loved and comforted in the bosom of his family, settled—like a Bayard, like a Milligan—a planter on his own estate. Like a Milligan! Yet poor

George Milligan had mortgaged his estate and then, driven by debt, had abandoned it and sought to make a new fortune in Louisiana.

Now in May, 1824, George expressed the hope that Louis would buy Bohemia; "lacerated and torn as his feelings are," Kitty told Louis, "he looks forward to it becoming your property with a satisfaction he [has] not for a length of days enjoyed." [53] Louis was instantly excited, but he feared that for some reason which is not clear Kitty's aunt, sister, and brother-in-law would baffle any arrangement. Yet, oh, the joy of the possession if it could become his. There might be very good reasons for having such a retreat—near Baltimore, near Washington. "If things go as they may do *here* within a few years," Louis's letter seemed almost to whisper his hopes to Kitty, "the acquisition of Bohemia will be immensely important to you and me and the children, and nothing should be neglected to effectuate it." [54]

V   TEMPTATIONS FROM BALTIMORE

Prospects in Washington may have seemed excellent, but there were times when Louis was tempted to leave Congress and abandon politics. Homesickness, loneliness for Kitty and the children, so affected him, of course, but so also did political reverses, or even the threat of them. In the winter of 1824 after Van Dyke and Thomas Clayton had been elected to the Senate, he was in such a mood. "I am sick of the men who now wield the power [in Delaware]," he told James Bayard. "If federalism in Del. is to be under the dominion of the Dover Junto I am off in the spring." [55] Perhaps he meant merely to leave the Federalist party; however, he had told the same correspondent within the month that public office required such sacrifice of his private concerns, especially his legal practice, that he "must resolve to retire either from Congress or the bar." [56]

By April, 1824, he declared himself determined to decline another election to Congress unless doing so would endanger Crawford's prospects. [57] As the spring progressed, he became convinced that his enemies in Delaware were plotting against his reelection. Senator Van Dyke, the Claytons, Thomas Stockton (a future governor), Kensey Johns, Jr. (a future chancellor), William Brobson, Joseph Bringhurst, John Wales, and Charles Thomas seemed to be the leaders of his opposition. [58] Kent was the home of his main opponents, the Claytons, and there his advocacy of a high tariff was said to hurt him; the tariff may also have been unpopular in his stronghold, Sussex, but Sussex folks used so little of foreign manufacture that by and large they would not care very much. [59]

Just at this time he was tempted once more to move to Baltimore. It was Isaac McKim now, rather than John Randolph or Sam Smith, who pressed him, and it was the death of General Winder, the vanquished commander at Bladensburg, that created a vacancy at the bar. McKim promised McLane he could count on an income of $3,000 the first year, "and then a gradual increase to 10,000." "How tempting, you will say," Louis put the words in Kitty's mouth, "to receive such a price in exchange for the ungrateful, ill blooded population of Del.!" McLane told McKim to inquire into the method of admission to a Maryland practice, the rental of a house in Baltimore, and other details. "Think of it, before I come," he asked Kitty as he was about to leave Washington, "for at my age, I shall require to be spurred on to so radical a movement. It requires *levers* to tear up an old tree by the roots, tho' it may have grown in a barren, uncongenial soil." [60]

VI REELECTION, 1824

The "barren, uncongenial soil" of Delaware nourished McLane's growth for a while yet. He came home in June, 1824, to good coffee, bad madeira, and confused politics, bearing with him as a douceur $565 he had collected from Congressmen and others in Washington for relief of those who had suffered in a fire that devastated part of New Castle.[61] Despite the Dover junto, he was renominated by the Federalists. Despite a high degree of confusion in the election as to which presidential candidate was the choice of which party, Louis McLane and the Federalist party triumphed as usual. They lost New Castle County, of course; and this despite efforts to foment a Democratic rebellion against a county ticket pledged for no one but against Crawford.[62]

Yet there was one ominous note in the election: the total vote fell off by 14 percent compared to the last congressional election in 1822; the Federalist vote declined 18 percent and the Democratic vote only 9 percent; and McLane's own margin of victory over Dr. Arnold Naudain, once again his opponent, was only about one third of what it had been.[63] This might mean that qualified voters and party workers were confused; the legislature would choose presidential electors but it was difficult to determine who was, or should be, for whom. McLane and his friends urged Federalists to support Crawford; the Claytons, on the other hand, told Federalists that Crawford was the most decidedly partisan of the four Republican candidates—for Federalists, they argued, anyone else was preferable. New Castle County, the Democratic-Republican stronghold, showed strong sentiment for Jackson.[64] Between McLane and Naudain no distinction on economic grounds was offered the voters, for the Democratic paper in Wilmington argued that Naudain was "a friend to National Industry" and a supporter of a protective tariff.[65]

The most important factor in holding down the number of voters was the absence of a gubernatorial contest. Not since 1818, when also there was no election of a governor, had McLane had so few votes; at the elections of 1820 and 1822 there had been closely contested gubernatorial contests—the governor's term was three years but death in office caused more frequent elections. This could explain the decrease in total votes, but not why McLane's support fell off proportionately much more than Naudain's. McLane not only got more votes when there was a race for the governorship, he outran the rest of the Federalist ticket. In fact, in both 1820 and 1822, years of heavy voting, the Federalist candidates for governor were defeated. Apparently the explanation of McLane's very good showing in years of gubernatorial contests, even though the Federalists lost them, is that the race for governor brought out more voters than the congressional, legislative, and county elections alone, and that a high percentage of the additional voters supported McLane. He profited particularly from the loyal support of the large Federalist electorate in Sussex, while his stand for a high tariff and internal improvements won him some votes from the Democrats in New Castle.[66]

After the election there was still one item of leftover business to worry the politicans, the choice of presidential electors. By statute the General Assembly chose these electors at its fall meeting, but the Democrats attempted to capitalize on grassroots Jackson sentiment by changing the law. The Federalists, even if divided, would not take a chance on losing the superiority they already had by their control of the legislature, and the motion for a popular choice of electors was tabled. But then the Federalists had trouble choosing electors; the votes were so divided among candidates that it is difficult to identify any solid bloc, even of the Democratic minority. One elector received a decisive majority, a Calhoun man who had shifted to Adams. Two Crawford electors got exactly half the votes, but were declared elected when the speaker of the state senate, who presided at the joint legislative meeting, declared he had a right to give a casting vote in this case. With this additional vote of the speaker—his second, for he had already cast one vote—the two Crawford electors were certified. McLane's friends had won this intra-party fight among Federalists, but their margin of victory was narrow.[67] At least some of their Federalist opponents felt Crawford to be "par excellence the democratic candidate," despite the urging of his cause by McLane and his friends.[68] And McLane himself admitted, "Mr. Adams's support, in this state, is for the most part, rather hostility to Mr. Crawford, than any cordial feeling for the former." "The most of his friends *here*," he added, "were originally the advocates of Mr. Calhoun, and partake liberally of all the bitterness, with which that restless, wicked man contrived to taint all his followers towards Mr. Crawford." [69]

VII   LAFAYETTE'S VISIT

The day following his reelection to Congress in October of 1824 afforded Louis McLane the opportunity for a second triumph when he welcomed Lafayette, the nation's guest, to Delaware. McLane acted as chairman of the state committee on arrangements and in the absence of Governor Samuel Paynter, who stayed at home in Sussex County. Within twenty-four hours McLane made four speeches: one at the Pennsylvania line, where he met Lafayette, a second at the Wilmington town hall, where a hundred men sat down to dinner with the marquis, a third at the Maryland line, when the marquis left Delaware, and a fourth at Frenchtown, Maryland, in the presence of Secretary of State John Quincy Adams, when Lafayette was boarding a bay steamer to continue his trip down the Chesapeake. Old Allen McLane won distinction on this day too. Nearing eighty as he was, he met Lafayette on horseback wearing a Revolutionary red, white, and blue cockade with a feather in it, and alone among the welcoming party was recognized by the Frenchman as an old comrade-in-arms. [70]

In Congress in December, Louis McLane gladly supported a bill appropriating a generous grant of money and land to Lafayette as an expression of the nation's gratitude. [71] But enough was enough, and McLane soon began to tire of the mania of politicians to have their names associated with the visitor. Two days before Christmas he preferred the pleasure of a walk to attendance at an evening party where Lafayette and General Jackson were to be "exhibited." [72] Yet on January 12 his mess joined the adulatory throng by giving Lafayette a dinner, and when Lafayette visited Wilmington a second time, in the following July, Louis McLane was one of those, Victor and Irénée du Pont included, who escorted the hero to the battlefield of the Brandywine, the scene where he had been wounded and thereby won America's heart. At the head of the retinue conducting Lafayette were "the two oldest revolutionary officers of the neighboring counties," a Captain Anderson and, of course, old Allen McLane. [73]

VIII   INTRIGUES

Louis McLane's messmates in Washington this winter were Martin Van Buren, Stephen Van Rensselaer, and Alfred Cuthbert, the four of them taking a furnished house together.[74] Such permanent arrangements could be made in advance because there was no hope of Kitty's coming to Washington: when Congress convened, Kitty was expecting another baby (a daughter, Juliette, was born on December 21), and this being the short session, it was not practical for her to plan a change of residence before Congress would disband on March 3.

But even without a wife and children to look after, this was certain to be a busy session for Louis McLane. Besides the ordinary business of Congress, particularly the duties incumbent on him as chairman of the Ways and Means Committee, Louis had a special burden. The new electoral college had no majority for any candidate and therefore could make no choice of a President. The election would depend upon the House of Representatives, with one vote to each state, however numerous its representation. Since Louis McLane was Delaware's sole Representative, he was equal in importance to the entire delegation of the most populous state.

If his candidate had a chance, McLane's course was clear. But he was for Crawford, and Crawford barely remained in the running. Jackson had received 99 votes in the electoral college, John Quincy Adams 84, Crawford 41, and Henry Clay 37. Since only the three top candidates could be considered, Clay was already eliminated. And since Crawford had narrowly beaten Clay and controlled only four state delegations, his followers could not feel very confident and were bound to reconsider their position.

In any such reconsideration the two lodging companions, Van Buren and McLane, held a central place—Van Buren because of his assumed leadership of the Crawford forces, and McLane because he was in himself a whole delegation, as well as because he held an important and independent position in the House. How much direction they received from Crawford himself it is difficult to know. Asbury Dickins, a clerk in the Treasury Department, was a go-between for them, according to Stephen Van Rensselaer, who should have known. The Patroon told Adams this and added that Crawford would not release his two companions.[75]

Certainly Crawford himself did not give up, He looked, one of his North Carolina supporters said, like "the ruins of Palmyra," but he could not now abandon the prize he had sought for more than eight years. Lisping, utterly unable to pronounce some words without careful physical preparation, he hung on to his hopes to the bitter end.[76] In meetings of the cabinet, he asked others to read his reports and confessed to difficulty in writing. But his spirit was strong: when the cabinet was considering admonishment of Commodore Porter for a foray into Spanish Puerto

Rico, Crawford broke forth in a declaration that Porter's fault was not one tenth as bad as Jackson's when he invaded Florida. The provocation was not only his jealousy of Jackson but also his anger at Monroe, who desired Porter's recall, and at Adams, who had just condemned Porter for "one of the most high-handed acts . . . ever heard of." [77]

"Would to God this country could see and know this man!" Louis McLane declared, confessing to becoming almost despondent "until I go to see Mr. Cd. and am there rebuked for my feelings"—rebuked by Crawford's unruffled good cheer, not by any scolding. [78] It was not new, this magnetism by which Crawford attracted support. McLane had felt it early in his congressional career. Benjamin F. Butler, of New York, a future Attorney General, meeting Crawford in May, 1823, found him "a plain *giant* of a man—very affable and talkative—seems to be a man of good sense and sound judgment." But, he added, "I should not think him (and his friends do not represent him as such) a man of brilliant talents." [79]

Albert Gallatin, a Crawford supporter, gave an intimate friend a different picture of the Treasury Secretary: After twelve years of searching for a man who could fill his place in the Treasury and replace Jefferson, Madison, and himself in the direction of national affairs, declared Gallatin, "only one man . . . appeared who fulfilled my expectations. This was Mr. Crawford, who united to a powerful mind a most correct judgment and an inflexible integrity; which last quality, not sufficiently tempered by indulgence and civility, has prevented his acquiring general popularity." Gallatin "would not even compare Jackson or Calhoun to him," dismissing Jackson as "an honest man" and military idol, but "altogether unfit for the office," and characterizing Calhoun as "a smart fellow . . . but of lax political principles and of a disordinate ambition." Adams seemed better to Gallatin—"a virtuous man, . . . he has very great and miscellaneous information and . . . is with his pen a powerful debater," but though his bad temper may be overlooked he lacks the essential quality of "sound and correct judgment." "Mr. Clay has his faults, but splendid talents and a generous mind"; yet Gallatin preferred Crawford to this more popular man. "Almost all the old Republicans (Mr. Jefferson and Mr. Madison amongst them)," Gallatin declared, "think as I do." [80]

In the early summer the Crawford campaign had still seemed to have vigor, as Gallatin viewed it hopefully and Adams fearfully. [81] But when months passed and Crawford's physical infirmities continued, the campaign lagged. Two influential officers of the government, Calhoun and John McLean, the Postmaster General, expected the Crawfordites to rally behind Clay, while some of Crawford's supporters—Van Buren declared he was one—hoped to win Clay to their candidate by offering him the vice-presidency.[82] Their desires were thwarted somewhat by the sudden withdrawal of Gallatin, the caucus nominee, from the contest for the vice-presidency without giving the Crawfordites opportunity to use his position on their ticket as a possible lure to rivals. Most damaging, however, was Clay's abrupt refusal to play their game. Clay was sufficiently younger than Crawford to accept a lesser position and become heir apparent to the Georgian. The hostility that both men had sometimes displayed toward Monroe's policies made such an alliance seem superficially natural; the difference in principles between the old republicanism of the one and the new republicanism of the other was not so apparent. But if ever Clay contemplated such an alliance favorably, Crawford's physical disability caused him to abandon it. An unprejudiced observer could hardly have concluded that Crawford was fit to be President.[83]

McLane would have preferred Van Buren for Vice-President, until he heard the results from New York, where Crawford and Clay men were outmaneuvered in the legislature.[84] The Crawfordites were the largest single party, though not a majority, in that legislature; yet in choosing electors it gave a stunning majority to Adams—the Clay and Crawford forces both outsmarting themselves.

It was a severe defeat for Crawford, but McLane did not want to admit it. "Tho' Mr. Crawford go the lowest man to the House," he counseled the editors of the influential Washington *Daily National Intelligencer,* "his health will not oppose a serious impediment to his election; at least it will not do, to say so, *just now.*" [85]

It will not do to say so in the daily press, but privately one can entertain doubt. "I think old Hickory has the best *chance,*" Louis wrote to Kitty a day after he had reached Washington, "tho' I am not without hopes. Cds. friends are undismayed, and if *Clay* behaves well, we may triumph." [86]

In the weeks that followed there were rumors galore of intrigues and alliances made or unmade over night. "On one occasion," according to Van Buren, "Francis Johnson, of Kentucky, . . . called, by appointment, upon Mr. McLane and myself," urging them to unite with Clay men to make Adams President. When they refused, he turned, hand on door, as he was leaving, and said that probably Clay men could effect Adams's election without help from the Crawfordites. "I think that very possible," responded Van Buren, or so he recalled the event thirty years later, "but, Mr. Johnson, I beg you to remember what I now say to you—if you do so you sign Mr. Clay's political death warrant. He will never become President be your motives as pure as you claim them to be." [87]

Albert Gallatin complained from his western Pennsylvania farm that he saw "coalitions of every description without the least regard to principle, . . . nothing but men and factions without caring whether Govt. shall be well or badly administered, the country exalted or disgraced, or anything but the fulfillment of personal views." [88] Van Buren too, after thinking it over, complained that "the country was overrun with personal factions" moved by "few higher motives . . . than individual preferences or antipathies." The fault, he thought, was chiefly Monroe's for failing to maintain union in his party—for the caucus candidate, Crawford, of course. [89]

What Monroe failed to do, Van Buren sought to do—to hold together the core of a party around Crawford. Soon after he arrived in Washington he called together the Crawford men in the New York congressional delegation and proposed that they remain aloof from all intrigue, let a choice be made without them, and "form a nucleus around which the old Republicans of the Union might rally if the new administration," be it Jackson's or Adams's, "did not act upon their principles." [90]

This account is testimony—written long after the event, to be sure—that Van Buren held little hope for Crawford when the decisive session of Congress opened. From the evidence it seems that Van Buren to the day of election adhered rather steadily to this plan of independence. He may, of course, have become more hopeful for Crawford's chances, once he recovered from the mortification of his party's loss of the electoral vote in New York and once he was sure, as he may not have been on the opening of Congress, that Crawford not Clay was the third candidate to be voted on in the House. [91]

"Crawford's friends," wrote Stephen Van Rensselaer, who was living with two of them, Van Buren and McLane, "are determined to remain firm"—note the significant closing phrase—"trusting that the yankees will prefer him to Jackson." [92]

Crawford's friends did remain firm. They met at least once, on January 18, and apparently resolved on their future course. But were they, was Van Buren sincere in disclaiming any desire to make a choice between Adams and Jackson? Possibly so; there was an undoubted advantage to be gained by taking no sides between Adams and Jackson. Romulus Saunders saw this clearly when he was writing a fellow North Carolinian. If Clay's friends are able to swing the election to Adams, he predicted, "this is the most fortunate result for us, because the public clamour of the Jackson men will fall upon Clay's party—and if we remain firm, as I think we shall[,] we avoid the odium and profit by it too." [93]

As Saunders predicted, this course did lead to a "fortunate result" for some Crawford men—for Martin Van Buren, in particular, who was chosen Secretary of State, Vice-President, and President within a dozen years of this election by the House. Moreover, their leader's jealousy of all rivals and their own distaste for both Adams and Jackson encouraged the Crawford men to follow an independent course. "May God preserve *me* from a choice between Adams and Jackson," Louis McLane had declared in November, when he heard of the wreck of Crawford's expectations in New York.[94] And after a month in Washington, he felt no happier about the choice: "I pray Heaven to preserve me from a choice between the Genl. & the Yankee." [95]

But granting this distaste for Crawford's rivals, does it give assurance that the Crawfordites were not willing, on any terms, to leave their hopeless candidate for Adams or Jackson? According to Rufus King, Samuel Swartwout, a shrewd New York merchant-politician who was a Jackson supporter, appeared in Washington late in January and proposed a reconciliation between Jackson and Crawford, "towards which purpose Mrs. Jackson made a visit to Mrs. Crawford, who returned it without delay." [96] But even if Swartwout schemed, it is no evidence that Crawford men would agree to his plans.

James Buchanan was another who suspected the Crawford forces would turn to an alternate candidate. "They believe," he wrote, "they hold the balance of power in their own hands & no doubt they wish to use it in such a manner as to aggrandize themselves & their friends." [97] But Buchanan expressed only his own suspicious nature.

Louis McLane, living with Van Buren and in close contact with Crawford, was at least willing to consider the possibility of supporting another candidate. "It is not at all improbable," he wrote Kitty on January 1, "that *I shall* ultimately elect J. *if I can*." He underlined "shall" because he was urging Kitty to let her brother John persevere in his belief that Louis preferred Jackson to Adams.[98] A week or so later he wrote James Bayard that he would vote for Adams in only one circumstance—if the Crawford men went to him in a body in order to "have the control of the admn." This was not likely. He would be willing to support Jackson under similar circumstances. But if Clay and his friends went to Adams, "to defeat so unhallowed a combination I wd. elect Jackson if possible." If Crawford's party broke up, Louis added, "& if the election should, in that way, depend on me, my present indication is, to continue my vote for Mr. Cd. & prevent an election." [99]

After the Clay-Adams coalition was announced, McLane concluded that only one course was open to him and his friends. The election of Adams, he felt, could not be prevented: "Our course is single, I think— We can only fall in with the mass, or stand firm & let an election be made without us. We could not do the former, without having the odium of the bargain. The latter will leave us free from all blame, & at liberty to act as we may please hereafter." [100]

The safe course, in other words, was to stick to Crawford. They could not elect Jackson if they wished; Adams would be chosen without them.

In the days that followed open confirmation of Clay's switch to Adams, the Crawford men regained some of their lost hopes. Walter Lowrie, a Crawfordite Senator from Pennsylvania, wrote on February 3—Clay's announcement had been made on January 24—that the Crawford men thought Clay could not deliver the election to Adams on the first House ballot as he hoped to do, and that the Crawford party still thought it had as good a chance of winning as its competitors.[101] On February 4 Stephen Van Rensselaer told Adams that Van Buren and McLane had not yet abandoned all hope of Crawford's success.[102] On February 6 Louis McLane hoped that "by a signal interposition of Prov." Crawford's virtues would yet triumph—"and stranger things than that have happened," he assured Kitty.[103] And on February 8, the day before the House was to vote, Romulus Saunders wrote, "the Adams and Jackson men are very bitter against each other & several of the latter have said they will go for Crawford to defeat the former. . . . It is yet possible we may succeed." [104]

The excitement that filled Washington through these winter weeks of anticipation worked on the nerves of Louis McLane. His health, usually so poor in the winter, held up fairly well—though a cold and his dyspepsia were bothering him late in January [105]—but he frequently could not sleep at night for concern, "not at the prospect of defeat," as he explained his state of mind to Kitty, "for that is familiar to me, but in the contemplation of the triumph of the Yankee, & the possibility of my being driven to prevent an election, or to submit to the obstinacy or treachery of some foolish man." [106] He did not waver—he was a fighter and a fighter's son— but in his excitement he began to feel treachery about him on all sides. The fourth member of his mess, Alfred Cuthbert, was late in arriving in Washington to Louis's regret, for he thought him "the most honorable & disinterested highminded man here—indeed the only one"— a strange, indirect commentary on Martin Van Buren.[107] By election time his jumpy nerves led Louis McLane to more direct charges, which Van Buren's reputation as a political manager could have stimulated, if there was no other reason for them: "The *New Yorker* is not free from suspicion, I regret to say—. He holds out for Mr. Cd. but leans as near as he can to the Yankee! Cuthbert reins him in with great difficulty, and the former stands on slippery grounds." [108]

By "the *New Yorker*" he could have meant Van Rensselaer, but he probably meant Van Buren. On the eve of the election he warned Kitty, unquestionably with Van Buren in mind: "distrust all men till severely tried, & be sure that no man is ever set down universally for intrigue & false friendships without *some* foundation for it." [109] In his nervous excitement, he even cautioned Kitty about receiving letters from Van Buren— "I do not think he is altogether a fit correspondent of a married lady; at least I do not wish the world to know or believe that he is in a familiar letter correspondence with my wife" [110]—but Kitty quickly took him to task for his apparent want of confidence in her.[111]

By February 20, Louis had heard a tale of Van Buren that finally led him to admit, "I am entirely convinced that he is both politically & morally licentious." The story ran that Van Buren was assigned by the Crawfordites to manage Samuel Eddy, one of Rhode Island's two Representatives, who was expected to vote for Crawford and by dividing his state's vote, prevent it from going to Adams. But on the first ballot Eddy deserted the Crawfordites. He claimed that Van Buren "made him a dishonorable proposition; admitting that Mr. Cd. could not be elected, & that A. ultimately would be, he desired Eddy to hold out, only that terms might be got! This shocked Eddy & he resolved not to be used for others schemes." [112]

The story does not sound unlikely; Van Buren would hardly have been so unrealistic as to prevent any election. The accusation of licentiousness arose in the aftermath of McLane's furious excitement of campaigning. He was, moreover, such an attached husband, even so puritanical a husband, that he was rather easily made jealous by the gallantry of a known bon vivant.

And this was, after all, his private wrath, poured out secretly and discreetly, with names hidden under such labels as "the *New Yorker*" and "the Pope." He emptied his heart to Kitty, and we must not misjudge him because we see him more clearly than other men. He was sensitive, suspicious, headstrong, but also intelligent, sensible, courageous. In his frequent letters he lays bare his worries of the moment. On the surface to his friends he wore a smoother countenance. Of Van Buren he told Kitty, "I told you our relations had not changed, nor have they." [113] And by the next fall, and another session of Congress, he was again on good terms with all his old messmates of election year and traveled to Washington with Van Buren.[114]

IX "LIKE THE STRICKEN BANQUO"

In this critical election year of 1824–25, Louis McLane was hospitably treated by the important folk of Washington. (This was the "personalist" election beyond compare, when personalities and personal relations meant more than ever before in national politics, and more than ever since.) He rode up to the door of the house he and his three colleagues were renting at five in the afternoon of Sunday, December 5, 1824—whereupon servant Hannah met him at the hearth with a cup of coffee—and two days later, on Tuesday evening, he attended "a pleasant party" at the home of John Forsyth, Senator from Georgia and fellow Crawfordite. This was but the first of a round of parties to which he was invited, far more than he cared to attend or had time for. At the Forsyths' "Mrs. Adams & her spouse were unusually civil and minute in all their inquiries & attention." And this civility too was but the first of a series of attentions Louis received from the Secretary of State. "On this occasion the old fellow has had the tact to volunteer the first visit," Louis told Kitty, "but all this must be thrown away:—as I opine." [115]

But Adams, ignorant of the depth of McLane's dislike of him or unwilling in any case to abandon all hope of a vote that meant a whole state, continued to woo McLane. On December 23 Louis dined with the Adamses and found "both the wine & company were unusually good." Adams's suit for McLane's vote had led him to include Louis in particularly good company—a dinner party that included Calhoun, Henry Clay, Edward Livingston, and Van Buren among the other guests. "Mrs. A. played her part as usual, making many kind inquiries after you," Kitty was told, "& expressing a vast many regrets at not seeing you here this winter." [116] Suspicious as Louis was, he did not think Mrs. Adams sincere, but her part of the campaign was far more successful than her husband's, "for the graces and fascinations of a man of ease & urbanity sit but badly on him—something like the lowering feathers of a city milliner on a raw country girl." [117]

On the day after he entertained McLane at dinner, Adams received a little encouragement from a New Hampshire Congressman, William Plumer, Jr., who told of a conversation he had had with McLane. Plumer felt that McLane would vote for Adams in the end—not that he had said so, but because his remarks implied that Crawford was out of the running, and showed great feeling against Jackson and Calhoun, and because he "said that he could not, at any rate, vote for Jackson." Plumer also understood McLane to say that Adams was not popular in Delaware, whereas Crawford was, that his constituents would be most pleased to see him stick to Crawford to the end, but that he did not regard popularity. "He inclines certainly to Adams," thought Plumer.[118] And by mid-January Adams was hopeful that most of the Crawford men and the Clay men would vote for him.

In a week, however, and after the Clay-Adams alliance had been an-

nounced, Adams felt sure the Crawford men were forming an alliance
with Jackson and Calhoun. "McLane," Adams said he was told, "would
overthrow the Capitol sooner than he would vote for Jackson." "But," he
added sadly, "[McLane] professed an intention almost as decided not to
vote for me." [119]

McLane's problem was to repress his naturally explosive spirit and avoid
antagonizing a likely future President, particularly because his father held
a federal appointment that expired in this year. If left to his own devices
—if he did not move to one side or other with the whole Crawford party
—he would probably have preferred Jackson to Adams. "I disapprove of
Jackson's character," he wrote, and he believed the scandalous tales circulated about pious Rachel Jackson, "an ordinary looking old woman
dressed in the height & *flame* of the fashion" when she visited the Senate.[120] But Louis had sympathized with Jackson when he was criticized
for the invasion of Florida, and in mid-January he told John Milligan:
"I am neither the advocate, [n]or the apologist of Genl. J. But with all
his sins, and the wildness of his former life has covered him with many,
he is nevertheless *honest, liberal* and *high minded*. If the coldness of Mr.
A. has saved him from similar transgressions, it has robbed him of the
latter qualifications, and he is liberally endowed with all the meanness
and duplicity of the Yankee."

These remarks, however, are not to be taken altogether at face value.
Through them McLane was scolding his brother-in-law for his close
friendship with McLane's political enemies. "At home," he explained,
"the friends I most value in both parties, who have stood by me, and
engaged actively in my behalf in the most perilous times are opposed to
Mr. A. Every bitter enemy I have is for him." [121] Adams, he told Kitty,
must "brush" these men "into oblivion, before I can march to his standard." As for Senator Thomas Clayton, who bragged he would be "cock
of the walk" in Delaware under Adams, why "A. says he does not know
him."

So perhaps Adams still had a chance, a very small chance, of winning
McLane's vote. But despite many speculations afoot in Washington as
to the course he would follow, McLane refused to commit himself. "I
delicately express my opinion of both [Adams and Jackson]," wrote Louis
to Kitty, "steadfastly maintaining that I cannot *think* of a *second* choice,
until it becomes necessary for *me* to elect one, or prevent an election." [122]

The two leading candidates were inspected together by McLane, Van
Buren, and Van Rensselaer on January 12, when these three messmates
gave a dinner at their bachelor establishment in honor of Lafayette. Besides Lafayette and his secretary, they had Adams, Jackson, Calhoun,
Clay, Rufus King, and Sam Smith as their guests. In the course of the

evening Jackson and Adams were sitting near each other beside the fire, a vacant chair intervening between them. Clay, who had been on the other side of the room, strolled over between the two men and took the vacant seat, "saying in his inimitably impudent significant manner, . . . 'Well, Gentlemen, since you are both so near the chair, but neither can occupy it, I will step in between you, & take it myself.'" In McLane's breast, hope stirred; Crawford might yet rise, like the stricken Banquo, and occupy the throne.[123]

X DEFENDER OF FEDERALISM

When Louis McLane referred to General Jackson as "honest, liberal, and high minded," he was thinking, at least in regard to his second complimentary adjective, of Jackson's counsel to Monroe, in letters written in 1816 and 1817 but published only in May, 1824, to appoint men to office regardless of their party—counsel that extended hope of position and influence to Federalists like McLane, who had otherwise no hope of national power.[124] For in his congressional years McLane never could forget his Federalist affiliation, however much he worked in cooperation with his Democratic friends.

To many politicians in the 1820's Federalism was a term of opprobrium, and years of association in Washington with such decided Democrats made McLane particularly sensitive on the subject. It was as a consequence of this sensitivity that he was impelled to defend his party in Congress in the first week of February, 1825.

The debate in the House was on conditions for the election of the President by that body. McLane urged that the galleries be closed to all except Senators and officials of the House, including the stenographers. "Members," he said, "should be left to act from the cool dictates of their judgment," free from any popular pressure. This was the precedent set in 1801, and it was a good precedent.[125]

Most Democrats did not think so. As James Hamilton, Jr., the future nullification governor of South Carolina, pointed out, the 1801 precedent had been set by the men who had passed the Alien and Sedition Acts—by Federalists, of course, though he did not say so.[126]

Hamilton's remarks brought McLane back to his feet—first to deny any suggestion that he sought to keep the presidential balloting a secret. What purpose could he have in this? His vote could not possibly be secret—he was the sole representative of his state. His purpose in desiring the galleries closed was to prevent any chance of popular intimidation of the Congressmen during the balloting. They ought, he insisted, to sit as judges, weighing the merits of the candidates and voting their own

convictions, even if these did not agree with the convictions of their constituents. If the members were all instructed by their constituents, the
House could no more give any one man a majority than the electoral college could. It was to guard against such failure that the Constitution set
up this last remedy, an independent tribunal.

And as to calumnies on the Federalists, those who set aside their precedent of 1801 must remember all the other precedents the nation owed
to this party. It had "organized the government, . . . put it in motion,
after building it up, and established the policy which . . . has made this
nation . . . prosperous at home and respected abroad." It is the party
"that established the judiciary, built up the navy, created an army, and
laid the foundations of the system of national defense, which has afforded
us security at home and protection abroad." Why, after adopting all these
measures of the Federalists, should anyone hesitate to follow another
precedent because it was a Federalist precedent?

John Floyd of Virginia patted McLane on the back, figuratively; not
a man in the House supposed McLane wanted secrecy for himself or
suspected he could be influenced by the galleries. (Perhaps Floyd and
other Southerners remembered McLane's independence when his constituents sought to instruct him to prohibit slavery in Missouri.) The
opinions of the old Federalist party were obnoxious to him, but not more
so than popular doctrines; indeed he thought he preferred the old ones.[127]

On the next day, George McDuffie disagreed with McLane's view of
the independence of Representatives. In voting for a President these Representatives should regard themselves as "mere organs of the popular
will." His personal choice would be Calhoun, but he had no right to go
against the expressed will of the people and try to prevent an election
so that Calhoun, as Vice-President-elect, would be forced to assume the
Presidency.[128]

McLane delayed his reply for several days as he nursed a headache
and Congress debated a member's libel of Henry Clay. To speak now,
said Louis, "would be like drawing the cork of still beer." When he did
finally answer McDuffie, on February 7, the speech had been well her-
alded beforehand. "For the first time in my publick career," Louis exulted, "[I] was honored with a Hall crowded with Ladies—as full as I
ever saw it." [129]

His reply to McDuffie was a triumph in popular esteem (a "most masterly appeal" that "cut McDuffie to the ground," according to Romulus
Saunders),[130] but a failure in immediate results. His immediate purpose
in this debate was to close the galleries during the election of a President
—or, what amounted to the same thing, to provide that the galleries would
be cleared at the request of any state delegation (it being understood that

he, a state delegation in himself, would make this request). But as soon as his speech was over, the House refused to accept this provision in its special rules for the election.

But in regard to his secondary purpose in speaking, he was more successful. For he insisted that the House had a right and an obligation to make its own independent choice among the three leading presidential candidates without any necessity of obsequiously following the election returns. (It was Crawford whom he wished to keep in the running, of course, but his argument served Adams too.) Incidentally he sought also to vindicate the Federalist party from the aspersions cast on it in the debate. The action of the House and the reaction of the Representatives indicated there was much sympathy with his opinions.

His strongest argument in urging an independent choice by the Representatives was his demonstration of the pointlessness of the whole constitutional procedure if any other view of it were taken. If, for instance, the Representatives were merely to ratify the people's preference (that is, to elect Jackson, who received the largest electoral vote), there would be no point in having the election devolve upon the House. And unless it were clearly intended that the Representatives should choose any one of the three leading candidates, the Constitution would not specify that in the absence of an electoral college majority a choice among the three leading candidates should be made by the House. He did not mention names, but obviously he meant that Crawford—and therefore Adams too, of necessity—was as eligible as Jackson. He respected the will of the people, he said, but any tyrant could make "lofty pretensions of regard for it." "He could imagine it to be sometimes a virtue to oppose even the wildest tumult."

As to the Federalist party, its survivors must be satisfied to observe "the wisdom and propriety of its works . . . daily triumphing over the bitterest prejudices." But old animosities yet lived, "the Monster Party was not dead but sleeping," and he could only hope that some day a Hercules would arise to slay the monster. Then at last he might hope to be freed of torment from "the arrows of the conqueror." [131]

After McLane closed with a tribute to the patriotism of the late James A. Bayard, the most revered figure in Delaware Federalism, his antagonist, McDuffie, confessed this speech to be "one of the most eloquent and imposing arguments ever delivered in this House." McDuffie would have gone on to answer McLane, but the Speaker cut him off, closed the discussion, and let the House ballot on its rules. [132]

No word of regret for the defeat of his effort to close the galleries entered into McLane's correspondence. If he felt disappointment at the House's decision in this regard, it was of minor importance in his excitement at other consequences of his speech. He was gratified, for instance, to receive a note from Joseph Hopkinson, one of the high priests of Delaware valley Federalism, expressing admiration for McLane's defense of the old party. He felt consolation, too, that he had given the lie to his enemies in Delaware, the Claytons and their friends, who had said he was two-faced, a Federalist in Delaware and a Democrat in Washington.[133] He was further pleased that Crawford's friends felt that the debate might be helpful to their candidate. Altogether it was a grand experience for Louis McLane. "My pride was excited by the immense crowd of fashion and taste," he told Kitty. "I would not have exchanged the moment of my exhibition for any other in my publick life.—I only wish you had been here to share my feelings with me." [134]

XI   THE KREMER COMMITTEE

As the date of the election neared, the excitement in Washington grew to a frenzy. The city was crowded with visitors, and a portion of them thronged into the theater on the night of Monday, February 7. The President was there, and Lafayette, the nation's guest, and all the candidates—Adams, Jackson, Crawford—and a hundred Congressmen. When Jackson entered, the people cheered and the orchestra played "See the Conquering Hero Comes." "Old Hickory bore off the palm," McLane reported, at second hand: "Old Q. they say looked desponding, and his fair help mate grined a ghastly smile." But "the real man of power & might & virtue"—this is Crawford, of course—"sat like himself self possessed and unmoved —the admiration of all around him." [135] In view of the testimony of his letters, it is difficult to doubt that McLane sincerely admired Crawford.

It is equally evident that Louis McLane was held in high regard by the other members of Congress. This is the session when Henry D. Gilpin, visiting Congress, found McLane in reputation "equal if not superior to any member here." [136] Further proof of the high regard of his colleagues was furnished by his election, against his will, to the so-called Kremer committee.

An eccentric Pennsylvania Congressman named George Kremer, conspicuous in Washington because of his leopard coat, had publicly claimed responsibility for a libel against Henry Clay—a claim that Clay threw his support to Adams in return for a promise of the succession. Clay insisted on a congressional investigation of the charge, and the House determined to elect a committee for the purpose. Although McLane spoke and voted for the inquiry, he did not wish to be upon the committee and have "the loathsome labour of purging J.Q.A. and Mr. Speaker." Hearing that "all sides" planned to vote for him, he rose and publicly requested not to be chosen. His excuse, which he regarded as "the most plausible" one he could give, was that members who had participated in the debate about the inquiry should be kept off the committee. He was not, however, afraid of being prejudiced: "if I know myself," he wrote, "I have no feeling that will prevent me from doing full justice to all parties, should I be so *unfortunate* as to be a *successful candidate*." [137]

His argument against his own election was not effective. On February 5 he was chosen to the committee by a majority vote on the first ballot, despite the fact that he had persuaded most of his personal friends not to vote for him.[138] Ahead of him in the balloting were Philip P. Barbour—the man who had defeated McLane for the Speakership in 1821—and Daniel Webster; the other members of the committee were John W. Taylor, John Forsyth, Romulus Saunders, and Christopher Rankin, of Mississippi.[139] That a majority were Crawford men probably reflected the House's desire to make the committee impartial in a quarrel between Jackson and Adams partisans.

The investigation never amounted to anything. Kremer refused to come before it—possibly because he was not the true author of the libel he took credit for—and on the day of the election the committee reported it could not proceed. The effect was probably damaging to Clay in the long run, for though the charges against him would not die in any case, he was deprived of whatever advantage a careful investigation of them might have given him. Perhaps it was to assure the Adams-Clay alliance this advantage that Daniel Webster, according to McLane, schemed for a place on the committee, entreated McLane himself to serve, and after the election sought a private interview with McLane on this committee's business. But Louis refused the interview on the grounds that all conversations on the subject ought to be before the whole committee. He hid from Webster the depth, at least, of the anger he felt at news of Webster's conversion to Adams. "There never lived an honest yankee," he told Kitty, charging that Webster had played a double role, pretending to Jackson men to be for Jackson and to Crawford's friends to be for Crawford, till he supposed Adams's election certain.[140]

Useless as the committee was, it did Louis McLane a disservice because to attend its last meeting he was obliged to part from a friend at a critical moment. The friend was his oldest messmate, Stephen Van Rensselaer; the time was ten in the morning of Wednesday, February 9, 1825; the moment was critical because this was the day of the presidential election and Van Rensselaer was wavering.

XII   THE PATROON

Louis McLane and Stephen Van Rensselaer had lived on very close terms through the winter of 1824–25. With Van Buren and Cuthbert, they had shared a home, and McLane at least, though normally quick to find fault, had exhibited no emotion but pleasure at his close contact with Van Rensselaer. The friendship of a man of his patrician background flattered Louis McLane, and the Patroon's kindly amiability completed the conquest. At Christmas time, for instance, Louis and Kitty were pleased at Van Rensselaer's thoughtfulness in sending a present to Louis, Jr., now nearly six, apparently because he had taken a liking for the little boy when Kitty brought him to Washington the previous winter. "God bless him," said Louis, in telling Kitty that the Patroon was kept an invalid by some trouble with his leg. At the same time in suggesting that a Scottish cousin of Kitty's should visit Washington, Louis declared she would "eclipse" any belle there, especially with Van Rensselaer as her patron. A few days later, rejoicing in the comfort of their bachelor quarters, Louis acknowledged that "few men can live together in difficult times happily & safely." [141]

But the reign of happiness in these comfortable bachelor quarters was destined to be short. Three of the residents—Van Buren, Cuthbert, and McLane—were pronounced Crawfordites; the old Patroon (at sixty he was twenty years older than McLane) had no allegiance so decided. His letters reveal that at the beginning of the session he thought Jackson would win, and they suggest that he personally favored Jackson and was particularly concerned at the prospect that New York's delegates would be evenly divided and his state lose its vote. As late as January 22 he wrote (to Solomon Van Rensselaer), "I feel inclined for 'Old Hickory' myself." But by this date he knew that Clay had taken Adams's side, and he felt sure Adams would win, if not on the first ballot, then on the second or third.[142]

In spite of his sympathy for Jackson, Van Rensselaer could not give Jackson the vote of New York, for the division in his state's delegation was between Crawford and Adams. If Van Rensselaer voted for Crawford or Jackson, New York would probably lose its vote, since the Adams men were thought to make up exactly half of the delegation of thirty-four men. Only by voting for Adams could Van Rensselaer prevent what he had referred to as the "disgraceful result" of a tie in the New York delegation on the first ballot.[143] And other influences besides his distaste for a tie led him toward this choice. He had, he told Rufus King, been favorable to Henry Clay till Clay was eliminated from the race. Then he had asked Clay what course to pursue but was put off for several weeks, probably because Clay was not ready to reveal his decision. Finally, according to Rufus King, Clay asked Van Rensselaer for assurances that New York would vote for Adams, and when he received them "Clay came out explicitly and said that he would vote for Adams," and, moreover, that with New York's vote Adams would win.[144]

This story is related at second hand, and therefore has special likelihood of error, but the major points in it—that Van Rensselaer respected Clay and allowed himself to be strongly influenced by Clay's support of Adams —are not contradicted by other evidence. They are supported, indeed, by another sign of his leaning to Adams in the days after Clay's public announcement of his support. On the evening of February 3 Daniel Webster called on Adams to get his assurance that Federalists would not be proscribed in his administration. After Webster secured Adams's approval of a letter to two Maryland Federalists, he told Adams that Stephen Van Rensselaer wanted similar assurances and would, at Webster's suggestion, stop to see Adams.

Van Rensselaer did call on the next day, five days before the election, and received from Adams's mouth the assurances he wanted. He said these entirely satisfied him, but confessed that his messmates, Van Buren and McLane, were still hopeful of Crawford's election. Adams was able to sow a little discord in this domestic circle by telling the Patroon he thought Van Buren had been wrong—"too much warped by party spirit" —in opposing the appointment of Solomon Van Rensselaer, a distant cousin of Stephen, as postmaster at Albany.[145]

These conversations with Clay, Webster, and Adams went far to commit Van Rensselaer to their support. Still, he was torn by conflicting loyalties. Personally he preferred Jackson—to Adams, at least—possibly because of a connection through his first wife with Hamilton, an enemy of the Adamses. And to further complicate matters, he resided in what was almost the Crawford headquarters—with McLane, Van Buren, and Cuthbert, all ardent supporters of the Treasury Secretary. Quite naturally he said little or nothing to them of his disagreement. He was an amiable man, a lover of good friends and good cheer, not the sort who would willingly overturn a household by expressing a personal opinion.

So as the election approached, Van Rensselaer pondered his vote. He was shocked, probably, by talk he heard from the Crawford men of sticking by their candidate even if they prevented an election. He had preferred Jackson, but he thought he could elect Adams and end any chance of chaos; now that he had personal assurances of Adams's liberality of view he was disinclined to be the cause of any indecisive result.

But as the day of election came, he began to lose his nerve. A vote for Adams would anger his messmates. He said later that he had mentioned the possibility to Van Buren, but Van Buren could not recollect any such incident, and McLane's separate testimony supports Van Buren. Van Buren was sure Van Rensselaer expressed his opinions frankly and without reserve and that he never contemplated voting for Adams, but Van Buren was wrong. He was deceived, either by himself or by Van Rensselaer, and so was McLane.[146]

On the morning of February 9, before they left their lodging, Van Buren and Van Rensselaer talked of the election, and Van Rensselaer asked whether it would matter if he voted for Jackson. It would not have mattered to the New York vote, which, without Van Rensselaer, was tied, half for Adams, half against him. But Van Buren argued—successfully, he thought—to convince the Patroon that he should vote for Crawford, as was expected, or people would think him fickle and he would have done Jackson no good anyway. Since Van Buren was a member of the Senate and Van Rensselaer of the House, they could not remain together through the morning. Under normal circumstances Louis McLane might have accompanied the Patroon to the House chamber and kept him reasonably well apart from alien influences. But at ten in the morning, an hour before the time when Congress was to convene, Louis McLane had to be off to a meeting of the Kremer committee.

"Up to . . . 10 OClk. when I left him," wrote McLane a few hours later, "he was firm for Crawford." [147] Probably it was in the next hour that Van Rensselaer conferred with Van Buren, who told him there was no point in voting for Jackson, for New York would still be tied. But if a vote for Jackson would leave New York disgracefully neuter, so would a vote for Crawford. Only a vote for Adams would be decisive. And he had just talked with Adams and found him sensible on some subjects that mattered.

These thoughts made Van Rensselaer all the more indecisive at a moment when neither Van Buren nor McLane was beside him. Snow fell heavily in the rutted roads as Van Rensselaer arrived at the Capitol. In the three or four hours that passed before the election was complete, arguments and ideas swirled around the old Patroon like the snowflakes outside. According to one story, Webster and Clay called him into the Speaker's room and plied him with earnest solicitation for Adams. If Adams was not chosen, chaos might result, established order and property might be endangered. The wealthy Patroon, of all people, with his extensive stake in the material prosperity of the country, should be one to appreciate the value of a peaceful succession, of law and order uninterrupted.[148] "There was no man," a contemporary wrote, "whose personal address gave him so absolute a control over the human heart as Henry Clay." He understood "the views, wishes, principles and prejudices of every individual member, and no man knew better than he how to turn those interests and prejudices to a good account." [149]

No wonder that when Louis McLane reached the House chamber he found Van Rensselaer "in tears litterally," acknowledging himself "*dreadfully* frightened—the vote of N. York he said depended upon him—if he gave it to A. he could be elected most probably on the first ballot." McLane talked to him much as Van Buren had: his hostility to Adams was so well known that no one could expect him to support that candidate; if he deserted his friends now, they could never feel the same affection for him. With that they parted. It was still not quite noon, for at that hour the Senators filed into the House chamber behind their sergeant at arms and their president pro tempore to hear the electoral votes counted. Mr. Speaker Clay invited Mr. President Gaillard to a seat beside him, and Louis McLane seized the opportunity to scratch out a woeful note to Kitty of "the womanish fears and miserable wavering" of Van Rensselaer: "Great God, what is human nature! How few of thy works are worthy of thy hands!" [150]

It took two and a half hours for the electoral college votes to be read and counted—a dreary business since the results were known beforehand. But while Senator Littleton Waller Tazewell and Representatives John W. Taylor and Philip P. Barbour were going through the routine of counting the returns, Van Rensselaer lost whatever resolve he had gained from his talk with McLane. During the afternoon a number of men were reported to have spoken to him about his vote—John Scott, an Adams man who held the vote of Missouri; Charles Fenton Mercer, a Virginia Crawfordite; his fellow lodgers, McLane, Cuthbert, and Van Buren. In his memoirs, Van Buren denied talking with Van Rensselaer in the Capitol. Van Buren was in the Senate and consequently was not as close to the Patroon as Representatives McLane and Cuthbert, although the Senators were on the floor of the House during the counting of the electoral vote. Twice, Van Buren said, William S. Archer came to him from McLane, urging him to speak to Van Rensselaer and dissuade him from voting for Adams. As he was going into the House chamber to make himself available, Van Buren was met by Cuthbert, who told him the Patroon had just pledged himself not to vote for Adams on the first ballot.[151]

McLane said he and Archer received a similar pledge, but he became worried when he heard that the Speaker was seen whispering with the Patroon. Therefore still another pledge was extracted from Van Rensselaer at half past two as he walked with the New York delegation to the seats they were to occupy when they voted as a state.[152] The electoral count had by now been completed, Calhoun's election as Vice-President had been announced, the Senate had withdrawn, and a thousand persons packed in the galleries became tense with excitement. The delegates were seated by states in the order in which they would be polled, north to south along the seaboard and then roughly south to north through the

Mississippi Valley—an order similar to the old practice of the Continental Congress. A separate ballot box was provided for each state, into which each delegate placed a secret written ballot. When all had voted, the state delegations appointed tellers to count their ballots and then prepare a state ballot, in duplicate, for the candidate who was the favorite of the delegation. The state ballots were turned in at the front of the chamber, where a committee of tellers was divided into two groups, as a check on each other. One group had appointed Daniel Webster as its spokesman, the other John Randolph, and Webster was the first to speak. The House was breathlessly still when his deep, sonorous tones announced Adams's election by the bare majority of 13 votes to 7 for Jackson and 4 for Crawford. As soon as he was seated, the shrill voice of John Randolph repeated the same results but with a slight change in the phraseology, saying "thirteen states" and "seven states" rather than so many votes.[153]

The crowded galleries were so separated from the body of the House that Webster's announcement was the first hint to the spectators that the election had been completed on the first ballot. "The effect was electric." A few Adams partisans clapped their hands, "a few scarcely audible hisses were heard as if in reply"—but perhaps only fifteen or twenty of the thousand people made any sound. Still Clay stopped the proceedings and cleared the galleries.[154]

It was now three o'clock. As the crowd streamed from the Capitol, a few friends of William Crawford's sorrowfully made their way to his house to break the news. Plain Nathaniel Macon told the Georgian of the total wreck of his ambition. Crawford was shocked, but in a few minutes he seemed himself again, conversing easily with his guests.[155]

McLane could not hide his feelings so easily. He had expected Adams to win the New England states and, with Clay's help, a good share of the Mississippi Valley. But Maryland and New York surprised him as each went to Adams by one vote. "Mitchell gave him Md.," he told young James Bayard, who had been reared in the Maryland county where Dr. Mitchell lived, "and I groan to say old Genl. Van Rennsselaer [*sic*] N. York." [156]

Van Rensselaer made no attempt to disguise the fact that it was his vote that had thrown New York to Adams. As McLane left the House, he saw Van Rensselaer coming toward him: "I hurried forward to avoid him, he hurried after me, when I reached the door I saw a hack in which were three gentlemen. I jumped in knowing he could not follow." As soon as McLane was home he ran up to his bedroom, but Van Rensselaer came after him as fast as he could. When he entered McLane's room, he looked wretched, tears once again coursing down his cheeks. "Forgive me, McLane," he said, extending his hand. But Louis turned away from him.[157]

A little later Van Buren entered the house to find the Patroon and Cuthbert sitting at opposite ends of the sofa, both much excited but stone silent till they saw him. "Well, Mr. Van Buren," the Patroon broke the silence, "you saw I could not hold out." With a few words Van Buren passed on to McLane's room, where he found Louis still more excited than the others—"and it required," Van Buren wrote in his memoirs, "the greatest effort on my part and a plenary exercise of Gen. Van Rensselaer's amiability to prevent a breaking up of our mess." [158]

McLane lay on his bed for an hour or two till he was a little calmed. Then he arose and poured out his feelings and "the whole history" in a letter to Kitty—a letter that unfortunately does not survive.[159] The next day he held up his head "as became a man defeated but not subdued," went to the House, and carried his appropriation bill through—"in triumph," he thought. In the evening at about dusk he and Van Buren rode to Crawford's, where they found the defeated candidate playing whist with his children and Mrs. Samuel H. Smith.

"No one could have conjectured that he had lost the election," Louis reported to Kitty. When a game of whist was finished, Van Buren took Mrs. Smith's hand and she came over to the sofa to talk with McLane, Mrs. Crawford, and Mrs. Crawford's daughter Caroline. Mrs. Crawford and McLane both showed plainly their indignation, particularly at Van Rensselaer's conduct. Mrs. Smith thought McLane bore the defeat worse than anyone she had seen; he confessed he was "sick at heart." "Oh, Mrs. Smith," he said "defeat I could have borne as philosophically as any one, but falsehood, deceit, treachery, from one in whom I had trusted, with as much fullness and confidence as I trusted myself, that *I could not* bear."

McLane stayed late at the Crawfords', and when he did come home, he could not rid his mind of agonizing thoughts of the failure of his hopes and of the treachery of Van Rensselaer. "As with a piece of indian rubber, I wiped him from my heart last night on a sleepless pillow," he wrote to Kitty the next morning.[160]

XIII   GALL AND WORMWOOD

"All this mischief falls on the head of Genl. V.R.!" [161] So Louis McLane thought, forgetting the one-vote margins Adams had enjoyed in Maryland, Louisiana, Illinois, and Missouri, in his dismay that a man with whom he had lived on the closest terms for two sessions of Congress would have voted for Adams. Yet even in his anger, McLane never suspected Van Rensselaer of any dishonorable purpose behind his vote. "I do not impeach his purity," McLane told Mrs. Smith; "it was sheer weakness of mind." And he repeated a tale circulating in Washington that the second Mrs. Van Rensselaer had been urging her husband, in her letters, to vote for Adams.[162]

"I could not hold out," Van Rensselaer had said to Van Buren. And in a letter to DeWitt Clinton, he explained, "Mr. Clay's combination could not be resisted and to allay the excitement we agreed to vote for Adams," who would have been elected on a second or third ballot anyway. To Van Buren the Patroon confessed that as a man of property he wanted a quick decision in order to avoid any chance of anarchy. Before voting he bowed his head in prayer for guidance, and his eye fell on a ballot marked Adams on the floor. This he took to be a divine inspiration, and accordingly he cast his vote for Adams.[163]

Van Buren kept this story, told him in secrecy, to himself for a long time. A quarter of a century later he told Henry Clay, when the latter teased him with the memory of the struggle for Van Rensselaer's vote. Whether or not divine inspiration guided the Patroon, the election of Adams on the first ballot was clearly a victory for the wiles of Henry Clay over the equally subtle arts of Martin Van Buren. But Van Buren would not be downed. In future years he would reverse the verdict of 1825, and indeed it is possible that his loss in 1825 was absolutely necessary to his later success. For it may be, as Louis McLane seems to have suspected—and as other men felt sure—that Van Buren wished to be the President-maker in 1825, to turn the election to Adams, or possibly to Jackson, after several ballots. Then, though he would never say it, Van Buren could clearly transfer to others his thought: I could and did make a President, when Henry Clay could not.[164]

Van Buren could pass off his disappointment suavely and wait and plan for another day. To Louis McLane, who had entered the election as his father had entered a battle—"Now is the moment of proud triumph of Del."—the defeat rankled like gall and wormwood. The battle left him scarred: "I have at least the satisfaction to have sustained myself reliantly in the fight, and to have escaped without any mortal wound. I have learned to esteem myself more, and mankind less." [165]

It was thought of the triumph of his enemies at home—of the Claytons and the Dover junto, of Wales and Bradford and the Wilmington Quakers —that embittered him. But he would put on a calm face and hide his suspicions of friends near at hand. "There has been no abatement of my intimacy with Mr. VB," he wrote Kitty. "He still professes great friendship, and it *may be* soon put to the test. But I doubt whether his vanity does not suffer somewhat from the knowledge of many things which he laughs off. . . ." [166]

7

A New Opposition

I   THE OLD COLLECTOR RETAINED

However Van Buren may have felt, Louis McLane always preferred Jackson to Adams. On February 11, 1825, when he described to Kitty how Jackson walked up to Adams and congratulated him on his victory at President Monroe's first reception after the election, McLane's preference was clear. "It showed [Jackson's] superiority," he wrote, "over A. for I assure you he could not have done such a thing to be a King." [1] And the next evening at the theater McLane took a malicious glee in finding Adams and his family present when a tremendous roar of approval greeted the singing of "The Hunters of Kentucky," which lauded the exploits of Jackson at New Orleans. [2]

Publicly, however, McLane bided his time, waiting to see how Crawford men in general and a Crawford Federalist in particular would be treated by the victorious faction. Besides his own ambitions, it was a matter of great importance to McLane to see his father reappointed to the collectorship he had held for thirty years. The collector was eighty years old now, and the attempts to replace him that had been made on every change of administration were quickly renewed. [3]

Federalist Senator Thomas Clayton was not the man to discourage these reports. "Why cannot the people of Wilmington unite," he wrote to a Democratic politician in that city, "in fixing on some one man as the successor of McLane." As long as Democrats continued to fight each other for the collectorship, McLane would be able to hold onto his post. If they united, they might succeed. And if anything was going to be done to displace him, "it should be done immediately." [4]

But in view of Louis McLane's standing in Washington, it was unlikely

187

that any attempt to replace his father would succeed, however united the Democrats might be. By sticking to Crawford, one Crawfordite said, his party had won "universal respect"—and he added, "Adams has caused it to be announced that they shall have no cause to be dissatisfied." [5] This man was overcheerful, but his party did occupy an advantageous position. Crawford had turned down an invitation from Adams to remain at the head of the Treasury, and by doing so left his party free to support or oppose the administration as it chose.[6]

McLane saw clearly that Adams could not control Congress without the Crawford men, and, consequently, he looked for a movement, even after Crawford's rejection of the Treasury appointment, to include some member of this party in the cabinet.[7] In a few days he was pleased to hear from Henry Clay that Adams wanted to offer the place of Secretary of the Treasury to him, Louis McLane. But Clay "had the candour" to add that he was opposed to the appointment, feeling it would be impolitic for Adams to put a Federalist in the cabinet. To which McLane responded that it was easier for Adams to make the offer than for him to accept it unless he had the backing of Crawford's friends as their representative in the cabinet. Even if Clay was stretching the truth in speaking of Adams's wish to appoint McLane to the cabinet, a possibility McLane did not mention, it was gratifying to hear this testimonial to his standing. "Sooner or later," he told Kitty, "my labours and integrity will be duly appreciated." Meanwhile, his father's enemies would be disappointed in their hope for his position. "But be *still* and discrete." [8]

To make sure of his father's reappointment, Louis called on Adams on February 24 and probably got Joseph Anderson, Crawford's comptroller and a transplanted Delawarean who had once been a Senator from Tennessee, to speak in the old man's behalf.[9] Several other Delawareans saw Adams in the weeks between the election and his inauguration, probably to urge other candidates for the office. "Great interest was made," the new President confided to his diary on March 5, "against the reappointment of Allen McLane, Collector at Wilmington, Delaware, and two persons were strongly recommended for his place; there were complaints against him, but of a character altogether indefinite." Thereupon Adams reappointed him and "every person against whom there was no complaint which would have warranted his removal." [10] The old collector was safe in his post for four more years if he should live that long.

II   A MISERABLE INSECT AND A POISONOUS SPIDER

In spite of his shock at the manner of Adams's election, the last weeks of the Eighteenth Congress were high spots in the career of Louis

McLane. He was respected and courted by all sides in Washington for the influence he would have in the next Congress. Clay later made a point of the fact that he had gone to McLane for advice on whether to accept appointment to the State Department.[11] An admirer sent McLane a favorable notice of one of his speeches from a Virginia paper and a copy of the speech in pamphlet form. His hero, Crawford, quizzed him on his attitude toward an invitation to enter Adams's cabinet, but McLane answered he was determined to refuse the place if it was offered him.

The Georgian was pleased with the answer. "This led to a conversation on his part of *me*, in which he was greatly affected. I believe I have not a warmer friend in the world than he, and have fresh cause to lament his failure." [12]

Compliments from Crawford were priceless, but compliments from sources less esteemed could also bolster McLane's ego. His mess entertained three visiting members of parliament on February 25, and though Louis thought them decidedly second rate, he did not forego repeating to Kitty that one of the visitors said he had found it "a matter of general regret" that Adams had been kept from gratifying his desire to make McLane Secretary of the Treasury. It was more pleasing to hear Rufus King—"old King Rufus," for Kitty's eyes—complain that Adams "had not the firmness 'to gratify the nation in my appointment!' " [13]

Doubtless he could have heard more compliments of this sort—and have pleased Kitty by relaying them—had he given more time to evening sociability. But he went out little this winter. One dinner party that did please him was given by Joel Poinsett, who had the judges of the Supreme Court as his guests, and McLane found that the time passed "very agreeably between the solid sense of the old Chief Justice, and the light garulity [*sic*] of Story." [14] But normally he stretched out on a sofa at home after the labors of the day, and he was beginning to gain weight until the pressure of his work and "the poisonous atmosphere" brought back his dyspepsia and a cold and made him "a fitter subject for my bed, than the House, to which my duties hourly confine me." [15]

The duties, of course, were mainly those of the Ways and Means Committee, for which he made numerous reports, including some important public measures and more private bills, such as one on behalf of Colonel William Duane.[16] However oppressive these duties were, they were lightened by the hope that a still grander position might be his in the future. "I think Mr. Clay will be Secy. of State!" he told Kitty three days after the election. "If not, a bold effort will be made next winter to dislodge him from the chair." [17]

Either way, the speakership would be vacant. For a few days there were only rumors about the new cabinet; among them an unhappy one that John Forsyth, according to McLane "the least popular" of the Craw-ford party, would become Secretary of War.[18] But by February 15 Clay's appointment seemed sure, and McLane stood ready to take Clay's place.

"My fds. in all parts of the House have put me forward," he explained to Kitty, "and there would be no hesitation with any one but the Ad [Adams or Administration?] men but for my *federalism*." The number of men who did pledge him support was surprising—Alfred Cuthbert, William Archer, Forsyth, George McDuffie, Joel Poinsett, Langdon Cheves, Robert Hayne, James Hamilton, Jr.—a bevy of South Carolinians. But two close associates steered shy of supporting him—Andrew Steven-son and Martin Van Buren.

Stevenson, with whom McLane had been on close domestic terms, coveted the office of Speaker for himself, and in mid-February Louis fore-saw clearly that Stevenson's candidacy, even if unsuccessful, would prob-ably "defeat the hopes of a federalist" by drawing away some of the old Crawford party. As to Van Buren—"I doubt his democ[rac]y is too rank for his friendship," Kitty was told, and a few days later Louis added: "The Pope—fights shy—liberal in professions, but stunted in action." [19]

Van Buren's suavity, like Van Rensselaer's timidity, may have misled Louis McLane. It was Van Buren's intention to strengthen the old Repub-lican party, and this was not to be done by exalting Federalists. So long as McLane as sole Delaware Representative had the strength of a delega-tion in a presidential election, one must be careful not to emphasize the Republicanism of the Crawford party. But there were limits in what the party should do for a Federalist who was so daring—if also so courageous —as to defend Federalism on the floor of the House of Representatives. This was hardly the substance with which Van Buren could knit his de-sired alliance of "the planters of the South and the plain Republicans of the North." [20]

And if Van Buren hung back from supporting a Federalist, what could be expected of the other factions? "Indeed," Louis McLane lamented, "it seems now to be a contest between the Adams and Jackson men, who can be the most unqualified Democrats." [21] Oh, well, a pox on all these factions of Republicans! "I will . . . next winter . . . take a ground which will put all these gossamer tribes in their appropriate sphere. I shall rely upon my talents, integrity and patriotism, and by cultivating these virtues climb to a more enviable destiny." [22]

He would not, Louis promised, wait around Washington for the in-auguration of John the Second. That would have meant subjecting his patriotism to an unnecessary trial; he had too much of Cato's blood to wish to walk in the triumph of Caesar. Caesar?—"that miserable insect, wrapped up in the wiley toils of that poisonous spider from the western regions"!

As he made plans to leave Washington on the day before the inaugura-tion he could not resist a bitter jest. John Randolph, he told Kitty, had sent Thomas Hart Benton to carry a challenge to Webster. But no surgeon would be needed because Webster was gun-shy, and "the crazy old Knight of Roanoke" probably knew it. "The genuine courage of both of them might be crammed into the socket of a fly's eye." [23]

The McLanes had tempers.

III   THE SPEAKERSHIP

Fleeing Washington on the day before Adams's inauguration, Louis McLane was soon enmeshed in other business, domestic and legal. After the initial excitement of rejoining his family—except for Rebecca, the oldest child, who was at Mme Sigoigne's school in Philadelphia [24]—Louis was soon directing the planting of thorn trees at the Mount Jones estate near Drawyers Creek which Kitty had inherited,[25] joining a new Masonic lodge,[26] commuting to New Castle to attend chancery court and orphans' court,[27] and taking care of various other affairs, from ordering wine from Simon Gratz as a friendly service for Van Rensselaer [28] (once more his friend despite the contretemps of February) to making provision for the 200 shares of stock he owned in the Bank of the United States. Inciden-tally, it is not clear when and how he came into possession of this stock—presumably he bought it with the proceeds of his law business—but it is known that he did not sell it until February, 1832, by which time he was Secretary of the Treasury and the Bank was under attack.[29] However, it was in Louis McLane as a politician rather than in Louis McLane as a stockholder that Nicholas Biddle, president of this bank, was chiefly inter-ested when he entered McLane's name on a list he compiled of selected members of Congress. In a second column beside the names of the Con-gressmen appeared another list of names, wholly unexplained except by inference from the fact that they were associates of Biddle—the inference being that the second group of men, Biddle's associates, could influence these Congressmen. McLane's name and that of his Delaware colleague, Senator Van Dyke, were both followed by the same entry:

> Lewis McLean—E. I. Dupont (Victor better)
> Vandyke   —E. I. Dupont (Victor better)[30]

And it is Louis McLane, the politician, who cannot become so entirely absorbed in his legal business but that he can "amid the hurry of . . .

Court," despatch a plea to his congressional associate Willie Mangum for news of North Carolina, where half of the Crawford Congressmen (but not Mangum) had been defeated when they sought reelection. "What has occasioned all this slaughter among you?" he asked. "What is the complexion of your new delegation?" [31]

Not only in North Carolina were politics unsettled in 1825. In one sense Delaware presented a remarkably unchanged political front, since in this state alone the two old parties still waged statewide contests. But even in Delaware change was evident, for the onetime dominant Federalists lost control of the lower house of the legislature and with it the power to choose a new Senator when Van Dyke's term expired. Louis McLane's disappointment at the result was somewhat assuaged by the fact that the Federalist defeat was due to the party's failure to carry Kent County, home of his enemy Thomas Clayton.[32] But though he might have agreed with the Democratic claim that "a tyrannical set of office holders and office hunters" had been defeated in Kent,[33] the election had touched his family too—his brother Dr. Allen had been defeated almost 2-to-1 in an attempt to be elected a state senator from New Castle on the Federalist ticket.[34] And when the new legislature organized itself, Louis McLane's erstwhile rival for Congress, Dr. Arnold Naudain, was chosen speaker of the Democratic lower chamber.[35]

Naudain's speakership was a poor prize compared to the office Louis McLane was seeking, in a campaign that began in the fall before he returned to Congress. McLane's goal was a speakership too, but in the federal Congress, and to achieve this goal he begged Van Rensselaer for the support of the Federalists of New York, at least as a second choice after the New Yorker John Taylor. Arguing ad hominem, McLane pledged himself to be a Federalist still: "I have not lived to the present period to abandon the principles of my youth, the cause of the fathers of my Country, and the best consolations of my own heart." "I suppose," McLane added, "there are more than twenty federalists in the next Congress, and their vote would probably decide the contest."

Obviously to have any chance to be Speaker he would have to draw his major support from Republicans, but "a portion of the most liberal" of them seemed "willing to be generous." Therefore he had to caution Van Rensselaer: "In yr. exertions with the Feds of N.Y. be cautious not to rouse the temper or fears of the opposite side." [36]

These efforts to unite the Federalists on his candidacy did not succeed, because, as McLane discovered when back in Washington, Daniel Webster led the New England Federalists to Taylor's support.[37] Webster himself was said to hunger after the post, even though it would interfere with his practice before the Supreme Court. But Adams persuaded Webster not to split the administration forces, for the Speaker's power to appoint all committees made the position extremely important to the administration.[38]

John W. Taylor's candidacy was formidable not only because Taylor had once been Speaker, and a good one too, but mainly because he had the united support of the administration. The opposition was not united. Generally, the Crawford men, or at least some of the Crawford men, supported McLane. "McLane is the most formidable opposer [of Taylor]," wrote one of them, "and would certainly succeed but for a few Jackson men from the West who are pressing Campbell from Ohio." [39] According to Adams's diary, Pennsylvania and Tennessee opponents of the administration supported Campbell, while some Virginians and North Carolinians backed a fourth candidate, Andrew Stevenson.[40] Henry Storrs, an upstate New York Federalist, testified that when Congress met, the "parties were not organized," and that "the running . . . of separate candidates by the Crawford and Jackson parties tended to unite many on Taylor. Besides," he added, "Mr. McLane was a Federalist and Campbell of Ohio very incompetent." [41]

Whatever was said of McLane, no one ever said he was incompetent. But the accusation of Federalism was one he could not combat.

He was most hurt at finding Andrew Stevenson as well as the Richmond *Enquirer* pressing this charge against him—assailing him, as he put it, "principally for my federal principles and *supposed agency in Mr. Clay's acceptance of the office of Secy. of State!*" [42] The latter charge involved nothing more serious than advising Clay to accept the cabinet post when offered it. In the extant McLane correspondence he neither denies nor avows such advice. But he does comment clearly on Stevenson's candidacy. As early as February 20, 1825, he declared: "Stevenson has indeed strung his long bow. . . . Whether he succeed or not himself, he will in all probability defeat the hopes of a federalist." [43]

The premonition was justified by the event. Before Congress convened in December, 1825, President Adams had heard that the strategy of the opposition was to start several candidates against Taylor and after three or four days' balloting to concentrate on one of these candidates and elect him. The President also heard that McLane was "very sanguine in his expectations of success." [44]

But alas for Louis! On the second ballot Taylor was elected Speaker with 99 votes to McLane's 44, John Campbell's 42, Stevenson's 5, and 3 scattered. The result was the harder to bear because McLane's strength was just beginning to show. He gained eight votes between the first and second ballots and passed Campbell to become runner-up; in the same interval Stevenson lost twelve votes.[45]

It was all an accident caused by absences and divisions, said Louis. Of nineteen absentees, most of them ill, seventeen were opposed to Taylor. As to divisions, "Mr. Stevenson insisted on trying his strength on one ballot, and the Jackson men were equally determined to give Campbell their votes for a time. The understanding was that they would come to me, whenever my vote should exceed Campbell's."

"But," he added, writing to his friend James Bayard, "it is folly to review these things. This whole admn. is the creature of accident—its progress will be a chapter of accidents. . . ." [46]

IV   FEDERALIST STILL

Though fearful John Quincy Adams had heard that Louis McLane was "very sanguine" about his chance of being elected Speaker, on the day before the election Louis told Kitty to "be prepared for the worst." He was then in Baltimore with Van Buren, passing a pleasant day on his leisurely way to Congress. The two travelers made morning calls on Isaac McKim, McLane's former colleague on the Ways and Means Committee, and on Albert Gallatin, whom McLane had never met. Louis was impressed. "I was more struck with this man," he told Kitty, "than with any other I ever met with. His genius is wonderful and instructive beyond any thing I ever heard." The evening they passed at the home of old Charles Carroll of Carrollton, "a wonder of another kind—possessing at the age of 89 all the elasticity and vivacity of youth." [47]

In Washington, despite his disappointment about the speakership, McLane remained a very influential member of Congress. Taylor conferred with Adams about the appointment of committees and decided "he could not displace the chairmen . . . who had been such in the last Congress" (the words are Adams's from his diary), but that he could arrange the composition of the committees "so that justice [might] be done as far as practicable to the Administration." [48]

As a result of this decision, McLane was reappointed chairman of Ways and Means. He was also appointed second, after Webster, to a Committee on the Organization of the Executive Departments, an ad hoc committee established to consider a portion of the President's message. [49] McLane took his reappointment to the Ways and Means Committee as a matter of course, but nevertheless complained of "the miserable composition of Mr. Taylor's Committees." [50]

On the Ways and Means Committee, only three members were left of the seven appointed at the beginning of the previous Congress, the Eighteenth: McLane, Andrew Stevenson, and George McDuffie. Samuel Ingham, Churchill Cambreleng, Isaac McKim, and Wiley Thompson of

Georgia—largely Crawford or Calhoun men—were replaced, though only McKim had left Congress, by a delegation that would give Adams control of the committee: Daniel Cook, of Illinois, Henry Dwight, of Massachusetts, Dudley Marvin, of New York, and William L. Brent, of Louisiana. Furthermore, Daniel Cook, who had so greatly irked the Crawfordites but a short time before, was named to second place on the committee, ahead of Stevenson and McDuffie.[51] If McLane should resign, the administration could count on a friendly chairman in his place. The entire arrangement rankled McLane's "aversion to Yankee power and ascendancy," he confessed to Kitty,[52] and to James Bayard he predicted that the administration's "exclusive and proscriptive policy" would "of itself . . . form and organize an opposition." [53]

But soon life took a happier turn for Louis McLane—through developments domestic not political. For Kitty came to Washington to join her husband, trailing her vivacity, her joy, her sympathy with Louis, not to mention a representative delegation of her children—three of the seven.

Plans for her coming had been carefully laid, perhaps in anticipation of increased social prestige for Louis as Speaker of the House. At any rate, he had traveled to Washington in October, 1825, hunting housing for his family and the Van Rensselaers.

The expense frightened him. Gadsby would furnish a parlor and two bedrooms at fourteen dollars a week for each adult (including meals), one dollar a day for each servant, and four dollars a week for each horse. Williamson, another Washington tavernkeeper, offered an entire house— dining room, drawing room, and two bedrooms—plus meals for a family of three and two servants at sixty dollars a week. Edward Livingston, of Louisiana, had already rented one of the four houses Williamson had, and Alfred Powell, a new Virginia member from the Shenandoah Valley and "a Federalist of the old school," was taking another. Arrangements for liquors and guests were the same with both Gadsby and Williamson— the usual tavern rates, one dollar a bottle corkage and one dollar for each guest.[54]

Louis made some arrangements with Williamson for rooms in his tavern —not for a house—but after Congress began (and before Kitty arrived) he found something better. It was a furnished two-story house owned by a gentleman who was going south for his health. The rental was only twelve dollars and a half a week, and servants, wood, food, and so forth, would cost only about twenty-five dollars a week more. Surely this was better than Williamson's rooms, which were next to the bar and accessible only through the common barroom passage. "I have a good man servant," he wrote Kitty, "who will take all trouble off of you, and old Hannah wants to come as a cook. . . . I know of nothing you need bring but towells and such like." The Van Rensselaers would be directly opposite.[55]

Once Kitty approved the plan, Louis was eager that she hurry and "heartily tired" of being alone. There was room now for two of the girls, Sally and Lid, who were to have been left with a governess in Wilmington, but Louis told Kitty she could decide whether to bring them—"tho' I should rejoice to have them, when I have you and the others I can do without them." He was "getting an attack of dyspepsy from cold with the sudden changes." He would give her the news when she arrived; "for God's sake let it be soon." [56]

So Kitty came. With her she brought six-year-old Louis, two-year-old Allan, baby Juliette, and at least one servant, a colored boy, Francis Hillery. "The old Gentleman," the collector, came too as an escort. A spry and alert veteran, if an aged one, he made a morning call on President Adams soon after his arrival to acknowledge gratitude for his reappointment.[57]

It was a grand winter for Kitty to pass in Washington. Her husband's constantly increasing stature, if nothing else, made her time in the city a great joy. For with all the other pleasures of Washington, the House of Representatives, one intelligent visitor said, "was the most interesting sight that the capital had to offer . . . in 1826." The raised platform serving as a gallery around the House was divided by huge pillars that made it difficult to find a seat with a view of the whole assembly.[58] But Kitty probably picked her seat with care so that she could watch a member who sat in the center of the section at the left hand of the Speaker— "a member whose bodily height may scarcely exceed five feet five inches," a political sketch of this winter declared, and it continued: "Disdaining the little arts of some aspirants after fame, . . . his manner is without pretension, his movements are without affectation. . . . When he arises . . . it is evident from his manner, that he considers his effort as the discharge of his duty. His is never a gratuitous and ostentatious display of talent to court approbation while it consumes time." Well, hardly ever.

"If he has the stature only of a David," the same panegyrist continued, "he has made all his power felt by many a political Goliath: among the Philistines of the House, there are few willing to conduct an encounter with him. [This was the son of a Jesse who had raided the camps of the Gentiles on the Schuylkill and the Hudson.] He presents to the eye a felicitous combination of the *suaviter in modo* and the *fortiter in re*." [59]

All this was exactly as Louis wanted it. He had become the kind of Congressman he had set out to be when he entered the House in 1817 and saw that reputations were gained by persuasion not argument, by logic not metaphors. It had been a House of one party and he was not of it; his party had withered and yet he had grown stronger. And now, in the winter of 1826, Kitty saw him at the acme of his powers under the old circumstances, in the one-party Congress.

And while she watched, conditions were changing; two new parties were being born. Young Josiah Quincy, fresh from Massachusetts that winter and full of loyalty to an Adams, saw that "a combination of brilliant, if unscrupulous, political leaders . . . had opened its batteries upon the administration and was thundering forth the grossest charges." [60]

Kitty saw the new dichotomy as clearly, perhaps more clearly, than Quincy. But she may have welcomed rather than feared it. After all, had the great Georgian become President instead of Adams, as under the old caucus scheme of things he should have been, her Louis might now have been Secretary of the Treasury, and perhaps destined for something more. [61] Since events had gone wrong, how could it be helped if McLane's financial genius outshone the talents of Mr. Secretary Rush. [62]

And everywhere that Kitty went, she could hear praise—even if but grudging praise—of her husband. And since it was a gay season and she was a gay body, Kitty went everywhere and met everyone. This was the year when at a public ball at Carracci's Assembly Rooms, Baron von Stackelberg, the Swedish chargé, introduced the waltz to American society, whirling around the floor with huge dragon spurs on his heels, startling and shocking many of the guests. This was the year when Mrs. Florida White, so-called because she was the wife of Joseph M. White, the delegate from the Florida Teritory, was for her remarkable beauty the most talked-of woman in Washington, and when Miss Cora Livingston, daughter of Representative Edward Livingston, and Miss Catherine Van Rensselaer, daughter of the Patroon, were the reigning belles. This was the season of evening parties galore, with the company assembling at eight and leaving before twelve after an evening of dancing, cards, music, or conversation—one room usually being reserved for men who chose to gamble. The finest ball of the season was given by the English minister and featured dancing on the second floor and on the first a supper spread on a large table and constantly replenished. [63]

At least three times this season the McLanes were invited to dine at the President's mansion. The first time they were apparently unable to accept. [64] Illness, as always, was prevalent in Washington, and Kitty McLane, busy distributing "Possets and Cordials to the surrounding beaux and belles," caught a cold herself. [65] This was in January. In February, Kitty and Louis apparently were able to be at the mansion, along with Albert Gallatin, Senator John Eaton, of Tennessee, and Senator and Mrs. Levi Woodbury, of New Hampshire, and about twenty-five other guests. Again on March 31 the McLanes were at the presidential mansion, along with the Benjamin Crowninshields, the Van Rensselaers, John

Geddes, Joseph Hopkinson, and many more.[66] If Kitty was a "leaky vessel," as her brother charged, she had many opportunities to learn and relay fashionable gossip.[67]

The gossip that suited her best was composed of compliments to Louis. Of these there were plenty, for within a few days of debate in April Daniel Webster, Samuel Ingham, and Edward Everett praised her husband in one way or another. Said Webster: "I have a habitual and very real respect for the opinions of the gentleman from Delaware." [68] Everett declared that he could not disagree with McLane without distressing himself.[69] Ingham, the leading Calhounite in Pennsylvania, drew a distinction between the two Federalists, Webster and McLane, that was wholly to McLane's credit. In the War of 1812, he said, "When the enemy was at our doors," Webster was in Congress doing all he could to withhold supplies from our troops and prevent a vigorous prosecution of the war; McLane, on the other hand, "shouldered his musket and marched to meet and fight the enemies of his country." [70] Perhaps Ingham overdid this a bit, for McLane, through no fault of his own, did not meet or fight the enemies of his country. But Ingham, who coupled Buchanan with McLane in his praise, was more interested in knitting together an opposition party than in knitting together threads of the history of the late war.

All these remarks Kitty could hear—at least she could if they really were spoken in the House and not merely written for the record of debates. Undoubtedly, Louis showed her similar compliments that he received by mail, such as Nicholas Biddle's note of thanks "for the admirable and triumphant manner in which you have vindicated the military policy of this Country." [71] And her own pleasure would have been greater than Louis's in reading a comment from her brother John on a recent McLane speech: "I read it with attention, and am fully prepared to join in the general approbation of it. His whole course on this occasion, has served to confirm what I have always thought, perhaps said; that however he may fret and fume in private about particular men, it will not affect his conduct in relation to measures; and that when he comes to act on any great public question, his judgment will be found to preponderate over prejudice." [72] This was half nonsense, but Kitty probably liked it. She may even have believed it.

V   A GREAT NATIONAL SYSTEM

As chairman of Ways and Means, it was Louis McLane's duty to steer appropriation bills through the House. His political principles made these chores generally congenial, for he was, as he acknowledged, "the advocate of the great national system, which combined the Navy, Army, Fortifications, Internal Improvements, and the Militia." It was his defense of the fortifications bill in the Nineteenth Congress that called forth the encomiums of Nicholas Biddle and John Milligan. This bill came under fire from a group of vigilant Republicans. John Floyd, of Virginia, for example, proposed changing the name of Fort Monroe to Fort Powhatan, but McLane was upheld by the House when he answered that it would be shameful to change the name now that Monroe had retired.[73]

John Forsyth, of Georgia, offered a more serious objection: why appropriate half a million dollars for Boston and nothing for Savannah or Charleston?[74] McLane's answer was to present a long defense and history of the fortifications system. He demonstrated that the current appropriations bill was just one stage in the development of a systematic plan that was originated in 1816 when the Board of Engineers invited General Bernard from Europe to advise them and that was embodied in a series of reports subsequently laid before Congress. In future years Congress could delay progress on this plan as it pleased, but this year it should support the board fully because of the contracts already made.

McLane viewed fortifications and other defense measures as connected to the internal improvements policy to which he was devoted. When he entered Congress, he said, advocacy of such a policy was unusual and unpopular, but in eight years he had enjoyed seeing "this doctrine gradually gaining ground." The men who favor such a policy, he declared, "are my men, because [their] measures are my measures; and I will sustain any Administration that will take hold and cherish those measures; and I will sustain none that will not."

One might assume from this declaration of principles that McLane would become an Adams-Clay supporter, but principles gave way to personalities. McLane seized this occasion to eulogize his hero. Crawford, McLane claimed, was "one of the principal founders of the system of permanent defence," having called General Bernard to America and set the Board of War to its studies. "I am not one of those who sit down and grieve and grumble over what has passed," declared McLane; "I look to the future, and would so act here, that, when the future comes, it may find the People happy and the country prosperous."[75]

VI   THE PANAMA MISSION

Through the winter of 1825–26 Louis McLane hid his anger at the administration and pursued a reasonably independent path. "The administration," he had told James Bayard in December, "are determined . . . to preserve an exclusive and proscriptive policy," advancing their friends and degrading their enemies; "in the number of the latter they include all who do not submit to their system of management." [76] He was such a one, and he would now mark time.

Because McLane did not throw down the gage of battle, the administration was inclined to treat him somewhat tenderly. In the latter part of February and in March, 1826, McLane presided over the House while it met in Committee of the Whole to discuss McDuffie's proposal of a district voting system for presidential elections. [77] The Jackson-Calhoun forces were angrily determined to prevent any future election from going to the House of Representatives. McLane did not share these fears of an election by the House for he and his little state were exalted in importance by such an election. Yet he remained quiet, even when McDuffie made a remarkably vigorous attack on the administration and the method of its election. Calhoun's biographer finds it "noteworthy" that no effort was made in the House to call McDuffie to order for his remarks, and that neither Adams nor his partisans saw fit to criticize the conduct of the presiding officer, whereas they had bitterly denounced Calhoun in a similar situation. [78]

Apparently the administration had no hope of Calhoun, whereas McLane and the old Crawfordites yet remained a kind of third force between Adams and Jackson. And besides, McLane was a very useful man in the House, where Speaker Taylor appointed him to various ad hoc committees—to fix the Michigan-Ohio boundary, to examine the laws regarding the accountability of receivers of public moneys, to confer with a Senate committee on an appropriation to carry out a treaty with the Creek Indians, and to determine what business was to be considered in the remainder of the session. [79] His review of a report by Treasury Secretary Richard Rush was so ably prepared that, at least in one Congressman's mind, it brought about "a very general distrust of the financial ability of the Secty." [80]

He was also a thorn in the administration's flesh in one of the main debates of the session, the debate over the Panama mission. President Adams proposed sending two American delegates to a conference of the newly liberated Latin American republics to be held at Panama. For a variety of reasons—because the conference might lead to foreign alliances, because it might involve some undesired relationship with the Negroes of Haiti, because it offered an opportunity to harass Adams and Clay—Congress was very hesitant to appropriate the necessary funds.

At the beginning of the debate McLane seemed to be following the independent course he claimed for himself, when he urged the importance of an appearance of unity in our foreign relations: "we should not come forward in a crippled state with one branch of the Government for a measure and another branch against it." [81] On March 25, he reported an appropriation bill for the delayed mission, but it is possible the motion may have represented the will of the administration's majority on the Ways and Means Committee more than it represented McLane's desire to be cooperative.[82]

A few days later, on April 3, 1826, McLane stood forth as a leader in the policy of impediment that became an opposition tactic when he moved to forbid American ministers at Panama from discussing a foreign alliance or any bilateral declaration binding the United States to resist European interference or committing the neutrality of the United States.[83]

In a long speech the following day, McLane argued for preserving the traditional neutral policy of the United States and for keeping the Monroe Doctrine unilateral. He denied Adams's contention that we were bound to have closer political connections with these sister American nations than with other countries, declaring he saw no superiority in the Latin American peoples "to drive me from my moorings."

Probably the issue reminded McLane of his early years in Congress and the opposition he then took to Henry Clay's eager championing of Latin American independence. Now he had new reasons for disliking Clay, and he did not pretend to any warm affection for the administration. "He professed to feel," the congressional reporter noted, "and he did feel, all proper respect to the functionaries of the Government—all that it became him to feel as a member of this House: he did not profess more, nor did he feel any more." [84]

Webster complained that McLane's proposal was unconstitutional because the House had no power to instruct ministers, but James Buchanan came to McLane's aid by suggesting new wording that met Webster's objections.[85] The debate continued for two weeks, with McLane insisting that the powers and purposes of the Panama delegation be fully discussed before the House voted on the appropriation bill he had reported.[86] In the debate an interesting comment was made by John Campbell, of Ohio, McLane's erstwhile rival for the speakership, who declared that McLane's proposal, which he liked, was "evincive of a want of confidence in the Executive." [87]

Finally the House narrowly approved McLane's proposal, which was an amendment to a resolution to approve the mission to Panama.[88] But when this resolution, as amended, came to a vote, it was defeated, 143 to 54, by the combined opposition of those men, like James Polk, of Tennessee, who were altogether opposed to United States representation at Panama, and of some Representatives who preferred to let the resolution die rather than accept McLane's restriction on the mission.[89]

After the vote, McLane proposed immediate consideration of the appropriation for the mission the House had just refused to approve. And following a desultory debate, in which George McDuffie and John Forsyth opposed the mission and Daniel Webster and Edward Livingston defended it, the appropriation was passed by the House on April 22 by a vote of 134 to 60.[90] "Thus ends," McLane wrote to a friend at home, "our Congressional Sport with this bubble. Bubble I think it will be, in its progress and termination."[91]

The Panama mission was the one decided administration victory in the first session of the Nineteenth Congress. Yet the victory was so long delayed (by dilatory tactics such as McLane's) and the ministers were so slow to move that it did turn out to be what McLane called it, "a bubble."

VII   GETTING AWAY

Kitty McLane rushed home in May of 1826 upon hearing that Bob, her oldest son, had had an accident—apparently a broken collarbone in a fall from a gig.[92] Home was where Louis, too, now longed to be, but a few bills that required his attention kept him in Washington for two weeks more.[93]

The most important of these—to Louis, at any rate—was the bill establishing a commissioner of customs in the Treasury Department to oversee all receivers of public money. As a customs collector's son, McLane recognized the need for such a measure, and despite a bilious attack that sent him to bed he allowed his friends to take him to the House on May 16 so he could participate in the debate and help the bill's passage. Though successful in the House, the bill failed of enactment until the 1830's, when a customs house scandal helped reawaken interest in it.[94]

Other bills that occupied his attention in the closing days of this session included his friend Mrs. Decatur's claim against the government ("if we had *sea room*," he told Mrs. Decatur, meaning if time did not run out, "we would gain the victory")[95] and an appropriation to the Creek Indians to compensate them for lands abandoned and to encourage them to move beyond the Mississippi.[96] "I am," he wrote Kitty on May 13, "now more constantly employed than you can imagine."[97]

One rumor that circulated through the boardinghouses in these closing days of the session was bound to gratify McLane, however little stock he put in it. It was that he was to be named minister to England to succeed Rufus King, who had resigned. It was not beyond the bounds of probability that the post might go to a Federalist, for King was one and his appointment had been the one Federalist appointment Adams and his friends had dared make. Nor was it altogether unlikely that a Crawford man might be appointed to the place; in fact, one was, for Adams and Clay passed over McLane and offered the post to Albert Gallatin, who had been the caucus nominee for Vice-President on the ticket with Crawford and against Adams.

It is interesting to consider what would have happened had the post been offered to McLane. If he had accepted, he could hardly have become a Jacksonian, and if he had not become a Jacksonian, his whole future career would have been changed. But it is unlikely he would have accepted the position, though the temptation might have been strong. Probably McLane's sympathies were well understood by his Crawfordite colleague Romulus Saunders, who had written of McLane during the Panama mission debate: "His feelings are with us, but he will not go the full-length." The "us" that Saunders mentioned was the new opposition to the administration, to what he called a "union between the East [that is, New England] and West," and probably McLane was coming to the same conclusion as Saunders—and Van Buren—about the proper role for the Crawford party. "If Jackson was to die," wrote Saunders, "I cannot say how things might turn—rely on it, *he* is the only man that can break down this union. If he can be placed under an honest Cabinet it is the best we can do for the Country at present. . . . Any thing to get clear of this cursed union of '*puritan and blackleg.*' " [98]

The one thing that held McLane back was undoubtedly his Federalism. Given his Federalism, would the Jackson party accept him, would a place be found for him in that "honest Cabinet" around Jackson as easily as a place—the Treasury Department, probably—might have been found for him in the Crawford cabinet? The Jacksonians, he recalled, had not been willing to support him for Speaker. Why rush to join the new opposition party if he could not be a leader in it? Might not more honor rest in an independent course?

William S. Archer, of Virginia, hearing the rumor that McLane was to be offered the London post, insisted on "a grave interview" to urge McLane to declare at once his entire unwillingness to accept any office under this administration. Louis McLane's answer was a little coy: "I very promptly informed him, that it would be in time for me to determine, when the offer should be made, and that in the mean time no one had a right to suppose the offer *would* be made, or that my determination would be inconsistent with my own honor, or the just expectations of my friends." He clearly implied that he would refuse the appointment, but he did not exactly say so. As to a public statement, "I could not be silly eno' to place myself in the attitude of declining, what might well be said was never at my disposal." Besides, Louis thought he knew who would get the appointment: "I have no doubt the visits of old Gallatin this winter had this for their object, and not fruitlessly." [99] He was right. "What wd. A. and C. do," he asked Kitty, after the announcement was made, "but for the Crawford men?" [100]

All this he told Kitty and much more—news of the great world at Washington and of their acquaintances, great and small. Of Mrs. Van Rensselaer and her beautiful Cora, whose departure from Washington he had missed even though he rose at seven, an hour earlier than usual. Of his "old Negro Man, . . . the finest old fellow in the world, . . . a Cook, a Nurse—quack, body servant and every thing else; pompous and methodical as can be," who "has been the steward of Crowninshields famous Barge, the Cleopatra, with which he visited Europe some years ago, and which the old man calls the Cleopatrick, and recurs to with great self satisfaction." [101] And of James Buchanan, a most eligible match, a man of "good fortune and fair prospects," who "informed me very significantly today voluntarily" that he had "resolved to pay us a visit in July"—thus nibbling at "your hook bated with the Scotch Lassie," Kitty's cousin, Mary Christie, who was living in Wilmington.

Sometimes Kitty, whose role it was now to stay at home and watch the children, the house, the garden and farm, while in her biennial delicate condition—sometimes Kitty grew a bit short-tempered. "Patience dear Kate," Louis then wrote; "be not so testy." [102]

"Patience," Kate answered, "I have often times invoked; so often, that her Ladyship has almost consented to take up her residence within sight, at least, of so *ardent a votary.*" But, she added, "my own dear husband," say what you will; from such a source "*good* only is prone to flow *to all,* [and] to me—love and kindness in abundance." And the Van Rensselaers had come and spent a delightful two hours with her, giving up a day in Philadelphia for this visit. And three-year-old Allan has the whooping cough and sits quietly all day, rousing only when he is told "his pa is coming and will bring him some chesnuts and Mr. Cambreleng with a gun." And "Mrs. Tindle is still the chief cook and it is impossible to have more perfect order, cleanliness and economy—*or,* more *wretched* cooking —tis well that I am trying to see on *how little* we can *sustain life*—for realy, she can only make bread, butter, and pies and boiled puddings— her dried peach pies sweetened with Uncle George's syrup, dear Bob says he is sure he could sleep on without mashing them." [103]

After spending a day in bed with a bilious attack, Louis fled home on May 19.[104] George Baldwin McLane was born at Wilmington on June 21, 1826.[105]

VIII GETTING BACK

Kitty was weak for months after George was born, but she scorned all advice to employ a wet nurse. Louis's health was no better than his wife's; so bad, indeed, was his dyspepsia that he determined to try a treatment at the springs and set off to Saratoga in August. He dosed himself liberally, taking six glasses of the water as well as a horseback ride every morning before breakfast, but in the long run he saw no improvement in his health.

The trip's failure to improve his physical condition may have been compensated for by its contribution to his political ambitions, for on the way to and from Saratoga and during his stay, there was time for sociability and politicking that were often intimately connected. In the previous spring Louis McLane had thought of himself still as a Crawford man. When he returned from Saratoga and plunged into state political campaigning, he was considered to be a Jackson man. The state conventions and elections practically forced him to take a new position, but it is possible that the Saratoga trip helped the decision.

On the way north he saw Cambreleng, dined with the Patroon, met the Magician and was made "an exhibition for his bucktails." At Saratoga he met a son of Alexander Hamilton, the DeWitt Clintons, and, at nearby Ballston Spa, where he rode each day, the Otises, Mrs. Robert Hayne, and Mrs. Adams. With society at Saratoga he was not altogether pleased: "at Saratoga the company is not generally genteel, though there are a great many of the best New Yorkers. . . . I confess to a strong suspicion that the state of society in this great state is looser than I had ever supposed and that the tricks in politics have tainted the more sacred relations."

Louis McLane was a devoted husband and loved Kitty, but he liked pretty girls too. So though merely "a looker on of the flirtations of others," he was not too ill to notice that "Miss S. Ann," daughter of a friend of his named Gordon, was the prettiest girl at the Springs. And not too ill to take Miss S. Ann on his arm at the "hop" and introduce her "to some of the gentlemen of Congress Hall," observing to Kitty: "She might have been the best dancer too, if she cld. have been persuaded to take the floor, for excepting a dau. of Tom Morris, of N.Y., who probably learned in Phila., I didn't see a graceful step." [106]

Whether well or not, Louis McLane on his return was forced to resume his active role in Delaware law and politics. In September he narrowly escaped a violent death. He had dined with Jean Garesché, at his home, Eden Park, formerly an estate of Robert Morris's, just south of

Wilmington on the New Castle Road. Garesché, son of a French refugee from Haiti, had married the daughter of Pierre Bauduy, E. I. du Pont's onetime partner, and had settled in Wilmington as a powder manufacturer. After dinner Garesché took McLane on a tour of his powder mill, pointing with pride to his installations. A few minutes after McLane and his host had left the mill, there was a terrific explosion and the mill was left in ruins.[107]

Another French immigrant, Victor du Pont, was believed to be a moving spirit in a Democratic act of friendship to McLane this fall. McLane had, of course, been renominated by the Federalists; as Hezekiah Niles noted, Delaware was the only state in the Union in which the old parties were still kept up "with pretty much their original force."[108] But when the Democratic nominating convention met at Dover, it too was presented with a proposal to nominate McLane, a petition signed by fifty residents of New Castle County urging McLane on the convention for his "manly, candid, and independent course," which was, the petitioners claimed, "essentially republican."[109]

The convention dismissed the petition at once and nominated Dr. Arnold Naudain, the speaker of the lower chamber, to oppose McLane for the third time.[110] Nevertheless McLane did make inroads on the Democratic strength in New Castle County, which Niles called the old "strong hold of democracy" in Delaware.[111] Charles I. du Pont, Victor's son, who had been nominated on the county ticket for the state legislature, was opposed by William McCaulley, whose friends proclaimed him the candidate of the anti-McLane Democrats of Brandywine Hundred and likewise declared that Charles du Pont, like his father, would support McLane rather than Naudain for Congress. Charles denied the allegation, but the denial did not save him. McCaulley outpolled him, but their contest allowed a Federalist candidate for the legislature to beat them both.[112]

The Federalists won control of the legislature, 17 to 13, narrowly held the governorship by electing Charles Polk over David Hazzard by a 96-vote plurality, and rather easily reelected McLane, by a plurality of about 700 votes in 8,000.[113] Still the reelection was not as easy as the friendly editor of the *Delaware Gazette* suggested when he claimed "the great and respectable body" of Delaware Democrats had "no expectation and . . . no desire" to defeat McLane, but were forced to a congressional nomination to aid "other parts" of their ticket. This editor was glad to find his enthusiasm for McLane shared by another journalist, Congressman Miner, of nearby West Chester, Pennsylvania, editor of the *West Chester Village Record*. In this paper Miner declared that few men in Congress were heard with as much respect as McLane, that by his representation

McLane made Delaware "morally a great state," and that Delaware should follow the example set by Boston in relation to Daniel Webster— "lay aside all party feelings and local division, and unite to place him in the National Councils, sustained and cheered by an unanimous vote." [114]

This would have suited McLane fine. But it did not suit all the Delaware Democrats, not even all the Federalists—certainly not the Claytons.

IX PROMOTION AT LAST

For three weeks following his reelection, illness—a "severe bilious intermittent"—kept McLane in bed.[115] But from his bed by correspondence he arranged a mess with Van Buren and Van Rensselaer at Mrs. Cottringer's on F. Street, and he was there for the opening of Congress on December 4, when he also made a courtesy call on President Adams. When committees were named, McLane was once again chairman of Ways and Means, but on his committee there was one change—Peleg Sprague of Maine replaced George McDuffie, possibly a measure of punishment for Calhoun, McDuffie's mentor, because of the part he was playing in the opposition. And Sprague was inserted at third place on the committee, ahead of Andrew Stevenson, another leader of the opposition.[116]

For once McLane's heart was not in his congressional business. He waited a few days, time enough to report out of committee an appropriation for Revolutionary War veterans and to send into committee—into Ways and Means, just as Nicholas Biddle wished—a petition from the Bank of the United States for a revision of its charter. Then he rushed home—"on private business," he told Biddle.[117]

In a little over two weeks he had returned to Washington and Senator Thomas Clayton was speculating about the trip: "Our representative," he wrote an ally in Wilmington, "has lately paid a long visit to Delaware. Can you inform me whether he succeeded in making any arrangement by which he can accomplish his desire? It is said that he and Dr. Black are about to come to terms by which they will both be gratified. In regard to myself I care very little about this business but I should like to see matters fairly conducted." [118]

No matter what he said, Thomas Clayton did care about this business. For McLane was seeking Clayton's seat in the Senate, and Clayton knew it. There was another seat vacant, the deceased Senator Van Dyke's, temporarily filled by the governor's appointment of Daniel Rodney, a former governor and former Congressman, who was to serve till the Delaware General Assembly met in January.

Until the Assembly met, and after it met, the intrigue was furious. The

Federalists had a 17 to 13 majority, but the Federalist party had many factions, not least of which were the Clayton and McLane wings. Louis McLane was appalled by Governor Paynter's appointment of Daniel Rodney and blamed it on the influence of Judge Kensey Johns, probably abetted by Thomas Clayton. McLane thought Johns wanted to force an Adams supporter on the legislature, and perhaps hoped himself to become Senator.[119] And Clayton would, of course, want an Adams man for his colleague. Obviously national politics would complicate the selection of Senators from Delaware. Another complication arose because although the Federalists could control the total of the two houses of the General Assembly, the Democrats controlled the state senate and could keep it from meeting with the lower house.[120] If the two houses did not meet together, there could be no election.

From Washington, McLane sent instructions almost daily to James Bayard. He projected a ticket of himself, for the long term, and Thomas Cooper, the Georgetown attorney who had been turned out of the House with Clayton at the time of McLane's first election. Apparently Cooper was now a Jackson man, like McLane. Representing a different county and a different wing of the party, Cooper would bring strength to the combination. McLane's ace in the hole was that some of the Democratic assemblymen, notably Henry Whiteley, speaker of the state senate, were Jackson supporters and would lend their aid to see an election take place if they could be sure Jackson men would be chosen. Knowing they were not strong enough to be able to elect Democrats for Jackson, they would prefer Jacksonian Federalists—McLane, for example—to no election at all.[121]

At Dover things did not go just as McLane planned, but he could hardly have been more pleased at the result. With Henry Whiteley's vote, the state senate agreed to meet with the house to elect United States Senators on January 12, 1827. Balloting on the short term took place first, after three men were nominated: Thomas Cooper, Daniel Rodney, the interim appointee, and Henry M. Ridgely, a Federalist member of the legislature from Dover who was a Jackson supporter and had years earlier been a Congressman. One ballot was enough; Ridgely was elected with 16 votes, a bare majority, while five ballots (Democratic ballots probably) were cast blank, and Cooper and Rodney divided the Sussex vote.

Immediately the assembly proceeded to elect a Senator for the long term and again only one ballot was necessary. Senator Thomas Clayton was nominated, and so were James R. Black, a New Castle Democrat, and McLane—by Archibald Hamilton, a Wilmington lawyer who was speaker of the lower house. The election was decisive; McLane received 20 votes of the 28 that were cast.[122] Clayton was put down.

So was Adams. The election created some excitement in Washington because it meant the replacement of two administration Senators, Thomas Clayton and Daniel Rodney, by two opposition men. "The intelligence from Dover," McLane reported to Bayard, in thanking him for his help, "reached us by . . . handbills, which the P.M. Genl. [John McLean] distributed in advance of the mail, and created a sensation almost equal to the news of the victory of New Orleans. It came most seasonably to chill the exultation at Randolph's defeat. . . . Unless [Thomas Hart] Benton lose his election, . . . the election of Del. gives the opp. the majority in the Senate in the next Congress." [123]

Monday, January 15, 1827, was the day the news arrived in Washington. To his wife, McLane declared it was the most important day of his life, a day of many emotions, of gratification first, and then, on a second thought, of doubt, "if not regret."

He was held up in the Ways and Means Committee, he explained, and had not heard the news until his friend James Hamilton, Jr., of South Carolina, sought him out. "When I entered the House it had been in session for nearly an hour, and my entrance resembled that of some hero just from the field of victory. Very gratifying and in some instances sincere gratulations poured in from all quarters, and continued till they became almost oppressive. To myself individually it was a moment of real triumph and enjoyment. I wanted nothing but your presence," this was to Kitty, of course, "to have completed my happiness." Dining at the Robert Haynes' with the Langdon Cheves family and others, he went through the same sort of triumph over again.[124]

But he could not leave the House of Representatives without regret. In the House he had found that despite his being a Federalist, his ability could carry him to a high position—not to the highest, not to the speakership, there was the rub. And now suddenly, as he was about to depart, the speakership was opened to him. It was on Monday, January 15, that he had learned of his election to the Senate. Three days later, on Thursday, January 18, the opposition party met and offered him a nomination for the speakership in the next House.

But "the die is cast," he decided, "and I must now climb another ladder." [125] Perhaps it was this very casting of the die that led the opposition to agree thus tardily to support McLane. Perhaps they were never before quite sure he was one of them. But now his acceptance of election to the Senate, made possible by Democratic connivance, at the least, in the Delaware legislature, was also an acceptance of identification with the new Jackson party. If and when he left the House, he would leave also the elevated position that assured him an opportunity for independence of action.

This he recognized clearly, but in his own mind he had long ago committed himself to the opposition. "I am giving my talents and wasting my health for my enemies and against my friends," he decided, thinking of the Ways and Means Committee in particular: "I can acquire little more character—and may lose much by the machinations of those who are reaping the fruits of my toil." Besides, he thought, he could not stand still. "A man loses character by remaining too long, without change in one place, and six years more in public will be eno' of Congressional life. The speakers chair offered some temptations, but the struggle would have been severe, it might have been unsuccessful and in that event fatal." It would have been fatal if his Federalism had once again prevented him from getting the united opposition vote. "Success even might have injured my health, and would have withdrawn me entirely from my courts." [126] And the courts were the source of his income. He must risk his health to attend them, he told Kitty in a later letter, "or starve." [127]

There was another risk that McLane was taking with less hesitation than he showed about risking his health. This was the political risk that he took in seizing Thomas Clayton's Senate seat. It was the risk of breaking to pieces the political machine that had kept him in Congress, the Federalist party of Delaware, for he could hardly expect Clayton to take his demotion lying down. After all, it was the second time McLane had stepped over Clayton into office.

The first time was in 1816, when the Federalists pushed Clayton aside for McLane because of Clayton's vote on the Compensation bill, and this replacement had started McLane off on his congressional career. But Clayton had not remained in the outer darkness of rejection by his party. Though never strong enough—or, possibly, never rash enough—to prevent McLane from securing in each biennium a Federalist renomination, Clayton had gained sufficient influence in the legislature to see to it that he was returned to Congress and to a higher and more select chamber, the Senate, than the one where McLane had succeeded him. Not only had he won this advancement for himself; his influence in the legislature and the party had helped keep McLane from a similar elevation, as witness McLane's complaints about the "Dover junto."

And despite McLane's success, with the help of Democrats and of Clayton's Kent County rival Henry Ridgely, in January, 1827, the Clayton faction was by no means left without influence. When Henry Ridgely resigned as Governor Paynter's secretary of state late in 1826, it was Thomas Clayton's young relation John M. Clayton who succeeded him.

And when Charles Polk succeeded Paynter as governor early in 1827, he retained John M. Clayton in this post. Nor was Polk himself merely accidentally friendly to the Claytons. As a state senator from Kent County it was he who nominated both Daniel Rodney and Thomas Clayton for the Senate at the joint legislative session on January 12 when Ridgely and McLane were elected. In other words, Polk was hand-in-glove with the Claytons, and though McLane for the moment might have won, the Dover junto that he hated remained in position to threaten the security of his political base.

For the moment, though, the friends of McLane, of Ridgely, and of Jackson were in control at Dover, and all was "feasting and rejoicing." Wilmington postmaster Williamson, a Democrat who owed his position to McLane, congratulated the assemblymen on their work. Speaker White-ley would be the next governor, he said, and another good Jackson Democrat would be the next Congressman. These men who made a Jackson victory possible were "the finest fellows in the world." [128]

In Washington, Louis McLane was inclined to agree. Whether he liked it or not, he was a Jackson man now. So, ho, for the next campaign, for the war against the corrupt combination.

"O Johnny Q. my jo, John, when you at first began
To fish in troubled waters, John, you found I was your man.
I nibbled at your bait, John, you canna tell me no,
Though you've found at last 'twas but a bite, O Johnny Q. my jo. . . .

"O Johnny Q. my jo, John, you play'd a canny game,
You won by *tricks* alone, John, and ye dinna think it shame:
For *honors* you had none, John, nor even I, I trow;
'The Chief' and Crawford hold them all, O Johnny Q. my jo." [129]

8

Senator and Supplicant

I LEAVING WAYS AND MEANS

A week after his election to the Senate, Louis McLane resigned from the Committee on Ways and Means, of which he had been chairman for four years. When the Speaker read McLane's letter of resignation, a committee member, Henry Dwight, of Massachusetts, praised McLane's work as chairman and urged the House to reject the resignation in the hope that he would still occasionally attend committee meetings, for he would not be moving to the upper chamber until March 4, 1827. Dwight's compliments were the more pleasing because he was an Adams supporter. But when he finished, James Buchanan rose and persuaded the House that McLane should be relieved from the committee assignment in the course of which "his health had fallen a sacrifice to his devotion." [1]

A few days later the *Daily National Intelligencer* paid McLane a tribute. "Unwarped by party zeal, he has been found," declared this paper, now friendly to the Adams administration, "in the most turbulent debates, the steady and unwavering supporter of the Constitution—the firm advocate of his own convictions of right—the mild but clear expositor of the concerns peculiarly committed to his charge—the unbiassed Legislator for the public interest. . . . The resignation of his station . . . was demanded by a regard to the state of his health, which is delicate." [2]

On the last point Kitty had already been given warning. "I propose to allege," Louis wrote her, "my health as the ground of this step. Not that I cannot get along in my present state, or because it is worse than it has been; but my duties are exceedingly arduous, and I have now no object to submit to so much pain and drudgery and responsibility." [3]

The duties were arduous. Daniel Cook, who succeeded McLane as chairman, soon broke under the strain.[4] Perhaps McLane left the job just in time. But as if to punish him for exaggerating his ill health, "a fit of dyspepsy," his ancient "fearful enemy," struck McLane at the end of January—"and brought with it all the old symptoms which always make me feel so miserable; especially that tight destroying headache, and sleepless nights." [5]

Well or ill, he found the session unusually dull, once his promotion to the Senate was assured. The one principal business of the session was political canvassing,[6] and in such an environment it was comforting to have a colleague from Delaware with whom he was in full political amity. As soon as he knew Henry Ridgely was in town, McLane called on him and carried him off to become a permanent member of the mess with Van Buren and Van Rensselaer at Mrs. Cottringer's.[7]

A new friend made during this session was William C. Rives, the best man in the Virginia delegation, according to McLane, and one who was building a solid reputation in Congress. Mrs. Rives too won McLane's approbation as a lady of great refinement. She agreed with McLane in condemning "the state of things" in Washington this winter: "She aimed principally . . . at the *waltz,* which is now the *only* dance, and amuses herself and me not a little at the excessively awkward figure made by these raw country girls. . . . Imagine to yourself a scene between two awkward dancers going thro' a *waltz,* in a crowded levee, and be assured that before its over they have got as closely knit and bound together as by a cord of hemp." [8]

A closer friend than Rives was Major James Hamilton, Jr., the former mayor of Charleston, who entreated McLane to come visit him along with Van Buren, who was planning a trip to the South and West—"for objects important no doubt." The idea interested McLane, but he preferred to save his money and time to take Kitty to Cape May or elsewhere. And he needed to attend to his business in the courts, particularly since the past year had been "a losing one" to him.[9]

Although at home the friendly Federalist newspaper argued that McLane had heretofore been one of the most effective supporters of the Adams administration—having, for instance, directed the course of the appropriation bills through Congress—McLane thought, as the winter of 1827 passed by, that the administration began to despair of coaxing him into their ranks.[10] Whether or not he would recognize the fact, his resignation from the Ways and Means Committee cut his last major tie to the administration. "Surely," he had persuaded himself, "*they* had no reason to expect *me* to make sacrifices of time and health for their purposes."

Perhaps McLane thought he had kept an appearance of independence by rejecting an opposition promise of support for the Speaker's chair at the same time that he abandoned whatever responsibility to the administration the committee chairmanship had thrust upon him.[11] But his votes and his remarks on the floor of Congress indicate his increasing identification with the Jackson party. He did not deceive Thomas Clayton.

"I want you to attend to the ayes and noes . . . on the bill to re-model the tariff in regard to woollen cloths, and observe how McLane voted on it," Clayton wrote to an associate in Wilmington. "While the votes of the manufacturers were of importance to him at a popular election he was their staunchest friend; but those votes being no longer useful to him (Senators being chosen by the legislature), he joins the coalition of the south against the north, because by doing so he may reap some advantage at a future day if that party should prevail." [12]

Clayton referred to a series of votes recorded in early February on a proposal to raise the tariff on woolen goods. In these votes, McLane, heretofore almost always a supporter of bills to raise tariffs, had demurred and voted in the negative.[13] But his speeches had made his position somewhat clearer and more defensible than Clayton wished to believe it. "He was," McLane had said on January 22, "and ever had been, an advocate for the tariff system." "But," he added on January 25, "he was not willing to advocate prohibition." The protection offered by the tariff of 1824 had led to a doubling of the capital invested in woolen manufacturing and therefore to a sudden excess of production. At the same time the British, because of developments elsewhere, had dumped a large amount of woolens on the American market for what they could get. But this was "a transient state of things" that would soon right itself without a prohibition of imports. The manufacturers "had a right to a steady, though moderate protection," but not to anything more.[14]

Thomas Clayton himself offers evidence that McLane had some reason to regard the current proposition as a prohibition. "The contemplated measure," Clayton wrote, "if carried into effect, must produce the utmost distress [in Great Britain]; because it would amount almost to a prohibition to import the articles." [15]

If McLane's hesitance about going all the way with high tariff enthusiasts had political overtones, so possibly did his attitude toward road and canal surveys. It was customary for the government to have surveys for important road and canal projects made by army engineers, even when the projects were to be undertaken by private companies. But when, in January, a Kentucky Jacksonian suggested that a study be made of all the applications for road and canal surveys, McLane agreed. "He was willing to carry on this system of surveys, etc., as far as was consistent with the means at the disposal of the government." But right now there was a deficit in the Treasury even for the ordinary annual expenses of the government.

When William Rives proposed that an appropriation for surveys made at the discretion of the executive branch should be stricken from the military appropriations bill in favor of specific appropriations for only those surveys authorized by Congress, McLane declared he too favored confining appropriations to specific objects. However, he went on to explain that "no blame attached to the present administration" for the deficit in the public treasury on January 1. It was the result of appropriations made in former years, and did not betoken anything more than a temporary difficulty; the Treasury was not in worse condition than in past years, but "unquestionably better." And while he thus sought to calm the injured feelings of Treasury Secretary Richard Rush, McLane went on to declare that he had been the first to acknowledge an error concerning the amount of the revenue in the Ways and Means Committee's report of the last year.[16]

His basic unfriendliness to the administration was apparent, however, when he voted to take the appointment of a group of ad hoc committees away from the Speaker and when he encouraged an investigation of the newspapers employed to publish federal statutes.[17] As Thomas Clayton saw, McLane had made his choice. But sometimes he worried about it: "I only regret that a more palatable candidate than Gen. J. were not destined to be the victor, for tho' he himself is a chivalrous honest independent man, he is badly surrounded. I do not expect the lines of old parties to be entirely disregarded, but there is a great choice, and much wisdom required in the selection from the republicans, and the Genl. I suspect will be under as strong an obligation to reform his friends as his enemies. We must trust in Providence however, and with the consideration that matters can not well be worse." [18]

II   THE DEATH OF THE FEDERALIST PARTY

Matters could have been worse, though. At least political matters in Delaware could have been worse than they were for Louis McLane, and Thomas Clayton sought to make them so. By emphasizing McLane's vote against the woolens bill, Clayton sought to "open the eyes of some very late admirers" of McLane, and on the day McLane returned home from this session of Congress a Wilmington paper carried a call, signed by "A Weaver," for a meeting of manufacturers and others who had advocated McLane's election because of his devotion to the protection of American manufactures.[19] This meeting may never have taken place, but in June

Chief Justice Kensey Johns presided at a meeting in the Wilmington town hall which voted approval to the protective tariff in general and to the woolens bill in particular—the bill McLane had opposed in the last Congress.

This action was not taken without opposition. A group of Jackson partisans had first seized control of the meeting and tried to rush through some resolutions of their own. But Dr. Arnold Naudain, McLane's perennial opponent for Congress, spoke up for the opposition. There was a threat of riot; the Jackson men proved to be a minority and lost control, though only after one of them insulted some of the high-tariff advocates by shouting that "no foreigner, hireling, or day-laborer had a right to interfere"—probably directing his remark at E. I. du Pont and his workers.

Before adjourning, the meeting appointed delegates to a protectionist convention to be held at Harrisburg on July 30, the delegates to consist of eight men—four of them manufacturers, including E. I. du Pont, and four of them politicians, including Louis McLane. "Some might wonder," wrote "A Looker-On" in a Wilmington paper that was pro-Adams, "why three Jackson men and two of them who voted against the Woolens Bill should be appointed to go to Harrisburg, but the Adams party did not want to trample on a fallen enemy, and permitted the names of McLane, Ridgely, and Black to be associated with Canby, Naudain, Kirk, and Young, who are men favorable to agriculture and manufactures and the best interests of their country." E. I. du Pont should have been listed with the presumably pro-Adams majority of the delegation.[20]

Louis McLane felt he could neither accept nor ignore this appointment. In a letter to the editor of the newspaper in which he read of it, he explained that he had already told a deputation he could not represent them at Harrisburg because he did not wish to commit himself on measures that would later come before him in the Senate. The unruly character of the Wilmington meeting did not induce him to change his mind.

His record in Congress for the last ten years, he added, would show his attitude toward the protection of American labor against foreign competition. His vote against the woolens bill indicated no change of opinion but only a conviction that passage of this particular measure was not justified. He thought "any administration" would consider a protective tariff essential to prosperity, unless the friends of protection, "consenting to use it as an engine of *party* purposes, involve it in the fate of *party* struggles." [21]

All Delawareans did not accept McLane's assurances. Thomas Clayton had already accused Louis of being a turncoat on the tariff issue. "As it is known that Kent and Sussex are decidedly opposed to the encouragement of manufactures by high duties," Clayton had written of McLane, "he means now exclusively to pay his court to those two counties from whom alone hereafter he can expect to be continued in his present situation"—that is, in the Senate.[22]

Though correct in noting McLane's sudden loss of enthusiasm for high tariffs, Clayton was probably wrong in attributing its cause to political realities in Delaware. It would have been better for McLane's political career if that had been the case. In reality, McLane's loss of enthusiasm for the tariff grew out of his dislike of the Adams administration and his disinclination to see their measures succeed; he did not like the administration nor the necessity of working closely with it, but while he was chairman the bills that emanated from the Ways and Means Committee were, by the force of his talents and his industry, his bills, and he worked vigorously for their success. But the woolens bill came from the Committee on Manufactures and was not his responsibility.

Had McLane been as aware as Clayton thought of the necessities of Delaware politics, he might have avoided the debacle which now overtook him. A decade in Washington had led him to put Washington politics first, something the member of Congress dares to do only at peril of his political life.

After he was elected Senator, McLane determined to work for the election of one of his friends to the seat he vacated in the lower house. "My mind is made up," he told Kitty, "and my preferences stand in this order —Bayard—Black—Hamilton. . . . This is a subject on which I must not be expected to, and *will not* be *neutral*." [23] Probably this was written for the indirect information of John Milligan, Kitty's brother, who was the friend of McLane's enemies. But Louis meant his remarks to be passed on, via Kitty and John, to other factions of his party. His letter was written January 19, 1827, and this early, a week after his election, he was throwing down the gage of battle, challenging his enemies, daring them to dispute his ability to fill his place with a man of his own choosing.

He was buoyed by success, of course. Four days earlier, when the news of his election reached Congress, he had enjoyed "a moment of real triumph and enjoyment," and an action taken in the overconfidence born of this success is not difficult to understand. But he was unwise to try at this time to dictate the choice of a man from his own law office to Delaware's only seat in the House of Representatives. If it was most important to him to have a Jackson man in Congress, it would have been more politic to support one from Kent or Sussex. He seems to have forgotten the political adage that suggests choice of a candidate who can both satisfy his own party and draw votes from the opposition.

Perhaps this is what McLane thought Bayard could do; perhaps he thought that Bayard, being from New Castle County, could weaken the Democratic majority there while assured of the customary heavy Federalist majority in Sussex. If so, he was overconfident about Bayard's chance of winning the Federalist nomination. But since his second choice was James R. Black, a New Castle Democrat, it seems that he had either completely lost touch—momentarily, at least—with political realities in Delaware, or that as early as January, 1827, he was confident that Jackson and Adams parties would arise in Delaware to replace the ancient alignments.

This is what did occur. A Federalist state convention was held in Dover on August 7. Fearing an unsatisfactory choice, Attorney General James Rogers, a friend of McLane's, moved it was inexpedient to make any nomination; his object undoubtedly was to provide opportunity for a combination of the Jackson men from both parties. But the convention rejected his proposal and proceeded to nominate another New Castle lawyer, Kensey Johns, Jr., son of the chief justice.

This was a solid rejection of McLane's claims to leadership. McLane's friends, however, had already set in motion plans for an amalgamation of like-minded men. On the day Johns was nominated at Dover, a group of Sussex County friends of Jackson met in Georgetown and took steps to set up Jackson tickets on both a county and a state basis.[24]

Perhaps this group absorbed most of the Democratic leadership in Sussex. At any rate, no Sussex delegation was present when Democratic delegates from New Castle and Kent met in Dover on August 28 and nominated Dr. Arnold Naudain for Congress.[25] The new nomination presented McLane with an odd situation. Two candidates for his seat were in the field—Naudain (nominated for the fourth time) and Johns— and neither was his man, and neither was a Jackson man.

More complications followed. The Sussex Federalists favorable to Jackson met on August 28 at Georgetown, where they nominated James Bayard for Congress, rejecting Kensey Johns, Jr.[26] But a week previously another group of Sussex County Jacksonians—probably mainly Democrats—had appointed delegates to a state Jackson convention scheduled for Dover on September 4.[27] When this convention met—and among its members was McLane's friend Attorney General Rogers—it nominated not Bayard, but a Democrat, Colonel Henry Whiteley.[28]

This would not do. Apparently Whiteley was not a candidate who could win many votes for the Jackson cause. "He does not possess a single qualification," wrote an Adams Democrat, "to represent the State in Congress with credit. . . . It would be mortifying to be Represented in Congress by any man friendly to the election of Genl. Jackson however respectable his talents, but to be represented by Whitely [*sic*] would be a disgrace to the State."

Whiteley apparently was a Ridgely candidate and was being rewarded for his assistance to Ridgely's senatorial election in the winter.[29] He was not McLane's man. McLane had wished to have the nominee of the Sussex Jacksonians—Bayard—accepted by the Jacksonians of each county without running the risk of a state convention. But the convention was held, and on the evening of the day Whiteley's nomination became known in Wilmington "a Federal Caucus was held at an obscure tavern in a back street, for the sake of secrecy, and it was resolved not to support Col. Whiteley, but to get up the amalgamation scheme, to try a new conference and run all hazards to wheel Bayard in."[30]

The plan worked. Another state convention—the fourth—replaced Whiteley with Bayard on the very eve of the election. "Louis McLane," said a critic, "the great magician who works all the wires, . . . is not the least respected for his Machiavelian tact."[31] Machiavellian or not, Mc-Lane's tactics made sense. In view of their subsequent careers, Bayard seems to have been a more suitable man than Whiteley—at least he made an outstanding Senator thirty years later. Furthermore McLane was being consistently loyal to a friend if also unpleasantly stubborn in insisting on controlling the nomination. In view of Bayard's father's fame and popularity, and also because of his Federalism, Bayard probably made a more attractive candidate for the Jackson party than Colonel Henry Whiteley could have been.

Yet McLane could not "wheel Bayard in" to Congress. For the Adams forces, probably directed by the Claytons from behind the scenes, were a step ahead of McLane. They won the first round by capturing both the Federalist and Democratic nominations. Then as soon as the Jacksonians began to organize, the Adams men moved to consolidate their own strength. New county meetings were held by Adams men of both parties, delegates once again were sent to Dover, and there on September 18 Dr. Naudain was induced to withdraw from the race (later the new party would reward him with a Senate seat), allowing the Adams strength to be concentrated on Johns.

"The old names 'Democrat' and 'Federalist,'" reported a Wilmington journal, "are, for the present at least, entirely lost sight of in Delaware, where they have been adhered to with such remarkable tenacity. You hear of no party names here but Adams-men and Jackson-men. An amalgamation of old parties has taken place."[32]

Earlier in the month a peculiar obituary notice had appeared in the same journal, with reference to a meeting of McLane's friends at Christiana, the customary place for Federalist county conventions:

DIED—and was buried, on Saturday the 8th inst., in the woods near the town of Christiana "the old and respectable Principles of Federalism."

The funeral was attended by a large concourse of the citizens of Newcastle County, among which were his honor the Senator of the United States, the Attorney General of the State of Delaware, and all the principal Generals, Colonels, Captains and Subalterns of the Old Hickory tribe—who did (in the presence of the few surviving heirs to the name,) deposite their last pretensions to the same; refusing longer to participate in the glories of seventy-six.

By this untimely death in Newcastle County, the State has met with a loss long to be deplored. That name which has shone, like the star of the morning, in the political horizon, since the day independence was declared—is no more.[33]

III   THE MANAGER AND HIS PROSPECTS

The election of 1827 destroyed the Federalist party in Delaware, its last state stronghold. When the Jackson men of both the old parties joined to support Bayard, their action prompted a merger of the anti-Jackson forces. "I hope we shall get Delaware," Henry Clay had written on September 7, 1827; "but for the division between our Federal and Republican friends I presume it would be certain." [34]

Henry Clay's Federal and Republican friends united and made Delaware certain. Kensey Johns, Jr., won the election. Johns's majority over Bayard was only 395, in contrast to McLane's 699 majority in 1826, but still Johns won by a larger majority than McLane in 1824 or Governor Polk in 1826 or Governor Paynter in 1823.[35] Not as many voters turned out as in 1826, and this suggests that despite the excitement about Jackson and Adams, the Delaware voters cared less about national politics than about the election of a governor.

If the voters were not aroused, it was not Louis McLane's fault. He had campaigned furiously, rushing around the state to organize his Jackson party. From the meeting of Federalists for Jackson in Sussex County in late August he had rushed to New Castle County for a "bush meeting" at Brandywine Springs, a spa southwest of Wilmington. Here he sought to have the New Castle County Jackson men agree to accept any nominee of the Sussex Jacksonians, but he was overruled by those who insisted on a state convention.[36] The convention led to Whiteley's nomination and more work for McLane in "wheeling Bayard in."

On Sunday morning, September 23, 1828, Louis McLane started off again for Sussex. Just before time for church services he and Attorney General Rogers embarked in a bateau at New Castle to confuse their enemies about their destination. They were rowed down the river to

Delaware City, where McLane's carriage was waiting for them, and from there they were driven to Sussex by back roads (for secrecy's sake) in a great hurry, without an overnight stop.

This, at least, is an enemy's account of the trip. Its aim is still mysterious; possibly it was to effect a change in the legislative ticket. Contemporary accounts vouchsafe only one more glimpse of the activities of these two travelers: on Tuesday, September 25, while an Adams meeting is being held in Georgetown, McLane is in the long room that adjoined the bar in Short's tavern, addressing as many people as can be inveigled inside and away from the other meeting.[37]

But in the long run all McLane's activity profited him nothing. Besides the stark fact of Bayard's defeat, there was the personal mortification of seeing his brother-in-law John Milligan, an openly active member of the opposition as secretary of a political meeting and a candidate (unsuccessful) for the General Assembly.[38]

John Milligan's activity was the harder for McLane to stomach because of the personal vilification he suffered during the campaign. Comparatively little was said about Bayard—that was one advantage of being nominated late in the campaign. McLane was the chief target of the opposition.

For example, a writer styling himself "Common Sense" declared in a Wilmington newspaper that McLane had once declared Jackson unfit for the Presidency and was now supporting him only because he hoped to be appointed to the cabinet. "How much money has Louis McLane had from the public treasury?" the same writer asked. "How much has his worthy father had from the public treasury? Has it amounted to 1, 2, or 300,000 dollars?"

Another letter in the same paper, this one signed "Many Manufacturers," mentioned "golden harvests" and took off on the same theme:

Who holds the office of *Collector?*
Who had a general charge of *Light Houses* and *Light Boats* in our Bay? Etc.
Who holds the appointment of *U.S. Senator*, with a compensation of *eight* dollars per day? [39]

It was a discouraging election, but McLane would not give up. Next year, 1828, would be the important time. For then would come the opportunity to oust Adams from the Presidency and replace him with Old Hickory. For this great purpose McLane must redouble his efforts to organize the Jackson forces in Delaware. One defeat must not be taken too seriously; Adams men had controlled both of the old parties, and new parties are not created overnight.

Yet the election statistics reveal a problem that would be difficult to solve. Bayard had carried New Castle County by a majority of 369 votes; Johns had carried Kent and Sussex by majorities of 409 and 355 respectively. Usually the Democrats had carried New Castle and the Federalists had carried Sussex and Kent, the former by a lot and the latter by a little. If the Jackson party of 1827 is equated with the pre-1827 Democrats and if the Adams party of 1827 is equated with the pre-1827 Federalists, then the election differs from those in the past only to a slight extent—the majority in Sussex is much smaller than the usual Federalist majority there, and the majority in Kent is much larger than the usual Federalist majority there. Perhaps McLane's personal visits to Sussex helped keep down the margin of his opponents' victory. In Kent the increased majority can be explained by the support for the Adams ticket given by the Claytons and their Federalist following and by the Democratic leader, Dr. Arnold Naudain. (Though Dr. Naudain had given way to Kensey Johns, Jr., another Naudain, Elias, was on the Adams county ticket.) [40]

This strange coincidence of the 1827 election results with those of past years suggests either (1) that the old parties essentially were retained, only the leaders and the names suffering a change, or (2) that though new parties came into existence there was something in the Delaware political climate that prevented the party of the majority in New Castle County from being the majority party in the two downstate counties— perhaps a natural division of interests between the more urban, more commercial north of Delaware, and the more rural, more agricultural south.

Whichever explanation is accepted, and the second seems the more likely, Louis McLane had committed political suicide. Whether or not he had founded a new party, he had exchanged a leading position in the party that usually controlled two of the three Delaware counties—and the state—for a leading position in the party that controlled only one of the counties—and therefore could not normally win a state office.

When he had time to think matters over a few years later, McLane regretted the decision to "take up" Bayard against Kensey Johns. He knew better, he claimed, but let himself be overruled by James Rogers and their friends in Sussex, who insisted on what turned out to be a premature movement to elect a Jackson man. Johns should have been allowed to run as the Federalist candidate against Naudain. Probably Johns would have lost, and then the Jackson men could have taken over the Federalist party. But whether Johns or Naudain won, "the possibility of coalition between their friends after such a struggle would not have existed." Bayard's nomination was a costly mistake. "When . . . we rashly tore away the corner stone, we might have expected the whole superstructure to tumble about our ears." [41]

IV "NO PARTY SHALL USE ME"

When Senator Louis McLane came to Washington in December, 1827, he was accompanied by Robert his oldest son, who was placed in a boarding school in the capital. Kitty could not come; she was expecting again. Louis was duly sworn in on December 3, and on the next day cast his vote for Duff Green as printer in what was practically a party vote— the opposition succeeding in retaining Green as printer by 25 to 19. On December 6 McLane was appointed to a special committee of seven on a bill for the abolition of imprisonment for debt. On December 10 he was elected to two standing committees: the Committee on Commerce, on which he was the fourth of five members, and the Committee on Finance, on which he was the second of five.[42]

This last assignment was an important one. Once again he was named second to Sam Smith, the Baltimore merchant who had preceded him as chairman of the House Ways and Means Committee, and though the Senate committee had not the responsibility for originating financial legislation that devolved on the House committee, McLane's election to this position shows the high opinion held of his fiscal acumen. Since Senate committees were elected, McLane's high post suggests he had the backing of a party, the same opposition party that had chosen Duff Green printer.

Then Louis was off to Wilmington to be with Kitty when their tenth child was born on December 23. When he had returned to Washington, immediately after Christmas, Andrew Jackson called to offer congratulations and inquire "how young Andrew was." Apparently Van Buren was spreading a story, whether facetiously or seriously is not clear, that the baby would be named for the family's politics. Someone—perhaps Kitty—suggested naming the child for James Bayard or one of the Bayards.

Louis opposed both suggestions: "I think," he wrote Kitty, "you had better put all this matter out of doubt by giving him a name most agreeable to your own feelings. Considering the number of Mr. Byd's family, the constant changes that are taking place in the world, and the handle which might be made of it elsewhere, you had better select some fancy name tho' I submit the whole matter to you."[43]

The child was named Charles Eugene—a fancy name, not in the McLane or Milligan tradition.

Meanwhile Bob, this child's oldest brother, almost burned down the Washington boardinghouse, Mrs. Miller's on Seventh Street, where McLane was living. Bob had gone there to celebrate Christmas, and the twelve-year-old boy celebrated vigorously. He and one of South Carolina

Major Hamilton's sons opened the window "to return the huzzas to old Hickory of some boys in the street." Their candle set fire to the curtains and the window casing blazed.[44]

By New Year's Day his indulgent father had forgiven Bob. Together they went with the crowd to the White House; together they were turned away by a sentinel who said, "No boys"; together they called on Mrs. Van Rensselaer and Mrs. Decatur, finding John Randolph at Mrs. Decatur's house talking of his European trip and of the Duke of Dorset and Mr. Canning.[45]

Half a century later Robert Milligan McLane, an ex-Congressman, ex-governor of Maryland, ex-minister to France, remembered the members of his father's mess as Van Buren, Cambreleng, Forsyth, Archer, and Colonel Drayton of South Carolina, and, not living in Mrs. Miller's house but yet "in the same intimate association," McDuffie, Hayne, Major Hamilton, Cuthbert, Speaker Stevenson, Rives, Buchanan, William King, of Alabama, Edward Livingston, Hugh White, and John Eaton. Historical knowledge of the founders of the Crawford-Jackson coalition may have led Robert to exaggerate the intimacy of some of these men—particularly those outside the old Crawford party. It was the time, Robert recalled, "when the final coalition was effected between the original friends of General Jackson, who had supported him for the Presidency in 1824, and the friends of Mr. Crawford." [46]

In reality the coalition was pretty well effected before this session began. The McLane banners had certainly been moved to the Jackson camp; even Bob, on being refused admission to the President's home, expressed the wish that General Jackson would open it to little boys when he arrived there, as arrive he must.[47] But sometimes Louis wondered about the step he had taken and felt uneasy about his colleagues in the Jackson cause.

It gave him no delight to see Andrew Stevenson elected to the speakership of the House. Despite the social graces of Mrs. Stevenson, Dolley Madison's cousin, Louis had never forgiven her husband for running against him for the speakership in 1825. At news of Stevenson's election, McLane lamented that Philip Barbour had not been chosen, though he hoped Stevenson would "be so sensible of his own incapacity . . . as to seek counsel of wiser heads." [48] Just in thinking of "this pompous hypocrite" Louis fumed: "His election at best was a bitter pill to a majority of the House and he owes his elevation to the arts of the Magician." [49]

The Magician himself continued to arouse McLane's suspicions as he had in the winter of 1825. "I am entirely convinced of his exclusively selfish views," Kitty was informed in the spring of 1828, "and in this state of things I am not disposed to hold out any association [with Van Buren] which will not leave me perfectly free in any event." [50]

So when Van Buren in leaving Congress proposed to escort Mrs. Edward Livingston and the beautiful Cora from the Frenchtown wharf to Wilmington on their way to Philadelphia and to spend a night with the McLanes, Louis was put to it to find an excuse for avoiding the visit. "I do not see well how I am to avoid it," he told Kitty, though he had one idea to suggest: "I shall do it however in some such way as this;— if you are afraid of the varioloid Mrs. McL. will be happy etc. . . . Both Mrs. L. and her daughter are very agreeable." [51]

Whether the varioloid scared off Van Buren and the agreeable Livingston ladies is not known, but another instance of McLane's suspicion of Van Buren dates back to the previous summer and fall. At Van Buren's request McLane had sent him the details of a conversation with Webster on February 9, 1825, the day of Adams's election, when Webster offered to show McLane a letter approved by Adams and intended to encourage Federalists to support him. McLane had refused to read the letter, but now an account of Webster's overtures to Federalists had appeared in a New York newspaper. Both Churchill Cambreleng and Gulian Verplanck sent clippings to McLane, who was disturbed because he thought Van Buren might have put the story in circulation through the press. The details in the newspaper were not as McLane remembered the incident, but whether the reconstruction was true or false, McLane did not want to be involved. [52]

"I cannot consent to stand forth as the accuser of any one," he told Kitty, months later, and his hesitance was not due to shyness. "No party shall ever use me as the instrument to break down one set of men to elevate another."

This was the rub; he would not be used. And it was Van Buren, the Magician, whom McLane at once admired for his skill and feared for his management. When their mess gave a large dinner to pay off debts before adjournment in the spring of 1828, McLane looked at Henry Clay, who seemed a physical wreck, and wondered whether it was not the parlous state of his political fortunes that vexed him. Watching Clay, Louis told Kitty, he wondered whether those who built their futures on Clay's ruined fortunes would "possess his high tone and generosity to his friends." It seemed unlikely. [53]

V   "CALM AND DIGNITY AND LEISURE"

This mood of discouragement, however, grew on McLane when spring came and his eagerness to get home to his law practice, his family, and his strolls "over the hills and on the Brandywine" made the session seem interminable. Congress, he told Kitty, should never sit later than April 1; thereafter Congressmen became tired "of each other, of the place, of those in it and they of us." [54]

Earlier in the session he was more easily pleased, though bored by the "calm and dignity and leisure" of the Senate in contrast with "the boisterous, stirring, busy scene of the other house." [55] Except that his room was small, Mrs. Miller's establishment was as good a boardinghouse as he had ever known. "Tranquillity and cleanliness" pervaded the house; the table was "excellent and the coffee not to be excelled"; of his fellow lodgers only Colonel Drayton of South Carolina was new to the group, and he, "by his gentlemanly feelings and deportment," soon commanded "all respect." [56]

If the Senate was unexciting at first, so was social life in Washington without Kitty. After a month of it Louis declared that the three most agreeable things he had met all winter were the Dutch minister, the Chevalier Huygens, and his wife and his wine—though Kitty was immediately comforted by assurance that Mme Huygens was "old and ugly." [57]

At Edward Livingston's a week or two later, McLane found himself again at dinner with an agreeable group, Vice-President Calhoun, Colonel Hamilton, Van Buren, Cambreleng, Levi Woodbury, and others—all good company except for Speaker Stevenson, whom McLane found "more awkward and vulgar than ever," talking "of nothing but rules of order and . . . how he *sung* out when a debater violated their law." [58] Obviously Louis McLane, despite his promotion to the Senate, still felt pangs of regret for surrendering his long-nourished hope of being chosen Speaker himself.

He held more kindly sentiments for the presiding officer of the chamber he had recently entered than for the president of the chamber he had deserted. If personal jealousy may explain his disdain for Andrew Stevenson, it was party loyalty that led McLane, for the first time in his career, to have a kind word for John Calhoun. On February 11 he defended on the floor the Vice-President's ruling that he should not call a Senator to order for words spoken in debate. [59] Months later, on April 11, he was delighted to find "the V.P. came out like a hero" and cast the decisive vote to limit an appropriation for surveys to those with "national objects." What particularly delighted McLane was that Calhoun in a short address upheld the very points that McLane had already made on this subject in a "close and animated debate" with "the giant of the Adams party," Daniel Webster.

As Calhoun rose in McLane's estimation, Webster fell. He was "over rated," McLane decided, "hollow hearted and insincere." A letter, possibly one still extant from James Westcott, of Bridgeton, New Jersey, to Van Buren, convinced McLane that Webster had unfairly maneuvered to get Adams the votes of Stephen Van Rensselaer and Henry Warfield of Maryland on the fateful 9th of February, 1825. And though McLane himself would not make any public charge against Webster, this letter, if published, would expose him "in his nakedness."

As to his own debate with Webster, McLane thought he was benefited rather than harmed by it. "He [Webster] made one of his left handed Yankee speeches," Kitty was told, "which impliedly at least involved my [principles] and sick as I was I took the field. I had the most gratifying triumph I have ever enjoyed in Congress. I forced him to take back his words." [60]

Naturally McLane thought Calhoun "came out like a hero" when his casting vote helped McLane to a victory over such a Goliath. But there was one odd point about McLane's argument. In stressing that only surveys with national objects should be made at the expense of the national government, McLane chose "the Rail Road in Maryland" (because it was entirely within one state) as an example of the kind of survey he did not approve.[61] A strange choice indeed for a future president of the Baltimore & Ohio Railroad!

However, his future peace of mind could be eased by a speech he made in favor of permitting the B & O to import iron free of duty and a vote he cast for allowing any railroad to import iron and machinery duty free. In his speech he argued that domestic production fell far short of railroad needs and denied that any protection the Senate was likely to approve—or that he himself would endorse—would stimulate this production sufficiently to meet the need.[62] In his vote he was expressing his continued friendliness to internal improvements, even if he now set himself limits in the extent to which he was willing to carry such measures as were irritating to his new and old southern friends.

In the case of the B & O's future Maryland rival, the Chesapeake and Ohio Canal, McLane showed a similar attitude—at once acting as a leading advocate of internal improvements and yet insisting that limits should be set upon what the government could and should do. He suggested that a proposal to authorize a government subscription to Chesapeake and Ohio stock might be postponed a year or granted with a proviso that the government subscription should be paid only as work on the canal progressed. The sum of $1.5 million was all he felt the government could safely spend in any one year on internal improvements, if they were to be regularly supported; this year already almost $2 million had been appropriated for this purpose. On the other hand, this canal was not a common case of internal improvement. It was to aid Washington, and the federal government should not keep this city "in a ragged state." New York already had its canal; Baltimore was building a railroad; "the capital of the country should be allowed to share in these benefits." He never wished to see any inducement offered the government to remove the capital to another place.[63]

By May 21, when McLane spoke on the Chesapeake and Ohio appropriation, he was a veteran of more than a dozen Senate speeches, and one of them, in his opinion, his "most gratifying triumph" in a decade of congressional debates. But his Senate debut had been almost as nerve-wracking an affair for him as for an altogether new Congressman, for if he had gained years of experience in the House of Representatives, he was worried by the fear that he might not sustain in the upper house the good reputation he brought with him.

He chose a subject that was proper to him as a veteran's son and an ex-midshipman—a proposal to raise the pay of lieutenants in the Navy to equal that of Army lieutenants. He was for the proposal of course; like a good Federalist, he declared that "from the peculiar situation of the country, the Navy is the most important branch of our war establishment." [64] But on rising to speak, he later told Kitty: "I . . . almost repented of my temerity. I felt scarcely less pain than on my first embarcation in debate in the H. of R. and this necessarily chilled some of my ardour, and obstructed considerably the clear channel of my ideas. The Senate too was filled with a brilliant audience, which you may be sure . . . was not calculated to stimulate my enterprise. I got on, however, without a failure, and commanded as much attention as from the character of the debate I could have expected." [65]

Two days later he was on his feet again, opposing any decrease in the appropriation to pay federal pensions. Even, he argued, if the pensioners are slow to claim their money, the full appropriation should be voted, for the money should be available when claimed in order that these men should not be put to inconvenience.[66] After the speech was over, he explained to Kitty that neither of his speeches was likely to be properly reported, because "the Magician's attempt to improve the press"—that is, the Senate's replacement of the *Intelligencer* editor, Joseph Gales, by the editor of the *United States Telegraph*, Duff Green—"has deprived us of the chance of being reported, Gales having drawn all his forces into the House to take care of those who have taken care of him." It is not the first time Van Buren's machinations have recoiled on him, McLane added, "and I predict it will not be the last"; Van Buren's political prejudices grow more bitter every day, and he will find the United States cannot be treated like New York.[67]

McLane's other speeches concerned such topics as a breakwater to protect shipping at the mouth of Delaware Bay (a matter of importance to his state and to Philadelphia shipping), the military academy at West Point (of which he was a defender), an indemnity to South Carolina for wartime expenditures (he supported it, possibly because Delaware had already received such an idemnity, possibly because of his friendship for Hamilton and Drayton), and public land grants for the support of colleges. The last subject was a suggestion of his, made as an amendment to a proposal to appropriate public land to the benefit of Kenyon College in Ohio. Why just Kenyon, asked McLane? Why not make similar grants to other colleges in other states? [68]

There were more important measures on which he had little or nothing to say publicly. There was, for instance, the tariff of 1828, a subject on which he chose to be silent. He was moderating his old protectionist enthusiasm to suit his new stance as a Jackson man, just as he was now insisting that internal improvements must have national value to receive aid from Congress. He explained to Joshua Gilpin, the paper manufacturer, that he was "unwilling . . . to be drawn into any excess," and went on into an explanation that was devoid of enthusiasm: "This system of protection is not only artificial but defensive. We have been driven to it, to counteract the policy and measures of foreign nations. It is in its very nature also progressive; one act invites the employment of new capital which soon requires further protection." [69] Obviously McLane was not eager to be thought a supporter of the American System of Secretary Clay.

When the new tariff bill came before the Senate, McLane quietly cast his vote for it, but not without premonitions of perils ahead.[70] This tariff, he told Kitty, "is destined to do more mischief in the country . . . than all the other measures of the Government—to make friends enemies, and enemies friends, if not to scatter discord thro' the Union." [71] He was probably aware that an unfriendly newspaper published in the state capital of Delaware was accusing him of having supported the tariff only to win votes in New Castle County and keep his seat in the House, but this particular criticism was not the cause of his forebodings so much as the serious resentment of this "Tariff of Abominations" that he observed among his southern friends. They "put it so deeply as to make the whole affair one of mournful reflection. I trust in God the subject will not be revived again." [72]

On another, but a minor matter, McLane separated from most of his congressional friends with little or no hesitation. A newspaperman, Jarvis of the *United States Telegraph*, wrung the nose of young John Adams, the President's son and secretary, in the rotunda of the Capitol because he had fancied himself insulted by the young man at a reception at the presidential mansion. "What right," thought Louis McLane, "has an impudent editor to intrude himself upon the hospitality of a family of whom he is in the daily habit of abusing, and then complain of a rough reception—more especially what can excuse his committing an outrage upon a member of that family within the walls of the Capitol, in revenge for his treatment." In this case, he told Kitty, he voted against his friends, but after they thought it over, they agreed with him.[73]

On another matter McLane was able at once to vote his own prejudices and to support his friends. This was in reducing the duty on madeira, which was "almost a necessary of life" in the South, according to Levi Woodbury.[74] It was a wine that McLane dearly loved, and when the time approached to return home he sent careful requests before him: have father get three gross of the best wine corks in Philadelphia; have Henry (a servant) open the box of wine and set out the bottles so it will be clear and fit for use; have him clean all the empty bottles and demijohns; place the filled bottles carefully on their ends.[75]

VI   LORD OF BOHEMIA

Only the "Bill for the old Revolutionary officers and the internal improvement bill," both possibly dependent on his vote, held Louis McLane at Congress in the spring of 1828. The latter was the bill on which he had spoken in favor of limiting the surveys to be made by the United States Army Corps of Engineers.[76] Probably because of his remarks on this bill as well as because he was an important member of the Committee on Finance, through which it had passed, he was elected by the Senate to serve with Tazewell, of Virginia, and Sanford, of New York, on a committee to confer with House members on reconciling the House and Senate versions. The bill McLane reported for this committee, limiting surveys only by declaring they must be for objects of national importance, proved quite acceptable.[77] Besides this service in the old Federalist cause of internal improvements, McLane had continued to give his vote to the extension of the Cumberland Road.[78] But he warned a friend that "many of the most intelligent advocates" of internal improvements had been so startled by "the extravagant doctrines" of Adams's first message and the "still more extravagant projects" springing from it that they had "suspended all their zeal." [79]

The other bill that held McLane in Congress was one on which he never took the floor. It was the nature, not the degree, of his interest that kept him silent, for the purpose of the bill was to provide full pay to all the surviving officers of the Continental Army in the Revolution. Old Collector McLane was one of these survivors, of course, and the bill consequently promised a handsome income to the McLanes while the collector lived. It looked all the better from the fact that the veterans were to be paid retroactively from March, 1826.

For weeks it seemed very unlikely that the bill would ever pass. Bob McLane, now twelve, sat in the gallery while it was debated on January 22; if his grandfather got nothing else, Louis felt, he would at least have the pleasure of knowing that a grandson with spirit enough to enjoy it listened to the illustrious deeds of himself and his compatriots in the Revolution.[80] Bob had not only spirit but perspicacity. A few days later, after listening to a speech by Senator Ezekiel Chambers of Maryland, he observed, "Why, pa, that gentleman's speeches have a beginning, an end, but no middle." [81]

In his autobiography, Van Buren declared that the bill was saved by a speech he made almost by accident. It had been his plan to speak for the bill, but its defeat seemed so certain that a number of his friends, including "Louis McLane, . . . a son of one of the officers for whose relief it was the object of the measure to provide," pressed him to let it go. He intended to take this advice, but when he rose to explain his silence to two ladies in the gallery who had come to hear him speak, the Vice-President misunderstood his motion and called upon him. Changing his mind suddenly, Van Buren made his speech and by the force of his argument turned senatorial opposition into an attitude sufficiently reasonable to permit the bill's passage, once some amendments were accepted.[82]

Whether or not Van Buren's account is dependable, the bill was defeated so decisively on March 12 that McLane thought it could hardly be brought up again.[83] Yet by mid-April he thought his vote might tip the scale for the bill, and by the end of the month he dared to absent himself from the final vote and the bill was passed without him.[84] When it had passed the lower house also, McLane rejoiced: "This one act of generosity, tho' not all these noble men deserved, will atone for many sins of this Congress." [85]

The act of generosity came at the right moment for Louis. For at some time during this year he had contracted for a considerable financial expenditure; he had agreed to buy Bohemia, the Milligan estate. Exactly when the agreement was made is uncertain, but an undated letter of 1828 asks Kitty whether she would prefer visiting Washington for three or four weeks or going to Bohemia to attend to the planting.[86]

Other letters during the congressional term refer in various ways to his poverty, but probably the shoe pinched Louis all the more when he was taking a big step. In sending Kitty "the enclosed needful," at the end of January, for instance, Louis repined, "Alas! that in the cup of every man there should be mingled something of the bitter. But for this want of cash, mine would be all sweet." [87] And again early in May he was pressed for cash. Sending Kitty twenty-five dollars, he told her to apply to "the old gent." for the loan of as much more if she needed it. "He will [lend it] cheerfully I know; especially as the appropriation for the Brandywine Light House has passed." [88] This was a week before the Revolutionary officers bill passed the lower house.

On June 24, 1828, the purchase of Bohemia was completed. George Milligan, Kitty's brother, had mortgaged the property to Joseph Tatnall, a wealthy Brandywine miller. Tatnall died, and soon afterwards a public sale was held because the mortgage payments were in arrears. The sale brought only $10,000, which was insufficient to discharge the debt. Mc-Lane then bought the property for $10,000, but the only money he had to provide was enough to cover selling costs and to pay "the large amount of interest"—exactly how much is not known—that was due on the mortgage. The mortgage itself was extended to him for $10,000, enough to cover the nominal purchase price.[89] Thus the mortgages secured the payment of back interest by permitting the transfer of the property from George Milligan to Louis McLane. For the payment of Milligan's debts, McLane became lord of Bohemia in his brother-in-law's place.

Some time after the sale Louis and Kitty made a trip to Bohemia. "We arrived last night," Kitty wrote to a neighbor, ". . . and have been walking today all over the Hills and Valleys—to see that new beginners go on right. Mr. McLane looks about as much like a Farmer as you can well imagine." [90]

Not very much, probably. But he was serious about his plans for the farm. In August he wrote James Buchanan, reminding him of a promise of the past winter to find a good man to operate Bohemia. It was a sensible idea to look for a farmer in Buchanan's area, Lancaster County, site of the most careful husbandry in the country. McLane planned to furnish the necessary stock and labor (he estimated that eight or ten men or boys and twelve horses would be needed) and to farm it on his own account through a superintendent on an annual salary.[91]

Despite being the son of an abolitionist, McLane probably planned to employ slave labor. When he died, at any rate, he had eight male slaves—and two female—on the Bohemia property.[92] From the beginning he had many plans for the thousand acres and more—eight hundred and fifty cultivated—of the estate. He thought the soil particularly adapted to corn and clover and planned to send dairy and poultry products to both the Baltimore and Wilmington markets. But being busy and twenty-six miles away, McLane needed a good superintendent. And he wanted to get him before fall so that he could help procure the stock and farm tools and begin operations by March 25.[93]

Whether or not he looked like a farmer as he trod over the hills and valleys of Bohemia, certainly Louis McLane must have felt like a lord, a man at last come into his own, walking in the dreams he had envisioned when he first voyaged down the Chesapeake toward Congress in 1817. It had not come to him too soon, this status as a Chesapeake planter—like a Milligan, like a Bayard. Had not a sweet young matron, Mrs. Julia Dickinson Tayloe, honored him as the sixth most important man in Washington this past winter when she called on him to fill a page in her autograph album? On the first page was "a dull verse" by President Adams; on the second a prose composition by Vice-President Calhoun; and then, in succession, a quotation from Milton by Secretary of State Clay, "a doggerel piece" by Speaker Stevenson (it was annoying that he should be so far forward), some prose by Van Buren—and the next page was presented to him, Louis McLane.[94]

Nor were the attentions of a financial giant like Nicholas Biddle, president of the Bank of the United States, likely to deflate McLane's self-esteem. "While you are taking care of the country," Biddle wrote him in March of 1828, "your friends must take care of you. Your note [for $5,000] will be due on the 13th inst. and you wil consult only your own convenience as to paying it or renewing it." [95]

Despite his financial setbacks, the former lord of Bohemia, George Milligan, enjoyed the good opinion of his brother-in-law—and partner in the Rokeby venture—in 1828. George has "a sound heart and a well regulated head," Louis told Kitty, adding the opinion that his Louisiana business prospects might well make George the wealthiest man in the family.[96]

But of John Milligan and his brother-in-law Joseph Sims, Louis had nothing good to say in 1828. "I have so often felt humiliation at J. M.'s [John Milligan's] conduct towards me and my friends," McLane told James Bayard, "that I have long since learned to be prepared for any new manifestation of it and thereby avoid all mortification." [97] In the winter of 1828 John Milligan seemed to be courting approval of the Claytons for a place on the Delaware bench, but McLane refused to endorse him.[98] And when the desired appointment went to someone else, McLane was not sorry. "His last appearance as Secretary of a tariff meeting in opposition to the expressed opinions of his life, *when* he *supposed me a friend of the tariff*, caps the climax of his subserviency! And yet the boon falls to another!" [99]

The boon—that is, the appointment to the Delaware supreme court—fell to Dr. Arnold Naudain, there being no requirement that the judges be attorneys. McLane saw the appointment as part of a bargain made in the fall when Naudain gave way to Kensey Johns, Jr., in the congressional contest.[100] What irritated McLane was another of Governor Polk's appointments—that of Thomas Clayton as chief justice. Of James Booth, the chief justice whose death caused this vacancy, McLane declared, "he annoyed me all in his power during his life, and has consummated the injury by his death. He brings to the head of the Bench the bitterest personal enemy I have in the world." [101]

"Our remedy," he told Bayard, "must be sought in a reorganization of the Judiciary System: and to this, as soon as we have beaten the Adams men we should devote all our efforts." [102] And to Kitty, he made a pledge: "the rest of my days in Del. shall be devoted to bring about a change in the judiciary. . . . I will not believe that she [Delaware] is destined to be governed by such men as the Claytons, the Yankee interlopers [lawyer John Wales and editor Moses Bradford] and their miserable dependents and tools." [103]

VII   A FIGHT FOR LIFE

Informed men realized that the new judicial appointments in Delaware proceeded from the secretary of state, John M. Clayton, as much as from Governor Charles Polk.[104] But even informed men, including Louis McLane, did not properly appreciate the political genius of this convivial young giant. "As soon as we have beaten the Adams men" we shall do such and so, wrote McLane. But the Adams men in Delaware, under Clayton's leadership, were not to be beaten. And as to McLane's political plans for "the rest of my days in Del."—he had no idea how short that time was to be. Certainly he had no idea how very futile his attempt to overthrow the Claytons would prove.

He did know that he was in for a fight. "I look to a bitter contest next fall," he warned James Bayard in January, 1828, "and if success is to crown our efforts I do not much care . . . how bitter it may be." [105] The contest for control of Delaware, he told Kitty, had "become vital" to him, but however it came out he thought he would retire from politics.[106]

Probably McLane felt that the victory of his party would bring him some choice position by executive appointment. And defeat—defeat was a grim possibility he hated to consider. "The present contest in Del. is one of existence almost for me. . . . It is no longer to be disguised that my fall and the fall of *my friends,* rather than the elevation of Mr. Adams, is now the object, open, avowed and gloried in." [107]

By May, when he wrote these words, the Adams party in Delaware had aimed their heaviest artillery directly at Louis McLane, as the leader of their opposition. By 1828 Louis McLane had six times won statewide election contests in Delaware, more than any man before him and more than any man in over a century to come. By 1828 Louis McLane had attained more prestige in Washington than any Delawarean before him —possibly excepting James Bayard and Caesar A. Rodney. And whereas Bayard had labored in a hopeless minority cause, and Rodney's star had burnt itself out of the first magnitude quickly, McLane had built his reputation solidly and seemed about to rise to greater power with a new party.

Some Federalists in Delaware were shocked by McLane's Washington alliances in the same way William Gaston, a North Carolina Federalist, was astonished to see "such men as McLane and Ridgely, pure in principles, federalists in the legitimate sense of the term, representing a state so firmly attached to the Union and deeply interested in good order, united with the wildest disorganizers, the rankest anti-federalists, and the crudest radicals." [108] This was probably the way John Milligan felt, though by acting on his impulses—and perhaps his ambition—he was not very considerate of his brother-in-law's feelings, and perhaps not conscious of the extent to which McLane had based his future prospects on a political gamble.

"I really begin to tremble almost for the ferociousness which will scarcely fail to characterize this Presidential contest," declared Louis.[109] "The men in power," he thought, meaning Adams and Clay, "do not . . . calculate upon success," but they would fight vigorously nonetheless.[110] And in Delaware the outcome was anything but certain.

So bitter did feelings run here that the lower house of the state legislature was unable to organize in January, 1828.[111] From Washington, McLane sent orders to the editor of his Wilmington paper, the *Delaware Gazette,* and also advice to be passed through one of the Reads to the editor of the Democratic Jackson paper, the *Delaware Patriot.*[112] "We now have the press," he exulted, and he looked to his friends "to hold a tight rein" over the editors.[113]

If the Democrat who edited the *Patriot* needed to be spurred, the Federalist, Samuel Harker, who edited the *Gazette,* needed to be reined in. "Keep Harker quiet about [Representative] Johns," McLane instructed Bayard on one occasion; "he will drive [Johns] to exertion, which he else would not attempt." [114]

When Bayard planned to attend a political rally of the Jackson men in Sussex, McLane sent him suggestions for a preamble and resolutions to be submitted to the Sussex meeting for adoption. The preamble, said McLane, should set forth the dangers of cabinet succession. (This suggestion, he undoubtedly thought, should please the majority of voters in Federalist Sussex—and the majority of voters in Federalist Delaware—

for they had been struggling against cabinet succession through the long years of Democratic-Republican rule at Washington.)

Now for the first time since 1800 the Delaware electorate was given a real chance to participate in the choice of a President, and they must put aside old party divisions and unite to make their voice effective. In 1824 the choice of a large plurality of the American people had been set aside by a coalition which sought to give Adams eight years of patronage and power and then to make Clay his successor. Against this corrupt coalition stood the honest, manly figure of a hero who had his first office from Washington (perhaps this made him more appealing to Federalists). Hurrah for Jackson! [115]

So Louis McLane went about his task of constructing a Jackson party in Delaware. But canny politicians like the Claytons would not let him destroy their Federalist machine to the advantage of Jackson—and for the further advancement of McLane, who had moved into first the House and then the Senate over the body of Thomas Clayton.

"Our opponeants [sic] are Extreemly Busey," Jesse Green, a veteran Sussex Democrat, warned McLane, "Circulating Lieing Handbills etc. Which confuse the people much." [116] Besides these handbills, one hundred and twenty copies of the *Weekly Marylander* came to Delaware, mainly to Sussex, from the office of Hezekiah Niles and for the advancement of the Adams cause.[117] But the first big Clayton salvo was fired from Dover on April 12, 1828.

On that day appeared the first issue of *The Political Primer, or A Hornbook for the Jacksonites*, edited by John Robertson in open opposition to Harker's *Delaware Gazette*. The *Gazette*, the *Primer's* first number declared, is controlled by politicians of questionable principles. "At the head of this group stands Louis McLane," and with him are "three fragments of the Democratic party," George Read, his son the district attorney, and Wilmington postmaster Nicholas Williamson. Next on "this list of intriguers" were the names of Archibald Hamilton (speaker of the Delaware house of representatives when McLane was elected to the United States Senate) and James A. Bayard, who "humbly worships and hopes one day to imitate the man who gave him his lessons in law and politics." Last "but not least of the group," said the *Primer*, were "Captain (or if you please Colonel) Allen McLane" and his son, "the Doctor." By these men the *Gazette*, "though purporting to be a Federal paper," has been used "to widen, instead of to heal, the differences which unfortunately existed in the old Federal Party."

The *Gazette* had been so used, it could hardly be denied. After the Federalists had nominated an Adams supporter, Kensey Johns, Jr., in September, 1827, McLane had thrown down the gage of battle to the

Adams wing of his old party. Now the abuse of the *Political Primer* repaid him for his desertion of the party and his continued leadership in
organizing a new party around the Jackson standard.

A less hot-tempered man than Louis McLane would have been angered
by the *Primer*, which described his policies as "jealous, cruel, and vindictive" and called his father an old dotard who dreamed of Louis's becoming President.[118] Angry as he was at the sponsors of the *Primer*,
Louis McLane was furious when he discovered that Kitty's brother-in-
law, Joseph Sims, was receiving it. "It has poured out," he complained,
"all the low private scandal" its editors could invent, including a "coarse,
vulgar, and outrageous allusion" to "the solitary act of my life capable
of being used by my enemies, and that only because my delicacy re-
strains me from explanation"—an event in which "the feelings of my
wife, of my children, of my friends every where are closely associated." [119]
The "coarse, vulgar, and outrageous allusion" was a reference to a "man
who deserted an amiable and accomplished young lady of Newcastle
county," [120] which McLane understood—correctly, without doubt—to be
an allusion to the still-unexplained rupture of his engagement to Ann
Van Dyke not long before his marriage to Kitty Milligan.

This was but the beginning of the *Primer*'s abuse. "A man," it called
McLane, "who under the old distinction of parties was a Federalist in
Delaware and a Democrat at Washington." To win a House seat he had
favored the tariff and gained some votes in New Castle County. When
no wind from Adams had filled his sails, he had changed his course; he
opposed the American System and was promised a place in the cabinet
of Jackson. "Like a Machiavel, . . . confident of his skill in unprincipled
intrigue," McLane has turned to destroy the party that supported him,
and "has declared that [quoting from a Jackson party manifesto] 'the
terms "Federalist" and "Democrat" can no longer be the watchword of
party. Under the banners of Jackson and Adams every man *must* now
either directly or indirectly array himself.' " [121]

VIII   THE OUTCOME

Arrayed boldly in his Jackson robes Louis McLane struggled to construct a new party through the summer of 1828. When James Bayard,
his chosen successor, seemed reluctant to seek office, McLane gave him
encouragement. Bayard had adopted low tariff views which in the spring
of 1828 he thought might be an impediment to his political success, but
McLane reassured him. The tariff was not a major issue in this campaign,
and in the future the two men would probably see alike on this issue,
for McLane thought the tariff of 1824 went far enough and no more pro-

tection should be sought; "I believe a majority of the People of Del. are of the same mind." [122]

Robert McLane, who was then thirteen, tells in his *Reminiscences* [123] of attending a "great mass meeting of the citizens of Maryland and Delaware" that was addressed by his father, by General Samuel Smith, and by George Read, Jr. "McLane of Del.," Samuel Ingham reported in September to Van Buren, "is engaged heart and soul in Stump Speaking. All depends on Sussex for the Electoral ticket." [124]

McLane rode around Sussex in a gig, "mounting the stage" at almost every crossroads. Speakers for the opposition followed him to rebut his arguments, but the Jackson meetings, enlivened by refreshments as well as orations, outlasted the patience of the opposition speakers. [125] There is no evidence that McLane ever debated on the same platform with an opponent, but he could not escape the jibes of the press. "The Delaware Martin Van Buren *in miniature*," the *Primer* called him, and it termed his party the "McLanites" and its leaders "McLane and Co." [126]

Despite Bayard's reluctance, he had been persuaded once again to stand as the Jackson candidate for the United States House of Representatives, and against him, of course, Kensey Johns, Jr., sought reelection as the Adams candidate. But the choice of legislators was even more important than the choice of a Representative. For the new legislature would have the power to choose presidential electors and a new Senator (Henry Ridgely's term would end March 4, 1829) and also to decide many questions of state policy that were left in abeyance by the failure of the previous legislature ever to get to work or even, in the case of the lower house, to organize.

Despite Bayard's reluctance he ran, and despite McLane's efforts his ticket lost. As in 1827, Bayard was defeated by Johns and by almost the same margin—by a few more votes, in fact. And the Adams forces seized control of the legislature, electing fourteen of the twenty-one members of the lower house, and gaining a 5 to 4 advantage in the state senate. [127]

A month after the election a special session was called to choose electors—Adams electors, of course—and when the regular session of the legislature met in January, 1829, Secretary of State John M. Clayton was elected to Henry Ridgely's Senate seat. [128] The greatest politician in the history of Delaware was launched on his senatorial career.

This was retribution for McLane with a vengeance. "If federalism in Del. is to be under the domination of the Dover junto," he had written years earlier, "I am off in the spring." [129] Now the Dover junto was in control of the party, and he was distinctly left out of it.

What is more, it was his own doing. In attempting to construct a new party in Delaware around his own close associates and the magic figure of Old Hickory, McLane had left the powerful Federalist state organization in the hands of his enemies. They had transformed it into an Adams party, aided by the transfusion of some new Democratic blood— Arnold Naudain and the du Ponts, for instance (E. I. du Pont had been an unsuccessful Adams party candidate for the state legislature from New Castle County) [130]—and by new leadership in the able young Clayton, and thereby had strengthened it for another twenty years.

For all McLane's efforts, Delaware politics remained as before, controlled by the party that ruled Kent and Sussex. The only significant difference between the outcome of the congressional contests of 1827 and 1828 was that in the latter year the Adams majority declined in Kent County to a figure similar to the old Federalist majority there, while increasing in Sussex County to a figure (450) large enough to give this party the victory, a figure more closely approximating the old Federalist majority in Sussex.

Louis McLane had exchanged a position of leadership in the majority party that controlled Kent and Sussex—and Delaware—for the leadership of a minority party that could carry only New Castle County. He had attempted to reshuffle the deck of Delaware politics, and when the new hand was dealt, the face cards were changed about a bit, but the values remained as before.

From Washington Stephen Pleasonton, a Treasury Department auditor, commented to Thomas Rodney, Caesar Augustus's son: "I felt very sure that the Administration would have a majority this year, for the people of Delaware do not change suddenly. They are a steady thinking people, and take great pride in maintaining their opinions." [131]

IX AN EXPECTANT WINTER

Put my name, McLane wrote to the secretary of the Senate, on a seat "on the outer row in the same spot or as nearly so as practicable where I sat last session." [132] And so McLane prepared to return to Washington. Though defeated in Delaware, his party was triumphant in the nation. Soon its old chief would be President. Then for his loyalty McLane might expect compensation.

But the defeat rankled nonetheless, whatever great expectations he might hold. "Tom Clayton," he exploded to his father, "and every other Clayton in Delaware is a great scoundrel." [133] Had it not been for the Claytons, he might have returned to Washington with the new prestige of carrying his state for Jackson—as had Van Buren, for instance, who could now wait to return until he took his place at Jackson's side, because he had been elected governor of New York. By leading the Jackson ticket to victory in his influential state, Van Buren had assured himself almost certainly of the highest place in Jackson's cabinet if he wanted it.

Not so McLane. He had lost his state and seemed unlikely to be able to carry it again in the near future. He "has staked everything on his political measures," declared Margaret Bayard Smith; "his practice injured, his popularity in his own state gone—Jackson's election affords him something more than mere triumph. I have no doubt he builds on it hope, nay almost certainty of office." [134]

She was right. It was no pleasure for McLane to look forward to having John M. Clayton as a colleague. What he desired was an honorable way to escape from the Senate and from dependence for his situation upon the politics of Delaware. "I am not," he confessed, when a position was finally offered him, "in a situation to consult all my feelings, much less to be fastidious." [135]

But a session of Congress had to be endured before Jackson would be inaugurated and any hope of office could be realized. To help the session pass more happily, Kitty accompanied Louis to Washington, and with Kitty came her three youngest children, Allan, Juliette, and Charles, aged five, four, and one.

As usual, Kitty was in a delicate condition, but she was as jolly as ever. She talked so much—she said she brought three and a half children with her—that Margaret Smith thought she might have been called "a Rattle" were she not "something so much better"—a charming woman. She is "so entertaining and agreeable," Mrs. Smith added, "that time literally flies when I am with her." [136]

Kitty helped the time fly for Louis too, and he needed her cheerfulness as uncertainty about his future role in politics kept him all winter on an uneasy seat. Nor did the mail from Delaware bring him happy news. The election of John M. Clayton to the Senate was a discouraging event, even though it was expected. So was the condition of McLane's only brother, the bibulous doctor, whom the opposition press loved to ridicule.

The first issue of the *Primer*, for instance, had probed this weak spot in the McLane armor: "'An't my brother the greatest man in the nation,' hiccupped the greatest physician in the State." [137]

After receiving from her father-in-law a "distressing account" of the problem "the poor Doctor" was coming to be, Kitty tried to comfort the old collector. "From my Soul I pity you," she wrote, "and pray to God to support you through it, and let you yet have some hope of seeing him reclaimed, and restored to his stand in society—and usefulness to his poor children. [The doctor's wife had died a few years earlier.] I sometimes strongly hope that the Doctor will be reclaimed by the claims, and demands, of these children. They are all fine children, and when he finds he must advance them by *his exertions* he *surely* will rouse, and take resolution." For the moment Louis could not help them, "for it is *not pretended* to be *concealed* that *no Jacksonian whatever* could be advanced in *any way*." But an Army or Navy appointment might be possible after the 4th of March. "A new order of things will now very soon come about and I shall most ardently trust that poor Allan or Sam . . . could soon be provided for." (Sam died at seventeen, but Allan did secure a midshipman's appointment.) [138]

Louis told his father he would love to invite the doctor to Washington, but dared not. "After the State he has been in nearly all the winter, how could he bear the exposure of such a ride without falling a victim to such an oft repeated friend." One might suspect that Louis did not want a brother with such a "besetting sin" in Washington for fear of embarrassment, but apparently his family pride and attachment overcame his fears on that point. For he suggested that "if the *boats* were running, which would so *much* shorten the time exposed on the road," or if the collector came too, the doctor might be encouraged to make the trip. If he comes, Louis said, "I will do everything possible to amuse and interest him while here." Apparently he was confident he could keep his younger brother in line once he got to Washington. [139]

Old Collector McLane had a special responsibility this winter because he and a female cousin of Kitty's were looking after the four children who were left in Wilmington. "God knows what they would do without you," Kitty wrote him. Rebecca was at Mme Sigoigne's school in Philadelphia, in company with the daughter of another notable Jacksonian, Major William Lewis. When inauguration time came near, Rebecca sent the collector a more than gentle hint of her interest: "I suppose you intend to go and see your friend the General inaugurated, and I beg you not to forget that you have a granddaughter in Philadelphia who is as anxious as any one to go under her Grandpapa's wing." [140]

It was not Rebecca, however, but her brother Robert who went to Washington under Grandpapa's wing. This does not signify any great neglect of Rebecca; her oldest brother, who was attending St. Mary's College in Baltimore, could more easily be taken to Washington. [141] And later in the spring Rebecca received her chance to visit Washington and mingle in its society as her father's sole companion.

The one strange case of forgetfulness in the McLane family circle was in regard to the other Rebecca, Louis's sister, the wife of Edward Worrell, a Wilmington banker. Rebecca Worrell spent long years in the Pennsylvania Hospital, in Philadelphia, where she was listed among the insane.

There is not one reference to her in the surviving correspondence of Louis McLane and his wife, though there are a few, a very few, references to the Worrell family. The death of one of her children, George Washington Worrell, in 1828, is as unnoted in these letters as are the lives of his four brothers and sisters. The old collector probably remembered this daughter as affectionately as he remembered his sons and their families. Very likely he visited the Pennsylvania Hospital on his frequent trips to Philadelphia. Certainly he made her a gift of an undisclosed amount of real and personal property, for which her son George was trustee.[142]

But for some reason the Worrells remained out of the circle of Louis McLane's concern. His sister's long illness and her confinement in a Philadelphia institution contributed to this separation of the two families, of course. Besides, Louis had been but eleven when Rebecca had married and moved away. Perhaps Louis's lack of religious feeling kept him apart from the Methodist Worrells; maybe even a rivalry between the Farmers Bank, of which Louis and Dr. Allen were officers, and the Bank of Delaware, of which Edward Worrell was cashier, helped to widen the distance between the families. No enmity existed of the sort that poisoned Louis McLane's relations with some of his in-laws. And today it is the Worrells, not the children of Louis McLane, who lie beside the old collector in Asbury Methodist churchyard in Wilmington.

X   THE CHESAPEAKE AND DELAWARE CANAL
AND OTHER BUSINESS

In the lame-duck Congress that met in the winter of 1828–29, Louis McLane spoke in favor of a bill granting a drawback—of import duties previously paid—on re-exported sugar in order "to promote the carrying trade," and against a proposal to divide among the states all unappropriated funds in the Treasury—it was unconstitutional, McLane argued, to use the federal government as a tax collector for the states.[143] In another unreported speech McLane apparently opposed acting on President Adams's nomination of John Crittenden to the Supreme Court, in which action he was siding with his party, which put off confirmation till after March 4, when it could control the appointment.[144]

More important to McLane than any of these matters was his advocacy of bills for internal improvements, and most particularly of a bill for the federal purchase of additional stock in the Chesapeake and Delaware Canal. In an animated debate an attempt was made to recommit this bill in order to add to it a similar appropriation for the Dismal Swamp Canal, running from near Norfolk, Virginia, to Albemarle

Sound in North Carolina. McLane, arguing that a motion for recommittal would only lead to killing both projects for this short session, persuaded the sponsor to withdraw this motion and replace it by a motion to amend, which was defeated with little loss of time. And time was precious, both because the session was short and because failure to make the appropriation would have delayed work on the Chesapeake and Delaware Canal for a year—or so McLane argued.

He was perfectly willing to vote an appropriation to the Dismal Swamp Canal in its turn, he said; advocates of the Chesapeake and Delaware Canal "had never, in a single instance, opposed any similar bill, from any part of the country." [145] He probably had no right to speak for every advocate of the Chesapeake and Delaware Canal, but his own record on internal improvements was exactly what he claimed it was. At this session he not only voted for but spoke on behalf of a subscription to the Louisville and Portland Canal Company—the only private canal besides the Chesapeake and Delaware in which the government ever became a stockholder. Perhaps his zeal in taking the floor represented a quest for votes for his own project; he confessed he had opposed the Louisville and Portland Canal bill in committee because he doubted whether the bill would effect the object proposed. [146] On the Cumberland Road, McLane kept his record clear; he supported the proposed extension of the road westward from Zanesville, Ohio, as he had supported all similar bills in the past. [147]

In internal improvements, McLane reaped what he sowed. At the end of the session he was happy not only with the passage of the Chesapeake and Delaware Canal appropriation but also with such local measures as appropriations for piers at New Castle, a lighthouse at the northern end of Bombay Hook Island in the Delaware, and four buoys to be placed in the channel east of Pea Patch Island, on which a fort was being built. [148]

XI   PRESSING FOR PREFERMENT

Successful as he may have seemed in securing legislation satisfactory to his constituents, for Louis McLane this was not the important business at the second session of the Twentieth Congress. The important business was the formation of the new government which would take office under Jackson on March 4. With this business Louis McLane was ready and willing, even eager to help if Jackson or his lieutenants would ask him. But nobody did.

Jackson was a hero, Louis McLane felt, a man of great character. But he was not a statesman with the finesse of a Crawford—or a McLane—and the success of his administration depended upon his securing the proper sort of ministers to advise him. This circumstance gave cause for great concern, for "unfortunately his friends of habit and those accustomed to live around him are not," as Kitty McLane wrote, under Louis's influence, "the high men of the country, from whom he could take advice." [149]

The more McLane considered the quality of the men about Jackson, the more he feared for the success of the administration—and for the possibilities of preferment it might offer him. Yet, among "the high men of the country" he would be warmly recommended. According to editor Duff Green the contest was between Vice-President Calhoun and Governor-elect Van Buren to control the new cabinet,[150] and in both of these camps McLane had his advocates. "I have not forgotten McLane," declared the New Yorker,[151] and though the South Carolinian might have been happy to forget McLane, his followers were not. Duff Green, who was Calhoun's son-in-law, suspected that Van Buren himself might come into conflict with McLane over the Treasury Department and its huge patronage.[152]

In view of McLane's able leadership of the Ways and Means Committee it is not strange that he was thought a likely Treasury Secretary.[153] Even Van Buren made him his choice for that position. Not, however, till after he tried to content McLane with the post of Attorney General— possibly because the Magician thought appointment to it would be easier to arrange, and possibly because he knew of McLane's ambition for a seat on the Supreme Court and thought this cabinet post the natural stepping-stone to a Court appointment.[154]

William Rives suspected that McLane, though "sensible . . . of his own solid talent," shrank from the prospect of "constant collision as an advocate with Webster, Wirt and the leaders of the U.S. Bar." [155] Whatever the arguments for and against his taking the post, McLane declared he would not have it. He wrote Van Buren to this effect—"holding myself at liberty," he told James Bayard, "to accept or reject the other [the Treasury office], *if offered,* as circumstances may render proper." On January 22, 1829, at the time of his letter to Bayard, it seemed dangerous to remove a Jacksonian from the Senate lest control of that chamber fall to the opposition.[156] But early in February came news of a Jackson victory in New Jersey, news that to McLane meant that "now there is no embarrasment [sic] in taking a man from the Senate." [157]

February also brought the Old Hero to Washington. Kitty reported to the collector of the great bustle that was being made as the general approached: "the Boys are already crying out and shouting Huzza for Jackson. Allan roars out *that's him,* at every noise he hears in the Street." [158] Two days later she reported the arrival of Jackson's baggage, and remarked: "There is snow enough here, but no sleighs—and indeed every body is so *full* of *Jackson* that I do not think they could take the time *to sit still so long,* if they had them." [159]

When the general did come, on February 11, he stole into the city with John Eaton before breakfast, while the McLanes were still in their beds, and "when the central committee *started* to meet him, he was already seated in his rooms at Gadsby's." On this very day the electoral vote was counted in Congress, a spectacle Kitty went to see despite a snow storm. Cannon were fired by order of the district marshal as soon as the result was announced. Congress adjourned at three, and on the way home McLane stopped to see the general, "who gave him a most distinguished reception." [160]

Kitty was not long behindhand. In a few days she too called at Gadsby's hotel, taking young Allan with her and presenting him *"as the grand son* of a *Brother Soldier."* Jackson "recognized the *illusion* [sic] directly," she wrote the collector, "and asked how and where you were. I told him that you were detained a close prisoner by the Rheumatism and many years—otherwise *you* would have the pleasure I then enjoyed. He replied, with quickness, '*those were the only enemys* who had *ever ventured near enough to* attempt making *you* a prisoner, and that as they had *fairly* captured you, he hoped they might long hold you!'"

He was a man of unusual politeness, Kitty concluded:

> Polite as all his life in Courts had been,
> Yet good, as he the World had never seen.

But he was harassed by affairs, particularly friends pressing for preferment. When a gentleman told him a committee was waiting, he went off without another word. [161]

One of the friends being pressed upon General Jackson was Louis McLane. On the day of Jackson's arrival, two Hamiltons were among those who called upon the general. One was Major James Hamilton, Jr., of South Carolina, the other was James A. Hamilton, of New York, son of Alexander, and it is likely that both of them mentioned McLane's name.

They were not encouraged to think there was much hope for him. Major Hamilton and John Randolph called on Jackson together and concluded the cabinet was unsettled, except for Van Buren as Secretary of State. "I tremble for poor McLane," Major Hamilton told Van Buren. "So. Carolina will stand I fear almost alone in supporting himself and Cheves, and both I fear may go to the wall without an opportunity . . . for you to say a word for both of them." [162]

But Van Buren was consulted—through the agency of James A. Hamilton, who was representing him in Washington. This Hamilton reported that Samuel Ingham, Bucks County, Pennsylvania, manufacturer and Congressman, was most likely to be offered the Treasury Department. Hamilton expected Ingham to refuse out of a just estimation of his own limitations, whereupon he thought the place would be offered either to Postmaster General John McLean or to Louis McLane. Louis McLane, he hoped, for he looked upon John McLean as a Calhoun man and hated to see Calhoun controlling Treasury patronage.[163]

Ingham was a Calhoun man too, but Langdan Cheves, onetime president of the Bank of the United States, seems to have been the Calhoun candidate for the Treasury. Before Jackson arrived, Cheves came to Washington, presumably to electioneer and possibly to contradict a rumor that he was a drunkard.[164] Van Buren thought well of him, but made McLane his first choice for the Treasury. Indeed, according to Van Buren, the only difference between his cabinet selections and those of the South Carolinians was that he placed Cheves in the Navy Department and McLane in the Treasury, while they reversed the positions.[165] Even Louis McLane preferred Cheves in the Treasury Department if the appointment did not come to him.[166] But Cheves had moved from South Carolina to Pennsylvania, and the Pennsylvania delegation did not back him. Instead they recommended Ingham, and Jackson decided to give this position to the man Pennsylvania wanted, since the support of this state had been of great stategic importance in his campaign.[167]

Perhaps there was something about his first interview with Jackson that forewarned McLane. Somehow, on the day of Jackson's arrival McLane suspected—or, at least, pretended to suspect—that he was out of the running for a cabinet position. "The conflicting claims of large states," he told James Bayard, "Crawford and Calhoun interests and original Jackson men, are so obvious, pressed in the person of powerful individuals with so much pertinacity, that a man of real pride coming from a small state politically opposed to the Admn. would be unwise to expect distinction." [168] "Del.," reported James A. Hamilton, meaning McLane, "is extremely anxious and figity [sic]. He would after Cheves be the Choice of the Whole South." [169]

Probably this was so. James Iredell of North Carolina put McLane first. "The appointment to the Treasury," he wrote, "that would be most acceptable to men of all the parties that compose the heterogeneous Jackson ranks, not only in our own State but throughout the Union, would be that of McLane of Delaware. He is one of the finest men I have ever seen; open, candid, independent as he is able and diligent in the discharge of his duties." [170] James A. Hamilton, of New York, testified to a similar regard for McLane's high standing when he advised Van Buren that if given an opportunity by Jackson to express an opinion on the Treasury appointment Van Buren ought to suggest that "the question as between Ingham an the two McLanes" (Louis McLane and John McLean) ought to be left "to Hamilton [of South Carolina], Drayton, McDuffie, Archer, Dickerson, Tazewell, with divers others. They will decide, depend upon it, in favor of McLane of Del." [171]

It was too late. James Iredell had sensed that the movement for McLane faced underground opposition. "There is a powerful influence here in his favor," he wrote, "but I fear there is a counter-influence which will prevent his appointment. I say, *I fear,* because I have no other authority than rumor and certain secret consultations, to which if nothing had been intended but the general good or the good of the party, I ought to have been privy." It was McLane's Federalism, he suspected, that had risen to defeat his expectation of preferment once again—or if not Federalism then his record of loyalty to Crawford. These things were important to men "who never could and never did thrive but in the hot bed of party." [172]

Perhaps it was to reach directly to Jackson's side, to appeal to the original Jackson influence that Van Buren sent a letter via his agent Hamilton to John Eaton, Jackson's close friend and biographer. But Hamilton did not deliver the letter. It reached him on Thursday, February 19. On the morning of that same day Hamilton met McLane and learned that the cabinet was pretty well set and that there was no place in it for McLane or Cheves.[173] McLane, in turn, had his information from Major Hamilton, who had been to see Jackson the previous evening.

Hamilton and other South Carolina Congressmen had been waiting for an invitation to discuss appointments with Jackson. They were annoyed that he was surrounded by Tennessee friends, such as Eaton and Major William Lewis, who were of little standing in the party nationally, and they were shocked by an announcement in Duff Green's *Telegraph* that Jackson would be happy to "consult all, in relation to the formation of his Cabinet who might think proper to visit him." This was undignified and even insulting to men of standing, they thought, and they held back till Vice-President Calhoun brought them a specific invitation from Jackson. Then, on Wednesday evening, February 18, Hamilton and Hayne called on Jackson and found that "the game" was "up both as to Cheves and McLane" and that Jackson had decided on Ingham. Jackson told them "he considered McLane as one of the first men in the Country, and that 'he should have laid his hand upon him' (to use his own words) but from the fact of his coming from a State in opposition, which would send a man of different politics from McLane to the Senate, and in the present critical State of politics in that body he could not spare him." If this were so, the Claytons had hurt McLane more than they knew.

Major Hamilton added to his letter a correct version of the cabinet, given him on Thursday, he said, by "that notorious Liar," Rumor, and "that veracious and sagacious politician," Thomas P. Moore. He did not like it. "I am perfectly cool," he wrote, in words he attributed to Sir Anthony Absolute, "damn cool—never half so cool in my life." [174]

McLane was even more upset. "Our old Cheif [sic] has fallen into evil Councils," he blurted out to Bayard, and then listed the cabinet, underlining Ingham's name, double underlining Eaton's, calling Branch an "old woman," and adding a word of the malicious gossip that was on many tongues in Washington: "Eaton, you know, has just married his mistress—and the mistress of 11 doz. others!!" [175]

It is interesting that McLane thought the disappointing cabinet was the work of Calhoun—interesting particularly because it suggests that he thought it possible that such Carolinians as Hamilton and Hayne, who were his friends, were not in perfect accord with the Vice-President. Calhoun's intercourse with Jackson, McLane noted, had been "constant," whereas the congressional leaders from South Carolina and Virginia had received no attention until the cabinet had been filled. He understood that John Eaton was Jackson's own choice for the War Department and that John Berrien of Georgia was Eaton's choice as Attorney General, but how Branch "was ever dreamed of" for Secretary of the Navy, McLane declared, "no one can tell."

This cabinet could not command public confidence, McLane told Van Buren, strongly intimating that the Magician should have no part of it but leave "these strange occurrences to run their own race." [176] Senator Elias Kane of Illinois, a transplanted Pennsylvanian (and a Bayard relation), agreed with McLane, both in condemning the cabinet and in advising Van Buren to stay out of it. He, too, suspected that the cabinet was of Calhoun's making, but after hearing Hayne condemn it roundly, he thought that Calhoun, Hayne's friend, could hardly be to blame.[177]

From his New York cronies in Washington, Van Buren got different advice. James A. Hamilton told him that in the cabinet "instead of being stale mated" he would "check mate" Calhoun. And he advised Van Buren that Cambreleng did not like McLane and urged adding to the cabinet Drayton, who would prove Van Buren's friend, "*au fond,*" not Calhoun's. Without confessing to being influenced by Cambreleng, Hamilton withdrew his previous advice that Van Buren write a strong recommendation of McLane if Jackson gave him an opening. "I now think that is not wise," he said; "responsible you must not be." A few days later he repeated the advice and assured Van Buren that Eaton and Branch would prove devoted friends and that Calhoun was quite disappointed with the cabinet.[178]

Rudolph Bunner, another New Yorker, joined his voice to Hamilton's and declared he spoke for Verplanck too, advising Van Buren that if he did not accept, "another less scrupulous would be brought in and not unlikely one who is now loudest against the present men." [179] He could have meant Hayne or Hamilton of South Carolina—and he could have meant McLane!

Nevertheless Van Buren made another effort to get McLane appointed to head the Treasury, motivated probably by a feeling that Ingham would prove unsatisfactory either as an administrator or as a patronage-dispensing politician. He enclosed his letter of acceptance in a long letter to Eaton—who was acting as the general's aide—in which he urged McLane's appointment. Just what he said, however, remains a mystery, for after being shown to the New York Hamilton, Major Lewis, and one or two others, the letter was destroyed.[180] The first Van Buren letter to Eaton about McLane, the one that Hamilton did not deliver, has also disappeared.

As late as February 25, Margaret Bayard Smith, who as a Washington hostess knew what was going on, still heard rumors that a cabinet post might be found for McLane.[181] These rumors were probably connected with a movement to get Eaton replaced in the War Department by John McLean—to "the deep, deep disappointment of Eaton," according to Van Buren's informant.[182] The objection to Eaton, James Gallatin reported to his famous father, who was particularly interested in events because he wanted an appointment to France, "is his wife, whom [*sic*] it is said is *not* as *she* should be. Mrs. Calhoun has refused to return her visit and would you believe it, that the lady who creates all this commotion is no other, than Albert's [his brother's] old flame Miss Peggy O'Neal."

Jackson at one time consented to replace Eaton, James Gallatin said, but when he saw that pressures were being brought on him "to effect other changes in the cabinet," he reinstated Eaton and declared "nothing on earth [would] induce him to again make a change." [183] To put a stop to all such efforts Jackson with his own hands gave the cabinet list to Duff Green and it appeared in the *Telegraph* on February 26. And as it was read—Secretary of State, Van Buren; Treasury, Ingham; Postmaster General, John McLean; Secretary of War, Eaton; Navy, Branch; Attorney General, Berrien—a comment was passed from lip to lip: "This is the millennium of the minnows." [184]

Van Buren and John McLean were generally excepted from the scathing criticism the appointments aroused. Ingham, Eaton, Branch, and Berrien were scarcely national figures. Major Hamilton, of South Carolina, had told Jackson with some truth that he had the opportunity of picking a brilliant cabinet, that he came to office unfettered and "was strong enough to cast aside the miserable political geography" which handicapped some other administrations—his strength would allow him to appoint all four of the leading cabinet members from the smallest state if those four men happened to be the best qualified.[185] And Thomas Ritchie, the Richmond editor, complained that the cabinet was "not of that splendid sort, which merits the confidence of his friends or dazzles and overawes his enemies." [186] Jackson's choices were so far from the brilliant appointments he might have made that even young Bob McLane at St. Mary's College—a prejudiced observer, of course—thought the appointments, aside from Van Buren, were not much.[187]

In a few days, according to Cambreleng, the clamor against the cabinet was silenced—"none rail but the 'tell-tale women.'" The "democracy," he said, was satisfied; the "federalist phalanx" was not. Complaints from South Carolina and Virginia only decreased Jackson's opinion of the political leaders of those states. The talk now was of who would lead the opposition. And "when Mrs. L[ivingston?], Mrs. H[ayne?], Mrs. S[tevenson?], and Mrs. McL[ane?] hold one of their caucuses ye gods what a storm."

But McLane had gone home. He had packed up Kitty and the children and set off for Wilmington, telling friends he was called away by his father's illness.[188] Probably embarrassment drove him off, for he was back on the 4th of March to attend a special session of Congress, and with him were his father and Bob, come to see the inauguration.[189]

The old collector apparently did not arrive in time to join a group of veteran Revolutionary officers who met on March 3 and adopted an address. Probably he was too weak to march with them on the morning of inauguration day from Brown's Hotel to Gadsby's and form an honorary escort for General Jackson to the Capitol.[190] Yet the old collector was not too feeble to win a prize he came to Washington to secure, his reappointment to office for another four years. It was his last appointment, and it was fitting that like his first it came to him from a soldier. From a soldier, too, that he honestly admired, almost idolized, as he had admired and idolized Washington. For though old Allen McLane was crude and cranky he was also bold and frank, and he made Jackson his man long before his more discreet son Louis saw fit to support the general.

Except for the pleasure of his father's reappointment, Louis must have felt some twinges of regret in March, 1829, for his rash attempt to carry Delaware for Jackson. Before the end of March the special session of Congress was adjourned and McLane returned to Delaware. There

Martin Van Buren found him when that gentleman, having delayed in Albany to wind up some business and then resign the governorship, was at last proceeding to Washington to take his new position.

According to Van Buren's reminiscences, he had en route experienced other gloomy interviews with men disappointed by Jackson's appointments—with Levi Woodbury in New York and Edward Livingston in Philadelphia—before he met McLane. But Louis McLane was more upset than either of these. After all, Livingston had been offered the mission to France but had turned it down. And McLane's "personal expectations in regard to the composition of the Cabinet," these are Van Buren's recollections, "had been higher and, as he and his friends supposed, better founded than those of Mr. Woodbury."

McLane met Van Buren at New Castle, where the Magician was to disembark from the river boat that brought him down the Delaware to take the stage across the head of the Delmarva Peninsula to Frenchtown, Maryland, the landing place for the Chesapeake Bay steamers. Even before Van Buren landed, he recognized McLane in the crowd on the wharf and noted the marks of "disappointment and deep mortification" on his "intelligent countenance." McLane slipped his arm in Van Buren's as he reached him and proposed they stroll out on the New Castle and Frenchtown turnpike to have time for a private chat before the stage caught up with them. "The stagecoach . . . was sufficiently delayed," as Van Buren recalled the event, "to give us a tramp, not a little fatiguing to me in my state of health." While they walked McLane poured forth his feelings in an "excited harangue." The burden of his complaint was that under the influence of evil counselors Jackson had made appointments that degraded his administration. Knowing that Van Buren had resigned the governorship of New York to enter the cabinet, McLane could not urge him to refuse to serve with such second-rate ministers as Eaton, Branch, Berrien, and Ingham, but had to content himself with an earnest and emphatic plea for the necessity of great changes in the government if there was to be any hope of its success.[191]

Probably this passionate recommendation on the turnpike road had its effect. Even if Van Buren cast furtive glances over his shoulder in hope the stage would soon catch up and free him from his energetic companion, he still felt a sympathy for McLane's complaints that arose out of more serious substance than just his customary amiability. "There was probably not one of these malcontents," he wrote, thinking of Hamilton and Woodbury and Ritchie and others as well as McLane, "more disappointed than myself by the composition of the administration."[192] This was stretching the truth a bit, for he was in the cabinet and the others were not. But Van Buren proved the honesty of his pretensions—and the effectiveness of McLane's fervent harangue—by quickly arranging a cabinet opening for the Delawarean.

Some years later Van Buren regretted his friendliness to McLane. "He never had it in his power to be—neither did I ever believe he was or would be of service to me," Van Buren declared in his *Autobiography*, arguing that his motives in helping McLane were not selfish. Indeed, by his account, his partiality for McLane, the offer of the place of Attorney General and the appointments, "in regular succession and within a briefer period than any one man ever held them, to the distinguished posts of Minister to England, Secretary of the Treasury and Secretary of State of the United States," for all of which McLane was indebted to Van Buren— these "repeated and successful efforts to advance him," declared Van Buren, "produced an abundant crop of dissatisfaction and even alienation in the circle of my old political friendships."

How was it, Van Buren wondered to himself—and for public consumption, since his autobiography was his apologia—"that I should have overlooked indications of an overweening care for self that ought to have put me on my guard"? [193]

Was it merely an excess of geniality that led Van Buren to befriend McLane? More likely it was a sensible recognition of McLane's ability, a shared admiration of some common friends, a desire to strengthen the administration on which Van Buren built his own future by the proper employment of McLane's talents. It hardly occurred to him to be cautious. Was it likely that a man tainted with membership in a lost party, an open and avowed Federalist, representative of a state so tiny as to carry no political weight—was it likely that such a man could ever become a rival? It was not for immediate selfish personal advantage that Van Buren befriended McLane; it was to aid his cause and aid his country.

9

Mission to England

I THE APPOINTMENT

Jackson decided on appointments to the two most important diplomatic positions overseas without consulting Van Buren, who did not reach Washington until April, 1829. The mission to Great Britain was offered to Senator Littleton Waller Tazewell, a Norfolk lawyer who, though an eccentric (perhaps *because* an eccentric), seemed to his contemporaries to be the epitome of a high-minded Virginia statesman. The mission to France was offered to Senator Edward Livingston of Louisiana, the transplanted New Yorker who had won the affection of the Jackson family in New Orleans.

It was no disappointment to Van Buren when both of these men refused the appointments offered them. Tazewell suited Calhoun better than he did Van Buren [1] and would have proved a particularly difficult minister for the Secretary of State to control. His reputation as a member of Congress and as a diplomatist exceeded Van Buren's own; he had first entered Congress, in John Marshall's place, in 1800, he was now chairman of the Senate Committee on Foreign Relations, and he had been mentioned almost as prominently as Van Buren as a likely Jacksonian Secretary of State. As a Senator, he had disagreed with Van Buren on some questions concerning American relations with Great Britain, and he had published his views in a series of newspaper essays, republished in London as a pamphlet. [2] Tazewell's refusal and Livingston's gave Van Buren an opportunity to pay off some political debts and also to assure himself of agreeable colleagues to help develop his foreign policy.

Domestic politics, to Van Buren, came before foreign affairs. The vacancy at London seemed to him a chance to strengthen the cabinet by bringing in McLane at the post he had originally designed for him, Attorney General. If, that is, Jackson's first choice as Attorney General could be shifted to the London mission. Jackson consented readily enough; a message was sent off to the Attorney General-designate, John McPherson Berrien, who was in Georgia packing to come to Washington. Van Buren assumed that Berrien would be glad to go to London, a post generally considered very desirable.[3]

Before Berrien could answer, Van Buren despatched James A. Hamilton to Wilmington to quiet his excitable friend's complaints about the cabinet with an offer of Berrien's place. A letter could hardly be trusted to do the work in view of the passionate feeling McLane had shown in his walk with Van Buren on the Frenchtown turnpike. And he had already once spurned the suggestion of becoming Attorney General. Now, however, since nothing else was available he might take the position if Hamilton's personal attention could flatter him a bit and blunt the edge of his anger.

Hamilton traveled by stage with all the haste possible and reached McLane's Market Street house in Wilmington before breakfast. The two men talked the matter over at length.[4] McLane was—or seemed to be—reluctant to accept. But to reject the position of Attorney General was easier for McLane in January, when there was hope of getting something better, than in April, after the Jackson government had once completely passed him by. His Senate term still had four years to run, but reelection appeared unlikely. Besides, a man lost character, McLane thought, by staying too long in Congress. Better to accept the place Van Buren now made for him and take a gamble on moving from it to something better.

Was it altogether a gamble? According to James A. Hamilton, it was not, for he recollected being authorized to promise McLane that on the death of Supreme Court Justice Gabriel Duvall, "who was very aged and infirm," or upon the creation of any other vacancy on the Supreme Court bench, he, Louis McLane, would be appointed to the place. This was a most attractive prospect for a man with nine children to support and with a tenth expected within the month. It was especially attractive to a politician who had lost control of his state, for it meant security combined with prestige. It meant that Louis McLane could free himself from dependence on the electorate of Delaware and could settle his family at Bohemia on their ancestral acres—theirs if not his—while he divided his time between court and countryside. And in the latter, at Bohemia, he could stroll and ride to his heart's content, and play the country gentleman, like a Randolph or a Milligan.

After their talk, Hamilton returned to Washington, fairly sure of his man. "McLane hesitated," Hamilton told a friend, "but will consent by letter."⁵ McLane must have thought he had given Hamilton a contrary notion, for when he sent his acceptance to Washington, he enclosed it in a note to Hamilton in which he declared, "You will see by the enclosed that you are a better negotiator than you supposed." Hamilton's opinion of himself was such that there was little at which he was better than he supposed. But McLane was too much obsessed by his own problems. "I have taken this step reluctantly," he told Hamilton, "and with fearful forebodings. I am not . . . in a situation to consult all my feelings, much less to be fastidious. . . . I have launched my bark on a new sea."⁶ To Van Buren, McLane explained in detail that he acted for the sake of his large family and his friends. As to the latter, McLane meant that his acceptance of a cabinet post would strengthen Van Buren's hand in intraparty maneuvers as against the Calhoun faction and such original Jackson men as Eaton and Lewis.

McLane hinted to Van Buren that he would have preferred another post to the attorney generalship, but he was not specific about what he had in mind.⁷ It turned out, however, that Van Buren had acted too hastily in offering the cabinet post to McLane by special courier; Berrien, to everyone's surprise, turned down the English mission. Thereupon it was offered to McLane, under the impression, according to Van Buren's recollections, that it was the place he wanted. "But," wrote Van Buren, "we were destined to further disappointment," on receiving McLane's response.⁸

It was not a refusal that disappointed Van Buren, for McLane did not refuse the position in London. It was the manner of his acceptance that was disappointing. His letter was not gracious; it was condescending. McLane was proud, and it hurt him to have been neglected in Jackson's original appointments. He could not afford to refuse the positions thus tardily offered him, but to accept first one and then the other was to eat crow twice in two days. He confessed his embarrassment and his reluctance to Van Buren, but he made it clear that he thought his acceptance was not merely profitable to himself but to his party and his country as well. "Considering," he told Van Buren, "the impropriety of exposing *you* and the President to too many rejected offers as to this Mission at this period of the administration, and understanding from your letter that your individual views are in favor of this determination, I will accept."

But this time he made very clear what he eventually wanted; by accepting, he said, he hoped to conserve his chance "for what I will frankly tell you would make me happier than any other worldly honor—the bench." With remarkable candor he confessed to hopes of taking particular advantage of the position. Kitty was expecting a child in early May, so he would go abroad alone and "husband sufficient resources to *relieve* rather than embarrass my private affairs." If he succeeded in an unexplained "commercial arrangement" in that time, he wished to be allowed to come home; if public service demanded that he stay abroad, Kitty and the family could then join him, for his brother meanwhile could have advantageously closed out his business. What this business was remains a mystery, but he had, he confessed—indeed, he proudly claimed—taken "counsel of Mrs. McL. whose judgement has generally guided me in a correct path." [9]

McLane's appointment annoyed John Quincy Adams. "This," he wrote in his diary concerning it, "is the most painful incident to me which has occurred since the change of the Administration, and it proves the utter heartlessness of Van Buren. . . . McLane is utterly incompetent to the mission to London, and if he does not disgrace the country, will effect nothing for her interest. His only merit is the sale of himself and his Crawford stock to Jackson. But he will give him and Van Buren trouble. No Administration can make bad appointments abroad with impunity." [10]

Adams, as usual, thought his course and his cause sanctified. Not every New England observer agreed with him. One, Francis Baylies, writing before McLane's appointment, proposed him for the English mission because of his personal talents and his party connection. "His talents," Baylies wrote, "certainly are of a high order. In the H. of R. no man could compete so successfully with Webster as Mr. McLane. . . . He is correct, conciliating and spirited; he would give no insult, and he would receive none." As to his Federalism: "that is a circumstance in his favor. In the settlement of our difficulties with G.B. much depends on good will, and you well know that the Federalists labour under the stigma of British partialities." [11]

It was perfectly true as Adams suggested that McLane had no experience in diplomacy, but only Adams's bitterness about the turning of the Crawford party to Jackson blinded him to the talents that had advanced a member of a forlorn party from a tiny state to an important position in Congress. Moreover, McLane's very lack of experience abroad made the enterprise peculiarly challenging to him. He approached it with the same determination to learn and to succeed that had been his when he first entered Congress.

However Adams might snort, Van Buren had made a good appointment. Baylies had assessed McLane's capacity better than the embittered expert diplomatist.

II THE SECRETARY

Between appointment and departure four months intervened, busy months, anxious months. For the usual reasons, Catherine McLane had to stay at home when her husband traveled to the capital in April for preliminary conferences on his mission, but the social support that Kitty usually gave Louis could now be offered by Rebecca, their oldest daughter. Rebecca was fifteen, of an age to be introduced "gradually" to Washington society when she was invited by Major William Lewis to pass a few days with his daughter Mary Ann, Rebecca's schoolmate, at the President's mansion, where Major Lewis lived.[12] There McLane left Rebecca on Monday, April 27, 1829, while he rejoined Van Buren and James A. Hamilton at Mrs. Miller's boardinghouse.

For two days Louis McLane was too busy—with the President or at the State Department—to see his daughter. His business was preliminary to the preparation of instructions for the mission abroad. The main issues in the relations between the United States and Great Britain— trade with the British West Indies, navigation of the St. Lawrence, impressment and neutral rights in wartime—had a long and a tangled history, which McLane now had to master. Much of it was generally familiar to him through his service in Congress in all but two of the years since the end of the War of 1812, but a general familiarity was no longer enough. Now he must know individual notes and despatches, statutes and orders, in detail, and be able to thread his way among them so as to cite the passages most favorable to the American position.

And then there was the American position itself to be determined. This being a new administration, brought into office in opposition to its predecessor, an opportunity existed to change or modify old positions. These were but preliminary meetings; the details could be mastered later. But still his labors, he told Kitty, were "arduous and incessant," and he suspected he had "indiscretely assumed" a mission which had little chance of success.[13]

In addition to diplomatic affairs, there were various matters of politics to discuss. While McLane was in Washington the post of minister to France, refused by Edward Livingston, was offered to William Cabell Rives, of Virginia, and although there is no proof that McLane was consulted about the appointment, it seems likely that he was in view of the fact that the invitation to Rives came after McLane had been in Washington and living with Van Buren for one week.[14] Besides, it was planned, Van Buren told Rives, to send the two ministers abroad on the same ship.[15]

Some time must also have been devoted to the selection of a secretary of the legation, with Van Buren determining the final choice. Suggestions came from every direction, for the post in London, though expensive, was popular. At Baltimore, where McLane visited General Sam Smith on the way to the capital, Jaspar Lynch was pressed on him.[16] At home in Wilmington, he had been visited by a Judge John McLean, of Seneca, New York, who proposed himself for secretary and bore recommendations from Branch and Berrien of the new cabinet. Louis was not impressed, and the Albany Regency was absolutely hostile; a false rumor of the judge's appointment and confirmation was published, but it was quickly denied.[17]

Suggestions came from every direction, even from William Henry Crawford and Nicholas Biddle.[18] McLane's choice was Asbury Dickins, the chief clerk in the Treasury Department, a man of whose ability he had become well aware in times past. But Dickins, McLane was told, presumably by Van Buren, could not be spared from his present post. Finally the appointment was offered by Van Buren, with the permission of Jackson and the "cordial approbation" of McLane, to Theodore Lyman, Jr., a wealthy Bostonian, who was eager for a political position. Lyman, Van Buren thought, could as well afford London life as the incumbent, William B. Lawrence, a young New York lawyer.[19]

Apparently a position overseas was not to Lyman's choice. Soon Van Buren was addressing John Treat Irving, apparently at the suggestion of John Nicholson, of the Navy, supported by James Kirke Paulding, to ask whether Irving's brother, the distinguished writer, would accept the appointment. The President, Van Buren cautioned, had not been consulted, but McLane had. Apparently the answer was favorable. Early in June, announcement was made of the appointment of Washington Irving as secretary of the legation of the United States to Great Britain.[20]

We do not know what Louis McLane thought of the appointment initially. It added prestige to his mission to have such a man in his train, for the English knew Irving better than any other American writer except Cooper. On the other hand, this man was certainly not McLane's choice. He was a year older than McLane and more distinguished (except in political circles); would he not cast Louis in the shade? Louis McLane was not the man to enjoy such a situation.

Yet to hint at dissatisfaction is but to speculate. Not one word about the appointment survives from McLane's pen. After all, this appointment was less important to his career than to Irving's. That gentleman might well have declined. He was living in Spain and not eager to give up his quiet habits, for he had an unfinished book on his hands,

The Alhambra; he had sought life in an out-of-the-way corner because
he was somewhat horrified by the bustle of affairs in the great world.
But he was drawn to it, too, for the chance to observe important affairs
close at hand attracted him, and when friends counseled him to accept the appointment, he acted on their advice. When someone suggested to Irving that he should have been the minister, he answered
that he would rather have people think him in too low than in too
high a place.[21] It was, after all, as the New York *Argus* pointed out, a
subordinate position, without trying responsibility. "The appointment
. . . smacks of the sense of those good old times," the friendly *Argus*
continued, "when such men as Chaucer were sent abroad on embassies,
as a sample of the land." [22]

III   THE SCANDAL

Rebecca McLane had a gay time in Washington and seemed, her indulgent father thought, to have become "quite a favorite" at the President's mansion. "She sings for the President," Louis reported to Kitty,
"and has read to him and translated for him several of his french [*sic*]
letters which but for her assistance he could not have understood." On
Thursday evening Louis dined at the President's with Rebecca and a
large company of ladies. On Friday evening father and daughter dined
with Charles Richard Vaughan, the British minister, and then went
to the May ball. Rebecca was dressed "plain but well, having selected
. . . her own dress" from her father's purse "to the amount of a little
more than $15." On Saturday evening they dined with the Dutch
minister and his wife. On Sunday Rebecca, with Mary Ann Lewis, went
off on a jaunt to Woodlawn Plantation in Virginia, and from there on
Monday to neighboring Mount Vernon.

"She was quite an object of admiration. . . . She was thought quite
pretty," Louis assured Kitty. "Madame Huygens said she was very like
you." And he told Kitty of taking Rebecca to call on Mrs. Cornelius Van
Ness, wife of the newly appointed minister to Spain, and on Mrs. Decatur, widow of the naval hero, both of them leaders of Washington
society.[23] But he did not mention—at least not in the surviving letters—
another social call that Rebecca made in Washington. It was a visit to
Mrs. John Eaton, wife of the Secretary of War, and our record of it
comes from the pen of President Jackson. "Miss McLean of Delaware,"
he wrote, "by the instructions of her father, visited her." [24]

A visit to Mrs. John Eaton was important to President Jackson, because he was battling Washington gossips to preserve that lady's standing and reputation. "Slander has gone abroad," reported Postmaster

General Barry. The slander was directed at Mrs. Eaton, a recent bride
of a cabinet member and only slightly less recent widow of a purser in
the Navy. Mrs. Eaton's first husband, John Timberlake, had taken his
own life at the American Mediterranean headquarters, Port Mahon, in
the Balearic Islands. Slanderous rumor declared that the lady, as Mrs.
Timberlake, had been more friendly than she should have been to
General Eaton.

Such slander touched a sore point in the chivalric armor of President
Jackson. Eaton, who was his campaign biographer, was a favorite; so
was Mrs. Eaton, whom Jackson had known as Peggy O'Neale when as
a Congressman he stayed at her father's Washington hotel. When Eaton
had consulted Jackson about his plans to marry, Jackson urged him to
disregard gossip. Besides the fact that he liked both John Eaton and
Peggy, the President's defense of them was motivated by memory,
recent memory, of the gossip circulated during the campaign about his
late wife and her first marriage.

Peggy O'Neale Timberlake Eaton bore very little resemblance to
Rachel Donelson Jackson except that both had suffered from gossip
and innuendo. "There is an aristocracy here," Postmaster General Barry
explained, "claiming preference for birth or wealth, and demanding
obeisance from others. . . . Mrs. Eaton was the daughter of a Tavernkeeper belonging to the democracy; she has by good fortune (if it may
be so considered) moved into the fashionable world. This has touched
the pride of the self-constituted great, awakened the jealousy of the
malignant and envious, and led to the basest calumny" [25]

Jackson never lost faith in Peggy. "I will never abandon an old and
well tried friend for new ones for slight or trivial causes," he explained
to an old friend, Richard K. Call, who believed the gossip; "nor will I
ever be *silent* when female character is wantonly assailed, and my name,
or those of my family, falsely introduced to give weight as to the truth
of the charge." As evidence of the false stories that were being circulated, Jackson told his friend a story that was being passed around
about the McLanes. Rebecca McLane, according to this tale, concealed
from her mother the fact that she had visited Mrs. Eaton in Washington.
But the secret was not to be kept. In traveling through Baltimore, Mrs.
McLane heard of her daughter's indiscretion in calling on Mrs. Eaton,
"and so great was the shock that she . . . well nigh fainted."

"This is the story," wrote Jackson. But reconcile it if you can with
the fact that this same Mrs. McLane, when visiting in Washington with
her husband, called on Mrs. Eaton. So also did Mrs. Rives. "What a
ridiculous attitude," it seemed to Jackson, "must the conduct of such

ladies as these place those in, who think *they* are too *good* to visit Mrs. Eaton." [26]

Quite probably Jackson knew whereof he wrote. This letter of his was dated July 5, and there was sufficient time since the birth of Catherine Mary for her mother to have visited Washington and called on Mrs. Eaton. And certainly Kitty would have done so if she thought it would help her husband's career. Yet McLane, with his strict Methodist upbringing, confessed he was uneasy about the tone of Washington society.[27] Probably he agreed with William Barry, who wrote, "If rumour were to be credited, but few handsome ladies in the fashionable world in this city would be free from blemish." [28]

IV   THE COLLECTOR'S DEATH

Louis had been eager to get away from Washington in order to be with Kitty when their child was born. To get away all the sooner, he tried to avoid a diplomatic dinner that Jackson, who was "all kindness," planned to give for him.[29] Probably he did avoid the dinner, for Jackson fell ill. And he did return to Wilmington in time for Kitty's accouchement.

Catherine Mary was born May 12, 1829, the eleventh McLane child and the second to be named for her mother. Except for the first Catherine, all the McLane children were living. Yet, in this season, when the McLanes seemed particularly blessed with vitality the old collector came to the end of his days. "Your dear old grandfather . . . has changed very much in the last few days and is now rapidly going to his last and I devoutly pray and believe his happy rest," Louis informed Robert, at school in Baltimore, on May 20; "he is quite composed and resigned to the will of his maker." [30] In two days he was dead, in his eighty-third year. The trip to Jackson's inauguration had been his last campaign.

A long train followed his body in funeral procession to the little graveyard beside Asbury Methodist Church, at Third and Walnut Streets, Wilmington. For two days after his death flags were displayed at half-mast in the port of Wilmington and on the revenue cutter, Captain Polk commanding, lying at New Castle. State legislator, speaker of the house, member of the privy council, justice of the peace and, as such, a judge of the court of common pleas, federal marshal, and finally collector of customs, Allen McLane was preeminently remembered as his old political enemy, Hezekiah Niles, recalled him, "a gallant soldier of the revolution." Members of the Pennsylvania State Society of the

Cincinnati wore crape on the left arm for thirty days in his memory.[31]

Before he died, intrigues about his place were well under way. The collectorship was, one Democrat declared, the most reputable federal post in Delaware, worth, in perquisites and fees, $1,200 a year.[32] As the collector's health declined, his successor became the "general topic," according to the Wilmington postmaster, and even the possibility of some turnover in subordinate posts became a matter of speculation.[33] Speculation was soon hushed by the appointment of Henry Whiteley to the collectorship, probably a reward to Whiteley for his self-abnegation in the congressional election of 1827, when he stepped aside to allow the Jacksonians to concentrate on Bayard.[34]

What was left of the modest fortune of Allen McLane went mainly to Louis, it was discovered when the collector's will was probated on May 29. For Rebecca Worrell and her family "ample provision" had already been made, it said. Four properties—one only a lot—were left to Dr. Allen. To Louis went the collector's house on French Street, Wilmington, two other houses near it, and two groups of small lots nearby, with wooden tenements and a stable. And also to Louis went the residue of his father's estate.[35] Even if he could still realize nothing from the assignment of his father's claims on the ships from Amelia Island, this new bequest would help make life in England possible for the McLanes.

V   THE INSTRUCTIONS

Meantime work had to go forward on the official instructions of the minister to Great Britain. James A. Hamilton was assigned to help McLane review Anglo-American relations, and Cambreleng, for the House Committee on Commerce, as well as several merchants, was called on for advice. McLane had second thoughts about his wisdom in accepting the English mission and urged that Hamilton be sent with him, the two to form a special commission; when their main object was achieved, Hamilton would remain as resident minister and McLane could escape home. However, Hamilton soon left Washington to accept appointment as district attorney in New York.[36]

Besides the Northeast boundary problem, on which Albert Gallatin labored until it was submitted to the King of the Netherlands for arbitration, the chief issue between Great Britain and the United States was the trade of the British West Indian colonies. This was a trade that Americans had thrived on before the Revolution, but from which they found themselves repulsed—with some exceptions—after they became free. For some time after the Revolution the British were unwilling to make any kind of commercial treaty with the United States, and when they finally did make such a treaty, their West Indian colonies were exempted from its details. After the War of 1812 various attempts were made by American ministers at London—by Richard Rush, Rufus King, Albert Gallatin, James Barbour—to open this trade, but though the two countries came close to agreement on terms, acrimony fostered by the lengthy quarrel led Britain to close her West Indian ports to American ships in 1826. Thereupon President Adams put into operation American laws to the same effect.

Terms offered by the British in 1825 had come to seem fairly acceptable to the Americans, but when Adams's emissaries tried to treat with the British government on these terms, they met a cold reception. The last of Adams's three ministers to Great Britain, James Barbour, did report hearing George Hamilton-Gordon, fourth Earl of Aberdeen, the British Foreign Secretary, express a desire in 1829 to open the trade, but Barbour felt that the high American tariff of 1828 and the fear of British shippers that Americans would monopolize the carrying trade would prevent Aberdeen from taking any action.[37] Yet Barbour, like McLane a onetime Crawford supporter, was willing to stay in England and do what he could for the new administration.[38]

Rumors began to circulate—and to be published by anti-Jackson papers—that the new administration was instructing McLane to trade American tariff reductions for reciprocal advantages in British markets. One paper suggested that England would reduce the corn laws and the United States the tariff on manufactures. Hezekiah Niles heard that the British were expected to grant favorable duties on American tobacco. Could a treaty, Niles asked, be used to lower a tariff set by act of Congress? [39]

Niles need not have worried about reduction of the tariff by treaty. McLane himself was opposed to the idea. No tariff reduction should be offered the English as an equivalent for any concession, he told Van Buren. The tariff was a domestic matter; to offer to negotiate it would embarrass the administration at home and give the British a pretext for setting up new pretensions. But—they could be told "in *conversation*" that the present government was disposed to modify the tariff and ultimately to promote the kind of liberal trade policy avowed by Great Britain.

This was not the only advice McLane had for the Secretary of State. In a long letter of June 11 he practically gave Van Buren material for his instructions. On two issues, impressment of sailors and navigation of the St. Lawrence, nothing was necessary, wrote McLane, except to refer him to "the principles and general directions already given" to his predecessors —unless, that is, Van Buren or the President had new views.

On the question of trade with the British West Indies, it was desirable to get Britain to allow the United States once again the terms offered in 1825—terms that Adams had been too slow to accept. Whether these would be offered would depend on the temper and interest of the British government, on European affairs, on the effects of British colonial policy on the islands. This trade, after all, was not as important as the papers made it. (Niles would have agreed with McLane on this point.) By way of the British northern colonies and the neutral islands—particularly Danish St. Thomas and Swedish St. Bartholomew's—American trade with the British West Indies was as extensive as ever. It was, however, annoyingly indirect and liable to burdensome duties.

On a method of reviving the discussion of this trade, McLane's suggestion was one that angered the opposition when it became known—though it was then blamed on Van Buren, presumably the author of the instructions, rather than on McLane. Delicately, but candidly, disconnect this administration, he advised, from the errors of its predecessors. (This meant Adams's errors for the last twelve years, eight as Secretary of State and four as President.) Make clear to the British that foreign policy was an issue of the recent campaign, and that the people, by choosing Jackson over Adams, had applied a "constitutional corrective," selecting an administration with better views and a different policy. It is now up to Britain to seize this opportunity to subdue "inveterate prejudices" and lay the foundation of future harmony, including commercial reciprocity.

As to the method, said McLane, there was no need to insist on a treaty or a convention, as past administrations were inclined to do. If the British wished to settle arrangements by statute law, let us be satisfied. Then, if the British were sincere in offering to open their West Indian ports in 1825, we could get them to revive the offer. It should be of advantage to us, for opening these ports would strengthen our commercial interests and raise an adversary to the extravagant demands of the manufacturers. Otherwise, the advantages of this trade were worth no great concessions.

Finally, cautioned McLane, keep this letter out of State Department files. Knowledge that it would remain confidential allowed him to state that Tazewell, writing public letters over the signature of Senex, was damaging the American position, for he put the United States in the wrong throughout the negotiation.[40] Perhaps McLane, true to his nature, was speaking out of jealousy of the man who had first been offered the English mission. Probably not, however—or not solely for this reason. It was his nature to be shrewd and intelligent too, and we know that James Barbour, in London, reacted similarly to Tazewell's Senex letters.[41]

As finally written, a month later, the instructions reflected McLane's advice and enlarged upon it. Our aim, said Van Buren, is to put trade with the British colonies on the same basis as trade with Britain itself. There are grounds on which our position is assailable: we resisted British protective tariffs, though we do so no more; we would not allow British ships arriving here from the colonies to clear for any port except the ports they came from; we did not accept the reasonable terms offered by Britain in 1825. Master all the explanatory circumstances so as to put the best face possible on our position. Then frankly and fully explain Jackson's desire to end this protracted dispute. No long discussions are needed; Jackson wants to be able to make some report on this subject to Congress when its next session opens.

You can say that the United States will open its ports to British vessels from the colonies on the same basis as to vessels from Britain if American shipping is admitted to the colonies under the terms of the act of 1825. You cannot promise "most-favored-nation" status because some countries allow our ships to bring goods originating anywhere to their ports, as Britain does not, and of course we extend these countries the same privilege. If the British complain of our tariff, refer to their corn laws. If they complain of our slowness in accepting their 1825 offer, your experience in Congress will allow you to explain the situation as far as you think right and proper. Those responsible for the delay (Van Buren meant the Adams administration) themselves abandoned the claims they at first put forth, and we do not revive them. Our policy has the approval of the American electorate. And whereas we formerly sought an arrangement by treaty while the British desired one by statute law, we are now willing to make the arrangement in whichever way they prefer.[42]

Among the Van Buren papers are notes indicating that Van Buren may have been willing to consider permitting the British to restrict the exportation of sugar and coffee in American ships to one half of the inward cargo. Similarly he thought it might be specified that the United States would allow no drawback (that is, repayment of the tariff) on the reexport of West Indian products brought to the States in American vessels.[43]

Another issue between the two countries was the right of the United States to the navigation of the St. Lawrence and to a place of deposit on its bank. Avoid connecting it with the West India negotiation, Van Buren cautioned, but be careful to do nothing that would "countenance the supposition" that our government has yielded its ground. More instructions will be sent on this question if you need them, but instructions sent to Gallatin and Barbour on this matter still express our position correctly.

As for piracy and the issues of wartime, continued Van Buren, we have been awaiting an English proposition, for our proposals have been offered in vain. Without questioning the action of his predecessors, Jackson feels we should be more active. Declare our readiness to discuss these issues, particularly impressment, for if either country goes to war, the practice of impressment immediately causes trouble.[44]

It was Van Buren's clear desire to remove all existing differences between the United States and Great Britain. His instructions were like an olive branch that McLane was to carry across the sea.

VI   THE DEPARTURE

Late in his life Martin Van Buren reminisced about the missions of Louis McLane and William Rives. In August, 1829, when they sailed from New York on the frigate *Constellation,* they were both "capable young men," "covetous of fame," possessing the requisite "energy, industry, and perseverance" to succeed in their negotiations and bring them close to the great goal—the Presidency—to which they aspired as keenly "and perhaps as confidently" as any of their contemporaries.[45]

Perhaps, in hindsight, Van Buren transfers his own aspirations to these two men. Though McLane was always ambitious, it is likely that in 1829 his sights were set on a position less exalted than the Presidency. If we take him at his word, there is no question of what position he desired, for he expressed himself clearly to Major Lewis, Jackson's confidential adviser: "There is no office under our Constitution which I would prefer to the office of a judge of the Supreme Court." He accepted the mission to England, he told Lewis, in a spirit of sacrifice, in order not to embarrass an administration which had already received one refusal of this post: "I scarcely permitted myself to count the cost of the step I felt it my duty to take." [46]

It would cost McLane a pretty penny, no doubt of that. His salary was $9,000 a year, which had to cover all his expenses. He was allowed a sum equal to a year's salary for what was called his outfit—expenses that were incurred in changing his place of residence—and promised a quarter of that sum for his return. His salary, moreover, did not begin when he was appointed or when his appointment was confirmed or when he accepted the invitation, nor yet on April 27 when he reported to Van Buren in Washington to begin his work. Only from June 20 was his salary to be paid, because he had told the department he would be ready to go to England on that date.[47]

As long as McLane was in Congress, he could to some degree continue his law practice. Now he was forced to give it up completely, to transport his family abroad (Kitty and nine children were to follow him on a passenger ship), and to set up his domestic establishment in an expensive city, where he would be thrown into daily association with the most opulent society in the world. No wonder that McLane's friend, Major James Hamilton, Jr., of South Carolina, said that he almost regretted McLane's acceptance, notwithstanding his eminent qualifications for the London post, because "with his large family he can for the next four years do nothing for his children however much he may add, as I am sure he will, to his present reputation." [48]

McLane's plan, of course, was to complete his mission and return, his reputation enhanced, in much less than four years. Perhaps he heard from William Crawford the same advice that Van Buren received: "The salaries of our foreign ministers are so low" that no one should take an appointment abroad for more than twelve months.[49] However much the appointment would cost him, McLane would go through with it. He was pleased with the instructions and told Van Buren so. But immediately he began worrying about the trip. "For a truly great man," Van Buren thought, and this unnecessary praise is significant, "he has more littleness about him than usual." [50]

Van Buren was unsympathetic because he could not put himself in McLane's place. Not only was McLane exposing himself to serious financial loss, he was about to suffer a hard personal deprivation in being separated from all his family, except Robert, who was sailing with him. He had reason to worry about how his wife would cross the ocean with nine children, one just born. And he also had reason, serious reason, to worry about how he himself would weather the voyage.

"Soda powders, Seidlitz Powders, Saratoga water, lemmon syrup, orange syrup, and flour water, ginger syrup, etc.," were the remedies he urged on Kitty,[51] and it is likely that he similarly prepared himself for the voyage, for he knew the sea and his own physical inability to cope with it from his experience as a midshipman.

A special difficulty arose to interfere with McLane's departure when his son Louis—"his favorite son," Van Buren said—became seriously ill.[52] But the boy recovered in time for McLane to leave with his mind at peace in this regard, at least. At that, the departure was delayed several times. The original plan was to board the *Constellation* at Cape May, at the mouth of the Delaware. But for some reason the place of departure was changed to New York, and then there was a delay till Rives and his wife returned to the city from trips they made, first to Niagara Falls and Albany, and then to Boston.[53]

Before McLane left home, Van Buren came up from Washington to Wilmington to give him the formal written instructions and also to pass on some more confidential instructions orally. Van Buren had thought of having a little conclave if James A. Hamilton and Cambreleng could meet him in Wilmington and all go on down to Cape May together. But his own caution interfered with his plan. He was somewhat apprehensive, he told Hamilton, that a meeting of McLane and Cambreleng, "the anti-tariff champion," might stir up the opposition press in fright that McLane was being instructed to sacrifice protective tariffs for West Indian trade. "Cam," Van Buren wrote, "would turn up his nose at this in great contempt, but there is more in small matters than he is always aware of." [54]

Cambreleng took the hint, particularly after he heard that the *Constellation* would sail from New York, for then he knew that the "Cape May expedition" would be called off and that he would have a chance to see McLane in New York. As to Van Buren's fears, "I see the old ghost is still fliting before him," Cambreleng wrote in a letter he did not send: "I do not wish to increase his apprehensions or be an unwelcome visitor to any of the party." [55]

Even though Cambreleng did not come to Wilmington, rumors eventually became current about a Wilmington conspiracy, a secret meeting of Van Buren, McLane, and Cambreleng at which it was agreed to offer Britain a reduced tariff in return for trade concessions. [56] Had Cambreleng come to Wilmington and attended a public banquet in McLane's honor in the town hall on July 22, he would have been acutely unhappy, for prominent on the list of toasts was one to "domestic industry and internal improvements." Another toast was to "the middle states" and a third to "the memories of Jay and Hamilton—the able coadjutors of the venerable Madison"—a bit of Federal Republicanism that must have amused Martin Van Buren, if he read of it in the paper. [57]

When Van Buren arrived, he spent about a week in Wilmington, though for part of the time he may have been employed in social intercourse with the party that accompanied him, which included Mrs. Andrew Jackson Donelson, the President's niece and hostess, who made a visit to Philadelphia. There should have been plenty of time for Van Buren to talk politics and diplomacy with McLane, but the illness of young Louis distracted his father. [58] It occurred to Van Buren on returning to Washington that he had forgotten to suggest to McLane that in view of newspaper speculations regarding "the character" of his instructions, it would be important to inform the British foreign office of his views, informally, as soon as possible after his arrival. [59]

Van Buren could and did make this point in McLane's formal instructions, and also urged McLane and Rives to maintain friendly relations and keep in close touch with each other, particularly since London and Paris would be able to maintain a much closer contact than either could have with the State Department. [60]

When McLane got to New York, Cambreleng had opportunity enough to talk to him, and there was much he wanted to say: that the English were turning to free trade doctrines, that Adams had misunderstood America's interests and refused reasonable proposals, that when Gallatin attempted to reopen negotiations the English were unwilling to negotiate with an "American System" government, and that McLane, on the other hand, could negotiate under favorable circumstances because his party, or a majority of it, advocated the very trade and tariff policies that were considered in England to be to the mutual advantage of both countries. Cambreleng, representing the New York mercantile community, valued the West India trade so much that he would take it on almost any terms if it was obtainable; but he felt it would not be obtainable unless we could propose something new on the tariff.[61]

McLane was not made into a free trader by Cambreleng's arguments, but he was favorably impressed by the New Yorker himself. "He is a man of great worth," Kitty was told, "and of real sensibility and honor."

After he shopped in New York, purchasing "a diamond heart pin of small value" for Cambreleng, a valuable watch for convalescent young Louis, a locket for Kitty (sent with a lock of his hair), and various remembrances for the other children (little aprons for the girls), Louis McLane and Robert were seen on board by Van Buren's two sons, by Louis's brother, the doctor, and by his friend James Latimer, Jr., who was to wind up Louis's law practice.[62] As they passed through the Narrows and beside the fortifications, the McLanes made the acquaintance of the other passengers and of the ship's officers. Besides William Rives and his wife, the passenger list on the ship included Robert Walsh, Jr., McLane's private secretary, and Commodore James Biddle, on his way to take command of the Mediterranean fleet. One of the ship's officers was Franklin Buchanan, a friend of McLane's, and among the midshipmen was a schoolfellow of Robert's, a young Decatur, "about 13 years old and not larger," noted Louis, "than I was when I embarked under his grandfather."[63] That had been on a West Indies cruise and thirty years ago.

VII THE NEGOTIATION

Washington Irving had come overland from Barcelona to Paris in nine days. After spending a fortnight in Paris, he crossed to England and arrived in London on September 19, 1829, two days after the McLanes, who were staying in Thomas's Hotel, Berkeley Square. Irving took lodgings near the legation, which McLane soon established at 9 Chandos Street, near Portland Place and just off Cavendish Square, and he fell into the habit of dining with the McLanes at eight every evening.[64]

The McLanes were running a bachelor establishment when Irving first met the American minister. "My father was no housekeeper," Robert recalled later, explaining that he was therefore left at liberty to run the establishment, except for the first floor, where the legation's offices were. Irving "hated boys as much as he loved girls" and was therefore disconcerted "to see a youth just rid of his round-about taking charge of an English butler and ordering dinner," and "it nearly set him wild" that Louis allowed Robert to ride to school each day on a pony, which Robert made it a point to gallop through Hyde Park at a fashionable hour as he returned.[65]

Those who thought Irving an idler were surprised at the way he got to work and how tactfully and effectively he handled legation business when his "principal," as he called McLane, was ill and unable to attend to affairs.[66] For McLane was not well during his first weeks in England. He arrived ill, for that matter; the voyage was exhausting. It took a month, and McLane was seasick from an hour after the *Constellation* crossed the bar at Sandy Hook until after he disembarked on the Isle of Wight. Most of the time water lay on the floor of the cabins, so that McLane had to sleep in a cot elevated only a few feet over a pool. The drinking water was "putrescent and shockingly offensive." Robert thrived under these conditions, but Louis could not eat, suffered a perpetual nausea, and landed weak and emaciated.[67]

In his first weeks in London McLane suffered from stomach disorders that were probably intensified by his heavy responsibility, his loneliness, and his concern over how Kitty and the children would stand the trip.[68] His concern was certainly greatly magnified if he heard news of George Milligan's tragedy before Kitty reached England. Kitty's brother George, now a Louisiana planter, had been visiting in Delaware, and when he went with his wife and child to New York in early November to take ship for New Orleans, his wife was drowned when their coach ran off a New York pier into the river.[69]

Kitty wrote Louis to have no fears for her own well-being. Cambreleng had taken the entire ladies' cabin for her and her brood on the *Cambria*, which sailed to London, and he had assured her the ship was superior and the captain a gentleman. Dr. McLane, James Bayard, and James Latimer would help her to New York with the children and see her off. She had a good wet nurse for the baby and "Molly for the others." She had packed the sheeting, table linen, silver, and "some few eatables I think you would like." [70] Far from being afraid, to join Louis she would embark for Canton as readily as cross the bay to Baltimore.[71] On another occasion Kitty wrote Robert that his little sisters, Lid and Sally, wished they could fly to their father; "Lid is afraid to go in any other way, but

Sally, faithful Sally, says she would shut her eyes and go through the water to her Father _____ So would I." [72]

VIII   THE TRIUMPH

The fall was no season to accomplish a diplomatic mission in England. The magnates who ran the affairs of that country were off to their hounds, their horses, their country recreations on great estates with manor houses having sixty bedrooms and establishments of family, guests, and servants to match. "It is the great season of field sports," Washington Irving explained to Major Lewis, "when every English gentleman . . . makes a point of absenting himself as much as possible from town, to enjoy the hunting and shooting, which are pursued with a kind of mania from one end of the kingdom to the other. The frequent absence of cabinet ministers on excursions of the kind, have repeatedly delayed interviews and interrupted and protracted negotiations." [73]

When McLane arrived, James Barbour, his predecessor, was still there, and no time was wasted in presenting the new minister to the Foreign Secretary, Lord Aberdeen, a cultivated, peace-loving young Scottish earl. As soon as possible, on October 14, Aberdeen arranged for McLane to meet King George IV, a stout and friendly monarch to whom McLane gave assurance of President Jackson's favorable disposition in all the relations between the two countries. [74]

The dress McLane wore at the royal reception reflected another aspect of President Jackson's disposition. It was—or, at least, according to instructions it should have been—a black coat with a gold star on each side of the collar, "a three-cornered chapeau de bras" (a tricorn hat), a black cockade and eagle, and a steel-mounted sword with a white scabbard. This dress was not prescribed, Van Buren wrote, but "barely suggested" at the President's direction. [75] However, when Rives protested that an American diplomat so garbed might be confused at a European court with a doctor or a head servant, the bare suggestion came very near being a prescription. Van Buren took the matter up with the President, who was stubborn. Van Buren was willing to leave the matter of dress to Rives and McLane, as his letter said. But Jackson was not. He said Rives and McLane had been consulted earlier and had not objected except to ask that the coat be black instead of blue, as Jackson originally preferred. Except for the eagle and the form of the hat, it was precisely like the dress customarily worn by Washington. Thereupon Jackson took Van Buren downstairs to look at a portrait of the first President. Van Buren was persuaded. "A better standard you could not have," he declared:

"Your appearance in a simple black dress . . . may on the first impression excite surprise, but I am greatly mistaken if in a very short time the superiority of your dress is not acquiesced in by all whose good opinions are of any value."[76] This was nonsense. When Van Buren himself went abroad in 1831, the new Secretary of State (Edward Livingston) declared that a departure from the form of dress described in the printed regulations had been found indispensable; Livingston recommended a costume as consistent as possible with the principle of republican simplicity while yet not subjecting Van Buren to "the reproach of singularity."[77]

It was also rather a prescription than a bare suggestion that McLane should speedily get to the main point of his mission, the opening of the British West India ports. On October 16, almost as soon as he felt well, he had an interview of over two hours with Lord Aberdeen, bringing him the customary friendly assurances and then proposing a new arrangement in regard to the colonial trade. When Aberdeen declared the tariff of 1828 was viewed as a hostile measure, McLane said it was a matter of domestic concern, not to be considered by them unless Britain would offer an equivalent stipulation about the Corn Laws. Besides, knowledge in America of foreign opposition to the tariff would decrease the chance of modifying it. Aberdeen wanted the United States to show some concession before he went to Parliament, but McLane tried to persuade him that the United States did not object to the regulation of West India trade but to the fact that these regulations did not apply to the United States as to other nations. Finally Aberdeen said the matter should be taken up with the Board of Trade, and that McLane should talk with its president, William Vesey Fitzgerald. The board had opposed any change in colonial trade regulations when Barbour suggested it, but Aberdeen would present the subject to them in the most friendly way possible.[78]

Fitzgerald, an Irish landlord, was out of town, and it was more than two weeks before McLane could see him. When he returned, Aberdeen was away or busy, and a week passed before McLane could, in turn, see him. Anyway, Aberdeen objected to taking any action till the United States showed by more than words its desire to reopen a direct West India trade. McLane, feeling that British interests profiting from the existing circuitous trade were working against him, told Aberdeen he would be glad to recommend American legislation to conform with the British act of 1825—to recommend doing now what the United States should have done then—if he had any assurance Britain would open its colonial ports. The British interests McLane referred to centered in British North America (including the Maritime Provinces not yet united with the St. Lawrence valley as the Dominion of Canada), which had a unique opportunity to profit from a trade with the British West Indies as long as the merchants and shipowners of the United States were shut out of any direct competition in this trade.

Aberdeen was to submit this proposition to a cabinet council,[79] and McLane hoped to get an answer quickly which he could send Jackson before Congress met, or at least early in the session. But he was not very hopeful of a favorable answer, for he felt British North American (hereafter referred to as Canadian) interests and the shipowners were working against him. The best he hoped for was that the answer would not be final or absolute, but would instead leave room for further negotiation.[80]

However, he received no answer at all. The delay was explained politely, but a month passed with no response. Then McLane, to stir the ministry, repeated his proposition in the form of a letter. Would Britain open the colonial ports to American shipping on the same basis as to all other powers if the United States would remove its discriminatory duties on British vessels and cargoes in this trade? Delay would only make future adjustment more difficult, and the continuance of the existing invidious relations might lead to consequences more important than considerations of the colonial trade.[81]

Aberdeen answered courteously that he would lose no time bringing the proposal to the attention of his government, which had "the most friendly feelings toward the government of the United States." [82] But the proposition was not answered. Another month passed by. And another. And another.

Despite the delay there were propitious signs. Irving had seen them even in the fall, when he noted that the ministers had to be freed of existing prejudices and inspired with confidence in the desire of the American government for reciprocal trade and a friendly relationship generally. In two months he was convinced that "the whole tone of the ministers had changed," thanks to the "manly frankness" of McLane's manner, "the courtliness of his deportment, and the force and perspicuity of his reasoning." In this short time a real disposition had come to exist in the cabinet to arrange this West Indian trade on a basis of mutual advantage. Irving declared himself "pleased and proud that my country should have such a representative in this haughty and somewhat supercilious court." "I feel the more sensible of the favour done me by our government," he added, "in associating me by my office with a gentleman whom I find in every way so worthy of confidence, affection and esteem." [83]

McLane, in his turn, liked English society; "the difficulty of one's entrance into the society of England," he wrote, "is amply repaid by its real worth when that difficulty is overcome." Probably he was bragging a bit when he told friends at home that his favorites among the public men were the King, the Duke of Wellington, who was Prime Minister, and his brother, Richard Colley Wellesley, Marquis Wellesley.[84] In the same spirit of brag, McLane wrote Rives that it was an accomplishment to have persuaded Britain, as he had, even to consider a proposition twice rejected, particularly in view of the mess Adams had made of American diplomacy in the last twelve years and also in view of the opposition of the merchants and capitalists who were profiting from the indirect trade by way of the neutral islands and the northern colonies.[85]

When the President's message to Congress reached England—the message in which Jackson had hoped to be able to announce progress in the West India negotiations—it won a very favorable response. Never since Washington's day, said the *Times,* had a message included so much that was valuable and so little that was offensive.[86] McLane did not neglect to tell Jackson he had heard the message warmly praised by cabinet ministers and others at a large dinner party given by the Home Secretary, Robert Peel.[87]

Throughout the winter of 1829–30 McLane continued to confer with Wellington, Aberdeen, and John Charles Herries, who had succeeded Fitzgerald as president of the Board of Trade. In January, Wellington, who seemed very friendly, told McLane some decision should be reached when the ministers returned to the city and before Parliament met.[88] But no answer to his proposition was forthcoming, and McLane concluded that the Wellington ministry, though well disposed, was too weak to respond favorably to American overtures.[89]

One comfort to McLane was the official advice, sent him by Van Buren in the name of the President, that he could use his own judgment in allowing the British time for their reply. The President wanted to report to Congress "in due season," but would leave it to McLane to protect the interests of the country against long delay. The desire of the British North American colonies to thwart his proposition was "exciting much sensibility" in Washington, Van Buren reported, and there were proposals to prohibit all trade with these colonies in order to bring an end to their profit on the artificially circuitous West Indies trade. But for the present, such measures would be withheld for fear of embarrassing McLane.[90]

Through February McLane saw little reason to be hopeful. The *Times,* denying that the American tariff occasioned any animosity ("it is all self-love in America, as in England") and praising McLane as "a courteous gentleman, shrewd, dexterous and persevering," still expressed doubt that he would succeed. Worse yet, the *Times* expressed the belief that he should not succeed because it desired the prosperity of "the Canadas" and felt that this depended on the West Indies trade.[91]

At the end of the month, McLane was aware that the Board of Trade was at last preparing a report on his proposition. He tried to press the ministry to give him an answer that he could forward to America before Congress recessed, in order that any necessary legislative action could be taken promptly.[92] But the British continued to put him off—and continued to be friendly. In one of his interviews, it was suggested to McLane that he should commit to paper some of the points he was making, and so once again, as in December, he addressed to Aberdeen a statement of the case for opening the West Indies ports. He emphasized once again that the British answer to his proposition, once given, must be regarded as final. And he added a warning that the issue at stake was more important than the West India trade itself, for the issue was the future of friendly relations between the United States and England.[93]

This was, of course, his most telling argument, and exactly the point to be stressed. The ministry was well disposed toward McLane's country, but it was under constant pressure from Canadian interests—the lieutenant governor of New Brunswick was in London to argue his case [94]—and allied British interests to put aside its view of the proper procedure for the kingdom in order to protect the particular interests involved. Contrary interests worked to McLane's advantage; the circuitous purchase of supplies from the United States via Canada made them more costly to the West Indian planters, whose distress was argued in Parliament as a reason for opening the trade.[95] As the *Times* said, it was a matter of self-love, and the ministry carefully steered its path among the interests.

From their consistently friendly manner and apparent interest in understanding "the real Merits of the question," McLane began to have "whisperings of hope," as he told Rives on March 19.[96] When, therefore, he wrote to Van Buren a few days later to tell him of his last note to Aberdeen, he suggested "prospective legislation," authorizing the President, in case no answer came from Britain till after Congress adjourned, to issue a proclamation that would legally comply with the terms the United States had offered—that is, repealing discriminatory duties and opening American ports to British vessels from the West Indian colonies.[97]

He must have known that this advice would arouse expectations of his eventual success in the executive branch and in Congress, but he was willing to take the gamble. Possibly he had heard "whisperings of hope" in his extensive social exchanges with the English. He argued that there could be no motive for a delay in answering his proposition, unless it was to be accepted, but the logic is not so clear now as it was to McLane, particularly in view of the threat of further retaliatory action by the United States.

On April 10, for instance, Jackson addressed a memorandum to Van

Buren declaring that the national honor demanded prompt action if Britain rejected our overture. "Let a communication be prepared for congress," the President wrote, "recommending a non intercourse law between the United States and Canady." [98] If this was to be the American response, why would the British government hurry a negative answer?

Yet, somehow, McLane came to feel sure of his eventual success. On March 30 he wrote Cambreleng, *"inter nos, we shall recover the direct trade."* He added, "I think," and warned that new protective duties favoring Canada might diminish the value of this trade, but the tone of his letter was exultant. "If you could see and feel the influence brought to bear against me from Canada, New Brunswick, and the shipping interests here you would appreciate the arduous and delicate labour I have undergone, and not lightly reject another offer of the direct trade should it be made, even rather less advantageously than in 1825." In a postscript Cambreleng was advised to show this letter to Van Buren at once and to no one else without the Secretary's approval. But McLane hoped Van Buren would approve its being shown to General Sam Smith so that he for the Senate and Cambreleng for the House could begin to concert their measures—particularly so that they could "legislate prospectively" to authorize the removal of American restrictive laws if Britain reopened the direct West Indies trade to Americans on the same footing as to the rest of the world. [99]

Whether or not Sam Smith was shown this letter, which reposes in the Van Buren Papers, its substance was certainly communicated to administration leaders in Congress, who began to prepare a bill such as McLane requested. Did Van Buren mind the fact that McLane, his own subordinate, sent a message via Cambreleng, a Congressman? There is no hint that he did mind. But by communicating with Van Buren through Cambreleng in this fashion, McLane ran the risk of seeming a little overeager to retain his own ties in Congress, independent of his chief. Such an action as this, if repeated often, was apt to rouse the jealousy of an ambitious Secretary.

For the time being everything went McLane's way. On May 26 Jackson officially informed Congress that McLane felt he had a good prospect of success. Congress quickly passed, "without material opposition," the act requested of it, authorizing the President to open our ports to trade with the British West Indies whenever he had assurance that Britain would reciprocate. And Congress also passed an act sought by Cambreleng, reducing United States duties on some West Indian products. [100]

For some reason McLane received news of the action of Congress from newspapers and by private letters from Cambreleng and Sam Smith before he heard from Van Buren. McLane was getting anxious, for he believed that the British would take no action before Congress adjourned; if Congress had not acted, he felt that the whole negotiation would have been delayed for one year. In his anxiety he was even willing to see Congress give the President the right to place an interdict on trade with Canada if it seemed likely Britain would not admit Americans to the West Indies trade.[101] The British North American provinces were "untiring and importunate" in their opposition, and though apprehensive of some "countervailing" legislation by Congress, they sought by delaying British action to hold the trade and avoid paying any penalty.[102]

Van Buren, apparently, was too wise to risk proposing to Congress any prospective action based on the likelihood of British refusal. It would have aroused feelings quite the opposite of those he wished to encourage. Indeed, Louis McLane felt Congress was given somewhat more assurance of his success than he desired.[103] Nonetheless, Van Buren did not wish the possibility of American retaliation to be forgotten; he told McLane to use his own discretion about revealing to the British Jackson's determination to recommend an interdict on all trade with the British northern provinces in case the negotiation failed.[104] Probably Van Buren thought it much wiser to handle the matter through McLane's discretion than by allowing talk of retaliation to raise anti-British prejudices in Congress.

In April McLane declared that he had warned the British that if duties were so raised as to prohibit American imports to the West Indies, the opening of the West Indies trade would be nominal, not real, and consequently would be regarded by Jackson as "illusory and unsatisfactory." [105] But he did not wish to raise objections to moderate duties, since he expected that only with some increase of duties would the British ever assent to the trade.

Early in July, McLane called on Aberdeen and Wellington to inform them of the action of Congress. The duke expressed a belief that the act regarding trade would have a favorable effect on the negotiation, but suggested no answer could be given till Parliament was dissolved, an action that was imminent because of the death of George IV. Aberdeen asked McLane to send him an official statement of the American action, as McLane did when he had copies of the legislation. With this note, dated July 12, McLane advised Aberdeen that the British should decide promptly either to fulfill American expectations now or to quiet these expectations immediately if the negotiation was bound to terminate unsuccessfully.[106]

At last a British answer came, and it was favorable. On August 17 Lord Aberdeen declared that the proposition now before the British government had suddenly been changed "by the more specific and therefore more satisfactory" proposals of McLane's latest note. Observing that the claims urged by the Americans in 1825 had been abandoned, in McLane's words, "by those who urged them and [had] received no sanction from the people of the United States," Aberdeen declared that Gallatin in 1827 and McLane in his notes of December, 1829, and March, 1830, had asked the British government to pledge itself to revoke the orders closing the West Indies ports if Congress repealed the acts occasioning these orders. Now the United States had put a different cast on the affair by taking action itself and had empowered its President to remove restrictions on the trade as soon as he was assured of British reciprocity. This pledge could now be given: when the President gave effect to the act of Congress, all difficulties on the part of Great Britain that prevented a renewal of trade between the United States and the British West Indies would be removed.

But Aberdeen raised two problems in giving this pledge. The first was a matter of the interpretation of the American statute. The second was a caveat that though Britain viewed the reduction of American duties with approval as evidencing a sincere desire to encourage trade, these duties were to form no part of the agreement, for America was free to alter them as she pleased and Britain contemplated some modification of her own duties in favor of the interests of her northern colonies.[107]

McLane sent Aberdeen's letter home in exultation. "My negotiation for the Colonial trade is successfully closed," he chortled. He concurred in the interpretation Aberdeen suggested for the American statute. As to the duties, from Aberdeen's observations McLane gathered that they would not be increased as much as he had feared. If they were raised, the United States could raise duties too. And we could always count on having the West Indian planters on our side, for higher duties would hurt them.[108]

Van Buren agreed. Aberdeen's interpretation of the statute won his approval and Jackson's. Their delight was such that McLane was asked to assure the British government that the President appreciated their liberality in not suffering "the inadvertences" of legislation drafted in the "haste and confusion of the closing scenes of the session, to defeat or delay" the arrangement. The President's proclamation opening American ports was promptly issued on October 5, and a note was hurried to McLane so that Britain, which briefly had an advantage in the trade, might take similar action—and it did so two days after notification, on November 5, 1830.[109] A long-standing source of discord was at last removed.

Van Buren was not only happy to have this question settled but happy too that the settlement came when it did, for the news arrived in time to be made use of in some elections. The news was in Maine before the elections there and was confirmed by the fact that Canadian newspapers were dressed in mourning.[110] Jackson hurried back to Washington from Tennessee in anticipation of the news,[111] and McLane personally carried his despatches to Liverpool, confiding them to a ship captain himself, and with them some private letters announcing his success.[112] Quite possibly McLane hoped that one of his private letters, the one sent to his former Senate colleague, Henry Ridgely, might, by boosting the prestige of the Jackson party, help Ridgely in his contest for election to the House. A Ridgely victory, of course, would strengthen McLane's political base in Delaware.

In Baltimore a special handbill headed "GLORIOUS NEWS!" was issued when the mail arrived. In Washington, Duff Green published an extra edition of the *Telegraph* at noon on Sunday, October 3, celebrating the opening of the West Indies trade. Copies of the handbill and the extra were circulated in Maryland in hopes of influencing the October 5 elections. Whether they influenced any sizable number of voters was a matter of controversy for journalists, but certainly they did not have enough effect to give Jackson's party the victory. His opponents carried the election in both Maryland and Delaware.[113] Elsewhere apparently the news did not arrive on the eve of elections.

Whether or not the news of the successful negotiations helped the party, it decidedly helped McLane's prestige within the party. Van Buren congratulated him for the President on his "untiring zeal, patriotic exertions, and great ability."[114] McLane deserved these compliments, as he would have immodestly agreed. He had been zealous, and his zeal had brought him his success.

For it was zeal to accomplish his mission in the shortest time possible that led McLane in March to suggest the step—the "prospective" legislation, as he called it—that finally brought British agreement. Although the British might have been persuaded to open the West Indies trade anyway, there is an excellent chance that they would have still been delaying action in the fall of 1830 when the Wellington ministry fell. And if that had been the case, McLane would have had to start his negotiations over again with a new ministry, including a Foreign Secretary, Lord Palmerston, decidedly less friendly than Lord Aberdeen.

The "prospective" legislation made the difference, and it seems to have been McLane's idea. But the idea had to be put into effect, and to this degree McLane was dependent on his superior, Van Buren, and on his party's leaders in Congress. When McLane requested legislation, he got what he wanted. In summary, the success of the negotiation was due to good team work of the State Department, Congress, and the American minister in London.

IX   THE LIFE ABROAD

Louis McLane was a successful diplomat, although he felt diplomacy was not his proper role. He was too shy, he declared, and too reserved; "the forms of society and the etiquette of a court are too much of a labor to me." [115] Very likely, however, neither his shyness nor his reserve cost him as much concern in keeping up with the forms of English society as did the inadequacy of his salary.

From the beginning to the end of the English mission, finances worried McLane. When Kitty joined him, in December, 1829, he presided over a household of ten children, two child's nurses who came with Kitty, and seven domestic servants hired locally—probably a steward-butler, valet, coachman, footman, cook, housemaid, and kitchen maid.[116]

From January to August, 1830, there was another member of the Mc-Lane household—Robert Walsh, Jr. Walsh, the son of a well-to-do Philadelphia journalist, had come abroad with McLane as private secretary with an understanding that he would be paid no salary—for the good reason, according to McLane, that he was not needed. However, the boy arrived without enough money for his support, and his father informed McLane that he was expected to supply half of the son's expenses, or about $300 a year. If he could not be used, the father hoped he could get free passage home as a bearer of despatches. When young Walsh was taken seriously ill in January, 1830, McLane took him into his house and kept him there till he was well enough to take a packet home. The packet was the very one that carried the news of the British agreement, but Mc-Lane was so angry at Walsh, senior, for shifting this burden to him that he would not send the despatches with the boy.[117]

Whereas Robert Walsh, Jr., was a burden, Washington Irving was an asset. At times Irving felt like quitting because the business into which he was plunged cost him a sacrifice in terms of "pleasure, profit, and literary reputation." Certainly his salary of $2,000 a year did not meet his needs, even though he was a bachelor. But he quickly developed an enthusiasm for his job that kept him at it as long as McLane stayed in England, and even afterwards until his successor arrived. "What a stirring moment it is to live in," he wrote to a friend. "It seems to me as if life were breaking out anew with me." [118]

Though Irving did not live in the McLane household, he was so frequently a visitor that he came to feel a member of the family. Probably, considering his affection for girls in general, Rebecca, Sally, and Lydia exerted a particular attraction for him, although, except for Rebecca, they were children. Washington Irving's nephew, Theodore Irving, also came into contact with the McLanes, spending over a year in the legation while reading law under Louis's direction.[119]

Partly because of Irving's reputation, partly in recognition of their country and their role in London, the McLanes were entertained in fashionable English circles, both political and literary. William George Cavendish, the sixth Duke of Devonshire, had them at Chatsworth.[120] McLane was at Roehampton with William Lamb, Viscount Melbourne, and with the Russian ambassador, Prince Christopher Lieven, and his intriguing wife. There McLane was persuaded to give an account of Gallatin and pictured him as a man of humble origins who began life in America by setting up a "little huxtering shop." "A sensible man, with good American manners, which are not refined," the priggish diarist, Charles Greville, said of McLane on this occasion, adding, "even Irving, who has been so many years here, has a bluntness which is very foreign to the tone of good society."[121]

Among the things that surprised McLane in English society was "the cool and easy way" in which the English took their celebrities, a remark drawn from him at the first appearance in society of Lord Byron's daughter. "Nobody," McLane was reported to have said, "even looked at her; whereas, to an American the opportunity of seeing Lord Byron's daughter would be a sort of era in his life."[122] It was an era in the life of Louis McLane, and of Kitty. One view of her joy is preserved by Thomas Moore, who jotted a note in his diary for March, 1830, of seeing Washington Irving at a party. Irving proposed that Moore "accompany him back to a party of Americans he had just left (at Mr. Maclean's), which I accordingly did to his great delectation. Found the party numerous. A young American lady played the harp and I sang, while Mrs. Maclean sat by my side, exclaiming enthusiastically, 'Oh elegant! elegant!' Notwithstanding this Irish Americanism, however, a very nice woman."[123]

Kitty McLane saw much of two Maryland ladies who were prominent in London society. These were the Caton sisters from Baltimore, who had come to England for a visit and stayed. Miss Betsy Caton, according to Robert, had been a friend of his mother's from childhood. With Miss Betsy, in a Regent's Park villa, was her sister Marianne, the Marchioness of Wellesley, "and there was," as Robert remembered it, "a close intimacy between that family and the Legation during our stay in London." Quite possibly this intimacy helped McLane get on well with the Duke of Wellington, who was an admirer of his sister-in-law, Lady Wellesley.[124]

Another Londoner with American connections who was helpful to McLane was Joshua Bates, of the American branch of the house of Baring. Bates, who was a neighbor of the McLanes, had a son about Bob's age and a daughter a little younger with whom Bob fell, temporarily, in love, which Irving set down as "another boyish outrage." [125] McLane's personal regard for the helpfulness of the Caton sisters and Bates is exhibited in the advice he gave his successor at the London legation. After counseling him to employ one Shultz as a tailor, Adams as a hostler, and Lahee as house agent, he promised him, "Lady Wellesley and Miss Caton will instruct you in the mysteries of fashion, and Mr. Bates, your Banker, of Portland Place—whom you will find the kindest man in the world, will instruct and aid you essentially in all matters of business and housekeeping." [126]

In the literary and artistic circles that Irving drew to the legation were the poets Samuel Rogers and Thomas Campbell, the artists Charles R. Leslie and Gilbert Stuart Newton, and, of course, Tom Moore, "whose voice and touch at the piano, singing his own songs, constituted," in Robert's memory, "one of the greatest attractions at the Legation Receptions." Newton and Moore both fell in love with American girls, according to the same observant young witness, who added that Moore "was already billetted with as much as he could carry in domestic life." But, then, English social life in this period saw much roving of those bound by matrimony.[127]

In McLane's day it was easier for an American minister to be popular in England than it had been earlier—in the time of John Adams, for instance. Vaughan, the English minister in Washington, was popular there and helped to evoke an American friendship for England which he then made increasingly firm by reporting it abroad. But the kindliness with which McLane was met in England went beyond anything Vaughan's reports could have evoked. The royal family and the cabinet ministers, old and new, show "marked respect and friendliness," wrote Washington Irving, "and all this appears to be spontaneous; as, while we have fulfilled all the usual forms of mere civility and etiquette, we have never courted any favor or attention, but have rather held ourselves in reserve, and let the advance be made from the other party." [128] Soon after his accession King William IV had made such positive asseverations of friendship that McLane felt "nothing could be more cordial and gratifying than the observations of the king." [129] The monarch also saw fit to remind McLane that he had twice been in America as a young naval officer and indeed had participated in the taking of a French prize in Delaware Bay.[130] The reformer, Jeremy Bentham, was even more friendly than the King, telling McLane he was "at heart more a United-States-man than an Englishman." [131]

Of course, McLane's success in removing a long-standing grievance helped raise his popularity abroad with Englishmen and Americans. A Baltimore merchant, visiting London, declared nothing could "be more honourable to the country and to [McLane] himself, than the impression he has made and the footing he holds here." [132] From Paris, Robert wrote his father, "You can't think how popular you are here," and told of Rives's embarrassment and lack of enthusiasm for the praise of McLane by Americans recently come from London.[133]

X A BUSY MISSION

The years McLane was spending in England were exciting ones. The death of George IV in the summer of 1830 and the general election consequent on the accession of his brother William IV served as a prelude to the fall of the Duke of Wellington's Tory government in the autumn. Hard times led to demands for the reform of a government that was controlled by wealth and privilege, operating through pocket boroughs and a restricted franchise. Rebellion in Paris in July, 1830, intensified demands for parliamentary reform in England, and Wellington, opposed, in his own words, "to all reform," [134] lost office on a minor matter and turned the government over to the Whigs.

McLane was well aware that "the Spirit of insubordination" was abroad in England and that many complaints of "grievances, if not abuses," were well founded, but still he was surprised by the fall of the government when it occurred.[135] John Quincy Adams gloated to himself at McLane's failure to prophesy the change as he noted in his diary: "Mr. Van Buren told me that McLane . . . wrote to him on the 14th of November that the Duke of Wellington and his Administration were immovable. They were turned out two days after." [136]

When Charles Grey, second Earl Grey, came into power in November, 1830, he and his colleagues were pledged to reform and yet were as aristocratic a body of ministers as modern England had known. It seemed to McLane that the United States had "nothing to apprehend in the change," but after a month he was made uneasy by their failure to exhibit the same friendliness he had known from the Wellington government. Lord Palmerston, in particular, was much less pleasant to treat with than his predecessor as Foreign Secretary, Lord Aberdeen.[137] It was fortunate that McLane had pressed his main business sufficiently to conclude it while Aberdeen was in office. Even though McLane sympathized with the reform agitation, it was Wellington, Aberdeen, and Peel, members of the Tory government, who won his personal regard.[138]

As soon as his negotiation was successful, McLane traveled to Paris to see his son and to view what he could of the results of the July Revolution, and possibly also to look into a private claim of some sort of which he had written Rives.[139] The revolution seemed to McLane to be the beginning "of a series of struggles which must eventually embroil all Europe, and probably end in overthrowing most of the existing Governments." [140] He regretted that Lafayette had early lost influence in the new government; to him he had turned for advice on Robert's schooling when sending the boy to Paris in March, 1830.[141] The idea was that Robert should spend six months learning the French language and having the "opportunity of further observation"; then he should return to the United States to complete his schooling, the schools in England being passed over as "very bad and frightfully dear." [142]

Lafayette took young Robert under his protection and kept the boy by him during the stirring events of July. The hero's grandsons became Robert's intimate friends after he had taken a room at the Pension Garbaux, where another American boy was quartered, the brother of Charles Carroll Harper, secretary of the American legation in Paris. Not all Robert's time was devoted to his formal studies. The "further observation" his father planned for him came to include frequent attendance at the Théâtre-Français and at various social affairs of the American colony in Paris.[143] Besides learning the language, Robert learned to love the French; no other people seemed "so full of fun, so affable, so gay, and so brave." Among the friends the boy made were the Urquharts, relatives by marriage of his uncle George Milligan, and among his observations was the toilette of young gentlemen of fashion. Kitty sent him Louis's old clothes and Robert had them altered to fit—a pair of pantaloons, a waistcoat, three cotton shirts; for a time these had to serve him, along with a great coat he bought in Paris, but when he left, he ordered a dozen pairs of gloves, a pair of boots, another of pumps, two pairs of shoes, and he asked his mother to have a dozen shirts made for him of coarse linen, without collars (he preferred false ones), but "with full breasts and wristbands exactly like Papa's." He had had no new shirts of his own for three years, and granting a boy's normal growth from twelve to fifteen, the new ones were needed.[144]

On his return to England, Robert had "a terrible scene" with Irving because he thought himself too big to wear a "round-about" to the Princess Victoria's birth-night ball. Yet in his new dress coat "of the latest Parisian fashion" he was seated at the foot of King William's throne with the young sons of the other foreign ministers who were to take part in the quadrilles in which the twelve-year-old Victoria was to dance. Later in the year Robert accompanied his father on a trip conducted by John Campbell, the seventh Duke of Argyll, to the ancestral home of the McLanes. From Castle Inverary in the Scottish Highlands, Sir Fitzroy MacLean accompanied them to the Isle of Man, where some of Louis's ancestors had lived before coming to America.[145]

Kitty was with Louis on his jaunt to Liverpool in August, 1830, to send off the news of his success, but she did not accompany him to France or to the Highlands. Perhaps she was again in a delicate condition. On June 1, 1830, an American reported a rumor that the Duchess of Clarence was with child, adding he did not know about that, "but *Mrs. McLane is;* and that will do for the gossips at Washington." [146] If she was again pregnant, she lost the child. In December she was too ill to be out, but found that since the King went to the seashore, all society fled from the fogs of London, and she could stay there and be as retired as she wished. But perhaps it was another weakness that troubled her, for she wrote of going to Brighton to treat her rheumatism in heated baths of seawater as soon as the King left the resort. [147]

Rebecca was the only one of the children old enough to take part in adult social life, though Robert was at least equally eager. [148] But in the winter of 1831 Rebecca suffered seriously "under the influence of the climate," or so her father claimed when he was asking permission to terminate his mission. [149] After his initial spell of illness, it is remarkable how well Louis himself kept.

Even well enough to envy a king. A story was well circulated in England, where it was felt to add to the glory of the monarch, that McLane had said to him, "I little thought, sir, I should live to see the day when I should *envy* a monarch!" To antimonarchical Hezekiah Niles in Baltimore came a report of this event, so phrased that Niles was led to believe McLane envied the King his power to dissolve Parliament. Niles published the story in the *Register* with the insinuation that McLane's comment was unworthy an American. But in London, Thomas Moore, on a morning call at the McLanes', had already traced the story to its source. According to his diary, when he mentioned the currency of this anecdote; "Mrs. Maclean (who is a very amiable, natural person) said, 'It is very true that Mr. Maclean said he envied the King, but it was not on the Reform question; it was (I am ashamed to say) on seeing the King kiss Lady Lilford.'" [150]

XI   ITS SUCCESS

The courtier who could envy a king was himself embarrassed when John Randolph came to London in the fall of 1830. The erratic knight of Roanoke had abandoned his Russian mission shortly after arriving in St. Petersburg and fled to the more congenial climate of Western Europe, volunteering himself as eventual successor either to McLane or to Rives. According to a report repeated at third hand, McLane and Irving were bothered by Randolph's dress when they called to take him to the court.

He wore a black suit, a little black hat, white stockings, gold shoe and knee buckles, and a steel-cap sword, and his friends feared that with his odd personal appearance—gaunt figure, bright eyes, small features, no beard—he would attract undue attention. But he was proud of his clothes, convinced that love of display caused most foreign ministers to overdress. "I wear no man's livery," he boasted, but Irving persuaded him to unbuckle his sword and leave it in the carriage. Even then he was stopped by the usher till his identity was explained, and as he entered the reception room the foreign ministers eyed him curiously. The Duke of Sussex, brother of the King, asked Irving, after Randolph had passed by, "Who's your friend, Hokey Pokey?" [151] Irving responded in some irritation, but Randolph who, feeling ill, bought a leaden coffin to take with him on a trip to southern France, could never free himself from the reproach of singularity.[152]

McLane and Irving had no trouble adapting themselves and their dress to English society, though the cost of the adaptation was hard on the father of ten children. When the court was ordered to don mourning clothes for George IV, McLane saw financial ruin ahead. Black bombazines, plain muslin, or long lawn linen crape hoods, "shamoy" shoes and gloves, and crape fans for the ladies; black cloth without buttons on sleeves and pockets, plain muslin or long lawn cravats and "weepers," shamoy shoes and gloves, crape hatbands, and black swords and buckles for the men—the whole would cost seven hundred dollars, a substantial part of his salary.[153] Fortunately the government agreed to pay for these clothes, but McLane had to spend the money at once and wait months for assurance that he would be repaid.

Since six weeks was the normal time needed for McLane's despatches to travel from London to Washington, he could count on waiting about three months for the answer to any inquiry he made. Therefore he was peculiarly on his own whenever his negotiations proceeded beyond the letter of his instructions. Such was the case once an agreement was made with England and the West India trade opened to the United States. The British government at once set about raising duties on foreign imports to the West Indies in order to protect the trade there of the British North American provinces. McLane's instructions gave him no power to negotiate about duties, but when Wellington was overthrown, he warned the new government that they would be expected to adhere closely to the trading privileges offered in 1825 and not to close the market to Americans, for he felt it was certainly in his powers to preserve the agreement he had made.[154]

Lord Palmerston promised to let McLane know what duties Great Britain would propose, but, probably because of his preoccupation with the diplomatic embroglio growing out of the Belgian revolution, he failed to do so. Consequently McLane went directly to Lord Grey, the new Prime Minister, and conferred with him and with the president and vice-president of the Board of Trade. They denied that they were bound by Aberdeen's agreement with McLane.

However, when the government's schedule of duties was finally worked out (McLane's copy came *"unofficially and confidentially"* from George Eden, the second Baron Auckland, president of the Board of Trade), it was less harsh than McLane had feared. In fact, in one way the new schedule was distinctly advantageous to Americans, for it admitted American produce to British North America duty free, with the intent, however, of preserving the circuitous trade that had developed prior to 1830. On the other hand, it gave American produce entry to England also, duty free, via Canada.

What should McLane do? Should he seek to protect American shipping against the competition of the North American colonies both in the trade to England and in the trade to the West Indies? Or should he rejoice in the advantages for American agriculture and say no more?

Not till March 7, 1831, did he receive official approval of the position he had taken as long ago as November 30 in requiring that Britain hold to its agreement to open the West Indies trade in fact as well as in name.[155] But even then he was warned not to commit his government as to the course it would take if the British persisted in their plans to raise duties.[156] At the same time he was sent some diplomatic documents—protocols of 1818 negotiations—which he had requested almost a year earlier.

Thereupon McLane felt impelled to make another formal protest. He called on Palmerston, but found this minister so distracted by Belgium and by parliamentary reform that he did not seem to know that a new schedule of duties had been prepared.[157] Two months later, on May 17, Palmerston sent McLane the new colonial trade act, along with a letter purporting to answer McLane's note of November 30. McLane had received no further instructions on the subject and concluded that he should let it rest.[158] No further instructions were forthcoming, and when McLane's successor went to England later that year, he was told that "no good purpose would be served by any immediate attempt to produce a change" in the duties.[159] By that time McLane was home and undoubtedly influencing the instructions.

Other points mentioned in his instructions, such as the questions of impressment and of American rights to the navigation of the St. Lawrence, McLane postponed discussing in favor of the main object of his mission. When that was settled, he did begin, in October, 1830, to discuss with

Aberdeen the St. Lawrence navigation, but the fall of the Wellington government and the need of arriving at understandings with a new set of ministers prevented his recurring to this question, on which he never had any hope of making progress.[160]

On the other hand, progress was being made on one important issue, the Northeast boundary controversy. It was, however, not McLane's problem, for it had been referred to the King of the Netherlands for arbitration. Gallatin had prepared the American case, which William Pitt Preble, of Maine, was to present to the Dutch King. On the way, Preble passed through London, where McLane had assembled various documents for his use.[161] Aside from collecting these documents, McLane had no part in the arbitration and was out of touch with Preble until the winter of 1831, when he received a long letter of complaint that the decision, which had recently been made, was unduly favorable to the British. McLane agreed that the decision, which was a compromise of the American and British claims, was "capricious and arbitrary," and suggested that the Dutch King's independence of judgment was probably influenced by the revolt of his Belgian subjects, which made him somewhat amenable to the influence of powerful neighbors. But having no instructions in the case, he confined his agency to forwarding Preble's despatches to Washington.[162]

He forwarded despatches for various other American agents abroad, for Van Ness, in Spain, and Wheaton, in Denmark, for example.[163] So good were the relations between Britain and the United States that the use of British diplomatic mailbags was requested for American despatches.[164] Yet McLane was sometimes provoked, as when he exclaimed, "There is . . . a blunt obstinacy and sullen pride in the character of John Bull which spoils all he can do; if, indeed, he ever meant to do a favor or an act of peace in his life—which I doubt." [165]

Constantly he came to the English with minor complaints of his countrymen. There was, for instance, the complaint of Captain Edmund Bulkley of the brig *Rodney* of New York who went for a cargo of salt to Turks Islands, at the southeastern end of the Bahama chain, and found his ship would not be admitted to the port unless he paid tonnage duties of $155.28. Bulkley, who owned the brig, protested that this was contrary to the recent agreement on West Indian trade, because British ships were charged no duties at this port under similar circumstances.[166] McLane addressed a note of protest to Palmerston on May 2 and received an answer on May 18 that was entirely satisfactory: the duty was ordered discontinued and any bonds taken for its payment were canceled.[167] Other complaints were less satisfactorily and, especially, less promptly dealt with, but the British government seems to have looked into every case in good faith.

In some cases McLane found other means more effective than a formal note to the Foreign Minister. He called on John Charles Spencer, Viscount Althorp, the Chancellor of the Exchequer, when it seemed likely that increased duties on foreign cotton would harm American shipping. Althorp promised to require certificates of origin, which apparently would allow Americans to transship West Indian cotton to England without penalty.[168]

Though he had no official connection with the American consuls, of whom there were eleven in the British Isles, by custom McLane exercised a certain supervision over them. [169] On the consul at Liverpool, Francis B. Ogden, a New Jersey man, he was particularly dependent for the rapid transmission of his despatches to the United States.[170] To the consulate at Belfast he secured the appointment of Thomas Gilpin, son of his friend Joshua Gilpin.[171] And into the work of the consul at Cowes, Robert Hunter, he conducted a special investigation at the request of Van Buren—though Van Buren hoped Hunter, who was of a prominent Virginia family, would be cleared of the charges against him—charges made by insurance companies which accused him of permitting unduly expensive repairs to a vessel that should have been condemned.[172]

Among other duties, there were maps, periodicals, and books to be ordered for the State Department—complete sets of the *Edinburgh Review* and the *Quarterly Review*, for example, a missing volume of Hansard, Bentham's works.[173] There were distinguished visitors to be met and, sometimes, to be aided—Louis A. Cazenove, of Alexandria; Colonel Achille Murat (nephew of Napoleon), of West Florida; and, from his post at Copenhagen, Henry Wheaton, who found McLane "very civil, even friendly." [174] There was information to be collected on British and foreign affairs; for the latter he was particularly recommended to establish "friendly social relations" with other diplomats in London, including (in January, 1831) Prince Lieven of Russia, Prince Paul Esterhazy of Austria, Talleyrand, now also a prince, of France, and Baron Heinrich von Bülow of Prussia.[175]

To one diplomat, the Mexican minister, Manuel Eduardo de Gorostiza, who was fearful of the safety of Texas because of American military actions on the Texas frontier, McLane gave assurance that the United States had no hostile or aggressive intentions.[176] He gave Aberdeen the same assurances, alluding to the subject only casually but noting later that his assurances were made use of by the government in the debates in Commons on the evening after his interview. British capitalists and adventurers, he felt, were jealous of any American influence in Mexico, and the government, partaking of some of that jealousy, was particularly apprehensive of American designs on "the Texas."

To defend the reputation of Joel Poinsett, lately United States minister in Mexico, McLane sent a copy of Poinsett's printed defense to the editor of the *Westminster Review*. But in giving assurances about American ambitions, he was careful not to repudiate the peaceful acquisition of land by purchase. If a false confidence in British assistance led Mexico to hostile acts against the United States, McLane was sure what the issue would be, "whatever G.B. may say or do." [177]

XII   THE HIGH POINT

The success of Louis McLane as minister to England depended not on his handling of the ordinary chores of his office, such as the issue of passports, or the less ordinary chores, such as assistance to Henry N. Cruger, representing South Carolina, who sought access to the Public Record Office. Nor did it depend upon his performance of the more sophisticated obligation to transmit information regarding the policy and views of the British government and its relations with other powers. All these duties had to be performed, but they might have been performed well by a man of less political stature and of more diplomatic experience than McLane. He was sent to England with the primary objective of opening to Americans the trade with the British West Indies on a basis of equality and reciprocity—the same basis on which trade with the British Isles themselves had been placed by the treaty of 1815, since then twice extended. [178]

McLane was a success because he accomplished this objective. The trade was opened in the fall of 1830 on the terms he was instructed to secure. It is of no purpose to say that McLane was lucky, that Gallatin and Barbour had made Britain substantially the same offer as he, but had been repulsed—of no purpose to note that McLane succeeded because his government gave him complete cooperation by statutory enactment and presidential proclamation that afforded Britain absolute assurance of American good will.

He was fortunate, it is true, but in the role in which he was cast he took the needful steps to make his mission a success. He proposed enabling legislation and a presidential proclamation. He interpreted American laws and American intentions to the complete satisfaction of both the British and the American government. He correctly foresaw what was needful.

Though critics doubted that the agreement he made was a good agreement, it was the agreement he was instructed to make. And it was a popular agreement. Even Hezekiah Niles, one of its severest critics, admitted there was "a feverish anxiety" for the opening of the West Indies trade.[179]

Thomas Ritchie, of the Richmond *Enquirer,* Sam Smith, of Baltimore, Robert Hayne, of South Carolina, and Churchill Cambreleng, of New York, all rejoiced at the "Reciprocity of 1830," as the agreement was called. Opponents claimed, and with some reason, that in the trade between the United States, British North America, and the West Indies, the total of American shipping declined and the total of foreign shipping grew.[180] But Jackson had a correct view of the situation when in his message to Congress in December, 1830, he rejoiced that at last a question long and almost uninterruptedly in contention, the subject of no less than six negotiations, had been settled in a manner promising results favorable to both countries.[181] In the House of Commons, Herries spoke to the same effect, pointing to "the close of one of the longest and most interesting controversies which had ever occurred between two nations," and declaring in compliment to the American government and, incidentally, to McLane, "it was impossible for any party to have conducted a negotiation involving such important interests in a more friendly, civil, straightforward, conciliatory, and therefore, as he should say, in a more wise and prudent manner."[182]

"Between ourselves," exulted Cambreleng, "John Bull has made a dangerous bargain for his navigation."[183] John Bull was not so foolish as Cambreleng thought. The reciprocity agreement of 1830 was more helpful to American producers than American shipowners. By imperial preferential duties, Britain kept a good share of the carrying trade. But the advantages she retained were fairly hers, despite Adams's complaints of them. Jackson and Van Buren had examined the situation with broadminded common sense and got all the advantages America could expect from an agreement. Not least of the advantages was the fact that an agreement had been made, that a controversy that had been an irritant in the way of good relations for half a century had been ended.[184] As Jackson wrote privately, it indicated a disposition of the two countries "to meet . . . half way in establishing . . . relations . . . upon that fair and reciprocal basis which is the only sure guarantee" for future peace and prosperity.[185]

The warm glow of success surrounded Louis McLane as his mission drew to a close in the late spring of 1831. The London *Albion,* noting that because of the distance and slowness of communications between two continents it was "peculiarly incumbent" on the American government "to select men of superior talent" to represent it in Europe, declared that in this instance "a more prudent choice" could not have been made;

"points of difficulty and delicacy, requiring no ordinary intelligence and address" had been adjusted so happily that it was difficult to say whether this minister had "given more satisfaction to his own government or to that to which he had been accredited."

A group of nineteen Americans resident in London (including the consul, Thomas Aspinwall, Joshua Bates, Richard Blatchford, Richard Biddle, G. S. Newton, C. R. Leslie) in a public letter praised McLane's "private urbanity and politeness," his "kindness and hospitality," and his "high and honorable frankness of character," as well as his "distinguished public services." Thanking them, Louis McLane declined their invitation to a dinner in his honor, as he declined another invitation to a public dinner that was tendered on his arrival at New York when he finally returned to the United States.[186] He was rushing into a new and greater responsibility than he had ever known before. It was the high point of his career.

10

Beside the Chief

I   AMBITION

Martin Van Buren was a careful man. "I would rather pull a tooth," he wrote to James A. Hamilton, "than say a word to you about the [Eaton affair]. I think you have a little of McLane's fondness for gossip." [1] The course Van Buren steered so carefully was close in the wake of the Jackson ship. "Tell Mrs. Eaton," he wrote to Jackson on one occasion during the quarrel over that abused woman's social position, "if she does not write me I will give her up as a bad girl." [2]

This remark, had they seen it, would have titillated Kitty and Louis McLane. Louis would not have approved it, but he dared not disapprove either, for at the moment he was dependent on Van Buren, who was the chief custodian of McLane's hope for an appointment to the Supreme Court. Jackson had promised—at least, so Van Buren said—that the first "suitable" vacancy should go to McLane. Major Lewis had also applied to Jackson on McLane's behalf respecting a seat on the Court and was permitted to tell McLane before his departure for England that he would be given a place on the bench as soon as one was available.

The place that Lewis, Van Buren, and Jackson had in mind was that held by Gabriel Duvall, a man nearing eighty who was so deaf that he was believed not to have heard an argument for years. Duvall was a Marylander, and his circuit (in that day when the judges of the Supreme Court also served on circuit) included McLane's native Delaware. [3]

Before any promise was given McLane, Jackson had made one appointment to the Supreme Court, in March, 1829, when he selected John McLean, of Ohio, the Postmaster General, to fill the vacancy on the western circuit created by the death of Allen Trimble. The next vacancy,

293

at the death of Bushrod Washington, of Virginia, did not prove "suitable," because Jackson determined to rectify the geographical distribution of members of the Court by appointing someone who resided in the Pennsylvania-New Jersey circuit. His choice fell on Henry Baldwin, of Pittsburgh. James A. Hamilton was apparently entrusted with some announcement of the President's intentions to McLane, who responded that he understood. "I did not expect and could not have desired him . . . to go out of the *circuit* for a successor to the late Judge Washington. . . . I am quite content to look forward to the event [Duvall's resignation] in which you think a proper provision will be certain." In that case, Delaware, never having had a judge, would have a good claim to the appointment, besides whatever personal claim to it McLane had. "On that event I trust Van Buren will keep his eye." [4]

There is evidence that Van Buren did. Henry Baldwin was not long on the Supreme Court before he threatened to resign, and Van Buren reported to McLane, then abroad, that though there were serious difficulties in the way of appointing McLane to this place (because McLane did not reside in Baldwin's circuit), the President would "watch the movement of events with a lively zeal" for McLane's welfare. Jackson would be delighted if he found he could appoint McLane to this vacancy; perhaps Van Buren was implying that Delaware might be annexed to Baldwin's Pennsylvania-New Jersey circuit. At any rate, Van Buren declared that Jackson was "confident that the Country would have nothing to apprehend" from McLane's opinions, meaning his Federalism would not bar his appointment to Marshall's court. [5]

But Baldwin did not resign at this time. Neither did Duvall. The deaf Maryland justice held on to his seat purposely to exclude someone— probably McLane—whom he considered a good enough lawyer but too much of a politician for the Court. By the time a vacancy did occur the President had other favorites. [6]

II   ANTICIPATION

With or without an appointment to the Supreme Court, the longer McLane stayed in England the more eager he was to come home. His increasing dismay over the inadequacy of his salary played no minor part in this decision. "Would to God I had remained in the Senate," he complained to James A. Hamilton in March, 1830, "and suffered some other man to pine and starve at this court in the midst of pomp and splendor." In May, he repeated the same plea to the same correspondent: "I could be of infinitely more service to Van Buren, the President, and the country, if I were at home." [7] A reader wonders whether McLane's order—"Van Buren, the President, and the country"—shows progress to a climax or whether it represents a descending order of his usefulness. Obviously McLane expected Hamilton to carry this message to the Secretary of State, if not also to the President.

By this time events had led to a schism between President Jackson and Vice-President Calhoun, and had cost the latter his hope of becoming Jackson's successor. These were the Eaton affair, with Mrs. Calhoun one of the leaders in the social snubbing of Mrs. Eaton; Jackson's discovery that Calhoun when Secretary of War had, in cabinet counsel, been bitterly critical of Jackson's invasion of Florida in 1818; and Calhoun's identification with the nullification doctrine in South Carolina. Losing faith in Calhoun, Jackson at the same time lost his regard for Calhoun's friends, chief among them the Secretary of the Treasury, Samuel Ingham, whose wife had been a leader in the conspiracy, as Jackson regarded it, against Mrs. Eaton.

Discussing various problems with Jackson, Hamilton, McLane's confidant, advised the President to drop Ingham from the cabinet, though, as Hamilton reported to McLane, he made this suggestion to the President only after consulting Van Buren and Major Lewis and gaining their approval. Jackson's response was excellent. He concurred with the suggestion and proposed to get rid of Ingham by sending him to England as soon as McLane brought his mission there to a successful conclusion. From Hamilton's letter McLane had encouraging assurance that he would be able to return to America promptly when his work abroad was done. "After the Treasury, the Attorney-General must be changed," Hamilton added. McLane might fairly come to the conclusion that in so many changes, a role surely would be found for him. But this information was strictly confidential, Hamilton warned, and was passed on only because Van Buren was writing McLane on the same subject. [8]

Later in that summer of 1830, his mission successful, McLane began to anticipate his return. In August as he despatched news of his success he told a Delaware friend he had no reason "except public rumor" to expect a return to his country "within any short period." [9] One suspects that he was writing to friends at home of his wish to return, since in October two influential party leaders urged Van Buren to find a place for him—and noted his financial predicament in England, of which he probably had informed them. Urged Cambreleng: "Save our friend McLane from bankruptcy—he is the ablest cabinet counsellor I know—and he has besides a wife and—ten—aye—I believe eleven children." [10] And Robert Y. Hayne: "A seat on the Bench of the Supreme Court, or the first Secretaryship that becomes vacant, belongs to him, and I confess I have too much regard for him to desire that he should become merely a *resident* minister . . . to the inevitable ruin of his family." [11]

While pressing Van Buren through mutual friends, McLane sought to give him direct assurance—or reassurance—that his political principles were up to scratch. Van Buren had written privately to McLane, probably to tell him of the plans for Ingham and perhaps also to sound out McLane on some important issues. Van Buren's letter is lost, but McLane declared in his answer that he was "pursuing the general tenor" of the lost letter and in a hasty way expressing some opinions he had been forming over a long time. Jackson's Maysville Road veto was the first item he discussed, after a progress report on his West India negotiations. Everyone knew he favored some internal improvements, McLane wrote, but Adams, Clay, and Webster carried them too far, for the power of the federal government was not unlimited. He applauded the Maysville veto (and it was a good thing he did, since Van Buren had written it), but he confessed to dissatisfaction with the rule Jackson had set for judging what improvements were proper. This rule would not give latitude for works of military usefulness, such as the Delaware and Raritan Canal across New Jersey. Yet for his courage (here the diplomat speaks) in stopping the corrupting, spending policies of Clay and Webster, Jackson deserved comparison with Washington.

In general, McLane wrote as a known, recorded Federalist trying to make his policies as palatable to Van Buren as possible, to trim them to fit the party line as closely as he dared. After all, the party line itself was by no means fixed.

So, in referring to the Supreme Court, which the Democrats criticized for its extreme nationalism in cases involving the rights of the states (Van Buren had twice attacked the Court on the floor of the Senate), McLane agreed that the Court had gone too far and suggested giving the President the power to dismiss justices, with the approval of the legislatures of two thirds of the states. However, he blamed Justice Joseph Story (a Republican) more than Chief Justice Marshall (a Federalist) for the attitude of the Court.

If extinction of the public debt were made a primary consideration, as it should be (here McLane was catering to Jackson), many other problems of policy would be taken care of by being subordinated to this. Once the debt was paid, he would reduce revenue, including the tariff. He opposed the distribution of federal funds to the states to support improvements, because he thought its constitutionality doubtful and its tendency dangerous—it would make some states overdependent on the federal government.

As to the Bank of the United States, McLane felt it necessary to insist that he had no interest in it. Without questioning the President's views (which, one suspects, he did really question), he regretted the reference to the Bank in the President's message to Congress as arousing unnecessary public excitement and giving the enemies of the administration a pretext for closer and more efficient cooperation than ever before. He thought the Bank was constitutional, on the same basis as was the Cumberland Road. The only question was one of expediency.[12]

In a later letter, McLane was to say: "Nothing is more fatal in this country—perhaps in any—than a direct attack upon the *monied* interest." [13] It was probably his opinion at this time too, though now he did not speak so clearly; he contented himself with saying that charter renewal need not be considered yet. But he left little doubt he would favor some sort of renewal—for a shorter period, with an increased number of government directors and authority to name the president, and with "its brokering character . . . changed." The interest of the stockholders deserved consideration; fixed interests ought to be injured as little as possible.

The question of the Bank, its renewal, and its form, was, McLane correctly foresaw, potentially as exciting as the tariff and ought to be approached with the some moderation. But he had no sympathy for the sort of government-owned bank suggested in the President's message, for he knew that such an institution could be a very dangerous agency under bad leadership.

Before closing, McLane chided Van Buren for the language he had used; apparently Van Buren had twitted McLane for his Federalism. McLane insisted that he was a soldier's son and as attached to his country and to republican principles as anyone, even Jackson. That Van Buren, at this period of their friendship, "could seriously so speak and so doubt and so suspect" was very aggravating. McLane flung his irritation into the face of the Secretary of State: "I have made the most of my case [in England], tho' you have not had the courtesy to say so."

"Be sure Mr. VB.," Louis McLane wrote to the man he was depending on to look after his interests at home, "that your friend is an honest man, . . . and then trust him for the rest." And, concluding, he reminded Van Buren, "I am a politician of the school of Washington, and enough of a federalist to have undeviatingly and regardless of risk acted with such moderate *temperate* politicians as Wm. H. Crawford and Mr. VB.!!" [14]

III   A NEW APPOINTMENT

"Both the President and Mr. Van Buren know my opinion," wrote McLane to James Bayard in November, 1830, in reference to the Bank of the United States; "and I am not prepared to say that they will be ultimately opposed to the renewal of the charter." [15] Nor was he prepared to say with certainty that any important position in the United States would be available for him in the near future. Rumors were afloat that McLane was slated to replace Ingham as Secretary of the Treasury, but as the year 1831 began McLane had no definite offer.[16] All he could say was that he hoped the time was coming when party prejudices and jealousies would no longer restrain his country from rewarding "a disciple of the old federal school." [17]

McLane was well aware that references to his Federalism harmed his chances of advancement, as, for example, a quotation that Hezekiah Niles reprinted from the St. Louis *Beacon:* "the whole range of our country does not present a more decided 'up-to-the-hub' *federalist* than Louis Mc-Lane." [18] Yet he took comfort for a time from hints that he received from Hamilton and Van Buren, the latter in the form of a letter, now lost, written at the President's table and suggesting that there would be some satisfactory appointment awaiting him on his return home. These hopes were disappointed in March of 1831 when Jackson asked him to stay in England for a year more, or at least till fall, in order to deal with any difficulties arising out of the Northeast boundary arbitration, just completed, and for some other undisclosed reasons.[19]

Jackson declared that he had previously decided to allow McLane to return in the spring and had approved Van Buren's writing him to that effect. Very likely the trouble now was that though the Maine boundary arbitration made it necessary to have some minister in England, imminent changes in the cabinet had not progressed to a point where Jackson—or Van Buren—was willing to decide who should be McLane's successor. But it turned out not to be necessary to wait a year or even until fall for some decision. Before another month had passed the cabinet was broken up and McLane was called home to take Ingham's place at the head of the Treasury Department.[20]

The invitation caught McLane unprepared. In February he had formally asked permission to return, alleging that the health of his family, particularly that of Rebecca, his eldest daughter, suffered from the English climate, while the inadequacy of his salary, despite "the simplest habits and the strictest regard to economy," made further residence in England unnecessarily ruinous now that the principal business of his mission was settled.[21] This despatch had not yet arrived in America when McLane received Jackson's letter asking him to stay at least until fall. Thereupon he leased a house for that period and made other arrangements he could not easily undo on June 2 when he received an invitation to join the cabinet, despatched by Van Buren on April 26.

He accepted, however. He did not accept very graciously; it was not in his nature to do so. He was willing to trim his course a bit to his own advantage, but he insisted on doing it with an air of independence; he would not lick boots. And so he answered that if the emergency required his service and if his acceptance could "promote the harmony of the Cabinet, strengthen the administration and subserve the public interests" —in other words, if he, Louis McLane, were indeed needed—then when he returned he would enter upon the duties of this new office.[22] Then he hurried as fast as he could and boarded the packet ship *President* (never again a frigate) at Portsmouth with his wife, his ten children, and two servants on June 19, seventeen days after receiving the invitation. McLane arrived in New York on July 28 and in Washington, after leaving his family in Delaware, on August 6. Of course, seasickness had weakened him and delayed his departure from New York to Washington.[23] Another cause for delay was the necessity of a long talk in New York with Van Buren, who was off to London as McLane's replacement.[24]

IV   THE DISSOLUTION OF THE FIRST CABINET

There was a place for McLane in the cabinet in April, 1831, because all the ministers, the least important excepted, were being replaced. It was not their will—not the will of most of them—that they be replaced. In Jackson's mind they had been divided into two groups by the Eaton affair: those who accepted Mrs. Eaton socially and those who did not. In the former group were Van Buren and Postmaster General Barry; in the latter group were the other ministers, except Eaton himself—Ingham, Branch, and Berrien, as well as Vice-President Calhoun. As Calhoun lost the President's favor, Jackson tended increasingly to view the Eaton affair as a scheme of his enemies to strike at him and his friends, particularly Secretary of State Van Buren, whose availability for the succession to the Presidency became ever more apparent as the star of the Vice-President declined.

Yet there was one sticking point in the way of Van Buren's eventual promotion. In the 1824 election Jackson and his supporters had made a major point of their opposition to cabinet succession to the Presidency, particularly succession by the Secretary of State, a custom followed at the end of the Jefferson and Madison administrations, and then again, despite the Jacksonites' best efforts, at the end of the Monroe administration. Since Calhoun, aided by his son-in-law Duff Green, editor of the *Telegraph,* was eager to rally all discordant elements against Van Buren, a great deal might be made of this point unless the New Yorker gave up the State Department portfolio well before the election.

A resignation looked like a wise course to Van Buren on other grounds. Men who were hesitant to blame Jackson, still a military hero, for the unpopular acts of his administration, might be glad to make the Secretary of State a scapegoat, particularly since this official already had a reputation for political manipulation. By resigning, Van Buren might remove himself from easy visibility as a target for political fire. By resigning Van Buren might also give the signal for a complete recasting of the cabinet which could remove the disruptive influence of the Eaton affair and rid the cabinet of any influences that might be thought anti-Eaton or pro-Calhoun.

To establish harmony in the administration and in the party, it was desirable that Eaton should resign as well, but since Jackson would never drop him it was necessary to persuade Eaton to take the action himself. To this end Van Buren shrewdly consulted about his own resignation with a small group which designedly included Eaton as well as the President. As Van Buren made clear one of his aims, the attainment of harmony among the President's advisers, Eaton generously offered his own resignation. Jackson consented because he thought he could reward both men for their generous friendship—Van Buren by an appointment in London to succeed McLane, and Eaton by an exchange of his position for the Senate seat held by his fellow Tennesseean, Hugh White.

On the basis of these resignations, dated April 7 in the case of Eaton and April 11 for Van Buren, Jackson informed Ingham, Branch, and Berrien that he wished to reconstitute his cabinet, whereupon they resigned, though not with good humor.

Indeed, their humors became increasingly ill as party journalists discussed the resignations from various points of view. The Eaton affair, widely spoken of for two years, but generally kept out of the papers, was now given an airing, the correspondence of the resigned ministers with the President was published, and the tempers of many of the persons involved neared the breaking point. On June 21, the day he left Washington, Ingham addressed the President to complain that Eaton had lain in wait for him on the public street with intent to assassinate him.[25]

Louis McLane was fortunate not to arrive home till a month after the climax of this controversy.

V   THE NEW CABINET

The course of cabinet making did not run smooth. Van Buren, who had written his resignation on April 11, 1831, announced it to friends in New York and Virginia on April 16.[26] Ingham and Branch resigned on April 19, and on the same day John Quincy Adams heard as fact that

McLane was chosen to replace Ingham, a story Niles had reported on April 9 as "freely rumored for some time past." [27] On April 23 Niles announced the rumored new cabinet: Edward Livingston (State), McLane (Treasury), Hugh White (War), Levi Woodbury, a Senator from New Hampshire (Navy).[28] Two days later Van Buren confirmed this selection in a letter to a friend, adding that a Virginian would be chosen to succeed Berrien.[29]

An old friendship dating from the Battle of New Orleans dictated Jackson's choice of Livingston, but it was supported by Livingston's reputation as one of the old Democratic Republicans, which made him impeccable on party grounds, and his lack of identification with any of the recent party schisms. He had not intrigued for the position and was not sure he wanted it. He thought a voyage to Europe might be necessary for his wife's health, he felt out of touch with the details of diplomacy, and he hated to be involved in the political intrigues he knew would swirl about him. But he was told that Van Buren, as a candidate for the Presidency, insisted on leaving the cabinet, he was promised time for his decision, and he was flattered by Jackson's offer. "My friend Livingston," the President said, with a slap on the knee, "you must accept!" [30]

He did, but Hugh White was more difficult. His wife had died recently and his daughter was dying of tuberculosis—these reasons at least gave him an excuse for refusing Jackson's importunate request to join the cabinet.[31] With his refusal went the hope of getting an immediate Senate seat for Eaton. For the War Department, Jackson turned from White to Colonel William Drayton, of South Carolina, not without some hesitation at the idea of having a second Federalist in the cabinet.[32] But Drayton too refused the post, which was then offered to Lewis Cass, governor of the Michigan Territory. He accepted.

Since Woodbury accepted the Navy Department, thus giving New England representation, the cabinet was completed with McLane's acceptance, which was, of course, a long time arriving, and with the appointment of Roger B. Taney, a Baltimore lawyer, as Attorney General. Taney, who was offered the place instead of a Virginian, gave representation to the upper South. His appointment also meant the addition of one more ex-Federalist to the cabinet, but he had left the Federalists a long time ago, and Jackson seemed unaware of the connection.

The reorganized cabinet—in which Barry remained as Postmaster General, though he too offered to resign—seemed to most observers to be stronger than its predecessor. McLane's appointment was generally approved, at least for his personal qualities, though his Federalist opinions aroused fears in some quarters. A member of the Albany Regency, Van Buren's political faction in New York, not only approved of McLane's appointment but even suggested that as he was a more vigorous man he might make a better Secretary of State than Livingston.[33] Calhoun agreed, but he added that McLane brought no popular support to the administration.[34]

VI   THE NEW OFFICE

When Louis McLane arrived in Washington on August 6, 1831, his seasickness was forgotten and it was a man in vigorous health that Jackson welcomed to his cabinet. The initial impression of physical vigor was succeeded by one of intellectual vigor. "Mr. McLane's mind is a host to me," Jackson declared a month later.[35]

It was a busy time for the new Secretary of the Treasury. He had to acquaint himself with official routine before he could take the forward steps he planned. And, not least of his problems, he had housing to find for as many of his family as he could bring to Washington with him. "I have attempted," he confessed, "to bribe each proprietor of every respectable house in Washington to quit his habitation, until I believe every owner of a house became almost afraid to meet me." [36]

Catherine McLane, "frank, gay, communicative," as ever, came to Washington too, to help her husband in the search for housing and in other ways. It is quite possible that one of the ways in which Kitty sought to help Louis get established in Washington was by calling on Peggy Eaton. One Washington gossip declared that Kitty had made such a call; one Washington newspaper denied it.[37] It was, Calhoun had told Ingham, Van Buren's recipe given the McLanes for getting on in the world.[38] Louis, however, was exasperated by public discussion of the Eaton affair and sought, without success, to dissuade Eaton from a public exposition of his grievances against his recent colleagues.[39]

In settling into the work of his office, where clerical inefficiency was said to exist, McLane was fortunate in having the assistance of at least one able bureaucrat.[40] This was Asbury Dickins, chief clerk of the Treasury Department and acting Secretary from the time of Samuel Ingham's departure late in June until McLane's arrival in August.

Dickins, a native of North Carolina, was the sociable son of a pioneer Methodist preacher. An early association with publishing and bookselling in Philadelphia, where he took over William Cobbett's shop, had brought him a wide acquaintance among the literary circle there that included young Nicholas Biddle. After some years abroad, Dickins was brought into the Treasury Department by William H. Crawford, whom he had met in Paris.

Dickins and his wife, who was the daughter of a wealthy Scottish literary man, played a leading role in Washington society, despite the expenses of rearing nine children on a clerk's salary. One of the sons of the family was employed as a clerk in his father's office, and father and son together made $3,400 a year, a good income in the 1830's but hardly enough for the fashionable dances the Dickins family gave. As a consequence, Dickins was usually in debt, and it was to his old Philadelphia friends that he turned when he was in need.

McLane had wanted Dickins as his secretary in London, and now the two worked together as a completely compatible team, so much so that when McLane left the Treasury Department he took Dickins with him to his new post. Their compatibility can be explained in terms of their common backgrounds in religion and in politics. Both men were reared as Methodists and began their careers as Federalists; both men had been supporters of Crawford, for when McLane, as chairman of Ways and Means, was working closely with that Treasury Secretary, Dickins was Crawford's confidential clerk.

If these factors served to make initial relations easy between McLane and Dickins, it was probably Dickins's knowledge and usefulness that impressed McLane the most. It was this knowledge that kept Dickins in office through the Treasury administrations of Richard Rush and Samuel Ingham, long after Crawford had retired. Ingham's continuance of Dickins was questioned by some Calhoun men who doubted the wisdom of retaining an old Crawfordite.[41]

Obviously Dickins was just the person to acquaint McLane with official routine and the arrears of business, and as the new Secretary made his way about Washington, the impression he created was generally good. "McLane is a charming little fellow," a friend wrote Van Buren, "and we are all pleased with him." [42]

Not quite all, if McLane's senses informed him correctly. "Taney fights shy of me," McLane wrote of the new Attorney General, adding, "We were always on good terms and I know of no cause for separation now but his fears on a certain subject." The "certain subject" was Gabriel Duvall's seat on the Supreme Court, for which Taney, having the advantage in legal reputation and in friendship with the incumbent, was a formidable rival.

McLane raised the subject of his own ambition for the Court when, upon his return from England, he met Van Buren in New York. On that occasion Van Buren gave McLane a note of recommendation for Jackson, but when McLane arrived in the capital, he decided not to deliver the note, fearing the impression he would make by begging one position at the moment of entering into another. Consequently he wrote Van Buren, who was still in New York, requesting him to communicate directly with the President. Van Buren did write Jackson on the day before he sailed. But no vacancy occurred, and McLane soon became so absorbed in his work that the Court and his ambition for a seat on it lost priority in his mind. Perhaps it was as it seemed to Major Lewis, that "a change came over the spirit of his dream" and McLane became not Taney's rival for the Court so much as Van Buren's rival for the succession.[43]

The Treasury Secretary, McLane clearly saw, occupies a commanding position, "the natural point of control to be occupied by any statesman," according to Henry Adams, who also wrote that an "effort to control the whole machinery and policy of government . . . is necessarily forced upon the holder of the purse."[44] But the old McLane, who had boasted he was the advocate of a great national system, combining "the Navy, Army, Fortifications, Internal Improvements, and the Militia," had to adjust his policies to the realities of his political position. The Navy, Army, fortifications, and militia could be looked after under a soldier President if McLane could find the money, but internal improvements at national expense were taboo except when a very strong case could be made for them as national projects. The old McLane had also been an advocate of protective tariffs and a national bank. The Treasury Secretary must now subordinate these issues to the major Jacksonian goal, extinction of the national debt. But in pursuing this major goal, the new McLane might find a way to cater to his old prejudices and cherish measures he had for more than a decade supported on the floor of Congress.

Van Buren was uneasy. Despite his sponsorship of McLane, knowledge of McLane's principles led Van Buren, soon after his arrival in England, to send Jackson a warning about doctrinal inconsistencies that might arise from the fact that several members of the cabinet (he singled out McLane for particular mention) were not strict constructionists.[45]

VII   MC LANE AND BIDDLE

What made Van Buren uneasy, made Nicholas Biddle glad. Judge William Johnson, Jeffersonian dissenter on the Supreme Court but brother to an official of the branch bank in Charleston, visited Washington as the new cabinet assembled to discover their attitude to the Bank. He was pleased, sending word to Biddle that "the Bank have nothing to apprehend from the present Cabinet," but warning the stockholders against any movements to influence elections.[46]

McLane soon invited Biddle to Washington, but the conference had to be postponed until after a meeting of the Bank's stockholders (who accepted Biddle's suggestion that renewal of their charter be sought at the next session of Congress) and until after McLane had journeyed with the President, Major Lewis, and Postmaster General Barry to visit Charles Carroll of Carrollton and bring that aged statesman their congratulations on his ninety-fifth birthday.[47] At their meeting in September Biddle found McLane friendly to the Bank but skittish about any positive advocacy of it. Sensitive as McLane was to the Bank's great usefulness, he would try to soothe the President and at least put an end to open castigation. On the way to Carroll's McLane had sounded Jackson out and secured some crumbs, at least, of comfort. And with Livingston, on whom the President primarily depended for his forthcoming message to Congress, McLane had reached an agreement that no reference at all should be made to the Bank.

This was not enough for Biddle. He hoped Jackson would declare that the future of the Bank was up to Congress. And he hoped McLane, in his report to Congress, would go a step further and recommend renewal of the Bank charter. It would be a daring step for a minister of Jackson to take, but Biddle left papers in the hands of Asbury Dickins which this clerk was to show McLane—papers demonstrating that previous proposals for the charter and recharter of the Bank had originated with McLane's predecessors in the Treasury Department.[48]

The suggestion made to McLane flourished like a seed dropped on fallow soil. "If the old chief would consent to recharter the bank," McLane had told his friend General Sam Smith, a month earlier, "what a glorious operation I could make for him." [49]

However, McLane's main objective, to retire the debt as soon as possible, did not strike Biddle happily. Yet McLane was determined and officially notified Biddle on September 29 that the commissioners of the sinking fund had decided that all government securities due to be redeemed on January 1, 1832, would be paid off early, that they would indeed be redeemed in the month of October upon presentation at any office of the Bank of the United States. The value of these certificates was $6 million, a large amount for any bank to be called on to pay almost without notice, and an embarrassing amount for the Bank of the United States to pay at this time when it was experiencing a large outflow of specie to Europe.[50]

When the Bank was to be called on for the payment of large sums, Biddle explained to Dickins, and through him to McLane, it ought to be given enough advance warning to accumulate the specie reserves needed. Otherwise it was obliged to be ever ready to make payments and was thereby prevented from using its funds to the advantage of the community. At the moment the Bank was under such heavy pressure from its own operations that this additional demand was particularly burdensome. "When you gave the order," Biddle could admonish Dickins, "you really had not the money." Referring to a promise that Danish indemnity funds would be left undisturbed for three years, he called Dickins and McLane "gay deceivers" but immediately assured them he did not mean it seriously.[51] After all, as he had told Dickins previously, "McLane's conduct has been so handsome in the matters of the Bank, that he has put me in a mood to agree to anything not very unreasonable." [52]

The handsome conduct referred to must have meant an understanding Biddle and McLane had come to on October 19 at their second interview, when McLane, home in Delaware for a short visit, appeared at the Philadelphia office of the Bank at ten in the morning. What he told Biddle gave the Bank president immense pleasure, and a share of self-satisfaction too. The evidence he had left in Dickins's hands to show that past Secretaries had recommended the Bank to Congress and that they had felt an independent responsibility to report to Congress as more than the President's agent—this evidence had apparently had its effect on McLane. It was a matter of the first importance to Biddle, for if the Secretary were only an executive assistant to the President, reflecting the President's opinion, the outlook for the Bank was clouded. On the other hand, if the Secretary bore a responsibility to Congress to report his independent opinion, things would look better for the Bank.

On October 19 Biddle discovered that McLane had taken the independent position the Bank desired. Furthermore, McLane had discussed the matter with Jackson and explained his intentions forthrightly. McLane's plan was imaginative and breathtaking. It may not have taken Biddle's breath—or Jackson's—but it was thoroughly pleasing to the one and seemed to the other to be at least clear and straightforward and perhaps, at least momentarily, convincing.

The central feature of the plan as it was outlined to Biddle was to pay off all the debt by March 3, 1833—by the end, that is, of Jackson's first term.[53] Whether or not McLane knew it, Biddle had suggested just such a proposition in 1829 and the President had approved it. But since Jackson at the same time indicated his doubts of the constitutionality of the Bank, the project had come to nothing. It is a remarkable coincidence, if a coincidence, that the Biddle and McLane plans for redemption both provided that the Bank would purchase the government's portion of its stock, carrying a par value of $7 million. Biddle, to be sure, had proposed payment by January 8, 1833, the anniversary of the Battle of New Orleans, whereas McLane was content with the date of March 3, but then McLane had less time to spare when he made his proposal.[54]

Biddle's plan for redemption was primarily a fiscal suggestion, intended to allow Jackson to achieve his aim of a debtless nation while winning his friendship for the Bank. McLane's plan was much more comprehensive, the plan of a Treasury Secretary who was not just a fiscal official but a first minister of statecraft; it was a plan worthy of a Morris or a Hamilton.

"He thinks he can present the Tariff question strongly," noted Biddle after McLane had called; "he can then press with equal strength the Bank question, and if he can arrange the question of the public lands . . . the Bank would be put in such company and on such a footing that even Mr. Benton would not attack it."

The Bank, in other words, would receive a warm recommendation from the Secretary in connection with his proposal to sell to it the government stock. He would furthermore prefer the present Bank, with its charter amended to meet several particular objections, to any other bank. (Privately McLane told Biddle that the greatest danger was from those who in jealousy and greed wished to abolish this bank in order to establish another.) He was aware, too, that his report might lead the Ways and Means Committee, chaired by the Bank's friend—and Calhoun's—George McDuffie, to propose a bill for recharter. Such a bill—and McLane told Biddle he had made this clear to Jackson—he could not in good conscience oppose.

However, he still hoped that the Bank would not apply for recharter, and on this point he was more insistent in October than he had been in September. The present charter did not expire until 1836, and the issue should not be put to Jackson before the election lest he regard it as a test. "I think," McLane added, "he would be more disposed to yield when he is strong [that is, after he has been reelected] than when he is in danger." [55]

"Handsome" was the word in Biddle's mind to describe McLane's conduct toward the Bank, and Biddle was "in a mood to agree to anything not very unreasonable"—perhaps even to postponing an application for recharter.[56] When his cousin Roswell Colt thought of sending a paragraph to the papers about the unjustified pressure placed on the money market by the Treasury's sudden order to pay off debts before they were due, Biddle demurred. In view of McLane's friendliness, he advised, "do not . . . say a word—and do not write a word—above all do not publish a word against it." [57]

With a wish for "the full success which you deserve in the efforts you are making for the reconciliation of all the great interests of the country," Biddle sent McLane formal notice of the Bank's agreement to buy back the government's 70,000 shares of its stock for not less than $8 million, a sum that would allow McLane to pay off a substantial part of the national debt.[58]

In the month that followed, Louis McLane shaped his plans and the report that would present them to Congress and the people. Through Asbury Dickins, Nicholas Biddle kept in touch with the Treasury Department. "We are doing very well in Washington," he wrote, four days before he lent Dickins $3,000. And with a note of thanks for the loan, Dickins sent reassurance: "Every thing goes well here. The influence of our friend [McLane] upon the policy of the administration cannot fail to have the most happy effect upon all the great interests of the country, —and will contribute to the popularity of the administration, and, hereafter, to his own fame and eminence." [59]

Yet in a short time their friend's plans, and their own, met a slight setback. Early in December, Jackson called the cabinet members to the White House to hear a completed draft of the message he was preparing to send to the new Congress, which was to convene on Monday, December 5. It was Jackson's custom to ask different men for advice on specific sections of the message and to have their suggestions, if he approved them, incorporated into the message, sometimes in the very language in which they were sent to him. On this occasion the message so prepared was read to the assembled Secretaries, and one of them, the new Attorney General, Roger Taney, was quite surprised when the reader, Andrew Jackson Donelson, came to a section referring to the Bank of the United States. The President, the section read, had in two previous years brought the Bank and its future to the attention of Congress. Now he declared himself content to ignore this subject, leaving it to Congress to take such action as it chose.

What could this mean, Roger Taney wondered. Would not people think Jackson had changed his mind on the Bank?

What it did mean was that Louis McLane had taken Nicholas Biddle's suggestion (that Jackson should say he left the matter to Congress) and, as he had promised Biddle in the October 19 conference, had persuaded Jackson to adopt it. Needless to say, the President was in total ignorance of the origin of the idea.

Taney, despite his old Federalist connections, had become an advocate of the democratic concept of "free banking" and an enemy of the national Bank, and he now thought it his duty to point out the construction that would be put on Jackson's words. Alone in the cabinet he vigorously criticized this section of the address. It would, he argued, discourage those who had supported the President against the Bank. It would lend encouragement to the Bank's friends, who might feel that Jackson, surrounded now by new advisers, had been persuaded to adopt new opinions.

Livingston, Cass, and McLane opposed Taney. Cass, however, said but little. Livingston supported the message (of which he was a chief architect) as it stood and denied it would give the impression Taney suggested. But McLane took the leading role in defense of the message, arguing with a vigor and tenacity that made Taney sure that the idea and even the words were of McLane's contriving.

The discussion turned into a debate between Taney and McLane, with Woodbury interposing to suggest a few minor changes that might effect a compromise, till finally it was obvious that the President was becoming embarrassed by the affair. He did not want, he said, to lead people to think he would sign any bill that Congress passed relating to the Bank, nor did he need to threaten a veto. It was time enough to speak and to act when legislation was put before him.

Obviously Jackson did not want to hurt the feelings of either of his advisers. Taney was tormenting him with recollection of past messages. McLane would be hurt if the section he defended was changed. And Jackson was not wholly in agreement with either of them.[60]

Unlike McLane, Jackson did not grasp the utility of the Bank of the United States. Unlike Taney, Jackson did not concentrate his suspicion and dislike on the Bank of the United States; he suspected and disliked all banks. Under persuasion by his advisers it was possible that he might agree to a recharter. He admitted as much in a letter to James A. Hamilton, when he wrote, "Mr. McLane and myself understand each other, and have not the slightest disagreement about principles, which will be a *sine qua non* in my assent to a bill rechartering the Bank." [61]

Perhaps McLane and Jackson did not understand each other as well as Jackson—and McLane too—felt they did. The Jackson horse that McLane and other old Crawfordites had mounted was not a colt that could be broken to follow their commands; he was headstrong, and though he could be led, he could not be driven. Had McLane remained in Washington for the first two years of the Jackson administration, he might better have understood the President's character.[62] As it was, he could only resent bitterly the opposition Taney made to his plans.

Yet Taney's opposition did little more harm than to alert McLane to the presence of a contrary voice in the cabinet. Jackson did change his reference to the Bank in his message, but the change was so slight— merely a reference to his opinions "heretofore expressed in relation to the Bank . . . as at present organized"—that the whole passage remained quite ambiguous. It was far short of what Taney wanted, but he preferred the revision to the first draft because it did at least refer to Jackson's opinions on the Bank.[63]

There was no reaction of any consequence to this section of the President's message when it was read to Congress on December 6, but the following day the release of McLane's report created a sensation. The editors of the *Intelligencer* could recall no executive report that had ever created a sensation like it. "For ourselves," they wrote, "we have not been able to draw a long breath since we read it." [64] "It is able and comprehensive, fuller of bolder views and more original propositions than any other paper, which has emanated from [the Treasury] for thirty years," declared Thomas Ritchie, the ultra-Jeffersonian editor of the Richmond *Enquirer*, shocked into acknowledgment of "a masterly effort" with which he could not wholly agree.[65]

There was one reaction McLane was most concerned about, so concerned that he wrote two letters within eight days to try to soften the report's effect. It was the reaction of Martin Van Buren, his sponsor and erstwhile confidant, that bothered McLane. To Van Buren in London he sent an early copy of the report the day before it was issued, coupling it with this admonition: "You will not approve this report most probably unless you purge your mind not of your democracy but of your party prejudices." [66]

VIII THE TREASURY REPORT

McLane's Treasury report is his political *opus magnum*. "It is," wrote a Virginia Congressman, "the most federal message which has been issued since the days of the elder Adams, far exceeding Hamilton himself." [67]

There were, indeed, strong Federalist influences in the report, but most of all in the way, a statesmanlike way, in which McLane sought to use fiscal policy to adjust and settle the diverse interests of segments, sectional and otherwise, of the nation. The chief goal of the report was, however, Jeffersonian, the extinction of the national debt.

This debt consisted, McLane declared, of about $24 million and could be paid off in its entirety by March 3, 1833, the end of Jackson's term, by applying to it $16 million of anticipated revenue (over and above operating expenses) and $8 million that could be realized by sale of the government's stock in the Bank of the United States. The par value of this stock was but $7 million, and little more might be realized if it were thrown on the open market, particularly if "under circumstances calculated to shake public confidence in the stability of the institution." [68]

But a sale to the Bank could be effected to the advantage both of the Bank and of the government: to the advantage of the Bank because it would escape a public sale that would cause the price of the stock as well as public confidence to fall, and to the government because it would be getting a profit of $1 million on the transaction.

Though expressly dissociating the adoption of this proposal from the renewal of the charter, McLane went on to declare himself frankly in favor of such a step, just as Biddle had urged him to do—in favor of re-charter "at the proper time" and with "such judicious checks and limitations as experience may have shown to be necessary." [69]

With the debt paid off, an annual revenue after March 3, 1833, of $13.5 million would be sufficient for the customary annual expenditures, "as at present authorized." But this was a propitious moment to take care of other objects of concern which had to be postponed by the prior obligation of paying off the debt. Therefore, like a good Federalist, and, in general, like a responsible experienced statesman who had knowledge of what was necessary, McLane reeled off a list of new expenditures that came to $1.5 million a year—one ninth of the total of previous expenditures, minus the debt. A good many of the items on McLane's list were devised to augment our military defenses, as by building armories, arming state militia, bringing naval officers up to the level of army officers in salary and in opportunities for instruction ("the Navy, the child of Federal policy," a Federalist commentator might have declaimed two decades earlier), enlarging the naval hospital fund, and strengthening frontier defenses.

If these were natural recommendations for an old soldier's son to make, so were others proper for the son of a customs collector. McLane recommended the construction of customs houses and warehouses in the major ports (these buildings were usually rented), river improvements in the West, harbor improvements in the East, coastal surveys, and an adequate compensation for customs officers, based on the vigilance required, not the business done, and payable as salary, not in fees. Perhaps it was out of his experience as a lawyer or as a marshal's son that McLane recommended construction of federal courthouses. His own experience in Washington and abroad could account for recommendations to raise the salary of public ministers overseas (so as not "to throw these high trusts altogether into the hands of the rich") and to provide increased space for federal offices in Washington. Finally veteran Colonel McLane's son recommended "further provision . . . for . . . officers and soldiers of the revolution." [70]

Add this $1.5 million to the $13.5 million for current expenditures and an annual revenue of $15 million was called for. A revenue tariff should be—and could be—the sole and sufficient source of this.

Of the three chief sources of government funds McLane would eliminate two. One was the interest on Bank stock, which would, of course, cease to come to the government when the stock was sold. The second was the income from the sale of public lands, and this, McLane, in the next major recommendation of his report, proposed to nullify by selling all the lands to the states in which they lay and then distributing the proceeds at one swoop to all the states. In this fashion he proposed at once to solve the problem of how to make the lands available (this problem would be given to the states) and the problem of what to do with the proceeds (which problem would also be given to the states).

The McLane solution was a politic one, made within a Republican pattern of decreasing the responsibility of the central government. The public land had been viewed as a great source for paying off the national debt, but once the debt was gone the resource was not needed. Western politicians urged that the lands be made increasingly more accessible to settlers and sometimes complained that their states did not control land distribution, as had the original states within their own borders. In recommending cession of the public lands to the states, McLane was following the recommendation of such an old Republican as Senator Tazewell, of Virginia.[71] In recommending distribution of the sums to be received from the states in payment, McLane was following the President's suggestion, made in the presidential message of December, 1829, for the disposal of a Treasury surplus.[72]

If the tariff was to be used hereafter as the sole source of government revenue, McLane warned that it should be so levied as to produce only the sums required by federal expenditures, for if the states became dependent on the government for appropriations, tariffs would be set at higher rates than necessary and the independence of the states would be undermined. A revenue tariff was McLane's recommendation, but a revenue tariff that would be used for other ends than revenue alone. He conceded the propriety of granting reasonable protection to domestic manufacturing, but if a revenue tariff did not suffice for the purpose, he preferred outright bounties to the accumulation of a Treasury surplus. For the particular assistance of the shipbuilding industry and through it of American shipping, McLane recommended drawbacks of the duties charged on articles made of iron, hemp, flax, or copper used in the construction of ships.

Such recommendations as he made regarding the new scale of duties were to be received as suggestions only, not as "a digested scheme." In general, he urged a pragmatic adjustment of diverse interests rather than settlement on the basis of abstract doctrines of political economy. He was a politician, not a philosopher.

In supporting the use of revenue duties for incidental protection, McLane insisted that he was following a precedent of the first tariff act of 1789, since which time tariff duties had "quickened each branch of industry." He would not, he said, deny that this adaptation of duties to purposes of protection might have gone too far and that a present crisis required the confinement of protection to reasonable limits. In other words, he did not foreswear the Federalist and protectionist doctrines he had voiced in the past, but he now urged a course that would conciliate opponents of the high tariff—Southerners, for instance.

The commodities presently needing continued protection, McLane suggested, were wool, woolens, cottons, iron, hemp, and sugar. Any sudden reduction of duties on these goods would hurt their American producers, but a gradual reduction could be undertaken. To the extent that revenue was needed, duties could advantageously be retained on luxury articles, particularly those used by the wealthy classes and not produced in the United States, while removing duties from raw materials not competitive with American products.[73]

He had taken the ground from under Clay, McLane bragged when his report was completed. It was a pleasure to deal this blow to an old enemy who seemed to have taken a seat in the Senate with the express hope of earning reputation as a composer of quarrels and a compromiser. Now the merit of harmonizing conflicting political interests should belong, by McLane's scheme, to the administration.[74] The whole report, McLane insisted, complied with the principles he had avowed to Van Buren when still in London. And no step had been taken without the fullest and frankest understanding with the President.[75]

IX   REACTION

The President's comments to Van Buren verified this claim. The Treasury report, Jackson wrote, "is full and lucid . . . and a display of Talent honorable to its possessor. . . . McLane differs with me on the Bank; still it is an honest difference of opinion, and in his report he acts fairly, by leaving me free and uncommitted." And then, as though gritting his teeth, he added, "This I will be, on that Subject." [76]

"Mr. McLane and myself understand each other," Jackson had insisted,[77] but he longed to have Van Buren back at his side: "Had I you in the State Department and Eaton in the War, with the others filled as they are, it would be one of the strongest and happiest administrations that could be formed. We could control the little Federal leaven in that high minded honorable and talented friend of ours, Mr. McLane." Cass was too amiable, could not say no, and Livingston was getting forgetful and was eager to go abroad. Let Van Buren return in two years, if confirmed; if not confirmed, and Jackson was sure the Senate would reject him "if they durst," he would be run for Vice-President.[78]

"I have to labour hard, and constantly watchfull," Jackson had interjected, perhaps remembering the warning Van Buren had sent him: "without much care on your part, doctrines may be suggested and adopted which would expose you to the charge of inconsistency." [79] Now the "Federal leaven" in Louis McLane brought "pain and mortification" to Van Buren, as he read the Treasury report in London, or so he recalled in later years. Aware of his own agency in securing McLane's appointment, he felt the humiliation bound to fall upon the innocent President through the publication of this paper which seemed calculated to make McLane "the efficient head" of Jackson's administration.[80] Yet McLane lost no ground in Van Buren's personal regard, or, if he did, Van Buren was too canny to show it, even to Washington Irving, who was with Van Buren in the London legation and who reported to McLane that the Treasury report was "greatly extolled . . . by persons of whose good opinion you would be proud, and has added to that estimation in which you are universally held."[81]

To free-trader Churchill Cambreleng, who thought the Treasury report "as bad as it possibly can be," Van Buren confessed that he too worried whether the administration might be led off the "old Republican track." He assured Cambreleng of McLane's purity, constancy, and regard, but at the same time advised, "Talk plainly to the President," when clearly he meant that Cambreleng's doubts of McLane's course should be voiced.[82]

Other disconcerted Republicans included Calhoun and his old antagonist John Randolph. Calhoun called the Treasury report ultra-Federalist, "one of the most faulty documents" he ever saw.[83] Randolph, as a friend of the administration, cautioned Jackson that he was surrounded by evil counselors, including one who was "ultra Federal, ultra Tariff, ultra Bank." But on thinking the matter over, Randolph regretted making such a hard judgment on McLane, whom he did not wish to blame for his principles.[84]

"The Secretary has done a very disingenuous act," complained a New York Democrat; "his race will be short."[85] He "covers ground," wrote another, that "scrupulous and old fashioned" Democrats "will not be willing to occupy."[86] The report "is too high toned—too ultra federal for me," the secretary of the Senate declared to Van Buren.[87]

When Cornelius Van Ness, American minister to Spain, had read the Treasury report, he too sent word of his dissatisfaction to his friend in London. "A very strange document," he thought it. McLane goes "out of his sphere." How strange for a Secretary, whatever his individual opinion, to go out of his way to recommend a bank the President disapproves. "How inconsistent it would appear" for a cabinet member to recommend passage of a law and then for the President to veto that law. "I have much respect and esteem for Mr. McLane, but you know that persons who exhibit a desire to strike out a new course, and to do something that no other person has done under like circumstances, are very apt to overact, and thus to run into absurdities."[88]

Jackson editors were as surprised by the Treasury report as were Jackson politicians. Most of them praised the report in general terms, but attacked some special part of it. Thomas Ritchie greeted McLane's recommendation of a Bank recharter "with much regret." [89] The New York Regency's paper, the Albany *Argus,* dissented "unreservedly" on several points, notably the Bank recharter.[90] The New York *Evening Post,* a free trade organ, disagreed with McLane's statements about the desirability of retaining some protection in the tariff schedule.[91]

Francis Blair's *Globe,* as voice of the administration, was in a difficult position, bitterly opposed to the Bank recommendation, yet not completely free to attack a member of the cabinet. According to one story, the *Globe* originally planned to publish a paragraph so strongly opposing the Treasury report's recharter recommendation that McLane threatened to resign if the paragraph were printed.[92] Even the article that finally appeared infuriated McLane, because he felt the *Globe* should have done him justice by noting that he proposed radical modifications, entirely changing the organization of the Bank.[93] The modifications he had in mind, however radical they may have been, were not specifically projected in the Treasury report, and McLane was not just to Blair in his criticism.

But Blair had his revenge for any pressure McLane may have put upon him. With or without Blair's connivance, the *Globe* was used for a subtle blow at McLane, when, under the pretense that the speeches in Congress brought up reminiscences of that "Byron of orators," John Randolph, the paper reprinted the famous congressional exchange between Randolph and McLane. The high point of it was reached in McLane's angry remark that he would not take Randolph's head if he must take his heart with it, and Randolph's rejoinder that he refused McLane's "heart, however good it may be, if obliged to take such a head into the bargain."

The *Globe* article did not use McLane's name, referring to him only as "the most powerful antagonist" Randolph ever encountered.[94] But the story was a familiar one to Washington politicians, and McLane immediately demanded an explanation of its revival at this moment by a paper enjoying the support of the administration. Blair explained that Key— probably Francis Scott Key—gave it to him for the purpose of putting Randolph in a good temper. McLane had little choice but to accept the explanation, despite his suspicion that the story was intended to hurt him rather than to benefit Randolph, a suspicion that was probably invigorated by the knowledge that Key was a friend of Roger Taney's.[95]

While the *Globe* was embarrassing McLane by repeating an old tale that he insisted was much garbled, his political position was seriously threatened by the remarks of the *Intelligencer*, an antiadministration paper that almost killed McLane with its kindness. His report, it said, was "manly and independent," treating established doctrines of the Jackson party with "loftiest disdain" or with "sovereign contempt." "In short," chortled the *Intelligencer*, "there is no ground heretofore occupied by the present administration, which the honorable Secretary has . . . been able to reach by the longest stretch of his arm in which he has not given the *coup-de-grace* to all the prior emanations from the Cabinet." [96] Such praise was potentially ruinous, but worse was a short paragraph in Duff Green's *Telegraph* charging McLane, in effect, with a specific act of treason to the anti-Bank element of the Jackson party. Jackson, said the *Telegraph*, had already agreed to a recharter bill worked out jointly by the Treasury and the Bank. And when the *Globe* denied there was such a bill, Duff Green, eager to embarrass the administration, fired back by declaring that his information came from a member of Congress who had it from the Secretary of the Treasury himself.[97]

On the appearance of the first paragraph in the *Telegraph*, McLane shot off a denial of it to the *Globe:* no bill was prepared or projected jointly by the Treasury and the Bank, and nothing of the sort existed that could have Jackson's approval.[98] After the *Telegraph* claimed that its indirect source was McLane, it went on to explain that he had not spoken of an existing recharter bill but had "said that a bill could be prepared which would meet the approbation of all parties." This, too, McLane denied: he had made no such statement to any member of Congress, nor had he authorized any part of the comment in the *Telegraph*.[99]

Maybe he had not. But surely he felt such a bill was possible. For the moment he was riding high, secure in his own self-esteem and bolstered by the evident approval of his clerks, who thought his report "statesman-like and manly," praised by "the wise and good . . . in the highest terms." [100] Probably he saw a letter from Nicholas Biddle to Asbury Dickins in which Biddle said that the report was "enlarged, liberal, wise, . . . much fitter for a President's message than the President's message itself." "I wish with all my heart," Biddle added, "that the writer of it was President." [101]

This was a sentiment McLane could appreciate. Indeed, he shared it. At last he was being given an opportunity to display his talents on a broad scale. Even his enemies paid him the tribute of admitting that he had become in a few months the dominant figure in Jackson's cabinet.[102] Even his friends noticed his vaunting ambition. The McLanes do not willingly yield either political or social leadership to the Edward Livingstons, a Washington hostess observed, after noting McLane's anger over a question of precedence at a presidential dinner.[103]

11

Climax

I BIDDLE'S DECISION

In speaking of Louis McLane during the last year of Jackson's Presidency, Senator Hugh L. White, of Tennessee, paid tribute to "the vigorous and discriminating mind of this highly gifted and useful man." [1] Yet at the time White spoke, McLane's talents were no longer directly employed in the service of his country, but instead were hired out to a private and speculative business that removed him from the neighborly connections and the professional ambitions of a lifetime.

The climax of Louis McLane's career was reached in the seven weeks that followed the Treasury report he presented to Congress on December 7, 1831. Not one but two events in this brief period halted his career at the moment when his light was brightest. The first of these events was the decision Nicholas Biddle reached by January 4, 1832, to seek immediate recharter of the Bank of the United States. The second event occurred on January 25, when the Senate, through the casting vote of Vice-President Calhoun, rejected the nomination of Martin Van Buren as minister to Great Britain.

On December 7, 1831, there was reason to hope that the system of statecraft embodied in McLane's Treasury report might be adopted. Even the one specific recommendation that aroused most opposition, renewal of the charter of the Bank of the United States, seemed to have a chance of eventual success. The cabinet, Taney excepted, seemed willing to follow McLane's lead. "The Chief," too, Jackson himself, seemed to be wavering.

However, McLane and his friend Sam Smith, chairman of the Senate Finance Committee, felt they should not push this issue for the moment.

In recommending sale of the government Bank stock, McLane specifically denied that the sale should be tied to any pledge to recharter the Bank. He did express his personal opinion that the Bank should be rechartered —but in due time, not hastily. Not at this session of Congress, he was willing to say privately, lest the President feel himself challenged or "pressed into a corner." [2] When the Bank sent Joshua Whitney to Washington to sample opinion, he was told that McLane was so much opposed to recharter at this session that he would advise Jackson to refuse to sign the bill if it were pressed on him. If McLane ever said this—the story comes thirdhand—it is likely that he was trying not to move too far too fast for other Jackson advisers. Major William B. Lewis, the President's permanent house guest, said that Jackson's advisers would take any move toward recharter this winter as an attack on them.

Nevertheless Whitney came to the conclusion that a recharter had better be sought at once while so much New York and Pennsylvania support existed that Jackson would not dare apply his veto.[3] From upstate New York came advice that Jacksonite opinion there was running for the Bank and had better be taken advantage of while Van Buren was out of the country and unable to organize the Democrats for his own selfish purposes.[4] Charles Fenton Mercer of Virginia also counseled striking for recharter at once, when, as he argued, the Vice-President, the Secretary of the Treasury, and other Secretaries and congressional leaders were friendly to the Bank.[5] By the next Congress, even by the next session of this Congress, these officials might be changed.

For several weeks Biddle remained undecided. It was hard for him to postpone securing the future of his Bank by recharter when he was so confident of its virtues. Like the *Times* of London, commenting upon the Bank on December 9, Biddle found it hard to believe that the Bank was not appreciated.

There was also a new pressure upon him to seek recharter at once. This pressure came from a candidate for President and his supporters, a candidate nominated by National Republicans, meeting in Baltimore from December 12 to 16. Their candidate was Henry Clay (with Bank attorney John Sergeant as his running mate), and the Kentuckian, searching for issues on which to assail Jackson, decided that the Bank question gave him an opportunity to exploit Jackson's ignorance of finance and thus to reduce Jackson's public stature. The obvious way to win attention to this issue was to get a recharter bill before Congress. Clay believed, as he told Biddle, that Jackson would not dare veto the bill before the election; after the election it would be another matter.[6]

Since Clay's first interest was in his own prospects, rather than in those of the Bank, his advice must seem suspect. Another of Clay's points seems to have more substance: this is the argument that whatever the decision Biddle made it would have political significance. If McLane and company urged Biddle to delay a recharter bill because it would be politically damaging to them, the anti-Jackson men had an equal right to claim that postponement of rechartering procedures was politically unfriendly.[7] Webster agreed with Clay that this was the time for recharter.[8]

Biddle now had to choose between McLane, who counseled delay, and Clay, who demanded action. Feeling he needed more information, Biddle sent another emissary to Washington. This time he chose Thomas Cadwalader, a Bank director who was his most intimate associate and had the additional advantage of having been one of the young literary set that met in Asbury Dickins's Philadelphia bookstore early in the century.[9] Arriving in Washington on December 20, Cadwalader immediately sought out McLane. They were together on the morning of December 21 and again that evening. McLane's advice was clear—wait!

"If you apply now," Cadwalader quoted him as saying, "you assuredly will fail,—if you wait, you will as certainly succeed." Jackson would veto a recharter bill now even if sure it would cost him the election; "hereafter" he would sign the bill if persuaded a large portion of the people were for it. But if he once vetoed a recharter bill, he would never change.

As they talked, Cadwalader and McLane painstakingly went over the congressional prospects of a recharter bill, testing whether it could possibly secure a two-thirds vote to override a veto. McLane's views were discouraging to Cadwalader, as to the present session, at least, for McLane believed that a number of men who were themselves friendly to the Bank—John Forsyth, for instance, Willie Mangum, and Felix Grundy —would support the government against it at this session.[10]

A day later Cadwalader recovered from the discouragement of his conversation with McLane. He saw George McDuffie, of South Carolina, chairman of Ways and Means, who leaned toward immediate application on the theory that the President was more likely to give his assent now than after the election. McDuffie's opinion may have been colored by the fact that as a Calhoun man he was anti-Jackson and therefore had no hesitancy whatever about embarrassing the administration—indeed, the opposite.

On Friday, December 23, Cadwalader planned to dine at McLane's home with McDuffie and General Smith, and then to confer again with these three men at McLane's office on Saturday night, which was Christmas Eve.[11] But McLane was ill on Friday and took to his bed for the whole Christmas weekend, not to go out again till Thursday, when he went "in a Carriage,—cloaked up," to the President's.[12]

Meanwhile Cadwalader was busy. He talked with Webster, with John Quincy Adams, with Secretary Livingston's brother, with McDuffie, with Sam Smith. Smith discouraged him, agreeing with McLane on postponement of renewal and arguing that ten votes in the Senate would go against the Bank this year that might be for it another year. "Smith failing us," Cadwalader wrote Biddle, "you will think the question settled *for this session,* and so it is." Unless, that is, he could turn the administration men from their objection to "a present movement." Adams was also discouraging, favoring postponement unless the Bank was sure of strong support for recharter. Gulian Verplanck, the New Yorker who was second to McDuffie on the Ways and Means Committee, also counseled delay. But McDuffie and Webster remained encouraging, and Peter R. Livingston, who was staying with his brother, the Secretary of State, urged the Bank to seek renewal at this session, declaring his brother and McLane would dissuade Jackson from a veto if a recharter bill were passed, though quite naturally they were eager to save him from the necessity of any action on recharter till after the election.

Cadwalader himself was inclined to favor seeking recharter at once, but he put off any commitment until he could hold the postponed meeting with Smith, McDuffie, and the convalescing McLane on December 30. Then on New Year's Eve he returned to Philadelphia to report to Biddle.[13]

By the time Cadwalader reached home, Biddle was all but determined to seek recharter without delay. The decisive point with him was a report that Cadwalader had written on December 26. The Bank emissary had called on McLane to inquire after his health and found the Secretary so anxious about the Bank business that he saw Cadwalader in his bedroom, to which he was still confined. During a long talk, in a "frank and familiar spirit," McLane assured Cadwalader that he would not be angry but would do his best to assure their success if the Bank directorate, despite his advice, went ahead with recharter now. "I brought it out of him," reported Cadwalader, "by intimating the present *inclination* of my opinions—in order to prepare him for what I do suppose we shall conclude upon." [14]

Perhaps McLane, weakened by his illness, contemplating from his confinement for a weekend the great trials that lay before him in his attempt to guide a whirlwind, felt too dispirited to argue further with his Philadelphia visitor. At any rate, this report was good news to Biddle. "The question was almost settled in my mind," he told Cadwalader, "when I found that Mr. M. [McLane] though opposed, would not be vexed. In truth, I hope he will be friendly." [15]

What more could Biddle hope for? "Our friends in general," he wrote a Vermont banker, "think . . . that the present moment is the most auspicious for an application to Congress." [16] Perhaps it did not occur to him that most of his friends who were urging an immediate application were members of the anti-Jackson opposition whose interest in renewal of the Bank charter was no greater than their desire to embarrass the President, to show him up. It is hard to blame Biddle for falling in line with their advice, however. It seemed a much more parlous course to desert the rest of the fleet and sail in the wake of Louis McLane, who seemed at most to be only the viceregent of the absent and inscrutable Martin Van Buren.[17] Surely it was to the advantage of the administration to have the question postponed till after the election; who would give assurance that Louis McLane could then win Jackson's acquiescence to a renewal of the charter, even though the Bank directors were likely to agree to any modifications the administration insisted upon? [18] The best that Sam Smith, a friend of the Bank, was able to say was that "if they drive the Chief into a Corner he will veto the Bill. If time be allowed him he may Sign it, altho that is very doubtful." [19] And Smith had a very high opinion of the ability, persuasive and otherwise, of Louis McLane.

Always in Biddle's memory hung the frightening specter of the destruction of the first Bank of the United States, which had prepared a petition to recharter in January, 1807, four years before the charter expired, but let more than a year go by before presenting it.[20] When the new board of directors assembled at the Bank on Chestnut Street on Wednesday, January 4, 1832, the decision was made.

Cadwalader was not in attendance because of a stagecoach accident that had left him with fractured ribs. Biddle had visited him and talked matters over and was able to supply the directors with more details than were stated in the written report Cadwalader submitted. Jackson, this report said, was as likely to sign a recharter bill now as ever. Probably he would never sign, and the sooner the country was so informed the better. Voters could cast their ballots more intelligently than otherwise if they knew before the elections how men stood on this issue, particularly incumbent Congressmen seeking reelection. Moreover, if recharter was not sought now, friends of the Bank, such as McDuffie and Clay, might lose some of their zeal for it.

Two years would be very little time to prepare for the Bank's demise, yet only that time would remain if the issue of recharter was postponed to the next congressional session, which would mean no decision till

March, 1834. Biddle's only regret, he told General Smith, while informing him of the decision, was that this action did not have "the concur-
rence of Mr. McLane and yourself, to whom the Bank as well as myself
personally owe much for the manner in which you have both sustained
the institution." [21]

Years later Thurlow Weed published in his Albany paper a story to
the effect that in an interview in Washington before the Bank applied
for recharter McLane handed Biddle a list of modifications in the charter
which he was authorized by Jackson to say would make that document
acceptable to the President. Biddle submitted the list to John Sergeant
and one or two other confidential directors of the Bank when he returned
to Philadelphia. These men found the modifications entirely acceptable,
but it was agreed that friends of the Bank in Congress should be consulted before acquiescence was indicated. Consequently Biddle and
Sergeant called on Clay and Webster, only to be dissuaded from the
project, because Clay and Webster declared no compromise or change
of front was expedient. They could carry the recharter bill, even over a
veto, and resented the idea of the Bank's abandoning its friends to work
with its foes.

Weed had this story from Nicholas Devereux, a director of the Utica
branch of the Bank of the United States and a friend of Biddle's, from
whom Devereux heard it. After Weed published the story he was
attacked for falsehood by several Whig journals. However, the New
York merchant Richard Blatchford came to Weed's defense, saying that
he had heard the same story from his friend Louis McLane, who used
to visit him often in New York.[22] This story also fits the account Duff
Green printed in the *Telegraph* on December 12, 1831, to the effect that
President Jackson had already approved a recharter bill jointly composed by the Treasury and the Bank.

Yet it is very unlikely that this story is true in all its details. Biddle's
interview with McLane in Washington occurred in October, long before
his decision to seek recharter through his congressional friends rather
than through McLane and other administration allies. Among surviving
manuscripts there are no references to an accepted list of modifications
to the charter. Finally, it seems very unlikely that Jackson ever made
himself quite so agreeable to McLane as to promise to assent to renewal
of the Bank charter if a certain set of modifications were introduced in it.

On the other hand, Devereux was a friend of Biddle's, as was Blatchford of McLane's. McLane did believe he could get Jackson to accept
a modified charter if there were no pressure. Biddle had declared himself willing to accept any modifications the administration demanded.

It is likely, therefore, that McLane had given him an idea of what modifications he had in mind.

As Weed said, the Bank decided not to abandon its friends to clasp hands with its foes.

II RECHARTER INTRODUCED

The Bank's decision to seek recharter at once was a serious blow to the plans of Louis McLane, believing as he did that this meant that the Bank would be destroyed and that without it his department could not perform its functions satisfactorily even for one year. He could still carry on with his program, however, for he should be able to launch it successfully within the four years still left to the Bank under its original charter. And he contemplated no difficulty in disposing of the government stock in the Bank. The Bank directors were still willing to pay $8 million for this stock without a pledge and on the mere chance of recharter; with assurance of a new charter, as McLane told Adams, who had questioned the ethics or wisdom of the sale, the Bank would give $12 million for this stock that had a par value of only $7 million.[23] If the charter were renewed, McLane had another equal offer from the Barings.[24] Despite this talk of selling the stock, it was held till after 1836, and redeemed for a sum between $7 and $8 million by the Bank after it had become a Pennsylvania corporation.[25]

After Cadwalader's departure McLane contented himself with warning Biddle that to seek recharter at this session inevitably threw the Bank into politics and deprived the government of the time it might have expected to devote to judging the value of the Bank before deciding what modifications to seek in it. Perhaps this letter was written with thought that it might be read by all the directors, including those newly appointed to represent the government. He could not oppose the veto of a recharter bill, McLane made clear, unless the bill were presented "as one of and in connection with a series of measures" for settling all the great problems before the country—his great plan, of course.[26]

Biddle had already sent his petition to Washington, requesting McDuffie and George Dallas, a Pennsylvania Senator and son of the Treasury Secretary who was the progenitor of the Second Bank, each to introduce the motion for recharter in his chamber.[27] Dallas, in introducing the petition in the Senate on January 9, 1832, weakened his case by referring to the application as "dangerously timed" and explaining that he, though flattered to be called on for this duty, would have preferred to have seen the petition held back at least until after the election.[28]

But it was not. This precipitate action destroyed McLane's hope of averting the Bank War and thus at once advancing his own public position and the welfare of his country. Though he did not know it, he was but days short of receiving another blow to his prospects, a blow not connected with recharter except that it was also the work of the enemies of Andrew Jackson.

III   THE VICE-PRESIDENCY

As early as November, 1831, Jackson had expressed concern whether his enemies would strike at him by rejecting his nominations in the Senate.[29] The disruption of Jackson's first cabinet, his falling out with Calhoun, the replacement of Duff Green as editor of the administration newspaper, all these events had left enmities to add to those created by the bitter campaign of 1828. Since McLane had been out of the country for two years he was reasonably free of involvement in these events, except for the opposition he had roused in Delaware in the 1828 election and the feeling that he had been all too willing to play the role of a pawn, moved from one square (London) to another (Washington) on the chessboard of the Magician.

When Congress met, McLane anticipated no trouble. "I have not the slightest idea," he wrote to Van Buren on December 14, "that any serious opposition will be made to the nominations." [30] However, Hezekiah Niles was soon reporting in his *Weekly Register* that an inquiry was likely to be made into the instructions Van Buren as Secretary of State had sent to McLane, in London.[31]

On December 27 the appointments of Levi Woodbury and of Roger Taney were approved by the Senate without committal, but those of Van Buren, Livingston, McLane, and Aaron Vail, a New York Regency politician who went with Van Buren to London as secretary of the legation, were sent to the Committee on Foreign Relations. Cass, whose nomination had gone to another committee, was approved December 30, but Livingston, Van Buren, and McLane, were "suspended," as a New York editor, James Watson Webb, put it, "between wind and water for the enemy to let fly their shafts at." [32]

According to a rumor that was abroad, the new cabinet members would be approved and Van Buren alone would be rejected. This, however, was an outcome that some of his friends looked forward to as a way of getting him home, for they were quite concerned about the state of affairs in the absence of Van Buren's leadership.[33] For example, they thought McLane was getting too much power. And indeed until Biddle placed him in an untenable position by seeking recharter, McLane did hold the reins of the administration carriage. Not without challenge, though.

"We have now the strangest Cabinet imaginable," Cambreleng informed Van Buren. "The President stands alone. McLane has Livingston, Cass, Lewis, Campbell, etc. Woodbury keeps snug and plays out of all the corners of his eyes. Taney, strange as it seems, is the best democrat among them. He is with Kendall, Hill, Blair, etc. Barry I presume I should have put with the president or else in the last list. McLane has burnished all of his satellites with the Bank gold and silver. Somehow or other they all begin to think the Bank must be re-chartered. This is a pretty tone at the moment of extinguishment of the public debt and the beginning of reform." [34]

Cambreleng, of course, oversimplified things. Livingston and Lewis were not mere minions of McLane but men who honestly and independently saw the usefulness of the national bank. The "kitchen cabinet" opposition was quite formidable, and was bolstered by some fairly weighty financial interests too—such as David Henshaw and friends in Boston, Elisha Tibbets and associates in New York City, and the Farmers and Mechanics Bank in Albany and other Safety Fund banks in New York State, all of which had some reason for wanting to see the Bank of the United States weakened or destroyed.[35] This is not to say that anti-Bank Jacksonians were controlled by these financiers, any more than pro-Bank Jacksonians were creatures of Nicholas Biddle.

In fearing McLane's growing ascendancy within the administration and the direction in which he would steer the government, Van Buren's friends were underestimating the strength of the National Republican opposition in Congress. In respect neither to the public debt, nor to the public lands, nor to the tariff were McLane's policies satisfactory to the Clay party. Nor was his triumph in England a matter they would cheer about, for they argued that his West Indian negotiation left his country's merchants worse off than before and had been achieved only at the cost of his country's honor.

Since McLane's negotiations in England had been carried on under the general direction of Van Buren as Secretary of State, some observers, like the editor of the *Intelligencer*, felt that they would be made the basis of objection to senatorial confirmation of both men.[36] You are denounced, McLane warned Van Buren, "for giving me the instructions in the colonial negotiation; and I for obeying them." But he thought the effort was only to mortify and wound, not to reject. A similar torment was being visited on Livingston; the defalcation that had driven him from New York years ago was being paraded cruelly.[37]

Livingston, however, was confirmed by the Senate on January 12, 1832;

McLane and Vail on January 13. On the latter day a motion to suspend action on Van Buren's appointment was passed by the tie-breaking vote of Vice-President Calhoun. When a motion to reject Van Buren was considered on January 25, four more Senators voted, but again there was a tie, and only by the casting vote of the Vice-President was Van Buren's confirmation refused.[38]

Van Buren's instructions to McLane when the latter was sent to England as minister in 1829 were made the basis of the argument for his rejection. He was said to have violated the honor of his country by denouncing earlier administrations and by introducing party politics into foreign negotiations, and in the course of the debate much hostility was evident that stemmed from resentment over Van Buren's success as a party manager and as adviser of the President. Van Buren's instructions to McLane, which were fundamental to McLane's success, authorized him to repudiate the excessive claims regarding the West India trade that Adams had made in his own administration and in Monroe's. Perhaps McLane's nomination would have been rejected with Van Buren's had the Senate been aware that McLane himself, according to Van Buren's reminiscences, had suggested the details of these instructions.[39]

But McLane did not escape altogether. Of all the opponents of Van Buren's nomination, the one who gave most attention to disparaging McLane's role was his fellow Delawarean, Senator John M. Clayton, who declared that McLane was sent to England to "fawn and beg" and did just that. Senator Holmes of Maine had previously spoken of McLane's role as to "bow and cringe."

A month earlier Senator Samuel Smith had been angry with McLane, whom he blamed for leaking news of the conference in which the two of them had participated, along with McDuffie and Cadwalader. But now Smith rose to McLane's defense. "What!" he argued, "a native American, the son of a distinguished officer of the revolution, bow and cringe at the feet of any man? . . . McLane is not made of such pliant materials. . . . The truth is, Mr. President, . . . the negotiation has completely succeeded under the instructions given by Mr. Van Buren, and as completely failed under those of another—a crime that can never be forgiven by the opponents of General Jackson."[40]

If this is not what General Smith said, it is what he wished he had said, for, like other speakers in Congress, he had the chance to revise his remarks before they were printed. John Forsyth, who made a point of stating that the remarks he sent to the printer were but a rough sketch of what he had said, made a particularly favorable impression on administration men by his defense of the Van Buren-McLane diplomacy.[41]

But it was on Van Buren alone that the Senate took out its spite by refusing to confirm his appointment, by subjecting him to the indignity of returning from England, discredited. Yet this was, as Van Buren's friends knew, greatly to his advantage. Before Van Buren's rejection there were many likely candidates to succeed Calhoun in the vice-presidency: among them Richard M. Johnson, called Tecumseh Johnson because he killed the Indian leader in the Battle of the Thames; Senator Forsyth; Senator Mahlon Dickerson, of New Jersey; Philip Barbour, of Virginia; Judge William Wilkins, of Pennsylvania; the ever-willing Judge John McLean; even Louis McLane.[42] After the rejection, one candidate had an outstanding claim on this position—Martin Van Buren—for it seemed only just to allow the body politic a chance to redress the indignity of his treatment by the Senate.[43] To anyone of a vengeful mind it was particularly fitting to have the people choose Van Buren to preside over the body which had treated him spitefully.

That it was spiteful treatment there was no doubt, for the speech of Senator Stephen D. Miller, of South Carolina, was an open attack on Van Buren for intrigue, accusing him of making a breach between the President and the Vice-President,[44] and four partisans of Calhoun who voted against Van Buren made the tie possible.

But it was Calhoun who cast the deciding vote, saying as he did, according to Senator Benton, "It will kill him, sir, kill him dead. He will never kick, sir, never kick." Hindsight makes it easy to note this was a prediction that could hardly have been farther from reality.[45] The blow that was intended to fell Van Buren, exalted him.

Calhoun himself felt that he had little choice. "In giving my casting vote in the case of Mr. Van Buren," he explained, two weeks later, "I performed what I believe to be a high act of duty, without regard to personal consequences. He had done the country incalculable injury." [46]

But Calhoun's view was a short one. "By the Eternal! I'll smash them!" Jackson shouted when he heard the news.[47] "You have broken a minister and elected a Vice-President," Thomas Hart Benton told Gabriel Moore, a Calhounite who sat near him in the Senate. "Good God!" Moore answered, "why didn't you tell me that before I voted, and I would have voted the other way." [48]

Van Buren might well have been the Jackson party's candidate for Vice-President even if his appointment as minister to England had not been rejected. Jackson had spoken to him of the vice-presidency as early as the summer of 1830 and had recurred to the subject in December, 1831. But in accepting appointment to England, Van Buren himself felt he was relinquishing pretensions to the vice-presidency, though surely not relinquishing his hope of being the ultimate successor of Jackson.[49]

In a letter of December 17, 1831, Jackson warned Van Buren that

"The opposition would, if they durst, try to reject your nomination as Minister, but they dare not—they begin to know if they did that the people in mass would take you up and elect you Vice President without a nomination. Was it not for this, it is said Clay, Calhoun and Company would try it." [50]

Yet "Clay, Calhoun and Company" did dare reject Van Buren. The result was almost what Jackson said it would be. The people "in mass" did not take up Van Buren without a nomination, but the Democratic party did take him up at a convention in Baltimore in May.

"Your rejection has blown up many schemes here," wrote Cambreleng. "We had many cabinet candidates for the Presidency." But now all were for Van Buren for the eventual succession. About a dozen party leaders, including all of the cabinet, met at McLane's on February 2 and talked the situation over—resolving, among other things, to put Kendall in Blair's place as administration editor.[51] Perhaps McLane inspired the meeting as a way of striking at Blair for his unfriendliness over the Bank issue in December. If Blair knew that this meeting with intent to replace him was held in McLane's house, it is not strange that in his old age he recalled McLane in a very unfavorable fashion.

Come home in the spring, Cambreleng further advised Van Buren, and take bold, but constitutional ground to settle the tariff. "McLane has ruined himself by taking the opposite course presuming that he had taken the popular ground." In other words, encourage compromise of this great divisive issue by a lowering of the tariff and you will confound your rivals. And by rivals, Cambreleng referred not only to avowed opponents like Clay. "You know," he warned, "what ambition makes of some of our friends." [52]

McLane agreed with Cambreleng that Van Buren should return soon, but wished him to go to the Senate and defend himself on its floor immediately, rather than wait patiently for the revenge of election as Vice-President. Probably McLane did not himself make this proposal directly, but he sought to get friends, including the President, to give Van Buren this advice.[53] But most of Van Buren's New York friends thought McLane's advice was bad. "The coast is clear," wrote one of them, "the wind is up, and I am for sailing direct for the best port." [54] "Forward, is the word," counseled Thomas Hart Benton; "the vice-presidency is the only thing." [55]

Why, it was asked, should Van Buren alone suffer for the British negotiations? [56] McLane, Virginia Governor John Floyd confided to his diary, was equally unworthy.[57] It would have been to McLane's eventual advantage if he had shared in the blame, for he would have been brought that much closer to the President, who insisted that what was done was on his authority and that the blame, if there was any—and he was quite sure there was not—was his.[58]

Instead, McLane was in the uncomfortable position of being a potential rival for the vice-presidency of the man who was the President's choice. Moreover, McLane did not occupy an independent position in the party (his independence was lost when he left Congress and, by espousing Jackson, lost control of Delaware) but held cabinet position and the public prominence it gave largely by the influence of the man he wished to supplant.

Van Buren's acceptance of a mission abroad had seemed to open a place for others at home, and they, as Joel R. Poinsett put it, "were busily preparing the way for themselves—I mean McLane and Co." [59] James Iredell was convinced that if McLane were to run "he would receive an almost unanimous support in North Carolina." [60]

But Jackson, as Senator Marcy observed, was "rapped up in Van Buren," [61] and no one else could be seriously considered. This was comforting to the New York Regency, not only because of the prominence the vice-presidency gave to their candidate and the political capital that could be made out of the coupling of his name with Jackson's but also because Jackson seemed "an old man, . . . daily failing, . . . surrounded by men who are Jackson men only from policy." Surely, thought New York Congressman Charles Dayan, "this case [is] a general exception to that notion afloat in [the] community that the V presidency is not a stepping stone, but a warrant to lay on the shelf." He trembled when any other candidate was mentioned for the office.[62]

It was late in February before Van Buren received news of his rejection. He decided almost immediately to settle affairs at the legation and take the opportunity for his first tour of the continent before returning. He rejected McLane's advice solemnly and gracefully, as he had three years earlier when McLane urged him to refuse a seat in Jackson's cabinet. There was, after all, no vacancy in the New York delegation, and even should one be created for him not much of the session would remain by the time he could return.[63]

Meanwhile the Democratic nominating convention would have met in Baltimore and accomplished its work. Nomination by a party convention was something new for the Democrats, but it was a device they were driven to adopt as they sought party unity around Jackson and his vice-presidential running mate. Having renounced caucus nominations in 1824, it was but natural to adopt a device widely used in state politics and employed nationally in a small way by the Federalists in 1808 and 1812 and, in a larger way, by the Anti-Masons and the National Republicans in this very campaign. To ensure strong party agreement on the vice-presidency, a rule was adopted requiring the successful nominee to receive the vote of two thirds of the delegates to the convention.

On the eve of the convention there was still hesitation in some quarters, among Tennessee intimates of Jackson, for instance, about the nomination of Van Buren. John Eaton objected, not from dislike of Van Buren, but because he feared his nomination might cost Jackson some votes and possibly hurt his chances for reelection.[64]

Another Tennesseean, Judge John Overton, left Washington for Baltimore doubtful that Van Buren could be nominated and prepared to switch his vote to General Samuel Smith. In his attitude Major William Lewis, ever devoted to whatever Jackson wanted, suspected an intrigue of Louis McLane via Postmaster General Barry, a relative of Overton. Smith was very friendly to McLane and was himself so old (seventy-nine) that he would stand in no one's way after four years.[65] As defender of Baltimore in the War of 1812, he and his name evoked thoughts of the "Star Spangled Banner" and this would make him a popular and patriotic candidate. That Lewis's suspicion may have had some foundation is indicated by a comment made by a young Delawarean, a clerk who had a position in the Treasury Department through the influence of McLane. "We are looking forward with much anxiety to the approaching meeting of the Convention at Baltimore. Van Beuren I presume must be taken up. Delaware has not much reason to lend him her support." [66]

Major Lewis has left an account of "a long and rather excited conversation" with McLane, who alleged Van Buren's nomination would endanger Jackson's success. Lewis reminded him of the cabinet's unanimous agreement to take up Van Buren in case the Senate rejected him, but McLane denied it. Besides, he argued, there were other candidates in the field—naming Tecumseh Johnson and Judge Wilkins—over whom the cabinet had no control. Lewis was sure that these men were not candidates, but he was wrong about them and McLane was right. Van Buren was nominated in May, 1832, at Baltimore, and after the election was over that fall, McLane met Major Lewis at a dinner party at the Washington home of John and Peggy Eaton and acknowledged to the major that he had been wrong about the popularity of a Jackson-Van Buren ticket. "Our former friendship was renewed," the major wrote, "and he had no better friend at Washington than myself." [67]

IV   OFFICIAL AND DOMESTIC LIFE

Coming to the Treasury as he did in the middle of a presidential term, McLane had little chance to fill offices with men of his own choosing. Ingham's appointees presumably were good Democrats and were not easily to be removed. Such influential officials as Joseph Anderson, of Tennessee (and once, long ago, of Delaware), for decades the first comptroller of the Treasury, Major William B. Lewis, the second auditor, and Amos Kendall, the fourth auditor, were quite untouchable. Such patronage as his office had, McLane pontificated to Henry Ridgely, he wished to employ to promote the interests of his friends, but he was talking about the appointment of only a lighthouse keeper.[68]

Despite the reputation of the Jackson administration for playing politics with the civil service, it seems likely that the number of replacements was little more than 10 percent of the total of civilian officeholders, and a large share of these appointments were made before McLane entered the cabinet. Two of the important Treasury officials, Peter Hagner and Stephen Pleasonton, third and fifth auditor respectively, had held their places since 1817. Joseph Anderson had been first comptroller since 1815.

Almost all of the chief clerks in the Treasury Department had worked up to their positions after years of service. Asbury Dickins had worked for this department since 1817; William B. Randolph, clerk in the treasurer's office, had come to the Treasury in 1816; Michael Nourse, chief clerk to the register from 1820 to 1853, entered the department in 1795. Among the minor clerks many had likewise served long terms. The register, Joseph Nourse, had been promptly fired by Jackson, but of twenty clerks in the register's office as late as 1836, two had served since Washington's administration, three since Jefferson's, one since Madison's, five since Monroe's, and three since John Quincy Adams's.[69]

From the time McLane assumed the duties of Secretary of the Treasury in the summer of 1831 to the end of that year less than five new appointments were made in the department, which employed over one hundred and twenty clerks. In 1832 eleven men were added to the department—several as replacements for clerks who had died. Six or seven new clerks were hired in 1833 before May 28, when McLane officially left the department.[70]

One patronage appointment that was afforded McLane, a clerkship in matters regarding the relief of insolvent debtors of the United States, was awarded William Thompson Read, of New Castle, a young lawyer and Delaware state legislator whose sister was married to Dr. Allen McLane. Read had gone into debt to purchase a farm and stock and applied for appointment as chargé in Buenos Aires, where he had once traveled as secretary to a diplomatic mission. This place, McLane found, had been filled, but he offered what he termed "an important clerkship in my immediate office," which paid $1,400 a year and which he wished to fill with "a *personal friend* of education and capacity." Read was able to live in Washington with his family on a portion of his salary ($880 a year for board and washing for himself and his wife the first year) and apply the rest of his salary to his debts. On the death of his father and brother in 1836, after McLane had left the cabinet, Read came into an inheritance that allowed him to give up his Washington post, pay off all his debts, and move back to Delaware.[71]

Because of the rigid constructions put upon the insolvent debtors law by Attorney General Taney, Read was not kept very busy by his official duties, but McLane furnished him with much work of a political nature, which work explained his need for "a *personal friend* of education and capacity." With the help of an assistant to do the copying and recording, Read was put at various tasks "of a miscellaneous character" that he found occupied "all the office hours and frequently other parts of the day." He had nothing to do with the great Treasury report of December 7, 1831, "except to make a copy and assist in correcting the proofs." At other times he worked on confidential papers or was encouraged to prepare articles of his own, such as "Mr. Clay's Senility," which appeared in the *Globe* of February 9, 1832, signed "X," and was a criticism of Clay's speech on the tariff, in the course of which Clay had spoken with great bitterness of old General Smith, McLane's ally.

Another article that Read worked on, entitled "The Hartford Convention American and His Pretence," appeared in the *Globe* of February 6 and assailed Webster for his criticism of Van Buren's instructions to McLane during the debate over Van Buren's confirmation. "It was given to me in the rough, to make what I could out of it," Read confided to his family at home, "and I have had to father it to the printer. It must not tho' be even lisped that it came from our Department." [72]

At first Read was somewhat dissatisfied with McLane because McLane did not seem eager to introduce him about in Washington, but the two families did mix socially.[73] "A weak point in McLane's character," Read commented early in his Washington service, "is . . . over-caution, a morbid dread of committal and the imputation of straining points for his friends, so that I sometimes fear they are just the persons who will benefit least by his station and influence." In this regard, however, Read was a prejudiced observer, peculiarly sensitive to McLane's attitudes toward patronage. There is less reason to hesitate at accepting another of Read's early judgments on McLane: "he is, too, somewhat jealous, suspicious, and ready to *imagine* offence." [74] But as Read worked beside McLane he came increasingly to appreciate the latter's statesmanship, particularly in relation to the tariff, where he thought McLane "with great moral daring" avoided "the ultras" of either side and took the only ground that could save the union, the middle ground.[75] Read came closer to cabinet politics in the fall of 1832 when Postmaster General Barry came to board at his home.[76]

Read's letters furnish evidence of McLane's continuing interest in Delaware politics and of efforts to serve his friends at home. Besides appointments to government posts McLane felt obliged to help his friend Jean P. Garesché, a competitor of du Pont, sell gunpowder to the War Department. To this department he went on another occasion to try to keep a detachment of troops at New Castle, explaining that his enemies would blame him for their removal, which he had forestalled a year earlier (the year of Nat Turner's rebellion) by pleading "fear of the blacks." [77]

Despite the long service of the clerks, George Bancroft, coming to Washington in the interests of a Cleveland bank in which his wife's family had invested, found the work of the Treasury Department annoyingly slow. "The departments," he wrote, "are full of the laziest clerks, . . . paid large salaries for neglecting the public business." But perhaps all of Bancroft's complaints were really due to delays caused by the illness of Louis McLane in December, 1831.[78]

By June, however, McLane was in good health and Washington Irving commented on seeing him that he seemed to stand "the fatigues and annoyance of his station" well and to be in better spirits, generally, than at London.[79] Probably his health and his spirits, too, were improved when weather allowed him to follow his favorite sport, riding, whether with the Washington Hunt, of which he was a founder, or merely for exercise, as when he boasted of putting Secretary of the Navy Woodbury almost *hors de combat* "by a jolting ride" that led Woodbury to admit he was "better suited to bear the flag of the fleet than to be master of the horse." [80]

The conduct of Dr. Allen McLane continued to give his brother much concern. In May the doctor moved to Baltimore, intending to make a fresh start in the practice of medicine where, as William Read observed, "his high qualifications . . . insure him success . . . if he be true to himself." [81] From Baltimore he could conveniently visit Washington and be of professional assistance to the Secretary's large family. By fall, however, the doctor was unhappy again, selling his furniture in Baltimore and seeking a position in government, though Louis was loath to recommend him from knowledge of his weakness. One day in the fall when Louis was in Baltimore for the races he was mortified to have his brother call on him at Barnum's Hotel in a state of intoxication.[82]

The McLanes frequently gave dinners and entertained. Senator Johnston of Louisiana, Representative Gulian Verplanck of New York, and Nicholas Biddle when visiting in Washington were among their dinner guests, in addition to a constant flow of friends from home, such as General Thomas Marsh Forman and his wife, neighbors of the Bohemia plantation in Cecil County, whom Kitty McLane showed around Washington and introduced to the President. In January, 1832, two French visitors, Alexis de Tocqueville and Gustave de Beaumont, were invited to a ball at the McLanes', and Edward Everett, who was there, described it as a "Great Party." [83]

The oldest McLane son, Robert, remembered these Washington days as gay and social ones. He remembered the lively circle that the Andrew Jackson Donelsons and three young ladies from Tennessee made at the White House, where the evenings were enlivened by music, always including "Home, Sweet Home," and "Auld Lang Syne" for the President, who sat night after night, puffing his clay pipe, in the chimney corner of a parlor adjoining the dining room. Bob recalled as part of his circle the Livingstons with their daughter Cora and a lovely niece, and he felt particularly at home with the Cass, Woodbury, and Taney families—an indication that political rivalries did not seriously affect the younger generation. [84]

In 1831 Louis McLane appealed to Secretary Cass for a West Point appointment for Bob, who was then in school in Pittsfield, Massachusetts. [85] Bob, however, attributed to President Jackson not only his appointment but also the encouragement that twice led him to withdraw his resignation and stay at the academy despite his hatred of the confinement and discipline. Whenever he visited Washington, Bob was invited to bring his horse Tom Breeze, a gift from his father, and ride with the President's family, which included Donelson, Major Lewis, and the Major's daughter. Jackson delighted in seeing Bob jump Tom Breeze, who could take any ordinary post and rail fence with ease. [86]

After a year in Washington the ranks of the young McLanes were swelled once again by the birth of another daughter, Mary Elizabeth, the twelfth child (all living but one) and seventh of her sex. "Mrs. McLane . . . has resumed her fomer occupation at home," wrote Louis in the fall of 1832 in explaining her approaching confinement. [87] Probably Charles A. Davis, a journalist and banker, was thinking of this latest addition to the McLanes when he wrote that "the Secretary of the Treasury . . . has too large a family" to be independent. [88]

His large family, however, gave pleasure to some notable guests, most particularly the literary lion of the hour, Washington Irving. Irving returned to the United States in May and after a public dinner in New York traveled to Washington to settle his accounts as chargé and to report to the President, to whom he came as a herald of the favorite, Van Buren, with welcome accounts of the good impression the Magician had made abroad. He found a room waiting for him at the McLanes', where he was "received with acclamation" by all the family, "large and small," and, as he reported to his brother, "spent nearly a fortnight with them in the most delightful manner." [89]

Rumor had it that Irving was courting Rebecca McLane, but she was only eighteen and he was older than her father. One letter from Irving to Rebecca does survive in the McLane correspondence. Answering a letter from Rebecca, this letter was written in the summer of 1832, after Irving had left Washington. For "my dear Rebecca," as he addressed her, he described a trip he had just made to Boston and the White Mountains and then down the Connecticut. He discoursed at length on a Mr. Newton and "his intended" and how much in love they were. Perhaps, Irving suggested, they fell in love as they sang a duet together; it shows, he added, the importance of music to young ladies. After comments on the plans for convent schooling for Sally and Lydia, who, in Irving's opinion, would "make a couple of fascinating beings [they were then less than twelve] however they may be educated," the letter stops abruptly, the concluding page or pages being lost. [90] If any personal message followed, it is gone. Perhaps Irving was half in love with Rebecca. Or maybe this middle-aged man was merely grateful for some attention paid him by a girl of eighteen.

As Irving traveled about his native land, from which he had been expatriated for a decade, he called on various McLane connections. In Baltimore he dined with Dr. McLane. After journeying west to Missouri and Arkansas, he sojourned for a time in Louisiana on the sugar plantation of Kitty McLane's brother, George Milligan. [91] When he arrived back in Washington early in December, Irving intended to stay only a few days and then set off to spend Christmas with his relatives on the banks of the Hudson. Instead, he found Washington so interesting that he stayed for three months. "I have," he wrote, "a very snug, cheery cozy room in the immediate neighborhood of McLane's, and take my meals at his house, and, in fact, make it my home. I have thus the advantage of a family circle (and that a delightful one) and the precious comfort of a little bachelor retreat and sanctum sanctorum, where I can be as lonely and independent as I please." [92]

And for the winter the McLanes had Diedrich Knickerbocker.

V   RECHARTER AND VETO

After George Dallas in the Senate and George McDuffie in the House introduced petitions for recharter of the Bank, the cause that McLane had been striving for in the cabinet was taken from him and placed under these new generals on a new field, the Congress. Bitterly, McLane complained that the struggle was premature, that the Bank charter, after all, was not to expire during this session of Congress, nor during the next session of this Congress, nor even during the life of the next Congress.[93]

Biddle was sufficiently concerned about McLane's feelings to urge his current ambassador in Washington to try to "persuade Mrs. McLane to exorcise the demons" tormenting her husband.[94] There is no indication that the Bank representative went so far as this, and for some time there were conflicting reports of McLane's feelings. When the Committee on Ways and Means suggested he might offer proposals for changes in the Bank charter, he felt he could not officially speak on the subject at all or he would be bound to say he altogether opposed recharter now, on grounds both of principle and of expediency. His recommendation had been for recharter "at the proper time," which this was not. To Biddle's agent, Horace Binney, he was entirely gracious, insisting that for the Treasury's sake no change at all was needed in the Bank. There were changes he might have suggested in order to meet the objections of the President, but now there was no point in mentioning them.[95]

Within the cabinet, Livingston supplanted McLane as the chief spokesman for the Bank.[96] Although originally of the opinion that Jackson would veto any recharter bill to come before him, Livingston gradually came to have a more optimistic view of the chances for recharter and on February 23 suggested terms on which he thought Jackson might accept the Bank—if pressure was kept up through Congress, the press, and even "les dames du palais"—a reference not to any scandalous element but to the ladies of the presidential family, such as those at the Donelsons' breakfast table. But still he did not know where McLane stood, the man was so much a creature of moods.[97]

Charles Ingersoll, another Biddle legate, visited McLane for the first time on February 13 but continued to work most closely with Livingston. Fearing McLane might be jealous of Livingston's leadership in a matter so close to Treasury concerns as the Bank, Ingersoll advised Biddle to "get some one to deal" with McLane, though the advance must be careful and not seem forced. Perhaps General Cadwalader should be used, or Dr. McLane, who was reported to be his brother's "most confidential friend at home." [98]

At the end of February, Ingersoll had a long and reasonably free conversation with McLane and found him "hurt, sore, not satisfied with the bank application now, contrary to his views and what he supposed he had settled." Ingersoll thought but was not quite sure that McLane implied he had promised the President in return for his "yielding paragraph" in his message to Congress that the Bank question would be postponed till after the election. And so McLane still wished it could be.

But Livingston, Ingersoll was confident, was the "predominating influence" over Jackson. McLane was sure to be agreeable in the long run: "all his impressions and tendencies are favorable." Livingston was particularly valuable because of his great influence with the Attorney General —according to Ingersoll, who thought Livingston and Taney together could "overcome Amos Kendall or whoever the malign influence is." [99]

Ingersoll was wrong, Livingston's influence on Taney in this matter was nil, and whoever the malign influence was, Livingston could not obstruct him. Early in March the Secretary of State was still sure a Bank bill such as he and Ingersoll had arranged would be signed by the President, though, he confessed, "I have never heard him say so." Yet at this very time the Bank sustained a defeat in the House of Representatives when its champion, McDuffie, yielded to the importunities of Augustus Clayton, of Georgia, and permitted appointment of a House committee to investigate the Bank's activities. [100] Clayton had made numerous charges against the Bank and was eager to bring out whatever damaging evidence of charter violation he could find. His committee, appointed by the Speaker with an anti-Bank majority, made an unfriendly report, but probably affected few votes in a House that was pro-Bank. [101]

During the spring Biddle made two trips to Washington to confer with McLane. The first visit was at the end of March and was occasioned by a Treasury announcement that one half of the 3 percent bonds would be redeemed on the 1st of July. This disturbed Biddle on two grounds. First, it meant the Bank would need to contract loans during the spring and accumulate funds at a time when importers wanted easy credit to replenish their stocks and pay customs duties. Second, there was likelihood that a cholera epidemic raging in Europe would cross the Atlantic and strike the coastal cities with such fury that finance and business would be disarranged. For these reasons, Biddle urged the administration to postpone payment of the debt till fall. With Jackson's approval, McLane agreed to the postponement, but in Biddle's plea the President saw signs of weakness in the position of his adversary, signs that he interpreted to mean some serious weakness in the Bank. [102]

Biddle's second spring visit to Washington was more political than financial in its motive. In May when the Clayton committee's report on the Bank was received by the House and the Bank recharter bill was taken up again, Biddle came to Washington, hoping that some compromise could be worked out. [103] The first person he called upon was McLane, and the second was Livingston. He was pleased that McLane gave him a dinner and they had "a full and frank conversation." With

Livingston, too, he explored "the peculiarity of their position which makes them passive." "The awkardness was irretrievable," he found; they could or would do nothing for him. Biddle felt "on the best terms" in parting with Jackson's Secretaries, but he understood at last that there was nothing he could do with the administration except make the recharter bill "as unexceptionable as possible." [104]

Livingston was honestly eager to help Biddle if he could: after all, he had a note for $3,200 due at the Bank office on June 4 and he wanted to borrow $2,500 toward paying it.[105] McLane had more important fish to fry; he still needed Biddle's cooperation in what hope remained for the accomplishment of his grand project of using the Treasury office as the point from which to control administration policy.

That the administration esteemed him safe is indicated by a motion of Senator Thomas Hart Benton, Jackson's "right bower," made on June 6. Benton proposed that the recharter bill be submitted to McLane as a matter "of official courtesy and public advantage." Every bank charter granted had had its origin in the Treasury Department, Benton added. Why slight the present Secretary? He was known to be favorable to the Bank, but what did he think of this bill? [106]

What he thought of it is not necessarily suggested by the refusal of the Bank's advocates to countenance Benton's proposal. They wanted no delay in getting their bill through Congress before the election. They succeeded in getting final action on July 3, and their success won them the reaction they had good reason to expect. There was a spirit of bravado about these bankers as they cast their challenge before the Old Chief. General Thomas Cadwalader called on the lightning to strike: "I say *the veto*—for *veto it will be!*" [107]

What McLane thought of the recharter bill did become briefly a subject for comment in the public press after Congress had received Jackson's veto message. When Cambreleng proposed in the House that ten thousand copies of the veto should be printed, Elisha Whittlesey, an Ohio lawyer who had been General Harrison's secretary, moved that McLane's views on the Bank, as expressed in his annual report, should be republished with the veto message, as an appendix. Obviously Whittlesey intended to counteract Jackson's views on the constitutionality of the Bank with the Treasury Secretary's hearty endorsement of the institution.[108] In noting Whittlesey's proposal, the *National Intelligencer* commented, correctly: "Whoever else had a hand in the rejection of the bill for removing the Bank Charter, it is very clear that the Chief of the Financial Department did not." [109]

True though the comment was, McLane could not allow it to pass unnoticed. A verbose and heavy retort was inserted into the editorial column of the next day's *Globe,* declaring the President "was sustained by an united Cabinet" in deciding to veto the recharter bill. The views of the "Chief of the Financial Department" regarding "the impropriety and unconstitutionality" of this attempt to force through a recharter were made quite clear, and it was insisted that the officers of the Bank had been "early and constantly forewarned of the necessary consequences of forcing this application during the 22d Congress." [110] The author was probably McLane's confidential clerk, William Read. He assured his brother that the article could be relied on as authentic.[111]

Even in a united cabinet, it was not to the chief of the financial department but to his Attorney General that Jackson turned for assistance with his veto of the Bank bill. In a way this was peculiarly appropriate, since Jackson felt the bill was unconstitutional. But the reason he turned to Taney, summoning him from Annapolis, was that other members of the cabinet—and surely McLane would have been prominent among them—wanted Jackson to leave the door open for approval of some sort of recharter in the future. Amos Kendall agreed with Jackson that the veto should settle the Bank issue once and for all. He was working on the veto message before Taney returned and took over the job. Andrew Donelson also helped, and so, to some extent, did Levi Woodbury, the Navy Secretary.[112]

But not McLane. The whole affair was very damaging to his prospects. As this stage of the Bank war ended, McLane was still on the winning side. His tactics, however, had been abandoned, his suggestions turned aside, and another lieutenant, Roger Taney, had the ear of the Old Chief on a matter wherein McLane should have been the natural adviser.

Van Buren was to become Vice-President, and now Taney, a new rival, was becoming an intimate adviser. What was left for McLane? Obviously he must make the best of the position he still had. After all, his was still a featured role in the political drama.

VI THE PEACEABLE KINGDOM

While many of his enemies and some of his friends were pushing the Bank bill through Congress in the spring of 1832, the legislation of greatest interest to Louis McLane was a new tariff bill of which he was, in large part, the author. Since the conclusion of the War of 1812 the tariff had been gradually rising, with the major steps in that rise occurring in 1816, 1824, and 1828. Though McLane, like most men with an interest in manufactures, had been a staunch advocate of protective tariffs, he had concluded by 1828 that they were high enough. When Jackson, in his message to Congress, called for "material reductions in the import duties" to be effected with "equal justice to all our national interests," McLane was ready to address himself to this almost impossible task.

A less self-confident Secretary might have approached this subject more timidly than Louis McLane. Southerners were calling for the removal of all protection and went so far as to deny its constitutionality. But Louis McLane, like his father, was not the man to avoid a fight.

His tariff work as Secretary began, moreover, when all seemed possible —the whole grand fabric of policy that he planned for the Jackson administration and revealed in his message of December, 1831—including extinction of the debt, reduction of taxes, sale of bank stock, and distribution of the public domain. The tariff was central to his scheme because it was to become the sole and sufficient support of the government, and yet was to continue to yield some measure of protection.

Though everyone agreed that new tariff legislation was expected from the first session of the Twenty-Second Congress, there was no certainty as to where the responsibility for it lay. The section of the President's message relating to "modification" of the tariff was referred in the House of Representatives to the Committee on Manufactures, but the Committee on Ways and Means was assigned financial problems, including "the public debt and revenue" and arrangements to abolish "unnecessary taxation after the extinguishment of the public debt." [113] Nor was the Senate to be left out of the business, for though constitutionally "all bills for raising revenue" originate in the House of Representatives, Senate sophists argued that they had a right to introduce bills lowering or abolishing taxes.[114]

In the tariff battle two new members of Congress were to play a leading part, one in the Senate and one in the House. Neither was really new to Congress, but both were returning after a long absence, both had played very distinguished roles during their absence from Congress, and both were remarkably able men who were bound to take leading parts in any assembly. The first was ex-President John Quincy Adams, who took his seat in the Twenty-Second Congress as a newly elected Representative from Massachusetts. The second was ex-Secretary of State Henry Clay, who had earlier distinguished himself as Speaker of the House but now took a seat in Congress as Senator from Kentucky.

Both men were ambitious, but whereas Adams was a gloomy pessimist, an ex-President who felt the best part of his career was behind him, Clay was an active optimist, an open candidate for the Presidency, having been nominated for that office by the National Republicans in the very December in which the Twenty-Second Congress convened. For this reason he had precipitated a fight over recharter of the Bank, and he was equally ready to make an issue of the tariff and his idea of an American system resting on a protected market for domestic products. On January 9 Clay raised the issue in the Senate by moving that the Committee on Finance prepare a bill abolishing the tariff on imports that did not compete with American products, excepting only teas and wines, on which the duty should also be abolished, but by gradual steps rather than immediately. When he took the floor to defend his motion on January 11, Clay was gratified to find the Senate chamber crowded by a public which had enjoyed no opportunity of hearing him perform in Congress since he had left the House for the State Department in 1825. He apologized: "I am getting old [and] have nothing but a plain, unvarnished and unambitious exposition to make." [115]

Louis McLane probably felt that any such disclaimer of ambition on Clay's part was a plain, unvarnished lie. The issue of removing duties because of the imminent extinguishment of the public debt had already been raised in the Senate, which had heard Louis McLane's opinion on the subject. He was against any hasty reduction and had said so when General Smith, chairman of the Senate Finance Committee, asked about the practicability of an immediate removal of the duty on tea. McLane was opposed for two reasons: (1) an immediate reduction of the duty would seriously disturb his estimates of the revenue for the coming year, on which estimates his plans for extinguishing the debt were based; and (2) the future status of a tax on tea should be dealt with by Congress in connection with a general revision of the tariff and not handled separately. [116]

For Smith, who admired McLane, this answer was quite satisfactory, and Clay knew there was little chance of getting much action from Smith's Committee on Finance unless a lot of prodding was done. To save the protective tariff at a time when reduced debts decreased the need for revenue and encouraged demands for tax reduction, Clay felt that the purely revenue tariff had to be sacrificed. The quicker it was done, the sooner the principle of protection would be safe, he explained to a selected group of anti-Jackson Congressmen that met at Edward Everett's lodgings on December 28. Since their enemies would use the accumulation of revenue as an excuse to lower the tariff, Clay argued it was necessary to reduce the revenue immediately by giving up all tariffs levied on goods that were noncompetitive.

John Quincy Adams, who was among the group that heard Clay, was not convinced; to him Clay's plan seemed pure defiance of the President, who had a right to be indulged in a reasonable and honest course of action. Clay, in his turn, was greatly irritated to learn from Adams that the House Committee on Manufactures had committed itself to cooperation with the Secretary of the Treasury in drawing up a tariff reform to take effect after March, 1833, when the last of the national debt would be paid off.[117] McLane was one up on the Kentuckian, thanks to the honest impartiality of Adams.

The spectacle of Adams and McLane in close cooperation is like a scene from Edward Hicks's *Peaceable Kingdom* where natural enemies of field and forest are seen lying down together. Adams had ridiculed McLane as "the Dauphin," reared to great expectations, and had bitterly resented his diplomatic success in England because it was founded on a renunciation of the position Adams had taken. To McLane, Adams was an accidental President whose elevation had confounded McLane's friends and pleased his enemies. Now circumstances threw them into a union which was effective though never intimate.

Very likely the idea of a close cooperation originated among Democratic members of the Committee on Manufactures, which Adams, as chairman, called to its first meeting on December 14. He had tried to get out of this position, preferring an ordinary place on the Committee on Foreign Affairs, but the Speaker, Andrew Stevenson, a Virginia Democrat who made all committee assignments, refused to sanction a transfer. At his committee meeting Adams promised to inquire of the Secretary of the Treasury whether the administration had any plan for tariff reduction. He did call on McLane four days later on the way home from Congress, but their initial talk was notable for more differences than points of agreement.[118]

Very likely this meeting between the two old enemies was but a preliminary baring of teeth. Essentially they soon found themselves in agreement. Both were fervent nationalists and were eager for any reasonable compromise that would appease the South. Tariff reduction was reasonable because the country, prosperous and almost debt free, did not need the revenues it was collecting. Yet both men at heart were protectionists who would not wish to see all protective tariffs abandoned in whatever adjustments were made.

Adams's inquiry about an administrative plan for a tariff "readjustment" led the two men into a reasonably close cooperation. McLane pleaded that the Treasury Department lacked the information needed for a "digested scheme" of a new tariff, and he persuaded Adams and Adams's committee to ask the House to empower him to collect this information. He even prepared a resolution to this effect for Adams to read in Congress, and possibly he wrote out a similar resolution for George McDuffie, chairman of the Ways and Means Committee.[119]

In the House, McDuffie got ahead of Adams, presenting a resolution on January 16 empowering McLane to do two things: (1) collect information on the condition of American manufacturing, and (2) draw up a tariff bill. The Committee on Manufactures was jealous, because it felt McDuffie was encroaching on its functions, so it ordered Adams to present its resolution to the same effect, with the result that on January 19 the House passed both of them. Adams's resolution was somewhat broader, since it asked McLane not only for information on American manufactures but also for details regarding similar articles imported recently.[120]

In criticizing the resultant tariff months later, Clay declared that "the famous tariff *projet* of the Secretary of the Treasury" originated in a resolution in his own handwriting, "presented to and adopted by the House of Representatives." The points that Clay wanted to make were that the responsibility for the tariff was McLane's and that this same responsibility was not reluctantly assumed but might well have been voluntarily sought.[121]

VII   THE REPORT ON MANUFACTURES

Not only "the famous tariff *projet*" of McLane originated in this resolution. So also did the somewhat more famous McLane report on manufactures. The McLane tariff project was soon replaced by other tariff schemes, but the McLane report on manufactures is of permanent importance, being decidedly one of the most valuable sources in American industrial history. The report is a collection of individual returns from manufacturers, "raw material," one authority on the subject has written, "and at first sight forbidding, but . . . eternally fresh; in few government documents do we get so close to the economic life of the time." [122]

After the House called on him for information via the McDuffie and Adams resolutions of January 19, which he may have written himself, McLane appointed commissioners to gather data on manufacturing in each of the states north of Maryland and in Ohio. Each of these commissioners—in some states there were more than one—was sent a packet of materials, including copies of the resolutions, the annual Treasury report, a letter from McLane, and a list of forty queries on the state of manufacturing. In his letter, McLane asked the commissioners to pursue their inquiries in person or by correspondence and to employ assistants if they were needed, promising an adequate compensation. He asked for the utmost impartiality in the collection of information, in order that Congress would not be unfairly influenced. Commissioners were requested to condense the data in their replies but to submit everything they collected. They were not restricted to the prepared list of queries, but were urged to collect any pertinent information available and any suggestions that would help in the adjustment of the tariff on the principles stated in the Treasury report.

McLane himself interviewed some manufacturers and "other gentlemen acquainted with the subject," as he put it. Among the score of commissioners he employed were the Rhode Island manufacturer Samuel Slater and the Pennsylvania journalist Mathew Carey. McLane's forty queries began with questions on the location and type of factory and went on to ask about the power, labor, and capital employed, raw materials and their source, markets, profits, competition, and prospects under certain conditions, as, for instance, how the capital would be employed if the business were abandoned.[123]

The returns came to McLane at different times, of course, and were too slow in arriving to be of much use to him in drawing up a new tariff. Such returns as he had he sent to Congress with his tariff bill in 1832, but they were incomplete. As other returns arrived, he sent them on to Congress, and eventually, in 1833, they were all published as a government document—a magnificent array of industrial data filling two large volumes.[124]

Despite the little immediate use made of the data, McLane recognized their eventual value, as he made clear in a letter urging the chairman of the Ways and Means Committee to see that all his agents in the compilation were properly rewarded: "These returns contain a body of the most useful, valuable, and extensive information of the manufactures of the United States . . . ever . . . presented to Congress. They have been collected by intelligent and practical agents, are minute and much in detail and drawn from the proprietors of manufacturing establishments and other authentic sources. They should be printed for future use."[125]

VIII   THE ADAMS TARIFF

In January of 1832 Louis McLane and John Quincy Adams found themselves for the most part in agreement on the principles on which new tariff legislation should be based. It should be a compromise, making some concessions to the discontents of the South, yet retaining a measure of the protection demanded in the North. It should moreover be written in the Treasury Department.[126] They were also agreed that the tariff reductions contemplated should not take place until the public debt was paid off, and this happy event was expected to coincide with the end of Jackson's term.

Clay, of course, wanted to move faster in reducing the revenue—and in removing the temptation to withdraw all protection by abolishing all duties on noncompetitive goods. In the House, on the other hand, the Committee on Ways and Means supported a proposal presented by its chairman, George McDuffie, that all tariffs be reduced to an equivalent figure, about 12½ percent of the value of the goods imported. In the Senate McDuffie's fellow South Carolinian, Robert Hayne, countered Clay's proposal by suggesting tariff duties for revenue, similar on all goods.

Other proposals were made in each chamber, but though many speeches were delivered on the tariff issue, no legislation was enacted during the winter and early spring as McLane's agents were gathering information from northern manufacturers and the Secretary himself was preparing a report. Pressures gradually mounted as the debate went on. Manufacturers or their agents came to Washington to protest the slightest reduction, hanging over Adams's committee like an incubus.[127] At the other extreme, fire-eating Southerners declared protective tariffs entirely unconstitutional and found even Albert Gallatin, the venerable friend of Jefferson, too moderate, because he felt it was not practicable to abandon all protection.[128] Compromise, said Gallatin, was the only solution, and compromise was possible only with the good will of the administration and the active cooperation of the Secretary of the Treasury.[129]

The Secretary's desire to cooperate was great, but his flesh proved weak under the strain of his work. He was severely ill late in March, his illness beginning with a headache so violent that Dr. Huntt feared an "inflamation of the brain,' and then it moved to his stomach. William Read attributed the trouble to "overtasking" the mind. Mrs. Adams told her husband, then in Philadelphia with the Bank committee, that McLane's trouble was a "gloomy dyspepsia." McLane himself referred to an intense headache, his "old malady," brought on by his anxiety to complete his report on manufacturing.[130]

Finally, on April 27, the report was ready and McLane sent it, with a letter, by messenger to the Speaker. At the same time he sent a note to a friendly member of the House, Gulian Verplanck, asking him to move for the printing of the letter and the tariff bill enclosed with it, but not the mass of papers, the partial returns from his inquiries, that he also was sending; "I am now in the hands of my friends," he concluded, "and they must take care of me." [131]

He referred, of course, not to the information he was sending the House as part of his inquiry into manufactures, but to the tariff bill he was submitting. It was not designed as a perfect scheme, he confessed; he would be happy to have the House improve on it. But he did not think it possible to preserve the degree of protection hitherto afforded now that the need for a federal revenue was to be reduced by the extinguishment of the debt.

His plan was a compromise, falling midway between the protectionist plan of Clay and the revenue plan of McDuffie. McLane was recommending an over-all reduction of duties from approximately 45 percent (in 1828) to approximately 27 percent. He noted that there had already been some reduction in 1830, when the duties on tea, coffee, molasses, and salt were lowered. The greater part of the total reduction of $10 million was to come from items that he was placing on the free list or items that were to pay an almost nominal tariff. McLane himself would have preferred a gradual to a sudden reduction of the tariff on protected items, but he yielded to other opinions in the hope that an immediate reduction might prove permanent, and besides providing manufacturers with cheap raw materials, allow them a degree of security they would lack under a system of gradual reduction.

He recommended the complete abandonment of a system of minimums, which provided an extravagant duty by overvaluing goods and was open to many frauds. He was equally ready to abandon the very high duties on raw materials which had made the 1828 tariff particularly abominable. On most competitive manufactures a protective tariff was still to be provided, but a notable exception was coarse woolen cloth, as well as coarse wool, on both of which the duty was reduced drastically to the level of a tariff for revenue only, an admitted concession to the South and the Southwest.[132]

The reaction to McLane's tariff was about what could be expected— good in administration circles generally; poor among the ultras of either side, protectionists or free traders. The *Globe,* benefiting from a synopsis of the plan received directly from McLane, noted it was based on the principles of Jackson and "in the patriotic spirit of conciliation" he had recommended. With talent, sagacity, and boldness, continued the *Globe,* McLane had forged a revenue tariff with incidental protection, taxing but lightly the necessities of the poor, and highest on commodities used primarily by the wealthy.[133]

On the other hand Hezekiah Niles and Duff Green both thought the tariff bill unjust, ill-digested, and abominable; Niles because the duties were too low and Green because they were too high.[134] Where one critic found McLane hostile to the manufacturers another declared him wedded to the tariffites. "This is proof," wrote his clerk, "that he has with great moral daring taken the only ground that can save the Union, the *middle ground.*" [135]

McLane professed himself most concerned with the reaction in New York. The South, except for South Carolina, would support his bill, but there was a serious opposition in the New York delegation. Part of the New York opposition he laid to his old friend Cambreleng, a Manhattan free trader with southern roots; part came from protectionists who had allies in Pennsylvania. If responsibility for the defeat of his tariff bill or a similar compromise could be thrown on New York, he warned Jackson "it will not be in the power of man to connect any politician from that state with the coming election." [136] In other words, Van Buren's goose would be cooked.

Most likely this prognostication was just a bit of wishful thinking, a searching for some benefit that might be blown his way by otherwise ill winds. The nominating convention was about to take place, and McLane's jealousy of Van Buren was mounting to such a pitch that he saw New York as the source of all evils.

McLane's "middle ground" on the tariff appealed to Jackson, and it appealed also to John Quincy Adams. On May 3 he set his Committee on Manufactures at work on McLane's tariff, and despite many "dissentient opinions" he kept them at it until a revision of the bill was completed on May 16. In these two weeks there were many conferences—all friendly, so far as is known—between Adams and McLane.[137] When his work was done, Adams was fearful of the reception his bill might meet. "I expect to report a Bill tomorrow," he wrote his son, that "I suppose . . . will demolish me in the North." [138]

Despite Adams's fears, he had done more for the manufacturers than McLane. After defending the principle of tariff protection on constitutional grounds, Adams explained that his committee felt McLane's bill reduced the revenue too much. They had therefore raised a number of the duties, notably on woolens, where they felt McLane had gone too far, and had deleted a few articles, which were manufactured in this country, from McLane's free list. In general they sought to reduce duties on noncompetitive goods and retain protective duties elsewhere. They found in the Treasury bill a spirit congenial to their own, a desire to conciliate and harmonize, and though they could not agree with McLane in all details, they sought to change his bill as little as they possibly could while still fulfilling their function of defending manufactures.[139]

Though we do not have his word directly, it seems likely that McLane approved of Adams's tariff bill. His clerk declared it was "nearly a transcript of McLane's project, but not so favourable to the South." "It is not so good as McLane's," he wrote a few days later, "but as it takes off ten millions of duties, I trust it will so far satisfy the South as to avert the catastrophe of disunion." [140] Because the new bill had the sanction of Adams's name, as well as because it was less favorable to the South, it took the wind out of the pro-tariff opposition. A letter to the *Globe* from Philadelphia told of a noisy meeting, sponsored by manufacturers, to protest against McLane's tariff, and added, "Since Mr. Adams' report has come out, which was in the evening after they had convened, in which he substantially, in many things, agrees with Mr. McLane, these same people do not know what to say." [141]

For a time the main choice before Congress seemed to be between Adams's bill, which was accepted by the House, and a bill from the Senate committee on manufactures, introduced by its chairman, Mahlon Dickerson, of New Jersey, on March 30. The bills were somewhat similar, but the Senate bill was higher; its effect would be to double the tariff on British woolen goods because it provided for the retention and enforcement of the minimums system.[142]

But the Dickerson bill was first postponed and in June tabled on the motion of Dickerson himself, perhaps because he felt it wise, for the sake of his own political ambitions, to keep out of the tariff spotlight and leave it to Adams.[143] Or possibly this was all part of some administration maneuvering. According to Henry Clay, "a small man with red hair," named Moses Myers, had been "flitting about between the House of Representatives and the Treasury Department, using his exertions to cut down the protective system." [144] Myers was a merchant with Norfolk connections, and he may have been representing trading interests in a counter-lobby to the manufacturers. Apparently McLane was encouraging him.

When the Adams bill came to the Senate in July, the Senators passed it quickly, but not till they had added a number of high-tariff amendments with which it went freighted to a conference committee of the two houses. "Bad as was the scheme of the Secretary of the Treasury," stormed Senator Hayne, "the bill from the House was much worse, and this [the House bill, as amended in the Senate] is infinitely the worst of all." [145]

Surprisingly, the conference committee rejected every one of the Senate amendments, and yet the Senate accepted the committee's report. Inasmuch as two of the three Senators on the committee were protectionists, William Wilkins, of Pennsylvania, and Dickerson—Hayne was the third member—it is odd that they should have given way on every point. Daniel Webster attributed the result to Hayne's shrewdness in manipulating his colleagues so that one always agreed with him. Senator Holmes, of Maine, complained that Wilkins wanted to be Vice-President and Dickerson, who was in his sixties, was "an old bachelor who cared nothing for posterity." Clay may have been nearer the mark in commenting that both men were primarily interested in iron (it was Dickerson's main business) and since the Adams tariff protected iron they would not worry about hemp or woolens or sugar.[146]

It is, however, difficult to believe that some administration management was not at work, whether emanating from McLane's office or from some other government bureau. When a vote was finally taken on the bill, it was passed in each house by majorities that were impressive.

Though he felt bound to support the bill, McLane was not altogether pleased with it. He had a great project in mind, which was being only imperfectly realized. About him, he saw his rivals prospering, and often at his expense. On the success of their West India negotiations, and the objections raised against them, Van Buren was being exalted to the vice-presidency. Biddle's foolish insistence on pressing recharter led to Taney's rise in favor. And now McLane's tariff bill had been distorted by Adams so as to anger the South and to imperil McLane's grand national project.

His clerk, at least, appreciated him. "If the union be saved," William Read wrote his father, "McLane deserves much of the credit. He deserves the praise of honesty and boldness, since, instead of throwing himself into the arms of the ultras, . . . he nobly cast himself between the combatants, and exposed himself to the fire of both." [147]

Read was overromanticizing, but at the moment it did seem that the tariff controversy had been settled successfully. McLane had investigated the situation of the manufacturing interests and had seemed "conciliatory and judicious" to a South Carolinian like William Drayton as well as to a New Englander like Adams.[148] As Drayton knew, tariff men controlled Congress, and so Adams succeeded in skewing McLane's bill in the direction of the protectionists. But when his work on it was done, Adams assured his wife it was a very good bill—"in spite of all you have heard." "And so," he added, "say and think no small number of those who voted against it." [149]

Even Hezekiah Niles softened his criticism, admitting privately that there were "many good things" in this bill.[150] Perhaps Niles was hurt by the criticism of a writer calling himself "Franklin" who had contributed a series of articles to the *Globe* in defense of McLane's tariff bill. A friend in Delaware suggested to Niles that "Franklin" was Louis McLane, but Niles declared he did not believe McLane would be guilty of the insinuations of "Franklin," who argued that Niles was hopelessly mad on the tariff issue.[151] Probably not, but it seems quite possible that someone in McLane's office wrote the articles. McLane was most successful in getting favorable reports in the *Globe* when he planted them himself.

Adams, who had been a pessimist on the day he presented his bill to Congress, was greatly cheered by the time two months had passed. He saw his tariff now as a "universal anodyne" that all parties claimed as their own. Remembering that Clay and the National Republican caucus had been very unhappy when Adams declared he would work with

McLane for a compromise, the ex-President was annoyed to find Clay and company boasting that they had carried the tariff bill—"they and they only." [152] To McLane the satisfaction of Adams and Clay should have been an ominous portent. If only McLane could have persuaded Congress to accept the Treasury tariff bill, a confrontation between the President and South Carolina might have been avoided.

12

Denouement

The *Globe* correspondent who called himself Franklin had prophesied on May 30 that the adoption of his tariff would bring McLane "everlasting fame." And so, perhaps, it might have done. But like most of McLane's endeavors, his work on the 1832 tariff brought him no fame at all. What little fame was to be connected with the tariff accrued to Adams, not McLane, and it was precious little.

Clay and the National Republicans were satisfied by the Adams tariff, but the South Carolinians were not. Its passage was an affront to them, for it was admittedly protectionist in spirit and in detail. In the fall of 1832, the nullifiers, led by John C. Calhoun, who had abandoned the vice-presidency, carried the South Carolina elections and called a special state convention which in November declared the tariff laws of the United States null and void in South Carolina from and after February 1, 1833.

Forewarnings of the action South Carolina was to take came to McLane in August, "like distant thunder in the South." [1] But for the moment the Secretary of the Treasury was more occupied with the payment of the national debt than with the South Carolina situation. In July he had posted formal notice that the government intended to pay off two thirds of the outstanding 3 percent bonds on October 1 and the final one third on January 1. A day or two earlier he sent the same notice to Biddle in a friendly personal letter. [2]

These were the same bonds, with a par value of $13 million, that had caused an embarrassment in the relations between the Treasury and the Bank earlier in the year when the Treasury had suddenly decided to pay off half of them on July 1. Biddle had then successfully pleaded for more

time in order not to derange business.[3] Now he was in no wise shocked
at the Treasury's notice because he had assumed that all the bonds were
to be paid in the fall, instead of only two thirds.[4] "The Bank has taken
the necessary steps," he answered McLane.[5]

The steps the Bank took were to add seriously to Biddle's troubles
once they became known. Even before the Bank's arrangements became
known McLane was embarrassed by the interpretation given to certain
phrases used in his letter of notification to Biddle, particularly to a section
of the letter inserted at the suggestion of Asbury Dickins. This section
referred to an "understanding . . . that if it should happen that the
public moneys are insufficient to complete . . . payments, the Bank will
delay the presentation of any certificates of which it may have the control
until the funds are sufficient to meet them, the interest to be paid by the
United States during the interval." [6] What McLane found embarrassing
was the suggestion, drawn from his own words, that the government
would lack the necessary funds on October 1 and would be forced to
apply to the Bank for help. This was indeed what he had said, and it was
natural for the Treasury to turn to the national bank in such an eventuality.[7] But McLane did not expect to be out of funds on October 1, and
as an agent of a President who declared the Bank unconstitutional and
thought it unnecessary, the admission of any dependence upon it—particularly while the Bank was an issue in the presidential election—was
unwise.

Probably McLane's suggestion became known through one of the government directors of the Bank, most likely John T. Sullivan. Biddle had
seen nothing confidential in the letter, or so he claimed, and had read it
to his board as a matter of course. Nor was he very much concerned
about the matter. Take care of the rumors, he advised the Treasury
Department, "by being very full of Funds in October." [8]

He did not see fit to explain, however, that he had set negotiations in
motion that would make it difficult for the Treasury to redeem the 3 percents in October, however "full of Funds" it was. Since a large part of
the 3 percents, over half, were owned abroad, Biddle sent Thomas Cadwalader to London to arrange with Baring Brothers to act as agent for
the Bank of the United States in securing these bonds. The board of directors of the Bank was not officially informed of Cadwalader's mission,
which was kept confidential till the Barings' announcement to foreign
bondholders became known in the United States. When it did, there was
reason for criticism, for Cadwalader's arrangements with the Barings
were unwise and, in part, illegal.[9]

Cadwalader's arrangements were unwise because the Barings invited
bondholders to keep their certificates for a year (they were not legally

compelled to give them up), for which period the Bank agreed to pay the interest. This was, in effect, a negation of the Treasury Department's measures to extinguish the debt. In defense, it could be pleaded that this scheme cost the government nothing, but, as critics of the Bank were quick to point out, the Bank was not only countermanding the Secretary of the Treasury's policy but it was maintaining control of federal monies which might otherwise have been paid out in canceling a portion of the debt. And the arrangements were illegal to the extent that Cadwalader arranged with the Barings to buy some of the certificates on the Bank's account, because the Bank by its charter was forbidden to buy and sell federal securities except as agent of the government.

When McLane heard of Cadwalader's arrangements and of the comments being made regarding them—the New York *Evening Post,* for instance, spoke of "evasion of the laws and wishes of the country" [10]—he became anxious. He had Dickins write at once to Biddle, asking him to contradict some of the published statements concerning Cadwalader's arrangements, and on October 15, probably the very day of the receipt of Dickins's letter, Biddle sent the Barings a new proposal. Explaining that the Bank was forbidden to purchase any public debt whatever, he canceled this part of Cadwalader's arrangements.

Still dissatisfied, McLane pressed Biddle to redeem the 3 percents as fast as possible. And yet, working through Dickins, the Secretary mixed honey with vinegar, complimenting Biddle on the precautions taken in case of any emergency such as a sudden tightening of the money market. [11]

Biddle responded with alacrity. He asked the Barings to speed along the transmission of certificates to the United States without delay. He sent McLane an explanation of the whole transaction, including a promise to abide by the Treasury's wish to pay off the debt as soon as possible. And to chief clerk Dickins, who would receive this letter, Biddle enclosed an informal note, reading, in part: "Your counsels are commands. Now if after having taken this trouble your auditor and kitchen cabinet and Hickory Club insist on quarrelling about deposits—be it so." [12]

But of course the auditor and the kitchen cabinet and the Hickory Club did insist on quarreling about deposits, and every maladroit act of a Bank agent, however well-intentioned, armed them for the war they waged. Not least, it encouraged Jackson to act on his own prejudices against the Bank. So did his triumphant reelection in the fall of 1832, which, thanks to Clay's espousal of the Bank, seemed a popular endorsement of the veto message.

According to Taney, Jackson raised the issue of the Bank in a cabinet meeting soon after the result of the election became evident. One proposal was that the funds of the government be withdrawn from the Bank on the grounds of its misconduct, especially in the case of the 3 percent bonds. By this action the Bank would lose its favored position as a government depository long before its charter expired. McLane, however, favored an alternate proposal which seemed an even more severe stroke against the Bank. This was prosecution of the Bank in court on a writ of *scire facias,* a process leading to the complete abrogation of the Bank charter on the grounds of misconduct. It was also a process which the President, not the Secretary, would be obliged to institute.

Taney suspected McLane of a deceitful purpose, of playing for time knowing that a trial would be long and involved. It would, moreover, take place in Philadelphia before a Pennsylvania jury and in the circuit court of Henry Baldwin, a Pennsylvanian known to be sympathetic to the Bank.[13] But it is not necessary to attribute such Machiavellian tactics to McLane. He knew the worth of the Bank; he had few doubts of its safety; how could he, as the responsible Secretary of the Treasury, withdraw funds from the Bank without an investigation or some other support for his action? He was angry at the Bank leadership for their cooperation with Clay and the opposition, but even more he disliked certain of his colleagues of the kitchen cabinet, Hickory Club set. It was these men, not Biddle and Cadwalader and the Bank set, who stood in his way and were his rivals.

"The plan is War upon the Bank to be carried on in every form," a friendly Senator warned Nicholas Biddle.[14] Caught between the battle lines, the Secretary of the Treasury was hard put to keep his head upon his shoulders. "No British or American minister ever before retained his place under like circumstances," declared Hezekiah Niles, in noting the differences of opinion between McLane and the President on the Bank.[15]

II   A VAN BUREN MAN

Not many ministers were possessed of the address of Louis McLane, the talent of impressing those who worked with him of his capability and his high-mindedness. If Van Buren is to be believed, the strange, and frequently strained, relationship he bore to McLane is a case in point.

After Van Buren went abroad friends began sending him worrisome despatches regarding McLane's attitude and conduct. When Van Buren came home, they rushed to recount their stories in his ear. Major Lewis, for instance, repeated his suspicions of McLane's attempt to influence the vice-presidential nomination. Though Van Buren suavely passed the matter over, refusing to admit any great concern, the tales he was hearing must have had a cumulative effect.[16]

One of these tales came from Frank Blair on the day after Van Buren's return to Washington. Blair called on Van Buren at the White House (as the President's home was now being called), where he was staying, and there in the window niche of a little breakfast room Blair poured forth his complaints of McLane's double dealing. Blair and Van Buren were not old friends, for Blair was but newly arrived in Washington before Van Buren set off for England, and Van Buren may well have been concerned how far to put any stock in the irate editor's suspicions.

Van Buren carried the matter to the President, who had also heard from Blair and pronounced himself persuaded that both men, the Secretary and the editor, were honest. If McLane had preferred a different vice-presidential nomination, Jackson felt sure he had done so in the belief that it would be best for everyone concerned. Undoubtedly Blair had also talked to Jackson about McLane's course, but Jackson seems to have admired McLane's independence and he assured Van Buren that McLane was as much his friend as it was his nature to be anybody's.

In the wake of Lewis and Blair, Senator Elias Kane, of Illinois, came to Van Buren to soothe the troubled waters. Van Buren esteemed Kane and was glad to be comforted when Kane declared he believed the rumors attributing bad faith to McLane to be without foundation. Van Buren was never a man to allow partisan political differences to obstruct social intercourse, and the interview with Senator Kane and the assurances of President Jackson encouraged him to resume his old friendship with McLane, especially after McLane himself made overtures toward the reestablishment of their old relationship.[17]

Indeed when Van Buren arrived at New York from England, there had been a friendly note awaiting him from the Secretary, and in Washington McLane was not slow in calling on Van Buren and inviting him to a ride and to dinner *en famille*. With some hesitancy, Van Buren accepted, and a week later he visited the Treasury Department. Still, all was not quite as it had been, and McLane, annoyed by a rumor circulating in Baltimore to the effect that he was leaving the cabinet after quarreling with Van Buren, wrote the latter to ask who had made the charge of disloyalty. Only by knowing the source, McLane said, could he determine whether gossip, or malice, or honest solicitude for a friend was at the basis of the charge. Van Buren would not tell; surely, he replied, it was honest solicitude which raised apprehensions, plus a feeling that the course advocated for Van Buren—the vice-presidential nomination—was vitally necessary.[18]

Through the late summer and fall of 1832 McLane assiduously set about establishing the most friendly relations possible, particularly with the kitchen cabinet. Late in September he and Kitty traveled to West Point, and en route he may have seen Van Buren. Letters survive that he addressed to Major Lewis and Andrew Jackson Donelson, as well as Gulian Verplanck, during the trip.[19] By this time he had succeeded in persuading Blair of his right-mindedness. "The Secretary is now a good Support," Blair insisted, "an Anti-Biddle-Bank man, . . . and . . . a Van Buren man." [20] It took longer to convince suspicious Amos Kendall, but in another month he came round. "Our cabinet are *now* all anti-bank," he informed Van Buren. "I believe they are also all very friendly to yourself. At one time I had some doubt of their *unanimous* disposition to do you justice." [21]

Despite slippery going, McLane's fortunes were still on the rise.

III   FROM A DEAD MISER'S DESK

For several years Edward Livingston had been eager for a diplomatic appointment abroad.[22] It was the French mission that he most ardently coveted, for he had a French wife, he understood French himself, he was an authority on French law, and he long had been an admirer of French culture. Now in his sixties, he had finally become head of the foreign office, as his brother had been almost half a century earlier, and it would be the capstone of his career if he could take the post at Paris which the same brother had filled with distinction at the time of the Louisiana Purchase.

Jackson had offered this position to Livingston in 1829, but personal affairs then made it very difficult for him to go off in a hurry, and when Jackson's Secretary of State pressed him to go or decline, Livingston declined.[23] The post next fell vacant in September, 1832, when William Rives returned to America, and by this time Livingston was Secretary of State himself and better able to command the time of his going. It was assumed immediately that he would be Rives's replacement; he was known to be tired of his office and of Washington intrigues.

Rives left Paris on September 22, 1832. Well before this date Jackson had determined to send Livingston to France and to move Louis McLane to the State Department from the Treasury. On August 11 McLane wrote Van Buren vaguely of "certain changes of which we spoke" and of his desire to make "some suggestions both in regard to myself and others which appear to me important; and both more feasible and expedient than some that are in contemplation." [24] It is possible that these changes and suggestions have nothing to do with the translation of Livingston and McLane, but on September 16 Jackson, home in Tennessee on a visit, refers to this change in a letter to Van Buren as though the latter has known of it for some time. He wished to send Livingston to France as soon as Rives started home, he said, but the problem was to find "a fit,

proper, and competent head" of the Treasury Department to replace Mc-
Lane, and to that end he solicited Van Buren's advice.[25] Late in September, McLane sent some suggestions to Jackson via Major Lewis regarding
an appointment to be made and he seconded Van Buren's desire that it
be delayed until after the election, but it is as likely that this appointment was in the New York customs house as in the cabinet.[26]

Whether the election, the inability to settle on a proper choice for Secretary of the Treasury, or some other reason caused the delay is not clear,
but when November began, Jackson was no further along with his cabinet
rearrangements than he had been in September. At the President's request McLane talked the matter over with Van Buren on November 7,
when he went to New York to fix the site for a new customs house.[27] Van
Buren later recalled suggesting that Attorney General Taney be moved
to the Treasury, creating a cabinet opening for his onetime law partner
and Regency colleague, Benjamin Butler, but McLane was vigorously
opposed to the promotion of Taney. This promotion would be "gall and
wormwood" to him, McLane insisted in a letter three weeks later, and
would leave him no "inducement to continue in public life" except the
needs of his "large and helpless family." [28] One thing they did agree upon
was that the cabinet rearrangement should be deferred so that Jackson
might begin the new session of Congress "with a steady cabinet and without the embarrassment of change." [29] Why change in this case would
cause any embarrassment is uncertain.

Jackson did not like it, but he acquiesced as he was forced to do inasmuch as he had not yet found a new Secretary of the Treasury. He disliked leaving the French post unoccupied except by a chargé, but it was
still more undesirable to leave the Treasury untenanted at a time when
preparations had to be made for the resistance to the tariff laws which
was expected to begin in South Carolina on the 1st of February.[30] On
October 16, for instance, Jackson was told of the possibility of armed war
in Charleston and warned that "the custom house where the battle will
be fought is crowded with Nullifiers." [31] Early in November McLane sent
special instructions to the collectors of Beaufort, Charleston, and Georgetown, urging them to carry out their duties with the aid of additional
revenue cutters which were being supplied and authorizing the removal
of customs houses to secure places, such as Castle Pinckney, if any out-
rages were threatened.[32] The instructions to the collector at Charleston
were carried by a secret messenger, George Breathitt, brother of the governor of Kentucky.[33] It fell to McLane also to send instructions to the
district attorney at Charleston, urging him to stick to his post (he had
contemplated a trip to Washington) and to defend any seizure of ships
or cargoes the collector felt he must carry out.[34]

Meanwhile some consideration was given to a candidate for Secretary of the Treasury from New York, but Jackson thought it much more desirable that a Pennsylvanian be chosen, and if no Pennsylvanian seemed fitting, that a choice should be made from the South. Senator John Forsyth, of Georgia, deserved consideration, but his talents, in Jackson's words, were "not of the fiscal order," and anyway it seemed unwise to weaken the administration leadership in the Senate at the moment.[35] The President sought someone of talent, integrity, and national reputation who was in "constitutional and political" accord with the administration —a man opposed to government investment in private corporations and even to the creation of them by Congress anywhere except in the District of Columbia; a man favorable to reducing the tariff to a revenue basis with protection only for the means of national defense; and, finally, a man disposed to "harmonize" the administration in behalf of "the *whole Union,* extending justice to every part of it." After this explanation to Van Buren in a letter dated November 25, Jackson added a postscript to convey "a happy thought." "William J. Duane," he explained, "in whom every confidence can be placed, flashed into my mind, after writing the above." He had "named" Duane, he added, to Louis McLane, who thought him a very fitting choice.[36]

Perhaps Duane seemed a fitting choice, but he was a surprising choice too. He was not a man of national reputation, but he bore a name that did have political value throughout the land. His father, Colonel William Duane, was to the Jeffersonian party in Philadelphia what Franklin P. Blair was to the Jacksonian party in Washington—editor of the party paper. Duane's *Aurora* had made his name famous and associated that name with the old traditions of Republicanism, to which Jackson was making an appeal. The name Duane connoted anti-Federalist and anti-Bank policies, and the younger Duane had worked with his father, who was still living in 1832, before beginning a career of his own as a Philadelphia lawyer.

Duane seemed a peculiarly fit candidate because he was an anti-Bank Republican from Philadelphia, the home of the Bank. As evidence of experience if not talents "of the fiscal order," which Jackson had found wanting in Forsyth, Duane had served as chairman of a committee on banks of the Pennsylvania legislature and was the legal counsel of the richest of Philadelphia merchants, Stephen Girard.

Years later Van Buren heard from Frank Blair that it was Louis McLane who suggested Duane's name. McLane was eager to give the impression that Duane's appointment was Jackson's idea, Blair said, because of the way the appointment turned out. "He hinted it to me," Blair wrote in 1845, "and I made some allusion to it, when the General in his disappointment spoke of Duane as having been palmed off on him. . . . The General pronounced McLane's intimation a perfect piece of deception. He told me expressly that when McLane conversed with him about re-signing his station in the Treasury and taking the State Department to the way [*sic*] to the removal of the deposits, he (McLane) when invited to cast about for a successor named several . . . which being, *by both,* set aside as undesirable, at last clapt his hand on his thigh and said 'General I can tell you the very man' and named Duane." [37]

It is difficult to know whether to accept Jackson's statement of 1832 that Duane was his own idea or Jackson's later claim, as relayed by Blair, that the suggestion was McLane's. Blair saw Jackson's letter and argued it was "framed to keep McLane's agency as suggestor out of sight." [38] (Blair refers also to a second postscript, which does not appear in the copy printed in Van Buren's autobiography—and the original is apparently lost.) But Blair was angry with McLane in 1845 and wanted to believe the worst of him. His memory is probably fallible at least in reference to the removal of deposits as an issue in McLane's transferral, for this was not a major issue in 1832. Van Buren declared he saw no reason to doubt Blair's story, but he too was angry with McLane in 1845 and wanted to believe it. [39]

Amos Kendall later confessed he had no personal knowledge of how Duane's name was suggested but had heard in Philadelphia that the idea originated with McLane, who wanted to control two departments. [40] Admitting that his informant disliked both McLane and Duane, Kendall passed the information on to Jackson in August, 1833, and Jackson in turn passed the story on to Van Buren, making a reference to McLane's recommendation of Duane. [41] Levi Woodbury heard the President quoted as declaring that McLane's recommendation of Duane caused his selection, but Woodbury also believed that Van Buren had encouraged the selection in order to strengthen his influence in Pennsylvania. However, when Woodbury discussed the appointment with McLane, the latter assured him that Van Buren had no part in the appointment and that it originated with the President himself. [42] Woodbury's information came from conversations nine months to a year after the decision to appoint Duane, which had been made in November, 1832.

At that time McLane reported to Van Buren by letter that in conversation with Jackson a number of men had been considered, including Woodbury and Taney, who had been suggested or had occurred as possibilities to the President while McLane was out of town, and four Pennsylvanians, Dallas, Wilkins, Buchanan, and Duane. McLane was opposed to consideration of either of his cabinet colleagues, and Jackson preferred to look to Pennsylvania, being eager to reward that state for its loyalty to him in the election despite his veto of the Bank, a Pennsylvania institution. Serious objections, personal and political, were found to all of the Pennsylvanians except Duane. McLane declared he did warn Jackson that Duane was not a very prominent person, but Jackson waved this objection aside. Jackson had set his mind on Duane by this time and asked McLane to write Duane.

McLane also informed Van Buren that the President had reluctantly but necessarily agreed to their request that all the changes be postponed till spring, after the winter session of Congress was over and time was allowed for settlement of the crises developing over the tariff and nullification. Apparently Van Buren and McLane had agreed on such a recommendation at their meeting in New York, and it is further indication of the importance of Van Buren as a presidential adviser even when out of office and away from Washington that not only Jackson but also McLane wrote him about the choice of Duane and pleaded the case. McLane professed himself a bit concerned that Jackson might offer the post prematurely. Duane was said to be in Washington at the moment; McLane was about to urge the President to do nothing definitive if he happened to see Duane till Van Buren had been heard from.

McLane was himself sold on Duane as his successor; his one professed reason for any hesitance was what he called "an apprehension" that Van Buren would prefer to move Taney to the place and make room in the cabinet for Butler. And though Jackson had mentioned Taney as a possibility, McLane had not told the President that this solution would suit Van Buren, having, happily, an excuse for staying silent in the request Van Buren had made of him that he not mention this proposal till Van Buren had inquired whether Butler would be interested. McLane could hardly tolerate thought of Taney as his successor, but would be glad to make room for Butler by sending Taney to a diplomatic post abroad, to fill the vacancy in England, for instance.[43]

In responding to the President's letter, Van Buren did not hesitate to mention his plan for Taney, but he did not press it, having learned that Butler preferred to maintain his practice in New York. And he agreed that the proposal to appoint Duane seemed preferable to any other. There was only one point about it that Van Buren questioned, which was Duane's capability, and he trusted, or claimed to trust, that Jackson and McLane would not make a mistake about that.[44]

The exchanges between Van Buren and McLane are as though between two experts in diplomacy, each treading warily so as to lose no advantage. Van Buren had decided to stay away from Washington until March, when he would officially take office as Vice-President. With this prize in his grasp it behooved him to stay in the background and avoid antagonizing any portion of the President's party. He was already the heir presumptive, the logical successor to Jackson's position if no startling development took place and no rival was brought forward with a better claim. McLane fitted very well into Van Buren's plans. With his Federalist antecedents and opinions he was not likely to prove acceptable to broad strata of the Jacksonian party. He was experienced in public affairs, he had ability (Van Buren would have called it "capacity"), industry, and imagination. When he thought it worth his while to make the effort, he could win the friendship as well as the respect of the people he dealt with. He was indeed a splendid prime minister to work with the Old Chief while the heir watched from a distance.

Perhaps the most comfortable factor about McLane's usefulness was his dependence on Van Buren. As long as Van Buren retained the respect Jackson held for him, he could demolish McLane if he chose. If Van Buren lost Jackson's respect, his expectations would be totally lost, of course, but Jackson was loyal to his friends unless very greatly provoked, and so this eventuality was not a likely one.

Van Buren, through the strength of his Regency colleagues in New York, might remain a strong factor in national politics even without Jackson, but McLane had no such source of strength to fall back upon. His state was nearly the smallest and least consequential in national affairs. And even such as it was, he had lost it. Since the Federalist party of Delaware had been broken in the new alignment of parties around Jackson and Adams, Delaware had become a bulwark of the anti-Jackson forces. The Jacksonians hoped that 1832 would mean a redemption and were misled briefly by the news that an aged Revolutionary veteran, Caleb Bennett, had been elected governor on the Jackson ticket. But Bennett's victory proved to be an electoral caprice. Delaware turned out to be one of the six Clay states in 1832, and McLane could have no illusions about playing Calhoun and resuming his Senate seat if he lost confidence in the administration. The two Senate seats were occupied by his determined antagonists, John M. Clayton and Dr. Arnold Naudain, and the House seat he had occupied for ten years belonged to his unfriendly brother-in-law, John J. Milligan. "Jacksonism is almost defunct [in] Delaware," sadly concluded one of McLane's lieutenants.[45]

McLane knew that he was skating on thin ice, wholly dependent on presidential favor for his political standing, but he was encouraged by confidence in his own ability, by ambition, and by the lack of any acceptable alternative. Under these conditions it would not be strange if he suggested an acceptable Secretary of the Treasury to Jackson to avoid the encouragement of a potential rival like Taney or a cold enigmatic Yankee like Woodbury. In the spring, when the changes were still an unannounced secret, Biddle heard that McLane was supporting a Pennsylvanian for the Treasury position over Rives, the choice of Van Buren and the kitchen cabinet, and that the Bank question was the issue between the two candidates.[46]

There is no doubt that McLane liked the appointment and encouraged it. But this is not the same thing as originating it. Though never a close friend, he had employed Duane for some personal business. His father knew the elder Duane, but they had been traditionally of opposite parties, the elder McLane a violent Federalist and the elder Duane the most outspoken of Republicans. Nor is it at all likely that McLane wanted to trick Jackson into accepting a Secretary of the Treasury with whom he could not work. On the contrary, it was to McLane's advantage to have a good working team in the cabinet of which he now was to be the first-ranking member. And it was by no means McLane who was responsible for a government post Duane already held as a commissioner to settle claims against Denmark. Van Buren admitted that it was he who proposed Duane to Jackson for this post—and on his own responsibility, happening suddenly to think of Duane as he and Jackson were walking on the White House terrace.[47]

It seems also worth noting that one of Jackson's earliest and best biographers, James Parton, wrote that "this appointment was the President's own." Parton had discussed Jackson's career with Major Lewis, who also read and criticized the printed work and made no criticism of this comment. Possibly Lewis was the source of a story Parton tells—that Jackson had a very high opinion of old Colonel Duane and when speaking of his son would "exhaust compliment by saying, 'He's a chip of the old block, sir.' "[48] Indeed Jackson had already offered the young Duane three positions.

Whoever first suggested the name, it seems that Jackson decided on Duane impetuously in the same fashion in which he chose the members of his first cabinet, particularly his first Secretary of the Treasury, Samuel Ingham. McLane made a serious mistake in encouraging the selection of Duane, as it turned out, but he was unduly eager, not because of his regard for Duane or any secret knowledge of Duane's opinions, but simply because he wanted to exclude Taney and Woodbury, who would remain candidates as long as no choice was made. And the idea that Taney might become an ever stronger candidate the longer the vacancy lasted was by no means absurd. Speaker Stevenson, Frank Blair, and Major Lewis, all spoke to Taney, according to his own recollection, asking his permission to suggest his name—probably much in the way Van Buren sought Butler's permission. But Taney refused them, apparently preferring to aspire to a Supreme Court seat. Nevertheless he was hurt that through the entire fall Jackson never mentioned the Treasury vacancy to him.[49] If a candidate had not been quickly found, Taney might have gained attention.

On December 4, 1832, the day before Congress was to convene, Mc-Lane saw Duane and surprised him with the offer of a much more important political post than any he had filled heretofore. Duane's first inclination was to refuse, but McLane, probably fearful of an invitation to Taney in the event Duane declined, pressed him to accept, arguing that it was a duty he owed his country and emphasizing the President's "spontaneous preference" of him to other candidates. Duane had refused appointments before (as a government director of the Bank and as district attorney, for instance), but this was far the best post he had been offered. His elderly father, whose advice he leaned on heavily, urged him to accept, and despite some morbid fears of losing office he finally did accept on January 30, after almost two months of deliberation.[50]

In the long run the appointment was to prove an unhappy one for McLane and for Jackson. In their eagerness to persuade Duane to accept, they had learned very little about the attitude of this man of whom an enemy said that he was "fished up from the desk of a dead miser, and the bottom of the Philadelphia bar, to . . . the seat which was once filled by Alexander Hamilton." [51]

IV SUSTAINING THE HERO

Another appointment in December, 1832, seemed a more positive advantage to the retiring Secretary of the Treasury—the appointment of Gulian Verplanck as chairman of the House Committee of Ways and Means. Verplanck was on very friendly terms with McLane, so much so that Frank Blair, disliking them both, called Verplanck "the toad that always took his complexion from McL[ane]." [52]

The opportunity for Verplanck's appointment came about through a fortunate accident. Committee chairmen were appointed by the Speaker, and few changes were made between sessions. George McDuffie, who had served as chairman of the Ways and Means Committee, was late in returning to Washington from South Carolina in December, 1832, giving Speaker Stevenson an excuse to leave him off the committee and elevate the number two man on it, Verplanck, to the chairmanship, while filling the vacancy in numbers by shifting James K. Polk, an undeviating Jacksonian, from the Foreign Affairs Committee to Ways and Means.

This change seemed to be fortunate for both McLane and his party because McDuffie was a thoroughgoing low tariff man who insisted on a more nearly complete abandonment of tariff protection than Congress was ever likely to accept, while Verplanck, though a low-tariff New York, was apt to be less dogmatic and more inclined to harmonize divergent sectional interests on the critical tariff question. Polk too would prove a useful member, industrious and eager to help with legislation that would bind the nation together after South Carolina intransigence had posed a threat of schism.[53] Through the close contact of this committee with the Treasury, Polk learned to regard Louis McLane with a respect that lasted the rest of his life and led him to trust McLane with a critical mission in 1845.

Another appointment that McLane sought never came off. This was an arrangement for James Gordon Bennett to buy a half interest in the *Globe* and become its co-editor with Blair. The arrangement was suggested by McLane, but it depended on Blair's becoming printer to Congress, which would leave him less time for the paper, and on Bennett's raising money to buy a half interest. As a New York newspaperman, Bennett, a native of Scotland, had become known as an ardent Democrat, supporting Van Buren and Jackson and opposing the Bank. Perhaps McLane was thinking only of the good of the party in suggesting that Bennett become a partner of Blair. It is likely, however, that he also looked upon any dilution of Blair's control of the official party press as a personal advantage for himself.

At any rate, the proposal did not work out. Blair did not become printer to Congress at this session, and Bennett continued his career elsewhere until 1835, when he started the New York *Herald*, which made him famous. The *Herald* was begun as a politically independent paper, probably because Bennett was angry about his failure to get financial help in December, 1832, though he wrote to both Van Buren and Biddle in hope of assistance. It seems not unlikely that McLane had both suggested a *Globe* partnership for Bennett and advised him where to seek funds.[54]

When Washington Irving returned to the East in mid-December, he found McLane looking well. "McLane is hard worked by his office," he wrote, "but it is a kind of work that agrees with him." [55] To observers he seemed now to be a part, and a vital part, of a unified cabinet team. There were, of course, misgivings about his effectiveness. Cambreleng found McLane was not managing the Bank "with his usual ability." But Cam did not sneer as he passed along McLane's boast, "he says he'll lay B[iddle] on his back soon." [56]

McLane's annual report had shocked Biddle somewhat but was far from laying him on his back.[57] In comparison with the comprehensive report he had made in 1831, the report of the Secretary of the Treasury that was received by Congress on December 6, 1832, was very weak indeed, and almost a shadow of the President's message. So far had Mc-

Lane's role changed that whereas in 1831 he sought to set the pace for the administration, a year later he was content to follow the President's lead, happy to be considered a loyal lieutenant. The change that had come over McLane's outward expression measures the forcefulness of Jackson. The Old Chief was not so maneuverable as some men had thought. "The more I see of this old cock of the woods," Washington Irving wrote this winter, "the more I relish his game qualities." [58]

The report did not, of course, exactly toe the Jackson line; had it done so, McLane would not have been McLane. John Quincy Adams noticed the difference. Whereas the President called for a gradual end to all protective tariffs except on wartime necessities, the Secretary called only for moderation, for "liberal concession and compromise," declaring that a permanent system of *high* protective duties favored certain classes in a society over others. He did call for further reduction of duties after 1833 when revenue might safely be reduced by $6 million, and he hailed the forthcoming liquidation of the public debt, noting that it might have been extinguished in this year had Congress accepted his recommendation that the government sell its Bank stock. [59]

Of course he noted the threat to the collection of revenue in South Carolina which was posed by the state nullification ordinance passed on November 24. Extraordinary measures requiring special legislation might be necessary to deal with this situation, but for the time he wished only to note that his department was considering the remedies that might be required.

The part of his message that surprised Biddle the most was a review of the history of the Bank's negotiations with the Barings for the payment of the 3 percents. [60] The story was fairly told, but McLane added a note of condemnation: "It is not perceived that there is any sufficient justification . . . for an arrangement . . . by which so large an amount of the public funds should be retained by the bank, at the risk of the Government, after it had directed their application to the payment of the public creditor."

Despite the fact that the Bank had an excuse for its actions, the statement is a true indictment. The words that followed were ominous: in view of this arrangement and of the great amount of the Bank's transactions and other matters that had disturbed public confidence, as well as because of the forthcoming termination of the charter, an inquiry into the security of the Bank seemed called for. Any immediate change in the government depository seemed inexpedient, but the Treasury had instituted an inquiry, and it was up to Congress to decide whether to conduct a further examination of the Bank. [61]

"McLane, . . . you are by this time aware," wrote one of Biddle's congressional correspondents, "abandons all his old ground and sustains the 'Hero' in all things. Heaven help us!" [62] An administration supporter hailed the "good old republican doctrines" of the President's message and the Secretary's report and declared that the history of the 3 percents had made McLane a "complete convert" to the anti-Bank forces.[63]

The report proved no such complete conversion. It was indeed tailored to Jackson's message, which condemned the Bank's arrangements for withholding the 3 percents and asked Congress to look into the safety of the government deposits, declaring that the Secretary had done what he could but that his powers might be inadequate.[64] But McLane had thus far successfully resisted pressure for removal of the deposits, particularly by his action in appointing an agent, as he had announced in his report, to examine the safety of the Bank as a government depository. By the time Congress met, the agent, who was Henry Toland, a Jacksonian merchant and a former government director of the Bank, had completed his work and his report was on the way to McLane. After investigation of the general accounts at the Philadelphia office, Toland found the Bank solvent beyond any doubt and the government deposits in it absolutely safe.[65]

Biddle was pleased. Somehow he had foreknowledge of the contents of Toland's report, for he told Adams it was "in the highest degree satisfactory" before even McLane had received it.[66]

And McLane must have been equally pleased. The Toland report gave him some leeway for further maneuvering and justified the position he had taken. As the winter began, his stock stood high. He could hardly longer delude himself into thinking he might be the prime minister of a constitutional monarch, for McLane did not control his parliament nor would King Andrew desist from taking a hand in affairs himself. But due to Van Buren's absence from Washington and Livingston's disinterest in all affairs except the diplomatic, McLane was the leading man in the cabinet.

If he could keep the President's confidence, his role could be a very significant one. There were just two sets of opponents—on any grounds other than personal—that he had to cope with. The first set was the anti-Bank element, and so strong were they in the administration that McLane apparently decided he must join them. Since they had Jackson's sympathy he could not defeat them, but perhaps his knowledge of banking and finance could be advantageous to the government. The second set of opponents was composed of the ultra-tariff men, who regarded McLane as a traitor to their ranks. Their strength was particularly great at home in Delaware, where John M. Clayton was trying to whip the manufacturers into a fury at McLane's betrayal of them. The only course McLane could take against these ultras was to disregard them and their protests and to proceed with plans for a lowering of the tariff that would at once placate reasonable low-tariff men and yet avoid a complete loss of protection. He sought, indeed, to harmonize the sections.

V THE FORCE ACT

When Congress convened on December 3, 1832, the engrossing topic of Washington conversation was the critical situation in South Carolina.[67] Not least excited by the news of nullification was the President of the United States. "They are trying me," he told his old friend, General Sam Dale, "but by the God in heaven, I will uphold the laws." [68]

In a fever of excitement he dashed off pages of an appeal to South Carolinians to reverse their course. His draft and notes were handed to Livingston, who, probably with the help of Cass, Kendall, and Donelson, put the statement in final order for issuance on December 10.[69] The document that resulted was an argument and a warning—an argument that nullification was illegal and that the reasoning of the nullifiers was specious and misleading—a warning that the President would enforce the laws. There followed a passionate plea to those he regarded as fellow citizens of his native state not to disgrace their heritage by following false leaders on the path to treason. "Declare that you will never take the field," he charged them, "unless the star-spangled banner of your country shall float over you." [70]

The long proclamation was strongly nationalist in tone, as even observers sympathetic to Jackson noted. Cambreleng, for instance, declared it was applauded by every Federalist from Maine to Louisiana.[71] Perhaps Louis McLane felt like Daniel Webster, who, thinking of the proclamation, wrote, "It is sometimes said that, in so changing a world, if people will but stand still, others sooner or later will come to them." [72]

But McLane could not relax and enjoy the President's nationalist sympathies, for he was under the necessity of preparing a new tariff act. The President had called for it in his message to Congress.[73] McLane echoed the call in his report; now the proclamation confessed to its South Carolina audience that the tariff was unfair to them and promised it would be revised. Since it was the executive branch of the government that called for a new tariff, it was to this branch that men looked for its preparation, and particularly, of course, to McLane.

On December 3, the very day Congress met, Verplanck wrote of awaiting "McLane's project of a tariff in detail." [74] Probably it was still not completed by December 13, when Sam Smith, on behalf of the Committee on Finance, asked the Senate to direct McLane to furnish a new tariff bill with as little delay as possible. On a point of prerogative the Senate refused to make the request, but before the end of the month McLane's "project of a tariff" had reached the House Ways and Means Committee, for on December 17, Verplanck, its chairman, introduced the new tariff bill.[75]

It was to this committee that the tariff recommendation in the President's message had been assigned, rather than to the Committee on Manufactures, which had prepared the last tariff. Adams, still chairman, was now stymied by an anti-tariff majority on his committee and was powerless to do anything more than present a minority report which was an overlong defense of the constitutionality and the wisdom of the protective system.[76]

It is probable that the proposed tariff which became known as the Verplanck bill after its congressional sponsor was largely McLane's work, or at least very close to the bill prepared under his direction in the Treasury Department. Jackson later referred to it as "the Tarriff bill prepared by McLain under my view," but this was in 1841 and he may have forgotten.[77] Moses Myers, the ubiquitous Norfolk merchant, is said to have helped McLane, and Verplanck, Polk, and Archer cooperated either in the initial preparation of the tariff or in the adjustments that Silas Wright testifies were made in committee before the bill was reported.[78] But the greatest part of the burden rested on McLane, and he collapsed when the work was finished.[79]

The proposed tariff meant a considerable reduction in the duties—to an average of 10 to 20 percent, as Verplanck explained in introducing it. The percentage was set by figuring that an income of $12.5 million was needed from imported goods expected to be worth about $84 million. The committee was encouraged by the fact that the duties it proposed were similar to those of 1816, as amended in 1818, and they called attention to the fact that the 1816 tariff had been prepared by some eminent men (no names were mentioned, but in other ways Calhoun's role in 1816 was being given attention) and that it had been intended to raise revenue to pay off the new war debt and also to offer protection to manufactures that had been started during the preceding years of embargo and nonintercourse as well as war.

A few duties were raised rather than lowered. Such was the case with silks because the committee felt that importers of foreign luxuries had not been carrying their share of the tariff burden. Tea and coffee were removed from the free list and assessed a normal duty, giving the tariff a measure of elasticity because this duty on a noncompetitive product could quickly be abandoned if the revenue proved to be larger than necessary.

And there was a chance that it would. The tariff reductions were not to take effect immediately but over a two-year period, half of them in 1834 and the other half in 1835. There might well be a surplus revenue when the Adams tariff would go into effect in 1833, but the committee preferred to err on the safe side.[80]

The Verplanck tariff was not a complete reversal of McLane's attitude and policy toward protection, but merely a tactical retreat to an earlier position, his purpose being to tranquilize the nation and, according to a cynic, to "immortalize himself." Jackson does not seem to have been aware that the bill did not fit his recommendations for a tariff—a gradual abandonment of protection—as well as it fitted the policy embodied in the report of the Secretary of the Treasury. "He at this time possesses the confidence of the President in a higher degree than any other man whatever," wailed Senator Dickerson, inaccurately, as he complained that the bill would disrupt the administration party.[81]

To Dickerson, as to Daniel Webster and to Senator John Tipton of Indiana, the Verplanck bill was objectionable not only in itself but because it seemed a surrender to the nullifiers.[82] And indeed it was. With McLane's help Jackson was approaching the South Carolinians, his fellow South Carolinians, as he felt they were, with an olive branch in one hand and a sword in the other. The olive branch was the Verplanck tariff, which he thought a reasonable concession to reasonable complaints in the interest of national harmony. The sword was a measure that came to be called the Force Act, and in persuading Congress to accept it McLane had as important a role as in the preparation of the Verplanck tariff.

There is no evidence that McLane wrote the Force Act itself, but he helped prepare the message Jackson sent to Congress on January 16, 1833, explaining the need for further legislation to enable the government to deal with the South Carolina nullification ordinance, which was due to go into effect after February 1. According to Robert McLane, writing long after the event, this paper "was originally prepared by the Secretary of the Treasury as a Treasury report and adopted by the President as a Message."[83] It is unlikely, however, that the whole of the message was prepared as a Treasury report.

The message is a clear, reasonable statement of the situation, detailing the President's attempt via the proclamation of December 10 at once to assure South Carolinians that the tariff would be further revised and to warn them against the course they were taking. His proclamation had been met in South Carolina only by a counter proclamation of Governor Hayne and legislation to enforce the nullification ordinance. It was clear that South Carolina intended to seize all imports from federal customs under a writ of replevin, and Jackson asked for legislation permitting transfer to federal courts of any actions taken against customs officials or other agents of the United States. He also wanted provision made for the safekeeping of prisoners seized by United States marshals, the power to move customs houses to points of safety, and the definite authority to use military force if necessary.

In his message Jackson insisted he wished to remove all just cause of complaints, and he avoided a denial of all right of revolution. If there were long and intolerable oppression, if all constitutional remedies had been tried in vain, he wrote—or McLane did for him—the case might be different. But there was no sufficient cause in South Carolina. Had not the last chief magistrate, James Hamilton, Jr., just congratulated the legislature on their "great and abundant blessings," on a state of health "almost beyond former precedent," and added that he found, "not less reason for thankfulness in surveying our social condition"? Hardly an oppressed people! [84]

It took the clerk an hour and a quarter to read the long message in the Senate, and when he was through, an agonized, sweating Senator from South Carolina rose to reply. It was John C. Calhoun, who would have been presiding, except that he had resigned his vice-presidency to represent his state in the Senate in the place of Robert Hayne, now governor. He was out of order but so visibly upset, pounding on his desk as he spoke, that Senator Hugh White, presiding as president pro tem, indulged him. The message was full of inaccuracies, he argued; South Carolina had no constitutional recourse, in its military measures it was wholly on the defensive, consolidation was ruining the country, converting it into a military despotism. "We are threatened to have our throats cut, and those of our wives and children," he began to say. "No—I go too far. I did not intend to use language so strong." [85] He was distraught.

"What think you of the *Message?*" McLane asked Van Buren. "Your silence speaks your thoughts of the *Proclamation*. You too, I suppose, have cursed my old federalism an hundred times, and laid all the sins at that door!" [86]

McLane was becoming anxious. He had been sick again; rumor had it that three southern members, angry at his course, had cut him dead on a Washington sidewalk.[87] This was before the message was read, so no wonder he begged Verplanck "*not in any manner* [to] *hint* at my participation in the Message." To this warning, written January 16, the day the message was read, he added a strange sentence that may mean much or little: "Things have assumed a new form and the past should, by my friends at least, be consigned to *oblivion*." [88]

Perhaps the clue to what he meant is in a remark he made to Van Buren: "this is not the time for doctrine of any kind; and there is not eno' of party discipline to sustain either a genuine or spurious policy for any length of time." [89] Opposition papers and members could rally to the message with greater ease than many of the Democrats. The *Intelligencer* praised it.[90] So did Henry Clay, who found it "able and elaborate, freer from passion than the proclamation." [91]

The Senate Judiciary Committee produced the legislation Jackson requested on January 21, and the Senate then debated the issue for almost a month. In the meantime South Carolina was supposed to have acted, but cool heads prevailed there and in view of the fact that the Verplanck tariff was still under consideration in the House, the time for the nullification ordinance to take effect was postponed, in an irregular proceeding, from February 1 until March 4, when the session of Congress would necessarily have come to an end.[92]

When the Senate finally passed the Force Act, late in the evening of February 20, most Southerners showed their sympathy for South Carolina and their dislike of the legislation by refusing to vote. The only southern votes for the act were cast by the Tennessee and Louisiana Senators and by John Forsyth, of Georgia, who was encouraged to be faithful by Jackson's support of his state on Indian removal. Neither Benton nor Clay was recorded.[93]

VI THE VERPLANCK TARIFF BILL

Meanwhile the Verplanck tariff was having hard going in the House of Representatives. Debate on it had begun the 5th of January and the high tariff men were frantic, regarding this bill as a complete betrayal of northern interests. South Carolinians, on the other hand, found the bill too protective to suit them. The word got round, furthermore, that Mc-Lane had demanded the Force Act as compensation for revising the tariff,[94] and while this, in view of Jackson's nationalistic order, is not a likely explanation, it made some opponents of the Force Act disinclined to accept the tariff.

For a time it seemed the tariff would pass in the House but have trouble in the Senate. McLane thought so, and Verplanck did too.[95] But as time went on, McLane lost his hopefulness, though he blamed the situation partly on some changes the Ways and Means Committee had made in the tariff bill he had sent them.[96] One faction, for which Webster was a spokesman, wanted no concessions made to South Carolina until that state retreated from the position it had taken.[97] "The Nullifyers have over reached themselves," McLane concluded sadly, and Jackson, in agreement, felt that hope for the Verplanck tariff was lost after an intemperate speech, theoretically on the tariff but actually directed at the

Force bill, by Richard Wilde, a Georgia Representative sympathetic to the "Nullies." [98]

"Government is like iron, toughest when it is softest," Wilde had said; "if you harden it to make it stronger, it becomes brittle." And he quoted a couplet in French,

> O, le bel âge, quand l'homme dit à l'homme,
> Soyons frères! ou je t'assomme!

which angered administration men when he freely translated it,

> O blessed age! when loving Senates vote,
> Let us be brothers! or I'll cut your throat! [99]

Early in the winter rumors began seeping through Congress concerning Clay's attitude toward the Verplanck tariff. He was quiet, and some said he would support the bill to win friends in the South, and others that he would defeat it to embarrass the administration while maintaining his protectionist principles.[100] On January 23 McLane thought he saw "obvious signs of an understanding between Clay and Calhoun" and expected that if the Verplanck tariff ever reached the Senate Clay would "move to strike out and insert his own scheme." [101]

Representative Cambreleng saw obvious signs of intrigue too, but his signs pointed to McLane as an intriguer who was as eager as Clay and Calhoun that New York—and Van Buren—should not have an opportunity to solve the critical issues of the winter and gain credit thereby. "Our republican friend," he wrote Van Buren, sarcastically, "begins now to see the errors of precipitation." Cambreleng and Van Buren would have preferred to see the Force bill held back till the end of the session, hoping a tariff revision would placate South Carolina and end the crisis. Cambreleng blamed McLane for "superseding the tariff with a greater and more exciting question," which had the effect of "throwing the administration on its adversaries," like Webster and Adams, for support, and arraying many of its friends in opposition. "The Treasury has the whole credit," he said, "whether true or not." [102] If McLane was responsible—and those who knew thought he was dominating the President's council on these matters—he was disrupting the New York-Virginia axis that was the backbone of the Jackson party, the alliance between the plain Republicans of the North and the agrarians of the South to which Van Buren looked for the country's future safety—and his own advancement.

It must have been a worrisome winter for Martin Van Buren, who was being very discreet in staying away from Washington until nearly time for his inauguration as Vice-President. His intent, of course, was to keep free of blame for whatever steps were taken at this critical time. But he must have been kept constantly on the anxious seat by the news he received and the aspersions, direct and indirect, that were cast on his peculiarly independent lieutenant, Louis McLane.

Mahlon Dickerson, for example, whose views on the tariff were quite different from Cambreleng's, agreed that McLane was wrecking the party. "If I am not greatly mistaken," he warned, "you will have cause to repent of the agency you have had in placing him where he is." [103]

Perhaps it was a sign of Van Buren's magic that he had found such a splendid scapegoat to take responsibility for administration measures. For this purpose McLane was more visible than Amos Kendall. It was a basic Democratic rule of conduct at this time that within his party Jackson was not to be blamed. All intraparty difficulties had to be blamed on someone else, and for this purpose an ex-Federalist from an insignificant state was a natural scapegoat.

VII   MR. CLAY STEALS THE SCENE

Henry Clay did not wait for the Verplanck bill to come to the Senate. He introduced his own tariff bill there on February 9, employing the old argument that only bills to raise taxes needed to originate in the House. His proposal was to lower taxes on imports, but to do it by slow steps and, in the end, not so far as by the McLane-Verplanck plan, though this latter point was hardly noticed. Thus his plan appealed to manufacturers as much as any lowering of protective duties could, because it made no immediate change and only slight changes for a number of years. True, in 1842 there would come a very sharp decrease in the duties to a maximum of 20 percent ad valorem. But the comparison of a sharp decrease in 1842 under the Clay plan and a sharp decrease in 1834 and 1835 under the McLane-Verplanck plan offered an easy choice. Besides, if plans to decrease the tariff could be postponed now, further postponements might be possible a decade hence.

The plan of Clay's tariff proposal is said to have come from Eliakim Littell, a native of Burlington, New Jersey, who spent his life editing reprint periodicals but was seriously interested in public finance.[104] As Clay's bill took its final shape, it provided for the reduction of all tariffs over 20 percent in a series of steps, the first on December 31, 1833, the second on the same date in 1835, the third in 1837, the fourth in 1839, and fifth and sixth steps in 1841 and 1842, each as large as the total of the first three steps. By 1842 no duties would be higher than 20 percent.

Besides these, its most important provisions, the Clay tariff act had other interesting features. It raised the tariff on cheap woolen goods called kerseys to the same 50 percent rate, hereafter to be reduced, charged on other woolen goods. It placed many linen and silk goods on the free list at the end of the year and provided that in 1842 many other items were to be admitted free of duty, including indigo, quicksilver, sulphur, saltpeter, india rubber, and gum arabic. The intent obviously was to give manufacturers relief in acquiring these raw materials at cheaper cost as compensation for the reduced protection afforded their products after 1842. Another provision of this act, to come into effect in 1842, required payment of all duties in cash (credits had been allowed) and the assessment of imports—in order to ascertain the duties—at the port of entry.[105]

Assessment in the United States was expected to be higher than in the country in which imported goods originated, and this was, consequently, a provision held desirable by the manufacturers of goods competing with imports. Its inclusion in the Clay tariff was a strategic victory for Louis McLane's Delaware rival, Senator John M. Clayton.

When their sense of the importance of Clay's bill led the Senate to form a select committee to consider it, President Jackson asked Senator Hugh White, who as president pro tempore would make the appointments, not to include Clayton because he was such an enemy of McLane that he would certainly prefer Clay's bill to the McLane-Verplanck proposal. But White had already given the secretary of the Senate the names of his choices, including Clayton, and he refused the President's request that he drop the Delawarean.[106]

Although he was unable to prevent what was called the home valuation provision from being sliced from Clay's bill in committee, Clayton lined up the strength of the tariff element on the floor of the Senate, bringing some manufacturers to Washington to support them, and forced the reincorporation of this provision in the bill. By threatening the defeat of the bill otherwise, Clayton even persuaded Calhoun to vote with him, correctly gauging Calhoun's eagerness to end the crisis with a compromise that did not come from the administration. Thus Clay and Clayton cemented an alliance between the old opposition party and the nullifiers that was strong enough to seize leadership in tariff revision, and the credit for it, from McLane and the administration.[107]

Their work was completed on Monday, February 25. Late that afternoon, when members were collecting their papers and donning their coats to leave for dinner, Clay's close friend Robert Letcher moved in the House of Representatives to strike out all of the Verplanck bill after the enacting clause and substitute the Clay bill being debated in the Senate. Action came with surprising speed; before adjournment the amended bill had been passed to a third reading, and on the next day it passed the House by a vote of 119 to 85.[108] The McLane-Verplanck plan had been, in Benton's words, "arrested, knocked over, run under, and merged and lost." [109]

Passage of the Clay bill in the House opened the way for its success in the Senate, where it was now returned as a House bill to obviate any objection to having a tax measure originate in the Senate. The Senate accepted the Clay tariff on March 1, and somewhat earlier on the same day the House passed the Force Act by a decisive vote. To the President it was a matter of importance that enforcement was agreed upon before compromise. As to the latter, the Clay bill was not, he declared, "of the exact character" he preferred but he approved it because he hoped it would have a good effect [110] and because with the session of Congress necessarily at an end there was no hope of any other action on the tariff for almost a year.

Clay had seized an opportunity and by his proposal gained credit for pacifying the country. Had he not acted, it is at least possible, perhaps probable, that the Verplanck tariff would have failed, and as a result military measures would have been necessary in South Carolina. It seems likely that in such a situation McLane would have counseled Jackson to follow a policy of strength. John Tyler told friends that McLane was to blame for the Force Act.[111] Calhoun, too, credited McLane with administration leadership in the passage of this, to him, obnoxious bill. "It was passed," he wrote, "by the joint influence of Webster and McLane, aided by the influence of Jackson." [112]

But as old John Quincy Adams saw the situation, at the critical moment when nullification was "at its last gasp," Clay intervened to give it "the show of Victory." "Mr. Clay's Tariff or Anti-Tariff Bill," the ex-President insisted, "is an Act for the protection of John C. Calhoun and his fellow nullifiers." With it Clay seized upon the policy of Jackson's message and snatched "from Jackson all the merit with the South of his monstrous concessions." [113]

However the credit was shared, there was little of it left for Louis McLane. But gifted with reason and foresight, despite his handicaps of passion and ambition, the Secretary perceived that the nullification crisis was but a foreshadowing of graver troubles to come in the South, a region he much admired. "There are men in that quarter," he wrote in June, 1833, when all seemed tranquil, "who will not be satisfied short of . . . a Southern confederacy." [114]

VIII   ANOTHER INVESTIGATION

At the opening of Congress on December 4, 1832, the President had called attention to the government deposits in the Bank of the United States, telling Congress he thought the safety of these deposits ought to be investigated.[115] The Secretary of the Treasury, in his annual report, mildly echoed the President's recommendation, submitting the matter of an investigation "to the wisdom of Congress." [116] The occasion for an investigation was the Bank's overseas transactions regarding the 3 percent bonds, but behind this excuse lay the implacable hostility of the President toward the Bank. "The hydra of corruption is only *scotched*," Jackson wrote Polk; "an investigation kills it and its supporters *dead*." [117]

The President's angry insistence indicated his dissatisfaction with the report of McLane's agent, Henry Toland, who had found the Bank entirely sound as a government depository. In placing his reliance on Polk, his fellow Tennesseean, Jackson knew his man, for Polk was as set on destroying the Bank as the President himself. But Polk, with all the help the administration could give him, was unable to get a special committee to investigate the Bank. Sharing leadership in debate with Cambreleng and Jesse Speight, he did manage to get an investigation undertaken, but by the Ways and Means Committee, which was very busy with other matters and was headed by Verplanck, who did not share Jackson's and Polk's feelings about the Bank.[118]

The excuse for the investigation, the Bank's negotiation with the Barings regarding the 3 percent bonds, was a subject mildly embarrassing to McLane. The Bank's defense rested partly on his letter of July 19, in which, unhappily, he had suggested that the government might be unable to pay off these certificates on the dates he assigned for their payment—and that therefore the Bank might need to delay their presentation as a kind service to the Treasury. The government had been able to redeem the certificates, though the Bank's agents were quick to point out that this was so only through the use of funds otherwise appropriated, and especially through the lucky chance that a first installment of the Danish indemnity (for damages to United States shipping in the Danish sounds during the Napoleonic Wars) had fortuitously been received at the critical moment.[119]

On New Year's Day, 1833, McLane was greatly embarrassed by a story in the *Globe,* probably written by Reuben Whitney, a man Biddle described as a confidence man and common gambler who once operated a faro game near Andalusia, Biddle's home.[120] Entitled "An Exposition of the Conduct of the Bank of the United States in Relation to the Payment of the Public Debt," it was an account of Bank-Treasury relations over most of the period McLane had been in office and was written at such length that it filled almost eleven columns. In a four-page newspaper with six columns to a page, this article filled almost half of the total space on the day it appeared. Purporting to explain the doubts of the safety of the Bank as a government depository voiced by the President and the Secretary of the Treasury, the article apparently was a refutation of the conclusions of Henry Toland's recent investigation.

An attack on the Bank was nothing new in the *Globe*, which a pro-Bank Congressman had called a "national foundry of slander and calumny." [121] The unusual feature of this article, apart from its length, was that it concentrated upon the defense of the Secretary of the Treasury and implied special knowledge of his point of view. For instance: "If Mr. McLane has changed his opinion of the present Bank or its management, it does not follow that his views are at all altered in relation to the expediency and constitutionality of a well constructed and well managed Bank of the United States." And again: "Mr. McLane is willing for his countrymen to decide . . . whether the Bank has not given him ample reasons, since his Report of last year, to recal[l] the encomiums he then expressed."

The natural inference was that McLane or someone either in his office or acting with his cooperation had written the article. The rival *Intelligencer* declared itself unwilling to believe that McLane would degrade himself by libeling Biddle as the author of this article did. Plainly, the *Intelligencer*'s editor continued, this was a disguise, preparing the way for the removal of the government deposits.[122]

As the *Intelligencer* leaped to the attack, Blair was retreating. On the same day he denied that the Secretary or anyone in his office had written the "Exposition," but insisted its facts were authentic and the implications just.[123] Not unnaturally, some readers concluded that McLane had demanded this denial, and Blair became sensitive on this point. He was, he said, accused of having lost the confidence of the President, of having offended McLane, of being in disgrace with the whole cabinet and about to be superseded by Mordecai Noah—all of which he contradicted. The President was paternally kind. Not a solitary member of the cabinet held an unkindly sentiment towards the *Globe*, not even McLane. Blair had issued his denial of McLane's authorship of the "Exposition" not in response to any demand but on his own as soon as the possible imputation was noted.

Blair would not deny, however, that McLane had made some response to the rumor connecting him with the "Exposition." [124] A few letters exchanged between the two men survive to indicate McLane's displeasure with Blair's conduct.[125] In one somewhat mysterious letter from McLane dated Tuesday, January 15, Blair was asked not to use a certain article until Thursday so that McLane might first see it.[126] Despite McLane's request, Blair proceeded on Wednesday to publish the article, which denied that McLane had any connection with Matthew L. Davis, who reported from Washington under a pseudonym, "The Spy," for the New York *Courier and Enquirer*.[127]

Perhaps McLane had seen Blair's story in the meantime and had approved it before it was published. At any rate, embarrassing inquiries were appearing in the opposition press. In whose hands are the keys of the Treasury?" asked the *Intelligencer*. In the hands not of the proper cabinet but of the improper cabinet, it suspected.[128] Yet despite the influence of the anti-Bank element among Jackson's unofficial advisers, McLane was still holding his own.

Another topic in the President's annual message to Congress that was related to his request for an investigation of the safety of the deposits was Jackson's recommendation that the government sell all the stock it held in private corporations. This, of course, included the government's one-fifth part of the stock of the Bank of the United States, which was more valuable than the total of all other such stocks—in the Louisville and Portland Canal Company, for instance—held by the government. When Samuel Jaudon, the Bank's cashier, was sent to Washington as a lobbyist in January—chosen because he was the son-in-law of the wife of Senator White, who was the Tennessee colleague of the aggravating Representative Polk—he soon reported to Biddle that Jackson was pressing this issue.[129]

However, the sale of stock, so far as it related to Bank stock, had been referred to the Ways and Means Committee, and the tariff kept this committee so busy that it did not get around to any Bank problems until January 23. Perhaps it never did give much attention to disposal of the stock.[130] McLane, however, prepared a bill for this purpose and sent it to Polk (not to the committee chairman) on February 8.[131] Five days later, Polk reported the bill in the House as a committee measure with only one minor change from McLane's draft.

The bill did not get far. Charles Wickliffe moved to reject it on first reading, arguing that the sale would help no one but the stockjobbers on Wall Street. It was merely a preliminary, he argued, to withdrawal of the deposits, which would be so pleasing to the state banks that they could then "be enlisted as soldiers in the next campaign."

Polk defended the bill, declaring the government should not be the partner of a "moneyed monopoly," but Ralph Ingersoll, of Connecticut, struck a blow at the measure by noticing how it differed from McLane's recommendation of a year earlier when he hoped to sell the stock at a million dollar bonus to the Bank itself, not, as now, to drop it into the market at not less than par and with bearish effects on the Bank's securities.

When a vote was taken, the pro-Bank forces carried the day and the sale was stymied. The margin of the administration's defeat was not great, 102 to 91, but the manner was unusual, for bills from standing committees were rarely rejected on a first reading without as much as twenty-four hours for reflection.[132]

Nicholas Biddle rejoiced at "a signal triumph for the Bank," but it was but one skirmish won in a long war.[133] An investigation by the Ways and Means Committee into the 3 percent transaction and into the safety of the Bank as a government depository had begun on January 31 and lasted for three weeks. At Reuben Whitney's suggestion, Polk tried to get McLane to appoint Amos Kendall a Treasury agent to go to the Bank office in Philadelphia and make a personal investigation, but McLane rejected the idea. Whitney, who was Polk's confidential adviser during the inquiry, did go to Philadelphia, but the committee stayed in Washington, where it interviewed a number of the Bank officials, including all five of the government directors and Thomas Cadwalader, the erstwhile agent to the Barings.[134]

During the investigation, McLane was on close, friendly terms with Polk, who was the most inquisitive of the Bank's inquisitors.[135] At the same time McLane gradually fell out with Verplanck, who was generally friendly to the Bank, declaring he personally despised the continued haranguing about the 3 percent bonds and thought McLane's conduct in this regard contemptible.[136] In coming into a closer association with Polk than with Verplanck, McLane was following the Jackson party line, for Verplanck, a lame-duck Congressman, not only displayed independence on the Bank question but dared to vote against Blair as printer for the House of Representatives and by that action won the condemnatory attention of the *Globe.* Oddly, Verplanck's announced reason for opposing Blair as printer to the House was Blair's printing the "Exposition" of the Bank's 3 percent transactions worded so as to appear to be by McLane.[137]

More poignantly than Verplanck, Biddle felt there was a "cruel injustice" in the course of McLane, who at once cast innuendoes upon the policies and soundness of the Bank while relying upon it as an ever-present aid with his fiscal problems.[138] He was, Biddle was advised, not hostile in his heart but a prisoner "*in* Irons" of the kitchen cabinet.[139] However friendly in his heart McLane might be, Biddle toyed with the idea of exposing a loss McLane had suffered in a recent transaction.[140]

This transaction—like the Secretary—was not so simple as Biddle pretended. The note McLane wanted to sell was an order on the French government for the first installment of the indemnity payments arranged for in the treaty recently negotiated by Rives. McLane received two bids, the first from the Bank of the United States and the second from Prime,

Ward, and King, a New York banking house that was a correspondent of Baring Brothers, in London. The Bank's bid was the better of the two, but McLane held off accepting it, hesitant to do further business with the Bank and hoping that Prime, Ward, and King would match the Bank's offer, or that he would get a third bid, equally good.[141] When neither of his expectations was realized, McLane sold the bill to the Bank and was disappointed to find that the Bank's price had fallen by $8,000 with a fall in the exchange rate.[142]

Though he risked making an enemy of McLane by trying to make capital of this incident, Biddle nevertheless sent an account of it to friends in Congress.[143] Somehow the story got to George McDuffie, undoubtedly to Biddle's satisfaction, and McDuffie made use of it to belittle the Treasury on March 2 on the floor of the House.

The occasion was a debate on a resolution presented by Verplanck from the Ways and Means Committee, following its investigation of the Bank. Declaring the safety of the deposits in the Bank, the resolution passed the House easily, as had been expected, though Polk made a valiant effort to dismiss the committee and postpone the matter until fall, arguing that there had been too little time to collect information.[144] For a minority of three members of the seven-man committee, Polk presented a long report that he had labored like a beaver to write in the last week of the session.

The testimony showed that in the investigation Representative Ingersoll tried to throw blame for the Bank's 3 percent transaction upon McLane, whereas Asbury Dickins, in testifying, and Polk, in the minority report, defended him.[145] In the debate, Ingersoll attacked McLane again before George McDuffie exposed the Treasury's loss of money on the French bill due to McLane's delay.[146] Hearing that the South Carolinian had "handled McLane with gloves off," Biddle resorted to doggerel to express his delight:

> Some would hang poor McDuffie for being a nully
> And others abhor him for acting the bully:
> But bully or nully he may be, for me,
> When the Bank is in danger—no bully like he.[147]

IX   THE TREASURY FIRE, MARCH 31, 1833

Once Congress had adjourned Biddle became more considerate of McLane than he had been at the end of the session. Perhaps Biddle recalled a rumor he had heard in mid-February, that Jackson's advisers were suggesting two projects: (1) that McLane remove the deposits after Congress adjourned, and (2) that the President issue a *scire facias* to proclaim that the Bank by its actions had forfeited its charter.[148] When his friend John Watmough wanted to print the Bank's correspondence with McLane on the French note as a footnote or appendix to Mc-Duffie's speech, Biddle urged him not to.[149] "Poor, contemptible Mc-Lane," responded Watmough, agreeing, "must either sink to the lowest possible level and become the most infamous of tools, or give up a situation which feeds and clothes him and his family."[150] If you have space to fill up, counseled Biddle, print Smollett's "Ode to Independence" for McLane's benefit.[151]

At the moment the Bank and McLane were working together on a plan to lend the French indemnity funds on interest until commissioners agreed what claims of American citizens for losses during the Napoleonic Wars should be paid from these funds. Though it was the Secretary who was to lend the funds at interest, it was the Bank which had displayed interest in the idea and secured its insertion as an amendment to the general appropriations bill at the very end of the congressional session. Despite the executive's eagerness to cut connections with the Bank, the law passed March 2, 1833, permitting the indemnity funds to be lent, provided that only government bonds or stock of the Bank of the United States would be acceptable as security—what one friend told Biddle was "a powerful expression of Congress in your favor."[152]

McLane wasted no time in advertising the money for loan, issuing a notice to that effect on March 6. Most of the money was applied for and except for two calamities loans probably would have been made promptly, despite a protest, apparently politically motivated, of some claimants of French indemnities against the use of stock in the Bank of the United States as security.[153]

The first of the two calamities was, in a political sense, the more serious—France failed to pay the installment that was due on the indemnity debt. All McLane's trouble in selling a note on the French government and in arranging to lend the proceeds seemed likely to be in vain, for he was counting his chickens before they hatched. It was all very well to say that France had agreed by treaty to pay 25 million francs to the United States as indemnity for losses due to French confiscation during the wars. There still had to be an appropriation voted by the French legislature, and in March of 1833 the United States government was astonished to hear from its chargé in Paris that the French executive had not yet even requested an appropriation from the two chambers of the legislature.[154]

The government heard from a chargé because there was no proper American minister in Paris, the apparently triumphant Rives having returned in the summer of 1832. Jackson had been eager to send Livingston off in Rives's place, but one thing after another had caused delay. First, there was the problem of finding a new Secretary of the Treasury to replace McLane when he switched offices. Then the threat to the Union imposed by South Carolina's nullification made it seem desirable to postpone all cabinet rearrangements until March. Now there was Livingston's lethargy in getting under way to overcome, plus a great fire at the Treasury building that disarrayed department records and further delayed cabinet reorganization.[155]

About 2:30 on the morning of Sunday, March 31, 1833, some people in the neighborhood noticed that windows on the second or main floor of the Treasury building were lighted up, and when they also saw smoke, they quickly turned in an alarm. Fire engines arrived in about twenty minutes, but the fire by then had spread to the garret, which was full of old papers and cases, and to the roof, which was quickly ablaze. Sufficient water could not be found, and soon the fire spread to the whole building except a fireproof section. Charred fragments of paper and wood were carried over the whole city, even over the Eastern Branch into Prince George's County, though the wind was so gentle that the fire itself was not spread. By nine in the morning the building was a fire-swept hulk.

A great crowd of Washingtonians turned out for the fire, and many of them, together with some of the Treasury clerks, got busy at once rescuing papers from the holocaust. McLane was among the early arrivals and rushed into the building to help save as many of the records as possible. He saw that the whole building would be lost and directed the clerks to concentrate on saving the records in the accounting offices and the register's office, and he had the papers placed under proper guard as they were brought out. Asbury Dickins and one of his sons climbed a ladder to a semicircular window through which they got to McLane's office and rescued his library and the papers in his desk.

Before noon of the same day McLane had rented some buildings on the south side of Pennsylvania Avenue, opposite Strothers' Hotel, for the accommodation of his department, and soon the clerks were busy sorting and arranging the rescued papers. A company of marines and a company of soldiers were put on duty around the wrecked building to prevent pilfering. By two in the afternoon an investigation of the blaze was under way at the President's order and at McLane's request, under the direction of Chief Justice William Cranch of the circuit court of the District of Columbia.

A report signed by Livingston, McLane, Cass, Taney, and Barry—all the cabinet ministers who were in town—revealed the results of the investigation but left the cause of the fire undetermined. The building superintendent, who was, according to Mrs. Adams, an "antient, . . . spirited and favourite member of the Hickory Club," was at home, sick, the night of the fire, and the young man he left in his place, employed regularly as a laborer in the building, fell asleep and was lucky to escape being seriously burned. He had checked the rooms and grates, where anthracite coal was the fuel, at ten, as he was supposed to do, and then was permitted to go to sleep. The fire had begun in a room used by clerks that was part of McLane's own suite. Despite the loss of the entire building the destruction of papers was comparatively small. The official report did not comment on a rumor that the firemen gave less than their best service because they were angry that the government had not relieved them from militia duty.[156]

Various rumors of the cause of the fire swept through Washington—naturally including one that agents of the Bank of the United States were to blame. As time passed, most of these rumors were forgotten, but in 1836 the city was stirred by news that a former clerk, one Richard H. White, was arrested for starting the fire to destroy fraudulent pension papers. He was brought to trial, but no conviction could be secured because of the statute of limitations.[157]

After the fire, the *Globe* reprinted from the Richmond *Enquirer* an exceedingly laudatory article about McLane's action during and just after the conflagration. The fact that Frank Blair called this article "a just tribute" indicates that the Secretary of the Treasury was still in good standing amid the waves of intrigue that swirled around the President's office.[158]

A ballad of the time included McLane (as "Lou") among the chief advisers of Jackson, according to Benjamin Perley Poore:

> King Andrew had five trusty squires
>   Whom he held his bid to do;
> He also had three pilot fish
>   To give the sharks their cue.
> There was Mat and Lou and Jack and Lev
>   And Roger, of Taney hue,
> And Blair, the book,
> And Kendall, chief cook,
>   And Isaac, surnamed the true.

Poore's memory was obviously faulty, since not all of the "five trusty squires" he mentions (and identifies as Van Buren, McLane, Branch, Woodbury, and Taney) were in Jackson's cabinet family together, but substitute William Barry for Branch and the list is improved. The third pilot fish, of course, was Hill, of New Hampshire.[159]

X   RELIEF AT LAST

In the spring of 1833 the pilot fish were relentlessly leading McLane into channels he did not wish to follow. Soon after the inaugural ceremonies were over he asked his nominal subordinate, Amos Kendall, the fourth auditor, to explain why a change of depositories was urged so incessantly. For an hour they talked, and at the end, according to Kendall's account, McLane said he was still opposed to removal but he would carry it out if the President made up his mind on the measure. If this is indeed what McLane said, he was being disingenuous, for there seems little doubt that the President had already made up his mind. "If the President insisted," seems a more likely condition for McLane's action.

After the interview Kendall wrote out his opinion at length and sent it to McLane, with a copy to Jackson.[160] Kendall hardly needed to work on Jackson to stir the President up, but he did need to convince him that removal of deposits was the proper course. Early in March when Henry Gilpin saw the President he was incoherent in violent denunciation of the Bank management for keeping the government directors uninformed, and he talked of exposing these conditions in court through a *scire facias* proceeding, which McLane was urging.[161] But by the end of March, when Duane visited Washington, the President indicated he himself was agitating for removal.[162] Perhaps the President's preference for removal was a tribute to the persuasiveness of Amos Kendall.

At any rate, on March 12 Jackson asked Taney for facts that would justify forfeiture proceedings, confessing that removal had to be left up to McLane.[163] Within a week he had received Kendall's memorandum favoring removal, whereupon he addressed a questionnaire to the members of his cabinet. Had anything occurred to lessen confidence in the Bank? Could the Bank be relied on as a Treasury agent? Should its charter be renewed under any circumstances? Should a new bank be established? Where should the public moneys be placed?

And what he asked he answered, including with his questionnaire his own "reflections" on some of his questions. The Bank should not be rechartered under any conditions. No new bank should be chartered outside the District of Columbia. An experiment should be made in carrying on affairs without a national bank and in employing state banks as government depositories.[164]

From Roger Taney the President soon had the sort of answer that he wanted, but from the Secretary of the Treasury, on whom removal depended, no answer was forthcoming for a long time.[165] Despite his promise to Kendall, McLane probably wanted to hold out as long as he could, or at least as long as he had any hope of converting Jackson to his point of view. Ahead of him, at any rate, was the security of the State Department, in which he expected soon to take refuge from the pressures being brought to bear on the Secretary of the Treasury.

He was also comforted in these days by the knowledge that he had the Vice-President on his side. As long as Van Buren opposed removal, it was unlikely that Jackson could be persuaded to demand it. When Van Buren visited Washington this spring, he sent for Kendall and protested against continued agitation for removal after the formal resolution voted in the House of Representatives. Kendall urged reasons financial and political why no further forebearance should be shown the Bank, and when Van Buren was still unconvinced, the fourth auditor declared he was sure that the opposition would win the next presidential election and recharter the Bank unless the Bank was stripped now of the power the government deposits gave it. Thereupon he left the Vice-President to contemplate his own ambitions. When they met the next time, some weeks later, Van Buren had come round to Kendall's point of view.[166]

McLane meanwhile was doing what he could to prevent removal. At his request James A. Hamilton called together a number of the leading bankers of New York and found them agreed that a transfer of government funds to the state banks would be disastrous. One prominent New York moneylender, Isaac Bronson, wrote Hamilton at length in response to queries sent him and argued that the community, not the Bank of the United States, would be the victim of such a transfer. When Hamilton consulted Albert Gallatin and explained that Jackson might be motivated by resentment of its actions in his attitude toward the Bank, the old banker became upset. "Resentment! Resentment!" he remonstrated; "the affairs of Government can only be successfully conducted by cool reasoning and the lessons of experience."[167]

An awareness of the part McLane was playing in delaying destruction of the national banking system gradually grew. The *Intelligencer* in mid-March declared it absolved the Secretary of the Treasury of blame for the renewed assault on the Bank: "We believe it to be the work of inferior persons."[168] Biddle's correspondents kept him informed of McLane's role in delaying removal, and though they declared McLane did not act from love of the Bank but out of honest fear of the results of removal, they felt the Bank should appreciate his position and do nothing to embarrass the Treasury.[169]

It was not till May 20 that McLane responded to Jackson's questionnaire of March 19, with the Treasury fire furnishing some excuse for the delay. The response that McLane finally made was in the form of a long letter of over fourteen thousand words. He agreed with Jackson that the Bank should not be rechartered, admitting he had changed his mind on this point. It was, however, almost the only point on which he did agree with the President. Concerning the constitutionality of the Bank, he still entertained no doubt, and he wished to see a new bank established rather than an experiment in the use of state banks. He attempted to explain the elemental point that bank notes, not coins, were now the chief form of currency and that control over bank notes was necessary to the maintenance of a safe, uniform medium of exchange.

Confessing he did not agree with every point in Jackson's veto of the recharter bill, McLane insisted that only the Secretary of the Treasury could remove deposits and that he was, in a sense, the agent of Congress in this respect since Congress by law gave him this authority and might take it away. Unless a new and more thorough investigation discovered a want of security in the Bank, the Secretary could hardly move contrary to the recent decisive vote in the House of Representatives on this subject. Withdrawal would lead to many calamities, such as a run on the banks, the suspension of specie payments, the loss of a circulating medium, a want of credit, the absence of facilities for transferring public moneys, and bank failures, all of which evils would cause suffering to the public at large.[170]

As always, McLane's arguments won some respect from Jackson. "There are some strong points in this view—all ably discussed," was the penciled note the President added to McLane's letter. Then he moved from the parlor to the kitchen and sent the letter to Frank Blair, who responded with a commentary attempting to refute some of McLane's arguments.[171]

As Biddle had heard, the position McLane was taking risked his standing in the party.[172] Consciousness of this risk probably had delayed his reply to Jackson's questionnaire and had also led him to reply at great length in an effort to make the best possible presentation of his views. He was so busy that it was only by driving himself—despite his dyspepsia—that he could accomplish all he did. A letter published in the New York *Evening Post* described the travail of a cabinet member with such close correspondence to McLane's problems that its author might have been inspired by the Secretary of the Treasury. A cabinet Secretary's job was "painfully laborious" and "deeply responsible," according to this letter, which continued, "The continual and often unnecessary calls for information made by Congress—the increase and diffusion of the land sales—the great extension of the pension system—the vast and important ramifications of the Post Office establishment—the important interests connected with the Indian relations—and, not least, a rigid scrutiny over the national currency and a jealous regard for the integrity of the fiscal agents, require the performance of immense labour by the sub-ordinate agents and clerks, and a severely arduous supervision by the principals." All of these problems were McLane's except the Post Office and Indian relations, and as the *Post*'s correspondent declared, little allowance was made for necessary increases in expense, for the miscarriage of a mail, or for any delay in the completion of a report.[173]

In the spring of 1833 when McLane was closing out his activities in the Treasury office he was absorbed by such major policy problems as relations with the Bank and such a calamity as the Treasury fire, but he had also a host of other items of business to attend to. The sale of public lands was a function of his department, and in this connection there were not only the customary fiscal and personnel problems of such an operation but a succession of such unusual chores as, for example, the selection of lands to be assigned to the University of Michigan.[174] In this same spring McLane was seeking bids for the construction of a bridge across the Potomac,[175] preparing a speech for the President to make at the laying of a cornerstone for a monument to Washington's mother in Fredericksburg, Virginia,[176] and supervising a study of the culture and refining of sugar cane by Professor Benjamin Silliman, who found McLane "honorable and very intelligent." [177] The pressure of other business and his imminent departure from the Treasury may have been factors in preventing McLane from ever carrying out a recommendation adopted by the Senate in May of 1832 that a plan for the reorganization of his department be prepared and laid before Congress with a view to simplifying accounts, redistributing duties fairly among the clerks, and reducing their number.[178] Perhaps the heavy burdens of business made the executive departments loath even to attempt to comply with any resolution suggesting a decrease in the number of clerks.

The Clay tariff left McLane with an especially difficult problem in that it made no special provision for specific duties but yet apparently intended that they should be reduced according to the formula set up for ad valorem duties. It was up to the Secretary of the Treasury to provide a method for the determination of ad valorem equivalents of specific duties; according to Hezekiah Niles, McLane was thus made "commander-in-chief" over the tariff. The construction of the tariff act adopted by McLane in April and approved by the President was protested vigorously in the next Congress because it eliminated minimum valuations on cotton goods.[179] Though Niles was usually a severe critic of McLane, the Secretary's promptness in issuing a report on American commerce and navigation in 1832 won even Niles's congratulations.[180]

From his office in Baltimore, Niles was reasonably close to events in Washington, and it is a measure of the secrecy in which Duane's appointment was kept that not till May did Niles announce it, and then only as a fresh rumor, along with news of the shift of Livingston and McLane to new offices.[181] The Livingston and McLane moves were really old rumors, widely spread in the winter, but even in mid-April Biddle's confidential informant did not know who the new Secretary of the Treasury would be and could only report he was a Pennsylvanian, backed by McLane, who had been chosen over William Rives. Incorrectly, the informant thought this appointment and McLane's forthcoming promotion were evidence of the triumph of McLane's struggle against removal of the deposits.[182]

The determining factor in finally bringing about the cabinet shift so long planned was Jackson's eagerness to get Livingston off to Paris.[183] McLane was commissioned as Secretary of State on May 29, with the official announcement of his appointment and of the appointment of Livingston and Duane appearing in the *Globe* on the next day. The reaction to the cabinet changes was generally favorable. As the *Intelligencer* noted, McLane had an advantage over both of his State Department predecessors in the Jackson administration—Van Buren and Livingston —in that he had previously been in the diplomatic service abroad. And in one way the State Department was a better place for an old Federalist than the Treasury Department because it had less connection with party politics.[184] Livingston's appointment to France also seemed very suitable, but Duane was generally unknown and taken on faith as his father's son.[185] The journalists would have been troubled, however, could they have seen a confidential opinion of Duane that James A. Hamilton sent to Van Buren in 1829: "a respectable man, not much of a lawyer."[186]

It was an ominous sign, however, that the *Globe* pointedly refrained from making any comment whatever on the new appointments for a period of two weeks. Then Blair's reserve broke down, and he published a laudatory article on McLane. But it was one that he copied from the New York *Journal of Commerce*.[187] The kitchen cabinet itself was not in a mood to sing hosannas to McLane's elevation.

13

Secretary of State

I ON TOUR WITH JACKSON

Soon after entering upon his new duties as Secretary of State on May 29, 1833, Louis McLane temporarily forsook them to accompany his Old Chief on the first stages of a trip to the Northeast. A month earlier, as Secretary of the Treasury, McLane had been forced by the pressure of business to give up plans to make another trip with the President, a short jaunt into Virginia for the laying of the cornerstone of the Fredericksburg memorial to Mrs. Augustine Washington, for which occasion he had written Jackson's speech.[1] Missing the trip, McLane had missed the excitement incident to it when a cashiered naval officer named Randolph attempted to pull the President's nose.

The trip north, into what might have been regarded as the country of Jackson's political enemies, was, unlike the Virginia trip, one long triumph. When the presidential party left Washington on June 6, McLane, Secretary of War Cass, Alexander Jackson Donelson, the President's nephew and secretary, and Ralph Earl, a painter who lived in the White House as the President's companion and aide, accompanied Jackson. The President intended to follow approximately the route President Monroe had taken in 1818 when he journeyed north to Maine and then west to Ohio. At the time he set out, Jackson was not feeling well, and in Philadelphia he consulted the famous Dr. Philip Syng Physick. But when McLane left the party, at New York, Jackson's health and spirits had gradually improved, perhaps under the influence of what McLane described as "the enthusiasm and cordial outpouring of the kindest feelings of the heart with which he was every where greeted." [2]

On the first day of his trip, Jackson had a new experience. As he and his companions crossed Maryland, they were met by a welcoming committee led by General Smith at the point where the Washington Turnpike intersected the Baltimore and Ohio Railroad, which then went directly westward and not through Washington. Here cars were waiting, and when the presidential party had boarded them Jackson was taken on his first train ride.

Two days were spent in Baltimore, where the President met the Indian chief Black Hawk, and attended the Front Street Theatre. On June 8 he left Baltimore on a Chesapeake Bay steamer for Chesapeake City, where he and his party boarded a canal barge drawn by six horses. As they proceeded slowly along the fifteen-mile course of the Chesapeake and Delaware Canal, Jackson sat on the upper deck of the barge, conversing freely, and McLane and Cass moved about, mingling with the people and then joining the President as fancy dictated. Both men seemed remarkably affable, perhaps because they were, in a sense, on home ground. Not only McLane was traveling near the scenes of his youth; Cass, too, had spent part of his boyhood in Delaware.

As the barge passed the hamlet of St. Georges, a six-pound cannon was fired in salute. At Delaware City the canal ended and the party boarded a steamer again, this time the *Ohio*, which stopped briefly at New Castle, where a crowd had gathered and the President went ashore to meet the elderly governor of Delaware, Caleb Bennett. A banner was stretched across a street bearing the words, "The Union—it must be preserved," and the crew of a revenue cutter, the cutter formerly commanded by Collector Allen McLane, fired a salute.[3]

The stop at New Castle must have been very gratifying to Louis McLane, who may have remembered one spring day in 1829 when he was one of the crowd here on the wharf awaiting the arrival of Martin Van Buren, en route to Washington to be commissioned Secretary of State. Then McLane was complaining that President Jackson had found no place for him. Now he was returning to New Castle at Jackson's side and in Van Buren's place. The thought was enough to turn a man's head.

On the way from New Castle to Philadelphia a splendid dinner was served in the *Ohio*'s cabin. The President sat at one end of the table, McLane at the other, members of the Philadelphia welcoming committees on either side of them. In Philadelphia the President and his party landed at the Navy Yard to the cheers of twenty-five thousand people and proceeded to the City Hotel, where they spent three nights. On Monday morning, June 10, the visitors went to Independence Hall, where the President stood for over two hours greeting all who could press into the building and get to him. So thick was the mob outside that some who had met the President found their only exit was through a window.

At noon Jackson mounted a horse and, with McLane and Cass, also on horseback, to the right and left of him, rode off to review a military parade on Arch Street. He was in the saddle five hours and still had enough energy in the evening to attend a military ball.

The next morning Jackson, McLane, Cass, and Donelson drove through crowded streets in a barouche behind a pair of "spanking grays" to Arch Street wharf, where they boarded the steamboat *Philadelphia*. At the next stop, Burlington, where the presidential party visited Garrett Wall, some women presented Jackson with a bouquet of roses, which he handed to McLane, saying this treasure could be entrusted to no one less than the Secretary of State.

Near Trenton they left the river and rode in a barouche into the New Jersey capital, where they dined, and then went on to Princeton for the night. On the next day, June 12, they were met at Perth Amboy by a welcoming committee from New York and taken aboard a steamboat to be dined as they proceeded up the bay to the din of salutes from the forts and vessels they passed. The landing took place in mid-afternoon at Castle Garden, then separated from the Battery by water over which ran a foot bridge. Jackson and McLane had just crossed the bridge when the Battery end of it collapsed, plunging several score of people, including Cass, Donelson, and careful Levi Woodbury, who had just joined the party, into the water. Fortunately it was but three or four feet deep here and no one was seriously hurt, though Cass had bruises on his forehead and shoulder.

Here in New York Van Buren joined Jackson's party and, as Vice-President, replaced McLane as the second ranking person in the President's entourage, which moved slowly through the throng estimated at a hundred thousand people gathered at the Battery. After reviewing troops, the President mounted a horse and rode in procession up Broadway, bowing to right and left, especially to the ladies, in response to handkerchiefs they waved at him.[4]

Jackson stayed in New York three nights, but McLane did not. According to plan, he hurried back to Washington to take up his new duties.[5] But before leaving he put in Donelson's hands a brief note for Van Buren which he had written on June 4 but apparently had no opportunity to deliver personally when Van Buren met the presidential party on June 12. It is odd that he should have written the note on June 4, carried it with him for eight days, and then not handed it over personally. It is understandable that he may have feared to trust this note to the mail, and he may have given it to Donelson to deliver even before June 12, not being sure whether he would himself have any opportunity to talk with Van Buren privately.

The note is important. In it McLane spoke of his long May 20 letter to Jackson on removal of federal deposits from the Bank, begging the Vice-President to read it carefully before finally disposing of the removal question. "God knows I have no love for the present Bank," McLane declared, explaining that he had nevertheless felt impelled to note the probable effects of removal on the country. What McLane particularly desired was postponement of any action till Congress had met, though it is not altogether clear why this seemed so important to him. The President could then make his views known in his message, McLane did explain, and the Senate would have a chance to confirm the new Secretary of the Treasury before he was forced to order withdrawal of the deposits.[6]

McLane's fear of action on removal before the meeting of Congress may have been based on the likelihood that if removal were pressed on Duane he would have a short tenure in office, whatever he did. If he refused, he could himself be removed; if he ordered removal, the Senate might refuse to confirm his appointment. This was a possibility that had not escaped Biddle, who was informed by the cashier of the Washington Branch that the cabinet changes gave the Bank an element of security because any Secretary who dared remove the deposits would lose his chance of being confirmed by the Senate.[7]

Any further change in the Treasury was bound to worry McLane, for if Duane were ousted, the way would be opened for the appointment of an enemy, of Taney, for instance. So it is not strange that McLane wished to see the new Secretary safely settled in his office and confirmed by the Senate before removal was demanded. To effect this postponement of the removal controversy it was of the utmost importance to McLane that he have Van Buren's continued support.

He did not get it. Van Buren wanted to avoid getting into the center of the removal controversy. By 1833, Van Buren was an avowed enemy of the Bank, opposed to its recharter and favoring its replacement by a set of state banks. As he later explained to Frank Blair, "we had not then raised the Independent Treasury standard but were all under the delusion that banks of some kind were indispensable."[8] Probably he was encouraged to rely on private banks by the success of such banks in New York state, where they were united and protected by the so-called safety-fund system. There was a suspicion also that he was motivated as a New Yorker to oppose a national bank centered in Philadelphia and that he could therefore have been persuaded to look with approval upon a New York-centered national bank or even one in the District of Columbia in which the government would essentially give direction, removing any possibility of the subjugation of New York capital to Philadelphia.[9]

But in whatever action was taken concerning the Bank it was of great importance to Van Buren not to upset the party apple cart. Under Jackson a strong national party had been constructed. As Vice-President, Van Buren was now heir apparent to the chief magistracy of the nation, and it was of fundamental importance to him that the party be held together. For an astute party manager like Van Buren the Bank War was an issue to be handled with great care, a conflict in which he had little to gain and much to lose by taking a public, prominent part.

Van Buren was as much of a party manager as a lawyer by trade; in fact, he gave up his latter business for the former. As a "magician" in party politics, the shrewd course, the clever course, often seemed to him to be the wise course. So it had been in the nullification crisis of the previous winter when Van Buren thought Congress and the administration were too slow to offer compromise and too quick to threaten punishment.

And so it was now. He was opposed to recharter, but he was also opposed to removal of the deposits on the ground that the Bank was not safe. Characteristically, he favored a gradual smooth change rather than precipitate action. Twenty years later he declared he had never changed either opinion.[10] Probably he never had, but as a practical politician, he was willing to muffle his opinion for the sake of party unity.

II A SURPRISE

In the late winter and early spring of 1833 it was fairly clear to informed men of affairs that Van Buren's counsel on removal of the deposits was "Go slow," particularly after the House of Representatives declared itself convinced of the safety of the deposits where they were.[11] "The wily *magician* is for throwing the responsibility on Congress," wrote one of Biddle's correspondents, adding, "Were it left to Kendall and [Jackson] they would withdraw the deposits immediately."[12]

To the truth of this statement William J. Duane's experiences offer testimony. Van Buren was in Philadelphia late in April and evidently saw Duane but said not one word regarding withdrawal that Duane considered significant enough to notice in the account he later published under the title of *Narrative and Correspondence concerning the Removal of the Deposites, and Occurrences Connected Therewith.* On the other hand, Jackson, conferring with Duane late in March, intimated that he was himself agitating for removal. Still Duane did not know till after entering office that the cabinet was discussing removal and that he would be expected to take some action soon.[13]

What Van Buren and McLane did not tell Duane, Amos Kendall and Reuben Whitney were quick to bring to his attention. Duane took his

Louis McLane: Federalist and Jacksonian

oath of office on June 1, and that evening Reuben Whitney called on him. Whitney, a former Bank director and a bankrupt merchant, now holding a job in the Treasury, implied he was calling at the President's request to apprise Duane of Jackson's decision to direct the Secretary of the Treasury to transfer the deposits from the Bank of the United States to a group of state banks. Whitney also told Duane of the opinions members of the cabinet had expressed in response to Jackson's questionnaire and further informed him that Amos Kendall, the fourth auditor in Duane's department, was preparing an order to the Secretary of the Treasury from the President which would settle the matter. Whitney read from a memoir on the subject that he had prepared himself.

Duane was mortified by these proceedings and complained to McLane of being treated like a figurehead. But the very next evening, Whitney was back, accompanied this time by Amos Kendall, whom Duane had never met. Whitney explained that Kendall could provide any further information Duane might desire as to what proceedings were planned in relation to the Bank; he added that he brought Kendall around because the latter was leaving for Baltimore and would not be available again for several days.

Duane was once again startled at the way the subject of the deposits was being thrust on his attention by Whitney and Kendall, both Duane's subordinates. Before Duane could even begin work (these interviews occurred on Saturday and Sunday) he was told by these men what he was expected to do on a major policy matter. Whitney may not have felt Duane's hesitation, but Kendall observed that the subject of the Bank and the deposits was not a welcome one, so he changed the subject and ended the interview as soon as he could. But inasmuch as he knew Duane to be an anti-Bank man, he apparently assumed that Duane would fall in with the plans for removal.[14] The next morning Duane complained to Jackson, who denied commissioning Whitney to speak for him but readily admitted his point of view had been represented correctly. Duane demurred, but Jackson was polite. In three days he left Washington on his northeastern tour, first telling Duane he would send his views from New York along with the opinions submitted by the cabinet members he had questioned. This would give the information Duane would need in order to come to a conclusion about withdrawal.

Before Duane heard from Jackson he heard again from Whitney, who had the gall to suggest he be employed as Duane's agent in superintending the transfer of deposits. At certain seasons of the year when the department was pressed he might help out with some of Duane's other responsibilities, "particularly those connected with the tariff." Duane's reply was frigidly correct.[15]

It was Duane's great misfortune that he came into office at the moment he did, when Jackson had made up his mind to a policy Duane was to be called on to execute with little previous preparation. It was a mistake for the administration to put in this post a man who was out of the mainstream of political developments as much as Duane was; and for the error McLane must take a share of the blame. However, it is almost inconceivable that Duane did not use the time at his disposal between December 4, when he was offered the secretaryship (or January 30, when he accepted it), and May 30, when he came to Washington, to find what were the main problems before the Treasury. Dozens of people could have told him that removal was a major and pressing issue.

Unfortunately Duane was indeed an independent choice, preferred by Jackson and McLane because the former admired his father and the latter wanted anyone who would save him from the gall and wormwood of being succeeded by an enemy. They had, by chance, selected a political innocent, a man of high principles but of little experience who proved neither wise enough to influence affairs nor weak enough to be swept along supinely by them.

III   THE END OF AN ALLIANCE

The government deposits were very much on Jackson's mind as he started north on June 6, 1833, and he wrote Van Buren that he wanted to talk with him about their removal before any final action was taken.[16] Jackson's aim was, as he had put it, to kill the Bank dead. The deposits he saw as blood in the Bank's veins, nourishing that evil monster's tentacles and keeping it a constant threat to the republic. If the deposits were removed, it would be as though the carotid artery were cut—the Bank would die. Jackson thought, and Blair and Kendall and lesser men shared his belief and stimulated him to act on it, that as long as the Bank had a plentiful supply of money it might possibly bribe its way to recharter. That the public money should thus be turned against the public good was a scandalous situation.

After conversing with McLane in Baltimore and with Dickins and others in Washington, a Virginia politician, James Barbour, concluded that all intention of removing the deposits was abandoned—if, indeed, it had ever seriously been entertained.[17] How wrong he was! Amos Kendall knew better. "I shall take it for granted that the deposits will be removed," he wrote Van Buren, explaining that Jackson had left Washington fully determined on that point but eager to talk to Van Buren about the "manner and time . . . and perhaps upon the expediency of the whole measure." Recognizing Van Buren's influence, Kendall went on to present him with a plan to have all government income deposited in a selected group of state banks while government funds were gradually withdrawn from the United States Bank to meet expenditures. Thus a smooth transfer would be effected, but Kendall deemed it important to begin very soon, preferably on the 1st of August, so that the change would have been accomplished and the Bank have lost the deposits by the time Congress met in December. Presented with a *fait accompli,* with a mammoth drained of its strength, the fearful and the mercenary friends of the Bank would proclaim their independence.[18]

Kendall's letter suggests that he and Van Buren had come to some understanding. In his recollections, Major Lewis also offers testimony that by this time Van Buren was persuaded that removal was a settled matter, and to Lewis's surprise Van Buren sought to justify it.[19] But this was more than McLane knew, and as he traveled northward in June, 1833, he hoped he had waiting in New York an ally who would help dissuade Jackson from the measures leading to removal that others pressed upon him.

However determined he was, Jackson was still worried about his decision. Not, certainly, about the evil nature of the Bank but about the proper strategy to pursue. Against his will he had been impressed by the points made in McLane's letter of May 20, and he did not wish to dismiss lightly the counsel of so many of his advisers—of McLane, of Cass, of Major Lewis, of the not yet departed Livingston. This is why Kendall in his note to Van Buren declared in one sentence, "the President seems to have made up his mind," and in the next warned Van Buren he might be consulted not only on the manner and time but "perhaps upon the expediency of the whole measure." [20] After all, by the time Van Buren met Jackson the latter would have been traveling with McLane and Cass by his side for six days.

But these were not the men from whom Jackson could get the advice he wanted, so he kept his own counsel till he got to New York. There by his choice he had James Hamilton, the district attorney, sit next to him at dinner and before they separated gave Hamilton several papers and asked him for an opinion on them, in writing. When Hamilton read them, he found they were arguments in favor of removal, written by several different authors, and he returned them with a brief note explaining that the subject needed more time than he had, that he suspected the measure might lead to great disturbances in commerce and therefore that he would like to consult with some distinguished bankers.[21]

There was no time. Jackson was off to Connecticut and probably would not have cared for Hamilton's advice anyway unless it strengthened the resolution he had already formed. And at hand he had a wiser and more prudent counselor, Martin Van Buren. Among the papers he carried, Jackson had brought the draft of a letter, possibly prepared by Kendall, to William Duane, asking him to begin making plans for the transfer. At intervals as they traveled, Jackson and Van Buren went over this letter, and when they were in Boston, a two-day illness that confined Jackson to his hotel room gave opportunity for Major Donelson to make a final copy and send the letter off—"with such modifications," according to Van Buren's recollection, "as I persuaded him to make in it." Cass and Woodbury were consulted sufficiently to keep them informed but were not committed. Their approval would have been difficult to win anyway, because Cass was opposed and Woodbury, jealous of everyone, was a master at saying yes and no at the same time.[22]

In fact, two letters were sent to Duane from Boston. The first asked him to appoint Kendall as agent to arrange with certain state banks to serve as depositories and to begin depositing the revenue with them not later than September 15. The second letter was a long argument in favor of the removal policy, indirectly a refutation of McLane's memorandum against removal. It was also clearly a statement that the President himself took responsibility for the course he called on the Secretary of the Treasury to follow.[23]

Meanwhile the President had written Kendall asking him to discover Duane's attitude toward removal, but Kendall got nowhere with the inquiry. He made official business a pretext for calling on Duane and brought up the subject of removal three times, but each time Duane evaded the issue.[24] To Duane, Kendall and Whitney and some others who called upon him while the President was away were representatives of "an influence . . . unknown to the Constitution and to the country," about which he had previously heard some rumors. He meant the kitchen cabinet, of course, and saw them as men "whose intercourse with the President was clandestine"; he dismissed as "factious and selfish" their arguments that Congress was corruptible and might thwart the President unless the Bank were crippled. "It is in my nature to be repelled or attracted at once," Duane wrote to a friend, and he did not find Kendall attractive.[25]

Duane was more willing to talk to McLane, who had returned to Washington from New York on June 13.[26] It seemed more fitting to Duane to discuss matters of high policy with McLane, the Secretary of State, than with Kendall, a Treasury Department underling. McLane's views at this time are indicated by a letter he sent to Buchanan in which he said the Bank was the only disturbing question in domestic politics, the only issue threatening the unparalleled influence of the President on the people. And the Bank, "after all its iniquities," could be overthrown without a jar except that the President, out of his own hostility to it and the advice given by many of his friends, seemed likely to transfer the deposits prematurely and thereby "seriously derange the business and currency."[27]

To McLane's surprise, the President and Van Buren arrived back in Washington on July 4. They had cut the tour short in Concord, New Hampshire, because of Jackson's debility, and giving up their plans to continue eastward to Portland, Maine, and then west to Albany and beyond, had hurried back to Washington in rapid stages. Even more of a surprise to McLane was the discovery that Van Buren had been persuaded to go along with Jackson's desire for removal. McLane himself had gone far in opposing the President's eagerness to strike again at the Bank, an eagerness that he attributed to the President's ignorance of the possible financial repercussions as well as to his willingness to listen to some unsound advisers. McLane knew that Van Buren did not share his own former feeling for the national Bank, and he had come to Van Buren's view that this Bank must go. But he counted on Van Buren's support against the pressure for removal of deposits, and he was crushed to find that the Vice-President had surrendered. A suspicious man and a jealous man, he had long entertained doubts of Van Buren, but up to this point he had thought of himself as an ally of Van Buren—though notably as an ally, not just a follower. Now he felt betrayed, and he later told friends that it was from this time and this occasion that he dated his separation from Van Buren.[28] But for a year he masked his feelings.

IV   KENDALL'S ACTIVITY

"So intense is the anxiety of Mr. Van Buren to succeed," concluded William Duane, "that he favours those who have private access to the President's ears."[29] Duane exaggerated, but only slightly. Van Buren found Jackson so set on removal that the best the Vice-President could do was to make the transfer as undisturbing to business and politics as possible.

In mid-summer at Jackson's order Kendall was commissioned to discover what state banks were willing to accept the government deposits on the government's terms, and he soon set out to visit the major commercial cities on the east coast. In New York he was surprised to run into Van Buren and McLane at the breakfast table of his hotel and somewhat disconcerted when they urged him to postpone the transfer—that is, the date when the government would begin using state banks as depositories —until January 1. This delay, they said, would help unite the friends of the administration. If the deposits were moved earlier, Congressmen might be insulted that their resolution declaring the Bank to be safe had been set aside.

Kendall was suspicious of the suggestion. It seemed likely to him that McLane had run to New York to get Van Buren's help in one more effort to delay removal. However, it was hard to withstand the Vice-President and Secretary of State together, and Kendall consented to write the President in favor of such a delay as long as McLane and Van Buren agreed to use their influence in Congress to support the administration in moving the deposits and particularly if they could get Duane to support the measure, too.[30]

Kendall's suspicion was probably justified—very likely it was McLane who was behind this proposal—though it is known he had gone to New York, ostensibly at least, to confer with Livingston, who had not yet departed, rather than to interrupt Kendall's mission.[31] But any suspicion that McLane was merely trying to delay removal out of a desire to help the Bank is as wrong as Taney's opinion that McLane never ceased to seek recharter.[32] McLane's proposal was attractive on two grounds, one partisan and one personal. On partisan grounds his proposal was attractive because it might unite the cabinet, and, as Kendall admitted to Jackson, if the whole cabinet could be rallied to support the President on removal, it was highly unlikely that his action could be upset by his enemies in Congress.[33]

This was a factor of equal appeal to Van Buren and McLane and Kendall. But there was another argument for McLane's plan that appealed to him alone. If he could bring about unity in the administration, he could sustain his own position as a leader in it, retrieving himself from the dangerous position in which he was left politically by Van Buren's desertion and Duane's recalcitrance. The administration that would carry this issue to Congress would be an administration in which McLane would rank high and in which he might be able to influence subsequent policies to the benefit of the nation—and to the enhancement of his own prospects.

But Jackson was too strong-minded to be won by McLane's arguments. He was like a horse that could be led only in the direction he wanted to take. And in this case he was being urged along the course he wanted by Kendall and Taney and Blair. Kendall was permitted to write his own instructions as Treasury agent, despite Duane, and as he traveled he sent Jackson news to stir up the old soldier's fighting spirit. In Baltimore he heard that Henry Toland, McLane's investigator, was deeply in debt to the Bank; in Philadelphia he heard that Duane was McLane's choice for his Treasury post; in New York he heard the proposal of McLane and

Van Buren, and though he kept his promise to them to write Jackson in its favor, the best he could say was that it would be a fine plan if it worked. He would be delighted to delay removal till January 1, he told Jackson, if McLane and Duane would "exert their influence to sustain the measure," but if they used their influence to defeat removal, they might, united with the Bank's supporters, be able to get a two-thirds majority against the administration—and the significance of a two-thirds majority was that it could carry a recharter bill over a veto. Leaving this implication that McLane could not be trusted in Jackson's mind, Kendall went on to say that the only certain course was "to make up an issue at once." [34]

Far off in South Carolina President Thomas Cooper of the college at Columbia somehow divined the fourth auditor's strength: "Amos Kendall is a man of no common talent; bold; active, with no character at stake; and he will succeed against Duane." [35] Kendall had a great deal of character in the modern sense, of course; Cooper meant it in the sense of reputation, or prestige.

From the Rip Raps, at Fortress Monroe, Old Point Comfort, Virginia, where he had fled in the hope that rest and sea bathing would restore his health, Jackson sent Van Buren the opinions that cabinet members had submitted regarding removal and asked the Vice-President's advice, not *whether* it should take place, but *when*. As to *whether,* there should be no doubt at all, and in this regard Jackson thought it necessary to warn Van Buren that a rumor associated him with the enemies of removal: *"This must be removed or it will do us both much harm."* [36]

In answering Jackson about *when* to remove the deposits, Van Buren stalled; he wanted to consult Silas Wright and some other friends. But as to *whether* to remove, perish all ugly doubts: "I go with you agt. the world, whether it respects men or things." [37]

V   JACKSON'S DECISION

While Van Buren was consulting his New York friends, Duane and McLane were both on duty in Washington, and Frank Blair was vacationing with the President at the Rip Raps. When Blair heard of McLane's proposal to postpone removal till January 1, he was furious and urged Van Buren to have no part in it. Procrastination would only give the Bank a chance to work on Congress. What trust could be put in the vows of McLane to turn into an enemy of the Bank on January 1? He had promised this before, after Biddle betrayed him by permitting recharter to become a political issue, and yet he had given the Bank a number of "good lifts"—for example, "hooking up a favorable report" through Toland; getting Verplanck, who proved "thoroughly treacherous," appointed head of Ways and Means; issuing a Treasury report on the losses of state banks and thus reducing confidence in them; selling French bills in a lump to the Bank on its terms; being "an underwriter" for Duane's appointment. "The fact is, disguise it as you may, Mr. McLane cannot be true to his own principles and to those of the President. He knows that the Bank power is the last hope of Federalism and he is fighting for it." Nevertheless, Blair would not drop McLane; just cut the ties between the Bank and the government and, presto, the administration would be in harmony once more, the cause of conflict gone.[38]

When Van Buren finally advised Jackson regarding the time of removal, he was well coached on what to say. Despite the fact that McLane had attempted to associate Van Buren with the proposal he made to Kendall in New York, Van Buren now disowned any part in it: "I could not for a moment think of advising such a course," he protested. But what he did advise was a halfway measure, very close to the McLane scheme against which the Vice-President was protesting so vigorously. Complete arrangements with state banks, he wrote, and order deposits in them to begin, but to begin on January 1, not before Congress meets.[39]

When Jackson answered that he dared not delay, because if he did the Bank could use government deposits to corrupt Congress, Van Buren tried to explain carefully how his plan, which he laid to Silas Wright, differed from McLane's. But he would not stand in the President's way— no, not he. "Do as you think best," he sagely counseled a President very likely to do exactly that. And off the elusive Van Buren went, with Washington Irving as his nonpolitical companion, on a four-week jaunt into the wilds of New England. The climactic battle of the Bank War was about to begin, and the Red Fox of Kinderhook shrewdly made himself scarce.[40]

Yet he sent back a letter urging the President to keep McLane in the cabinet. Apparently Van Buren felt that when Duane resigned or was dismissed, as seemed likely soon, McLane might also leave the administration. Perhaps Van Buren pleaded for McLane out of genuine friendliness, bulwarked by knowledge that faithfulness to a friend was a quality with which Jackson would not quarrel. Furthermore, Van Buren was in the company of Irving, who was well disposed toward McLane.

McLane and I differ wholly on the Bank, warned Van Buren, and on almost all public questions we tend to go in opposite directions. (This being so, was it not strange of Van Buren to have procured McLane's advancement to so high a place as he held?) "Still, I entertain the strongest attachment for him, and have been so long in the habit of interceding in his behalf, that I cannot think of giving it up." If he resigned with Duane, he would be ruined, for his former Federalist friends would feast on his lost prestige. But if Jackson asked him to stay, then he could do so. And Van Buren was sure McLane had made it explicit that he had not known of Duane's views on removal when Duane was appointed.[41]

Now Duane was stubborn beyond measure. In mid-summer he promised to remove the deposits or resign, but now he would do neither. Early in September McLane asked Duane to agree to remove the deposits on some certain day, probably January 1, subsequent to the meeting of Congress, in case Congress took no action. Again he refused. Unless persuaded there was reason to remove the deposits, or ordered to do so by Congress, he would not act.[42]

On September 9 Jackson officially received, through the Treasury Department, a copy of Kendall's report, showing that state banks were ready to accept federal deposits. The cabinet met September 10, when Jackson gave the report and attached correspondence to McLane to be shown to them all. In a brief address the President declared himself convinced that the state banks were ready to offer a safe depository and should be used at once before the United States Bank employed powers recently given to Biddle to spend money lavishly on his own responsibility.[43]

In the week that elapsed before the cabinet met again, Jackson spoke to many of the ministers individually, informing McLane and Taney of his fixed intention to shift the deposits speedily and trying to part amicably with Duane by suggesting his appointment as Buchanan's successor in the Russian mission. But Duane would not agree to go to St. Petersburg any more readily than to return to Philadelphia.[44]

At the cabinet meeting on September 17 Jackson called on the members one after another, beginning with McLane, who reviewed his objections to removal "in detail," as Duane reported, "in an emphatic and lucid manner." Duane urged that the matter be left to Congress. Cass would leave it to the Secretary of the Treasury. Woodbury was on both sides, against removal but with the President, whatever he decided. Taney briefly answered he was for removal from the beginning.[45] Jackson then adjourned the meeting overnight.

The next day Jackson read the cabinet members a lengthy exposition, on which Taney and Van Buren had helped, of reasons for abandoning the national bank in favor of state banks as government depositories. Duane borrowed the paper to study it, and the next morning when Jackson sent to him for his decision he wanted two days more to get his father's opinion of what he should do. But Jackson, who had been waiting all summer for Duane to make up his mind on removal or resignation, had had enough. The President's decision to begin using selected state banks on October 1 appeared in the *Globe* on September 20, 1833. When Duane refused to order this transfer or to resign, the President dismissed him on September 23 and appointed Attorney General Taney to his place.[46]

"Mr. Taney is a sterling man," Jackson assured Van Buren; "he has, I am told, drawn high encomiums from Mr. McLane, who in the evening after my final decision, was in good spirits." [47] This was on September 19, prior to Taney's appointment to succeed Duane, but McLane must have known it was coming. If he seemed in good spirits, either he was putting on a brave front to hide his dejection or Jackson was so insensitive that he saw only the emotions that he wanted to see.

At any rate, Jackson remained confident of his ability to prevail on McLane to stay in the cabinet despite their disagreement on withdrawal of the deposits.[48] When it was suggested to Jackson that publication of the paper he had read to the cabinet on September 18 would drive McLane and Cass to resign lest they be thought to have acquiesced in it, Jackson had a statement published in the *Globe* of September 23, declaring that he begged "his Cabinet to consider the proposed measure as his own, in the support of which he shall require no one of them to make a sacrifice of opinion or principle."

Perhaps it was knowledge of this face-saving insertion, in which he may have been an agent, that allowed Major Lewis to deny rumors that a number of cabinet members were resigning.[49] Lewis was pleased that only Duane was being lost, but Taney would have been very willing indeed to see McLane go, too. On September 23 Blair called on Taney to read him the published exposition. Donelson was there and Taney sat back in his chair, his feet on his desk, happily puffing on a cigar till Blair got to the passage on responsibility, when Taney stopped the reading to ask, "How under heaven did that get in?"

The explanation did not cheer him. "This has saved Cass and McLane," he told Blair. "But for it they would have gone out and have been ruined —as it is, they will remain and do us much mischief." [50]

Jackson's taking the responsibility did not, however, satisfy McLane and Cass as easily as Taney and others, including Jackson, thought it would. The day after Jackson's paper to the cabinet was printed, Cass called on Major Lewis to notify him, as a close friend, that he had decided to resign in order not to embarrass the President by his opposition to the measures the President was now taking. McLane was of the same opinion, Cass said.

Lewis was concerned because he thought it likely the Congress would try to overrule Jackson on the deposit question, and if McLane and Cass left the cabinet, their resignation might strengthen the opposition, for he knew they were both very well regarded in Congress. Consequently he urged Cass to see the President, assuring him there was no need for his resignation or McLane's.

Cass did go to see the President and returned to Lewis in half an hour, greatly encouraged and willing to stay in the cabinet if McLane would. Acting at Lewis's suggestion again, Cass persuaded McLane to go to the White House. Jackson told McLane, as he had told Cass, that he did not see how his feelings or delicacy could be involved; the truth could be told that he had heard McLane's full opinion frankly given, had disagreed and taken all responsibility on himself. He asked no support from them on this measure but only that they attend to their own departments and refrain from taking open ground with the opposition when the removal became a party question.

When McLane and Cass came to see Jackson twenty-four hours later and told him they would stay, he was pleased. The requirements of public duty were more powerful than the desires of private friendship, he wrote Van Buren, but after his duty was done it was "the first pleasure" of his life to know he would not lose those friends.[51] Van Buren, in turn, continued to give advice from a distance and reassured Jackson that he had treated McLane and Cass exactly right.[52]

William Henry Harrison declared himself well pleased with the way McLane and Cass had got out of "that sad Bank affair," but Louis McLane could not be pleased.[53] Gall and wormwood were his lot with Roger Taney promoted to the Treasury Department and the administration committed to a policy Taney had urged and McLane had vigorously opposed. Others might see him as did John Quincy Adams, who, after reading Duane's apologia, castigated McLane and his fellow Secretaries as a group of "supple and submissive assentators." [54] And he could not but be dismayed at news of mass meetings, including one in Wilmington, to protest the removal policy of an administration with whose fortunes his own were closely linked.[55]

Washington Irving, moved by his natural kindliness and perhaps by his very particular interest in the McLane family, left Van Buren's side to go to Washington and offer McLane encouragement during the cabinet crisis. Once it was over, McLane seemed to cheer up (he would not have wished Irving to know how hurt he was) and set off on a short excursion to Delaware, apparently "relieved from the fogs and glooms" that had lowered about his spirits.[56] "It will do him no harm to mix a little more with the people," Van Buren commented, when he heard of McLane's trip, thinking perhaps of the trip he had just enjoyed with Irving and of the enthusiastic support he had found for Jackson and Jackson's policies among the people.[57]

VI ORGANIZING A DEPARTMENT

There were some encouragements to staying in the State Department besides salary and prestige and a mode of life, political and social, to which both Louis and Kitty McLane had become accustomed. His old congressional colleague, James Buchanan, now in St. Petersburg, was delighted to hear of McLane's appointment. His talents, his industry, and his "just view of things," Buchanan thought, would bring new vigor to the very department of government where reform was most needed. Having received not one word from the State Department in six months, Buchanan appreciated McLane's instituting regular semimonthly despatches to all of the principal ministers abroad. Perhaps, however, in his eagerness to get out of Russia and home to Pennsylvania Buchanan was too critical of Livingston ("either too old or too much engrossed in other affairs," Buchanan complained); St. Petersburg was a long way off, and despite McLane's good intentions, State Department despatches were often delayed for months in reaching Buchanan's successor.[58]

But when due allowance is made for Buchanan's special problems and prejudices, it is still evident that McLane brought new vigor to the State Department. The desire of the aged chief clerk, Daniel Brent, to go to Paris as consul with Livingston, opened a place for Asbury Dickins, allowing McLane at once to keep a trusted associate in his office while shielding this friend of Nicholas Biddle's from participation in any anti-Bank maneuvers that might be expected in the Treasury—though it should be noted that Dickins's translation from Treasury to State was arranged while Duane was Secretary and before Taney's appointment seemed imminent.[59]

For Dickins, McLane would do a good deal. He sought, in vain, to have Dickins's salary raised from $2,000 to $3,000 while he was still in the Treasury.[60] After his transfer to State, McLane urged that he be included at diplomatic dinners.[61] Despite the storm over removal, Dickins remained a friend of Nicholas Biddle's, a fact of which McLane was probably well aware.[62] Another principal clerkship in the State Department was bestowed on Aaron Ogden Dayton, a friend of New York customs collector Samuel Swartwout, whose defalcations were still undetected.[63]

The weakness of McLane's political position made him particularly careful in handling personnel problems so that he could not easily be accused of unfair decisions. In theory his position gave him control of a large number of appointments, but in practice his authority in patronage matters was not great. To one aspirant for office he spoke "candidly and freely" on this matter: "he stated . . . that the appointment properly belonged to his office—but as matters were—He thought that the New York delegation . . . would determine on the individual." [64] He announced the selection of newspapers in each state that were to print the federal laws, he received recommendations for district attorneys and marshals, but the President controlled these appointments, as he did appointments to posts overseas. [65] When a close associate sought appointment as secretary of the claims commission being established under the Spanish treaty, McLane wrote him: "Whether the P. [President] is committed I have no reason to know, though . . . it is not improbable that he is at least in some degree prepos[ses]sed. I see no impropriety in your sending him an application backed by such support as you may be able to get, and of a character likely to be useful. You may safely rely upon my friendship as far as it may avail; but I owe it to my regard for you frankly to say that I do not myself in such a case rate it high." [66] And when a clerk named Carton, whom he had appointed to a Treasury post, was being discharged by Taney, McLane was reduced to begging Cass to find a place for him in the pension office of the War Department, where he had previously worked. [67]

These examples, however, come from the spring of 1834, when McLane's political star was noticeably on the wane. In the spring of 1833, before final decisions had been made in the removal phase of the Bank War, McLane was more confident of his influence. In April, 1833, for instance, he sought to win an appointment for John Nelson, a Marylander who had recently successfully negotiated a claims convention at Naples. The chief opposition he ran into was provided by Taney, who sought the post for "his relation Heath," a Federalist. "God knows these family concerns have been carried far enough," McLane exclaimed, thinking not only of Taney but of Livingston, who was taking his son-in-law to Paris as secretary of his legation and already had his brother-in-law stationed at the Hague. [68] And in the fall of 1833, McLane made inquiries for the President and Van Buren about the opinions of Thomas Ruffin, who was being considered for the attorney generalship that went eventually to Van Buren's ally Benjamin Butler. [69]

The Patent Office, a bureau of the State Department, was the source of several personnel problems during McLane's tenure as department head. Dr. John D. Craig, the bureau superintendent, complained about the work of one of the clerks, Charles Bulfinch, Jr., probably a son of the architect. McLane gave Bulfinch a chance to defend himself, with full access to the records, but finally McLane dismissed Bulfinch after the case had dragged on from June to November. [70] In the next month charges were brought against Craig—that he issued conflicting patents for the same invention, never reading specifications and never submitting conflicts to arbitration, that he failed to keep proper records, and that he was rude and uncouth. Distinguished men, such as Senator Gabriel Moore, of Alabama, and the old comptroller, former Senator Joseph Anderson, of Tennessee, testified in this case, in which the organization and rules governing the operations of the Patent Office were called to McLane's attention.[71] As an efficient administrator, McLane wished to set things right. "Courtesy is the indispensable duty of all persons employed in the offices," he cautioned Craig, while he set to work on a thorough revision of the rules of the bureau.

McLane ordered the new clerk, Aaron O. Dayton, to conduct an investigation of all the charges against Craig, and Dayton heard testimony at the Patent Office from February 12 to 24.[72] He found abundant evidence of Craig's guilt on many of the charges, but it was not clear what Craig's responsibility was under the law. McLane contented himself with censuring Craig for his conduct and with laying down specific rules for future guidance—among others, that all official correspondence should be preserved and filed, that all conflicts should be resolved by arbitration before a new patent was issued, and that no original papers should be removed from the office. Failure to comply with any detail of these rules, he warned Craig, would constitute reason for dismissal.[73]

McLane also found it necessary to tighten administrative authority over American representatives abroad. No presents, he ordered, should be accepted without the specific approval of Congress; the department already had problems enough with such gifts as the ornamental sword given to Commodore James Biddle by the Viceroy of Peru, the gold snuffbox set with diamonds presented by the Czar to Leavitt Harris, consul at St. Petersburg, the lion and two horses given to R. J. Leib, consul at Tangier, by the Sultan of Morocco.[74] McLane placed definite limits on the contingent expenses of missions abroad, ranging from a high figure of $2,000 allowed the legation at London to the modest $500 expenditure permitted at the Hague.[75] He reminded the Mexican minister, who was summering in Philadelphia, that foreign representatives were asked to reside in Washington so they could be reached easily when needed; and from him and all other heads of missions lists of all personnel were requested.[76] At least one American representative abroad was advised how to use the diplomatic cipher and particularly instructed to acknowledge each despatch received and to send despatches in duplicate to ensure delivery.[77] To many such representatives abroad McLane sent requests that they furnish the department with files of the best newspapers and journals as well as copies of pamphlets referring to American diplomacy, and in turn he promised to send copies of leading American newspapers.[78]

McLane as Secretary of State showed an awareness of the value of historical documents. During his administration the State Department completed publication of a seven-volume collection of the diplomatic correspondence from the end of the Revolution to the adoption of the Constitution,[79] and began gathering material for a still larger and more general documentary history of the United States. The latter project, however, ran into opposition from Congressmen who feared the eventual cost and suspected that printers of the political opposition, such as Duff Green or Gales and Seaton, would profit from the contract.[80]

McLane made an effort to carry out the dictates of Congress by having British documents copied in London, but the man he chose as his agent, one J. Walter Barry, turned the proposal down.[81] Efforts to get early Florida and Louisiana records copied from Spanish archives in Havana were also unsuccessful,[82] but McLane did succeed in setting under way negotiations that led to the purchase of Washington's papers for $25,000 in the summer of 1834.[83]

Acquisition of historical records was only one part of the archival problem McLane faced on becoming head of the State Department. He found the diplomatic archives, a peculiarly useful collection, housed in only one room and that room too small to permit proper arrangement and preservation of documents, let alone convenient and speedy access to them. Nor was expansion easy, because almost every section of the department was similarly pinched for space. Though the six more rooms that were needed were unobtainable, McLane fortunately knew that Treasury Department plans to rent a new building would allow the fifth auditor to be moved from three rooms he occupied contiguous to State Department offices and thus allow some elbow room for State Department operations.

Jackson approved this expansion and other adjustments in department operations that were recommended by McLane—approving them all the more readily, surely, because Jackson himself had called for some reorganization of the State Department in his first annual message and because McLane had carefully prepared the way for his recommendations. Immediately on entering his new office he had called for a report on the business and conditions of labor in each office of the department. On the basis of this report McLane provided a new organization for the department that featured division of labor and a clear assignment of responsibilities.

Asbury Dickins, the chief clerk, was to be an undersecretary, superintending all bureaus, of which there were to be eight. First among them was the diplomatic bureau, with three main clerks, one supervising the missions to England, France, Russia, and the Netherlands, the second supervising all other European missions (including Spain, Portugal, Belgium, Sicily), and a third supervising missions in North and South

America. Registers were to be kept of all transactions, properly indexed, and weekly correspondence was anticipated.

After this strategic bureau, the others seemed less important, consisting of a consular bureau; a home bureau (authenticating certificates, listing seamen and passengers arriving from foreign ports); a bureau of archives, laws, and commissions; a bureau of pardons, copyrights, and the library; a disbursing and superintending bureau (with custody of the Great Seal of the United States); a translating and miscellaneous bureau; and, somewhat independently, the Patent Office. If this organization did not provide a complete metamorphosis from chaos to order, it was at least a long step in that direction.[84]

However, all his skill as an administrator was insufficient to bolster McLane's weakened standing in the administration and he was reported "ill at ease" and doubtfully able "to sustain himself." [85] John Quincy Adams noted in his diary that McLane was "in a perilous condition"; Adams had no confidence in McLane and thought whoever trusted in him would be betrayed.[86] Kendall, for once, would have agreed with Adams. It had been a damper on his spirits when McLane had not resigned in September; in his autobiography Kendall explained that he did not see how a man could honorably remain in the cabinet if he believed, as McLane apparently did, that the President had committed a "gross usurpation." [87]

Washington Irving saw things differently. "Your high and clear standing in the eyes of the world," he assured McLane, "must console you for any temporary embarrassments resulting from honest differences in opinion with the friends with whom you are officially connected." "Yours is a reputation that will wear well," Irving added, but at the moment McLane's reputation was not wearing well at all.[88] To be sure there were those who thought of him as a possible presidential or vice-presidential candidate of elements in the Jackson party that were unfriendly to the anti-Bank policy of the administration.[89] Even if Van Buren had, as one politician put it, "well nigh petted McLane into a rival," Van Buren himself had nimbly kept his footing—and his place in the succession—while the cabinet was racked by dissension.[90] Besides the Taney-McLane feud, Biddle heard that McLane's relations with Barry and Woodbury were so poor that they had refused to attend a dinner he gave for the cabinet. Probably Biddle was misinformed; Barry had, in fact, become unfriendly to the kitchen cabinet of Lewis, Kendall, and Blair, to the ambitious course of Van Buren ("I owe him nothing and care nothing for him"), and to Taney's "foolish plan, . . . if plan he had any." [91]

There is evidence that McLane talked with both Jackson and Van Buren early in January about resigning his office.[92] By the middle of

February knowledgeable men, such as Willie Mangum, John Tyler, and Hezekiah Niles, were expecting to hear of his resignation momentarily.[93] Nicholas Biddle heard that McLane would move to Baltimore in the hope that he might occupy the prominent place at the bar there that was vacated by the recent death of William Wirt.[94]

Very likely McLane did submit his resignation, only to be persuaded that for the good of the party and for his own good, too, he should not desert the Jackson team when it faced a hostile Senate majority and factional opposition in the House.[95] Martin Van Buren gave Kitty Mc-Lane credit for persuading her husband to keep his place, though only "after a severe trial, in which he was brought to the brink of a fatal precipice." [96]

"His sacrifice of feeling must be great," wrote Irving on hearing the news; "yet his continuance in the Cabinet at this crisis is of great importance to his friends. . . . It is also important to his own welfare. His retirement at this moment would be made a handle of by the opponents of the Administration, and he would be forced, in spite of himself, into a wretched collision with his late friends." [97]

McLane not only stayed in the cabinet, but for the time being—in March, 1834—he remained on close terms with Van Buren.[98] Kitty, who had won Van Buren's approval for influencing her husband's decision, had come out splendidly this season as lady Secretary of State, giving a dinner and an evening party each week.[99] Nor had McLane lost anything of the impressive demeanor that had won him respect both in Washington and London. A North Carolina lawyer visiting the capital was taken about to meet the most distinguished men—Jackson, Van Buren, Webster, the cabinet members, and so forth. And though Webster had the most intellectual look, it was McLane who made the best impression on the visitor: "I am more pleased with him than any gentleman I have yet seen here." [100]

In Scotland, at about this time, an American journalist was talking with Lord Aberdeen, who made a thousand inquiries about America. He had known McLane intimately, he said, and seldom had he been so impressed with a man's honesty and straightforwardness—never had he done business with anyone with more pleasure. Aberdeen spoke flatteringly of Gallatin and Richard Rush also, but "recurred continually to Mr. McLane, of whom he could scarce say enough." [101]

VII DIPLOMACY

If his political prospects were not very encouraging in the year 1833–34 when Louis McLane was tormented with doubts as to what step he should take next, he could, at least, find temporary refuge in the diplomatic problems that were his responsibility and with which he anticipated little or no interference from alien elements in the administration. He entered upon this responsibility with some advantages—first, from his long service in Congress, and second, and most important, from the two years he had spent as American minister in England. English relations, nevertheless, posed a problem with which he could make very little progress. The problem was the Northeastern boundary, which could not be run exactly as described in the Treaty of 1783. In the spring of 1832 the Senate rejected an arbitral award made by the King of the Netherlands in 1831, and no further progress in drawing a boundary was made in these years despite much correspondence on the subject.

The strangest event in Louis McLane's relationship to this diplomatic controversy occurred in May, 1832, before he had become Secretary of State. In an imaginative effort to gain a free hand to negotiate the boundary with Great Britain, the Jackson administration drew up an agreement, a sort of treaty, with the state of Maine. By its terms Maine provisionally surrendered its claim to the northeastern part of the disputed frontier area in return for a quid pro quo that included the proceeds from the sale of a large tract of public lands in the Michigan Territory. On behalf of Maine this agreement was signed by three commissioners, including William Pitt Preble, who had been American minister to the Netherlands at the time of the Dutch King's arbitration award and had protested against it. Three commissioners also signed the agreement for the federal government: Edward Livingston, Secretary of State; Levi Woodbury, Secretary of the Navy; and Louis McLane, Secretary of the Treasury. Had the agreement held, the Jackson administration should have been able to negotiate a settlement to this old boundary dispute in a short time, granting the good relations existing between it and the British government. However, Maine repented its share in any such agreement, and this state's recalcitrance, plus the strength of the opposition party in the Senate, ruined the hope of any negotiated settlement before McLane took office as Secretary of State.[102]

Immediately on taking office, it became McLane's duty to explain the American argument that acceptance of any compromise boundary line without consent of Maine would be unconstitutional because the federal government lacked power to take land from a state without its permission. After Maine insisted on the right to approve the cession of any part of the American claim, Edward Livingston had proposed fresh surveys in an effort to draw a boundary on the 1783 terms, however difficult this might be. McLane took up Livingston's suggestion, arguing in a series of letters that until every possible effort had been exhausted to settle the boundary on the treaty terms there was no likelihood that Maine—or the Senate either—would accept a compromise boundary line. McLane's letters were very persuasive, but at the time he left office the matter rested in this indeterminate state.[103] So did his hope of removing impressment and the right of search as issues between the two countries.[104]

In relations with another European neighbor, Spain, mistress still of an island empire in the West Indies, some progress was made, but by virtue of negotiations initiated under Van Buren's administration of the State Department. In a treaty signed at Madrid on February 17, 1834, Spain agreed to pay $600,000 for damages resulting from illegal seizures in the closing years of the Spanish-American wars for independence. McLane's contribution to the successful completion of this negotiation lay in the authorization he gave the American minister, Cornelius Van Ness, to settle for less—by more than half—than the total sum originally claimed by the United States. Van Ness thought he might have coaxed the Spanish into raising the sum a bit had not King Ferdinand VII died late in 1833. And though McLane had warned Van Ness not to settle prematurely for a smaller sum than necessary, he must have been happy to close the matter, particularly in view of the civil tumult of the Carlist wars which caused lasting confusion in Spanish affairs following the King's death.[105] Efforts that McLane made to improve the conditions of trade with Cuba and to persuade Spain to recognize the independence of the Latin American states were not immediately successful.[106]

Nor was McLane successful in securing ratification of a treaty drawn up between the new Kingdom of Belgium and the United States in the winter before he took office, but the failure does not seem to have been his fault. The treaty was approved by the American Senate, but held up by the Belgian government, which felt its minister to the United States, Baron Désiré Behr, had acted precipitately and exceeded his instructions in signing this treaty. Specifically the Belgians objected to terms in the treaty defining legal blockades for the good reason that Belgium was at the very moment being defended by England and France against the Dutch by the use of just such a blockade as the treaty condemned. Hugh Legaré, who represented the United States at Brussels, asked McLane to have the time for ratification extended. His request was granted, but the treaty was never approved, and the United States had no formal agreement with Belgium for almost twenty-five years.[107]

On the other hand, treaties with Chile, Muscat, and Siam were completed during McLane's administration and approved with a fair degree of despatch. The treaty with Chile, which was signed September 1, 1833, was actually an addition to an earlier treaty, completed in 1832 and approved by the Senate but not yet proclaimed. The new treaty extended the time allowed for the original one to go into effect and contained some new matters that Chile had introduced in ratifying the original treaty, notably a provision to the effect that slaves on American ships touching at Chilean ports should not thereby become automatically free as they might otherwise be under Chilean law, which did not recognize slavery. John Hamm, who was, like Louis McLane, a native of Kent County, Delaware, negotiated both the original treaty and the addition. McLane had nothing to do with the appointment of Hamm, an Ohio resident, nor with his success, except insofar as McLane influenced the Senate to accept the additional treaty in April, 1834.[108]

The treaties with Muscat and Siam, intended to open the way to American commerce with these Asiatic states, were negotiated by Edmund Roberts, who went out as a special envoy for this purpose before McLane entered the State Department. The significance of a treaty with the Sultan of Muscat was that he ruled the rich spice island of Zanzibar, off the east coast of Africa, as well as a more barren and larger kingdom, Oman, on the coast of Arabia. The Senate ratified both treaties in June, 1834.[109]

A treaty negotiated by John Nelson with the Kingdom of the Two Sicilies in the fall of 1832 demanded some attention from McLane after the exchange of ratifications in June, 1833, because it provided for the payment of claims made by Americans for seizures by the Neapolitan government while allied with Napoleon. McLane had to see that commissioners were appointed, plus a secretary and clerk, and to instruct them how to set about their work when they met in Washington in September. The presence in the group, although only as a substitute, of McLane's North Carolina friend Romulus Saunders suggests that the Secretary had some influence in these appointments. In his annual message of December 1, 1834, Jackson was happy to announce that the first installment of money due under the Sicilian treaty had been received.[110]

Despite, or perhaps because of the President's own intense personal interest in the subject, McLane failed to bring such a happy conclusion to the relations of the United States with Mexico. The responsibility, however, was not his. The American representative in Mexico was Colonel Anthony Butler, a onetime comrade-in-arms of the President who had gone to Mexico with instructions for the minister, Joel Poinsett, and remained there as chargé when Poinsett returned home.[111] Butler, who had personal speculative interests in Texas, was neither diplomatic nor scrupulous, but enjoyed the privilege of corresponding directly with the President and behaved more like a personal emissary of Jackson than like a representative of the State Department.

Jackson regretted the 1819 treaty with Spain which had fixed the boundary of the United States at the Sabine River and definitely established Texas within Spanish territory. In 1828 the United States had signed a treaty with Mexico, ratifying the old Spanish border and providing for its survey by a joint Mexican-American commission. Butler and Jackson nursed a hope that the "western bank of the Sabine," as mentioned in the treaty, could be so interpreted as to bring the boundary up a river which met the Sabine near the Gulf and thus provide a notable territorial addition to Louisiana. And Butler also was empowered to offer Mexico up to $5 million for a further share of Texas.[112]

As Secretary of State, McLane could do little more than urge Butler to get on with his work of establishing the boundary and of getting recognition of damage claims of American citizens against Mexico. McLane's hope of inducing Butler to follow normal diplomatic procedures in his correspondence proved vain.[113] On October 12, 1833, McLane did send Butler a list of charges of bad conduct made against him by the American consul at Mexico City—and with the charges the President's hope that Butler could refute them. A month later McLane announced the consul's replacement, and in May he declared Butler's answer to the charges was considered wholly satisfactory.[114]

Despite the assurance given Butler in May, everyone's patience with him was wearing thin. In August, 1833, Butler had been hopeful of acquiring Texas by negotiation.[115] In October he had suggested bribery.[116] Jackson responded indignantly that he authorized no corruption, but Butler continued scheming.[117] Santa Anna would deal, he wrote, but was afraid of a public outcry; if the commissioners running the boundary (who were still unappointed) got into a quarrel, this might be an excuse for Mexico to give up a portion of Texas.[118]

In January, 1834, McLane sent Butler the President's orders to conclude a convention extending the time for the boundary survey—and then come home.[119] But Butler was incorrigible. The sum of $200,000 would bribe the Mexican President, he informed Jackson. And then, a month later, he begged to be put at the head of a filibustering expedition to invade Texas. "What a scamp," Jackson wrote at the end of this letter; "The Secretary of State will reiterate his instructions to ask an extension of the treaty for running boundary line and then recall him, or if . . . the Mexican Govt. has refused, recal [sic] him at once."[120]

And at the time he left office, in June, 1834, this was exactly what McLane was trying to do—to get Butler to conclude his negotiations and come home.[121] However, Butler did as he pleased, relying on the President's zeal for Texas, and he stayed in Mexico for another year, his roguery unabated.

VIII   THE FRENCH SPOLIATIONS AFFAIR

For McLane, Mexican relations were not a matter of intense personal interest; and there are no indications that he resented the President's domination of this aspect of foreign policy. French relations were a different matter. Not only had McLane been to Europe and lived two years in London in the midst of gossip about European state affairs but the main issue of French payment of the spoliations claims was a matter that had already concerned him as Secretary of the Treasury.

It was, consequently, most irritating to him when on May 17, as acting Secretary of State (in the absence of Livingston, presumably preparing for his trip abroad), McLane heard the French combine a complaint regarding the American method of collection with their explanation of the delay in the appropriation.[122] His irritation was evident in the instructions, dated June 3, that he gave Livingston.

The explanations of the French minister, McLane wrote, were unsatisfactory. The French government could not hide behind its legislature to escape blame for failing to make a payment it had agreed to, particularly since the government confessed that it had not yet called on the legislature for the appropriation. Since the legislature had been in session when ratification of the treaty had been completed and then had met again in the fall of 1832 and continued in session all winter, this failure to make any effort to pay the debt at the time agreed on was astonishing.

This was McLane's comment on the main point. The French complaint about the method of collection was, McLane declared, irrelevant.[123] They were annoyed that eagerness for the indemnity money had led the American government to sell a bill of exchange on Paris, instead of waiting to collect directly from the French government. The bill had been resold in Europe and presented to the French government, which could not pay, by a third, or fourth, party.[124]

Aware that it reflected on him personally because as Secretary of the Treasury he had been responsible for the method of collection, McLane pointed out to the French minister, Louis Sérurier, in a letter of the same date as the instructions to Livingston, that after the Louisiana Purchase Treaty of 1803 France had disposed of its claims to a banker who received the American payment. By another 1803 convention the private claims of French citizens on the United States were paid by bills of exchange drawn by the United States minister at Paris on the United States Treasury. Other examples were cited, including the recent collection of the Danish indemnity by bills of exchange at Hamburg. He, Louis McLane, had acted in this case under authority of an act of Congress, and if the French minister saw any fault in the method of collection, he should have raised the point at the time; he might also have then expressed a doubt that the funds would be available on time if he had any hint of the state of things.[125]

McLane had thus begun his career in the State Department in a peremptory fashion by demanding explanations from the French and rejecting any imputation that he had acted improperly as Treasury Secretary in his attempt to collect 5 million francs, the first installment of the 25 million franc debt. On his trip to the Northeast he may have grown concerned about the possibility of affronting the French; after his return he wrote Leavitt Harris, the American chargé in Paris, telling him of the correspondence with Sérurier and asking him to delay any negotiations till Livingston's arrival, though he should not hesitate to assure the French of the American desire to maintain friendly connections.[126]

Obviously McLane was eager to get Livingston off to the French capital, but Livingston still had not departed at the end of July, when McLane was disappointed to read a newspaper despatch reporting that on June 18 the Chamber of Deputies had postponed to its next session any action on the debt owed to the United States.[127] Leavitt Harris had led McLane to anticipate this development, but insisted the debt would be acted on early at the next session. "Where there is so much shuffling," McLane observed, skeptically, to Jackson, "the whole subject may be considered to be more or less doubtful." [128]

At last Livingston did leave on August 14, after a final conference in New York with McLane and probably also with Van Buren and John Forsyth, of the Senate Committee on Foreign Relations. While Livingston was en route to his new station, the French minister came to McLane to explain that the French government had felt it important to allow time for the eradication of some popular prejudices against paying the American claims before it asked the Chamber of Deputies to carry out the terms of the spoliations treaty. Interest would be paid and the American government in the long run should be able to see that the French would live up to their engagements.[129]

McLane rejected Sérurier's explanation as nothing more than a reiteration of statements previously made, though in the meantime the hope once proffered that the French legislature would soon take action had been destroyed by news that the legislature had postponed the matter to another session.[130] Because McLane had seemed to listen sympathetically to the French explanation, his note disappointed Sérurier, particularly the assertion in it that any obstacle the French legislature placed in the way of execution of the spoliations treaty would be a violation of the public faith. It was odd that a minister of a foreign government, "and moreover a representative Government," should have the nerve to tell the Chamber of Deputies exactly what its constitutional duties were.[131]

Soon after his arrival in France, Livingston reported that he had met with a most cordial reception and had assurances from King Louis-Philippe and his ministers that French tardiness in carrying out the treaty terms would soon be remedied by favorable action in the legislature.[132] The Foreign Minister, Achille-Victor, Duke de Broglie, went so far as to promise that the government would introduce a request for the necessary appropriation on the second day of the next session—the day after the legislature organized.[133] Other Americans in France were also sure that the appropriation would soon be provided.[134]

As a consequence of the hopeful appearance of affairs in the fall of 1833, Jackson showed no sign of anger in the account of Franco-American relations that he incorporated in his annual message to Congress on December 3. The President recounted the course of events up to the postponement of the appropriation in June and then added that he had assurances the delay proceeded from no indisposition to fulfill the treaty and that the appropriation would be sought, "with a reasonable hope of success," at the next meeting of the French legislature. He was concerned, however, about the failure of France to provide documents useful to the American commissioners who were trying to settle individual damage claims that were to be paid from the indemnity. Jackson and McLane continued to argue that these documents were to be provided free; the French interpreted the treaty otherwise.[135]

Shortly before the President sent his message to Congress, McLane received despatches from Livingston, who recommended suspending the reduction in the duty on French wines that Congress had adopted in the summer of 1832 in accordance with the new treaty. Livingston felt that some measures must be taken to make the French understand that the United States took seriously the French failure to pay the indemnity promptly; raising the duties would immediately show the French that something was to be gained by carrying out their part of the agreement. McLane and Jackson rejected his advice. Their hand was strengthened, they felt, if they could argue that their part of the agreement had been kept. If the United States were driven to coercive measures, McLane warned Livingston ominously, it was not likely that they would be "of so mild a character" as the tariff rearrangement Livingston suggested.[136]

As matters developed, the American government may have made a mistake in not following Livingston's advice to raise the wine duty. Through the winter the administration expected good news from France, but the expected news did not come. A bill providing for the indemnity payment was introduced into the Chamber of Deputies as promised, but it rested in committee for two months without further action. At last, on March 10, 1834, it was favorably reported out of committee. Debate began on March 28 and lasted five days; when it was over, the Chamber defeated the measure by a narrow margin, 176 to 168.

Americans were shocked, and so was the French government. Broglie resigned at once, accepting the vote as a rebuke to the ministry, members of which were charged with possessing a personal pecuniary interest in the American treaty. The chief French opposition, however, was to the amount of the indemnity, which French critics argued was too large, and to the precedent it set for claims on France by other countries.[137]

In sending news of the French action, Livingston reported that he had called on the new French Foreign Minister, Henri Gauthier, Count de Rigny, and had his pledge that the government would bring this issue before the new Chamber of Deputies as soon as practical. This meant the following December. The new Chamber would meet in the summer to organize but would quickly adjourn and no important business could be brought before it until it would reconvene in December. The French must be shown that the United States was not to be trifled with, Livingston counseled, and he suggested that an embargo on all imports from France might serve the purpose very well.[138]

This suggestion of commercial coercion was entirely in character for an old Jeffersonian like Livingston, but it was not a suggestion likely to appeal to a man with the Federalist background of McLane. He informed Livingston that his news was a "most painful surprise" to the President. What measures would be taken had not been decided and would not be decided until more was known about the proceedings in the Chamber of Deputies and the plans of the ministry. Friendship with France was a fundamental object of American foreign policy, but if the new ministry did not offer satisfactory assurances, the President would feel called upon to recommend measures vindicating the rights and honor of his country.[139]

McLane's letter masked a quarrel within Jackson's cabinet about the proper American response to the French defalcation. One of Nicholas Biddle's correspondents sensed the two conflicting reactions when he reported that Jackson at first "breathed nothing but War and Vengeance [and] talked loudly of sending a Message to Congress recommending the issuing of Letters of Marque forthwith," but in a few days was calmly reporting that assurances had been received that the vote would be reconsidered and reversed.[140]

An inside story of cabinet dissension is provided by Taney, but it depends on his memory in 1860, twenty-six years after the event. According to Taney's account, shortly after Jackson heard of the failure of the French appropriation bill he told his cabinet that he would send Congress a special message on the subject and request authority to issue letters of marque, which would permit Americans to indemnify themselves by attacking French shipping. Cass and McLane supported Jackson to such an extent that Taney, who was completely surprised by this proposal, concluded that McLane and Jackson had discussed the matter before the cabinet met. Taney thought allowance should be made for the problem of liaison between the French executive, which drew up treaties, and the French legislature, which made appropriations, and noting that the American government was still involved in war with the Bank, which had recently tightened credit, he urged that this was no time for a war with France.

McLane argued for Jackson's proposal of strong measures, claiming that the French King and his ministers were procrastinating and seeking ultimately to evade any payment because they found it would be unpopular and they did not wish to endanger their government's popularity with the French people. They could have saved the United States from having its bill protested had they cared very much. Now they must be shown that the United States would not quietly submit, and for this purpose letters of marque and reprisal would do very well.

Taney and McLane monopolized the conversation, arguing in particular whether letters of marque would mean war. McLane pointed out that France had recently employed this device against Portugal. Taney protested that though Portugal had submitted, a strong nation like France would not submit to commerce raiding. Jackson interposed a comment only occasionally, but though he avoided giving an opinion, it was evident he was inclined toward McLane's point of view.

After the meeting Taney was worried. He was not so much concerned about the war itself—it could hardly be more than a naval war—as he was about the possibility that warlike measures would shake the faith of Congress in Jackson's prudence and cost him his majority against the Bank. Obviously his arguments, Taney thought, had had little effect on Jackson.

In desperation he sought an interview with the Vice-President, who was soon closeted with Taney in the latter's private office. When he heard about the discussion at the cabinet meeting, Van Buren, true to his normally fearful instincts, took the same view as Taney, that a French war or even only quasi-war could ruin the major program of the administration—and, Van Buren must have also perceived, hurt his chance of succeeding to the Presidency.[141] Even if the Jackson party maintained its standing in the country a war could produce new and rival aspirants to succeed Jackson in 1837.

For a moment events seemed strangely like those of 1798, when naval war had erupted between France and the United States. And just as the events of 1798 had strengthened the Federalists and played into the hands of Hamilton, it seemed possible that the events of 1834 would strengthen a neo-Federalist bloc and play into the hands of one who was a disciple of Hamilton—McLane. How splendid it would be for him if out of the wreck of his domestic policy he could yet rise on the strength of his foreign policy, featuring friendship for England and enmity toward France.

Levi Woodbury, who sensed much and said little, saw the dangers of this situation. He regretted, he wrote, that the action of the French had hurt the party which had hitherto defended the French Revolution—meaning the July Revolution of 1830, probably. The President had never seemed more disappointed nor more resolute to vindicate American rights, and reprisals seemed likely. "We all regret such a prospect," Woodbury added, "except the old enemies of France." [142]

IX   A MILITANT BAFFLED

A man more likely to be able to change prospects than Martin Van Buren was hard to find. After Taney appealed to him, he asked Rives, who had written the French treaty and was acquainted with the French leadership, for his opinion. Rives's response was much to Van Buren's liking, for Rives, too, opposed any violent reprisals, such as attacks on property. He did urge some action, in particular commercial sanctions by increased duties on silk (then free of duty) and other goods not specifically protected by treaty. With the new treaty provisions for French wines, Rives would not interfere, for like McLane, Rives thought it well to show high regard for treaties. The King was sincere, he added, and the deputies did not mean to act in bad faith. As to the latter point, he explained to Van Buren that the opposition in the Chamber of Deputies was based on a misapprehension supported by sophistries which could easily be exploded.[143] Rives also wrote Woodbury, assuring him he had confidence in the course on which enlightened counselors would lead Jackson. He took it for granted that the President would do nothing until Sérurier, the resident minister, had time to present the explanations that his government was known to be sending.[144]

This is precisely what the President decided to do. Sérurier appealed to McLane to delay any action that was contemplated till the French government had an opportunity to send explanations. At the same time he informed Paris that Jackson was extremely irritated and that the opposition leader, Clay, was also excited; drastic action by the American government would have popular support. As it happened, a corvette of the French Navy was already en route to Sérurier with despatches, and with Van Buren and Taney advising moderation Jackson was persuaded to await its arrival.[145]

It was probably fortunate—though not for McLane—that the corvette made a remarkably slow crossing, arriving only on June 2. Sérurier hurried to McLane to express the French government's regrets at the failure of the indemnity appropriation; its assurance that it continued to adhere to the treaty of 1831, calling attention to the speech of Broglie in the Chamber of Deputies in defense of the treaty; its intention of appealing to the new Chamber for passage of the rejected bill at as early a time as possible; and its conviction that a more mature examination would change the minds of many delegates and that the bill would consequently be enacted.[146]

This communication apparently arrived in the middle of the cabinet struggle over whether the United States should insist on reprisals. Sérurier saw McLane on June 4 and presented his explanations in writing on June 5. On May 30 McLane had expected Jackson to send a message to Congress, probably calling for authorization for reprisals by letters of marque, for on that date McLane informed Livingston that he had had the debates on the appropriation in the Chamber of Deputies printed so as to send them to Congress with Jackson's message.[147]

But no message was sent. Van Buren had had several weeks to work on the President, and that was all he needed. "My strong dissent . . . produced momentary embarrassments," Van Buren recalled, years later, "but as between the President and myself they soon disappeared." [148] But while the differences between the President and Van Buren decreased, McLane's embarrassments grew.

This was the last straw. As Secretary of State, he could pretend to ignore the fact that the President pursued a policy of financial management that he vigorously opposed—though as a former Secretary of the Treasury, this course was a hard one for him. But as Secretary of State, it was more than his pride could stand to be overruled on a major matter of foreign policy.[149] Three weeks passed before he responded to Sérurier's note or gave Livingston, who was beginning to fret, any instructions. Sérurier was notified that Jackson had decided to wait until the new Chamber of Deputies had a chance to receive the recommendation of the French government to reconsider the indemnity appropriation—but that the President wished it known he hoped to announce the Chamber's decision to Congress at the opening of its next session in December.[150]

At the same time McLane wrote Livingston at greater length, informing him that the French assurances of their intent to adhere to the treaty were so strong that they could not be altogether rejected, but instructing him to urge the French government to convoke the new Chambers in time to permit Jackson to be informed of their decision before the opening of Congress. "The President cannot and will not . . . permit the next session of Congress to terminate without asking for their definitive and energetic action" if France has not lived up to its obligations. France should be aware that "the responsibility for the consequences will be all its own." [151]

These letters were written by McLane in good faith and drafted with great care, although they announced a decision he had opposed. But by the time they were sent he had made his decision, which was to leave the cabinet but to maintain, outwardly at least, his friendly relations with the administration. His private relations were another matter. He was so angry at the role Van Buren had played in siding with Taney both in the matter of the withdrawal of the deposits and now in the spoliations claims affair that he kept his intentions secret from this man with whom he had previously been on very intimate terms.

McLane handed in his resignation as Secretary of State on Monday, June 16, 1834, but Van Buren knew nothing of it till he arrived at a dinner party given by Mrs. Benjamin Ogle Tayloe a day or two later. Here he saw Mrs. McLane talking to John Sergeant and heard her say, "Well, thank Heaven! it is over at last." Van Buren stopped to ask her what happy deliverance had occurred and was startled when she replied, "Why, I referred, of course, to Mr. McLane's resignation," adding that she was surprised the Vice-President did not know of it.

Seeing Major Donelson, Jackson's secretary, Van Buren asked him to confirm the news. When Donelson did, Van Buren hurried off to see Jackson, who was relieved to learn Van Buren had no intimation in advance of McLane's decision. Jackson had Donelson read McLane's letter of resignation to Van Buren and then a reply which Donelson had just drafted. Van Buren thought the reply Donelson had prepared went too far in conceding errors on the President's part, and Jackson asked Van Buren to rewrite it forthwith, as he did. Donelson did not agree with Van Buren's criticism of his letter but agreed it might be misconstrued. Once the new draft was written, Van Buren completed his work by agreeing with Jackson on John Forsyth as a successor to McLane.

The next day he called on the McLanes, but Louis, though admittedly in his study, never appeared. It was the beginning of a lifelong coldness, for the two men never spoke to each other hereafter. Once they passed in their carriages without recognition, and again at the funeral of General Sam Smith they were close to each other but did not speak. [152]

At least once, possibly as late as 1836, the sentimental President made an effort to heal the rift between McLane and Van Buren. He called upon Senator William R. King, of Alabama, to act as intermediary, but King, though a friend to both men, was unsuccessful. McLane told his son Robert to tell the President that he could not support Van Buren for the Presidency, for he felt that his policies would lead to bankruptcy and ruin of banks and individuals. Bob gave both the President and Senator King the message, and the latter, Bob thought, repeated it to Van Buren. Bob was pleased that Jackson nonetheless sent affectionate greetings to his father.[153]

But Jackson could be gracious in an interview of this sort even though boiling inwardly. In the fall of the election year, angered by some action of Cass's, Jackson revealed his later opinion in a memorandum, "keep me from such advisers as Govr. Branch, Mr. McClain, and Governor Cass." [154]

At the time, however, his natural instincts led Jackson to the side of the fiery McLane rather than that of the calm Van Buren. "I am obliged to forbear for the present a communication to the present Congress," he wrote to Livingston on June 27, 1834, "from the assurances of the French minister here that the Chambers will be called immediately after their elections . . . and that the treaty will be carried into effect. . . . Should I be disappointed in this you will find me speaking to Congress as I ought —I cannot recommend a war thro' the Custom Houses. . . ." [155] In March of 1835 Jackson praised McLane's last letter as Secretary of State by calling it to Livingston's attention.[156]

It is quite likely that Livingston in advising Jackson to raise the tariff was wiser than either McLane or Van Buren. In June, 1834, Livingston alone seems clearly to have foreseen that France would not take any action that could be reported in the United States before the end of the next Congress, and for this reason he recommended an embargo on importations from France. "This can not injure us," he explained, "for we take nothing from France that we cannot do without, and whatever we send, is indispensible for their manufactures." [157] Rives, too, thought some vigorous step was needed to get action from the French.[158]

But neither Livingston nor Rives wished to go as far as Jackson and McLane were willing to go. "I have never had the slightest fear of war," McLane explained, a year and a half after leaving office; "and if I had seen it probable I should have felt rather indifferent, for I conscientiously believe a war would not be as injurious to the country as peace under the reign of the K.C. [Kitchen Cabinet]." [159]

But Van Buren had triumphed, recalling Jackson from any precipitate action in June of 1834. His own view was probably similar to that of Albert Gallatin, that reprisals and war should both be avoided.[160] By letting

Jackson postpone action in the hope, for which he had little basis, that the French legislature would have voted the indemnity appropriation by December, 1834, he was taking a chance that Jackson's fury would be uncontrollable in the winter. But Van Buren was also taking a course that was practical, that would allow him to retain his influence with the President; and in his own wisdom and powers of persuasion Van Buren had enormous confidence.

14

A Chapter on Morris

I   APPOINTMENTS AND REJECTIONS

In leaving office, McLane told Lewis Cass, he took as his model the first Earl of Shaftesbury, who had left all those he had worked with, their concerns, their actions, their purposes, and their counsels, perfectly behind him, so no one "could complain . . . he had any memory of what he had known when one of them." [1]

To behave as a man of honor, to leave office with dignity, was of great importance to McLane. The immediate cause of his resignation was rebuff of his advocacy of a sterner policy toward France (like Hamilton in 1799, he was less patient with the French than his President was willing to be), but the immediate occasion for it was the President's decision to submit McLane's name and the names of all his recess appointees to the Senate for confirmation. There were those who said McLane resigned because he feared he would not be confirmed, but this seems very unlikely. Even the unfriendly Hezekiah Niles termed this report nonsense, adding that McLane would have been confirmed without a division. [2]

Though Martin Van Buren's surprise is evidence that McLane's resignation was not expected at the moment when it came, political gossips had been anticipating it for months. [3] Biddle heard rumors of it throughout the spring, and Lydia Sims, Kitty's sister, reported in May that wherever she went "the first question was, if McLane had resigned." [4] As Van Buren testified, McLane was "never at ease in his official seat" after the withdrawal crisis that led to Duane's ouster in September. [5] He was "among the friends of Jackson, but not of them," as a newspaperman reported. [6]

425

Perhaps the wonder was why McLane had stayed so long rather than why he departed from the cabinet now. He had stayed in office mainly because he was ambitious. In the fall of 1833, after his major defeat in the controversy over the deposits, he had William Read make notes regarding his congressional services—notes that could be very useful if he were a candidate for elective office.[7] But when he was overborne again in June in the crisis over whether to call for reprisals against France, and this time in a matter that fell distinctly within the responsibility of his department, McLane decided that as a man of spirit and honor he could not continue to hold office. He might have withheld his resignation until Congress had adjourned or until he had planned what he would do next, but the fact that his appointment was to go to the Senate determined him to act immediately, a decision that suited his mood and his character anyway.

Jackson's decision to ask for Senate confirmation of his appointments could not very well be put off longer. McLane had been installed as Secretary of State on May 29, 1833, at a time when the Senate was not in session. His appointment should have come before the Senate in the following December or January, but it had been held back because the appointment of a new Attorney General and a Secretary of the Treasury should have been submitted also. McLane and Butler, the Attorney General, would probably have been confirmed as a matter of course, but the Senate, controlled by opponents of the administration who had Clay, Webster, and Calhoun to give them leadership, would certainly not confirm Roger Taney as Secretary of the Treasury, particularly not after he shifted the public deposits from the Bank of the United States to pet banks. The desire to give Taney tenure in his office, the hope that the anger of the Senate would die down, had led Jackson to postpone submission of these appointments to the Senate. Recess appointees could hold appointments without confirmation to the last day of the next session of Congress, and as that day approached, Jackson's enemies began to fear he intended to spurn the Senate altogether and to reappoint his favorites in the next recess, a procedure that they declared unconstitutional.

To John Tyler the President's action in delaying submission of the appointment for several months was in itself obnoxious, "a violation of the true intent of the Constitution as flagrant as any ever committed."[8] Frank Blair attempted to defend Jackson in the *Globe,* but criticism mounted as the congressional session went on through the spring and half the cabinet ministers continued on recess appointments.[9] Daniel Webster, Horace Binney, and Horace Everett, of Vermont, joined in the attack, which included criticism of an appropriation requested for ministers to Britain and Russia though no appointments had been made to these posts since Van Buren's rejection in 1832 and Buchanan's resignation in 1833.[10] To the House of Representatives William Archer, chairman of the Foreign Relations Committee, pledged that "it was the intention of the President, at present, to nominate a minister to England, and also one to Russia, during the present session, unless something should occur in the meantime, connected with the public interests, which, in my judgment, may render it unnecessary."

Archer was very precise about this wording, reading from notes he had taken exactly as the Secretary of State, Louis McLane, had given Jackson's pledge.[11] But the pledge seemed no pledge at all to John Quincy Adams. It is like an oracle, he suggested—like predicting "you will conquer the Romans or the Romans will conquer you." Adams criticized not only the failure to appoint ministers but their failure to stay at their posts for any length of time when they were appointed.

It would not matter so much that the ministers ran home as soon as they signed treaties if their negotiations were indeed successful, argued Adams, but they were not, despite all the panegyrics he heard about the agreements that Jackson's agents had made. Take the British West Indies trade agreement, for instance. Since one of the gentlemen involved with it was now presiding over the other house (Van Buren) and the other gentlemen implicated was now in the State Department (McLane), Adams would not be critical, for he would not wish to speak behind their backs. But let the Representative from Georgia who eulogized this agreement go to that portion of the Union affected by it (Adams probably meant the northeastern ports) and ask people what they thought of it.[12]

Jackson kept the oracular pledge that he made through McLane and Archer, appointing Senator Mahlon Dickerson and Speaker Andrew Stevenson to the Russian and British missions respectively. But as it happened, neither man served under this appointment. Dickerson became Secretary of the Navy instead, and the Senate rejected Stevenson on the very day (June 24) it turned down Roger Taney.[13]

II SO SHORT A TIME

By the date of Stevenson's rejection, Louis McLane's resignation was known. Speculations ranged widely. He was forced out, an enemy thought.[14] He wanted to do something for his family, declared a cabinet colleague.[15] He could no longer reconcile it with his conscience to remain in the administration, guessed the *Intelligencer*, with some truth.[16] Few people suspected the chief reason for the resignation, the disagreement within the administration over French policy. Even Robert McLane in his *Reminiscences* is wrong in ascribing the resignation to his father's disappointment at passage by the House of Representatives of a series of anti-Bank resolutions presented by Polk in defense of removal.[17] The House approved these resolutions on April 4, after McLane had withdrawn one resignation and apparently before he had determined on another. Robert was away at West Point at the time and hardly likely to know all the details, and if he had known them, he still might not have remembered them half a century later when writing his reminiscences.

One of the factors that made it hard for McLane to leave the cabinet was that in doing so he was depriving himself of his best chance of an appointment to the Supreme Court, a prize that he had long desired and that rumor had assigned to him for a year or more.[18] Gabriel Duvall, the octogenarian Marylander whose seat was considered most appropriate for McLane, finally resigned, in January, 1835, but only after he was informed that Taney would be his successor.[19] The Senate would not confirm Taney's appointment to this place, postponing action rather than rejecting him, but later in 1835 Marshall died, and the next Senate, with a Jacksonian majority, approved Taney's appointment to the first judicial position in the land.

It was thus McLane's misfortune to have missed a second major appointment by a narrow margin and after a similar set of circumstances. In 1832 the Senate failed to confirm Van Buren's appointment as minister to Great Britain and Van Buren became Vice-President instead. In 1834 the Senate failed to confirm Taney as Secretary of the Treasury and he became Chief Justice of the United States instead. Those men who became so closely identified with Jackson that an unfriendly Senate took revenge upon them were subsequently given the highest honors at his disposal by a grateful President. McLane, unfortunately for his ambitions, never was enough of a Jacksonian to suffer for it at the hands of the Senate; failing that test, he was not esteemed enough of a Jacksonian to realize the goals of his ambition.

He was, however, permitted to leave office with praise from the administration press. This was against Frank Blair's will, but Senator Silas Wright, probably participating because of his friend Van Buren's known patronage of McLane, persuaded Blair to print in the *Globe* a friendly announcement of the resignation that Donelson had written, referring to the President's "high sense of Mr. McLane's patriotism, talents, and eminent services" and to the "sincere friendship" he bore McLane and his reluctance to yield to the latter's wish to retire.[20]

Blair came later to feel that this paragraph was forced on him for his "estoppel" from any later attack on the resigning Secretary. Van Buren was able to block another document praising McLane and drafted by Donelson from being used as written. It was a letter that was to be sent by the President to the departing Secretary, but before Jackson signed it he had it read to Van Buren, who thought it was weak—too open to be construed as admitting errors on the President's part. Therefore Van Buren took a pen and made changes in the letter (which does not survive) that were probably sufficiently significant to keep McLane from ever making use of it.[21]

Washington society assumed that McLane was leaving office on good terms with the President, just as the *Globe* article claimed.[22] And so he was. On the issue that led McLane to resign, the spoliations controversy, the President was very sympathetic to McLane's view; if he was more willing than McLane to be patient, perhaps it was because he was more secure than McLane.

In reporting the resignation to his son, Van Buren did not say that McLane was parting in good feeling, but merely that, "He insists upon his determination to remain with us (politically)." And in directing his son to see to it that the Regency's Albany newspaper treated McLane kindly, Van Buren probably was motivated less by a desire to help McLane than by a wish to preserve the appearance of a united front before the opposition. "*We shall before long*," he advised Prince John, "get a united and strong cabinet." [23]

Margaret Bayard Smith took a more personal view of events. "Poor Mr. McClane," she commented; "after all the sacrifices of private and domestic comfort, after all his labours and strivings, to retain his hard earned place for so short a time!" [24]

III   STANDING POISED

Seventeen years of public life were at an end on July 21, 1834, when Louis McLane loaded his family and possessions on a Potomac River steamer for the trip to Baltimore.[25] His career had opened before him in the fall of 1817 when he boarded another river steamer at Frenchtown en route to Baltimore. Then Baltimore was a way station on his road to honor and glory, and he had dreamed as he traveled down the Elk River of becoming at once a statesman of national reputation and a gentleman, master of a country estate on the Eastern Shore like his preceptor at the bar, his father's friend James Bayard. On the Potomac, coming home, Baltimore loomed as a way station on the road to security and obscurity —as he hoped in the one case and feared in the other. Much that he sought had been obtained. A measure of fame had been his, the honor of being in the first place in the President's cabinet, the second or third or fourth man in the nation. A country estate had become his, too, but whatever good the possession of Bohemia did to McLane's ego and the quiet of Bohemia to McLane's nerves, it would not support his numerous family. There were eleven children already, and though one, Robert, now at West Point, was no longer much expense, the further education of the girls, for example, Sally, who was at Mme Sigoigne's school in Philadelphia, was a matter of concern. And faithful Kitty was again expecting.

A family of this size and of this standing constituted a pressing demand on Louis McLane to be up and doing. Not for him was there yet the prospect of a dignified retirement to Bohemia's bowers. At fifty he must seek a new career in law or business to replace the prospects he had given up for politics.

Perhaps Baltimore might offer the opportunities he sought. This was the home of his dear old friend Sam Smith, who thought no post too good for McLane, not even the Presidency.[26] Baltimore was also the home of his uncherished new enemy, Roger Taney, to whom the city's ardent Jacksonians were giving a public dinner to express their loyal friendship despite the senatorial rejection of his appointment as Secretary of the Treasury. An invitation was sent to McLane, as to all prominent Jacksonians in Baltimore and many in Washington. Of the latter, few could attend. Van Buren, Woodbury, Barry, and Forsyth sent with their regrets a toast or some other expression of their esteem. McLane's response was curt and unflattering. He was in Baltimore when he replied, and he remained there until July 27, three days after the dinner. "It will be out of my power to accept," he wrote, and Hezekiah Niles, delighted to observe rancor in the enemy camp, termed McLane's response a "cold cut" before dinner.[27]

From Baltimore the McLanes may have traveled to Bohemia, but they did not tarry there and were soon in guest quarters at the spa called Brandywine Springs, near Wilmington, a convenient and healthful place for Kitty to await her accouchement. On September 2 she delivered a late and final addition to the McLane clan, a son who was named James Latimer for his father's old friend.[28]

Meanwhile McLane used Brandywine Springs as an eminence from which to survey the future. At first the unaccustomed rest and relaxation, together with the chagrin he had been storing for months past, encouraged him to talk freely. Robert Walsh, the wealthy and cultivated Baltimorean who had become a Philadelphia editor, came to the Springs, conversed with McLane, and was so delighted with what he heard that he concluded McLane should be made President. "There must be a dinner got up for McLean in Philadelphia," Walsh told Samuel Jaudon and Samuel Jaudon told Nicholas Biddle.[29]

No dinner had been "got up" for McLane in Wilmington, but Wilmington, alas, was in the hands of Democrats of strong anti-Bank convictions. At best, McLane seemed a controversial character they could hardly take up with impunity—at least not until they saw what his course would now be. And the other Delaware party, the Whigs, though the Bank party, was composed of McLane's old enemies, including the Claytons, men he had spurned in 1827 when he bent all his efforts at the erection of a Jackson party. Some Delawareans did not dare honor McLane as a fallen statesman; others did not care to honor him, however sympathetic they might be with his position on the Bank.

At Brandywine Springs, McLane found himself in a more sympathetic circle than he could find elsewhere in Delaware. The owner of the resort was Matthew Newkirk, a wealthy New Jerseyman, who was a director of the Bank of the United States and therefore predisposed to friendliness toward McLane. No expense had been spared by Newkirk after he took over the Springs in 1833. Thomas V. Walter had been hired as architect to remodel the hotel; John Stewart had been procured to landscape the grounds. Running water was piped into the hotel and to fountains on the lawn. Opposite the hotel, basically a four-story Greek revival parthenon, with a row of dormers and a captain's walk, Newkirk had an Italianate palace built for himself, flanked on either side by a small temple cottage for his children's families.[30]

Under Newkirk's care, the Springs were fit for a prince, and late in the summer a prince arrived to sample the fare. This was Nicholas Biddle, a prince of taste and of finance, recently home from a Newport holiday, who graced a gathering of invited guests at the Springs that included most of the directors of his bank.

"We know a hawk from a handsaw," wrote the editor of the anti-Bank *Pennsylvanian*, who saw the occasion as a Whig convention to uncover a new presidential prospect to replace such old favorites as Clay, Webster, Calhoun, Benjamin Watkins, Leigh of Virginia, and Judge John McLean.[31] The *Pennsylvanian* and other elements of the Jackson press stood poised, ready to loose a broadside against McLane, but publicly he kept his peace and gave the journalistic bombardiers no opportunity.[32] "He must . . . best understand his own position," declared Biddle, regretting McLane's decision to preserve silence.[33]

His own position, McLane knew, was one that required his best efforts to extricate his affairs and provide properly for his family. The birth of her last child had left Kitty weak, too weak to spend a winter in the country at Bohemia. So McLane rented a snug, small house in Wilmington for the winter, intending to set his affairs in order before deciding on his future course. "I have every reason to know," he assured Lewis

Cass, "that I could very soon, with little or no effort, regain all my professional business here, and also any political object that I might desire." But he did not care to make the effort. "I find the law practice in Del. lower than I could have believed it possible," he wrote Buchanan. The practice of his profession, in Delaware, at least, held no charms for him, and he denied having any "popular political ambition," though he admitted "too many partialities and friendships" to refrain from taking a hand in any political row that was "knocked up." [34]

He protested too much. The plain truth of the matter was that he had few friends left in Delaware.[35] The local Jackson party rode with the winning faction in national politics. Its organ, the *Delaware Gazette,* lauded Taney at the same time that it reprinted the *Pennsylvanian's* aspersions on McLane. It hailed James Bayard, McLane's onetime protégé, now a candidate for Congress, as an "uncompromising" foe of the Bank.[36]

A compromising friend of the Bank like McLane could hardly endorse such a candidate, particularly after Bayard and his friends in the Delaware democracy had refused to support McLane in his cabinet quarrels or even to offer him a dinner upon his retirement. If they chose Taney and Van Buren, so be it; they could then expect no help from McLane.[37]

Nor could he link arms with his old enemies in the Whig camp. Henry Ridgely assured Sam Smith that John M. Clayton would support McLane for President, but talk was cheap when a nomination was unlikely.[38] For his part McLane did not easily forgive old foes like the Claytons, nor did his regard for old Democratic friends, including the President himself, allow him "to give countenance to their enemies." [39]

Perhaps McLane still retained some small hope of a judicial appointment. Justice William Johnson, of South Carolina, died in the summer of 1834, and one Southerner suggested to Van Buren that McLane could be a worthy successor to the place if he would move to Georgia.[40] Van Buren, however, advised Jackson to use the opportunity to enlarge some of the old circuits and establish a new circuit in the West, a plan that left no place for McLane.[41] Johnson's place eventually went to James M. Wayne, of Georgia, and the expected vacancy in McLane's home circuit was, as has been said, saved for Taney.

That the expectation of deaf Gabrial Duvall's resignation was on McLane's mind is proved by a letter McLane sent to Buchanan in November, 1834, in which McLane claimed to be the victim of "a scheme of . . . duplicity and turpitude" involving men who feared "that the President might not be disposed wholly to forget our relations, and his own often repeated assurances, in filling up the vacancy which Judge Duvall's resignation will soon make on the bench!" [42]

But the President was now disposed to forget his "often repeated assurances," and the blame for this forgetfulness was fastened by McLane on his erstwhile friend, Van Buren. The thought that this latter aspirant to the purple might be defeated by "simple, honest, open and republican" Judge Hugh White of Tennessee delighted McLane, who forgot his ancient loyalty to Crawford, a caucus candidate, in denouncing successions arranged by caucus or cabal, as Van Buren's was.[43] Van Buren himself was uneasy about the depth of McLane's prejudice against him and the finality of the rupture in their relations; Henry D. Gilpin, visiting Washington, found the Vice-President very inquisitive about the McLanes and their plans.[44] Van Rensselaer was another who, like Gilpin, maintained contact with both of these rivals. McLane, however, found the Patroon "too much a VB–ite" for confidences, and to the question, "When I had [heard] from VB.," McLane answered, "Not since I quit W[ashington] and had no great desire ever to see him again." [45]

The schism that ended the once close relations between McLane and James Bayard was due not merely to Bayard's adherence to Van Buren and Taney. Bayard also challenged McLane by joining his sister and brother in a suit in chancery, in which they claimed a share of McLane's inheritance from the Amelia Island cases. A moiety or half of the double duties paid on the cargoes of two of the ships that the collector had seized in 1812 was finally awarded by the United States Supreme Court in January, 1832, to Louis McLane, as heir to his father's claim. But the Bayards then instituted suit for a share of the money on the basis of a contract the senior James A. Bayard had made with old Collector McLane. Bayard was to share in the award for his efforts in the case. His death in 1815, his heirs claimed, did not destroy the contract, and Richard Bayard began to press his claim on Louis McLane in February, 1832, immediately after McLane was awarded half of the double duties. Expensive outside counsel, including Reverdy Johnson for the Bayards, John Sergeant and William Meredith and Walter Jones for McLane, were eventually drawn into the case, in which a sum running into the tens of thousands of dollars was involved, but no final decision was reached until the winter of 1840–41. Then McLane's rights were upheld, but meanwhile, in 1834 and 1835, when McLane was seeking a new career that would enable him to support his large family, the threat this suit posed to his inheritance was very real.[46]

Like McLane, his friend Washington Irving refused any part in politics in the fall of 1834. The Jackson party in New York appealed to Irving to run for Congress, but he declined "mingling in any way in the feuds of party, not even giving a vote." It was the "coarseness and vulgarity and dirty trick[s]" of politics of which Irving complained,[47] though very likely his continued close adhesion to the McLane family and his observance, through them, of how politics could distort a career and destroy a friendship cooled the ardor for public affairs that had once kept Irving in Washington through a congressional season.

Irving's fondness for the McLanes, or at least for some of them, continued through the early years after Louis retired from politics. In June Irving was in Philadelphia and saw Sally at her school, where he begged the family to continue her. She "has grown finely, . . . looks charmingly, . . . and is improving in her studies," he wrote, adding that she thought the family lacked confidence in her in giving her no intimation of her father's intent to resign. Sally was the family beauty, but Irving did not forget his friend, her elder sister. He complained that Rebecca owed him one or two letters but supposed she was "so much immersed in politics and entangled with foreign and domestic relations that she has no time to think of any one out of Washington." [48]

Whether Irving visited the McLanes in the winter of 1834 is doubtful, but in July, 1835, he traveled to Wilmington to see them, and meanwhile he had given a singular pledge of his affection for McLane: "I have lately become a bank director!" he wrote his brother. "This was for the sake and at the solicitation of Mr. McLane, who has taken the presidency of the Morris Canal and Banking Company, with a salary of six thousand dollars." [49]

IV THE MORRIS CANAL AND BANKING COMPANY

The Morris Canal and Banking Company was but ten years old when McLane was elected its president on May 5, 1835. The canal that it operated had two primary purposes: (1) to enrich northern New Jersey, through which it passed, and (2) to connect the coalfields of northeastern Pennsylvania with the port of New York. Its sponsors, however, had found themselves without sufficient political influence to secure a charter when they first applied to the New Jersey legislature in 1822 and 1823. Thereupon they made common cause with some merchants endeavoring to secure a banking charter, and the new canal company was floated through the New Jersey legislature on a bank. [50]

Such a combination was not unique. In New York the Bank of the Manhattan Company was a combination of a bank and a water company. The Delaware and Hudson Canal Company, chartered in New York in 1823, had banking privileges for twenty years. There was a Central Railway and Banking Company in Georgia, a Southwestern Railroad Bank in South Carolina, a Canal and Banking Company in Louisiana, a Blackstone Canal Bank in Rhode Island, a Texas Railroad, Navigation, and

Banking Company—some predating the Morris and others established later. New Jersey had previous experience with such double-purpose enterprises, having recently incorporated the New Jersey Manufacturing and Banking Company, the Salem Steam-Mill and Banking Company, and the Hoboken Banking and Grazing Company.[51]

The Morris was unusual among canals in that it received no direct financial assistance from the state government. It raised all its own money by private subscriptions, but fell into the hands of speculators, and in 1826 four of its directors resigned after indictment for conspiracy to defraud. Despite this and other future scandals that eventually made "curses on Morris" a familiar Wall Street expletive, the company in 1831 completed its canal from the Delaware at Phillipsburg to Newark, where there were natural maritime connections with New York. En route the canal crossed rugged country, climbing nine hundred feet above sea level at Lake Hopatcong, higher than any other canal. For the heights it crossed, the Morris employed a series of ingenious inclined planes on which the canal barges were hauled up and over summits that seemed too expensive to grade down to water level. Altogether twenty-three planes and twenty-three locks were built along the ninety miles of the original canal.[52]

By the spring of 1835 the Morris, which had never yet paid a dividend, needed new money for enlargement and extension, struggled to meet payments on a foreign loan secured by a mortgage, and had still to realize its hope of developing a profitable banking business. Strong, able leadership was an obvious necessity.

Enlargement and extension were necessary because the dimensions of the canal were too narrow for barges carrying the most economical payloads, and because expensive transshipments were required from Newark to New York since the bay was too rough for canal barges. Eventually these deficiencies were corrected by widening the canal and extending it from Newark across Bergen Neck to Jersey City, providing a terminal on the Hudson directly opposite New York.[53]

Although originally oversubscribed, the Morris faced financial problems as soon as the initial enthusiasm was spent, for the subscribers reneged on their payments. As was usual in such enterprises, costs were greater than expected and revenues were smaller. Among the devices adopted to save the company was a loan of $750,000 secured in 1830 from a Dutch banker, Willem Willink, Jr., on a mortgage of the canal, and this loan and mortgage remained a threat to the financial well-being of the company throughout the brief administration of Louis McLane.

In January, 1835, a few months before McLane's administration began, a group of speculators effected a corner on Morris stock, driving its price up from 32 to 188 in less than a year. This first famous—or infamous—corner in Wall Street history collapsed when the Board of Brokers, on grounds of conspiracy, freed sellers of their engagements to produce stock. However, the price of Morris stock stayed reasonably high and the company was able to dispose of the forfeited stock it had repossessed as well as a new issue of $1 million.[54]

Gradually attention turned from the canal to the banking operations that the company conducted, ostensibly from its official headquarters in Jersey City, but really from its true headquarters in New York. The Morris charter gave the company broad banking and investment powers. It could issue notes, hold trusts, buy and sell securities for itself or on commission. At a time when restraining laws limited the number of companies that could engage in banking in New York state and preserved a monopolistic situation for existing banks and such would-be bankers as possessed enough political influence to secure charters from the legislature—at such a time the Morris Canal and Banking Company, as a Jersey corporation with remarkably broad powers, became very attractive to the merchants of New York and seemed to have great potential usefulness.[55]

In 1835 a group of these New York merchants took control of the Morris and invited Louis McLane to become its president. Perhaps Nicholas Biddle had something to do with McLane's appointment. Martin Van Buren certainly thought so. "He obtained," Van Buren wrote of McLane and his appointment to the Morris presidency, "thro' the direct influence of [Biddle], a position which afforded him for several years a liberal salary with little labor." [56] The reference to "little labor" is gratuitous and unfair. Van Buren was writing decades after the event, and he probably remembered very little about the problems faced by the Morris, if he ever had understood them. Van Buren's reference to Biddle's influence may be equally unjustified. Certainly there is little direct evidence connecting Biddle with McLane's appointment, though there is much evidence to show Biddle's interest in the Morris after McLane became its president. Charles Augustus Davis, a friendly correspondent of Biddle's, apparently knew of no possible Biddle connection with the offer to McLane when he wrote Biddle from New York on April 17, 1835, to explain that "A circle of Gentlemen here desirous of securing for Mr. McLane—(late Secy of Treasy) a situation in this quarter—are about taking hold of the 'Morris Canal and Banking Co.' as Directors and placing Mr. McLane at the head of it as President." [57] The gentlemen sought Davis to join them on the board of the Morris, but he eventually turned them down, preferring to stay on the board of the New York branch of the Bank of the United States rather than he connected with an enterprise of soiled reputation, even though it now had respectable direction.[58]

The most likely explanation is that Nicholas Biddle recommended McLane to the New York merchants who were taking over the Morris and attempting to clean its tarnished reputation, but that Biddle himself lacked the power to place McLane in the Morris position. The usefulness of the Morris to Biddle seems to have become apparent only after McLane's appointment to its presidency. Six months later, indeed, in November, 1835, his cousin Edward R. Biddle informed Nicholas that the Morris charter was very comprehensive and could possibly be used to great advantage as a means of extending or supporting the power of the Bank of the United States when the latter institution lost its federal charter. "The circumstances of this Institution," by which Edward Biddle meant the Morris, "having hitherto been unpopular and unprofitable opens the Door wide to make a good bargain." [59]

A correspondent warned Van Buren of the possibility that Edward Biddle saw. The stockholders and former directors of the Morris, Van Buren's correspondent wrote, induced a number of rich, respectable men to become directors, perhaps by giving them stock at a very low price, and the next step was to buy out the New York branch of the Bank of the United States.[60]

One of the great advantages of the Morris Canal Bank to New York merchants was its branch in New York City. Such interstate banking was unusual but, like other features of the Morris, not unique. Another New Jersey bank, the State Bank of Camden, opened a Philadelphia agency shortly after securing a charter in 1812.[61] The Bank of the United States, of course, had branches in New York and elsewhere.

But in these other cases, the branches were only branches, whereas in the case of the Morris the branch was the tail that wagged the dog. It was to New York, not to Jersey City or any other point in New Jersey, that Louis McLane came when he was being interviewed about the Morris presidency in the spring of 1835. And it was from New York that he sent home to Kitty announcement of his acceptance. "My destiny," he wrote, "for good or for ill, is fixed. The company is now under good auspices and appears to be rising gradually and surely into public confidence." Most important, the salary of $6,000 was "fixed with a liberal cordiality and there appears to be with the new directors, and indeed, with the old and the community generally a kindly disposition towards me, and a desire to promote my fortunes." [62] It was ironical that after fleeing from the cabinet McLane should wind up as a banker in Van Buren's state.

V   MUTUAL ATTRACTIONS

Up to this time McLane apparently was intending to recommence the practice of law in Wilmington—probably because he had no other good alternative. A Wilmington gossip, Sally Black, who passed on this rumor, spoke of McLane's intention to reopen his law office as a "dernier resort." [63] One advantage, however, that Louis McLane could derive from a Wilmington location was the opportunity to take his family for long visits on their Bohemia estate and to see that this estate, which he had long looked to as a quiet retreat, was put back in order.[64]

Meanwhile, as he marked time through the fall and winter of 1834–35 McLane had begun to involve himself once again in local activities. When the Newark Academy, which he had attended, was at long last given a college charter in 1833, McLane became a member of the new board of trustees; and in September of 1834, after he had returned to Delaware, he was appointed chairman of an ad hoc committee appointed to inquire into the details of a student rebellion.[65] Louis, his second son, was duly entered as a student at the college in November, 1834, as was his cousin George Read McLane, but there must have been embarrassment when Louis was expelled from this institution on February 23, 1835 —for profanity and intemperance,[66] according to rumor. The rumor seems likely, because the boy was rushed off into the Navy as a midshipman, and his mother, writing him, urged that he should, "for once, reflect upon the necessity of obedience and strict attention to . . . duty." [67] To add to the parents' embarrassment, a still younger son, George, was expelled in May from Miss Smith's elementary class of twenty-three pupils which met in the session room of the Presbyterian church, his expulsion being, in one contemporary's opinion, "a very necessary step for the good of her little charge[s]." [68] Louis settled down in time and had a very distinguished career, but poor George never made out. He had one failure after another until finally he was killed chasing an Indian band in New Mexico.

In March the McLanes left one rented house in Wilmington and moved to another, near the Market Street mansion where they used to live, across the street from Miss Milligan, Kitty's aunt and former guardian. Kitty resumed her place in her old world, probably with far greater ease than the prouder Louis. In January her Eastern Shore neighbor Phoebe Bradford saw her at a benefit concert by blind musicians and remarked she was very civil and not much changed; in April at Kentmere, Joshua Gilpin's mansion, Kitty was all civility, but the Wilmington editor, Moses Bradford, left the house to avoid her.[69]

Louis McLane's brother, the ne'er-do-well doctor, was also on the scene, having moved back to Wilmington in 1834 to reopen his practice there. To everyone's surprise he found someone willing to share his burdens when, late in February, 1835, by a marriage ceremony performed in Baltimore, Anna Pearce, an Eastern Shore acquaintance of the Milligans, became Dr. Allen McLane's second wife.[70]

None of these connections was of a sort to endear Wilmington to Louis McLane, and he must have welcomed the opportunity to move to New York. The one regret he may have had was in putting so many miles between himself and Bohemia, but he hoped his new position would bring him the means to stock this estate for the future. At the moment, when even his inheritance was being challenged in court, he needed money to support his family in the fashion he desired for it—the fashion a former Secretary of State's family might expect.

"If the concern succeed," he wrote Kitty about the Morris, "we may have comfort and wealth; and if it fail something else may grow out of it. . . . Six thousand dollars will be an ample income here for a decent mode of living, and I do not doubt that we may occupy the best stand in the best society—So that our children will now have the advantages of a liberal community and of future advantageous employment." [71]

Six thousand dollars was indeed a good salary and is a measure of the desire of the company to secure McLane's services. There is no doubt that it was the salary that was the primary attraction of the job to McLane. He could now afford to educate his children, however his suit with the Bayards came out. As a first measure in this respect, he planned to take young Louis out of the Navy, but he was too late. When he arrived in New York to accept the position, he found Louis's ship had sailed for Brazil the day before.[72] By such a narrow margin did this son enter on a career that led him from naval service to interests in shipping, the express business, banking, and railroads.

If it is obvious what attracted McLane to the Morris, it is equally obvious what it was about McLane that made the company eager to engage his services. His name was an advantage to them because, like the names of the new directors, it would help give respectability to an enterprise in danger of having none. But McLane was not of mere figurehead importance to the Morris. He had an excellent reputation as a man of affairs, as one who got things done, whether in congressional committees, in a London legation, or in a cabinet ministry. He was a mover and a doer, and he made a good impression on the people who worked with him. At this very time George Ticknor, an American abroad, was dining at Holland House in London in the usual distinguished company there when Lord Melbourne, the Prime Minister, spoke of American ministers he had known and in particular of Van Buren and the likelihood of his becoming the next President. "He said he was a pleasant and agreeable man," Ticknor noted in his journal, "but he did not think him so able as Mr. McLane, who preceded him." [73]

VI   PROBLEMS OF THE MORRIS

Louis McLane presided at his first Morris board meeting on May 15, 1835, at the New York office of the company, 21 Wall Street.[74] For the next several months Louis stayed in New York alone. Kitty would occasionally come to New York to visit with him, bringing some of the children, but she divided her time between Wilmington and Bohemia until the summer, preparing to leave the one place, where Dr. McLane and his bride were to take over her house, and seeking to improve the other. At the end of August Louis returned to Wilmington to look into the progress of his chancery suit with the Bayards and to spend some days at Bohemia with his own family as well as with Kitty's brother George Milligan, who had come with his second wife on a visit from Louisiana. Then all the McLanes moved to New York, where Louis had rented a house at 1 Greenwich Street, near the Battery. It was intended to enroll young Allan in the grammar school connected with Columbia College, but in the end he and George were left at Bullock's school in Wilmington. Bob, at West Point, was now closer to the family circle than he had been, and though he was not entirely happy with the military life it was decided to leave him where he was at least another year so that he could profit by training as an engineer.[75]

Not all elements in New York welcomed McLane. His acceptance of the Morris presidency was the occasion for a blistering attack from the editor of the New York *Evening Post*, who reminded Democrats of McLane's opposition to the President's course in the Bank War and went on to find all manner of flaws in the proceedings of the Morris, accusing the new directors of selling the use of their names and reputations in return for an opportunity to buy Morris stock below market price. When the directors published a resolution of gratitude to their retiring president, James B. Murray, the *Post* ridiculed the statement, declaring that Murray was so far from a success as president that the company had paid him to resign. Yet angry as the *Post* was, it could find no specific fault with McLane other than to charge him with duplicity in statements he had released to the press regarding the location of the New York custom house.[76]

Even in its anger, the *Post* confirmed the value to the Morris of the reputations of McLane and the new members of the board. Two who were elected to the board on May 5, the same day as McLane, were Jonathan Goodhue and Henry Hicks. Goodhue, the son of a Senator, was a native of Salem, Massachusetts, who had moved to New York and founded Goodhue and Company, one of the major general commission businesses of the city, with agents all over the world. Hicks was a member of a shipping firm founded by his father, who till his death in 1830 had been a principal sponsor of the Liverpool packet line.

Other directors were of similar background. John Crary was a leading dry goods merchant; George Griswold, a tea importer and real estate speculator; John Haggerty, senior partner in New York's largest auction house; Daniel Jackson, a government contractor for Indian supplies; Joseph L. Joseph, a New York agent for the Rothschilds; Stephen Whitney, a New York merchant of Connecticut origins; Samuel R. Brooks and Edwin Lord, merchants whose offices faced each other on William Street; and Henry Yates, a junior partner in the firm of Yates and McIntyre, lottery managers, in which his brother, John B. Yates, was the senior partner. Archibald McIntyre, of the same firm, presided at the meeting of the Morris board at which Louis McLane was elected to the presidency and then resigned at the next meeting to make room for a new director.

Only four of the fifteen directors of the Morris who formed McLane's first board did not fall into the single category of New York merchants. One was McLane himself. Another was John Moss, a merchant, but a Philadelphian rather than a New Yorker. A third was Peter M. Ryerson, of Pompton, New Jersey, who was engaged in his family's iron business. The fourth was Washington Irving.[77]

Clearly the Morris was under New York control in the spring of 1835 when McLane assumed its presidency. And despite the fact that the canal was being extended to Jersey City to put it closer to New York, it seems clear that the New York directors cared more about the Morris as a bank than as a canal. One of the ablest New York financiers, Robert Lenox, credited McLane with insisting on a first-class board as a condition to his accepting a post with the Morris.[78] But New York direction was not new to this company. The retiring acting president, James B. Murray, who received a salary of $2,500 a year pro-rated for the period of his administration and who now resigned from the board when he left the presidency, was a New Yorker. Most of the other men who left the board in the spring of 1835 to make way for new directors were New Yorkers. The previous president, Cadwallader Colden, who had died on February 7, 1834, was a New Yorker—in fact, he had served several terms in the New York legislature and had been mayor of New York from 1818 to 1820. But in Colden's time things were different with the Morris. New Yorker or not, he had lived in New Jersey while president of the Morris and died in Jersey City. And he was primarily interested in transportation and internal improvements, rather than banking, and was the author of a life of Robert Fulton.[79]

The climactic step in this transformation of the Morris from a canal primarily to a bank primarily, from a local institution to an enterprise with a national, even an international view, had occurred on May 5, 1835, the day McLane was elected to the presidency, when the Morris board of directors also agreed to rent an office on Wall Street, next to the National Bank. Since Albert Gallatin was president of the latter company (which, despite its name, was not one of New York's larger banks), it seems symbolic that these two former ministers to England and Secretaries of the Treasury, an old Republican and an old Federalist, were thus made Wall Street neighbors. The nineteenth century apparently made the money market more attractive for some old politicians than the hustings.

Yet for the moment it was the canal that attracted the attention of the new president of the Morris. He found eighty-eight new boats contracted for when he came into office, a necessary step because the Morris Canal was so narrow that boats used elsewhere would not fit it.[80] Originally it had been thought that the company would provide only the canal and others would supply boats, but soon it was seen that if the full potential of the canal was to be realized, particularly in view of the encouragement the Morris brought to manufacturing and commerce in northern New Jersey, it was up to the Morris management to provide some barges and operate them.[81]

Another immediate problem of the canal was to acquire a basin for the docking of boats and the landing of cargoes at the new canal terminus that would be located at Jersey City when the extension of the Morris Canal was completed.[82] Before contracts for the new basin were let, McLane in late May and early June traveled the length of the canal, from the Hudson to the Delaware and then up the Lehigh to Mauch Chunk, where the cargoes of coal the Morris anticipated first became waterborne.[83] On his return he reported to his board on the state of the canal and its locks and planes, with various suggestions for improvements and repairs, for increased water supply, for the reconstruction of boats, and for "greater Oeconomy in the employment of lock and plane tenders."[84] Probably as the result of this trip, the board authorized McLane to negotiate with the Lehigh Company to "enlarge" the existing contract for coal transportation.[85]

The company hoped that necessary repairs could be covered by the proceeds from a new issue of stock, authorized in January and subscribed to before McLane took office; the subscriptions were to be paid as called for, 25 percent at a time.[86] A mortgage held by Yates and McIntyre was paid off by having the cashier call in a sufficient number of 5 percent loans.[87] The Dutch loan was a greater problem. Hope of paying it off had to be deferred for other needs, such as purchases of rolled and cast iron, probably for the planes, and construction of a new feeder canal from Long Pond, now Greenwood Lake, where McLane and three other directors traveled on an inspection trip.[88]

One function of the Morris is to be observed in the decision to accept a new deposit of $100,000 from John S. Crary, a director, as a demand deposit on five days' notice, with 5 percent interest to be paid per annum. Crary, who had already deposited another $100,000, was to receive a certificate for the money. The presence of a note on this transaction in the minutes—and the lack of any similar notices—indicates that this was an unusual occurrence.[89]

Despite new emissions, new deposits, new directors, new plans, and a new president, the bad reputation of the Morris was hard to live down. In refusing a seat on the Morris board, Charles Augustus Davis referred to "Some Circumstances indicative of bad faith—or *bad taste*," and declared he preferred a directorship in another company that was "clean and new," adding, in an obvious contrast of this second company to the Morris, "tho' it may grow old I sh'd hope it will not grow dirty." [90]

Morris Canal stock, though temporarily banned from the Board of Exchange after the attempted corner early in 1835, was traded actively as the summer wore on.[91] It was a season of overtrading, observers thought.[92] Morris stock was reported at a high of 93¼ on September 17 but reached a low of 72 ten days later.[93] Among various rumors on the exchange was one published by James Gordon Bennett to the effect that the Bank of the Manhattan Company was negotiating to buy the New York branch of the Bank of the United States.[94] However, just at the time that Bennett concluded that the United States Bank branch was not for sale, the Morris began to negotiate for it. McLane and a committee of three directors were ordered to propose a scheme of using the personal guaranty of members of the Morris board as security for a purchase offer, and McLane and Joseph L. Joseph were authorized on October 12 to conduct the negotiation.[95] They went to Philadelphia and met with a United States Bank committee to whom they proposed taking over "the whole of the discounted debt, the loans and other Securities and Specie" at the New York branch, offering bonds or post notes in payment, to be guaranteed, as aforesaid, by members of the Morris board individually. The banking house in New York was to be included if the United States Bank wished to dispose of it.[96]

This was a bold effort to lift the Morris Canal Bank immediately into a commanding position where its very liberal charter could be fully utilized. But it failed. As the possibility of keeping the United States Bank in business through a Pennsylvania state charter grew more likely, Biddle and his cohorts felt it desirable, while shutting down minor branches, to keep their agency in the city that had become the nation's commercial capital. Besides, the security offered by the Morris did not seem acceptable, at least not to Robert Lenox, a leading member of the branch's directorship. The legislature, he wrote, "certainly will not allow them to bank here." On the other hand, "the Manhattan could and would buy but God forbid it should fall into such hands." [97]

Lenox probably was revolted by the fact that the White family, dominating the Manhattan Company bank, were associated with Democratic party politics, one member, Campbell White, being a New York Congressman. Van Buren, on the other hand, was being warned at the same time that the Morris was conducted by his enemies, and he was entreated to block an effort it was making to acquire government deposits. Unsafe, its stock greatly inflated, it was a creature of the Josephs and the Biddles, who were linked in a variety of speculations—a connection noted also by a correspondent of the *Globe*.[98] The Morris pleaded for a deposit "as due to New Jersey," continued Van Buren's friend, "but if New Jersey is to be benefited then give the Banks in New Jersey deposits and Not a Bank . . . smuggled into New York in Wall Street paying no tax nor subject to any of our laws, and directed by New York men and their Stock owned by Stock Jobbers *entirely*." "This institution," he charged, "has never made a [dividend] and from their business are never likely to make one." [99]

Under McLane the Morris would make a dividend, but the rest of the indictment seems fair. The Morris had applied to be made a deposit bank for government funds and had sent a delegation to Washington to plead its case. The delegation did not include McLane, undoubtedly in recognition of the fact that he had enemies in the cabinet, but did originally include Washington Irving, who refused the assignment.[100]

But the mission was sent in vain. The known connection of the Biddles with the Morris, of whatever sort it was, surely was enough to defeat the bid of the Morris to become a pet bank of the government. And at this moment Nicholas Biddle was strongly interested in the Morris, with the encouragement of his cousin Edward R. Biddle, who pointed out that the charter of the Morris conveyed "trust powers, full powers to borrow money, etc.," and that the Morris had over a million dollars worth of forfeited stock "that responsible capitalists can get on favorable terms." Even the canal, hitherto unproductive, was likely to yield a profit in the future, according to statistics Edward Biddle had for receipts in the last three years: 1833, $27,300; 1834, $48,000; 1835, $70,000 (estimated).[101]

VII   LOBBYING IN TRENTON

Before winter forced the closing of the canal, McLane, with a committee of the board of directors, made another trip along it. On the committee's recommendation it was agreed to use the winter months for alterations that would decrease the number of accidents and delays on the inclined planes. November 10, an earlier date than usual, was set for the closing, so that there would be time to have the planes in operation by spring. It was also agreed that the New Jersey legislature should be asked to authorize construction of the new feeder and grant a number of other privileges, including the right to open a banking office in Newark.[102]

The decision to go to the New Jersey legislature may have seemed rash. This same fall, in October, 1835, Governor Peter Vroom had warned the legislators that from past experience with banks, all petitions for new banking establishments should be regarded with jealousy, and he congratulated the members of the last assembly for their rejection of the only petition of this sort that they received. Other voices informed the legislators that banking corporations should be disallowed because they were privileged monopolies, subversive of democracy.[103]

Nevertheless, the Morris directors proceeded with their plans, and their petition, prepared by a committee consisting of Samuel R. Brooks, Edwin Lord, and Henry Yates, was presented to the legislature on January 15, 1836.[104] There were four main points to the petition: (1) that the company be permitted to construct a feeder canal to Long Pond and to charge tolls on it; (2) that the company be allowed to sell the water used to operate its inclined planes to anyone needing water power for manufacturing; (3) that the board of directors be made self-perpetuating in order to give greater security to anyone depositing funds in trust with the company; and (4) that it be allowed to open a branch bank in Newark.[105]

Legislative committees viewed the petition favorably, but opposition soon became evident. Manufacturers feared that the Morris would monopolize water rights. The idea of a board that was self-perpetuating (that is, not elected by stockholders) aroused opposition.[106] To stifle possible objections in Newark to the projected branch, McLane was directed by the trustees to promise that the Morris would allocate to the Newark branch any funds it was permitted to raise by sale of new stock for its banking operations.[107]

As the legislative struggle reached the critical stage two additional

directors, Peter M. Ryerson and Henry Hicks, the former the only New
Jerseyman in the group, were sent to Trenton to reinforce the original
lobbying committee with authorization to hire the prominent New Jersey
lawyer David B. Ogden as their counsel and to bring along McLane's
predecessor in the presidency, James B. Murray, for whatever help he
could offer. McLane himself was busy negotiating agreements on water
rights with various manufacturers, as a means of softening their opposition, but in February he, too, was off to Trenton.[108] "We have a new
member of the lobby," Governor Vroom reported to a friend; "I mean
Louis McLane, the President of the Morris Canal and Banking Company.
That Co[mpan]y is, as usual, asking new favors, and some of them this
year are rather of an extraordinary character, insomuch that the Legislature, tho' rather good natured, hesitate; and I believe they will fail for
once." [109]

The special correspondent of the Newark *Daily Advertiser* was in
agreement with Governor Vroom that the fate of the Morris Canal bill
was doubtful though the legislature was not unfriendly.[110] Yet to his
surprise, the bill was passed—without provision for a branch bank at
Newark, for that was deleted in the upper house of the legislature, but
with most of the requested changes. These were not granted exactly as
requested—some limitations were placed on the new privileges that were
granted—but on the whole the new bill pleased the company very well
indeed. The feeder from Long Pond was authorized, along with tolls on
it and on other feeder canals. The water used on the inclined planes could
be employed also to work other machinery between Newark and the
village of Boonton, but the Morris itself was forbidden to enter any
manufacturing business. The board of directors was rearranged and
enlarged to consist of twenty-three persons, named in the bill, who were
to be divided into five classes. The terms of directors of one class would
expire each year, and their reelection or replacement would then be up
to the stockholders. Since not more than one fifth of the directors were
to be chosen in any one year, there was a new assurance of continuity
in the direction of the company. And since the legislature named every
one of the existing fifteen-man board to the new directorship of twenty-
three (with McLane's name leading all the rest) the new arrangement
provided stability.

The legislature did add a New Jersey flavor to the board by naming
seven Jerseymen to the eight new places. (James B. Murray, of New York,
the former president, was the eighth new member.) It also provided that
the new arrangement of the board must be approved within a month
by three fourths of the stockholders, in number and in amount of stock.

Furthermore, the New Jersey supreme court was given the right to remove any director against whom a complaint was raised.

As a further favor to the Morris, it was permitted to issue 6,000 new shares of stock to sell at $100 each to finance land purchases and new construction of reservoirs, basins, and feeders. None of the new funds could be used for banking purposes, however, and a new limit was placed on these activities by limitation of the bank note issue to $2 million. An attempt to reduce the limit to $1 million was defeated in the lower house, and the new limit did not seem very confining when the outstanding notes amounted to only $70,000. One final method of public control was introduced by a provision that at any time the legislature chose, an investigation of Morris affairs could be carried out by a special three-member ad hoc commission.[111]

In the house of assembly, the lower house of the legislature, which gave final approval of this bill, its chief sponsor, Andrew Parsons, declared that the company asked "for no new powers but for privileges that would enable them to carry out the powers" they already had—noting at the same time that the request for a branch bank had been deleted. He praised the company as "pioneers of internal improvement in New Jersey" and declared, probably with truth, that "their work had been an immense advantage to the State."

New Jerseymen were apparently quite willing to overlook the New York directorship of the Morris and the Manhattan-oriented banking activities of the company in their satisfaction with its achievement in constructing a water connection from the Lehigh valley to Newark Bay, with a new shortcut under way across Bergen Neck to a $200,000 basin terminus directly on the Hudson. What if the enterprise was under New York direction? Was it not made possible by New York capital? And indeed was this not one of the arguments for the grant of banking privileges in the first place—that such a grant would attract money to New Jersey from out of state to help in the construction of a New Jersey facility? It mattered to the legislators that the Morris had, as Parsons informed them, already paid a tax of $5,000 into the common school fund, and that a similar tax was to be paid every year.[112]

VIII   THE MORRIS PAYS A DIVIDEND

The Morris leadership hurried to take advantage of the new legislation by calling a stockholders meeting for March 26 at Jersey City, where the new arrangement of the board of directors was approved. In a few days the directors divided themselves into five classes. McLane, of course, was placed in the fifth class—in other words given a five-year term on the board—and was reelected to the presidency.[113] "He is remarkably well in Health & Spirits," Kitty had written from New York in the middle of the contest for the new charter; "and tho he works very hard yet I think we have great reason indeed to rejoice, that he ever came here. He has been treated with unexampled kindness by everyone. The Bank, which he took the charge of, has revived wonderfully in character; the stock has risen from 54 to 95—and is still going up." [114]

This was indeed a high point in Louis McLane's business career. His standing among New York men of affairs was very high. "Mr. McLane," Philip Hone confided to his diary, "is one of the ablest and most agreeable men I ever knew"; New Yorkers found his residence among them to be "to the sincere gratification of all . . . who have the pleasure of his company." Even the house McLane occupied at 1 Greenwich Street, which he rented from Abraham Schermerhorn, gave him a certain standing because it was still remembered as the residence of the prominent merchant Dominick Lynch. Through Philip Hone and through Washington Irving, McLane was entertained in the home of such a lord of finance as old John Jacob Astor, who lived near Hell Gate, where Irving resided for a time while he was writing his history of Astoria.[115] The merchant Richard Blatchford and the collector Samuel Swartwout were more intimate with the McLane family.[116]

Besides the pride McLane could take in the success of his efforts to win new privileges for the Morris from the New Jersey legislature, as well as in the private negotiations he had carried on regarding water rights in order to avoid gaining the enmity of North Jersey merchants and manufacturers, he also had reason to be proud of his success in disposing of the company's securities. The Morris had already managed to dispose of a new million dollar stock issue in 1835, after McLane's appointment but before he turned his attention to an even larger amount ($1,134,000) in forfeited stock, part of the original capitalization that had come back to the company when the original subscribers failed to complete their payments. In December he offered these shares for a small 10 percent down payment with the opportunity of purchasing a 6 percent Morris bond after one year as an added inducement.[117]

Whether or not the bond was any incentive to the sale, the forfeited stock was quickly sold. With the market price of Morris shares hovering in the 90's, the opportunity to secure forfeited shares for a down payment of only ten dollars was not to be missed. By June, 1836, McLane was able to brag of disposing of 10,000 new shares authorized in 1835, 11,340 forfeited shares, and 6,000 shares authorized in March, 1836.[118]

By June McLane could also report that water rights and land had been acquired for the new feeder canal from Long Pond via the Pompton River. The first sale of water rights at one of the inclined planes was to a factory in Newark employing two hundred men. A contract with the Lehigh Company had been changed to provide for the transportation of 60,000 instead of 40,000 tons of coal in 1836. Never had the Morris done so much business or had such good prospects, McLane concluded in his report to the stockholders.

He confessed that the canal had previously yielded an inadequate return—indeed it had never paid a dividend—but now he took pride in his accomplishments. The annual tax of $5,000 due to New Jersey had been paid, a sum of $1,332,000 in trust funds had been received since March to be held for ten years, and a further sum of $1,536,000 in trust funds had been arranged for. Now at last the company had the means to discharge the Dutch loan of $750,000, which was not due till 1846 but was a heavy incumbrance on revenues in the meantime. With the reconstructed planes able to pass six boats an hour each way, the canal was now capable of a traffic of 1,833,600 tons a year. If used to only one eleventh of its capacity, it would yield more than ordinary interest, and with trust and banking profits, sale of water rights and valuable building lots available beside the new basin being constructed at Jersey City, Morris directors could be very optimistic.[119]

Optimism is the prevailing tone of all corporation reports, and McLane's hopefulness is therefore to be accepted at something less than face value. But the situation of the Morris did seem in the spring of 1836 to be better than ever before. Nicholas Biddle thought so, for on April 11 he asked Samuel Swartwout to buy him 1,000 or 1,500 shares. "I do not wish to connect myself with the Company ostensibly," he warned Swartwout, "and therefore whatever you do, you must do entirely in your own name."[120]

In a few days, after only 400 shares had been procured at his price, Biddle stopped Swartwout from making further purchases for him.[121] Perhaps, however, in view of the secrecy insisted on in this purchase (by the head of one bank in the stock of a rival bank), Nicholas Biddle was interested in the purchase of 3,000 shares of new Morris stock by Thomas Biddle and Company a week later. A further proposal from Thomas Biddle and Company to invest $3 million in 6 percent Morris bonds payable in twenty years in London was apparently rejected in June.[122]

No such bonds are noted in the June statement of Morris finances that accompanied McLane's report, though there is an item of somewhat more than $200,000 listed by the name of Morrison, Cryder, and Company, a London house which had recently agreed to act as agent for the

Morris.[123] Rumors began circulating that the Morris was about to pay a dividend "from its vast operations in foreign and domestic exchanges," as was reported by the *Herald,* which also declared that McLane, as "manager" of the Morris, "bids fair to become a rival to Nicholas Biddle in finance operations." [124]

It is amusing to note that the very man to whom McLane was being compared was himself receiving rumors of the contemplated Morris dividend—from those who were likely to know his eagerness to hear this news. Edward R. Biddle reported to his cousin Nicholas that he had talked with McLane, "who voluntarily broached the subject of a dividend and expressed his decided opinion in favor of $2\frac{1}{2}$ pr.ct. and possibly 3 pr.ct. and remarked that he considered three pr.ct. would certainly be divided next January and that afterwards it would be an eight or nine pr.ct. Stock." That very afternoon the Morris board met and declared a 3 percent dividend.[125]

While fair winds blew, McLane and that "great number of the first merchants" of New York, as the *Herald* appraised the Morris directors, dared hope once again that their institution might be granted a share of the government deposits. Legislative appointment of a group of New Jersey directors in March seemed to offer a new route to administrative favor, and before the month was out a committee of three of the new directors—Christian Zabriskie, of Bergen, John S. Darcy, of Newark, and John Travers, of Paterson—were despatched to Washington with a letter from Governor Vroom, an application from members of the legislature, and a memorial signed by sundry New Jersey citizens asking that the Morris be made a deposit bank.[126]

The mission was undertaken in vain, but the Morris did not give up. Three months later, on June 25, a new application was decided on. McLane was instructed by the board to address Levi Woodbury, the Secretary of the Treasury, once again, calling his attention to the company's application and the documents accompanying it, on which no decision had yet been announced. A copy of McLane's report was also to be sent and a pledge of satisfactory security for any government funds deposited with the Morris. As a final stroke of persuasiveness—or so it was hoped—three more of the New Jersey directors of the Morris were pressed into service to support the application. Senator Garrett D. Wall (of Burlington), Representative Philemon Dickerson (of Paterson), and Representative James Parker (of Perth Amboy) had the useful advantage of being Democrats and members of the Congress of the United States— which is very likely the reason they had been added to the Morris board.[127]

How solicitous these three Congressmen were for the company of which they were directors is not known, but Edward R. Biddle, at least, thought they had been active in the cause they were asked to plead. "As regards the Deposits," he wrote to Nicholas Biddle, "I beleive the Secy, of the Treasury has so far committed himself, to the New Jersey members, that he will be in a very awkward position if he does not give them to the Morris Canal, as may be at some future day proven by their correspondence," and Biddle went on to speak of the "determined perseverance" of the New Jersey members.[128]

But donning the mask of New Jersey Democrats was insufficient disguise for the Morris, and no government deposits came its way. Secretary Woodbury answered McLane's application by explaining that deposit banks were authorized only where public funds were collected or disbursed; in New Jersey such transactions occurred only in Trenton, where pensions were paid and where a bank would soon be selected.[129] The outcome could hardly have been surprising to McLane, who avowed himself long indifferent to the "personal hostility" of Van Buren and "his immediate tools" and disgusted at the Vice-President's "new associations . . . with the tribe of parasites which have so long exerted such a dangerous sway in the politics of the country, and with the Bentons and Johnsons, '*et id omne genus.*'"[130]

"After all, the opposition to the Bank of the United States," McLane was convinced, "was mere party opposition—and many in their hearts friendly to it, were found battering it down." How, from such men, could the Morris expect consideration? "I believe it to be true," he confided to his old Alabama friend, William King, "that Party has been a greater and a more merciless destroyer than the sword."[131]

In the case of the Morris application, as in the Bank War of 1833–34, party had reared its head. "This Morris affair is in a great measure in the hands of our enemies," Van Buren and Woodbury had both been warned, though "a few of our political friends . . . aid them in their speculations."[132] Under these circumstances, it was not likely that the national administration would make a pet of the Morris.

When McLane allowed himself to think of politics, he saw terrible omens of future trouble. In the long run, he was sure, there would be a division between North and South, and when that division came he would regret having accepted a position in New York. "For in that division," he explained to a friend, "I am 'South of Mason and Dixon's line,' and I mean to keep up my farm, dilapidated as it is, in Maryland, as a place of retreat in future emergencies."[133]

IX   LEASING THE CANAL

Despite McLane's preference for the South, despite his intellectual spurning of his father's abolitionism and the craftsman, mercantile background of his youth in favor of some idealistic plantation chivalry, compounded of Walter Scott and southern political bombast, Louis McLane functioned in New York affairs as a useful citizen. After fire destroyed a portion of the city, including many warehouses, on December 16, 1835, McLane attended a meeting of leading citizens—city officials, bankers, brokers, manufacturers, and merchants—and there became a member of a committee, including Albert Gallatin and Mayor Cornelius Lawrence, to solicit aid in Washington. Whether McLane went to the capital is not clear, but he did urge at least one of his friends to support legislation providing for the remission of duties on unsold imports destroyed by fire, an act that he thought long overdue. Congress accepted this proposal and another granting importers an extension of time for the payment of duties.[134] In printing these two proposals as well as another suggesting that the federal government invest a portion of the surplus revenue in municipal securities, the New York *American* ascribed to McLane's pen the memorial in which these ideas were draughted for presentation to Congress by the Mayor.[135] McLane was also responsible for a proposal that another New York committee carried to Albany—that the state of New York buy from the federal government the public stock of the Bank of the United States, using for the purpose an issue of scrip paying 3 or 4 percent, with profits on the transaction somehow being devoted to the needs of the sufferers from the great fire. It was an ingenious scheme, according to Charles Augustus Davis, whose appetite for bank stock was whetted by the thought that the government stock might be thrown on the market by the state. "Whoever gets that Govt. Stock and it gets into private hands by *Contract* with the State—and the Bank gets a new Charter—its a dish worth sitting down to"—Davis was so eager that he was incoherent.[136]

Perhaps McLane and the Morris directorate had also given some thought to the government stock in the Bank of the United States; there were few such opportunities that they missed. Already a committee of Morris directors had sought to borrow $500,000 to $1 million from Biddle on the security of Morris post notes for the relief of New York.[137] Apparently they were unsuccessful.

But the Morris never failed in business for want of trying. The opinion of counsel was sought in the winter on the legality of continuing to maintain an office and transact business in New York.[138] Apparently the advice was favorable, because before long new office space was secured on

William Street.[139] And in this year the Morris began the large purchases of Indiana state bonds that were later, after McLane's time, to be a source of new embarrassments. In July, 1836, the Morris Canal Bank and Thomas Biddle and Company jointly bought $19,000 worth of the 5 percent bonds Indiana issued to finance the Wabash and Erie Canal. Apparently this was an initial purchase. In September the same two firms bought $440,000 worth of the same bonds at a premium of $4,400, and before the end of 1836 the Morris is said to have received $898,824 of Indiana bonds, on which, in February, 1837, it still owed the state a payment of $584,890. Dr. Isaac Coe, who was one of the commissioners charged with disposing of the Indiana bonds, became a Morris stockholder in the fall of 1836. In the next three years it is estimated that Dr. Coe made $100,000 on bond transactions, while Indiana lost $3.5 million, mainly through its dealings with the Morris.[140]

But these losses occurred after McLane had left the bank, and his only serious responsibility for them seems to be the fact that he encouraged the Morris to be active in the business of interstate and international banking and exchange. In July, 1836, for instance, he urged the governors of Mississippi and Alabama to employ the Morris Canal Bank as official agent to receive and remit in the New York area funds transmitted from New York banks to these state governments under the Surplus Distribution Act. Offering interest of 3 to 5 percent on deposits, McLane pleaded, "Our vicinity to New York, and our agency in that City, for such business as we may lawfully perform there, give us equal facilities with the Banks encorporated by the State of New York" [141] These particular letters may never have been sent, but they do correctly represent the efforts McLane and the other Morris directors were making to stimulate business.

At this time the Morris Canal showed a profit for the year of $273,229, but this profit was too good to last.[142] On October 12, 1836, there was a panic on the stock market and values began to tumble. From 93 on October 12 the Morris stock declined to a low of 74 on November 2, but then it rallied.[143] Nicholas Biddle foresaw the turning point before it occurred. On November 1 he advised Edward Biddle that it was safe to "operate to any extent at present rates." "If you retain your good opinion of Morris," the Philadelphia banker advised, "there is no limit—scarcely half a million—which you might not go to at 60 or 90 days—and so of almost all the good stocks." [144]

Between November 3 and November 9 Nicholas Biddle acquired 650 shares of Morris stock at prices ranging from 78 to 84; at the time he was purchasing on the low market 2,350 shares of Delaware and Hudson and 1,000 shares of Mohawk Railroad stock.[145] The substantial new Biddle interest in the Morris was recognized on December 1, when Edward R.

Biddle became a director in place of James Parker, who resigned. Philemon Dickerson also resigned from the board, after his election to the governorship of New Jersey, and was replaced by another New Jerseyman, Andrew Parsons, who happened also to be from Paterson, and had been the chief sponsor of company legislation in the house of assembly.[146] This thoughtfulness for the interests of Paterson may not have been unconnected with the fact that Paterson citizens were seeking a branch of the Morris Canal Bank for their city, as well as an increase in the Morris capitalization of $500,000 for the projected branch—an idea the Morris administration, thwarted in its effort to start a Newark branch, encouraged.[147]

After the stock market break on October 12, Attorney General Butler visited New York, presumably to consult with bankers about the currency problems that were attributed to the Specie Circular, an order requiring payment for western lands in gold or silver. This order, issued in July and effective in August, had reversed the tendency toward easy money and inflation that had been encouraged by the "pet bank" deposit system and the weakening of the controls over bank note issues previously exercised by the Bank of the United States. Land speculation suddenly ground to a halt, and the tightness of the money market led to the failure of more than a dozen New York mercantile firms, including the Higginsons, formerly of Boston.

When Butler, as agent of the government, came to New York, he called representatives of four banks, including the Morris Canal Bank, into consultation with him at the Astor House. However, it was not McLane but George Griswold who appeared at Butler's hotel to represent the Morris. Perhaps McLane was out of town; more likely it was felt someone else, and particularly a bona fide New York merchant, might be more effective in conversing with a cabinet minister who happened also to be a member of the Albany Regency. To the Regency Griswold was thought to have particular appeal because he had been known as a strong anti-Bank man —anti-Bank of the United States, that is.[148]

There was particular reason for the Morris to fear the designs of Albany politicians in the fall of 1836, for it was rumored that the New York legislature was about to pass a law forbidding agencies of out-of-state corporations from operating in New York. Such legislation would have been aimed directly at the Bank of the United States and the Morris, and for a time these two institutions may have entertained the idea of purchasing control of the Dry Dock Bank, a New York corporation, in order to retain a Manhattan foothold. In January, however, the legislature reconsidered, possibly moved by rumors that outstanding loans of the Morris Canal Bank and the New York branch of the Bank of the United

States equaled approximately $12 million, a sum large enough to produce very severe pressures in the local money market if the two agencies were driven from New York. Perhaps as a consequence of these calculations the legislature reenacted existing laws that included restraints on foreign corporations but permitted agencies to deal in paper and securities.[149]

Twice within a half year scandal struck the Morris through the actions of its cashiers. One cashier, Pierre Bacot, committed suicide in a New York hotel room on August 31. His despondency apparently had nothing to do with the affairs of the Morris Canal Bank, where he had worked for only a few weeks.[150] But his predecessor, Robert Gilchrist, was found to be a defaulter to the extent of more than $120,000. However, seizure of his securities, real estate, and cash, reduced the total loss to $28,000, and Morris earnings covered this sum before another dividend, this time of 4 percent, was paid on February 10, 1837.[151]

The ability of the Morris to pay another dividend was a proud achievement for Louis McLane. In a report presented to the board on March 2 and to the stockholders a few days later, McLane summarized the condition of the company on February 1, and the first item he chose to mention was the declaration of two dividends in the past twelvemonth, the first dividends in the history of this company, the first of 3 percent and the second of 4 percent. And these profits, he declared, were the fruits of only a partial possession of the capital and "but a small contribution from the Canal." For the coming year he expected profits to be considerably larger, with the whole capital available and the canal busier than ever before. In expectation of these profits, the Dutch creditors had been informed that both principal and interest would be paid on July 1, 1837, canceling the mortgage.[152]

One of the reasons the canal was looked to in 1837 as a source of more profits than in 1836 was the completion of the extension through Bergen Neck to Jersey City. Louis McLane was probably one of the directors of the Morris who were aboard the packet boat *Maria,* along with the mayor and aldermen of Newark, when this boat passed through the new section of the canal and arrived in Jersey City on November 29. Close behind the *Maria* followed other boats laden with coal from the Lehigh valley and its environs and with firewood from northern New Jersey. Their arrival seemed to presage future business, though it was noted that only the extreme exertions of Roswell B. Mason, the chief Morris engineer, managed to get these boats through ice that was already two inches thick.[153]

In announcing completion of this extension in his annual report, McLane predicted that the new feeder canal from Long Pond would be completed by summer and that new reservoirs would also be constructed soon. At the same time he confessed that the enlarged banking activities of the company were absorbing the attention of its officers and directors to the disadvantage of the canal, which needed constant supervision. After considering establishing a separate board for the canal, the directors had decided instead to lease it to another transportation company, one naturally interested in the promotion and extension of trade. This company was the Little Schuylkill & Susquehanna Rail Road, which had agreed to rent the Morris Canal for five years and to pay annually a sum equal to 6 percent of the total cost of the canal. The lessee would have full right to water power and real estate along the canal and could buy the company barges at cost or an assessed valuation if it chose.[154]

What McLane did not emphasize in his report was that the Little Schuylkill & Susquehanna was not a functioning railroad as yet, but only a planned and incorporated railroad. Its intention was to build a line from Williamsport on the Susquehanna to Beaver Meadow, an anthracite coalfield in the mountains above Mauch Chunk. The Morris was already in touch with the Beaver Meadow coalfield through the Lehigh Navigation Canal, which assisted coal barges to come down the Lehigh River from Mauch Chunk, and through the short Beaver Meadow Rail Road, running fourteen miles from Mauch Chunk to Beaver Meadow—a railroad of which Samuel Ingham was president and the Morris Canal Bank was a stockholder.[155] The Little Schuylkill & Susquehanna planned to connect these fields, as well as the coalfield to the southwest in the upper Schuylkill valley, with the Susequehanna and the various canals and railroads running northward into New York and westward toward Lake Erie. In the expansive terms of promoters, all the interior of America was opened to the Morris Canal by this connection.

By this prospective connection, that is. This was the rub. The Morris Canal had been rented to a railroad that was a prospectus rather than a reality. It has authority to build a railroad, McLane reported; it has authority to hold five thousand acres of coal land; of its capital "it is understood an amount has been already subscribed by the Bank of the United States and responsible individuals sufficient to ensure the early completion of the Rail Road and the seasonable development of the mines."

The Bank of the United States connection is not surprising since the Little Schuylkill & Susquehanna was essentially a Philadelphia-oriented line—despite this ephemeral relationship with the Morris. It is said that it was founded after two promoters from northern Pennsylvania, Christian Brobst and Joseph Paxton, of Catawissa, compiled traffic statistics on the North Branch of the Susquehanna and persuaded officials of the Bank of the United States to ride over the projected route and discover for themselves how this traffic might be diverted toward Philadelphia.

When the company was organized a Jaudon—Ashbel G. Jaudon—became its secretary, and prominent Philadelphia capitalists—including Thomas Biddle, Matthew Newkirk, and William D. Lewis—formed the major part of its board of managers.[156]

For the moment, the lease looked like a splendid arrangement for the Morris. Morris stock was bought avidly at the end of December when the news got around, and soon its price was raised nearly to par; it was now, the *Herald* said, "as good a stock as any in the street." [157]

When Louis McLane reported execution of the detailed contract, he could not fail to be exultant. The rental meant a return of $4\frac{1}{2}$ percent on the total capitalization of the Morris, and if the banking business continued as in the past year, this income would guarantee even larger dividends than those just paid. Moreover, the fact that the Little Schuylkill & Susquehanna had a financial interest in the Morris Canal should ensure that the Canal would be used as a major route to New York for Pennsylvania coal. In the immediate past, the share of the Morris in this coal business had been disappointing. For instance, in 1836, only 23,000 tons of Lehigh valley coal had been transported on the Morris Canal, whereas 112,082 tons had been carried via the Delaware Division Canal through Bucks County to Philadelphia. These statistics were particularly discouraging because the 23,000 tons carried by the Morris in 1836 were less than the 40,000 tons carried by the same canal in 1835.[158]

"I would rather purchase Morris shares than anything else," chortled Edward Biddle; "we will certainly get . . . 100,000 Tons of coal." [159] He went so far in his bullish spirit as to encourage Nicholas Biddle to sell his own 2,500 shares in the Bank of the United States and invest in "the low priced Stocks such as Morris, Vicksburg—and all the good cotton Banks." [160] It is not likely that Nicholas took this advice, but he had been dealing heavily in Morris Canal securities during the winter. In January, when the Bank of the United States was very hard pressed for funds it owed to other banks, Biddle threw 3,525 shares of Morris on the market —though it is not positive that they were sold. In late February, on the other hand, he bought 950 shares of the same stock, probably for the Bank.[161]

X A NEW POSITION

The splendid record that McLane was making as president of the Morris Canal and Banking Company may have stimulated the invitation that led him to leave New York. In December, 1836, he was offered another administrative position in an American business, the presidency of the Baltimore & Ohio, the country's premier railroad. Even his old enemy,

Hezekiah Niles, greeted the news with pleasure, convinced that McLane's "energy, talents and weight of character" would assure this railroad of realizing "the warmest wishes of its friends." [162]

The Morris stockholders did not willingly let McLane go. They "spared no pains," as Edward Biddle put it, "to induce him to stay," and a month after the B & O invitation was issued they still had some hope he would not accept it.[163] Even on January 31, when McLane sent his resignation to the board of directors, a special committee of four was appointed to confer with him and "make any arrangement necessary" to persuade him to stay with the Morris.

The attraction that drew McLane to the Maryland position was too great to permit him to change his mind. This was, as he told the directors —and there is no reason to doubt his frankness in this case—"the proximity of Baltimore" to his "landed property and native home." They were not quite the same thing, since he was born in Delaware and his estate was in Maryland, but they were so close that he thought of them together. It had become clear, he wrote, that his duties to the Morris required his services full time, excluding any chance of giving reasonable attention to his Bohemia property. He had, consequently, concluded sometime earlier that he would be obliged to resign before long, but he had not wanted to leave until the future of the Morris looked so bright that his resignation could not possibly be interpreted as arising from any want of confidence in the company.

Now that the leasing of the canal and the declaration of a second semi-annual dividend demonstrated the success of the Morris, he could leave his post without arousing any misconceptions. And though he desired to move to Baltimore and assume his new responsibilities as soon as possible, his new directors understood that he must allow the Morris board time to make provisions for his replacement.[164]

Perhaps in the back of his mind for the last year he had been nourishing the thought he had once expressed that someday a division would occur between North and South and when it did he wished to be south of the Mason-Dixon Line. If this appears to be an extreme statement, born of some momentary despair, it should be noted that his disdain for the course of political affairs seems to be consistent through these years. It was the tone of affairs with which he found fault, "tone" being his way of characterizing the influence in the Democratic party of men distasteful to him. The cure of this "blighting influence" he foresaw only in heroic actions. For instance, after declaring that no one could regret the preservation of peace with France, inasmuch as it saved lives, he confessed "a good active rousing war would not have filled me with great horror."

And why not? Why because it would have swept away those blighting influences that have nearly extinguished "manly independence and patriotic virtue in public men." McLane assumed, probably, that a war would bring new men to the fore in place of Van Buren and Taney and Kendall. Even his friend Lewis Cass, as Secretary of War, spent his talents "ministering to the bloated vanity of the dispenser of patronage" with his pen while neglecting the national defenses that were his responsibility.[165]

There was no higher compensation to be anticipated from the new position than from the one McLane was relinquishing, for the B & O offered $6,000, the same as his Morris salary. That this was not such a great sum is suggested by the fact that Biddle was advised his cashier, Joseph Cowperthwaite, could not be tempted to leave the Bank of the United States for the Morris presidency for less than $7,000 or $8,000. The point was being made that a salary of $6,000 from the Morris Canal would not be as desirable as whatever Cowperthwaite received—undoubtedly something less than $6,000—from the Bank of the United States.[166]

That the Morris presidency was not deemed as desirable as even a lesser post in the Bank of the United States was probably because the future of the Morris was reckoned to be the more doubtful of the two, despite the dividends just paid. A comparison of the current standing and expectations of the Morris and the B & O would similarly have been to the disadvantage of the Morris.

Besides other attractions of the B & O presidency, McLane would have an advantage in being close to Dover, where his lawsuit with the Bayards had recently been transferred on appeal from the chancellor's decision in McLane's favor. The suit was important to McLane because the funds involved would free him from the annoyance of some debts, such as the $5,150 he owed to the Bank of the United States in 1837. The counsel he now employed were expensive—James Rogers, of New Castle, John Sergeant, of Philadelphia and Walter Jones, of Washington. The whole affair was also distracting; in the winter of 1836 it had drawn him to New Castle at a time when he was busy lobbying for the Morris with the New Jersey legislature.[167]

At Bohemia, in 1836, he had set an English gardener and two assistants to work improving and adorning the estate, if rumors heard in Wilmington were true. His arrangements for the farming apparently had not worked out well, for in the spring of 1837 he was once again looking for a man to run his farm, preferably "a first rate Pennsylvania farmer," a "skilful, . . . sober, industrious *managing* man, who would make the most of everything," assisted by "a wife capable of taking charge of house affairs and the dairy." To a man who would look after Bohemia, McLane promised not only his "support" but also "a reasonable salary," and a commission on sales.[168]

However eager McLane might be to return to the Maryland farm where his heart was, it seemed when he accepted the Baltimore & Ohio's call that the Morris job had been good both to him and for him. "Your Father has recovered his spirits and grown very fat," Kitty reported to an absent son in July; "he is constantly employed and tho' he sometimes looks back upon the past and gives a sigh, to the empty honors he has left behind, yet I consider his situation much more prosperous than it ever was." [169]

Kitty appreciated the prosperity; Louis sighed for the honors left behind. Perhaps a move to Baltimore was a step toward Washington and those honors that were forsaken but not forgotten. In Maryland an old Federalist could not only make a living; he might even make a political career. In New York, with the Regency his enemy, he had no political future. In Maryland, with friends like the Smiths, anything was possible. And if not in Maryland, then Bohemia might be a base for a political career in Delaware, as the neighboring Bohemia Manor estate had been for Bayards and Claytons.

XI PANIC

Meanwhile he had promised not to leave the Morris until provisions for a smooth transfer of his responsibilities to a successor had been completed. And as he lingered on, the Morris's bright prospects of early 1837 gradually dimmed and catastrophe approached.

When the annual meeting was held in March, no successor to McLane had yet been found, and so he was reelected to the presidency. There were changes in his board of directors, however, changes apparently brought about by the Biddle interests. "I have just returned from the election of the Morris at Jersey City," Edward R. Biddle reported to his cousin Nicholas on March 6. "I put in T. Cadwalader, Washington Jackson, S. Draper and myself as New Directors." Simeon Draper represented no new interest on the board, for he was merely another New York merchant and replaced his father-in-law, John Haggerty, who resigned. But Cadwalader, Washington Jackson, and Biddle represent the enlarged Philadelphia interest in the Morris. Most of the candidates for directorships were chosen by unanimous vote, but two candidates, both board members seeking reelection, were defeated. One of the two was the New York merchant John Crary, who was known to have been an enemy of the Bank of the United States. The other was Andrew Parsons, the New

Jersey legislator who had helped steer the Morris charter amendments through the house of assembly in 1836.[170]

Edward Biddle was so sure McLane's report to the stockholders would enhance the value of Morris stock that he started buying again, even though the price was quoted at over 100. Nicholas Biddle warned Edward to go easy, that a brilliant retreat was the test of a good general, but the tumbling market caught him unprepared.[171] From a high of 102 on March 13, the Morris stock declined to a low of 77 on March 31. A day earlier two Morris directors resigned, one of them Joseph L. Joseph, whose Wall Street banking house had collapsed on March 13.[172]

The tight money market led a self-appointed committee of merchants to invite Nicholas Biddle to New York for a conference on their problems. Probably McLane was one of the bankers who sat in on the conference with Biddle and his cashier, Samuel Jaudon, at the Merchants' Bank on March 28. To fill the void caused by a lack of specie, it was agreed that the Morris and some other banks would issue several million dollars worth of what were called post notes, interest-paying, short-term transferable bonds that were purchased for shipment to London in place of specie or bank notes.[173]

The post notes might have helped, but nothing averted the coming panic. The market stringency was enough worry for a retiring president, but two other problems, the Dutch loan and the canal lease, compounded McLane's troubles. In March the directors had thought it advisable for McLane to go abroad to straighten out their embarrassed relations with Morrison, Cryder, and Company in London, hopefully by helping the sale of the Indiana bonds the Morris was floating or by application of them to satisfaction of the Dutch banker's mortgage on the canal. Other problems spared McLane this trip, but the mortgage, on which a payment was due the 1st of July, was a constant worry.[174]

One of the stated purposes for leasing the canal was to rid the Morris management of concern for it, but when time came to turn the management over to the lessee, the Little Schuylkill & Susquehanna Rail Road, the president of this company complained that the canal was not in good and complete repair. Consequently further expenditures were necessary at the very time when the Morris could least afford them. The canal remained, after all, the main property of the company, and, as one adviser said, the reputation of the canal would have an effect on the confidence the public would put in the company's other interests.[175]

At a meeting of bankers and merchants in the office of Mayor Cornelius Lawrence on April 8, McLane was appointed to a committee of ten that was to seek aid for hard-pressed firms from the New York governor and legislature. Albert Gallatin served as chairman of the committee, which proposed that the state issue a 6 percent stock to merchants on good security so that these merchants would be able to pay their foreign debts and encourage a flow of foreign capital into the American economy.[176] Banks chartered in New York were particularly concerned by the shortness of the supply of specie, because their charters were automatically voided if they suspended specie conversion. Although the Morris, as a New Jersey institution, was not immediately subject to this New York law, its relations to New York banks were so close that it was bound to be affected by their fate.

On May 9, however, the banks of New York City decided they could no longer withstand the inevitable, that they must suspend specie payments for the time being. On May 11, the Morris Canal Bank came to the same decision, after New Yorkers crossed the river in numbers and caused a run on it. Baltimore and Philadelphia banks, including the Bank of the United States, were forced to suspend specie payments at the same time.[177]

In writing of the Morris Canal Company James Gordon Bennett of the New York *Herald* claimed that over 50 percent of its stock was now owned by Thomas Biddle and Company, of Philadelphia, which firm had lost about $700,000 on this stock in approximately two months. Bennett was quoting the stock at 60, but in the next few days it was quoted first at 30 and then, rallying, at 47. Under these circumstances it became increasingly difficult for McLane to leave the Morris for his new position, but also hard for him to justify neglecting the interests of the Baltimore & Ohio. Three directors of the Morris served as a committee that made a last-ditch effort to persuade him to continue permanently with their company, but on June 1, at a board meeting which McLane did not attend, they acknowledged their failure, complimenting him on his valuable services as well as his "honorable and dignified course" in staying with his responsibilities through a difficult period.[178]

And still he stayed on in New York for another two weeks and more to see negotiations carried through with the Bank of the United States and with Thomas Biddle and Company. The Bank agreed to help the Morris and the Biddle firm meet the obligations they had jointly undertaken to the Indiana commissioners when arranging to purchase that state's bonds. By a further agreement Richard Blatchford, who had been serving as a confidential emissary from the Morris to the Biddles, went to London to deal with Morrison, Cryder, and Company. These agents of the Morris were balking at paying the interest due July 1 on the Dutch debt, and indeed at making any payments on behalf of the Morris. Fortunately, the help of the Bank of the United States could be counted on abroad as well as at home.[179]

One other major problem had remained in June, the problem of finding a successor to McLane, and that was a problem for the directors and the stockholders, particularly for the Biddles, rather than for McLane. Nicholas Biddle himself interviewed and offered the position to the man finally determined upon—Samuel Southard. Like McLane, Southard was a former cabinet minister and Senator; unlike McLane, he had also the advantage of being a New Jerseyman. It was felt, however, that much as his name might contribute to the respectability of the Morris, this company's problems might be too much for him, and therefore it was decided to create a new position, the vice-presidency, to which Edward R. Biddle was appointed at the same salary as the president. Biddle could be counted on to look after the investment of his Philadelphia colleagues; Southard would provide a Jersey coating of respectability to the enterprise. Biddle was to provide efficiency; Southard, a façade.[180]

And now, at last, McLane could depart. His resignation was finally accepted on June 15 by a board that gratefully remembered how the resources and credit of the Morris had seemed exhausted when the directors, convinced the privileges of their charter were too valuable to be abandoned, had "almost as a last hope fully unfolded" the situation to McLane. They recalled that after a deliberate examination he had accepted their invitation, "not certainly without some hazard," and had efficiently led the company to a position of growth, respectability, and profit. And particularly they appreciated McLane's willingness to stick with the Morris, at the sacrifice of personal convenience and domestic arrangements, when new perils menaced the company after he had accepted another position. Finally, the cashier was directed to credit Louis McLane on the books of the company with the sum of $9,312.95 in consideration of extra services, in addition to his salary.[181]

XII RETROSPECT AND PROSPECT

In the life of Louis McLane, the Morris Canal episode seems to resemble his diplomatic missions abroad. He went to New York as he had gone to London to accomplish a particular task. He succeeded, and once the task was accomplished he moved on to other responsibilities.

McLane had brought respectability as well as profitability to the Morris, once the toy of speculators. When he left this company, the canal had been leased to a management presumably devoted to transportation, a friendly legislature had granted almost every adjustment desired in the company charter, and the New York mercantile interest had been reenforced—not yet overpowered—by the investments of Philadelphia capitalists. Unfortunately a financial crisis in 1837 delayed McLane's departure from New York and darkened the prospects of his new venture before he began upon it.

Baltimore offered Louis McLane no serene and comfortable haven after a storm. Unlike the canal he was leaving, the railroad he came to was decidedly incomplete. Physical and financial barriers blocked its way; the wide Appalachians had to be crossed and the money to support construction had to be found in a depressed economy.

15

The Baltimore & Ohio

I BALTIMORE, THAT LAGGARD

Baltimore, that laggard among coastal cities, a mere village in colonial times, leaped into prominence and prosperity in the first half century of the republic. In that period it grew faster than any other major American port, and it was the first to tie its future prospects to a new transportation device, the railroad.

It was not that Baltimore ignored the possibilities of the railroad's older rivals, the canal and the turnpike. The turnpike, or improved highway, had already been utilized by Baltimoreans, and by way of a turnpike they had access to the most ambitious highway in all the United States, the National Road, federally sponsored, that led from Cumberland, Maryland, across the mountains to Ohio and the Mississippi valley. But at a time when the opening of a canal through New York from the Hudson to Lake Erie promised a new and advantageous route for bulky commodities, Baltimore was not to be satisfied with a wagon road westward.

The lower Ohio River, not the Great Lakes, was the seat of western settlement. Cincinnati was a metropolis before Cleveland, and St. Louis before Chicago. To Cincinnati and St. Louis Baltimore was closer than Boston or New York or even Philadelphia. Because of the southwestward trend of the Atlantic coast and the indentation formed by the Chesapeake Bay, Baltimore had a geographical advantage in reaching the Mississippi valley over its major rivals.

To the west, it was clear, lay America's future and the enterprising American's profit. Baltimoreans of the 1820's were enterprising Americans who knew better than to relax in smug satisfaction with their proximity to the West. The Appalachian Mountains were the great barrier to west-ern trade. It was of little advantage to be nearer the Ohio if the easy route there led from—and to—some rival harbor.

With the Erie as a model, Baltimoreans thought also of a canal and investigated whether the canal long projected beside the Potomac could be extended across Maryland to Baltimore. It could, of course, but the cost would be exorbitant, and at any rate this canal already had a termi-nus in the District of Columbia. A railroad seemed the best way of en-suring Baltimore's future.

When the logical course to be taken was made clear, Baltimore capital-ists did not shrink from the adventure. Eleven merchants or mercantile firms, led by the Hoffman Brothers, Alexander Brown and Sons, Robert Oliver, William Patterson, and Philip E. Thomas quickly pledged half a million dollars in the new enterprise, and the last named of them, a Quaker banker, became president of the new company. He was a particu-larly fitting choice since his brother Evan Thomas had been chiefly re-sponsible for starting a railroad fever in Baltimore when he returned from England enthusiastically touting the advantages of this new mode of transport.[1]

Under the leadership of Philip Thomas, the railroad built a line west-ward from Baltimore to Ellicott City, Frederick (reached by a short branch), and the Potomac, where it came to a halt in 1834 after crossing to the Virginia side at the town of Harper's Ferry. There it was to be met by the Winchester & Potomac Railroad, and as a result of this con-nection it hoped to realize a profitable trade in the produce of the fertile Shenandoah valley.

This Main Stem, as it was called, of the Baltimore & Ohio, was eighty-one miles long from Baltimore to Harper's Ferry. Much of its construc-tion was later found unsatisfactory, including inclined planes installed at a hill, Parr's Ridge, where the cars were supposed to be drawn up the height by stationary engines. A major branch of this road, separately capitalized, led directly to Washington, a distance of forty miles, parting from the Main Stem at an old stage stop called the Relay House.[2] Decades later the Washington Branch was incorporated into the main line of B & O passenger traffic westward when another line was built from Washing-ton northwestward to intercept the old Main Stem at Point of Rocks.

But when Louis McLane assumed the presidency of the Baltimore & Ohio in 1837, the Main Stem and the Washington Branch met only at the Baltimore end, and construction westward had ceased at Harper's Ferry, where the rivalry of the Chesapeake and Ohio Canal seemed to doom the B & O to a long period of waiting. The great difficulty was the narrowness of the Potomac River valley. To follow the river was the logical route west, both for the railroad and the canal. Yet where the river broke its way through Appalachian ridges and foothills, its shores were precipitous and there was little room for construction of canal or railroad—still less for them both.

Consequently the natural rivalry of the two transportation systems grew as they struggled for priority on the river bank. Their agents in western Maryland vied in seeking out landowners and purchasing a right-of-way; their agents in Annapolis sought legislative favors and fought every prejudicial law that might prove a handicap or give the rival an advantage. Baltimore sentiment naturally favored the railroad over the canal, but the legislature was so apportioned that Baltimore was seriously underrepresented, and to some rural Maryland delegates the canal was successfully presented as having a prior claim on the Potomac passageway—as, in chronological terms, indeed it did. After the canal had won approval of its priority from the courts, a compromise was reached whereby canal and railroad were constructed simultaneously along the Potomac from Point of Rocks to Harper's Ferry, but from there on westward the canal was to be given priority to build to Cumberland.[3]

II   STOPPED AT HARPER'S FERRY

In 1836 the Baltimore & Ohio Railroad was bogged down at Harper's Ferry by more problems than its agreement to give priority to the Chesapeake and Ohio Canal. The initial enthusiasm Baltimoreans had felt for this railroad had run its course, and they were now turning pessimistic about its prospects. The stock market reflected their gloom; B & O stock had fallen from 65 in June to 40 by September of 1836.[4] Shrewd capitalists who bought the stock as a speculation were disappointed that the company was having trouble making its receipts equal its expenses.[5]

The incomplete state of the railroad, halted at Harper's Ferry, far short of its goal on the Ohio, could explain the failure of the enterprise to produce a sizable profit. Moreover, the capital outlay ahead was greater than that already expended, for the major part of the road was not yet built and the highest part of the Appalachian Mountains, where construction costs would be greatest, was not yet surmounted. Bridges and viaducts over streams and valleys were turning out to be very expensive, particularly the bridge crossing the Potomac at Harper's Ferry. The road already constructed was largely unsatisfactory, being in great part experimental. Finally, the required use of horses at Parr's Ridge, where stationary engines had not yet been installed, and in Baltimore, where steam locomotives were not allowed on tracks laid through the streets, proved to be particularly expensive. Since maximum fees were fixed by statute, the B & O could not increase income by raising rates, even when expenses rose.

Money, moreover, was needed for the construction westward from Harper's Ferry. The original capital of the company, which included half a million dollars from the state of Maryland and another half million from Baltimore City, had largely been expended. There were still installments due on the $3 million of stock that had been privately subscribed, but most of this money was already pledged to cover debts incurred in construction.[6] What was probably worse, the statutes granting the B & O necessary privileges were expiring. The railroad could always hope to raise money by its own endeavors, but it could secure a new charter only by the grace of a state legislature. It was not likely that Maryland would hesitate about renewing the privileges of the B & O, though a new Maryland charter might have stipulations added to it that were not to the advantage of this railroad. But other states, specifically Virginia and Pennsylvania, might be much more difficult because rival interests, if they were local, would have a first call on the attention, and affection, of their legislators.

Virginia and Pennsylvania charters were of essential importance to the B & O because Maryland did not extend to the Ohio River, and it was therefore only by building through Virginia or Pennsylvania that this Baltimore railroad could reach its destination. A corporation of one state must be recognized by another state, but to construct a railroad special legislative favors are necessary, such as the right of eminent domain, empowering a railroad to buy property in its way. Virginia, like Maryland, had granted the B & O this right in 1827 for ten years. Both of these grants were consequently about to expire. The Pennsylvania charter, granted in 1828, was for fifteen years, but at the current rate of progress of the B & O it was unlikely that it would reach Pennsylvania by 1843. Meanwhile Virginia and Pennsylvania were spawning their own transportation schemes. Clearly, diplomacy would be needed to retain the privileges previously granted the B & O.

It was natural for investors to blame the administration of the Baltimore & Ohio for the cessation of construction after 1834, and perhaps even more so for the failure to pay dividends regularly. (The company paid a small dividend in October, 1835, but none in 1834 or 1836.) In June of 1836 President Thomas resigned, discouraged with his job and tired of devoting so much time and effort to an enterprise that was becoming unpopular. He consented, however, to remain on the board, although half of the directors quit, including George Brown, the original treasurer of the company. Though bad health was generally reported as the cause of the president's resignation, the real difficulty was that the private stockholders in the B & O, once overenthusiastic about its prospects, were now fearful that their money was in a losing enterprise. Private investors, many of them speculators, subscribed to two thirds to three fourths of the original B & O capitalization of $3 million (raised to $4 million in 1828), and Thomas became the scapegoat for the failure of their dreams of quick returns on their investment. He lived, however, to see the road completed and to be honored for his vision.[7]

A member of another prominent mercantile family of Baltimore, Joseph W. Patterson, succeeded Thomas in the presidency. He was the brother of Betsy Patterson Bonaparte and son of William Patterson, a Scotch-Irish immigrant grown wealthy in trade who was one of the principal original investors in the B & O. But Patterson consented only to an interim term in the presidency, and so a search began at once for a permanent successor to Thomas.

It is likely that John C. Calhoun was seriously considered for the position, but if so, he decided not to leave the Senate. Asbury Dickins was, like Barkus, willing, when he heard his name mentioned in connection with this post.[8] The railroad directorate apparently sought a man with wide political connections, someone who could effectively influence state and perhaps national legislators on behalf of the B & O. Calhoun, a promoter of South Carolina railroads and a sponsor of the Bonus Bill of 1816, seemed a likely prospect, with many friends in the key states of Virginia and Pennsylvania. Dickins, a former Philadelphian and now secretary of the United States Senate, was a possibility because of his friends. But Louis McLane outranked Dickins in importance and was held in particularly high esteem by the Smith family, which had many connections in Baltimore mercantile circles, and by the old Bank of the United States circle. Nicholas Biddle himself was but a moderately small stockholder in the B & O Railroad at the time, having only 615 shares in July, 1835, but his associate, Roswell Colt, was more deeply involved in the B & O, and Biddle took a great interest in this railroad, partly because of his general interest in railroad companies and partly because it was hoped that a junction with the B & O might be arranged for the new Baltimore & Port Deposit Railroad, which seems to have been controlled by Biddle and Matthew Newkirk, who were associated in many ventures.[9]

McLane's record as the executive who made the Morris Canal profitable enough to pay dividends assured his popularity in Baltimore. The preliminary maneuvers in the hiring of McLane are unknown, but some assurance of his interest and willingness to accept the post must have been received by the B & O directors before December 20, 1836, when they unanimously elected him president and at the same time raised the salary to make the position attractive. Acting President Patterson, railroad counsel John H. B. Latrobe, and board member James Swan, a connection by marriage of the Smiths, traveled to New York by stagecoach to dine with McLane and formally offer him the presidency. Acting President was not the correct title for Joseph Patterson by the date of this trip, for he resigned the presidency at the same meeting at which McLane was elected, and Philip E. Thomas consented to take over once again as interim president until McLane could come to Baltimore. The proceedings of this meeting suggest strongly that the board of directors had reason to take McLane's acceptance for granted, the new salary voted for the president just before the election of McLane undoubtedly being part of a bargain.[10]

There was much reason for optimism in the fall of 1836 about the future prospects of the B & O, for energetic directors had been at work solving some of the problems that had stopped the railroad's westward progress at Harper's Ferry. The biggest problem of all, raising funds for further construction, seemed to be solved, for the city of Baltimore had agreed in the spring to subscribe $3 million to the B & O, and the state of Maryland in June had promised to subscribe an exactly similar amount. Moreover, the state extended the time given the B & O for completion of its line by five years, from 1838 to 1843, and freed it from any requirement to wait upon the extension of the canal. Both the railroad and canal, however, were required to approve this law, and to conciliate the canal company, which also was promised a $3 million state subscription, the B & O felt required to enter into a written agreement that its construction westward would not be so planned as to impair the permanence or usefulness of the canal. The railroad was not given complete freedom in choosing its route; this statute directed that the B & O should make its course from Harper's Ferry to Cumberland pass through Boonsboro and Hagerstown, in Washington County, Maryland, or else forfeit a million dollars of the state subscription. This legislative dictation of the route eventually caused much trouble.

The new state subscription was to be a preferred stock, with a guaranteed annual dividend of 6 percent, payable semiannually; but to help pay the dividend passenger fares were raised one cent a mile.[11] This requirement of a preferred return on its investment was not altogether an innovation for the state of Maryland. In setting up the Washington Branch of the railroad, the state had subscribed $500,000, a third of the total capitalization, but required that it receive, as a sort of bonus, one fifth of the gross passenger receipts on this branch.

The Washington Branch itself had been completed in 1835, just late enough to avoid some of the experimental errors committed on the Main Stem. The B & O had purchased two thirds of the stock, through a million-dollar loan secured by a mortgage on the Main Stem. Though established by a separate charter, the Washington Branch had no board or other corporate officials of its own, and its surplus annually went into the treasury of the parent company.[12]

III   MC LANE ARRIVES

The bright prospects that seemed opening for the Baltimore & Ohio Railroad at the end of 1836 when McLane was offered the presidency had clouded by the time Louis McLane entered actively upon his new job in July, 1837. He was in Baltimore briefly in February and was inducted into office on February 8. Thereafter until July 5 Joseph Patterson, succeeding Thomas for a second time, presided at meetings of the B & O board of directors, while McLane kept in touch with them only by mail nearly until July 5, when he finally was present to preside at a meeting of the board.[13]

The collapse of the money market in the spring of 1837 made it difficult for either Baltimore City or the state of Maryland to raise the money recently promised to the B & O. Maryland sent commissioners abroad to try to sell state bonds for internal improvements, but they found so little market that the state determined to issue bonds directly to the Baltimore & Ohio and the other transportation companies it had promised to help. These companies would then be responsible for selling the bonds themselves.[14]

Meanwhile, in April, 1837, eleven miles of track west of Ellicott City were so defective that reconstruction had to be undertaken immediately. In May the new viaduct at Harper's Ferry was found to be rotting and to need reconstruction. The one happy new development in the B & O story in the spring months was news that Virginia had voted to extend assistance to the amount of $302,100 to the B & O, but this promise of funds was just another case of fair prospects and was no help immediately.[15]

It was both immediate and long-range help that McLane sought through a committee he appointed at the first board meeting after his arrival in Baltimore in July. As an experienced administrator, responsible successively for the conduct of affairs in the federal Treasury Department, the State Department, and the Morris Canal, he saw the value of a thorough study and possible reorganization of the operation of the railroad company. Therefore he chose three directors, including a past president, Joseph Patterson, to serve with him on a committee to investigate B & O organization and management.[16]

One of the first problems to concern them was the high cost of horse power required in Baltimore and at Parr's Ridge. Little could be done about Baltimore for the moment; the city was not yet sufficiently acquainted with steam power to permit locomotives on public streets. But something could be done at Parr's Ridge, and the committee consulted Moncure Robinson, who had supervised construction of the Allegheny Portage Railroad on the main line of the Pennsylvania state canal system.[17] The eventual solution was a new road around the ridge that eliminated all need of either stationary engines or horse power. Even though the new road added three miles to the distance, it reduced travel time between Baltimore and Harper's Ferry by one hour upon its completion, two years later, and the expected savings amounted to $50,000.[18]

Other early decisions following recommendations from the new committee on organization and management recognized McLane as a professional administrator by giving him the power to appoint and dismiss employees of the company when the board was not in session and sought to cut expenses by rescinding a contract for the construction and repair of locomotives held by George Gillingham and Ross Winans, who leased the Mount Clare shops of the B & O in Baltimore for this purpose. Hereafter, the company would operate these shops and make its own repairs; purchases would be made competitively to get the best equipment available.[19]

Despite increased passenger and freight charges since April, McLane admitted in the fall that revenues had not increased as expected and therefore that there would be no dividends. At this time, however, when he had spent only a few months in his new office, the failure to pay a dividend cannot have bothered him very much. The financial panic of the spring was excuse enough. Meanwhile his committee on organization and management was studying means of reducing costs, including such questions as the comparative efficiency of wood and anthracite as fuel (decided in favor of wood) and the best means of repairing machinery and of reconstructing the road.[20]

In January, 1838, the same committee proposed to the board a reorganization plan that originated with McLane, with the implication that it arose from observations made by him and by the company engineers in the course of visits they had made to most of the railroads then in operation. Company business by this plan was to be divided among three departments: (1) construction and repair, which would have the duty of keeping the road in order; (2) transportation, in charge of the rolling stock and of scheduling use of the road; and (3) accounts. The object was to provide efficiency, accountability, and conformity to orders, centralizing authority in functional departments, with the president responsible for vigilant supervision over all.[21]

As these suggestions were put into effect, they seemed to have worked out to mean four departments rather than three. Accounts were handled by the house department, which came directly under the president, but the work of the other two divisions was spread three ways. The engineer department was in charge of construction and directed by the chief engineer, Jonathan Knight, a Pennsylvanian who had formerly been chief engineer on the National Road. A machinery department had charge of all repairs, and a transport department operated the rolling stock. This division of responsibilities continued in effect until a grand reorganization scheme was adopted in 1847.[22]

A new source of income in McLane's first year with the B & O came from a two-year contract he made with the Postmaster General for the transportation of mail between Baltimore and Washington. A federal statute of July 7, 1838, making all railroads post routes and authorizing their use, opened further possibilities of revenue from this business, at the same time that the B & O was being tied into a network of railroads by the completion of the Philadelphia, Wilmington, & Baltimore Railroad, which used a new depot on Pratt Street jointly with the B & O. Not without some opposition, however. Baltimore draymen were unhappy to lose their transshipment business, and some Baltimore merchants felt that this connection threatened to rob Baltimore of its status as a terminal for western produce and turn it into a way station on the road to Philadelphia.[23]

Such men must have been appalled by a toast offered to Matthew Newkirk, the railroad entrepreneur, at a celebration in July, 1837, marking the opening of a section of his road between Baltimore and Wilmington: "By his aid Philadelphia had grappled the city of Baltimore to her bosom with hooks of steel."[24] In 1838 the B & O board determined to sever this close connection by declaring it needed exclusive use of the Pratt Street depot. But somehow joint occupancy was continued until 1842, when it was the P W & B that announced it would end the previous arrangement and build a station of its own, as it eventually did.[25]

IV   FURTHER CONSTRUCTION

It was by design and not just by chance that the B & O long eluded an interior connection with Pennsylvania railroads leading eventually to Philadelphia. The Cumberland Valley Railroad from Harrisburg to Chambersburg was to be extended by a spur called the Franklin Railroad to Hagerstown, and through Hagerstown the B & O was committed to build. But before the B & O continued westward McLane wished to be sure the way was clear before it to the Ohio. A preliminary survey directed by Jonathan Knight and completed in October, 1837, showed construction over the mountains to Wheeling, with a branch going to Pittsburgh, to be entirely practicable for railroad traffic, without resort to inclined planes.[26] A branch had to be planned to Pittsburgh because Pennsylvania demanded it in allowing the B & O a right-of-way. And a right-of-way through Pennsylvania was important because the most likely route from Harper's Ferry to Wheeling led, like the National Road, across the southwestern corner of Pennsylvania.

The immediate problem, however, was Virginia, because the rights of the B & O to extend its line in Virginia expired in 1837, whereas its rights in Pennsylvania were good until 1843. Virginia was particularly important to the B & O because the railroad management decided in December, 1837, to build on the Virginia side of the Potomac from Harper's Ferry to Cumberland. In doing so (and avoiding Hagerstown) they knew they stood to forfeit a million dollars of the Maryland sub-scription, but they hoped to get help of an even larger figure from Virginia. They must also have hoped to get this provision changed in the Maryland legislature, where McLane and some of his directors spent several days lobbying for the company in January, 1838.[27]

At any rate, with the preliminary surveys on hand as a basis, the B & O directors were able to compare estimated costs of various possible routes westward. The Virginia route avoided competition with the Chesapeake and Ohio Canal, which would have the north shore of the Potomac to itself. Another advantage, apparently unstated at the time though referred to later, was the avoidance of a junction with the Franklin Railroad at Hagerstown. The western business that the extended B & O brought to Harper's Ferry would be directed to Baltimore, not funneled off toward Philadelphia at Hagerstown.

A route across Virginia from Harper's Ferry to Cumberland was shorter, too, and cheaper than building through Hagerstown, which involved some backtracking to the north before proceeding westward—though in this mountainous area the straightest route was not necessarily the cheapest. Most important, if the railroad were built across Virginia, Virginia might be called upon for a substantial stock subscription by way of subsidy—most likely for two fifths of costs, a proportion Virginia had offered to other internal improvements.

With this in mind, a lobbying party of the B & O set off for Richmond on March 12, 1838, consisting of Louis McLane and the two members of his board of directors with notable Virginia connections—John Pendleton Kennedy, lawyer and litterateur, and John Spear Nicholas. They traveled overnight by the new bay steamer *Alabama* to Norfolk and there took the James River steamboat *Patrick Henry* to Richmond, where they met their chief engineer Jonathan Knight, who had preceded them. Knight was able to give them details of a favorable Virginia statute, approved March 9, which allowed the city of Wheeling to subscribe for 10,000 shares of B & O stock, which meant $1 million, an important incentive to extension of the railroad through Virginia.

The journal of the trip kept by Kennedy affords an unusual glimpse of lobbying methods of this day. Kennedy prepared for the Virginia legislature a formal statement of the argument for assisting this railroad, accompanying it with statistical tables. The major effort, however, seems to have been made through the informal interviews and conversations of these B & O delegates and various important Virginians. Spear Nicholas, himself a Baltimore lawyer, was the son of Judge Philip Norborne Nicholas, a leading member of the political clique called the Richmond Junto, and both Judge Nicholas and his son Robert Carter Nicholas entertained the Baltimore visitors at dinner. Judge Nicholas had about twenty men in to meet them—including Judge Henry St. George Tucker (half brother of John Randolph of Roanoke) and a Brockenbrough, a Cabell, and a Daniel—and Robert Nicholas, too, had "a large company" to meet them. They also dined in a party of twenty at Judge Tucker's and in a party of twenty-three at the home of Judge Brockenbrough—probably John Brockenbrough, president of the Bank of Virginia—and they supped with Conway Robertson, president of the railroad from Richmond to Fredericksburg, and with Governor David Campbell. One evening they held a levee in their rooms at the Eagle Hotel, entertaining fifty or sixty members of the legislature. On other occasions legislators called on them separately.

McLane complained of rheumatism, but perhaps he was even more bothered by the intrigues of John Bruce, president of the Winchester & Potomac Railroad, who had promised the B & O delegation every assistance beforehand but actually embarrassed their efforts in Richmond by trying to persuade them to buy his unprofitable railroad—probably at the instance of Judge Tucker, a Winchester man, who was said to have $5,000 invested in it. When Kennedy and McLane left Richmond on March 25, Nicholas and Knight remaining behind, they felt their plans were succeeding. So they were, for on April 2 Virginia extended the privileges of the B & O to 1843 and promised a subscription of $1,058,420, two fifths of the estimated cost of construction from Harper's Ferry to Cumberland. The Virginia statute required the road to proceed on Virginia soil to within six miles of Cumberland and to make Wheeling a terminus, but this route was apparently the one the B & O had decided on anyway, and Wheeling had been thought of as one of several terminal points from the beginning.[28]

V   CUMBERLAND SOUGHT

The journey of March, 1838, to Richmond was but one of many such trips undertaken by McLane for the Baltimore & Ohio Railroad, though thanks to John Pendleton Kennedy's diary this trip is documented as few if any other trips are. Whether because of his political and diplomatic experience or merely from some unusual personal aptitude, McLane was able to perform such missions with value to the railroad and credit to himself. The B & O counsel, John H. B. Latrobe, declared he never met anyone, not even excepting Daniel Webster, "who possessed in the same degree [as McLane] the faculty of stating a case clearly" and of making an argument in support of his case without seeming to do any more than present the facts. "He was not a pleasant person to get along with," Latrobe added. "He was peremptory and at times uncertain, and would not abide opposition or differences of opinion." [29] But just as on coming to Congress, a young and unknown Federalist, he won respect for his opinions, so as B & O president McLane proved able still to argue a case forcefully when he found it necessary.

McLane found it necessary to argue forcefully for the B & O in Washington in the fall of 1838 before he could hope to extend the road through Virginia from Harper's Ferry to Cumberland. The Winchester & Potomac, apparently angry because it could not sell its line to the B & O, refused the latter road the use of its right-of-way out of Harper's Ferry. The only suitable alternative was to get War Department approval for use of part of a military reservation beside the Harper's Ferry arsenal for B & O trains going westward after leaving the Potomac River bridge. This meant that McLane had to go to Washington and negotiate with officials of the Van Buren government. Fortunately, the Secretary of War was Joel Poinsett, with whom his relations had never been difficult, and War Department approval of the desired B & O right-of-way was assured before a stockholders' meeting in November, 1838, was asked to approve the Virginia grant, including its limitations on both the route and the terminus of the western extension. [30]

Several trips were necessary to Annapolis for every one to Richmond or Washington. In the winter of 1840–41 McLane was so often away lobbying that he apologized to his son Louis for his "constant absence at Annapolis." "Your father," Kitty wrote Lou, who was in Philadelphia preparing for midshipman's examinations, "is all the time at this Seat of Government. Came up yesterday, goes down this afternoon, so as to be ready for the meeting of the Legislature in the morning." [31]

The Maryland state government was, of course, of great importance to the B & O, more even than the municipal government of Baltimore. To raise the charge for hauling flour, its principal freight, eastward, the B & O had to secure an amendment of its charter from the Maryland legislature.[32] To reduce fares on the Washington Branch in order to meet the competition of steamboats and stagecoaches, the railroad again needed Maryland's approval.[33] When the authorities of Washington County sued the B & O for not building its main stem westward through Hagerstown, McLane successfully sought statutory permission to avoid Hagerstown without the threatened forfeit of $1 million of the state aid —which had not yet become fully available to the B & O anyway.[34]

Most critical of McLane's missions to Annapolis were those concerned with financing the road. The $3 million state subscription to the B & O was a tremendous resource nominally, but it came in the form of state bonds that first the state and then the B & O failed to market. The B & O wanted to get face value or nearly face value for them—and the fact that they were part of an $8 million internal improvement loan made them all the less desirable to investors. Advised by George Peabody that sterling bonds, payable in London, would have an advantage in the overseas market, the state converted the dollar bonds to sterling. In April, 1839, $3.2 million worth of 5 percent sterling bonds, payable, principal and interest, in London, were issued directly to the B & O, which was compensated by the extra $200,000 for guaranteeing the interest for three years. Security for the interest payments for these three years was to be furnished by a mortgage on the railroad, which mortgage was executed in June, 1839.[35]

McLane, who had personally lobbied for this measure in Annapolis, despite an attack of gout, felt that his company now had the "go ahead" signal. Perhaps he had hoped for something more than he had achieved— the estimated cost of extending the road from Harper's Ferry through Cumberland to Wheeling and, by a branch, to Pittsburgh, was $9.5 million, and the funds earmarked for the B & O ($3 million from Maryland; $3 million from Baltimore; $1,358,000 from Virginia; and $1 million from Wheeling) were short by more than $1 million. But something could be hoped for from Pittsburgh or the state of Pennsylvania, and it was always possible to knock on Maryland's door again. Private investors could hardly be counted on for a direct investment; the last installments on B & O stock had just been collected, and the state and city bonds would now flood the capital market, offering what looked like a secure investment.

The immediate problem was to get the road to the Ohio built in a hurry before the Pennsylvania and Virginia charters expired, as they were to do in 1843. The B & O board of directors, meeting on May 1,

1839, adopted what they called the northern route from Cumberland through Pennsylvania, near Connellsville, to Wheeling, and a stockholders' meeting on May 10 heard McLane speak and then formally accepted the provisions of the Maryland sterling bond subscription. When McLane returned to his office from the stockholders' meeting, he felt confident. "The prompt and vigorous prosecution of the work," he wrote, ". . . is no longer uncertain, and can only be retarded by an unfavorable state in the stock market." [36]

The city of Baltimore required that its subscription to the B & O should be used in extending the road in an unbroken line westward from Harper's Ferry, because it wanted to be sure that the trade of the railroad was led directly to Baltimore. Since the Virginia subscription was not to be forthcoming until the line through Virginia was completed, the Baltimore grant, which was intended to be paid in cash at not more than $1 million a year, became the chief reliance for the expenses of construction between Harper's Ferry and Cumberland. Despite his confident tone in public, McLane was oppressed by the tightening of credit in the summer of 1839 and he warned the directors that contracts should not be let until money to pay them was in hand or in immediate prospect. Because of his fears, the B & O board decided to ask Baltimore city banks to advance a loan of $500,000 on the security of city bonds.[37] Upon assurance that the money would be raised, the railroad gave out contracts for the line to Cumberland and urged its surveyors to complete their work on the other side of the mountains, including the final stretch from Brownsville, Pennsylvania, to Wheeling.[38]

It was disappointing to the B & O interests that they were offered no help from Pennsylvania, not even an extension of their charter except on terms so demanding that they could not be accepted.[39] Therefore it was doubly important to raise money and rush construction of the whole line at once. After traveling to Philadelphia and New York in a vain effort to market Maryland state bonds, McLane prepared for a still longer trip, for he heard the bonds could be disposed of at a decent price in London.

Considering his previous experience in London, he was the logical man to go there for the company, but he did not relish the trip and absolutely refused to make it in the winter. He could not, of course, forget his propensity to seasickness. He had been ill, and he was greatly concerned by his lawsuit with the Bayards, which had been argued in the early winter but was not to be decided until the May term. Kitty, who had been living at Bohemia ever since she left New York in 1837, came down to Baltimore to nurse him and found him in dreadful spirits, worried where the money would come from if he lost the suit and had to pay the Bayards from his inheritance, which, what was left of it, was tied up in land. He

had participated in the speculative schemes of his friend Samuel Swartwout, but Swartwout's bubble had burst and Swartwout himself had fled
abroad. Out of the office McLane lived like a hermit, taking no society
and no pleasure, according to Kitty.[40]

But his own correspondence shows that he was concerned about Kitty's
health and that he tried to use his influence with the Secretary of War
to have Bob transferred to Baltimore after long service in the Seminole
campaign in Florida—a favor Secretary Poinsett was glad to perform.[41]
To a lady from a neighboring estate on the Eastern Shore of Maryland
McLane was the personification of courtesy when she was passing
through Baltimore on her way to Washington on an errand concerned
with her son's status in the Army. McLane took her into his parlor,
attended her to the depot, "was not merely the high bred gentleman but
an old and kind friend." [42]

This was in July of 1839, and perhaps by this time McLane was more
content and more cheerful. As yet, at any rate, he had escaped financial
ruin. No decision had been released in the Bayard case because one of
the judges was ill.[43] The terms on which he was going abroad had been
decided upon by the directors, and were not unfavorable: $8,000 certain
for his expenses and a second $8,000 if he disposed of the bonds; his
salary not to be cut while he was away (for his family expenses would
be the same as if he were at home); no restrictions at all upon his negotiating authority, and he could, therefore, sell all or part of the bonds or
borrow on them, as he saw fit. A few of the directors, led by John White,
the former cashier of the Baltimore branch of the Bank of the United
States and now one of the directors representing the stock held by the
city of Baltimore, wished to limit the sale price of the bonds to a minimum of 90 percent of par, but they were outvoted. The directors understood that in McLane they had a man uniquely suited for this mission
by his wide acquaintance in banking and political circles, in England
as well as at home.[44]

VI   MISSION TO LONDON

There was every reason for McLane's spirits to be roused by this journey to London for the B & O. Everybody in Maryland was waiting for
news of it, his son Robert wrote, "and should you succeed in your mission—so great is their idea of the difficulties you have to encounter—I
have no doubt in the world it will produce the greatest enthusiasm of
feeling in your favor—and fate only can tell to what it may lead." [45]

To what it may lead! These were words to excite old, forgotten aspirations in McLane. But, alas, the trip was made at the wrong time. McLane

arrived in Liverpool on September 8, 1839, "shattered and reduced by sea sickness and starvation," having lived on soda powders and dry toast soaked in coffee for the last nine days of a fourteen-day voyage.[46] As soon as possible he was off for London, where he found American securities had become a drug on the market. Indiana 5 percent bonds would not sell, even when offered at 66. Samuel Jaudon, agent of the Bank of the United States in London, had sold at 85 some Maryland sterling bonds he got from the Susquehanna and Tidewater Canal, and another agent (probably Peabody) had "huckstered off," in McLane's words, a few thousand of the same bonds from the Chesapeake and Ohio Canal at the same rate or less. But these were small sales; if McLane threw a large quantity of the bonds on the market, they "would not bring any price whatever."

The great problem facing McLane in his effort to sell bonds was the immense quantity of American securities available. In the three years between 1836 and 1838, inclusive, the individual American states, largely out of their enthusiasm for internal improvements, had issued more bonds than in the previous half century. The $3 million in sterling bonds that McLane sought to market was less than half of the total Maryland issue, and McLane's attempt to work jointly with the Chesapeake and Ohio Canal Company agent failed because the canal needed money so desperately that it could not delay sales to keep the price high.

A panic, of which the 1837 crisis was but the forerunner, struck the American economy in the fall of 1839, and the depression deepened over the next three years. Even before the Bank of the United States suspended specie payments on October 9, McLane saw that the depression in the security market would last for years. He negotiated, therefore, with the Barings—he was well acquainted with Joshua Bates, the American partner in this firm—and arranged for them to take all the sterling bonds assigned by Maryland to the B & O, using them as security for such advances as the B & O might need to push construction. None were to be sold at less than 85, and the bonds could be withdrawn from the Barings (except insofar as pledged for any loan) or sold at home at any time. The Barings did finally succeed in getting from George Peabody the unsold Maryland sterling bonds that had been assigned to the Chesapeake and Ohio Canal and thereafter controlled the major part of this issue and sustained the credit of Maryland—until 1842 when the state ceased paying interest on its obligations.[47]

The arrangement that McLane made was probably a brilliant one, conserving the bonds as a resource that eventually enabled the B & O to reach its goal. But he was unhappy with his journey. Apparently he sought to market some securities of his own, some "coal shares," and was unable to get rid of them; apparently a short trip to Holland was of no help to him; and news that his agent Finley had failed and cost him the income from his crops at Bohemia, perhaps $1,200, was one more depressing event. London was "unusually thin"; "indeed," he wrote, "so entirely deserted is it that where I expected to find so many acquaintances not one of those to whom I had the pleasure of being particularly known is in the city, and I really feel quite desolate." On October 19 he boarded the *Great Western*, and he was in New York on November 3.[48]

Although a Baltimore newspaper celebrated "a much more flattering and gratifying result of his mission than could have been anticipated," McLane was depressed to find financial prospects at home very gloomy.[49] In October the stringency in the money market and uncertainty of disposing of city or state bonds had led the Baltimore & Ohio Railroad to call in all its surveying parties from west of Cumberland, even though their work was not complete. Construction work on the section between Harper's Ferry and Cumberland, which had been begun in September, was continued, though at a circumscribed rate, with 1,495 men and 466 horses employed at the end of the year and one eighth of the work accomplished. Money was available, from the sum loaned by Baltimore banks on a pledge of city stock, to keep the work going on until the 1st of February.[50]

McLane had a plan to keep construction going even if, for the moment, no more bonds could be sold and no bank loans negotiated. At the first meeting of the B & O board of directors after his return he proposed an inquiry into the possibility of issuing "small notes payable in the City Stock." Six directors, led by John White, opposed the proposal and insisted that their opposition be recorded in the minutes, but McLane had his way; his plan was sent to the committee on finance with instructions to consult John H. B. Latrobe, the company counsel.

Apparently Latrobe's opinion was favorable, for on December 4 only White and one other director continued in opposition when the directors voted to empower McLane to issue up to $100,000 worth of $5 and $10 certificates. On the same day John White alone opposed a resolution that it would be injurious to stop any part of the work in progress on the railroad. White, apparently, thought construction should be stopped at Hancock, which was approximately halfway between Harper's Ferry and Cumberland.[51]

This was not the first time the B & O had considered issuing certificates that would circulate like currency. Shortly after McLane took office, at a time when "shinplasters" or fractional currency were being widely used in the currency shortage resulting from the Panic of 1837, the directors authorized McLane to issue certificates for any money the company needed to borrow in the emergency. A sum of $141,768.94 was borrowed for construction necessities by the end of November, but it is not clear whether shinplasters or any sort of circulating paper furnished even a small part of this sum. Payment of the final installments due from subscribers to B & O stock was to wipe out this debt, and business recovery by the end of 1837 probably obviated any necessity of appealing to the Bank of the United States for a guarantee of B & O notes, as was at one time contemplated.[52] Late in 1838, however, the Baltimore *Sun* was complaining, "Why are railroad and canal companies permitted to issue shinplasters?" and since "railroad" generally meant the B & O to Baltimoreans, this note suggests that B & O certificates, issued under the authorization given by the directors in July, 1837, were still circulating. The *Sun* may have had no thought at all of the transformation of the Morris from a canal to a banking company when it reviewed the status of the B & O and protested against its being granted banking privileges or allowed to fall "into the grasp of cormorants" who would sacrifice "this great national work" to their worship of the almighty dollar.[53]

Considerable opposition appeared when the B & O board of directors in December, 1839, set about carrying out McLane's scheme for the stock orders, as these "small notes payable in the City Stock" were called. Interest-paying city of Baltimore bonds (called "stock" then) were to be turned over to two commissioners in the amount of stock orders that were issued, and these commissioners would serve as trustees, holding the bonds and paying them out to anyone presenting stock orders in the amount of $100. By this device of placing the city bonds in a trust, the stock orders would be known to have secure backing and therefore might be circulated easily until someone finding himself possessed of $100 in these $5 and $10 certificates took the trouble to exchange them for a bond, in order to be getting interest. In this way, McLane explained to the stockholders in his annual report, a great enterprise can be prosecuted on the basis of the distribution of city bonds at par, while the state bonds, in the hands of the Barings, are held for a good market and the credit of the state is maintained. "The expedient may not be successful," he confessed, "but the stake is too great and the crisis too urgent to warrant the board in leaving it untried." [54]

VII   THE STOCK ORDERS AND A STRIKE

Governor William Grason, a Federalist farmer from the Eastern Shore who had turned Jacksonian, viewed the stock order scheme with foreboding. Neither Baltimore city bonds nor Maryland state bonds were presently a suitable foundation for a circulating medium. They were not valued at par; had they been, they would have been sold. A certain amount of paper could, he admitted, be issued by a company like the B & O, constantly paying and receiving money, because some paper could be kept in circulation (like tokens for a city transit system) by answering the needs of money in the normal transactions of this company. But once more paper is issued than will freely circulate, its value falls below the value of the stock in which it is convertible. Brokers will buy the certificates at a discount and sell them to capitalists, still at less than the value of the bonds in which the capitalists will invest. And, of course, these bonds have already depreciated, because only their depreciation has suggested the idea of issuing certificates, not in just a small amount for circulation, but to such an excess as to coerce their conversion into depreciated bonds. A particular evil of the use of certificates, Governor Grason saw clearly: they "will be distributed in small sums, along the line of the works, among laborers and others, who do not deal in stocks and . . . are not able to make permanent investments." [55] The governor did not see clearly that the alternative to McLane's use of stock orders was no work at no pay.

Yet his criticism so disturbed the railroad directorate that it appointed a committee to prepare an answer. Membership in the committee was carefully arranged to include three directors who were Democrats, like Governor Grason, and two Whigs, Samuel Donaldson and Fielding Lucas, Jr., who were the commissioners holding the city bonds as a trust. But the company's retort was written by none of these men but by a sixth director, John Pendleton Kennedy, who as a political opponent of the governor was carefully kept in the background though acknowledged to be the most literary member of the board.

Kennedy's long response, published separately as a forty-four-page pamphlet, could not very effectively rebut the governor's arguments regarding the stock orders, but on many other points it did answer the governor. He had for instance claimed that the B & O was proceeding to extend its line without money or means, and Kennedy noted that $500,000 had been raised on the city bonds by a loan; the governor criticized the arrangements made abroad with the Barings, and Kennedy defended these arrangements, particularly in comparison with the sale of bonds by the Chesapeake and Ohio Canal. A paper war followed, in which the governor was assisted by John White, the recalcitrant city director who wished, according to Kennedy, to be made president of the B & O. Even McLane was driven to enter the squabble with a letter defending his negotiations abroad. [56]

In defense of the B & O it was pointed out that all its construction contracts contained clauses permitting their cancellation if financial resources proved wanting. Furthermore, it was argued with much truth that in pressing on to Cumberland the B & O was merely following public demand, not in advance of it. Mayor Leakin of Baltimore professed himself entirely sympathetic to the steps taken by the railroad leadership, including the use of stock orders, which he noted the B & O would gladly abandon if the city could pay its subscription in any form that would permit rapid completion of the work.[57]

Even the governor had confessed that the B & O was the only internal improvement aided by the state government that kept all its engagements and paid the state regularly (5 percent of gross profits plus dividends from the Washington Branch) from its income. Friends of the B & O were encouraged when they could report that the Barings had some success in disposing of state bonds—at 85, the minimum permitted—early in 1840. Unfortunately the market fell then, instead of rising, and no further sales could be anticipated in the near future.[58]

But the B & O pushed on, regardless of sales of the Maryland bonds, despite criticism. Stock orders became the chief reliance, once the $500,000 loan from Baltimore banks was spent. On March 4, 1840, smaller certificates—for only $2 and $3—were approved, to a total of $100,000. On April 1 another issue of $500,000 was approved over the objections of John White and two other directors.[59] Soon $1 and $100 notes were also being issued, so many of the former that McLane was authorized to hire a clerk to help him sign them.[60]

By the end of September, 1840, over half of the extension to Cumberland was complete, and work was moving ahead rapidly with 1,600 men and 500 horses on the job and completion expected in 1842. The cost per month was reckoned at $75,000, mainly provided through stock orders, of which $515,000 had been issued, largely ($354,000) in the smallest ($1) certificates. The stock orders had been supplemented by another method of financing construction—the issuance of city bonds (the amount being just under $140,000) directly to contractors at par, with an understanding that these bonds would be sold only at prices approved by the railroad and by a mutual agent so as to prevent a rapid depreciation.

Because most of the stock orders were in very low amounts and only $10,000 out of the total of $515,000 had been funded in city bonds it is evident that these certificates were circulating in some manner and not coming into the hands of investors, who would have hurriedly funded them in $100 units in order to collect interest on the bonds. McLane dared even to boast of the low rate of funding, arguing that unfunded certificates meant a large annual savings in interest.[61] Apparently forgotten was the argument that the use of stock orders allowed ordinary people a chance to invest in a savings fund paying 6 percent, once they converted their certificates into city bonds.[62]

However, ordinary people in the depression year of 1840 apparently did not often retain the stock orders till they had the $100 worth they needed for funding. Poor Richard to the contrary, saving one of the lowest-valued certificates did not easily lead to the acquisition of ninety-nine more. Nevertheless, the use of stock orders seems to have created no immediate problems between the B & O and the people who received them. Of course, the B & O itself was not dealing with the laborers who were working on the extension of the road. They were employed by contractors, and it was to the contractors that their complaints would be addressed. Still, if the laborers had complained effectively, the contractors would have hesitated to receive stock orders or to undertake the railroad jobs. The depression made laborers and contractors alike glad to get any pay at all. And the early issues of stock orders were absorbed in circulation with little depreciation in a time of money stringency.

The B & O did have labor troubles in 1840, but the cause was not the stock orders but the attempt of management to make employees pay for any damages due to their agency. According to McLane, dismissal was not punishment enough to ensure carefulness in an employment where mistakes could easily lead to fatalities. He told of cases such as one in February, 1840, when the conductor and engineer of a freight train from Washington decided not to wait on a siding for the passenger train from Baltimore but to beat it to the Relay House. They did not quite succeed; the two trains "came in contact" and $1,200 in damages occurred. The two men at fault were fired and their wages retained, but the engineer sued for his back wages and won his case.

After other similar cases, McLane had his counsel, John H. B. Latrobe, prepare a new contract authorizing the B & O to retain wages in such cases—just as a 20 percent forfeit was written into all grading contracts for the new extension. The new contract, which was put to use in July, 1840, was not offered to common laborers, but only to men in responsible positions where neglect could cause fatalities—switchmen, depot agents and clerks, drivers, shop foremen, and the like.

A good many of them refused to sign, and the leader of these recalcitrants, a man named Ziegler who was head of the machine shops, was called in by McLane on the evening of July 15. McLane reminded Ziegler, who had twice forfeited wages for damages due to his neglect, that a workman always could appeal a fine to the board and told him further that he could take to the end of the month to sign the new contract. But Ziegler said he might as well quit at once and on returning to the shops talked to the workmen with such effect that they all went on strike the next morning.

Ziegler, in particular, was a hard man to replace, and when men outside the shops followed the example of the shop workers, even the mail trains ceased to run from Baltimore. On McLane's application, police were sent to the Baltimore depots, and after a week a few loyal engineers, supplemented by men brought from Philadelphia, had the trains running again.

On July 24, before workmen had been imported from Philadelphia, McLane called the problem to the attention of the board of directors at a special meeting and asked for their backing. They closed ranks, approved McLane's course unanimously, and instructed him to protect the property.[63]

A few days later when a committee of the workmen called on McLane to propose terms on which they would return to work, he refused all negotiations. The majority of the workmen, he told the committee, were welcome to return to work at any time, but the strike leaders, those "chiefly active in fomenting the troubles and instrumental in misleading others would not be reemployed upon any terms."

Apparently he had his way—helped, of course, by the bad times which made jobs relatively scarce. The contract the men were asked to sign was altered a bit—simplified but left as comprehensive as before.[64] By the fall of 1840 McLane was able to report a successful year of operations. A surplus allowed a 4½ percent dividend on the Washington Branch (and this would have been 7 percent had not one fifth of gross receipts from passengers gone to the state as bonus) and a 2 percent dividend on the Main Stem (the first since McLane had been president). To McLane's particular delight as an administrator he could announce that freight costs had been reduced one cent per ton mile on the entire system, and that outstanding debts of $114,125 had been paid off in the fiscal year—as had over $67,000 of the $500,000 borrowed from Baltimore banks to finance the extension. If the B & O had not been legally required to carry flour at a loss, his record of management might have been even better than it was. But he could take great pride in his success in making his business pay, for under his administration the net profits had grown from $12,176 in the year ending September 30, 1837, to $157,694 in 1840.[65]

VIII   THE TROUBLED FATHER

One of the developments that made the winter of 1840–41 a happy one for Louis McLane was the news that had come to him at Christmas-

time of a favorable decision in his long suit with the Bayards over the
Amelia Island ship forfeitures. At last on December 24, 1840, after more
than a week of argument and study, a three-judge court of errors and
appeals, from which his antagonist Chief Justice Richard Bayard and
his brother-in-law Judge John Milligan had been excused from serving,
had ruled unanimously that the chancellor's decision in favor of McLane
should be upheld, that there was no need to pay the children of James
Bayard anything out of the forfeiture money Louis McLane had received
by the will of his father.[66] It was a great relief because the money was
long ago invested and, to some extent, lost in speculations.

"I am poor and in debt," he had written Bob in November before the
Bayard suit was decided, explaining why he could not afford to give his
grown sons an independent allowance. "If my lawsuit should terminate
favorably for me," he added, "I will have it in my power to do more for
my children."[67]

Whether he gave them an allowance is unknown. The great demands
that a large family made on McLane were met, in part, by securing Army
or Navy commissions for the older boys. Bob, in the United States Army
Topographical Corps, received assignments in various parts of the country but managed to spend the winter of 1839–40 exhibiting a taste for
politics and studying law in Washington, where he was admitted to the
bar.[68] In the summer he was out in the field on surveys, and in September of 1840 he managed to get to Wisconsin to look into the status of
some investments his father had made in land there, including lots in the
city of Madison.[69] In the winter of 1841 he was sent abroad by the Army
to study canal construction in Western Europe.[70]

The third son, Allan, studied briefly at Princeton and then followed
Lou into the Navy. Their younger brothers, George and Charles, went
to St. Mary's College (a preparatory school) in Baltimore, while Juliette
followed her sisters to Mme Sigoigne's school in Philadelphia.[71] Many
young men came calling on the older girls at Bohemia, where the family
lived, or at the Exchange Hotel in Baltimore, when they were visiting
their father.

Sally, who was generally considered the family beauty, was the first
to marry. Her husband was Henry Tiffany, son of a Baltimore merchant.
The Tiffanys came from New England and set up the first large jobbing
house in Baltimore, where they made a great fortune and were, in the
words of Kitty McLane, an Eastern Shore aristocrat at heart, "advancing
slowly in society." Sally and Henry Tiffany presented Kitty with her first
grandchild, named Kate for both Kitty and her Aunt Milligan. Later
Sally and Henry had two other children, another Henry and a Louis Mc-
Lane Tiffany, but the marriage did not turn out happily for Sally in the

long run. Nevertheless, in the winter of 1841 the Tiffanys were frequently a comfort and a refuge for other McLanes, and the family correspondence furnishes a vignette of Sally and Henry visiting her father's rooms in the Exchange Hotel and playing "a sober game of wist" for her father's amusement after tea.[72]

Kitty found a winter in Baltimore "wearing and wearesome" in these years when she was growing fat and rheumatic, and she was happiest at her Bohemia home, where she was comforted by familiar surroundings, such as the little parlor's red furniture that had grown somewhat shabby till she covered it with gray linen, the "beautiful New York carpet" in the dining room and the cosy chair and English sofa that converted it into a "comfortable sitting room as well as a *salle à manger.*"[73] But the girls, including Lydia, who "made her debut" there in the winter of 1840, found Baltimore "very gay." Besides Baltimore they frequently visited in Washington and Wilmington, where young Charles was sent to John Bullock's Quaker school and Juliette frequently stayed with the Gareschés. There were also occasional visits to Philadelphia, New York, and even such distant spas as Saratoga. The older McLane children, Rebecca particularly, were friendly with the Hamiltons of New York, and there was much visiting back and forth between the family estates, Bohemia and Nevis. Allan brought a South Carolina Petigru home from Princeton; Bob brought an Army friend home from the Florida campaign, a Virginian named Joseph Eggleston Johnston who showed particular interest in Lydia.[74]

All of the McLanes were saddened by the death in Louisiana in the spring of 1841 of Kitty's favorite brother, George Baldwin Milligan, Louis McLane's onetime partner in a milling venture on the Brandywine. Lydia Sims rushed off to Louisiana and reached her brother before his death.[75] His orphan son, Bayard, was at the time in Europe with his Urquhart grandfather; and Bob McLane, spending much time with the Urquharts in France and Italy, followed in his uncle's footsteps by falling in love with one of the Urquhart girls.

Before Bob and Georgine Urquhart were married early in August in Paris, Bob's sisters and mother sent their love and his father sent advice. However well intentioned he was, Louis tended to be heavy-handed and overserious when writing to his children. His advice had not been asked, he admonished Bob, and having never met the girl he could do nothing but trust Bob, approve his choice, and welcome his bride. With the usual complaints about his poverty—the financial burden of his large family was a problem Louis McLane could never forget—he assured Bob that the welfare of his children was the only thing in life that still interested him, and that "deprived of the means of affording . . . pecuniary assistance," he was all the more solicitous of advancing the happiness of his children by all the other means in his power. "Mutual love and affection—pure and ardent enough to outlive and defy all the vicissitudes" of life were the most essential ingredients to a marriage. And in the next paragraph, he added: "I take it for granted that both the Lady and her Parents know that with my scant means and large family you will be necessarily dependent upon your own exertions." In his next letter McLane made more explicit his advice "to be sure of some aid from Mr. U. [Urquhart] who has ample ability to grant it, or of the Lady's disposition and ability to be reconciled to the altered condition to which in case he should refuse," she will be compelled to accustom herself.[76]

Heavy and sober as his manner was, McLane wrote truthfully when he spoke of his solicitude for his sons. He not only followed their careers with personal advice but used such influence as he had to get them assignments they chose. If some of the children did not learn to love him, this was the fault of his nature, for this intelligent, ambitious, industrious man was too clever, too vain, too hard, to be easily loved.

If his ambitions for his children were very high, they were hardly higher than his father's had been for him. If John Quincy Adams's story that Louis McLane was named for the dauphin of France and was expected to succeed to Washington's throne was not wholly true, it is still true that his father had the highest aspirations for him. And it was Louis's aspirations for his eldest son that led him to an unkind remark about Bob: "He has, I fear, played the fool with a little *creole!* However, if he is happy I ought to be content tho' it is a bitter pill." [77]

IX POLITICAL POSSIBILITIES

The victory of the Whigs in the presidential election of 1840 must have brought some pleasure to Louis McLane. It was not that he loved Harrison so much, but that he disliked Van Buren more. Bob, who was particularly sensitive to his father's opinions as well as sympathetic with them, reported from Europe that he had told Andrew Stevenson, now minister at London, "what a dog" he thought Van Buren was—a statement that indicates not only what Bob thought of Van Buren but what he thought his father wanted to hear about the President.[78]

Yet according to Robert McLane's *Reminiscences,* written many years later, he himself remained "a steady Democrat," though doubting that Van Buren had "the moral and intellectual force to breast the storm that swept over the country." [79] It may seem that his memory was convenient, but probably in this case it was correct. Louis McLane's enemies in Delaware were in the Harrison camp, and therefore Louis was not likely to feel any enthusiasm for the Whigs other than a desire to see Van Buren humiliated. Certainly Kitty did not sound like a Harrison admirer when she wrote of seing the "renowned hero of Tippecanoe" pass through Baltimore in February, 1841, on his way to Washington and his death, "very much broke and looking much older" than she expected. Looks are not important if only the man himself is what he should be, she added; *"of this,* I have my doubts." [80] After Harrison's death McLane was reported to have said the old general was a habitual drunkard and to have given several instances to support the charge.[81]

Yet Harrison's election and Harrison's death brought McLane unanticipated political opportunities. The new president, Tyler, like McLane, was more a disgruntled Democrat than a Whig. The reasons Tyler deserted the Democrats and the troubles that arose to divide him from the mass of the Whigs were not McLane's reasons for leaving the cabinet or the troubles that prevented any close relationship between McLane and the Whigs. Tyler opposed Jackson's personal leadership as McLane never did; Tyler opposed a national bank, whereas McLane tried to be a friend to the Bank of the United States; Tyler was for states' rights, and McLane was a nationalist. Yet they had been acquainted since they served together on the 1819 congressional committee to investigate the Bank, and now that both were in political limbo, why should they not get together?

The first tentative rapprochement between McLane and Tyler probably came in May, 1841, a month after Harrison's death. Joshua Bates, the Barings' American partner, had visited Baltimore and together with McLane concocted "a plan for putting things right . . . in regard to currency and credit" which Bates presented to the President. The plan called on the states to limit banking capital, forbid issuance of small bank notes, and provide for payment of interest and principal on all state indebtedness. In return the federal government would distribute revenues from public lands to the conforming states. If the loss of this revenue made new federal taxes necessary, they would be imposts on luxury items, such as silk. When more banking capital was needed, a small national bank acting as the government's fiscal agent would provide it.[82]

How much of the plan was McLane's and how much originated with Bates is not clear, but we do know that McLane believed the "unnatural, extravagant" expansion of credit was an evil that had to be regulated. "Can any attempt to regulate currency be effective that doesn't attempt to limit credit?" he asked a correspondent, and then answered for himself, "I think not." [83]

Nor do we know what Tyler thought of these ideas when Bates

"broached" them on being invited by the President to speak freely.[84] Perhaps, though it is unlikely, Bates hid McLane's part in the proposals. And perhaps these proposals have no connection, or no significant connection, with Tyler's action in August, 1841, in calling McLane to Washington and offering him the chief position, the State Department, in a reorganized cabinet.

McLane was hesitant. According to one story, he discovered, upon his arrival in Washington, that the President was at Attorney General Crittenden's drinking hot punch; the news convinced McLane that Tyler was not to be trusted if he could be so hypocritical as thus to partake of the hospitality of a man he was about to dismiss from office.[85] No hint of this story is to be found in the surviving McLane correspondence. It seems more likely that McLane's main fear was that permanent estrangement from the Democratic party would be the price of entering into what he had recently called "the worst of all penitentiaries, a dependent office in Washington." [86]

It is said that McLane sought, as a sine qua non of his acceptance, a public pledge from Tyler that he would not run for another term, and that Tyler refused to give such a pledge. If Tyler had removed himself from future consideration, McLane might have considered this an interim nonpartisan administration in which he could serve without any long-term commitment.[87] In other words, he would serve Tyler only if he could still keep his standing as a Democrat—and as a potential candidate for President himself.

Kitty felt that the main objection to her husband's accepting the chief cabinet post in the Tyler administration was the President's adamant opposition to a national bank, as expressed in his veto message of August 16, 1841.[88] On the last weekend of that month, she came down from Bohemia to Baltimore to be with McLane while he worried over his decision. On Monday, August 30, he sent Tyler a courteous note of refusal.[89]

Apparently Tyler did not immediately accept McLane's decision. The precise order of events is not clear. It seems that McLane was called to a consultation with the President but still persisted in his refusal to return to his old post in the State Department.[90] "The offer had a good deal in it that was tempting," he confessed to Bob, "but after having enjoyed that and all other public honors short of the highest I could not be induced to embark in the same way again but for motives of public necessity, and with better chance of serving the country, than, as it appeared to me, existed in the present instance." [91]

McLane expected Tyler's second veto of a bank bill (he regretted that men insisted on pressing Tyler on this issue), he expected the cabinet dissolution that followed, but he was surprised at Webster's retention of the State Department, and particularly at the announcement that Webster stayed on "in compliance with the wishes of the President." [92] Perhaps he did, in view of the important boundary negotiations then under way with Great Britain, but Tyler had been and seems to have remained willing to drop Webster if he could be replaced by McLane, who had a record of successful negotiations with the British.

Meanwhile McLane had additional reason to be grateful to the President and Major Lewis in the spring of 1842 when their influence secured a midshipman's appointment for young Allan. Later in the year Allan and his brother Louis were kept out of the African squadron by Major Lewis at their father's request.[93]

But despite such favors and despite a lively sympathy for Tyler in his troubles with an unfriendly Congress, McLane still was hesitant to be drawn into the Tyler camp. Politics itself did not lack interest for him. In August, 1842, he felt it was his conscientious course to quit the railroad for "a new line of march," and waited only for political issues to be clearly defined.[94] A month later rumors were widespread that McLane was to replace Webster, but though confessing there was some truth in these rumors McLane assured his eldest son that the State Department was not more attractive to him than it had been a year earlier—if anything, the passage of a year had robbed the post of some of its "apparent, not real, advantages." If he could get away from the railroad, he would greatly prefer a seat in Congress to a place in Tyler's cabinet.[95]

The truth of the matter was that McLane was too canny to be caught on a limb with Tyler, an exile from two parties. Politics did attract him—and business repelled him. "One thing I am sure of," he wrote Bob, "that if I were *without debt,* I should prefer a crust on the farm, or elsewhere, to my present condition." [96] When Louis Cass visited Baltimore in December, 1842, he and McLane spent the afternoon and the evening, till "a late bed time," closeted together. They were similar in being highly ambitious men, set aside at the moment from any line of progress toward the power and position for which they yearned. After the long conversation McLane concluded sadly that Van Buren still held the driver's seat in the Democratic party—unless, as seemed unlikely, Calhoun could unite the South against him. Cass's only chance would be in a crisis, when a compromise candidate might be called for. Such a crisis, which might open new opportunities for McLane, as well as for Cass, seemed very unlikely.[97]

X   CUMBERLAND ATTAINED

One reason that a humble life on his farm seemed (if only for rhetorical purposes) better to Louis McLane than the presidency of his railroad was the strain he underwent in extending the B & O line to Cumberland. By December, 1842, this work had been completed. On November 3, McLane and his board of directors, accompanied by leading state and city officials and by the editors of Baltimore newspapers, rode an experimental train over the new line, on which regular service, with one passenger train daily each way, was begun on November 5.[98] The Main Stem was now 178 miles long, the new extension from Harper's Ferry to Cumberland being 97 miles, over half of the road west from Baltimore.[99]

The completion of this work was one of the major achievements of McLane's career. The technical problems were not his chief concern; he was able to leave them to his engineers, under the direction of Jonathan Knight and Benjamin Latrobe. But the financial and political problems rested primarily on his shoulders and were particularly difficult because, as to politics, two states were involved plus the municipal government of Baltimore, and, as to finance, the extension was constructed during the greatest and most prolonged depression in the history of the nation to date.

Throughout 1841 and part of 1842 McLane's chief reliance was upon the stock orders.[100] However, as their numbers increased, their popularity —and their exchange value—gradually declined until finally the railroad was forced to give up their use. Early in 1841 the acceptability of stock orders was greatly aided by actions of the state and municipal governments. McLane first persuaded the state legislature to approve the receipt and reissue of stock orders by Maryland banks.[101] When some banks still refused to accept the stock orders, McLane secured passage of a city ordinance making the stock orders receivable in payment of city taxes.[102] In return for this favor, the B & O directorate agreed to a request from the municipal government that it issue the stock orders in amounts smaller than one dollar to satisfy a need for fractional currency or "shinplasters' in ordinary commercial transactions.[103] Before long, however, rumors circulated that the B & O was refusing to pay out its fractional shinplasters in exchange for its $1, $2, and $3 stock orders in order to retaliate against banks refusing its stock orders. Merchants needing the B & O shinplasters for their business were forced to exchange bankable money for them.[104]

Despite these attempts to raise the market value of the stock orders, they continued to depreciate. The state, having legalized the acceptance of the orders by banks, refused to take the further step of requiring their acceptance. Nor would the state go so far as the city and receive the orders in payment of taxes or fees.[105] One reason for this reluctance of the state to honor the orders was the devaluation of the Baltimore city bonds on which they were based; at the beginning of March, 1841, these bonds were traded at a discount of approximately 8 percent. By this time $830,488 in stock orders were in circulation, including $3,000 in fractional notes with a face value of fifty, twenty-five, and twelve-and-a-half cents. About $63,000 worth of orders was being issued each month, mainly in the value of $1, $2, and $3.[106]

A further blow against the stock orders fell in July when a judge ruled they could be refused in payment of any debt where current notes were called for, and he added that the B & O orders being exchanged at a discount of 2½ percent below face value, were not a fair equivalent in payment of a debt.[107] Nevertheless the rate of issuance of the stock orders was slightly increased till the total amount in circulation stood, at the beginning of October, 1841, at $1,435,339. In response to public demands, the directors then agreed to place a limit of $1.5 million on these certificates, but McLane defended them in his annual report as chiefly beneficial not to the railroad but to the city government and the community at large. Unlike bank paper, McLane pointed out, these stock orders brought no individual profit to members of the board of the issuing company. Their issuance allowed the city government to pay its subscription in the railroad without ruining its credit by the sale of securities at a great loss and without necessitating a great increase in taxes either to pay the subscription or to pay the interest on these same securities. They furnished a circulating medium so much needed that the city had appealed for further issues in fractional parts of the dollar. Whereas the normal circulation of bank paper in Baltimore, even under the specie standard, ran at about $2.3 million, the depression had reduced this paper to $1 million and the stock orders supplied the deficiency. The value of the orders was upheld by the fact that they were acceptable both to the city and to the railroad, which two institutions had a combined annual revenue of about $1.1 million, only slightly below the total of orders in circulation.[108] Most important, use of stock orders made possible continued construction and employment of labor during a depression.

Yet fear of the orders was growing in the Baltimore community—fear not only of the orders in circulation but also fear of orders yet to be issued. A mass meeting in Union Hall on September 30 was somewhat calmed by news that McLane had ordered a complete cessation of the issuance of stock orders for the time being, which order would give opportunity for the absorption of quantities of orders that had been driven back into Baltimore by the issuance of small bank notes in neighboring states. A committee was appointed to confer with the mayor, the banks, and the railroad.[109]

The B & O directors, in subsequent meetings, agreed not only to put a limit on the amount of stock orders to be issued but also to reduce those in circulation by almost 10 percent to $1.3 million if Baltimore city would pay the next installment on its subscription in bankable paper.[110] According to the *Sun* the fall currency crisis arose because Baltimore had to sell a large amount of the stock orders on October 1 to get funds needed to pay the interest due on the city debt. Most taxes had been paid in stock orders, but banks would not receive these orders as interest payments. The sale of so many stock orders caused them to depreciate in value, to the dismay of all who had an interest in them.[111] Committees from every ward in Baltimore met in convention and proposed that the banks should be penalized for not receiving stock orders by agreements of citizens to boycott notes of offending banks and pay all debts two thirds in stock orders and one third in specie.[112]

McLane obviously could work on good terms with committees making such plans as these, and he received their thanks for his cooperation.[113] To McLane, the goal of these negotiations must have been to assure the B & O of the wherewithal to pay for the year of construction work that in the fall of 1841 was still ahead. At his recommendation the B & O board of directors asked the city to pay off the balance of its $3 million subscription in equal monthly payments—in specie or bankable paper, he hoped, but bonds were satisfactory as long as contractors would accept them.[114]

In January the city government took one step toward complying with the railroad's request by agreeing to use dividends received on its B & O stock as well as any other sums of money that could be spared toward payment of the installments due on its subscription to the B & O.[115] A few weeks later the city agreed to help reduce the number of stock orders in circulation by authorizing a $500,000 loan to be used in buying them up.[116]

The city also offered a premium, payable in city scrip, to all banks funding the orders, but one day after this ordinance was passed its operation was negated by repeal of the state law authorizing banks to receive stock orders. Nor did the state's effort to inhibit the circulation of stock orders stop here. All further issuance of stock orders in denominations less than $5 or in any denomination when intended to circulate as currency was forbidden. No scrip, stock orders, notes, bills, or checks of any sort intended to circulate like currency could henceforth be issued by any corporation unless, as in the case of a bank, such an issue was expressly authorized in the corporation's charter.[117]

With this law, approved March 5, 1842, a definite limit was placed upon McLane's use of stock orders, though those already issued could continue in circulation without penalty. But even their circulation was soon drastically restricted by the decision of first the city (on March 17) and then the railroad (on March 21) not to receive stock orders any longer.[118] It was a decision they were driven to in order to avoid being stuck with stock orders or bonds they could not get rid of. Of course the orders could still be converted into bonds, and therefore individuals holding them did have security, but the railroad and the city wanted to dispose of bonds, not to accumulate them.

Indeed, instead of selling these bonds at a loss, the city ordered its register to raise money by a short-term loan to meet its installments due to the B & O. At the same time, it sought to ensure the economical use of the moneys it was borrowing by suggesting that the B & O might dispense with the services of some of its officers and reduce the salary of others.[119] In response the B & O set up a retrenchment committee which reported on the possibility of reducing expenses. Only one official could be discharged, and this was the clerk of the commissioners employed to receive and change stock orders. His duties being nearly at an end, he could be dropped on April 1, as could a number of men employed in the machine shop. Apparently no attempt was made to reduce salaries, of which the highest by far was McLane's $6,000. The next best paid were the two engineers, Jonathan Knight and Benjamin Latrobe, who received $3,000, followed by the heads of the transport and machinery departments, William Woodside and James Murray, who received $2,000, as did the company's secretary, J. I. Atkinson. Apparently none of these salaries was reduced at this time, nor were the lesser stipends received by the counsel, J. H. B. Latrobe ($1,000), the foreman in the machine shop, Thatcher Perkins ($1,000 plus free house rent), the clerks ($500 to $700), draftsmen ($3 a day), and other employees.[120]

The idea of economizing by reductions of salaries and of the number of employees appealed to McLane's sense of good management as long as his own salary was not threatened. Hs had proposed combining the duties of ticket and forwarding agents as early as the fall of 1840, with the expectation that a man could be hired for $1,000 to perform two jobs, each previously compensated at $800; not till July, 1841, did the board accept this proposal.[121] Then in February, 1842, he proposed reductions in the salaries paid assistant engineers and superintendents of construction; but after Benjamin Latrobe was called before the directors and questioned about these men, who were employed in his department, the idea of salary reductions was given up. McLane also proposed dismissal of some "vanemen and axemen" employed in the construction to Cumberland, but this suggestion too seems to have been rejected for the time being.[122]

Perhaps Latrobe, who was nominally second to Jonathan Knight in the engineering department but was paid an equal salary, had a closer relationship to many of the directors than McLane and was, therefore, able to get what he wanted from the board, for whom his brother John served as counsel. Knight, a Pennsylvanian who had fewer Baltimore connections than Latrobe, retired from his post as chief engineer in March, 1842, and was succeeded by Latrobe. The loss of Knight, who returned to farming in Washington County, Pennsylvania, may have been a more severe loss than was anticipated. He was, of course, respected as one of the few veterans of trans-Appalachian highway and railroad construction. But he was also a man of political influence in Pennsylvania, where he had already sat for six years in the legislature and was to be elected to Congress in 1854.[123] The B & O needed political friends in Pennsylvania.

Possibly Knight's retirement was stimulated by the inquiries being made into possible reductions in personnel and in salaries; when Latrobe moved into Knight's position, no one was appointed to Latrobe's former place. At about the time of this change more reductions were suggested in a resolution the city government ordered its representatives on the B & O board of directors to present. This resolution struck directly at McLane by demanding that his salary be reduced to $4,000 and some others proportionately and that seventeen employees (one porter, one clerk, five resident engineers, five vanemen, and five axemen) be discharged.

A bare majority of the eight city directors favored this resolution, and one of the minority immediately offered a resolution, speedily passed, to the effect that the general interest of the company would be affected adversely by a reduction in McLane's salary before Cumberland was reached. The obvious inference is that McLane had threatened to resign if his salary was reduced. In this case, as in many others, John White was opposed to McLane, voting here with the small minority insistent on reducing McLane's salary.

The directors contented themselves with instructing McLane and his department heads to reduce expenses as much as possible and with setting up a committee to study the possibility of discharges and salary reductions. In May the committee reported there had been significant reductions of expenses in the last three years in all departments but engineering and that expenses here could be reduced on June 1 by laying off all the men employed on the extension between Harper's Ferry and Hancock, Maryland, which should then be completed. This was approved, but a further recommendation that all salaries in the engineering department be reduced 20 percent was rejected.[124]

Perhaps the move to reduce McLane's salary had some basis in the illness which incapacitated him in the late winter of 1842. While at Annapolis on January 22 he was attacked by what Kitty called "inflimation of the Kidneys" and from early in February never left his rooms and seldom his bed till past the middle of March.[125] He missed meetings of the B & O directors on March 2, 16, and 21 through a period when his great reliance, the stock orders, were becoming increasingly unpopular. Drygoods dealers and grocers, for instance, announced in February that they would accept stock orders only at their market value.[126] Lumber contractors informed the company they would discontinue deliveries unless paid in a currency that their employees would accept. When, in McLane's absence, the directors voted to pay all railroad employees in stock orders, such resistance arose that the directors rescinded their order.

One reason for giving in was fear that the workmen would win if they sued in court against being paid in the depreciating stock orders.[127] Apparently an attempt was made to pay workmen at Mount Clare depot in Wheeling scrip, which they also refused. A committee that called on McLane reported he favored their payment in good current funds, and they were so paid subsequently.[128]

The financial condition of the company continued to bedevil McLane through the remainder of 1842. Yet the extension to Cumberland was completed with only one new loan to augment the resources of the B & O. The new loan came as a result of a new arrangement with the Barings. In order to avoid selling the Maryland state bonds they held for the railroad at a sacrifice, the Barings agreed to pay for iron rails ordered in England in return for annual payments of $50,000 plus 6 percent interest for seven years. First, a Baring partner made a trip over the line to report on its condition, and it is accordingly a compliment to McLane's management that the loan was made. McLane took advantage of the occasion to offer to conduct stock transactions in Baltimore for the Barings, but there is no evidence that his offer was accepted.[129]

In his annual report in the fall of 1842 McLane bragged that expenses on the B & O, down $23,000 from 1841, were now not half what they had been in 1837 and were indeed less than the expenses on any other railroad in the United States or Europe. The extension, he added, had been constructed at less expense ($3,450,000), than anticipated—because of depressed prices—and yet promised to be of more permanent construction than originally planned. The year's revenues, up $35,000 over the previous year, had been used for construction, and so there were no dividends except for 5 percent paid on the separately financed Washington Branch.[130]

When Cumberland was reached, McLane wanted to avoid any public ceremony in order to save money and emphasize that the railroad was still incomplete.[131] Ohio was the goal, not Cumberland, and unless advantage was taken of the shortest, cheapest route to the West other cities would win the advantage from Baltimore.

An immediate problem was to encourage the interest of both western Virginia and western Pennsylvania in the B & O so they would adopt it as their own, while the railroad, ever advancing, would with every step open new trade to help pay its cost. The first step should be into Allegany County, just beyond Cumberland. Here iron was waiting for transportation, and coal offered a valuable new commodity for Baltimore trade.[132]

XI   THE COAL TRADE

The directors agreed with McLane's plan of procedure, but the railroad did stop at Cumberland all the same.[133] For seven years it halted here at the eastern side of the Appalachians, while the management gathered its strength, determining its route for the next plunge forward, the final dash to the Ohio.

Meanwhile railroads were built from Cumberland into the Maryland mining region, which was but ten miles away. It was not the B & O which thrust its rails to the mouths of the mines, however, but the mining companies which connected their enterprises to the railroad.

At first the B & O took a minimal interest in the coal industry. For one thing, this Allegany County coal was bituminous, and the popular coal of the time was anthracite from eastern Pennsylvania. Then, too, coal was a bulk commodity which the canal hoped to carry, and it may be that railroad men had been influenced by canal propaganda to the extent that they felt doubtful about their ability to compete for carriage of these goods. Coal is not our major interest, declared McLane's annual report in 1844, and when we reach the Ohio, we will leave it to others; yet while we are stopped at Cumberland we must consider every business possibility.[134]

As soon as the extension to Cumberland was opened, two enterprises, the Maryland Mining Company and the Mount Savage ironworks of the British-owned Maryland and New York Iron and Coal Company, asked the B & O its terms for carrying coal.[135] At first the B & O was interested in carrying coal from Cumberland, whither it was brought from the mines in wagons, only to the end of the Chesapeake and Ohio Canal.[136] Early in 1844, the president of the Maryland and New York Iron and Coal Company informed the B & O that he had the capital to build a railway from his mines to Cumberland and offered to sign a five-year contract for coal transportation by rail all the way from Cumberland to Baltimore. His terms were accepted when he guaranteed to ship at least one hundred seventy-five tons a day for three hundred days each year.[137]

Before long other mining companies made similar inquiries of the B & O, including the Union Company through the intermediacy of Duff Green.[138] Two major feeder lines and several minor ones were built within the next decade to cover the stretch of about ten miles between the mines and the city of Cumberland.[139] The B & O, for its part, purchased new cars for the coal trade and a fleet of heavy new locomotives, constructed by Ross Winans, the Baltimore engineer who was responsible for many of the innovations that had already marked this line as a laboratory in railroad science.[140]

The rails for one of these lines leading out of the valley of the Savage River were made at the Mount Savage ironworks and were probably the first rails manufactured in the United States.[141] This new branch of the iron industry furnished an example of the mutual advantages derived from the extension to Cumberland, for by the stimulation it furnished to the Mount Savage ironworks the B & O helped provide an alternate source of supply that liberated it from complete dependence on imports from England.

The stimulation that the B & O offered the iron industry, however, was nothing like as great as its effect on the Maryland coal business. If any coal was carried by the B & O before 1843, it is hidden under the category of miscellaneous commodities. But the total of these miscellaneous commodities was only 4,133 tons in 1842, whereas 4,964 tons of coal were carried in 1843 and the quantity mounted rapidly to 66,289 tons by 1848, when coal was still growing in popularity and had just passed flour to become the major bulk commodity handled by the B & O. The popularity of Cumberland coal may have been encouraged by a report made to the Navy in 1844 indicating that Cumberland coal was the best available fuel for naval use. But the growth of the B & O coal business survived a second report that led the Navy to shift to Pennsylvania anthracite, and throughout the 1850's the coal business represented over half of the total freight tonnage carried by the B & O.[142]

XII. STATES' RIGHTS

The coal and iron fields of Allegany County, Maryland, that furnished a profitable cargo for the Baltimore & Ohio Railroad seemed likely also to furnish the grave of that railroad's expectation of extending farther westward. In the fall of 1842, exhilarated by completion of the road to Cumberland, McLane hoped to press on ahead to both Wheeling and Pittsburgh with little delay. "The promptness and regularity with which everything is conducted [and] the happy results which continue to attend the exertions of the Board" testified, according to the *Sun,* to the efficiency and influence of McLane at all levels of B & O operations.[143] How could an enterprise with such good leadership be halted short of its goal?

For one thing, a breathing spell was necessary. In seeking to complete the Cumberland extension with the limited resources available, McLane had felt required to stop the surveys and all other costly work beyond Cumberland. Second, some revision of previous planning had to be carried out. It had been thought that the B & O, like the National Road, would be built through the southwest corner of Pennsylvania to reach the Ohio at Wheeling or nearby. But it now seemed unlikely that this route could be followed, for the B & O charter to build through Pennsylvania expired in 1843 and the prospects of its renewal were poor.

McLane had not put this matter off to the last moment. In 1839 he secured an extension from 1843 to 1847 of the time allowed the B & O for the completion of its line through Pennsylvania. But the statute granting an extension did not limit itself to this one provision, and McLane found other terms that made the new law unacceptable. It provided no money for construction of the track to Pittsburgh which Pennsylvania demanded but which the B & O regarded as only a branch of its main line. Yet it levied a heavy tax, set a fixed rate of tolls, and discriminated in favor of traffic to Philadelphia, along with a requirement that the B & O permit the Franklin Railroad to intersect its line between Hancock and Martinsburg, a junction that McLane feared might divert western trade to Philadelphia.[144]

In the fall of 1842, when the B & O had reached Cumberland, McLane was still hopeful of building through Pennsylvania what he declared would be the shortest and cheapest route from Pittsburgh to the Atlantic. It was Pittsburgh interests that had secured for the B & O the countenance of Pennsylvania; if these interests were not served, Pennsylvania would not be likely to grant any further favors to the B & O. There were, moreover, formidable enemies to the B & O in Pennsylvania, and, true to McLane's warning, they were soon at work, reducing the charges on the Pennsylvania system of internal improvements so as to discourage Ohio River traffic from taking the turnpike from Wheeling to Cumberland and the B & O. In the annual report he issued to stockholders in the fall of 1843 McLane said nothing about any plans to build to Pittsburgh or even through Pennsylvania, though he had devoted a paragraph to this subject in his report a year earlier.[145] He understood that though Pittsburgh wanted the B & O, it did not want to have its trade monopolized by any one railroad; it looked also to the Pennsylvania canal-railroad system, a formidable rival of the B & O.

In the meantime McLane ordered the chief engineer, Benjamin Latrobe, to survey routes westward from Cumberland that would avoid Pennsylvania. Latrobe's surveys proved the practicality of a Virginia route to the Ohio, considerably to the south of the National Road.[146] Thereupon McLane concentrated his attention on Maryland and Virginia and refused to enter into any engagement with Pittsburgh authorities about extension west of Cumberland.[147]

By coincidence all B & O charter rights to extend the road onward to the Ohio expired in 1843, the charter extension offered by Pennsylvania having been rejected. McLane was well aware of this problem and strove to rectify it in the winter of that year, when he devoted much attention to lobbying, directly or through intermediaries, in Annapolis and in Richmond. He sought not only legislative blessing on further extension of the B & O but also approval of whatever route westward would promise to be the easiest and cheapest when all surveys were complete. He also sought money, and for this purpose he was authorized in December, 1842, to appeal to Congress. Here he was quickly discouraged.[148]

"I went down to Washington yesterday, to change the scene, and relieve my mind, but there I found a bad atmosphere," he reported to Robert. "What an occupation is that of the aspiring politician and busy demagouge! . . . How devoutly would I thank Heaven for a small competence to pass the few years remaining to me in the quiet of my farm. . . ." McLane's growing distaste for lobbying was evident. "Going to Annapolis has always been a bore to him," wrote one of his associates, noting that McLane stayed in his rooms there and avoided mixing with legislators.[149]

Public complaints about the high fares of the B & O led to proposals in the Maryland legislature and the Baltimore city council that the railroad to pare expenses should reduce McLane's salary.[150] Inquiries about the salaries of all the officers of the B & O had been made by the house of delegates in January, 1840, in February, 1842, and now again in 1843.[151] As a response to Maryland complaints and Pennsylvania action, fares were lowered on the B & O in the spring of 1843, but not salaries. McLane saw this criticism as a movement aimed at him by what he called "the radical VB. party," combining with representatives of the canal interest. He had blundered, he felt, in not foreseeing before he came to Maryland that the railroad would be drawn into the vortex of party politics. It could be made "an Engine of great power" in politics, and therefore the politicians were not content to have it administered for the benefit of its stockholders. Some partisans, according to McLane, hoped to get control of the company in order to provide a place—McLane's place, evidently—"for a *lame duck,* who would otherwise be clamorous for another place that they do not wish to give him." So McLane intended to look without delay for other employment in a more congenial atmosphere.[152]

There is evidence in the Baring correspondence that early in 1843 Kitty McLane, desperately anxious because of her husband's worries about the B & O, suggested to Joshua Bates, whom she had known in England, that Louis give up the railroad presidency in favor of an agency for Baring Brothers.[153] Louis himself, in August of the same year, told Bates that his railroad connection might terminate soon because of "intensiveness of party Heat." [154]

To McLane's great concern, attempts were made to withdraw the aid given the B & O in the form of unsold state bonds deposited with the Barings, but these attempts were unsuccessful, for the B & O board of directors flatly refused to surrender the bonds.[155] Maryland did finally extend the company's charter rights for twenty years, but it did so in a statute in which it attempted to sell the state interest in all internal improvements, the B & O included. Such a sale might have helped Maryland with its mounting financial problems, but when railroad stock was offered for the bonds, the offer was ignored.[156]

From the Virginia legislature in 1843, the B & O secured no new legislation at all. Yet events in other states impelled the B & O to hurry to its goal. Three formidable rivals were mentioned by McLane in his report to B & O stockholders in the fall of 1843: the Erie Canal across New York, the canals and other internal improvements of Pennsylvania, and the railroad from Boston to Albany. In addition, two of these routes were greatly aided in periods of low water in the Ohio by the development of a route of travel up the Illinois River and across land (where a canal was in progress) to Chicago, then by the lakes to Buffalo, and finally to Boston or New York.[157]

Once again in the winter of 1843–44 McLane directed vigorous lobbies in Richmond and Annapolis, and once again the B & O was denied the legislation it sought. From Virginia the B & O desired the right to build to any point on the Ohio not farther south than Parkersburg, at the mouth of the Little Kanawha River, for the surveyors had found a number of possible terminal points between Parkersburg on the south and Fishing Creek, which met the Ohio just forty miles downstream from Wheeling, and seemed to McLane a preferable terminus. If construction was to be wholly through Maryland and Virginia, avoiding Pennsylvania, Wheeling itself declined in attractiveness as a terminus because its location in the

Virginia panhandle made it farther from Cumberland and more difficult to reach than other towns on the Ohio.[158]

But Wheeling was not so easily eliminated. Its influence in the Virginia legislature blocked the B & O from getting any choice of terminus such as the first charter had granted, and Wheeling hired Jonathan Knight in 1844 to find how it could be reached from Cumberland without crossing Pennsylvania. Knight was successful, and despite the likelihood of high grades and expensive excavation McLane directed the B & O surveyors to consider this route in their plans. After all, Wheeling promised financial assistance to soften the fit of the political straightjacket it sought to put on B & O expansion.[159]

McLane and Latrobe both went to Richmond early in 1845 to see what they could do with the Virginia legislature.[160] Though supported by the growing enthusiasm for a Baltimore connection in such western Virginia towns as Clarksburg and Parkersburg, they found the legislature determined to direct the B & O to Wheeling, not only because of Wheeling's influence but because there were Virginia transportation interests that were reluctant to see the B & O expanding southward. The statute enacted by Virginia on February 19, 1845, required the B & O to make Wheeling its Ohio River terminus, provided for its annexation of the Winchester & Potomac Railroad, and repealed the subscription of more than a million dollars that Virginia had previously promised to the B & O on completion of its line.[161]

McLane found the act unacceptable and recommended its rejection by the B & O stockholders, who followed his advice when called to a special meeting in July, 1845.[162] His efforts in this same year to persuade Pennsylvania to authorize a B & O extension met no success.[163]

XIII   FARES AND FINANCES

By the time stockholders of the Baltimore & Ohio Railroad met and rejected the Virginia statute of February, 1845, McLane was on leave from his railroad job on a diplomatic mission for his old congressional colleague James K. Polk, whose accession to the Presidency brought McLane new political opportunities. But if the railroad stood still at Cumberland when he left it in 1845, this did not indicate that McLane had been unsuccessful as an executive or innovator in the years since its westward expansion had been halted in 1842.

A constant problem to the infant railroad industry of America was the establishment of a scale of rates, a problem complicated by the limitations set upon the railroads by the statute law of each of the states through which they passed. McLane's basic approach to this problem, determined after some investigation, was revealed in a recommendation to his board in June, 1841: "a tariff of rates for transportation regulated and averaged according to distances and seasons." [164] But such a principle was easier to enunciate than to abide by.

Competition was a major factor in provoking rate changes. Sometimes a desire to get its share of the available traffic led the B & O to reduce its tariffs, as in the spring of 1843, when competition of the Pennsylvania system led the B & O to lower rates to Cumberland, thus encouraging traffic from the Ohio to use the combination of the National Road and the B & O rather than the canal-rail system across Pennsylvania. [165] Competition could, however, occasion higher rates, and so it did when the B & O set fees for transportation across the Harper's Ferry viaduct so high as to discourage its use as a feeder for the Chesapeake and Ohio canal. [166] The idea of a through ticket over several transportation lines was also born of a competitive challenge, as when in 1844 a $13 fare from Wheeling to Philadelphia was accepted by the B & O in order that, in cooperation with the Philadelphia, Wilmington, & Baltimore Railroad and a stage line west of Cumberland, goods bound from the Ohio to Philadelphia could be enticed to use this route rather than the Pennsylvania canals. For special situations, special fares were offered, as for delegates to political conventions and immigrants traveling westward en masse. [167]

Up and down the line McLane himself made frequent tours of inspection. "Your father has been absent since the 16th," wrote Kitty to Robert on June 18, 1841, "on his usual summer excursion over the Mountains," meaning that he had gone to view the progress on the Cumberland extension and would be away, by his own testimony, about ten days. [168] Such trips allowed him to add weight to his recommendations, when, for example, he could confirm the reports of the engineers from his own observations. [169] Winter was the season for lobbying; summer for inspection trips, possibly with time out for politicking en route. McLane's diligence in overseeing his road may have been partly responsible for the administrative efficiency that led a newspaper, reporting an accident, to claim it was "something rare to record an accident upon this road, so very careful are its agents." [170] To ensure employees against accidents, McLane secured the establishment in 1844 of an "Invalid Fund," a self-insurance scheme to recompense employees disabled by injuries received in the service of the B & O and to aid the families of those killed in company service. Employees accepting the plan could be assessed up to one half of 1 percent of their wages, but the fund was started with a $1,250 payment from the Postmaster General for distribution of the President's message, heretofore carried free. This money was invested in B & O 6 percent bonds, and the fund thus formed, to which McLane declared he would himself contribute, was to save current funds that would otherwise be reduced whenever an employee was injured.[171]

Another special fund set up during the McLane administration of the B & O was a sinking fund to redeem the $1 million loan floated by the company for the Washington Branch and due to be paid in 1854.[172] As soon as the Cumberland extension was completed, McLane began making a modest annual contribution to this fund intended to provide for the future solvency of the railroad (in case 1854 turned out to be an unfortunate year for refunding) and for the establishment of its credit.[173] In these same years of the early 1840's McLane lent his efforts to the cause of those seeking to persuade Maryland to resume payment of interest on the state debt.

The lavish help Maryland offered several internal improvement companies in the 1830's was not accompanied by plans for increased revenues other than the expectation that the improvements themselves would recompense the state, primarily in dividends, for the funds advanced. Only the Baltimore & Ohio Railroad did bring any considerable return to the state, and by the end of 1841 Maryland was unable to meet interest payments on state obligations. Suspension of these payments lasted for six years, until January 1, 1848, and in the meantime the poor credit standing of the state was a major factor in the inability of McLane to prosecute the line of the B & O beyond Cumberland, because until Maryland resumed interest payments he could hardly hope to sell the Maryland state bonds he had left with the Barings in 1839.[174]

The Barings exerted their influence to persuade Maryland to resume repayment. John H. B. Latrobe, the B & O counsel, directed their lobbying efforts in Maryland, and McLane helped through letters signed "Q.E.D." in the Baltimore press in 1844. McLane had reason to cooperate in this campaign because the Barings refused any further loans to the B & O until Maryland resumed interest payments on the state debt. The Barings also refused to cancel a personal debt of $4,200 which McLane owed them, though their American agent suggested that this might be a way of procuring McLane's full and sympathetic cooperation. They were interested in McLane's idea of reaching untapped sources of revenue through a state income tax, but they never were able to persuade him to spell out his plan in detail.

Canal-railroad rivalry made it difficult for the English bankers to unify in a concerted campaign the two Maryland companies that would have been most interested in the credit rating of the state bonds. Finally, however, with the Barings and George Peabody offering substantial support to Whig candidates friendly to resumption, a Whig legislature was elected that voted, on March 8, 1847, to resume interest payments at the beginning of the next year.[175] This decision, supported by a new tax structure developed by Maryland over the last few years, helped strengthen the financial position of the B & O by reestablishing the credit standing of Maryland state bonds.

While Maryland's failure to make good on its obligations handicapped the B & O, McLane sought to conserve railroad resources by paying debts to the state in stock orders. In 1842, when the company was receiving stock orders but they were coming into disrepute, the B & O offered them to Maryland authorities in payment of the one fifth share of all passenger fares on the Washington Branch that was due to the state. Maryland refused the offer.[176] Later, beginning in 1846, McLane had more success with the distribution of bonds as a dividend.[177]

XIV   THE ELECTROMAGNETIC TELEGRAPH

Meanwhile McLane had sought to improve the efficiency of the railroad by the introduction of labor-saving machinery at Mount Clare and by the enlargement of the shops there and the construction of a roundhouse.[178] Through the fall of 1844 he negotiated, without any immediate success, for the purchase of the Winchester & Potomac, which was finally incorporated into the Baltimore & Ohio in 1848.[179] New central offices were planned to be built in Baltimore, and a continual struggle was waged for permission to draw trains through the city streets by steam power instead of by horses, the use of which was both expensive and inconvenient. Some success was achieved in 1845 in limited permission to use steam power in bringing coal to the Baltimore docks.[180]

An innovation that turned out to be a tremendous success was permitted by McLane in 1843, when he allowed Samuel F. B. Morse to lay the wires of the first electric telegraph along the line of the B & O between Washington and Baltimore. One story has it that McLane first sought John Latrobe's opinion, telling Latrobe of a visit by a crazy man who believed he could send messages over a wire. In Latrobe's memoranda there is a note in which Latrobe, without reference to any statement regarding a crazy man, represents McLane as saying, "You know more of these things than I do. I wish you would have a talk with him [Morse] and let me know what you think of his scheme. Come at such an hour and I will introduce you to him, and you can tell me afterward if the company is authorized under its charter to allow him to put his line upon the road."

Latrobe, who already knew of Morse's achievements as a painter, became enthusiastic about his plans for the telegraph, for which he had obtained a $30,000 appropriation from Congress. In recommending the telegraph, Latrobe told McLane his greatest fame might come from this association with Morse. "Mr. McLane," Latrobe wrote, "took in the whole subject on the instant, and, when I told him there was no legal difficulty, granted to Mr. Morse the privilege he desired." [181]

Whether or not John Latrobe's recollections were accurate, it is certain that the B & O board received an application from Morse in the spring of 1843 for permission to use its right-of-way and that it granted the permission provided McLane and the chief engineer, Benjamin Latrobe, agreed that the experiment would not injure the road or embarrass the company's operations and provided Morse would grant the B & O use of his telegraph without expense. McLane and Benjamin Latrobe reported favorably, though Morse was at first hesitant to concede free use.[182]

If, in making their request for free use of the wire, the B & O officials foresaw how significant to railroad development the telegraph was to prove, they were far more perspicacious in this respect than most early promoters either of railroads or of telegraphs. B & O property had been chosen as the site of this first interurban telegraph line simply because it offered a convenient right-of-way. Morse hoped eventually to dispose of his telegraph not to the railroad or to other private interests but to the government itself, which was, after all, proprietor of the existing medium for interurban communication, the postal system. But this was not to be.

Despite some problems in laying the wire before Morse turned to stringing his line through the air on poles, the telegraph was completed and demonstrated on May 24, 1844, and two days later it brought to Washington the news of the choice of Polk, the first dark-horse nominee for President, and of Silas Wright by the Democratic convention at Baltimore—and it carried back to the convention Wright's rejection of his nomination.[183] This dramatic exchange of news helped make the telegraph known, but its true value was still to be learned. The B & O directorate had insisted that Morse must agree to remove the telegraph whenever requested, and though they found no reason to demand removal, neither did they discover the uses of the wire until Charles Minot had proved its value in managing traffic on the Erie Railroad in 1850.[184]

Though his connection with Morse did not add to McLane's fame to the degree Latrobe had predicted, McLane did help the inventor along with his work. He did not secure from the board the reduced fees Morse sought for transportation of materials used in constructing and maintaining the telegraph, but McLane did offer reduced fares to Morse and his associates and he did have the wisdom to request and secure the use of the telegraph in transmitting messages on railroad business. If he did not see the marriage of the railroad and the telegraph consummated, McLane at least saw them affianced.[185]

16

The Oregon Cession

I   FAMILY AFFAIRS

It was a joy for Louis McLane to welcome his eldest son, Robert, back to America in January, 1842. Stationed first at New Orleans, then at Lewes, Delaware, and finally at Philadelphia, where his first child was born, Bob used these last years of his Army service to prepare himself for the life in law and politics which he undertook in the fall of 1843, when he left the Army and moved with his little family to Baltimore.[1] Even before he left Philadelphia, Bob had begun writing pieces for the newspapers, articles supporting Calhoun (and possibly showing the influence of his southern in-laws, the Urquharts). His political interest was always keen—even as a boy, it will be remembered, he had enjoyed hearing the debates in Congress—and two years after his return to Baltimore, he ran, successfully, as a Democratic candidate for the state legislature.[2]

Meanwhile two more of the McLane children had been married. Rebecca, the oldest, was twenty-nine when she was married in December, 1842, to Philip, the youngest and perhaps the least prepossessing of Alexander Hamilton's sons. For some reason, Louis McLane was unhappy about the possibility of any marital alliance between his children and the Hamiltons; he feared at one time that young Louis might fall in love with a Hamilton. But he approved Rebecca's marriage, again deciding he had no choice, gave sententious advice (Rebecca should devote herself to her husband's welfare and should not neglect her religious duties), and in due time anxiously awaited news of the children born to Rebecca and Philip, hoping they would name a child for Rebecca's grandfather, old Colonel McLane, whose favorite she had been.[3] Faithful Rebecca named children for both her father and grandfather, and though Louis McLane Hamilton met an early death as a soldier in the Indian Wars Allan McLane Hamilton lived to win distinction as the leading psychiatrist, or "alienist," as he was usually called, of his day. But when Kitty suggested to Louis that he give Rebecca's firstborn $250, Louis demurred: if he did this for one grandchild, he must do it for the others, and he simply could not afford to take $250 a year from the costs of his family and the interest on his debts; the time for the winding up of his affairs was closer, he was sure, than Kitty realized.[4]

Joseph E. Johnston, who married Lydia McLane on July 10, 1845, suited Lydia's father better as a son-in-law than Philip Hamilton did, despite the distinction of Hamilton's family. For one thing, Johnston was a Southerner, for another, he was a soldier, and for a third, he was a friend of Bob's, who had first brought him home. Johnston had been visiting the McLanes occasionally for years, but he had disclaimed rumors that he might settle down in a nonmilitary career: "No, no, . . . women are pleasant and attractive creatures, beyond denial, when one has nothing else to think of, or to excite him, but . . . there are not—never were— women enough in the world to allure me from the chance of one hostile shot."[5] After his marriage, Johnston took Lydia along with him to many of his Army posts.

One of the youngest of the McLane boys, George Baldwin McLane, who was fifteen in 1841, was already causing his father concern. Possessed of a violent temper, he could not be left alone on the farm with his sisters, yet was withdrawn from boarding school, partly because of the "ruinous drafts" he made on his father's purse, and was frequently in rebellion against authority, particularly that of his father, who had no patience with him. He was sent to sea when he was seventeen, in the expectation he would become a purser, but it did not work out.[6] Eventually George made the Army his career.

For the next son, Charles, who was only slightly more amenable, though neither so violent nor such a spendthrift as George, McLane sought a West Point nomination from his old associate William Wilkins, the Secretary of War, and went even so far as to suggest to Kitty that she keep the application alive by writing to Mrs. Wilkins. But the application failed and Charles became a civil engineer on the B & O, the first of McLane's sons not to enter the armed services.[7]

Ambitious, impatient, and possibly overworked in these years when railroad business weighed heavily on him in his office and sent him frequently on journeys up and down the line, Louis McLane, commuting weekends from Baltimore to Bohemia, was an impatient and often an unsympathetic father to the children who remained at home, except to his pet, James, the youngest child, who was only nine in 1843.[8] When

Catherine Mary came home from convent school with a first premium for "excellence in the common catechism," her father was wild. "Though no sectarian and incapable of doing violence to my children in matters of conscience," as he told her, he would not allow a child of her age "to abandon the church of her fathers and pass under the domination of nuns and priests." She must not go to the cathedral; he would not return her to the convent school. Nevertheless young Kitty (she was fifteen at this time) became a Catholic, and so did her older sister Juliette and her younger sister Mary.[9]

Holidays may have helped Louis McLane keep his composure and his health in sufficiently good condition for the continuance of his work; they also helped the whole McLane family escape Bohemia in the fever season of middle and late summer. In 1842 they took an especially long holiday, going from one favorite retreat, Cape May, to another, Brandywine Springs. In another year, 1843, they went to the mountains, to Martinsburg on the line of the B & O.[10]

By 1843 McLane had become convinced that the family would have to give up residence at Bohemia, where malaria was a threat every summer. He could not afford every year the expensive vacation at seashore and springs which the family enjoyed in 1842. Kitty, as her health declined, grew increasingly to think of her residence at Bohemia as an exile from a more social life—and at the same time she became less able to cope with the problems of management that were hers during her husband's absence. Nor could Louis keep up with weekend commuting between his work in Baltimore and his domestic affections and responsibilities at Bohemia. "Luckless speculations" with Urquhart, Robert's father-in-law, probably in New Orleans property, made McLane especially sensitive to the need of economizing by bringing his family to Baltimore, where its needs required him to anticipate "dying in harness." Room and board at the Exchange Hotel would be about $2,800 a year for the family, including three children (the others would be away at school) and two servants, probably slaves. The estate at Bohemia was not to be sold but to be farmed more thoroughly and economically and used also for family gatherings in the safe season.[11]

Following an apparently brief stay at the Exchange Hotel after the McLanes left Bohemia in July, 1843, they had moved into a town house at 70 Franklin Street, not far from the Washington Monument, by the fall of 1844.[12] In the spring of this year Kitty spent a month in Wilmington with her sister, Lydia Sims, who was desperately ill. Louis McLane had frequently been annoyed by the talk and the actions of his sister-in-law; on one occasion, two years before her death, he declared his hope that he had atoned for his worst sins by putting up for twenty years with the "tiresome and vexatious twaddle" of Mrs. Sims. He was particularly irritated by her continued association with Wilmingtonians who had been his opponents in politics, including her brother John Milligan and the editor Moses Bradford, whom she appointed her executor. And though Lydia Sims was a great admirer of McLane's when he was in his glory of high public position, he found she rarely took his advice; when, for example, he urged her to sell her Philadelphia, Wilmington, & Baltimore Railroad bonds in 1843 and invest instead in Baltimore city bonds, she did nothing of the kind. But after her death in August, 1844, her will revealed that her namesake, Lydia McLane, was her residuary legatee and some small gift—such as $150 to Robert for a watch—was left to all but two of the McLane children.[13]

Within a year of his sister-in-law's death, Louis McLane lost his brother, the friendly but intemperate Dr. Allen McLane. Perpetually unsuccessful, perpetually ambitious, perpetually reforming, the unfortunate doctor's last aspirations were as unrewarded as his earlier hopes. He had stuck with Van Buren in the late thirties in expectation of some reward— and possibly through conviction too—but in 1843 he heard the collectorship might be vacant and sought to get his brother to recommend him to President Tyler—indirectly, through his nephew Bob, in consequence, as he wrote, "of your Father's supposed reluctance upon former occasions to aid my wishes." Louis remained reluctant to recommend this embarrassing brother.

As soon as Polk was nominated, the doctor, abandoning his hopes of preference under Tyler, sought to ingratiate himself with this dark-horse candidate. He had, he immodestly declared, procured Polk's nomination in Delaware for the vice-presidency in 1840. In a second letter he hinted at the value of customs house patronage. But alas, poor Allen! His frailty betrayed him. He died in February before the new President he was assiduously cultivating could be inaugurated. Probably his death, at the age of fifty-four, saved him from one more disappointment. His four children were left with a strange inheritance—lands and "book accounts" and securities and debts, debts to John Janvier and to the Bank of Delaware and to the Union Bank of Delaware and to the Farmers and Mechanics Bank of Philadelphia.[14]

While the doctor had accumulated debts, his lawyer brother had accumulated honors. Besides the important positions Louis had held, he had been elected to membership in the American Philosophical Society and in the Philadelphia Society for Promoting Agriculture; he had been invited to lecture at the Maryland Institute; and shortly before setting out on his second official mission to England in July, 1845, he was awarded an honorary LL.D. by Delaware College, successor institution to his alma mater, the Newark Academy.[15]

II APPOINTMENT AND DEPARTURE

Like his brother, Louis McLane had rallied to Polk; unlike the doctor, Louis lived to profit from his allegiance. "I have formed no new party connections," he assured Polk in November, 1844, and Kitty testified to young Louis of her husband's delight at Polk's victory.[16]

The fact that Louis McLane had formed no new party connections stood him in good stead in the administration of a Tennesseean who sought to restore the old Jackson party and was most friendly to those politicians who had never joined the opposition to the Old Chief.[17] A principal renegade, Calhoun, was eased out of the State Department with an offer of the English mission, an offer he twice refused, first in February and again in May. To gain his consent and with it the support of his faction, Calhoun was offered the opportunity to conduct in London the important negotiations that were called for with Great Britain to settle the future of the Oregon Territory. Calhoun's interest in these negotiations was great, but he was not sympathetic to the President's position on Oregon as stated in the inaugural address. Through the campaign Polk had insisted on the validity of the claim of the United States to all of Oregon, from Mexican California north to Russian Alaska; and in his inaugural he declared that the benefits of American laws and republican institutions should be extended to the people who had settled there.

It was Calhoun's opinion that the American claim to all of Oregon could best be realized not by talking about it, but by continuing the existing treaties for joint occupation with Britain until American migrants had so filled the land that settlement rather than diplomacy determined possession.[18] But Polk wished speedier action. When Calhoun first refused the London post, the President turned to Franklin Elmore and to Francis Pickens, Calhoun lieutenants, who successively declined the appointment. Thereupon, Polk veered to the north and offered Van Buren the place. The ex-President was tempted but finally submitted a qualified rejection; he did not care to take the post unless he could convince himself that the good of the country made his acceptance necessary, and this he could not do. Polk turned to another old Jacksonian, Levi Woodbury, but he too refused.[19]

Polk had not approached these Jacksonians entirely out of pique at the failure of his efforts to confer the British mission on a South Carolinian. The British response to his inaugural claim to all Oregon had been firm and even threatening, so much so that the President had concluded he must be represented in London by the ablest man available, without regard to geography.[20] It was when Polk was in this frame of mind that Secretary of State Buchanan received a letter from one of Polk's chief North Carolina lieutenants, Romulus Saunders, proposing Louis McLane. McLane was peculiarly well qualified for the mission, Saunders wrote, enjoying the respect of leading English statesmen, able and patriotic beyond question, yet for years removed from all party conflicts.[21]

It was all true, except for the last point. Partly through the activities of his son Bob, Louis McLane had, since his departure from office in 1834, been moving gradually closer to the Calhoun wing of the party. He was certainly no friend of Van Buren or Blair, and their estrangement from the Polk administration made it easier for McLane to accept office from it than otherwise would have been the case. A correspondent of Thomas Ritchie's new administration organ, the *Union,* successor to Blair's *Globe,* defended McLane's record, but on the subject of McLane's relations with Van Buren, particularly in the 1840 election, "I presume not to speak," was all he chose to write.[22]

When McLane was offered the English mission early in June, 1845, he did not hesitate long about accepting, for he was eager to escape from the railroad and, despite the expense of residing in London and the misery of traveling there, the position had obvious advantages. The chief of them was that the prestige of the post and the critical nature of British relations gave a thoroughly satisfactory explanation for relinquishing the railroad presidency.[23] Tyler, to be sure, had offered an even more distinguished post, but an alignment with Tyler would have amounted to a break with the Democratic party that McLane, already tainted by his Federalist and Bank connections, could not afford. Accepting office from Polk, on the other hand, put McLane back in the untainted Jackson and Tennessee center of the Democracy.

To the B & O, McLane sent his resignation, but it was not accepted. The directors declared they acquiesced in his departure from a sense of public duty and hoped he would not be away long, and they proceeded to choose a president pro tem. Their first choice, William Cooke, a Baltimore merchant, declined the position, and they then chose Samuel Jones, Jr., a banker and politician, who accepted.[24]

The B & O directors hoped McLane could preside at a meeting of stockholders scheduled for July 12, but he could not, for he had taken passage on a steamer that left New York on July 15. Four children were to go along, the three youngest girls—Juliette, now twenty, Kitty, who was sixteen, and Mary, twelve—and the baby of the family, Jim, who was not yet eleven. On the same ship with them, without prearrangement, traveled two other Marylanders, Whig Senator Reverdy Johnson and his wife.[25]

Before McLane left Baltimore, the exigencies of party politics caused him one disappointment—a harbinger of troubles ahead. In accepting the post, McLane asked for a share of responsibility in the appointment of a legation secretary. What response he received is unknown, for it was given to him orally, via Robert, but his choice was turned down. This was unfortunate, for McLane's choice, John Randolph Clay, was an excellent man for the position. Clay was a Philadelphian with Delaware connections who had accompanied his godfather, John Randolph, to St. Petersburg in 1830 and remained in the diplomatic service there and in Vienna under a succession of ministers for the next fifteen years. London particularly appealed to Clay because his wife was English, but he was told he was needed in Russia.[26] The secretaryship was offered first to a Pennsylvania politician named Benjamin Brewster, a Cameron lieutenant who turned down the place for one where he could "hear the jingle of cash." [27] If Brewster was Buchanan's choice, as he probably was, the next proffer of the secretaryship was probably dictated by Polk himself—or by his chief New York lieutenant, Secretary of War Marcy. This second choice was Gansevoort Melville, a presumptuous young New York attorney (elder brother of Herman Melville) whose strange qualifications for the post were his campaign services as a stump speaker notorious for fiery anti-British declamations.[28]

Melville's appointment must have come as a shock to McLane. On July 8, a week before McLane's departure, the Baltimore *Sun* announced that John R. Clay would be the secretary, and the *Sun*'s information must have come directly or indirectly from McLane. On the same day the authoritative Washington *Union* announced the appointment of Melville, and two days later the *Sun* corrected its error.

McLane had to go to Washington to be instructed regarding the state of Anglo-American affairs, and apparently these briefing sessions began on or soon after June 20, for it was on this day, when he left home to prepare for his departure, that his salary of $9,000 began. Besides his salary he was to get another $9,000 as an "outfit," to take care of his extraordinary expenses in starting out in this new post, and a further sum of $2,250, one quarter of a year's salary, was to be his at the end of his mission to take care of the expenses of his return.[29]

While preparations for departure were under way, McLane was annoyed by a newspaper debate about the extent of his responsibility and authority. A portion of the unfriendly Whig press charged that he was being sent abroad to make a treaty that would enhance the reputation of Polk and Buchanan, and Ritchie through the *Union* hastened to explain that this was not so, that the negotiations were to remain in Washington and McLane was merely to be on the ground in England to answer questions and expedite affairs. To the new minister it seemed that the *Union* went too far in robbing him beforehand of any possible credit for developments and threatened to "mar the general effect" of his appointment.[30]

The general effect of the appointment seems to have been good—on both sides of the Atlantic. From abroad Charles Augustus Davis, who was visiting in England, congratulated Polk on the appointment, declaring that McLane was just the man for this post.[31] Arnold Harris, a Tennessee Democrat and adviser of the President, reported from Liverpool in the same vein: McLane's appointment was the best that could have been made and was "hailed with general satisfaction" in England, where he had left an excellent reputation.[32]

At home Henry Gilpin in the North and Joel Poinsett in the South were friendly to the appointment. Poinsett, thinking of the party welfare, called the appointment the least objectionable one possible, while Gilpin declared he had more faith in McLane's ability as a negotiator than in Polk's or Buchanan's, though he knew there was an element in the Democratic party that would watch McLane's every action jealously.[33]

Gilpin's correspondent, Van Buren, angered by the cabinet appointment given his New York enemy, Marcy, was one of this element; the displaced editor, Frank Blair, was another. John Quincy Adams was moved by McLane's departure to set a jaundiced account of the man's whole career in his diary: "Louis the Dauphin," he concluded, "is precisely the man to cower before the British lions." [34]

Adams was wrong, of course; McLane was not a man to cower before the British. But there was a natural element that struck fear in him, the waves of the Atlantic, and between his departure from New York, where the board of aldermen voted him the hospitalities of the city, and his arrival in Liverpool on July 29 he experienced his usual misery on the high seas.[35]

In Liverpool the McLanes were greeted by a representative of the restored Tennessee dynasty, General Robert Armstrong, friend of President Polk and recently appointed to this rich consulship, worth $18,000 a year. In two days they were in London, where they met a relic of the Tyler administration, the retiring minister, Edward Everett, who arranged for McLane's presentation to Queen Victoria on August 8, and on the same day took his audience of leave, officially terminating his mission.[36]

III   AN AMERICAN PROPOSAL

The Oregon question, the subject that drew McLane away from his railroad back into diplomacy, had been under negotiation intermittently since 1818. At stake was dominion over the Pacific empire between California and Alaska, an empire still largely unexplored but of obvious strategic value as a foothold on the western shore of the continent for both the United States and British North America. In 1818 and several times thereafter the United States offered to divide this territory on the line of the 49th parallel, this being the boundary on the eastern side of the Rockies. In 1818 and several times thereafter the British offered to divide this same territory by the course of the Columbia River, which was, for the most part, considerably to the south of the 49th parallel. Consequently the essential area in dispute was the land between the Columbia and the 49th parallel, mainly the western part of the present state of Washington. This land was valued not for itself alone but for the possibilities it afforded, or seemed to afford, for inland navigation and deepwater ports on the Columbia River and on Puget Sound.

At the beginning of 1845 Americans dominated the area south of the Columbia, where transcontinental migrants were establishing farms in the rich valley of the Willamette; and British subjects dominated the area north of the Columbia, where the Hudson's Bay Company and its subsidiary, the Puget Sound Agricultural Company, had established trading posts, farms, and ranches.[37] The publicists and pioneers of Oregon settlement had aroused a new interest among Americans in this far frontier, and politicians found it profitable to cater to American expansionism and prudent to insist on American rights. In his presidential campaign, Polk had called for the "reoccupation" of all of Oregon (as well as the "re-annexation" of Texas), and his inaugural address claim to title to the whole territory was consistent with his campaign declarations.

In the case of Oregon, however, Polk's bark was louder, designedly, than his bite. While talking of an American claim to all of Oregon, he authorized his Secretary of State to repeat once again the old American offer of a boundary on the 49th parallel, plus ports on Vancouver Island south of 49°, thus ensuring British access to the Strait of Juan de Fuca which connected the mainland harbors on Puget Sound and Georgian Sound with the ocean. Polk justified this compromise of what he declared to be a clear title to Oregon by the fact that previous administrations, beginning with Monroe's, had offered as much—or almost as much, for the proffer of Vancouver Island ports was a new wrinkle, intended to replace a previous offer of free navigation on the Columbia.[38]

Had McLane been permitted to carry this proposal with him to London, he might well have been able to bring his mission to such a successful and rapid conclusion as to make himself a factor in national politics once again, with "McLane and Oregon" as the rallying cry of his partisans. But Polk and Buchanan—and it is not clear which is chiefly responsible—had, as they took pains to explain, no intention of transferring the negotiations away from their hands in Washington. Sir Richard Pakenham had come to Washington as the British envoy to conduct these negotiations, and it was with him that Polk and Buchanan would treat. Still, it was assumed that Pakenham would remain in constant touch with London, and there McLane was sent to use his persuasive powers with his old friend, the Earl of Aberdeen, British Foreign Minister.

Once McLane had accepted the mission, the Polk administration timed its steps well. Buchanan sent his government's proposal to Pakenham on July 12, and on the same day officially informed McLane, who was then about to leave this country, of the terms of the proposal and of the government's expectation that he would "enforce" the proposition upon the British ministry.[39] No matter how fast Pakenham acted in transmitting the proposal, McLane would arrive in London as soon as Pakenham's despatch. With McLane at Aberdeen's elbow, America's cause would have a powerful advocate, for these two men had taken the measure of each other fifteen years earlier and been well satisfied. When Robert McLane had visited England in 1841, Aberdeen spoke of the high regard he held for Robert's father and of a wish to see him back in England as American minister.[40]

But when Louis McLane arrived in London, he found, to his intense disappointment, that the negotiation had not only started in Washington but had stopped there. Pakenham, to the general surprise, rejected Buchanan's proposition without referring it to London. And then, to make matters worse, Polk ordered Buchanan to withdraw the proposition. By this action, Polk once again took the high ground of his inaugural address: he claimed all of the Pacific Coast beyond the Rockies from California to Alaska.[41]

IV   HAMSTRUNG BY THE PRESIDENT

McLane was surprised, alarmed, disgusted at the news. Why, he asked himself, had he consented to come to England, if his mission was hopeless? Indeed, it was worse than hopeless, it was a non-mission; he was a minister with no role to play, to do nothing, say nothing, that could possibly commit Polk.[42]

It seemed to McLane that the administration was desperately afraid he would distinguish himself. And so he could and would if given half a chance. McLane and I could settle the Oregon problem in half an hour, the British Foreign Minister told the Prime Minister, and to his son McLane declared he was "*absolutely* and *positively* certain" he could bring about a settlement on terms that were acceptable when he left America to both Polk and the cabinet.[43]

Somehow the American Whig press got news of McLane's dissatisfaction and pounced on the tidbit with glee as a sign of disagreement in the Polk administration. The publicity irked McLane, who wondered where the leak could be and assured Polk he would not abandon his post.[44] But he was tempted.

London had lost much of its old charm for him, perhaps because he was too old to enjoy its society. His friends, when he arrived, were out of town, or dead. The anti-American spirit of the British press was appalling, far beyond anything he had observed in 1829, and it was made worse by a particular prejudice against Polk and the Democratic party that had probably been inspired by the agents of the outgoing administration, such as Edward Everett, his predecessor in the London legation, and Webster, the former Secretary of State, who had many friends in England.[45]

To add to his troubles, McLane found, or claimed, that Everett had left him a deskful of unsettled business.[46] And as he set about attending to it, his daily routine was poisoned by the dislike he developed for the obstreperous young politician fastened on him as secretary, Gansevoort Melville.

Move Melville, he begged. Constantinople might be a fine spot for him. Or Paris, in place of Robert Walsh. But in London he was "not the thing" —vain, vulgar, regarding John Van Buren as his only rival among the young New York Democrats, a York State politician on the make. Even the children disliked Melville, a sentiment, according to Kitty, "not to be wondered at." [47]

Worst of all, McLane heard rumors that Buchanan was giving up the State Department for a seat on the Supreme Court and would be succeeded by Andrew Stevenson. Such a succession would bring McLane home instanter, even without awaiting permission. "Old Ritchie" was behind this promotion for a fellow Virginian, McLane believed, and it would please only Van Buren, "to whom S. would sell himself anew." [48]

Meanwhile McLane prayed that the negotiations would be continued and sought to make his view clear to Buchanan and Polk by a series of private letters addressed to Polk, to Buchanan, or to his son Robert, but often intended for all three. In the long run Robert McLane proved of special value to his father as a transmitter of his views to the President, to the Secretary of State, or even to other influential figures in the government like Senators Benton and Calhoun. Robert McLane could be trusted to take a letter to Washington and read it to the President and Buchanan, retaining the letter in his possession so that there was no danger of its being made public at the call of Congress for the official correspondence or through the indiscretion of a public official, even a President, who desired to bolster his public image. McLane had two objects in mind in the increasing use he made of his son as a personal courier. First, he protected the confidence imposed in him by Englishmen, especially the Foreign Minister, who spoke freely to him but would not want their private opinions exposed to Congress as State Department files might be. And, second, McLane desired to protect his own public image; he wanted, avidly wanted, to help settle the Oregon problem, but in doing so he sought to prevent any attack by the Democrat extremists who called for the whole of Oregon and nothing less. Robert had another value as a courier. His father had sufficient faith in Robert's loyalty and his discretion to allow him to play the tune by ear—to decide for himself how to use his father's information for the purposes his father had in mind. Show my letter to Benton, he directed in regard to one epistle, and then, with such changes as Benton wishes made regarding his position in 1828, allow Polk to read the whole of it; "and after that I must have you show it *carefully* and discreetly if you deem it right to Calhoun, or others." [49]

Attempts to influence a few leading Senators developed as the year wore on, but in the beginning of his mission McLane's efforts at persuasion were directed at Polk and Buchanan. We never expected our first proposal to be accepted by the English just as it was, he reminded them, so why let it be dropped altogether. Arbitration or war were the only alternatives, and if war was to come, as it very well might, we should make sure we fought for reasonable ends. [50]

There was no doubt in McLane's mind that a claim to the whole of Oregon was not a reasonable ground for war. The old fire-eater was "quite prepared to stand upon a demand of our extreme right, if that should be desirable," but he was too wise a man, too experienced a diplomat, to think such a position made much sense. Somebody would have to take the responsibility for making concessions, and McLane thought the President might do so with less risk than ever before because Texas, not Oregon, now obsessed the public mind. [51]

Buchanan was sympathetic to McLane's viewpoint and had urged Polk repeatedly not to break off negotiations (and urged so vigorously that Polk decided to keep a diary to record this disagreement). But the headstrong President waved Buchanan's advice aside. Lord Aberdeen seems to have estimated the situation correctly. "Polk and his Government are more afraid of the Senate than they are of us," he advised his minister at Washington; "and . . . much management is required to accomplish what they really desire." [52]

The Senate and its Democratic extremists may have had more influence on Polk's behavior than did the English. But Pakenham's maladroitness in rejecting the American proposal gave Polk a bargaining advantage he was quick to realize. By withdrawing his proposal he forced the English to take the bargaining initiative, if, as he was assured, they wanted to bargain; by pretending to insist on extreme demands, he forced the British to come close to the one compromise he had offered to accept.

McLane saw that there were some advantages in the delay Polk's attitude caused, but he chafed at his own position of impotence. He was not as impotent as he felt himself to be in his most pessimistic moods. To Lord Aberdeen, and to such other members of the British governing circles as he saw, he could give assurances of the essentially friendly disposition of the American government and of its chief executive, and inasmuch as Polk was an unknown quantity to them this was important. What was galling to McLane was that he could not be precise, could not say exactly or even approximately what Polk would accept, could initiate no maneuver by which he could cover himself with a glory so transcendent that a better future would be assured for him than resumption of his railroad presidency.

So he pleaded with Buchanan to tell him without delay whether Polk would still accept what he would have accepted when McLane set off; if so he might bring Aberdeen to make such a proposal. But poor Buchanan, who also had a reputation to make, was also denied any leeway for negotiating. The best he could promise was that Polk, "as at present advised" in September, 1845, would submit a British proposition to the Senate if the British offered any proposition that might possibly be accepted. As to the nature of such a proposition he could say nothing. The impatient McLane ranted to his son of the "hollow pretenses" that had lured him abroad and declared the administration was simply not to be trusted.[53]

Polk's stratagem did succeed in forcing the British to take the initiative. Aberdeen's first step was a suggestion to Pakenham that he withdraw his rejection of the American proposition if Buchanan would withdraw his reply to that rejection. This message was not an order, for Aberdeen wanted Pakenham to use his own judgment on whether this could possibly lead to a renewal of negotiations. McLane's opinions were cited lavishly through Aberdeen's letter: McLane is entirely without instructions; is most anxious to contribute to a friendly settlement; regrets the present posture of affairs and tells me Polk and Buchanan do, too; seems to think such an approach to Buchanan might afford a solution.[54]

But it did not. Buchanan would have been glad enough to encourage a resumption of the negotiations when Pakenham called on him, but Polk absolutely forbade any commitment to negotiate, and without a commitment Pakenham would not proceed.[55] Polk explained his position in a private note to McLane on October 29, just after this exchange: the British were perfectly free to make a proposal, but he would give them no assurances about the answer. He could not accept any settlement less favorable to the United States than the proposition Pakenham had rejected; he was doubtful whether popular opinion or the Senate would go even that far.[56]

The British seem already to have been closer to the American position than most people knew. He was ready to compromise, Aberdeen told his Prime Minister, on a 49° line, the Strait of Juan de Fuca, navigation of the Columbia, and free ports between the Columbia and the boundary.[57] The last two points were in advance of the American position, but they were not the major points. Whether or not McLane understood precisely what the British wanted, he knew Aberdeen was eager to settle matters and was all the more exasperated at Washington's reluctance to give him any negotiating power. Though the Oregon settlement was the great object of his mission, he had also hoped to be able to increase the ease of commercial relations between Britain and America, and here too he felt shabbily treated. The Peel and Polk governments were both determined to lower tariffs, and a liaison man between the two might have found it easy to win some distinction by coordinating their plans, encouraging Britain to import more American wheat and the United States to import more British manufactures than heretofore. "This was one great subject," McLane claimed, "for which the P. *affected* to desire me to come here. Instructions . . . were promised, were to be sent after me, [but] nothing came from any quarter." To his consternation he found that the eager, ambitious little Secretary of the Treasury, Robert Walker, was himself negotiating with Pakenham in Washington.[58]

Fearing that Polk's message to the new Congress would press again the most extreme American territorial claims, McLane resolved to take a vacation in France at the time the message would arrive and save himself the embarrassment of having his assurances of Polk's pacific and reasonable intentions contradicted. But first he explained to his government that the next British move would be a proposal of arbitration, a proposal the British had been considering for months but which McLane had sought to convince them was not acceptable because the issue was too important to the Americans to be subjected to the uncertainty arbitration entailed.[59] Possibly his protestations had had some effect; at any rate he thought Aberdeen would be neither surprised nor hurt by a rejection of arbitration if the rejection were couched in terms encouraging the resumption of negotiations.[60]

By December McLane was calmer than he had been in September, when he heard of Polk's withdrawal of the American proposition, or in November, when he discovered his advice to invite a British proposal was disregarded. His son Robert had helped calm him by a letter, no longer extant, to which Kitty McLane referred when she wrote to Bob, "*Your letter*, tho *filled with truths*, was not less disagreeable." "I do not think," she added, in reference to her husband, "he meets any real grounds here, for *so much* dissatisfaction as he feels." Perhaps not, but it was annoying to see Webster made a hero in the English press and to know that because of Webster, and of Everett, the late minister, and of Joshua Bates, American partner of the Barings, the Democratic party, together with its agents, was held in odium by most Englishmen.[61] It was annoying to know that some Whigs were directly appealing to English sympathies by urging a reduction of American territorial claims, as Webster did in a Faneuil Hall speech, well circulated in England, in which he suggested Oregon be given up by the United States and allowed to become a new and independent country.[62] It was annoying to hear from the British that Buchanan was thought to have a plan, for McLane's immediate reaction was that he was being left in the dark while some important negotiation was set under way in Washington.[63]

However, Buchanan was as hamstrung as McLane by the President's policies, and as to Webster's suggestion, the British themselves had no interest in establishing an independent Oregon. Nor were they, McLane testified, in any way eager to bring on the armed conflict between the United States and Mexico which was threatening in the fall of 1845 following the American annexation of Texas. On the contrary, they counseled Mexico to keep the peace, if for no other reason, because Mexico was more useful to Britain as a threat to the United States than as an active adversary of the United States.[64]

V CLOSE TO INTRIGUE

When Polk's message to Congress, delivered December 2, finally reached London, it aroused no angry response from the government despite the fact that Polk called for an end of joint occupancy of the Oregon Territory, as well as for the extension of American laws to the Oregon settlers by establishment of courts.[65] It was possibly a tribute to McLane's powers of persuasion that in a private conversation with a friend Lord Aberdeen displayed no excitement about the President's message, expressing confidence that there was no disposition for war in America and that the Oregon question would be settled within the year. Aberdeen similarly assured Edward Everett, who had addressed him in fear of the British reaction, that Polk's message was not distressing.[66] Though McLane was happy about the general reaction and congratulated himself on preparing the government for a strong paper, he confessed there was one section of Polk's message that could cause trouble, Polk's resurrection of the Monroe Doctrine in prohibition of further European colonization, for this might unite the European countries in defense of their American claims and ambitions.[67]

The American government was not as sure about Britain's intentions as Aberdeen professed to be about America's, but this may have been, in part at least, McLane's doing. It was to his advantage, as a would-be peacemaker, to assure Aberdeen that Polk's bark did not mean he would bite, but it was also to his advantage to give Polk and the cabinet a little fright occasionally to put them into a bargaining mood. On December 1, for instance, in his official despatch he warned Buchanan that Aberdeen's offer to arbitrate might become an ultimatum if the Americans insisted on pressing a claim to all of Oregon.[68]

Buchanan, like McLane, thought it the part of statesmanship to keep negotiations active and proposed in cabinet meeting that McLane be permitted to tell Aberdeen a proposal of a 49° line continuing through the Strait of Juan de Fuca would be welcomed or at least would be transmitted to the Senate, but Polk refused to give such a specific guarantee. He would agree only to inform McLane that any proper proposal (and Polk alone would determine what was proper) would be submitted to the Senate. Yet bold as he was, Polk was properly concerned about rumors of British naval preparations, of which McLane had written him as early as September 18, and he had Buchanan ask McLane to make a direct inquiry of Aberdeen and send a personal opinion as well.[69]

Perhaps, on thinking matters over, Polk became increasingly concerned about relations with England, for he wrote McLane himself on December 29. Pakenham had now formally proposed arbitration, and Polk was determined to reject it. But he assured McLane that peace was his policy and that he would consult the Senate if the British offered any specific compromise. Speaking of specific compromises, Polk now went further into particulars than he had permitted Buchanan to go. If the British offer was only a slight modification of the last American proposal, he thought the Senate would accept it. At the same time Polk took the opportunity to assure McLane of the high regard in which he was held, informing him that he had been promptly confirmed as minister by the Senate when his name was submitted, and that he was the only nominee that the Senate had thus far approved, though many nominations had been made.[70]

It seems strange that McLane was not notably encouraged by Polk's letter, but apparently he was not. "They are afraid of me," he told Robert. Apparently he was persuaded that the "slight modification" Polk would accept in any British proposal allowed too little latitude for negotiation. He knew arbitration had been proposed and would be rejected, and whether or not the rejection would be couched in language encouraging renewed negotiation he sensed a conspiracy to keep him from getting any credit. "B. means to take the whole share," he declared, unjustly, as his pique mounted to the point where he complained that his name was misspelled in the *Union*—Christian name and surname both—and his confirmation announced with no more form than if he were appointed to a land office.[71]

I am "hors de combat as to the Oregon question," he informed Henry Wheaton, adding that he always favored an equitable partition, but Britain asked for too much. And to the question Buchanan sent him regarding Britain's military preparations he answered that though they were no doubt routine and part of general policy, as Aberdeen claimed, yet they were useful (for example, augmentation of the steam navy) in the event of war with the United States and should not be assumed to have no reference to that possibility.[72]

Ever more suspicious of his superiors, McLane gradually slid perilously close to private intrigue in his eagerness to make a success of his mission. Robert offered a willing ear and a helping hand across the sea, and McLane called on him unceasingly. For instance, early in December he asked Robert to get Ritchie and the *Union* to expose Webster as a venal politician without influence so that what McLane considered anti-American speeches by Webster would not be regarded too highly by the British press. And if Ritchie would or could not do it, Colonel Benton should expose Webster in the Senate. Robert was a friend of Calhoun's, and McLane hoped this influence could be used to keep Calhoun from falling in with Webster's proposals.[73]

In another month McLane was addressing Calhoun directly, explaining the terms on which the British would compromise—the 49° line, the Strait of Juan de Fuca, and navigation of the Columbia—holding out the promise of free trade, emphasizing the need for good sense and calm tempers, and praising Polk's "manly" message, this last point being important as evidence that McLane was on the administration team.

Thereafter, through the winter, McLane wrote to Calhoun by every steamer—twice a month—endlessly repeating the same message: good sense demanded a compromise, McLane could persuade the British to offer one if he knew what would be acceptable, Calhoun and the Senate might suggest appropriate terms. As time went on he increasingly urged the importance of Senate action to give Britain the year's notice Polk had called for of abrogation of the joint occupancy agreement on Oregon. Apparently he did not know Calhoun was opposed to this notice—or perhaps he did know and was feigning ignorance while seeking to win Calhoun to his point of view.[74]

It seemed clear to McLane that the Senate was hindering his chances of success by debating the notice Polk wanted sent to England. On the one side, extremists like Senators Allen, Hannegan, and Lewis Cass demanded all of Oregon; their views aroused moderates like Webster and Calhoun, who cast doubt on the American claim, and, in McLane's view, encouraged Britain to be more grasping than otherwise. Pakenham's offer of arbitration—actually there were two such offers, one regarding a territorial division and the second of the title itself—might have afforded another pretext for resuming negotiations had the American refusal been phrased in the proper terms.[75] Arbitration itself was unacceptable because, as the American government explained, arbitrators tried to please both sides, and the United States could not allow this subject, of first importance to itself but of less importance to Britain, to be settled in this fashion.[76]

McLane's warning regarding British military preparations and possibly also his eager assurance that he could persuade the British to make a satisfactory proposal finally led Polk, late in February, to have assurances sent to him that an offer of a boundary on the 49th parallel and through the Strait of Juan de Fuca (south of Vancouver Island), plus a limited use of the Columbia by the Hudson's Bay Company, would be deemed worthy of submission to the Senate.[77] But this encouragement came to London too late. Aberdeen had determined to wait for official notice of the abrogation of joint occupancy, with some thought, apparently, that the Senate debate on this measure would soften the American demand.[78]

VI   THE FAMILY

In February, at the time his renewed hope for an early compromise was collapsing, McLane fell ill. First he had a cold, then influenza, and finally an inflamed bladder confined him to the house at 38 Harley Street, near Cavendish Square, where he had established both his office and his family, "comfortably and handsomely fixed" in a thoroughly renovated, newly furnished, "magnificent" house, double the size of his former London house, at £540 a year.[79] Young Jim had been sent to a boarding school, seven miles in the country, but the three girls were at home, occupying their time with music, dancing, and drawing.[80] McHenry Boyd, a young Marylander accompanying McLane at his own expense, danced attendance on the whole family, even writing faithfully to Jim, and was suspected of being in love with Juliette. But Juliette had left her heart at Eden Park, in Delaware, with Peter Bauduy Garesché, to the distress of her father.

The distress arose not on account of the Garesché boy himself, for his was a notable family, but because Juliette had inclined not only to him but to his religion. Her father vigorously disapproved, but the only result was that Juliette became morose. "Occasionally," her mother wrote, "Lady Wellesley, who is very kind to her, takes her to see some Nun, or Priest, or Church, and that she enjoys—but all else is a blank,—and Papa may as well give in." [81]

If observation of Juliette's piety caused her father concern, rumors of George's waywardness were even more upsetting. George and Charles had been left to study law under their brother Robert's supervision, but accounts of their behavior that reached London were not encouraging. In the spring his parents heard that George had become engaged to a Serena Barroll, and McLane directed Robert to appeal to this young lady's mother against permitting an engagement to a young man still under age, without either a profession or expectations of wealth and in the absence of his parents. The headstrong George would not give up Serena, but he cut loose the strings of his dependence on his parents by joining a company of mounted dragoons that was being enlisted in Baltimore. [82]

George's mother, looking her age now, as indeed she had since her sister's death in 1844, partook of the pleasures of London society with much less joy than in earlier days. "The all of life, *in this life*, is love," she had decided, and would have preferred being at home in America where she could kiss her infant granddaughters rather than in England to be entertained by Sir Robert Peel and presented to the Queen. Only the determination that "*a total change*" (Kitty underlined freely) was needed for her husband's welfare and the confident belief "that *it was a singular blessing* . . . to have the opportunity of breaking up an unhappy home by an *honorable change of employment*" had won her consent to this trip abroad. Before they left America, she added, "*an unhappy state of temper*, preyed upon *all* around, to such a degree that hope herself was fast forsaking me." [83]

The long delay in negotiations did little to cure McLane's temper, but there were some palliatives to be found in being abroad, at least until February, 1846, when he fell ill. There was, for instance, his trip to Paris in December, taking Juliette to enjoy the society there. Juliette stayed, but Louis was soon back in England and off with Kitty for a visit at the country estate of Alexander Baring, Baron Ashburton, and from there he was called back to London by the arrival of Washington Irving, somewhat petulant about his replacement as minister to Spain. [84]

One heartening piece of news from America was the report of Bob's election to the Maryland legislature, but this did not bring Louis Mc-

Lane unalloyed pleasure, for he thought Bob should aim singlemindedly at a seat in Congress and refuse any other nomination from the party. The one service that could be performed at Annapolis was the restoration of the state credit by the resumption of interest payments on state bonds, and in this regard McLane referred his son to Joshua Bates, knowing that Bates's firm had an intense interest in this resumption. Otherwise the post may have had some value in giving Bob a standing in the party, but McLane does not seem to have thought this necessary.[85]

To him, Bob remained his most effective Washington liaison, as also the supervisor of the younger brothers, the manager of family business at home, chief contact with the B & O, and, as Kitty wrote, "a prop in all hours of trial." Bob and his sister Sally were also looked to as sources of supplies needed in London, including oysters, terrapins, and canvasback ducks, which might by their rarity "have helped to make amends for the paucity of an American Minister's table." [86]

VII   USING THE PRESS

In the long period of waiting while the Senate debated the notice Polk requested of abrogation of the joint occupancy treaty, both Aberdeen and McLane employed propagandists to strengthen their arguments for compromise. Both sought the same end, a reasonable solution of all the problems involved in partition of the Oregon Territory on the 49th parallel, but Aberdeen's efforts, as befitted his position, were more extensive and more successful than McLane's.

Articles planted in magazines and newspapers were utilized by Aberdeen to forward his ends. Early in December, for instance, he secured publication of an article in the *Times* to the effect that the Corn Laws were to be repealed. The announcement was premature—indeed the Peel ministry, Aberdeen included, was briefly ousted from office in this month—but Aberdeen wanted this news to reach America early in the congressional session, knowing it would have a pacific effect, especially on members of the dominant Democratic party.[87] In the new year, on January 3, another *Times* article of Aberdeen's inspiring called for partition on the 49° line and the Strait of Juan de Fuca. More such articles followed, and they were noted in America as evidence of Britain's peaceful intention, while in Britain, where the *Times* was known for its independence, they helped weaken partisan opposition to compromise and stiffen the will of Tories who might otherwise have feared to seem too willing to give up British claims.[88] On February 3, for instance, the leader of the Whig opposition, Lord John Russell, probably influenced by a letter he had recently received from Edward Everett, told Lord Palmerston that he was not opposed to partition on the 49° line and had already so informed Lord Aberdeen.[89]

The McLanes had not appreciated Edward Everett. He had seemed to them to hang on to his London post unduly long and to have prejudiced his English friends against the Democrats. Mrs. McLane referred to his "cold, cold, face," and another observer commented that Everett was bitter about being superseded by McLane in his negotiations.[90] Yet in the winter Everett gave McLane a large measure of assistance not only by his appeal to Russell, but also by a long, intelligent letter to Aberdeen urging that he accept settlement on the 49th parallel, and explaining that no American government could fail to insist on this boundary.[91] Another veteran diplomat who took up his pen in behalf of compromise was Albert Gallatin, whose strictures on the history of the Oregon negotiation appeared in the Washington *Intelligencer*.[92]

Neither Everett's assistance nor Gallatin's was welcome to the jealous McLane, though had he seen Everett's letter he would have found his predecessor's position very close to his own. A literary champion of the American position more to McLane's taste was Washington Irving, who was put to work on a pamphlet when he appeared in London in the middle of the controversy. The pamphlet was never completed, but Irving's very presence aided the American cause, since the high reputation he enjoyed in English literary circles helped dissipate the hostility displayed toward things American at the time of his arrival. Yet McLane, concerned whether he lose face with the administration for his employment of a recalled minister, explained to Buchanan that he had not brought Irving to London to write on the Oregon controversy, but had advised him to make use of his pen in Madrid or Paris if he wished to write on this subject.[93]

VIII   A PROPOSITION INVITED

Through March all negotiations on Oregon were stalemated. Congress was debating, and Aberdeen waited patiently to see the form of the notice Congress seemed certain to send. McLane on March 1 felt sufficiently recovered to ride out as far as the Archbishop's palace at Lambeth, where he was delighted with the gardens. But the excursion led to a relapse and he spent most of the month in bed.[94]

If the month of March brought no real physical recovery to McLane, at least there was a little intellectual comfort in the despatches that were carried to his bedroom on their arrival in midmonth. Among them were Buchanan's letters of February 26, giving assurance that a British proposition offering the 49° line and the Strait of Juan de Fuca would be sent to the Senate. This, on top of Polk's letter of January 28, seemed so important, though Polk himself had not been explicit, that McLane, feeble as he was, arranged an interview with Aberdeen at once.

Nothing was to be done immediately, for Aberdeen still waited for the abrogation notice, and therefore McLane only hinted at the terms the despatches had mentioned, but now at last he had the authority he wanted and was confident he could get a proposition in time. It would have to be offered through Pakenham in Washington—Buchanan was quite specific on that point; he was not about to transfer negotiations to London. The main problem, as McLane saw it, was no longer the reopening of negotiations but how to get the British to moderate their desire for navigation rights on the Columbia. Polk had been specific on this point—it was a privilege he would not concede—and Buchanan urged McLane to try to keep the British from insisting on it. A private letter from George Bancroft, Polk's Secretary of the Navy, further impressed upon McLane the idea that there was no chance Polk would cede the Columbia navigation permanently. McLane's diplomacy from this time forward was strongly influenced by the idea that the Columbia navigation might be the sticking point and that he must get the British to modify their demands.[95]

Buchanan's insistence on keeping the negotiations officially centered at Washington did not disguise from McLane the fact that it was with him and in London that the active part now lay. Nor could McLane fail to be stirred by the complaint of Buchanan that he would lose a chance to leave the State Department for a seat on the Supreme Court unless this major diplomatic problem could be solved speedily. This was a temptation McLane understood, for a seat on the Court he confessed— as he had confessed once long ago to Van Buren—was McLane's own ambition. "If I could have had the uncontrouled gratification of my highest ambition, at any period of my life," he wrote, "I should have found it in a seat on the Bench of the Supreme Court. . . ."[96]

It is not likely that McLane thought a Supreme Court seat a very probable assignment for him in the near future, but considering his overweening ambition, it is not impossible. After all, he did not know that Polk had declared himself unwilling to appoint anyone to the Supreme Court who had still been a Federalist when past thirty because such a man could not be trusted to be free of Federalist constitutional prejudices. Any decent government position with a salary sufficient to support his family would be preferable to McLane to a return to the railroad, where measures were being undertaken—mainly a reconstruction of the tracks—that he opposed.[97] The important objective for the B & O, in McLane's mind, remained completion of the route to the Ohio, but so many difficulties impeded that accomplishment that this new diversion of resources to reconstruction only proved to McLane that he should escape from his railroad responsibilities as soon as he could find another means of supporting his family.

IX   A PROPOSITION ACCEPTED

Finally, in April, Congress voted the notification Aberdeen was awaiting. McLane, fussing and fuming at the delay, became increasingly concerned about allocation of credit for the success he now envisaged. "For myself," he told Buchanan, "I am not particularly ambitious of responsibility or merit upon this subject," and he meant not one word of this.[98]

He was recovering now, riding out every day, but he had a new worry: the ministry seemed likely to fall and if the Whigs took over the Foreign Minister would be Lord Palmerston, who was likely to be much less tractable than Aberdeen. McLane thought he could possibly persuade Aberdeen to offer a proposition by May 1; indeed Aberdeen almost told McLane as much at a conference on April 17 at which the Foreign Minister made it clear he wanted only a pretext for resuming negotiations.[99]

Aberdeen was carefully flattering McLane with visions of a solution to the Oregon problem while at the same time softening the British public for a compromise by articles in the *Quarterly Review*, the *Times*, and the *Economist*. "The negotiation," McLane wrote, truthfully, "is already as much here, and must so continue, as elsewhere." [100] But it could not proceed in London or elsewhere unless the American government was willing, and McLane was alarmed to hear, from Bob and others, that Buchanan encouraged Polk to hold to the extreme line.[101] This was not so; Buchanan had generally favored compromise in his private conversations with Polk, but perhaps Buchanan wanted to seem an adherent to the 54° 40′ school and purposely led people to believe his weight was thrown on this side. Midwestern extremists were not easily to be placated, and Buchanan may have thought that his future in the party depended on their support.

Each country had to be prepared to give in a little, McLane thought, and he admired the reasonable position Thomas Hart Benton was taking. In fact, McLane went further in praising Benton, declaring that the latter had wanted to settle the boundary at the 49° line in 1827 and that he, McLane, had opposed such a partition then but now he knew Benton had been right. Show this to Polk and Benton, he told Bob in his eagerness to identify himself with the stalwarts of the party.[102] There were others in public life with whom he was becoming increasingly disenchanted: Cass, for instance, who sought popularity by demanding 54° 40′;

Gallatin, who was still meddling with a problem that he might have settled in 1827, in McLane's opinion; Robert Owen, who came to England with a proposal of his own and secured an interview with Aberdeen; even Calhoun, who had continued to oppose the notice in the Senate and had supported a call for McLane's correspondence despite McLane's private pleas to him.[103]

"Every man must take care of himself," McLane warned his son Robert, and there was no question but that the way Louis McLane wished to take care of himself was by making his mission so successful that public life would lie open to him again and he would not have to go back to the railroad—"Lord knows how gladly I would escape from it." Governor of Oregon would be an acceptable post, McLane admitted, and his wife speculated more widely on what the future might hold: "Gov. of Oregon, ViceRoy of Mexico, Secretary of State, or Judge on the Bench." [104] Rumor spoke of an even higher post.[105]

McLane stood "deservedly high in England, with both Whig and Tory," William King reported from Paris after talking with Henry Petty-Fitzmaurice, the third Marquis of Lansdowne, who described McLane in the most exalted terms.[106] This high standing, plus his April 17 conference with Aberdeen, may have made McLane overconfident, for he was now sure he could get the negotiation reopened.[107] For the moment he was wrong, but he had not long to wait. Within a week, notice of abrogation of the 1827 Oregon convention reached London in a form completely satisfactory to Aberdeen, and by the next steamer a proposal for settlement of the Oregon question was on the way to Washington.[108]

It was, as expected, an offer of the 49° line and Strait of Juan de Fuca as a boundary, with a guarantee of private British property between the Columbia River and 49°, and navigation rights on the Columbia. McLane had hoped to do better, but after the Senate debate, throwing doubt on the American position, this proposal was almost the best that could be hoped for. His accomplishment, he recognized, had been to keep relations with Britain in a state propitious to the reopening of negotiations. The terms themselves were not very new, being close to Everett's suggestions, but McLane had one minor triumph at the last minute before their despatch when Aberdeen sent for him to announce that on one point, at least, McLane had argued effectively. Because of all the arguments McLane had opposed to the British claim to navigate the Columbia, Aberdeen, on his own responsibility, had decided to restrict that right to the Hudson's Bay Company.

McLane thought a further limitation to the British use of the Columbia could be won, a limitation to a stated number of years, and he urged Buchanan to seek such a modification of the proposition. It was not an ultimatum, McLane noted, and he had prepared Aberdeen for its rejection, though other advice made the British sanguine of success. But McLane had Polk's own word that navigation of the Columbia could not be granted, and consequently he was astonished when the British proposal was submitted to the Senate and accepted exactly in the form in which it came from London to Washington.[109]

Saying he would ne'er consent, Polk consented, but he had some trouble with a surprisingly reluctant Buchanan at next to the last moment. The other cabinet ministers agreed in advising Polk to submit the British proposal to the Senate, and then Buchanan held back. There can be suspicion that Buchanan saw political hay to be made from a super-patriotic attitude at this moment when danger of strife seemed finally averted and compromise on some basis certain. Perhaps Buchanan was merely playing the role of a good diplomat who sees a chance to wrest a few additional advantages in the last moment of a negotiation. But to Polk, he seemed a popularity-seeker who feared the compromise would create some enemies to his further ambitions.[110]

Buchanan aside, the government was more eager to compromise on the Oregon issue than it might otherwise have been because of two developments. One was the imminent fall of the Peel ministry, which would mean the replacement of Aberdeen in the Foreign Office by his Whig rival, Lord Palmerston, notably less friendly to peaceful compromise of British claims. From fear of Palmerston's attitude, McLane begged Aberdeen that a vote on the critical issue of Corn Laws repeal (which might lead to a change of government) be delayed in Parliament till there was time for an exchange of messages with Washington on the new Oregon proposal. And in case the Peel ministry fell before Washington answered the British proposition, McLane begged Buchanan to send proposed modifications to him, McLane (rather than through Pakenham), with power to judge whether they might be acceptable and to withhold them in case further ministerial changes seemed likely.[111] This meant transferral of a portion of the negotiation from Washington to London, but it was justified by the necessity of adjusting American counterproposals to the likelihood of a ministerial change in Britain. Acceptance of the British proposition as offered made it unnecessary to consider McLane's shrewd procedural suggestions.

The second development that hastened American acceptance of Aberdeen's terms was the outbreak of war between the United States and Mexico. Polk signed the declaration on May 13, and when notice of it was being sent to American ministers abroad, Buchanan once again found himself out of step with the President. Our object in the war, Buchanan had written, was not to make conquests or to annex California,

New Mexico, or any portion of Mexican territory, but Polk insisted on a deletion of this disclaimer, for he frankly did hope for California and some other territory as an indemnity.[112] As Buchanan suspected he would, Aberdeen inquired whether the United States had any idea of territorial conquest, but McLane was able to answer at once honestly and evasively, saying the language of the American despatch must serve as answer, though it was only to be expected that after many Mexican provocations to war the United States would insist on laying the foundations for permanent peace. Although the answer sufficed, the war, McLane declared, certainly diminished the chance of improving the terms of the British proposal regarding Oregon. The best course of action in the war, he advised Buchanan, was to prosecute it vigorously and secure victory before any foreign power—particularly any new ministry in England—could interfere.[113]

The Mexican War and the threat of a new ministry in England help to explain the speed with which the British proposition on Oregon found acceptance by the United States Senate and by the executive. On June 15, 1846, in Washington, Buchanan and Pakenham signed a formal treaty exactly on the British terms. The treaty was written and signed in Washington, it is true, but insiders knew that the terms of the treaty had come from London, and that it was there that the most sensitive portion of the negotiations, namely, the diplomatic drama of coaxing a proposal from the British, had taken place. Louis McLane had achieved a diplomatic success once again, fifteen years after his first triumph in London, and he was eager for the credit of his achievement and for whatever rewards it might bring.[114] Anything rather than the railroad!

X   COMPLETING THE MISSION

On no account, however, could McLane remain long in London, for he simply could not afford it. He hoped the party would find him a good post in return for the service he had rendered, but in the despondency of a man facing the end of a political career he felt little optimism about his future or Polk's loyalty to a faithful minister. Neither a minor cabinet post nor the railroad sounded very inviting, and he considered the possibility of returning to the practice of law in New York or even in Delaware. But while he grumbled in letters to Bob, he continued to play his part in London, winding up the affairs of his mission by taking care of details neglected during his long illness and, in some cases, dating back to Everett's time in London—mainly private claims of American citizens against the British government.[115]

One old grievance was removed at last in the month of May, but the cure was a savage one that even McLane, sour as he was on this subject, would never have wished. Gansevoort Melville, his secretary, appointed because of Polk's obligation to settle a campaign debt, had been a thorn in McLane's side from the beginning—not only because he seemed a loud, crude, aggressive politician on the make, without the social grace to make friends with even the youngest and most impressionable members of the McLane household. Repeatedly McLane had protested this appointment to Buchanan, but the latter, aware of the intricacies of patronage awards among New York politicians, had not dared raise the subject with the President until May, when Buchanan intimated that McLane did not have sufficient confidence in Melville to leave him even temporarily in charge of the legation. This was an amazing display of discretion on Buchanan's part in view of McLane's continual complaints against Melville almost from the day of his arrival. But the complaints and the cause of them had alike terminated before Buchanan ever raised the subject, for Melville died in his bachelor lodgings, after a short illness, on May 12. Probably unaware of the dislike the McLanes felt for him, Melville had reveled in his one season in London society till a cancer or some other serious infirmity laid him low. Before he died he rendered one important service to his literary younger brother Herman by succeeding in marketing his first volume, *Typee,* with an American publisher, George Putnam, who was then resident in London.[116]

McHenry Boyd, who had won the hearts of all the McLanes except the girl he sought to win, now fell into Melville's place, and his appointment was soon made official by Polk at McLane's request.[117] But Boyd, though personally congenial, was a young man of independent wealth not accustomed to hard clerical labor and his work did not always suit McLane. The want of money and the disallowance of many expenditures by a Treasury auditor were also a constant annoyance. The fifth auditor, Stephen Pleasonton, had fixed the exchange rate so low that McLane claimed he was the loser by $900. It was all in the interests of reform, but McLane hoped the reform would be thorough enough to oust Pleasonton from his office. Why suddenly cut down on legation expenditures in 1845, McLane asked; he himself had persuaded Jackson to place limitations on these expenditures, but the intent was not to curtail allowances but merely to prevent unlimited discretion from being the rule. He was angered at the disallowance of bills he presented for office lamps, for new mail bags, for repairs to office furniture, for cab hire incurred in taking despatches to the railroad depot, and the like.[118]

Among the protested office expenditures of McLane were sums spent to buy books and maps and deal cases for the archives of the legation, items that suggest McLane's genuine interest in documentary materials.

As in other posts he filled, his interest was demonstrated on a number of occasions during this mission abroad. In October, for example, he called Buchanan's attention to a catalogue listing books for sale, some illustrating early American history, that he thought should be purchased for the State Department or the Library of Congress.[119] In November he helped the Historical Society of Pennsylvania acquire some needed papers and records.[120] In July, he forwarded another catalogue of books and manuscripts that he thought a desirable purchase for the Library of Congress.[121] And at the end of the year, after his return to America, he called Buchanan's attention, vainly, to the availability in England of a large collection of Franklin papers that went unclaimed until Henry Stevens, the leading dealer in Americana, bought them in 1850.[122]

Throughout his stay in London a persistent problem for McLane was the duties the British collected, apparently in contradiction to their treaty rights, on rough rice imported from the United States. When McLane arrived in England, Robert Barnwell Rhett was there representing South Carolinians who were seeking compensation for duties illegally collected. In time Buchanan and Pakenham worked out an agreement in Washington, but at the end of McLane's mission, as at the beginning, Rhett, now back in the United States, was complaining of British delays in refunding the duties.[123]

The most important service McLane gave his country in the last days of his mission was his parrying of British suggestions that they might offer their good offices as mediators in an effort to end the Mexican War. McLane instinctively understood how Polk would feel about any foreign interference with the progress of this war, because his own view toward it was identical with Polk's. In McLane's opinion, the war was entirely justified and should be prosecuted vigorously to the end that an honorable peace could be won before any European nation found a pretext to intervene. Victory, thought McLane, would inspire respect. So when Aberdeen hinted he would gladly offer mediation if it would be accepted, McLane deftly declined, explaining that intervention was precisely what Mexico wanted and that the Oregon question was looked to as the issue that would cause a rupture in British-American relations. Its successful solution was the best measure Americans could have taken to keep Britain neutral, and the amiability with which Aberdeen and McLane had worked together on this and other problems was an extra insurance against misunderstandings that could occasion British intervention. When, for example, McLane informed Aberdeen on June 6 of an intended blockade of Mexican ports, Aberdeen's protest against notice of a mere intention to blockade was so mild that he connived with McLane's quick change to notice of an existing blockade, which Aberdeen felt he could properly accept. Polk's approval of McLane's course was forthcoming as quickly as an exchange of correspondence could cross the Atlantic—which meant, in this case, about a month and a half.[124]

The issue of possible British intervention was important to McLane not only for its own sake but because British activity in this matter might make his post so important that he could not leave it until a successor arrived, and this could mean a long time, particularly after Senator John Dix, the first man to whom the post was offered, refused it.[125] Therefore McLane was eager to transfer from London to Washington all discussion of possible British connections with Mexican affairs, and from Polk himself he finally received permission, in a letter dated July 13, to return when he pleased as long as no European intervention seemed imminent.[126]

XI A NEW OPPORTUNITY

Besides his concern not to be held in London by British connections with the Mexican War, McLane had another reason for desiring to see any discussion of these possible connections transferred to Washington. It was, simply, that he expected to be in Washington and to be entrusted with this discussion. For suddenly the dark clouds in McLane's future lifted and a rainbow was in view with a pot of gold at the end of it.

A first rift in the dark clouds appeared when McLane began to reap the rewards of his successful diplomacy in public praise. In the House of Lords on June 29, Aberdeen, announcing American acceptance of his proposal regarding Oregon without the alteration of a word, graciously complimented McLane "as an act of duty and justice, as well as . . . pleasure," for his friendly and conciliatory course—this to the accompaniment of loud cheers for the Oregon settlement and cries of "hear, hear," that testified the peers' approval of Aberdeen's praise of McLane.[127] There was talk of a dinner in his honor to be given by the American community in London, with Peabody a promoter of the idea, but Joshua Bates and some other Americans were eager to have Webster and the Senate Whigs share in the credit. This, at least, is what McLane suspected, and one correspondent pandered to McLane's jealous disposition by suggesting that Buchanan would run off with the honors.[128]

Such robbery of the laurels he deserved McLane would not tolerate, and he set about getting the credit he thought was rightfully his. Everything was done in London, he told Bob, and this should be known. The papers in Baltimore on both sides should publish the true story of the negotiations. Bob McLane would be counted on to take care of the Baltimore papers, while Bob's brothers-in-law, Philip Hamilton and

Henry Tiffany, would be expected to see that the press in Philadelphia, New York, and Boston picked up the account. In Congress Dixon Lewis, of Alabama, and Thomas Hart Benton should be asked to see that Mc-Lane's work was appreciated. Yet it was vitally important McLane should not fall out with Polk—"not that I think he has any sincerity or that his friendship is of much importance"—nor with the party, for after his separation from Jackson and Van Buren he could not endure another exile from the inner circles. Instead, the Oregon settlement must fix his reputation firmly in the party.

To this end he wrote an account of the Oregon negotiations, in the form of a private letter that was probably never mailed but intended in whole or in excerpt for the press, with the *Journal of Commerce* particularly in mind.[129] He went abroad in 1845, this letter explained, to discuss Oregon and bring matters into shape for acceptance at Washington. When Pakenham failed to forward Buchanan's proposal to London, it became McLane's duty to get Britain to reopen the negotiations. After British offers of arbitration were rejected in such terms that further negotiations seemed unrewarding, McLane almost despaired, but he succeeded in persuading Aberdeen, against the advice of most of Peel's ministers, to use the excuse to reopen negotiations, as Aberdeen eventually did with an offer that was wholly acceptable. In other words, the actual negotiations would have quickly moved to London if Pakenham had forwarded Buchanan's original proposition; despite the fact that he did not, the necessary face-to-face negotiations took place in the long run in London, not in Washington.[130]

Although in the back of McLane's mind rested the hope that a grateful nation—or a grateful executive—might see fit to reward him properly, he was glad the railroad job was still open to him. However, a suggestion by the directors that he employ a Baltimore merchant named Gustav W. Lurman to help raise a larger loan abroad irritated McLane, who did not want a colleague to share either the credit of raising money or the profits offered by the company for successfully negotiating a loan. He felt insulted at the idea that anyone could improve on his own fund-raising efforts, and yet angered that he was put in the position of making an enemy of Lurman if he refused the man's help.[131]

In July of 1846, it suddenly looked to McLane as if the Lurmans and Joneses and other Baltimore merchant potentates could be forgotten, for a greater prize came into view. Robert Armstrong, the former Nashville postmaster who now held the lucrative consulship at Liverpool, had returned to the States in the late spring, presumably to bring his daughter to England, but in reality out of a concern to keep the party united and the President free of the influence of poor advisers till he was through the Oregon difficulty. Oregon was a settled matter by the time Armstrong arrived, for the treaty was signed by Buchanan and Pakenham on the day Armstrong landed in New York. The next evening, June 16, Armstrong had dinner with Polk at the White House, and at this dinner it is likely he told Polk of the high standing in which McLane was held in England and it is likely he bolstered Polk's pride by telling him how McLane had effectively sought to raise the prestige of the administration in London, where influential Whigs had once denigrated Polk and his party.

According to McLane, Armstrong wanted to see him in the State Department when Buchanan left it, and sought to counter the influence of Thomas Ritchie and the *Union* in behalf of Ritchie's fellow Virginian, Andrew Stevenson.[132] The idea that Buchanan would soon leave the State Department was widely held in Washington circles. He wanted a seat on the Supreme Court, as was generally known, and a vacancy existed, as if made to order for him. Indeed it had been offered to him in the fall, but he had then yielded to Polk's request that he stay in the cabinet because of the crisis in foreign relations. But the post had never been filled. The Senate rejected George W. Woodward, Polk's second choice, and early in June Polk offered the place to Buchanan again, suggesting that the formal nomination should wait till near the close of the Senate session. By that time a number of problems, including the Oregon issue, ought to have been solved, and Polk confessed to Buchanan that he did not know where to turn for a successor.[133]

If Polk did not know where to turn for a new Secretary of State, he need not lack advisers on a selection. One of those advisers was Armstrong, who reached the White House at a critical moment. On June 22, six days after Armstrong dined with him, Polk wrote McLane, very confidentially, offering him Buchanan's post. "Though he has not said to me positively nor have I asked him to say what his decision will be," Polk wrote, concerning his offer of a Supreme Court seat to Buchanan, "I have yet no doubt in my mind, that he will desire the appointment." In that case, he continued, "I know of no one in the country with whom my personal as well as my political relations would be more agreeable, or who would render more service to my administration and to the country than yourself." [134]

To think of the old Delaware Federalist McLane as being politically the most agreeable of colleagues for the old Tennessee Democrat Polk stretches the imagination. The combination suggests the linking of Hamilton with Jefferson or of Biddle with Jackson. But it is to be remembered, first, that McLane had successfully transformed himself into a Jacksonian in the early 1830's, and that his withdrawal from politics in 1834 resulted from disagreements over procedures, not over ideologies.

Furthermore, McLane had never quarreled with Jackson himself nor with his Tennessee advisers; McLane's bitter feeling was directed particularly at Van Buren, his erstwhile friend, not for very sound reasons but out of a kind of personal rivalry and emotional jealousy. In the same way, Polk, who had supplanted Van Buren as Democratic nominee in 1844, found his relations with the ex-President to be uneasy and tinged on both sides by some of the bitterness of jealousy.

If their relations with Van Buren cast McLane and Polk together in this negative manner, positive attractions also existed. One such attraction was their successful cooperation in the Oregon settlement. McLane had performed his role in London nobly, despite his complaints, which, after all, Polk never heard, and Polk was naturally inclined to think of him for further service. Furthermore, they were in complete agreement on Mexican policy, and this was now the major problem before a Secretary of State. "You are fully acquainted," Polk was able to say, "with the policy of my administration and with my opinions and views upon all the leading questions now before the country, and which have been before it, for the last twenty years, and I have no doubt the utmost harmony and accordance of views and opinions would exist between us." [135]

Polk's decision was, of course, his own, and it was kept very much a secret, even from Buchanan, for the time being. But those politicians who knew of Polk's offer to Buchanan were naturally speculating about his successor. Romulus Saunders, visiting McLane in London, declared the latter should be Secretary of State to foil the plans of Ritchie and Stevenson; and Saunders, who had suggested McLane for the London mission, may have influenced Polk by a letter once again. George Bancroft, writing to congratulate McLane on a settlement that was proving very popular, did not go so far as Saunders, but hoped McLane's counsel would be taken in the filling of "the post of Premier." [136]

XII OPPORTUNITY LOST

Armstrong brought Polk's invitation to McLane when he returned to England as bearer of the Oregon treaty, and McLane did not long delay his acceptance, assuring Polk that their opinions seemed to be in strict harmony. McLane did use the occasion to warn Polk that the Senate might feel encouraged to assume an undue power in the conduct of foreign relations, though he did not in this letter express his opinion that the origin of this senatorial presumption could be laid to Polk, who had called on the Senate not merely for approval but for advice on whether the terms Aberdeen offered for an Oregon settlement should be accepted.[137]

Telling Bob of the offer, McLane dropped all criticism of Polk and his administration. All his suspicions of the President's good faith were forgotten. The terms of the offer were handsome, McLane said, and the cabinet members, with only a few changes, would make agreeable colleagues. He saw the appointment as offering a position more reputable than a railroad presidency, as effectually reuniting him with the party, and as an opportunity to do something for such friends and relatives as Rebecca's husband, Philip Hamilton.[138]

When he thought the matter over, McLane began playing the game of cabinet building, deciding who must go, who could stay, and what new members should be invited. John Y. Mason was the man he most wanted to get rid of, because he was lazy, insincere, and a friend of Chief Justice Taney's, to boot. But Mason was also a personal friend of Polk's, and the worst McLane could plan for him was to give him a consular post in which he could get rich. Silas Wright was the man McLane would choose as Secretary of the Treasury, if he could be depended on not to reconstruct a Van Buren machine and punish its enemies. And McLane would make room if he could for William King, and for Saunders, and for Jones, of Virginia. Properly constituted, the cabinet could serve as a device to reinvigorate the Democratic party, sans Van Buren, whom he regarded as defunct.[139]

But the Whigs were not defunct, and McLane worried lest they make political profit out of calling him an extremist in the Oregon quarrel, for the Senate vote in favor of the Oregon settlement had demonstrated that the extremists, or Fifty-four Forties, were only a loud minority. The basis of the charge against McLane was his refusal to approve Lord Aberdeen's proposition, but his only objection to it was the grant of navigation rights on the Columbia River, a grant that seemed to him to be unimportant but which he had been assured, incorrectly, the American government would never allow. He was, he now insisted, always in favor of compromise and had urged compromise from the beginning of his mission.[140]

Meanwhile, back in Washington, Buchanan was performing in an indecisive manner, as those who knew him best thought he would. McLane, from the beginning, doubted that Buchanan would leave the State Department unless forced out, and Vice-President Dallas declared, unfairly, that all the talk of Buchanan's leaving the cabinet was "smoke—a method of keeping up his importance." [141]

"It is more than doubtful whether I shall accept it, and if I should it will not probably be until within a day or two of the close of the Session of Congress," Buchanan himself wrote concerning Polk's offer.[142] But after thinking the matter over, Buchanan decided it was not to his advantage to see the nomination delayed until shortly before the end of the session.

He feared the extremists of the party, like Senator Allen, of Ohio, who had resigned the chairmanship of the Foreign Relations Committee in anger that the administration had accepted a partition of Oregon. These rabid Fifty-four Forties were very likely to combine with the Whigs to take revenge on the Secretary of State who had concluded the Oregon treaty.[143] If Polk would propose the appointment at once, Buchanan could hold the portfolio of State while the issue was being decided and there would be several weeks leeway for negotiation (and for party pressure to be effective) on the appointment.

On June 28 Buchanan sent Polk a note saying he would accept the Supreme Court appointment, and on July 1, in answer to a question, Polk told him that McLane seemed a likely choice as next Secretary of State. Buchanan seemed to approve the idea, and Polk tried it out on William Marcy, who was more enthusiastic, saying he thought McLane "was to be preferred to any man in the country." But Buchanan, after thinking the matter over for two days, came back to Polk and requested that no intimation be given of any intention to appoint McLane to the cabinet, because the news might have an influence on the tariff bill and other important administration measures still before Congress. Polk agreed, quite willingly, but Buchanan was not told that Polk had already written McLane, offering him the place.[144] Five days later, on Sunday evening, July 12, they conferred on this matter again. Polk had called Buchanan in to get a definite answer because he wanted to write to McLane by the next steamer, but still Polk did not tell Buchanan that he had already written McLane. Buchanan requested immediate nomination to the Court, but Polk demurred. Such a nomination would lead every faction in the party to press its favorite on Polk as Buchanan's successor; no appointment would please everyone and the whole legislative program would be imperiled.

Buchanan did not disagree, but simply questioned the wisdom of appointing McLane, who would be an unpopular choice and would, since he lived in a southern state (Buchanan meant Maryland, of course), give the South a preponderant influence in the cabinet, together with Polk himself and Walker, of Mississippi, the Secretary of the Treasury, not to mention Mason and Cave Johnson. With McLane, answered Polk, according to his diary, "I was sure of one thing, and that was that I would have in my Cabinet a gentleman of high character and unblemished honour, a man of talents, and a man that the whole country would pronounce to be qualified and fit for the place." Buchanan could not contradict Polk and had no other candidate to suggest.[145] Or, rather, he did not care to suggest a candidate, possibly because he was not yet sure he would move. He did have a favorite candidate, William King, of Alabama, the minister to France, but apparently he did not think the time propitious to mention King to Polk—and if he objected to McLane's Maryland residence as too southern, how could he suggest King? [146]

Polk proceeded to write McLane, as he had told Buchanan he would do. All was still unsettled regarding the promotion, was the substance of his report. He had little doubt Buchanan would go on the bench, "though occasionally he seems to hesitate." [147] One important reason for Buchanan's hesitation is indicated in the letters William King was writing him from Paris at this very time. If you accept the judgeship you place yourself on the shelf, King advised; stay in your present position and the field will be open to you for the Presidency in 1848.[148]

Not satisfied with giving epistolary advice, King deputized Francis I. Grund, a German-born American journalist who had been consul at Antwerp and reporter for Ritchie's *Union* from Paris, to go personally to Buchanan and persuade him to hold on to his office. Grund naïvely explained his errand to McLane on their first meeting, confessing that his true intent was to obtain the Presidency for King, who could be greatly helped by the influence of Buchanan as long as the latter remained Secretary of State. Later King came to London, and from his niece McLane learned that Buchanan had led King to believe he might be the next Secretary of State.[149]

McLane's head was in a whirl. Was he at the last moment to be cheated of his reward? As soon as ratifications of the treaty were formally exchanged with Lord Palmerston, who was now Foreign Minister, McLane himself carried the documents to Liverpool, where he entrusted them to Armstrong. That gentleman, who had just returned from one round trip to America, was happy to undertake the trip once again and equally happy to put in a word with Polk in favor of McLane's ambitions. But though Armstrong's spirit was willing, his physique was greatly weakened by a long bout of drinking and McLane feared to trust him with a private commission to counteract Grund and, through Grund, King. In fact, McLane had to ask Grund to look after Armstrong, when he would far rather have asked Armstrong to watch out for Grund. Somehow destiny moved in to trip his friends at the very moment when they could be most helpful, concluded McLane, as he prepared to put the drunken Armstrong aboard the steamer *Hibernia*.[150]

Bob at any rate could still be counted on to see Polk and serve his father's interests. So to Bob, McLane sent a series of commissions. He was to hint to Polk of Grund's intent, which was to serve King's ambitions and not Polk's policy. He was entrusted with copies of a congratulatory address to McLane from the Liverpool Chamber of Commerce and with McLane's reply and asked to see that they were printed in the *Union* and in a Baltimore paper, while Philip Hamilton performed a similar errand in New York. Bob was asked to delay cabinet changes and the appointment of a successor at London, if he could, until the return of his father, so the latter might be able to influence these appointments to his own advantage. He was begged to prevent the change of official American bankers in England, despite the Whig sympathies of the incumbent agent, Joshua Bates, lest his father be made to feel the wrath of Bates and his Baring partners. He was to collaborate with Armstrong in persuading Buchanan that matters had gone too far to be recalled, to suggest —a foolish fancy—that Buchanan could no longer escape the seat on the Court he had been seeking. And, finally, Bob was to meet his father in person or through a letter setting out the state of affairs when his father would arrive in Boston on the *Britannia* early in September.[151]

Unfortunately for McLane's aspirations, when Robert McLane received these instructions and when Robert Armstrong, whether drunk or sober, arrived in America, Buchanan had already determined to retain his cabinet post and forego appointment to the Supreme Court. On August 1, 1846, he informed Polk of his decision, and Polk thereupon determined to appoint Robert Grier, of Pittsburgh, to the Supreme Court and to send George Bancroft to London, where he could further his historical research.[152] It was too late to get word of Buchanan's change of mind to McLane before his departure from England, but Polk wrote him nonetheless, just in case he, McLane, waited for a later steamer. "I preferred you to any other citizen" as Buchanan's successor, Polk reassured McLane, adding, "My estimate of your character and eminent qualifications to fill that or any Station under your Government remains undiminished."[153] But no other station was offered.

17

"This Cunning, Diplomatic President"

I   A DEATH OF HOPE

Just where and when McLane learned that there was no government post waiting for him is not known. In his last letter extant to Bob before leaving England, McLane confessed he expected the worst and was glad he had never hinted at quitting his railroad job since he had at least that position to return to. And perhaps, if proper advantage could be taken of his role in the Oregon settlement, the future need not be dark.

He was, however, merely being his suspicious self. Having heard that Buchanan hesitated and knowing that King was counseling Buchanan to hold his place, McLane suspected an intrigue was under way.[1] There was no opportunity for news of Buchanan's final decision to reach McLane before he left England. Having dispensed with a formal audience of leave (Queen Victoria was on the Isle of Wight and Palmerston could not get away from Parliament to escort him there) and leaving Boyd behind as chargé, McLane embarked his family on the *Britannia* at Liverpool on August 19, 1846.[2]

They arrived in Boston on September 3 and in New York on September 4.[3] If dutiful Bob was not himself in Boston to greet the *Britannia*, it is likely that a letter from him was there to tell his father how things had gone wrong. After disembarking at New York, McLane stayed at the City Hotel for several days, seeing friends and relatives, digesting the news, and recovering from the effects of the voyage. He had been ashore three days before President Polk despatched what he called a hasty note inviting McLane to Washington and explaining how it happened that things were not in the condition he had reason to expect. "I saw your son Robert," Polk wrote, "shortly after it was known that the office of Secretary of State would not at present become vacant and conferred with him fully on the subject." [4]

At the City Hotel various delegations of New Yorkers, public and private, called on McLane. One group, headed by the mayor, invited him to a public dinner, which he accepted with the proviso that he could set a later date after he had a chance to recover his health and return to his home. When a committee of the Chamber of Commerce presented him with a resolution of gratitude, Louis McLane made a formal reply that irritated the President. Defending himself against the charge of being an extremist on the Oregon issue, McLane explained that he was always in favor of partition, which had been the consistent American position. Though the American title to the whole territory was as good as to a part of it (according to McLane), the United States had never proposed more than the 51st parallel and never demanded more than the 49th parallel. Such was the design of the American government in 1828 when it agreed to renewal of joint occupation, and such, McLane was satisfied, was still his government's view when he went to England in 1845. "In earnestly and steadily laboring to effect a settlement upon that basis [partition at 49°], I was but representing the policy of my own government," McLane declared, "and faithfully promoting the intentions and wishes of the President." [5]

When McLane reported to Polk at the White House on September 11, the President asked him about this speech. It was particularly fresh in Polk's mind because the *Intelligencer* had just published it and called particular attention to McLane's statement that the President wanted to divide Oregon. This suggested that Polk's claim of the whole of Oregon to 54° 40′ was a great bluff, and Polk a hypocrite in pretending to demand so much while negotiating for less.

This seems a perfectly fair evaluation of Polk's diplomacy. He had played the game of brag and won, but there was no lightness in Polk's spirit and he did not want his tactics to be analyzed so frankly. Nor would McLane have been capable of chuckling at his methods, if the shoe had been on the other foot. Both men were serious, both were pressing, both were capable of subtle and devious tactics, but neither would admit it.

McLane was driven to explanations: the *Intelligencer* had placed a false construction on his language; in saying he was carrying out the views of his government and the wishes of the President in seeking partition, he never meant to deny that the President believed the United States had a right to all of Oregon but only that Polk, because of commitments made by his presidential predecessors, had offered in July, 1845, to divide the territory on the 49th parallel, and all McLane's subsequent efforts were aimed at bringing about a settlement on this basis. It was unfortunate, complained Polk, that from McLane's language people might think Polk held to one doctrine in his message to Congress and to another in his intercourse with McLane, whereas Polk's letters would show clearly that this was not so, that he held to the same doctrine in writing McLane as in addressing Congress and the country. Technically Polk was right, and McLane could hardly afford to press the subtleties of the case. Instead, he promised to have Robert insert a paragraph of correction in one of the Baltimore papers.

But before their ladies joined them at dinner, Polk and McLane discussed Buchanan's change of heart, or of mind, and McLane took the opportunity to air his suspicions of an intrigue. Buchanan, he argued, wanted King to be his successor, and when he saw this could not be, would not leave his place. Not so, said Polk; Buchanan had other reasons for his decision, and among them the fear that an opposition would appear to his nomination to the Supreme Court, and that this opposition might be sufficient to defeat him. Polk insisted he had never written to King about succeeding Buchanan and had not even thought of him in that regard, but in his diary he admitted it seemed likely that Buchanan raised the subject with King.[6]

Polk and the *Intelligencer* were not alone in reading political connotations into McLane's public remarks. The New York *Sun*, which was under the influence of Polk's appointee, Postmaster Robert H. Morris, declared that McLane, Buchanan, Cass, and Wright were the leading Democratic candidates for the Presidency, and that Cass and Wright men, having little fear of McLane, were promoting him as the principal Oregon negotiator in order to take the credit away from Buchanan, their most formidable opponent. Commenting on this *Sun* story, Philip Hamilton observed that he was glad to see McLane and Oregon connected in the public view.[7]

Another Democratic paper in New York, the *Evening Post*, dealt directly with the idea that McLane was being brought forward for the Presidency and argued that Democrats could never support him for this position because he had abandoned Jackson in the Bank War and joined the ranks of Jackson's opponents. This was not quite true, and neither was the *Post*'s declaration that Polk and Buchanan "were the Alpha and Omega" of the Oregon settlement, for this claim left too little credit for Louis McLane.[8]

Robert McLane succeeded in getting one of the Baltimore papers to print a refutation of that interpretation of his father's statement which Whigs thought convicted Polk of double dealing, but in Washington the *Union* and the *Intelligencer* kept up the argument. Probably the controversy destroyed Louis McLane's chance of any further appointment from Polk, who remained convinced that McLane's words were "not only erroneous . . . but . . . ill-timed and calculated to do mischief rather than good." [9]

And so despite his diplomatic success Louis McLane was relegated once again to the sidelines. No secretaryship of state, no governorship of Oregon would be offered him. With Robert McLane, things were different. Acting as his father's intermediary, he had impressed Polk favorably, and in October, 1846, he was called to the White House and entrusted with instructions to be taken to Taylor's army in northern Mexico. His mission, Polk stressed, "will be more important than as the mere bearer of despatches." [10] As Louis McLane's star set, his son's rose. The son went off to Mexico; the father returned to his railroad.

II   AN EFFORT FOR THE RAILROAD

The railroad was never completely out of Louis McLane's mind when he was in England. It was a possible refuge, a safeguard against financial ruin to which he could cling when the winds of diplomacy and politics were adverse. Look to my place on the railroad, he appealed to Robert again and again, convinced that enemies would try to dislodge him. Samuel Hoffman, Judge James Harwood, and John Pendleton Kennedy were the friends he relied on to save his position, and he feared lest Robert in assisting a Democratic candidate for the seat in Congress held by Kennedy might make an enemy of this influential Whig. [11]

The degree of trust and understanding between the acting president, Samuel Jones, and McLane is difficult to ascertain, but it was not in McLane's nature to trust a rival very far or very long. He was upset in the fall of 1845 because no one thought to send him a copy of the annual report of the B & O president, and he was unhappy with the decision made by the board of directors to borrow money for renovation on the existing line of the railroad east of Harper's Ferry. If the new coal business made this necessary, McLane would abandon it completely to the canal. The important task for the B & O, in McLane's mind, was to push on to the Ohio as soon as possible. This could best be done by refusing to encumber the revenue and the credit of the company for the sake of renovating the existing line. Once the Ohio was reached, increased trade would provide the wherewithal for repair. And if the Ohio were not soon reached, the politicians and merchants on the Baltimore city council would shortly be investigating company affairs and demanding, very likely, a sizable reduction in McLane's salary. [12]

In his failure to appreciate the possibilities of the coal traffic, McLane was not alone, for it had been generally accepted that such heavy commodities as coal and iron would be carried most economically by the canal. But the flour trade, which was the mainstay of the freight business of the B & O, was falling off in 1845 because of the competition offered by the canal and by the Cumberland Valley Railroad, running from Chambersburg east; and the development of a coal trade, despite the immediate demands it placed on the road in, for instance, the need for heavier locomotives, proved eventually to be a godsend.[13]

Despite his disapproval of the extensive renovation the directors decided upon, McLane sought to raise money for the company in England. He could hardly do otherwise after the Maryland legislature passed legislation on March 6, 1846, that empowered the B & O to issue noncirculating bonds on the security of its own property, but he had begun his efforts to raise money early in the winter, at the direct request of Acting President Jones. At that time, the uncertain condition of British-American relations, overshadowed by a threat of war, however faint, negated his efforts, but even later, after the relations of the two countries had improved, McLane found a formidable opposition in the existing distrust of American securities, and particularly of those from enterprises situated in states that had, like Maryland, defaulted on their bonds.[14]

The suggestion that he make an associate in fund-raising of Gustav Lurman, who had connections in Bremen, where he was born, spurred McLane on to seek success on his own, particularly since he had no desire to split the commission of 1 percent that he was promised. Even more important was his knowledge that a loan was necessary to the progress of the railroad and that if he were unsuccessful in raising money he must expect to be turned out of office at no distant period.[15]

In August, after the major work of his mission in England was done, McLane stayed abroad briefly in a final effort to market B & O bonds. Perhaps he would have stayed on until September and have taken his quest for a loan to the continent had he not been eager to get home and take the place he was led to expect at the head of Polk's cabinet. Probably he pinned his greatest hopes on the Barings, but when they turned him down on August 22, stating clearly that they would not grant a loan to the B & O as long as Maryland was in default, McLane was already on the high seas returning home to another disappointment.

The tactics of the Barings eventually led to success. Once McLane was home, he and his colleagues in the B & O pressed the legislature to resume payment on state debts, and thanks to the assistance of assemblyman Robert McLane and lobbyist John H. B. Latrobe, plus an election triumph by the Whigs, who were the resumption party, in the fall elections, a resumption law was enacted in March, 1847, to go into effect in January, 1848.[16]

III   A SEARCH FOR EFFICIENCY

On returning to the presidency of the B & O in the fall of 1846, McLane presided at a special meeting of the board of directors on October 1 and offered a plan for paying dividends and marketing bonds at one and the same time.[17]

The stockholders were due a dividend, he explained, and many of them, including the city of Baltimore, were counting on it. The coal trade seemed so little a part of the legitimate business of the railroad to McLane that he argued the money spent on it in equipment and repairs should be paid to stockholders in the form of bonds. To the larger stockholders only, however. Men with less than 50 shares would be paid in cash at 3 percent, or $3 a share; holders of 50 shares or more would receive two thirds of the dividend in bonds.[18]

For the cash part of the dividend, McLane succeeded in raising $105,-000 from two banks and three wealthy merchants of Baltimore, but he was not so successful in winning the approval of public bodies. The city of Baltimore ultimately agreed to accept bonds in payment of dividends on its railroad stock, but the Maryland state legislature was not amenable and brought suit for payment of its dividends in cash. Ultimately, however, the courts upheld McLane's procedure, though the matter was not finally decided until February, 1848.[19]

Meanwhile McLane had moved to cut unnecessary expenses by an extensive reorganization of the company. He had this reorganization under way before he went abroad in 1845 and he resumed the task soon after his return to the railroad in 1846. In March, 1845, for instance, he recommended a thorough reorganization of committees of the board and was allowed to appoint six new committees as he chose, giving preference to directors who were resident in Baltimore and could be counted on to attend meetings.[20] But revision of committees of the board did not touch operations, and to effect a significant improvement here he prepared a list of questions regarding the operations of the relatively new and efficient railroads of New England and asked Chief Engineer Latrobe to procure information for him there and elsewhere. The essential features of B & O organization had been adopted in 1838, at the beginning of McLane's tenure as president, but the growth of the railroad had led to departures from the system and these departures had impaired its efficiency. The system of repairs, in particular, had grown too loose. Delays on the road were frequent and were protested, particularly by the Post Office Department. The large engines being used were unwieldy and broke down often. Superintendents had become bureau heads, far removed from the activities that they were supposed to be supervising.

Again, as in 1837, a special committee was established, this time chaired by John P. Kennedy, to recommend what was to be done.[21] The reforms that were adopted, however, originated with McLane rather than with the committee. Possibly McLane's proposals were based in part on his observations of the management of English railroads; probably his proposals were also rooted in Latrobe's investigation of American railroads, particularly New England railroads. Kennedy reported to the board on Christmas Eve, 1846, that his committee had heard McLane's ideas on a general scheme of organization and recommended their adoption, with authority given McLane to prescribe the rules necessary to this new system, merely reporting them to the board.[22]

The report of the new system was made to the board on February 10, 1847. Its feature was that it divided the operations of the company into two parts, the working of the road and the collection and disbursement of revenue, whereas previously there had been three divisions: construction, transportation, and accounts. Now construction and transportation were combined under the authority of the chief engineer, who acted as a general superintendent and had three division heads under him: (1) the master of the road, who was in charge of construction and maintenance of the tracks and road bed; (2) the master of the machinery, who had charge of the shops and of all the repairs to the rolling stock; and (3) the master of transportation, who had charge of the scheduling and operation of all trains. Finances were made the responsibility of a hierarchy of officers reporting to the president and headed by a treasurer, a secretary, and a chief clerk.[23] All these officers were placed on annual contracts with renewal dependent on satisfactory performance. Other principles of organization worked out by McLane and Kennedy's committee included the restriction of B & O shop work to repairs, not construction, attempts to provide for economical purchasing, and the multiplication of checks on the collection and disbursement of money so as to effect a strict responsibility. The receipt of money was confined to as few agents as possible, with the establishment of a new and closely guarded system of handling tickets that featured daily accountability.[24]

Various problems arose in the establishment of the new system of organization, which was put in effect on May 1, 1847. Some of the stations were such simple affairs that enclosures for the safeguard of tickets were lacking. Scales had to be procured for each station to permit the weighing of freight, but even when the proper facilities were on hand the B & O often had to depend on inefficient part-time agents. Nevertheless the new system seemed essentially sound and, though suspended for a time, remained the basic plan of organization of this railroad for many years.[25]

IV   AND FOR A SOUTHERN TERMINUS

Next to the great problem of how to finance the extension of the railroad to the Ohio River came the problem of where the terminus of the road should be. Pittsburgh and Wheeling actively wooed the B & O, and ultimately the choice lay between them, though the B & O management preferred a third alternative, the village of Parkersburg, farther down the Ohio and on a more direct route to Cincinnati.

Since the Ohio valley was settled before the shores of the Great Lakes, Baltimore merchants considered a connection to Cincinnati and St. Louis preferable to a connection with Cleveland or Chicago. Because of this fixation on southern Ohio trade, the B & O hesitated to accept Virginia laws granting a right-of-way no farther south than to Wheeling, and tolerated thought of a line to Pittsburgh only as an alternative, or second, terminus.

Pittsburgh merchants, indeed, were more interested in Baltimore than Baltimore merchants in Pittsburgh, particularly after the winter of 1845–46, which showed the Pennsylvania canal system to be entirely undependable. First a drought had crippled the canals in the autumn and then the violent breaking up of the winter kept them inoperative until late in the spring.[26]

Under the impetus of these troubles Pittsburgh interests demanded that the Pennsylvania state legislature permit the B & O to acquire a right-of-way to connect their city to Baltimore. In complying with this demand, however, the legislators affixed a proviso to the law which in time negated it. If $3 million should be subscribed (and $900,000 paid in) by July 31, 1847, to the Pennsylvania Railroad for a Pittsburgh-Philadelphia connection, the B & O charter would be null and void. Furthermore, the B & O was required, if the charter was operative, to permit a fourteen-mile connection with the Franklin Railroad which would enable goods from Pittsburgh to be moved directly to Philadelphia without coming through Baltimore.

The necessary subscription to the Pennsylvania Railroad was forthcoming, so the B & O lost its entree to Pittsburgh. But the requirement of a Philadelphia connection via the Franklin Railroad had already removed the incentive to Baltimoreans of taking this route to the Ohio.[27] However, a kind of back door to Pittsburgh still remained open. This was via the Pittsburgh & Connellsville Railroad, which was authorized by the Pennsylvania legislature to extend its road well beyond Connellsville along any branch of the Youghiogheny River as far as the Maryland boundary; therefore connecting it to the B & O rails at Cumberland would be no great task. To encourage the P & C to begin construction and thereby to keep this route to Pittsburgh a possibility, the B & O directors had subscribed to 700 shares of P & C stock and paid a first installment of $1,750 before McLane returned from England. Acting President Jones was particularly enthusiastic about this opportunity to open up fertile districts of Pennsylvania and allow the shores of the Great Lakes "to pour their tribute of commerce and wealth into the lap" of Baltimore.[28]

A Philadelphia newspaper spread a rumor that McLane by a secret letter from London had encouraged B & O support for the P & C, which proceeded to hire Benjamin Latrobe as its chief engineer.[29] But when McLane returned, he soon made it clear that he regarded Pittsburgh as only a secondary goal, useful also as a threat or a decoy in which the B & O could display particular interest whenever Virginia legislators seemed unresponsive. The preferred route for the B & O, as he saw it, was through Virginia, to reach the Ohio at some point where the trade of Cincinnati and the lower Ohio valley could easily be tapped.

When Latrobe, in October, wrote McLane of the plans of the P & C, a special committee was established of six B & O directors, including Kennedy and Hoffman, to aid in negotiations with the Pittsburgh company. Despite this committee's existence, McLane tried to avoid a conference, writing to Pittsburgh to head off a P & C delegation that was rumored to be coming to Baltimore. But the letter was too late; the delegation was on its way. Apparently McLane and his six committeemen were caught unprepared when the Pittsburgh group, led by Congressman Harmar Denny, arrived at the B & O headquarters on November 1. Nevertheless a meeting was begun at 4 P.M. that lasted until late in the evening.

For the Pittsburghers the results were very disappointing. All the B & O committeemen professed themselves in favor of a Pittsburgh connection, but they would not give the P & C any financial aid or even make a further subscription for the present.[30] According to McLane, the P & C wanted $350,000 at once and a commitment that the B & O would subscribe $2 million in all, roughly two thirds of the cost of construction from Pittsburgh to the state line. They also wanted the B & O to connect with the Franklin Railroad at Hancock to give a route to Philadelphia, and they threatened to negotiate directly with Philadelphia interests if the B & O did not offer some immediate assistance.[31] Part of their concern, they told McLane, was a fear that the B & O was only using the P & C to its own advantage.[32]

McLane stalled, declaring the B & O stockholders would have to approve a large subscription (he mentioned $600,000) to P & C stock and that no further help should be given unless the P & C would agree to certain terms: e.g., that it not intersect with any other railroad unless the B & O approved, that its rates conform to those of the B & O, and that it not require a connection until the B & O main line was completed to some point on the Ohio south of Pittsburgh.[33] The Pennsylvania legislature was so unfriendly, McLane explained, that the B & O was not permitted to build a foot of road in Pennsylvania; certainly it would not use Baltimore capital to connect Pittsburgh with Philadelphia. Of course the P & C could profit by being part of two lines, but a Philadelphia connection would draw business away from Baltimore. His "first and great duty" was to reach a point farther down the Ohio than Pittsburgh, and the chance of doing so was less doubtful than it might seem.[34] "I am again at my old position in the railroad," he wrote to a son at the end of 1846, "bending my efforts to procuring the right of way through Virginia." [35]

Maryland Governor Thomas Pratt, in his annual message to the legislature, suggested a reason for optimism about a Virginia right-of-way. The retrocession of a portion of the District of Columbia to Virginia left the mouth of the Chesapeake and Ohio Canal (at Alexandria) in that state. In view of the benefits to Virginia from Maryland expenditures in the construction of this canal, the least that Virginia could do, Governor Pratt said, was concede to the B & O Railroad the right to seek a western terminus in Virginia.[36]

Virginia would indeed cede a terminus, but not the one the B & O wanted. There were competing Virginia interests which wanted to keep the B & O out of Parkersburg, and their strength was augmented by the influence of Wheeling, which wanted the B & O for itself.[37]

V   PITTSBURGH OBJECTS

The B & O lobbyists in Richmond, such as Thomas Swann, a Virginia native of increasing importance in Baltimore mercantile circles, found friendly reception among delegates from northwestern Virginia such as Andrew Hunter, an attorney from Charles Town, near Harper's Ferry, who introduced a bill that would grant the B & O a right-of-way to Fishing Creek, below Wheeling. McLane addressed a Richmond paper to deny rumors that the B & O would be satisfied with Wheeling if it had no other choice of terminus in Virginia, but this and other efforts he made to influence Virginia lawmakers were called "an offensive attempt of a corporation in which the State has no interest, to interfere with its legislation." [38]

At a stockholders' meeting on February 8, McLane explained the dissatisfaction of the board of directors with the Virginia acts of February 19, 1845, already rejected by the B & O, and of February 28, 1846, which the board thought not worth consideration. To remove any doubt about the acceptability of these acts, which permitted a right-of-way only to Wheeling, the stockholders by unanimous vote rejected them and declared they would not for any consideration approve construction on the route to which these laws confined the B & O. At the same time a committee was established, including Thomas Swann, to investigate the possibility of a connection with Pittsburgh via the Pittsburgh & Connellsville Railroad.[39]

Very likely McLane's interest in Pittsburgh was merely a bit of commercial coquetry intended to rouse Virginia to rivalry. The maneuver did succeed after a fashion, when Virginia passed a new right-of-way law on March 6, still requiring the B & O to make Wheeling its terminus but permitting use of a new and easier route and even providing that the Ohio River might be reached south of Wheeling at Fish Creek (13 miles north of Fishing Creek) under certain conditions. The conditions were complicated: the line to Wheeling was to be built on the route where it could be constructed, maintained, and worked at least expense; in case the Fish Creek route to the Ohio was the cheapest, another route could be chosen if the city of Wheeling would pay the difference. In any case Wheeling might subscribe up to $1 million in B & O stock. Besides giving Wheeling a chance to help the B & O move along rapidly (the act had to be accepted within six months, construction to be begun within three years, and a through line to be completed within twelve years), the act offered the B & O a terminus farther south than Wheeling, though not as far south as the B & O had desired. And whether the B & O could use this Fish Creek terminus was made to depend somewhat on Wheeling, which could, at some financial sacrifice, require the B & O to build farther north.[40]

At first McLane professed dissatisfaction with the new Virginia legislation. He declared to a member of his board of directors that the application to Virginia had been a failure and he suggested a subscription of $800,000, the largest authorized by the B & O charter, to the stock of the Pittsburgh & Connellsville Railroad. A subscription of this size would give the B & O "absolute control" of the Pittsburgh & Connellsville charter, and this certainty of a northern terminus, in his opinion, would materially strengthen a future B & O application "for a more southern and preferred route" through Virginia.[41]

To a Virginia route to the Ohio he was inalterably committed, and as time passed he persuaded himself that the Virginia application had not been altogether a failure. At a stockholders' meeting on March 22, he declared that the Virginia legislation of March 6 was the best the B & O ever secured from this state, removing every onerous restriction except the required connection with Wheeling, and even in this regard granting a southern terminus at Fish Creek if Wheeling approved.[42]

What McLane said was true enough, but the B & O had not needed a very generous right-of-way from Virginia in 1839, when it decided to build to Wheeling roughly on the route of the National Road. The difference was that in 1839 the B & O had the right to cut through southwestern Pennsylvania to Wheeling, the most direct route from Cumberland. In 1847, on the other hand, the B & O no longer had any right-of-way through Pennsylvania, except by utilizing the P & C connection, which led only to Pittsburgh. A Virginia route to Wheeling, which lies in the panhandle jutting north between Pennsylvania and Ohio, meant the expensive and awkward necessity of building around the southwestern corner of Pennsylvania, a kind of dog's leg detour from the direct route.

Perhaps McLane was led to be increasingly receptive to the idea of a Wheeling terminus, dog's leg and all, because of the criticism he received from Pittsburgh interests. The Pittsburgh *Gazette,* for example, on January 26, called on the B & O stockholders to rebel against the policies of McLane, and on the same date the Baltimore *American* published a letter berating McLane for procrastination on negotiations for a Pittsburgh terminus, declaring "he has argued us into more trouble than his skill in diplomacy may be of any avail in helping us out of." McLane's critics held that he was primarily responsible for the tactics of the B & O management. "He should know," one critic wrote, "that public sentiment outside of the RR office is inimical *in toto* to the course that has been pursued." [43] No wonder McLane was complaining to Buchanan at this time, "I am quite sure that those charged with the cares of state, are not the only men who do not lie upon a bed of roses; and mine, certainly, has its full proportion of thorns." [44]

When the select committee that had been appointed on February 8 to investigate a Pittsburgh connection reported to the B & O stockholders on February 22 that they thought Pittsburgh should not be made the terminus at this time, they were not in perfect agreement, for one member, Tench Tilghman, representing the stock held by the state of Maryland, presented a minority report in favor of cooperation with the P & C. The majority report was accepted, but the fact that it depended on statistics furnished the committee, in part, at least, by McLane, helped to increase his unpopularity with advocates of the Pittsburgh connection.[45]

All was harmony between the B & O and the P & C, declared "A Well Wisher of Both Roads," in a letter to the Pittsburgh *Gazette,* until McLane returned from Europe, and even now the only obstacle to continued harmony lies "in the preconceived notions of Mr. McLane himself. Should these continue to operate . . . I see no other mode left than that of making some one else the President of the Baltimore Company." [46] "A Large Stockholder," possibly Thomas Swann, defended McLane in print, arguing he had a "peculiar competency" for his position, in which he displayed "untiring zeal," and that "paramount interests connected with the road . . . have sustained the President in his disinterested efforts to carry out the objects of his trust." The Virginia law of March 6, 1847, this same writer explained, was distinctly preferable to the 1845 and 1846 Virginia charters which the B & O had rejected. The earlier charters prescribed a route surveyed by Jonathan Knight called "the route of tunnels" because it led around the corner of Pennsylvania across a series of mountain ridges. The 1847 act permitted a route that for four fifths of the way followed streams of easy grade. Wheeling would be closer to Baltimore by train on this route than to Pittsburgh by boat on the Ohio. [47]

Yet Pittsburghers continued to blame McLane for the collapse of negotiations, referring to his "apparent insincerity" and "want of candor." [48] At a B & O stockholders' meeting on March 22 a committee, of which the merchant Columbus O'Donnell was chairman, reported its opinion that the Pittsburgh & Connellsville Railroad now offered the best practical route to the Ohio River, whereupon John P. Kennedy moved the appointment of another committee to confer with P & C officials, particularly on the possibility of raising money in Pittsburgh as well as on the possibility of a large subscription to P & C stock by the B & O. Kennedy became chairman of this committee, which also included former and future presidents of the B & O (Joseph W. Patterson and Thomas Swann) as well as the prominent Baltimore merchant Johns Hopkins, but its efforts to cooperate with the P & C were made abortive by the intransigence of Pittsburgh officials, who insisted on a route of their own choosing and argued that they could have little faith in the B & O as long as McLane was at its helm. [49]

Even Kennedy was moved, for the last time, to expostulate with the Pittsburghers in defense of McLane, as the object of "a most unjust assault . . . for what is called his diplomacy." It was a "most mischievous mistake" to think McLane the only obstacle to satisfactory cooperation, for the citizens of Baltimore were overwhelmingly opposed to abandoning hope for a southern route to the Ohio and as long as that hope existed a Pittsburgh connection would be regarded only as a branch or secondary line. Within this pattern, McLane had always favored a Pittsburgh connection and was willing to spend up to a million dollars on it, in which respect, wrote Kennedy, "he has been in advance of a considerable portion of the Board of Directors." And admitting that McLane had declared a road to Pittsburgh incompatible with one to Wheeling, Kennedy denied that McLane had expressed a preference for the latter city.[50]

Whatever McLane had previously said regarding the relative merits of connections to Wheeling and Pittsburgh, he soon made himself quite clear—to the discomfiture of Kennedy. The scene was a B & O stockholders' meeting on April 5, where McLane made what the minutes call "a full and elaborate statement of his views," later published as a pamphlet. Southern Ohio, he declared, was the object of the B & O, and it should go there by the shortest, cheapest route. If any route could be taken, the best would be by the Shenandoah Valley and Winchester, but Virginia would not permit its use. He preferred any Virginia point on the Ohio to Pittsburgh, because at Pittsburgh the advantage Baltimore had elsewhere over Philadelphia and New York was lost.[51]

After McLane had read his statement, which proved thirty-two pages long when printed at the order of the directors, John P. Kennedy proposed that the Pittsburgh & Connellsville should be told that if it could raise $750,000 in subscriptions in Pittsburgh, the B & O would subscribe $800,000 and the city of Baltimore would provide whatever additional sum was necessary to build from Pittsburgh to the state line. But this was to be on a particular route that the B & O preferred because it would intersect conveniently with the roadway it intended to follow along the Potomac River westward toward the Ohio. This route had lower grades than the shorter northern route the P & C preferred (via Casselman River) and opened the valuable coal region at Westernport and the mouth of the Savage River, "the most valuable and productive mineral region in Alleghany." Though Kennedy was not willing to support the P & C on that railroad's own terms, he did desire to offer it cooperation, because he thought a Pittsburgh connection, which would lead to the Great Lakes area through Cleveland, was of great importance to the B & O—very little inferior to the main objective of the B & O, the connection to Cincinnati or Columbus via some point on the lower Ohio.

Before any action could be taken on resolutions embodying Kennedy's proposal, Thomas Parkin Scott, a representative of the city of Baltimore, substituted a series of resolutions declaring a desire to connect with Pittsburgh but refusing to make it the sole western terminus of the B & O, rejecting any thought of proceeding on the Casselman River route, and referring the whole subject back to the board with power to act subject to these restrictions. After considerable debate, Scott's resolutions were adopted and the idea of any compromise with the P & C was killed for the time being.[52]

When the meeting was over, Kennedy was gloomy, convinced that negotiations with Pittsburgh had been "so mismanaged as to leave us little hope of being able to do anything." [53] The resolutions he had offered might have led to further negotiations, Kennedy thought, but though the people at large would probably sustain him, the Baltimore city representatives on the railroad overruled him.[54] Kennedy's assurance about the people at large may have derived from a "numerously attended" mass meeting at the Merchants' Exchange on April 3 which urged construction of a railroad to Pittsburgh.[55] He probably did not attend this meeting, but he kept in close touch with what was going on and corresponded with leaders of the Pittsburgh & Connellsville.

On April 15, William Robinson, president of the P & C, visited Kennedy, who urged him to organize a mass meeting in Pittsburgh in favor of a Baltimore connection in the hope that this would lead to new negotiations. The resolutions Kennedy had offered to the B & O stockholders on April 5 were completely acceptable to the P & C directorate, according to Robinson, but Kennedy explained that he had refused to offer them again at a B & O board meeting on April 14 because he found the majority of the board hostile. Even McLane, who had heretofore always professed an interest in the Pittsburgh connection, was "silent and surly," and one of the city directors, Wesley Starr, spoke openly against arrangements with the P & C.[56]

At this April 14 meeting McLane was empowered to seek the advice of lawyers in Virginia and in Maryland regarding the meaning of the Virginia right-of-way law of March 6, and he was also authorized to confer with Wheeling authorities on possible modifications of this law and to visit Cincinnati and other cities regarding future operations of the B & O. These powers and duties were given to McLane at his own request, but it was another of McLane's recommendations that proved most surprising to John P. Kennedy. This was a recommendation that the B & O proceed with the "indispensable" task of reconstruction. This was a surprising recommendation because just two days earlier, according to Kennedy, McLane "told the finance committee, of which I was one, that the old portion of the road did not need the reconstruction, which we had begun a year ago." [57] And much earlier, when abroad, McLane had criticized the B & O management for expending their resources on reconstruction when the one task immediately necessary was to push on with every resource until the Ohio was reached.

Quite likely McLane still thought the reconstruction should be postponed till extension was completed. In this case he may have decided to give in because he lacked the support of a majority of the board and would, moreover, be taking issue with the interim president, Samuel Jones, who had begun the reconstruction. The one member of the board who finally voted against reconstruction was Samuel Hoffman, one of the largest stockholders and a man generally in agreement with McLane. If a majority of the private directors plus the city and state directors wanted reconstruction, McLane may have decided to go along with them in order not to alienate any of the support he needed in the quarrel about what Ohio River terminus to adopt. Or he may have been honestly influenced by Latrobe's report of March 16 on this subject—and by the fact that the anticipated surplus would be too low for a cash dividend anyway.[58]

"What has got into him?" Kennedy asked, and he thought he found a political explanation. In December, McLane told Kennedy's committee on reorganization that the workshop at the main depot was entirely too large and that he would reduce the size of this operation gradually as existing contracts were completed and bring it to the footing of a mere shop for repairs. Incidental to this change, many workmen would be discharged, though probably not till spring. And all this was part of a long-range plan to reduce the establishment, as McLane explained to Kennedy's committee—a plan of reduction that McLane had begun to put into effect before he went to England. On his return he was amazed to find that far from reducing the laboring force in the shops, Jones had actually increased its size.

"This was a ground of complaint against Jones," Kennedy commented, after noting that McLane now claimed (in April, 1847) that the laboring force was "no more than the repairs required." Kennedy wondered whether McLane's change meant that Robert McLane was planning to run for Congress—as Kennedy's opponent—and that McLane wished to keep men at work for fear that Bob would suffer at the polls if men were discharged by the B & O. Perhaps Bob's ambitions caused his father to be unfriendly to Kennedy.

Personal ambition had influenced McLane's actions all through his life, thought Kennedy, who wrote, not entirely accurately: "He was a Federalist, a Whig, a Jackson man, an anti-Jackson—a Loco, a democrat—a Tyler, and a Polk man—a little while, when it was necessary to get a foot upon the ladder, a Calhoun man—and now he is all agog for Taylor," but fears the Whigs will monopolize this military hero.

And Kennedy remembered the advice once given him regarding McLane: *"He is not to be trusted*—as Mr. Clay once told me." [59]

VI   PITTSBURGH REJECTED

In the spring and summer of 1847, the quarrel regarding the western terminus of the B & O moved rapidly toward its climax and denouement. Counsel in Virginia (Andrew Hunter) and Maryland (Reverdy Johnson) advised the B & O that the mouth of Fish Creek could be its terminus only if it was on the cheapest route to Wheeling and if the Wheeling authorities agreed. In any other case, Wheeling alone could be the terminus unless the Virginia legislature relented.[60] Meanwhile the right-of-way law must speedily be accepted or it was lost.

If the B & O insisted on a Virginia terminus, it was obviously dependent on Wheeling, not only for permission, under certain conditions, to build via Fish Creek, but also for support in the Virginia legislature if any modification of the right-of-way act was requested. A modification to permit a more southern terminus was desired—of that there was no question—and so McLane appointed an influential committee (including Samuel Hoffman, Joseph W. Patterson, Thomas Swann, and T. Parkin Scott) and proceeded, on April 29, to Wheeling.

In Wheeling the B & O representatives found great interest in their railroad but little willingness to agree that it could touch the Ohio at the mouth of Fish Creek or at any other desirable spot south of Wheeling. Representatives of various Ohio cities also appeared at Wheeling to meet McLane and his colleagues, perhaps invited there to persuade the Baltimoreans of the complete suitability of Wheeling as a western terminus. McLane and company decided that the first necessity before concluding any agreements was to discover whether the south of Fish Creek was on the cheapest route to Wheeling; if so, they would try to persuade Wheeling authorities to let the railroad come via this place; if not, the only hope of any terminus south of Wheeling lay with the Virginia legislature, and Wheeling was not likely to offer any help in influencing that body of men—quite the contrary. So the Baltimoreans returned home and sent out Benjamin Latrobe to find which route to Wheeling was the cheapest.[61]

While Latrobe went about this task, it became evident to close observers that the trip to Wheeling had influenced McLane and his companions to look upon a connection there more enthusiastically than before. Perhaps the Ohioans they had met—representatives of Columbus, Zanesville, Steubenville, and St. Clairsville—had contributed to this enthusiasm. At any rate, at a meeting of the B & O board on May 8, shortly after the committee returned from Wheeling, Kennedy was surprised at the change in their attitude. "McLane and his clique have . . . jumped Jim Crow, and are all for Wheeling," he wrote; "strange enough, this! After embroiling Virginia for ten years on this question, with so many protestations that nothing could induce him to recommend Wheeling . . . we have new lights upon it now." [62]

Meanwhile, the Pittsburgh & Connellsville board, alarmed at the developing relations between Baltimore and Wheeling, resolved on another effort to win B & O support by offering to reopen the issue of the route a connecting line should take in crossing the Pennsylvania–Maryland boundary to Cumberland.[63] It was on receipt of a letter from Robinson, president of the P & C, declaring a P & C board committee was eager to meet with a similar committee from the B & O, that McLane called the special May 8 meeting of the B & O board, and a B & O committee was appointed—with strict instructions to make no propositions but simply to hear what the P & C had to say. Kennedy and O'Donnell, both advocates of resumed negotiations with Pittsburgh, felt so hopeless they would not serve on the committee, and in the debate tempers began to boil. "McLane and myself make speeches—at daggers," Kennedy noted in his journal; "he black as thunder—I blacker." [64]

There was another angry quarrel between these two men at the regular board meeting four days later (May 12), when Kennedy proposed a set of instructions for the committee to confer with the P & C. He wanted the B & O to subscribe $800,000 to the P & C at once and to offer, once Pittsburgh had raised $750,000, to building the P & C to the Maryland line at whatever point suited the B & O for a connection. The issue, put in this fashion, was clearly a choice between Wheeling and Pittsburgh, and Kennedy was surprised to find more opposition to Pittsburgh than he expected. McLane's leadership was upheld and the Kennedy resolutions defeated, 16 to 7, but when the meeting adjourned, according to Kennedy, it was "with declarations of war." [65]

The victory of McLane was assured a few days later when the committee set up by the B & O board received a set of proposals from Pittsburgh that were completely unacceptable—because, for example, the P & C insisted on controlling the route and on having the Pittsburgh connection with Baltimore completed before the B & O built to any other Ohio River terminus. McLane sent his son Bob and Samuel Hoffman, the latter "mad as a Bedlamite," around to the trustees to drum up support, and when the board met on May 17 all but unanimous approval (a 24 to 1 vote) was given to a resolution McLane introduced declaring it inexpedient to give further help to the P & C on the terms it insisted upon. Even Kennedy and O'Donnell did not oppose this motion, and though the friends of a Pittsburgh connection did offer a series of compromise resolutions, they were defeated as soundly as on May 12.[66]

It is quite possible that, as Kennedy suspected, the Pittsburgh interests were led to make extravagant demands because they thought all hope was gone. Perhaps they thought that maintaining a strong public position would place them in a better situation for an appeal to the Pennsylvania legislature—making them appear Pennsylvania patriots rather than traitors to Philadelphia interests. At all events, their recalcitrance played into

McLane's hands, and Kennedy, hopeless at last, began to sell his B & O stock.[67]

McLane had his victory, but he had to take the blame for it. The Pittsburgh *Gazette* referred to the "iron control" of McLane over the B & O which made negotiations impossible. "We have been duped and played with," it added, "by this cunning Diplomatic President, who never, in our humble opinion, entertained any serious opinions of a connection" between Baltimore and Pittsburgh.[68]

With the B & O board taking a firm stand against the P & C, an attempt was made to get around the B & O by rousing public sentiment in Baltimore. At a mass meeting on May 25, a citizens' committee was appointed that went to Pittsburgh at once and returned to report at another meeting of interested citizens on June 8.[69] Much enthusiasm was exhibited, and the Baltimore city council was persuaded to instruct the city directors on the B & O board to support a large subscription to P & C stock. But even these instructions were won only by conceding certain conditions (that sizable other sums should first be raised by the P & C) which indicated there was little more hope of a quick commitment of Baltimore municipal aid to the P & C than there was of aid from the Baltimore & Ohio Railroad.[70]

VII   VICTORY—AND COLLAPSE

Meanwhile McLane, though waiting for Latrobe's report on comparative costs before concluding his Wheeling negotiations, was not standing pat. On June 9 he persuaded his board to support a major extension at each end of the Main Stem of the B & O. At the western end he proposed a fifty-six-mile continuation of the tracks from Cumberland to the Maryland–Virginia boundary. This extension would not only be a step toward the western goal of the B & O but would permit some intermediary profit by crossing an important coal and iron field near the mouth of the Savage River. Furthermore, it would be drawing near the Cheat River (a proper terminus for humbuggery, said the Pittsburgh *Gazette*), which Virginia proposed to make navigable to Pittsburgh, and, of more importance, the Northwestern Virginia Turnpike, leading to Parkersburg, which seemed likely to replace the ill-repaired National (Cumberland) Turnpike as the main wagon route west. This extension did not definitely commit the B & O to any one of several possible Virginia terminuses on the Ohio, but its adoption did mean a decisive rejection of the northern route to Pittsburgh via Casselman River.

At the eastern end of the road McLane recommended a shorter but almost equally important extension of the B & O, from its Mount Clare depot on the southwestern side of Baltimore to Locust Point, on the south shore of Baltimore harbor. Because the B & O was not allowed to use steam power on the streets of Baltimore it had been forced into an expensive business when it moved western cargoes of flour, stone, and coal, to the Baltimore docks. By McLane's proposal it would avoid Baltimore streets—indeed, avoid Baltimore City—by moving cargo directly by rail behind its steam locomotives to new docks on the south shore (Baltimore City was on the north shore) of the Patapsco. An engineer's report regarding this recommendation had been on file for several years, McLane explained, and he would have pressed it upon the directors two years ago had he not been away.

The major criticism leveled at McLane's proposal bore on the ability of the B & O to pay for this new construction. Admittedly it would tax the resources of the B & O severely, but McLane argued that it could be done, thanks to the earnings and the credit of the road plus possible use of the $3 million in state bonds that he had carefully held in reserve rather than sell at a sacrifice when the state's credit was low. The Locust Point extension would actually save money as well as attract freight, while the western extension was but another step toward the railroad's cherished Ohio goal.

Advocates of the Pittsburgh connection feared McLane's recommendations not only because they took the B & O away from the shortest route to Pittsburgh but also because they threatened to be such a load on the resources of the railroad as to leave little hope that it could also pay for a line to Pittsburgh—not, at least, till the other work was done. Yet the recommendation for the extension to the Maryland–Virginia line was adopted by the directors with but one dissenting vote, Columbus O'Donnell's. Some members who might have voted with O'Donnell were absent, however, and McLane did meet with more opposition to his proposal for the Locust Point extension, which was opposed by six directors though supported by fourteen.[71]

Another step in the extension of the B & O was taken at a board meeting on July 14, when surveys for the new construction were authorized. At this same meeting, McLane announced completion of an agreement with the municipal authorities of Wheeling, but the vote upon the agreement was put off to an adjourned meeting two days later.[72]

Agreement with Wheeling had followed Latrobe's return to Baltimore at the end of June and the assurances he brought that the cheapest route to Wheeling went, as McLane had hoped, via the mouth of Fish Creek. A Wheeling committee then visited Baltimore and worked out an understanding with McLane, Patterson, Swann, Hoffman, and Scott. Wheeling agreed to subscribe $500,000 to the stock of the B & O as soon as the railroad reached the banks of the Monongahela and announced its intention to commence the final stretch to Wheeling. In addition, it promised to provide grounds for a depot on the north side of Wheeling Creek and a free right-of-way through the city on which the B & O would be permitted to use steam locomotives. Most important, Wheeling agreed to waive its right to determine the route of the railroad; this meant the B & O could use the mouth of Fish Creek if, as Latrobe's report indicated, this was the cheapest route to Wheeling.[73]

Today, McLane wrote his son Robert on July 6, we "concluded an arrangement with the Wheeling committee quite satisfactory to every member of our committee." [74] In drafting an explanation of the agreement, the committee noted that their records and the records of the stage companies using the National Road proved that two thirds of all the passengers journeying from the Ohio to Baltimore continued on to Philadelphia and the North. If these passengers had gone to Pittsburgh, they would naturally have taken the road directly to Philadelphia and not have used the B & O at all. Obviously, the committee argued, it was wise for the B & O to reach these passengers at a point west of Pittsburgh, such as Wheeling, and bring this traffic profitably through Maryland.[75] By a 17 to 5 vote on July 16 the B & O board accepted the agreement with Wheeling and asked the stockholders to meet on August 25 to ratify it.[76]

Before the stockholders met, a hot fight was waged for proxies. "Our opponents boast," McLane wrote, "of having secured 12,000 proxies, which, if the boast be true, will undoubtedly give them the controul of the stockholder vote for all purposes." On the whole, he decided, victory by the opposition might be a relief for him, "as it would afford a sufficient pretext to quit a position absolutely odious." If McLane's administration carried the day, the opposition would continue and constantly embarrass the railroad management as well as throw on McLane the odium of delay or even of failure. "I do not perceive any abatement in the angry feelings to which this contest has so surprisingly given rise." [77]

Nor did they abate, and the strain of the quarrel told on Louis McLane. On August 2 the governor of Pennsylvania announced the nullification of the B & O right-of-way because the Pennsylvania Railroad had fulfilled the conditions prescribed to keep its charter alive and negate the one granted the Baltimore road.[78] This announcement was not startling, however, for the B & O had long ago discounted any hope of building in Pennsylvania under its own charter.

When the B & O stockholders convened on the morning of August 25, McLane submitted the proceedings of the July 16 board meeting, as well as the report of the committee that had conferred with the municipal authorities of Wheeling. Former Governor Samuel Sprigg, who was attending to represent the interests of the state of Maryland, asked that the meeting be adjourned till afternoon so that his colleague Tench Tilghman, whose presence was needed if the state stock was to be voted, could attend. The meeting was adjourned till 4 P.M., but when it reconvened McLane was missing. He had suddenly become ill, as Samuel Hoffman explained, and had been carried away unconscious.

By this sudden faint, McLane missed the outcome of the proxy battle. The Virginia law granting a right-of-way to Wheeling was accepted by the stockholders almost unanimously—only Robert Garrett, a Baltimore merchant with Pennsylvania connections, voting his stock in opposition. But on the crucial question of whether to accept the agreement with Wheeling the vote was closer. The B & O management was upheld, 54,718 shares to 35,520, when Tilghman proposed a committee be chosen, minus officers and directors of the B & O, to weigh the comparative merits of Pittsburgh, Wheeling, and other points as terminuses. The opposition vote was chiefly composed of the 35,000 shares of the state of Maryland, but it is likely that more private stockholders might have voted with the state had there seemed to be any hope of defeating the management. O'Donnell and Kennedy, for example, cast no votes and presumably were not present, while the largest private stockholder in opposition, William F. Murdock, left the meeting after the first vote was lost. Apparently Robert Garrett had also left the meeting early, for he did not vote on the Wheeling agreement, to which he was opposed. Still the opposition obviously had nothing like the 12,000 private-share votes McLane had heard they expected.

McLane's management was upheld because it had the support of the city of Baltimore and the chief private stockholders. The city's 35,000 shares countered the equal number of the state, and the private stockholders, such as Samuel Hoffman, who voted 8,978 shares, Edward Patterson, voting 2,167 shares, and Thomas Swann, voting 1,640 shares, made the difference. McLane's management was sustained because it did represent the ownership of the B & O, but his physical collapse suggested that he would not be able to stand continued agitation.[79]

VIII   THE MC LANES AT WAR

The concern that led to Louis McLane's physical collapse in August of 1847 was not completely caused by the problems of his railroad. He was also worried by the condition of his wife, who had been taken ill in October, 1846, shortly after their return from England, and had never completely recovered. Her illness, called inflammatory rheumatism, caused her acute pain, and gradually she grew increasingly emaciated until by the end of the year she was confined to her bed in the house McLane had rented at 45 Franklin Street, next to the Unitarian Church.[80]

It may have added to McLane's concerns that three of his sons and one son-in-law were in the midst of the Mexican War, but he was so strong a supporter of a militant policy that he seems to have been more excited by the gallantry of his boys than worried by their danger. He even apologized for Robert's absence from the war. Robert was eager to go, his father assured another son: only his wife and children held him back, and if the war lasted they would probably not be able to prevent his going.[81]

Of all the boys young Louis had the most unusual adventures during the war. In July, 1846, he was a passed midshipman on board the U.S.S. *Levant,* part of Sloat's squadron, which seized Monterey, the capital of California. Sloat appointed him first lieutenant, after he volunteered for service in a company of dragoons to reconnoitre the country, keep the Indians under control, and maintain communications by land between Yerba Buena (San Francisco) and Monterey.[82] Colonel John Frémont borrowed young Louis McLane to command the artillery in the troops he marched to southern California.[83] Subsequently Louis rose to the rank of captain and then of major, was one of the American signers of the Treaty of Cahuenga, January 13, 1847, and served under William T. Sherman in the pacification.[84]

Lou's difficult brother George, who had joined Taylor in Mexico as a lieutenant of mounted riflemen, declared himself "enchanted" with the life of a soldier and determined to make this service his profession. Transferred to Scott's expedition to Mexico City, he won distinction in the assault on Chapultepec and was cited for his gallantry in the despatches of General Quitman.[85]

A third brother, Allan, was thought even more eager for action by his prejudiced father, and it is a mark of the attitude of Louis McLane toward this war that he feared Allan might be less fortunate than George in having an opportunity for distinction in combat. But to Allan too an opportunity for gallantry came, and he seized upon it in the landing at Vera Cruz. In the words of one despatch, Allan answered "a call for volunteers to clear away some brushwood which obstructed the view to a battery on which we wished to direct our fire, . . . sprung through an embrasure, followed by two men, . . . and amidst a shower of balls, quickly removed the obstruction." Later, he was ordered to Annapolis, where he passed a year in further study for a naval career.[86]

The only member of the family seriously wounded in the war was

Lydia's husband, Joseph Johnston, but he recovered in time to participate in the capture of Mexico City.[87] His close friend, Robert McLane, never reentered the Army, though when he joined General Taylor in northern Mexico, bearing oral as well as written despatches from the President, he was offered a position on General Robert Patterson's staff. He did not accept.[88]

To have done so would have meant separation not only from his wife and infant children but also from his promising political career. His ambitions became evident in September, 1847, when he opened an active canvass as Democratic candidate for John P. Kennedy's seat in the House of Representatives. His theme was support of the administration and of this war that Kennedy thought "vile and odious." Despite the fact that Kennedy, a Whig, polled the largest number of votes ever given a Whig candidate in this district, McLane was victorious, aided, according to Kennedy, by strong support from the Democratic city government, the custom house, and federal authorities generally. In Congress, McLane quickly jumped to the defense of the administration in debate when opponents claimed Taylor's army had unduly provoked the Mexicans on a contested frontier.[89]

In his support of the war and the administration, Robert McLane was completely in step with his father. Congratulating Polk on his message to Congress, Louis McLane declared the opposition to be "neither more adroit nor more patriotic than their predecessors in 1813." This remark seems somewhat odd to come from an old Federalist, but McLane found it possible to support Polk's tariff views, emphasizing revenue as the object of a tariff law and protection as an incidental benefit, and argued they were founded on a principle Washington and Hamilton would uphold, whereas the Whig American System persisted in augmenting protection despite the fact that the labor of the country was in decreasing need of it.[90]

Learning from Robert that Calhoun was lukewarm toward the war policy of the administration, Louis McLane tried to persuade the South Carolinian that the future leadership of the party would be drawn exclusively from those supporting the government at this critical hour. "The war is popular with the great Masses," McLane wrote, "and public opinion will be very apt to visit those who are endeavouring to obstruct its progress with a condemnation scarcely less than that which followed the federal opposition to the War of 1813." [91] Calhoun's continued influence in the party seemed important to McLane, particularly for the sake of his son Robert, who was closer to Calhoun than Louis had ever been. Only a Federalist could be so sensitive to the public obloquy in store for men who opposed a war once the country had entered upon it.

"You men of the South must be careful," he warned Barnwell Rhett on another occasion, pleading for unity in the party, even in the face of such a popular candidate as General Zachary Taylor.[92] To Buchanan he lamented the lack of "a vigorous and united support of the President" which would invigorate the party and allow it to withstand "all the factions—abolition & everything else." [93] In respect to the war McLane's only complaint against the administration was its lack of vigor in subjugating Mexico and overdependence on civil diplomacy, and he hoped sufficient territory would be seized and held permanently to recompense the United States for the cost of the war and to give it a secure boundary for future years. As to the cause of the war, he did not blame Polk; the war was inevitable once Texas was annexed—and so he frankly told Calhoun, architect of the annexation.[94]

Probably it was, as he said, a sad disappointment for Louis McLane that in June, 1847, he was unable to accept the President's invitation to join his party on a tour north at least as far as to Boston, but this was the time when a decision regarding the railroad route to the Ohio was in the making and the engineers' reports on their surveys were daily expected. Even a brief absence, McLane felt, would be inexcusable.[95]

In March, 1848, McLane felt obliged to refuse a more important invitation from President Polk. The treaty negotiated between Mexico and the United States at Guadalupe Hidalgo was being debated in the Senate but seemed likely to be ratified shortly, and Polk desired to send it to Mexico in the care of a commissioner who would effectively urge its ratification upon the Mexican government. McLane was Polk's choice for the appointment, and the cabinet agreed, except for Buchanan, who objected to McLane on the grounds of his ignorance of Spanish as well as for other reasons not revealed in Polk's diary. But Polk had his way, and the offer was tendered through Congressman Robert McLane. He took the night train to Baltimore but returned the next morning with his father's declination; in view of his wife's protracted illness, Louis was unwilling to leave the country.[96]

Later that spring when the Democratic nominating convention met in Baltimore, there was some hope in the McLane family that in some way or other the nomination might fall on Louis McLane. Ever ambitious, now, though in his sixties, he particularly sought some position of distinction to which he might move from his railroad job. But the only definite statement implying that he had great expectations in the spring of 1848 is to be found in a letter of Louis McLane, Jr., written four years later. Addressing his wife, young Louis wrote in criticism of his brother Bob: "Robert always has & will fall between two stools—he vacillates while others are selecting their course—and at the last moment joins the losing side. Had he worked as hard for his Father in '48 as he did for Cass—Papa would have been the 'Nominee' of the Democratic party. But Robert allowed to leak out (or at least to my eye) the real difficulty or obstacle—with Cass he would have all he wanted—with Papa he thought he had nothing." "I would," young Louis added, "a thousand to one rather fail working for the advancement of my Father, than succeed by working for his political contemporary." [97]

But Louis was in California and could do nothing for his father. Nor, except by reports received secondhand, could he know how much Robert did—or could do—for any candidate. Their father, though greatly preferring the eventual nominee, Lewis Cass, to his competition, regarded the convention activities in Baltimore as "humbuggery." Perhaps there was some personal disappointment behind his statement that "The South are extravagant in their pretensions, and the man who places his hopes upon their course will soon lie a sheer hulk on the ocean." Cass, he declared, had more timidity than gratitude in his nature and would disappoint devoted friends while propitiating lukewarm supporters. "I am exerting my usual Phylosophy upon this subject," McLane added. "A very little time will effectually wean me from politics, and reconcile me to a determination to accept no office from the administration or the people." [98]

IX   AFTER A DECADE

In many important ways railroad affairs were going well in the spring of 1848, but McLane, always choleric, felt pressure from the enemies his policies had aroused—the Whigs in the Maryland legislature, for instance, and the partisans of a Pittsburgh connection—as well as from those friends who merely urged greater speed in carrying out the major policies of his administration.

His latest annual report, dated October 1, 1847, had summarized a decade of McLane's leadership with details that must have been a balm to the wounds of the doughty but quarrelsome old president. A railroad 82 miles long in 1837 had become one of 178 miles in 1847 and was about to launch upon its greatest extension yet. The 66,703 tons of freight carried in 1837 had risen to 263,334 in 1847. From 1835 to 1840 no dividends were paid and the largest previous dividend had been $1.12½ a share, whereas in 1847 a $3 dividend was declared. And though the 1847 dividend was paid in bonds, not cash, there did remain a substantial profit to be reinvested in the company, for while total receipts had more than tripled, from $301,000 in 1837 to $1,102,000 in 1847, expenses had only doubled, rising from $289,000 to $591,000. [99]

A measure of the increased business of the company, largely in freight rather than in passenger traffic, is to be found in the number of freight cars—983 in 1847, including 240 hopper cars for the transportation of coal, which was rapidly coming to be the most important item of freight, surpassing flour in 1848. Twelve locomotives in 1837 had become 38 in 1847, with six times as much total power.

But the record of his management, as Louis McLane saw it, was to be judged rather by efficiency than by size. The cost of repairs on the road itself had been reduced by 25 percent in ten years; the cost of repairs to machinery had been reduced 50 percent. Expenses had equaled 95 percent of receipts in 1837 but were only 52 percent of receipts in 1846.

McLane was particularly proud to make comparisons between the B & O and other railroads in terms of operating efficiency. Except in Britain, where rates were high, wages low, and passengers the main paying traffic, railroads rarely were run at less than 50 percent of receipts. This was the average expense of a group of eleven New England railroads that were relatively new and well constructed, that derived most of their receipts from passenger traffic in an area of dense population, and that were conceded to be well conducted; and if the B & O, which was older, had a smaller proportion of passenger receipts, and was required to use expensive horse power in Baltimore, could be run with expenses of only 52 percent of receipts, McLane felt he had reason for satisfaction with his record. If the cost of horse power in Baltimore was not counted, the running expenses of the B & O were 59.8 cents a mile, whereas the eleven New England railroads spent 78.1 cents a mile. The net earnings of the B & O equaled 7¼ percent of the capital, in McLane's figures, and he was quick to point out that the state of Maryland, thanks to its preferred stock in the Washington Branch, received a 7 percent return on its total railroad investment.

The reorganization of management which went into effect in May, 1847, should further improve the efficiency of the business, though after a year defects in the new system were still being corrected. For example, Chief Engineer Latrobe, who was serving also as general superintendent, was unable, according to his own report, properly to supervise all the details for which he was responsible, because he was frequently away from his office for long intervals on surveys or other engineering business. But Latrobe agreed that the principles of the reorganization were sound and that the advantages anticipated from it would eventually be realized.

An extensive reconstruction of the tracks east of Harper's Ferry had largely been completed by 1848, the old and unsatisfactory plate rail being replaced by stronger bridge rail, which was now manufactured by the Covington Company at its Avalon works on the line of the road. The development of the iron as well as the coal industry in the Maryland mountains had brought an unanticipated amount of business to the B & O, and its rolling stock was in heavy use on the mine railroads beyond Cumberland as well as on the newly acquired Winchester & Potomac Railroad south of Harper's Ferry.

Yet to all McLane's boasts regarding the performance of the B & O he had to append the note that the road was still unfinished. It had not yet reached its Ohio goal, and even for the portion constructed it still lacked some of the equipment and facilities needed to accommodate the public while operating economically. A constant problem, for example, arose from the fact that four times as much freight was offered for carriage eastward as for transportation westward. There was a bottleneck to the distribution of freight on arrival at Baltimore because of the necessity of using horse power in Baltimore streets. Some small concessions to the use of steam power had been won from the city authorities, but the concessions were accompanied with such restrictions that they proved to be useless, and only by working night and day could the congestion at the Baltimore depot be effectively reduced. Even then would-be shippers were suing the B & O because of the failure to transport livestock promptly upon its arrival at depots such as Harper's Ferry.

McLane successfully undertook measures to end the Baltimore bottleneck when, in April, 1848, the extension to Locust Point on the Patapsco was begun. But the major extension of the railroad, from Cumberland to the Ohio, presented greater difficulties. The decision had been made now, to proceed to Wheeling, but such a residue of bad feeling had been aroused by the attempt to draw the B & O to Pittsburgh that McLane feared the whole enterprise might be destroyed. Should competing lines complete their construction, trade might be diverted from the channels served by the B & O.

It was McLane's hope in the fall of 1847 that he could place the western extension under contract in 1848, but he was unable to move so fast. Three survey parties—to one of which young Charles McLane was attached—were sent out in the summer of 1847, and they were kept in the field all through the winter of 1847–48 as they moved on from Cumberland toward Wheeling. Jonathan Knight, the former B & O engineer, and John Childe, a prominent railroad surveyor in New England, were called in as consultants, and these two men and Benjamin Latrobe carefully examined the country and decided where to locate the line. Their report, submitted to the board of directors on September 13, 1848, left no doubt that a practicable railroad route existed to Wheeling, without traversing Pennsylvania.[100] It was not McLane, however, who was to direct the B & O to completion over this route.

X   TOO MANY PRESSURES

Thomas Swann joined the board of directors of the B & O as a representative of the private stockholders in July, 1847, having previously represented the public stockholders, and he rapidly became the most conspicuous of the directors in planning the future development of the railroad.[101] A native of Alexandria, Swann attended the University of Virginia before studying law with his father. Later President Jackson appointed him secretary of the United States commission to the Kingdom of the Two Sicilies. In 1834 he married the granddaughter of Robert Gilmor, a prominent Baltimore merchant, and thereafter he was identified with Baltimore mercantile interests.[102]

Perhaps because of his Virginia connections Swann had vigorously supported the idea of a Virginia rather than a Pennsylvania terminus for the B & O, and because of his knowledge of Virginia politics he had urged the B & O directors to accept the Virginia law of 1847 granting a terminus at Wheeling, for he thought this was the best possibility at the moment though he never gave up hope of getting a Parkersburg terminus. Eventually he became president of the Northwest Virginia Railroad, which provided a B & O connection to Parkersburg.[103]

In 1847 Swann became chairman of a special committee that included Samuel Hoffman and Johns Hopkins and was established by the board to help McLane find means of building the railroad westward from Cumberland. Through this committee and by his personal lobbying efforts in the Maryland legislature, Swann sought to abate legislative hostility toward the B & O that was directed particularly at McLane. The $3 million subscription of the state to the B & O was made, Swann pointed out, not for the sake of a private company and its stockholders but for the sake of Baltimore and its future growth, and the money could not be withdrawn without consideration of the effect it might have on Baltimore's prosperity. The B & O had carefully preserved the bonds representing this subscription, resisting temptations to throw them on the market as the rival canal had done with a similar subscription. By its restraint the B & O had preserved the credit of Maryland, and it would, therefore, be a hard blow to lose the bonds at the moment when Maryland was resuming payment on its debts and when the bonds might finally be marketed at a good price.[104]

McLane was not altogether in agreement. Buffeted by criticism from every angle, at the end of 1847 he was willing to give up the Maryland bonds, presumably in the hope that by cutting ties with the state he would protect himself and his position with the railroad from attack by a Whig legislature and the unfriendly B & O directors it might appoint. He looked to Virginia for a sizable grant toward construction expenses —two fifths was the amount he counted on—but this could be anticipated only when the line through Virginia had been completed. Wheeling's grant of $500,000 was more certain, but it was not to be paid till the Monongahela was reached and passed. A government mail contract for $150,000 or more a year was a further possibility, and McLane hoped the government might be persuaded to offer an advance payment in bonds for twenty years—a total of $3 million. The city authorities might also be appealed to, and subscriptions or loans be sought, particularly in Baltimore, but McLane preferred deferring such measures to a later and more desperate time. As to stock subscriptions, he had no choice, for the charter required stock to be sold at par and the market price of B & O shares was not half of that and was falling.

The one great resource of the B & O was the income it had as an efficient, functioning business. Put all net income into the extension, McLane proposed, and pay dividends in new stock representing the increased value of the corporation. Get rid of the state bonds so that no interest charges need divert income from its proper use.[105]

"The Directors of the Railroad Co. are set all agog by McLane's letter," noted John P. Kennedy in his diary. "McL. expects to make the road to Wheeling out of the profits of the road! . . . The marvel of the matter is that the Board believe him. He proposes to surrender the $3,000,000 subscription of the State, if they will withdraw the State Directors—in other words, he is willing to give up this subscription in order that he may be retained as President,—for the State is opposed to his maladministration and folly—and he is quite content the road shall linger along his life time and go to nothing then—if they will keep him in office." [106]

McLane insisted that the proposals he made did not originate with him alone, but when an ad hoc committee of the board, including Swann, began to inquire closely into the terms that might be expected in any arrangement with the state, McLane insisted the committee's powers were merely consultative.[107] For the moment McLane seemed successful. The mayor of Baltimore, a B & O director, told the city council that the mode of financing proposed by McLane—from surplus revenue—struck him as the only mode possible.[108] But McLane's troubles were mounting.

The directors were not so much in agreement with McLane that they rushed to turn back the state bonds. On the contrary, through the delicate mediation of Thomas Swann they managed to retain the confidence of the legislature and keep the bonds while at the same time supporting the rest of McLane's plans for the new extension.[109] By a stroke of good fortune Philip Thomas, a Democrat, who had been nominated at a party convention by Robert McLane, became governor in January, 1848, succeeding Thomas Pratt, a Whig, who in his last message urged the legislators to consider carefully whether the B & O had the means to build to Wheeling and, if not, to insist on selection of the less expensive route to Pittsburgh or forbid use of the state bonds.[110] Trouble arose on another front when the Baltimore city council called for a list of B & O officials and their salaries, such a demand being the usual prelude to a movement for economies, including the reduction of McLane's salary or his replacement by a less well-paid president.[111]

The enemies McLane had made in the quarrel over a western terminus were pursuing him and may have been responsible for the opposition manifest among politicians in both Annapolis and Baltimore. Kennedy, ousted from Congress by Robert McLane and from the B & O board by the efforts of Samuel Hoffman, who undoubtedly acted on Louis McLane's behalf, sold his and his mother's stock in the company and sought to persuade legislators and the public by private letters and anonymous newspaper articles that the B & O could achieve nothing till it replaced its "diplomatic" chief.[112] Friends of the Pittsburgh & Connellsville Railroad, which commenced construction on its line to Maryland in December, 1847, referred to McLane as "a one man power" and called on the Maryland legislature to charter a railroad from Cumberland to Pennsylvania that would meet the P & C.[113]

A bill to incorporate a Cumberland & Pennsylvania Railroad was introduced in the legislature and an attempt made, vainly, to slip it through quietly on the last day of the session. Another bill that threatened the B & O was one authorizing the Franklin Railroad to extend its line from Hagerstown across the Potomac into Virginia. Here it was intended to connect with the B & O, and through this connection the western traffic of the B & O could have been drawn off via Hagerstown to Philadelphia. This bill was defeated easily once the possibilities it would open were made known by friends of the B & O.[114] But the imminence of the enactment of such unfriendly legislation threatened the peace of Louis McLane as long as the assembly was in session.

Other annoyances included a strike of several hundred laborers who were dissatisfied with wages of 87½ cents a day,[115] the hesitancy of the board to accept McLane's choice of J. Dutton Steele as general superintendent in place of Benjamin Latrobe, who had been combining this position with that of chief engineer, and the decline in value of B & O stock, which by its fall hurt McLane's chances of selling bonds to finance construction.[116]

But these were, in themselves, minor matters. McLane's main trouble was that he had come to a major disagreement with the very directors who had been his staunch supporters in earlier difficulties. He was un-willing or unable to push ahead with the western extension as rapidly as they desired, and he felt that the demands they made on him were unfair. Given his choleric nature, it was but a step from thinking his fellow directors unfair to thinking them treacherous, and he parted from the B & O in the fall of 1848 with anger in his heart.

When in London McLane had urged that repairs and reconstruction of the existing road should be delayed in favor of the extension west-ward. He wished to complete the road from Baltimore to the Ohio before doing anything else. But he had been forced to consent to a reconstruc-tion program and to the ordering of new equipment for the livestock and coal trade. And now, he felt, this new equipment and the repairs and reconstruction should be paid for before the B & O got in debt over its head for the western extension. As far as possible he would pay debts in bonds, but he feared to sell bonds lest he destroy the market and ruin the credit of his company. He sought help from the Barings, hoping they would buy the state bonds they held for the B & O or lend money on their security. The most the Barings would do was to postpone payment of $50,000 remaining of an old B & O debt to them from October, 1848, to April, 1849.[117]

So in the end McLane was forced to rely on revenue, a good source but a slow one. Too slow, he felt, to warrant moving ahead rapidly with the extension. Too slow, his colleagues felt, to warrant continuance of their confidence in McLane, and when he finally offered his resignation on September 13, it was immediately accepted.

His colleagues knew, he declared in resigning, that he had long been determined not to participate permanently in the labor of extending the road to the Ohio. Only their solicitation had kept him from resigning in the winter—their solicitation and the hope he could assist in maturing plans for the extension. If he remained in office now he would have to take responsibility for disappointments he could not prevent, for unless a new source could be found to pay for equipment and repairs he, who was as eager as anyone to get to the Ohio, would not agree to contracts he considered premature. A delay of only a few months was called for, and if a temporary loan of $200,000 could be secured or if contractors could be persuaded to accept bonds of the company or of the state—in this case there need not be the delay of one day. But the directors were impatient, and therefore he would step aside.[118]

McLane's resignation was presented to the directors at a board meet-ing which he himself did not attend on September 13, 1848. A commit-tee was appointed that drafted a letter of acceptance, thanking him for the rapid renovation he had brought to the company in its hour of distress in 1837 and asking only that he retain office until a new president could be chosen after the annual stockholders' meeting on October 9.[119]

"It is a cowardly abandonment of his comrades in the moment of danger," growled Kennedy when he heard of the resignation.[120] But Mc-Lane's colleagues do not seem to have been notably upset. McLane was older now and less venturesome than when he first came to the B & O eleven years earlier. His leadership had then spurred the company on; now he threatened to hold it back. A new president, younger and more daring, might push the enterprise to completion as McLane, when smarting at his early retirement from politics, had ambitiously driven it to Cumberland.[121]

A new driver was found on October 11, when Thomas Swann was chosen as McLane's successor. There is some indication that Swann was not the first candidate or at least not the only candidate of the directors. The Cumberland *Civilian* heard that the post was first offered to Lieutenant Colonel Robert E. Lee, "the celebrated Topographical Engineer of Scott's division of the U.S. Army," but that he declined it. This may be so, for Lee had returned to Washington from Mexico late in June of 1848 and spent some time that summer in Baltimore, where he had a sister and where his next military assignment placed him in charge of the construction of a harbor fort.[122]

Swann, however, became McLane's successor, and the only question seemed to be whether he would take the post on a permanent basis or merely as an acting president, as some directors preferred, very likely fearing his youth and bumptiousness and his inexperience in administration. But the majority favored a permanent appointment and succeeded in winning a unanimous vote for appearance' sake, with Swann agreeing to quit if he proved incapable of the responsibilities of the presidency —and accepting a salary that was but half of McLane's.[123]

It was but a continuation of the same dynasty, according to John P. Kennedy, who predicted bankruptcy or at least cessation of the western extension within two years.[124] Kennedy was wrong. Blessed with a high degree of confidence in himself, Thomas Swann let contracts for the extension and sold the bonds McLane had feared to part with. Swann preferred to take a discount for them rather than delay construction, but the reaction was the reverse of what McLane had expected. The confidently aggressive policy of the B & O in pushing its western extension to completion steadied its value in the market and shored up its credit. In four years Wheeling was reached.[125]

Yet Swann's success and that of the B & O rested largely on the sound and efficient condition in which Louis McLane left the company on his resignation.

18

Retirement

I   THE CASS CAMPAIGN

No sooner had Louis McLane retired from the Baltimore & Ohio than he was invited to reenter politics. "The country has another claim upon him," the Washington Democratic paper declared, meaning that he should aid in the Lewis Cass campaign for the Presidency.[1] The Cass-McLane connection went back to the boyhood of both men, to a time when Major Cass, father of the presidential candidate, was stationed in Wilmington, where he organized a volunteer military society.[2] "I have known General Cass from my youth upward," declared McLane in endorsing the Democratic candidate.[3]

The endorsement came in response to a letter from a group of Delaware Democrats who invited McLane to send them his opinions on the issues and the candidates in 1848. Perhaps they hoped he would come to Delaware and actively participate in the campaign. If so, they were disappointed. All they could get from him was a letter, a very long letter that occupied four columns in the *Gazette*, defending the Democratic party in general and Lewis Cass in particular. The old issues between the two parties, such as the Bank, the tariff, and internal improvements, had disappeared, he argued, but the Whigs, formerly opposed to the candidacy of a military hero, had taken a strange course in nominating General Taylor. It was they who would upset the country, especially by challenging constitutional institutions (slavery was, of course, what McLane meant) in the states and territories.[4] McLane sounded like a Southerner, or a doughface.

To his enemies, at any rate, he also sounded like a job hunter trying to ingratiate himself with a party and a candidate who might have jobs to dispense. Using the pseudonym "Rodney," Nelson Poe, a Baltimore journalist, cousin of Edgar Allan Poe, castigated McLane in the Baltimore *Patriot*. McLane, Poe charged, was a man of intelligence and of administrative talent, energetic in freeing himself of former professions and opinions, gifted in the art of subjecting men of weaker minds and wills to his control. In Jackson's cabinet he must have learned of Cass's infirmity of will, despite his real ability, and on this basis hoped to be able to dominate Cass as his prime minister.[5]

When Poe's letter appeared, the election was over and Cass had been defeated. McLane's foes laughed at his discomfiture. According to a story they circulated, it was Bob who persuaded his father to write the Delaware Democrats on behalf of Cass in the hope—unproven, but not unlikely—of winning a political plum. Of this story and of its aftermath in the ignominy of Nelson Poe's letter, John P. Kennedy made a fable:

"Once upon a time a fox who had grown old, listening to the persuasion of a conceited young cub of his own, set a trap to catch a goose for his Christmas dinner. But he had hardly laid the bait before the trap sprung and caught the old fox by the tail. 'O you young rascal,' said the old fox to his son, 'see what you have done!' 'If you had been half as wise as you are cunning,' said the bystanders, 'you would never have allowed that foolish son of yours to put it into your head to get a goose for your Christmas dinner.'"

"Did you ever read that fable in Aesop?" Kennedy asked a correspondent, and went on, "'Poe, Poe,' says McLane, 'I hate fables.'"[6]

II A DOMESTIC LOSS

Why Louis McLane did no more for the Cass campaign than write a letter is not clear. Certainly he had considered doing more. In September, announcing his resignation from the B & O to young Lou, he wrote, "It is possible I may take some active part in the contest for the Presidency."[7]

And his interest remained strong, inactive as he was. A letter survives from February, 1849, in which he declared his willingness to make as great exertions and sacrifices as any man to restore and reunite the Democratic party after its defeat in the fall elections. The measures of the Polk administration, he argued, had had brilliant results, but the larger share of "the éclat of success" had gone to the opposition, and Polk and his cabinet had been driven into retirement, leaving the party that raised them to power, beaten, distracted, and disheartened.[8]

Perhaps an inactive role was forced on McLane by the disinterest of his party. It is difficult to resume the role of political leadership where no followers can be found. But McLane might have made greater efforts to plant his banner firmly where elements of his distracted party might rally to him had it not been for his wife's continued illness.

Kitty seemed at times to make a slight recovery, but never much and not for long. "I cannot tell you how much your Mother's situation oppresses me," McLane wrote to young Louis in April from Bohemia, where he was trying to make the farm a paying proposition but was depressed by the effect of the rigors of winter upon all his operations.[9]

Work on the farm was not only a form of exile or separation from politics for McLane; it was also a separation, far sadder to him, from his wife. Kitty was so ill that she perforce stayed in Baltimore through this first spring of her husband's retirement. It was to be the last spring of her life, for Kitty died in Baltimore on July 31, 1849, half a month short of her fifty-ninth birthday. Her body was brought to Bohemia for interment beside her parents in the Milligan family graveyard, and nine years later, when the farm was sold, her remains and those of her parents were removed to Greenmount Cemetery, in Baltimore.[10]

III   ITS EFFECT

It is difficult to exaggerate the effect of his wife's death on Louis McLane. For decades wife and children and the home that was where they were had been the center of McLane's world. In marrying Kitty, Louis married into a world of gentility and influence and decorum that fitted the Scott novels he read and the Eastern Shore plantation he purchased. The boy baptized in the rural Methodism of Duck Creek Crossroads had been married by Bishop White into the aristocracy of Maryland Episcopalianism. Through Kitty, a leather breeches maker's son became a cavalier.

Yet the Milligan marriage was no mere stepping-stone for a rough, talented, pugnacious McLane into the drawing rooms of the social élite; his marriage was an emotional attachment for McLane that provided him with an intelligent companion and confidante to share his aspirations and disappointments. And the children the union produced were so numerous that Louis had to keep employed, swallowing his easy resentments despite temptations to withdraw when vexed or to turn his back on those who disappointed him. Even without Kitty, McLane would have made his mark in the world; but without Kitty, his public career might well have been shorter and less distinguished than it was.

The children, as well as their father, recognized the loss he and they suffered. "I cannot tell you how wretched the thought of poor papa makes me," wrote Lydia; "his situation is appalling. What is to become of him & those *poor girls*, poor little things?"[11] With less sympathy for their father, Lydia's brother Louis recalled that his mother, in her last illness, expressed the keenest regret at leaving her husband with young children who would "be witnesses of ebullitions of temper" that she might have softened or stifled had she lived.[12]

The children at home when their mother died were the three youngest girls, Juliette, Catherine, and Mary, and the baby of the family, Jim, almost fifteen and away at boarding school much of the time. Juliette, who was twenty-four, did not tarry long in marrying her longtime sweetheart, Bauduy Garesché. Her parents' disapproval of a Catholic connection may have postponed the marriage while her mother lived, though a stronger reason for delay could have been Bauduy's efforts to establish himself in a law practice in St. Louis, where he had moved from Wilmington.[13] Parental disapproval had certainly not sufficed to keep Juliette from turning Catholic, and once her father was alone his influence was no sufficient deterrent to the marriage; if anything, his attitude encouraged Juliette to seek a home of her own.

"I always feared," she wrote to a sister-in-law, "that sorrow would have just the effect on him that it has—harden him," and so bitter did Juliette feel that when her father, hearing she needed a wet nurse at twenty dollars a month, sent her a hundred dollars to help with this expense she refused to accept the help thus offered—though Bauduy put the money aside for the child's eventual use.[14] Juliette heard that the girls still at home were self-indulgent and spoiled, but their routine of life with an old father at Bohemia was monotonous, sad, and lonely.[15] Baltimore, and occasional visits to Washington and watering places, afforded them welcome relief. Both girls eventually followed Juliette's path to Catholicism, to their father's dismay.[16]

Their brother Louis suggested that their course, which Lou, a low church Episcopalian, called "apostasy," resulted from his father's lack of faith, from his devotion to a religion of honor and gentility rather than a religion of a personal Savior. "In teaching his children to tell the truth and be upright in all their dealings, it was not that God would be pleased, & angered if they did not, but that truth & honesty were necessary to a gentleman, for in the same lesson we were taught to resent a slight or insult to death, to the shedding of blood." Young Louis also charged that his father "systimatically [*sic*] violated the Sabbath, and treated everything sacred with gross levity," but the latter charge may not so truly represent the father as it does the sober piety of this son who had left home in his teens and thereby lost whatever intimate contact he had known with a very busy parent.[17]

Young Kitty's life was short, for she died after a brief illness—an attack of dysentery, it was called—in August, 1853. McLane had been in Philadelphia and returned to find his daughter ill, with no previous hint that she was at all indisposed. He sent for Father Foley, her confessor, and watched by her bedside night and day for a week before she died. "A fresh calamity has befallen my old age," the heartbroken man wrote to his eldest son; all of life appeared "vain and empty." [18]

The one daughter left at home, Mary, in due time followed Juliette's course to marriage and the Middle West, though with Mary the order of these events was reversed. She visited Juliette in St. Louis and with the Gareschés went north for a holiday in Wisconsin, where she met and eventually married an English physican, Joseph Hobbins, who lived in Madison. Though Mary was geographically and spiritually far from home, her paternity was recalled by the naming of her only son for her father.[19] And if evidence seems to suggest that McLane was a harsh, insensitive father, it should be noted that three of his four daughters who had sons were proud to use his name; besides Mary's Louis McLane Hobbins, there were Rebecca's child, Louis McLane Hamilton, and Sally's son, Louis McLane Tiffany. Only Juliette, of those of his daughters who had children, failed to name a son for Louis McLane.

IV   THE BOYS

Of the McLane boys, Charles was still single but away from Baltimore working as an engineer on the railroad, happy enough with his job and his prospects to refuse his father's offer of Mount Jones, the farm his mother had inherited near Cantwell's Bridge (Odessa), Delaware.[20] George stayed in the Army after the Mexican War was over, and with the security his new commission gave him he was married in Baltimore in December, 1848, to Serena Barroll. Young Lou was married a half year later, on June 12, 1849, to Sophie Hoffman, daughter of Samuel Hoffman, the Baltimore merchant who had been the elder McLane's staunch supporter on the B & O board of directors.

On the whole, all the McLane boys led what would generally be termed useful as well as successful lives, but it was young Louis who was the steadiest, most consistent, and most industrious of the lot. Robert became better known; his career was the most brilliant, but this was partly because as a politician he lived in the public eye. He was suave, gregarious, personable, but he wanted a quick return for the effort he put into any endeavor and was unwilling to sustain a long persistent course of action toward a desired goal. As far as his career was concerned, he was handicapped by his marriage, for Georgine was, or was thought to be, a delicate woman who was apt to require a change of climate for her health's sake and was reared to think the south of France as likely a spot for a restorative rest as one of the McLane girls would have thought Cape May or Newport.

"Robert is a most vacillating white man," wrote his brother Lou; "He wants half a dozen things at once and don't know which to take hold of first." [21] "Poor fellow," Lou's mother-in-law exclaimed, "I pity any man with an inert wife." [22]

Mrs. Samuel Hoffman could judge Georgine without embarrassment on behalf of her Sophie, because she knew Sophie was neither an "inert wife" nor in any way a handicap to her husband. Indeed it was his marriage to Sophie that provided young Louis McLane with a second start in the world. His first start had come when his father procured him an appointment in the Navy as a midshipman. The boy had made good in the Navy, rising in rank and winning some distinction in the California campaign, but once the war was over, the possibilities of a career in the peacetime Navy seemed to offer a bleak prospect to an ambitious young man. They offered an even bleaker prospect to an ambitious young husband when he learned that his next assignment was likely to be a three-year cruise to the East Indies, and he made up his mind to renounce this prospect and his naval career when he took his bride.

But Louis McLane, Jr., was not improvident; like his father, he looked ahead. Samuel Hoffman made him a generous offer of assistance in setting out on a business career in California. The idea of California as the immediate locale of his enterprise brought no glee to the heart of this young McLane or his bride, for it meant a separation; in 1849 San Francisco was no place for Sophie. But Louis hoped that by one short separation he and Sophie would lay the foundation for a lifetime in close unity such as a naval career would never permit. He had seen California, and now that it was known to be golden he was sure it was the place for an ambitious young entrepreneur.

And so after a wedding trip to Niagara Falls, Louis McLane, Jr., set out for California in February, 1850, via Panama. At the same time a vessel bound around Cape Horn carried the disassembled parts of a steamboat, the *Erastus Corning*, which young Lou and nine partners planned to run from San Francisco to Stockton, the entrance to the goldfields.[23]

When Lou arrived at Panama City, he met his brother Allan, who had also resigned his commission in the Navy and was serving as first mate on the Panama Pacific Line. Allan too had marriage in prospect, and after a year he was able to return east to marry his fiancée, Maria Bache, in December, 1850.[24] The marriage culminated soon in tragedy. Allan accepted appointment as captain of the steamer *Frémont* for a voyage round the Horn to California, and he took his bride on the trip. She seemed well at Rio de Janeiro, but a few days out of that port she took sick and died.[25]

Before Allan arrived in California with his sad news, more of the McLane clan had gathered there. This new contingent, which arrived on June 1, 1851, consisted of the oldest McLane son, Robert, and his brother-in-law Philip Hamilton.[26] These two lawyers had come to California in the hope of making their fortunes, for in this regard their careers in the East did not seem to be progressing satisfactorily. "I am really anxious to extricate myself," Robert wrote at Washington in March, "from the expensive & ruinous life I am leading in politics, which could only be tolerated in view of the most commanding successes & the highest public consideration, neither of which in my judgment now concur to keep me where I am." [27] Consequent to this reasoning, Robert had determined not to seek reelection to Congress. Instead he would yield to the lure of rich fees to be won in California in the adjudication of private land claims, which conflicting Spanish, Mexican, and American grants and laws made a promising field for litigation. According to the testimony of his autobiography, he had been sought out as counsel by claimants to the valuable New Almadén mercury mine, but before long his general practice became more important to him than the New Almadén case. He was, it seems clear, an orator of ability and an attorney of such presence that he quickly won the friendship and the confidence of those who met him. His partner had little of Robert's popular charm, but Philip Hamilton knew admiralty law and was expected to excel at research.[28]

But Robert was too restless, and perhaps too lonely, to be satisfied in the California of 1851. Philip Hamilton, deaf and dour, was not a very agreeable companion, and young Louis was away on business too much to give Robert the company his gregarious nature needed. Robert's original enthusiasm for California law was transformed into an enthusiasm for California politics, until his ambitions in this field were quashed by the refusal of the legislature to send him to the United States Senate. Despite being a complete newcomer on the scene, he had a chance to gain such a political plum in this state of newcomers. Louis supported him with all the influence his old military associations of the 1846–47 campaigns could bring. Louis admired Robert as he could never admire their father, but yet he gave old Louis his due. "Robert takes to politics like a spaniel to water," his brother wrote; "he is peculiarly fitted in temper and manners to mix among & lead men and he has talents & virtue— not my Father's talents, but certainly Mama's temper & manner, and therefore better suited for public life." [29]

Perhaps a Senate seat appealed to Robert particularly, because it would give him an excuse to come east again. Win or lose, he planned

Louis McLane, circa 1848. Lithograph by E. Sacher & Co. from daguerreotype
by Whitehurst.

a trip east in the winter, and after he lost he decided never to return to California. Georgine must have been all the more lonely in the East because she lost a child in her husband's absence, and Robert explained his decision as due to "the impossibility of my controling the domestic influences that urge my course." But it is likely that the failure of his political aspirations had as much as domestic influence to do with Bob's decision to give up California permanently. Philip Hamilton, more morose in Bob's absence than before, closed the accounts of the firm and left California several months after his partner.[30]

But Louis—and Allan too—cast their lots more permanently in California. Louis returned to the East again and again through the next few years, but he came back each time to California until years after his father's death. And so did Allan, who eventually married again, his new bride being the sister of his first wife.

Both young men made a success of their California careers. Louis left the steamboat business for ventures in real estate and found his way upward in the world with Wells, Fargo & Company, where he advanced from San Francisco agent to president. Allan stayed in the shipping business, but he, too, made rapid progress, perhaps with help from his brother, rising to the presidency of the Pacific Mail Steamship Company. And still one more brother, Charles, was drawn to California, to become Wells, Fargo's San Francisco agent when Louis moved on to the company presidency.[31]

V   THE MARYLAND CONVENTION

Meanwhile old Louis McLane had found, briefly, a congenial occupation. In April, 1850, his nervous system, he claimed, was still shattered and prostrate as a result of his wife's death, and he had no heart to go anywhere except back and forth between Baltimore and Bohemia.[32] But by July he was sufficiently recovered to travel to New York, combining some family visits with an effort to raise capital for a "propeller scheme," whatever that meant, of his son Allan.[33]

This renewal of his vitality led him, later in the summer, to accept nomination on the Democratic ticket to represent Cecil County, where Bohemia was located, in a Maryland state constitutional convention. The Democratic ticket was the reform ticket, for the Democrats were urging revision of a constitution written in 1776. There were many complaints about this constitution, but chiefly they were centered on charges that the legislature, ill apportioned in terms of population distribution, was almost unrestricted in its power to create debt and to control the amending of the constitution; there were also serious complaints that the state judiciary was too large, too expensive, too arbitrary, and too independent. The old tobacco counties of southern Maryland, underpopulated, devoted to a slave economy, were opposed to change. Baltimore City and the yeoman-farmed, prospering wheat counties of northern and western Maryland favored change. Under the old order, Whigs controlled southern Maryland and the legislature; they were split on the reform issue, and in the northern counties many Whigs ran for the legislature on a Union ticket.

But Cecil was a progressive county, directly on the Philadelphia-Baltimore railroad axis, nearest of the Maryland counties to the commercial centers of Philadelphia and New York. If southern Maryland represented the old order, then Cecil, next after Baltimore City, represented the new.[34]

The Democrats carried Cecil, and their ticket had strength enough to carry Louis McLane, though he had the fewest votes of the five delegates chosen.[35] That McLane lagged a hundred votes behind the top man on his ticket is not strange, for though long associated with Cecil through his farm at Bohemia, he was normally but a part-time resident there, usually busy with affairs elsewhere. The B & O had as yet not entered Cecil, and McLane's farm was in the agricultural southern end of the county, at some distance from the center of population and of growth.

More honor was paid Louis McLane in the convention than at the polls. He was among those present in Annapolis when the convention opened on November 5, and he voted with his Cecil colleagues for Benjamin Chew Howard, the Democratic candidate for presiding officer. The balloting, however, dragged on for a week. The Democrats were in a minority, and the Whigs, though a majority, were divided, most of them supporting a candidate unfriendly to the convention, but some favoring a reform Whig, a supporter of the convention and of constitutional reform. When the deadlock seemed very serious, many of the delegates began shopping around for a compromise candidate, and in such a situation it is not strange that some of them thought of Louis McLane, who, in terms of national offices held, was the most distinguished man present. On November 12, McLane ran second to John G. Chapman, the majority Whig candidate, but he asked leave after the ballot to withdraw his name, and eventually Chapman was chosen to preside over a convention he did not approve.[36]

McLane's standing was recognized again by his appointment as chairman of the comittee on the treasury, one of the major standing committees of the convention—a natural post for the former head of the federal

Treasury Department. He served also on two special committees, one on miscellaneous business and the other to draft a statement regarding the recently enacted Compromise of 1850. The latter was a subject quickly attended to, for compromise was a popular subject in a border state like Maryland and the delegates most eager for reform were well aware of the delicacy with which they must treat the slave-owning planters of southern Maryland and the Eastern Shore. No one should be allowed to doubt that this convention was composed of moderate, responsible men who would tolerate no challenge either to the harmony and good order of the federal union or to the institution of slavery.

In ten days McLane and his fellow committeemen reported a series of resolutions praising the federal Constitution, declaring the duty of all states to support its provisions and the laws Congress passed in conformity with it, and acquiescing in the Compromise of 1850. The fugitive slave law they chose for particular attention as the only one of these measures protecting the peculiar institution of the southern states from wicked fanaticism in the North, a "tardy and meagre measure of compliance" with constitutional guarantees. The delegates unanimously approved this report, and in doing so went far toward mollifying the areas of Maryland most suspicious of reform.[37]

A month later the convention went further in this direction by unanimously inserting a provision in the new constitution absolutely forbidding the legislature from passing any laws that would disturb the existing master-slave relationship—in other words, abolition laws were made unconstitutional.[38] In approving such a defense of slavery Louis McLane demonstrated how far he had moved from the abolitionist sentiments of his father.

His attitude toward slavery helps to explain McLane's enthusiasm for the Compromise of 1850. In the summer of 1850, on the death of Taylor, once his hero, McLane had been hopeful that a change in the cabinet might avert a civil war which the administration of "an honest but weak old man" had made almost inevitable. He expressed hope then that the Vice-President, Fillmore, would be led, by his friendship with Clay, to support the compromise.[39]

In the convention, McLane castigated abolition: "We owe to it the spirit of discord, the spirit of hatred, the danger of disunion." Because of it he thought it had become necessary to remove the free colored population from Maryland "as soon as it can be done with propriety." He was "ready to adopt any humane provision for their removal," but while they were still in Maryland he would protect them, and he rose to object, unavailingly, to a motion specifically exempting them from the guaranties of due process and trial by jury in the state bill of rights.[40]

VI THE STATE TREASURY

McLane's major contribution to the new Maryland constitution came in the form of a report he presented on January 31 for the committee on the treasury department. He bore the brunt of the debate—on May 9—on this report, and it seems likely he was mainly responsible for it, drawing on his experience with the federal government for the organization he proposed.

Heretofore the Maryland treasury had operated on a very loose system, with two treasurers, one for the Eastern and one for the Western Shore, and an unpaid commissioner of loans who was a bank president and was willing to serve without stipend because his bank could profit from the use of state deposits.

Under this system Maryland's interests, McLane said, were "exceedingly insecure" and it was a near miracle that the state had suffered no serious losses. In twenty-three of the thirty-one states McLane's committee found a comptroller or similar official sharing responsibility for state funds with the treasurer, and this, too, was the example set by the federal government. McLane consequently proposed that there be two state officials, a comptroller, elected by the people, and a treasurer, chosen by the legislature, sharing responsibility for money management. Both would be paid a fixed stipend, but the money being paid yearly to London agents for the state bonds could be saved under the new system and the office of loan commissioner could be eliminated.

There was opposition to the proposal—for example, someone suggested that the governor serve as comptroller, and another delegate moved that the loan commissioner be retained—but McLane answered all opposition satisfactorily, assisted especially by Thomas Donaldson, of Anne Arundel, his second on the committee, and the report was written into the new constitution as Article VI with only minor changes.[41]

In the recorded debates on this issue there is more than a trace of the old McLane of congressional debates in the 1820's. He presented a clear, reasonable report, explained it to the satisfaction of the house, answered all queries and overcame all serious objections, winning both the votes and the respect of a majority of his fellow delegates. But he was feeling his age now—sixty-seven in the spring of 1851—and it took a special effort to care for the business entrusted to him. He had been confined to his bed with influenza in February and was forced to beg off serving on a special committee to reconsider the rules of the convention.[42]

Little over a week after recovering from influenza, McLane felt obliged to take a major role in the debate over the state debt. Placing some limit on the legislature's power to create debt was, he explained, the one great duty he felt when he came to Annapolis, and he asked the convention to hear him out without interruption because he was too frail to answer questions.

It was a subject close to his heart not only because of his experience in debt management as Secretary of the Treasury and chairman of the Ways and Means Committee but also because the Maryland state debt had largely been created for the benefit of internal improvements, including the Baltimore & Ohio Railroad. He would not deprecate these works, of course; Maryland, in his opinion, had a great system of internal improvements. The trouble was that Marylanders had falsely believed this system to be an El Dorado that would make taxes obsolete.

Then, too, the expenses of the system had been underestimated, and this was likely always to be the case. The remedy was simple: create no debt unless there is also a tax levied to pay off the debt. Then the people will think twice before they risk embarrassing their state as Maryland was embarrassed when it could not pay the interest due to its creditors. At a time when the nation and the individual states were uneasy under a vast load of debt (probably he referred to the early 1840's when states were reneging on their payments) he had urged, but "only through private channels," that the federal government assume all the state debts on one condition: that the states incorporate in their constitutions "an irrepealable provision" not to contract a debt without imposing a tax for its liquidation.

Of this proposal no other record is known to survive, but the idea of assumption, or a nationalizing of the debt, fits McLane's Federalist antecedents very well, and it comports, too, with his fears about the state debt at a time when he was unable to market the bonds turned over to the B & O. There is no reason to doubt his sincerity when he repeated his warning: "the great bane of our prosperity is the contraction of large debts under tempting circumstances; and . . . the greatest security we can afford to the people will be, that these debts shall no longer be contracted unless the urgency is so great as to justify a system of taxation to pay for it." [43]

His advice was well received. Into the new constitution was written just such a provision as he advocated.[44] And a majority of the delegates agreed with him in opposing any refunding measures, even at a halving of the interest rate, that would delay payment of the existing debt.[45]

Another area in which McLane contributed personally to the writing of the new constitution was in the provisions regarding the judiciary. Shortly after the work of the convention began, McLane proposed that common law and equity should be combined in one system of courts, which would also include all business pertaining to orphans and bankrupts, and that all judges and court clerks should be elected and paid fixed stipends. He also recommended provision for laws regulating fees charged by attorneys, for the revision of statutes so as to simplify suits, and for the restatement of criminal and penal laws in order to give courts no more discretion than was necessary.[46] In debate he explained that he was concerned that the chancery court had twenty-five hundred undisposed cases, through no fault of the chancellor himself, and he quoted a rhyme to the effect that

> If the counsel be apt, and the client clever,
> A chancery suit may last forever.

In debate he also supported a proposal to abolish the office of attorney general and turn the duties of this office over to state's attorneys elected in each county.[47]

Only part, but a large part, of his desires could be realized. The office of chancellor and the separate equity court system were abandoned, as was the office of attorney general, but orphans' courts with a judiciary of their own were retained in each county. Provisions were written into the new constitution for the election of judges and court clerks, and regular stipends were established for many but not all of these officials.[48]

VII A LAST SUCCESS

Occasionally when he clashed with other members in debate, McLane was chided for his Federalist and his Delaware origins. A Calvert County delegate, claiming to speak as a native Marylander, questioned whether, as he put it, "learned men from other states should be allowed to come here and teach us our duty." The question arose because McLane, speaking in regard to the necessity of laws to ensure honest elections, had declared that it was public opinion that had to be cured because if what was being said about bribery at Maryland elections was true the state was "rotten to the core." Gerrymandering was practiced and also the colonization of voters (the registration of voters in a district not normally their home), and large contributions were made by the wealthy in order to carry elections. Committees in Baltimore called on office-holders and other potential donors seeking contributions of ten and twenty dollars; he confessed he had himself contributed to the expenses of an election.

It was the "rotten to the core" comment that aroused Augustus R. Sollers, a fiery ex-Congressman, now representing Calvert County. He admitted that McLane "had, by his manner and his talents, done much to sustain the dignity of this Convention" but complained that Maryland did not deserve so severe a wound. McLane replied that the charge was not his; he had not heard of so much corruption till he came to Annapolis; and he did not believe all he heard. But if the evil was as great as was represented, "homopathic doses," such as a proposal that required voters to be resident in the election district, were not enough, for a way would be found to get around them. The new constitution kept the old franchise laws (requiring a voter to be free, white, male, twenty-one or older, and a Maryland resident for at least a year), which McLane had praised, but added a provision requiring six months' residence in the election district.[49]

Generally he voted with his party: for example, for allocating representation on the basis of population (which was thought likely to give the Democrats control of the legislature) and against a provision allowing a part of the state to secede and join a neighboring state (a popular idea with Eastern Shore and southern Maryland Whigs who thought Delaware or Virginia might offer them a comfortable haven if reform forces in Baltimore and northern Maryland became overbearing). It is interesting that the latter resolution was offered by Thomas Hicks, who as war governor in 1861 helped prevent Maryland from leaving the Union.[50]

On one occasion Ezekiel Chambers, of Kent County, became irate because McLane intimated Chambers opposed majority rule and thereby criticized Chambers's republicanism. Chambers declared he was "a thorough-bred republican" and "had been so all the days of his life"; the first speech he ever made and the first vote he ever gave were for the Republican party, which was dating him "beyond some gentlemen who had attached themselves to later schools of republicanism." McLane granted Chambers the priority in republicanism and admitted they had started far apart, but suggested that the present course of Chambers in opposing reform and representation based on population meant that they interpreted Jeffersonian republicanism differently and remained far apart.[51]

On representation, McLane was willing to compromise, hoping that the constitution would make provision for future conventions to consider necessary changes at reasonable periods.[52] Not all of his comments were recorded because he seldom kept his promises to give the reporter a revised version of his speech.[53] Probably it was his health that was at fault, for besides the spell of influenza he suffered in February he found it necessary to absent himself again for three weeks in April because of his physical condition.[54] At the final session late in the evening of May 13, McLane urged that the convention rise and go home and voted against all motions for a delay. In these final hours he voted steadily with the majority to ratify the constitution over the vain objections of such conservatives as Ezekiel Chambers and Chapman, the president of the convention.[55]

After McLane had returned to Bohemia he was delighted to see the new constitution approved by a decisive popular vote, 29,025 to 18,616. He complained of his "laborious and disagreeable duties" at Annapolis, but a visitor, Samuel Hoffman, found him "in more than usual good health and spirits." [56] Very likely the experience of sharing in a political victory was an invigorating one for Louis McLane, even if it confirmed his almost constant fears about his physical resilience.

VIII   THE LAST YEARS

A lovelier spot than Bohemia was scarcely to be found, thought Hoffman after his visit there in June, 1851, and he praised both its high state of cultivation and the prospect it offered of a good return for the labor expended on it. But it was no place to rear girls, those who knew the situation agreed, and they were sorry for Mary and Kitty who had to endure the solitude of Bohemia after the joys of a winter at Annapolis.[57]

Whether for his own pleasure or for the sake of his children, Louis McLane used his leisure in the years immediately following the Annapolis convention to do some traveling. He never went far—to New York, for the Crystal Palace exhibition, or to Cape May, for instance—but he dreamed of more extensive excursions. At one time he talked of going to Cuba for the winter, at another time of California.[58] In the fall of 1853 he seriously considered moving to New York, where he might find "agreeable and lucrative employment" or at least enjoy associating with intelligent friends and "be relieved from the distressing and mortifying dearth" that in this respect he experienced in Baltimore.[59] He went so far as to rent rooms somewhere on Broadway for one to four months and planned to move there with Mary on January 1, 1854, but apparently he never carried out this plan.[60]

The beauty of Bohemia was often a joy even at the season when malaria made residence there dangerous to health.[61] Baltimore, on the other hand, remained an uncongenial and unattractive residence, and he put up with it only for the sake of Mary and James—so the former could "carry on her devotion to Saints and 'graven Images'" and the latter, pursue his studies.[62] Moreover, a Baltimore residence—and Bohemia, too, in the healthy season—furnished a headquarters where his family—children, and grandchildren, and in-laws—could gather round the patriarch for short or long visits. Lydia, in particular, came for long visits when her husband, Joseph Johnston, was sent by the Army to stations where she could not join him.

Interest in the careers of his sons and sons-in-law enlivened these last years of Louis McLane, who remained very eager for their success. "I am afraid," he wrote Lydia, "I will grow selfish enough not too inconsoleably [*sic*] to repine at an occasional Indian war, especially if it brought in its train honor and promotion"—to Joseph Johnston, of course.[63] George was once again a source of grief to his father when during the 1852 campaign the Whigs made use of a story George told about the Democratic candidate, Franklin Pierce. It was, simply, that during the occupation of Mexico City in 1848 George McLane and Pierce had been playing cards together and Pierce had allowed another officer to slap his face and had done nothing about it. The implication, of course, was that Pierce was a coward, and it can be believed that George would have thought this, for the McLane boys were taught to resent any slight on their honor. Pierce's explanation was that the man who slapped him was drunk when he did it and that the incident was forgotten because the man apologized the next day. But Robert McLane and his father were upset by the publicity, feeling that unfriendly Democrats spread the story in Baltimore to humiliate them.[64]

And indeed there were unfriendly Democrats who did not appreciate Robert's willingness to resume his career in Maryland politics after his return from California. In 1853 they were responsible for defeating his bid for the Democratic nomination to his old seat in Congress.[65] (Maryland still held its congressional elections in odd-numbered years.) It was, perhaps, symptomatic of Robert's cavalier attitude that he was not himself in Maryland at election time, having accompanied Georgine to France, where she suffered another miscarriage.[66]

Despite George's gaffe, the Pierce administration was friendly to the McLanes. As President-elect, Pierce seriously considered offering old Louis appointment as Secretary of State, and Robert, who had been one of Maryland's Pierce electors in 1852, did receive a diplomatic post in the fall of 1853, when he was appointed United States commissioner to China with the rank of minister plenipotentiary, the highest rank then awarded in the American foreign service, and was accredited also to the governments of Japan, Siam, Korea, and Cochin China. His main task was to draw up a commercial treaty with China, then devastated by the Tai Ping rebellion but thought likely, for this very reason, to be more favorable than previously to the commercial demands of foreign countries. If Commodore Perry failed to persuade the Japanese to agree to a treaty, Robert McLane was to take over this negotiation, too.

The China mission promised to be long and difficult, and he was not Pierce's first choice for it.[67] But being second, or third, or even fourth choice did not, at this moment, matter. Robert McLane was eager to get away from Maryland politics and the embarrassment his defeat had caused him, and since Georgine wished to spend at least a year in France "for the improvement and education of the children," as Robert explained to his father, this was a peculiarly fit time to accept overseas employment.[68]

When Robert arrived in Paris en route to China, two others of Louis McLane's numerous children were there, for Sally Tiffany had taken her children abroad and was accompanied by her young brother Jim McLane.[69] The father, whether in Baltimore or in Bohemia, did not cease to bewail the fate that scattered his family far over the globe. According to his own view, he did all he could for them, furnishing a home for Mary and Jim, lending money to Lou and Allan, running political errands for Bob, and providing a gathering place for other members of the clan when they were able to return to the area.[70]

His financial resources consisted of his real estate and the return he regularly got from it and 100 shares in the Bank of North America, in Philadelphia, worth $14,000 in the fall of 1854 and paying $15 a share yearly. The stock represented the remnant of his patrimony after, according to his account, $90,000 had been lost on endorsements for George B. Milligan and Outerbridge Horsey in mutual enterprises. He would not sell this stock, but he tried to raise money on it for the California enterprises of Allan and young Lou, until he found he could do so only on what he regarded as unacceptable terms.[71] Investments that he did make through Louis in San Francisco real estate, including the Custom House block, brought him regular returns, though he was disturbed and querulous when the amount of the dividend declined.[72]

He continued to be interested in public affairs. In the Crimean War, his sympathies were with Russia, largely because, still an ardent nationalist, he feared control of the seas by France and England in combination.[73] He thought the Democrats made a mistake in underrating the strength of the Know Nothings and instead of making use of them threw them into the arms of the Whigs.[74] He was concerned at hearing of a "Vigilance Committee" in San Francisco and feared it might not be restricted within proper limits.[75] He approved Philip Hamilton's interest in going to Congress, largely because Philip's success would bring Rebecca into "a theatre where her virtues and talents and power would be appreciated." [76]

Increasingly, he was obsessed with the effect events would have on the fortunes of his children. It was well, he thought, that Robert was in China when the Know Nothings were disturbing the course of politics. Young Louis must beware of taking any part in the California vigilante movement that his conviction would not justify and that would not in future redound to his "patriotism and honor and conservative character."

Yet every day this veteran found himself becoming "so much more and more separated in political preferences and sympathies" from all the children living near him that he was "becoming shy of any allusion" to such subjects.[77]

In the winter of 1856–57 he arranged daguerreotypes of his children and grandchildren over the mantel in the library of his Baltimore house.[78] There were seventeen grandchildren now—"a patriarchal number," he confessed.[79] He must appear in character, he thought, and in ordering new clothes he directed his tailor: "make and send me a *dress coat,* and a *frock* coat, vest, and pantaloons *of the best black* cloth,—the vest of the best black *cassimere.* The cut and fashion I leave to your direction, only cautioning you not to indulge in an *extreme* cut on either side, but to remember my *time of life.*"[80]

IX   THE END

By the end of his seventieth year, in May of 1854, Louis McLane was increasingly suffering the infirmities of his age. Sometimes he could use but one eye because gout—or, at least, so he thought—had affected the other.[81] His fingers were so stiff that he had trouble writing, and occasionally he was incapacitated by attacks of vertigo.[82] He spoke of escaping Baltimore and its climate for the warmth of Cuba or of California. In the fall of the year he sought a companion for the California voyage but failed to find one, and in view of his dizzy spells he dared not go alone.[83]

He was willing to leave Mary and Jim for the winter; they were no longer children, and Sally was at hand. But a problem greater than that of a companion was what to do about Bohemia. The income from this farm and Mount Jones were essential to him, though barely sufficient to cover expenses—according to him, and he may have made himself seem poorer than he was. He felt keenly the results of a drought that cost him half his corn crop. With no one to oversee Bohemia properly in his absence, the only solution was to sell it and invest the proceeds in more lucrative enterprises that did not anchor him to Maryland.[84]

Bob objected to the idea of selling Bohemia. He had returned from his China mission to France by the spring of 1855 and was about to bring his family home to Maryland. When he did, he wanted Bohemia, with its "sacred associations," to belong to the family still. His father could afford to give James an allowance and, taking Mary with him, make trial of a New York residence or travel in Europe; it would cost him but $400 or $500 a month.[85]

Nevertheless the father, despite Bob's advice, did try to sell Bohemia. Worse lands in Sassafras Neck were bringing sixty to eighty dollars an acre, but McLane decided not to insist on this much and hoped to find a market in Philadelphia, since farms on the upper Eastern Shore were becoming popular there.[86] He felt he was failing rapidly and would have gone to Cuba for the winter had Bob and Georgine, now resident in Maryland again, chosen to go there instead of to New Orleans, where the father probably did not want to make himself dependent on Georgine's relatives.[87]

When spring came in 1857, McLane was sorry he had stayed in Baltimore, for the cold had tested his remaining strength, and he particularly regretted that he had been deprived of the exercise he normally enjoyed through a morning walk. Even if he could not sell Bohemia he was determined to avoid the heat of another summer and the cold of another winter by fleeing to some milder climate—"if I do not take a longer and the last journey." [88] In May he declined an invitation to the opening of the railroad lines that brought the B & O by way of Parkersburg to Cincinnati and St. Louis, the farthest goal he had set for the B & O when he was its president. The excuse he gave was that he had other engagements, but it is more likely that he simply did not feel up to attending this celebration.[89]

He was an invalid for more than six weeks in May and June, but his health did not keep him from Bohemia, where he particularly enjoyed a family reunion in June. Rebecca, Sally, and Lydia were all there, the first two probably with their children, and of course Mary and Jim, the only two children still unmarried. Bohemia was particularly beautiful; "the old place never looked half so well as it does this season," McLane wrote. Besides the twenty-five acres devoted to ornamental planting, McLane was particularly proud of the improvements on the farm, which he thought in cleanliness and fertility and production rivaled the best-kept farms anywhere.[90]

In July he was confined to his Baltimore home at the corner of Mount Vernon Place and St. Paul Street, with little pain but "distressing debility and failing strength." Dr. Thomas Buckler, a close friend, promised that if he rested for a while he could soon throw his medicine vials out the window and go somewhere for fresh air, and go, he did, in August, to New York, but it was his last trip. An old acquaintance who saw him in Philadelphia in the course of this journey thought he looked reasonably well and in good spirits.[91]

On his return to Baltimore, however, kidney trouble forced him to his bed for what turned out to be his terminal illness. Now when he was seriously ill he amazed his children by his good temper—as Rebecca noted, a "wonderful and blessed change . . . took place" in his disposition. His mind remained clear, and though he prayed frequently he re-

fused Robert's entreaties that he see a minister. Mary, Lydia, Sally, Rebecca, Robert, and James—six of his eleven surviving children—were
frequently at the bedside, and the quarrelsome old statesman caressed
and kissed them often before he died on October 7, 1857, in his seventy-
fourth year.[92] He was buried with Protestant Episcopal rites in Greenmount Cemetery.[93]

Well might he have thought of his children in his final days, for they
were a remarkable group and their careers must have seemed in these
last hours to be their father's chief claim to fame. Robert was to go on
to be a Congressman again, a commissioner to Mexico, a governor of
Maryland, an ambassador to France. Young Louis was to become the
president of an express company, of banks, and of railroads. Allan rose
to the chief position in the largest American shipping firm on the Pacific
coast. Lydia's husband, Colonel Johnston, although pledged to a losing
cause, became the most famous of them all. Juliette became a missionary
in New Zealand. George, the family scapegrace, met a hero's death.

This was the future. If Louis McLane in his last hours surveyed his
own career, the record was disappointing. He had been a distinguished
Congressman, an outstanding chairman of the Ways and Means Committee, but his services in Congress were forgotten. In Jackson's cabinet
he had been, briefly, the first minister, but the Bank War and the Van
Buren ascendancy had set him and his reputation to one side. On two
missions to England he had accomplished almost exactly what he had
set out to do, but his role on each occasion was unappreciated and unknown. In business, he had developed the Morris Canal and Banking
Company to the point where it paid a dividend, but an economic depression coupled with the wild policies of his successors destroyed the
firm's reputation. Despite hard times, he had carried the extension of the
B & O westward to Cumberland, significantly increased its operating
efficiency, and husbanded its financial resources to permit completion
of the line to its Ohio River goal—but the completion was effected under
a younger, more ebullient successor, who reaped the glory of the successful enterprise.

The problem was that few people could love Louis McLane; few
could mourn his passing. He was intelligent and able, clear-minded and
efficient, but to the average man and even to some of his children, he
was not lovable. He was almost sinfully ambitious, as his father had encouraged him to be. He was often meanly suspicious, and life had encouraged him to be ever mindful of his welfare and that of the large family
dependent on him. He was easily affronted, and he held grudges almost
with glee against those who crossed him. He was immensely persuasive,
but in the long run he abandoned in disgust each of the successive scenes

of his triumphs—Delaware, which elected him to national office; Congress, where he became an influential leader in spite of being without a party; the cabinet, where by force of mind and will he had become the President's chief adviser; diplomacy, where his successes were, he hoped, to be parlayed into high domestic office; and business, where his talents were great but his choler could not stand opposition. In the long run it was to Kitty and the children that he was true, and the children learned to admire but not all to love this stern, busy, handsome, sensitive man.

In the old dispensation, the first American party system, Louis McLane was a Federalist. He outlived his party and adjusted his politics to the new dispensation of the second party system, but he could not adjust his temperament, his personal amalgam of the four humors, blood, phlegm, choler, and melancholy. A Delawarean, exalted in the national sphere by his neighbors, he lost his power base when he abandoned his party and his state. From a Federalist Congressman representing little Delaware he made a metamorphosis into a diplomat and statesman representing nothing at all except the friends who appointed him to office. When he lost their favor, he had no place to go in politics unless he wished to start his climb over again from the state level. The transportation revolution offered an alternative employment for administrative talents, and the significance of this biography may be that it demonstrates there was a use in society for a discarded minister and a politician who lost his party. He was not forced to return to his farm or his law office; instead he found a profitable and important role before him as a business executive engaged in assisting the American economy to begin its phenomenal nineteenth-century growth. In this new role he accomplished the miracle of making the Morris Canal profitable, and he doubled the length of the country's premier railroad. Yet to McLane, as to many men of his generation, a business career seemed anticlimactic, a sad though salaried decline for a statesman. To a later generation, his early career might seem to be the waste of time and talent. The ablest of his sons went into business; the only one to follow his father's steps in politics became a political dilettante.

Louis McLane, son of a Revolutionary, reared on tales of martial glory, seeking political distinction, reading Scott and dreaming of a chivalric élite, was forced by circumstances to turn to a business career, even as America turned its attention gradually and reluctantly from politics to industry. Like his nation, Louis McLane made the change successfully, but he was not altogether happy about it.

Notes

Abbreviations Used in Notes

AMcL	Allen McLane (1746–1829)
CMcL	Catherine (Mrs. Louis) McLane (1790–1849)
DAB	*Dictionary of American Biography*
DSA	Delaware State Archives, Dover
EMHL	Eleutherian Mills Historical Library, Greenville, Del.
HSD	Historical Society of Delaware, Wilmington
HSP	Historical Society of Pennsylvania, Philadelphia
LC	Library of Congress, Washington
LMcL	Louis McLane (1784–1857)
NA	National Archives, Washington
NYHS	New-York Historical Society
NYPL	New York Public Library
PAC	Public Archives of Canada, Ottawa
PMHB	*Pennsylvania Magazine of History and Biography*

CHAPTER ONE: THE OLD COLLECTOR AND HIS SON

1. *Directory and Register for the Year 1814 of the Borough of Wilmington and Brandywine,* p. 66.

2. *American State Papers* (Washington, 1832–1861): Class X, *Miscellaneous,* I, 272. *Cf. Senate Document* No. 141, 20th Cong., 1st sess., p. 40.

3. Act of March 27, 1801, in *Laws of the United States of America from . . . 1789 to . . . 1815* (Philadelphia, 1815), III, 623. *Cf. Senate Document* No. 141, 20th Cong., 1st sess., p. 40.

4. Act of March 2, 1799, in *Laws of the U.S.,* III, 237–240.

5. Schmeckebier, *The Customs Service,* pp. 3–4, 141.

6. *Ibid.,* pp. 9–10, 12.

7. *Ibid.,* pp. 7–8.

8. *Ibid.,* pp. 7, 10–13.

9. *American State Papers: Misc.,* I, 272.

10. H. Niles to C. A. Rodney, Feb. 7, 1804, Rodney Papers, Society Collection, HSD; P. Jaquett to C. A. Rodney, Nov. 8, 1804, Clayton Papers, LC; J. R. Black to H. M. Ridgely, April 12, 1829, Ridgely Papers, DSA; de Valinger and Shaw, *Calendar of Ridgely Family Letters,* II, 240.

11. AMcL to T. Pickering, June 3, 1799, Pickering Papers, Massachusetts Historical Society; AMcL to C. A. Rodney, June 24, 1801, Gratz MSS, HSP; Cunningham, *Jeffersonian Republicans in Power,* pp. 44–49.

12. T. Clayton to W. P. Brobson, Feb. 17, 1825, Brobson Papers, HSD.

13. Will Book S-1-280, Register of Wills, Wilmington.

14. AMcL to A. Jackson, Jan. 28, 1819, Jackson Papers, 1st ser., LC.

15. Wilmington *Political Primer,* April 16, 1828.

16. AMcL to H. M. Ridgely, Jan. 23, 1815, McLane Papers; inventories, 1809–1881, Register of Wills, Wilmington.

17. [William Maxwell,] "The Late Commodore Barron," *Virginia Historical Register,* IV (1851), 167; W. S. Morton, "Revolutionary Officers of Virginia," *William and Mary College Quarterly,* 2d ser., I (1921), 291.

18. *Niles' Register,* XXX (Nov. 18, 1826), 179.

19. Levasseur, *Lafayette in America,* I, 159; II, 236.

20. Wilmington *Political Primer,* April 16, 1828; R. M. McLane, *Reminiscences,* p. 158.

21. Adams, *Memoirs,* XII, 204.

22. McLane family genealogical notes compiled by D. K. Este Fisher, Jr., Baltimore, with some additions from the late Reverend James Latimer McLane, Los Angeles.

23. Will of Allen McLeane, Jan. 25, 1775 (probated May 13, 1776), Register of Wills. Philadelphia.

24. McLane genealogical notes; R. M. McLane, *Reminiscences,* pp. 32–33.

25. McLane genealogical notes.

26. Pemberton Papers, XX, 60, HSP; W. A. Newman Dorland, "The Second Troop, Philadelphia City Cavalry," *PMHB,* XLVII (1923), 274n; genealogical material by Frank Willing Leach in *The North American* (Philadelphia), June 21, 1908, in scrapbook at Pennsylvania Genealogical Society (kindness of John A. H. Sweeney); undated letters [Dec., 1779, and Dec., 1780] in "The Norris-Fisher Correspondence," ed. John A. H. Sweeney, *Delaware History,* VI (March, 1955), 199, 216–217; "Washington's Household Account Book, 1793–1797," *PMHB,* XXX (1906), 43, 309, 472; XXXI (1907), 186.

27. R. M. McLane, *Reminiscences,* p. 33.

28. McLane genealogical notes.

29. McLane family Bible, seen by courtesy of the late Reverend James Latimer McLane.

30. Extracts from AMcL's journal, McLane Photostats, HSD.

31. McLane family Bible; Scharf, *History of Delaware,* II, 1039.

32. Leon de Valinger, Jr., to the author, April 1, 1957; Scharf, *History of Delaware,* II, 1048.

33. McLane family Bible; McLane genealogical notes; *DAB,* XII, 112; Scharf, *History of Delaware,* II, 1099; petition from residents [1778], Legislative Papers, DSA; H. Lloyd Jones, Jr., "Sic Transit . . . The Story of Duck Creek Landings," *Delaware Folklore Bulletin,* I (Oct., 1951), 5–6.

34. Munroe, *Federalist Delaware,* pp. 53–54; Asbury, *Journal and Letters,* I, 277–278.

35. Munroe, *Federalist Delaware,* pp. 167–168.

36. McLane family Bible.

37. Extract from Mrs. Freeborn Garrettson's journal, McLane Papers; George Dangerfield, *Chancellor Robert R. Livingston of New York, 1746–1813* (New York, 1960), chart opp. p. 516.

38. Extract from Mrs. Freeborn Garrettson's journal, McLane Papers.

39. John Lednum, *A History of the Rise of Methodism in America* (Philadelphia, 1859), p. 260n; Henry Boehm, *Reminiscences, Historical and Biographical, of Sixty-four Years in the Ministry* (New York, 1865), p. 88; Scharf, *History of Delaware,* II, 1102.

40. Richard Whatcoat, "Journal," in W. W. Sweet, ed., *Religion on the American Frontier, 1783–1840,* IV (*The Methodists*) (Chicago, 1946), 86; F. Asbury to J. Dickinson, Dec. 10 [1786], in Asbury, *Journal and Letters,* III, 47–48; bond of Thomas White, A. McLane, and Francis Many, June 1, 1789, Logan Papers, XXXVI, 110, HSP.

41. Thomas Ware, *Sketches of the Life and Travels of Rev. Thomas Ware* (New York, 1839), pp. 185–186; Phoebus, *Beams of Light on Early Methodism in America,* p. 236.

42. Hanna, *The Centennial Services of Asbury Methodist Episcopal Church,* p. 145.

43. Asbury, *Journal and Letters,* II, 129, 301, 336, 356, 440, 468.

44. *Ibid.,* p. 754; Boehm, *Reminiscences,* p. 88.

45. LMcL to Dr. Allen McLane, July 23, 1806, Fisher Collection.

46. Boehm, *Reminiscences,* pp. 151–152.

47. Scharf, *History of Delaware,* II, 1099.

48. Copy of articles of association, Nov. 1, 1774, AMcL Letterbook, Society Collection, HSP; Irvine Papers, XVI, 45, HSP. Sketches of AMcL's career in the Emmet Collection, NYPL, the Irvine Papers, HSP, the Society Collection, HSP, the McLane Papers, NYHS, and AMcL's journal, Morristown National Historic Park, have been largely utilized in the account of his career and will not be cited hereafter. The account in the Historical Society of Pennsylvania may be the earliest of these. See also Watson, *Annals of Philadelphia,* II, 321–324.

49. AMcL, commission, Sept. 11, 1775, Letterbook, Society Collection, HSP. AMcL papers cited from the Society Collection at the HSP are usually also to be found in the McLane Papers at the NYHS, of which photostatic copies are in the HSD. Copy of C. Rodney's note, Oct. 10, 1775, Letterbook, Society Collection, HSP.

50. Ennion Williams to AMcL [Sept.] 3, 1824, Society Collection, HSP, and in "Original Letters and Documents," *PMHB,* VI (1882), 114; Willard M. Wallace, *Appeal to Arms* (New York, 1951), p. 111.

51. AMcL to unknown addressee, Gratz MSS, case 4, box 21, Officers of the Revolution, HSP; Washington, *Writings,* XII, 82–83; J. McHenry to AMcL, June 18, 1778, Letterbook, Society Collection, HSP; A. Scammell to AMcL, April 10, 1778, *ibid.;* Watson, *Annals,* II, 322; P. Jaquett to C. A. Rodney, Nov. 8, 1804, Clayton Papers, I, LC.

52. Jean L. Brockway, "James Peale," *DAB,* XIV, 347; Sellers, *Portraits and Miniatures by Charles Willson Peale,* p. 138; Watson, *Annals,* II, 322; Ward, "The Germantown Road and Its Associations," *PMHB,* V, 17; Alexander Garden, *Anecdotes of the American Revolution* (Brooklyn, 1865), III, 77.

53. S. Weir Mitchell, *Hugh Wynne* (1897), and Howard Fast, *Conceived in Liberty* (1939).

54. Unidentified newspaper clipping, Dreer Collection, HSP.

55. H. Lee to AMcL, July 2, 1779, Letterbook, Society Collection, HSP; Garden, *Anecdotes,* III, 74; Wallace, *Appeal to Arms,* p. 198.

56. Charles H. Lincoln, ed., *Naval Records of the American Revolution, 1775–1788* (Washington, 1906), p. 258; Garden, *Anecdotes,* III, 75; Lewis, *Admiral de Grasse and American Independence,* p. 126; Gardner W. Allen, *Naval History of the Revolution* (Boston, 1913), II, 565–567; AMcL to T. Clark, June 25, 1813, Society Collection, HSP.

57. Washington, *Writings,* X, 283n; J. Fitzgerald to AMcL, Jan. 8, 1778, Letterbook, Society Collection, HSP; AMcL to T. Clark, June 25, 1813, *ibid.;* unidentified newspaper clipping [*c.* 1848], Fisher Collection; William B. Clark, *Gallant John Barry* (New York, 1938), pp. 151–153.

58. AMcL, Account of the Fort Wilson Riot, Joseph Reed MSS, VI, item 90, NYHS.

59. AMcL to T. Clark, June 25, 1813, Society Collection, HSP.

60. Heitman, *Historical Register of Officers of the Continental Army*, p. 373; McLane Papers, NYHS; L. de Valinger, Jr., to author, March 13, 1970.

61. Heitman, *Historical Register*, p. 373; *Journals of the Continental Congress, 1774–1789* (Washington, 1904–1937), XII, 1212; XIV, 822–823; Washington, *Writings*, VIII, 327n; XV, 297; XIX, 486; AMcL to [C. Rodney], April 20, 1779, Gratz MSS, case 4, box 21, HSP; J. Dickinson to C. Rodney, May 10, 1779, in George H. Ryden, *Letters to and from Caesar Rodney* (Philadelphia, 1933), p. 301; Washington to AMcL, June 9, 1779, Letterbook, Society Collection, HSP.

62. AMcL's anecdotes, July 2, 1826, Society Collection, HSP.

63. AMcL to J. Reed, May 20, 1780, Gratz MSS, case 4, box 21, HSP.

64. AMcL to H. Lee, Jan. 15, 1780, Washington Papers, CXXV, LC; H. Lee to Washington, Jan. 26, 1780, *ibid.;* Washington to H. Lee, Jan. 30, 1780, in Washington, *Writings*, XVII, 471.

65. *Journals of the Continental Congress*, XVI, 159, 164; B. Stoddert to Washington, April 3, 1780, Washington Papers, CXXXII, LC; H. Lee to Board of War, April 3, 1780, *ibid.;* Washington, *Writings*, XVIII, 234–235, 478–479, 486–487; J. Duane to Washington, May 21, 1780, Washington Papers, CXXXVI, LC; J. Shee to J. Duane [n. d.], *ibid.;* H. Lee to Washington, Aug. 31, 1780, *ibid.,* CXLVIII.

66. *Journals of the Continental Congress*, XXV, 786.

67. James Tilton to James Monroe, Aug. 2, 1785, Monroe Papers, I, LC.

68. Washington, *Writings*, XXIV, 44.

69. AMcL to unknown, Dover, Jan. 13, 1790, Stauffer Collection, VII, 599, HSP.

70. Munroe, *Federalist Delaware*, passim.

71. "State of the General Election in Delaware Anno 1785," MS in Clymer-Meredith-Read Papers, NYPL.

72. George H. Ryden, *Delaware—The First State in the Union* (Wilmington, 1938), pp. 24, 26.

73. Wilmington *Delaware Gazette*, Jan. 10, 1789; Philadelphia *Pennsylvania Packet*, Jan. 15, 1789.

74. Wilmington *Delaware and Eastern Shore Advertiser*, Sept. 3, 1794.

75. Peter Jaquett to C. A. Rodney, Nov. 8, 1804, Clayton Papers, I, LC.

76. *Delaware Gazette*, July 5, 1796.

77. Washington to AMcL, Sept. 30, 1789, McLane Letterbook, Society Collection, HSP.

78. *American State Papers: Misc.*, I, 60.

79. See summons signed by Allen McLane, J.P., Feb. 22, 1796, McLane Papers.

80. Legislative Papers, DSA; Munroe, *Federalist Delaware*, p. 161; Scharf, *History of Delaware*, II, 827; *Pennsylvania Packet*, Aug. 22, 1788; Delaware Abolition Society minutes, HSP.

81. Scharf, *History of Delaware*, II, 1097.

82. McLane genealogical notes.

83. *American State Papers: Misc.*, I, 272; Conrad, *History of Delaware*, I, 343.

84. LMcL to Dr. Allen McLane, Dec. 11, 19, 1806, Fisher Collection.

85. Managers' accounts, Pennsylvania Hospital, microfilm (kindness of William H. Williams); will of Edward Worrell, dated July 4, 1829, Will Book S-1-374, Register of Wills, Wilmington; will of Allen McLane, dated Nov. 24, 1821, Will Book S-1-280, Register of Wills, Wilmington.

86. LMcL to Louis McLane, Jr., May 17, July 2, 1857, Fisher Collection; Scharf, *Chronicles of Baltimore*, p. 557; Baltimore *Sun*, Oct. 8, 9, 1857; Greenmount Cemetery records (Baltimore).

87. J. Bayard to R. Bassett, Feb. 16, 1798, in Bayard, *Papers*, p. 49.

88. Wilmington *Political Primer*, April 16, 1828.

89. Scharf, *History of Delaware*, II, 1099.

90. Scott, *Geographical Description of . . . Maryland and Delaware*, p. 183.

91. AMcL to Washington, June 9, 1794, U.S., Applications for Office under Washington, XIX, LC.

92. Act of May 8, 1792, in *Laws of the U.S.*, II, 298.

93. AMcL to Washington, June 9, 1794, U.S., Applications for Office under Washington, XIX, LC.

94. R. Bassett to Washington, Feb. 25, 1797, *ibid.;* Washington, *Writings*, XXXV, 404.

95. Letters of J. Tilton quoted from William Currie, *An Historical Account of the Climates and Diseases of the United States* (Philadelphia, 1792), pp. 207–221; Munroe, *Federalist Delaware*, pp. 178–179.

96. Washington, *Writings*, XXXV, 404.

97. John Fisher to C. A. Rodney, Oct. 4, 1795, John Fisher Papers, HSD. See also Timothy Pickering to AMcL, Aug. 10, 30, 1798, Pickering Papers, Massachusetts Historical Society.

98. AMcL to T. Pickering, Dec. 6, 10, 1798, Pickering Papers, Massachusetts Historical Society.

99. Wilmington *Mirror of the Times*, Oct. 1, 4, 11, 1800.

100. William Cobbett, *Porcupine's Works* (London, 1801), I, 9.

101. AMcL to Nicholas Ridgely, Nov. 14, 1800, McLane Papers.

102. [Bringhurst,] *The Wilmingtoniad*, p. 8.

103. H. Niles to C. A. Rodney, Feb. 7, 1804, Rodney Papers, Society Collection, HSD.

104. P. Jaquett to T. Rodney, Nov. 8, 1804, Clayton Papers, I, LC.

105. [Bringhurst,] *The Wilmingtoniad*, pp. 7–8.

106. Morton Borden, "The Election of 1800: Charge and Countercharge," *Delaware History*, V (March, 1952), 58.

107. *Ibid.*, p. 59; Matthew L. Davis, *Memoirs of Aaron Burr* (New York, 1836–1837), II, 132, 135–136.

108. Borden, "Election of 1800," p. 60; Davis, *Memoirs of Burr*, II, 136.

109. J. Bayard to AMcL, Feb. 17, 1801, in Bayard, *Papers*, p. 127.

110. AMcL to Joseph Eggleston, Jan. 1, 1801, Jefferson Papers, CVIII, LC.

111. Samuel Miller to A. Gallatin, June 22, 1801, Gallatin Papers, NYHS. *Cf.* Cunningham, *Jeffersonian Republicans in Power,* pp. 44–49.

112. AMcL to C. A. Rodney, June 24, 1801, Gratz MSS, case 4, box 21, HSP; undated letter of C. A. Rodney in Wilmington *Mirror of the Times,* June 29, 1803.

113. Undated letter of C. A. Rodney in Wilmington *Mirror of the Times,* June 29, 1803.

114. David Hall to T. Jefferson, May 31, 1802, Jefferson Papers, CXXIII, LC.

115. Address of Democratic Republican Convention to T. Jefferson [June 5, 1802]; Jno. Bird to Jefferson, June 8, 1802; David Hall to Jefferson, June 9, 1802; unknown to unknown, Kent County, June 8, 1802, *ibid.*

116. AMcL to John Steele, June 12, 1802; AMcL to A. Gallatin, June 12, 1802, *ibid.*

117. T. Jefferson to David Hall, July 6, 1802, in Jefferson, *Works* (ed. Paul Leicester Ford) (New York, 1892–1899), VIII, 157n; Jefferson to C. A. Rodney, June 14, 1802, *ibid.,* pp. 154–155.

118. AMcL to A. Gallatin, Jan. 11, 1803, Jefferson Papers, CXXVIII, LC; AMcL to John Steele, Oct. 25, 1802, *ibid.,* CXXVII; AMcL to Gallatin, Nov. 3, 1802, Gallatin Papers, NYHS; H. Niles to C. A. Rodney, Feb. 7, 1804, Rodney Papers, Society Collection, HSD; extract from Wilmington *Mirror of the Times* [Aug. 27, 1804], Jefferson Papers, CLXIII, LC; Peter Jaquett to C. A. Rodney, Nov. 8, 1804, Clayton Papers, I, LC; John Bird to C. A. Rodney, Nov. 5, 1804 (photostat), Morse Autograph Collection, I, HSD.

119. AMcL to Joseph Eggleston, Jan. 1, 1801, Jefferson Papers, CVIII, LC; Powell, *History of Education in Delaware,* p. 44.

120. *Delaware and Eastern Shore Advertiser,* Dec. 17, 1794.

121. Powell, *History of Education in Delaware,* pp. 43, 47; Benjamin Ferris, *A History of the Original Settlements on the Delaware* (Wilmington, 1846), pp. 286–287; [Augustus Longstreet,] *Georgia Scenes* (New York, 1855), pp. 73–82.

122. Report by Thomas J. Coleman, Navy Branch, War Records Division, National Archives, in Elbert L. Huber to author, April 1, 1957; *Naval Documents Related to the Quasi-War Between the United States and France,* VII (Washington, 1938), 340.

123. Allen, *Our Naval War with France,* pp. 178, 217–218; Allan Westcott, "Stephen Decatur (1752–1808)," *DAB,* V, 186–187.

124. Report by Thomas J. Coleman, cited in n. 122.

125. Memoir by Catherine M. McLane, a granddaughter, Louis McLane Collection, HSD; unidentified printed biographical sketch in Roberts Collection, Haverford College; Scharf, *Chronicles of Baltimore,* p. 557.

126. Minutes of the Trustees of the Newark Academy, *passim* (microfilm in Morris Library, University of Delaware); William D. Lewis, "University of Delaware: Ancestors, Friends and Neighbors," *Delaware Notes,* 34th ser. (Newark, Del., 1961), pp. 20–21.

127. James A. Bayard to C. A. Rodney, Dec. 10, 1803, in Bayard, *Papers,* pp. 6–7.

128. George Strawbridge, "Memoirs," pp. 31–33 (typescript), Princeton University.

129. *Ibid.,* p. 32.

130. John Fisher to C. A. Rodney, July 7, 1805, John Fisher Papers, HSD; advertisement of Bayard's house in *Museum of Delaware,* Dec. 5, 1807.

131. LMcL to Allen McLane, Jr., Aug. 28, 1805, Fisher Collection.

132. LMcL to Allen McLane, Jr., Sept. 11, 1805; July 23, Dec. 19, 1806; Jan. 28, 1807, *ibid.*

133. LMcL to Allen McLane, Jr., Sept. 11, 1805, *ibid.;* Count de Grouchy to C. A. Rodney, Sept. 24 [1804?], Rodney Papers, Society Collection, HSD.

134. LMcL to Allen McLane, Jr., Sept. 11, 1805; Jan. 28, 1807, Fisher Collection.

135. LMcL to Allen McLane, Jr., Dec. 3, 1806, *ibid.*

136. LMcL to Allen McLane, Jr., Dec. 19, 24, 1806, *ibid.*

137. *Delaware House Journal,* 1800, p. 14.

138. Conrad, *History of Delaware,* III, 895.

CHAPTER TWO: A RISING YOUNG FEDERALIST

1. Scott, *Description of Maryland and Delaware,* p. 108.

2. Cecil County Land Records, Lib. 7, fol. 290, collection of the late J. D. Otley, formerly at Bohemia.

3. Mary L. Milligan, Family Scrapbook, April 10, 1899, pp. 41–43, Batchelder Papers.

4. M. Jane (Nuckols) Garrett, "The Philadelphia and Baltimore Spheres of Influence: Their Relationships and Points of Contact, 1790–1840" (unpublished honors thesis, University of Delaware, 1957).

5. Mary L. Milligan, Family Scrapbook (no page), Batchelder Papers; Joseph Towne Wheeler, "Reading Interests of the Professional Classes in Colonial Maryland, 1700–1776," *Maryland Historical Magazine,* XXXVI (1941), 282; "Notes and Queries," *PMHB,* XIV (1890), 98; William S. Baker, ed., "Washington after the Revolution," *PMHB,* XIX (1895), 185; "Extracts from Washington's Diary . . . 1787," *PMHB,* XI (1887), 304; *American Museum,* V (1789), 425.

6. Mary Tilghman to Mary Pearce, Chestertown, May 8 [1789], in J. Hall Pleasants, ed., "Letters of Molly and Hetty Tilghman," *Maryland Historical Magazine,* XXI (1926), 238.

7. John P. Nields to Mrs. Francis Crowninshield, Wilmington, June 1, 1925, Batchelder Papers; Dyre Family Chart, Delaware Branch, *ibid.;* John A. H. Sweeney, *Grandeur on the Appoquinimink: the House of William Corbit at Odessa, Delaware* (Newark, Del., 1959).

8. Clark, *The Eastern Shore of Maryland and Virginia,* I, 520.

9. John P. Nields to Mrs. Francis Crowninshield, Wilmington, June 1, 1925, Batchelder Papers; Mary L. Milligan, Family Scrapbook, *ibid.*

10. Will Book Q-1-196, Register of Wills, Wilmington.

11. J. Bayard to Catherine Milligan, Feb. 20, 1812, Batchelder Papers.

12. Mrs. E. I. du Pont to E. I. du Pont, June 19, 1812, in du Pont, *Life of E. I. du Pont,* IX, 41; [Francis Sims McGrath,] "A Letter to Eileen," *Maryland Historical Magazine,* XXIV (1929), 323–324; "The Diaries of Sidney George Fisher," *PMHB,* LXXVI, 190–191; LXXIX (1955), 220; William B. Rawle, "Laurel Hill and Some Colonial Dames Who Once Lived There," *PMHB,* XXXV (1911), 388.

13. Mary L. Milligan, Family Scrapbook, Batchelder Papers.

14. CMcL to Catherine Milligan, Paterson, N.J. [*c.* Aug. 2–3, 1812], Fisher Collection.

15. Mary L. Milligan, Family Scrapbook, Batchelder Papers.

16. John A. Munroe, "Senator Nicholas Van Dyke of New Castle," *Delaware History,* IV (1951), 207.

17. LMcL to [N. Van Dyke], June 30, 1812, copy, Van Dyke Papers, EMHL.

18. Mary Read to W. T. Read, New Castle, Dec. 1, 1812, Richard S. Rodney Collection, HSD.

19. Munroe, "Senator Nicholas Van Dyke of New Castle," pp. 207–226.

20. Elizabeth Booth, *Reminiscences* (New Castle, 1884), pp. 74–75; *Delaware Gazette,* Oct. 4, 1814.

21. Clipping from *Federal Gazette,* Jan. 4, 1813, in Horizontal File, Maryland Historical Society; Maria Read to William T. Read, Jan. 6, 1813, R. S. Rodney Collection, HSD.

22. LMcL to Dr. Allen McLane, Aug. 28, 1805, Fisher Collection.

23. Thomas Cope, "My Own Mirror and Record of Events" (typed MS), IV (1807–1813), 105 (courtesy of Professor David B. Tyler, Wagner College, Staten Island, N.Y.).

24. *Ibid.,* pp. 106–108.

25. *Ibid.,* p. 108.

26. John B. McMaster, *Life and Times of Stephen Girard,* II (Philadelphia, 1918), 172–194.

27. J. Bayard to C. A. Rodney, May 6, 1812, Ann Bayard *et al.* v. Louis McLane, Harrington, *Reports of Cases,* III, 156.

28. McMaster, *Girard,* II, 196.

29. Harrington, *Reports of Cases,* III, 157.

30. McMaster, *Girard,* II, 196, 358.

31. Harrington, *Reports of Cases,* III, 139, 151–152.

32. *Ibid.,* pp. 140–142, 157.

33. *Ibid.,* pp. 154, 155–156, 158, 204; McMaster, *Girard,* II, 359; C. A. Rodney to J. Monroe, Feb. 14, 1819, Monroe Papers, XXVII, LC; Will Book S-1-280, Register of Wills, Wilmington.

34. Harrington, *Reports of Cases,* III, 239.

35. Boorstin, *Delaware Cases,* III, 183, 219–340.

36. Deed L-3-465, Recorder of Deeds, Wilmington.

37. Record of the Title of Louisa d'A. du Pont Copeland to Land on the Brandywine, EMHL.

38. *Ibid.;* Allan J. Henry, *Life of Alexis I. du Pont* (Philadelphia, 1945), II, 28; *Delaware Gazette,* Feb. 21, 1823.

39. View between pp. 16 and 17 in Gentieu, *History of Mount Salem Methodist Church.*

40. Scharf, *History of Delaware,* I, 304–305; W. Young to E. I. du Pont, March 31, 1813, Longwood MSS, box 61, EMHL; Minutes, Meeting of Manufacturers, Nov. 25, Dec. 9, 1815, and Jan. 10, 1816, Joseph Bringhurst Papers, HSD.

41. *Delaware Gazette,* April 2, 1816; *Niles' Register,* XIV (March 21, 1818), 64.

42. *Delaware Gazette,* Sept. 22, 1820.

43. 1820 Census, p. 465; *Delaware Gazette,* Feb. 26, 1822; Feb. 21, 1823.

44. LMcL to John Torbert, Wilmington, Oct. 6, 1822, McLane Papers, HSD; *Delaware Gazette,* Feb. 21, 1823; *American Watchman,* July 4, 1826.

45. Henry, *Life of Alexis I. du Pont,* II, 50n.

46. *McLane Report,* pp. 796–797.

47. Offer of sale, Smith's Tavern, Wilmington, Oct. 6, 1832, McLane Papers, HSD.

48. Record of the Title of Louisa d'A. du Pont Copeland to Land on the Brandywine, EMHL; see also Longwood MSS, Group 5, ser. B, box 27, EMHL.

49. Power of attorney, June 1, 1835, in deed book V 4, pp. 171–172, in Longwood MSS, Group 5, ser. B, box 27, EMHL.

50. Petition to Delaware legislature for extension of charter of Bank of Delaware, Legislative Petitions, 1811, DSA.

51. Lunt, *Farmers Bank,* p. 54.

52. Conrad, *History of Delaware,* I, 347–348; Munroe, *Federalist Delaware,* pp. 248–250; Lunt, *Farmers Bank,* pp. 58, 69.

53. Conrad, *History of Delaware,* I, 348.

54. *Delaware Gazette,* Feb. 22, April 23, 1816; Lunt, *Farmers Bank,* pp. 72, 81.

55. Conrad, *History of Delaware,* I, 347; Deed P-3-100, Recorder of Deeds, Wilmington; Wilmington *Morning News,* Jan. 12, 1881.

56. Henry C. Conrad, "Gunning Bedford, Junior," *Papers of the HSD,* III, No. 26 (1900), 9; Montgomery, *Reminiscences,* pp. 287–289.

57. MS Life of Louis McLane, McLane Papers.

58. AMcL to C. A. Rodney, July 21, 1807, Gratz MSS, HSP.

59. AMcL to Peter B. Porter, Feb. 28, 1812, Peter A. Porter Collection of Peter B. Porter Papers, Buffalo Historical Society; statement of association, June 30, 1812, Letterbook, Society Collection, HSP; Conrad, *History of Delaware,* I, 163; Allen, *Naval History of the Revolution,* II, 567; Lincoln, ed., *Naval Records of the American Revolution,* p. 258; Scharf, *History of Delaware,* II, 815–816; *Wilmington Directory,* 1814, p. 78; *Niles' Register,* IV (March 27, 1813), 68.

60. AMcL to William Jones, March 21, 1813, Uselma Clarke Smith Collection, William Jones Papers, HSP.

61. AMcL to James Monroe, Jan. 25, 1814, Monroe Papers, LIV, LC.

62. *Delaware Gazette*, Aug. 25, 1814; quoted in Albert H. Hadel, "A Review of the Battle of Bladensburg," *Maryland Historical Magazine*, I (Sept., 1906), 197–198.

63. Bayard, *Letters*, p. 24.

64. LMcL to CMcL [*c.* Sept., 1814], McLane Papers.

65. MS Life of McLane, McLane Papers.

66. *Delaware Archives* (Wilmington, 1911–1919), V, 761, 770; *Delaware Gazette*, Sept. 19, 1814.

67. LMcL to G. Read, Oct. 5, 1814, R. S. Rodney Collection, HSD.

68. LMcL to G. Read, Nov. 11, 1814, *ibid.*

69. Furlough signed by Capt. George Read, Dec. 2, 1814, *ibid.*

70. Payroll signed by Capt. George Read, *ibid.; Delaware Archives*, V, 906.

71. Louis McLane, *Oration Delivered Before the Artillery Company of Wilmington*, July 5, 1813, pp. 3, 18n, 22.

72. *Ibid.*, pp. 10, 16.

73. *Ibid.*, pp. 19–21.

74. *Ibid.*, p. 2.

75. *Wilmington Directory*, 1814, p. 62.

76. Munroe, *Federalist Delaware*, pp. 265, 268.

77. Charles Evans, ed., *Report of the Trial of the Hon. Samuel Chase* (Baltimore, 1805), p. 5.

78. *Niles' Register*, XXV (Oct. 25, 1823), 121; Munroe, *Federalist Delaware*, pp. 231–259.

79. Frederic R. Kirkland, ed., *Letters on the American Revolution in the Library at "Karolfred,"* I (Philadelphia, 1941), 93.

80. *American Watchman*, Oct. 2, 1810.

81. Wilmington *Delaware Statesman*, Sept. 5, 1812.

82. *Governor's Register, State of Delaware*, I, 104.

83. *Delaware Gazette*, Oct. 12, 1815.

84. Scharf, *History of Delaware*, I, 304.

85. Broadside, "To the Federalists of the State of Delaware," Sept. 14, 1816, Broadside Collection, Wilmington Institute Free Library; *Delaware Gazette*, Sept. 16, 1816.

86. *Delaware Gazette*, Aug. 12, Sept. 16, 1816.

87. *Ibid.*, Aug. 19, 1816.

88. *Ibid.*, Sept. 16, 1816.

89. *Ibid.*, Sept. 19, 1816.

90. *Ibid.*, Aug. 26, 1816.

91. *Ibid.*, Sept. 9, 1816.

92. E. I. du Pont to wife, Sept. 26, 1816, in du Pont, *Life of E. I. du Pont*, X, 174–175.

93. Willard Hall to N. G. Williamson, Oct. 14, 1816, Hall Letters, HSD; *Governor's Register*, I, 138–139.

94. James M. Smith, "The Enforcement of the Alien Friends Act of 1798," *Mississippi Valley Historical Review*, XLI (1954), 98.

95. Affidavit of Victor du Pont, Jan. 17, 1814, in du Pont, *Life of E. I. du Pont*, IX, 156–164.

96. Boorstin, *Delaware Cases*, III, 227.

97. *Delaware Gazette*, Oct. 7, 1816.

98. *American Watchman*, Sept. 30, 1809.

CHAPTER THREE: A VILLAGER IN WASHINGTON

1. LMcL to CMcL, Dec. 2, 1817, McLane Papers.

2. *Niles' Register*, XIII (Nov. 8, 1817), 163.

3. LMcL to CMcL, Dec. 2, 1817, McLane Papers.

4. *Ibid.;* Young, *Washington Community*, pp. 98ff.

5. LMcL to CMcL, Jan. 8, 1818, McLane Papers.

6. *Ibid.*

7. LMcL to CMcL, Dec. 19, 1817, *ibid.;* Young, *Washington Community*, p. 220.

8. LMcL to CMcL, Jan. 8, 1818, McLane Papers.

9. LMcL to CMcL, Feb. 7, 1818, *ibid.*

10. LMcL to CMcL, Jan. 1, 1818, *ibid.*

11. LMcL to CMcL, Dec. 2, 1817; Jan. 15, 1818, *ibid.*

12. LMcL to CMcL, March 1, 20, 1818, *ibid. Cf.* LMcL to J. J. Milligan, March 15, 1818, Fisher Collection.

13. LMcL to CMcL, Jan. 20, 1819, McLane Papers.

14. LMcL to J. J. Milligan, Dec. 4, 1817, Fisher Collection; Rufus King to Jeremiah Mason, Jan. 3, 1818, in *Memoir of Jeremiah Mason*, p. 173.

15. LMcL to J. J. Milligan, Dec. 4, 1817, Fisher Collection.

16. LMcL to CMcL, Feb. 19, 1818, McLane Papers.

17. LMcL to CMcL, Dec. 19, 1817, *ibid.*

18. LMcL to CMcL, Feb. 9, 1819, *ibid.*

19. LMcL to J. J. Milligan, Feb. 12, 1818, Fisher Collection.

20. LMcL to J. J. Milligan, March 15, 1818, *ibid.*

21. LMcL to J. J. Milligan, Feb. 12, 1818, *ibid.*

22. White, *Jeffersonians*, pp. 101ff.; Young, *Washington Community*, pp. 202–206.

23. Joseph Story to Ezekiel Bacon, March 12, 1818, in William W. Story, ed., *Life and Letters of Joseph Story* (Boston, 1851), I, 311.

24. Jeremiah Mason to Rufus King, Dec. 10, 1817, in *Memoir of Jeremiah Mason*, pp. 170–171.

25. John Quincy Adams to Abigail Adams, May 25, 1818, in Adams, *Writings*, VI, 338.

26. *Annals of Congress*, 15th Cong., 1st sess., p. 443.

27. *Ibid.*, p. 445.

28. *Ibid.*, p. 400.

29. LMcL to J. J. Milligan, Dec. 4, 1817, Fisher Collection; LMcL to CMcL, Dec. 19, 1817, McLane Papers; LMcL to a Mr. Smith, July 13, 1818, Misc. Papers, NYPL.

30. LMcL to CMcL [*c.* Jan. 10, 1818], McLane Papers.

31. LMcL to CMcL, Jan. 15, 1818, *ibid.*

32. LMcL to J. J. Milligan, Jan. 19, 31, 1818, Fisher Collection; LMcL to CMcL, Jan. 19, 1818, McLane Papers.

33. LMcL to CMcL, Jan. 8 [10], 1818, McLane Papers. *Cf.* Marshall Smelser, "Legislative Investigations: . . . The Problem in Historical Perspective: The Grand Inquest of the Nation," *Notre Dame Lawyer,* XXIX (1954), 170.

34. *Annals of Congress,* 15th Cong., 1st sess., p. 684.

35. *Ibid.,* pp. 684, 775–777.

36. LMcL to CMcL, Jan. 15 and 16, 1818, McLane Papers.

37. LMcL to J. J. Milligan, Jan. 19, 1818, Fisher Collection.

38. LMcL to CMcL, Jan. 21, 1818, McLane Papers.

39. *Delaware Gazette,* Jan. 31, 1818.

40. LMcL to CMcL, Jan. 21, 1818, McLane Papers.

41. *American Watchman,* Feb. 14, 1818.

42. John Bellach to LMcL, Feb. 3, 1818, McLane Papers; LMcL to CMcL. Feb. 19, 1818, *ibid.*

43. LMcL to CMcL, Jan. 15, 1818, *ibid.*

44. LMcL to CMcL, Feb. 11, 1818, *ibid.*

45. *Annals of Congress,* 15th Cong., 1st sess., pp. 1054–1066.

46. LMcL to CMcL, March 1, 1818, McLane Papers.

47. LMcL to CMcL, March 8, 1818, *ibid.*

48. *House Journal,* 15th Cong., 1st sess., pp. 46, 127, 207.

49. *Annals of Congress,* 15th Cong., 1st sess., pp. 1394, 1399.

50. *House Journal,* 15th Cong., 1st sess., pp. 334–342, 348.

51. LMcL to CMcL, Dec. 18, 1817, McLane Papers.

52. *House Journal,* 15th Cong., 1st sess., pp. 109, 111–112, 120.

53. LMcL to CMcL, Jan. 8, 1818, McLane Papers.

54. LMcL to CMcL, Sat. morning [*c.* March 14, 1818], Fisher Collection.

55. *House Journal,* 15th Cong., 1st sess., pp. 318, 350, 379, 390, 391.

56. *American Watchman,* Jan. 7, 1818; *Delaware Gazette,* Jan. 7, 1818.

57. LMcL to CMcL, March 20, 1818, McLane Papers.

58. LMcL to CMcL, March 8, 1818, *ibid.*

59. *Delaware Gazette,* Aug. 8, 1818.

60. *American Watchman,* Sept. 5, 1818.

61. *Ibid.,* Sept. 16, 1818.

62. *Ibid.,* Sept. 26, Oct. 3, 6, 1818.

63. *Governor's Register,* I, 157–158.

64. *American Watchman,* Sept. 26, 1818; *Delaware Gazette,* Oct. 3, 1818; LMcL to H. M. Ridgely, Oct. 2, 1818, McLane Papers.

65. LMcL to CMcL, Dec. 28, 1818, *ibid.*

66. LMcL to CMcL, Feb. 7, 1818, *ibid.*

67. LMcL to CMcL, Dec. 28, 1818, *ibid.*

68. LMcL to CMcL, Jan. 15, 1818, *ibid.*

69. LMcL to CMcL, Sat. afternoon [Feb. 15, 1818?], *ibid.*

70. Boorstin, *Delaware Cases,* I, 534–536.

71. Will Book S-1-280, Register of Wills, Wilmington.
72. *Ibid.*
73. LMcL to CMcL, Dec. 19, 1817; Jan. 21, 24, 1818, McLane Papers.
74. LMcL to CMcL, Jan. 24, 1818, *ibid.*
75. LMcL to CMcL, Feb. 7, 1818, *ibid.*
76. LMcL to CMcL, Sat. afternoon [Feb. 15, 1818?], *ibid.*
77. J. Bellach to LMcL, Feb. 4, 1818, *ibid.*
78. LMcL to CMcL, Feb. 24, 1818, *ibid.*
79. LMcL to CMcL, Nov. 19, and Sun. afternoon [Nov. 22], 1818, *ibid.*
80. LMcL to CMcL, Dec. 5, 1817, *ibid.*
81. LMcL to CMcL, Dec. 19, 1817, *ibid.*
82. LMcL to CMcL, Jan. 29, 1818, *ibid.*
83. LMcL to CMcL, Nov. 19, 1818, *ibid.*
84. *Annals of Congress,* 15th Cong., 2d sess., p. 291.
85. *Ibid.,* p. 311; *House Journal,* 15th Cong., 2d sess., p. 30.
86. *Annals of Congress,* 15th Cong., 2d sess., p. 319.
87. LMcL to CMcL, Nov. 25, 1818, McLane Papers.
88. LMcL to CMcL, Dec. 2, 1817, *ibid.*
89. *Annals of Congress,* 15th Cong., 2d sess., p. 319.
90. *Ibid.,* pp. 325–331, 333.
91. *Ibid.,* pp. 335, 340.
92. Power of attorney, LMcL to George B. Milligan, Feb. 4, 1817, Misc. Papers, NYPL.
93. Lists of stockholders in *House Document* No. 92, 15th Cong., 2d sess., pp. 169–493; Lunt, *Farmers Bank,* p. 78.
94. LMcL to [George Read], March 24, 1816, Read MSS, HSP.
95. *Ibid.;* LMcL to H. M. Ridgely, Jan. 13, 1816, Misc. MSS, NYHS.
96. *Delaware Gazette,* Jan. 15, 1817; Lunt, *Farmers Bank,* p. 82.
97. LMcL to J. J. Milligan, Jan. 31, 1818, Fisher Collection.
98. John Tyler to Dr. Curtis, Dec. 18, 1818, in Tyler, *Letters and Times of the Tylers,* I, 302–303.
99. Tyler, *The Tylers,* I, 303–304; Catterall, *The Second Bank of the United States,* p. 58; LMcL to CMcL, Dec. 28, 1818, McLane Papers. Catterall mistakenly lists Burwell Bassett instead of William Burwell as a member of the committee.
100. LMcL to CMcL, Dec. 31, 1818, McLane Papers.
101. LMcL to CMcL, Jan. 16, 1819, *ibid.*
102. R. King to C. King, Jan. 23, 1819, in King, *Correspondence,* VI, 195.
103. *House Document* No. 92, 15th Cong., 2 sess., p. 15; Catterall, *Second Bank,* p. 58; Hammond, *Banks and Politics,* p. 258.
104. Hammond, *Banks and Politics,* pp. 256–258, 260–262.
105. R. King to C. King, Jan. 16, 1819, in King, *Correspondence,* VI, 193.
106. LMcL to CMcL, Jan. 16, 1819, McLane Papers.
107. *House Committee Report* No. 92, 15th Cong., 2d sess., pp. 14, 15, 16.
108. LMcL to CMcL, Feb. 12, 1819, McLane Papers.

109. LMcL to CMcL, Feb. 21, 1819, *ibid.; Annals of Congress,* 15th Cong., 2d sess., pp. 1330–1331, 1350–1351.

110. *Annals of Congress,* 15th Cong., 2d sess., pp. 1411–1412, 1415.

111. LMcL to CMcL, Jan. 18, 1819, McLane Papers.

112. Adams, *Memoirs,* IV, 214–215, 239–240, 242.

113. LMcL to CMcL, Jan. 24, 1819 [incorrectly dated Jan. 23], McLane Papers.

114. LMcL to CMcL, Jan. 20, 1819, *ibid.*

115. LMcL to CMcL, Jan. 23, 1819, *ibid.*

116. LMcL to CMcL, Jan. 26, 1819, *ibid.*

117. *Annals of Congress,* 15th Cong., 2d sess., pp. 1135–1138; *House Journal,* 15th Cong., 2d sess., pp. 240, 241, 243, 245.

118. LMcL to CMcL, Feb. 9, 1819, McLane Papers.

119. LMcL to CMcL, Jan. 18, 1819, *ibid.*

120. LMcL to CMcL, Jan. 23, 1819, *ibid.*

121. LMcL to CMcL, Jan. 24, 1819 [incorrectly dated Jan. 23], *ibid.*

122. LMcL to CMcL, Feb. 12, 1819, *ibid.*

123. LMcL to CMcL, Feb. 21, 1819, *ibid.*

124. *House Journal,* 15th Cong., 2d sess., pp. 155, 177, 186, 210, 237.

125. LMcL to CMcL, Jan. 24, 1819, McLane Papers.

126. LMcL to John Way, Jan. 9, 1819, McLane Papers, HSD. *Cf.* LMcL to John C. Calhoun, March 15, 1819, Misc. Papers, NYPL.

127. LMcL to CMcL, Feb. 11, 1819, McLane Papers. *Cf.* LMcL to CMcL, Feb. 9, 12, 1819, *ibid.*

128. Bayard v. McLane, Harrington, *Reports of Cases,* III, 142, 145, 158.

129. McMaster, *Girard,* II, 359.

130. C. A. Rodney to James Monroe, Feb. 14, 1819, Monroe Papers, XXVII, LC.

131. McMaster, *Girard,* II, 359; Bayard v. McLane, Harrington, *Reports of Cases,* III, 155–156, 158.

132. Bayard v. McLane, Harrington, *Reports of Cases,* III, 154, 158.

133. LMcL to J. J. Milligan, Jan. 2, 1819, Milligan Papers, HSD.

134. LMcL to CMcL, Sun. afternoon [Feb. 14, 1819], Fisher Collection.

135. LMcL to CMcL, Feb. 16, 1819, McLane Papers.

136. LMcL to CMcL, Feb. 21, 1819, *ibid.*

137. LMcL to CMcL, Sun. afternoon [Feb. 14, 1819], Fisher Collection; Quincy, *Figures of the Past,* pp. 230–231.

138. LMcL to CMcL, Jan. 26, Feb. [6], 11, 16, 1819, McLane Papers.

CHAPTER FOUR: MISSOURI—AND MAKING ONE'S WAY

1. J. Bellach to LMcL, Feb. 4, 1818, McLane Papers.

2. LMcL to J. Bayard, Jan. 12, 1820, Hilles Collection.

3. Washington *National Intelligencer,* Dec. 7, 1819; Cooley, *Etiquette at Washington City,* pp. 37–38, 40, 49.

4. Smith, *First Forty Years,* pp. 148–149.

5. Cooley, *Etiquette,* pp. 43–46, 52–53.

6. *National Intelligencer,* Dec. 6, 1819.

7. LMcL to CMcL, March 23, 1820, Fisher Collection; LMcL to CMcL, Feb. 17, 1822, McLane Papers; CMcL to LMcL, Feb. 20, 1822, Fisher Collection; LMcL to J. A. Bayard [n.d., probably 1822], Hilles Collection.

8. LMcL to CMcL, Jan. 4, 1819, McLane Papers.

9. LMcL to Joseph S. Gibbs, Jan. 10, 1821, Vertical File, Maryland Historical Society.

10. LMcL to Lydia Johnston [Baltimore, 1856?], incomplete, Fisher Collection.

11. Catherine Milligan McLane's Memory Book, by courtesy of Louis McLane Hobbins, Madison, Wisconsin, now deceased.

12. LMcL to J. A. Bayard, Jan. 12, 1820, Hilles Collection.

13. LMcL to J. J. Milligan, Feb. 11, 1820, Fisher Collection; Young, *Washington Community,* pp. 216–217.

14. LMcL to J. A. Bayard, Jan. 12, 1820, Hilles Collection.

15. Garland, *John Randolph of Roanoke,* II, 217–218.

16. LMcL to CMcL, April 10, 1820, Fisher Collection.

17. LMcL to J. J. Milligan, Feb. 11, 1820, *ibid.*

18. John Randolph to LMcL, May 16, 1820, *ibid.*

19. Moore, *Missouri Controversy,* pp. 66, 342. I am indebted to Moore's work for the general thread of this story.

20. *Ibid.,* p. 34; *House Journal,* 15th Cong., 2d sess., p. 30; *Annals of Congress,* 15th Cong., 2d sess., p. 311.

21. *Annals of Congress,* 15th Cong., 2d sess., pp. 1214–1216; *House Journal,* 15th Cong., 2d sess., pp. 273, 275.

22. Moore, *Missouri Controversy,* pp. 34–35; Scharf, *History of Delaware,* II, 827; *Governor's Register,* I, 141.

23. LMcL to CMcL, Jan. 26, 1819, McLane Papers.

24. *Annals of Congress,* 15th Cong., 2d sess., pp. 1227–1235; Moore, *Missouri Controversy,* p. 64.

25. *House Journal,* 15th Cong., 2d sess., pp. 284–286, 289, 291, 294, 337, 340.

26. Moore, *Missouri Controversy,* pp. 67ff.

27. LMcL to J. A. Bayard, Jan. 12, 1820, Hilles Collection.

28. LMcL to [C. A. Rodney], Jan. 14, 1820, Rodney Papers, Society Collection, HSD.

29. *Delaware House Journal,* 1820, p. 14.

30. *Ibid.;* Moore, *Missouri Controversy,* p. 73.

31. LMcL to William T. Read, March 24, April 27, 1854, Richard S. Rodney Collection, HSD.

32. *Delaware House Journal,* 1820, pp. 26–27, 32, 48, 50; *Delaware Senate Journal,* 1820, pp. 25–26, 43.

33. LMcL to [C. A. Rodney], Jan. 31, 1820, Brown Collection, HSD.

34. *Delaware Gazette,* Feb. 23, 1820.

35. John A. Munroe, "Willard Hall," *Delaware History,* XI (1964–1965), 36–39.

36. *Annals of Congress,* 16th Cong., 1st sess., pp. 1138–1169; Moore, *Missouri Controversy,* p. 122.

37. *Annals of Congress,* 16th Cong., 1st sess., p. 1409.

38. *House Journal,* 16th Cong., 1st sess., pp. 240, 242, 243, 261, 263, 264, 266, 270, 276, 278.

39. LMcL to CMcL, April 22, 1820, Fisher Collection.

40. Moore, *Missouri Controversy,* p. 221; *Delaware House Journal,* 1820, p. 60; *Niles' Register,* XVII (Jan. 22, 1820), 343.

41. LMcL to [C. A. Rodney], Jan. 31, 1820, Brown Collection, HSD.

42. C. A. Rodney to LMcL, Feb. 5, 1820, *ibid.*

43. LMcL to J. J. Milligan, Feb. 11, 1820, Fisher Collection.

44. LMcL to CMcL, Feb. 16, 1819, McLane Papers.

45. LMcL to J. J. Milligan, March 24, 1820, Fisher Collection.

46. LMcL to CMcL, April 13, 1820, *ibid.*

47. LMcL to CMcL, May 3, 1820, *ibid.*

48. LMcL to CMcL, April 10, 1820; John Randolph to LMcL, May 16, 1820, *ibid.*

49. LMcL to CMcL, May 8, 1820, *ibid.;* LMcL to Victor du Pont, March 12, 1820, V. du Pont Papers, EMHL. *Cf.* Ninian Edwards to William H. Crawford, Jan. 11, 1821, in Edwards, *The Edwards Papers,* p. 184.

50. [Bringhurst,] *The Wilmingtoniad,* p. 7.

51. *Niles' Register,* XVII (Dec. 11, 1819), 233.

52. Quoted by Edmund Quincy, *Life of Josiah Quincy* (Boston, 1867), p. 374.

53. William Plumer, Jr., to William Plumer, April 10, 1820, in Plumer, *Missouri Compromise and Presidential Politics,* p. 49; Adams, *Memoirs,* V, 57–58, 60.

54. John M. Clayton to James Black, Jr., Aug. 9, 1820, Roberts Collection, Haverford College.

55. John Fisher to C. A. Rodney, Sept. 13, 1820, Rodney Papers, Society Collection, HSD.

56. "Charity," in the *Delaware Gazette,* Sept. 1, 1820.

57. *Delaware Gazette,* Aug. 29, 1820.

58. John Fisher to C. A. Rodney, Sept. 13, 1820, Rodney Papers, Society Collection, HSD.

59. *Delaware Gazette,* Sept. 22, 1820.

60. *Ibid.,* Oct. 3, 1820.

61. Dr. Allen McLane to Ezekiel Cooper, Sept. 11, 1820, Cooper MSS, XV, Garrett Biblical Institute, Evanston, Illinois.

62. *Delaware House Journal,* 1820, pp. 21–22; Scharf, *History of Delaware,* I, 306, 307; *Governor's Register,* I, 174–175.

63. LMcL to [William Hill Wells?], Oct. 10, 1820, Roberts Collection, Haverford College.

64. Scharf, *History of Delaware,* I, 306; *Governor's Register,* I, 174–175.

65. John Fisher to C. A. Rodney, Sept. 13, 1820, Rodney Papers, Society Collection, HSD.

66. LMcL to C. A. Rodney, Sept. 23, 1820, *ibid.*

67. Stephen Pleasonton to C. A. Rodney, Oct. 11, 1820, Brown Collection, HSD.

68. LMcL to CMcL, Nov. 20, 1820, Fisher Collection.

69. *Annals of Congress*, 16th Cong., 2d sess., p. 439; *House Journal*, 16th Cong., 2d sess., p. 9.

70. LMcL to CMcL, Nov. 20, 1820, Fisher Collection.

71. LMcL to CMcL, Jan. 17, 1821, *ibid.*

72. LMcL to CMcL, Jan. 12, 1821 [incorrectly dated 1820], Batchelder Papers, HSD.

73. LMcL to CMcL [*c.* Feb. 5, 1821], Fisher Collection.

74. Moore, *Missouri Controversy*, Chap. V.

75. LMcL to CMcL, Nov. 23, 1820, Fisher Collection.

76. LMcL to CMcL, Nov. 24, 1820, *ibid.*

77. LMcL to CMcL, Dec. 12, 1820, *ibid.*

78. LMcL to CMcL, Jan. 10, 1821, *ibid.*

79. *Annals of Congress*, 16th Cong., 2d sess., pp. 608, 610–611, 614–615, 619–620, 621, 626.

80. *Ibid.*, pp. 635, 638.

81. LMcL to CMcL, Dec. 12, 1820, Fisher Collection.

82. LMcL to C. A. Rodney, Jan. 9, 1821, McLane Papers, HSD.

83. *Annals of Congress*, 16th Cong., 2d sess., pp. 842, 844.

84. *Ibid.*, pp. 999–1000, 1002.

85. *Ibid.*, pp. 1007–1024; *House Journal*, 16th Cong., 2d sess., p. 193.

86. William Plumer, Jr., to William Plumer, Feb. 2, 1821, in Plumer, *Missouri Compromise and Presidential Politics*, p. 31.

87. Moore, *Missouri Controversy*, pp. 154–157.

88. *Delaware Senate Journal*, 1821, p. 58; *Governor's Register*, I, 178.

89. H. F. du Pont Winterthur MSS, EMHL; *House Journal*, 16th Cong., 2d sess., p. 254.

90. LMcL to CMcL, Feb. 16, 1821, Fisher Collection.

91. LMcL to CMcL, Jan. 12, 1821 [incorrectly dated 1820], Batchelder Papers.

92. LMcL to CMcL, April 13, 22, 1820, Fisher Collection.

93. LMcL to CMcL, May 3, 1820, *ibid.*

94. LMcL to CMcL, Jan. 10, 1821, *ibid.*

95. William Plumer, Jr., to William Plumer, Nov. 24, 1820, in Plumer, *Missouri Compromise and Presidential Politics*, pp. 57–58.

96. LMcL to CMcL, Jan. 10, 1821, Fisher Collection.

97. LMcL to CMcL [*c.* Feb. 5, 1821], *ibid.*

98. LMcL to CMcL, Feb. 9, 1821, *ibid.*

99. LMcL to CMcL, Nov. 13, 1820, *ibid.*

100. LMcL to CMcL, Nov. 20, 1820, *ibid.*

101. LMcL to CMcL, Jan. 10, 1821, *ibid.*

102. LMcL to CMcL, Jan. 13, 1821, *ibid.*

103. *Delaware Senate Journal,* 1821, pp. 23, 91, 120.

104. LMcL to CMcL, Jan. 17, 1821, Fisher Collection.

105. LMcL to CMcL, Feb. 9, 1821, *ibid.*

106. LMcL to CMcL, Nov. 23, 1820, *ibid.*

107. LMcL to CMcL, Jan. 12, 1821 [incorrectly dated 1820], Batchelder Papers.

108. LMcL to CMcL, Feb. 9, 1821, Fisher Collection.

109. Boorstin, *Delaware Cases,* II, 593, 598, 611, 644, 651, 653; Bates, *Delaware Chancery Reports,* I, 146–149, 177–184.

110. For the Bauduy–du Pont litigation, see Boorstin, *Delaware Cases,* III, 219–340.

111. LMcL to E. I. du Pont, Sept. 21, 1815, Old Stone Office Records, Accession 500, EMHL; James Rogers to E. I. du Pont, April 15, 1824, *ibid.* Also in du Pont, *Life of E. I. du Pont,* X, 113; B. G. du Pont, *E. I. du Pont de Nemours and Company* (Boston, 1920), p. 45.

112. Bates, *Delaware Chancery Reports,* I, 77–88; LMcL to E. I. du Pont, July 14, 1818, in du Pont, *Life of E. I. du Pont,* X, 294–295.

113. Holland, *The Garesché, de Bauduy, and des Chapelles Families,* p. 131.

114. LMcL to Victor du Pont, Feb. 20, 1821, H. F. du Pont Winterthur MSS, EMHL.

115. Boorstin, *Delaware Cases,* III, 308.

116. *Ibid.,* p. 3.

CHAPTER FIVE: A MAN OF REPUTATION

1. Wiltse, *Calhoun, Nationalist,* pp. 235–236.

2. *Niles' Register,* XXI (Dec. 15, 1821), 242; Adams, *Memoirs,* V, 428.

3. William Plumer, Jr., to William Plumer, Dec. 3, 1821, in Plumer, *Missouri Compromise and Presidential Politics,* p. 65.

4. *House Journal,* 16th Cong., 2d sess., pp. 157, 161; *Annals of Congress,* 15th Cong., 2d sess., pp. 514, 1165; 16th Cong., 2d sess., p. 937.

5. *Niles' Register,* XXI (Dec. 15, 1821), 242.

6. Stephen Pleasonton to C. A. Rodney, July 26, 1821, Brown Collection, HSD.

7. Adams, *Memoirs,* V, 428; *Niles' Register,* XXI (Dec. 15, 1821), 242.

8. Adams, *Memoirs,* V, 437.

9. LMcL to CMcL, Dec. 4, 1821, McLane Papers.

10. Romulus M. Saunders to Thomas Ruffin, Dec. 15, 1821, in Ruffin, *Papers,* I, 255.

11. Adams, *Memoirs,* V, 451.

12. William Plumer, Jr., to William Plumer, Dec. 3, 1821, in Plumer, *Missouri Compromise and Presidential Politics,* p. 66.

13. LMcL to CMcL, Dec. 4, 1821, McLane Papers.

14. LMcL to CMcL, Jan. 1, 1822, *ibid.*

15. *Delaware Gazette,* Oct. 9, 1821.

16. *Ibid.*, Sept. 28, Oct. 2, 5, 1821.

17. John Fisher to C. A. Rodney, Jan. 2, 1822, John Fisher Papers, HSD.

18. LMcL to CMcL, Jan. 5, 1821, McLane Papers.

19. CMcL to LMcL, Jan. 4, 1822, Fisher Collection.

20. John Fisher to C. A. Rodney, Jan. 2, 1822, John Fisher Papers, HSD; CMcL to LMcL, Jan. 4, 1822, Fisher Collection.

21. *Delaware Senate Journal*, 1822, pp. 30–31; *Delaware House Journal*, 1822, pp. 56–57.

22. John Fisher to C. A. Rodney, Jan. 11, 1822, John Fisher Papers, HSD.

23. *Delaware Gazette*, Jan. 25, 1822.

24. LMcL to CMcL, Jan. 7, 1822 [incorrectly dated 1821], McLane Papers.

25. LMcL to J. J. Milligan, Feb. 9, 1822, Milligan Papers, HSD.

26. LMcL to CMcL, Jan. 7, 1822 [incorrectly dated 1821], McLane Papers.

27. LMcL to J. J. Milligan, Jan. 19, 1822, Milligan Papers, HSD.

28. CMcL to LMcL, Jan. 9, 1822, McLane Papers.

29. LMcL to J. J. Milligan [Jan. 30, 1822], Milligan Papers, HSD; J. J. Milligan to LMcL, Jan. 31, 1822, Batchelder Collection.

30. *House Journal*, 17th Cong., 1st sess., p. 29.

31. *Ibid.*, 17th Cong., 1st sess., p. 81; LMcL to CMcL, Dec. 23, 1821; Jan. 5, Feb. 7, 1822, McLane Papers.

32. *Annals of Congress*, 17th Cong., 1st sess., pp. 807, 881.

33. *House Journal*, 17th Cong., 1st sess., p. 145.

34. *Annals of Congress*, 17th Cong., 1st sess., pp. 1013–1015.

35. LMcL to CMcL, Dec. 23, 1821, McLane Papers.

36. LMcL to CMcL, Dec. 29, 1821, *ibid.*

37. CMcL to LMcL, Dec. 25, 1821, Fisher Collection.

38. LMcL to CMcL, Dec. 29, 1821, McLane Papers.

39. Van Buren, *Autobiography*, p. 574.

40. LMcL to CMcL, Jan. 2, 1822 [incorrectly dated 1821], McLane Papers.

41. LMcL to CMcL, Dec. 25, 1821, *ibid.*

42. LMcL to CMcL, Dec. 29, 1821, *ibid.*

43. LMcL to CMcL, Dec. 4, 19, 23, 28, 29, 1821, *ibid.*

44. LMcL to CMcL, Dec. 28, 1821, *ibid.*

45. CMcL to LMcL, Dec. 4, 1821, *ibid.*

46. LMcL to CMcL, Jan. 9, 1822, *ibid.*

47. LMcL to CMcL, Dec. 23, 1821, *ibid.*

48. LMcL to CMcL, Dec. 25, 1821, *Ibid.*

49. LMcL to CMcL, Dec. 23, 1821; Feb. 14, April 28, 1822, *ibid.*

50. Van Buren, *Autobiography*, p. 574.

51. LMcL to CMcL, Feb. 17, 1822, McLane Papers.

52. LMcL to CMcL [Feb. 23, 1822], *ibid.*

53. *Ibid.*

54. LMcL to CMcL, March 18, 1822, *ibid.*

55. LMcL to CMcL, May 3, 1822, *ibid.*

56. LMcL to CMcL, April 23, 1822, *ibid.*

57. LMcL to CMcL, March 3, 1822, *ibid.*

58. LMcL to CMcL, March 2, 1822, *ibid.*
59. LMcL to CMcL, Feb. 14, 1822, *ibid.*
60. LMcL to CMcL, April 18, 1822, *ibid.*
61. LMcL to CMcL, April 21, 1822, *ibid.*
62. LMcL to CMcL, April 19, 1822, *ibid.*
63. LMcL to CMcL, April 25, 1822, *ibid.*
64. Quoted in Lynch, *Fifty Years of Party Warfare,* p. 251.
65. LMcL to CMcL, Feb. 9, 1822, McLane Papers.
66. LMcL to CMcL, Feb. 7, 1822, *ibid.*
67. LMcL to CMcL, Jan. 4, 1822, *ibid.*
68. CMcL to LMcL, Jan. 5, 1822, Fisher Collection.
69. *House Journal,* 17th Cong., 1st sess., p. 284.
70. *Annals of Congress,* 17th Cong., 1st sess., pp. 620–621.
71. *American State Papers: Public Lands,* III, 538; White, *Jeffersonians,* pp. 523–525; H. Warren, "Replication," in C. W. Alvord, *Governor Edward Coles* (Springfield, 1920), p. 340; Edwards, *History of Illinois,* p. 258.
72. Adams, *Memoirs,* V, 482–483; J. C. Calhoun to N. Edwards, Oct. 5, 1822, in Edwards, *History of Illinois,* p. 493.
73. Alexander Davidson and Bernard Stuve, *A Complete History of Illinois from 1673 to 1873* (Springfield, 1874), p. 337n; Adams, *Memoirs,* V, 483.
74. *House Journal,* 17th Cong., 1st sess., p. 284.
75. *American State Papers: Public Lands,* III, 538–540, 543.
76. R. M. Saunders to Bartlett Yancy, April 3, 1822, in Saunders, "Letters of Romulus M. Saunders to Bartlett Yancy," *North Carolina Historical Review,* VIII, 432.
77. *American State Papers: Public Lands,* III, 538.
78. *Ibid.,* pp. 538, 540.
79. LMcL to CMcL, March 21 and 22, 1822, McLane Papers.
80. *Annals of Congress,* 17th Cong., 1st sess., pp. 1405–1407, 1887.
81. *National Intelligencer,* March 30, 1822. The *Annals,* apparently incorrectly, have McLane making the select committee report. Niles agrees with the *Intelligencer.*
82. LMcL to CMcL, April 19, 1822, McLane Papers.
83. Edwards, *History of Illinois,* p. 271.
84. LMcL to CMcL, April 16, 1822, McLane Papers.
85. LMcL to CMcL, April 18, 1822, *ibid.*
86. LMcL to CMcL, April 30, 1822, *ibid.*
87. LMcL to CMcL, April 21, 1822, *ibid.*
88. LMcL to CMcL, May 4, 1822, *ibid.*
89. LMcL to CMcL, Sun. morning [May 5, 1822], *ibid.*
90. LMcL to CMcL, Jan. 7, 1822 [incorrectly dated 1821], *ibid.*
91. CMcL to LMcL, Jan. 9, 1822, *ibid.*
92. CMcL to LMcL, Jan. 11, 1822, *ibid.*
93. LMcL to J. J. Milligan, Feb. 26, 1822, Milligan Papers, HSD.
94. LMcL to CMcL, Feb. 22, 1822, McLane Papers.
95. LMcL to Rebecca McLane, May 14, 1822, *ibid.*

96. "To the Conscientious Freemen of the State of Delaware," Delaware Broadside Collection, Wilmington Institute Free Library.

97. 1820 Census, Delaware, p. 201.

98. *Delaware Gazette,* Oct. 1, 1822.

99. *Governor's Register,* I, 190–191.

100. *Delaware Gazette,* Oct. 8, 1822.

101. *Ibid.,* Feb. 7, 18, 1823.

102. C. A. Rodney to James Monroe, Feb. 7, 1823, Monroe Papers, XXXII, LC.

103. William P. Brobson to [C. A. Rodney], Feb. 5, 1823, *ibid.*

104. *Delaware Gazette,* Feb. 11, 1823.

105. Victor du Pont to the editor, *American Watchman,* April 25, 1823, from notes at EMHL.

106. LMcL to V. du Pont, Feb. 20, 1821, H. F. du Pont Winterthur MSS, EMHL.

107. LMcL to E. I. du Pont de Nemours and Co., March 30, 1820, Du Pont Company Papers, EMHL.

108. LMcL to unknown addressee [V. du Pont?], Feb. 11, 1823, H. F. du Pont Winterthur MSS, EMHL.

109. *Diary of George Brydges Rodney,* p. 14.

110. Romulus M. Saunders to Thomas Ruffin, Dec. 15, 1821, in Ruffin, *Papers,* I, 255.

111. CMcL to [AMcL], Dec. 22 [1822], Fisher Collection.

112. Mary K. Sims to LMcL, Jan. 29, 1823, McLane Papers.

113. CMcL to AMcL, Dec. 12, 1822, Fisher Collection.

114. LMcL to unknown addressee, Feb. 11, 1823, H. F. du Pont Winterthur MSS, EMHL.

115. *Ibid.*

116. LMcL to CMcL, April 29, 1820, Batchelder Papers, HSD; *Annals of Congress,* 16th Cong., 1st sess., p. 2116.

117. *Annals of Congress,* 16th Cong., 1st sess., pp. 2093–2115.

118. LMcL to J. J. Milligan, April 13, 1824, Milligan Papers, HSD.

119. Garland, *John Randolph of Roanoke,* II, 216.

120. LMcL to J. J. Milligan, April 13, 1824, Milligan Papers, HSD.

121. *Annals of Congress,* 18th Cong., 1st sess., pp. 2314–2316; Bruce, *John Randolph of Roanoke,* I, 492–495; Garland, *John Randolph of Roanoke,* II, 215–218.

122. Garland, *John Randolph of Roanoke,* II, 217.

123. LMcL to J. J. Milligan, April 13, 1824, Milligan Papers, HSD.

124. *Annals of Congress,* 18th Cong., 1st sess., pp. 2316, 2342, 2429.

125. LMcL to CMcL, May 7, 1824, McLane Papers.

126. LMcL to CMcL, May 8, 1824, *ibid.*

127. LMcL to CMcL, May 13, 1824, *ibid.*

128. LMcL to CMcL, May 15, 1824, *ibid.*

129. LMcL to CMcL, Dec. 24, 1824, *ibid.*

130. *Annals of Congress,* 16th Cong., 1st sess., p. 2115.

131. *Ibid.*, 15th Cong., 2d sess., pp. 1150, 1152; 17th Cong., 2d sess., pp. 1029–1030, 1072–1075; 18th Cong., 1st sess., pp. 1217–1232.

132. *Ibid.*, 18th Cong., 1st sess., pp. 1217–1231.

133. *Ibid.*, pp. 1309–1336.

134. *Ibid.*, p. 1469.

135. *Ibid.*, pp. 1231–1232.

136. *Ibid.*, 15th Cong., 1st sess., p. 445.

137. *Ibid.*, pp. 1394–1399.

138. *Register of Debates*, 20th Cong., 2d sess., pp. 60–61.

139. Gilpin, *A Memoir on the Rise, Progress, and Present State of the Chesapeake and Delaware Canal;* Livingood, *The Philadelphia–Baltimore Trade Rivalry, 1780–1860,* Chap. IV; Gray, *The National Waterway: A History of the Chesapeake and Delaware Canal, 1769–1965.*

140. Joshua Gilpin to Paul Beck, Sept. 10, 1821, M. Carey, Correspondence on Internal Improvements, Library Company of Philadelphia (kindness of Ralph Gray).

141. *Register of Debates,* 18th Cong., 2d sess., pp. 216–218, 220.

142. *Ibid.*, pp. 290–297.

143. *Ibid.*, pp. 298, 333–334.

144. *Ibid.*, p. 679.

145. Henry D. Gilpin to Joshua Gilpin, Feb. 28, 1805, Henry D. Gilpin Collection, HSD.

146. Henry D. Gilpin to Joshua Gilpin, March 2, 1825, *ibid.*

147. Henry D. Gilpin to Joshua Gilpin, March 3–4, 1825, *ibid.*

CHAPTER SIX: THE CRAWFORD CAMPAIGN

1. LMcL to M. Van Buren, April 30, 1823, in Van Buren, *Autobiography,* p. 575.

2. Jeremiah Mason to Christopher Gore, April 17, 1823, in *Memoir of Jeremiah Mason,* pp. 264–265.

3. Morison, *Life of Harrison Gray Otis,* II, 243.

4. *Delaware Gazette,* Jan. 21, Oct. 10, 1823.

5. John Brinckloe to Victor du Pont, Sept. 15, 1823, Victor du Pont Correspondence, Old Stone Office Records, Accession 500, EMHL.

6. LMcL to J. A. Bayard, Dec. 16, 1823, Hilles Collection.

7. LMcL to J. A. Bayard, Dec. 22, 1823, *ibid.*

8. LMcL to J. A. Bayard, Jan. 14, 1824, *ibid.*

9. LMcL to J. A. Bayard, Dec. 16, 1823, *ibid.*

10. LMcL to J. A. Bayard, Dec. 22, 1823, *ibid.*

11. Romulus Saunders to Bartlett Yancy, Dec. 7, 1823, in "Saunders-Yancy Letters," *North Carolina Historical Review,* VIII, 439.

12. LMcL to J. A. Bayard, Jan. 4, 1824, Hilles Collection.

13. Adams, *Memoirs,* VI, 237, 246–247.

14. Van Deusen, *Clay,* p. 174; Adams, *Memoirs,* VI, 236, 241.

15. Romulus Saunders to Bartlett Yancy, March 1, 1824, in "Saunders-Yancy Letters," *North Carolina Historical Review*, VIII, 443.

16. *Niles' Register*, XXV (Feb. 21, 1824), 392.

17. George M. Bibb to J. J. Crittenden, March 8, 1824, in Mrs. Chapman Coleman, *The Life of John J. Crittenden* (Philadelphia, 1871), I, 61.

18. Wiltse, *Calhoun, Nationalist*, pp. 282–283.

19. Albert Gallatin to Albert R. Gallatin, March 10, 1824, Gallatin Papers, NYHS.

20. LMcL to J. A. Bayard, Feb. 22, 1824, Hilles Collection.

21. Daniel Webster to Jeremiah Mason, Feb. 15, 1824, in *Memoir of Jeremiah Mason*, pp. 275–276.

22. Adams, *Memoirs*, VI, 267.

23. LMcL to J. J. Milligan, April 10, 1824, Milligan Papers, HSD.

24. William Plumer, Jr., to William Plumer, April 1, 1824, in Plumer, *Missouri Compromise and Presidential Politics*, p. 108.

25. Daniel P. Cook to Ninian Edwards, April 17, 1824, in Edwards, *Papers*, p. 224.

26. LMcL to J. A. Bayard, April 12, 1824, Hilles Collection.

27. *Annals of Congress*, 18th Cong., 1st sess., pp. 2474–2477.

28. LMcL to J. Gales, April 22 [1824], Misc. Papers, NYPL.

29. LMcL to CMcL, May 7, 1824, McLane Papers.

30. *Annals of Congress*, 18th Cong., 1st sess., pp. 2552–2555.

31. LMcL to CMcL, May 8, 1824, McLane Papers.

32. LMcL to CMcL, May 11, 1824, *ibid.;* LMcL to J. A. Bayard, May 11, 1824, Hilles Collection.

33. LMcL to CMcL, May 22, 1824, McLane Papers.

34. Lynch, *Fifty Years of Party Warfare*, pp. 288–289; Wiltse, *Calhoun, Nationalist*, pp. 262–263, 292.

35. D. Webster to J. Mason, May 9, 1824, in *Memoir of Jeremiah Mason*, p. 285.

36. CMcL to LMcL, May [20], 1824, McLane Papers.

37. LMcL to CMcL, Sun. [May 23, 1824], Fisher Collection.

38. Lydia Sims to CMcL, Jan. 10 [1824], *ibid.*

39. *Ibid.*

40. Mrs. Edward Livingston to Mrs. Montgomery, Feb. 16, 1824, in Hunt, *Memoir of Mrs. Edward Livingston*, pp. 75–76.

41. Mrs. Jackson to Mrs. Kingsley, Dec. 23, 1824, in Parton, *Jackson*, III, 52–53.

42. LMcL to CMcL, May 21, 1824, McLane Papers.

43. LMcL to Robert McLane, May 16, 1824; LMcL to CMcL, May 12, 1824, *ibid.*

44. LMcL to CMcL, May 7, 8, 1824, *ibid.*

45. CMcL to LMcL, May 13, 1824, *ibid.*

46. LMcL to CMcL, May 11, 15, 1824, *ibid.*

47. LMcL to CMcL, Sun. [May 23, 1824], Fisher Collection.

48. Henry D. Gilpin to Joshua Gilpin, May 29, 30, 1823, Henry D. Gilpin

Letters, HSD; LMcL to M. Van Buren, April 30, 1823, in Van Buren, *Autobiography*, p. 576.

49. CMcL to LMcL, May 14, 1824 [incorrectly dated 1823], Fisher Collection.

50. LMcL to CMcL, May 15, 1824, McLane Papers.

51. CMcL to LMcL, May 18, 1824, *ibid.*

52. LMcL to CMcL, May 22, 1824, *ibid.*

53. CMcL to LMcL, May 15, 1824, *ibid.*

54. LMcL to CMcL, May 17, 1824, *ibid.*

55. LMcL to J. A. Bayard, Feb. 1, 1824, Hilles Collection.

56. LMcL to J. A. Bayard, Jan. 4, 1824, *ibid.*

57. LMcL to J. A. Bayard, April 12, 1824, *ibid.*

58. LMcL to J. A. Bayard, May 11, 1824, *ibid.;* LMcL to CMcL, May 15, 1824, McLane Papers.

59. J. G. Brincklé to W. P. Brobson, May 19, 1824, Brincklé Collection, HSD.

60. LMcL to CMcL, Mon. morning [May 24 or 31, 1824], McLane Papers.

61. *American Watchman*, June 8, 1824 (clipping inserted in MS by William T. Read, "Report on the Destruction of A Large Part of New Castle, Delaware, by Fire," April 26, 1824, in HSD); LMcL to J. Howard March and Co., Nov. 29, 1824, Batchelder Collection.

62. *American Watchman*, Oct. 1, 15, 1824.

63. *Governor's Register*, I, 190–191, 211–212; *American Watchman*, Oct. 12, 1824.

64. J. G. Brincklé to W. P. Brobson [1824], Brincklé Collection, HSD; J. G. Brincklé to J. M. Clayton, Sept. 24, 1824, Clayton Papers, LC.

65. *American Watchman*, Oct. 5, 1824.

66. *Governor's Register*, I, 157–158, 174–175, 190–191, 211–212; Scharf, *History of Delaware*, I, 307; *Delaware Senate Journal*, 1822–23, pp. 23–24.

67. *Niles' Register*, XXVII (Nov. 20, 27, 1824), 186–187, 194–195; *Delaware Gazette*, Dec. 9, 1824.

68. J. G. Brincklé to J. M. Clayton, Sept. 24, 1824, Clayton Papers, LC.

69. LMcL to Samuel Smith, Nov. 17, 1824, Roberts Collection, Haverford College.

70. J. G. Brincklé to J. M. Clayton, Sept. 24, 1824, Clayton Papers, LC; Joseph H. Rogers, "Recollections," pp. 47–48; *Niles' Register*, XXVII (Oct. 16, 1824), 101–102; *American Watchman*, Oct. 5, 8, 19, 1824; Levasseur, *Lafayette in America*, I, 159–160; Scharf, *History of Delaware*, I, 308; Adams, *Memoirs*, VI, 425.

71. LMcL to CMcL, Dec. 6, Thurs. [Dec. 9], Dec. 24, 1824, McLane Papers; Levasseur, *Lafayette in America*, II, 13–15, 18–19; *House Journal*, 18th Cong., 2d sess., pp. 28, 29, 73.

72. LMcL to CMcL, Dec. 24, 1824; Jan. 2, 4, 1825, McLane Papers.

73. LMcL to CMcL, Jan. 13, 1825, *ibid.; American Watchman*, Aug. 30, 1825; Levasseur, *Lafayette in America*, II, 234–236.

74. Van Buren, *Autobiography*, p. 149.

75. Adams, *Memoirs*, VI, 493.

76. Romulus Saunders to Bartlett Yancy, Dec. 10, 1824, in "Saunders-Yancy Letters," *North Carolina Historical Review*, VIII, 447.

77. Adams, *Memoirs*, VI, 453–454.

78. LMcL to CMcL, Jan. 31, 1825, McLane Papers.

79. B. F. Butler to Mrs. Butler, May 7, 1823, Butler Papers, box 2, folder 3, New York State Library, Albany.

80. A. Gallatin to Jean Badollet, July 29, 1824, Gallatin Papers, NYHS.

81. Adams, *Memoirs*, VI, 391.

82. John C. Calhoun to Joel R. Poinsett, July 8, 1824, in Calhoun, *Correspondence, American Historical Association Annual Report*, 1899, II, 224; John McLean to John W. Taylor, Oct. 25, 1824, Taylor Papers, NYHS; Walter Lowrie to A. Gallatin, Sept. 25, 1824, Gallatin Papers, NYHS; LMcL to Gales and Seaton, Oct. 21, 1824, Misc. Papers, NYPL; Van Buren, *Autobiography*, pp. 665–666.

83. Shipp, *Giant Days*, pp. 176–177; Parton, *Jackson*, III, 59.

84. LMcL to Gales and Seaton, Oct. 21, 1824, Misc. Papers, NYPL; LMcL to Samuel Smith, Nov. 17, 1824, Roberts Collection, Haverford College; LMcL to Samuel Smith, Nov. 19, 1824, Samuel Moyerman Collection, University of Delaware.

85. LMcL to Gales and Seaton, Nov. 19, 1824, Misc. Papers, NYPL.

86. LMcL to CMcL, Dec. 6, 1824, McLane Papers.

87. Van Buren, *Autobiography*, p. 150.

88. Albert Gallatin to Frances Gallatin, Nov. 26, 1824, Gallatin Papers, NYHS.

89. Van Buren, *Political Parties*, p. 3.

90. Van Buren, *Autobiography*, p. 150.

91. Lynch, *Fifty Years*, p. 293.

92. S. Van Rensselaer to DeWitt Clinton, Dec. 18, 1824, quoted in Fink, "Van Rensselaer and the House Election of 1825," *New York History*, XXXII, 327.

93. Romulus Saunders to Bartlett Yancy, Jan. 18, 1825, in "Saunders-Yancy Letters," *North Carolina Historical Review*, VIII, 450–451.

94. LMcL to J. A. Bayard, Nov. 18, 1824, Hilles Collection.

95. LMcL to CMcL, Dec. 29, 1824, McLane Papers.

96. R. King's notes, Jan. 29, 1825, in King, *Correspondence*, VI, 583.

97. J. Buchanan to Thomas Elder, Jan. 2, 1820, in Buchanan, *Works*, I, 120.

98. LMcL to [CMcL], [Jan. 1, 1825], [incorrectly dated 1826 in margin], McLane Papers.

99. LMcL to J. A. Bayard, Jan. 9, 1825, Hilles Collection.

100. LMcL to J. A. Bayard, Jan. 24, 1825, *ibid.*

101. Walter Lowrie to A. Gallatin, Feb. 3, 1825, Gallatin Papers, NYHS.

102. Adams, *Memoirs*, VI, 493.

103. LMcL to CMcL, Feb. 6, 1825, McLane Papers.

104. Romulus Saunders to Bartlett Yancy, Feb. 8, 1825, in "Saunders-Yancy Letters," *North Carolina Historical Review,* VIII, 451.

105. LMcL to CMcL, Jan. 28, 1825, McLane Papers.

106. LMcL to CMcL, Jan. 19, 1825, *ibid.*

107. LMcL to [CMcL], [Jan. 1, 1825], [incorrectly dated 1826], *ibid.*

108. LMcL to CMcL, Feb. 6, 1825, *ibid.*

109. LMcL to CMcL, Feb. 8, 1825, *ibid.*

110. LMcL to CMcL, Feb. 11, 1825, *ibid.*

111. LMcL to CMcL, Feb. 15, 1825, *ibid.*

112. LMcL to CMcL, Feb. 20, 1825, *ibid.*

113. LMcL to CMcL, Feb. 20, 1825, *ibid.*

114. LMcL to CMcL, Fri. evening [Dec. 4, 1825], *ibid.*

115. LMcL to CMcL, Dec. 7, 1824, and Thurs. evening [Dec. 9, 1824], *ibid.*

116. LMcL to CMcL, Dec. 24, 1824, *ibid.;* list of guests, Dec. 23, 1824, in J. Q. Adams, "Rubbish III," Adams Papers, reel 51, Massachusetts Historical Society; Adams, *Memoirs,* VI, 453.

117. LMcL to CMcL, Dec. 29, 1824, McLane Papers.

118. William Plumer, Jr., to William Plumer, Dec. 25, 1824, in Plumer, *Missouri Compromise and Presidential Politics,* pp. 125–126; Adams, *Memoirs,* VI, 453, 455.

119. Adams, *Memoirs,* VI, 470–478; William Plumer, Jr., to William Plumer, Jan. 24, 1825, in Plumer, *Missouri Compromise and Presidential Politics,* p. 136.

120. LMcL to CMcL, Thurs. evening [Dec. 9, 1824], McLane Papers.

121. LMcL to J. J. Milligan, Jan. 18, 1825, Milligan Papers, HSD.

122. LMcL to CMcL, Jan. 13, 1825, McLane Papers.

123. *Ibid.;* Adams, *Memoirs,* VI, 466.

124. Parton, *Jackson,* III, 15.

125. *Register of Debates,* 18th Cong., 2d sess., pp. 420–422.

126. *Ibid.,* p. 428.

127. *Ibid.,* pp. 428–431.

128. *Ibid.,* pp. 445–454.

129. LMcL to CMcL, Feb. 5, 7, 1825, McLane Papers.

130. Romulus Saunders to Bartlett Yancy, Feb. 8, 1825, in "Saunders-Yancy Letters," *North Carolina Historical Review,* VIII, 451.

131. *Register of Debates,* 18th Cong., 2d sess., pp. 498–508.

132. *Ibid.,* pp. 509–510.

133. LMcL to CMcL, Feb. 7, 1825, McLane Papers.

134. LMcL to CMcL, Feb. 8, 1825, *ibid.*

135. *Ibid.*

136. Henry Gilpin to Joshua Gilpin, March 3–4, 1825, Henry D. Gilpin Collection, HSD.

137. *Register of Debates,* 18th Cong., 2d sess., pp. 443–484, 486; LMcL to CMcL, Feb. 5, 1825, McLane Papers; Parton, *Jackson,* III, 104.

138. LMcL to CMcL, Feb. 6, 1825, McLane Papers.

139. *House Journal,* 18th Cong., 2d sess., p. 208.

140. LMcL to CMcL, Feb. 6, 1825, McLane Papers.

141. LMcL to CMcL, Dec. 24, 27, 1824; [Jan. 1, 1825], *ibid.*

142. Fink, "Van Rensselaer and the Election of 1825," *New York History,* XXXII, 326–327.

143. S. Van Rensselaer to DeWitt Clinton, Dec. 18, 1824, *ibid.,* p. 327.

144. R. King's memoranda, Feb. 10, 1825, in King, *Correspondence,* VI, 586.

145. Adams, *Memoirs,* VI, 492–493.

146. R. King's memoranda, Feb. 10, 1825, in King, *Correspondence,* VI, 587; Van Buren, *Autobiography,* p. 150.

147. LMcL to CMcL, Feb. 9, 1825, McLane Papers.

148. Van Buren, *Autobiography,* pp. 151–152.

149. Hammond, *History of Political Parties in the State of New-York,* II, 189.

150. LMcL to CMcL, Feb. 9, 1825, McLane Papers.

151. Van Buren, *Autobiography,* pp. 150–151.

152. Smith, *First Forty Years,* pp. 191–192; R. King's memoranda, Feb. 9, 1825, in King, *Correspondence,* VI, 585.

153. *National Intelligencer,* Feb. 10, 1825; Cobb, "A Review of the Life and Times of William H. Crawford," in *Leisure Labors . . .* (New York, 1858), p. 225.

154. *National Intelligencer,* Feb. 10, 1825; *Niles' Register,* XXVII (Feb. 12, 1825), 384; S. G. Goodrich, *Recollections of a Lifetime* (New York, 1856), II, 400.

155. Cobb, "Crawford," pp. 227–228.

156. LMcL to J. A. Bayard, Feb. 9, 1825, Hilles Collection.

157. Smith, *First Forty Years,* p. 192.

158. Van Buren, *Autobiography,* p. 151.

159. Smith, *First Forty Years,* p. 190.

160. *Ibid.;* LMcL to CMcL, Feb. 11, 1825, McLane Papers.

161. LMcL to CMcL, Feb. 11, 1825, *ibid.*

162. Smith, *First Forty Years,* pp. 192–193.

163. Van Buren, *Autobiography,* pp. 151, 152; Dangerfield, *Era of Good Feelings,* p. 342.

164. Van Buren, *Autobiography,* p. 153; Hammond, *Political History of New-York,* II, 190.

165. LMcL to CMcL, Feb. 9, 1825, McLane Papers.

166. LMcL to CMcL, Feb. 12, 1825, *ibid.*

CHAPTER SEVEN: A NEW OPPOSITION

1. LMcL to CMcL, Feb. 11, 1825, McLane Papers.

2. LMcL to CMcL, Feb. 12, 1825, *ibid.*

3. LMcL to Mr. Canby [Feb. 15 or 16, 1825], copy, *ibid.*

4. T. Clayton to W. P. Brobson, Feb. 17, 1825, Brobson Papers, HSD.

5. Cobb, "A Review of the Life and Times of William H. Crawford," in *Leisure Labors* . . . (New York, 1858), p. 229.

6. Daniel Webster to Jeremiah Mason, Feb. 14, 1825, in *Memoir of Jeremiah Mason*, p. 291.

7. LMcL to CMcL, Feb. 12, 1825, McLane Papers.

8. LMcL to CMcL, Feb. 16, 1825, *ibid.*

9. Adams, *Memoirs*, VI, 511, 514.

10. *Ibid.*, p. 521.

11. H. Clay to W. H. Crawford, Feb. 18, 1828, in Calvin Colton, ed., *Private Correspondence of Henry Clay* (New York, 1856), p. 193; H. Clay to Francis Brooke, Feb. 18, 1825, *ibid.*, p. 115.

12. LMcL to CMcL, Feb. 20, 1825, McLane Papers.

13. LMcL to CMcL, Feb. 26, 1825, *ibid.*

14. LMcL to CMcL, Feb. 14, 1825, *ibid.*

15. LMcL to CMcL, Feb. 22, 25, 1825, *ibid.*

16. *House Journal*, 18th Cong., 2d sess., pp. 232, 240, 254, 260, 268, 279, 287, 288.

17. LMcL to CMcL, Feb. 12, 1825, McLane Papers.

18. LMcL to CMcL, Feb. 14, 1825, *ibid.*

19. LMcL to CMcL, Feb. 15, 20, 1825, *ibid.*

20. Remini, *Martin Van Buren and the Making of the Democratic Party*, p. 138 and *passim*.

21. LMcL to CMcL, Feb. 15, 1825, McLane Papers.

22. LMcL to CMcL, Feb. 20, 1825, *ibid.*

23. LMcL to CMcL, Feb. 21, 1825, *ibid.*

24. Adèle Sigoigne to CMcL, July 8, 1825, *ibid.*

25. LMcL to CMcL, Feb. 22, 1825, *ibid.*

26. Charles E. Green, *History of the M. W. Grand Lodge of Ancient, Free, and Accepted Masons of Delaware* (Wilmington, 1956), p. 330.

27. Boorstin, *Delaware Cases*, III, 118, 123.

28. LMcL to Simon Gratz, April 4, 1825, Gratz MSS, case 2, box 19, HSP.

29. LMcL, grant of power of attorney to Hall and Davidson, June 24, 1825, "L. McLane" folder, Gratz MSS, HSP.

30. Undated list headed "Members of Congress" in Biddle Papers, XXXVIII, LC.

31. Mangum, *Papers*, I, 195–196.

32. *Delaware Gazette*, Oct. 7, 1825; Stephen Pleasonton to W. P. Brobson, Oct. 20, 1825, Brobson Papers, HSD.

33. *American Watchman*, Oct. 11, 1825.

34. *American Watchman*, Aug. 30, Oct. 7, 1825.

35. Scharf, *History of Delaware*, I, 310.

36. LMcL to Stephen Van Rensselaer, Oct. 18, 1825, Gratz MSS, HSP. See LMcL to M. Van Buren, April 10, 1825, Van Buren Papers, LC.

37. LMcL to CMcL, Fri. evening [Dec. 4, 1825], McLane Papers.

38. Adams, *Memoirs*, VII, 68–69; William P. Brobson Diary, Dec. 17, 1825, Pennsylvania Historical and Museum Commission, Harrisburg.

39. Romulus Saunders to Bartlett Yancy, Dec. 4, 1825, in "Saunders-Yancy Letters," *North Carolina Historical Review*, VIII, 452.

40. Adams, *Memoirs*, VII, 71.

41. Henry Storrs, Private Journal, I, Dec., 1825, Buffalo Historical Society.

42. LMcL to Stephen Van Rensselaer, Oct. 18, 1825, Gratz MSS, HSP.

43. LMcL to CMcL, Feb. 20, 1825, McLane Papers.

44. Adams, *Memoirs*, VII, 68, 70.

45. *Register of Debates*, 19th Cong., 1st sess., p. 795.

46. LMcL to J. A. Bayard, Dec. 6, 1825, Hilles Collection.

47. LMcL to CMcL, Fri. evening [Dec. 4, 1825], McLane Papers.

48. Adams, *Memoirs*, VII, 70.

49. *American Watchman*, Dec. 13, 1825.

50. LMcL to CMcL, Sun. evening [Dec. 11 or 18, 1825], McLane Papers.

51. *House Journal*, 18th Cong., 1st sess., p. 23; 19th Cong., 1st sess., p. 27.

52. LMcL to CMcL, Sun. evening [Dec. 11 or 18, 1825], McLane Papers.

53. LMcL to J. A. Bayard, Dec. 15, 1825, Hilles Collection.

54. LMcL to Stephen Van Rensselaer, Oct. 15, 1825, Gratz MSS, HSP.

55. LMcL to CMcL, Dec. 10, 1825, McLane Papers.

56. CMcL to LMcL, Dec. 13 [1825], Fisher Collection; LMcL to CMcL, Sun. evening [Dec. 11 or 18, 1825], McLane Papers.

57. *Ibid.;* Adams, *Memoirs*, VII, 91.

58. Quincy, *Figures of the Past*, pp. 234, 241.

59. *Delaware Gazette*, March 17, 1826.

60. Quincy, *Figures of the Past*, p. 174.

61. John F. May to Thomas Ruffin, Feb. 10, 1826, in Ruffin, *Papers*, I, 341.

62. Willie P. Mangum to John Haywood, Feb. 16, 1826, in Mangum, *Papers*, I, 248–249.

63. Quincy, *Figures of the Past*, pp. 224–226, 228–230, 283.

64. List dated January 5, 1826, in J. Q. Adams, "Rubbish III," Adams Papers, reel 51, Massachusetts Historical Society.

65. Mary C[hristie] to CMcL, Jan. 28, 1826, McLane Papers.

66. Lists dated Feb. 17 and March 31, 1826, in J. Q. Adams, "Rubbish III," Adams Family MSS, box 51, Massachusetts Historical Society.

67. J. J. Milligan to CMcL, Feb. 17, 1826, Fisher Collection.

68. *Register of Debates*, 19th Cong., 1st sess., p. 2256.

69. *Ibid.*, p. 2432.

70. *Ibid.*, p. 2366.

71. N. Biddle to LMcL, Feb. 21, 1826, Biddle Papers, LC.

72. J. J. Milligan to CMcL, Feb. 17, 1826, Fisher Collection.

73. *Register of Debates*, 19th Cong., 1st sess., pp. 1150–1151, 1192–1208.

74. *Ibid.*, pp. 1176–1177.

75. *Ibid.*, pp. 1196, 1201, 1206.

76. LMcL to J. A. Bayard, Dec. 15, 1825, Hilles Collection.

77. *House Journal*, 19th Cong., 1st sess., pp. 262, 264, 267, 275, 283, 290, 306, 318, 324, 327, 341, 342, 371, 375, 395, 400.

78. Wiltse, *Calhoun, Nationalist*, pp. 331, 335.

79. *House Journal,* 19th Cong., 1st sess., pp. 305, 444, 527, 556.

80. Willie P. Mangum to John Haywood, Feb. 16, 1826, in Mangum, *Papers,* I, 248–249.

81. *Register of Debates,* 19th Cong., 1st sess., pp. 1251–1252.

82. *Ibid.,* p. 1764.

83. *Ibid.,* pp. 2009–2010, 2011, 2249; Dexter Perkins, *The Monroe Doctrine, 1823–1826* (Cambridge, 1932), pp. 218–219.

84. *Register of Debates,* 19th Cong., 1st sess., pp. 2011–2021.

85. *Ibid.,* pp. 2021, 2029, 2368–2369.

86. *Ibid.,* pp. 2371–2372, 2376.

87. *Ibid.,* p. 2414.

88. *Ibid.,* pp. 2457–2458.

89. *Ibid.,* pp. 2473–2490.

90. *Ibid.,* pp. 2508–2514, 2550–2551.

91. LMcL to [Dr. James Tilton?], May 3, 1825, McLane Papers.

92. LMcL to Robert McLane, May 2, 1826, Fisher Collection.

93. LMcL to [Dr. James Tilton?], May 3. 1826; LMcL to CMcL, May 2, 12, 1826, McLane Papers.

94. *House Journal,* 19th Cong., 1st sess., pp. 464, 521; *Register of Debates,* 19th Cong., 1st sess., p. 2653; LMcL to J. Buchanan, May 19, 1826, Buchanan Papers, HSP; White, *The Jacksonians,* p. 171.

95. LMcL to CMcL, May 3, 1826, McLane Papers; *Register of Debates,* 19th Cong., 1st sess., p. 2600.

96. *Register of Debates,* 19th Cong., 1st sess., pp. 2606–2607, 2622, 2626, 2628.

97. LMcL to CMcL, May 13, 1826, McLane Papers.

98. Romulus Saunders to Bartlett Yancy, April 17, 1826, in "Saunders-Yancy Letters," *North Carolina Historical Review,* VIII, 456–457.

99. LMcL to CMcL, May 4, 1826, McLane Papers.

100. LMcL to CMcL, May 9, 1826, *ibid.*

101. LMcL to CMcL, May 2, 1826, *ibid.*

102. LMcL to CMcL, May 4, 1826, *ibid.*

103. CMcL to LMcL, May 6 [incorrectly dated May 5], [1826], *ibid.*

104. LMcL to J. Buchanan, May 19, 1826, Buchanan Papers, HSP.

105. McLane genealogical notes.

106. LMcL to CMcL, Aug. 11, 17, 1826, McLane Papers.

107. William P. Brobson Diary, Sept. 8, 1826, p. 99, Pennsylvania Historical and Museum Commission.

108. *Niles' Register,* XXXI (Sept. 2 and Oct. 14, 1826), 1, 101.

109. Broadside, "To the Democratic Voters of New Castle County," Sept. 29, 1826, HSD.

110. Martin W. Bates to W. P. Brobson, Aug. 23, 1826, Brobson Papers, HSD.

111. *Niles' Register,* XXXI (Oct. 14, 1826), 101.

112. *American Watchman,* Sept. 29, Oct. 3, and Oct. 10, 1826.

113. *Governor's Register*, I, 226; Scharf, *History of Delaware*, I, 310; *Delaware Gazette*, Oct. 10, 1826.

114. *Delaware Gazette*, Sept. 5, 1826.

115. LMcL to S. Van Rensselaer, Nov. 2, 1826, MS Accession 11617, New York State Library, Albany.

116. M. Van Buren to C. C. Cambreleng, Nov. 7, 1826, Van Buren Papers, LC; H. M. Ridgely to Mrs. Ridgely, Jan. 24, 1827, in de Valinger and Shaw, *Calendar of Ridgely Family Letters*, II, 218; Adams, *Memoirs*, VII, 196; *House Journal*, 19th Cong., 2d sess., pp. 5, 23.

117. *House Journal*, 19th Cong., 2d sess., pp. 26, 34; LMcL to N. Biddle, Dec. 7, 1826, Gratz MSS, HSP.

118. T. Clayton to W. P. Brobson, Dec. 27, 1826, Brobson Papers, HSD.

119. LMcL to J. A. Bayard, Nov. 14, 1826, Hilles Collection.

120. *Delaware Gazette*, Oct. 10, 1826.

121. LMcL to J. A. Bayard, Dec. 26, 1826; Jan. 1, 6, 8, 9, 1827, Hilles Collection.

122. *Delaware Senate Journal*, 1827, pp. 45–47. See also Scharf, *History of Delaware*, I, 310.

123. LMcL to J. A. Bayard, Jan. 18, 1827, Hilles Collection.

124. LMcL to CMcL, Jan. 16, 1827, McLane Papers.

125. LMcL to CMcL, Jan. 19, 1827, *ibid.*

126. LMcL to CMcL, Jan. 16, 1827, *ibid.*

127. LMcL to CMcL, Feb. 5, 1827, *ibid.*

128. Presley Spruance, Jr., to W. P. Brobson, Jan. 19, 1827, Brobson Papers, HSD.

129. *United States Telegraph*, Feb. 5, 1827, from the Pittsburgh *Mercury*.

CHAPTER EIGHT: SENATOR AND SUPPLICANT

1. *Register of Debates*, 19th Cong., 2d sess., pp. 751–752.

2. *National Intelligencer*, Jan. 22, 1827.

3. LMcL to CMcL, Jan. 16, 1827, McLane Papers.

4. John McLean to Ninian Edwards, March 19, 1827, in Edwards, *History of Illinois*, p. 486; Edwards, *Papers*, p. 123n.

5. LMcL to CMcL, Jan. 30, 1827, Fisher Collection; LMcL to Dr. James Tilton, Jan. 30, 1827, McLane Papers.

6. LMcL to Dr. James Tilton, Jan. 30, 1827, McLane Papers.

7. LMcL to J. A. Bayard, Jan. 31, 1827, Hilles Collection; H. M. Ridgely to Mrs. Ridgely, Jan. 24, 1827, Ridgely Collection, folder 271, DSA.

8. LMcL to CMcL, Feb. 10, 1827, McLane Papers.

9. LMcL to CMcL, Feb. 19, 1827, Fisher Collection.

10. *Delaware Gazette*, Jan. 30, 1827; LMcL to CMcL, Feb. 5, 16, 1827, McLane Papers.

11. LMcL to Dr. James Tilton, Jan. 30, 1827, McLane Papers.

12. T. Clayton to W. P. Brobson, Feb. 10, 1827, Brobson Papers, HSD.

13. *Register of Debates,* 19th Cong., 2d. sess., pp. 995, 1028, 1087, 1098, 1099.

14. *Ibid.,* pp. 785–786, 822–823.

15. T. Clayton to W. P. Brobson, Feb. 10, 1827, Brobson Papers, HSD.

16. *Register of Debates,* 19th Cong., 2d sess., pp. 643–645, 1267, 1306, 1345–1346, 1352.

17. *House Journal,* 19th Cong., 2d sess., pp. 252, 274.

18. LMcL to CMcL, Feb. 16, 1827, McLane Papers.

19. T. Clayton to W. P. Brobson, Feb. 10, 1827, Brobson Papers, HSD; *American Watchman,* Feb. 27, 1827.

20. *Niles' Register,* XXXII (July 7, 1827), 315; *American Watchman,* July 6, 1827.

21. *Niles' Register,* XXXII (July 7, 1827), 315.

22. T. Clayton to W. P. Brobson, Feb. 10, 1827, Brobson Papers, HSD.

23. LMcL to CMcL, Jan. 19, 1827, McLane Papers.

24. *Delaware Gazette,* Aug. 10, 1827.

25. *American Watchman,* Aug. 31, 1827.

26. *Delaware Gazette,* Aug. 31, 1827.

27. *Ibid.,* Aug. 28, 1827.

28. *American Watchman,* Sept. 4, 7, 1827.

29. P. Spruance, Jr., to W. P. Brobson, Sept. 5, 1827, Brobson Papers, HSD.

30. *American Watchman,* Sept. 25, 1827.

31. *Ibid.*

32. *Ibid.,* Sept. 21, 1827.

33. *Ibid.,* Sept. 11, 1827.

34. H. Clay to John W. Taylor, Sept. 7, 1827, Taylor Papers, NYHS.

35. *Governor's Register,* I, 250–251.

36. *American Watchman,* Sept. 25, 1827.

37. *Ibid.,* Sept. 28, Oct. 1, 1827.

38. *Ibid.,* Sept. 14, 21, 1827.

39. *Ibid.,* Sept. 21, 1827.

40. *Ibid.*

41. LMcL to Joshua Gilpin, Jan. 20, 1831, James Maury Deposit, University of Virginia.

42. LMcL to CMcL, Dec. 7, 1827, McLane Papers; *Senate Journal,* 20th Cong., 1st sess., pp. 5, 24, 26, 28.

43. LMcL to CMcL, Dec. 27, 1827, McLane Papers.

44. *Ibid.*

45. LMcL to CMcL, Jan. 1, 1828, *ibid.*

46. R. M. McLane, *Reminiscences,* pp. 1–2.

47. LMcL to CMcL, Jan. 1, 1828, McLane Papers.

48. LMcL to CMcL, Dec. 7, 1827, *ibid.*

49. LMcL to CMcL, Jan. 1, 1828, *ibid.*

50. LMcL to CMcL, Thurs. afternoon, April [17 or 24], 1828, *ibid.*

51. LMcL to CMcL, Sat. morning [c. May 3, 1828], *ibid.*

52. LMcL to M. Van Buren, June 18, Oct. 14, 1827, Van Buren Papers, LC; LMcL to Gulian Verplanck, Oct. 22, 1827, Verplanck Papers, NYHS; *New-York Evening Post*, Oct. 9, 1827.

53. LMcL to CMcL, Wed. morning [May 14–25, 1828?], Fisher Collection.

54. LMcL to CMcL, Sun. morning [*c.* April 27, 1828], *ibid.*

55. LMcL to CMcL, Sat. morning [Jan. 26, 1828], McLane Papers.

56. LMcL to CMcL, Dec. 7, 1827, *ibid.*

57. LMcL to CMcL, Sun., Jan. [13 or 20], 1828, Fisher Collection.

58. LMcL to CMcL, Sat. morning [*c.* Jan. 26, 1828], McLane Papers.

59. *Register of Debates*, 20th Cong., 1st sess., pp. 287–295.

60. LMcL to CMcL, Wed. morning [April 9, 1828], McLane Papers; J[ames] D. W[estcott] to Van Buren, Jan. 18, 1828, Van Buren Papers, LC.

61. *Register of Debates*, 20th Cong., 1st sess., p. 606.

62. *Ibid.*, pp. 687–688; *Senate Journal*, 20th Cong., 1st sess., p. 326.

63. *Register of Debates*, 20th Cong., 1st sess., pp. 798–799, 803, 804.

64. *Ibid.*, p. 99.

65. LMcL to CMcL, Jan. 22, 1828, McLane Papers.

66. *Register of Debates*, 20th Cong., 1st sess., p. 111.

67. LMcL to CMcL, Jan. [27], 1828, Fisher Collection.

68. *Register of Debates*, 20th Cong., 1st sess., pp. 344, 415, 419–420, 467–468, 542–543.

69. LMcL to Joshua Gilpin, Jan. 27, 1828, James Maury Deposit, University of Virginia; LMcL to J. A. Bayard, April 8, 1828, Hilles Collection.

70. *Senate Journal*, 20th Cong., 1st sess., pp. 406, 409, 410.

71. LMcL to CMcL, Sun. [May 11, 1828?], McLane Papers.

72. Wilmington *Political Primer*, May 5, 1828; LMcL to CMcL, Tues. evening [May 13, 1828], McLane Papers.

73. LMcL to CMcL, April 15, 1828, Fisher Collection; LMcL to CMcL, Sat. [April 19, 1828], McLane Papers; *Register of Debates*, 20th Cong., 1st sess., p. 672.

74. *Register of Debates*, 20th Cong., 1st sess., pp. 804, 805.

75. LMcL to CMcL, May 14, and Wed. morning [May 21?], 1828, Fisher Collection.

76. LMcL to CMcL, Sat. [April 19, 1828], McLane Papers.

77. *Register of Debates*, 20th Cong., 1st sess., pp. 734, 787.

78. *Ibid.*, p. 675.

79. LMcL to Joshua Gilpin, Jan. 27, 1828, James Maury Deposit, University of Virginia.

80. LMcL to CMcL, Jan. 22, 1828, Fisher Collection.

81. LMcL to CMcL, Fri., Feb. [8], 1828, Batchelder Papers.

82. Van Buren, *Autobiography*, pp. 211–212.

83. LMcL to CMcL, Thurs. [March 13?], 1828, Fisher Collection; *Register of Debates*, 20th Cong., 1st sess., pp. 448, 449.

84. LMcL to CMcL, Sat. [April 19, 1828], McLane Papers; *Senate Journal*, 20th Cong., 1st sess., pp. 330, 335.

85. LMcL to CMcL, Tues. evening [May 13, 1828], McLane Papers.

86. LMcL to CMcL, Sun. [Feb. 10 or later, 1828], Fisher Collection.

87. LMcL to CMcL, Jan. 30, 1828, McLane Papers.

88. LMcL to CMcL, Sat. morning [May 3, 1828?], *ibid.*

89. Cecil County Land Record, XXXIII (J. S. No. 8), 515–517; LI (J. S. No. 26), 109–115; LV (J. S. No. 30), 346–349; LXVI (J. S. No. 41), 433–442, Court House, Elkton, Maryland.

90. CMcL to Mrs. Thomas Forman [n.d.], Forman Papers, Maryland Historical Society.

91. LMcL to J. Buchanan, Aug. 12, 1828, Buchanan Papers, HSP.

92. Inventory of goods, chattels, and personal estate of Louis McLane in Cecil County, Nov. 7, 1857, Baltimore City Inventories No. 75, p. 241, Baltimore City Court House.

93. LMcL to J. Buchanan, Aug. 12, 1828, Buchanan Papers, HSP.

94. LMcL to CMcL, Jan. 30, 1828, McLane Papers.

95. N. Biddle to LMcL, Oct. 23, 1827; March 4, 1828, Biddle Papers, LC.

96. LMcL to CMcL, Fri. morning [April 18?], 1828, Fisher Collection.

97. LMcL to J. A. Bayard, March 16, 1828, Hilles Collection.

98. LMcL to CMcL, Fri., Feb. [8], 1828, Batchelder Collection.

99. LMcL to CMcL, Thurs. [*c.* March 13, 1828], Fisher Collection.

100. LMcL to CMcL, Sun. morning, Feb. [17], 1828, Batchelder Collection; LMcL to J. A. Bayard, March 16, 1828, Hilles Collection.

101. LMcL to CMcL, Wed. [*c.* Feb. 13, 1828], Fisher Collection.

102. LMcL to [J. A. Bayard], [Feb., 1828], Hilles Collection.

103. LMcL to CMcL, Thurs. [*c.* March 13, 1828], Fisher Collection.

104. Jesse Green to LMcL, March 25, 1828, Hilles Collection.

105. LMcL to J. A. Bayard, Jan. 20, 1828, *ibid.*

106. LMcL to CMcL, Sun. afternoon [*c.* March 30], 1828, Fisher Collection.

107. LMcL to CMcL, Sun. morning [May 4 or later, 1828], *ibid.*

108. W. Gaston to John H. Bryan, March 1, 1828, quoted in Connor, "William Gaston," *Proceedings of the American Antiquarian Society,* n.s., XLIII, 442–443.

109. LMcL to CMcL, Sun. morning, Feb. [17?], 1828, Batchelder Collection.

110. LMcL to J. A. Bayard, Jan. 20, 1828, Hilles Collection.

111. *Delaware House Journal,* 1829, p. 6; LMcL to J. A. Bayard, Jan. 9, 1828, Hilles Collection.

112. LMcL to J. A. Bayard, Jan. 9, 1828, Hilles Collection.

113. LMcL to J. A. Bayard, Jan. 20, 1828, *ibid.*

114. LMcL to J. A. Bayard, March 16, 1828, *ibid.*

115. LMcL to J. A. Bayard, April 1, 1828, *ibid.*

116. Jesse Green to LMcL, March 25, 1828, *ibid.*

117. N. Niles to W. P. Brobson, June 18, 1828, Brobson Papers, HSD.

118. Wilmington *Political Primer,* April 16, 28, 1828.

119. LMcL to CMcL, Sun. morning [May 4 or later, 1828], Fisher Collection.

120. Wilmington *Political Primer,* April 12, 1828.

121. Wilmington *Political Primer*, April 28, May 5, 1828.

122. LMcL to J. A. Bayard, April 8, 1828, Hilles Collection.

123. R. M. McLane, *Reminiscences*, p. 4.

124. S. Ingham to M. Van Buren, Sept. 26, 1828, Van Buren Papers, LC.

125. Wilmington *Political Primer*, Sept. 15, 17, 29, 1828.

126. *Ibid.*, May 21, Sept. 8, 1828.

127. *Niles' Register*, XXXV (Oct. 11, 1829), 99; *Governor's Register*, I, 262.

128. *Delaware House Journal*, 1828, pp. 7–8; 1829, p. 47.

129. LMcL to J. A. Bayard, Feb. 1, 1824, Hilles Collection.

130. *American Watchman*, Oct. 14, 1828.

131. S. Pleasonton to T. M. Rodney, Oct. 10, 1828, Brown Collection, HSD.

132. LMcL to Walter Lowrie, Nov. 5, 1828, Vertical File, Maryland Historical Society.

133. LMcL to [AMcL], Feb. 5, 1829, Fisher Collection.

134. Smith, *First Forty Years*, p. 251.

135. LMcL to James A. Hamilton, April 14, 1829, in Hamilton, *Reminiscences*, p. 131.

136. Smith, *First Forty Years*, pp. 251, 260–261, 275.

137. Wilmington *Political Primer*, April 12, 1828.

138. [CMcL] to [AMcL], Sun. [Feb. 8, 1829], McLane Papers.

139. LMcL to [AMcL], Feb. 15, 1829, *ibid*.

140. *Ibid.*; LMcL to Louis McLane, Jr., Jan. 22, 1829, *ibid.*; Rebecca McLane to AMcL, Sun. [Feb. 8], and Feb. [21], 1829, *ibid.*

141. R. M. McLane, *Reminiscences*, p. 7.

142. Wills of Edward and George Washington Worrell, Will Books S-1-240 and S-1-374, Register of Wills, Wilmington; Conrad, *History of Delaware*, I, 343.

143. *Register of Debates*, 20th Cong., 2d sess., pp. 14–15, 41.

144. *Ibid.*, pp. 87, 91.

145. *Ibid.*, pp. 60–63.

146. *Ibid.*, pp. 48–49.

147. *Ibid.*, p. 44.

148. *Ibid.*, appendix, pp. 62, 63.

149. [CMcL] to [AMcL], Mon. noon [Feb. 16, 1829], Fisher Collection.

150. Duff Green to John Pope, Dec. 11, 1828, Duff Green Papers, LC.

151. M. Van Buren to C. C. Cambreleng, Oct. 18, 1828, Van Buren Papers, LC.

152. Duff Green to Ninian Edwards, Dec. 22, 1828, in Edwards, *Papers*, p. 378.

153. R. Bunner to J. A. Hamilton, Jan. 14, 1829, in Hamilton, *Reminiscences*, p. 88.

154. M. Van Buren to C. C. Cambreleng, Dec. 17, 1828, Van Buren Papers, LC.

155. G. C. Verplanck to M. Van Buren, Dec. 6, 1828, Van Buren Papers, LC.

156. LMcL to J. A. Bayard, Jan. 22, 1829, Hilles Collection.

157. CMcL to AMcL, Feb. 2, 1829, Fisher Collection.

158. [CMcL] to [AMcL], Feb. 5, 1829, *ibid.*

159. CMcL to [AMcL], Feb. 7, 1829, McLane Papers.

160. [CMcL] to [AMcL], Thurs. morning [Feb. 12, 1829], *ibid.*

161. [CMcL] to [AMcL], Mon. noon [Feb. 16, 1829], Fisher Collection.

162. James Hamilton, Jr., to M. Van Buren, Feb. 12, 1829, Van Buren Papers, LC.

163. James A. Hamilton to M. Van Buren, Feb. 13, 1829, *ibid.*

164. [CMcL] to [AMcL], Feb. 7, 1829, McLane Papers.

165. M. Van Buren to James A. Hamilton, Feb. 2, 1829, in Hamilton, *Reminiscences,* p. 92; James Hamilton, Jr., to M. Van Buren, Jan. 23, 1829; Robert Hayne to M. Van Buren, Feb. 14, 1829, Van Buren Papers, LC.

166. LMcL to J. A. Bayard, Feb. 12, 1829, Hilles Collection.

167. James Hamilton, Jr., to M. Van Buren, Feb. 19, 1829, Van Buren Papers, LC.

168. LMcL to J. A. Bayard, Feb. 12, 1829, Hilles Collection.

169. James A. Hamilton to M. Van Buren, Feb. 16, 1829, Van Buren Papers, LC.

170. James Iredell to Thomas Ruffin, Feb. 16, 1829, in Ruffin, *Papers,* I, 474.

171. James A. Hamilton to M. Van Buren, Feb. 18, 1829, Van Buren Papers, LC.

172. James Iredell to Thomas Ruffin, Feb. 16, 1829, in Ruffin, *Papers,* I, 474.

173. James A. Hamilton to M. Van Buren, Feb. 19, 1829, Van Buren Papers, LC.

174. James Hamilton, Jr., to M. Van Buren, Feb. 19, 1829, *ibid.*

175. LMcL to J. A. Bayard, Feb. 19, 1829, Hilles Collection.

176. LMcL to M. Van Buren, Feb. 19, 1829, Van Buren Papers, LC.

177. E. K. Kane to M. Van Buren, Feb. 19 and 20, 1829, *ibid.*

178. James A. Hamilton to M. Van Buren, Feb. 19, 21, 1829, *ibid.*

179. R. Bunner to M. Van Buren, Feb. 21, 1829, *ibid.*

180. James A. Hamilton to M. Van Buren, Feb. 25, 1829, *ibid.;* Hamilton, *Reminiscences,* p. 99.

181. Smith, *First Forty Years,* p. 282.

182. James A. Hamilton to M. Van Buren, Feb. 25, 1829, Van Buren Papers, LC.

183. James Gallatin to Albert Gallatin, Feb. 28, 1829, Gallatin Papers, NYHS.

184. Parton, *Jackson,* III, 174, 179.

185. James Hamilton, Jr., to M. Van Buren, Feb. 19, 1829, Van Buren Papers, LC.

186. Thomas Ritchie to M. M. Noah [March 14, 1829], *ibid.*

187. Robert McLane to CMcL, Sun. evening [March 1, 1829], McLane Papers.

188. C. C. Cambreleng to M. Van Buren, March 1, 1829, Van Buren Papers, LC.

189. R. M. McLane, *Reminiscences,* p. 7; *Senate Journal,* 21st Cong., special session, p. 196.

190. *United States Telegraph,* March 4, 5, 1829.

191. Van Buren, *Autobiography,* pp. 229–230.

192. *Ibid.,* p. 231.

193. *Ibid.,* p. 577.

CHAPTER NINE: MISSION TO ENGLAND

1. Wiltse, *Calhoun, Nullifier,* p. 24.

2. W. C. Rives to Thomas P. Moore, March 18, 1829, Van Buren Papers, LC.

3. Van Buren, *Autobiography,* pp. 251, 257.

4. Hamilton, *Reminiscences,* p. 130.

5. *Ibid.*

6. LMcL to James A. Hamilton, April 14, 1829, *ibid.,* p. 131.

7. LMcL to M. Van Buren, April 14, 1829, Van Buren Papers, LC.

8. Van Buren, *Autobiography,* pp. 257–258.

9. LMcL to M. Van Buren, April 15, 1829, Van Buren Papers, LC. *Cf.* LMcL to M. Van Buren, April 15, 1829, State Dept., Diplomatic Despatches, Great Britain, XXXVII, NA.

10. Adams, *Memoirs,* VIII, 139.

11. F. Baylies to unknown [April, 1829], in "Baylies Papers, 1821–1831," *Proceedings of the Massachusetts Historical Society,* XLVI (1912–1913), 331. *Cf.* T. Ward to J. Bates, April 28, May 5, 1829, Baring Papers, HC 512, Part I, Baring Brothers and Co., London.

12. LMcL to M. Van Buren, April 21 and 22, 1829, Van Buren Papers, LC.

13. LMcL to CMcL, Mon. afternoon [April 27, 1829], Fisher Collection; and April 29, 1829, McLane Papers.

14. M. Van Buren to W. C. Rives, May 5, 1829, Van Buren Papers, LC.

15. M. Van Buren to W. C. Rives, May 5, 1829, Rives Papers, LC.

16. LMcL to CMcL, Mon. afternoon [April 27, 1829], Fisher Collection.

17. LMcL to M. Van Buren, April 21, 1829, Van Buren Papers, LC; LMcL to CMcL, May 1, 1829, McLane Papers; Azariah Flagg to M. Van Buren, May 6, 1829, Van Buren Papers, LC; Philadelphia *National Gazette,* May 9, 1829; *Niles' Register,* XXXVI (May 2, 1829), 150; (May 9, 1829), 163.

18. W. H. Crawford to M. Van Buren, May 12, 1829, Van Buren Papers, LC; N. Biddle to M. Van Buren, May 15, 1829, Biddle Papers, LC.

19. M. Van Buren to Theodore Lyman, Jr., May 2, 1829; A. Jackson to M. Van Buren, May 3, 1829, Van Buren Papers, LC; Theodore Collier, "William Beach Lawrence," *DAB,* XI, 53.

20. M. Van Buren to John Treat Irving [May, 1829], Van Buren Papers, LC; *National Gazette,* June 4, 1829; *Niles' Register,* XXXVI (June 6, 1829), 234; Williams, *Washington Irving,* I, 370–372.

21. Williams, *Washington Irving,* I, 368–372; Washington Irving to Peter Irving, July 25, 1829, in P. M. Irving, *The Life and Letters of Washington*

Irving, II, 111–112; Washington Irving to Henry Brevoort, Aug. 10, 1829, in *Letters of Washington Irving to Henry Brevoort*, II, 219–220.

22. Quoted in the London *Times*, July 18, 1829.

23. LMcL to CMcL, May 1, 1829, McLane Papers; LMcL to CMcL, Sat. afternoon [May 2, 1829], Fisher Collection.

24. A. Jackson to Richard Call, May 18, 1829, in Jackson, *Correspondence*, IV, 35–36.

25. W. T. Barry to Mrs. Susan B. Taylor, May 16, 1829, William T. Barry Letters, Filson Club, Louisville.

26. A. Jackson to Richard Call, July 5, 1829, in Jackson, *Correspondence*, IV, 52.

27. LMcL to M. Van Buren, April 21, 1829, Van Buren Papers, LC.

28. W. T. Barry to Mrs. Susan B. Taylor, May 16, 1829, Barry Letters, Filson Club, Louisville.

29. LMcL to CMcL, May 1, 1829, McLane Papers.

30. LMcL to Robert McLane, May 20, 1829, Fisher Collection.

31. *Delaware Gazette*, May 26, 1829; *National Gazette*, May 26, 1829; *Niles' Register*, XXXVI (May 30, 1829), 223.

32. James R. Black to H. M. Ridgely, April 17, 1829, in de Valinger and Shaw, *Calendar of Ridgely Family Letters*, II, 240.

33. Nicholas G. Williamson to H. M. Ridgely, May 21, 1829, *ibid*.

34. *National Gazette*, June 9, 1829.

35. Will Book S-1-280, Register of Wills, Wilmington.

36. Hamilton, *Reminiscences*, pp. 136, 137; M. Van Buren to C. C. Cambreleng, June 4, 1829; J. A. Hamilton to M. Van Buren, June 6, 19, 1829, Van Buren Papers, LC.

37. M. Van Buren to LMcL, July 20, 1829, State Dept., Diplomatic Instructions, Great Britain, XIV, NA.

38. J. Barbour to M. Van Buren, May 13, 1829, Van Buren Papers, LC.

39. *Niles' Register*, XXXVI (July 18, 1829), 330–331; (July 25, 1829), 345; (Aug. 8, 1829), 386–387; (Aug. 22, 1829), 418–419; Benns, *The British West India Carrying Trade*, p. 163.

40. LMcL to M. Van Buren, June 11, 1829, Van Buren Papers, LC.

41. J. Barbour to M. Van Buren, May 13, 1829, *ibid*.

42. M. Van Buren to LMcL, July 20, 1829, State Dept., Diplomatic Instructions, Great Britain, XIV, NA.

43. M. Van Buren, notes for McLane's instructions, July 20, 1829, Van Buren Papers, LC.

44. M. Van Buren to LMcL, July 20, 1829, State Dept., Diplomatic Instructions, Great Britain, XIV, NA.

45. Van Buren, *Autobiography*, p. 274.

46. LMcL to William B. Lewis, July 17, 1829, Blair-Lee Collection, Princeton University.

47. M. Van Buren to LMcL, July 20, 1829, State Dept., Diplomatic Instructions, Great Britain, XIV, NA; LMcL to M. Van Buren, June 11, 1829, Van Buren Papers, LC.

48. James Hamilton, Jr., to M. Van Buren, April 28, 1829, Van Buren Papers, LC.

49. W. H. Crawford to M. Van Buren, Sept. 9, 1829, Van Buren Papers, LC.

50. M. Van Buren to J. A. Hamilton, July 13, 1829, in Hamilton, *Reminiscences*, p. 142.

51. LMcL to CMcL, Sept. 13, 1829, McLane Papers.

52. M. Van Buren to W. C. Rives, July 28, 1829, Rives Papers, LC.

53. W. C. Rives to M. Van Buren, Aug. 1, 1829, Van Buren Papers, LC; LMcL to CMcL, Aug. 11, 1829, McLane Papers.

54. M. Van Buren to J. A. Hamilton, July 18, 1829, in Hamilton, *Reminiscences*, p. 143; M. Van Buren to C. C. Cambreleng, July 19, 1829, Van Buren Papers, LC.

55. C. C. Cambreleng to LMcL, July 24, 1829, rough draft, Van Buren Papers, LC. Final letter, not extant, was not identical.

56. *Niles' Register*, XXXVIII (May 8, 1830), 201; Benns, *The British West India Carrying Trade*, pp. 163–164.

57. *Niles' Register*, XXXVI (Aug. 8, 1829), 387–388; *Delaware Gazette*, July 28, 1829.

58. *Niles' Register*, XXXVI (Aug. 1, 1829), 361; M. Van Buren to W. C. Rives, July 28, 1829, Rives Papers, LC; M. Van Buren to A. J. Donelson, Aug. 3, 1829, Donelson Papers, LC.

59. M. Van Buren to LMcL, Aug. 5, 1829, State Dept., Diplomatic Instructions, Great Britain, XIV, NA.

60. M. Van Buren to C. C. Cambreleng, Aug. 5, 1829, Van Buren Papers, LC; M. Van Buren to W. C. Rives, July 28, 1829, Rives Papers, LC.

61. C. C. Cambreleng to LMcL, July 24, 1829 (draft), Van Buren Papers, LC.

62. LMcL to CMcL, Frigate *Constellation*, off New York, Aug. 11, 1829, McLane Papers.

63. *Ibid.*; R. M. McLane, *Reminiscences*, pp. 12–13.

64. Williams, *Washington Irving*, I, 378; W. Irving to M. Van Buren, Sept. 21, 1829; LMcL to M. Van Buren, Sept. 22, 1829, State Dept., Diplomatic Despatches, Great Britain, XXXVII, NA; W. Irving to Henry Brevoort, Oct. 6, 1829, in Irving, *Letters to Brevoort*, II, 225.

65. R. M. McLane, *Reminiscences*, pp. 17–18.

66. Williams, *Washington Irving*, II, 10–11.

67. LMcL to CMcL, Sept. 13, 1829, McLane Papers; R. M. McLane, *Reminiscences*, p. 13.

68. Williams, *Washington Irving*, II, 3; LMcL to M. Van Buren, Oct. 14, 1829, State Dept., Diplomatic Despatches, Great Britain, XXXVII, NA.

69. George B. Milligan to CMcL [Nov. 5, 1829], Fisher Collection; *Niles' Register*, XXXVII (Nov. 14, 1829), 182.

70. CMcL to LMcL, Nov. 6, 1829, Batchelder Papers.

71. CMcL to LMcL, Oct. 3, 1829, Fisher Collection.

72. CMcL to Robert McLane, Sept. 19 and after, 1829, Fisher Collection.

73. W. Irving to William B. Lewis, Nov. 20, 1829, Washington Irving Papers, NYPL.

74. LMcL to M. Van Buren, Oct. 14, 1829, State Dept., Diplomatic Instructions, Great Britain, XXXVII, NA.

75. M. Van Buren to LMcL, July 20, 1829, State Dept., Diplomatic Instructions, Great Britain, XIV, NA.

76. M. Van Buren to W. C. Rives, July 28, 1829, Rives Papers, LC.

77. Edward Livingston to M. Van Buren, Aug. 1, 1831, State Dept., Diplomatic Instructions, Great Britain, XIV, NA.

78. LMcL to M. Van Buren, Oct. 17, 1829, State Dept., Diplomatic Despatches, Great Britain, XXXVII, NA.

79. LMcL to M. Van Buren, Nov. 14, 1829, *ibid.*

80. LMcL to M. Van Buren, Nov. 28, 1829, *ibid.*

81. LMcL to M. Van Buren, Dec. 14, 1829; LMcL to Aberdeen, Dec. 12, 1829, *ibid.*

82. Aberdeen to LMcL, Dec. 14, 1829, *ibid.*

83. W. Irving to W. B. Lewis, Nov. 20, 1829, Irving Papers, NYPL.

84. LMcL to Joshua Gilpin, Dec. 14, 1829, James Maury Deposit, University of Virginia.

85. LMcL to W. C. Rives, Jan. 2, 1830, Rives Papers, LC.

86. London *Times,* Jan. 8, 1830.

87. LMcL to A. Jackson, Jan. 22, 1830, Jackson Papers, 1st ser., LC.

88. LMcL to M. Van Buren, Jan. 14, 1830, State Dept., Diplomatic Despatches, Great Britain, XXXVII, NA.

89. LMcL to J. A. Hamilton, Feb. 4, 1830, in Hamilton, *Reminiscences,* pp. 160–161; LMcL to A. Jackson, Feb. 6, 1830, Jackson Papers, 1st ser., LC.

90. M. Van Buren to LMcL, Dec. 26, 1829, State Dept., Diplomatic Instructions, Great Britain, XIV, NA.

91. London *Times,* Feb. 11, 1830.

92. LMcL to M. Van Buren, Feb. 26, 1830, State Dept., Diplomatic Despatches, Great Britain, XXXVII, NA.

93. LMcL to Aberdeen, March 15, 1830; LMcL to M. Van Buren, March 22, 1830, *ibid.*

94. LMcL to W. C. Rives, March 19, 1830, Rives Papers, LC; *Niles' Register,* XXXVII (Feb. 20, 1830), 430.

95. London *Times,* Feb. 24, 1830.

96. LMcL to W. C. Rives, March 19, 1830, Rives Papers, LC.

97. LMcL to M. Van Buren, March 22, 1830, State Dept., Diplomatic Despatches, Great Britain, XXXVII, NA.

98. A. Jackson to M. Van Buren, April 10, 1830, in Jackson, *Correspondence,* IV, 133.

99. LMcL to C. C. Cambreleng, March 30, 1830, Van Buren Papers, LC.

100. Benns, *The British West India Carrying Trade,* pp. 173–174; M. Van Buren to LMcL, June 18, 1830, State Dept., Diplomatic Instructions, Great Britain, XIV, NA.

101. LMcL to M. Van Buren, April 6, 1830, State Dept., Diplomatic Despatches, Great Britain, XXXVII, NA.

102. LMcL to M. Van Buren, April 14, 1830, *ibid.*

103. LMcL to M. Van Buren, June 29, 1830, *ibid.*

104. M. Van Buren to LMcL, June 18, 1830, State Dept., Diplomatic Instructions, Great Britain, XIV, NA.

105. LMcL to M. Van Buren, April 14, 1830, State Dept., Diplomatic Despatches, Great Britain, XXXVII, NA.

106. LMcL to M. Van Buren, July 6, 14, 1830; LMcL to Aberdeen, July 12, 1830, *ibid.*

107. Aberdeen to LMcL, Aug. 17, 1830, *ibid.*

108. LMcL to M. Van Buren, Aug. 20, 1830, *ibid.*

109. M. Van Buren to LMcL, Oct. 5, 1830, State Dept., Diplomatic Instructions, Great Britain, XIV, NA; Benns, *The British West India Carrying Trade,* pp. 178–181, 184.

110. *Niles' Register,* XXXIX (Oct. 9, 1830), 109.

111. A. Jackson to John Overton, Sept. 30, 1830, in Jackson, *Correspondence,* IV, 181.

112. LMcL to H. M. Ridgely, Aug. 19, 1830, McLane Papers; LMcL to J. A. Hamilton, Aug. 19, 1830, in Hamilton, *Reminiscences,* p. 172; *Niles' Register,* XXXIX (Oct. 9, 1830), 109.

113. *Niles' Register,* XXXIX (Oct. 9, 1830), 105, 110; (Oct. 16, 1830), 121; (Oct. 23, 1830), 151; Benns, *The British West India Carrying Trade,* pp. 178–179.

114. M. Van Buren to LMcL, Oct. 5, 1830, State Dept., Diplomatic Instructions, Great Britain, XIV, NA.

115. LMcL to Joshua Gilpin, Jan. 20, 1831, James Maury Deposit, University of Virginia.

116. M. Van Buren to Palmerston, Oct. 11, 1831, Van Buren Papers, LC; Williams, *Washington Irving,* II, 7; CMcL to LMcL, Nov. 6, 1829, Batchelder Papers.

117. LMcL to M. Van Buren, Aug. 6, 1830, Van Buren Papers, LC; *Niles' Register,* XXXIX (Oct. 9, 1830), 109.

118. Williams, *Washington Irving,* II, 5, 11; W. Irving to H. Brevoort, March 31, 1831, in Irving, *Letters to Brevoort,* II, 228–229.

119. W. Irving to LMcL, Jan. 20, 1834, Fisher Collection.

120. R. M. McLane, *Reminiscences,* p. 14.

121. Greville, *Memoirs,* I, 344–345.

122. Moore, *Memoirs, Journal and Correspondence,* VII, 157.

123. *Ibid.,* VI, 112.

124. R. M. McLane, *Reminiscences,* pp. 15–16.

125. *Ibid.,* pp. 18–19.

126. LMcL to M. Van Buren, Aug. 10, 1831, Van Buren Papers, LC.

127. R. M. McLane, *Reminiscences,* pp. 14–15, 19–21.

128. W. Irving to Peter Irving, Dec. 3, 1830, in P. M. Irving, *Washington Irving,* II, 130–131.

129. LMcL to M. Van Buren, Nov. 6, 1830, State Dept., Diplomatic Despatches, Great Britain, XXXVII, NA.

130. LMcL to M. Van Buren, July 6, 1830, *ibid.*

131. J. Bentham to A. Jackson, June 14, 1830, in Jackson, *Correspondence,* IV, 146.

132. Christopher Hughes to M. Van Buren, June 1, 1830, Van Buren Papers, LC.

133. Robert McLane to LMcL [Jan.] 16, 1831 [incorrectly dated 1830], McLane Papers.

134. Quoted in Elie Halévy, *The Triumph of Reform* (New York, 1961), p. 11n.

135. LMcL to M. Van Buren, Nov. 6, 13, 1830, State Dept., Diplomatic Despatches, Great Britain, XXXVII, NA.

136. Adams, *Memoirs,* VIII, 261.

137. LMcL to M. Van Buren, Nov. 22, Dec. 22, 1830, State Dept., Diplomatic Despatches, Great Britain, XXXVII, NA.

138. R. M. McLane, *Reminiscences,* pp. 30–31.

139. LMcL to W. C. Rives, April 20, 1830, Rives Papers, LC.

140. LMcL to M. Van Buren, Oct. 6, 1830, State Dept., Diplomatic Despatches, Great Britain, XXXVII, NA.

141. Robert McLane to LMcL [Dec., 1830], McLane Papers; LMcL to W. C. Rives, March 14, 1830, Rives Papers, LC; R. M. McLane, *Reminiscences,* p. 22.

142. LMcL to George Read, Jr., April 18, 1830, Richard S. Rodney Collection, HSD.

143. R. M. McLane, *Reminiscences,* pp. 25–29.

144. Robert McLane to LMcL, Oct. 5, Dec. 9, 1830; Feb. 10, March 3, 1831, McLane Papers.

145. R. M. McLane, *Reminiscences,* pp. 32–33.

146. Christopher Hughes to M. Van Buren, June 1, 1830, Van Buren Papers, LC.

147. Robert McLane to LMcL, Dec. 9, 1830, McLane Papers; CMcL to Catherine Milligan, Jan. 3, 1831, Fisher Collection.

148. R. M. McLane, *Reminiscences,* p. 31.

149. LMcL to M. Van Buren, Feb. 22, 1831, State Dept., Diplomatic Despatches, Great Britain, XXXVII, NA.

150. *Niles' Register,* XL (June 25, 1831), 294; Moore, *Memoirs,* VI, 190.

151. Bruce, *John Randolph of Roanoke,* I, 642; II, 446–447; P. M. Irving, *Washington Irving,* II, 129–130.

152. LMcL to J. A. Hamilton, Oct. 6, 1830, in Hamilton, *Reminiscences,* p. 188.

153. LMcL to M. Van Buren, June 29, 1830; Lord Chamberlain's orders, June 26, 1830, State Dept., Diplomatic Despatches, Great Britain, XXXVII, NA.

154. LMcL to M. Van Buren, Dec. 16, 1830, *ibid.*

155. LMcL to M. Van Buren, March 14, 1831, *ibid.;* LMcL to M. Van Buren, Feb. 14, 1831, Van Buren Papers, LC.

156. M. Van Buren to LMcL, Feb. 4, 1831, State Dept., Diplomatic Instructions, Great Britain, XIV, NA.

157. LMcL to M. Van Buren, March 14, 1831, State Dept., Diplomatic Despatches, Great Britain, XXXVII, NA.

158. LMcL to M. Van Buren, May 21, 1831, *ibid.*

159. E. Livingston to M. Van Buren, Aug. 1, 1831, Van Buren Papers, LC.

160. LMcL to M. Van Buren, May 29, Oct. 6, 1830, State Dept., Diplomatic Despatches, Great Britain, XXXVII, NA.

161. M. Van Buren to LMcL, Oct. 31, 1829, State Dept., Diplomatic Instructions, Great Britain, XIV, NA.

162. LMcL to M. Van Buren, Feb. 14, 1831, Van Buren Papers, LC; LMcL to W. Preble, Feb. 15, 1831, William Pitt Preble Papers, LC.

163. LMcL to M. Van Buren, April 14, 1830, State Dept., Diplomatic Despatches, Great Britain, XXXVII, NA; M. Van Buren to LMcL, Oct. 20, 1830, State Dept., Diplomatic Instructions, Great Britain, XIV, NA.

164. M. Van Buren to LMcL, Oct. 1, 1830, State Dept., Diplomatic Instructions, Great Britain, XIV, NA.

165. LMcL to M. Van Buren, Aug. 6, 1830, Van Buren Papers, LC.

166. M. Van Buren to LMcL, March 26, 1831, State Dept., Diplomatic Instructions, Great Britain, XIV, NA.

167. LMcL to Palmerston, May 2, 1831; Palmerston to LMcL, May 18, 1831; LMcL to M. Van Buren, May 21, 1831, State Dept., Diplomatic Despatches, Great Britain, XXXVII, NA; *National Gazette,* July 7, 1831.

168. LMcL to M. Van Buren, March 14, April 14, 1831, State Dept., Diplomatic Despatches, Great Britain, XXXVII, NA.

169. M. Van Buren to LMcL, July 20, 1829, State Dept., Diplomatic Instructions, Great Britain, XIV, NA.

170. Daniel Brent to LMcL, Jan. 5, 1830, *ibid.*

171. *Niles' Register,* XXXIX (Jan. 8, 1831), 322.

172. M. Van Buren to LMcL, Dec. 27, 1830, State Dept., Diplomatic Instructions, Great Britain, XIV, NA.

173. M. Van Buren to LMcL, Oct. 2, 1830; N. P. Trist to LMcL, March 26, 1831, *ibid.*

174. M. Van Buren to LMcL, Oct. 2, Dec. 23, 1830, *ibid.;* Baker, *Henry Wheaton,* p. 110.

175. M. Van Buren to LMcL, July 20, 1829, State Dept., Diplomatic Instructions, Great Britain, XIV, NA; London *Times,* Jan. 5, 1831.

176. LMcL to M. Van Buren, Dec. 22, 1829; May 29, 1830; M. E. de Gorostiza to LMcL, Dec. 12, 1829, State Dept., Diplomatic Despatches, Great Britain, XXXVII, NA.

177. M. Van Buren to LMcL, April 6, 1830, State Dept., Diplomatic Instructions, Great Britain, XIV, NA; LMcL to M. Van Buren, May 21, 1830, State Dept., Diplomatic Despatches, Great Britain, XXXVII, NA; LMcL to Joel R. Poinsett, June 14, 1830, Poinsett Papers, HSP.

178. M. Van Buren to LMcL, July 20, 1829, State Dept., Diplomatic Instructions, Great Britain, XIV, NA.

179. *Niles' Register*, XXXIX (Sept. 4, 1830), 17.

180. *The Political Mirror* (New York, 1835), p. 162.

181. Richardson, *Messages and Papers of the Presidents*, II, 501–504.

182. *Niles' Register*, XXXIX (Jan. 8, 1831), 351.

183. C. C. Cambreleng to M. Van Buren, Oct. 11, 1830, Van Buren Papers, LC.

184. Benns, *The British West India Carrying Trade*, pp. 186–188.

185. A. Jackson to Anthony Butler, Oct. 6, 1830, in Jackson, *Correspondence*, IV, 182.

186. *Niles' Register*, XL (Aug. 13, 1831), 428, 431–432.

CHAPTER TEN: BESIDE THE CHIEF

1. M. Van Buren to J. A. Hamilton, Sept. 24, 1829, in Hamilton, *Reminiscences*, p. 146.

2. M. Van Buren to A. Jackson, July 25, 1830, Van Buren Papers, LC.

3. Van Buren, *Autobiography*, pp. 577, 583–584; Charles Warren, *The Supreme Court in U.S. History* (Boston, 1923), II, 257.

4. LMcL to J. A. Hamilton, Feb. 4, 1830, in Hamilton, *Reminiscences*, p. 160.

5. Undated letter, M. Van Buren to LMcL, in Van Buren, *Autobiography*, p. 578.

6. Swisher, *Taney*, pp. 311–312.

7. LMcL to J. A. Hamilton, March 22, May 27, 1830, in Hamilton, *Reminiscences*, pp. 163, 165.

8. J. A. Hamilton to LMcL, June 27, 1830, *ibid.*, pp. 169–170.

9. LMcL to Joshua Gilpin, Aug. 25, 1830, James Maury Deposit, University of Virginia.

10. C. C. Cambreleng to M. Van Buren [Oct. 3, 1830], Van Buren Papers, LC.

11. Robert Y. Hayne to M. Van Buren, Oct. 23, 1830, *ibid.*

12. LMcL to M. Van Buren, July 20, 1830, *ibid.;* Warren, *Supreme Court in U.S. History*, II, 168, 169, 177, 179.

13. LMcL to M. Van Buren, Feb. 14, 1831, Van Buren Papers, LC.

14. LMcL to M. Van Buren, July 20, 1820, *ibid.*

15. LMcL to J. A. Bayard, Nov. 22, 1830, Hilles Collection.

16. Duff Green to Ninian Edwards, Nov. 8, 1830, in Edwards, *Papers*, p. 553; Adams, *Memoirs*, VIII, 289.

17. LMcL to Joshua Gilpin, Jan. 20, 1831, James Maury Deposit, University of Virginia.

18. *Niles' Register*, XXXIX (Nov. 20, 1830), 201.

19. LMcL to J. A. Hamilton, Oct. 6, 1830, in Hamilton, *Reminiscences*, p. 188; A. Jackson to LMcL, March 8, 1831, in Jackson, *Correspondence*, IV, 246–247.

20. M. Van Buren to LMcL, April 26, 1831, State Dept., Diplomatic Instructions, Great Britain, XIV, NA.

21. LMcL to M. Van Buren, Feb. 22, 1831, State Dept., Diplomatic Despatches, Great Britain, XXXVII, NA.

22. LMcL to A. Jackson, June 6, 1831 [incorrectly dated 1830], Jackson Papers, 1st ser., LC.

23. LMcL to the Secretary of State, June 13, July 28, 1831; LMcL to A. Jackson, July 28, 1831, State Dept., Diplomatic Despatches, Great Britain, XXXVII, NA; *Niles' Register*, XL (Aug. 13, 1831), 417; *National Gazette*, July 30, 1831; W. Irving to E. Livingston, June 22, 1831, *Catalogue of Sale at American Art Association, Dec. 2–3, 1925.*

24. M. Van Buren to J. A. Hamilton, Aug. 1, 1831 [probably earlier], in Hamilton, *Reminiscences*, pp. 226–227; G. C. Verplanck to A. C. Flagg, July 28 [1831], A. C. Flagg Papers, NYPL; Van Buren, *Autobiography*, pp. 422–423, 482; M. Van Buren to A. Jackson, July 29, 1831, Van Buren Papers, LC.

25. Bassett, *Life of Jackson*, pp. 520–528; *Niles' Register*, XL (June 18, 1831), 268; (June 25, 1831), 289, 302–304; (July 9, 1831), 331–333.

26. M. Van Buren to B. F. Butler, April 16, 1831; M. Van Buren to Thomas Ritchie, April 17, 1831, Van Buren Papers, LC.

27. *Niles' Register*, XL (April 9, 1831), 90; Adams, *Memoirs*, VIII, 357; Jackson, *Correspondence*, V, 264–266.

28. *Niles' Register*, XL (April 23, 1831), 129.

29. M. Van Buren to J. A. Hamilton, April 25, 1831, in Hamilton, *Reminiscences*, p. 214.

30. E. Livingston to wife [April 16, 1831], in Hunt, *Memoir of Mrs. Edward Livingston*, pp. 97–99.

31. Parton, *Jackson*, III, 361; Scott, *Memoir of Hugh Lawson White*, pp. 247–251.

32. A. Jackson to H. L. White, April 29, 1831, in Jackson, *Correspondence*, IV, 272.

33. Benjamin F. Butler to M. Van Buren, April 22, 1831, Van Buren Papers, LC.

34. J. C. Calhoun to S. Ingham, May 25, 1831, Calhoun-Ingham Letters, Calhoun Papers, South Caroliniana Library, Columbia, South Carolina.

35. A. Jackson to M. Van Buren, Aug. 8, Sept. 5, 1831, in Jackson, *Correspondence*, IV, 328, 347; *Niles' Register*, XL (Aug. 13, 1831), 417.

36. LMcL to M. Van Buren, Sept. 6, 1831, Van Buren Papers, LC.

37. Smith, *First Forty Years*, pp. 319–321; *United States Telegraph*, Sept. 20, 1831, quoted in *Niles' Register*, XLI (Sept. 24, 1831), 66.

38. J. C. Calhoun to S. Ingham, May 4, 1831, Calhoun-Ingham Letters, Calhoun Papers, South Caroliniana Library.

39. LMcL to M. Van Buren, Sept. 6, 1831, Van Buren Papers, LC.

40. J. C. Calhoun to S. Ingham, April 23, July 26, 1829, Calhoun-Ingham Letters, Calhoun Papers, South Caroliniana Library.

41. Ruth K. Nuermberger, "Asbury Dickins (1780–1861): A Career in Government Service," *North Carolina Historical Review*, XXIV (July, 1947),

281–314; *Report of Clerks in the Department during the Year, 1831 . . . ,* *House Document* No. 47, 22d Cong., 1st sess.; Duff Green to S. Ingham, July 3, 1829, Duff Green Papers, LC.

42. John Campbell to M. Van Buren, Oct. 4, 1831, Van Buren Papers, LC.

43. Van Buren, *Autobiography,* pp. 578–580, 583.

44. White, *The Jeffersonians,* p. 147; Adams, *Life of Gallatin,* p. 267.

45. M. Van Buren to A. Jackson, Oct. 11, 1831, in Jackson, *Correspondence,* IV, 358.

46. R. Smith to N. Biddle, Aug. 9, 1831, Biddle Papers, LC.

47. LMcL to N. Biddle, Aug. 21, 1831; N. Biddle to LMcL, Aug. 23, 1831; A. Dickins to N. Biddle, Sept. 19, 1831, Biddle Papers, LC; Catterall, *Second Bank,* p. 208.

48. N. Biddle, Memorandum, Oct. 19, 1831; A. Dickins to N. Biddle, Sept. 19, 1831, Biddle Papers, LC.

49. Quoted in Swisher, *Taney,* p. 173.

50. Govan, *Biddle,* p. 206; Ralph Hidy, "The House of Baring and the Second Bank of the United States, 1826–1836," *PMHB,* LXVIII (July, 1944), 274; Smith, *Economic Aspects of the Second Bank,* pp. 152–153.

51. N. Biddle to A. Dickins, Nov. 29, 1831, Biddle Papers, LC.

52. N. Biddle to A. Dickins, Oct. 28, 1831, *ibid.*

53. N. Biddle, Memorandum, Oct. 19, 1831, *ibid.*

54. Govan, *Biddle,* p. 120; Catterall, *Second Bank,* pp. 189–192.

55. N. Biddle, Memorandum, Oct. 19, 1831, Biddle Papers, LC.

56. N. Biddle to A. Dickins, Oct. 28, 1831, *ibid.*

57. N. Biddle to R. Colt, Nov. 4, 1831, *ibid.*

58. N. Biddle to LMcL, Oct. 21, 25, 1831, *ibid.*

59. N. Biddle to A. Dickins, Nov. 14, 1831; N. Biddle to John Potter, Nov. 17, 1831; N. Biddle to A. Dickins, Nov. 20, 1831; A. Dickins to N. Biddle, Nov. 22, 1831, *ibid.*

60. Roger B. Taney, Bank War MS, pp. 67–71, 73, 75–77, 80–85, 87–89, LC; Hammond, *Banks and Politics,* pp. 335–338, 383–384.

61. A. Jackson to J. A. Hamilton, Dec. 12, 1831, in Hamilton, *Reminiscences,* p. 234. *Cf.* Parton, *Jackson,* III, 395–396.

62. Taney, Bank War MS, pp. 78–79, LC.

63. *Ibid.,* p. 94; *House Executive Document* No. 2, 22d Cong., 1st sess., p. 14.

64. *National Intelligencer,* Dec. 10, 1831.

65. Quoted in Washington *Globe,* Dec. 12, 1831.

66. LMcL to M. Van Buren, Dec. 6, 1831, Van Buren Papers, LC.

67. Charles C. Johnston to John B. Floyd, Dec. 16, 1831, *William and Mary College Quarterly,* 2d ser., I (1921), 203.

68. *House Executive Document* No. 3, 22d Cong., 1st sess., pp. 5–8.

69. *Ibid.,* p. 10.

70. *Ibid.,* pp. 11–12.

71. Roy M. Robbins, *Our Landed Heritage* (Princeton, 1942), pp. 41, 47;

Gates, *The Farmer's Age, 1815–1860*, p. 66; Hibbard, *History of Public Land Policies*, p. 177.

72. Richardson, *Messages and Papers of the Presidents*, II, 452.

73. *House Executive Document* No. 3, 22d Cong., 1st sess., pp. 13–16.

74. LMcL to M. Van Buren, Dec. 6, 1831, Van Buren Papers, LC.

75. LMcL to M. Van Buren, Dec. 14, 1831, *ibid.*

76. A. Jackson to M. Van Buren, Dec. 6, 1831, in Jackson, *Correspondence*, IV, 379.

77. A. Jackson to J. A. Hamilton, Dec. 12, 1831, in Hamilton, *Reminiscences*, p. 234.

78. A. Jackson to M. Van Buren, Dec. 17, 1831, Van Buren Papers, LC.

79. M. Van Buren to A. Jackson, Oct. 11, 1831, in Jackson, *Correspondence*, IV, 358.

80. Van Buren, *Autobiography*, p. 581.

81. *Ibid.*, p. 601; W. Irving to LMcL, Feb. 22, 1832, Fisher Collection.

82. C. C. Cambreleng to Jesse Hoyt, Dec. 29, 1831, in Mackenzie, *Van Buren*, p. 230; M. Van Buren to C. C. Cambreleng, Jan. 19, 1832, Van Buren Papers, LC.

83. J. C. Calhoun to S. Ingham, Dec. 22, 1831, Calhoun-Ingham Correspondence, Calhoun Papers, South Caroliniana Library.

84. J. Randolph to A. Jackson, Dec. 19, 1831; Jan. 3, March 28, 1832, in Jackson, *Correspondence*, IV, 386, 395, 429.

85. N. S. Benton to A. C. Flagg, Dec. 28, 1831, A. C. Flagg Papers, NYPL.

86. A. G. Danby to A. C. Flagg, Dec. 27, 1831, *ibid.*

87. Walter Lowrie to M. Van Buren, Jan. 27, 1832, Van Buren Papers, LC.

88. Cornelius Van Ness to M. Van Buren, March 19, 1832, *ibid.*

89. Quoted in Washington *Globe*, Dec. 12, 1831.

90. *Ibid.*, Dec. 19, 1831.

91. *New-York Evening Post*, Dec. 12, 1831.

92. Robert M. Gibbes to N. Biddle, Dec. 11, 1831, Biddle Papers, LC.

93. LMcL to M. Van Buren, Dec. 14, 1831, Van Buren Papers, LC.

94. Washington *Globe*, Dec. 17, 1831.

95. LMcL to Francis P. Blair, Dec. 19, 1831, Blair-Lee Collection, Princeton University.

96. *National Intelligencer*, Dec. 13, 1831.

97. *United States Telegraph*, Dec. 12, 16, 1831; Washington *Globe*, Dec. 14, 1831.

98. L. McLane's contradiction of the *Telegraph* [Dec. 12, 1831], MS in McLane's hand in Blair-Lee Collection, Princeton University; Washington *Globe*, Dec. 17, 1831.

99. *United States Telegraph*, Dec. 16, 1831; Washington *Globe*, Dec. 20, 1831.

100. W. T. Read to George Read, Jr., Dec. 15, 1831, Richard S. Rodney Collection, HSD; A. Dickins to N. Biddle, Dec. 13, 1831, Biddle Papers, LC.

101. N. Biddle to A. Dickins, Dec. 20, 1831, Biddle Papers, LC.

102. Taney, Bank War MS, pp. 73–82, LC; T. W. Ward to Baring Brothers, Oct. 23, 1831, Baring Papers, HC 512, Part III, London.

103. William B. Lewis to M. Van Buren, April 22, 1859, in Van Buren, *Autobiography*, p. 583; Smith, *First Forty Years*, pp. 325–327.

CHAPTER ELEVEN: CLIMAX

1. Scott, *Memoir of Hugh Lawson White*, pp. 208–209.

2. Samuel Smith to N. Biddle, Dec. 7, 1831, in Biddle, *Correspondence*, pp. 138–139; *House Executive Document* No. 3, 22d Cong., 1st sess., p. 8; LMcL to M. Van Buren, Dec. 14, 1831, Van Buren Papers, LC.

3. R. Smith to N. Biddle, Dec. 14, 1831, Biddle Papers, LC; Govan, *Biddle*, p. 171.

4. N. Devereux to N. Biddle, Dec. 16, 1831, Biddle Papers, LC.

5. C. F. Mercer to N. Biddle, Dec. 12, 1831, *ibid.*

6. Van Deusen, *Clay*, p. 257; H. Clay to N. Biddle, Dec. 15, 1831, Biddle Papers, LC.

7. S. H. Smith to N. Biddle, Dec. 17, 1831, Biddle Papers, LC.

8. D. Webster to N. Biddle, Dec. 18, 1831, *ibid.*

9. Govan, *Biddle*, pp. 10, 79–80, 172.

10. T. Cadwalader to N. Biddle, Dec. 21, 1831, Biddle Papers, LC.

11. T. Cadwalader to N. Biddle, Dec. 22, 1831, *ibid.*

12. T. Cadwalader to N. Biddle, Dec. 29, 1831, *ibid.*

13. T. Cadwalader to N. Biddle, Dec. 23, 25, 26 (two letters), 1831, Biddle Papers, LC; Govan, *Biddle*, p. 172.

14. T. Cadwalader to N. Biddle, Dec. 26, 1831, Biddle Papers, LC.

15. N. Biddle to T. Cadwalader, Dec. 30, 1831, *ibid.*

16. N. Biddle to Heman Allen, Dec. 26, 1831, *ibid.*

17. *United States Telegraph*, Dec. 12, 1831.

18. N. Biddle to Edward Shippen, Dec. 23, 1831, Biddle Papers, LC.

19. S. Smith to W. C. Rives, Jan. 3, 1832, Rives Papers, LC.

20. N. Biddle to T. Cadwalader, Dec. 23, 1831, Biddle Papers, LC.

21. T. Cadwalader to N. Biddle [Jan. 4, 1832]; N. Biddle to S. Smith, Jan. 4, 1832; T. C. Cadwalader, Jr., to G. McDuffie, Jan. 4, 1832 [incorrectly dated 1831], *ibid.*

22. Thurlow Weed, *Autobiography* (Boston, 1883), pp. 373–375.

23. Adams, *Memoirs*, VIII, 457.

24. T. Cadwalader to N. Biddle, Dec. 26, 1831, Biddle Papers, LC.

25. Catterall, *Second Bank*, pp. 372–375.

26. LMcL to N. Biddle, Jan. 5, 1832, Biddle Papers, LC.

27. N. Biddle to G. McDuffie, Jan. 5, 6, 1832, *ibid.*

28. G. Dallas to N. Biddle, Jan. 9, 1832, *ibid.*; *Register of Debates*, 22d Cong., 1st sess., pp. 54–55; Belohlavek, "Dallas, the Democracy, and the Bank War of 1832," *PMHB*, XCVI, 381.

29. A. Jackson to M. Van Buren, Nov. 14, 1831, Jackson Papers, LC.

30. LMcL to M. Van Buren, Dec. 14, 1831, Van Buren Papers, LC.

31. *Niles' Register,* XLI (Dec. 24, 1831), 297.

32. *Senate Journal,* 22d Cong., 1st sess., pp. 494, 500, 501; James Watson Webb to M. Van Buren, Dec. 31, 1831, Van Buren Papers, LC.

33. Gabriel Moore to Ninian Edwards, Dec. 31, 1831, in Edwards, *History of Illinois,* p. 509; J. W. Webb to M. Van Buren, Dec. 31, 1831; C. C. Cambreleng to M. Van Buren, Jan. 4, 1832, Van Buren Papers, LC.

34. C. C. Cambreleng to M. Van Buren, Jan. 4, 1832, *ibid.*

35. Hammond, *Banks and Politics,* pp. 387–392.

36. *Niles' Register,* XLI (Jan. 7, 1832), 339; (Jan. 21, 1832), 378; Abel C. Pepper to John Tipton, Jan. 12, 1832, in Tipton, *Papers,* II, 497–498.

37. LMcL to M. Van Buren, Jan. 12, 1832, Van Buren Papers, LC.

38. *Senate Journal,* 22d Cong., 1st sess., appendix, pp. 494, 500, 505, 507–508.

39. *Register of Debates,* 22d Cong., 1st sess., pp. 1309–1386; Van Buren, *Autobiography,* pp. 530–531.

40. *Register of Debates,* 22d Cong., 1st sess., p. 1360; *Niles' Register,* XLI (Feb. 11, 1832), 425; S. Smith to N. Biddle, Jan. 4, 7, 1832, Biddle Papers, LC.

41. Isaac Hill to M. Van Buren, Jan. 29, 1832, Van Buren Papers, LC.

42. Louis R. Harland, "Public Career of William Berkeley Lewis," *Tennessee Historical Quarterly,* VII (1948), 132–133.

43. W. B. Lewis to A. C. Flagg, Feb. 14, 1832, in Van Buren, *Autobiography,* p. 591.

44. W. L. Marcy to M. Van Buren, Jan. 26, 1832, Van Buren Papers, LC; *Register of Debates,* 22d Cong., 1st sess., pp. 1367–1375.

45. Wiltse, *Calhoun, Nullifier,* pp. 127–128; Benton, *Thirty Years' View,* I, 219.

46. J. C. Calhoun to S. Ingham, Feb. 11, 1832, Calhoun-Ingham Correspondence, Calhoun Papers, South Caroliniana Library.

47. Wikoff, *Reminiscences of an Idler,* p. 30.

48. Parton, *Jackson,* II, 379; Benton, *Thirty Years' View,* I, 215.

49. Van Buren, *Autobiography,* pp. 506–508.

50. A. Jackson to M. Van Buren, Dec. 17, 1831, *ibid.,* p. 508; Jackson, *Correspondence,* IV, 385.

51. C. C. Cambreleng to M. Van Buren, Feb. 4, 1832, Van Buren Papers, LC.

52. C. C. Cambreleng to M. Van Buren, Feb. 5, 1832, *ibid.*

53. Van Buren, *Autobiography,* pp. 502–503.

54. Charles Dayan to A. C. Flagg, Jan. 29, 1832, A. C. Flagg Papers, NYPL.

55. T. H. Benton to M. Van Buren, Jan. 28, 1832, Benton, *Thirty Years' View,* I, 219.

56. W. A. Duer to M. Van Buren, Feb. 1, 1832, Van Buren Papers, LC.

57. John Floyd, "Diary," pp. 173–174.

58. C. J. Ingersoll to N. Biddle, Feb. 3, 1832, Biddle Papers, LC; *Register of Debates,* 22d Cong., 1st sess., p. 1359.

59. J. R. Poinsett to Dr. J. Johnson, Feb. 4, 1832, in Poinsett, *Calendar,* pp. 4–5.

60. James Iredell to Willie P. Mangum, Feb. 4, 1832, in Mangum, *Papers,* I, 473.

61. W. L. Marcy to A. C. Flagg, Feb. 6 [1832], Flagg Papers, NYPL.

62. Charles Dayan to A. C. Flagg, Feb. 12, 1832, *ibid.*

63. M. Van Buren to A. Jackson, Feb. 20, 21, 1832, in Jackson, *Correspondence,* IV, 407–408.

64. Parton, *Jackson,* III, 421; John Eaton to William B. Lewis [May 21, 1832], in Van Buren, *Autobiography,* pp. 590–591.

65. William B. Lewis, Notes, in Van Buren, *Autobiography,* p. 588.

66. W. T. Read to George Read, May 19, 1832, Richard S. Rodney Collection, HSD.

67. William B. Lewis, Notes, in Van Buren, *Autobiography,* pp. 589–590.

68. LMcL to H. M. Ridgely, Sept. 15, 1831, McLane Papers.

69. White, *Jacksonians,* pp. 308, 350–353, 355.

70. *House Executive Document* No. 47, 22d Cong., 1st sess.; *House Executive Document* No. 42, 22d Cong., 2d sess.

71. W. T. Read, Statement, Aug. 1, 1867; W. T. Read to George Read, Jr., Nov. 8, 1831; LMcL to W. T. Read, Nov. 15, 1831; W. T. Read to LMcL, Nov. 19, 1831; W. T. Read to George Read, Jan. 17, 1832, Richard S. Rodney Collection, HSD.

72. W. T. Read to George Read, Jr., Dec. 15, 1831; W. T. Read to George Read, Jan. 17, 18, Feb. 7, 1832, *ibid.*

73. W. T. Read to George Read, Jan. 24, 1832; W. T. Read to George Read, Jr., Dec. 15, 1831, *ibid.*

74. W. T. Read to George Read, Jan. 18, 1832, *ibid.*

75. W. T. Read to George Read, Jr., May 31, 1832; W. T. Read to George Read, June 20, 1832, *ibid.*

76. W. T. Read to George Read, Dec. 1, 1832, *ibid.*

77. LMcL to Lewis Cass [June 24, 1832], Cass Papers, Clements Library, Ann Arbor; W. T. Read to George Read, Jr., June 18, 1832, Richard S. Rodney Collection, HSD.

78. George Bancroft to his wife, Dec. 27, 1831, in Howe, *George Bancroft,* I, 196–197; B. F. Butler to his wife, March 17, 1832, Butler Papers, New York State Library, Albany; W. T. Read to George Read, Jr., March 20, 1832, Richard S. Rodney Collection, HSD.

79. W. Irving to Peter Irving, June 16, 1832, in P. M. Irving, *Washington Irving,* II, 160.

80. H. W. Smith, *Sporting Family of the Old South* (Albany, 1936), pp. 269, 410; LMcL to A. Jackson, Aug. 3, 1832, Jackson Papers, 1st ser., LC.

81. W. T. Read to George Read, May 19, 1832, Richard S. Rodney Collection, HSD.

82. W. T. Read to George Read, Jr., July 28, Nov. 12, 1832, *ibid.*

83. B. F. Butler to wife, March 12, 1832, Butler Papers, New York State Library; B. F. Butler to J. S. Johnston, Feb. 18 [1832], Johnston Collection,

HSP; B. F. Butler to G. C. Verplanck, Mon. morning [no year], and other undated letters, Verplanck Papers, NYHS; N. Biddle to T. Cadwalader, May 30, 1832, Biddle Papers, LC; C. A. Porter Hopkins, ed., "A Marylander Visits President Jackson, 1832," *Maryland Historical Magazine*, LIV (March, 1959), 112–113; George W. Pierson, *Tocqueville and Beaumont in America* (New York, 1938), p. 670.

84. R. M. McLane, *Reminiscences*, p. 51.

85. LMcL to Lewis Cass, May 7, 1832, Cass Papers, Clements Library.

86. R. M. McLane, *Reminiscences*, pp. 52–53.

87. LMcL to W. C. Rives, Nov. 21, 1832, Rives Papers, LC.

88. C. A. Davis to N. Biddle, Dec. 6, 1832, Biddle Papers, LC.

89. Williams, *Washington Irving*, II, 29; P. M. Irving, *Washington Irving*, II, 159–160.

90. [W. Irving] to Rebecca McLane, Aug. 1, 1832, Fisher Collection.

91. Dr. Allen McLane to Robert Gilmor, June 18, 1832, Dreer Collection, HSP; Williams, *Washington Irving*, II, 43.

92. P. M. Irving, *Washington Irving*, II, 171; Williams, *Washington Irving*, II, 48.

93. LMcL to N. Biddle, Jan. 13, 1832, Biddle Papers, LC. *Cf.* Horace Binney to N. Biddle, Jan. 23, 1832, *ibid.*

94. N. Biddle to Horace Binney, Jan. 25, 1832, *ibid.*

95. LMcL to G. C. Verplanck, Jan. 24, 1832, Verplanck Papers, NYHS; Horace Binney to N. Biddle, Jan. 28, 1832, Biddle Papers, LC.

96. Swisher, *Taney*, p. 186.

97. C. J. Ingersoll to N. Biddle, Feb. 9, 10, 17, 21, 23, 1832, Biddle Papers, LC.

98. C. J. Ingersoll to N. Biddle, Feb. 13, 28, 1832, *ibid.*

99. C. J. Ingersoll to N. Biddle, Feb. 29, March 1, 1832, *ibid.*

100. C. J. Ingersoll to N. Biddle, March 6, 1832, *ibid.*

101. G. Dallas to N. Biddle, March 15, 1832, *ibid.;* Govan, *Biddle*, p. 198.

102. Govan, *Biddle*, pp. 207–208; Parton, *Jackson*, III, 496–498; Taney, Bank War MS, pp. 143–144, LC; Swisher, *Taney*, p. 208; *New-York Evening Post*, April 10, 1832.

103. Govan, *Biddle*, p. 198.

104. N. Biddle to T. Cadwalader, May 30, 1832, Biddle Papers, LC.

105. R. Smith to N. Biddle, May 31, 1832, *ibid.*

106. *Register of Debates*, 22d Cong., 1st sess., pp. 1045–1047.

107. T. Cadwalader to N. Biddle, May 31 [1832]; N. Biddle to T. Cadwalader, July 3, 1832, Biddle Papers, LC.

108. *Register of Debates*, 22d Cong., 1st sess., pp. 3913–3914.

109. *National Intelligencer*, July 19, 1832.

110. Washington *Globe*, July 20, 1832.

111. W. T. Read to George Read, Jr., July 21, 1832, Richard S. Rodney Collection, HSD.

112. Taney, Bank War MS, pp. 122–126, LC.

113. *House Journal*, 22d Cong., 1st sess., pp. 39, 40.

114. Stanwood, *American Tariff Controversies in the Nineteenth Century*, I, 373–374.

115. *Register of Debates*, 22d Cong., 1st sess., pp. 55, 57, 66–67.

116. *Ibid.*, pp. 12–13.

117. Adams, *Memoirs*, VIII, 444–448.

118. *Ibid.*, pp. 437, 438, 439.

119. *Ibid.*, pp. 457–458; LMcL to J. Q. Adams, Jan. 14, 16, 1832, Adams Papers, Part IV, reel 495, Massachusetts Historical Society.

120. *House Journal*, 22d Cong., 1st sess., pp. 195, 206.

121. *Register of Debates*, 22d Cong., 1st sess., p. 1293.

122. Day, "The Early Development of the American Cotton Manufacture," *Quarterly Journal of Economics*, XXXIX, 451.

123. *House Executive Document* No. 222, 22d Cong., 1st sess., pp. 1, 6–10.

124. *Documents Relative to Manufactures in the United States, House Executive Document* No. 308, 22d Cong., 1st sess., 2 vols. (Washington, 1833), known as the *McLane Report on Manufactures*.

125. LMcL to G. C. Verplanck, June 28, 1832, Verplanck Papers, NYHS.

126. Adams, *Memoirs*, VIII, 460.

127. *Register of Debates*, 22d Cong., 1st sess., p. 186.

128. J. R. Poinsett to Joseph Johnson, Feb. 4, 1832, in Poinsett, *Calendar*, pp. 44–45; Walters, *Gallatin*, p. 360; *Register of Debates*, 22d Cong., 1st sess., pp. 1178–1179.

129. A. Gallatin to William Drayton, March 19, 1832 (not sent), Gallatin Papers, NYHS; A. Gallatin to William Drayton, April 7, 1832, in Gallatin, *Writings*, II, 457.

130. W. T. Read to George Read, Jr., March 20, 1832, R. S. Rodney Collection, HSD; Mrs. J. Q. Adams to J. Q. Adams, March 24, April 13, 1832, Adams Papers, Part IV, reel 495, Massachusetts Historical Society; LMcL to B. C. Howard, April 26, 1832, Dreer Collection, HSP.

131. LMcL to G. C. Verplanck, April 27 [1832], Verplanck Papers, NYHS.

132. *House Executive Document* No. 222, 22d Cong., 1st sess.

133. Washington *Globe*, April 30, 1832; LMcL to F. P. Blair, April 28, 1832, Blair-Lee Papers, Princeton University.

134. *Niles' Register*, XLII (May 26, 1832), 227; Washington *Globe*, May 9, 1832.

135. W. T. Read to George Read, Jr., May 31, 1832, Richard S. Rodney Collection, HSD.

136. LMcL to A. Jackson, May 5, 1832, Jackson Papers, 1st ser., LC; LMcL to G. C. Verplanck, April 30 [1832], Verplanck Papers, NYHS.

137. J. Q. Adams, Diary, May 4, 5, 7, 9, 10, 12, 15, 16, 1832, Adams Papers, reel 49, Massachusetts Historical Society.

138. J. Q. Adams to C. F. Adams, May 16, 1832, *ibid.*, reel 495.

139. *House Committee Report* No. 481, 22d Cong., 1st sess.

140. W. T. Read to George Read, June 20, 26, 1832, Richard S. Rodney Collection, HSD.

141. Washington *Globe*, June 1, 1832.

142. Draft of speech by J. Q. Adams in House of Representatives, June 6, 1832, Adams Papers, reel 496, Massachusetts Historical Society.

143. *Senate Journal,* 22d Cong., 1st sess., pp. 218, 261, 345.

144. *Register of Debates,* 22d Cong., 1st sess., p. 1180.

145. *Ibid.,* p. 1217.

146. *Ibid.,* pp. 1275, 1289.

147. W. T. Read to George Read, June 20, 1832, Richard S. Rodney Collection, HSD.

148. William Drayton to A. Gallatin, April 11, 1832, Gallatin Papers, NYHS.

149. J. Q. Adams to his wife, June 29, 1832, Adams Papers, reel 496, Massachusetts Historical Society.

150. H. Niles to J. Q. Adams, July 14, 1832, *ibid.*

151. *Niles' Register,* XLII (June 9, 1832), 279; Washington *Globe,* May 25, 1832.

152. J. Q. Adams to wife, May 23, 1832, Adams Papers, reel 495; July 19, 1832, *ibid.,* reel 496, Massachusetts Historical Society.

CHAPTER TWELVE: DENOUEMENT

1. LMcL to A. Jackson, Aug. 3, 1832, Jackson Papers, 1st ser., LC.

2. LMcL to N. Biddle, July 19, 1832, U.S. Finance Papers, Misc., 1827–1897, LC.

3. Catterall, *Second Bank,* pp. 268–269.

4. N. Biddle to Thomas W. Ludlow, July 23, 1832, Biddle Papers, LC.

5. N. Biddle to LMcL, July 26, 1832, Adams Papers, reel 496 (enclosed with N. Biddle to J. Q. Adams, Nov. 19, 1832), Massachusetts Historical Society.

6. LMcL to N. Biddle, July 19, 1832, U.S. Finance Papers, Misc., 1827–1897, LC.

7. A. Dickins to N. Biddle, Aug. 4, 1832, Biddle Papers, LC.

8. N. Biddle to A. Dickins, Aug. 7, 1832, *ibid.*

9. Catterall, *Second Bank,* pp. 269–272; *House Committee Report* No. 121, 22d Cong., 2d sess., pp. 19, 50–52, and *passim.*

10. *New-York Evening Post,* Oct. 11, 1832.

11. N. Biddle, Memorandum, Oct. 19, 1831 [to Dec., 1832], Biddle Papers, LC; *House Committee Report* No. 121, 22d Cong., 2d sess., pp. 182–184.

12. *House Committee Report* No. 121, 22d Cong., 2d sess., pp. 119–120; N. Biddle to LMcL, Oct. 27, 1832, copy in Adams Papers, reel 496, Massachusetts Historical Society; N. Biddle to A. Dickins, Oct. 28, 1832, Biddle Papers, LC.

13. Taney, Bank War MS, pp. 147–158, LC.

14. J. S. Johnston to N. Biddle, Dec. 2, 1832, Biddle Papers, LC.

15. *Niles' Register,* XLIII (Oct. 13, 1832), 99.

16. C. C. Cambreleng to M. Van Buren, Jan. 4, Feb. 4, 1832, Van Buren Papers, LC; Joel R. Poinsett to Joseph Johnson, Feb. 4, 1832, in Poinsett, *Calendar,* pp. 44–45; Van Buren, *Autobiography,* p. 590.

17. Van Buren, *Autobiography*, pp. 568–571.

18. *Ibid.*, pp. 570–573; M. Van Buren to F. P. Blair, Oct. 15, 1845, Van Buren Papers, 2d ser., LC; LMcL to M. Van Buren, July 7, 1832, *ibid.*, 1st ser.

19. LMcL to W. B. Lewis, Sept. 22, 1832, Jackson-Lewis Papers, NYPL; LMcL to G. C. Verplanck, Sept. 28, 1832, Verplanck Papers, NYHS; LMcL to A. J. Donelson, Oct. 1, 1832, Donelson Papers, LC.

20. F. P. Blair to M. Van Buren, Sept. 30, 1832, Van Buren Papers, LC.

21. A. Kendall to M. Van Buren, Nov. 2, 1832, *ibid.*

22. A. Jackson to M. Van Buren, Dec. 17, 1831, *ibid.*, and quoted in Van Buren, *Autobiography*, p. 705n.

23. Hatcher, *Edward Livingston*, pp. 4, 35, 51, 119, 122, 333–334.

24. Van Buren, *Autobiography*, p. 572.

25. A. Jackson to M. Van Buren, Sept. 16, 1832, Van Buren Papers, LC.

26. LMcL to W. B. Lewis, Sept. 22, 1832, Jackson-Lewis Papers, NYPL; LMcL to A. J. Donelson, Oct. 1, 1832, Donelson Papers, LC.

27. LMcL to M. Van Buren, Nov. 1, 1832, Papers of the Secretaries of State, II, HM4699, Huntington Library, San Marino, California; [R. Colt?] to N. Biddle, Nov. 17, 1832, Biddle Papers, LC.

28. Van Buren, *Autobiography*, pp. 593–594, 596.

29. M. Van Buren to A. Jackson, Nov. 18, 1832, Van Buren Papers, LC.

30. Van Buren, *Autobiography*, p. 595.

31. Joel R. Poinsett to A. Jackson, Oct. 16, 1832, in Jackson, *Correspondence*, IV, 481.

32. *House Executive Document* No. 45, 22d Cong., 2d sess., pp. 92–97.

33. A. Jackson to George Breathitt, Nov. 7, 1832, in Jackson, *Correspondence*, IV, 484–485; to Poinsett, Nov. 7, 1832, *ibid.*, pp. 485–486.

34. *House Executive Document* No. 45, 22d Cong., 2d sess., pp. 97–99.

35. A. Jackson to M. Van Buren, Nov. 18, 1832, Van Buren Papers, LC.

36. A. Jackson to M. Van Buren, Nov. 25, 1832, in Van Buren, *Autobiography*, p. 595.

37. F. P. Blair to M. Van Buren, Oct. 10, 1845, Van Buren Papers, 2d ser., LC.

38. F. P. Blair to M. Van Buren, Oct. 22, 1845, *ibid.*

39. M. Van Buren to F. P. Blair, Oct. 15, 1845, *ibid.*; Van Buren, *Autobiography*, p. 594.

40. Kendall, *Autobiography*, p. 377.

41. A. Kendall to A. Jackson, Aug. 11, 1833; A. Jackson to M. Van Buren, Aug. 16, 1833, in Jackson, *Correspondence*, V, 152, 159.

42. See Ari Hoogenboom and Herbert Ershkowitz, "Levi Woodbury's 'Intimate Memoranda' of the Jackson Administration," *PMHB*, XCII (Oct., 1968), 510.

43. LMcL to M. Van Buren, Nov. 26, 1832, in Van Buren, *Autobiography*, pp. 596, 597.

44. M. Van Buren to A. Jackson, Nov. 29, 1832, *ibid.*, p. 598.

45. W. T. Read to George Read, Jr., June 26, 1832, Richard S. Rodney Collection, HSD.

46. Richard Smith to N. Biddle, April 15, 1833, Biddle Papers, LC.

47. Van Buren, *Autobiography*, pp. 598–600; LMcL to W. J. Duane, Aug. 6, 1829, Collection of Louis McLane, Phoenix, Arizona.

48. Parton, *Jackson*, III, 486; W. B. Lewis, "Notes and Corrections on the Third Volume of Parton's Life of Jackson," in Flower, *James Parton*, pp. 233–235.

49. R. B. Taney to M. Van Buren, March 3, 1860, in Bernard C. Steiner, "Taney's Letters to Van Buren in 1860," *Maryland Historical Magazine*, X (March, 1915), 15–16.

50. Parton, *Jackson*, III, 509–511; letter of W. J. Duane, Oct. 23, 1833, from *New Orleans Bulletin*, in *Niles' Register*, XLV (Dec. 21, 1833), 272; Duane, *Narrative and Correspondence Concerning the Removal of the Deposites*, pp. 2–4, 127–129.

51. Bassett, *Jackson*, p. 633.

52. F. P. Blair to M. Van Buren, Oct. 10, 1845, Van Buren Papers, 2d ser., LC.

53. Sellers, *Polk, Jacksonian*, p. 158; Michael Hoffman to M. Van Buren, Dec. 9, 1832, Van Buren Papers, LC; *Register of Debates*, 22d Cong., 1st sess., p. 1764.

54. J. G. Bennett to N. Biddle, Dec. 1, 1832, Biddle Papers, LC; J. G. Bennett to M. Van Buren, Dec. 1, 1832, Van Buren Papers, LC; Allan Nevins, "James Gordon Bennett, 1795–1872," *DAB*, II, 195–199.

55. P. M. Irving, *Washington Irving*, II, 171.

56. C. C. Cambreleng to M. Van Buren [between Dec. 10 and 18, 1832], Van Buren Papers, LC.

57. N. Biddle, Memoranda, dated Oct. 19, 1831, Biddle Papers, LC.

58. W. Irving to James K. Paulding, Jan. 3, 1833, in P. M. Irving, *Washington Irving*, II, 172.

59. *House Document* No. 3, 22d Cong., 2d sess., pp. 7–10; *House Document* No. 2, 22d Cong., 2d sess., pp. 8–9; *Register of Debates*, 22d Cong., 2d sess., p. 1090.

60. N. Biddle, Memorandum, dated Oct. 19, 1831, but continued at later date, Biddle Papers, LC.

61. *House Document* No. 3, 22d Cong., 2d sess., pp. 11–14.

62. John G. Watmough to N. Biddle [Dec., 1832], Biddle Papers, LC.

63. Quoted in *National Intelligencer*, Dec. 8, 1832.

64. *House Document* No. 2, 22d Cong., 2d sess., p. 10.

65. *House Document* No. 8, 22d Cong., 2d sess., p. 3; Catterall, *Second Bank*, p. 289; Sargent, *Public Men and Events*, I, 253.

66. N. Biddle to J. Q. Adams, Dec. 5, 1832, Adams Papers, Part IV, reel 496, Massachusetts Historical Society.

67. W. T. Read to George Read, Dec. 8, 1832, Richard S. Rodney Collection, HSD.

68. Quoted from Dale in Parton, *Jackson*, III, 462.

69. *Ibid.*, p. 466; Longaker, "Was Jackson's Kitchen Cabinet a Cabinet?" *Mississippi Valley Historical Review*, XLIV, 103–104.

656 *Notes to Pages 367 to 371*

70. Richardson, *Messages,* II, 640–656.
71. C. C. Cambreleng to M. Van Buren, Dec. 18, 1833, Van Buren Papers, LC.
72. D. Webster to Chief Justice Livermore, Jan. 5, 1833, Fletcher Webster, *Private Correspondence of Daniel Webster,* I, 530.
73. Richardson, *Messages,* II, 652–653.
74. G. C. Verplanck to A. Gallatin, Dec. 3, 1832, Gallatin Papers, NYHS.
75. *Register of Debates,* 22d Cong., 2d sess., pp. 6, 7, 8, 11, 926.
76. Adams, *Memoirs,* VIII, 504, 510; J. Q. Adams to Charles F. Adams, Dec. 25, 1832, Adams Papers, Part IV, reel 496, Massachusetts Historical Society; *House Report* No. 122, 22d Cong., 2d sess.
77. A. Jackson to F. P. Blair, Aug. 12, 1841, in Jackson, *Correspondence,* VI, 118.
78. Mahlon Dickerson to M. Van Buren, Jan. 11, 1833; C. C. Cambreleng to M. Van Buren, Dec. 18, 29, 1832, Van Buren Papers, LC; Sargent, *Public Men and Events,* I, 233; Tyler, *The Tylers,* I, 446; Sellers, *Polk, Jacksonian,* p. 158; Silas Wright, Jr., to A. C. Flagg, Jan. 27, 1833, A. C. Flagg Papers, NYPL.
79. C. C. Cambreleng to M. Van Buren, Dec. 18, 1832, Van Buren Papers, LC; LMcL to A. Jackson, Dec. 27 [1832], Jackson Papers, 1st ser., LC.
80. *House Report* No. 14, 22d Cong., 2d sess.
81. C. C. Cambreleng to M. Van Buren, Dec. 18, 1832; Mahlon Dickerson to M. Van Buren, Jan. 11, 1833, Van Buren Papers, LC.
82. John Tipton to Calvin Fletcher, Jan. 11, 1833, in Tipton, *Papers,* II, 772.
83. LMcL to G. C. Verplanck, Jan. 16 [1833], Verplanck Papers, NYHS; *United States Telegraph,* Jan. 8, 1833; R. M. McLane, *Reminiscences,* p. 43.
84. *House Document* No. 45, 22d Cong., 2d sess., pp. 1–19; Richardson, *Messages,* II, 640-656; Freehling, *Prelude to Civil War,* pp. 280–285.
85. *Register of Debates,* 22d Cong., 2d sess., pp. 100–103; W. T. Read to George Read, Jr., Jan. 19, 1833, Richard S. Rodney Collection, HSD.
86. LMcL to M. Van Buren, Jan. 23, 1833, Van Buren Papers, LC.
87. *Ibid.;* Washington *Globe,* Jan. 19, 1833.
88. LMcL to G. C. Verplanck, Jan. 16 [1833], Verplanck Papers, NYHS.
89. LMcL to M. Van Buren, Jan. 23, 1833, Van Buren Papers, LC.
90. *National Intelligencer,* Jan. 17, 1833.
91. H. Clay to Francis Brooke, Jan. 17, 1833, in Colton, *Works of Clay,* V, 348.
92. Wiltse, *Calhoun, Nullifier,* pp. 180–181.
93. *Ibid.,* p. 190; *Register of Debates,* 22d Cong., 2d sess., p. 688.
94. Wiltse, *Calhoun, Nullifier,* p. 449.
95. LMcL to Joel Poinsett, Jan. 4 [1833], Poinsett Papers, HSP; W. B. Lawrence to A. Gallatin, Jan. 6, 1833, Gallatin Papers, NYHS; Mahlon Dickerson to M. Van Buren, Jan. 11, 1833, Van Buren Papers, LC.
96. LMcL to M. Van Buren, Jan. 23, 1833, Van Buren Papers, LC; Silas Wright to A. C. Flagg, Jan. 27, 1833, A. C. Flagg Papers, NYPL.
97. Van Buren, *Autobiography,* p. 557.

98. LMcL to M. Van Buren, Jan. 23, 1833, Van Buren Papers, LC; A. Jackson to Joel Poinsett, Jan. 24, 1833, in Jackson, *Correspondence*, V, 12.

99. *Register of Debates*, 22d Cong., 2d sess., pp. 1250–1251, 1256.

100. Silas Wright to M. Van Buren, Jan. 13, 1833, Van Buren Papers, LC; W. T. Read to George Read, Jr., Jan. 19, 1833, Richard S. Rodney Collection, HSD.

101. LMcL to M. Van Buren, Jan. 23, 1833, Van Buren Papers, LC.

102. C. C. Cambreleng to M. Van Buren, Feb. 5, 1833, *ibid.*

103. Mahlon Dickerson to M. Van Buren, Jan. 11, 1833, *ibid.*

104. Bryant, *A Discourse on the Life, Character and Writings of Gulian Crommelin Verplanck*, pp. 28–29.

105. *Laws of the United States*, VIII (Washington: W. A. Davis, 1835), 788–792.

106. *Register of Debates*, 22d Cong., 2d sess., pp. 484–486; testimony of Hugh L. White, Feb. 13, 1837, in Scott, *Memoir of Hugh Lawson White*, pp. 299–300. *Cf. ibid.*, pp. 239–240.

107. J. M. Clayton, speech in Wilmington, June 15, 1844, in Colton, *Works of Clay*, II, 252–259; Benton, *Thirty Years' View*, I, 342–344; Sargent, *Public Men and Events*, I, 237–239; *Register of Debates*, 22d Cong., 2d sess., pp. 697–701, 715–716; J. M. Clayton to E. I. du Pont, Feb. 13, 1833, Eleuthera Bradford du Pont Collection, file 120, EMHL; J. M. Clayton to J. A. Bayard, Jan. 6, 1833 [incorrectly dated 1832], Hilles Collection.

108. *House Journal*, 22d Cong., 2d sess., pp. 415–428; *Register of Debates*, 22d Cong., 2d sess., pp. 1772–1811.

109. Benton, *Thirty Years' View*, I, 309.

110. A. Jackson to Joel Poinsett, March 6, 1833, in Jackson, *Correspondence*, V, 28–29.

111. Ambler, *Life and Diary of John Floyd*, p. 214.

112. J. C. Calhoun to S. Ingham, March 25, 1833, Calhoun-Ingham Correspondence, Calhoun Papers, South Caroliniana Library.

113. J. Q. Adams to C. F. Adams, March 26, 1833, Adams Papers, Part IV, reel 497, Massachusetts Historical Society.

114. LMcL to J. Buchanan, June 20, 1833, Buchanan Papers, HSP.

115. *House Document* No. 2, 22d Cong., 2d sess., p. 10.

116. *House Document* No. 3, 22d Cong., 2d sess., p. 14.

117. A. Jackson to J. Polk, Dec. 16, 1832, in Jackson, *Correspondence*, IV, 501.

118. *Register of Debates*, 22d Cong., 2d sess., pp. 824–833, 840–853, 861–862.

119. N. Biddle to G. McDuffie, Jan. 9, 1833, Biddle Papers, LC.

120. N. Biddle to W. B. Shepherd, Jan. 26, 1837; N. Biddle to J. G. Watmough, Jan. 8, 1833, *ibid.*

121. *Register of Debates*, 22d Cong., 2d sess., p. 859.

122. *National Intelligencer*, Jan. 3, 1833.

123. Washington *Globe*, Jan. 3, 1833.

124. *Ibid.*, Jan. 16, 1833.

125. F. P. Blair to LMcL, Jan. 4, 1833, draft, and LMcL to F. P. Blair, Jan. 4, 1833, Blair-Lee Collection, Princeton University.

126. LMcL to F. P. Blair, Jan. 15 [1833], *ibid.*

127. Washington *Globe,* Jan. 16, 1833.

128. *National Intelligencer,* Jan. 4, 8, 1833.

129. N. Biddle to John G. Watmough, Jan. 13, 1833; S. Jaudon to N. Biddle, Jan. 21, 1833, Biddle Papers, LC.

130. Sellers, *Polk, Jacksonian,* p. 189.

131. LMcL to J. Polk, Feb. 8 [1833], Polk Papers, LC.

132. *House Journal,* 22d Cong., 2d sess., pp. 325–328; *Register of Debates,* 22d Cong., 2d sess., pp. 1707–1716; Manuel Eyre to N. Biddle, Feb. 4, 1833, Biddle Papers, LC.

133. M. Eyre to N. Biddle, Feb. 14, and Biddle to P. P. F. Degrand, Feb. 20, 1833, Biddle Papers, LC.

134. Sellers, *Polk, Jacksonian,* pp. 191–192.

135. LMcL to J. Polk, Feb. 3, 4, March 2, and undated note marked "Sunday," 1833, Polk Papers, LC; J. S. Johnston to N. Biddle, Feb. 3, 1833, Biddle Papers, LC.

136. John G. Watmough to N. Biddle, Feb. 27, 1833, Biddle Papers, LC.

137. Washington *Globe,* March 14, 1833.

138. N. Biddle to H. Clay, Feb. 8, 1833; N. Biddle to C. A. Wickliffe, Feb. 8, 1833, Biddle Papers, LC.

139. R. Willing to N. Biddle, Feb. 10, 1833, *ibid.*

140. N. Biddle to M. Eyre, Feb. 8, 13, 1833, *ibid.*

141. LMcL to W. C. Rives, Jan. 7, 1833, Rives Papers, LC.

142. N. Biddle to M. Eyre, Feb. 8, 1833, Biddle Papers, LC.

143. N. Biddle to J. G. Watmough, Feb. 22, 1833; N. Biddle to H. Clay, Feb. 28, 1833, *ibid.*

144. *House Journal,* 22d Cong., 2d sess., p. 450; *Register of Debates,* 22d Cong., 2d sess., pp. 1898–1899, 1922–1925.

145. *House Committee Report* No. 121, 22d Cong., 2d sess., pp. 42, 89–90.

146. *Register of Debates,* 22d Cong., 2d sess., pp. 1927–1935.

147. Samuel Carson to N. Biddle, March 2, 1833, Biddle Papers, LC; enclosure with N. Biddle to J. Q. Adams, March 9, 1833, Adams Papers, Part IV, reel 497, Massachusetts Historical Society.

148. N. Biddle to J. G. Watmough, Feb. 19, 1833, Biddle Papers, LC.

149. J. G. Watmough to N. Biddle, March 12, 1833; N. Biddle to J. G. Watmough, March 13, 1833, *ibid.*

150. J. G. Watmough to N. Biddle, March 16, 1833, *ibid.*

151. N. Biddle to J. G. Watmough, March 18, 1833, *ibid.*

152. *Laws of the U.S.,* VIII (1835), 787–788; John Connell to N. Biddle, March 5, 1833; Silas E. Burrows to N. Biddle, March 5, 1833, Biddle Papers, LC.

153. *Niles' Register,* XLIV (March 9, 1833), 29; R. Smith to N. Biddle, April 12, 1833, Biddle Papers, LC.

154. McLemore, *Franco-American Diplomatic Relations*, pp. 99–102; N. Biddle to J. McKim, Jr., April 27, 1833, Biddle Papers, LC.

155. A. Jackson to M. Van Buren, April 25, 1833; LMcL to M. Van Buren, April 25, 1833, Van Buren Papers, LC; N. Biddle to Robert Lenox, May 10, 1833, Biddle Papers, LC.

156. *United States Telegraph*, April 1, 1833, Washington *Globe*, April 1, 16, 1833; *National Intelligencer*, April 3, 4, 16, 1833; J. Q. Adams to C. F. Adams, April 1, and Mrs. J. Q. Adams to Mrs. C. F. Adams, April 4, 1833, Adams Papers, Part IV, reel 497, Massachusetts Historical Society; R. S. Briscoe to Comptroller of the Treasury, April 11, 1833, U.S. Boxes, folder "1832–1833, U.S. Treasury," NYPL; *Niles' Register*, XLIV (April 6, 1833), 84, and (April 20, 1833), 120–122.

157. Ambler, *Life and Diary of John Floyd*, p. 230; *New-York Evening Post*, April 15, 1833; Washington *Globe*, April 22, 1833; *Niles' Register*, L (April 2, 1836), 74, and (June 18, 1836), 276; *Register of Debates*, 24th Cong., 2d sess., p. 1412; Wilhelmus Bogart Bryan, *A History of the National Capital* (Washington, 1914–1916), II, 242; *National Intelligencer*, March 28, 1836; *Baltimore American*, March 28, 29, 1836.

158. Washington *Globe*, April 8, 1833.

159. Poore, *Perley's Reminiscences*, I, 103.

160. Kendall, *Autobiography*, p. 375.

161. Govan, *Biddle*, p. 227.

162. Duane, *Narrative*, p. 38.

163. "Letters of Andrew Jackson to Roger Brooke Taney," *Maryland Historical Magazine*, IV, 297.

164. *Ibid.*, 298–299.

165. Jackson, *Correspondence*, V, 33–41.

166. Kendall, *Autobiography*, p. 376.

167. Hamilton, *Reminiscences*, pp. 253–258.

168. *National Intelligencer*, March 14, 1833.

169. Anonymous to N. Biddle, April 13 [1833]; R. M. Gibbes to N. Biddle, April 13, 1833; R. Smith to N. Biddle, April 15, 1833, Biddle Papers, LC.

170. Jackson, *Correspondence*, V, 75–101.

171. *Ibid.*, 101, 102–104.

172. R. Smith to N. Biddle, April 15, 1833, Biddle Papers, LC.

173. *New-York Evening Post*, March 20, 1833.

174. E. Hayward to LMcL, March 11, 1833, Clarence E. Carter, ed., *Territorial Papers of the United States* (Washington, 1934–1962), XII, 585.

175. *National Intelligencer*, April 15, 1833.

176. Draft, *c.* May 8, 1833, Jackson Papers, 2d ser., LC.

177. Fisher, *Life of Benjamin Silliman*, I, 374–377.

178. *Senate Journal*, 24th Cong., 1st sess., p. 272; *National Intelligencer*, Feb. 16, 19, 1833.

179. *Niles' Register*, XLIV (May 4, 1833), 145; (June 29, 1833), 283; XLV (Jan. 11, 1834), 329; (Jan. 18, 1834), 346; (Jan. 25, 1834), 365; Washington *Globe*, April 29, 1833; *Register of Debates*, 23rd Cong., 1st sess.,

pp. 199–205; Taussig, *Tariff History of the United States,* p. 111; LMcL to A. Jackson, April 20, 1833, in *Senate Document* No. 43, 23d Cong., 1st sess.; J. M. Clayton, speech, June 15, 1844, in Colton, *Works of Henry Clay,* II, 257n.

180. *Niles' Register,* XLIV (June 8, 1833), 233.

181. *Ibid.* (May 4, 1833), 150.

182. R. Smith to N. Biddle, April 15, 1833, Biddle Papers, LC.

183. LMcL to M. Van Buren, April 25, 1833, Van Buren Papers, LC.

184. *National Intelligencer,* May 31, 1833.

185. Washington *Globe,* June 3, 1833; *New-York Evening Post,* May 31, 1833.

186. J. A. Hamilton to M. Van Buren, Feb. 27, 1829, Van Buren Papers, LC.

187. Washington *Globe,* June 12, 1833.

CHAPTER THIRTEEN: SECRETARY OF STATE

1. LMcL to A. J. Donelson, May 6, 1833, Blair-Lee Collection, Princeton University; Washington *Globe,* May 7, 1833.

2. LMcL to J. Buchanan, June 20, 1833, Buchanan Papers, HSP; Green, "On Tour with President Andrew Jackson," *New England Quarterly,* XXXVI, 214; Washington *Globe,* June 7, 1833.

3. Green, "On Tour with Jackson," p. 214; Washington *Globe,* June 12, 14, 1833; *National Intelligencer,* June 8, 1833.

4. Green, "On Tour with Jackson," pp. 215–220; Washington *Globe,* June 12, 13, 14, 1833; *National Intelligencer,* June 12, 14, 17, 19, 1833.

5. Washington *Globe,* June 17, 1833; *National Intelligencer,* June 18, 1833.

6. Van Buren, *Autobiography,* p. 602.

7. N. Biddle to R. Smith, April 8, 1833; R. Smith to N. Biddle, April 12, 1833, Biddle Papers, LC.

8. M. Van Buren to F. P. Blair, Oct. 15, 1845, Van Buren Papers, LC.

9. N. Biddle to Thomas Cooper, May 6, 1833, Biddle Papers, LC; Hammond, *Banks and Politics,* pp. 331–332.

10. M. Van Buren to F. P. Blair, Oct. 15, 1845, Van Buren Papers, LC.

11. W. B. Lewis, "Narrative," in Parton, *Jackson,* III, 504; D. Webster to N. Biddle, April 8 [1833], Biddle Papers, LC.

12. R. M. Gibbes to N. Biddle, April 13, 1833, Biddle Papers, LC.

13. LMcL to M. Van Buren, April 25, 1833; M. Van Buren to A. Jackson, May 2, 1833, Van Buren Papers, LC; Duane, *Narrative,* pp. 5–7.

14. Duane, *Narrative,* pp. 5–7, 38; Kendall, *Autobiography,* p. 377.

15. Duane, *Narrative,* pp. 7–9.

16. A. Jackson to M. Van Buren, June 6, 1833, in Jackson, *Correspondence,* V, 106.

17. J. S. Barbour to N. Biddle, June 12, 1833, Biddle Papers, LC.

18. A. Kendall to M. Van Buren, June 9, 1833, in Jackson, *Correspondence,* V, 106–108n.

19. Lewis, "Narrative," in Parton, *Jackson,* III, 505.

20. A. Kendall to M. Van Buren, June 9, 1833, in Jackson, *Correspondence,* V, 107n.

21. Hamilton, *Reminiscences,* p. 253.

22. M. Van Buren to F. P. Blair, Oct. 15, 1845, Van Buren Papers, LC; Van Buren, *Autobiography,* p. 602; James, *Andrew Jackson, Portrait of a President,* pp. 345–346; Hoogenboom and Ershkowitz, "Levi Woodbury's 'Intimate Memoranda,' " *PMHB,* XCII, 512–513.

23. Duane, *Narrative,* pp. 12–35.

24. Kendall, *Autobiography,* p. 377.

25. Duane, *Narrative,* pp. 9–10, 130.

26. Washington *Globe,* June 17, 1833.

27. LMcL to J. Buchanan, June 20, 1833, Buchanan Papers, HSP.

28. Hamilton, *Reminiscences,* p. 258; "A Calm Observer," in *National Intelligencer,* Oct. 9, 1845.

29. Duane, *Narrative,* p. 130.

30. Kendall, *Autobiography,* p. 383; A. Kendall to A. Jackson, Aug. 14, 1833, in Jackson, *Correspondence,* V, 156.

31. LMcL to A. Jackson, Aug. 1, 1833, Blair-Lee Papers, Princeton University.

32. R. Taney to M. Van Buren, March 8, 1860, Van Buren Papers, LC.

33. A. Kendall to A. Jackson, Aug. 14, 1833, in Jackson, *Correspondence,* V, 156.

34. A. Kendall to A. Jackson, Aug. 2, 11, 14, 1833, *ibid.,* pp. 146, 152, 156; Kendall, *Autobiography,* p. 379.

35. T. Cooper to N. Biddle, Aug. 9, 1833, Biddle Papers, LC.

36. A. Jackson to M. Van Buren, July 24, Aug. 16, 1833, in Jackson, *Correspondence,* V, 142–143, 159.

37. M. Van Buren to A. Jackson, Aug. 19, 30, 1833, *ibid.,* pp. 159–160, 173.

38. F. P. Blair to M. Van Buren, Aug. 17, 1833, Van Buren Papers, LC.

39. M. Van Buren to A. Jackson, Sept. 4, 1833, in Jackson, *Correspondence,* V, 179–181.

40. A. Jackson to M. Van Buren, Sept. 8, 1833; M. Van Buren to A. Jackson, Sept. 11, 14, 1833, *ibid.,* pp. 182–184, 185.

41. M. Van Buren to A. Jackson, Sept. 14, 1833, *ibid.,* p. 186; M. Van Buren to C. C. Cambreleng, Jan. 25, 1833, Van Buren Papers, LC.

42. Duane, *Narrative,* pp. 90, 92–94.

43. *Ibid.,* pp. 96–98.

44. *Ibid.,* pp. 98–99; A. Jackson to R. Taney, Sept. 15, 1833, in Jackson, *Correspondence,* V, 188; Swisher, *Taney,* p. 231.

45. Duane, *Narrative,* pp. 99–100; Woodbury, Opinion Concerning the Removal of the Deposits, Sept. 18, 1833, Woodbury Papers, XIII, LC.

46. Duane, *Narrative,* pp. 100–112; Jackson, *Correspondence,* V, 192–203, 206.

47. A. Jackson to M. Van Buren, Sept. 19, 1833, in Jackson, *Correspondence,* V, 204.

48. J. S. Barbour to N. Biddle, Sept. 21, 1833, Biddle Papers, LC.

49. W. B. Lewis to J. A. Hamilton, Sept. 22, 1833, in Hamilton, *Reminiscences*, p. 266.

50. F. P. Blair to M. Van Buren, Nov. 13, 1859, in Van Buren, *Autobiography*, p. 608.

51. Lewis, "Narrative," in Parton, *Jackson*, III, 501–503; A. Jackson to M. Van Buren, Sept. 24, 25, 1833, in Van Buren, *Autobiography*, pp. 603–604.

52. M. Van Buren to A. Jackson, Sept. 27, 1833, in Van Buren, *Autobiography*, p. 606.

53. Frank B. Woodford, *Lewis Cass, the Last Jeffersonian* (New Brunswick, 1950), p. 180.

54. Adams, *Memoirs*, X, 115.

55. Sargent, *Public Men and Events*, I, 264.

56. W. Irving to M. Van Buren, Oct. 5, 1833, in Van Buren, *Autobiography*, p. 610; W. Irving to Peter Irving, Oct. 28, 1833, in P. M. Irving, *Washington Irving*, II, 177–178.

57. M. Van Buren to A. Jackson, Sept. 27, 1833, in Van Buren, *Autobiography*, p. 606, and Oct. 2, 1833, in Jackson, *Correspondence*, V, 214.

58. Joseph O. Baylen, "James Buchanan's 'Calm of Despotism,'" *PMHB*, LXXVII (1953), 309; LMcL to J. Buchanan, June 20, 1833, Buchanan Papers, HSP; R. G. Beasley to W. C. Rives, Sept. 19, 1833, Rives Papers, LC; J. R. Clay to LMcL, Jan. 7, March 14, 1834, State Dept., Diplomatic Despatches, Russia, XII, NA.

59. *National Intelligencer*, June 5, 1833; *Register of the Department of State* (Washington, 1874), p. 56; Hunt, *Department of State*, p. 201.

60. LMcL to J. Polk, Feb. 3 [1833], Polk Papers, LC.

61. LMcL to A. J. Donelson, Dec. 4, 1833, Donelson Papers, VI, LC.

62. A. Dickins to N. Biddle, July 3, 1834, Biddle Papers, LC.

63. LMcL to A. O. Dayton June 17, 1833, collection of the late J. D. Otley, formerly at Bohemia.

64. N. Hall to R. Swartwout, Feb. 13, 1834, Robert Swartwout Papers, box 1, NYPL.

65. LMcL to John Ervin, Feb. 5, 1834; LMcL to Isaac Hill, Feb. 12, 1834; LMcL to C. C. Clay, Feb. 12, 1834, State Dept., Domestic Letters, XXVI, NA.

66. LMcL to W. T. Read, April 22, 1834, Richard S. Rodney Collection, HSD.

67. LMcL to L. Cass [May, 1834], Cass Papers, Clements Library.

68. LMcL to M. Van Buren, April 25, 1833, Van Buren Papers, LC.

69. Romulus G. Saunders to Thomas Ruffin, Nov. 4, 1833, in Ruffin, *Papers*, II, 105–106.

70. LMcL to Charles Bulfinch, Jr., June 20, 1833; D. Brent to C. Bulfinch, June 29, 1833, State Dept., Domestic Letters, XXV, NA; LMcL to John D. Craig, July 9, 17, Nov. 11, 1833, *ibid.*, XXVI.

71. *Senate Document* No. 398, 23d Cong., 1st sess., pp. 3–6.

72. LMcL to William P. Elliot, Dec. 17, 1833; LMcL to J. D. Craig, Dec.

16, 1833; Jan. 6, 7, 25, 27, Feb. 2, 4, 1834, State Dept., Domestic Letters, XXVI, NA.

73. LMcL to J. D. Craig, March 28, 1834, *ibid.; Senate Document* No. 398, 23d Cong., 1st sess., pp. 26–33; Weber, *The Patent Office,* p. 7.

74. A. Jackson to Congress, Jan. 6, Feb. 12, 1834, in Richardson, *Messages,* III, 37–38, 41; LMcL, circular letter, Jan. 6, 1834, State Dept., Diplomatic Instructions, Great Britain, XIV, NA; *Senate Document* No. 49, 23d Cong., 1st sess.

75. LMcL to J. Buchanan, July 12, 1833, State Dept., Diplomatic Instructions, Russia, XIV, NA.

76. LMcL to J. M. de Castillo y Lanzas, July 13, 1833, *House Executive Document* No. 351, 25th Cong., 2d sess., pp. 686–687.

77. LMcL to Anthony Butler, July 5, Nov. 28, 1833; June 11, 1834, *House Executive Document* No. 351, 25th Cong., 2d sess., pp. 106, 114, 142–143.

78. LMcL to J. Buchanan, July 5, 1833, State Dept., Diplomatic Instructions, Russia, XIV, NA; LMcL to Aaron Vail, July 27, 1833, *ibid.,* Great Britain; LMcL to A. Butler, Aug. 7, 1833, *House Executive Document* No. 351, 25th Cong., 2d sess., p. 107.

79. *The Diplomatic Correspondence of the United States of America from the Signing of the Definitive Treaty of Peace . . . to the Adoption of the Constitution* (Washington: Francis Preston Blair, 1833–1834); LMcL to William A. Weaver, April 14, 1834, State Dept., Domestic Letters, XXVI, NA.

80. *Register of Debates,* 23d Cong., 1st sess., pp. 2044–2045, 2054, 2063.

81. LMcL to J. Walter Barry, July 17, Oct. 13, 1833; LMcL to A. Vail, July 20, Oct. 14, Dec. 5, 1833, State Dept., Diplomatic Instructions, Great Britain, XIV, NA.

82. LMcL to B. F. Butler, Jan. 24, 1834, State Dept., Domestic Letters, XXVI, NA; Jackson, Annual Message, Dec. 1, 1834, in Richardson, *Messages,* III, 98; LMcL to Cornelius Van Ness, Sept. 27, 1833, in Manning, *Diplomatic Correspondence, Inter-American Affairs,* XI, 8–11.

83. J. M. Toner, "Some Account of George Washington's Library and Manuscript Records and Their Dispersion from Mount Vernon . . . ," *Annual Report of the American Historical Association, 1892* (Washington, 1893), pp. 80–81; *House Committee Report* No. 381, 23d Cong., 1st sess.; Hunt, *Department of State,* p. 323.

84. LMcL to A. Jackson, Aug. 20, 1833, State Dept., Domestic Letters, XXVI, NA; Hunt, *Department of State,* pp. 203–207, 210–211, 279–280; "The Following Arrangement of the Gentlemen Employed . . . in the Department of State from . . . the 30th of June, 1833" (printed 7-page pamphlet with proper names inserted by hand), collection of the late J. D. Otley, formerly at Bohemia.

85. J. G. Watmough to N. Biddle, Nov. 28, 1833, Biddle Papers, LC.

86. Adams, *Memoirs,* IX, 36.

87. Kendall, *Autobiography,* pp. 386–387.

88. W. Irving to LMcL, Jan. 20, 1834, Fisher Collection.

89. Philip Kearney to W. C. Rives, Oct. 8, 1833, Rives Papers, LC; John Tipton to Calvin Fletcher, Oct. 31, 1833, in Tipton, *Papers,* II, 840.

90. Thomas P. Moore to W. C. Rives, Nov. 7, 1833, Rives Papers, LC.

91. [R. Colt] to N. Biddle [Dec. 26, 1833], Biddle Papers, LC; W. Barry to Mrs. Susan Taylor, Feb. 22, 1834, in "Letters of William T. Barry," *William and Mary College Quarterly,* 1st ser., XIV, 238–239.

92. LMcL to M. Van Buren, Jan. 8 [1834], Van Buren Papers, 2d ser., LC.

93. W. P. Mangum to Duncan Cameron, Feb. 9, 1834, in Mangum, *Papers,* II, 76; John Tyler to Mrs. Tyler, Feb. 17, 1834, in Tyler, *The Tylers,* I, 485; *Niles' Register,* XLV (Feb. 15, 1834), 410.

94. Anonymous to N. Biddle [Feb. 20, 25, 1834], Biddle Papers, LC.

95. Wiltse, *Calhoun, Nullifier,* pp. 231–232; [R. Colt] to [N. Biddle], [Feb. 19, 1834], Biddle Papers, LC.

96. M. Van Buren to W. Irving, March 6, 1834, in Van Buren, *Autobiography,* p. 611.

97. W. Irving to M. Van Buren, March 11, 1834, *ibid.*

98. LMcL to M. Van Buren, March 14, 18 [1834], Van Buren Papers, LC.

99. Smith, *First Forty Years,* pp. 343–344.

100. James Graham to William A. Graham, Jan. 5, 1834, in Graham, *Papers,* I, 280.

101. N. P. Willis, quoted in *Quarterly Review* (London), LIV (Sept., 1835), 462–463.

102. John Bassett Moore, *History and Digest of the International Arbitrations to Which the United States Has Been a Party* (Washington, 1898), I, 138; Callahan, *Canadian Relations,* pp. 152–155.

103. Callahan, *Canadian Relations,* pp. 155–156; McCormac, "Louis McLane," in *American Secretaries of State and Their Diplomacy,* IV, 294–296; LMcL to Sir Charles R. Vaughan, June 5, 1833; March 11, 21, 1834; C. R. Vaughan to LMcL, Feb. 10, March 16, 24, 1834, in Manning, *Diplomatic Correspondence, Canadian Relations,* II, 248–250, 258–273, 946–952, 956–961.

104. C. R. Vaughan to Palmerston, Dec. 4, 1833; Feb. 12, March 28, April 4, 1834; LMcL to C. R. Vaughan, March 31, 1834, Foreign Office Transcripts, 5th ser., LC.

105. LMcL to C. Van Ness, Aug. 27, Dec. 5, 1833; May 28, 29, 1834; C. Van Ness to E. Livingston, June 17, 1833; C. Van Ness to LMcL, Nov. 28, Dec. 21, 1833; Feb. 18, 1834, *Senate Document* No. 147, 23d Cong., 2d sess., pp. 20–24, 64–68, 79–85.

106. LMcL to H. L. Pinckney, April 12, 1834, State Dept., Domestic Letters, XXVI, NA; LMcL to J. M. de Castillo y Lanzas, April 30, 1834, *House Executive Document* No. 351, 25th Cong., 2d sess., p. 694; Richardson, *Messages,* III, 23–24; LMcL to C. G. De Witt, April 20, 1834; C. Van Ness to LMcL, Feb. 18, April 15, 1834, Manning, *Diplomatic Correspondence, Inter-American Affairs,* III, 12–13; XI, 263–264, 272–273.

107. H. Legaré to LMcL, Oct. 9, 1833; March 23, 1834, in Legaré, *Writings,* I, 177–184, 188–196; Richardson, *Messages,* III, 25.

108. Richardson, *Messages,* III, 27, 41, 51; LMcL to L. Woodbury, May 5, 1834, State Dept., Domestic Letters, XXVI, NA; William M. Malloy, *Treaties . . . and Agreements Between the United States of America and Other Powers* (Washington, 1910), I, 181–183.

109. Richardson, *Messages,* III, 53; Malloy, *Treaties,* I, 1228; II, 1626.

110. LMcL to B. Silliman, Livingston, and Cabot, Sept. 18, 1833; LMcL to Cabot, Saunders, and Overton, March 7, 14, 1834, State Dept., Domestic Letters, XXVI, NA; Richardson, *Messages,* III, 48, 50, 98; *Niles' Register,* XLIV (Aug. 10, 1833), 388–389; XLV (Sept. 7, 1833), 32.

111. Stenberg, "Jackson, Anthony Butler, and Texas," *Southwestern Social Science Quarterly,* XIII, 264–265; Callahan, *Mexican Relations,* pp. 63–65; Rives, *United States and Mexico,* I, 235–237.

112. Malloy, *Treaties,* I, 1083; Stenberg, "Jackson, Butler, and Texas," p. 264.

113. LMcL to A. Butler, July 5, 1833, *House Executive Document* No. 351, 25th Cong., 2d sess., p. 106.

114. LMcL to A. Butler, Oct. 12, Nov. 18, 1833; May 26, 1834, *House Executive Document* No. 351, 25th Cong., 2d sess., pp. 109, 112–113, 142.

115. A. Butler to LMcL, Aug. 5, 1833, in Manning, *Diplomatic Correspondence, Inter-American Affairs,* VIII, 263.

116. A. Butler to A. Jackson, Oct. 28, 1833, in Jackson, *Correspondence,* V, 219–220.

117. A. Jackson to A. Butler, Nov. 27, 1833, *ibid.,* pp. 228–230.

118. Stenberg, "Jackson, Butler, and Texas," p. 277.

119. LMcL to A. Butler, Jan. 13, 1834, in Manning, *Diplomatic Correspondence, Inter-American Affairs,* VIII, 27.

120. A. Butler to A. Jackson, Feb. 6, March 7, 1834, in Jackson, *Correspondence,* V, 244–247, 249–253.

121. LMcL to A. Butler, June 24, 1834, *House Executive Document* No. 351, 25th Cong., 2d sess., p. 144.

122. L. Sérurier to LMcL, May 19, 1833, *House Executive Document* No. 40, 23d Cong., 2d sess., pp. 63–65; LMcL to L. Sérurier, May 18, 1833, State Dept., Notes to Foreign Legations, V, 240, NA.

123. LMcL to E. Livingston, June 3, 1833, *House Executive Document* No. 40, 23d Cong., 2d sess., pp. 5–6.

124. Govan, *Biddle,* p. 233; McLemore, *Franco-American Relations,* pp. 100–101.

125. LMcL to L. Sérurier, June 3, 1833, *House Executive Document* No. 40, 23d Cong., 2d sess., pp. 65–74.

126. LMcL to L. Harris, June 18, 1833, *ibid.,* pp. 7–8.

127. LMcL to E. Livingston, July 25, 1833, *ibid.,* p. 9; McLemore, *Franco-American Relations,* p. 108; LMcL to A. Jackson, July 31, 1833, Blair-Lee Papers, Princeton University.

128. LMcL to A. Jackson, Aug. 1, 1833, *ibid.;* A. Kendall to A. Jackson, Aug. 11, 1833, in Jackson, *Correspondence,* V, 152.

129. L. Sérurier to LMcL, Aug. 31, 1833, House Executive Document No. 40, 23d Cong., 2d sess., pp. 75–76.

130. LMcL to L. Sérurier, Sept. 5, 1833, ibid., pp. 77–78.

131. L. Sérurier to LMcL, Sept. 10, 1833, ibid., pp. 79–80.

132. E. Livingston to LMcL, Sept. 29, Oct. 4, 1833, State Dept., Diplomatic Despatches, France, XXVII, NA; Richardson, Messages, III, 130; McLemore, Franco-American Relations, pp. 108–110; Hatcher, Edward Livingston, p. 426.

133. Broglie to L. Sérurier, Oct. 12, 1833, House Executive Document No. 40, 23d Cong., 2d sess., p. 81.

134. R. G. Beasley to W. C. Rives, Sept. 29, 1833, Rives Papers, LC.

135. Richardson, Messages, III, 21–22; LMcL to E. Livingston, March 15, 1834, House Executive Document No. 40, 23d Cong., 2d sess., pp. 11–12.

136. LMcL to E. Livingston, Dec. 11, 1833, House Executive Document No. 40, 23d Cong., 2d sess., p. 10.

137. McLemore, Franco-American Relations, pp. 111–114.

138. Ibid., pp. 115–116; E. Livingston to LMcL, April 3, 8, 13, 1834, State Dept., Diplomatic Despatches, France, XXVII, NA.

139. LMcL to E. Livingston, May 17, 1834, House Executive Document No. 40, 23d Cong., 2d sess., p. 13.

140. [R. L. Colt] to N. Biddle [May 14, 1834], Biddle Papers, LC.

141. R. Taney to M. Van Buren, April 9, 1860, in Bernard Steiner, ed., "Taney's Letters to Van Buren in 1860," Maryland Historical Magazine, X (1915), 16–22.

142. L. Woodbury to Nathaniel Niles, May 16, 1834, Woodbury Papers, LC.

143. W. C. Rives to M. Van Buren, May 15, June 16, 1834, Van Buren Papers, 2d ser., LC.

144. W. C. Rives to L. Woodbury, May 26, 1834, Woodbury Papers, LC.

145. McLemore, Franco-American Relations, p. 117; LMcL to E. Livingston, May 29, 1834, House Executive Document No. 40, 23d Cong., 2d sess., pp. 13–14.

146. L. Sérurier to LMcL, June 5, 1834, House Executive Document No. 40, 23d Cong., 2d sess., pp. 81–82.

147. LMcL to E. Livingston, May 30, 1834, ibid., p. 14.

148. Van Buren, Autobiography, p. 612.

149. McCormac, "Louis McLane," in American Secretaries of State, IV, 287.

150. LMcL to L. Sérurier, June 27, 1834, House Executive Document No. 40, 23d Cong., 2d sess., pp. 83–84.

151. LMcL to E. Livingston, June 27, 1834, ibid., pp. 15–17.

152. Van Buren, Autobiography, pp. 612–614; M. Van Buren to John Van Buren, June 22, 1834, Van Buren Papers, 2d ser., LC.

153. R. M. McLane, Reminiscences, pp. 54–56.

154. A. Jackson, memorandum, Nov. 15, 1836, in Jackson, Correspondence, V, 437.

155. A. Jackson to E. Livingston, June 27, 1834, ibid., p. 272.

156. A. Jackson to E. Livingston, March 10, 1835, *ibid.*, p. 329.

157. E. Livingston to A. Jackson, June 23, 1834, *ibid.*, pp. 270–271.

158. W. C. Rives to M. Van Buren, May 15, 1834, Van Buren Papers, 2d ser., LC.

159. LMcL to William R. King, Dec. 25, 1835, "Louis McLane" folder, Misc. Papers, NYPL.

160. A. Gallatin to E. Everett, Jan. 5, 6–22, 1835, Gallatin Papers, NYHS; Van Buren, *Autobiography*, p. 612.

Chapter Fourteen: A Chapter on Morris

1. LMcL to [L. Cass], Nov. 20, 1834, Cass Papers, Clements Library.

2. *National Intelligencer*, July 19, 1834; *Niles' Register*, XLVI (July 5, 1834), 313.

3. M. Van Buren to John Van Buren, June 22, 1834, Van Buren Papers, 2d ser., LC; Van Buren, *Autobiography*, p. 612.

4. D. A. Smith to N. Biddle, May 9, 1834, Biddle Papers, LC; [Lydia Sims] to CMcL, May 14 [1834], Fisher Collection.

5. Van Buren, *Autobiography*, p. 609.

6. Sargent, *Public Men and Events*, I, 276.

7. LMcL to W. T. Read, Oct. 15, 1833, Richard S. Rodney Collection, HSD.

8. J. Tyler to Henry Curtis, March 28, April 6, 1834, Tyler Papers, 1st ser., LC.

9. Washington *Globe*, April 29, 1834.

10. *Niles' Register*, XLVI (May 3, 1834), 162–163; *Register of Debates*, 23d Cong., 1st sess., pp. 3894–3895, 3897–3898.

11. *Register of Debates*, 23d Cong., 1st sess., p. 3876.

12. *Ibid.*, pp. 3883–3885.

13. Francis F. Wayland, *Andrew Stevenson* (Philadelphia, 1949), pp. 106–107; Swisher, *Taney*, pp. 287–288; Richardson, *Messages*, III, 53–54; LMcL to Mahlon Dickerson, May 29, June 26, 1834, State Dept., Diplomatic Instructions, Russia, XIV, NA.

14. Thomas Corwin to John McLean, June 19, 1834, in *Boston Public Library Bulletin*, VII (June, 1902), 273.

15. B. F. Butler to his wife, June 19, 1834, Butler Papers, New York State Library.

16. *National Intelligencer*, June 20, 1834.

17. R. M. McLane, *Reminiscences*, pp. 47, 50, 51.

18. [Lydia Sims] to CMcL, June 22 [1833?], Fisher Collection; W. Irving to LMcL, Jan. 20, 1834, *ibid.*; Thomas Corwin to John McLean, June 19, 1834, in *Boston Public Library Bulletin*, VII (June, 1902), 273.

19. Samuel Tyler, *Memoir of Roger Brooke Taney* (Baltimore, 1872), pp. 239–240; Swisher, *Taney*, pp. 311–312; Warren, *Supreme Court*, II, 258.

20. Washington *Globe*, June 19, 1834.

21. Van Buren, *Autobiography*, pp. 613, 614.

22. B. F. Butler to his wife, June 19, 1834, Butler Papers, New York State

Library; William S. Archer to a Mr. Skinner, June 19, 1834, Misc. Papers, NYPL; *National Intelligencer,* June 20, 1834.

23. M. Van Buren to J. Van Buren, June 22, 1834, Van Buren Papers, LC.

24. Smith, *First Forty Years,* p. 353.

25. *National Intelligencer,* July 22, 1834; *Niles' Register,* XLVI (July 26, 1834), 361.

26. S. Smith to H. M. Ridgely, Aug., 1834, in de Valinger and Shaw, *Calendar of Ridgely Family Papers,* II, 249.

27. Washington *Globe,* July 31, 1834; *Niles' Register,* XLVI (Aug. 16, 1834), 418.

28. McLane genealogical notes.

29. S. Jaudon to N. Biddle, Aug. 11, 1834, Biddle Papers, LC.

30. Weslager, *Brandywine Springs,* pp. 35–41.

31. Quoted in the *Delaware Gazette,* Sept. 9, 1834.

32. H. M. Ridgely to S. Smith, Sept. 12, 1834, in de Valinger and Shaw, *Calendar of Ridgely Family Papers,* II, 250; *National Intelligencer,* Sept. 19, 26, 1834.

33. N. Biddle to R. M. Blatchford, Sept. 30, 1834, Biddle Papers, LC.

34. LMcL to J. Buchanan, Nov. 18, 1834, Buchanan Papers, HSP; LMcL to L. Cass, Nov. 20, 1834, Cass Papers, Clements Library.

35. Phoebe George Bradford diary, Jan. 20, 1835, HSD.

36. *Delaware Gazette,* Sept. 2, 5, 12, 1834.

37. LMcL to L. Cass, Nov. 20, 1834, Cass Papers, Clements Library.

38. H. M. Ridgely to S. Smith, Sept. 12, 1834, Ridgely Papers, DSA.

39. LMcL to L. Cass, Nov. 20, 1834, Cass Papers, Clements Library.

40. Romulus M. Saunders to M. Van Buren, Aug. 20, 1834, Van Buren Papers, LC.

41. M. Van Buren to A. Jackson, Aug. 7, 1834, *ibid.*

42. LMcL to J. Buchanan, Nov. 18, 1834, Buchanan Papers, HSP.

43. LMcL to William S. Archer, Feb. 25, 1835, in Mangum, *Papers,* II, 315–316.

44. H. D. Gilpin to Joshua Gilpin, March 22, 1835, H. D. Gilpin Collection, HSD.

45. LMcL to CMcL, Tuesday Morning [April, 1835], McLane Papers.

46. Bayard v. McLane, Harrington, *Delaware Reports,* III, 139, 148, 151, 158; Phoebe George Bradford diary, Jan. 20, 1835.

47. P. M. Irving, *Washington Irving,* II, 182.

48. W. Irving to CMcL, June 26, 1834, Batchelder Collection.

49. W. Irving to Peter Irving, May 16, July 16, 1835, in P. M. Irving, *Washington Irving,* II, 186, 188.

50. Cranmer, "Internal Improvements in New Jersey," *Proceedings of the New Jersey Historical Society,* LXIX, 333–335.

51. Smith, *Development of Trust Companies,* p. 248n; Redlich, *Molding of American Banking,* II, 326; Callender, "Early Transportation and Banking Enterprises of the States," *Quarterly Journal of Economics,* XVII, 160, Jones,

The Anthracite-Tidewater Canals, p. 75; Cadman, *The Corporation in New Jersey,* p. 68; Winfield, *History of the County of Hudson,* pp. 372–373.

52. *Niles' Register,* XXXVI (Feb. 28, 1829), 3; Veit, *The Old Canals of New Jersey,* pp. 31–32; Vermeule, *Morris Canal and Banking Company,* pp. 54–57, 72; Lane, *Indian Trail to Iron Horse,* pp. 226, 232; Harlow, *Old Towpaths,* p. 196.

53. Lane, *Indian Trail to Iron Horse,* pp. 230, 232; Vermeule, *Morris Canal and Banking Company,* pp. 54, 57.

54. Lane, *Indian Trail to Iron Horse,* pp. 234–236; *New York Transcript,* Feb. 12, 1835; Clews, *Twenty-Eight Years in Wall Street,* pp. 104–105; Medbery, *Men and Mysteries of Wall Street,* p. 91; Shaw, *History of Essex and Hudson Counties,* I, 192.

55. Redlich, *Molding of American Banking,* I, 50; II, 341; Lane, *Indian Trail to Iron Horse,* p. 236; Knox, *History of Banking,* pp. 391–392, 398, 404, 406; Hammond, *Banks and Politics,* pp. 159, 184.

56. Van Buren, *Autobiography,* p. 617.

57. C. A. Davis to N. Biddle, April 17, 1835, Biddle Papers, LC.

58. C. A. Davis to N. Biddle, May 9, 1835, *ibid.*

59. E. R. Biddle to N. Biddle, Nov. 18, 1835, *ibid.*

60. J. D. Beers to M. Van Buren, Nov. 21, 1835, Van Buren Papers, LC.

61. French, *Banking and Insurance in New Jersey,* p. 27.

62. LMcL to CMcL, Tues. morning [spring, 1835], McLane Papers.

63. Phoebe G. Bradford diary, Jan. 20, 1835, HSD.

64. LMcL to L. Cass, Nov. 20, 1834, Cass Papers, Clements Library; T. M. Forman to wife, Feb. 21, 1835, Forman Papers, Maryland Historical Society, Baltimore.

65. Newark College (later Delaware College), trustees' minutes, Sept. 22–23, 1834, I, 19–22, University of Delaware, Newark.

66. Newark College, faculty minutes, Feb. 23, 1835, University of Delaware, Newark; Phoebe G. Bradford diary, March 17, 1835, HSD.

67. CMcL to Louis McLane, Jr., April 10 [1835], Fisher Collection.

68. Phoebe G. Bradford diary, May 12, 1835, HSD.

69. *Ibid.,* Jan. 16, March 20, April 29, 1835.

70. *Ibid.,* Feb. 26, March 4, 1835.

71. LMcL to CMcL, Tues. morning [spring, 1835], McLane Papers.

72. LMcL to Louis McLane, Jr., Aug. 28, 1835, Fisher Collection.

73. George Ticknor, *Life, Letters, and Journal* (Boston, 1909), I, 408–409.

74. Morris Canal and Banking Company minutes, May 12, 15, 1835, Department of Conservation and Economic Development, Trenton, New Jersey.

75. Phoebe G. Bradford diary, Aug. 19, Oct. 26, 1835, HSD; CMcL to Louis McLane, Jr. [June 14, 1835]; LMcL to Louis McLane, Jr., Aug. 28, 1835; CMcL to Louis McLane, Jr., Aug. 28 [1835], Feb. 24 [1836], Fisher Collection; LMcL to John Sergeant, Sept. 1, 1835, Dreer Collection, HSP; Henry D. Gilpin to Joshua Gilpin, Aug. 31, 1835, H. D. Gilpin Collection, HSD.

76. *New-York Evening Post,* May 7, 9, 11, 12, 14, 1835.

77. Scoville, *Old Merchants of New York City, passim; Longworth's New York . . . City Directory for 1837–1838; National Cyclopedia of American Biography,* I, 499; III, 359; V, 200; XIX, 124; John Ezell, *Fortune's Merry Wheel* (Cambridge, 1960), p. 86; Aitken, "Yates & McIntyre," *Journal of Economic History,* XIII, 41, 56; Richard I. Shelling, "Philadelphia and the Agitation in 1825 for the Pennsylvania Canal," *PMHB,* LXII (1938), 182n; *The Wealth and Biography of the Wealthy Citizens of the City of New York,* 13th ed. (New York, 1855), p. 56; Ann H. Benson to author, March 2, 1966; W. Irving to Peter Irving, May 16 [1835], in P. M. Irving, *Washington Irving,* II, 186; Morris Canal minutes, May 5, 7, 1835.

78. R. Lenox to N. Biddle, Nov. 17, 1835, Biddle Papers, LC.

79. *DAB,* IV, 287–288.

80. Morris Canal minutes, May 5, 1835.

81. Lane, *Indian Trail to Iron Horse,* p. 235.

82. Morris Canal minutes, May 12, June 6, July 28, 1835.

83. LMcL to S. Ingham, June 2, 1835, Drew University Autograph Collection, Drew University Library, Madison, New Jersey.

84. Morris Canal minutes, June 13, 1835.

85. *Ibid.,* June 15, 1835.

86. *Ibid.,* May 7, 22, 1835.

87. *Ibid.,* May 15, 18, June 30, 1835.

88. *Ibid.,* June 10, Sept. 10, 29, 1835.

89. *Ibid.,* July 28, 1835.

90. C. A. Davis to N. Biddle, May 9, 1835, Biddle Papers, LC.

91. *New-York Evening Post,* May 12, 1835; *New York Herald,* Aug. 31, 1835; account of sales and purchases by R. L. Colt, July 29, Aug. 20, 1835; N. Biddle to C. S. Huntt, Aug. 24, 1835, Biddle Papers, LC.

92. *New York Herald,* Sept. 8, 1835.

93. *Ibid.,* Sept. 17, 28, 1835.

94. *Ibid.,* Sept. 22, 23, 26, 1835.

95. Morris Canal minutes, Sept. 29, Oct. 9, 12, 1835.

96. *Ibid.,* Oct. 16, 1835.

97. R. Lenox to N. Biddle, Nov. 17, 1835, Biddle Papers, LC.

98. Washington *Globe,* Oct. 8, 1835.

99. J. D. Beers to M. Van Buren, Nov. 21, 1835, Van Buren Papers, LC.

100. Morris Canal minutes, Nov. 11, 16, 24, 1835; McFaul, *Politics of Jacksonian Finance,* pp. 152–156.

101. E. R. Biddle to N. Biddle, Nov. 18, 1835, Biddle Papers, LC.

102. Morris Canal minutes, Oct. 30, 31, Nov. 3, Dec. 8, 11, 1835.

103. Smith, *Development of Trust Companies,* pp. 265–266.

104. Morris Canal minutes, Dec. 8, 11, 1835; Jan. 2, 5, 13, 1836.

105. *Memorial of Morris Canal and Banking Company to Council and General Assembly of State of New Jersey, Jersey City, January 15, 1836* (printed copy among Robert Swartwout Papers, box 3, NYPL).

106. *Newark Daily Advertiser,* Feb. 11, 12, 13, March 2, 1836; Cadman,

Corporation in New Jersey, p. 303n; Smith, *Development of Trust Companies,* p. 266.

107. Morris Canal minutes, Jan. 19, 1836.

108. *Ibid.,* Feb. 11, 12, 15, 1836.

109. P. D. Vroom to F. S. Schenck, Feb. 23, 1836, F. S. Schenck Papers, Rutgers University Library.

110. *Newark Daily Advertiser,* Feb. 25, 1836.

111. *Ibid.,* March 4, 7, 1836.

112. *Ibid.,* March 5, 1836.

113. Morris Canal minutes, March 7, 15, 28, 30, 1836.

114. CMcL to Louis McLane, Jr., Feb. 24 [1836], Fisher Collection.

115. Hone, *Diary,* I, 165, 204–205; Williams, *Washington Irving,* II, 76.

116. R. M. Blatchford to N. Biddle, Aug. 10, 1835, Biddle Papers, LC; LMcL to Louis McLane, Jr., Aug. 28, 1835, Fisher Collection.

117. Morris Canal minutes, Dec. 2, 11, 1835.

118. *Report of the President and Directors of the Morris Canal and Banking Co. . . .* June, 1836, pp. 9–10.

119. *Ibid., passim.*

120. N. Biddle to S. Swartwout, April 11, 1836, Biddle Papers, LC.

121. N. Biddle to S. Swartwout, April 14, 1836, *ibid.*

122. Morris Canal minutes, April 21, June 9, 10, 13, 1836.

123. *Ibid.,* March 15, 24, 1836.

124. *New York Herald,* June 21, 1836; *Newark Daily Advertiser,* June 24, 1836.

125. E. R. Biddle to N. Biddle, July 14, 1836, Biddle Papers, LC; Morris Canal minutes, July 14, 1836.

126. *New York Herald,* June 21, 1836; Morris Canal minutes, March 24, 1836.

127. Morris Canal minutes, June 25, 1836.

128. E. R. Biddle to N. Biddle, July 14, 1836, Biddle Papers, LC.

129. L. Woodbury to LMcL, June 28, 1836, Treasury Department, General Records, NA.

130. LMcL to William R. King, Dec. 25, 1835, McLane folder, Misc. Papers, NYPL.

131. LMcL to W. R. King, Sun. [spring, 1836], *ibid.*

132. J. D. Beers to M. Van Buren, Nov. 21, 1835, Van Buren Papers, LC.

133. LMcL to W. R. King, Dec. 25, 1835, McLane folder, Misc. Papers, NYPL.

134. Hone, *Diary,* I, 185–187; Nathan Miller, *The Enterprise of a Free People* (Ithaca, 1962), p. 175; LMcL to W. R. King, Dec. 25, 1835, McLane folder, Misc. Papers, NYPL.

135. *Newark Daily Advertiser,* Dec. 30, 1835.

136. C. A. Davis to N. Biddle, Dec. 28, 1835, Biddle Papers, LC.

137. Morris Canal minutes, Dec. 19, 1835.

138. *Ibid.,* Jan. 9, 1836.

139. *Ibid.,* March 15, 1836.

140. Kettell, "Debts and Finances of the States . . . Indiana," *Hunt's Merchants' Magazine,* XXI, 150–153; Esarey, *State Banking in Indiana,* p. 258; Logan Esarey, *Internal Improvement in Early Indiana* (Indiana Historical Society *Publications,* V, No. 2, 1912), pp. 124–126; McGrane, *Foreign Bondholders and American State Debts,* pp. 131–133; Heydinger, "Railroads of the Lehigh Valley," *Railway and Locomotive Historical Society Bulletin,* No. 109, p. 29.

141. LMcL to Governors Lynch and Clay, July, 1836, McLane folder, Misc. Papers, NYPL.

142. *Newark Daily Advertiser,* July 1, 1836.

143. [R. Colt] to N. Biddle, Oct. 12, 1836, Biddle Papers, LC; *New York Herald,* Oct. 12–14, Nov. 2, 1836.

144. [N. Biddle] to [E. R. Biddle], Nov. 1, 1836, Biddle Papers, LC.

145. List of "Purchase of 5000 Shares of Stock," Nov. 3–9, 1836, *ibid.*

146. Morris Canal minutes, Nov. 17, Dec. 1, 1836; Smith, *Economic Aspects of the Second Bank,* p. 211.

147. Morris Canal minutes, Oct. 29, 1836.

148. *New York Herald,* Oct. 12, 14, 20, 22, 24, 1836; R. M. Blatchford to N. Biddle, June 11, 1836, Biddle Papers, LC.

149. [R. L. Colt] to [N. Biddle], Oct. 18, 1836; E. R. Biddle to N. Biddle, Jan. 20, 1837, Biddle Papers, LC; A. C. Flagg to S. Maison, Nov. 15, 1836, A. C. Flagg Papers, NYPL; C. L. Livingston to Jesse Hoyt, Jan. 12, 25, 1837, in Mackenzie, *Van Buren,* pp. 178, 181.

150. *National Intelligencer,* Sept. 5, 1836.

151. Morris Canal minutes, Jan. 26, 1836.

152. *Ibid.,* March 2, 1837. *Cf. Report of the President and Directors of the Morris Canal and Banking Co.,* March, 1837.

153. *Newark Daily Advertiser,* Nov. 29, 30, 1836; New York *Observer,* Dec. 3, 17, 1836.

154. Morris Canal minutes, March 2, 1837.

155. Heydinger, "Railroads of the Lehigh Valley," pp. 16–19.

156. *Report of the President and Managers of the Little Schuylkill and Susquehanna Rail Road Co.* (Philadelphia, 1838); Heydinger, "Little Schuylkill," *Railway and Locomotive Historical Society Bulletin,* No. 108, pp. 21–22.

157. *New York Herald,* Dec. 27, 1836; New York *Observer,* Dec. 31, 1836; R. L. Colt to N. Biddle, Dec. 26, 1836, Biddle Papers, LC; Morris Canal minutes, Dec. 24, 1836.

158. Jones, *Anthracite-Tidewater Canals,* p. 58; Morris Canal minutes, Jan. 19, 1837.

159. E. R. Biddle to N. Biddle, Feb. 24, 1837, Biddle Papers, LC.

160. E. R. Biddle to N. Biddle, March 1, 1837, *ibid.*

161. List of Purchases, Feb. 20–25, 1837; N. Biddle to E. R. Biddle, Jan. 25, 1837, *ibid.*

162. *Niles' Register,* LI (Dec. 31, 1836), 274.

163. E. R. Biddle to R. L. Colt, Jan. 27, 1837, Biddle Papers, LC.

164. Morris Canal minutes, Jan. 31, 1837.

165. LMcL to W. R. King, Sun. [spring, 1836], McLane folder, Misc. Papers, NYPL.

166. [R. L. Colt] to N. Biddle [Feb. 4, 1837], Biddle Papers, LC.

167. CMcL to Louis McLane, Jr., Feb. 24 [1836]; Allan McLane to CMcL, Feb. 21 [1836], Fisher Collection; LMcL to John Sergeant, June 24, 1836, McLane folder, Misc. Papers, NYPL; LMcL to John Sergeant, May 30, 1836, Roberts Collection, Haverford College; Biddle, *Correspondence*, p. 358.

168. Phoebe G. Bradford diary, April 20, 1836, HSD; LMcL to Samuel McKean, April 27, 1837, Gratz MSS, HSP.

169. CMcL to Louis McLane, Jr., July 30, 1836, Fisher Collection.

170. R. M. Blatchford to N. Biddle, June 11, 1836; E. R. Biddle to N. Biddle, March 6, 7, 1837, Biddle Papers, LC; Morris Canal minutes, March 9, 1837; Scoville, *Old Merchants of New York*, I, 115–116, 179.

171. E. R. Biddle to N. Biddle, March 6, 21, 1837; Brooks Bros. and Co. to E. R. Biddle, March 11, 1837, Biddle Papers, LC.

172. *New York Herald,* March 13–31, 1837; Morris Canal minutes, March 30, 1837.

173. *New York Herald,* March 29, 30, 1837; McGrane, *Foreign Bondholders,* p. 16; Jenks, *Migration of British Capital,* p. 90; Morris Canal minutes, March 23, 26, 30, 1837.

174. Morris Canal minutes, March 11, April 22, 1837.

175. *Ibid.,* March 31, April 6, June 9, 1837; R. M. Blatchford to N. Biddle, June 20, 1837, Biddle Papers, LC.

176. Walters, *Gallatin,* p. 364; Minutes of Emergency Meeting, April 8, 1837; Report of Committee of Ten, April 13, 1837; Gallatin's observations, April 13, 1837, Gallatin Papers, NYHS.

177. *Newark Daily Advertiser,* May 8, 12, 1837; *New York Herald,* May 10, 11, 1837.

178. *New York Herald,* May 9, 10, 1837; *Newark Daily Advertiser,* May 11, 15, 1837; Morris Canal minutes, June 1, 1837.

179. Morris Canal minutes, June 6, 12, 1837; LMcL to N. Biddle, June 10, 1837; R. M. Blatchford to N. Biddle, June 10, 1837, Biddle Papers, LC; LMcL to Joshua Bates, June 19, 1837, Baring Papers, C-1371, PAC.

180. N. Biddle to LMcL, June 5, 1837; LMcL to N. Biddle, June 6, 10, 1837; S. Southard to N. Biddle, June 15, 1837; R. M. Blatchford to N. Biddle, June 20, 1837; N. Biddle to E. R. Biddle, June 21, 1837, Biddle Papers, LC; Morris Canal minutes, June 7, 15, 29, 30, July 1, 1837.

181. Morris Canal minutes, June 15, 1837.

CHAPTER FIFTEEN: THE BALTIMORE AND OHIO

1. *Niles' Register,* XXXVI (July 25, 1829), 349; Latrobe, *The Baltimore and Ohio Railroad,* p. 5.

2. [Smith], *History and Description of the B & O,* p. 98.

3. Reizenstein, *Economic History of the B & O,* p. 36; Scharf, *History of Baltimore,* p. 326.

4. R. L. Colt to N. Biddle, Sept. 14, 1836; Charles Oliver to N. Biddle, June 6, 1836; William Woodville to R. L. Colt, Aug. 18, 1836, Biddle Papers, LC.

5. Charles Oliver to N. Biddle, June 14, 1836, *ibid.*

6. Reizenstein, *B & O*, pp. 42–43.

7. *Objections to Yielding to Northerners the Control of the Baltimore and Ohio Rail Road . . . by a Marylander* (Baltimore, 1860), p. 7; Charles Oliver to N. Biddle, June 14, 1836; R. L. Colt to N. Biddle, July 29 [1836]; B. H. Latrobe to M. Newkirk, Oct. 6, 1836; M. Newkirk to N. Biddle, Oct. 8, 1836, Biddle Papers, LC; Scharf, *History of Baltimore*, p. 327; Semmes, *John H. B. Latrobe and His Times*, p. 359; Reizenstein, *B & O*, pp. 19, 22.

8. Wiltse, *Calhoun, Nullifier*, p. 472; A. Dickins to N. Biddle, July 23, 1836, Biddle Papers, LC.

9. R. L. Colt to N. Biddle, July 21, 1835; William Woodville to R. L. Colt, Aug. 18, 1836, Biddle Papers, LC.

10. Semmes, *Latrobe*, p. 360; Baltimore and Ohio Rail Road Company, minutes, Dec. 20, 1836, Baltimore & Ohio Railroad Company, Baltimore; R. Oliver to N. Biddle, Dec. 4, 1833, Biddle Papers, LC.

11. Reizenstein, *B & O*, p. 39.

12. *National Intelligencer*, March 15, 1833; Scharf, *History of Baltimore*, p. 324; Poor, *History of Railroads and Canals*, p. 596; Smith, *B & O*, pp. 43–44.

13. B & O minutes, Feb. 4, 7, 8, 21, 1837.

14. Muriel E. Hidy, "George Peabody, Merchant and Financier, 1829–1854" (unpublished Ph.D. dissertation, Radcliffe College, 1939), pp. 150–152; Hanna, *Financial History of Maryland*, pp. 88–89; Thomas Marian to Joshua Bates, March 7, 1837; Robert Gilmor to Baring Brothers and Co., May 17, 1837, Baring Papers, C-1371, PAC.

15. *B & O Annual Report* (1837), p. 5; Reizenstein, *B & O*, p. 44.

16. B & O minutes, July 5, 1837.

17. *Ibid.*, Sept. 11, 1837; Osborne, "Moncure Robinson," *William and Mary College Quarterly*, 2d ser., I, 245–253; *American Railroad Journal*, VI (1837), 547.

18. Bateman, *The Baltimore and Ohio*, p. 9; *B & O Annual Report* (1838), p. 5; Baltimore *Sun*, May 21, July 9, 1838; June 4, 21, 1839.

19. B & O minutes, Sept. 11, 1837; Hungerford, *Story of the B & O*, I, 192, 218.

20. *B & O Annual Report* (1837), pp. 4, 6, 8; B & O minutes, Nov. 7, 1838; Baltimore *Sun*, June 14, 1839.

21. B & O minutes, Jan. 10, 1838.

22. *Ibid.*, March 16, 1842.

23. Baltimore *Sun*, Jan. 3, 1838; Meyer, *History of Transportation*, pp. 592, 595; Baltimore *Sun*, July 7, 1837; N. Biddle to John McKim, Jr., March 8, 1837; M. Newkirk to N. Biddle, May 4, 1837, Biddle Papers, LC; *Baltimore American*, March 31, 1837; *B & O Annual Report* (1837), p. 26; *B & O Annual Report* (1838), p. 6.

24. *Baltimore American*, July 24, 1837.

25. B & O minutes, July 11, Nov. 7, Dec. 5, 1838; Sept. 7, 1842; July 15, 1843; Scharf, *History of Baltimore,* p. 349.

26. Scharf, *History of Baltimore,* p. 326; *B & O Annual Report* (1837), pp. 8–9, 17–22; *Baltimore American,* July 18, 1837; Baltimore *Sun,* July 19, Sept. 6, 1837.

27. B & O minutes, Jan. 3, 10, 19, Feb. 7, 1838; Baltimore *Sun,* Jan. 25, 1838; *B & O Annual Report* (1837), p. 21.

28. J. P. Kennedy, Journal of Trip to Richmond, March 12–26, 1838, Kennedy Papers, Peabody Institute Library, Baltimore; Howard Braverman, "The Economic and Political Background of the Conservative Revolt in Virginia," *Virginia Magazine of History and Biography,* LX (1952), 266-267; Baltimore *Sun,* March 24, 1838; Scharf, *History of Baltimore,* pp. 325–326; Reizenstein, *B & O,* p. 44; *B & O Annual Report* (1838), pp. 9–11; *Laws and Ordinances Relating to the Baltimore and Ohio Rail Road Company* (Baltimore, 1850), pp. 229–232; T. K. Cartmell, *Shenandoah County Pioneers and Their Descendants* (Berryville, Va., 1963), pp. 60–61.

29. Semmes, *Latrobe,* pp. 361–362.

30. Scharf, *History of Baltimore,* p. 326; B & O minutes, July 11, Aug. 1, 1838; Reizenstein, *B & O,* p. 45; LMcL to Joel R. Poinsett [Oct. 24, 1838], Poinsett Papers, XI, HSP; Baltimore *Sun,* Nov. 15, 1838; March 21, 1839; [Smith], *B & O,* pp. 59–60.

31. LMcL to Louis McLane, Jr., Jan. 31, 1841; CMcL to Louis McLane, Jr., Jan. 24, 1841, Fisher Collection.

32. *B & O Annual Report* (1839), pp. 3–4; Baltimore *Sun,* Jan. 24, 1840; Jan. 28, Feb. 1, 16, March 13, 1841; *B & O Annual Report* (1840), p. 8; B & O minutes, Jan. 6, March 3, 1841; CMcL to Louis McLane, Jr., Jan. 24, 1841; LMcL to Louis McLane, Jr., Jan. 31, 1841, Fisher Collection; *Laws Relating to the B & O* (1850), pp. 113, 154–155; Reizenstein, *B & O,* p. 88; Poor, *Railroads and Canals,* p. 584.

33. Meyer, *History of Transportation,* p. 406; *B & O Annual Report* (1843), p. 9; Baltimore *Sun,* Dec. 28, 1843; Jan. 15, March 11, 1844; *B & O Annual Report* (1844), pp. 22–23; *B & O Annual Report* (1845), p. 20.

34. Baltimore *Sun,* June 7, 19, 1839; Feb. 23, 24, 26, March 3, 11, 1841; Jan. 28, March 24, 1843; Feb. 10, 1845; B & O minutes, Jan. 1, March 4, 1840; Jan. 6, 18, 1841; Jan. 4, Dec. 6, 1843; *Laws Relating to the B & O* (1850), p. 122.

35. Reizenstein, *B & O,* pp. 48–49; Donaldson, *Speech on the Subject of . . . Maryland's Relations with the Baltimore & Ohio Railroad Company, . . . March 9, 1876,* pp. 14–15; Bowen, *Rambles in the Path of the Steam-Horse,* p. 76; Garrett, *Letter and Accompanying Documents . . . to the Comptroller of Maryland,* p. 5; Baltimore *Sun,* April 6, 8, 1839; Hidy, "George Peabody," pp. 159–165.

36. Baltimore *Sun,* May 2, 11, 1839; B & O minutes, May 10, 1839; LMcL to Andrew Stewart, April 10, 1839, Batchelder Collection; *B & O Annual Report* (1839), p. 8.

37. B & O minutes, June 5, 1839; *B & O Annual Report* (1839), pp. 8–9; Baltimore *Sun*, April 3, 1839.

38. Baltimore *Sun*, July 6, Aug. 3, 19, 1839.

39. Reizenstein, *B & O*, p. 54.

40. LMcL to Louis McLane, Jr., Jan. 20, 1839; CMcL to Louis McLane, Jr., March 6, April 10, 1839, Fisher Collection; CMcL to Robert McLane, June 6, 1839, McLane Papers; LMcL to Joshua Bates, April 23, 1839, Baring Papers, C-1371, PAC.

41. LMcL to Robert McLane, June 12, 1839, McLane Papers; LMcL to Joel Poinsett, March 26, 1839, Poinsett Papers, XII, HSP.

42. Augusta Forman to her uncle, July 9, 1839, Forman Papers, Maryland Historical Society.

43. LMcL to Robert McLane, June 12, 1839, McLane Papers.

44. B & O minutes, July 3, 1839; LMcL to Joshua Bates, July 30, 1839, Baring Papers, C-1372, PAC.

45. Robert McLane to LMcL, Sept. 9, 1839, McLane Papers.

46. LMcL to CMcL, Sept. 8, 1839, *ibid.*

47. Taylor, *The Transportation Revolution, 1815–1860*, pp. 344–345; LMcL to Robert Gilmor, Sept. 20, 1839, Dickinson College Collection, Carlisle, Pennsylvania; LMcL to Louis McLane, Jr., Sept. 28, 1839, Fisher Collection; Hidy, *House of Baring*, pp. 281, 290; LMcL to Joshua Bates, Oct. 15, 1839, Baring Papers, C-1372, PAC; Hidy, "George Peabody," pp. 160–170.

48. LMcL to CMcL, Sept. 20, 1839, McLane Papers; LMcL to Louis McLane, Jr., Sept. 28, 1839, Fisher Collection; B & O minutes, Nov. 6, 1839.

49. *Baltimore Patriot*, quoted in Baltimore *Sun*, Nov. 6, 1839.

50. *B & O Annual Report* (1839), pp. 7–9.

51. B & O minutes, Nov. 13, Dec. 4, 1839.

52. *Baltimore American*, July 10, 12, 1837; R. L. Colt to N. Biddle, July 29 [1837]; N. Biddle to Robert Gilmor, Jan. 2, 1838, Biddle Papers, LC; *B & O Annual Report* (1837), p. 5; Baltimore *Sun*, Aug. 4, 1837; Hungerford, *Story of the B & O*, I, 191.

53. Baltimore *Sun*, Oct. 22, Dec. 19, 1838.

54. B & O minutes, Dec. 11, 18, 1839; *B & O Annual Report* (1839), p. 12.

55. Buchholz, *Governors of Maryland*, pp. 130–135; Baltimore *American*, Jan. 4, 1840.

56. J. P. Kennedy, journal, V, Jan. 26, Feb. 1, 1840, Kennedy Papers, Peabody Institute Library; B & O minutes, Jan. 13, 1840; Baltimore *Sun*, Jan. 15, 16, 21, 29, Feb. 1, 1840; *Report of the Select Committee of the B & O Appointed to Prepare an Exposition on the Governor's Message of January 2, 1840 . . .* (Baltimore, 1840); Bohner, *John Pendleton Kennedy*, pp. 128–131.

57. *Baltimore American*, Jan. 7, 1840.

58. Baltimore *Sun*, Jan. 4, March 13, 1840; Reizenstein, *B & O*, pp. 49–50; *B & O Annual Report* (1840), pp. 7–8.

59. B & O minutes, March 4, April 1, 1840.

60. *Ibid.*, Sept. 2, 1840; *B & O Annual Report* (1840), p. 11.

61. *B & O Annual Report* (1840), pp. 9–12.

62. Mayor Leakin's message, Jan. 6, 1840, in *Baltimore American,* Jan. 7, 1840.

63. B & O minutes, July 24, 1840; Baltimore *Sun,* July 24, 1840.

64. B & O minutes, Sept. 2, 1840.

65. *B & O Annual Report* (1840), pp. 3–8; Poor, *Railroads and Canals,* p. 584.

66. Harrington, *Reports of Cases,* III, 139–241; *Governor's Register,* I, 373–374.

67. LMcL to Robert McLane, Nov. 6, 1840, McLane Papers. *Cf.* LMcL to J. Bates, May 21, 1840, Baring Papers, C-1372, PAC.

68. LMcL to Robert McLane, Dec. 6, 1839; William C. Barney to R. McLane, Jan. 10, 1840, McLane Papers; R. M. McLane, *Reminiscences,* p. 83.

69. Robert McLane to LMcL, Sept. 10, 17, 1840, McLane Papers.

70. Robert McLane to LMcL, Jan. 25, 1841, *ibid.*

71. Allan McLane to LMcL, Tuesday [Jan., 1841], Fisher Collection; A. P. Upshur to Allan McLane, May 24, 1842, McLane Papers; catalogue of St. Mary's College of Baltimore for 1840–1841; CMcL to Louis McLane, Jr., April 25 [1841], Fisher Collection.

72. Howard, *The Monumental City,* pp. 467–469; Kitty and Juliette McLane to Louis McLane, Jr., Feb. 6, 1840, Fisher Collection; McLane genealogical notes; conversations with McLane descendants; CMcL to Louis McLane, Jr., Feb. 10 [1841], Fisher Collection.

73. CMcL to Louis McLane, Jr., April 10, 1839, Fisher Collection; Sally to Robert McLane, Thurs. [Oct.] 3 and Fri. [Oct. 4], [1839]; Rebecca to Robert McLane, April 8, 1841, McLane Papers; CMcL to Mary Christie, Fri. evening [1841], Fisher Collection.

74. Juliette to Louis McLane, Jr., Feb. 6, 1840; CMcL to Louis McLane, Jr., April 10, 1839; June 10, 1840; Jan. 24, 1841, Fisher Collection; Charles McLane to CMcL, Nov. 21, 1841; Rebecca to Robert McLane, April 8, May 2, 1841; Sally to Robert McLane, Fri. [Sept. 28, 1839], Fisher Collection; "Diaries of Sidney George Fisher," *PMHB,* LXXVI, 458 (entry for March 20, 1839).

75. CMcL to Mary Christie, Fri. evening [1841], Fisher Collection; Rebecca to Robert McLane, April 8, 1841, McLane Papers.

76. CMcL to Catherine Milligan, April 17 [1841]; CMcL to Louis McLane, Jr., April 25 [1841]; Robert McLane to Sally Tiffany, June 14, 1841, Fisher Collection; LMcL to Robert McLane, April 28, June 15, 1841, McLane Papers.

77. LMcL to Louis McLane, Jr., June 9, 1841, Fisher Collection.

78. Robert McLane to LMcL, Jan. 25, 1841, McLane Papers.

79. R. M. McLane, *Reminiscences,* pp. 73–74.

80. CMcL to Louis McLane, Jr., Feb. 10 [1841], Fisher Collection.

81. Augustus James Pleasonton diary, April 25, 1841, HSP, as quoted in unpublished seminar paper by Arthur Leibundguth.

82. J. Bates to Baring Brothers, May 13, 1841, Baring Papers, C-1373, PAC.

83. LMcL to T. W. Ward, Feb. 22, 1841, *ibid.*

84. J. Bates to Baring Brothers, May 31, 1841, *ibid.*

85. Chitwood, *John Tyler,* p. 280; Adams, *Memoirs,* XII, 214.

86. LMcL to [John Campbell], July 4 [1839], Campbell MSS, Duke University Library, Durham, North Carolina.

87. Oscar D. Lambert, *Presidential Politics in the United States, 1841–1844* (Durham, N.C., 1936), p. 79n; S. S. Nicholas to John Crittenden, Jan. 12, 1842, Crittenden Papers, LC.

88. CMcL to Louis McLane, Jr., Aug. 22, 1841, Fisher Collection.

89. LMcL to William B. Lewis, Aug. 26, 30, 1841, Jackson-Lewis Papers, NYPL; CMcL to Louis McLane, Jr., Aug. 31 [1841], Fisher Collection.

90. LMcL to William B. Lewis, Sept. 9, 1841, Jackson-Lewis Papers, NYPL.

91. LMcL to Robert McLane, Sept. 9, 1841, McLane Papers; LMcL to William B. Lewis, Sept. 15, 1841, Jackson-Lewis Papers, NYPL; J. P. Kennedy, journal, V [*c.* Sept. 26, 1841], 82, Peabody Institute Library.

92. John Tyler to LMcL, May 25, 1842; A. P. Upshur to Allan McLane, May 24, 1842, McLane Papers; LMcL to W. B. Lewis, May 26, 1842, Jackson-Lewis Papers, NYPL.

93. W. B. Lewis to LMcL, Dec. 20, 1842; LMcL to Louis McLane, Jr., Dec. 22, 1842, Fisher Collection.

94. LMcL to Robert McLane, Aug. 18, 1842, McLane Papers.

95. *New York Herald,* Sept. 16, 1842; Washington *Globe,* Sept. 19, 1842; LMcL to Robert McLane, Sept. 20, 23, 1842, McLane Papers.

96. LMcL to Robert McLane, Dec. 15, 1842, *ibid.*

97. LMcL to Robert McLane, Dec. 19, 1842, *ibid.*

98. B & O minutes, Oct. 7, Nov. 2, 1842; Baltimore *Sun,* Nov. 3, 4, 1842; Scharf, *History of Baltimore,* p. 327; *Baltimore American,* Nov. 7, 1842.

99. Smith, *B & O,* p. 98.

100. *B & O Annual Report* (1840), p. 12.

101. B & O minutes, Jan. 6, 1841; Baltimore *Sun,* Jan. 12, 23, 26, 1841; *Laws Relating to the B & O* (1850), p. 112.

102. Baltimore *Sun,* Feb. 1, 3, 4, 9, 10, 1841; *Laws Relating to the B & O* (1850), p. 154.

103. B & O minutes, Feb. 10, 1841; Baltimore *Sun,* Feb. 11, 16, 17, March 11, 1841.

104. Baltimore *Sun,* March 18, 1841.

105. *Ibid.,* May 7, 1841.

106. *Ibid.,* March 11, 1841.

107. *Ibid.,* July 17, 30, 1841.

108. *B & O Annual Report* (1841), pp. 14–18.

109. Baltimore *Sun,* Oct. 1, 2, 1841.

110. B & O minutes, Oct. 6, 8, 1841.

111. Baltimore *Sun,* Nov. 8, 1841.

112. *Ibid.,* Oct. 30, Nov. 5, 1841.

113. *Ibid.,* Nov. 5, Dec. 10, 1841.

114. B & O minutes, Nov. 3, Dec. 1, 1841.

115. *Laws Relating to the B & O* (1850), p. 156.

116. *Ibid.*, pp. 157–158.

117. *Ibid.*, pp. 113–115, 158–159; Baltimore *Sun*, Feb. 18, 19, 1842.

118. *Laws Relating to the B & O*, p. 161; Baltimore *Sun*, March 16, 18, 22, 1842; B & O minutes, March 21, 1842.

119. *Laws Relating to the B & O*, pp. 160–161.

120. B & O minutes, March 16, 1842.

121. *Ibid.*, July 7, 1841.

122. *Ibid.*, Feb. 2, 1842.

123. *Ibid.*, March 2, 1842; Dorwart, "Biographical Notes on Jonathan Knight," *PMHB*, LXXV, 76–90; Baltimore *Sun*, April 8, 1842.

124. B & O minutes, April 6, 13, May 4, 1842.

125. CMcL to Louis McLane, Jr., March 31 [1842], Fisher Collection.

126. Baltimore *Sun*, Feb. 24, 1842.

127. B & O minutes, March 2, 16, 21, 1842.

128. Baltimore *Sun*, April 2, 4, 1842.

129. B & O minutes, April 6, 1842; Baltimore *Sun*, July 9, 1842; Hidy, *House of Baring*, pp. 291, 548; *B & O Annual Report* (1842), pp. 7–8; J. Bates to Baring Brothers, April 26, May 31, 1841; J. Bates to Mildmay, May 13, 1841, Baring Papers, C-1372–73, PAC.

130. B & O minutes, Oct. 7, 1842; Jan. 4, 1843; *B & O Annual Report* (1842), p. 4.

131. B & O minutes, Oct. 7, 1842.

132. *B & O Annual Report* (1842), pp. 12–13.

133. B & O minutes, Oct. 10, 1842; Baltimore *Sun*, Oct. 19, 1842.

134. *B & O Annual Report* (1844), pp. 20–21; Scharf, *History of Baltimore*, p. 327; Baltimore *Sun*, Feb. 20, 1844; LMcL to J. Bates, Feb. 27, 1844, Baring Papers, C-1374, PAC.

135. B & O minutes, Dec. 7, 1842; Thistlethwaite, *The Anglo-American Connection in the Early Nineteenth Century*, p. 24; Harvey, *The Best-Dressed Miners*, pp. 9–11.

136. *B & O Annual Report* (1843), p. 6.

137. Meyer, *History of Transportation*, pp. 407–408; B & O minutes, Feb. 1, 10, 1844; Baltimore *Sun*, Feb. 14, 1844; *B & O Annual Report* (1844), p. 16; W. Young to Charles B. Penrose, Feb. 28, 1845, Robert Swartwout Papers, box 3, folder "Maryland and New York Iron and Coal Company, 1845–1848," NYPL.

138. B & O minutes, April 3, Sept. 4, 1844.

139. Poor, *Railroads and Canals*, pp. 573–574; Fisher, *Gazetteer of the State of Maryland*, pp. 47, 48, 69, 84.

140. B & O minutes, April 18, June 5, 1844; *B & O Annual Report* (1845), p. 13; Scharf, *History of Baltimore*, p. 328.

141. Bowen, *Rambles*, p. 255; James M. Swank, *History of the Manufacture of Iron* (Philadelphia, 1884), pp. 343–344; Irene Neu, *Erastus Corning*

(Ithaca, 1960), p. 48; Temin, *Iron and Steel,* pp. 48, 73; Harvey, *The Best-Dressed Miners,* p. 11.

142. Poor, *Railroads and Canals,* p. 582; Reizenstein, *B & O,* p. 88; Binder, "Pennsylvania Coal and the Beginnings of American Steam Navigation," *PMHB,* LXXXIII, 442–443.

143. Baltimore *Sun,* Nov. 7, 1842.

144. LMcL to Andrew Stewart, April 10, 1839, Batchelder Papers; Clark, "Railroad Struggle for Pittsburgh," *PMHB,* XLVIII, 2.

145. *B & O Annual Report* (1842), p. 14; *Annual Report* (1843), p. 12.

146. *B & O Annual Report* (1844), pp. 30–33.

147. B & O minutes, June 7, 1843.

148. *Ibid.,* Dec. 7, 1842, Feb. 1, 27, 1843; Reizenstein, *B & O,* p. 51.

149. LMcL to Robert McLane, Feb. 13, 1843, McLane Papers; J. H. B. Latrobe to T. W. Ward, Dec. 7, 1844, Baring Papers, C-1387, PAC.

150. Baltimore *Sun,* Dec. 27, 1842; Jan. 10, 28, 30, Feb. 20, March 28, April 5, 1843.

151. B & O minutes, Feb. 14, 1843.

152. *B & O Annual Report* (1843), p. 4; LMcL to Robert McLane, Jan. 17, 1843, McLane Papers.

153. LMcL to J. Bates, March 25, 1843, Baring Papers, C-1373, PAC.

154. LMcL to J. Bates, Aug. 28, 1843, *ibid.*

155. Baltimore *Sun,* Dec. 30, 1842; Jan. 12, Feb. 14, 24, 28, 1843; B & O minutes, Feb. 27, 1843.

156. *Laws Relating to the B & O* (1850), pp. 116–117; Reizenstein, *B & O,* p. 82; Hidy, *House of Baring,* p. 310; McGrane, *Foreign Bondholders,* p. 95; *Hunt's Merchants' Magazine,* XX (1849), 488; LMcL to J. Bates, March 15, 25, April 27, 1843, Baring Papers, C-1373, PAC.

157. *B & O Annual Report* (1843), pp. 11, 14.

158. B & O minutes, Dec. 6, 1843; Hungerford, *Story of the B & O,* I, 247; LMcL to J. Bates, Aug. 28, Oct. 13, 1843, Baring Papers, C-1373–74, PAC; LMcL to Charles J. Faulkner, Feb. 24, Aug. 15, 1844, C. J. Faulkner Papers, West Virginia University, Morgantown.

159. *B & O Annual Report* (1844), p. 33; B & O minutes, July 3, 1844.

160. B & O minutes, Jan. 8, Feb. 5, 1845.

161. Baltimore *Sun,* Aug. 3, 1844; Feb. 1, 1845; B & O minutes, Sept. 4, 20, Oct. 9, 1844; *B & O Annual Report* (1844), p. 39; *Laws Relating to the B & O* (1850), pp. 238–244.

162. B & O minutes, June 11, July 9, 1845; Baltimore *Sun,* July 14, 1845; *B & O Annual Report* (1845), p. 21; J. H. B. Latrobe to T. W. Ward, July 12, 1845, Baring Papers, C-1387, PAC.

163. Baltimore *Sun,* Feb. 7, 19, March 18, 20, 21, April 4, 7, 12, 14, 16, 1845; *B & O Annual Report* (1845), p. 22.

164. B & O minutes, June 2, 1841.

165. Baltimore *Sun,* April 10, 1843.

166. Sanderlin, *The Great National Project,* p. 195.

167. B & O minutes, April 21, 1843, March 25, 1844.

168. CMcL to Robert McLane, June 18 [1841]; LMcL to Robert McLane, June 15, 1841, McLane Papers.

169. B & O minutes, July 7, 1841.

170. Baltimore *Sun,* July 13, 1842.

171. B & O minutes, April 3, June 5, Dec. 4, 1844.

172. *Ibid.,* Sept. 23, Oct. 8, 1841.

173. *B & O Annual Report* (1843), p. 7; *Annual Report* (1844), p. 7; *Annual Report* (1845), p. 9; *Annual Report* (1846), p. 9; *Annual Report* (1847), p. 4.

174. Baltimore *Sun,* Jan. 2, 1845; Hanna, *Financial History of Maryland,* pp. 105, 124; Joshua Bates to Baring Brothers, May 31, 1841; John Gittings to Baring Brothers, Nov. 27, Dec. 4, 1841; George Mackubin to Baring Brothers, July 30, 1842, Baring Papers, C-1373, PAC.

175. McGrane, *Foreign Bondholders,* pp. 96–97, 100; Hidy, *House of Baring,* pp. 322–326, 329; Scharf, *History of Baltimore,* p. 329; J. H. B. Latrobe to Baring Brothers, Sept. 27, 1842; Nov. 28, 1844; J. H. B. Latrobe to T. W. Ward, Feb. 25, Aug. 14, Sept. 14, 1843; LMcL to J. Bates, May 21, 1840, Baring Papers, C-1372–74, PAC. See also J. H. B. Latrobe to T. W. Ward, April 4, Dec. 17, 1844; Jan. 4, 1845; T. W. Ward to Baring Brothers, Aug. 12, 29, 1844; T. W. Ward to J. H. B. Latrobe, Dec. 10, 1844, *ibid.,* C-1386–87.

176. B & O minutes, Feb. 2, 1842.

177. *B & O Annual Report* (1846), p. 9; B & O minutes, Oct. 1, 1846.

178. B & O minutes, Aug. 4, 1841; March 5, 1845.

179. *Ibid.,* Nov. 6, Dec. 4, 1844; Jan. 1, 1845; Hungerford, *Story of the B & O,* II, 117.

180. B & O minutes, Nov. 6, 1843; Jan. 3, June 5, 1844; May 14, 1845; Baltimore *Sun,* March 7, 1843; Jan. 5, 1844; *B & O Annual Report* (1844), pp. 7–8; Scharf, *History of Baltimore,* p. 331.

181. Semmes, *Latrobe,* pp. 321, 553–554.

182. B & O minutes, April 5, June 7, 1843.

183. Mabee, *The American Leonardo,* p. 264; Prime, *Life of Samuel F. B. Morse,* pp. 477, 492, 497; Edward L. Morse, *Samuel F. B. Morse,* II, 209–215.

184. B & O minutes, June 7, 1843; Thompson, *Wiring a Continent,* pp. 204–207.

185. B & O minutes, June 5, 1844; May 14, 1845; S. F. B. Morse to Francis Thomas, Oct. 19, 1843, "A Letter from Samuel Morse," *Maryland Historical Magazine,* XXXIV (1939), 40.

CHAPTER SIXTEEN: THE OREGON CESSION

1. LMcL to Louis McLane, Jr., Jan. 18, 1842; Robert McLane to Sally Tiffany, Feb. 3 [1843], Fisher Collection; LMcL to Robert McLane, July 29, 1842; Robert McLane to CMcL, April 9 [1843]; Rebecca Hamilton to Robert McLane, Oct. 15, 1843, McLane Papers.

2. LMcL to Robert McLane, July 12, 1843; Robert Hunter to Robert McLane, July 25, Sept. 19, 1843; LMcL to CMcL, July 1, 4, 1844, McLane

Papers; Baltimore *Sun,* June 30, Oct. 1, 2, 3, 1845; R. M. McLane, *Reminiscences,* p. 91.

3. CMcL to Louis McLane, Jr., Aug. 31 [1841], Fisher Collection; Rebecca McLane to Robert McLane, May 2, 1841; LMcL to Robert McLane, Nov. 22, 1842; LMcL to Philip Hamilton (copy), Nov. 22, 1842; LMcL to CMcL, July 1, 21, 23, and undated (Sunday), 1844, McLane Papers; McLane genealogical notes; LMcL to Rebecca Hamilton, Jan. 1, 1843, Batchelder Collection.

4. LMcL to CMcL, July 26, 1844, McLane Papers.

5. McLane genealogical notes; Joseph E. Johnston to John Preston Johnston, April 4, 1843, in Robert M. Hughes, "Some Letters of General Joseph E. Johnston," *William and Mary College Quarterly,* 2d ser., XI (1931), 321.

6. CMcL to Louis McLane, Jr., Aug. 22, 1841; Nov. 20, 1844, Fisher Collection; LMcL to Robert McLane, July 29, Aug. 2, 1842; March 30, Aug. 1, 7, 1843; George McLane to Robert McLane, March 16 [1843]; CMcL to Robert McLane [April 6], July 16 [1843]; Robert McLane to CMcL, April 9 [1843]; LMcL to James McLane (c/o Robert), July 5, 1843, McLane Papers.

7. LMcL to CMcL, July 4, 7, 10, 1844, *ibid.*

8. LMcL to Robert McLane, June 20, 28, 1843; LMcL to James McLane, July 5, 1843; CMcL to Robert McLane, July 5 [1843], *ibid.*

9. LMcL to CMcL, July 21 [1844], *ibid.;* Holland, *The Garesché, de Bauduy, and des Chapelles Families,* pp. 192, 246; Mrs. Sophie McLane to Louis McLane, Jr., May 22–June 1, Aug. 6–18, 1853, Fisher Collection.

10. LMcL to Louis McLane, Jr., July 29, 1842; CMcL to Louis McLane, Jr., Aug. 13 [1843], Fisher Collection; LMcL to Robert McLane, July 29, Aug. 18, Sept. 20, 1842; CMcL to Robert McLane, Sept. 13, 1842, McLane Papers.

11. LMcL to Robert McLane, July 29, Dec. 15, 1842; June 20, 1843, McLane Papers; LMcL to Louis McLane, Jr., June 29, 1843, Fisher Collection.

12. CMcL to Robert McLane, July 5, 1843, McLane Papers; CMcL to Louis McLane, Jr., Nov. 20, 1844, Fisher Collection; *The Baltimore Directory for 1845* (Baltimore, 1845), p. 79.

13. LMcL to Robert McLane, Sept. 20, 1842; CMcL to Robert McLane, Feb. 12, 1843; will of Lydia C. Sims, probated Aug. 16, 1844; Joshua E. Driver to LMcL, Oct. 16, 1844, McLane Papers; LMcL to Louis McLane, Jr., Nov. 20, 1844, Fisher Collection.

14. Dr. Allen McLane to Robert McLane, March 14, 1843, McLane Papers; Dr. Allen McLane to J. Polk, May 31, Sept. 6, Nov. 15, 1844, Polk Papers, LC; will of Dr. Allen McLane, Oct. 30, 1844, probated Feb. 14, 1845, Book U-1-295, Register of Wills, Wilmington.

15. American Philosophical Society minutes, April 15, 1831 (kindness of Dr. Whitfield J. Bell, Jr.); *Memoirs of the Philadelphia Society for Promoting Agriculture,* VI (1939), 288; Baltimore *Sun,* Oct. 18, 1841; July 1, 1845; LMcL to unknown, Oct. 30, 1841, Mercantile Library autograph book, p. 116, Maryland Historical Society.

16. CMcL to Louis McLane, Jr., Nov. 20, 1844, Fisher Collection; LMcL to J. Polk, Nov. 28, 1844, Polk Papers, LC.

17. John C. Calhoun to R. M. T. Hunter, March 26, 1845, in Hunter, *Correspondence,* p. 76.

18. Wiltse, *Calhoun, Sectionalist,* pp. 218, 220, 222, 226; J. Calhoun to Francis Pickens, May 6, 1845; J. Calhoun to Mrs. T. G. Clemson, May 22, 1845; J. Calhoun to John Y. Mason, May 23, 1845, in Calhoun, *Correspondence,* pp. 653–654, 656, 660–661; Richardson, *Messages,* IV, 381.

19. *New York Herald,* Sept. 12, 1846; Sellers, *Polk, Continentalist,* p. 292; M. Van Buren to George Bancroft, May 12, 1846, Van Buren Papers, LC.

20. J. Polk to B. F. Butler, May 5, 1845, Polk Papers, LC.

21. R. M. Saunders to J. Buchanan, May 20, 1845, State Dept., Appointment Papers, NA.

22. *Washington Union,* July 7, 1845.

23. LMcL to J. Polk, June 12, 1845, Polk Papers, LC.

24. B & O minutes, June 19, 1845; Baltimore *Sun,* June 20, 1845; Howard, *Monumental City,* pp. 464–466.

25. B & O minutes, July 9, 1845; *Washington Union,* July 9, 18, 1845; LMcL to J. Polk, July 16, 1845, Polk Papers, LC.

26. LMcL to J. Polk, June 12, 1845, Polk Papers, LC; LMcL to J. Buchanan, June 27, 1845, Buchanan Papers, HSP; Oeste, *John Randolph Clay,* p. 259.

27. Klein, *President James Buchanan,* p. 168.

28. G. Melville to J. Polk, May 7, 1845, Polk Papers, LC. Parker, "Gansevoort Melville's Role in the Campaign of 1844," *New-York Historical Society Quarterly,* XLIX, 143–173.

29. J. Buchanan to LMcL, July 8, 1845, State Dept., Diplomatic Instructions, Great Britain, XV, NA.

30. *Washington Union,* June 20, July 1, 14, 1845; LMcL to J. Buchanan, June 21, 1845, Buchanan Papers, HSP.

31. C. A. Davis to J. Polk, July 18, 1845, Polk Papers, LC.

32. Arnold Harris to J. Polk, July 18, 1845, *ibid.*

33. J. R. Poinsett to Gouverneur Kemble, July 5, 1845, in Poinsett, *Calendar,* pp. 196–197; H. D. Gilpin to M. Van Buren, July 7, 1845, Van Buren Papers, LC.

34. Van Buren, *Autobiography,* p. 614; Adams, *Memoirs,* XII, 204.

35. Baltimore *Sun,* July 17, 1845; *Washington Union,* July 18, 1845; *Niles' Register,* LXVIII (Aug. 23, 1845), 400; CMcL to [daughters Sally Tiffany and Lydia Johnston], July 18–28 [1845], Fisher Collection.

36. E. Everett to J. Buchanan, Aug. 2, 8, 1845, State Dept., Diplomatic Despatches, Great Britain, LI, NA; LMcL to J. Buchanan, Aug. 4, 1845, *ibid.,* LII; LMcL to J. Buchanan, Aug. 4, 1845 (private); LMcL to J. Polk, Aug. 4, 1845 (copy), Buchanan Papers, HSP; Sellers, *Polk, Continentalist,* p. 270.

37. Frederick Merk, "The Oregon Pioneers and the Boundary," *American Historical Review,* XXIX (July, 1924), 681–699.

38. J. Buchanan to LMcL, July 12, 1845, State Dept., Diplomatic Instructions, Great Britain, XV, NA; also in Buchanan, *Works,* VI, 186–194.

39. J. Buchanan to R. Pakenham, July 12, 1845, *House Executive Document No. 2,* 29th Cong., 1st sess., pp. 163–169.

40. R. M. McLane, *Reminiscences,* p. 79.

41. R. Pakenham to J. Buchanan, July 29, 1845; J. Buchanan to R. Pakenham, Aug. 30, 1845, *House Executive Document* No. 2, 29th Cong., 1st sess., pp. 170–192.

42. John Y. Mason to LMcL, Aug. 12, 1845, Polk Correspondence, Bancroft Transcripts, NYPL; LMcL to Robert McLane, Sept. 3, 16, 1845, McLane Papers; LMcL to J. Buchanan, Sept. 18, 1845, State Dept., Diplomatic Despatches, Great Britain, LVI, NA.

43. LMcL to Robert McLane, Oct. 10, 18, Nov. 2, 1845, McLane Papers; Miller, ed., *Treaties and Other International Acts of the United States of America,* V, 48.

44. Baltimore *Sun,* Nov. 18, 1845; *Niles' Register,* LXIX (Nov. 1, 1845), 132; LMcL to Robert McLane, Nov. 30, 1845, McLane Papers; LMcL to J. Polk, Dec. 1, 1845, Polk Papers, LC.

45. CMcL to Lydia Johnston, Oct. 3, 1845, Fisher Collection; LMcL to Henry Wheaton, Oct. 14, 1845, McLane Papers, Pierpont Morgan Library, New York; LMcL to Robert McLane, Aug. 22, Sept. 26, 1845; LMcL to Allan McLane, Oct. 18, 1845; CMcL to Robert McLane, Dec. 1, 1845, McLane Papers.

46. LMcL to J. Buchanan, Oct. 18, 1845, Polk Papers, LC; LMcL to Robert McLane, Oct. 18, 1845, McLane Papers.

47. LMcL to Robert McLane, Sept. 3, Oct. 10, Nov. 2, 18, 1845, McLane Papers; LMcL to J. Buchanan, Sept. 18, 1845, Buchanan Papers, HSP; CMcL to Lydia Johnston, Oct. 3, 1845, Fisher Collection; LMcL to J. Buchanan, Oct. 10, 1845, Polk Papers, LC; CMcL to Rebecca Hamilton, Oct. 22, 1845, Batchelder Collection.

48. LMcL to Robert McLane, Sept. 3, Oct. 18, Nov. 18, 1845, McLane Papers.

49. LMcL to Robert McLane, May 4, 1846, *ibid.*

50. LMcL to J. Buchanan, Sept. 3, 1845, Buchanan Papers, HSP; LMcL to Robert McLane, Sept. 3, 1845, McLane Papers.

51. LMcL to J. Buchanan, Oct. 3 [incorrectly dated Sept. 3], 1845, Buchanan Papers, HSP.

52. Polk, *Diary,* I, 1–12; Aberdeen to R. Pakenham, Dec. 3, 1845, in Miller, *Treaties,* V, 48, and in Clark, *History of the Willamette Valley,* I, 847.

53. LMcL to J. Buchanan, Sept. 18, Oct. 3, 1845, Buchanan Papers; LMcL to Robert McLane, Oct. 3, 10, Nov. 2, 1845, McLane Papers; J. Buchanan to LMcL, Sept. 13, Oct. 14, 1845, Polk Correspondence, Bancroft Transcripts, NYPL.

54. Aberdeen to R. Pakenham, Oct. 3, 1845, in Miller, *Treaties,* V, 39–40.

55. R. Pakenham to Aberdeen, Oct. 25, 1845, *ibid.,* pp. 40–41; Polk, *Diary,* I, 62–82; J. Buchanan to LMcL, Oct. 28, 1845, in Buchanan, *Works,* VI, 285–286.

56. J. Polk to LMcL, Oct. 29, 1845, Polk Papers, LC.

57. Aberdeen to R. Peel, Oct. 17, 1845, in Miller, *Treaties,* V, 698–699.

58. LMcL to Robert McLane, Nov. 2, 1845, McLane Papers.

59. LMcL to J. Buchanan, Aug. 22, Sept. 3, 18, 1845, Buchanan Papers, HSP; LMcL to Robert McLane, Oct. 3, Nov. 18, 1845, McLane Papers.

60. LMcL to J. Buchanan, Dec. 1, 1845, State Dept., Diplomatic Despatches, Great Britain, LVI, NA.

61. CMcL to Robert McLane, Dec. 1, 1845; LMcL to Robert McLane, Dec. 1, 2, 1845, McLane Papers.

62. LMcL to J. Polk, Dec. 1, 1845, Polk Papers, LC.

63. LMcL to Robert McLane, Dec. 1, 2, 1845, McLane Papers.

64. J. Buchanan to John M. Read, Dec., 1845, J. H. Powell, Report on the Read Family Papers in the Library Company of Philadelphia (1944), p. 21; LMcL to J. Buchanan, Sept. 26, Dec. 1, 1845, State Dept., Diplomatic Despatches, Great Britain, LVI, NA.

65. *House Executive Document* No. 2, 29th Cong., 1st sess., pp. 11–14.

66. Greville, *Memoirs,* V, 272; Aberdeen to E. Everett, Jan. 3, 1846, in Clark, *History of the Willamette Valley,* I, 849–850.

67. LMcL to J. Buchanan, Jan. 3, 1846, State Dept., Diplomatic Despatches, Great Britain, LVI, NA; LMcL to George Bancroft, Jan. 15, 1846, Bancroft Papers, Massachusetts Historical Society.

68. LMcL to J. Buchanan, Dec. 1, 1845, State Dept., Diplomatic Despatches, Great Britain, LVI, NA.

69. Polk, *Diary,* I, 122–123; LMcL to J. Buchanan, Sept. 18, 1845, State Dept., Diplomatic Despatches, Great Britain, LVI, NA; J. Buchanan to LMcL, Dec. 13, 1845, State Dept., Diplomatic Instructions, Great Britain, XV, NA.

70. J. Polk to LMcL, Dec. 29, 1845, Polk Papers, LC.

71. *Ibid.;* LMcL to Robert McLane, Jan. 17, 1846, McLane Papers; J. Buchanan to LMcL, Dec. 29, 1845, State Dept., Diplomatic Instructions, Great Britain, XV, NA.

72. LMcL to H. Wheaton, Jan. 15, 1846, McLane Papers, Pierpont Morgan Library; LMcL to J. Buchanan, Jan. 3, 1846, State Dept., Diplomatic Despatches, Great Britain, LVI, NA.

73. LMcL to Robert McLane, Dec. 1, 2, 1845, McLane Papers.

74. LMcL to J. C. Calhoun, Jan. 2, 3, 17, Feb. 3 [16], March 3, 1846, Calhoun Papers, Clemson University; Polk, *Diary,* I, 159.

75. LMcL to J. Buchanan, Feb. 3, 1846, State Dept., Diplomatic Despatches, Great Britain, LVI, NA; LMcL to J. Buchanan, Feb. 3, 1846, Buchanan Papers, HSP; LMcL to J. C. Calhoun, Feb. [16], 1846, in Boucher and Brooks, "Correspondence Addressed to Calhoun," pp. 322–323.

76. J. Buchanan to R. Pakenham, Feb. 4, 1846, *House Executive Document* No. 105, 29th Cong., 1st sess., pp. 8–10.

77. J. Buchanan to LMcL, Feb. 26, 1846, State Dept., Diplomatic Instructions, Great Britain, XV, NA; Polk, *Diary,* I, 244–245; J. Buchanan to LMcL, Feb. 26, 1846, Buchanan Papers, HSP.

78. LMcL to J. Buchanan, March 17, 1846, State Dept., Diplomatic Despatches, Great Britain, LVI, NA.

79. LMcL to R. Armstrong, Feb. 5, 1846, State Dept., Misc. Correspondence (London), V, NA; CMcL to Henry Wheaton [Feb. 11, 1846], McLane

Papers, Pierpont Morgan Library; Catherine Mary McLane to her brother Louis [spring, 1846]; CMcL to Sally Tiffany, March 15, 1846; CMcL to Lydia Johnston, March 16, 1846, Fisher Collection; LMcL to J. Buchanan, April 3, 1846, Buchanan Papers, HSP; LMcL to Robert McLane, Sept. 3, 1845, McLane Papers; Baltimore *Sun*, Sept. 22, 1845.

80. LMcL to Allan McLane, Oct. 18, 1845, McLane Papers.

81. CMcL to Lydia Johnston, Oct. 3, 1845, Fisher Collection; CMcL to Lydia Johnston, Dec. 25, 1845, Batchelder Collection; CMcL to Louis McLane, Jr., June 2, July 17, 1846, Fisher Collection.

82. LMcL to Robert McLane, Aug. 22, 1845; June 14, 18, 1846, McLane Papers; CMcL to Lydia Johnston, March 16, 1846, Fisher Collection.

83. Catherine Mary McLane to Louis McLane, Jr. [March or April, 1846]; CMcL to Louis McLane, Jr., Sept. 14, 1845; CMcL to Lydia Johnston, April 7, 1846, Fisher Collection.

84. LMcL to Sally Tiffany, Jan. 3, 14, 1846, *ibid.;* Williams, *Washington Irving,* II, 121.

85. LMcL to Robert McLane, Sept. 3, Nov. 2, 1845, McLane Papers; Baltimore *Sun*, Sept. 10, 1845; J. Buchanan to LMcL, Feb. 26, 1846, Buchanan Papers, HSP.

86. LMcL to Robert McLane, Oct. 18, 1845, McLane Papers; CMcL to Louis McLane, Jr., Sept. 14, 1845; LMcL to Sally Tiffany, Jan. 14, 1846, Fisher Collection.

87. Greville, *Memoirs,* V, 246, 247.

88. Frederick Merk, "British Government Propaganda and Oregon," *American Historical Review,* XL (1934), 55–57.

89. *Ibid.,* "British Party Politics and the Oregon Treaty," *American Historical Review,* XXXVII (1932), 656–658.

90. CMcL to Robert McLane, Aug. 22, 1845, McLane Papers; R. Armstrong to J. Polk, Sept. 3, 1845, Polk Papers, LC.

91. E. Everett to Aberdeen, Jan. 28, 1846, in Clark, *History of the Willamette Valley,* I, 851–854.

92. A. Gallatin to Gales and Seaton, Feb. 27, 1846, in Gallatin, *Writings,* II, 621–625.

93. Williams, *Washington Irving,* II, 191–192, 386; LMcL to J. Buchanan, March 3, 1846, Buchanan Papers, HSP.

94. CMcL to Sally Tiffany, March 15, 1846, Fisher Collection.

95. CMcL to Lydia Johnston, March 16, 1846, *ibid.;* J. Buchanan to LMcL, Feb. 26, 1846, State Dept., Diplomatic Instructions, Great Britain, XV, NA; J. Buchanan to LMcL, Feb. 26, 1846, Buchanan Papers, HSP; J. Polk to LMcL, Jan. 28, 1846, Polk Papers, LC; LMcL to J. Buchanan, March 17–18, 1846, State Dept., Diplomatic Despatches, Great Britain, LVI, NA; LMcL to J. Buchanan, March 17–18, 1846, Buchanan Papers, HSP; G. Bancroft to LMcL, March 29, 1846, in Howe, *Life and Letters of George Bancroft,* I, 282–284.

96. LMcL to J. Buchanan, March 17–18, 1846, Buchanan Papers, HSP.

97. Polk, *Diary*, I, 137; LMcL to Robert McLane, April 18, 1846, McLane Papers.

98. LMcL to J. Buchanan, April 10, 1846, Buchanan Papers, HSP; Miller, *Treaties*, V, 69.

99. CMcL to Louis McLane, Jr., April 17, 1846, Fisher Collection; LMcL to J. Buchanan, April 17, 1846, State Dept., Diplomatic Despatches, Great Britain, LVI, NA; LMcL to J. Buchanan, April 18, 1846; A. Dudley Mann to J. Buchanan, April 18, 1846, Buchanan Papers, HSP.

100. LMcL to J. Buchanan, April 18, 1846, Buchanan Papers, HSP.

101. LMcL to Robert McLane, April 18, 1846, McLane Papers.

102. LMcL to Robert McLane, May 3, 4, 1846, *ibid.*

103. LMcL to Robert McLane, May 4, 7–8, 1846, *ibid.*; LMcL to J. Buchanan, May 4, 1846, Buchanan Papers, HSP.

104. LMcL to Robert McLane, May 7–8, 1846; CMcL to Robert McLane, May 5 [1846], McLane Papers.

105. T. W. Ward to Baring Brothers, Oct. 21, 1845; J. H. B. Latrobe to J. Bates, Aug. 18, 1846; J. H. B. Latrobe to T. W. Ward, Sept. 12, 1846, Baring Papers, C-1388–89, PAC.

106. W. R. King to J. Buchanan, April 30, 1846, Buchanan Papers, HSP.

107. LMcL to Robert McLane, May 7–8, 1846, McLane Papers; Aberdeen to R. Pakenham, May 4, 1846, in Clark, *History of the Willamette Valley*, I, 858.

108. Aberdeen to J. W. Croker, May 11, 1846, *ibid.*, p. 858; Miller, *Treaties*, V, 75–81.

109. J. Polk to LMcL, Jan. 28, 1846, Polk Papers, LC; LMcL to J. Buchanan, May 18, 1846, State Dept., Diplomatic Despatches, Great Britain, LVI, NA; LMcL to Robert McLane, May 18, 1846, McLane Papers; LMcL to J. C. Calhoun, May 18, 1846, Calhoun Papers, Clemson University.

110. Polk, *Diary*, I, 447–448, 451–454, 455–456, 459.

111. LMcL to Robert McLane, June 3, 1846, McLane Papers; LMcL to J. Buchanan, June 18, 1846, State Dept., Diplomatic Despatches, Great Britain, LVI, NA.

112. Polk, *Diary*, I, 397.

113. LMcL to J. Buchanan, May 29, June 3, 1846, State Dept., Diplomatic Despatches, Great Britain, LVI, NA; LMcL to Robert McLane, June 3, 1846, McLane Papers.

114. LMcL to Robert McLane, June 3, 18, 1846, McLane Papers.

115. LMcL to Robert McLane, July 3, 6, 1846, *ibid.*; LMcL to J. Buchanan, July 13, 1846, State Dept., Diplomatic Despatches, Great Britain, LVI, NA.

116. Polk, *Diary*, I, 432; Melville, *London Journal*, pp. 12–14; J. McHenry Boyd to [James L. McLane], May 13, 1846; CMcL to Robert McLane, May 16, 1846, McLane Papers; LMcL to Allan Melville, May 18, 1846, State Dept., Misc. Correspondence (London), V, NA; LMcL to J. Buchanan, May 4, 1846, Buchanan Papers, HSP.

117. CMcL to Robert McLane, May 16, 1846, McLane Papers; LMcL to J. Buchanan, June 1, 1846, State Dept., Diplomatic Despatches, Great Britain,

LVI, NA; CMcL to Louis McLane, Jr., June 2, 1846, Fisher Collection; J. Buchanan to LMcL, June 5, 1846, State Dept., Diplomatic Instructions, Great Britain, XV, NA; J. McHenry Boyd to J. Buchanan, July 18, 1846, State Dept., Diplomatic Despatches, Great Britain, LVI, NA.

118. LMcL to Robert McLane, Aug. 22, 1845, McLane Papers; LMcL to J. Buchanan, Aug. 5, 1846, State Dept., Diplomatic Despatches, Great Britain, LVI, NA.

119. LMcL to J. Buchanan, Oct. 12, 1845, State Dept., Diplomatic Despatches, Great Britain, LVI, NA.

120. LMcL to Daniel J. Desmond, Nov. 7, 1845, State Dept., Misc. Correspondence (London), V, NA.

121. LMcL to J. Buchanan, July 6, 1846, State Dept., Diplomatic Despatches, Great Britain, LVI, NA.

122. LMcL to J. Buchanan, Jan. 27, 1847, *ibid.;* W. J. Bell, Jr., to author, Jan. 10, 1967.

123. LMcL to J. Buchanan, Aug. 16, Dec. 31, 1845; LMcL to Palmerston, Aug. 6, 1846, State Dept., Diplomatic Despatches, Great Britain, LVI, NA; Polk, *Diary,* I, 21–22; Aberdeen to R. Peel, Sept. 17, 19, 1845, in Clark, *History of the Willamette Valley,* I, 843–844; J. Buchanan to LMcL, Nov. 27, 1845; July 13, 1846, State Dept., Diplomatic Instructions, Great Britain, XV, NA.

124. LMcL to J. Buchanan, June 18, Aug. 15, 1846, State Dept., Diplomatic Despatches, Great Britain, LVI, NA; J. Buchanan to LMcL, July 27, 1846 (extract); LMcL to J. Buchanan, June 18, 1846, Buchanan Papers, HSP; J. Buchanan to LMcL, July 27, 1846, State Dept., Diplomatic Instructions, Great Britain XV, NA; LMcL to J. Polk, Aug. 2, 1846, McLane Papers; J. Polk to LMcL, June 22, 1846, Polk Papers, LC.

125. Polk, *Diary,* II, 18–19; John A. Dix to A. C. Flagg, July 17, 1846, A. C. Flagg Papers, NYPL; J. Buchanan to LMcL, July 27, 1846 (extract), Buchanan Papers, HSP.

126. J. Polk to LMcL, July 13, 1846, Polk Papers, LC; LMcL to J. Polk, Aug. 2, 1846, McLane Papers.

127. London *Times,* June 30, 1846; Cunningham, British Response to the Cry of "54–40 or Fight" (M.A. thesis, University of Washington, 1928), p. 126; B. Hawes to LMcL, June 30, 1846, McLane Papers; Baltimore *Sun,* July 20, 1846; *Washington Union,* July 21, 1846.

128. LMcL to Robert McLane, July 3, 6, 1846; William Brown to [LMcL], July 1, 1846, McLane Papers.

129. LMcL to Robert McLane, July 3, 1846, *ibid.*

130. LMcL to [Charles A. Davis], June 28, 1846, *ibid.*

131. Samuel Jones, Jr., to LMcL [May 1, 1846]; LMcL to Samuel Jones, Jr., May 28, July 15 (copy), 1846; LMcL to Robert McLane, May 29, July 3, 1846, *ibid.;* LMcL to John P. Kennedy, June 18, 1846, Kennedy Papers, IX, Peabody Institute Library.

132. LMcL to Robert McLane, May 29, 1846, McLane Papers; Polk, *Diary,* I, 470–471, 474.

133. J. Buchanan to John M. Read, June 11, 1846, Read Family Papers, III, LC.

134. J. Polk to LMcL, June 22, 1846, Polk Papers, LC.

135. *Ibid.*

136. LMcL to Robert McLane, June 18, 1846, McLane Papers; G. Bancroft to LMcL, June 23, 1846, in Howe, *Life and Letters of George Bancroft,* I, 285–287.

137. LMcL to J. Polk, July 17, 1846, McLane Papers.

138. LMcL to Robert McLane, July 15, 1846, *ibid.*

139. LMcL to Robert McLane, July 24, 1846, *ibid.*

140. LMcL to J. Buchanan, July 15, 1846, Buchanan Papers, HSP; LMcL to Robert McLane, July 15, 18, 1846, McLane Papers; *Delaware Gazette,* July 24, 1846.

141. LMcL to Robert McLane, July 15, 1846, McLane Papers; George M. Dallas to his wife, June 14, 1846, in R. F. Nichols, ed., "The Mystery of the Dallas Papers," *PMHB,* LXXIII (1949), 384.

142. J. Buchanan to John M. Read, June 11, 1846, Read Family Papers, III, LC.

143. George M. Dallas to his wife, July 17, 1846, in Nichols, "The Mystery of the Dallas Papers," *PMHB,* LXXIII, 385.

144. Polk, *Diary,* II, 2, 4–5, 7.

145. *Ibid.,* pp. 21–24.

146. W. R. King to J. Buchanan, Feb. 28, 1846, Buchanan Papers, HSP.

147. J. Polk to LMcL, July 13, 1846, Polk Papers, LC.

148. W. R. King to J. Buchanan, July 3, 15, 1846, Buchanan Papers, HSP.

149. LMcL to Robert McLane, July 18, 19, Aug. 2, 1846; LMcL to J. Polk, Aug. 2, 1846, McLane Papers.

150. LMcL to J. Buchanan, July 17, 1846, State Dept., Diplomatic Despatches, Great Britain, LVI, NA; CMcL and Mary McLane to Louis McLane, Jr., July 17, 1846, Fisher Collection; LMcL to Robert McLane, July 18, 19, 1846, McLane Papers.

151. LMcL to Robert McLane, July 18, 19, 24, Aug. 2, 1846, McLane Papers.

152. Polk, *Diary,* II, 60–61, 67; Baltimore *Sun,* Aug. 4, 1846.

153. J. Polk to LMcL, Aug. 12, 1846, Polk Papers, LC.

CHAPTER SEVENTEEN: "THIS CUNNING, DIPLOMATIC PRESIDENT"

1. LMcL to Robert McLane, Aug. 2, 1846, McLane Papers.

2. LMcL to J. McHenry Boyd, Aug. 18, 1846, State Dept., Misc. Correspondence (London), V, NA; LMcL to J. Buchanan, Aug. 18, 1846, State Dept., Diplomatic Despatches, Great Britain, LVI, NA.

3. Baltimore *Sun,* Aug. 28, Sept. 4, 5, 1846; *New York Herald,* Sept. 4, 1846.

4. J. Polk to LMcL, Sept. 7, 1846, Polk Papers, LC.

5. *New York Herald,* Sept. 8, 11, 1846; *National Intelligencer,* Sept. 11, 1846.

6. Polk, *Diary,* II, 133–137.

7. Philip Hamilton to LMcL, Sept. 9, 1846, with clipping from New York *Sun,* McLane Papers.

8. *New-York Evening Post,* Sept. 14, 1846.

9. Polk, *Diary,* II, 139, 168, 170, 172–173; *National Intelligencer,* Sept. 18, 23, Oct. 1, 1846.

10. Polk, *Diary,* II, 198–200, 203, 204–206.

11. LMcL to Robert McLane, Oct. 18, Nov. 2, 1845, McLane Papers.

12. *B & O Annual Report* (1845), p. 10; LMcL to Samuel Jones, Jr., May 28, 1846; LMcL to Robert McLane, May 29, 1846, McLane Papers; J. H. B. Latrobe to T. W. Ward, May 28, 1845; J. H. B. Latrobe to Thomas Baring, Oct. 20, 1845, Baring Papers, C-1375, C-1387, PAC.

13. *B & O Annual Report* (1845), pp. 14–16, 25.

14. *Laws Relating to the B & O,* p. 119; Donaldson, *Maryland's Relations with the B & O,* p. 5; LMcL to Samuel Jones, Jr., May 28, 1846, McLane Papers.

15. LMcL to J. P. Kennedy, June 18, 1846, Kennedy Papers, IX, Peabody Institute Library; LMcL to Robert McLane, July 3, 6, 1846, McLane Papers; Dieter Cunz, *The Maryland Germans, a History* (Princeton, 1948), p. 312.

16. LMcL to Robert McLane, Aug. 2, 1846, McLane Papers; LMcL to J. Bates, Aug. 1, 4, 1846; J. H. B. Latrobe to T. W. Ward, March 2, 1847, Baring Papers, C-1375, C-1389, PAC; McGrane, *Foreign Bondholders,* pp. 100–101.

17. B & O minutes, Oct. 1, 1846.

18. *B & O Annual Report* (1846), pp. 5–9.

19. B & O minutes, Oct. 8, 1846; *Baltimore American,* May 21, 1847; Baltimore *Sun,* March 10, Dec. 3, 1847; Feb. 15, 1848; *Laws Relating to the B & O,* pp. 120–121; Steiner, *Life of Reverdy Johnson,* p. 11n.

20. B & O minutes, March 5, April 2, May 14, 1845.

21. *Ibid.,* Nov. 11, 1846.

22. *Ibid.,* Dec. 24, 1846.

23. *Ibid.,* Feb. 10, March 17, 1847; *Organization of the Service of the Baltimore & Ohio R. Road under the Proposed New System of Management: Submitted by the President* . . . (Baltimore, 1847).

24. *B & O Annual Report* (1847), pp. 13–14; Bateman, *B & O,* p. 9.

25. *B & O Annual Report* (1848), pp. 17–18; Reizenstein, *B & O,* p. 55.

26. *B & O Annual Report* (1846), p. 15.

27. Clark, "Railroad Struggle for Pittsburgh," *PMHB,* XLVIII, 7–12; Baltimore *Sun,* April 20, 22, 24, 1846; McCarrell, "The Coming of the Railroad to Western Pennsylvania," *Western Pennsylvania Historical Magazine,* XVI, 5–6.

28. *B & O Annual Report* (1846), pp. 10–11, 25.

29. Baltimore *Sun,* May 9, 1846; *Pittsburgh Gazette,* Dec. 8, 1846.

30. Backofen, "Congressman Harmar Denny," *Western Pennsylvania Historical Magazine,* XXIII, 77; *Pittsburgh Gazette,* Dec. 8, 1846; B & O minutes, Oct. 14, 1846.

31. B & O minutes, Nov. 11, 1846.

32. H. Denny *et al.* to LMcL, Nov. 10, 1846, in *Pittsburgh Gazette,* Dec. 8, 1846.

33. B & O minutes, Dec. 9, 1846.

34. LMcL to William Robinson, Dec. 26, 1846, unidentified clipping in Kennedy Papers, LXIII, Peabody Institute Library.

35. LMcL to Louis McLane, Jr., Dec. 28, 1846, Fisher Collection.

36. Baltimore *Sun,* Dec. 30, 1846.

37. Scharf, *History of Baltimore,* p. 329; *B & O Annual Report* (1847), pp. 16–17.

38. Unidentified clipping in Kennedy Papers, LXIII, Peabody Institute Library; *Baltimore American,* Feb. 1, 1847; [Smith], *History of the B & O,* p. 70.

39. B & O minutes, Feb. 8, 1847; Baltimore *Sun,* Feb. 9, 1847; *Baltimore American,* Feb. 9, 1847.

40. *Laws Relating to the B & O,* p. 245; *B & O Annual Report* (1847), pp. 108–110; Reizenstein, *B &O,* p. 53; Baltimore *Sun,* Feb. 26, 1847.

41. LMcL to T. Parkin Scott, March 19, 1847, Personal Miscellaneous Papers, LC.

42. Baltimore *Sun,* March 23, 1847; unidentified clipping in Kennedy Papers, LXIII, Peabody Institute Library.

43. *Pittsburgh Gazette,* Jan. 29, 1847.

44. LMcL to J. Buchanan, Jan. 27, 1847, Buchanan Papers, HSP.

45. B & O minutes, Feb. 22, 1847.

46. *Pittsburgh Gazette,* March 2, 1847.

47. "The Railroad—Its Extension to the West," by "A Large Stockholder" [Thomas Swann?], unidentified clipping in Kennedy Papers, LXIII, Peabody Institute Library; [Smith], *History of the B & O,* p. 70.

48. *Pittsburgh Gazette,* March 22, 1847.

49. B & O minutes, March 22, 1847; *Baltimore American,* March 23, 29, 1847; *Pittsburgh Gazette,* March 24, 27, 30, April 1, 1847; T. W. Ward to Baring Brothers, April 15, 1847, Baring Papers, C-1389, PAC.

50. J. P. Kennedy to Neville B. Craig, April 1, 1847 (copy), Kennedy Papers, XVIa, Peabody Institute Library; Baltimore *Sun,* March 23, April 2, 1847.

51. B & O minutes, April 5, 1847; McLane, *Address . . . Respecting . . . a Proposed Subscription to the Capital of the Pittsburgh & Connellsville Rail Road Co.*

52. B & O minutes, April 5, 1847; Baltimore *Sun,* April 6, 1847.

53. J. P. Kennedy, journal, April 10, 1847, Kennedy Papers, V, Peabody Institute Library.

54. J. P. Kennedy to S. I. Bigham, April 6, 1847, Kennedy Papers, XVIa, Peabody Institute Library.

55. *Baltimore American,* April 5, 1847.

56. J. P. Kennedy, journal, April 12, 13, 14, 15, 1847, Kennedy Papers, VIIa, Peabody Institute Library.

57. B & O minutes, April 14, 1847; J. P. Kennedy, journal, April 14, 19, 1847, Kennedy Papers, VIIa, Peabody Institute Library.

58. B & O minutes, April 14, 1847.

59. J. P. Kennedy, journal, April 14, 19, 1847, Kennedy Papers, VIIa, Peabody Institute Library.

60. Andrew Hunter to LMcL, April 20, 1847, and Reverdy Johnson to LMcL, April 27, 1847, in *B & O Annual Report* (1847), pp. 111–114.

61. Bowen, *Rambles,* p. 87; *Report and Documents Submitted by the Committee Appointed to Confer with the Authorities of the City of Wheeling Respecting the Late Law of Virginia Granting the Right of Way to the Baltimore & Ohio Rail-Road Co.* (Baltimore, 1847), pp. 3–4; *Pittsburgh Gazette,* May 3, 8, 1847.

62. *Report by the Committee to Confer with the Authorities of Wheeling,* p. 3; B & O minutes, May 8, 1847; J. P. Kennedy, journal, May 8, 1847, Kennedy Papers, VIIa, Peabody Institute Library; [Smith], *History of the B & O,* p. 159.

63. *Pittsburgh Gazette,* April 28, 1847; Baltimore *Sun,* May 1, 5, 1847; J. P. Kennedy, journal, May 2, 1847, Kennedy Papers, VIIa, Peabody Institute Library.

64. B & O minutes, May 8, 1847; J. P. Kennedy, journal, VIIa, May 8, 1847; J. P. Kennedy to Neville B. Craig, May 9, 1847 (copy), Kennedy Papers, XVIa, Peabody Institute Library.

65. J. P. Kennedy to Neville B. Craig, May 9, 1847 (copy), *ibid.;* J. P. Kennedy, journal, May 12, 1847, *ibid.,* VIIa; *Baltimore American,* May 14, 1847; J. P. Kennedy to William Robinson, May 15, 1847, Kennedy Papers, XVIa, Peabody Institute Library.

66. B & O minutes, May 17, 1847; J. P. Kennedy, journal, May 15, 16, and Mon. [May 17], 1847, Kennedy Papers, VIIa, Peabody Institute Library.

67. J. P. Kennedy, journal, May 15, 19, 20, 1847, Kennedy Papers, VIIa, Peabody Institute Library.

68. *Pittsburgh Gazette,* May 26, 29, 1847.

69. J. P. Kennedy to Neville B. Craig, May 25, 1847 (copy), Kennedy Papers, XVIa, Peabody Institute Library; *Baltimore American,* May 26, June 9, 1847; *Pittsburgh Gazette,* June 1, 1847; J. Gardiner to R. Garrett and Sons, June 7, 1847, Garrett Papers, LXVIII, LC.

70. Baltimore *Sun,* June 9, 1847; *Baltimore American,* June 11, 18, 19, 1847; *Pittsburgh Gazette,* June 11, 18, 1847.

71. B & O minutes, June 9, 1847; *Baltimore American,* June 12, 16, 17, 1847; Baltimore *Sun,* June 12, 1847; *Pittsburgh Gazette,* June 23, 1847; G. Lurman to T. W. Ward, July 9, 1847, Baring Papers, C-1389, PAC.

72. B & O minutes, July 14, 1847.

73. *Report by the Committee to Confer with the Authorities of Wheeling,* pp. 21–22; *B & O Annual Report* (1847), pp. 71–83.

74. LMcL to Robert McLane, July 6, 1847, McLane Papers.

75. *Report by the Committee to Confer with the Authorities of Wheeling,* pp. 16–17; *B & O Annual Report* (1847), p. 81.

76. B & O minutes, July 16, 1847; Baltimore *Sun*, July 17, 19, 1847.

77. LMcL to Robert McLane, Sun. morning [July 11, 1847], McLane Papers.

78. *Pennsylvania Archives*, 4th series, VII (Harrisburg, 1902), 189–192; Clark, "Railroad Struggle for Pittsburgh," *PMHB*, XLVIII, 11–12.

79. B & O minutes, Aug. 25, 1847; Baltimore *Sun*, Aug. 26, 27, 1847; LMcL to Robert McLane, July 11, 1847, McLane Papers.

80. LMcL to J. Buchanan, Nov. 23, 1846, Buchanan Papers, HSP; LMcL to Louis McLane, Jr., Dec. 28, 1846; Feb. 21, 23, 1848, Fisher Collection; LMcL to Robert McLane, Aug. 3, 1847, McLane Papers.

81. LMcL to Louis McLane, Jr., Dec. 28, 1846, Fisher Collection.

82. Log of the U.S.S. *Levant*, May 29–July 7, 1846, typescript, Bancroft Library, Berkeley; Thomas C. Lancey, "Cruise of the *Dale*," mounted clippings from San José *Pioneer*, Bancroft Library, p. 89; Monterey *Californian*, Aug. 22, 1846.

83. Walter Colton, *Three Years in California* (New York, 1850), p. 98; Edwin Bryant, *What I Saw in California* (New York [1848]), pp. 366, 367.

84. William H. Davis, *Seventy-five Years in California* (San Francisco, 1929), p. 292; Hubert Howe Bancroft, *History of California* (San Francisco, 1886), IV, 725; V, 404–405, 434; William T. Sherman, *Memoirs* (New York, 1875), I, 35.

85. George McLane to Robert McLane, Oct. 24, 1846; George McLane to Mrs. Robert McLane, Nov. 8, 1846, McLane Papers; Baltimore *Sun*, Nov. 18, 1847.

86. LMcL to Louis McLane, Jr., Dec. 28, 1846, Fisher Collection; unidentified newspaper clipping in CMcL's Sentiment Book (owned by Louis McLane Hobbins, Madison); J. Y. Mason to Allan McLane, July 28, 1847; Aug. 5, 1848; Louis McLane, Jr., to Robert McLane, April 3, 1847, McLane Papers.

87. Mrs. Ellen Lee to Lydia Johnston, May 14, 1847, Fisher Collection; Robert S. Henry, *The Story of the Mexican War* (Indianapolis, 1950), p. 280.

88. Rives, *The United States and Mexico*, II, 284–286, 288; J. Polk to Robert McLane, Oct. 20, 1846; Robert McLane to J. Polk, Oct. 30 [1846], Polk Papers, LC; George McLane to Mrs. Robert McLane, Nov. 8, 10, 1846, McLane Papers.

89. J. P. Kennedy, journal, Sept. 13, Oct. 7, 1847, Kennedy Papers, VIIa, Peabody Institute Library; R. M. McLane, *Reminiscences*, p. 93; Baltimore *Sun*, Jan. 5, 7, 1848.

90. LMcL to J. Polk, Dec. 13, 1846, Polk Papers, LC.

91. LMcL to J. C. Calhoun, Dec. 17, 1846, Calhoun Papers, Clemson University.

92. LMcL to R. B. Rhett, June 19, 1847, *ibid.*

93. LMcL to J. Buchanan, Jan. 27, 1847, Buchanan Papers, HSP.

94. LMcL to J. C. Calhoun, Jan. 18, 1848, Calhoun Papers, Clemson University.

95. J. Polk to LMcL, June 19, 1847; LMcL to J. Polk, June 19, 21, 1847, Polk Papers, LC.

694 Notes to Pages 569 to 576

96. McCormac, "Louis McLane," in Bemis, *American Secretaries of State,* IV, 297–298; Polk, *Diary,* III, 372–373, 375, 381; L. Cass to LMcL, March 25, 1848, Gratz MSS, HSP; Baltimore *Sun,* March 16, 1848.

97. Louis McLane, Jr., to his wife, July 31, 1852, Fisher Collection.

98. LMcL to Louis McLane, Jr., May 31, 1848, *ibid.*

99. Reizenstein, *B & O,* pp. 87–88; *B & O Annual Report* (1847), pp. 8–9.

100. *B & O Annual Report* (1847), and *Annual Report* (1848), *passim; Baltimore American,* March 5, 6, 9, 1847; B & O minutes, March 17, 1847; Baltimore *Sun,* Dec. 30, 1847.

101. B & O minutes, July 14, 1847.

102. *Biographical Cyclopedia of Representative Men of Maryland and the District of Columbia,* pp. 239–240.

103. Bowen, *Rambles,* p. 84.

104. B & O minutes, Nov. 10, 1847; address of T. Swann to citizens of Baltimore, Sept. 17, 1847, unidentified clipping in Kennedy Papers, LXIII, Peabody Institute Library.

105. B & O minutes, Nov. 10, 1847; LMcL to T. Swann and others of select committee, Dec. 15, 1847, unidentified clipping in Kennedy Papers, LXIII, Peabody Institute Library; Baltimore *Sun,* Jan. 8, 1848.

106. J. P. Kennedy, journal, Jan. 13, 1848, Kennedy Papers, VIIb, Peabody Institute Library.

107. B & O minutes, Jan. 5, 12, 1848.

108. Mayor Davies' address to City Council, Jan. 17, 1848, unidentified clipping in Kennedy Papers, LXIII, Peabody Institute Library.

109. Bowen, *Rambles,* pp. 83–84.

110. Baltimore *Sun,* June 25, 1847; *Baltimore American,* Dec. 29, 1847; Jan. 3, 1848.

111. B & O minutes, Jan. 12, 1848.

112. J. P. Kennedy, journal, Oct. 12, 20, 23, Dec. 2, 1847, Kennedy Papers, VIIa, Peabody Institute Library; Jan. 20, 21, 24, 1848, *ibid.,* VIIb; J. P. Kennedy to Thomas Ducket, Dec. 26, 1847 (copy), *ibid.,* XVIa.

113. Baltimore *Sun,* Dec. 7, 1847; *Baltimore American,* Jan. 4, 1848; letter of "Franklin," unidentified clipping in Kennedy Papers, LXIII, Peabody Institute Library.

114. Richard Lennon to editor of *Baltimore American,* March 22, 1848, clipping in Kennedy Papers, LXIII, Peabody Institute Library.

115. Baltimore *Sun,* March 2, 6, 1848.

116. B & O minutes, Nov. 10, 1847; April 12, July 12, 1848; J. P. Kennedy, journal, July 18, Sept. 19, 1848, Kennedy Papers, VIIb, Peabody Institute Library; Bowen, *Rambles,* p. 82.

117. LMcL to directors of the B & O, Sept. 12, 1848, in B & O minutes, Sept. 13, 1848; LMcL to Louis McLane, Jr., Sept. 30, 1848, Fisher Collection; Hidy, *House of Baring,* p. 387; LMcL to Baring Brothers, May 12, June 23, Aug. 3, 1848, Baring Papers, C-1375, PAC.

118. LMcL to board of directors, Sept. 2, 1848, in B & O minutes, Sept. 13, 1848.

119. B & O minutes, Sept. 18, 1848.

120. J. P. Kennedy, journal, Sept. 14, 1848, Kennedy Papers, VIIb, Peabody Institute Library.

121. Baltimore *Sun,* Sept. 14, 1848; Semmes, *Latrobe,* pp. 361–363; Bowen, *Rambles,* p. 82.

122. Baltimore *Sun,* Oct. 14, 1848; Douglas S. Freeman, *Robert E. Lee* (New York, 1935), I, 301–303.

123. B & O minutes, Oct. 11, 1848; Baltimore *Sun,* Oct. 12, 1848.

124. J. P. Kennedy, journal, Sept. 16, 1848, Kennedy Papers, VIIb, Peabody Institute Library.

125. Scharf, *History of Baltimore,* pp. 329–330; Charles L. Wagandt, *The Mighty Revolution* (Baltimore, 1964), p. 192.

CHAPTER EIGHTEEN: RETIREMENT

1. *Delaware Gazette,* Oct. 6, 1848, quoting the *Washington Union,* Oct. 5, 1848.

2. Wilmington *Mirror of the Times,* Feb. 26, 1800.

3. *Delaware Gazette,* Oct. 24, 1848.

4. *Delaware Gazette,* Oct. 24, 1848; Wilmington *Blue Hen's Chicken,* Oct. 27, 1848; Baltimore *Sun,* Oct. 25, 1848.

5. *Baltimore Patriot,* Nov. 21, 1848; J. P. Kennedy, journal, Nov. 22, 24, 1848, Kennedy Papers, VIIc, Peabody Institute Library; Scharf, *Chronicles of Baltimore,* pp. 91, 96.

6. J. P. Kennedy to P. L. Pendleton, Nov. 26, 1848 (copy), Kennedy Papers, XVIa, Peabody Institute Library.

7. LMcL to Louis McLane, Jr., Sept. 30, 1848, Fisher Collection.

8. LMcL to Robert McLane, Feb. 12, 1849, McLane Papers.

9. LMcL to Louis McLane, Jr., April 19, 1849, Fisher Collection.

10. Baltimore *Sun,* Aug. 6, 1849; Greenmount Cemetery tombstone inscription and records, Baltimore.

11. Lydia Johnston to Sally Tiffany, Sept. 5, 1849, Fisher Collection.

12. Louis McLane, Jr., to his wife, Aug. 16–30, 1850, *ibid.*

13. Holland, *The Garesché, de Bauduy, and des Chapelles Families,* p. 161; Juliette Garesché to Louis McLane, Jr., Feb. 15, 1850, Fisher Collection.

14. Juliette Garesché to Sophie McLane, May 22, 1850; Juliette Garesché to Louis McLane, Jr., March 23, 1851, Fisher Collection.

15. Catherine Mary McLane to Sally Tiffany, April 8, 1850, *ibid.*

16. Louis McLane, Jr., to his wife, May 24, 1853; Sophie McLane to Louis McLane, Jr., July 16, 1853, *ibid.*

17. Louis McLane, Jr., to his wife, May 24, 1853, *ibid.*

18. LMcL to Robert McLane, Aug. 12, 1853, McLane Papers; Sophie McLane to Louis McLane, Jr., Aug. 9, 1853, Fisher Collection.

19. Interview with Louis McLane Hobbins, Madison, Wisconsin, spring, 1952.

20. Samuel Hoffman to Louis McLane, Jr., Aug. 26, 1851; Charles McLane

to Louis McLane, Jr., Feb. 1, 1850; James L. McLane to Louis McLane, Jr., Sept. 7, 1850, Fisher Collection.

21. Louis McLane, Jr., to his wife, Aug. 18, 1853, *ibid.*

22. Mrs. Samuel Hoffman to Louis McLane, Jr., April 17 [1850]; Louis McLane, Jr., to his wife, June 20, 1851, *ibid.*

23. Louis McLane, Jr., current expense account, 1849–1850; Louis McLane, Jr., to his wife, Feb. 17–24, April 22–27, May 16–June 1, 1850, *ibid.*

24. Louis McLane, Jr., to his wife, Feb. 28–March 2, 1850, March 13–14, 1851; Louis McLane, Jr., to Sally Tiffany, March 9–10, 1850, *ibid.;* CMcL, Sentiment Book (seen by courtesy of the late Louis McLane Hobbins, Madison).

25. Louis McLane, Jr., to his wife, June 21, 1851; Mrs. Samuel Hoffman to Louis McLane, Jr., June 25, 1851; Samuel Hoffman to Louis McLane, Jr., June 25, 1851, Fisher Collection.

26. Louis McLane, Jr., to his wife, June 4, 1851, *ibid.*

27. Robert McLane to Louis McLane, Jr., March 1, 1851, *ibid.*

28. R. M. McLane, *Reminiscences,* pp. 116–119; Robert McLane to Louis McLane, Jr., March 24, 1851; Samuel Hoffman to Louis McLane, Jr., April 9, 1851; Louis McLane, Jr., to his wife, June 4–13, 18–30, 1851, Fisher Collection.

29. Louis McLane, Jr., to his wife, Aug. 19, Sept. 5–6, 22, Nov. 14, 28, 1851, Fisher Collection.

30. Louis McLane, Jr., to his wife, Dec. 15, 1851; Jan. 2, 14, June 27, 30, July 9, 15, 1852, *ibid.;* R. M. McLane, *Reminiscences,* pp. 121–122; Allan McLane Hamilton, *Recollections,* p. 83; Samuel Hoffman to Louis McLane, Jr., July 11, 1851; Robert McLane to Louis McLane, Jr., July 4, 1852, Fisher Collection.

31. Edward Hungerford, *Wells Fargo* (New York, 1949), pp. 64–65; Otis, *History of the Panama Rail Road and Pacific Mail Steamship Company,* pp. 155, 168, 230; Cross, *Financing an Empire,* I, 412–418; Wells Fargo Organization (typescript in Wells Fargo Museum, San Francisco), I, 6–7; *San Francisco News Letter and California Advertiser,* Sept. 29, 1866; Hubert Howe Bancroft, *Works,* XXI (*History of California,* IV) (San Francisco, 1886), 725; San Francisco *Alta California,* Aug. 26, 1866, and Aug. 26, 1881; San Francisco *Call,* Dec. 23, 1891.

32. LMcL to Sally Tiffany, April 10, 1850, Fisher Collection.

33. LMcL to Robert McLane, July 1, 1850, McLane Papers; Allan McLane to Louis McLane, Jr., July 31, 1850, Fisher Collection.

34. Harry, *Maryland Constitution of 1851,* Chap. 1.

35. *Baltimore American,* Sept. 6, 1850; James L. McLane to Louis McLane, Jr., Sept. 7, 1850, Fisher Collection.

36. *Baltimore American,* Sept. 9, Nov. 5, 6, 12, 1850; *Proceedings of the Maryland State Convention to Frame a New Constitution* [hereafter referred to as Riley and Davis, *Proceedings*], pp. 6–7, 15, 17, 25–30, 32–38.

37. Riley and Davis, *Proceedings,* pp. 97, 127–129; Harry, *Maryland Constitution of 1851,* pp. 37–38.

38. *Debates and Proceedings of the Maryland Reform Convention to Revise*

the State Constitution [hereafter referred to as McNeir, *Debates*], I, 149–150; Thorpe, *Federal and State Constitutions*, III, 1700.

39. LMcL to Robert McLane, July 12 [1850], McLane Papers.

40. McNeir, *Debates*, I, 194, 197–198.

41. *Ibid.*, I, 166–167; II, 815–817, 828–836; Thorpe, *Federal and State Constitutions*, III, 1735–1736.

42. LMcL to J. Buchanan, Feb. 16, 1851, Buchanan Papers, HSP; McNeir, *Debates*, I, 293.

43. McNeir, *Debates*, I, 343–345.

44. *Ibid.*, 346, 347, 349; Thorpe, *Federal and State Constitutions*, III, 1723–1724.

45. NcNeir, *Debates*, I, 411–418, 423.

46. Riley and Davis, *Proceedings*, pp. 93–94.

47. McNeir, *Debates*, I, 520, 531, 534–535; II, 657–658.

48. *Ibid.*, II, 7; Thorpe, *Federal and State Constitutions*, III, 1727–1734.

49. McNeir, *Debates*, I, 29–30, 46–49, 60–61; Thorpe, *Federal and State Constitutions*, III, 1716–1717.

50. McNeir, *Debates*, I, 157, 372; Harry, *Maryland Constitution of 1851*, pp. 29, 35, 39, 43–44.

51. McNeir, *Debates*, I, 507–515.

52. *Ibid.*, I, 127–128, 177–186.

53. *Ibid.*, I, 169, 412, 524.

54. *Ibid.*, II, 219.

55. *Ibid.*, II, 585–586, 870.

56. Harry, *Maryland Constitution of 1851*, pp. 84, 86; Samuel Hoffman to Louis McLane, Jr., June 11, 1851, Fisher Collection.

57. Samuel Hoffman to Louis McLane, Jr., June 11, 1851; Mrs. Samuel Hoffman to Louis McLane, Jr., June 25, 1851; James L. McLane to Louis McLane, Jr., Sept. 7, 1850; Louis McLane, Jr., to his wife, Jan. 6–15, 1851, Fisher Collection.

58. LMcL to [Robert McLane], July 5, 1853; Robert McLane to LMcL, Jan. 1, 1854, McLane Papers; Sophie McLane to Louis McLane, Jr., July 4, 16, 1853; LMcL to Louis McLane, Jr., July 4, Oct. 3, 1854, Fisher Collection.

59. LMcL to Louis McLane, Jr., Sept. 17, 1853, Fisher Collection.

60. Sophie McLane to Louis McLane, Jr., Dec. 3, 1853, *ibid.*

61. LMcL to Louis McLane, Jr., June 18, 1854, *ibid.*

62. LMcL to Louis McLane, Jr., March 3, 1856, *ibid.*

63. LMcL to [Lydia Johnston], undated, *ibid.*

64. Robert McLane to C. H. Peaslee, Sept. 23, 1852; C. H. Peaslee to Franklin Pierce, Sept. 24, 1852; Robert McLane to C. H. Peaslee [Sept. 18, 1852], Franklin Pierce Papers, reel 5, LC; Roy F. Nichols, *Franklin Pierce* (Philadelphia, 1931), pp. 212–213.

65. Baltimore *Sun*, June 18, 20, 22, 24, 25, 28, 1853; Robert McLane to LMcL [May 30, 1853], McLane Papers.

66. Robert McLane to LMcL, June 14, July 4, 1853; LMcL to Robert McLane, July 5, 1853, McLane Papers; LMcL to Louis McLane, Jr., June 15, 1853, Fisher Collection.

67. R. M. McLane, *Reminiscences,* p. 126; LMcL to Louis McLane, Jr., Sept. 17, 1853, Fisher Collection; W. L. Marcy to Robert McLane, Nov. 9, 1853, McLane Papers; Nichols, *Pierce,* pp. 228, 268; Baltimore *Sun,* June 7, 24, 27, 1853.

68. Robert McLane to LMcL, Jan. 1, 26, 1854, McLane Papers [2d letter incorrectly dated 1853].

69. Sophie McLane to Louis McLane, Jr., Oct. 10–18, 1853, Fisher Collection; Robert McLane to LMcL, Jan. 1, 1854, McLane Papers.

70. LMcL to Louis McLane, Jr., Sept. 3, 1853; June 18, Dec. 2, 18, 1854; March 18, 1855; Sophie McLane to LMcL, Nov. 4, 1853, Fisher Collection; Robert McLane to LMcL, Jan. 1, 1854, McLane Papers.

71. LMcL to Louis McLane, Jr., Sept. 3, 17, 1853; Oct. 3, 1854, Fisher Collection.

72. LMcL to Louis McLane, Jr., April 4, 1854; Sept. 3, 1856, *ibid.*

73. LMcL to Louis McLane, Jr., Dec. 2, 1854, *ibid.*

74. LMcL to Louis McLane, Jr., Oct. 16, 1854, *ibid.*

75. LMcL to Louis McLane, Jr., Sept. 3, 1856, *ibid.*

76. LMcL to Allan McLane, Oct. 29, 1854, *ibid.*

77. LMcL to Lydia Johnston, March 9, 1857, *ibid.*

78. LMcL to Louis McLane, Jr., Dec. 18, 1856, *ibid.*

79. LMcL to Louis McLane, Jr., Dec. 3, 1856, *ibid.*

80. LMcL to W. and L. Carpenter, Dec. 17, 1855, Vertical File, Maryland Historical Society.

81. LMcL to Louis McLane, Jr., April 4, 1854, Fisher Collection; Robert McLane to LMcL, May 8, June 15, 1854, McLane Papers.

82. LMcL to Louis McLane, Jr., July 4, Oct. 16, Dec. 2, 1854, Fisher Collection.

83. Robert McLane to LMcL, Jan. 1, 1854, McLane Papers; LMcL to Louis McLane, Jr., July 4, 17, Oct. 3, Dec. 2, 1854; LMcL to Allan McLane, Aug. 3, 1854, Fisher Collection.

84. LMcL to Louis McLane, Jr., Sept. 4, 1854; LMcL to Allan McLane, Oct. 29, 1854, Fisher Collection.

85. Robert McLane to LMcL, April 11, May 3, 1855, McLane Papers.

86. LMcL to Louis McLane, Jr., Jan. 1, March 3, 1856, Fisher Collection.

87. LMcL to Louis McLane, Jr., Dec. 3, 1856, *ibid.*

88. Robert McLane to LMcL, June 15, 1854, McLane Papers; LMcL to Louis McLane, Jr., March 18, May 17, 1857, Fisher Collection.

89. LMcL to W. P. Smith, May 18, 1857, Garrett Papers, CVII, LC.

90. LMcL to Louis McLane, Jr., July 2, 1857, Fisher Collection.

91. LMcL to Louis McLane, Jr., July 19, 1857, *ibid.;* Rebecca Hamilton to Allan McLane, Oct. 14, 1857, Batchelder Papers; "Diaries of Sidney George Fisher," *PMHB,* LXXXVI, 465.

92. Memorandum on conversation of LMcL and Robert McLane, Sept. 29, 1857; Rebecca Hamilton to Allan McLane, Oct. 14, 1857, Batchelder Papers; *Baltimore American,* Oct. 10, 1857; Baltimore *Sun,* Oct. 10, 1857.

93. *Baltimore American,* Oct. 10, 1857; Baltimore *Sun,* Oct. 10, 1857.

Bibliography

MANUSCRIPT SOURCES

McLane Papers

Just as there has long been a misunderstanding about the date of Louis McLane's birth, so there has long been a misunderstanding regarding his personal papers. These have been commonly thought to have been destroyed in the Baltimore fire of 1904. I believe that there were indeed McLane papers destroyed in the Baltimore fire. The story, as I heard it from the late Reverend James Latimer McLane, is that his father, Judge Allan McLane, acting because of Woodrow Wilson's interest in the family papers, placed in a Baltimore bank vault the surviving correspondence between Louis McLane and distinguished contemporary statesmen, and that these letters were destroyed in the fire that ravaged downtown Baltimore but did not reach Judge Allan McLane's house.

Probably these lost manuscripts were mainly letters to Louis McLane, for in the papers that survive there is a lack of the many letters that might be expected from Van Buren, Buchanan, Jackson, Washington Irving, Lewis Cass, and men of similar stature. But the family did preserve what might be called Louis McLane's domestic letters, and in this correspondence, particularly with his wife and his oldest son, Robert, it is likely that McLane's character, objectives, and opinions are revealed much more clearly than in correspondence with his eminent contemporaries, with whom he would have been guarded. It is, of course, chiefly their letters that are lost, for his letters to them turn up in collections of their papers.

The two major collections of McLane correspondence I have entitled the McLane Papers and the Fisher Collection. Both are in private hands. The former belonged, when I saw them, to the Reverend James Latimer McLane, now deceased, a descendant of Louis McLane's youngest child. They were then stored in a Bekins warehouse in Denver, but were temporarily removed for my use to the home of Father McLane's brother-in-law, James Day, Esq., and were subsequently arranged and microfilmed for me by the kindness of Miss Dolores Renze, state archivist of Colorado. For the most part these are papers that had been owned by Robert Milligan McLane, Louis McLane's oldest son.

The second collection is in the possession of another McLane descendant, Mr. D. K. Este Fisher, Jr., of Baltimore, who called my attention to them after they were found in the apartment of his aunt, Miss Elizabeth Curzon McLane, following her death in 1952. Miss McLane was the daughter of Louis McLane, Jr., whose papers these seem to have been. They were microfilmed for me through the kindness of Dr. Leon de Valinger, Jr., state archivist of Delaware, after my notes had been made from the original manuscripts. I also had the privilege of using genealogical notes on the McLanes compiled by Mr. Fisher.

A third collection of McLane papers, smaller than the others but the key to my discovery of them, I have entitled the Batchelder Collection. I saw them through the kindness of Mrs. George Batchelder, Jr., of Moraine Farm, Beverly, Massachusetts. Mrs. Batchelder, who is a descendant of Louis McLane's daughter Sally, has generously given these papers to the Historical Society of Delaware, Wilmington.

My first discovery of Louis McLane papers was among the James A. Bayard papers belonging to the late Mrs. Florence Bayard Hilles. I examined them at her home, Ommelanden, south of New Castle, Delaware, but Mrs. Hilles kindly permitted me to take them to my home and to have copies made of them. These copies, as well as copies of most of the Louis McLane papers in private hands, including microfilm of the two large collections previously mentioned, are deposited in the Morris Library of the University of Delaware.

Papers of Louis McLane's father, Allen McLane, turn up in many places, but the major collection of them is in the New-York Historical Society. (I used photostatic copies in the Historical Society of Delaware.) Louis McLane's father commonly spelled his name "Allen," the *Dictionary of American Biography* to the contrary notwithstanding; however, the descendants of Louis McLane who bear the name spell it "Allan."

Small additional collections of Louis McLane papers are deposited at the Historical Society of Delaware and at the University of Delaware. Miscellaneous McLane items were provided by the libraries of Dickinson College (Carlisle, Pennsylvania), Drew University (Madison, New Jersey), and West Virginia University (Morgantown), and especially by the Pierpont Morgan Library (New York). I am indebted to the kindness of Mrs. J. D. Otley, of Haverford, Pennsylvania, and the late Mr. Otley for use of various items relating to the history of Bohemia, which the Otleys restored to its present handsome state.

Through the kindness of the late Louis McLane Hobbins, of Madison, Wisconsin, I was permitted to examine the commonplace book of his grandmother, Mrs. Louis McLane, and to learn something of the migration of McLanes to the Middle West. Mr. and Mrs. Thomas Hurst, of Kansas City, Missouri, and their grandson Allan McLane Hurst, Jr., had a microfilm copy made for me of the surviving journals of Mr. Hurst's grandfather, who was a nephew of Louis McLane. The late Judge Richard S. Rodney, of New Castle, Delaware, allowed me to examine at my leisure his collection of papers of the Read family, now housed at the Historical Society of Delaware. I was enabled to examine the diary of Phoebe George Bradford through the kindness of Mrs. Harry Clark Boden, a descendant of Mrs. Bradford.

A typescript of "My Own Mirror and Record of Events," by Thomas Cope, was lent me by Professor David B. Tyler, of Wagner College. The "Recollections" of Joseph H. Rogers were examined through the kindness of Mrs. Laussat R. Rogers and the late Mr. Rogers, of Boothhurst, near New Castle.

Other Manuscript Sources

Adams Papers (microfilm). Massachusetts Historical Society, Boston.

William Barry Papers (typed copies). Filson Club, Louisville.

Baltimore & Ohio Railroad Company Minutes. Baltimore & Ohio Railroad Company, Baltimore.

Baring Papers. Baring Brothers & Company, London.

Baring Papers (microfilm). Public Archives of Canada, Ottawa.

Bayard Papers. Library of Congress, Washington.

Nicholas Biddle Papers. Library of Congress, Washington.

Blair-Lee Papers. Princeton University, Princeton, N.J.

Phoebe George Bradford Diary. Historical Society of Delaware, Wilmington.

Bradford Papers. Maryland Historical Society, Baltimore.

Breck Collection. Library Company of Philadelphia.

William P. Brobson Diary. Pennsylvania Historical and Museum Commission, Harrisburg.

H. Fletcher Brown Collection. Historical Society of Delaware, Wilmington.

Buchanan Papers. Historical Society of Pennsylvania, Philadelphia.

Benjamin F. Butler Papers. New York State Library, Albany.

Calhoun Papers (photostats). Clemson University, Clemson, S.C.

Calhoun Papers (microfilm). South Caroliniana Library, Columbia, S.C.

Lewis Cass Papers (microfilm). Clements Library, Ann Arbor, Mich.

John M. Clayton Papers. Library of Congress, Washington.

Clymer-Meredith-Read Papers. New York Public Library.

Ezekiel Cooper Papers. Garrett Biblical Institute, Evanston, Ill.

W. W. Corcoran Papers. Library of Congress, Washington.

Dallas Papers. Library Company of Philadelphia.

Mahlon and Philemon Dickerson Correspondence. New Jersey Historical Society, Newark, N.J.

Andrew J. Donelson Papers. Library of Congress, Washington.

Dreer Collection. Historical Society of Pennsylvania, Philadelphia.

Du Pont Papers. Eleutherian Mills Historical Library, Greenville, Del.

Emmet Collection. New York Public Library.

A. C. Flagg Papers. New York Public Library.

Foreign Office Transcripts, 5th series (from Public Record Office, London). Library of Congress.

Thomas Marsh Forman Papers. Maryland Historical Society, Baltimore.
Gallatin Papers. New-York Historical Society.
Gallatin Papers. Library of Congress.
Garrett Family Papers. Library of Congress.
Gilpin Papers. Historical Society of Delaware, Wilmington.
Gist Papers. Maryland Historical Society, Baltimore.
Gratz Manuscripts. Historical Society of Pennsylvania, Philadelphia.
Duff Green Papers. Library of Congress.
Howard Papers. Maryland Historical Society, Baltimore.
Samuel D. Ingham Papers. South Caroliniana Library, Columbia, S.C.
Samuel D. Ingham Papers. University of Pennsylvania, Philadelphia.
Irvine Papers. Historical Society of Pennsylvania, Philadelphia.
Washington Irving Papers. New York Public Library.
Jackson Papers. Library of Congress.
Jackson-Lewis Papers. New York Public Library.
Johnston Collection. Historical Society of Pennsylvania, Philadelphia.
John Pendleton Kennedy Papers. Peabody Institute Library, Baltimore.
Latimer Papers. University of Delaware, Newark, Del.
Logan Papers. Historical Society of Pennsylvania, Philadelphia.
Madison Papers. Library of Congress.
James Maury Deposit. University of Virginia, Charlottesville.
John J. Milligan Papers. Historical Society of Delaware, Wilmington.
Miscellaneous Papers. New-York Historical Society.
Miscellaneous Papers. New York Public Library.
Monroe Papers. Library of Congress.
Morris Canal and Banking Company Minute Books. New Jersey Department
    of Conservation and Economic Development, Trenton.
Morse Autograph Collection. Historical Society of Delaware, Wilmington.
Newark Academy and College Records. University of Delaware, Newark.
Noah Noble Collection. Indiana Historical Commission, Indianapolis.
Franklin Pierce Papers (microfilm). Library of Congress.
Poinsett Papers. Historical Society of Pennsylvania, Philadelphia.
Polk Papers. Library of Congress.
Peter A. Porter Collection. Buffalo Historical Society, Buffalo, N.Y.
Preble Collection. Library of Congress.
George Read Papers. Historical Society of Delaware, Wilmington.
Read Manuscripts. Historical Society of Pennsylvania, Philadelphia.
Read Family Papers. Library of Congress.
Joseph Reed Manuscripts. New-York Historical Society.
Ridgely Papers. Delaware State Archives, Dover.
William C. Rives Papers. Library of Congress.
Charles Roberts Autograph Collection. Haverford College, Haverford, Pa.
Richard S. Rodney Collection. Historical Society of Delaware, Wilmington.
Rush Correspondence. Library Company of Philadelphia.
Margaret Bayard Smith Papers. Library of Congress.
Society Collection. Historical Society of Delaware, Wilmington.

Society Collection. Historical Society of Pennsylvania, Philadelphia.

State Department, Appointment Papers. National Archives.

State Department, Diplomatic Despatches. National Archives.

State Department, Diplomatic Instructions. National Archives.

State Department, Domestic Letters. National Archives.

State Department, Miscellaneous Correspondence (London). National Archives.

State Department, Notes to Foreign Legations. National Archives.

Henry Storrs Private Journal. Buffalo Historical Society, Buffalo, N.Y.

George Strawbridge, Memoirs. Princeton University, Princeton, N.J.

Robert Swartwout Papers. New York Public Library.

Roger B. Taney Papers. Library of Congress.

John W. Taylor Papers. New-York Historical Society.

John Tyler Papers. Library of Congress.

United States Boxes. New York Public Library.

United States Finance Collection. Library of Congress.

Vail Family Papers. New York State Library, Albany, N.Y.

Van Buren Papers. Library of Congress.

Van Dyke Papers. Eleutherian Mills Historical Library, Greenville, Del.

Gulian C. Verplanck Papers. New-York Historical Society.

Warden Papers. Maryland Historical Society, Baltimore.

Elisha Whittlesey Papers. Western Reserve Historical Society, Cleveland.

Levi Woodbury Papers. Library of Congress.

Other libraries that I used included the Bancroft Library of the University of California (Berkeley), the California Historical Society, the California State Library, the Charleston (South Carolina) Historical Society, the Chicago Historical Society, the Columbia University Library, the Detroit Public Library, the Duke University Library, the Henry E. Huntington Library, the Massachusetts Historical Society, the Missouri Historical Society, the Oregon Historical Society, the Rutgers University Library, the San Francisco Public Library, the Southern Historical Collection of the University of North Carolina Library (Chapel Hill), the State Historical Society of Missouri, the State Historical Society of Wisconsin, the University of Chicago Library, the University of Rochester Library, the Virginia Historical Society, the Wells Fargo Bank Museum, the William and Mary College Library, and the Wilmington Institute Free Library. In some cases my searches were made fifteen or more years ago.

PUBLISHED WORKS

Adams, Henry. *The Life of Albert Gallatin.* New York, 1943.

Adams, John Quincy. *Memoirs of John Quincy Adams.* Ed. Charles Francis Adams. 12 vols. Philadelphia, 1874–1877.

―――. *Writings of John Quincy Adams.* Ed. Worthington C. Ford. 7 vols. New York, 1913–1917.

Aitken, Hugh G. J. "Yates and McIntyre: Lottery Managers." *Journal of Economic History*, XIII (1953), 36–57.

Albjerg, Victor L. "Jackson's Influence on Internal Improvements." *Tennessee Historical Magazine*, n.s., II (1931–1932), 259–269.

Allen, Gardner W. *Our Naval War with France.* Boston, 1909.

Ambler, Charles H. *The Life and Diary of John Floyd.* Richmond, 1918.

Ammon, Harry. *James Monroe.* New York, 1971.

Asbury, Francis. *Journal and Letters.* Ed. Elmer E. Clark, J. Manning Potts, and Jacob S. Payton. 3 vols. London, 1958.

Backofen, Catherine. "Congressman Harmar Denny." *Western Pennsylvania Historical Magazine*, XXIII (1940), 65–78.

Baker, Elizabeth Feaster. *Henry Wheaton, 1785–1848.* Philadelphia, 1937.

Baltimore & Ohio Rail Road Company. *Annual Reports of the President and Directors to the Stockholders.* Baltimore, 1837–1849.

———. *Laws and Ordinances Relating to the Baltimore and Ohio Rail Road Company.* Baltimore, 1850.

———. *Report of Documents Submitted by the Committee Appointed to Confer with the Authorities of the City of Wheeling, Respecting the Late Law of Virginia Granting the Right of Way to the Baltimore & Ohio Rail Road Company Through That State. Passed 6th March, 1847.* Baltimore, 1847.

Barker, E. C. "President Jackson and the Texas Revolution." *American Historical Review*, XII (1906–1907), 788–809.

Barroll, Hope H. *Barroll in Great Britain and America, 1554–1910.* Baltimore, 1910.

Barry, William T. "Letters of William T. Barry." *William and Mary College Quarterly*, 1st ser., XIII (1904–05), 236–244; XIV (1905–06), passim.

Bassett, John S. *Life of Andrew Jackson.* New York, 1916.

———. "Major Lewis on the Nomination of Andrew Jackson." *Proceedings of the American Antiquarian Society*, n.s., XXXIII, pt. 1 (1923), 12–33.

Bateman, Carroll. *The Baltimore and Ohio: The Story of the Railroad That Grew Up with the United States.* Baltimore [1951].

Bates, Daniel M., ed. *Reports of Cases Adjudged and Determined in the Court of Chancery of the State of Delaware*, I. Wilmington, 1917.

Bayard, James A. *Letters of James Asheton Bayard, 1802–1814. Papers of the Historical Society of Delaware*, XXXI. Wilmington, 1901.

———. *Papers of James A. Bayard, 1796–1815.* Ed. Elizabeth Donnan. Annual Report of the American Historical Association, 1913, II. Washington, 1915.

Belohlavek, John M. "Dallas, the Democracy, and the Bank War of 1832." *Pennsylvania Magazine of History and Biography*, XCVI (1972), 377–389.

Bemis, Samuel Flagg. *John Quincy Adams and the Foundations of American Foreign Policy.* New York, 1949.

———. *John Quincy Adams and the Union.* New York, 1956.

Benns, F. Lee. *The American Struggle for the British West India Carrying Trade.* Bloomington, 1923.

Benton, Thomas H. *Thirty Years' View.* 2 vols. New York, 1854–1856.

Biddle, Nicholas. *The Correspondence of Nicholas Biddle Dealing with National Affairs, 1807–1844.* Ed. Reginald C. McGrane. Boston, 1919.

Binder, Frederick M. "Pennsylvania Coal and the Beginnings of American Steam Navigation." *Pennsylvania Magazine of History and Biography,* LXXXIII (1959), 420–445.

Binns, John. *Recollections of His Life, Written by Himself.* Philadelphia, 1854.

The Biographical Cyclopedia of Representative Men of Maryland and District of Columbia. Baltimore, 1879.

Blue, George Verne. "France and the Oregon Question." *Oregon Historical Quarterly,* XXXIV (1933), 39–59, 144–163.

Bohner, Charles H. *John Pendleton Kennedy, Gentleman from Baltimore.* Baltimore, 1961.

Bonny, Mrs. Catharina V. R. *A Legacy of Historical Gleanings.* Vol. I: Albany, 1875.

Boorstin, Daniel J. *Delaware Cases, 1792–1830.* Vol. III: St. Paul, Minn., 1943.

Boucher, Chauncey S., and Brooks, Robert P., eds. "Correspondence Addressed to John C. Calhoun." Annual Report of the American Historical Association, 1929. Washington, 1931.

Bouldin, Powhatan. *Home Reminiscences of John Randolph of Roanoke.* Danville, Va., 1878.

Bourne, Kenneth. *Britain and the Balance of Power in North America, 1815–1908.* Berkeley, 1967.

Bowen, [Eli] Ele. *Rambles in the Path of the Steam-Horse.* Philadelphia, 1855.

[Bringhurst, Joseph.] *The Delawariad, or a Second Part of the Wilmingtoniad: Being a Touch at the Times. A Dialogue.* Wilmington, 1801.

[———.] *The Wilmingtoniad, or, A Touch at the Times. A Dialogue.* Wilmington, 1800.

Brocker, Galen. "Jared Sparks, Robert Peel and the State Paper Office." *American Quarterly,* XIII (1961), 140–152.

Brown, George R. *Washington: A Not Too Serious History.* Baltimore, 1930.

Brown, Richard H. "The Missouri Crisis, Slavery, and the Politics of Jacksonianism." *South Atlantic Quarterly,* LXV (1966), 55–72.

Bruce, William C. *John Randolph of Roanoke, 1773–1833.* 2 vols. New York, 1922.

Bryant, William Cullen. *A Discourse on the Life, Character and Writings of Gulian Crommelin Verplanck.* New York, 1870.

Buchanan, James. *Works of James Buchanan.* Ed. John Bassett Moore. 12 vols. Philadelphia, 1908–1911.

Buchholz, Heinrich Ewald. *Governors of Maryland from the Revolution to the Year 1908.* 2d ed. Baltimore, 1908.

Butler, William Allen. *A Retrospect of Forty Years, 1825–1865.* Ed. Harriet Allen Butler. New York, 1911.

Cadman, John W. *The Corporation in New Jersey: Business and Politics, 1791–1875.* Cambridge, 1949.

Calhoun, John C. *Correspondence of John C. Calhoun*. Ed. J. F. Jameson. Annual Report of the American Historical Association, 1899, II. Washington, 1900.

Callahan, James M. *American Foreign Policy in Canadian Relations*. New York, 1937.

———. *American Foreign Policy in Mexican Relations*. New York, 1932.

Callender, G. S. "The Early Transportation and Banking Enterprises of the States in Relation to the Growth of Corporations." *Quarterly Journal of Economics*, XVII (1902–1903), 111–162.

Cassell, Frank A. *Merchant Congressman in the Young Republic: Samuel Smith of Maryland, 1752–1839*. Madison, 1971.

Catterall, Ralph C. H. *The Second Bank of the United States*. Chicago, 1903.

Chambers, William N. *Old Bullion Benton, Senator from the New West*. Boston, 1956.

Chandler, Alfred D., Jr. "Patterns of American Railroad Finance, 1830–50." *Business History Review*, XXVIII (1954), 248–263.

Chitwood, Oliver P. *John Tyler, Champion of the Old South*. New York, 1939.

Clark, Charles B. *The Eastern Shore of Maryland and Virginia*. 3 vols. New York [1950].

Clark, Joseph S., Jr. "The Railroad Struggle for Pittsburgh. Forty-three Years of Philadelphia-Baltimore Rivalry, 1838–1871." *Pennsylvania Magazine of History and Biography*, XLVIII (1924), 1–37.

Clark, Robert C., ed. "Aberdeen and Peel on Oregon, 1844." *Oregon Historical Quarterly*, XXXIV (1933), 236–240.

———. *History of the Willamette Valley, Oregon*. Vol. I: Chicago, 1927.

Clay, Henry. *The Papers of Henry Clay*. Ed. James F. Hopkins. Vol. III: [Lexington], 1963.

Cleveland, Frederick A., and Powell, Fred Wilbur. *Railroad Promotion and Capitalization in the United States*. New York, 1909.

Clews, Henry. *Twenty-Eight Years in Wall Street*. New York, 1888.

Cobb, Joseph B. "A Review of the Life and Times of William H. Crawford." In *Leisure Labors: or, Miscellanies, Historical, Literary, and Political*, pp. 131–247. New York, 1858.

Colton, Calvin, ed. *The Works of Henry Clay*. 10 vols. New York, 1904.

Commager, Henry. "England and the Oregon Treaty of 1846." *Oregon Historical Quarterly*, XXVIII (1927), 18–38.

Connor, R. D. W. "William Gaston." *Proceedings of the American Antiquarian Society*, n.s., XLIII (1933), 381–446.

Conrad, Henry C. *History of the State of Delaware*. 3 vols. Wilmington, 1908.

Cooley, E. *A Description of the Etiquette at Washington City*. Philadelphia, 1829.

Cox, Issac Joslin. "Selections from the Torrence Papers." *Quarterly Publications of the Historical and Philosophical Society of Ohio*, I (1906), 65–96; II (1907), 5–36, 97–120; III (1908), 65–102; IV (1909), 93–138; VI (1911), 3–88.

Crall, F. Frank. "A Half Century of Rivalry between Pittsburgh and Wheeling." *Western Pennsylvania Historical Magazine*, XIII (1930), 237–255.

Cranmer, H. Jerome. "Internal Improvements in New Jersey: Planning the Morris Canal." *Proceedings of the New Jersey Historical Society*, LXIX (1951), 324–341.

Crosby, Nathan. *Annual Obituary Notices of Eminent Persons Who Have Died in the United States. For 1857*. Boston, 1858.

Cross, Ira B. *Financing an Empire: History of Banking in California*. Vol. I: Chicago, 1927.

Crouthamel, James L. "Three Philadelphians in the Bank War: A Neglected Chapter in American Lobbying." *Pennsylvania History*, XXVII (1960), 361–378.

Cunningham, Gertrude. "British Response to the Cry of '54–40 or Fight.'" M.A. thesis, University of Washington, 1928.

Cunningham, Noble E., Jr. *The Jeffersonian Republicans in Power: Party Operations, 1801–1809*. Chapel Hill, 1963.

Curtis, George Ticknor. *Life of James Buchanan*. 2 vols. New York, 1883.

Curtis, James C. "Andrew Jackson and His Cabinet: Some New Evidence." *Tennessee Historical Quarterly*, XXVII (1968), 157–164.

Dangerfield, George. *The Awakening of American Nationalism, 1815–1828*. New York, 1965.

———. *The Era of Good Feelings*. New York, 1952.

Day, Clive. "The Early Development of the American Cotton Manufacture." *Quarterly Journal of Economics*, XXXIX (1925), 450–468.

de Valinger, Leon, Jr., *Calendar of Kent County, Delaware, Probate Records, 1680–1800*. Dover, 1944.

de Valinger, Leon, Jr., and Shaw, Virginia E., eds. *A Calendar of Ridgely Family Letters, 1742–1899, in the Delaware State Archives*. 3 vols. Dover, 1948–1961.

A Directory and Register for the Year 1814 . . . of the Borough of Wilmington and Brandywine. [Wilmington, 1814.]

Domett, Henry W. *A History of the Bank of New York, 1784–1884*. 3d ed. [1884.]

Donaldson, John J. *Speech of John J. Donaldson, of Howard County, on the Subject of the State of Maryland's Relations with the Baltimore & Ohio Railroad Company. Delivered in the House of Delegates, Thursday, March 9th, 1876*. Baltimore, 1876.

Dorwart, Harold L. "Biographical Notes on Jonathan Knight (1787–1858)." *Pennsylvania Magazine of History and Biography*, LXXV (1951), 76–90.

Duane, W. J. *Narrative and Correspondence Concerning the Removal of the Deposites, and Occurrences Connected Therewith*. Philadelphia, 1838.

du Pont, Eleuthère I. *Life of Eleuthère Irénée du Pont from Contemporary Correspondence*. Ed. Bessie G. du Pont. 11 vols. Newark, Del., 1923–1927.

Duvall, Marius. *A Navy Surgeon in California, 1846–1847: The Journal of Marius Duvall*. Ed. Fred B. Rogers. San Francisco, 1957.

Eaton, Margaret L. O'Neale Timberlake. *The Autobiography of Peggy Eaton.* New York, 1932.

Eckman, Jeannette, ed. *Delaware, a Guide to the First State.* 2d ed. New York, 1955.

Edwards, Ninian. *The Edwards Papers.* Ed. E. B. Washburne. Chicago, 1884.

Edwards, Ninian Wirt. *History of Illinois from 1778 to 1833; and Life and Times of Ninian Edwards.* Springfield, Ill., 1870.

Ellet, Charles, Jr. *Report on the Location of the Western Portion of the Baltimore and Ohio Rail Road to a Committee of the City Council of Wheeling.* Philadelphia, 1850.

Elliott, Orrin Leslie. *The Tariff Controversy in the United States, 1789–1833.* Palo Alto, 1892.

Eriksson, Erik M. "Official Newspaper Organs and Jackson's Reelection, 1832." *Tennessee Historical Magazine,* IX (1925), 37–58.

———. "Official Newspaper Organs and the Campaign of 1828." *Tennessee Historical Magazine,* VIII (1924), 231–247.

———. "Official Newspaper Organs and the Presidential Election of 1836." *Tennessee Historical Magazine,* IX (1925), 115–130.

Esarey, Logan. *State Banking in Indiana, 1814–1873.* Indiana University Studies, No. 15. Bloomington, 1912.

Fenhagen, Mary Pringle, comp. "John Ashmead and Some of His Descendants in Pennsylvania and South Carolina." *South Carolina Historical and Genealogical Magazine,* XLVII (1946), 133–142, 232–242.

Fink, William B. "Stephen Van Rensselaer and the House Election of 1825." *New York History,* XXXII (1951), 323–330.

Fischer, David Hackett. *The Revolution of American Conservatism.* New York, 1965.

Fish, Carl Russell. *The Civil Service and the Patronage.* New York, 1905.

Fishbein, Meyer H. *Early Business Statistical Operations of the Federal Government: National Archives Accessions,* No. 54 (1958), 1–29.

Fisher, George P. *Life of Benjamin Silliman.* . . . 2 vols. New York, 1866.

Fisher, R. S. *Gazetteer of the State of Maryland.* New York, 1852.

Fisher, Sidney George. *A Philadelphia Perspective: The Diary of Sidney George Fisher Covering the Years 1834–1871.* Ed. Nicholas B. Wainwright. Philadelphia, 1967. (Cited from first publication as "The Diaries of Sidney George Fisher" in the *Pennsylvania Magazine of History and Biography,* beginning with volume LXXVI [1952], 177.)

Flower, Milton E. *James Parton, the Father of Modern Biography.* Durham, 1951.

Floyd, John. "Diary of John Floyd." *John P. Branch Historical Papers of Randolph-Macon College,* V (1918), 119–233.

Fowler, Dorothy Ganfield. *The Cabinet Politician: The Postmasters General, 1829–1909.* New York, 1943.

Freehling, William W. *Prelude to Civil War: The Nullification Crisis in South Carolina, 1816–1836.* New York, 1968.

French, Bruce H. *Banking and Insurance in New Jersey: A History.* Princeton, 1965.

Fuess, Claude Moore. *Daniel Webster.* Vol. II (1830–1852): Boston, 1930.

G., H. B., of Charlotte. "Sergeant Champe." *Virginia Historical Register and Literary Note Book,* III (1850), 93–99.

Gallatin, Albert. *The Writings of Albert Gallatin.* Ed. Henry Adams. 3 vols. New York, 1960.

Gammon, Samuel Rhea, Jr. *The Presidential Campaign of 1832.* Johns Hopkins Studies in Historical and Political Science, XL, No. 1. Baltimore, 1922.

Garland, Hugh A. *The Life of John Randolph of Roanoke.* 2 vols. New York, 1850.

Garrett, John W. *Letter and Accompanying Documents, from John W. Garrett, President of the Baltimore and Ohio Railroad Company to the Comptroller of Maryland. . . .* Baltimore, 1865.

Gatell, Frank Otto. "Sober Second Thoughts on Van Buren, the Albany Regency, and the Wall Street Conspiracy." *Journal of American History,* LIII (1966), 19–40.

Gates, Paul W. *The Farmer's Age: Agriculture, 1815–1860.* New York [1960].

Gentieu, Frank P. *History of Mount Salem Methodist Church, Wilmington, Delaware, 1847–1947.* Wilmington, 1948.

Gilpin, Joshua. *A Memoir on the Rise, Progress, and Present State of the Chesapeake and Delaware Canal.* Wilmington, 1821.

Goodrich, Carter. *Government Promotion of American Canals and Railroads.* New York, 1960.

Goodrich, Carter, and Segal, Harvey H. "Baltimore's Aid to Railroads." *Journal of Economic History,* XIII (1953), 2–35.

Govan, Thomas Payne. *Nicholas Biddle, Nationalist and Public Banker, 1786–1844.* [Chicago, 1959.]

Governor's Register, State of Delaware. Vol. I. [No other printed.] Wilmington, 1926.

Graebner, Norman A. *Empire on the Pacific: A Study in American Continental Expansion.* New York [1955].

Graham, William A. *The Papers of William A. Graham.* Ed. J. G. de Roulhac Hamilton. Vol. I (1825–1837): Raleigh, 1957.

Gray, Ralph D. *The National Waterway: A History of the Chesapeake and Delaware Canal.* Urbana, 1967.

Green, Constance M. *Washington, Village and Capital, 1800–1878.* Princeton, 1962.

Green, Fletcher M. "On Tour with President Andrew Jackson." *New England Quarterly,* XXXVI (1963), 209–228.

Greville, Charles. *The Greville Diary.* Ed. Philip Whitwell Wilson. Vol. II: Garden City, 1927.

———. *The Greville Memoirs.* Ed. Lytton Strachey and Roger Fulford. 8 vols. London, 1838.

Hagner, Alexander B. "History and Reminiscences of St. John's Church,

Washington, D.C." *Records of the Columbia Historical Society,* XII (1909), 89–114.

Haller, Mark H. "The Rise of the Jackson Party in Maryland, 1820–1829." *Journal of Southern History,* XXVIII (1962), 307–326.

Hamilton, Allan McLane. *Recollections of an Alienist, Personal and Professional.* New York [1916].

Hamilton, James A. *Reminiscences of James A. Hamilton; or, Men and Events, at Home and Abroad, during Three Quarters of a Century.* New York, 1869.

Hammond, Bray. *Banks and Politics in America from the Revolution to the Civil War.* Princeton, 1957.

Hammond, Jabez D. *The History of Political Parties in the State of New York.* Vol. II: Albany, 1842.

Hanaford, Phebe A. *The Life of George Peabody.* . . . Boston, 1870.

Hanna, H. S. *A Financial History of Maryland, 1789–1848.* Johns Hopkins University Studies in Historical and Political Science, XXV, Nos. 8–10. Baltimore, 1907.

Hanna, John D. C., ed. *The Centennial Services of Asbury Methodist Episcopal Church, Wilmington, Delaware. October 13–20, 1889.* Wilmington, 1889.

Harlow, Alvin F. *Old Towpaths: The Story of the American Canal Era.* New York, 1926.

Harlow, Ralph Volney. *The History of Legislative Methods in the Period before 1825.* New Haven, 1917.

Harrington, Samuel M. *Reports of Cases Argued and Adjudged in the Superior Court and Court of Errors and Appeals of the State of Delaware.* 5 vols. Dover, Del., 1837–1856.

Harry, James W. *The Maryland Constitution of 1851.* Johns Hopkins University Studies in Historical and Political Science, XX, Nos. 7–8. Baltimore, 1902.

Harvey, Katherine A. *The Best-Dressed Miners: Life and Labor in the Maryland Coal Region, 1835–1910.* Ithaca, 1969.

Hatcher, William B. *Edward Livingston: Jeffersonian Republican and Jacksonian Democrat.* University, La., 1940.

Hazzard, David, *et al. Address to the People of Delaware on the Approaching Presidential Election: Prepared in Obedience to a Resolution of the Convention of the Friends of the National Administration Assembled at Dover, on the Fifteenth Day of July, 1828.* Dover, 1828.

Heitman, Francis B. *Historical Register of the Officers of the Continental Army during the War of the Revolution, April, 1775, to December, 1783.* Washington, 1914.

Heydinger, Earl J. "The Little Schuylkill." *Railway and Locomotive Historical Society Bulletin* No. 108 (1963), 19–28.

———. "Railroads of the Lehigh Valley-Pennsylvania Railroad Group." *Railway and Locomotive Historical Society Bulletin* No. 109 (1963), 16–29.

Hibbard, Benjamin Horace. *A History of the Public Land Policies.* New York, 1939.

Hidy, Muriel Emmie. "George Peabody, Merchant and Financier, 1829–1854." Ph.D. dissertation in economics, Radcliffe College, 1939.

Hidy, Ralph W. "The House of Baring and the Second Bank of the United States, 1826–1836." *Pennsylvania Magazine of History and Biography*, LXVIII (1944), 269–285.

————. *The House of Baring in American Trade and Finance*. Cambridge, Mass., 1949.

History of the Railway Mail Service; A Chapter in the History of Postal Affairs. Washington, 1885.

Holland, Dorothy Garesché. *The Garesché, de Bauduy, and des Chapelles Families: History and Genealogy*. St. Louis, 1963.

Hollander, J. H. *The Financial History of Baltimore*. Baltimore, 1899.

Hone, Philip. *The Diary of Philip Hone, 1828–1851*. Ed. Bayard Tuckerman. 2 vols. New York, 1889.

Howard, George W. *The Monumental City, Its Past History and Present Resources*. Baltimore, 1873–1876.

Howe, M. A. De Wolfe. *The Life and Letters of George Bancroft*. Vol. I: New York, 1908.

Hunt, Gaillard. *The Department of State of the United States*. New Haven, 1914.

Hunt, Louise Livingston. *Memoir of Mrs. Edward Livingston with Letters Hitherto Unpublished*. New York, 1886.

Hunter, Robert M. T. *Correspondence of Robert M. T. Hunter, 1826–1876*. Ed. Charles H. Ambler. Annual Report of the American Historical Association, 1916, II. Washington, 1918.

Irving, Pierre M. *The Life and Letters of Washington Irving*. Vol. II: New York, 1883.

Irving, Washington. *The Journals of Washington Irving*. Ed. William P. Trent and George S. Hellman. Vol. III: Boston, 1919.

————. *The Letters of Washington Irving to Henry Brevoort*. Ed. George S. Hellman. Vol. II: New York, 1915.

Jackson, Andrew. *Correspondence of Andrew Jackson*. Ed. John S. Bassett. 7 vols. Washington, 1926–1935.

————. "Letters of Andrew Jackson to Roger Brooke Taney." *Maryland Historical Magazine*, IV (1909), 297–313.

James, Marquis. *Andrew Jackson: Portrait of a President*. Indianapolis, 1937.

Jenks, Leland H. *The Migration of British Capital to 1875*. London, 1963.

Jones, Chester Lloyd. *The Economic History of the Anthracite-Tidewater Canals*. Publications of the University of Pennsylvania: Series in Political Economy and Public Law, No. 22. Philadelphia, 1908.

Jones, Wilbur Devereux. *Lord Aberdeen and the Americas*. University of Georgia Monographs, No. 3. Athens, 1958.

————, and Vinson. J. Chal. "British Preparedness and the Oregon Settlement." *Pacific Historical Review*, XXII (1953), 353–364.

July, Robert W. *The Essential New Yorker: Gulian Crommelin Verplanck*. Durham, 1951.

Keller, William F. *The Nation's Advocate.* [Pittsburgh, 1956.]

Kendall, Amos. *The Autobiography of Amos Kendall.* Ed. William Stickney. Boston, 1872.

Kennedy, John Pendleton. *Memoirs of the Life of William Wirt.* Philadelphia, 1854.

Kettell, Thomas P. "Debts and Finances of the States of the Union . . . Chapter VI. The Western States-Indiana." *Hunt's Merchants' Magazine,* XXI (1849), 147–163.

Kibler, Lillian Adele. *Benjamin F. Perry, South Carolina Unionist.* Durham, 1946.

King, Rufus. *The Life and Correspondence of Rufus King.* Ed. Charles R. King. Vol. VI: New York, 1900.

[Kirkland, Elizabeth Cabot.] "Letters of Mrs. John T. Kirkland." Comp. Henry Cabot Lodge. *Proceedings of the Massachusetts Historical Society,* 2d ser., XIX (1905), 440–504.

Klein, Philip S. *President James Buchanan.* University Park, 1962.

———. *Pennsylvania Politics, 1817–1832: A Game Without Rules.* Philadelphia, 1940.

Knox, John Jay. *A History of Banking in the United States.* New York, 1900.

Lane, Wheaton J. *From Indian Trail to Iron Horse: Travel and Transportation in New Jersey, 1620–1860.* Princeton, 1939.

———. "The Morris Canal." *Proceedings of the New Jersey Historical Society,* LV (1937), 214–231, 251–263.

Latrobe, John H. B. *The Baltimore and Ohio Railroad. Personal Recollections. A Lecture, Delivered before the Maryland Institute, . . . March 23d, 1868.* Baltimore [1868].

Legaré, Hugh Swinton. *Writings of Hugh Swinton Legaré, Late Attorney General . . . Edited by His Sister.* Vol. I: Charleston, 1846.

Levasseur, A[uguste]. *Lafayette in America in 1824 and 1825; or, Journal of a Voyage to the United States.* 2 vols. Philadelphia, 1829.

Lewis, Charles Lee. *Admiral De Grasse and American Independence.* Annapolis, 1945.

Little Schuylkill and Susquehanna Rail Road Co. *Report of the President and Managers . . . to the Stockholders.* Philadelphia, 1838.

Livermore, Shaw, Jr. *The Twilight of Federalism: The Disintegration of the Federalist Party.* Princeton, 1962.

Livingood, James W. *The Philadelphia-Baltimore Trade Rivalry, 1780–1860.* Harrisburg, 1947.

Longaker, Richard P. "Was Jackson's Kitchen Cabinet a Cabinet?" *Mississippi Valley Historical Review,* XLIV (1957–1958), 94–108.

Lunt, Dudley. *The Farmers Bank, 1807–1957.* Farmers Bank of the State of Delaware, 1957.

Lyell, Charles. *A Second Visit to the United States of North America.* 2 vols. London, 1850.

Lynch, William O. *Fifty Years of Party Warfare (1789–1837).* Indianapolis [1931].

Mabee, Carleton. *The American Leonardo, a Life of Samuel F. B. Morse.* New York, 1944.

McCabe, James O. "Arbitration and the Oregon Question." *Canadian Historical Review,* XLI (1960), 308–327.

McCarrell, David K. "The Coming of the Railroad to Western Pennsylvania." *Western Pennsylvania Historical Magazine,* XVI (1933), 1–12.

McCormac, Eugene I. "Louis McLane." In *The American Secretaries of State and Their Diplomacy,* IV. Ed. Samuel Flagg Bemis. New York, 1928.

McCormick, Richard P. *The Second American Party System: Party Formation in the Jacksonian Era.* Chapel Hill, 1966.

McFaul, John M. *The Politics of Jacksonian Finance.* Ithaca, 1972.

McGrane, Reginald C. *Foreign Bondholders and American State Debts.* New York, 1935.

Mackenzie, William L. *The Life and Times of Martin Van Buren.* Boston, 1846.

McLane, Louis. *Oration Delivered before the Artillery Company of Wilmington Commanded by Captain Rodney, on the 5th of July, A.D. 1813.* Published by request of the company. [Wilmington, 1813.]

[———.] *Address of Mr. McLane, President, to the Stockholders of the Baltimore & Ohio R. Road Company . . . 5th of April, 1847, Respecting a Proposed Subscription to the Capital of the Pittsburg & Connellsville Rail Road Co.* Baltimore, 1847.

[———.] *Two Replies of the Baltimore & Ohio R. Road Company to Interrogatories Propounded . . . by the House of Delegates of Maryland* [on January 25 & February 10, 1844]. Baltimore, 1844.

McLane, Louis [Jr.]. *The Private Journal of Louis McLane, U.S.N., 1844–1848.* Ed. Jay Monaghan. Los Angeles, 1971.

McLane, Robert M. *Reminiscences, 1827–1897.* Privately printed. 1903.

McLane Report on Manufactures, Documents Relative to Manufactures in the United States. House Document No. 308, 22d Congress, 1st Session. 2 vols. Washington, 1833.

McLemore, Richard Aubrey. *Franco-American Diplomatic Relations, 1816–1836.* University, La., 1941.

———. "The French Spoliation Claims, 1816–1836: A Study in Jacksonian Democracy." *Tennessee Historical Magazine,* 2d ser., II (1931–1932), 234–254.

Mangum, Willie P. *Papers of Willie P. Mangum.* Vols. I–II. Ed. Henry T. Shanks. Raleigh, 1950–52.

Manning, William R. *Diplomatic Correspondence of the United States: Canadian Relations, 1784–1860.* Vol. III, *1836–1848.* Washington, 1943.

———. *Diplomatic Correspondence of the United States: Inter-American Affairs, 1831–1860.* 12 vols. Washington, 1932–1939.

Marbut, Frederick Browning. "The History of Washington Newspaper Correspondence to 1961." Ph.D. dissertation, Harvard University, 1950.

Marine, William M. *The Bombardment of Lewes by the British. Papers of the Historical Society of Delaware,* XXXIII. Wilmington, 1901.

Marryat, Capt. C. B. *Second Series of a Diary in America, with Remarks on Its Institutions*. Philadelphia, 1840.

Martin, Thomas P. "Cotton and Wheat in Anglo-American Trade and Politics, 1846–1852." *Journal of Southern History*, I (1935), 293–319.

——. "Free Trade and the Oregon Question, 1842–1846." *Facts and Factors in Economic History: Articles by Former Students of Edwin Francis Gay*. Cambridge, Mass., 1932.

[Maryland State Convention.] *Debates and Proceedings of the Maryland Reform Convention to Revise the State Constitution*. 2 vols. Annapolis: William M'Neir, Official Printer, 1851.

[——.] *Proceedings of the Maryland State Convention to Frame a New Constitution. Commenced at Annapolis, November 4, 1850*. Annapolis: Riley and Davis, 1850 [1851].

Mason, Jeremiah. *Memoir, Autobiography, and Correspondence of Jeremiah Mason*. Kansas City, 1917.

Mayo, Robert. *Political Sketches of Eight Years in Washington*. Baltimore, 1839.

Mearns, David C. *The Story Up to Now. The Library of Congress, 1800–1946*. Washington, 1947.

Medbery, James K. *Men and Mysteries of Wall Street*. New York, 1878.

Melville, Gansevoort. *Gansevoort Melville's London Journal and Letters from England, 1845*. Ed. Hershel Parker. New York Public Library, 1966.

Merk, Frederick. *The Oregon Question: Essays in Anglo-American Diplomacy and Politics*. Cambridge, Mass., 1967.

Meyer, Balthasar Henry, MacGill, Caroline E., *et al*. *History of Transportation in the United States before 1860*. Peter Smith, 1948.

Miller, [David] Hunter, ed. *Treaties and Other International Acts of the United States of America*, V, 1846–1852. Washington, 1937.

Moore, Glover. *The Missouri Controversy, 1819–1821*. University of Kentucky Press [1953].

Moore, Thomas. *The Letters of Thomas Moore*. Ed. Wilfred S. Dowden. Vol. II (1818–1847): Oxford, 1964.

——. *Memoirs, Journal, and Correspondence of Thomas Moore*. Ed. Lord John Russell. Vols. VI, VII: London, 1853–1856.

Montgomery, Elizabeth. *Reminiscences of Wilmington, in Familiar Village Tales, Ancient and New*. Philadelphia, 1851.

Moran, Benjamin. *The Journal of Benjamin Moran, 1857–1865*. Ed. Sarah Agnes Wallace and Frances Elma Gillespie. Vol. I: Chicago, 1948.

Morison, Samuel Eliot. *The Life and Letters of Harrison Gray Otis, Federalist, 1765–1848*. Vol. II: Boston, 1913.

Morris Canal and Banking Company. *Charter of the Morris Canal and Banking Company, and the Several Acts of the Legislature in Relation Thereto*. New York, 1836.

——. *Memorial of the Morris Canal and Banking Company to the Council and General Assembly of the State of New Jersey*. [N.p.], 1836.

————. *Reports of the President and Directors of the Morris Canal and Banking Company to the Stockholders.* June, 1836, and March, 1837. New York, 1836–37.

Morse, Edward Lind. *Samuel F. B. Morse, His Letters and Journals.* Vol. II: Boston, 1914.

Motte, Jacob Rhett. *Journey into Wilderness. An Army Surgeon's Account of Life in Camp and Field during the Creek and Seminole Wars, 1836–1838.* Ed. James F. Sunderman. Gainesville, 1953.

Munroe, John A. *Federalist Delaware, 1775–1815.* New Brunswick, 1954.

————. "Senator Nicholas Van Dyke of New Castle." *Delaware History,* IV (1951), 207–226.

Nussbaum, Frederick L. "The Compromise Tariff of 1833—A Study in Practical Politics." *South Atlantic Quarterly,* XII (1912), 337–349.

Oeste, George I. *John Randolph Clay, America's First Career Diplomat.* Philadelphia, 1966.

Osborne, Richard B. "Professional Biography of Moncure Robinson." *William and Mary College Quarterly,* 2d ser., I (1921), 237–260.

Otis, F. N. *History of the Panama Railroad; and of the Pacific Mail Steamship Company. . . .* New York, 1867.

Parker, Hershel. "Gansevoort Melville's Role in the Campaign of 1844." *New-York Historical Society Quarterly,* XLIX (1965), 143–173.

Parton, James. *Life of Andrew Jackson.* Vol. III: New York, 1861.

Pessen, Edward. *Jacksonian America: Society, Personality, and Politics.* Homewood, Ill., 1969.

Phoebus, George A. *Beams of Light on Early Methodism in America, Chiefly Drawn from the Diary, Letters, Manuscripts, Documents, and Original Tracts of the Rev. Ezekiel Cooper.* New York, 1887.

Plumer, William, Jr. *The Missouri Compromise and Presidential Politics, 1820–1825, from the Letters of William Plumer, Junior, Representative from New Hampshire.* Ed. Everett S. Brown. St. Louis, 1926.

Poinsett, Joel R. *Calendar of Joel R. Poinsett Papers in the Henry D. Gilpin Collection.* Ed. Grace E. Heilman and Bernard S. Levin. Philadelphia, 1941.

The Political Mirror: or Review of Jacksonism. New York, 1835.

Polk, James K. *The Diary of James K. Polk during His Presidency.* Ed. Milo M. Quaife. 4 vols. Chicago, 1910.

————. "Letters of James J. Polk to Andrew J. Donelson, 1843–1848." Ed. St. George L. Sioussat. *Tennessee Historical Magazine,* III (1917), 51–73.

————. "Letters of James K. Polk to Cave Johnson, 1838–1848." Ed. St. George L. Sioussat. *Tennessee Historical Magazine,* I (1915), 209–256.

Poor, Henry V. *History of the Railroads and Canals of the United States.* New York, 1860.

Poore, Ben Perley. *Perley's Reminiscences of Sixty Years in the National Metropolis.* 2 vols. Philadelphia, 1886.

Porter, Sarah Harvey. *The Life and Times of Anne Royall.* Cedar Rapids, 1909.

Powell, Lyman P. *The History of Education in Delaware.* Bureau of Education, Circular of Information No. 3, 1893. Contributions to American Educational History, No. 15. Ed. Herbert B. Adams. Washington, 1893.

Pratt, Julius W. "James K. Polk and John Bull." *Canadian Historical Review,* XXIV (1943), 341–349.

Prime, Samuel Irenaeus. *The Life of Samuel F. B. Morse, LL.D., Inventor of the Electro-Magnetic Recording Telegraph.* New York, 1875.

Putnam, George Haven. *George Palmer Putnam, a Memoir.* New York, 1912.

Quincy, Josiah. *Figures of the Past; From the Leaves of Old Journals.* Boston, 1883.

Ratchford, B. U. *American State Debts.* Durham, 1941.

Redlich, Fritz. *The Molding of American Banking: Men and Ideas.* 2 vols. New York, 1951.

Reed, H. Clay, ed. *Delaware: A History of the First State.* 2 vols. New York, 1947.

Reed, William B. *Life and Correspondence of Joseph Reed.* 2 vols. Philadelphia, 1847.

Reiser, Catherine E. *Pittsburgh's Commercial Development, 1800–1850.* Harrisburg, 1951.

Reizenstein, Milton. *The Economic History of the Baltimore and Ohio Railroad, 1827–1853.* Johns Hopkins University Studies in Historical and Political Science, XV, Nos. 7–8. Baltimore, 1897.

Remini, Robert V. *Andrew Jackson and the Bank War.* New York [1967].

———. *Martin Van Buren and the Making of the Democratic Party.* New York, 1959.

———. "Martin Van Buren and the Tariff of Abominations." *American Historical Review,* LXIII (1958), 903–917.

Richardson, James Daniel, ed. *A Compilation of the Messages and Papers of the Presidents.* 10 vols. Washington, 1896–1899.

Rippy, J. Fred. *The United States and Mexico.* New York, 1926.

Rives, George L. *The United States and Mexico, 1821–1848.* 2 vols. New York, 1913.

Rives, William C. "Letters, 1823–29, to Thomas Gilmer." *Tyler's Quarterly Historical and Genealogical Magazine,* V (1924), 223–237; VI (1924), 6–15, 97–105.

Rodney, George Brydges. *Diary of George Brydges Rodney.* Published by the Committee for Preservation of Existing Records, National Society of the Colonial Dames of America in the State of Delaware. N.p., n.d.

Royall, Mrs. Anne. *Mrs. Royall's Pennsylvania, or Travels Continued in the United States.* 2 vols. Washington, 1829.

Ruane, Joseph William. *The Beginnings of the Society of St. Sulpice in the United States (1791–1829).* The Catholic University of America Studies in American Church History, XXII. Washington, 1935.

Rubin, Julius. *Canal or Railroad? Imitation and Innovation in the Response to the Erie Canal in Philadelphia, Baltimore, and Boston.* Transactions of the American Philosophical Society, n.s., LI, pt. 7. Philadelphia, 1961.

Ruffin, Thomas. *The Papers of Thomas Ruffin.* Ed. J. G. de Roulhac Hamilton. 4 vols. Raleigh, 1918–1920.

Sagle, Lawrence W. "Baltimore & Ohio Stations in Baltimore." *Railway and Locomotive Historical Society Bulletin* No. 106 (April, 1962), 24–27.

Sanderlin, Walter. *The Great National Project: A History of the Chesapeake and Ohio Canal.* Johns Hopkins University Studies in Historical and Political Science, LXIV, No. 1. Baltimore, 1946.

Sargent, Nathan. *Public Men and Events from the Commencement of Mr. Monroe's Administration, in 1817, to the Close of Mr. Fillmore's Administration, in 1853.* 2 vols. Philadelphia, 1875.

Saunders, Romulus M. "Letters of Romulus M. Saunders to Bartlett Yancy, 1821–1828." Ed. A. R. Newsome. *North Carolina Historical Review,* VIII (1931), 427–462.

Scharf, J. Thomas. *The Chronicles of Baltimore; Being a Complete History of 'Baltimore Town' and Baltimore City.* . . . Baltimore, 1874.

———. *History of Baltimore City and County.* . . . Philadelphia, 1881.

———. *History of Delaware, 1609–1888.* 2 vols. Philadelphia, 1888.

Schlesinger, Arthur M., Jr. *The Age of Jackson.* New York, 1945.

Schmeckebier, Laurence F. *The Customs Service; Its History, Activities and Organization.* Institute for Government Research: Service Monographs of the United States Government, No. 33. Baltimore, 1924.

Scott, Joseph. *A Geographical Description of the States of Maryland and Delaware.* . . . Philadelphia, 1807.

Scott, Nancy N. *A Memoir of Hugh Lawson White.* . . . Philadelphia, 1856.

Scoville, J. A. [Walter Barrett]. *The Old Merchants of New York City, by Walter Barrett, Clerk.* 3 vols. New York [c. 1889].

Scudder, H. E., ed. *Recollections of Samuel Breck, with Passages from His Note-Books (1771–1862).* London, 1877.

The Seligman Collection of Irvingiana: A Catalogue of Manuscripts and Other Material by or about Washington Irving Given to the New York Public Library by Mrs. Isaac N. Seligman and Mr. George S. Hellman. New York, 1926.

Sellers, Charles Coleman. *Portraits and Miniatures by Charles Willson Peale. Transactions of the American Philosophical Society,* XLII, pt. 1. Philadelphia, 1952.

Sellers, Charles Grier, Jr. *James K. Polk, Jacksonian, 1795–1843.* Princeton, 1957.

———. *James K. Polk, Continentalist, 1843–1846.* Princeton, 1966.

Semmes, John E. *John H. B. Latrobe and His Times, 1803–1891.* Baltimore [1917].

Shaw, William H., comp. *History of Essex and Hudson Counties, New Jersey.* 2 vols. Philadelphia, 1884.

Shipp, J. E. D. *Giant Days, or the Life and Times of William H. Crawford.* Americus, Ga., 1909.

Sioussat, St. George L. "James Buchanan." In *The American Secretaries of State and Their Diplomacy,* V. Ed. Samuel Flagg Bemis. New York, 1928.

———, ed. "Selected Letters, 1844–1845, from the Donelson Papers." *Tennessee Historical Magazine,* III (1917), 134–162.

Skinner, Frederick G. "Reminiscences of an Old Sportsman." In Harry Worcester Smith. *A Sporting Family of the Old South.* Albany, 1936.

Smith, James G. *The Development of Trust Companies in the United States.* New York [1928].

Smith, Justin. "Great Britain and Our War of 1846–1848." *Proceedings of the Massachusetts Historical Society,* 2d ser., XLVII (1913–1914), 451–462.

Smith, Margaret Bayard. *The First Forty Years of Washington Society, Portrayed by the Family Letters of Mrs. Samuel Harrison Smith.* Ed. Gaillard Hunt. New York, 1906.

Smith, Walter B. *Economic Aspects of the Second Bank of the United States.* Cambridge, Mass., 1953.

[Smith, William P.] *A History and Description of the Baltimore and Ohio Rail Road . . . by a Citizen of Baltimore.* Baltimore, 1853.

Sparks, W. H. *The Memories of Fifty Years.* 3d ed. Philadelphia, 1872.

Stanwood, Edward. *American Tariff Controversies in the Nineteenth Century.* Vol. I: Boston, 1904.

Steiner, Bernard C. *Life of Reverdy Johnson.* Baltimore [1914].

Stenberg, Richard R. "Jackson, Anthony Butler, and Texas." *Southwestern Social Science Quarterly,* XIII (1932–1933), 264–286.

———. "The Texas Schemes of Jackson and Houston." *Southwestern Social Science Quarterly,* XV (1934–1935), 229–250.

Still, William. *The Underground Rail Road.* Philadelphia, 1872.

Swisher, Carl Brent. *Roger B. Taney.* New York, 1935.

Taney, Roger B. "Roger B. Taney's 'Bank War Manuscript.'" Ed. Carl Brent Swisher. *Maryland Historical Magazine,* LIII (1958), 103–130, 215–237.

———. "Taney's Correspondence with Van Buren." *Maryland Historical Magazine,* VIII (1913), 305–326; X (1915), 15–24.

Tanner, H. S. *A Description of the Canals and Rail Roads of the United States.* New York, 1840.

Taussig, F. W. *The Tariff History of the United States.* 6th ed. New York, 1914.

Taylor, George Rogers. *The Transportation Revolution, 1815–1860.* New York [1951].

Temin, Peter. *Iron and Steel in Nineteenth-Century America.* Cambridge, Mass., 1969.

Thacher, James. *A Military Journal during the American Revolutionary War, from 1775 to 1783.* Boston, 1827.

Thistlethwaite, Frank. *The Anglo-American Connection in the Early Nineteenth Century.* Philadelphia [1959].

Thompson, Robert Luther. *Wiring a Continent: The History of the Telegraph Industry in the United States, 1832–1866.* Princeton, 1947.

Thorpe, Francis Newton. *The Federal and State Constitutions.* . . . Vol. III: Washington, 1909.

Tipton, John. *The John Tipton Papers,* II. Comp. and ed. Nellie Armstrong Robertson and Dorothy Riker. Indiana Historical Collections, XXV. Indianapolis, 1942.

Trotter, Alexander. *Observations on the Financial Position and Credit of Such of the States of the North American Union as Have Contracted Public Debts.* London, 1839.

Tyler, Lyon G. *The Letters and Times of the Tylers.* Vol. I: Richmond, 1884.

Van Buren, Martin. *The Autobiography of Martin Van Buren.* Ed. John C. Fitzpatrick. Annual Report of the American Historical Association, 1918, II. Washington, 1920.

———. *Inquiry into the Origin and Course of Political Parties in the United States.* Edited by his sons [Abraham and John Van Buren]. New York, 1867.

Van Deusen, Glyndon G. *The Jacksonian Era, 1828–1848.* New York [1959].

———. *The Life of Henry Clay.* Boston, 1937.

Veit, Richard F. *The Old Canals of New Jersey: A Historical Geography.* Little Falls, N.J. [1963].

Vermeule, Cornelius C., Jr. *Morris Canal and Banking Company: Final Report of Consulting and Directing Engineer, June 29, 1929.* Trenton, 1929.

Walters, Raymond. *Albert Gallatin: Jeffersonian Financier and Diplomat.* New York, 1957.

Ward, Townsend. "The Germantown Road and Its Associations." *Pennsylvania Magazine of History and Biography,* V (1881), 1–18, 121–140, 241–258, 365–392; VI (1882), 1–20, 129–155, 257–283, 377–401.

Washington, George. *The Writings of George Washington from the Original Manuscript Sources, 1745–1799.* Ed. John Fitzpatrick. 39 vols. Washington, 1931–1944.

Watson, John F. *Annals of Philadelphia and Pennsylvania, in the Olden Time.* . . . Enlarged by Willis P. Hazard. 3 vols. Philadelphia, 1927.

Weber, Gustavus A. *The Patent Office: Its History, Activities, and Organization.* Institute for Government Research: Service Monographs of the United States Government, No. 31. Baltimore, 1924.

Webster, Daniel. *The Private Correspondence of Daniel Webster.* Ed. Fletcher Webster. 2 vols. Boston, 1857.

Wellington, Raynor G. *The Political and Sectional Influence of the Public Lands, 1828–1842.* Boston, 1914.

Weslager, C. A. *Brandywine Springs: The Rise and Fall of a Delaware Resort.* Wilmington, 1949.

White, Leonard D. *The Federalists: A Study in Administrative History.* New York, 1948.

———. *The Jacksonians: A Study in Administrative History, 1829–1861.* New York, 1954.

———. *The Jeffersonians: A Study in Administrative History, 1801–1829.* New York, 1951.

White, Ray Barton. *At Baltimore on December 7, 1842—being extracts from a railroad Minute Book.* A Newcomen Address. [Princeton,] 1942.

Wikoff, Henry. *The Reminiscences of an Idler.* New York, 1880.
Williams, Stanley T. *The Life of Washington Irving.* 2 vols. New York, 1935.
Wiltse, Charles M. *John C. Calhoun, Nationalist, 1782–1828.* Indianapolis, 1944.
———. *John C. Calhoun, Nullifier, 1829–1839.* Indianapolis [1949].
———. *John C. Calhoun, Sectionalist, 1840–1850.* Indianapolis, 1951.
Winfield, Charles H. *History of the County of Hudson, New Jersey.* New York, 1874.
Winther, Oscar O. *Express and Stagecoach Days in California.* Palo Alto [c. 1936].
Winthrop, Robert C. "Memoir of Hon. Nathan Appleton." *Proceedings of the Massachusetts Historical Society,* 1st ser., V (1860–1862), 249–308.
Woodbury, Levi. "Levi Woodbury's 'Intimate Memoranda' of the Jackson Administration." Ed. Ari Hoogenboom and Herbert Ershkowitz. *Pennsylvania Magazine of History and Biography,* XCII (1968), 507–515.
Young, James S. *The Washington Community, 1800–1828.* New York, 1966.

NEWSPAPERS

Baltimore	*Baltimore American*
	Sun
London	*The Times*
New York	*New-York Evening Post*
	New York Herald
Newark, N.J.	*Newark Daily Advertiser*
Philadelphia	*National Gazette*
Pittsburgh	*Pittsburgh Gazette*
Washington	*Globe*
	National Intelligencer
	United States Telegraph
	Washington Union
Wilmington, Del.	*American Watchman*
	Blue Hen's Chicken
	Delaware and Eastern Shore Advertiser
	Delaware Gazette
	Delaware State Journal
	Delaware Statesman
	Mirror of the Times
	Museum of Delaware
	Political Primer

Index

Aberdeen, George Hamilton-Gordon, earl of, 263, 271, 283, 288, 410; American trade reopening (1829) and, 272, 274, 275, 277–78, 279, 287; Mexico and, 289, 533–34, 536–37; Oregon and, 518, 520–26 *passim*, 528–34 *passim*, 536, 537, 538, 540, 541

Abingdon, Maryland, 11

abolitionist movement, *see* slavery

Adams, Henry, quoted, 304

Adams, John, 33, 63, 79, 310

Adams, John (son of John Quincy Adams), 229–30

Adams, John Quincy, 116, 133, 207, 208, 209, 212, 218, 219, 220–22, 233, 242, 331; Bank of the United States recharter (1832) and, 320, 323, 366; cabinet appointments of, 188, 189–90, 193; Chesapeake and Delaware Canal and, 148, 150; "Dauphin" story and, 7, 489; election of 1824 and, 155, 156, 160, 164, 166, 167, 168, 169, 170–71, 172, 173, 174–75, 177, 178–79, 180–86, 187, 188, 197, 225, 227; election of 1828 and, 57, 221, 234, 235, 236–39; English ministry appointments of, 203, 263, 282; House speakership races and, 122, 123, 132, 192, 193, 194; Jackson's Florida campaign and, 90, 91; McLane

(Louis) on, 70, 154, 157, 170–71, 173, 174, 187, 190–91, 199–200, 201, 213, 296; on McLane cabinet posts, 300–301, 404, 409, 427; on McLane diplomatic posts, 256, 283, 291, 342, 427, 516; as Secretary of State, 76, 98; tariff issue and, 216, 217, 237, 263, 264, 269, 274, 326, 340, 341–43, 344–50, 351, 365, 368, 372, 375

Adams, Mrs. John Quincy, 94, 98, 117, 173, 205, 349; on McLane illness (1832), 345; on Treasury fire (1833), 383

Agricultural Society of New York, 88

Alabama (vessel), 474

Alabama, 77, 453; Congressmen, 129, 224, 407

Alaska, 513, 517, 518

Albany, New York, 181, 251, 322, 325, 398, 503. *See also* New York State. Legislature (Albany)

Albany *Argus*, 259, 315, 429

Albemarle Sound, 242–43

Alexander II, czar of Russia, 407

Alexandria, Egypt, 289

Alexandria, Virginia, 554, 573

Alhambra, The (Irving), 259

Alien and Sedition Acts (1798), 5, 175

Allegany County, Maryland, 499, 500–501

ABOUT THE AUTHOR

John A. Munroe is H. Rodney Sharp Professor of History at the University of Delaware, where he has taught since 1942, serving as chairman of the history department from 1952 to 1969. He received his B.A. and M.A. from the University of Delaware and his Ph.D. from the University of Pennsylvania. He is the author of *Federalist Delaware, 1775–1815* (1954).

The text of this book was set in Caledonia Lino-type and printed by Offset on P & S Special Book L manufactured by P. H. Glatfelter Co., Spring Grove, Pa. Composed, printed and bound by Quinn & Boden Company, Inc., Rahway, N.J.

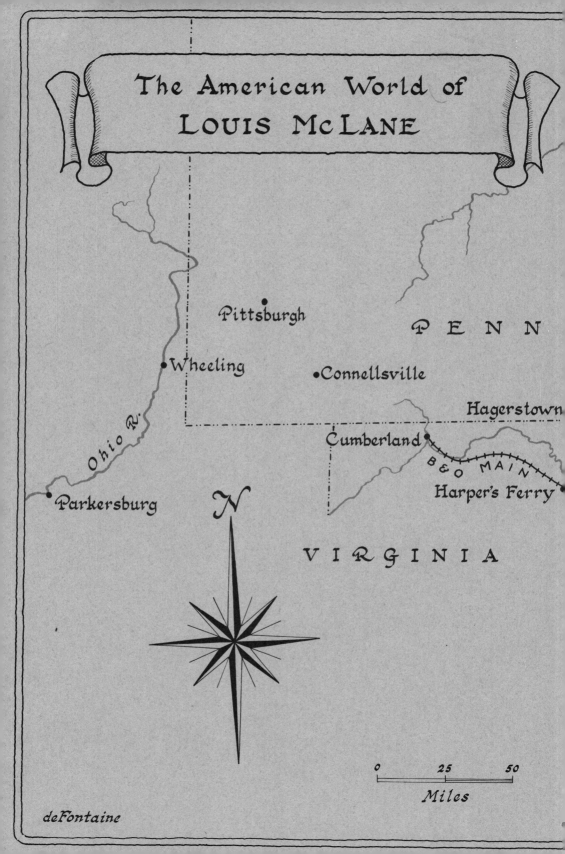

The American World of
LOUIS McLANE

P E N N

Pittsburgh

Wheeling

Connellsville

Hagerstown

Cumberland

B&O MAIN

Ohio R.

Harper's Ferry

Parkersburg

N

V I R G I N I A

0   25   50
Miles

deFontaine